When he was inaugurated on January 5, 1985, James Grubbs Martin became only the second Republican to serve as governor of North Carolina during the twentieth century. As a member of the state's minority political party, Martin sometimes clashed with a General Assembly dominated by Democrats. Wary lawmakers appeared to reject some of his legislative initiatives, such as the gubernatorial veto and a school construction bond referendum, as a partisan reflex. While it seldom adopted the governor's proposals exactly as he had envisioned, the legislature nevertheless enacted measures that were inspired by his recommendations: the tax relief package of 1985 and the "Roads to the Future" program of 1986 are two examples.

There was more to Martin's first term than his relationship with the General Assembly, however. A desire to make government more accountable led him to open the proceedings of the Council of State and Advisory Budget Commission to reporters. The governor insisted that an increasing percentage of the General Fund be devoted to education, established the state's first foreign language institutes, and vigorously supported increased local control of schools. He focused widespread attention on the plight of abused and missing children, the condition of the state's prison system, school dropouts, substance abuse, illiteracy, and the needs of families and older adults. Although his administration's concerted efforts to attract the superconducting super collider to North Carolina went unrewarded, record-setting levels of economic growth and employment were achieved by assisting traditional industries and recruiting a mix of manufacturing and high-technology businesses. Martin also demonstrated a commitment to the completion of Interstate 40, announced a strategic highway corridor concept to strengthen the rural economy, and devised the Coastal Initiative plan.

(continued on back flap)

ADDRESSES AND PUBLIC PAPERS

OF

JAMES GRUBBS MARTIN

ADDRESSES AND PUBLIC PAPERS

OF

JAMES GRUBBS MARTIN
GOVERNOR OF NORTH CAROLINA

Volume I

1985-1989

Jan-Michael Poff, Editor

Raleigh
Division of Archives and History
Department of Cultural Resources
1992

DEPARTMENT OF CULTURAL RESOURCES

Patric Dorsey
Secretary

DIVISION OF ARCHIVES AND HISTORY

William S. Price, Jr.
Director

Larry G. Misenheimer
Assistant Director

NORTH CAROLINA HISTORICAL COMMISSION

ISBN 0-86526-250-0

STATUTORY AUTHORIZATION

Section 121-6(b) of the *General Statutes of North Carolina* requires that a copy of "all official messages delivered to the General Assembly, addresses, speeches, statements, news releases, proclamations, executive orders, weekly calendars, articles, transcripts of news conferences, lists of appointments, and other official releases and papers of the Governor" be provided to the Department of Cultural Resources. From these records a selection is made by "a skilled and competent editor" who "shall edit according to scholarly standards the selected materials which shall be published in a documentary volume as soon as practicable after the conclusion of the term of office of each Governor."

2,500 copies of this volume were printed at a cost of $56,400.00, or $22.56 each.

FOREWORD

In 1971 the North Carolina General Assembly gave the then State Department of Archives and History statutory authority to compile, edit, and publish each governor's public papers. G.S.121-6(b) merely formalized a policy that had been initiated by the North Carolina Historical Commission a half century earlier. In 1923 the Historical Commission issued *Public Letters and Papers of Thomas Walter Bickett, Governor of North Carolina, 1917-1923*. Since then each governor has had a selection of his public papers edited and published. Publication of *Addresses and Public Papers of James Grubbs Martin, Governor of North Carolina, 1985-1989*, is the latest in this series.

Under the skillful editorship of Jan-Michael Poff, the public papers of Governor James G. Martin have been collected, selected, edited, and annotated for publication. Mr. Poff also edited Volume II of the *Addresses and Public Papers of James Baxter Hunt, Jr., Governor of North Carolina, 1981-1985*. His careful research and close working knowledge of the issues and events affecting political discourse in North Carolina are reflected in the headnotes and footnotes to Governor Martin's speeches. Mr. Poff also has been compiling an appointments section. Because of Governor Martin's reelection in 1988, the appointments section will not appear until Volume II of his papers is published. That same editorial procedure was followed in publishing the two volumes of Governor Hunt's papers.

Over the years the documentary volumes devoted to the public papers of North Carolina's governors have received high praise from reviewers. The volumes are indispensable to researchers of twentieth-century North Carolina history. Writing in the October, 1988, issue of the *North Carolina Historical Review*, one scholar commented: "Other states would do well to follow the example set by North Carolina." As a compendium of the complexities of running a state government in the late twentieth century, the *Addresses and Public Papers of James Grubbs Martin, Governor of North Carolina, 1985-1989*, provides an essential record.

Jeffrey J. Crow
Historical Publications Administrator

May, 1991

ACKNOWLEDGMENTS

No matter how fixed his vision or firm his grasp, an editor cannot bring a documentary project to conclusion single-handedly. The process whereby a loose collection of official typescripts was transformed into the first volume of the *Addresses and Public Papers of James Grubbs Martin, Governor of North Carolina* bears the imprint of many minds. That liberality of effort is hereby acknowledged: Everyone who contributed in any way to the completion of this book deserves, and has, my sincere thanks.

Although it is impossible to name each person who assisted this editor in the execution of his duties, the generous participation of a number of individuals merits special recognition. I am most grateful to the following members of the Martin administration for their unstinting cooperation: Tim Pittman, director, Karen Hayes Rotterman, his predecessor, and Mary Ann Dusenbury and Nancy Pekarek, of the Governor's Communications Office; Jane Bolin, assistant director for legislative affairs, Office of the Governor; Sarah Lofton, executive assistant, and Betty F. Dean, personal secretary and administrative assistant to First Lady Dorothy M. Martin; and Barbara R. Marsh, senior research analyst, Governor's Office of Research.

Jeffrey J. Crow, administrator of the Historical Publications Section, Division of Archives and History, read the manuscript closely and offered characteristically thoughtful suggestions and corrections. He also navigated the governmental channels necessary to ensure the typesetting, printing, and binding of this volume. As always, I greatly appreciate the benefit of his experience.

Lisa Bailey, the section's proofreader, thoroughly searched the copy for all manner of grammatical errors and mechanical inconsistencies. Her diligence is laudable.

Others in state government and the university system who were particularly helpful include Robert G. Anthony, Jr., Alice R. Cotten, and the staff of the North Carolina Collection, University of North Carolina at Chapel Hill; Jane W. Basnight, librarian, Department of Environment, Health, and Natural Resources; Carolyn B. Honeycutt, Department of Public Instruction; Charles E. Jones, Department of Transportation; Butch Matthews, West Forehand, Vickie Guin, Larry Perry, and Jimmy Stallings, University Graphics, North Carolina State University; Cheryl W. McLean, Division of State Library, Department of Cultural Resources; Dianne Parrish, assistant to the director, Division of Forest Resources, Department of Environment, Health, and

Natural Resources; and Louise Stafford, assistant librarian, North Carolina Supreme Court Library.

Finally, special thanks are due to Peter A. Pantsari, general manager, Southern Educational Communications Association, Columbia, South Carolina, for permission to reprint the "Firing Line" transcript; Kyoko Mimura, a graduate student at the University of North Carolina School of Journalism, Chapel Hill, who cheerfully provided the Japanese-to-English translations used in this volume; Deborah Dunn, of the *Charlotte Observer*'s newsroom library; J. P. Freeman, executive director, North Carolina Association of Colleges and Universities, Raleigh; Jerry Huff, *News and Observer*, Raleigh; Robin Pendleton, Veterans of Foreign Wars State Headquarters, Raleigh; and Margaret A. Sullivan, editor and publications officer, Southern Regional Education Board, Atlanta.

Jan-Michael Poff

May, 1991

EDITORIAL METHOD

Texts or notes exist for more than 960 of the addresses James Grubbs Martin delivered during his first administration as governor. Add to them the scores of news releases issued by his Communications Office, and one has amassed a body of material too large to be reprinted in the single-volume documentary permitted each of the state's chief executives, per four-year term, by North Carolina law. Materials ultimately selected for inclusion in the *Addresses of Martin* most comprehensively reflect the scope of the governor's official activities during the 1985-1989 period; they discuss the aspirations and accomplishments of his administration, explain policies, focus on developments in the state and the issues he confronted, effectively illuminate some aspect of his occupational or political philosophy, or contain significant autobiographical elements. Whenever possible, transcripts of speeches meeting those criteria were published. If transcripts were unavailable or multiple versions of an address were prepared for a single event, the text bearing Governor Martin's handwritten emendations was favored over unadorned copy.

Because many of the texts the editor received bore the governor's personal revisions, the diplomatic transcription of those speeches initially was considered; that is, a system of textual symbols would have enabled researchers using the *Addresses of Martin* to distinguish his additions to, and deletions from, the material prepared for him. But discussion of the merits of such an arrangement with William S. Price, director of the Division of Archives and History, and Jeffrey J. Crow, administrator of the Historical Publications Section, determined that the editorial barbed wire characteristic of diplomatic transcription would impede comprehension of the documents themselves. Consequently, the clear text method generally was followed. Researchers can, however, examine evidence of the governor's fine tuning of one of his speeches in the diplomatic transcription prepared as Appendix I, pages 1014-1016.

While most of the governor's textual emendations were incorporated silently into the documents reprinted in the *Addresses of Martin*, there have been exceptions to the rule. Marginalia and interlinear notes that Martin added to his speeches, but which could not be incorporated elegantly into the body of a published document, were reprinted as annotations, their corresponding footnote numbers placed at the point in the text where the governor made his original insertion. Some of his jottings were so fragmentary that they defied accurate interpretation; these were not reproduced. Extrapolation was kept to an absolute minimum, and all of the editor's supplemental words have been placed in square brackets.

Naturally, it is inevitable that some of the same conceptual currents flow through more than one address, thus demonstrating the continuing importance Governor Martin assigned to specific issues. Annotations accompanying the documents reprinted herein mention textually identical and thematically similar items that were omitted. Deleted speeches and statements, and speaking engagements for which there was no prepared text, are listed by date, title, and place of delivery, on pages 971-1006.

Overall, the documents were edited to ensure consistent spelling, capitalization, punctuation, and use of numbers. Headings were standardized, and salutations of addresses were deleted unless they contained information or a particular nuance that greatly enhanced a reader's understanding of the audience, occasion, or of the main text of the speech. Ampersands and esoteric abbreviations have been expanded, and typographical errors in the originals have been corrected. Generally, the lack of uniformity in textual mechanics of addresses is the norm. Although Governor Martin wrote all of the addresses he delivered before the General Assembly and the 1986 Report to the People, he also depended upon other speechwriters throughout state government to generate accurate and reliable copy in terms of content. With so many different hands producing texts, editorial inconsistencies frequently occur.

Every effort was made to identify persons, legislation, reports, and quotations the first time they appear in the documentary. Presidents of the United States, the founding fathers, and others whose names are immediately recognizable did not receive biographical annotations. The editor mailed letters requesting biographical information to individuals the governor mentioned but for whom such data could not be found in standard directories. Those who failed to reply were not footnoted. Although extensive measures were employed to locate and cite all bills, laws, and studies to which the governor referred, and to check the accuracy of quotations he used, unfortunately not every one could be verified.

Finally, some will question the relative absence of materials from Martin's 1988 campaign for reelection and other political events. Because the governor's purely political speeches were not written by state employees on state time, the administration contended that such items were considered private papers and therefore did not qualify as official documents to be submitted for publication under G.S. 121-6(b), the state law authorizing the governors' papers project. While all governors are statutorily required to deposit their official papers with the Department of Cultural Resources—and it is upon official papers, like Governor Martin's, that documentaries such as this are based—the manner of disposal of personal records is left to the discretion of the chief executive. Governor Martin had not announced the repository chosen for his private papers by the time this volume went to press.

TABLE OF CONTENTS

LIST OF ILLUSTRATIONS

JAMES GRUBBS MARTIN
By Tim Pittman*

The election in 1984 of James Grubbs Martin as the sixty-fifth governor of the state of North Carolina, and only the second Republican in the twentieth century to hold that office, signaled the emergence of competitive, two-party politics in a statehouse dominated by the Democratic party. His upset victory over the Democratic candidate, Attorney General Rufus Ligh Edmisten, had less to do with partisan politics, at least initially, than it did with the arrival of a new personality on the state's political scene. As a former county commissioner and United States congressman, Jim Martin clearly arrived as a well-connected North Carolina political veteran. But he entered the Raleigh establishment with an outsider's perspective on state government, an intellectual's view of the political world, and a county commissioner's appreciation for issues that made a difference in people's lives.

Martin brought to the Capitol a platform to open government and make it more accountable. As he demonstrated in his first year, the administration would be framed by the twin themes of reform and responsibility. These ideals became part of the governor's oft-repeated pledge to fashion "one united state"—to bring North Carolina together, urban and rural, east and west, areas with good jobs and those without; to move beyond regional and political jealousies—where opportunity and progress were within the reach of every citizen.

A student of North Carolina history, Governor Martin saw in his election not only the revival of two-party politics but also the inauguration of an age of progress, a period similar in many respects to the

*Tim Pittman, director of communications for Governor Martin, graciously furnished this essay. The opportunity for an administration spokesman to provide an introduction describing the accomplishments of the chief executive, as well as his personal and political background, traditionally has been extended as a courtesy by the editors of previous volumes of modern governors' papers. The essay represents the views of the writer and is a supplement to, and not an official part of, the documentary.

Timothy Ralph Pittman (1955-   ), born in Smithfield; B.A., University of North Carolina at Chapel Hill, 1977. Newspaper reporter, *Winston-Salem Journal*, 1978, *Fayetteville Observer*, 1978-1981, and for *Greensboro News and Record*, 1985-1988; press secretary, 1985-1988, and director of communications, 1988-1991, for Governor James Grubbs Martin; also served as press secretary for Governor Martin's 1988 reelection campaign; media relations director, Whittle Communications, Knoxville, Tennessee, since 1991. Timothy Ralph Pittman to Jan-Michael Poff, August 10, 1990; telephone conversation with Timothy Ralph Pittman, May 17, 1991.

fourteen years of Whig party leadership between 1837 and 1851. Characterized by vast transportation improvements and social, economic, and education reforms, the Whigs awakened a state deadened by the dulling effects of single-party dominance. Martin's first inaugural address called attention to the need for a progressive, unified agenda that would move North Carolina forward.

Not disposed to making vague promises, his vision for North Carolina was anchored in the realities of solving the multitude of problems it faced. Early in his first term, the governor proposed elimination of the intangibles tax and the gradual reduction of the inventory taxes, cuts that would fuel the state's economy with new business investment.

Martin recognized in North Carolina a crumbling infrastructure that hampered new investment. He set to work immediately to secure improvements in prison construction, strategic highway building, the delivery of human services, and environmental regulation. He saw the dangerous lack of planning given to handling hazardous wastes generated by the state's industries and began to address those problems.

He brought a new idea to education in North Carolina: putting schools first in the list of budget priorities. In his initial term, the governor reversed a trend of reduced spending on education by insisting that greater percentages of the state's General Fund be allocated to education each year. Teachers' salaries turned upward.

The governor's strong scientific background—he was a Davidson College professor and held four patents in the chemistry of synthetic detergents and butyl rubber vulcanization—enhanced his reputation as a nontraditional leader independent of the influence of lobbyists and organizations that was so common among predecessors who emerged from the state's orthodox political structures. James E. Holshouser, Jr., the first Republican chief executive to be elected in twentieth-century North Carolina, said Martin demonstrated in his first term a "thinking man's approach to problem solving."

When the governor faced unusual problems, he demonstrated his disciplined approach to management by spending hours in personal study of the the issues. He used computers extensively in his Capitol and Executive Mansion offices. Memos on work assignments, draft speeches, letters to the editor—any or all might show up on a workday morning in the Governor's Office from a chief executive who labored through the night on a special project. His staff often encountered a man who knew more than government experts about the issues of the day; experience gained in county government and at the federal level proved valuable on a daily basis in the state Capitol. From setting budget priorities to building waste-water treatment plants, Martin was comfortable with the tasks of governing.

Jim Martin approached state government with a novel perspective shaped by his own intellect, independent in spirit and thoughtful in outlook. His belief in empirical study and factual analysis placed him at odds with the public on some issues. Given more to careful review and action than political expediency, the governor often endured open criticism while working instead for what he believed was best for North Carolina. He viewed these stands—opposing a state lottery despite widespread support, for example, or advocating limited tax increases despite opposition from his own party—as issues of honor for the good of North Carolina.

Important early signals from the new governor demonstrated his willingness to take the responsibility to rehabilitate institutions and change practices that symbolized the abuses in the state's political process: a bloated political personnel system, deteriorating prisons, and unfulfilled highway promises. Within the first few months of his administration, this theme of reform took shape in several key areas.

In a state where gubernatorial elections usually meant upheaval and mass firings in state government, Martin replaced only top administrators and refused to allow widespread partisan reprisals. He halved the number of state employees subject to political firings. In the previous administration, the number of such jobs had swelled to more than 1,500. The new governor reduced that level to 875.

In a state where hollow highway promises were as common as leaves changing in election-year Octobers, Martin made only one pledge during the 1984 campaign: to complete Interstate 40 from the coast to the mountains. It was a promise he kept. He also restored reliability to the Transportation Improvement Program and developed the strategic corridors network, a long-term, nonpolitical approach to road building designed to coax new businesses beyond city limits and deep into job-hungry rural sectors of an economy sharply divided between rich and poor.

In a state where the prison system tottered on the brink of a federal takeover after years of neglect, Martin accepted the challenge of restoring it to a condition that protected the public and ensured that criminals would serve their sentences. In addition, he emphasized ideas that strengthened the state's alternative punishment programs. It was symbolic of Martin's sense of responsibility that he would undertake the rebuilding of the state's corrections system, which brought little political gain and, in fact, enjoyed no constituency of advocates.

In a state where open meetings were talked about more often as campaign rhetoric, Martin kept his word. He opened the meetings of the Council of State and the Advisory Budget Commission, an unprecedented step for political reporters accustomed to waiting outside closed doors to learn of decisions by elected leaders.

In a state where the arbitrary awarding of pork barrel projects had long dominated the General Assembly's budget process, the new governor promised to correct those abuses. He pointed out that local appropriations bills, known as pork barrel, were used as a tool by a small group of Democratic legislative leaders to maintain party discipline and enforce vote guarantees. Martin criticized the practice and the secret meetings where the final budget was assembled. Over the course of his first term, significant changes emerged in both the method of awarding local projects and opening up the budget process.

As part of a reform package he carried to the General Assembly in 1985, the governor kindled anew the old debate on the issue of veto power for North Carolina's chief executive.

These broad reform themes resonated throughout the first term of Governor James G. Martin. Framed by his willingness to accept responsibility for the tough issues of the day, he brought an instinct for change to a government in need of it.

A Family Tradition of Service

A minister's son of modest circumstances by birth, Jim Martin's boyhood was an active one where leadership came naturally in the classroom and on the athletic field. In his youth he developed the inquisitiveness about people and issues that marked his career. Even as governor, this wide-ranging intellectual curiosity transcended his interest in the next election.

James Grubbs Martin was born December 11, 1935, in Savannah, Georgia, the second of four sons born of the Reverend and Mrs. Arthur M. Martin. While the young Jim Martin's first lessons in politics came from learning to get along with his brothers, the earliest lessons about service and commitment came from his parents. In his first inaugural address, the newly elected governor was moved to recall the words delivered by his father, a Presbyterian minister, at a family reunion in 1967: "Our future grows from our past. Looking back, we can see generations of farmers who planted more than cotton and corn. By the grace of God, they planted the seed of His word in the hearts of their children. With a conscience enlightened by that word, problems became calls to great achievement."

An active student leader who served as president of the South Carolina Beta Club, the young Martin was also an accomplished athlete. He played varsity basketball and football in the Winnsboro, South Carolina, public schools. His gridiron talents won him the honor of second-team all-state end in the days before the modern wide-receiver formation had evolved—the days when high school players worked both sides of the ball.

His passion for music and the fine arts was nurtured while in Winnsboro, where he developed an interest in the tuba. "It was the only instrument that was provided free of charge by the school," Martin remembered. As a Davidson College senior, he joined the Charlotte Symphony Orchestra and later described himself, in jest, as a "semi-pro" tuba player. The governor varied the tuba joke occasionally to report that he had held first chair with the Charlotte Symphony—where, of course, there was only one tuba chair.

Playing the tuba and singing in church choirs and barbershop quartets inspired Martin to study the piano and learn to write music as well. He composed a work based on the Jude Benediction that was performed at his father's funeral. In March, 1986, the Covenant Presbyterian Church choir in Charlotte performed sacred music written by the governor during the preceding ten years: two anthems and ten short pieces, including offertories, choral amens, and calls to worship.

Graduating from high school in 1953, Jim Martin entered Davidson College, where he continued to demonstrate the talent for leadership that he discovered as a student in Winnsboro. He participated in athletics, the chemistry and musical fraternities, and served as president of the college concert band. Martin was inducted into Omicron Delta Kappa, the national honorary leadership fraternity, and joined Beta Theta Pi, a social fraternity, serving as its national president from 1975 to 1978.

Martin earned a bachelor's degree in chemistry from Davidson in 1957, and Princeton University awarded him a doctorate in 1960. Afterward, he accepted a position as associate professor of chemistry at his undergraduate alma mater. While such a background might seem unusual for a man destined to enter politics, Martin explained to an interviewer his reasons for pursuing one of the most difficult of sciences: "Chemistry proceeds from mystery to understanding through orderly processes, and metaphor, and mathematics. I thought I had some aptitude for those requirements."

Martin's interest in politics became more evident upon his return to Davidson. In 1963 he ran unsuccessfully for a seat on the Davidson Town Board. "At that time, I didn't know much about politics," he told a reporter during the 1984 campaign for governor. "I learned that I had to do more than declare my intent and vote for myself." It was the only political race Jim Martin ever lost.

Characteristically, he learned from that losing experience and prepared more carefully for a countywide race two years later. In 1965 Martin won a seat as Mecklenburg County commissioner, the first of three terms he served on the commission. During those six years—three as chairman—he learned the importance of setting budget priorities, and he was part of trend-setting developments in local government. While arguments over how to spend education dollars raged during his first term as governor, Martin often recalled his days as commissioner to point out that he helped persuade Mecklenburg officials that education spending should be the priority in the county budget.

He also took great pride in two other accomplishments while he served as a commissioner: Mecklenburg County established the first mechanism for enforcement of environmental regulations and the first county zoning ordinances in the state. His commitment to effective local government won him election as president of the North Carolina Association of County Commissioners; and in 1971 he was the founder and first chairman of the Centralina Council of Governments, one of the state's first regional organizations created to improve the workings of local government. It was this interest in government, and in the good it could do for people, that attracted the county commissioner to the United States Congress.

An unusual opportunity presented itself in 1972. Ninth District congressional veteran Charles Raper Jonas announced he would retire that year after unbroken electoral success despite repeated attempts at gerrymandering his district. Looking for an attractive candidate with sympathetic views and youthful potential, Jonas offered his organization and fund-raising contacts to the Davidson College chemistry professor and county commissioner. Withstanding a challenge from the right wing of his own party in 1972, Martin won the primary handily. He went on to defeat Jim Beatty, a state legislator and former Olympic miler, in the general election.

Described as "soft-spoken" by the 1982 edition of *Politics in America*, Martin built a congressional office that excelled in constituent service. Although his district had supported Democratic statewide candidates in previous years, he proved extremely popular with the electorate through six congressional campaigns. Charlotte, North Carolina's largest and most business-oriented city, held much of the population of the Ninth Congressional District. Martin fashioned a voting record in the United States House of Representatives that allied him with that business community.

Congressman Martin was an ardent defender of supply-side economics and worked consistently to lower the federal budget deficit by reducing spending, a position often characterized as partisan. Much of his congressional record also reflected his interest in the impact of government policy on the individual. He rose to the position of sixth-most-senior member of the powerful House Ways and Means Committee, which formulated tax law for the nation. (Every few years, Martin insisted on preparing his own returns in order to gauge the complexity of federal tax regulations.)

Politics in America observed of Martin that, "Over the years, he has been most active when the argument has turned to science." This subject of academic interest had become a passion for him in the world of politics. The congressman's understanding of the chemical industry helped him make national news during the debate on the use of saccharin as a sugar substitute. Martin worked against efforts to ban it, challenging the claim that tumors found in rats given massive doses of the substance meant that humans faced a great health risk. Typical of his tendency to analyze an issue, Martin stood on the floor of the House to argue that the use of saccharin shortened life by only twenty-three minutes.

Martin became known in Congress as an expert on topics related to toxic wastes, and his ability to bring a reasoned intelligence to the tough, often emotional issues of chemical and hazardous waste management earned him the praise of regulators and the companies that were regulated. He realized the daily dilemma the United States faced as its population grew ever more accustomed to a life-style that demanded goods and services that generated hazardous wastes. More importantly, Martin understood that the nation must come to terms with the methods of managing that waste.

Many recognized Congressman Martin's grasp of these complex issues. He became the first elected official to receive the American Chemical Society's Charles Lathrop Parsons Award for outstanding public service by an American chemist, and his reputation prompted the Reagan administration to approach him about becoming the Environmental Protection Agency chief in 1983. However, Martin

declined the post. By that time, he had started to think of returning to
North Carolina. No decision had been made on the governor's race, but
Martin knew it would be an open seat. Governor James Baxter Hunt, Jr.,
had all but announced his intent to run for the United States Senate in
1984, and the North Carolina Constitution did not allow him to seek a
third term in the state's highest office. Friends, political supporters, and
North Carolina's Republican establishment began to see in Jim Martin
a formidable candidate to win the Executive Mansion. For Martin, the
governorship offered an opportunity to return home to serve the state
he loved.

Competitive, Two-Party Politics

In the early 1960s, North Carolina's state government was the exclusive domain of a single party. Then an associate professor of chemistry
without strong ties to either political entity, Martin viewed Democratic
dominance in Raleigh as a barrier to new ideas and competition, while
the minority party offered the challenge of working for the underdog.
Drawn to politics by his sense of civic involvement and a view that
North Carolina government would benefit from strong interparty
rivalry, Jim Martin registered in his home county of Davidson as a
Republican.

Jim Martin's decision to join the GOP might have been a humble
decision by a young professor, but in retrospect, it was a remarkable
event in the history of a state just beginning to engage in two-party
politics on a grand scale. As a county commissioner, a United States
representative, and finally as the first Republican governor elected in
North Carolina with a chance to succeed himself, Martin brought
vibrancy and competitiveness to a political party that had suffered the
indignities of back-row seats in the General Assembly for more than
eighty years. He received more votes in 1984 than any previous gubernatorial candidate in North Carolina and came to Raleigh with a mainstream Republican agenda that was characterized by his tax policies;
the commitment to limit the growth of the state bureaucracy; his desire
for increased governmental openness and efficiency; and a promise to
reform state personnel practices. Martin shunned an agenda dominated by narrow ideological concerns.

The governor seized the Republican party as a catalyst for change in
North Carolina. Under his leadership, areas for political reform were
identified early and emphasized often in his first term: securing veto
power for state's chief executive; challenging the autocratic leadership
of a secret subcommittee that ruled budget negotiations; and ending

pork barrel abuses. Martin made the very structure of the "single-party" legislature, in which Republicans played no significant role, a campaign issue in the 1986 General Assembly elections, and his heavy schedule of appearances in support of GOP candidates helped the party essentially hold its own—a noteworthy outcome in an off-year political contest that saw the party lose its bid to return James Broyhill to the United States Senate.

For a Republican party accustomed to growing in influence during presidential election years and shrinking dramatically in mid-term elections, Martin's first term in office as a governor constitutionally able to succeed himself offered the promise of sustained influence. His leadership accounted for the steady growth of the GOP across North Carolina, inspired active candidate recruitment by the GOP, attracted the increasing involvement of young people in the party's political campaigns, and led to the more frequent election of Republicans to local office. The number of Republicans elected to district court judge-ships, for example, increased from eleven, in the 1986 elections, to twenty-three in the 1988 elections; county commissioners registered as GOP members increased from 141, in 1986, to 157, in 1988.

His victory rejuvenated Republican interest in legislative races and even opened the door for reform of the judiciary. For the first time in more than a century, Republicans made the 1986 state supreme court races competitive and set the stage for genuine consideration of a merit selection plan for judges. Under the single-party legislature, this idea had never gathered political strength.

His style of leadership, so remarkably different from previous Demo-cratic governors, became an unexpected asset in the political climate of the mid 1980s. Instead of making backroom deals with legislators, Martin insisted on a more open process, presenting his administra-tion's plans publicly and trying to make his case by proving points of merit to legislators. He eschewed the image of good-old-boy politics for a more modern approach that followed closely the codes of conduct observed during congressional debates. While some argued that his open style was less effective, Martin believed government served best when the public saw the full range of proposals from both sides. His was a sort of merit system, a political arena in which he presented good ideas, argued his case, and hoped his leadership opened new doors of debate for state policy.

Economic Growth

Jim Martin's first term as governor will be remembered as a period of broad, balanced economic growth that came at a time when national naysayers warned of the end of the *buffalo hunt,* a term characterizing easy pickings for Sunbelt governors as they courted the commercial and manufacturing giants that wanted to leave colder climates in the Northeast and Midwest. While other state officials lamented the passage of those glory days of industrial recruiting, Martin's well-publicized commitment to rebuild North Carolina's infrastructure and strengthen the public schools and community college system paid off among carefully selected business clients. He also launched an ambitious and aggressive economic development plan with two elements: First, help existing industries expand and strengthen; second, convince national and international prospects that North Carolina's work force, quality of life, and commitment to new business offered the finest location in the United States.

Despite an often stormy national business outlook, the Tar Heel State thrived while Martin served as governor. The years from 1985 to 1988 were a time of unprecedented economic growth. More than 380,000 jobs were created, and new and expanding investment totaled more than $21 billion. Helped by the Department of Commerce's *Blueprint for Economic Development,* a review of recruiting strategies ordered by Martin as he came to office, his administration steered the state toward new directions in targeting defense contractors, a mix of high-tech and manufacturing companies, and firms that would locate in rural settings.

Jim Martin's personal salesmanship and hardworking approach to industry hunting made North Carolina the envy of the nation during his first term. Publications covering the recruiting business routinely gave the state top ratings in efforts to court new industries. A survey released in 1988 by the highly respected trade journal, *Site Selection and Industrial Development Handbook,* showed that North Carolina placed first in the country as the preferred location for new manufacturing plants, with 113 having been announced in 1987.

Rather than just seeking out new businesses, the governor offered a hand to North Carolina's traditional industries—furniture, agriculture, textiles—and helped strengthen their attempts to modernize and expand. He created the first deputy secretary for traditional industry within the Department of Commerce, thus underscoring his commitment to assist the businesses that kept the North Carolina economy strong through the years.

As an economic centerpiece of much of North Carolina, agriculture remained one of its most significant traditional industries. Martin formed a task force to study the economic health of the state's farms. He also developed a plan for agricultural parks in geographically diverse regions in order to help farmers market their products more effectively.

Among his long list of accomplishments in the arena of economic expansion, Governor Martin was especially proud of his administration's work to promote rural development. In 1987 southeastern North Carolina enjoyed $122 million in new manufacturing investment; another $156 million was invested in the twenty-one northeastern counties. During that year, 68 percent of the jobs announced went to the state's outlying communities. To stimulate the rural economy further, Martin proposed a strategic corridor network that would bring a four-lane highway within ten miles of every citizen in the state. Costly in the short term but sweeping in its impact over the long run, the plan provided highways envisioned as avenues for quality growth, paving the way for progress into the twenty-first century.

Martin's chronicle of good news in rural development owed a great deal to teamwork in the local communities, and the governor touted state-local partnerships to help attract economic growth. As a result, new industry was directed into areas where plants were needed desperately. Indeed, as a one-time county commissioner, Martin often spoke directly with former colleagues across North Carolina when problems needed personal solutions, and he held a deep appreciation for the high quality of local government in the state. Instead of crowing about personal accomplishments in business recruiting, the governor nurtured local efforts by passing the praise on to local leaders. He knew that in the end, industrial development success rested with the community, not with state government.

The governor's intellectual interests also prompted him to pursue North Carolina's ambitious quest for a high-technology research center: the superconducting super collider. While the bid for the SSC was unsuccessful, the spin-offs in research and development continued to pay dividends for state government and set the tone for an aggressive, pro-science approach toward investment. This emphasis led to new ventures in aquaculture, the supercomputing center, and high-technology research, all encouraged by the governor's personal enthusiasm and willingness to work for futuristic goals.

Despite a first-term record that set new standards in North Carolina's history of business development, Martin's most impressive industrial recruiting legacy was his personal salesmanship. Always willing to board a predawn flight for a breakfast meeting with out-of-state executives, the governor was just as enthusiastic about huddling with business representatives after a twelve-hour day of speeches and other public events. His high energy level and willingness to work around the clock during trade missions to the Far East and Europe became the stuff of legends among recruiters who tried to keep up with him. He favorably impressed Japanese business contacts with his knowledge of their native language. As the closer of the deal, the man who understood the client and what it took to convince the prospect of North Carolina's quality, Martin had no equal.

The Tobacco Summit

Even though his congressional constituents had not demanded great tobacco expertise during his years in Washington, as governor, Jim Martin became a quick expert on what was then North Carolina's number-one agricultural commodity. His involvement in the historic tobacco industry summit at the Executive Mansion in November, 1985, as much as any single issue, symbolized his ability to resolve thorny problems.

The Flue-Cured Tobacco Cooperative Stabilization Corporation stood at a dangerous crossroads in 1985. The cooperative's higher operating costs were hurting tobacco growers, and the price support system faced a debt-ridden future.

Taking under loan any tobacco that sold for less than one penny per pound above support levels, Stabilization bolstered the tobacco price support program by purchasing leaf the manufacturers would not buy. As the organization's warehouses filled, the poundage fees, assessed all tobacco growers for storing the massive surpluses, also rose. After steady increases in the assessment required to support the Stabilization program, tobacco farmers had grown weary and discouraged, and their incomes were tumbling.

Not quite in office one year, the governor summoned manufacturers, representatives of growers' organizations, and much of the state's political leadership to a series of meetings at the Executive Mansion. In July, 1986, they announced from the Mansion's front steps a buy-down of the $1.2 billion in surplus tobacco being held in Stabilization warehouses. Manufacturers agreed to purchase the stockpiles and reduce the huge surplus, thus restoring the financial viability of the Flue-Cured Tobacco Cooperative Stabilization Corporation. The agreement also dropped the per-pound assessment from a record-high 25 cents to only 2.5 cents, a dramatic decrease for hard-pressed tobacco farmers.

For the tobacco manufacturers, the historic agreement protected the industry's warehousing stalwart, the Stabilization Cooperative, and ensured the longevity of the program. For growers, the agreement meant income protected from increasing assessment charges, and it lessened the dark clouds of uncertainty about the future of Stabilization. For Jim Martin, it was an early opportunity to demonstrate his ability to bring together diverse interests and work successfully toward compromise.

An Educator as Governor

While other governors talked about education or sought highly visible, national roles, Jim Martin quietly brought North Carolina's commitment to education back where it belonged: at the top of the priority list. With little fanfare, he sought achievement in important educational yardsticks such as teacher pay, accountability, and recruiting; funding flexibility for local school boards; minority initiatives; and language training. As an educator himself, he believed the best way to improve the teaching profession was to offer better pay linked to better performance. That way, he reasoned, good teachers would be attracted to remain in the profession, and students would be rewarded with better educations.

Jim Martin changed a course that had hamstrung educational achievement. State spending on public education, as a percentage of the General Fund, had decreased every year, save two, during the twenty-four years preceding 1985; only in 1966 and 1984 was that negative trend reversed. Following his election as governor, appropriations for schools increased each year as a measured percentage of the General Fund. Martin viewed that indicator as one of the most critical because it reflected his budgetary commitment to education improvements.

With each new budget, the governor held firm to annual increases for teacher pay. Late in his first term, his steady, responsible effort paid off handsomely. Teachers' salaries jumped from fortieth to thirty-first in the nation.

Despite vocal opposition from teachers' lobbying groups, Governor Martin continued to push for a career ladder program in which educators who passed evaluations were rewarded with increased pay as they advanced into higher career levels. "The public demands teacher accountability and better schools," the governor often said. "The career ladder will give them both."

While the governor endorsed the Basic Education Program and its $700 million price tag in 1985, he questioned the lack of flexibility the plan afforded school boards in each district. His challenge drew the immediate ire of some education groups, but his reasons for seeking change held up over time. In less than four years, school boards across the state demanded and got from the General Assembly exactly what Martin had recommended in 1985: BEP funding with a promise that each school board could set its own priorities to meet local needs.

Ever watchful of impediments to North Carolina's educational excellence, in 1986 Governor Martin called attention to the poor quality of many of the state's school buildings. At that time, more than half were constructed before 1959. The governor proposed a statewide bond referendum to finance $1.5 billion in new school construction, but the General Assembly refused to adopt his solution.

Martin also pushed for resolution of the long-standing struggle over the governance of public education. With lines of authority sometimes tangled among two elected officials—the governor and the state school superintendent—and an appointed state school board handling day-to-day issues, no single office could be held responsible. Martin argued that either the governor or state board should select the superintendent, who then would assume direct accountability for guiding the public education system.

In 1987 an historic opportunity arose to reform the issue of education governance. A. Craig Phillips, who had held the office of state school superintendent since 1969, announced his intention to forego reelection in 1988. Although the Martin administration asserted that the time was ripe for amending the constitution to create an appointed superintendent, the General Assembly would not accept such a change. The cumbersome triumvirate remained.

Governor Martin could, however, point with great pride to encouraging education developments that had grown from his own recommendations. An office of teacher recruitment, proposed during his first year as chief executive, became the Teacher Enhancement Program enacted by the General Assembly in 1986.

One of his most significant achievements, the governor thought, was the development of the state's first foreign language institutes. Located across North Carolina, the institutes trained promising foreign language instructors to impart more effectively the communications skills their students would need to compete in a competitive, global economy. Martin announced the plan in 1987, and summer schools were held in both French and Spanish the next year.

Another of Martin's priorities was to attract minority teachers into public schools, and he set in motion early the concepts that led to the creation of the North Carolina Consortium on Minority Teachers, which flourished in his second term. In 1986 he signed an executive order establishing the Governor's Program to Strengthen Historically Black Colleges and followed up that commitment by pledging budget dollars to improve programs at those institutions. Finally, as honorary chairman, the governor presided over the United Negro College Fund during the first year in which it raised more than $1 million.

Pursuing an Environmental Agenda

Early in his first term, before public sentiment crystallized around such issues, Jim Martin signaled his environmental priorities. As a former county commissioner who took pride in his role in creating Mecklenburg's pro-environmental land-use and zoning regulations, the first in the state, he wanted the same progressive record as governor. Martin pledged a new vigilance in environmental enforcement, offered solutions to protect coastal and inland waters, and worked to develop a plan to acquire more parkland and use it more wisely.

As a chemist, he understood the complexities of solving the problems caused by the runoff of storm water into streams and rivers, by discharges from unregulated industry, and by agricultural residue drifting from farmland and into water supplies. The governor instructed his team at the Department of Natural Resources and Community Development to adopt an aggressive posture toward violators and to pursue strategies that would afford long-term protection for the environment. Within two years, his administration had imposed more fines than any other; by 1988, enforcement activity was up 300 percent in some programs. During the first term, 563 civil penalties, seeking $10.9 million in fines, were levied. Waste-water discharge compliance stood at 85 percent and air quality compliance at 98 percent. The highest environmental damage award in North Carolina history, $5.6 million, was assessed in 1986 against Texasgulf, Incorporated, for violation of air purity standards by its plant near Aurora. Eventually, the fine was reduced to $1 million plus the cost of the investigation as part of an environmentally sound settlement.

These aggressive protection efforts grew from the governor's insistence that the regulatory staff perform its duties without influence from any outside source. This pro-environment stance, often over-looked in the daily press coverage of the administration, mirrored the governor's sense of reform and responsibility.

Fines and enforcement represented but one element of the Martin administration's environmental record. By 1986 a more activist environmental presence was emerging in North Carolina, and the state faced more and tougher regulatory challenges each year, with the public demanding even greater accountability from fewer staff. Martin made sure the state stayed abreast of new regulatory demands, and he responded with creative solutions of his own. Hallmarks of his progressive environmental agenda included:

—A new standard of protection for water supplies, Outstanding Resource Waters, was created as a shield to prevent high-risk development in ecologically sensitive areas.

—A model program to control agricultural runoff, Best Management Practices, grew in the first term of the Martin administration from a humble pilot program to a statewide initiative. More than 7,000 landowners have participated, implementing the program on over a half million acres. Conservative estimates indicated that at least one million tons of soil would be saved annually over a ten-year period.

—The Coastal Initiative, conceived by Martin personally, recognizes that North Carolina must balance economic development with preservation. The program offered grants to shoreline communities to direct growth where it would not have major environmental consequences. At the same time, it prevented development in pristine areas.

Martin knew that the greatest challenge to protecting the environment rested in the state's ability to manage the consequences of steady economic growth. In 1987, the governor made good on a commitment to help communities better manage that growth with a proposal for a state revolving loan fund that would help local government pay for high-cost waste-water treatment plant projects and improve water supply facilities. More than $21 million was appropriated for 1987-1988, the beginning of the state's first major improvement for local infrastructure devoted to water quality.

The governor understood from prior experience that most environmental successes would be based in local government. With that in mind, he proposed a policy of gradually reducing dependence on landfill use by 90 percent by the year 2000. This goal would be achieved by promoting and assisting the development of conservation, resource recovery, composting, and incineration.

While legislators worried publicly about the threat to groundwater supplies from leaking petroleum tanks, Martin proposed a state-mandated, shared responsibility system in which the state's costs would be financed by annual tank charges and would include third-party damages for contaminated wells.

Early in his first term, the governor outlined to legislators a state parks act that would have mandated a statewide plan to address park resources and needs. Despite a $50 million bond proposal in 1985, the General Assembly appropriated only $25 million. But to Martin, unafraid to present worthy proposals even if they became the property of other political groups, increased funding for state parks was a symbolic victory.

Human Resources

While the governor remained focused on his major priorities—improving schools, stretching highways into rural areas, and luring high-quality industry—he also encouraged innovations that would help disadvantaged North Carolinians. Martin established the first veterans preference system for state government hiring that gave former servicemen and women genuine advantages over citizens who lacked military experience. Responding to the shortage of nurses in North Carolina, he set up a task force that worked with hospitals and universities to improve recruiting and solve personnel problems at rural medical centers. The governor hosted the state's first Conference on Aging, in 1988, where he announced plans for new and expanded programs for senior citizens.

The North Carolina Center for Missing Persons, a successor of the Missing Children's Information Center created in 1984, offered professional assistance in locating lost children and adults. Headquartered within the Department of Crime Control and Public Safety, the center grew from handling 174 cases in 1985 to more than 3,500 in 1988. It gained national attention for its efforts.

When state government reorganized the way it managed unemployment insurance contributions, the Martin administration championed a plan to offer a tax cut to businesses and simultaneously set up a state-directed fund that offered more help for job-skill retraining projects. The tax-reduction program was designed to save employers $250 million over five years, money they could plow back into reinvestment and thus help to foster the state's economic expansion.

The General Assembly approved the governor's plan, including the unemployment insurance tax cut, in March, 1987. The change in regulations protected employee benefits at existing levels, while the interest accruing to the state from its oversight of unemployment monies permitted the establishment of the Worker Training Trust Fund— which paid for new training for people to learn new technical skills, qualifying them for better jobs. North Carolina's state-managed unemployment insurance program was unique in the nation.

As he looked at the preparedness of North Carolina's work force to tackle the employment challenges of the twenty-first century, the governor saw the tragedy of illiteracy. Martin set in motion a series of measures to identify solutions, including the creation of the Governor's Commission on Literacy. He also worked with the departments of Correction and Cultural Resources to establish Motheread. That nationally recognized program encouraged incarcerated women to learn to read so that they, in turn, could teach their own children to read, consequently breaking the cycle of illiteracy that threatened productive lives.

A Commitment to Family and the Spirit of Fun

During his junior high years, Jim Martin met Dorothy Ann McAulay at a church youth conference. The daughter of Benson Wood McAulay and the former Dorothy Louise Gill of Charlotte, she married Martin in 1957. They eventually had three children: Jim Jr., Emily, and Ben.

The families of North Carolina governors live in the very public Executive Mansion, where every coming and going can be viewed by interested press and citizens. A specially trained team of Highway Patrol officers provided personal security, safe passage, and the convenience of day-to-day logistical planning. Every governor establishes his own relationship with the executive protection team at the Mansion, but Jim and Dottie Martin and their youngest son, Ben, who was thirteen when they moved in, made it clear early on that they would treat the patrol like family.

Early in 1985, when a North Carolina Highway Patrol trooper dropped the new governor off at his home on Lake Norman, the driver settled down patiently for a long wait in his patrol car. For those on executive protection duty, this solitary vigil was commonplace—a part of the job, something a trooper gets used to. He had not waited long before North Carolina's new First Lady poked her head out of the modest dwelling and strolled over to the patrolman. "I don't know how this was done in the past," Mrs. Martin explained, "but we don't allow company to wait out in the car." She invited him in for coffee and refreshments.

With that friendly gesture, she set a new tone that defined the relationship between the Martins and the rest of officialdom. The First Family developed strong bonds with the men and women who worked with them. When the governor traveled, his staff knew to make accommodations for security that were comfortable and similar to his own. When the governor ate at an event, arrangements were effected to make sure security did the same. Martin often praised the patrol publicly, but his private signals of support for them and appreciation for their jobs forged a strong bond between the men in the detail and the man they served.

Mrs. Martin, like her husband, shaped her own public agenda and worked hard in her third-floor office at the Mansion. A popular First Lady, she pursued an active schedule as a speaker and representative of causes related to family life, literacy, and child care. Her advocacy of the antidrug, pro-family message of Parent to Parent, a new program that she expanded from a tiny pilot project to a statewide initiative, reflected the First Lady's deep concern that public officials should serve as role models and be involved in problems that state government could not solve by itself.

Her personal commitment to issues related to the family kept her busy through the first term, but she also was determined to have fun; to make the experience at the Mansion pleasurable and memorable despite the public nature of the First Family's life. At Halloween the First Lady and her husband joined in the festivities by displaying a front porch full of jack-o-lanterns, helping arrange elaborate displays for the kids, and handing out candy themselves. During the first Halloween at the Mansion, Governor Martin entertained a local television station by making frightening faces with a flashlight.

Such antics characterized the Martins. They were public servants, certainly, but they understood, often more than their staff, the importance of keeping their own sense of family amidst the official clamor around them. Even during the hectic pace of the last months of the 1988 reelection campaign, the governor insisted on attending a professional wrestling match with Ben to see one of his son's favorite wrestlers.

Plus Ultra: More Beyond

The last year of Jim Martin's first term was filled with the challenges and opportunities of a reelection campaign. The inaugural theme of 1985, "One United State," resonated through his first administration and found voice in the reelection. The governor's theme in the 1988 campaign was printed proudly on a banner displayed behind him at each rally: "Better Schools, Better Jobs, Better Roads."

As the campaign marched toward November, Martin modified his message to reflect his accomplishments more accurately. By mid-summer he added "A Better Environment" to his campaign addresses, and he made adjustments to parallel his political goals as well. Acknowledging the campaign of former United States representative Jim Gardner of Rocky Mount in his bid to win the state's second-highest elective office, Martin plugged another idea into his speeches: "A Better Lieutenant Governor."

The 1988 gubernatorial race offered a referendum on the leadership of Jim Martin, and his mainstream, progressive campaign themes produced successes both tangible and historic. His convincing reelection margin, capturing 56 percent of the more than 2 million votes cast, marked the first time a Republican governor had won reelection in modern North Carolina. He led a ticket that produced the state's first twentieth-century Republican lieutenant governor; elected Robert Orr, a Republican, to the North Carolina Court of Appeals; and shored up the party's strength in the General Assembly. To a chief executive who identified with the reform principles of the Whigs, his reelection symbolized the growing influence of two-party politics in North Carolina. Martin believed the campaign proved that the public understood the importance of interparty competition and voted to continue his gradual but critical reforms.

Reform, however, is an ongoing process. Governor Martin knew the improvements of his first term, accomplishments built on his desire for constructive change and his willingness to face tough issues responsibly, had laid the bedrock for a brighter future. The theme of his second inaugural reflected that promise for the years ahead; Martin chose a Latin motto inscribed on coins of the Spanish empire: *Plus ultra,* meaning "More beyond."

Top: When inaugurated on January 5, 1985, James G. Martin became North Carolina's second Republican governor of the twentieth century. State Supreme Court Chief Justice Joseph Branch administered the oath of office. Dorothy Martin stood on her husband's right. *Bottom*: The governor outlined his legislative proposals for the ensuing biennium in his first "State of the State" message to the General Assembly, February 28, 1985. (Unless otherwise specified, all photographs courtesy of the Office of the Governor.)

Ben Martin, the governor's youngest son, attempts a bold gambit in a chess game with his father at the Executive Mansion. Dorothy Martin, the First Lady, looks on.

INAUGURAL ADDRESS:
OUR FUTURE CALLS US TOGETHER—AS ONE UNITED STATE

My Fellow Citizens:

Throughout our four centuries of settled history, North Carolina has prospered through a blend of rivalry and unity. We have known the rivalry of east against west—against piedmont; of planter against frontier settler—against native Indian; of business competition, of team against team, and party against party. Yet, we have reached our greatest achievements when called to a unity of purpose: to weather a colonial winter; to throw off a colonial oppressor; to bind the wounds of a torn nation; to share the combined intellectual resources of a great university system. Here today, after a time of rivalry, our future calls us together in that spirit of unity, for today we are all Democrats, and we are all Republicans; we are all from east and west and piedmont. Today, we are all North Carolinians: one united state.

As the third Martin to be governor of North Carolina, it is my honor to be the first Martin elected by the people. It was Josiah Martin who had to make a forced departure as the last of the royal governors. He reported his circumstances to be "most despicable and mortifying," with "the whole constitution unhinged and prostrate."[1] Indeed.

Shortly after statehood, the popular Alexander Martin was chosen governor by the General Assembly—incidentally, he served seven terms! It was Alexander Martin's privilege to herald a new day for North Carolina. Upon hearing in 1783 that the Treaty of Paris had been signed, recognizing the United States as independent, he proclaimed to the General Assembly: "I congratulate all my fellow citizens of the state of North Carolina. . . . Nothing now remains but to enjoy the fruits of uninterrupted constitutional freedom, the more sweet and precious as the tree was planted by virtue, raised by toil, and nurtured by the blood of heroes."[2] Now I, too, have come to herald a new day for North Carolina.

While preparing for this day, I have been thinking about certain unifying ideas that have persisted throughout North Carolina's history.

I have been thinking about economic development. That is what spurred Sir Walter Raleigh to colonize these shores four hundred years ago. It led yeoman farmers to the fertile, black earth of the Albemarle in the 1650s and on to mountain frontiers soon after. It triggered North Carolina's gold rush[3] and the growth of its railroad network. It was economic development that inspired nineteenth-century North Carolina businessmen to found our state's early industries, to make products that became household words throughout this nation and beyond. It was economic development that inspired in Concord the founding of the first mill in the South that black businessmen capitalized, owned, and operated.[4] There also developed, in Durham, the largest black-managed financial institution in the world.[5] It was economic development based on tourism that, in turn, forged a popular commitment to environmental stewardship and historic preservation, and it was economic development that brought our brilliantly successful Research Triangle Park into being—and with it a constellation of high-technology industries. So, I have been thinking a great deal about economic development as an essentially competitive force that unites us.

I have been thinking, too, about political freedom—that ideal of political freedom that inspired colonial rebellions in North Carolina. It moved the ladies of Edenton to hold a "tea party" that was one of the first women's political protests in this country's history,[6] and it inspired the men of Halifax and Mecklenburg to frame important resolves about liberty and, finally, to take up arms for their belief.[7] It was our state which had the largest population of free blacks, before 1860, and would continue to extend and enhance freedom for all citizens a century later. So, I have been thinking about political freedom, a competitive force that unites us.

I have been thinking long and seriously about education. Our constitution of 1776 provided for institutions of learning, and the first state university in the nation opened its doors at Chapel Hill in 1795.[8] Even before independence, in 1772, Salem had the only school of its kind for women in the South.[9] Now we have an impressive array of excellent private liberal arts colleges, a great consolidated university system, and a network of community colleges in every part of North Carolina.

Public schools to educate all children grew from the vision of Archibald DeBow Murphey, and every governor since Charles Aycock has been an "education governor."[10] That vital tradition continues! With special schools to develop the most unusually creative talents in the performing arts and math and science, we have affirmed our belief in the cultivation of excellence.[11] If universal public education is the rising tide that lifts all boats, then a high order of academic rigor for our most gifted young scholars may well be that essential, gravitational, lunar force that lifts the tide! So, I have been thinking a great deal about education as an intellectually competitive force that continues to unite us.

Economic development. Political freedom. Public education. What, then, do we believe about these traditions today?

This is what I believe about economic development: I believe deeply in our system of private enterprise, based on traditional principles of self-reliance. I believe the most powerful economic force for maximizing the greatest good for the greatest number is the act of investing one's own resources, at the risk of losing it all, in the hope of realizing a profitable return and thereby creating jobs for others. Yes, I am for business. We all should be. That's where jobs come from.

I have a special concern for jobs in our traditional industries— textiles, furniture, tobacco, agriculture—which have provided so many entry-level jobs for generations of North Carolinians and have sustained so many families and communities in our state. We must make a special effort to champion their interests as they face a rising level of subsidized competition from other nations. At the same time, we must continue to reach out to the future and its high-technology ventures that are finding a welcome climate for growth in North Carolina, and we must support our farmers with a major effort to recruit more food-processing businesses. All these objectives will benefit from strategic tax reforms to remove unique taxes that impose a competitive disadvantage on North Carolina businesses and workers. Elimination of such anti-jobs taxes is imperative if we are to restore our rural border counties to the economic vitality of one united state.

This is what I believe about political freedom: We are a varied people in North Carolina—Republicans, Democrats, independents, conservatives, liberals, moderates. I believe in an open political marketplace, where alternative ideas and their consequences can be debated and can compete for our allegiance. I believe in a strong two-party system as the best way to promote that competition of ideas, and to encourage good people to compete for public office, and to ensure greater accountability for those who serve. I intend for my party to build its strength through inspiration, not intimidation; through addition, not subtraction; and through continued respect for those who register under a different persuasion.

I believe that we will have more open government these next four years, because of the degree of healthy, two-party tensions that will exist. I intend, however, for bipartisan cooperation to characterize our relationship. That has been reflected in my leadership appointments, as well as in the cooperation we have enjoyed during a productive transition period—for which I commend my predecessor, Governor Hunt.[12] There is surely a time for partisanship, and there is also now a time for bipartisanship. Once again, paradoxically, this competitive force must unite us to serve the people.

This is what I believe about education: Today's students will be adults when this century turns into the next millennium in the year 2000, and they must be equipped with a good basic education. The basics of reading, writing, arithmetic, and respect—the ultimate vocational courses—will be the survival skills in an increasingly specialized world. One must learn to read before one can read to learn. Beyond the basics, I want our graduates to have enough understanding of science that they will face our technological future with confidence. I want them well grounded in history, literature, and social studies so they will understand where we have come from, as a people, and appreciate the values of civilization.

I believe that, to strengthen our schools, we must strengthen the teaching profession and promote teaching as a career. We must provide better pay for better teachers. We must carefully develop incentives for excellence that will win the confidence of teachers: that the better they are, and the better they become, the better they will be paid. Achieving that goal will win the confidence of all parents and taxpayers. By pulling together to strengthen our schools throughout North Carolina, we will surely harness a powerful force to unite us.

Running through all these remarks is the theme of unity. We will achieve unity by beginning with goodwill toward each other and building a sense of responsibility for one another. Ultimately, we will have the satisfaction that comes from our efforts to help one another. In practical terms, this means a unity achieved by balanced economic growth in our state, a growth that takes place from the mountains to the sea. It means a unity achieved by a public school system that offers high-quality preparation to children in every part of our state. It means a unity achieved by knowing each other culturally—that may begin with such simple acts as traveling in other regions of the state; in doing so, we learn about the needs for highways and bridges and jobs in communities beyond our own. In our own communities, where we know every corner, every pothole, and every tree, we know what the needs are. We must learn to understand and support the needs of others in this united state of North Carolina.

In closing, I want to share a private view of this event. The Bible upon which I took my oath of office was given to me by my wife, Dottie,[13] for our first Christmas together, twenty-nine years ago, as teenaged sweethearts. This book marks the distance we have traveled together. Today our mothers,[14] our children[15]—in fact, dozens of members of the extended Martin family—are here to share this memorable day with us. One Martin who is not here is my father.[16] He was a good man, a Presbyterian minister. In a sermon to our family reunion in 1967, he said something like this to us: "Our future grows out of our past. Looking back, we can see generations of farmers who planted more than cotton and corn. By the grace of God, they planted the seed of His word in the hearts of their children. With a conscience enlightened by that word, problems become opportunities for service, and challenges become calls to great achievement."

With its problems, its opportunities, and its challenges, the future calls us together. In that spirit, my friends, I begin my service to you today as governor of this great united state of North Carolina.

---

[1]Josiah Martin (1737-1786), born in Antigua; died in London, England; British army officer, 1757-1769; last royal governor of North Carolina, 1771-1775. Rendered powerless by the provincial congress and committees of safety, and physically threatened by revolutionary elements emboldened by the outcomes of the battles of Lexington and Concord, Martin abandoned the capital at New Bern for Fort Johnston, where he arrived on June 2, 1775. Part of his letter of June 30, 1775, to the Earl of Dartmouth, and quoted, above, by Governor James Martin, indicates both his personal powerlessness and that of royal authority in North Carolina generally: "The situation in which I find myself at present is indeed My Lord most despicable and mortifying to any man of greater feelings than a Stoic. I daily see indignantly, the Sacred Majesty of my Royal Master insulted, the Rights of His Crown denied and violated, His Government set at naught, and trampled upon, his servants of highest dignity reviled, traduced, abused, the Rights of His Subjects destroyed by the most arbitrary usurpations, and the whole Constitution unhinged and prostrate, and I live alas ingloriously only to deplore it." The following July, Martin fled from the fort to a British ship, *Cruizer*, anchored in the Cape Fear River. Allen Johnson, Dumas Malone, and others (eds.), *Dictionary of American Biography* (New York: Charles Scribner's Sons, 20 volumes, 1928; index and updating supplements), XXI, 343; William L. Saunders (ed.), *The Colonial Records of North Carolina* (Raleigh: State of North Carolina, 10 volumes, 1886-1890), X, 47, hereinafter cited as Saunders, *Colonial Records*.

[2]Alexander Martin (1740-1807), native of Hunterdon County, New Jersey; died in Stokes County, North Carolina; was graduated from College of New Jersey (later Princeton University), 1756; served in Second North Carolina Regiment, Continental Army, 1775-1777. Began Guilford County law practice, 1772; member, colonial North Carolina Assembly, 1774-1775; member, 1779-1782, 1785-1788, and Speaker, 1780-1782, North Carolina Senate; acting governor, 1781-1782, and governor, 1782-1784, 1789-1792, of North Carolina; delegate to state convention for ratification of United States Constitution, 1787; member, United States Senate, 1793-1799. *Biographical Directory of the American Congress, 1774-1989* (Washington: United States Government Printing Office, 1989), 1427, hereinafter cited as *Biographical Directory of Congress*.

Seeking an end to the War of the Revolution, British negotiators concluded preliminary peace treaties with their American counterparts in November, 1782, and with the French on January 20, 1783. Alexander Martin referred to the consequent acknowledgment of American independence, as stated in these agreements, in his April 19, 1783, address to the General Assembly: "For this happy and auspicious event, which involves in it a precious inheritance for ages, and all the blessings that can flow from Independent empire, with the most lively, fervent & heart-felt joy I congratulate you, and through you all my fellow Citizens of the State of North Carolina." After thanking the French for their aid in the conflict with Britain and speculating upon the implications that American independence held for other oppressed peoples, he concluded, "nothing now remains but to enjoy the fruits of uninterrupted Constitutional freedom, the more sweet and precious, as the Tree was planted by virtue; raised by the toil and nurtured by the blood of Heroes." The Treaty of Paris, officially ending hostilities and recognizing American independence, was signed September 3, 1783, and ratified by Congress on January 14, 1784. Mark Mayo Boatner III, *Encyclopedia of the American Revolution* (New York: David McKay Company, Inc., 1966), 848-849; Walter Clark (ed.), *The State Records of North Carolina* (Winston and Goldsboro: State of North Carolina, 16 volumes, numbered XI-XXVI, 1896-1906), XVI, 773-774, hereinafter cited as Clark, *State Records*.

³Gold was discovered on John Reed's Cabarrus County farm in 1799; when active mining commenced in the area three years later, the North Carolina gold rush was on. The 1837 opening of the Charlotte branch of the United States Mint and the removal, by 1860, of between $50 million and $65 million in gold from mines scattered across the western two thirds of the state attested to North Carolina's importance as a primary antebellum source of the precious metal. However, the discovery of California's vast and more easily accessible gold deposits in 1848 led to the decline of the mining industry in North Carolina during the 1850s. Brent D. Glass, "'Poor Men with Rude Machinery': The Formative Years of the Gold Hill Mining District, 1842-1853," *North Carolina Historical Review*, LXI (January, 1984), 1-35; Hugh Talmage Lefler and Albert Ray Newsome, *North Carolina: The History of a Southern State* (Chapel Hill: University of North Carolina Press, third edition, 1973), 394-395, hereinafter cited as Lefler and Newsome, *North Carolina*.

⁴Warren Clay Coleman (1849-1904), native of Concord; attended Howard University, 1873-1874. Emancipated slave; Concord merchant and property developer; president, North Carolina Industrial Assn.; cofounder, National Negro Protective Assn., and of the Coleman School, Welford, South Carolina; founder, Coleman Manufacturing Co., Concord, the nation's first black-owned and operated textile mill. Coleman Manufacturing opened ca. 1896 and was sold at auction in June, 1904. William S. Powell (ed.), *Dictionary of North Carolina Biography* (Chapel Hill: University of North Carolina Press, projected multivolume series, 1979—), I, 401-402, hereinafter cited as Powell, *DNCB*.

⁵The North Carolina Mutual and Provident Association was organized in Durham, in 1898, and received its state charter February 28, 1899. Known as the North Carolina Mutual Life Insurance Company after 1919, it is the largest black business in the United States. Walter B. Weare, *Black Business in the New South: A Social History of the North Carolina Mutual Life Insurance Company* (Urbana: University of Illinois Press, 1973), 4n, 29, 31.

⁶Unlike the Boston Tea Party of December 16, 1773, when colonists disguised as Indians protested Parliament's power of taxation by dumping £15,000 worth of East India Company tea into Boston Harbor, the Edenton version was a sedate, but still significant, affair. Taking a cue from patriotic male counterparts who agreed to eschew British cloth and tea, fifty-one women from at least five North Carolina counties gathered at the Edenton home of Mrs. Elizabeth King, vowed never to use the East India Company beverage again, and burned a quantity of dry tea leaves to cement their pact. The Edenton Tea Party, October 25, 1774, is often referred to as the earliest example of women's political activism in the thirteen colonies. Hugh Talmage Lefler (ed.), *North Carolina History Told by Contemporaries* (Chapel Hill: University of North Carolina Press, fourth edition, 1965), 97; Lefler and Newsome, *North Carolina*, 201.

⁷An alleged meeting of the Mecklenburg County Committee of Safety, May 20, 1775, declared the independence of the county's citizens; eleven days later a set of resolves was adopted in Charlotte announcing the termination of royal authority in Mecklenburg. However, the Halifax Resolves, approved by the Fourth Provincial Congress in its April 20, 1776, meeting in Halifax, provided the first official state endorsement of independence from Britain. Lefler and Newsome, *North Carolina*, 205, 218.

⁸For general provisions on education, see Constitution of the State of North Carolina, 1776, Section XLI, reprinted in Clark, *State Records*, XXIII, 984. Although the University of Georgia was the first state university granted a charter, the University of North Caro-

lina at Chapel Hill, in 1795, was the first such institution to admit students. Lefler and Newsome, *North Carolina,* 262.

[9]Elisabeth Osterlein began a school for little Moravian girls in Salem in April, 1772. Its success led to the opening of the Girls' Boarding School—known later as Salem Female Academy and ultimately as Salem Academy and College—in 1805. Johanna Miller Lewis, "A Social and Architectural History of the Girls' Boarding School Building at Salem, North Carolina," *North Carolina Historical Review,* LXVI (April, 1989), 129, 138, 142, 148.

[10]Archibald DeBow Murphey (1777-1832), native of Caswell County; resident of Hillsborough; was graduated from University of North Carolina, 1799. Lawyer in private practice, from 1802; state senator from Orange County, 1812-1818; state superior court judge, 1819-1820; champion of North Carolina's first coherent internal improvements program; first Tar Heel politician to devise and promote a system of state-directed and funded education for all white children, 1817. Samuel A. Ashe and others (eds.), *Biographical History of North Carolina: From Colonial Times to the Present* (Greensboro: Charles L. Van Noppen, 8 volumes, 1906-1917), IV, 340-348, hereinafter cited as Ashe, *Biographical History;* John L. Cheney, Jr. (ed.), *North Carolina Government, 1585-1979: A Narrative and Statistical History* (Raleigh: North Carolina Department of the Secretary of State, second, updated edition, 1981), 361, hereinafter cited as Cheney, *North Carolina Government.*

Charles Brantley Aycock (1859-1912), native of Wayne County; was graduated from University of North Carolina, 1880. Lawyer; cofounder, *Goldsboro Daily Argus,* 1885; U.S. attorney, Eastern District of North Carolina, 1893-1897; North Carolina governor, 1901-1905; Democrat. A proponent of sweeping improvements in public education, Aycock enacted measures resulting in marked increases in teacher salaries, school construction and the growth of the public school system in rural areas, and student enrollment and attendance; a decrease in the rate of illiteracy; improvement of standards at training schools for black teachers; and proposals for three colleges that eventually were established: Appalachian State University (1903), Western Carolina University (1905), and East Carolina University (1907). Beth G. Crabtree, *North Carolina Governors, 1585-1974: Brief Sketches* (Raleigh: Division of Archives and History, Department of Cultural Resources, third printing, revised, 1974), 112-113, hereinafter cited as Crabtree, *North Carolina Governors;* Powell, *DNCB,* I, 73-75.

[11]Governor Terry Sanford recommended, in 1963, and the General Assembly approved, the founding of the first state-supported high school for the performing arts in the United States. The North Carolina School of the Arts opened in 1965. *North Carolina Manual, 1987-1988* (Raleigh: State of North Carolina [issued biennially, 1903 to present]), 975, hereinafter cited as *North Carolina Manual,* with appropriate year.

The North Carolina School of Science and Mathematics was dedicated October 11, 1980. The nations' first tuition-free residential high school for scientifically and mathematically gifted students grew from an idea vigorously pursued by Governor James B. Hunt, Jr. Memory F. Mitchell (ed.), *Addresses and Public Papers of James Baxter Hunt, Jr., Governor of North Carolina, Volume I, 1977-1981* (Raleigh: Division of Archives and History, Department of Cultural Resources, 1982), 832, hereinafter cited as Mitchell, *Addresses of Hunt, 1977-1981;* Jan-Michael Poff and Jeffrey J. Crow (eds.), *Addresses and Public Papers of James Baxter Hunt, Jr., Governor of North Carolina, Volume II, 1981-1985* (Raleigh: Division of Archives and History, Department of Cultural Resources, 1987), xxi, 368, hereinafter cited as Poff and Crow, *Addresses of Hunt, 1981-1985.*

[12]James Baxter Hunt, Jr. (1937-   ), born in Greensboro; resident of Wilson County; B.S., 1959, M.S., 1962, North Carolina State College (later University); J.D., University of North Carolina at Chapel Hill, 1964. Attorney in private practice, 1966-1972, and since 1985; economic adviser to Nepalese government, 1964-1966; North Carolina lieutenant governor, 1973-1977, and governor, 1977-1985; chairman, Democratic National Committee Commission on Presidential Nomination, Education Commission of the States, National Task Force on Education for Economic Growth, National Governors' Assn. Task Force on Technological Innovation, and of other boards and commissions; Democrat. *North Carolina Manual, 1983,* 463.

[13]Dorothy McAulay Martin (1937-   ), born Dorothy Ann McAulay, in Charlotte; permanent residence at Lake Norman, near Mooresville, Iredell County; was educated at Queens College and University of South Carolina; was married to James Grubbs Martin, June 1, 1957. Assistant, Industrial Relations Department, Princeton University, 1957-1960; Davidson kindergarten teacher, 1960-1972; realtor, Mount Vernon Realty, Inc., Alexandria, Virginia, during husband's six terms representing North Carolina's Ninth Congressional District, 1972-1984. As First Lady, Mrs. Martin served as chairwoman, Governor's Commission on Child Victimization, and of Governor's Commission for the Family; member, Governor's Council on Alcohol and Drug Abuse among Children and Youth. Betty F. Dean, personal secretary and administrative assistant to First Lady Dorothy McAulay Martin, to Jan-Michael Poff, September 22, 1988, hereinafter cited as Dean Correspondence.

[14]Mary Julia Grubbs Martin (1912-   ), born in Savannah, Georgia; resident of Lexington, South Carolina; married Arthur Morrison Martin, June 21, 1932; mother of Governor James Grubbs Martin. Dean Correspondence.

Dorothy Louise Gill McAulay (1912-   ), born in Chester, resident of Chapin, South Carolina; was educated at University of South Carolina and Columbia College. Retired elementary school teacher and reading supervisor, Richland County Public Schools, Columbia, South Carolina; married Benson Wood McAulay (1907-1969) in February, 1935; mother of Dorothy McAulay Martin. Dean Correspondence.

[15]Governor and Mrs. Martin had three children: James Grubbs, Jr. (1959-   ), Emily Wood (1962-   ), and Arthur Benson (1972-   ). Dean Correspondence.

[16]Arthur Morrison Martin (1902-1982), born in Savannah, Georgia; died in Columbia, South Carolina; A.B., 1925, D.D., 1965, Davidson College; B.D., Louisville Presbyterian Seminary, 1928; was also educated at New College, Edinburgh, Scotland, and Protestant Faculty, University of Paris, France. Ordained Presbyterian minister, 1928; pastor, Thunderbolt, Eastern Heights, and Bryan Neck Presbyterian churches (Savannah, Georgia, and vicinity), 1928-1938, and of Sion (Winnsboro, South Carolina), Union Memorial, and Mount Olivet Presbyterian churches (Winnsboro vicinity), 1938-1953; executive secretary, 1953-1973, moderator, 1961, Synod of South Carolina, Presbyterian Church in the United States; founding trustee, South Carolina Presbyterian Home for the Elderly; founding chairman, South Carolina's first ecumenical council of churches; cofounder, South Carolina's first biracial ministerial assn.; member, trustee, of numerous boards. Dean Correspondence; see also *Charlotte Observer*, January 1, 1983, and *State* (Columbia, South Carolina), January 12, 1983.

MESSAGES TO THE GENERAL ASSEMBLY

STATE OF THE STATE

FEBRUARY 28, 1985

Mr. President,[1] Mr. Speaker,[2] members of the North Carolina General Assembly, your distinguished guests, and fellow North Carolinians:

Nearly eight weeks ago, on a cold Saturday morning, you honored me with your presence for my inauguration and kindly received my remarks at that time regarding the unity of our state. Today you have honored me, again, with this opportunity to address this joint session on the "State of the State" and to present my first biennial message.

In many respects, our state and its economy have shown strength and resilience. We continue to see improvements in retail sales; in wages, relative to inflation; in productivity; in housing and other construction; in new investment; and in overall optimism. At the same time, there are strategic weaknesses in many sectors. The strength of the U.S. dollar has generated a severe, chronic, trade deficit, as cheaper imports flood American markets and our exports are priced out of foreign markets. This threatens our vital textile and apparel manufacturing in North Carolina, as well as our tobacco stabilization program.

At a time when our economic development resources have been focused on recruiting new industries, especially in high technology and services—an effort I intend to continue—I have added a new commitment to emphasize also the need to sustain existing, traditional industries. I intend to be measured not only by the familiar yardstick of success at recruiting new investment, which is relatively easy and seems now destined to reach new heights, but also by the more difficult standard of how well we help sustain existing businesses. For that reason, I have established a new program under an assistant secretary of commerce for traditional industries[3] to coordinate our efforts to support these businesses that have been historically important to our job market.

It is for this reason, also, that my proposals to phase out the intangibles tax and inventory tax, and to replace any lost revenue for local governments, are so eminently justifiable.[4] At the same time, our pattern of unemployment, which clearly correlates with rural border counties, is a compelling argument for eliminating these virtually unique, self-inflicting handicaps on North Carolina businesses and the jobs they provide. We are indeed fortunate that many profitable businesses can prosper in North Carolina; we are unfortunate that too many marginally profitable businesses cannot. When that investment goes elsewhere or goes under, it is our workers who pay a hidden tax of unemployment.

In the past years, the majority of you favored efforts to repeal these taxes. It was never possible to do so before because the recommended budget proposed to spend all the accelerating revenue growth. With this governor that will not be a problem, because my budget for fiscal 1985-1987 will not spend all the growth in revenues, reserving enough to give tax cuts to our people. The plan I submit to you fulfills my chosen obligation, endorsed by the voters of this state by a larger total vote than any other North Carolina candidate has ever received, to use part of that healthy revenue growth for a tax cut so that we give part of it back to the people.[5]

My plan will include not only these two strategic anti-jobs taxes—beginning on January 1, 1986, six months earlier than my proposal of last October—but also the elimination of the 3 percent state sales tax on food and nonprescription medicine at the point of sale.[6] My plan shows, in the "General Fund" attachment, that this is feasible not only for the 1985-1987 biennium, but also for the following two years until the last stage of relieving the inventory tax is complete beginning January 1, 1988.

Today those three taxes extract $340 million a year, not to mention the corollary cost in lost jobs and buying power. If continued, by 1988 they would rise to almost $500 million. By adopting my schedule for phasing in these cuts, you can save our taxpayers the combined four-year total of almost $1.2 billion in reduced taxes. That will greatly improve their buying power and savings rate. It can be done, as I will show you, without cutting any existing programs, although because of a specific belief and commitment, I do propose to greatly reduce funding for abortions, by eliminating payments for elective abortions.

Sales Tax on Food and Medicine

I propose to eliminate only the 3 percent state tax on food and nonprescription medicines, without affecting the local sales tax on these items. The state 3 percent tax would cease to be collected for all food items purchased in retail grocery stores for home preparation. It would continue to be collected for restaurants, carry outs, and ready-to-eat home deliveries, as well as some vending machines. Of the forty-six states which have a sales tax, twenty-eight exclude food from the sales tax, and two provide some relief from the food tax through a credit. Only sixteen states tax food.

Other groups of citizens, merchants as well as consumers, have a legitimate interest to express as to how this tax relief on life's necessities can best be implemented. Let me make clear that my essential goal is to relieve a tax burden of $178 million a year. How to do it is of secondary importance, but I would not dodge that issue. So, I have told you how I would propose to do it: just stop collecting it, like dozens of other states.

Intangibles Tax

Eliminating this irrevered "nuisance tax" will greatly boost the attractiveness of North Carolina to investors and retirees who have substantial assets. That will remedy a severe problem in that our state is now capital deficient. It will also deprive local governments of $87 million in 1987-1988 which is remitted to them from the North Carolina Department of Revenue, which actually collects the tax and deducts 6.5 percent for overhead.

To offset this lost source of revenue, I propose to distribute a like amount of money to the localities from excess state revenues. Each county would get a fixed share in 1985. The amount would increase each year at the same rate as the state sales tax, adjusted to prevent any penalty arising from the elimination of the food and medicine tax. Historically, the intangibles tax has increased at an average rate of 9.3 percent, while the sales tax has grown at a 9.3 percent rate. Other formulas were considered, but this one has the profound advantages that (a) no county or its municipalities will get less than each receives from its own prior share of the intangibles tax; and (b) the future will be as bright as before because of tying the replacement revenue to the growth of the sales tax.

The intangibles tax would not be reported or paid on assets for the 1986 tax year and thereafter. It would be collected for the last time in April, 1986, upon the 1985 tax return, and local governments would receive their share of that tax as in the past. The replacement would thus begin in mid 1987.

Business Inventory Tax

My proposal is to make a 50 percent rebate to businesses for the tax year beginning January 1, 1986, continuing in 1987, and then going to a 100 percent rebate on January 1, 1988. Those businesses having a tax liability for that or any subsequent year could elect a tax credit instead of a rebate and realize an earlier cash flow advantage. With these tax cuts on schedule, revenues will continue to grow, but to the extent of 23 percent over the next four years instead of a 33 percent increase with no tax relief. Once again, the important thing to keep clearly in mind is that our objective is to cut those taxes.

Base Budget

As the accompanying charts will show, this can be done without reducing any continuation level of funding for any program in the Base Budget. That means that for all programs but one, I propose funding at levels that will continue the present levels of service. In a few instances, identified in the appendix, present levels of service are possible at reduced cost, so those savings are incorporated as "Adjustments to Continuation Budget" (the appendix). For example, a reduced reimbursement allowed for use of one's personal auto- mobile is appropriate in light of reduced fuel costs from the peak years for which current allowances are pegged.

Abortion

I propose to continue limited state funding for abortions only for those cases involving rape or incest, promptly reported, or where two medical opinions agree that continuing a pregnancy to term would endanger the life or physical health of the pregnant woman. Some view such limited exceptions as amounting to self-defense. Other abortions of an elective nature would not be financed by state funds.[7]

Otherwise, my budget allows for continuation of all existing gov- ernment services and programs. During the course of the next year my new administration will be examining existing programs to find areas for savings. We expect that my newly announced Efficiency Study Commission, chaired by Mr. Tom Storrs, will identify many improvements that we can implement administratively.[8] Others will require legislation. You can be sure that I will want to share as many such ideas with you as quickly as I can. This means, then, that my tax-cut proposals will not necessitate any spending cuts in existing programs. To the extent any are proposed later, by you or me, on their own merits, that will certainly free up flexibility for some new spend- ing or reserves, a rainy-day fund or the like.

Expansion, New Programs, and Pay Increases

My tax-cut proposals will still leave room for major improvements. Previously, I had indicated to you in my acceptance of your kind invitation to speak that my specific proposals for the Expansion Budget and compensation improvements would be presented to you just a few legislative days after the biennial address. Indeed, I have completed those recommendations and will be ready to share the itemized specifics with you on Monday.

Accordingly, I have indicated to the Speaker and the president, the Speaker pro tem[9] and the president pro tem,[10] that I am prepared to appear before a joint session of the full Appropriations Committee on next Monday evening at 7 o'clock in the House Appropriations Committee Room. This would be a less formal situation suitable for our purposes in a location that can accommodate the attendance of all members. That will be a historic innovation for presenting to you and the people of North Carolina my specific recommendations for improvements.

Those can be summarized at this time as providing expansions, compensation improvements, and capital outlays totaling $519 million in 1985-1986. For 1986-1987, my proposal provides $760 million in improvements over this current year. For the biennium, instead of spending the entire excess revenue, I propose $1.28 billion for program improvements, along with $328 million in combined tax cuts!

What that means is that, thanks to the same healthy revenue growth forecast which Governor Hunt presented to you in December,[11] there is room to use most of it for improvements in state programs, and use a smaller part of it to cut taxes as I have proposed, and do that without having to cut any existing programs except the ones I have already identified. It can be done, and it should be done.

Now, some have already raised the specter of possible federal budget cuts. If the Congress of the United States were somehow to enact a fiscally responsible federal budget and reduce the growth of federal spending, it would so strengthen our economy that we would have no great trouble financing those lost programs that we would agree on the need to keep as a state responsibility. It is simply not realistic to postpone our overdue tax cuts on the remote, hypothetical possibility that federal spending is going to be cut substantially.

The question before us is not really whether Congress might surprise us and cut spending. The question is whether we are going to take all of that revenue growth over the next four years and spend it all, or whether we are going to give a fourth of it back to our taxpayers.

Many of the so-called federal cuts are, in reality, just smaller increases than some would want. For example, what the National Governors' Association claims to be a 13 percent cut in Medicaid for North Carolina means, in fact, that we get only a 15 percent increase in place of a 28 percent increase!

Keep in mind that there are several significant factors that serve to protect my budget proposals that are not reflected in the numbers I've shown you. For one, there is the efficiency study with a potential saving upwards of $200 million, none of which is yet projected in my budget—nor should it be until we receive the specifics. If that achieves one half of its potential, it will more than offset the federal cuts in state programs. For another, there is the likelihood that my strategic tax cuts will generate more investment, more jobs, more tax base, and therefore a stronger budget balance; nothing of this effect is reflected in my revenue projections, however, for they use the same cautious, static assumptions that predicted little economic growth in 1983-1984 after President Reagan's tax cuts. But if you want a bigger cushion in the budget numbers for a specific rainy-day fund greater than the annual balances I've shown, I will be happy to work with you to identify where cuts might be made in the Base Budget. This proposal reflects my belief that none are needed to accommodate the tax cuts.

Other Legislative Initiatives

I am pleased to use part of this time to put before you a select number of other legislative intiatives for which I respectfully invite your consideration. You will recognize in them some ideas that many of you have championed in the past. My purpose is not to usurp your authorship, but to add my support along with modifications I believe are desirable.

Education

The greatest number of funding improvements in my budget over this current year, as well as the majority of the dollars budgeted for improvements, are for education. That is as it should be. Public schools especially represent the greatest area of need. These improvements will be documented in detail on Monday evening. Let me emphasize for now that I propose salary improvements for certified and noncertified personnel, a two-step reduction in class size for grades seven through nine, remedial summer school for third graders scoring poorly on the competency test, the teacher advancement center at Western Carolina University,[12] and microcomputer laboratories to completely establish your computer literacy initiative.

In addition, I wholeheartedly endorse the start-up of the career ladder pilot program to develop incentives for better pay for better teachers.[13] Almost no one closely associated with this vitally important experiment is advocating that the results of only one year of pilot development should be promptly imposed statewide in 1986-1987. The consensus, with which I agree, is that at least a second year and maybe a third will be needed to work out the organizational and preceptual difficulties of so profound a change. We must not force this prematurely if we want to build confidence both inside as well as outside the classroom. I therefore propose to fund it in 1986-1987 at the level needed for the second year of a two-year pilot program for the intial sixteen school systems. Without prejudging 1987-1988, I have reserved an additional amount for that and the next year in the general reserve, for compensation improvements, the amount needed for full statewide implementation beginning in the fall of 1987. In all, I project over the biennium $116 million in improvements for our public schools, with $75 million of that coming in the first year.

The Year of the Child

One of the most gratifying developments in this session is the emphasis which so many of you have given to the problems of the abused, abducted, and victimized children. Many of you have highlighted this as the year of the child. My wife, Dottie, has promoted family awareness of child safety practices. I hope that you will welcome me to this crusade. Accordingly, I am proclaiming that, for North Carolina, 1985 is the "Year of the Child."[14]

My administration, working with Dottie, Senator Hipps,[15] Representatives Easterling,[16] Keesee-Forrester,[17] and others, has put together an eleven-part package of firm measures for dealing with the tragedy of abducted, lost, disappeared, or otherwise missing children. That will be submitted to you as my Missing Children Act of 1985.[18] A companion bill, the Child Protection Act of 1985, proposes seven important steps to combat the exploitation and sexual or other physical abuse of children. It also provides for videotaped testimony of children to be admitted as evidence in criminal trials, to at least minimize the further traumatization of victimized minors.[19]

Together, these two bills will move North Carolina well into the forefront of states in responding to the modern horror of at least 50,000 American children disappearing every year without a trace and many thousands more brutalized and murdered. You are to be commended for your progress in earlier years. Let's push ourselves to get all the basic protections in place this year.

Let me add that in my budget improvements I have proposed additional support for prevention of pregnancy, prenatal care, and more adoption—and less abortion—as a plan for dealing with the problem of unwanted pregnancy.

DOPE FAST

The rising tide of drug traffic assaults us almost daily as more and more families find themselves infected by this epidemic plague. It is widely recognized today as nothing less than a terrorist invasion of our very homeland, and it is time for us to declare war on those who seek to destroy us by psychochemical guerrilla warfare.

I repeat my 1984 proposal for a Drug Observation, Prevention, and Education (DOPE) program to interdict the international supply routes, catch the dealers and their suppliers, and educate our young people to the horrible danger they face. We must work on both the supply and the demand. We must employ modern surveillance, including our most sophisticated military assets. We must double the number of undercover agents, as Attorney General Thornburg[20] and I separately and jointly have proposed, and we must bring Families and School Together (FAST) in a community effort to rescue those who have begun a chemical dependency and to help others to avoid that first fateful step.

I will share with you briefly four more initiatives before closing this address:

Open Meetings

I am submitting to you legislation to tighten up certain exceptions to the Open Meetings Law and to provide for nullification of official actions taken in unlawfully closed meetings of public bodies. This legislation was inspired by and tracks earlier proposals by Senator Ballenger.[21] It is time for us to assure the people that, with few justifiable exceptions, public business must be done in public. Already we have demonstrated that the Council of State and the Advisory Budget Commission can function very well and meet their responsibilities with only a modest additional burden of time. If anything, members of these important bodies find greater reassurance that their views will be less misrepresented when they can speak for themselves rather than risking having an adversary characterize their participation after a secret session. In a time of bipartisan government, both our rivalries and our collaborations deserve the public confidence and awareness of open meetings.

State Personnel Act Amendment

I have previously announced my commitment to state employees to reduce the number of state jobs that are exempt from the protection of the State Personnel Act.[22] In fact, my senior assistant for personnel policy[23] has begun a review with all my cabinet secretaries of the 1,529 individual exempt positions. By law, those designations can be added or subtracted at the discretion of the governor, provided notice is given. I intend to make substantial reductions in the number of such exempt positions, and deeply appreciate the forbearance of the General Assembly until that review is completed. Most understand and agree with the absolute need for a new governor to make key managerial changes, without which one cannot govern.

I submit to you a related measure, which I expect you will welcome and enact with suitable dispatch. I am proposing that for all other personnel, the initial trial period until their rights are vested in the State Personnel Act be reduced from five years to three years.[24] Democrats and Republicans and independents alike, our new employees can understand a reasonable apprenticeship, but reducing that to three years and keeping it there will vastly reduce unnecessary political pressure. I believe that after a three-year vulnerability, they are entitled to full protection so that they can settle down to do their job with pride. I am also particularly interested in the initiative introduced by Representatives Jones, Warren, Allran, and Anderson to put teeth into legislation to protect state employees from being coerced by their supervisors into making involuntary campaign contributions.[25]

Merit Selection of Judges

It is becoming increasingly clear that many leaders in the legal profession are concerned about our process for selection and retention of judges in our state courts. Chief Justice Joseph Branch[26] and I have proposed a plan which we believe deserves serious consideration. It would modify the plan established in Missouri, which would improve the merit selection and retention of judges. In the weeks to come, we will be calling attention to the advantages of such a system.[27]

Veto Power

I am convinced, also, that it is time for serious consideration of a constitutional amendment to grant the veto power to the governor of North Carolina.[28] Let me just leave three points with you:

1. The constitutional system of checks and balances between executive and legislative branches of government has been so successful in America that every other state has enshrined it, and every one of the original thirteen colonies has long since overcome any residual phobia against royal governors in the two centuries since they were driven from our shores. Is our system so enviable that even one other state is moving to revoke veto authority?

2. As several editorial commentators have observed, there is, after all, a responsibility which we alone in North Carolina do not require of our governor: the obligation to be involved in some degree of leadership on every important issue of the state, and be held accountable for his views. That is a profound point worth considering. You and your predecessors have experienced days of high honor when you have risen to confront a difficult issue, to meet it head on without your governor sharing that public burden, other than whispering words of encouragement from the cool shade while you had to take the heat.

3. Check it out, and you will find that the people of this state are ready for it.

Think about it. Really think about it. Can we not do more of genuine value for North Carolina if we are compelled to share responsibility and accountability for the tough decisions through a system that works in every other state? Is it really so uniquely and exclusively alien to North Carolina?

Distinguished members of the North Carolina General Assembly, you have honored me with your attendance and your attention to these thoughts. In coming months, as you react to and speak of these proposals—and you will—be confident in the assurance that I have prepared and brought them to you in a sincere commitment to work honorably and cooperatively with you. I will do my best to try to fulfill the kind of leadership that the people of North Carolina expect from their governor, and I will always do my best to respect your jurisdiction and prerogatives so as to help you carry out the kind of responsibility that they have come to expect from their legislature. If, together, we can just reaffirm those vows and endeavor to keep them, the people of North Carolina are going to be well served during these coming years.

---

[1]Robert Byrd Jordan III (1932-   ), born in Mt. Gilead; B.S., North Carolina State College (later University), 1954; U.S. Army, 1955-1957, and Reserve, 1957-1962. President, Jordan Lumber and Supply; member, Mt. Gilead Town Board, 1957-1968; chairman, Montgomery County Planning Board, 1964-1974; state senator, 1977-1984; elected lieutenant governor, 1984; unsuccessful candidate for governor of North Carolina, 1988; Democrat. The lieutenant governor serves as Senate president. *News and Observer* (Raleigh), November 9, 1988, hereinafter cited as *News and Observer; North Carolina Manual, 1987-1988,* 567, 570.

[2]Liston Bryan Ramsey (1919-   ), native of Madison County; was educated at Mars Hill College; served in U.S. Army Air Force during World War II. Retired merchant; member, Marshall Board of Aldermen, 1949-1961; member, state House of Representatives, 1961-1963, reelected in 1966 and returned in subsequent elections; Speaker of the House, 1981-1989; Democrat. *News and Observer,* January 12, 1989; *North Carolina Manual, 1987-1988,* 375.

[3]Governor Martin appointed White G. Watkins as assistant secretary of commerce for traditional industries.

[4]Martin described his tax reduction plan in *Governor's Supplemental Budget and Tax Relief Package, 1985-1987* (Raleigh: Office of State Budget and Management, March, 1985). The General Assembly cut taxes in 1985, but not entirely in the manner or to the extent that the governor wished. Martin's proposal would have reduced taxes approximately $400 million by 1987, but legislators approved a cut estimated to reach only $179 million by the end of the biennium. Taxes on business inventories were reduced; the tax on intangible personal property was removed from money on deposit, money on hand, funds on deposit with insurance companies, and from credit balances with investment brokers and securities dealers. "An Act to Provide Broad-Based Tax Relief to North Carolina Citizens," ratified July 9, 1985, mandated these and other changes in the state's tax structure; see *Session Laws of North Carolina, 1985,* c. 656, hereinafter cited as *N.C. Session Laws,* with appropriate year. For an overview of the revisions, see Robert P. Joyce (ed.), *North Carolina Legislation, 1985* ([Chapel Hill]: Institute of Government, University of North Carolina at Chapel Hill, 1985), 3-4, 296-299, hereinafter cited as Joyce, *North Carolina Legislation, 1985.* The General Assembly repealed the tax on manufacturers', retailers', and wholesalers' inventories under the "School Facilities Finance Act of 1987" (short title), ratified July 16, 1987. *N.C. Session Laws, 1987,* I, c. 622.

[5]More North Carolinians went to the polls in November, 1984, than in any previous electoral contest in the state's history. Of the ballots cast for gubernatorial candidates from the two major parties, Martin won election by a difference of 54.4 percent to 45.6 percent over his Democratic rival, Attorney General Rufus L. Edmisten. However, the largest margin of victory in the race for governor since 1960 belongs to James B. Hunt, Jr., who in 1976 defeated Republican candidate David T. Flaherty by winning 64.9 percent of the total vote. *North Carolina Manual, 1987-1988,* 1313-1319.

[6]The General Assembly exempted only food and other items purchased with food stamps from the state retail sales tax. *N.C. Session Laws, 1985,* c. 656, s. 25.

[7]"An Act to Make Appropriations for Current Operations of State Departments, Institutions, and Agencies, and for other Purposes," ratified June 27, 1985, set eligibility criteria for the State Abortion Fund. Women who met certain other requirements were eligible for state-funded abortions if they were minors, victims of rape or incest, or mentally ill; if the pregnancy jeopardized the mother's health; or where "a fetal deformity" existed. *N.C. Session Laws, 1985,* c. 479, s. 93.

[8]Executive Order Number 2, signed February 12, 1985, established the Governor's Efficiency Study Commission. *N.C. Session Laws, 1985*, 1420-1422. The team's 162-page report was published as *Governor's Efficiency Study Commission, State of North Carolina, Findings and Recommendations* ([Raleigh: The Commission], 1985). Press releases bearing on the commission include one untitled, Raleigh, February 12 [1985], describing the body's creation, purpose, and membership; "Governor Announces Kick-off of Governor's Efficiency Study Commission," Raleigh, March 21, 1985; "Governor Martin Initiates Efficiency Study," Raleigh, March 25, 1985; and "Governor Announces Improved State Efficiency Saves Taxpayers Money," April 29, 1985, Governors Papers, James G. Martin, Archives, Division of Archives and History, Raleigh, hereinafter cited as Governors Papers, James G. Martin.

Thomas I. Storrs (1918-   ), born in Nashville, Tennessee; was graduated from University of Virginia, 1940; M.A., Ph.D., Harvard University; U.S. Navy, 1941-1945, 1951-1952. Former economist, vice-president in charge of research, and vice-president in charge of Charlotte branch, Federal Reserve Bank, until 1960; appointed executive vice-president, 1960, president, 1969, and chief executive officer, 1973, NCNB National Bank; became chairman and chief executive officer, NCNB Corp., 1974; president, Federal Advisory Council of the Federal Reserve System, 1975-1976, and of the Assn. of Reserve City Bankers, 1980; chairman, Governor's Efficiency Study Commission. Thomas I. Storrs to Jan-Michael Poff, October 11, 1988.

[9]John Jackson (Jack) Hunt (1922-   ), native of Cleveland County; B.S., Wake Forest College (later University), 1943; D.D.S., Emory University, 1946; U.S. Army, 1943-1948, 1950-1952. Dentist; merchant; farmer; Lattimore city alderman, 1958-1964; member, since 1973, Speaker pro tem, since 1985, of the state House, and chairman, Committee on Rules and Operations of the House, 1981-1982; Democrat. *North Carolina Manual, 1985*, 367, *1987-1988*, 377.

[10]Joseph Julian (Monk) Harrington (1919-   ), native of Bertie County; was educated at Lewiston-Woodville High School; U.S. Army, 1942-1945. Retired businessman; member, 1963-1988, and president pro tem, 1985-1988, state Senate; chairman, Committee on Rules and Operations of the Senate; Democrat. *News and Observer*, January 25, 1987, July 14, 1988; *North Carolina Manual, 1987-1988*, 285.

[11]Governor Hunt's estimate of the rate of expansion of state revenues appears in *Summary of Recommended State Budget, 1985-1987 Biennium* (Raleigh: Office of State Budget and Management, December, 1984), 6-23.

[12]The North Carolina Center for the Advancement of Teaching was established under *N.C. Session Laws, 1985*, c. 479, s. 74.

[13]*N.C. Session Laws, 1985*, c. 479, secs. 39-53, established the Career Development Plan, launching career-growth pilot programs for teachers and administrators in sixteen education districts for the 1985-1987 biennium.

[14]See "Year of the Child, 1985, by the Governor of the State of North Carolina: A Proclamation," February 28, 1985, Governors Papers, James G. Martin.

[15]Charles William Hipps (1943-   ), native of Haywood County; A.B., 1965, J.D., 1968, University of North Carolina at Chapel Hill. Attorney; member, state Senate, 1983-1988; chairman, Senate Constitution Committee; Democrat. *News and Observer*, February 1, 1988; *North Carolina Manual, 1987-1988*, 303.

[16]Ruth M. Easterling (1910-   ), born in Gaffney, South Carolina; resident of Mecklenburg County; was educated at Limestone College and Queens College. Executive assistant to the president, Radiator Specialty Co., 1947-1985; member, Charlotte City Council, 1972-1973; president, N.C. Women's Political Caucus, 1974; elected to state House of Representatives, 1976, and returned in subsequent elections; chairwoman, House Committee on Children and Youth; Democrat. *North Carolina Manual, 1987-1988*, 416.

[17]Margaret Pollard Keesee-Forrester (1945-   ), born in Greensboro; B.A., Guilford College, 1967. Retired classroom teacher; account executive, Keesee and Associates; elected to state House of Representatives, 1972, and returned in subsequent elections; member, Child Protection, Child Video Testimony Legislative Study Commission, 1985-1987; vice-chairwoman, House Committee on Children and Youth; Republican. *North Carolina Manual, 1987-1988*, 454.

[18]On February 7, 1985, Senator Hipps introduced Governor Martin's Missing Child Act of 1985, as it was then called, as S.B. 18, "A Bill to Establish the North Carolina Center for Missing and Exploited Children." It was ratified by the General Assembly on July 15, 1985, as "An Act to Establish the North Carolina Center for Missing Children." *Journal of the Senate of North Carolina, 1985,* 25, 27, 68, 75, 77, 806, 811, hereinafter cited as *N.C. Senate Journal,* with appropriate year; *N.C. Session Laws, 1985,* c. 765; telephone conversation with Barbara Marsh, senior research analyst, Governor's Office of Research, January 25, 1990, hereinafter cited as Marsh conversation.

[19]The Child Protection Act took the form of identical bills introduced in both houses of the General Assembly on April 1, 1985. Thirteen representatives joined Margaret Keesee-Forrester in support of H.B. 332, "A Bill to Be Entitled an Act to Authorize Electronic Transmission or Recording of the Testimony of Children in Cases of Physical or Sexual Abuse of Children." It was referred to the House Committee on Courts and Administration of Justice, where it remained through the end of the session. Meanwhile, Senators Hipps and William W. Redman, Jr. (R-Iredell) brought forth S.B. 165, that, as a committee substitute bill, was incorporated into "An Act Authorizing Studies by the Legislative Research Commission, Making Technical Amendments Thereto, and to Make Other Amendments," ratified July 18, 1985. *Journal of the House of Representatives of North Carolina, 1985,* 140, hereinafter cited as *N.C. House Journal,* with appropriate year; Marsh conversation; *N.C. Senate Journal, 1985,* 145, 685; *N.C. Session Laws, 1985,* c. 790, s. 1(23).

[20]Lacy Herman Thornburg (1929-   ), born in Charlotte; A.B., 1951, J.D., 1954, University of North Carolina at Chapel Hill; U.S. Army, 1947-1948. Attorney; staff member, Congressman David McKee Hall, of Jackson County, 1959-1960; member, state House, 1961-1966; superior court judge, 1967-1983; elected state attorney general, 1984, reelected in 1988; Democrat. *News and Observer,* November 9, 1988; *North Carolina Manual, 1987-1988,* 619.

[21]Thomas Cass Ballenger (1926-   ), native of Hickory; B.A., Amherst College, 1948; U.S. Navy Air Corps, 1944-1945. Founder, board chairman, Plastic Packaging, Inc.; member, 1966-1974, chairman, 1970-1974, Catawba County Board of Commissioners; member, state House, 1975-1976, and Senate, 1977-1986; elected to U.S. House from North Carolina's Tenth Congressional District, 1986, was reelected in 1988. *News and Observer,* November 6, 1986, November 9, 1988; *North Carolina Manual, 1987-1988,* 253.

Ballenger and other senators introduced unsuccessful proposals to strengthen the state Open Meetings Law during the 1985 legislative session; see S.B. 326, "A Bill to Amend the Open Meetings Law" and S.B. 392, "A Bill to Provide the North Carolina Government-in-the-Sunshine Law." H.B. 170, "A Bill to Be Entitled an Act to Provide Additional Remedies for Violations of the Open Meetings Law," cleared the House and was sent to the Senate, while H.B. 725, "A Bill to Be Entitled an Act to Amend the Open Meetings Law," remained in committee through the end of the session. *N.C. House Journal, 1985,* 75, 250, 670, 704, 750; *N.C. Senate Journal, 1985,* 208, 234.

[22]"State Personnel System," *General Statutes of North Carolina,* Chapter 126, hereinafter cited as G.S.

[23]John Higgins was the governor's senior assistant for personnel policy at that time. Charles Duckett, Boards and Commissions, Office of the Governor, to Barbara Marsh, Governor's Office of Research, February 5, 1990; information courtesy of Ms. Marsh.

[24]See "An Act to Amend the State Personnel Act," ratified July 5, 1985. *N.C. Session Laws, 1985,* c. 617, secs. 3, 4.

[25]"An Act to Further Define the Appropriate Political Activity of State Employees" was ratified June 26, 1985, and became effective October 1, 1985. *N.C. Session Laws, 1985,* c. 469. It was introduced as H.B. 94 on February 20, 1985, and sponsored by fifty-six legislators, four of whom the governor mentioned above; see *N.C. House Journal, 1985,* 51.

Walter Beaman Jones, Jr. (1943-   ), native of Pitt County; A.B., Atlantic Christian College, 1967. Business consultant; elected to state House of Representatives, 1982, and returned in subsequent elections; chairman, Committee on Commissions and Schools for the Blind and Deaf; Democrat. *North Carolina Manual, 1987-1988,* 452.

Edward Nelson Warren (1926-   ), native of Pitt County; A.B., Atlantic Christian College, 1951; M.A., East Carolina College (later University), 1953; U.S. Air Force, 1945-1948. Farmer; investor; chairman, Pitt County Board of Commissioners, 1973-1979; elected to state House of Representatives, 1980, and returned in subsequent elections; chairman, House Appropriations Base Budget-Education Committee; Democrat. *North Carolina Manual, 1985*, 477, *1987-1988*, 491.

Austin Murphy Allran (1951-   ), born in Hickory; B.A., Duke University, 1974; J.D., Southern Methodist University, 1978. Attorney; legislative assistant to Governor James E. Holshouser, Jr., 1974; member, state House of Representatives, 1981-1986; appointed by Governor Martin to complete unexpired N.C. Senate term of Thomas Cass Ballenger, December 30, 1986; Republican. *North Carolina Manual, 1987-1988*, 290.

Gerald L. Anderson, (1939-   ), native of Craven County; was graduated from New Bern High School, 1958; was also educated at Deaver Realty Institute, 1974. Businessman; Craven County commissioner, 1978-1980; elected to state House of Representatives, 1980, and returned in subsequent elections; chairman, House Appropriations Base Budget Committee on Justice and Public Safety; Democrat. *North Carolina Manual, 1987-1988*, 382.

[26]Joseph Branch (1915-   ), native of Halifax County; LL.B., Wake Forest College (later University), 1938; honorary degrees; U.S. Army, 1943-1945. Attorney in private practice, 1938-1966; member, state House of Representatives, 1947-1953; legislative counsel to Governors Luther H. Hodges, 1957, and Daniel K. Moore, 1965; associate justice, 1966-1979, and chief justice, 1979-1986, North Carolina Supreme Court; Democrat. *News and Observer*, July 31, 1986; "Next Chief Justice: All Joe Branch Aspired to Be Was Just a Small Town Lawyer," *We the People of North Carolina*, XXXVII (July, 1979), 16; *North Carolina Manual, 1985*, 831.

[27]Missouri's practice of filling judicial vacancies was widely copied. The plan called for the chief executive to make appointments to the bench from a list of nominees selected for each vacancy by a judicial nominating committee. When the judge's term concluded, the electorate determined whether or not he or she should be retained. *News and Observer*, January 13, February 27, 1985.

The General Assembly enacted no judicial merit selection system during Martin's first administration. Court-related legislative proposals that were rejected during the 1985 session included S.B. 676, "A Bill to Amend the Constitution of North Carolina to Provide for Nonpartisan Selection of Justices and Judges of the General Court of Justice," and S.B. 677, "A Bill to Create a Judicial Nominating Commission and to Implement the Nonpartisan Plan for the Selection of Judges as Required by Article IV, Section 16, of the North Carolina Constitution"; S.B. 551, "A Bill to Amend Section 11, Article IV of the North Carolina Constitution to Abolish the Practice of Rotation of Superior Court Judges," and H.B. 1015, similarly titled; S.B. 44, "A Bill to Require Regular Superior Court Judges to Be Both Nominated and Elected in Their Resident Judicial Districts," H.B. 350, "A Bill to Be Entitled an Act to Amend the Constitution of North Carolina to Provide for Four-Year Terms for Members of the General Assembly, and to Make Conforming Changes to Other Statutes and to Other Sections of the Constitution Concerning Elections for Other Officers and Filling Vacancies," and H.B. 1199, "A Bill to Be Entitled an Act to Amend the Constitution to Allow Regular Superior Court Judges to Be Elected in Their Judicial Division, and to Implement That Amendment"; and H.B. 1197, "A Bill to Be Entitled an Act to Allow District Court Vacancies to Be Filled by Members of Any Party." *N.C. House Journal, 1985*, 150, 391, 431, 473, 569, 724, 740; *N.C. Senate Journal, 1985*, 44, 51, 328, 357; *News and Observer*, July 3, 1985.

[28]The General Assembly did not approve legislation bearing on the veto during 1985. S.B. 53, "A Bill to Grant Veto Power to the Governor," sponsored by Senator Wendell H. Sawyer, a Republican, received its first reading before the upper house on February 22, 1985, and was assigned to the Judiciary I Committee for study; on March 28, the chairman, Senator Henson P. Barnes, a Democrat, announced that the committee would not support the measure. Another Republican, Laurence A. Cobb, unsuccessfully attempted to resurrect the bill on March 29 and place it before the full Senate for immediate consideration. *N.C. Senate Journal, 1985*, 46, 132, 136.

With the failure of S.B. 53 in the Senate, veto proponents shifted their focus to the House. Seventeen Republican representatives sponsored H.B. 375, "A Bill to Be Entitled an Act to Give the People of North Carolina the Right to Vote on a Constitutional Amendment Providing for a Gubernatorial Veto," introduced on April 5, 1985. The Democrat-controlled Committee on Constitutional Amendments rejected the bill; and a minority report supporting the measure, signed by GOP committee members Walter H. Windley III, Raymond A. Warren, Larry T. Justus, and James M. Craven, was defeated in a House vote on April 24. *N.C. House Journal, 1985*, 164, 269-170.

STATE OF THE STATE

FEBRUARY 16, 1987

Mr. Speaker, Lieutenant Governor Jordan, members of the 137th North Carolina General Assembly, distinguished guests, ladies and gentlemen:

I am here this evening at your kind invitation—and in obedience to our state constitution, which for 211 years has manifested the sovereignty of our state in a proud and virtuous people. It is to you their representatives, directly, and to them, indirectly, that I am pleased to present my biennial budget message and report on the "State of the State," which I may supplement from time to time.[1]

Economy of the State

Overall, our economy has had a relatively strong year. The total number of jobs broke above 3 million for the first time in December, 1985, and throughout 1986 averaged above that 3 million mark. Correspondingly, the rate of unemployment, which had dropped from 7 percent in 1984 to 5 percent in 1985, averaging 5.4 percent for the year 1985, has held to that level, averaging 5.3 percent throughout 1986 and is currently below 5 percent. Certainly, there's still room for improvement, but it's worth noting that only a couple of states ranked better throughout this past biennium—none in the Southeast.

Our so-called gross state product, consequently, has steadily outpaced the gross national product. One of the most reassuring reports was the resurgence of manufacturing jobs, especially among textiles and apparel, which regained more than 6,000 jobs in a dramatic reversal from the previous decade's trend. Average personal income showed only modest improvement, clearly an area which will command greater attention in the next few years.

Our greatest concern regarding the economy is the increasing difficulty experienced [in] recruiting new business investment to North Carolina. The competition from other states is tougher and more aggressive than before, and there are fewer known prospects in the field to satisfy all this competition. So, our pipeline is not as full as in years past. Surely, this is no time for complacency or negativism.

Blueprint[2]

That is why our Commerce Department has laid out a bold plan to set fresh targets of opportunity for our recruiting efforts. With all our high-tech successes, we have not scratched the surface of the aerospace and defense-related industries. They are eager to expand our way.

My administration discovered early on that with all our efforts to recruit new industry to North Carolina, there previously wasn't much of an effort, or have much of a program [sic], for the hundred thousand businesses already here. Our new office for traditional industries is a pioneering effort that we are sharing with other states.

North Carolina's traditional industries have gotten—indeed, have sought—very little of the business for supplying the needs of America's armed forces. Surely, we can improve on this. We are making progress attracting manufacturers of automotive components, and many other targets appear attractive for us. We have had some spectacular successes bringing foreign companies to invest here, and we can do much more.

With the U.S. dollar finding a truer exchange rate with foreign currencies, the time is ripe. The next two years should also be a prime time for us to become more aggressive about exporting North Carolina's many quality products into their markets, for a welcome change. That's why we propose a bolder commitment of state offices overseas to help sell North Carolina. That's why I proposed new summer institutes for foreign languages: to help North Carolina compete in world markets. It just makes good sense.

Our regional offices in state will also be strengthened, and our State Library's new telecommunications network will give every county immediate access to vital business information. Far exceeding any other state, this will share a powerful weapon for recruiting and helping technology-dependent business in rural areas far removed from resource centers.

We will strengthen our North Carolina Film Office to assist movie makers in taking advantage of the attitudes and skills of our workers;

our climate; our natural lighting so admired by Steven Spielberg for *The Color Purple*.[3] Currently, we have three production studios with fifteen sound stages. That far exceeds what any other state has to offer, with the giant exception of California, of course, which explains why we're already being called the "Hollywood of the East." Of the top ten films at the box office last month, three were "Made in North Carolina."[4]

There is so much we can do to help build a brighter future for North Carolina's small businesses. They have two major problems. One is the vast and complicated array of permits that are required to do business—too much red tape. Another is access to adequate capital.

Here's what we should do with the red tape: give them a break, with a one-stop permit office that will develop a complete checklist with simplified directions of all the permits and licenses that are needed from all levels of government.[5] Time is money in business, and anything we can do to save time for a business saves money. Now that makes good sense, doesn't it?

We are establishing such an office in a bipartisan effort to get businesses the information they need quickly, so they can accomplish what they want to do by knowing what is expected of them for compliance with our laws and regulations. We will offer the same special help to counties to shorten the delays they have encountered with landfill permits. I am establishing an inter-agency task force to give them quicker, better coordinated, on-site decision making.[6]

Your own task force on jobs and economic growth has identified a number of areas needing legislation to give us the weapons to win new victories in economic development, especially with existing businesses and especially in rural areas.[7] I ask you to join with me in a coordinated assault from both our branches of government. Some improvements we can do internally, and some will need your legislative approval. In many ways, the two plans are complementary. That's good.

Your proposal for a rural economic development corporation deserves support as an excellent mechanism for giving long-term direction and stimulation for investment in those small cities that can serve as growth centers in rural areas.[8] It avoids setting up an uncoordinated rival that might undermine the main strength of our Commerce Department and confuse prospective investors as to who negotiates for North Carolina.

Even in the single, solitary area where we have found some disagreement, I believe we can agree on the goal and work out our differences. It is not disputed that, while many venture capital funds are actively investing in homegrown businesses, there is considerable need for early seed money. The sticking point has to do with the means of solving this need.

My concern is with the notion of creating a state-funded authority for doling out the money and for choosing the winners who would receive the capital boost. Such a mechanism would always be suspected of political favoritism and would be unable to function without a typical governmental overlay of formulas and extraneous, unbusinesslike factors. It would probably find itself unable to replenish its capital from profits, relying instead on never-ending doses of tax dollars. There is a better way: it's called free enterprise.

Drawing on the expertise of North Carolina investment specialists, we have developed no less than six new financing mechanisms to help increase the availability of both capital and credit for new businesses and expansions, with special emphasis on small business ventures and with special attention to rural North Carolina.[9] I invite you to work with me to make these innovative ideas into a productive reality:

1. To increase the availability of fixed-rate, long-term financing for small business;

2. A secondary market for small business loans under various Small Business Administration loan guarantees;

3. To make industrial revenue bonds more widely accessible to small businesses, especially in rural counties that previously had been left out;[10]

4. To authorize, but not require, state trust funds to be able to invest in private, investment-quality venture capital funds;[11]

5. To create a private, early venture capital fund for seed capital in North Carolina which might include tax credits or similar incentives for investors;[12]

6. A statewide "504" certified development corporation to act as loan originator and facilitator in those 48 counties that now lack those services.[13]

Farming

No sector of our economy has had to endure a heavier burden longer than our small family farms. The number of farms has been steadily declining for over twenty years, so it is not a recent phenomenon as some have tried to portray it for political purposes. Excessive credit accumulated in the seventies is now crushing our farmers, and pressure to undermine the tobacco stabilization program has threatened the commodity that once was our number-one source of farm income.

This has been a major focus of attention for me and my administration. Working with Agriculture Commissioner Graham,[14] I have organized a task force of financial institutions to assist farmers in restructuring their credit along more affordable terms. Another series of meetings at the Executive Mansion brought together farm organizations, cigarette manufacturers, bankers, and most of our Congressional delegation. Together we forged an agreement that produced the largest business deal in the history of North Carolina: to buy out the surplus of stockpiled tobacco and eliminate the oppressive assessment that faced our farmers.[15]

Together, during the long drought, we mobilized the resources of our state, public and private, for an orderly and fair distribution of donated hay that had come to us in a magnificent, outpouring example of neighbors helping neighbors.[16]

By my order, job training programs that had been designed for dislocated factory workers were extended for the first time to dislocated farm workers, as well as to our Vietnam veterans.

To strengthen the markets for our farm commodities, I am asking you now to establish three innovative agricultural parks, one in our northeastern area, one in our southeastern counties, and a third at the Western Farmers' Market in Asheville. In addition to the more conventional tailgate retail operations, modern food processing services would be available to improve the marketability of our field crops.

I have commissioned a Task Force on Rural Economic Growth, headed by former lieutenant governor Jimmy Green,[17] to work closely with your rural economic development corporation to develop these and other ideas and to renew the agricultural vitality of rural North Carolina.

Transportation

Crucial to our *Blueprint for Economic Development* is transportation. Thanks to your adoption of my proposal for major strengthening of our highway construction program, as amended, our major funding commitment is now in place. As soon as the United States Congress gets its Highway Act together we can begin to schedule long-awaited improvements in every highway district.[18]

More Roads to the Future

There are a couple of missing pieces that will be submitted for your approval. North Carolina can save time and a great deal of money with a permanent state construction fund, avoiding many of the costly federal requirements for federally matched projects. At the same time, local governments need greater authority to identify, protect, and/or acquire costly rights-of-way so that developers can be kept from encroaching with buildings that we later would have to condemn and purchase at great cost. These two bits of unfinished business would soon be able to save us $50 to $60 million a year, which is already anticipated in our current Transportation Improvement plan. The Senate passed both measures last year, and I ask you to join with me to complete our roads to the future. It means a lot of dollars, and it makes a lot of sense.

Fair Roads Law

For years our mountain counties have suffered an unfair distribution of secondary road construction. Giving each county the same percentage of secondary road money as its percentage of total unpaved miles shortchanges those in the mountains where road-building costs are naturally much higher. They don't get much mileage out of that. I will ask you to join with me to adopt a fairer formula, a fair roads law, with a bonus provision so that no county will receive less than it gets this year.

Public Schools

Now let's face up to our weakest record as a state: public schools. This is the largest and most important responsibility of state and local governments, and hardly any measurement has earned us satisfaction or pride. Our students' performance on standardized tests is falling behind; the dropout rate is embarrassing and unacceptable; we have had great difficulty attracting enough talented teachers to our classrooms and keeping them there. On this subject, without a doubt, North Carolina needs improvement.

Our state must pull together to strengthen our support for public schools. Responsibility for this situation falls not on our schools, but on all of us, together; and that means that we, the people, must join together to revitalize North Carolina's schools. The Southern Growth Policies Board will report to you tomorrow on its efforts to invigorate schools in all southern states, in the belief we can make our schools competitive with any in America.

We have made a start. In 1984 and 1985 you made a monumental commitment to strengthening our basic state funding of local schools through the first two years of the Basic Education plan.[19] Together, we rallied behind the sixteen pilot programs for the career ladder concept to develop, for the first time, a fair and effective system for evaluating and rewarding good teaching, to provide a way to give promotions to good teachers without their having to leave the classroom—to offer better pay for better teachers.

The budget which I am submitting to you clearly spells out a renewed commitment to public schools as the highest priority for our available resources. For the twenty-four years before my administration, spanning five "education governors," the percentage of the General Fund budgeted for public schools declined every year except two, 1966 and 1984. Even with my tax-cut proposals, school spending was increased even as a percentage of the General Fund, and if you will join with me to approve my budget for the next biennium, we will improve it five years, back to back.

It is fitting for you to show pleasure that my budget supports some of your best ideas—and why not? The same bipartisan spirit should earn your support for the bold initiatives in my budget.

Basic Education Plan

It begins with a giant step forward to add another $375 million to the Basic Education Program over the biennium. That will fully fund your goals for the fourth year of this eight-year plan for boosting state financing of public schools by one third. Of vital importance, my proposal will keep us moving steadily forward to reduce classroom size, by hiring the extra teachers needed to lower the critical pupil-teacher ratio. It avoids the suggestion of skipping even one year, for that would break the stride of our momentum and would miss the full advantage of this year's college graduating talent.

You will recall my earlier questions related only to the order of priorities within the Basic Education plan. Its chief virtues have been (1) that it increase, in a substantial way, our state funding of public schools statewide, and (2) its strong allocation of resources to remedy the conditions that contribute to so high a dropout rate. Yet, even if it were an ideal plan for the average condition of our schools, that would not make it ideal for the typical school, which is not average at all.

Local Control

Some will need to allocate even more of these resources to counter-ing "dropitis," while others may have better-than-average dropout rates and might need to allocate more resources for college prepara-tory work, if that fits their situation better. For such reasons, I propose that you join with me to provide a greater degree of local flexibility. Local school boards need to be able to initiate a variance from the standard program, subject to the approval of the State Board of Edu-cation. In this way a major advantage will be won for all our schools by strengthening their local control. It is well established that more effective schools result from a greater degree of local control and local determination of priorities. It just makes sense!

Career Ladder

At the same time, I am proposing that we strengthen our commit-ment to the Career Development program, which holds the brightest promise for heightened excellence in education by raising the stature and appeal of classroom teaching as a profession and career. The first year of the experimental pilot project did not meet all the goals we had set, but it demonstrated clearly a high degree of success in help-ing our teachers improve their skills and their effectiveness. Some schools had difficulty with the evaluation methods, particularly if they had little prior experience, but it appears that will be overcome with practice and familiarity, just as with any other academic undertaking.

I am proposing that we continue with the third and fourth year of the pilot projects in the sixteen school systems that are now in their second year. They have prepared their participating teachers for Career Level I, and a high percentage of them qualified, as expected. This year, these sixteen systems are moving forward to prepare for the next promotions to Career Level II, while at the same time making some necessary adjustments in Career I, based on last year's findings.

To validate the revised first-year step of preparing for Career Level I, I propose that we add an additional twelve school systems to initiate the revised procedures from a fresh start. They will have the benefit of the research from the first sixteen and will give us a much truer example of the adaptation of new schools to the revised pro-gram under more normal—that is, nonexperimental—conditions. They will bring a larger, more representative sample of new teachers starting afresh with the revised first year than would be likely among the new candidates available in the original sixteen pilot systems. Certainly they should be allowed more flexibility and a lot less paperwork!

I am confident that we will have plenty of new school systems eager to become an early part of this bold, new concept offering promotions to outstanding teachers. Indeed, I am concerned that if we prolong the experimental steps without moving forward with the rest of North Carolina, great stress and pressures will build among those schools left behind and unable to offer the enhanced pay and promotions available in the pilot systems. Already, superintendents have told me that their nonpilot schools risk losing their best teachers to neighboring pilot systems where they can qualify for promotions and better pay. For that reason, and because I have full faith and confidence in the ability of our schools and teachers to generate the full potential of this program, I am proposing to begin in the second year of the biennium to move all the remaining 113 school systems into the first year of preparing their participating teachers to qualify for Career Level I. That would be the best way to provide another 5 percent better pay for the 95 percent or so who would qualify for this promotion, and it would surely break away from the status quo!

I propose that we go only just that far, withholding until the next budget cycle the decision whether to continue on to levels II and III. The first sixteen pilots will have reached Career Level III, with their highest-qualified teachers drawing salaries at the highest level, in 1988-1989. The twelve additional pilot systems will have completed the demonstration of their adaptation of the first year of preparation for Level I, giving us three full years of experience with that crucial first year of preparation, and I say let's move forward. Failure to do so will only risk bogging down what ought to be the most dynamic improvement in our public schools since Governor Charles Brantley Aycock welded the state to public schools at the turn of the century.

Of course, there will be some who would be timid and wait, and wait, and wait. There are also some who have never wanted this career promotion concept to work, or even to be attempted, and who would argue for delay after delay until we give up in despair. I say, let's go forward; let's have the courage of our convictions and the total commitment to this major and well-conceived reform to strengthen the most strategic educational resource for which we have responsibility, our classroom teachers. Of all the good ideas that have been advanced for better schools, none has had the tremendous prospect that this career ladder has for profoundly improving the output performance of our schools. Nothing will or can do more to raise the scholastic achievement of our elementary and secondary students than this commitment to reinvigorate the profession of classroom teacher.

Adoption of my budget will dramatically lock North Carolina into the most important boost in public support of public schools in eighty years. That will be our most lasting legacy. Even in a year of mild revenue growth, we will have shown that public schools are clearly our first priority. I call on you to join with me to make it so.

Building Schools

There is another monumental responsibility facing us and our schools. We are more than $1 billion behind in school buildings all across North Carolina. For many years, we have depended upon county governments, with their traditionally limited tax base, to build the schools in our state. Some have done well, with modern facilities to which they can point with pride. Many other counties, however, have lacked the resources to meet their construction needs.

I ask you to join with me to authorize and promote a school bond issue on the order of $1.5 billion, the amount to be based on a current survey of county commissioners and their school boards. Proceeds from the sale of these bonds would be available to loan to counties at the state's most favorable interest rate to share with them the advantage of our triple-A bond rating. Counties would pay [the money] back to the state over a twenty-year period, using the proceeds from their current sales tax already allocated to public schools. In this way, the half-cent sales tax already earmarked for schools or for school debt service could finance as much as $1.5 billion.[20]

This plan has strong, widespread support, including the state associations of school boards and of county commissioners, and notably the state treasurer[21] and superintendent,[22] both of whom made great contributions to this bold and innovative proposal. The key to it is the decision you made in recent years to allocate the proceeds from the local option sales tax on a per-capita basis, thus providing each county the same revenue base per pupil. You should take credit for that feature.

It's your call whether to require a separate, local referendum, or you may want to authorize a local vote simultaneously with the statewide issue. State Treasurer Boyles and I believe it's not required by the constitution and therefore don't propose it. The main thing is not to let that consideration be an excuse for the status quo.

This plan will get the job done, and it is affordable. It preserves the historic responsibility of counties for school buildings, yet it assists them in keeping this responsibility affordable. It means that we will be able to build now the schools that we need now, including those required for the expanded programs under the Basic Education plan. It will be fiscally sound because we will not risk paying the next future round of inflation, and won't have to wait so long to upgrade our communities, and can pay for the new schools as we go and use them.

It just makes such good sense, that I invite you and urge you, every one, to join with me to present to the people for their approval this timely plan to modernize our school buildings at the same time that we modernize the programs and strengthen the teaching that will be offered in them. If we are going to upgrade our educational system to prepare North Carolina for its future, then let us not undercut ourselves. Let us not defeat our own best efforts. If you will join with me, together we can assure our people of the best system of public education in America and ensure that every community will have the school facilities to match those programs and to be worthy of those teachers. Then, every county will point with pride.

Governance

This session is also the critical window of opportunity for making the state superintendent appointive. The reason for doing this is to improve the line of responsibility and accountability. For that reason, if the appointive power is to be given to the State Board of Education, I urge you not to dilute that accountability by eroding the responsibility of the governor to appoint the board.[23]

Four Pillars

Here, then, is my proposal for building four strong pillars under education. With your help, it can be done.[24]

Prisons

Last year I recommended to you a major expansion of our prison capacity, coupled with a variety of alternative punishments, such as intensively supervised probation and parole, to reduce the prison population.[25] I wish to commend the legislative leadership for offering to work together with me in a bipartisan front to meet this emergency.

We have encountered some typical governmental delays, just as in the previous administration, and yet our Correction Department has developed a number of steps that can help to expedite the facilities we need: metal or concrete buildings that are quicker and cheaper to build are suitable in many applications, and for conventional construction we propose to make repetitious use of a new design that has helped us move swiftly and under budget in meeting the South Piedmont consent decree.[26] We are now ready to move forward on those and have recruited an experienced and professional contractor to "ride herd" on these projects so that we will have the benefit of his business skills in driving construction projects to prompt completion.

Capital Improvements

North Carolina must meet other responsibilities. I am proposing major improvements for our two seaports,[27] construction of a new judicial center and a revenue building, additional improvements at our college campuses, and $120 million in state and federal money for a new fund to provide low-interest loans to local governments for water, sewer, and solid waste facilities.[28] Capital improvements of $415 million can be financed primarily through appropriations and partly—$77.5 million of it—through the two-thirds bond authority.[29]

Environment

Protection of our fragile water resources is among the most vital challenges facing us. Consequently, I am asking for more environmental specialists to handle the growing backlog of waste-water discharge permits; to monitor and evaluate groundwater quality; to reclassify coastal waters that are unsuited for shellfishing; and to locate leaking underground storage tanks to be cleaned up. I am also requesting additional funding to improve our state parks.

Pay Increase

Even in a tight budget year, we must not neglect to make some progress in improving pay for state employees. Based on January revenue statements, I have shown that money is available, after major program improvements, to provide a 4.5 percent increase in com-

pensation for school and state employees. Part of this should be
devoted to across-the-board scale increases, to offset inflation, and
part should be used for a round of performance increments. Later on,
if revised revenue estimates permit, you may find that an additional
increment could be made available—in which case you will find that I
would welcome you to outbid me, again.[30] Our Office of State Personnel has prepared a new pay plan for your consideration which will
greatly improve the equity and the job security of our state workers.

Veto

The constitutional amendment to provide for the veto was quickly
buried in the last session, despite the strong popular support for this
historic measure. This issue deserves full debate and should be submitted to a referendum.[31] North Carolina should not continue to be
the only state in America where the people have never been allowed
to vote on whether to give their governor the veto. How's that for the
status quo?

Nonpartisan Judicial Election

There is also strong sentiment and logic favoring nonpartisan election of judges. Let me suggest a useful distinction between trial
judges and appellate judges that might help move this issue forward.
Trial judges, those before whom you or I might stand in the courtroom, should be elected in their own districts, in a nonpartisan election, for both district court and superior court judges. The time is ripe
to act on that and all but the most partisan among us should see the
virtue of that reform.

For the supreme court and court of appeals, I propose that you
authorize the lieutenant governor and the Speaker of the House of
Representatives to join with me in appointing a bipartisan blue-
ribbon committee of lawyers and nonlawyers to devise a plan for
nonpartisan election and meritorious selection.[32] Judges on these
appellate courts are not as well known in the local communities, and
voters have so little to go on in the voting booth. This approach
makes sense and might help break the logjam.

Currently, partisan judicial elections are required by statute, but in
truth hardly anyone wants them to be partisan. The people of North
Carolina are much more interested, I believe, in having qualified,
competent judges sitting on the bench no matter what their political

affiliation. There's a time to study and a time to act. This way, we could study one level while we act on the other before the federal courts decide it for us.

Abortions

In 1985 you approved some restrictions on state funding of elective abortions. Again, I will recommend that we discontinue paying for abortions where the pregnancy is not associated with a felony or a risk of death or serious physical injury to the mother.[33]

Workfare

I am proposing additional increases in the "Workfare" program which assists families in breaking out of the cycle of poverty.[34]

Legislative Reforms

Your leaders are to be commended for proposing reforms in the legislative process. In a spirit of harmony I will simply say that anything you can do to open up the process—so that the public, the press, even the loyal opposition can examine legislation, before it is voted on—will strike a blow for good government.

Unifying Themes

There are other such topics on which there may be dissension and which ultimately will yield to majority wisdom. I will not parade them all out this evening. It has been my intention here mainly to emphasize those subjects on which there is a great potential for bipartisan agreement. Those unifying themes need our strong support and will take us further along on our journey toward the vision we share for North Carolina. North Carolina's future depends upon us and upon our ability to overcome our differences and unite our efforts to build the brightest future for our people.

Year of the Reader

Each year I have directed my administration to devote special emphasis to one unifying theme for the year. The "Year of the Child" in 1985 built upon a number of children's issues, including the Missing Children's Center, culminating in the hearings and report of the

Governor's Commission on Child Victimization, chaired by our First Lady, and the creation of the North Carolina Fund for Children and Families.[35] The "Year of the Family," 1986, keyed many departmental programs to ways to strengthen the family as a self-supportive unit.[36] Special attention was directed at innovations for breaking the cycle of poverty.

What special direction should we set for 1987? I propose that together we make this the "Year of the Reader" and pledge our special emphasis to the rescue of so many of our citizens from the anemia of functional illiteracy.[37] Our community colleges have pioneered a strong remedial reading program offered in adult basic education, yet it reaches no more than 6 percent of the potential population.

The State Library is working with the Department of Correction to develop a remedial reading program for women inmates, especially those with children. Called Motheread, it will allow them to visit with and read to their children on weekends outside the prison, and we believe this will present a powerful motivation for learning to read.[38]

At the same time, it is troubling that our schools are turning out a fresh crop of dropouts every year to replenish the supply of illiterates faster than we can save them. Many of our school systems have made a special effort to reduce their dropout rates—some with notable success, such as Weldon, Pender, Currituck, Hertford, Pamlico, Mooresville, and Granville. Their results need to be emulated all across North Carolina.

Already, sixty literacy councils have been organized locally. Burlington Mills has a reading program for employees and their children. Charlotte businesses helped pioneer the exciting Cities in Schools program which other business leaders are planning to extend to Rocky Mount and two or three other cities.

One key to this will be how well we involve the strength of the people, by calling on them for help as tutors, in that same volunteer spirit that has made North Carolina great.

To pull this all together in a coordinated assault on illiteracy, I will ask the heads of these and other pertinent agencies and groups to serve on a new North Carolina literacy council, and I have asked former UNC president Bill Friday to serve as its first chairman.[39] We must mount a sustained, nonpartisan effort if we are to succeed.

Preparation for our challenging and bright future depends upon a population of workers who are trained and trainable; who can read; who can read to learn because they have learned to read. What a tremendous challenge for North Carolina! Surely you remember the national thrill that responded to President Kennedy's exciting call to greatness when he said we are going to the moon![40] It was an enormously difficult task, but America did it. A courageous few Americans actually made it—"One giant step" for precious few of us.[41]

Would it not be a reachable and exciting goal for us to say, we are going to read! Could we make that simple challenge into a mighty and dedicated undertaking, but one which would seek to take all of our people along on the mission to become readers?

If we fail, North Carolina will suffer more generations of inadequately prepared workers, and yet, if we succeed, it would truly be one giant step for a million of us. It is one of the most worthy objectives we could set for our state. I ask you to join with me to direct our minds and energies to solving this problem. Together, we can chart our course and boldly proclaim on behalf of everyone in this one united state: We are going to read, all of us! We are going to learn to read!

Thank you, and generations yet to come will thank you.

North Carolina Is My Home

In one of the most remarkable collaborative contributions to our contemporary culture, two brilliant North Carolina native sons, Charles Kuralt and Loonis McGlohon, have composed a splendid musical tribute entitled, *North Carolina Is My Home*.[42] In its lyrics and its melodies and rhythms it captures the heritage and natural splendor of this magnificent land of ours, its waters, its mountains, its cities and towns, and most of all, its people.

With a reverence for North Carolina, they have distilled the essence of a state "where the weak grow strong and the strong grow great."[43] They have used their considerable talents so effectively to remind us of who we are and where we have come from. Along with a humorous counterpoint about how we named some of our places,[44] they have reminded us, too, of how we named our noblest aspirations with a pledge to integrity in our state's motto, *Esse quam videri*, "To be rather than to seem."

North Carolina is our home. We are truly blessed with all that North Carolina has to offer. A large part of that is a God-given natural resource, ours to enjoy and protect. A good part of it can be said to be a God-given human resource. That, too, is ours to enjoy, but also ours to build for future generations. We must make the most of our time and opportunities here. We must join together as representatives of this one united state to build that home.

There will always be issues and causes that divide us. There will be rivalries and the usual kinds of suspicions that one team has for another. There is, surely then, a time for partisanship, as when we compete for electoral trust and favor. That's healthy. Yet, there is just as surely a time for bipartisanship, when we must set aside partisanship to unite for the good of all of North Carolina.

Such a time is now, and the goals and objectives which I have addressed with you this evening are surely the issues around which we ought to unite. Education, transportation, and vocation: schools for the future, roads to the future, and jobs of the future. Join with me, then, and let us build together those schools, those highways, those jobs, and that future for what must become, increasingly, one truly united state.

---

[1]Constitution of the State of North Carolina, 1971, Article III, Sections 5(2), 5(3), hereinafter cited as Constitution, 1971.

The governor's fiscal proposals are contained in *The North Carolina State Budget, 1987-89 Biennium* (Raleigh: Office of State Budget and Management, 6 volumes, January, 1987), hereinafter cited as *North Carolina State Budget, 1987-89*; and *The North Carolina State Budget, 1987-89 Biennium: Summary of Recommendations* (Raleigh: Office of State Budget and Management, January, 1987), hereinafter cited as *North Carolina State Budget, 1987-89: Summary of Recommendations*. *Post-Legislative Budget Summary, The North Carolina State Budget, 1987-89 Biennium* (Raleigh: Office of State Budget and Management, October, 1987), hereinafter cited as *Post-Legislative Budget Summary, 1987-89*, is a guide to legislatively authorized state spending. *North Carolina Legislation, 1987*, edited by Joseph S. Ferrell ([Chapel Hill]: Institute of Government, University of North Carolina at Chapel Hill, 1987), hereinafter cited as Ferrell, *North Carolina Legislation, 1987*, describes significant measures passed by the General Assembly.

[2]*North Carolina's Blueprint for Economic Development: A Strategic Business Plan for Quality Growth* ([Raleigh: Department of Commerce, 1986]).

[3]Steven Spielberg (1947-   ), born in Cincinnati, Ohio; B.A., California State College at Long Beach. Motion picture director, screenwriter, producer, executive producer; noted for films such as *Jaws* (1975), *Close Encounters of the Third Kind* (1977), *Raiders of the Lost Ark* (1981), *E.T. The Extraterrestrial* (1982), and *The Color Purple* (1985). *Who's Who in America, 1988-1989* (Wilmette, Illinois: Marquis Who's Who, A Macmillan, Inc., Company, 2 volumes, 1988), II, 2934, hereinafter cited as *Who's Who in America*. *The Color Purple*, starring Whoopi Goldberg, Danny Glover, and Adolph Caesar, was shot in Union and Anson counties during the summer of 1985. The film was based on Alice Walker's Pulitzer Prize-winning novel of the same name. *News and Observer*, July 28, 1985.

[4]The trio of motion pictures to which Martin referred were: *The Bedroom Window* (De Laurentiis Entertainment Group), starring Steve Guttenberg, Elizabeth McGovern, and Isabelle Huppert, filmed in Winston-Salem and Wilmington; *Crimes of the Heart* (De Laurentiis Entertainment Group), starring Jessica Lange, Dianne Keaton, and Sissy Spacek, filmed in Southport; and *Critical Condition* (Paramount Pictures), starring Richard Pryor, filmed in High Point, Winston-Salem, and Greensboro. Press release, "Three North Carolina Movies in Box Office Top Ten," Raleigh, January 29, 1987, Governors Papers, James G. Martin.

[5]"An Act to Establish the Business License Information Office" was ratified August 13, 1987. *N.C. Session Laws, 1987*, II, c. 808.

[6]For related press release, see "Governor Martin Announces Inter-Agency Task Force on Landfill Permitting," Raleigh, Februrary 12, 1987, Governors Papers, James G. Martin.

[7]"An Act to Appropriate Funds for Various Statewide Projects, to Specify How Certain Appropriated Funds are to Be Used, and to Make Various Changes in the Law," *N.C. Session Laws, 1985*, c. 757, s. 52(a), established the North Carolina Commission on Jobs and Economic Growth; see *North Carolina Commission on Jobs and Economic Growth: Report, November, 1986* (Raleigh: [The Commission], 1986), for recommendations.

[8]"An Act to Appropriate Funds to State Departments, Institutions, and Agencies for Aid to Certain Governmental and Nongovernmental Units," *N.C. Session Laws, 1987*, II, c. 830, s. 110, authorized financial support for the Rural Economic Development Center.

[9]For a brief discussion of the six business assistance proposals the governor listed, see *North Carolina Development Report, 1987* ([Raleigh]: North Carolina Department of Commerce, [1988]), 13.

[10]"An Act to Amend Chapter 159D of the General Statutes Pertaining to Industrial and Pollution Control Facilities Pool Program Financing Act" was ratified June 30, 1987. *N.C. Session Laws, 1987*, I, c. 517.

[11]"An Act to Expand and Clarify the Investment Authority of the State Treasurer" was ratified August 7, 1987. *N.C. Session Laws, 1987*, II, c. 751.

[12]Martin established the Governor's Task Force on Development of Private Seed Venture Capital Sources to investigate such funding mechanisms; see Executive Order Number 41, signed March 20, 1987, *N.C. Session Laws, 1987*, II, 2354-2356.

[13]See "An Act to Assist Small Business Development," ratified May 19, 1987. *N.C. Session Laws, 1987*, I, c. 214, s. 1(3).

[14]James Allen Graham (1921-   ), native of Rowan County; B.S., North Carolina State College (later University), 1942. Farmer; vocational agriculture teacher, Iredell County, 1942-1945; head, Beef, Cattle, and Sheep Dept., North Carolina State Fair, 1946-1952; superintendent, Upper Mountain Research Station, 1946-1952; manager, State Farmers Market, 1957-1964; elected state agriculture commissioner, 1964, and returned in subsequent elections; Democrat. *North Carolina Manual, 1987-1988*, 633.

[15]For related press release, see "Governor Martin, Tobacco Leaders Announce Buy-Out Agreement," Raleigh, July 2, 1986, Governors Papers, James G. Martin.

[16]A severe drought afflicted farms throughout the Southeast in 1986. For related press releases, see "North Carolina Begins Airlift of Hay for Drought-Plagued Farmers," Raleigh, July 23, 1986; "Governor Martin Announces Intention to Apply for Presidential Declaration of Disaster," Raleigh, July 25, 1986; "Governor Martin Announces Address for Monetary Contributions to 'Operation Hay' Efforts," Raleigh, July 29, 1986; "Governor Martin Sends Message of Thanks via Satellite to Those Who Sent Drought Relief to N.C.," Raleigh, July 31, 1986; "Martin Announces Disaster Designation," Raleigh, August 12, 1986; "N.C. Turkey Producers Join in Hay Effort," Raleigh, August 29, 1986; "Governor Martin, Commissioner Graham Discuss Drought Problems, Farm Programs with U.S. Agriculture Secretary Lyng," Washington, D.C., December 18, 1986, Governors Papers, James G. Martin. Executive Order Number 26, "Emergency Drought Relief," signed July 23, 1986, implemented "Operation Hay." *N.C. Session Laws, 1987*, II, 2307-2309.

[17]James Collins Green (1921-   ), born in Halifax County, Virginia; was educated at Washington and Lee University; U.S. Marine Corps, 1944-1946. Farmer; owner, operator, tobacco warehouses in Chadbourn and Clarkton, North Carolina, Brookneal, Virginia, and Greenville and Newport, Tennessee; member, state Senate, 1967, and House, 1961-1966, 1969-1976; House Speaker, 1975-1976; elected lieutenant governor, 1976, reelected 1980; candidate for Democratic gubernatorial nomination, 1984. *North Carolina Manual, 1983*, 483.

[18]Congress passed P.L. 100-17, "Surface Transportation and Uniform Relocation Assistance Act of 1987" (short title), *United States Statutes at Large*, Act of April 2, 1987, 101 Stat. 132-261, over President Reagan's veto.

[19]The Basic Education Program, first named as such under *N.C. Session Laws, 1985,* c. 479, s. 55, actually grew out of the "Elementary and Secondary Reform Act of 1984" (short title), *N.C. Session Laws, 1983, Extra and Regular Sessions, 1984,* c. 1103, ratified July 6, 1984. The impetus for both pieces of legislation was generated by the report of the North Carolina Commission on Education for Economic Growth; see *Education for Economic Growth: An Action Plan for North Carolina* ([Raleigh: The Commission], April, 1984). Governor Hunt signed Executive Order Number 98, creating the commission, on October 13, 1983. *N.C. Session Laws, 1983,* 1448-1450.

[20]Describing his school construction financing plan to the North Carolina Retail Merchants Association, February 4, 1987, the governor asserted: "It is a bold program, and it will get the job done. Five years ago, facing this same need, the previous administration considered but backed away from a $600 million bond issue! They had two problems with it: (1) It was too big, and (2) it wasn't nearly big enough!"

Martin had no qualms championing a much larger bond proposal; Senator Paul S. Smith (R-Rowan) introduced the governor's plan, as S.B. 434, on April 15, 1987. However, the bill remained in committee through the 1987 session, and the General Assembly passed a compromise measure of its own. See *N.C. Session Laws, 1987,* I, c. 622; see also S.B. 434, "A Bill to Establish the Public School Facilities Loan Fund, to Authorize the Issuance of $1.5 Billion in Bonds of the State, Subject to Approval by the Qualified Voters of the State at a Bond Election, to Provide Funds for Public School Facilities through Loans to Counties, and to Amend Certain General and Special Laws," *N.C. Senate Journal, 1987,* 223, 656.

[21]Harlan Edward Boyles (1929-   ), born in Vale; resident of Raleigh; B.S., University of North Carolina at Chapel Hill, 1951. Certified public accountant; elected state treasurer, 1976, and returned in subsequent elections; Democrat. Alumni Office of the General Alumni Association (comp. and ed.), *The University of North Carolina at Chapel Hill Alumni Directory* (Chapel Hill: Alumni Office, University of North Carolina at Chapel Hill, 1976), 119, hereinafter cited as *UNC Alumni Directory; North Carolina Manual, 1987-1988,* 593.

[22]Andrew Craig Phillips (1922-   ), native of Greensboro; B.S., 1943, M.A., 1948, Ed.D., 1955, University of North Carolina at Chapel Hill; U.S. Naval Reserve, 1942-1946. Teacher, assistant principal, principal, assistant superintendent, and superintendent, 1946-1962, Winston-Salem City Schools; superintendent, Charlotte-Mecklenburg Schools, 1962-1967; administrative vice-president, Smith Richardson Foundation, 1967-1968. Elected state superintendent of education, 1968, and returned in subsequent elections; retired from post in 1989; Democrat. *News and Observer,* January 6, 1989; *North Carolina Manual, 1987-1988,* 607.

[23]With the retirement of longtime state school chief A. Craig Phillips. to become effective early in 1989, proponents of an appointed, rather than popularly elected, state superintendent of public instruction attempted to rewrite the constitution in their favor. They did not succeed. See H.B. 230, "A Bill to Be Entitled an Act to Amend the Constitution and the General Statutes to Change the Terms of the Members of the State Board of Education and to Make the Office of the Superintendent of Public Instruction Appointive," *N.C. House Journal, 1987,* 112; H.B. 331, "A Bill to Be Entitled an Act to Provide a Unitary Governance Structure for the Department of Public Education," *N.C. House Journal, 1987,* 161, 859, *N.C. Senate Journal, 1987,* 605; and S.B. 149, "A Bill to Amend the Constitution and the General Statutes to Change the Method of Selecting the Members of the State Board of Education and to Make the Office of the Superintendent of Public Education Appointive," *N.C. House Journal, 1987,* 296, 918, *N.C. Senate Journal, 1987,* 90, 226, 235.

[24]Speaking to members of the Marion Rotary Club on August 20, 1987, the governor described the reception his education proprosals received from the 1987 General Assembly. "In the legislative session, I continued to press for programs designed to upgrade our school plants, attract and hold good teachers, reduce class size, and provide timely remediation to stem the flood tide of illiteracy and school dropouts," Martin

said. "Unfortunately, partisanship reared its unruly head, causing defeat of a number of educational initiatives in the legislature. One victim of the legislative veto was my proposal for a bond referendum to establish a construction fund that would make it possible for school districts to obtain low-interest construction loans. The dog-in-the-manger attitude of key Democratic legislators, with one eye on the pork barrel and the other on the next gubernatorial election, resulted in no school construction program at all."

He continued: "I proposed a $32.8 million remedial summer school program for 1988-1989 to help alleviate learning deficiencies among our students. The General Assembly provided only $21.8 million over both years of the biennium.

"Another of my programs, a $95.4 million Career Development program, which included a $10.7 million appropriation for the effective teacher training program, was mugged on its way through the legislature. Though bloodied and covered with contusions, the Career Development program did manage to get out of the legislature alive, although less than half of what it could have been: at a funded level of $47.1 million over the biennium.

"Another casualty was my proposal for a career ladder for teachers. In the teaching profession, as in any other, there is nothing quite so unequal as the equal treatment for unequal. Excellence in teaching is not rewarded; mediocrity is."

[25]Martin announced, on March 6, 1986, a ten-year plan targeting overcrowding in state prisons; see "Corrections at the Crossroads: Plan for the Future" (Raleigh: Department of Correction, 1986), hereinafter cited as "Corrections at the Crossroads."

[26]The consent judgment affecting the state's South Piedmont prison region, approved September 16, 1985 in *Hubert* v. *Ward* (Case No. C-C-80-414-M, U.S. District Court, Western District of North Carolina), ordered increases in staff and space per inmate and abolished the practice of triple bunking. Standards established in *Hubert* and two other lawsuits against the state correction system markedly increased the cost of incarceration and limited the number of inmates held at a given prison to a proportion of the available staff and facilities. Ferrell, *North Carolina Legislation, 1987*, 245-246.

[27]For related press release, see "Martin Announces Design Funding for New Morehead Berth," Raleigh, February 12, 1987, Governors Papers, James G. Martin.

[28]The General Assembly passed "An Act to Create the North Carolina Clean Water Loan and Grant Program," *N.C. Session Laws, 1987*, II, c. 796, on August 12, 1987. However, legislators appropriated only $21.5 million for the ensuing biennium—$5.7 million for 1987-1988 and $15.8 million for 1988-1989—instead of the $120 million the governor had recommended. The difference in funding levels between his proposal and the legislatively approved package threatened the growth and prosperity of some municipal economies, according to the governor. Speaking in Hickory, on May 20, 1988, Martin said that "requests this year for waste-water treatment assistance alone totaled more than $58 million, yet this year we had less than ten percent of that, only $5.7 million, to fund both the water supply and waste-water treatment requests." Consequently, thirty-eight projects in thirty-three counties received no money; Martin called on representatives of the affected communities to join him in urging state legislators to approve supplemental water-sewer appropriations during the 1988 short session.

[29]The state constitution empowers the legislature "to authorize the issuance of bonds to the extent of two-thirds of the amount by which the state's total indebtedness has been reduced during the preceding biennium." Martin noted that the 1985-1987 period saw a decrease in the state's indebtedness sufficient to permit issuing $77.5 million in two-thirds bonds. *North Carolina State Budget, 1987-89: Summary of Recommendations*, 2.

[30]*N.C. Session Laws, 1987*, II, s. 30, provided 5 percent average pay increases for many state employees.

[31]All ten Senate Republicans sponsored S.B. 456, "A Bill to Amend the Constitution to Secure to the Governor the Power of Veto." Introduced on April 16, 1987, the proposal was relayed to the Senate Constitution Committee, where it was defeated. *N.C. Senate Journal, 1987*, 229, 456.

[32]"An Act to Authorize Studies by the Legislative Research Commission, to Create and Continue Various Committees and Commissions, to Make Appropriations Therefor, and to Amend Statutory Law," ratified August 14, 1987, established the Judicial Selection Study Commission. *N.C. Session Laws, 1987,* II, c. 873, s. 19A.1.

[33]*N.C. Session Laws, 1987,* II, c. 738, s. 75, maintained the abortion fund restrictions established under *N.C. Session Laws, 1985,* c. 479, s. 93.

[34]The Community Work Experience Program, known more commonly as Workfare, furnished job "training and work for families receiving assistance under the Aid to Families with Dependent Children (AFDC) Program." *N.C. Session Laws, 1987,* II, c. 738, s. 76; c. 830, s. 23, expanded the Workfare concept to Halifax, Pasquotank, and Transylvania counties.

[35]The Governor's Commission on Child Victimization was established under Executive Order Number 5, signed May 20, 1985. *N.C. Session Laws, 1985,* 1426-1429. Executive Order Number 27, signed September 8, 1986, established the North Carolina Fund for Children and Families Commission; see also Executive Order Number 47, signed April 28, 1987. *N.C. Session Laws, 1987,* II, 2310-2313, 2373-2377.

[36]"Year of the Family, 1986, by the Governor of the State of North Carolina: A Proclamation," January 24, 1986, Governors Papers, James G. Martin.

[37]"Year of the Reader, 1987, by the Governor of the State of North Carolina: A Proclamation," February 16, 1987, Governors Papers, James G. Martin.

[38]For related press release, see "Governor Announces New Literacy Program," Raleigh, August 25, 1987, Governors Papers, James G. Martin.

[39]Executive Order Number 32, signed February 16, 1987, established the Governor's Literacy Council; its name was changed to the Governor's Commission on Literacy, under Executive Order Number 38, signed March 12. *N.C. Session Laws, 1987,* II, 2326-2328, 2345-2346.

William Clyde Friday (1920-   ), born in Raphine, Virginia; resident of Chapel Hill; B.S., North Carolina State College (later University), 1941; LL.B., University of North Carolina at Chapel Hill, 1948; honorary degrees; served in U.S. Navy during World War II. President, 1956-1986, president emeritus, since 1986, University of North Carolina system; chairman, federal Task Force on Education, under Presidents Johnson and Carter; served on numerous state and national educational boards and commissions. *News and Observer,* June 19, 1985; *North Carolina Manual, 1985,* 915.

[40]Prompted by the Bay of Pigs fiasco and the successful orbiting of the earth by Soviet cosmonaut Yuri Gagarin, President Kennedy recommended a significantly larger space program, one primarily devoted to lunar exploration. "First, I believe that this nation should commit itself to achieving the goal, before this decade is out, of landing a man on the moon and returning him safely to earth." John F. Kennedy, "Message to the Congress on Urgent National Needs," May 25, 1961, as quoted in John W. Gardner (ed.), *To Turn the Tide* (New York: Harper and Brothers, Publishers, 1962), 74-75; Arthur M. Schlesinger, Jr., *A Thousand Days: John F. Kennedy in the White House* (Boston: Houghton Mifflin Company, 1965), 361.

[41]"That's one small step for man, one giant leap for mankind," stated Neil A. Armstrong on July 20, 1969, as he stepped onto the lunar surface, becoming the first astronaut to walk on the moon. John Gordon Burke and others (eds.), *Dictionary of Contemporary Quotations* ([N.p.]: John Gordon Burke, Publisher, Inc., 1987), 11; *New Encyclopaedia Britannica: Micropaedia,* 15th ed., s.v., "Armstrong, Neil (Alden)."

[42]Charles Bishop Kuralt (1934-   ), born in Wilmington; A.B., University of North Carolina at Chapel Hill, 1955. Award-winning journalist; reporter, columnist, *Charlotte News,* 1955-1957; writer, 1957-1959, correspondent, since 1959, CBS News; correspondent, host, "CBS News Sunday Morning"; author. *Who's Who in America, 1988-1989,* I, 1769.

Loonis McGlohon (1921-   ), born in Ayden; resident of Charlotte; B.S., East Carolina University, 1942; honorary degrees; U.S. Army Air Force, 1942-1945. Pianist; music composer, arranger; band leader; recording artist; television producer, 1970-1985; music director, WBT Radio, and Jefferson Standard Broadcasting Co., Charlotte; two-time winner, George Foster Peabody Award; recipient of North Carolina Award. *Charlotte Observer*, July 30, 1972; Loonis McGlohon to Jan- Michael Poff, January 18, 1990; *News and Observer*, December 3, 1963, July 11, 1964.

Governor Hunt initially suggested that Kuralt and McGlohon collaborate on a musical tribute to their native state, and *North Carolina Is My Home* was the result. See *North Carolina Is My Home: A 400th Birthday Gift to the Tar Heel State* [sound recording], by Charles Kuralt and Loonis McGlohon (Winston-Salem: Piedmont Airlines, MR-19001, [1985?]), hereinafter cited as *North Carolina Is My Home* [sound recording].

[43]The quotation is from the first stanza of the state toast, as approved by the 1957 General Assembly:

> Here's to the land of the long leaf pine,
> The summer land where the sun doth shine,
> Where the weak grow strong and the strong grow great,
> Here's to "Down Home," the Old North State!

Quoted from *North Carolina Manual, 1987-1988*, 80.

[44]"Tar Heel Places," *North Carolina Is My Home* [sound recording], side one, track three.

LETTER TO STATE LEGISLATORS CONCERNING MARTIN LUTHER KING, JR., HOLIDAY

RALEIGH, MAY 7, 1987

To the Honorable Members of the 1987 General Assembly:

Article III, Section 5(2) of the constitution directs that from time to time I give you information of the affairs of the state and recommend to your consideration measures that I find to be expedient. This letter is written for that purpose.

You have enacted, and there has been signed into law, a bill directing that the third Monday in January be a state holiday honoring the late Reverend Martin Luther King, Jr. According to your enactment, the holiday (1) is to be a paid holiday for state employees; (2) the holiday is not to increase the number of paid holidays for state employees beyond the number of paid holidays for state employees in 1986; and (3) should it be necessary to meet this requirement to eliminate a holiday that has been traditionally observed as a paid holiday for state employees, the State Personnel Commission shall designate the holiday to be eliminated—but it may not be the Veterans Day holiday.[1]

In the course of the debate that preceded your enactment of this law, I observed what I perceived to be disquietude among the state employees concerning the bill. It was my feeling that there were feelings among them that, rather than being mandatory, the holiday should be optional; and, if a traditionally observed holiday was to be given up so that the Reverend Martin Luther King, Jr., holiday could be observed as provided in the bill, the state employees should have a voice in the decision as to which holiday was to be given up. With this in mind, I asked the state personnel director[2] to poll the state employees concerning the issues and to make the results of the poll known to me. He has done so.

Questionnaires were distributed to the 69,698 state employees subject to the State Personnel Act. To date, 73.62 percent of those polled have responded. There were no questionnaires returned by the State Auditor's Office or the Department of Labor. Responses to the questionnaire were as follows:

Holiday should be optional:	37,363
Holiday should not be optional:	12,024
No choice indicated:	1,466
Altered questionnaires:	458
	51,311

Preferred holiday to be given up:

New Year's Day	3,383
Easter Monday	4,417
Memorial Day	6,840
Independence Day	1,059
Labor Day	2,828
Thanksgiving	117
Day after Thanksgiving	5,700
Christmas Eve	401
Christmas Day	843
No choice expressed	23,424*
Altered questionnaires	2,299

*Of these, 14,709 expressly protested giving up any holidays.

The results of the questionnaire make clear at least three things:

(a) The response to the questionnaire, almost 75 percent, was unexpectedly high, indicating a high interest by the state employees in the subject of the questionnaire;

(b) If there is to be a paid holiday for state employees honoring the late Reverend Martin Luther King, Jr., the state employees prefer that the holiday be an optionally observed holiday rather than a mandatorily observed holiday; and

(c) There is no clear-cut preference among the state employees as to which traditionally observed holiday should be given up in favor of the Reverend Martin Luther King, Jr., holiday. It is clear, however, that a substantial number do not want to give up any of the traditionally observed holidays. Half chose none at all.

For the above reasons, I am submitting to you the results of the survey so that you will have information regarding the opinions of state employees on this matter.

One related issue is that the law enacted by you does not make clear whether 1988 and other years in which Christmas does not fall on Tuesdays, Wednesdays, or Thursdays should have ten holidays or be expanded to eleven. The debate made clear that no net cost was intended by this law, yet an added day off with pay is estimated to cost $4 million in additional work force to make up for it. Accordingly, so that the State Personnel Commission can comply with your intent in this regard, I recommend that you, by resolution, make clear whether it is your intent that there be ten or eleven holidays in years that traditionally have had ten holidays.[3]

> Respectfully submitted,
> [signed] James G. Martin
> Governor

---

[1]"An Act to Change the Date for the Martin Luther King, Jr., Legal Public Holiday to the Same Date Provided by Federal Law and to Provide for a Paid Holiday for State Employees on that Date" was ratified Marh 25, 1987. *N.C. Session Laws, 1987*, I, c. 25.

State employees received eleven paid holidays in 1986, thanks to a government policy that established a three-day observance for Christmas when it fell on Tuesday, Wednesday, or Thursday. The State Personnel Commission ultimately decided that, during those years, one of the three Christmas holidays was to be abolished in favor of the Martin Luther King, Jr., birthday commemoration, thus holding to eleven the number of days state offices were closed. The regulation granting two days off when Christmas fell Friday through Monday remained unchanged. *News and Observer*, October 21, 1987.

[2]Richard V. Lee

[3]The General Assembly adjourned its 1987 session without passing a resolution determining the number of annual, paid holidays to be granted state employees. The State Personnel Commission later authorized eleven such days per year. *News and Observer*, October 21, 1987.

MESSAGE FROM THE GOVERNOR TO THE GENERAL ASSEMBLY

June 2, 1988

Our constitution directs that from time to time I shall give to you information on the affairs of the state and recommend for your consideration such measures as I deem expedient. This message is being sent to you pursuant to that direction.

I am pleased to report to you that, overall, the affairs of the state are in good order. Our economy continues to outperform that of the nation and most of the world. Median family income is higher than ever before; the number of our people at work is at an all-time high; unemployment is at an all-time low. According to April statistics, only seven counties have unemployment greater than 7 percent; only two exceed 10 percent. Our state, like our nation, is at peace, and our citizens go about their daily businesses free of interruption or interference. The Almighty has, indeed, blessed us.

The good order our state enjoys notwithstanding, there are still legislative matters that need your attention, matters by which we can further improve the lives of our citizens. Many of these are matters that will require the public debate and full consideration that can come only during a regular legislative session, and, therefore, must wait. But there are, also, matters which need immediate attention. It is these that I present to you today.[1]

The Budget

You have received a copy of my *Recommended Changes to the 1988-89 State Budget*.[2] Its contents are self-explanatory and require no additional explanation here. The recommendations were arrived at after thorough investigation and study. It is my hope that you will accept the recommendations as presented and that you will not allow partisan political considerations to affect your decisions. In preparing my recommendations, I have put the interests of the citizens of the state first.

Veto

For a fourth time, I ask that you allow the people of North Carolina to vote upon whether they wish for their governor to have a legislative veto.[3] Survey after survey shows that the people want the opportunity to express themselves on this issue. I cannot think of a reason why they should not be allowed to do so. Our democratic form of government is based upon the freely given consent of the governed. Only in North Carolina have the people repeatedly been denied the chance to express themselves upon this issue. In prior years, this was seen as a partisan issue. That is no longer valid. Both candidates for governor now favor the veto.[4] It is time for this issue to be placed on the ballot. If the people don't want their governor to have a legislative veto, they will say so. If they do want him to have it, they will so express themselves. It is my hope that you will demonstrate enough trust in the electorate to put this issue on the ballot this November.

Drug Trafficking

Almost daily we learn of the destruction of our young people by drugs—the children of our friends and neighbors, and sometimes, our own. It is heartbreaking. Yet, we do not seem to be able to do anything about it. Our police tell us that drugs are everywhere.

Trafficking in drugs is profitable. Drug traffickers are willing to risk the punishments handed them because they know that despite the severity of the sentences given them by the judges, they will get out of prison much sooner. A sentence for years does not mean that the felon will be in prison for the years to which he was sentenced, it only means that he will serve that sentence minus credits given him for good time and for gain time. It is no wonder that our citizens are losing faith in our system.

The law has to be changed. Penalties for drug trafficking have to be made tougher if we are to rid ourselves of drug dealers in North Carolina. These felons must be taught to respect the law.

To get tough on drugs in North Carolina, I am asking that you eliminate parole as well as good-time and gain-time benefits from sentences given in drug trafficking cases. If that is done, the offender will serve the sentence given him by the sentencing judge. A trafficker given ten years will remain in prison for ten years; one given twenty years will stay in prison twenty years. There will be no early releases.[5]

Further, I am asking that the drug kingpin, the big dealer, the one responsible for bringing drugs into our state, be given life imprisonment for his crimes—again, without parole, good time, and gain time. Life imprisonment will mean just that: real life. If convicted, these kingpins will die in prison. There are not many who will take that risk just to earn some easy money.

Some may say that these proposals are too harsh. I say that they are not. We have got to end the reign of drugs in North Carolina, and this is what it will take to bring it to an end.

Driving While Impaired

There is no issue on which people are more agreed than the need to remove the hazard of drunken drivers from our roads. The subject can be studied to death—literally. While study proceeds at a ponderous pace, the carnage on our highways continues. It is time to act. If only one life is saved by your action, it will have been better to act than only to study.

Expert testimony indicates that two measures will have a greater effect on reducing DWI on our state's highways than any other. They are:

1. Increased visible enforcement; and
2. Extending the period of immediate license revocation for DWI offenses.

In the 1987 long session, I requested 100 additional Highway Patrol troopers. You provided forty.[6] In my budget recommendations, I propose you grant the balance of sixty troopers requested. I urge you to respond favorably to that recommendation. DWI enforcement has been pushed to the limit of our resources. We need the additional manpower.

Also in the 1987 long session, I proposed that the period of immediate license revocation in DWI cases be extended from ten to thirty days.[7] You will have the opportunity to consider that proposal again in this session, and I urge you to act on it.

In 1987, you enacted legislation providing severe penalties for operation of an aircraft with blood alcohol level of .04 or more.[8] No action was taken on my proposal to subject drivers of commercial vehicles on our roads—heavy trucks and buses—to the same blood alcohol content level. I hope you will take the opportunity that will be offered in this session to remedy that deficiency.[9]

Restoration of Merchants' Sales-Tax Discount

During the 1987 long session, you saw fit to repeal the 3 percent merchants' sales-tax discount. I propose that it be substantially restored. My recommended budget anticipates restoration of the discount while providing sufficient funds to carry out the programs and perform the services reflected therein. Specifically, I ask that you re-store the 3 percent merchants' sales-tax discount on the first $60,000 of taxes collected by each merchant, the amount that would be col-lected on $1.2 million in sales. This will fully restore the discount to 95 percent of the merchants in the state.[10]

Consolidation of Environmental Agencies

Over the past several months, my administration has worked coop-eratively with your Consolidation of Environmental Regulatory Agencies Study Commission on the subject of consolidation of envi-ronmental agencies.[11] In February I presented to that commission my proposal for the creation of a new department of health and environ-ment, essentially combining the Division of Health Services from the Department of Human Resources with the natural resource and environmental regulatory functions of the Department of Natural Resources and Community Development. This structure bolsters support for both environmental and health functions of state government by highlighting the historic close relationship that exists between them. It eliminates the duplication and overlap which plague current environmental regulation. It obviates the long-perceived conflict between development and resource protection by transferring the community development aspects of NRCD to the Department of Commerce. Equally important, its basic structure represents a broad consensus between environmentalists, business, local government, health professionals, and state administrators that has never been achieved before. That consensus, like most consen-sus[es], is fragile. It is the fact that gives urgency to the need to act now. I urge you to take up this issue and act to correct an organiza-tional problem which we have allowed to continue for too long.[12]

Prisons

During the 1987 long session, I recommended to you a major expansion of the state's prison capacity, together with a variety of alternative punishments to incarceration. My recommendations were directed towards bringing our correctional system into compliance with the requirements of the federal courts. While not all of my recommendations were accepted, you did accept many of them, and much has been done in the interim to bring our correction system into compliance.[13]

Noncompliance with federal requirements exposes the state to the risk of having its correctional system taken over by the federal courts. To avoid such a take-over, I am recommending capital and operating expenditures that I believe will meet current federal court challenges. If you enact all of my recommendations, these challenges will have been met. If you enact only part of my recommendations, the state will continue to risk having its correctional system taken over by the federal courts. None of us wants that. I urge you, therefore, to accept my recommendations.

Programs for the Aging

All of us know that, today, people are living longer and that our older people are becoming an ever-larger part of our population. While there has been a variety of state programs designed to help our older citizens, not enough is being done. What the state's obligations to, and opportunities for our senior citizens are, is a subject that, as a whole, I suggest be deferred to your 1989 regular session. But we should not wait to get started.

With that in mind, I am asking that you appropriate $5 million as earnest money on a program for the aging that should ensure a later, substantial commitment by the state to those in their retirement years. In many ways, appropriating the $5 million that I request is like asking for the modest pledge that leads to the tithe. I recommend it to you and ask that you not turn your backs on these of our citizens who, in the past, have done so much for us.[14]

Early Childhood Development Program

One of the things that has been learned from the child victimization program conducted for the past three years by our First Lady is that most children in North Carolina are born into homes of loving and nurturing parents. These children have normal childhood and school experiences and mature into adulthood as caring and responsible persons who, in turn, give their children similiar childhood experiences.

But not all of our children are so fortunate. Many are born into broken homes, homes in which there is alcohol, drug, spouse, and child abuse. These children tend to carry their early year experiences into their adulthoods. Children raised in deprived environments tend to become our dropouts, our criminals, and our alcohol, drug, spouse, and child abusers.

What can be done, that is not now being done, to help? While we cannot, without the state becoming a surrogate parent, remove these children wholly from the unfortunate environments into which they were born, we can, for a portion of each day, introduce them to an environment akin to the home atmosphere in which most of our children are raised. What I propose is that the state sponsor a pilot program, administered at the local level, by which disadvantaged four-year-olds spend a portion of each day in publicly or privately operated early childhood development centers where they can receive the care and attention that other children get at home.

What I envision is a warm and loving environment where each day the child can be fed, read to, play, and nap the same as four-year-olds do in normal homes. I am not talking about mandatory state-supported day-care centers in our public schools, as some advocate. These four-year-olds will not benefit from an institutional environment. Nor am I proposing a system of state-supported day-care centers for the use of all, irrespective of need; what I am proposing is that we focus on where the need is greatest, the truly disadvantaged child, and that we give to him that which he otherwise will not get. The need for developing a system of early childhood development centers such as I have described is upon us and requires your attention now.[15]

Roads

Secretary of Transportation Jim Harrington has laid before our Highway Study Commission the state's short- and long-range road and highway needs. The needs are large and the ways of meeting them will require extensive legislative consideration and debate, but that does not mean that we should put off beginning to meet those needs until the 1989 legislative session. So that no more time will be wasted and we can get recognized needed projects under way, Secretary Harrington has proposed a $450-million bond issue to step up our construction timetable by six to twelve months.[16]

Secretary Harrington's plan is a good one. There will be no new taxes, no lost revenues, and we can be at work by the end of the year. There may be other options available which will allow us to build while we study. I and Secretary Harrington stand ready to explore those options with you.

Why Now?

As elected officials, all of us are aware that 1988 is an election year. Many of us are standing for election. Given the election pressures during your session, the temptation will be great to observe partisan interests in what is said and done. There will be those who will play the role of the cynic and dismiss my proposals as election-year politics. If you will give these and the other proposals that I recommend your careful consideration, I do not believe that you will be caught up in that cynicism. Rather, you will recognize that each proposal represents a need of our people that should be enacted into law and enacted in law now.

The needs of the people do not cease in an election year, nor should leadership. If we can work together, even in an election year, to meet those needs and provide that leadership, no one will earn any political advantage because all will have shared in the effort. Let us put aside our differences and put North Carolina first, so North Carolina can continue to be first.

---

[1]For an overview of the laws the General Assembly passed during its short session, as well as the noteworthy bills that were not approved, see Joseph S. Ferrell (ed.), *North Carolina Legislation, 1988* (Chapel Hill: Institute of Government, University of North Carolina at Chapel Hill, 1988).

[2]*Recommended Changes to the 1988-89 State Budget, 1987-89 Biennium* (Raleigh: Office of State Budget and Management, June, 1988), hereinafter cited as *Recommended Changes to the 1988-89 State Budget*; for a review of state spending as authorized by the General Assembly, see *Post-Legislative Summary of the 1988-89 State Budget, 1987-89 Biennium* (Raleigh: Office of State Budget and Management, September, 1988), hereinafter cited as *Post-Legislative Budget Summary, 1988-89*.

[3]The Senate Constitution Committee tabled S.B. 456, "A Bill to Amend the Constitution to Secure to the Governor the Power of Veto," on May 20, 1987. Attempts to resurrect it during the 1988 session, via S.J.R. 1866 and subsequent Senate and House substitute bills, proved futile. A veto referendum was not included on the November ballot. *N.C. Senate Journal, 1987, Regular Session, 1988,* 116, 134, 187, 189, 308, 317.

[4]Martin defeated Lieutenant Governor Jordan, his Democratic opponent in the 1988 gubernatorial election, by a 56 percent to 44 percent margin. *News and Observer,* November 9, 10, 1988.

[5]Both good-time and gain-time credits reduce the length of a convict's prison term. Good-time credits shorten an inmate's sentence by one day for each day served on good behavior, but can be revoked for disciplinary reasons. Inmates earned gain-time and meritorious-time reduction credits by participating in work or program assignments, or for behavior or specific acts, not normally required of an inmate. *News and Observer,* September 6, 1986; telephone conversation with Patsy Woodlief, Classification Services, Division of Prisons, Department of Correction, January 10, 1990.

[6]*N.C. Session Laws, 1987,* II, c. 738, s. 121.

[7]S.B. 509, "A Bill to Increase the Immediate Civil License Revocation for Certain Persons Charged with Implied-Consent Offenses from Ten Days to Thirty Days and for

Certain Other Persons from Thirty Days to Sixty Days," was transformed into a study of the Safe Roads Act. *N.C. Senate Journal, 1987*, 239, 838; *N.C. Session Laws, 1987*, II, c. 873, s. 2.1(38); see also press release, "Martin Administration DWI Legislation to Be Introduced in General Assembly," Raleigh, April 15, 1987, Governor's Papers, James G. Martin, for other proposals.

[8]"An Act to Provide for Effective Measures to Combat the Operation of Aircraft while Impaired and to Combat Tampering with Aircraft or Airport Facilities" was ratified August 13, 1987. *N.C. Session Laws, 1987*, II, c. 818.

[9]"An Act to Establish the Offense of Impaired Driving in Commercial Motor Vehicles, To Assess a Fee for License Revocation for the Offense, and to Increase the Fee for a Class A or Class B License," was ratified July 12, 1988. *N.C. Session Laws, 1987, Regular Session, 1988*, III, c. 1112.

[10]S.B. 1594, "A Bill to Allow a Three Percent Discount to Merchants for Collecting State Sales and Use Taxes," passed the Senate and was sent to the House, where it was assigned to the Finance Committee. Two other proposals, S.B. 1609 and H.B. 2223, which also would have restored the merchants' discount, were less successful. *N.C. House Journal, 1987, Regular Session, 1988*, 86, 315; *N.C. Senate Journal, 1987, Regular Session, 1988*, 15, 20, 21, 27, 31. The 3 percent provision was repealed to generate additional revenue under *N.C. Session Laws, 1987*, I, c. 622.

[11]The study commission was established under "An Act to Amend the Fee Schedule Applicable to Generators and Transporters of Hazardous Waste and to Hazardous Waste Facilities; to Revise the Name of the Hazardous Waste Regulation Study; to Make Technical Amendments to the Marine Fisheries Act of 1987; and to Amend the Business Corporation Act," *N.C. Session Laws, 1987*, II, c. 773, s. 9, ratified August 12, 1987.

[12]The governor's plan to reorganize specific state agencies into a new governmental entity did not meet with legislative favor in 1988. S.B. 1577, "A Bill to Create the Department of Health and Environment and Reappropriate Funds for its Operation; to Consolidate Environmental Programs; to Make Transfers to the Department of Health and Environment, Department of Human Resources, and the Department of Commerce; and to Make Conforming Statutory Changes," was introduced by Senator Donald R. Kincaid (R-Caldwell) on June 6, 1988. The proposal did not clear the Senate Appropriations Committee. *N.C. Senate Journal, 1987, Second Session, 1988*, 13.

However, as the 1989 session waned, the General Assembly granted Martin his belated wish. "An Act to Create the Department of Environment, Health, and Natural Resources and to Provide for its Organization, to Consolidate Environmental Programs, to Abolish the Department of Natural Resources and Community Development and Transfer the Divisions, Agencies, Powers, Duties, and Functions of the Department of Natural Resources and Community Development, to Provide for Further Study of Environmental Agency Consolidation and Reorganization, to Amend Various Related Laws, and to Make Technical and Conforming Statutory Changes," was ratified August 3, 1989. *General Statutes of North Carolina, 1989, Advance Legislative Service, Pamphlet Number 4* (Charlottesville, Virginia: The Michie Company, 1989), c. 727; see also press release, "Department of Environment, Health, and Natural Resources Formed," Raleigh, August 11, 1989, Governors Papers, James G. Martin.

[13]See *North Carolina State Budget, 1987-89*, Volume 4, Section Q, and *North Carolina State Budget, 1987-89: Summary of Recommendations*, for prison spending proposals Martin submitted to the regular session of the General Assembly; for approved measures, see *Post-Legislative Budget Summary, 1987-89*, 40-42. The topic of state prisons was also included among the governor's speaking points to North Carolina Citizens for Business and Industry, Raleigh, December 1, 1988.

[14]The governor's proposed plan for the aged was outlined in his *Recommended Changes to the 1988-89 State Budget*, 29-30, and introduced into the Senate by Laurence A. Cobb (R-Mecklenburg) as S.B. 1777, "A Bill to Provide Assistance to North Carolina's Aging Population;" see *N.C. Senate Journal, 1987, Second Session, 1988*, 65. However, the General Assembly adopted its own package to assist the aged, totaling approximately $6.5

million for fiscal year 1988-1989. See "An Act to Provide for the Urgent Needs of Older Adults, to Begin Building an In-Home and Community-Based System of Services for Older Adults, and to Appropriate the Necessary Funds," c. 1095, ratified July 11; "An Act to Create and Continue Various Committees and Commissions and to Make Changes in the Budget Operations of the State," c. 1100, s. 40.3, ratified July 12; and "An Act to Make Further Appropriations for the 1988-89 Fiscal Year," c. 1101, s. 8, ratified July 12. *N.C. Session Laws, 1987, Regular Session, 1988,* III.

[15]A pair of bills respecting early childhood education were introduced in the Senate on June 17, 1988, and neither one had come to a floor vote by the end of the short session. J. Richard Conder (D-Richmond) backed S.B. 1720, "A Bill to Establish 16 Pilot Centers for Prekindergarten Children to Be Administered by the State Board of Education," while Senator Cobb supported S.B. 1773, "A Bill to Initiate an Early Childhood Education Pilot Program." *N.C. Senate Journal, 1987 Session, Regular Session, 1988,* 60, 65, 87.

[16]James E. Harrington (1927-   ), born in Bethlehem, New Hampshire; B.S., Virginia Military Institute, 1949; U.S. Army, 1949-1952; N.C. National Guard, 1953-1974. President, Pinehurst, Inc., 1967-1972, and of Cambridge Properties, since 1976; secretary, North Carolina Department of Natural and Economic Resources, 1973-1976; appointed state transportation secretary, 1985; Republican. *North Carolina Manual, 1987-1988,* 817.

The General Assembly did not approve a highway bond issue in 1988. S.B. 1712, "A Bill to Authorize the Issuance of Four Hundred Fifty Million Dollars of General Obligation Bonds of the State, Subject to a Vote of the Qualified Voters of the State, to Provide Funds for Highway Facilities," introduced June 16, 1987, was assigned to the Senate Finance Committee before becoming stalled in the Transportation Committee. Companion bill H.B. 2491, introduced June 17, received an indefinite postponement report from the House Committee on Appropriations. *N.C. House Journal, 1987, Regular Session, 1988,* 118, 338; *N.C. Senate Journal, 1987, Regular Session, 1988,* 55, 72, 185, 197.

PUBLIC ADDRESSES AND STATEMENTS

PRESS RELEASE: MARTIN PROPOSES TRUCE, AGREES TO DATE FOR BIENNIAL MESSAGE

RALEIGH, FEBRUARY 11, 1985

[North Carolina governors customarily delivered biennial State of the State messages before the General Assembly on the first Monday after a new session convened. Initially, Governor Martin had been invited to appear before both houses of the legislature on the evening of February 11, 1985. Unable to accept, Martin then suggested February 19 as an alternative, but the legislative leadership declined, citing its prerogative to establish its own calendar. With the disagreement surrounding the date of the State of the State address stoking "partisan bickering" over his legislative proposals, the governor called for a truce and complied with a joint resolution granting him the opportunity to deliver his biennial message on February 28. Martin presented his completed budget proposals on March 5. Joyce, *North Carolina Legislation, 1985*, 3; *News and Observer*, February 12, 14, 23, 1985. The disagreement between Governor Martin and the Democratic-controlled General Assembly over the scheduling of his first State of the State address was a harbinger of the nature of the relationship between the chief executive and the legislature for the ensuing four years.]

On Friday afternoon, February 8, I met with Lieutenant Governor Robert Jordan and House Speaker Liston Ramsey at the Executive Mansion to discuss and resolve the impasse that was shaping up over the scheduling of my first biennial message to the General Assembly. I believed that the dispute over procedural timing had run its course and therefore was concerned that the dispute was about to become a bitter quarrel distracting us from more substantive issues. All the necessary debate points had been made on both sides; it was time to reach a solution and to demonstrate that we could work together, legislative and executive, Democrat and Republican, to reach agreement on a question about which we clearly disagreed. Therefore, at the suggestion of veteran senator Cass Ballenger, R-Catawba, I invited the lieutenant governor and the Speaker to have coffee at the Mansion.

I proposed to them a truce: I would withdraw my position favoring an earlier date, February 19, to present my message, often called the State of the State address, and make the presentation at their joint session at noon, Thursday, February 28. (This assumes that the House of Representatives agrees to the date already adopted in a Senate resolution.)[1] I further informed them that my recommendations regarding the so-called Base Budget, which continues funding of existing programs, would be made available with the biennial message. By doing this, the General Assembly would not be delayed in its consideration of ongoing programs. I have not quite concluded all my recommendations for increases or new programs in what is known as the Expansion Budget, but I expect to have that ready for legislators within a few days after the biennial message. As requested by the Speaker, I will also press my efforts to conclude certain detailed features of my tax-cut proposals so that their tax-writing committees will have those measures before them for study.

While the earlier date of February 19 would have suited my own plans better by allowing me to present my complete budget and legislative initiatives to the General Assembly at the earliest possible date, I respect their right to schedule their own calendar. No one's interest could be served by prolonging the stand-off. Accordingly, upon receipt of the formal Senate and House resolutions regarding the date of the biennial message, I am prepared to accept formally the date of February 28.

---

[1]S.J.R. 4, "A Joint Resolution Informing His Excellency, Governor James G. Martin, that the General Assembly is Organized and Ready to Proceed with Public Business and Inviting the Governor to Address a Joint Session of the Senate and House of Representatives at 12 o'Clock Noon on Thursday, February 28, 1985," passed its third reading in the state Senate on February 5, 1985. The House approved the resolution on February 13. *N.C. House Journal, 1985,* 42; *N.C. Senate Journal, 1985,* 20; for the text of the resolution, see *N.C. Session Laws, 1985,* 1363-1364.

INDIAN UNITY CONFERENCE

FAYETTEVILLE, MARCH 15, 1985

I'm delighted to be with you once again. My last appearance before you was at your unity conference in Raleigh, when I spoke as a candidate for the office I now occupy. Today, because of the encouragement and support given me by you and a great majority of other North Carolinians, I am here as the state's chief executive. How many times our former governor, Jim Holshouser,[1] has told me of how close he felt to you, individually, and your tribal organizations, and this unity conference that began at that time.

I have looked at your agenda for this tenth annual conference, and I'm impressed. You're here to talk about serious issues and to plan for the future. I'm even more impressed that you have chosen as your theme for this meeting, "Memories of our past, visions of the future."

This theme has great meaning. Personally, I have a great belief in the linkage between time and history. In my "Inaugural Address," quoting [my] late father, [I said,] "Our future grows out of our past." Today is not possible without yesterday, just as tomorrow is not possible without today.[2]

So, we come together at this conference in the spirit of building unity: Indian unity forged out of different tribal customs, and traditions, and leadership, and the unity of one united state; the unity without which we cannot achieve a better system of government based upon solid programs in health, education, economic development, and the welfare of our children and youth.

I addressed all of these issues in my campaign, and just recently I placed my program before the General Assembly of North Carolina in my "State of the State" address and budget message to the Joint Appropriations Committee. That program relates directly to the many workshop sessions that are taking place at this conference, and, with your indulgence, I'd like to deal with some of the specifics of that program as it relates to the affairs of our Native North Carolinians.

I've noted that you're holding two workshops in the area of economics: "Economic Concerns of Indian Women" and "Economic Development for Indian Communities." Both of these topics relate directly to my proposal to achieve major tax reductions for our citizens without sacrificing services provided them by the state; both of the objectives can be reached because of continued growth in revenues. For example, I have asked the General Assembly to remove the state's 3 percent sales tax on food and nonprescription medicines. The elimination of that tax will greatly affect the well-being of Indian women and families in a positive way. That same proposal includes elimination of the intangibles tax and provides for the reimbursement by the state of any revenue that would be lost by local governments. This would benefit retirees and others who have spent many years accumulating savings, so they would not become burdens upon society, and encourage them to invest in North Carolina and provide jobs here—not Florida [or] Texas.

The third part of my total tax-reduction package includes providing a corporate income tax rebate or credit to offset inventory taxes paid by businesses. In effect, this virtually eliminates the tax on business inventories and stimulates the economy and creates new jobs. This total tax relief package deserves your full support, for it makes positive strides for our people. Let your senators and representatives know that you want this program implemented.

I am not unmindful of your economic development program in Robeson County[3] and other areas in which there are concentrations of Native Americans. Unemployment is a border county problem in North Carolina. Last year, I spoke of my support of the proposed Indian cultural center; last year, the General Assembly provided funds to acquire property for this center, and I plan in the near future to ask the Council of State to allocate funds for preparation of a development plan.[4] Upon completion of this plan, we can work together to find ways and means of moving forward with this project, which will build tourism and provide new jobs for area residents.

While we are focusing on culture and history, I want to remind you that 1986 has been designated the "Year of the Native American" as part of North Carolina's quadricentennial celebration.[5] This is an excellent time to acquaint all citizens with a knowledge of the rich and viable heritage the descendants of the first Americans add to the dimensions of the state.

Another workshop that has captured my interest is the one of "Indian Health Issues." I realize that Indians have a life expectancy ten years less than the rest of our population. I also know that Indian infant mortality is excessively high. On those points, I have asked the General Assembly to channel more funds into prenatal care and premature birth prevention. These are positive approaches to dealing with the health problems of Indian people, as well as all citizens of the state.

Our secretary of human resources, Phil Kirk, is a member of the North Carolina Commission of Indian Affairs. He has already taken steps to continue the biennial reports on Indian health statistics. The latest report will be available within a short time, and it will provide us a sense of direction in handling those problems.[6]

The two workshops you are holding on education will be of great benefit. At the state level, the largest share of public funding goes to this area. From the public school system to the community colleges and our public universities, many dollars are spent to enable our children to acquire learning and skills. I have proposed increased funding of education during the biennium, and I will continue to be a strong advocate of those programs that have proved workable.

The Indian people have a long history of educational involvement. Pembroke State University, for example, was the first four-year Indian college in the nation. It has a history of 100 years of service to our youth—and many of you who used to be our youth! Now as part of our consolidated university system, its stature will grow even more as an outstanding institution for young people. By becoming part of the state system under the University of North Carolina, its programs and facilities will be enlarged, and enhanced, and made secure.[7]

Much has been said about minority participation in state government. I want to assure you that Indian people will not be left out of my consideration of appointments to boards and commissions, the judiciary, jobs in state government, and funding of Indian scholarships and other programs. As an illustration, I have appointed my longtime friend and Greensboro city councilman, Lonnie Revels, as chairman of the Commission of Indian Affairs, and I will be working with him to ensure that Indian concerns are addressed.[8]

Today, I have touched on some of our problems and concerns, but not all of them. I firmly believe that these problems can be solved through unity of purpose. Together, with sincerity, dedication, and goodwill, North Carolina people will help write a new and exciting chapter in our future history. I'm going to give it my best effort, and I know that you will, also.

---

[1]James Eubert Holshouser, Jr. (1934-   ), born in Boone; resident of Southern Pines; B.S., Davidson College, 1956; LL.B., University of North Carolina, 1960. Attorney; member, state House, 1963-1971; chairman, Republican State Executive Committee, 1966-1972; governor of North Carolina, 1973-1977, and the state's first Republican chief executive in the twentieth century. Memory F. Mitchell (ed.), *Addresses and Public Papers of James Eubert Holshouser, Jr., Governor of North Carolina, 1973-1977* (Raleigh: Division of Archives and History, Department of Cultural Resources, 1978), xvii-xxx.

[2]The governor inserted into his prepared text, at this point, "What greater expression of tribute, 'Raleigh and Roanoke' exhibition and its testimony to earliest friendships," a reference to the state Museum of History exhibit commemorating the 400th anniversary of the Roanoke voyages.

[3]Martin was referring to the Lumbee Regional Development Association. A. Bruce Jones, executive director, state Commission of Indian Affairs, to Jan-Michael Poff, October 11, 1988.

[4]"An Act to Appropriate Funds for Various Statewide Projects," ratified July 7, 1984, authorized $360,000 for the state to obtain the remaining interest in 386.89 acres of Robeson County land for the Indian cultural center. It also appropriated $125,000 to purchase nearly 100 additional acres, adjoining U.S. 74, for the project. *N.C. Session Laws, 1983, Extra and Regular Sessions, 1984*, c. 1116, s. 14.

[5]"Year of the Native American, 1986, by the Governor of North Carolina: A Proclamation," December 9, 1985, Governors Papers, James G. Martin.

[6]Phillip James Kirk, Jr. (1944-   ), born in Salisbury; resident of Raleigh; B.A., Catawba College, 1967; was also educated at North Carolina State University. Former teacher, Boyden High School, Salisbury; state chairman, N.C. Young Republicans, 1969-1971; elected to state Senate, 1970, reelected 1972, but resigned to serve in administration of Governor James E. Holshouser, Jr.; administrative assistant to Governor Holshouser, 1973-1976; secretary, Department of Human Resources, 1976, 1985-1987; administrative assistant to Congressman James T. Broyhill, 1976-1984. *North Carolina Manual, 1985*, 745; *North Carolina Manual, 1987-1988*, 787. The statistical survey to which the governor referred was "Update on the Health Status of American Indians in North Carolina," by Kathryn B. Surles, *SCHS Studies* (Raleigh: State Center for Health Statistics, Division of Health Services, Department of Human Resources, June, 1985).

[7]Croatan Normal School, a teacher training academy, was established in Robeson County in 1887. It underwent a number of name changes, expanded its curriculum, and in 1940, offered its first bachelors' degrees. Known as Pembroke State College after 1949, the school was designated a regional university by the General Assembly twenty years later. Pembroke State University became part of the University of North Carolina system in 1972. *North Carolina Manual, 1987-1988*, 989-990.

[8]William Lonnie Revels, Sr. (1935-   ), born in Pembroke; resident of Greensboro; B.S., Wake Forest University, 1958; U.S. Army, 1958-1960. Salesman, branch manager, Ditto, Inc., 1961-1965; president, co-owner, Safety Distributors, Inc.; owner, Revels Printing Co., Greensboro; member, Greensboro City Council, since 1983; former chairman, Guilford Native American Assn.; organizer, former chairman, Greensboro City Schools Indian Education Parent Committee; chairman, N.C. Commission of Indian Affairs, 1985-1990; Republican. *News and Observer*, September 9, 1990; William Lonnie Revels, Sr., to Jan-Michael Poff, December 21, 1988.

PRESS RELEASE: STATEMENT FROM GOVERNOR MARTIN CONCERNING VETO POWER

RALEIGH, APRIL 1, 1985

Events of this past week show clearly the need for strengthening the relationship between the governor and the General Assembly of our state. The need for the executive veto has been clearly demonstrated as legislative leaders continue to assault the office of governor and its constitutional prerogatives. They have shown little or no reluctance to whittle away at this office, and little regard for its comparative weakness of authority and responsibility—ranked as "weak" by Chapel Hill political scientist Thad Beyle in his analysis of the organizational powers of fifty governors.[1] This is no new phenomenon, but it is getting worse.

On Tuesday, two co-chairmen of the Base Budget committees announced they had frozen authority to hire new employees without prior consent of their legislative committee. Even as they clarified that they meant no claim of executive jurisdiction for themselves, the Speaker of the House of Representatives was echoing precisely that earlier version: that any vacant positions that we filled without legislative clearance would be summarily abolished.[2]

On Thursday, action was hastily completed in the Senate to strip the governor's appointive power over the elections chief, once again repeating the highly partisan stand that had deprived Governor Holshouser of this authority that all Democratic governors have been responsible for.[3]

Legislation is quickly brewing to transfer the new Missing Children's Center away from its home in the Department of Crime

Control and Public Safety over to the Justice Department—without consulting those who worked to create this program.[4]

The pattern is clear. Either out of an attitude of partisan intransigence or cavalier disrespect, legislative leadership is not content with the traditional and constitutional separation of powers. This will only get worse until the people of North Carolina insist upon giving their governor the same power of veto that every other governor in every other state has had since 1920. This right of executive veto has been normal for most states since the early nineteenth century. Previous governors have generally favored it, but none risked investing political capital into it. The growing pattern of legislative intrusion into the executive branch compels me now to do so, to make it into a clear political issue. Only in this way can further attempts to weaken the governor's responsibilities be seen for what they are.

On last Tuesday, there could have been an opportunity to let the Senate vote on submitting to the people a constitutional amendment establishing the veto power. That was unceremoniously crushed by hastily calling up the bill in committee and killing it without any hearing or any consideration of the will of the people. This arrogantly repulsive act apparently was engineered by the Senate's increasingly partisan leadership. Only one Democrat voted against using this committee quickstep to kill consideration of the veto amendment.[5]

On the very same day, the Senate completed action on another constitutional amendment to repeal the new two-term succession amendment, again by essentially a party-line vote. The Democratic pretext of this stripping action was to allow the people to vote again on succession just one year after its first trial was completed.[6] It is nothing more than pious posturing, however, to argue that the people can be trusted to decide what's best regarding succession, when the same leadership does not trust the people to decide whether their governor should have the veto. It will be ridiculed as self-serving hypocrisy unless both issues are placed before the people.

There is yet a way. New legislation can be introduced differing sufficiently to justify further consideration in the Senate, but the same leadership that disregards its parliamentary principles once will simply do so again, with impunity. For that reason, I call upon the Speaker of the House to see to it that the House of Representatives gives fairer consideration to this issue and shows greater respect for the people. I challenge him to let the bill be brought out, and debated and voted on, as the serious, historic issue that it is. The constitution is the people's mechanism to check and balance the conflicts between the respective branches of government. So, let the people decide.

Do the people of North Carolina really want a weak office of governor to be further weakened and regularly eroded, or do they want it strong enough to carry its share of their popular sovereignty? Do the people of North Carolina really want to deny themselves the right to choose whether a future governor should be reelected to a second term, or do they want this new measure of strength taken away from future governors? The issue is whether the office of governor of North Carolina should continue to be among the weakest in the nation. I say it is time to let the people decide.

---

[1]Thad L. Beyle (1934-   ), born in Syracuse, New York; A.B., 1956, A.M., 1960, Syracuse University; Ph.D., University of Illinois, 1963. Political science professor; taught at University of Illinois, 1960-1961, Denison University, 1963-1964, and at University of North Carolina at Chapel Hill since 1967; director, Center for Policy Research and Analysis, National Governors' Conference, 1974-1976; member, since 1977, chairman, since 1980, Board of Directors, N.C. Center for Public Policy Research; cofounder, Southern Growth Policies Board; consultant; author; editor; managing editor, *Inside Politics: NC.*

The governor was referring to one of two studies by Beyle; see "How Powerful is the North Carolina Governor?" *N.C. Insight,* 4 (December, 1981), 3-11; and "Governors," in Virginia Grey and others (eds.), *Politics in the American States* (Boston: Little, Brown, fourth edition, 1983), 193-203. Thad L. Beyle to Jan-Michael Poff, October 10, 1989.

[2]Senate Base Budget Committee chairman Tony Rand and his collaborator from the House, fellow Democrat Bobby Etheridge, announced on March 26, 1985, that 3,087 vacant state government jobs would be abolished "unless officials justified their need." The positions were budgeted at $60 million, and some had remained empty for nine years. Martin viewed the hiring freeze as "an unconstitutional usurpation of the responsibility of the office of governor to administer the budget," and Secretary of Human Resources Kirk branded it "a clearly partisan move" and "another attempt to involve the legislature in the day-to-day management of state government." Rand countered: "If it's partisan politics to hold down spending, . . . we plead guilty." *News and Observer,* March 27, 28, 29, 1985.

Anthony Eden (Tony) Rand (1939-   ), native of Garner; resident of Fayetteville; A.B., 1961, LL.B., 1964, University of North Carolina at Chapel Hill. Attorney; member, state Senate, 1980-1988, majority leader, 1987-1988, and chairman of its Base Budget Committee; unsuccessful Democratic candidate for lieutenant governor, 1988. *News and Observer,* November 10, 1988; *North Carolina Manual, 1987-1988,* 287; *UNC Alumni Directory,* 945.

Bobby R. Etheridge (1941-   ), born in Sampson County; resident of Harnett County; B.S., Campbell College (later University), 1965; U.S. Army, 1965-1967. Owner, Layton Supply Co.; president, WLLN Radio, and of Angier Hardware and Home Center; member, state House, 1979-1988, and chairman of its Appropriations-Base Budget Committee; elected state superintendent of public instruction, 1988; Democrat. *News and Observer,* November 10, 1988; *North Carolina Manual, 1987-1988,* 420.

[3]"An Act to Provide for Nomination of Members of the State Board of Elections by the State Political Party Chairmen, and Concerning the Term of Office of the Executive Secretary-Director," was ratified April 5, 1985. Section 1.1 instructed the governor to fill any vacancy on the state board with a nominee from the departing member's political party; section 2 extended the expiration date of the term of the state director, Alex K. Brock, a Democrat, to 1989. Although he had not intended to replace Brock, whose term normally would have ended in 1985, the latter provision prevented Martin from doing

so during his first—and only, some lawmakers hoped—administration. *N.C. Session Laws, 1985,* c. 62; *News and Observer,* March 29, 1985. The legislation echoed an earlier measure that extended Brock's term until May 15, 1977, thereby eliminating Governor Holshouser's chance to appoint a new state elections chief. See "An Act to Provide that the State Board of Elections Shall Be an Independent Agency," *N.C. Session Laws, 1973, Second Session, 1974,* c. 1409, s. 3, ratified April 13, 1974.

[4]Governor Hunt signed Executive Order Number 112 on October 25, 1984, establishing the North Carolina Missing Children's Information Center within the Department of Crime Control and Public Safety. *N.C. Session Laws, 1983, Extra and Regular Sessions, 1984,* 469-474. However, some members of the 1985 General Assembly, on the advice of Robert B. Morgan, supported transferring the center to the Department of Justice. Morgan, director of the State Bureau of Investigation, an agency of the state Justice Department, recommended the change out of concern that law enforcement professionals retain sole access to the Police Information Network, a database used in investigating reports of missing children. The Department of Crime Control and Public Safety naturally disputed the SBI chief's position on the center and PIN. In the end, legislation ratified July 15, 1985, statutorily authorizing the North Carolina Center for Missing Children, assigned the entity to the Department of Crime Control and Public Safety. *N.C. Session Laws, 1985,* c. 765; *News and Observer,* March 30, 1985.

[5]S.B. 53, the proposed amendment granting veto power to the governor, met its demise in the Senate Judiciary I Committee on Thursday, March 28, not Tuesday, March 26. Weldon Robert Price was the lone Democrat on the committee who supported the bill. *N.C. Senate Journal, 1985,* 132; *News and Observer,* March 29, 1985.

Weldon Robert Price (1928-   ), native of Rockingham County; A.B., Elon College, 1957; U.S. Army, 1950-1952. Superintendent, American Tobacco Co.; Reidsville City Council member, 1966-1972, mayor pro tem, and mayor; member, Rockingham County Board of Commissioners, 1972-1984; elected to state Senate, 1984. *North Carolina Manual, 1985,* 300.

[6]North Carolinians approved gubernatorial succession in a 1977 referendum authorized under "An Act to Amend the Constitution of North Carolina to Empower the Voters to Elect the Governor and Lieutenant Governor for Two Consecutive Terms," *N.C. Session Laws, 1977,* c. 363. Nevertheless, in 1985 the General Assembly decided to give the state's electorate the opportunity to reconsider its earlier decision. Lawmakers ratified, on April 5, "An Act to Amend the Constitution of North Carolina to Provide that Future Governors and Lieutenant Governors May Not Succeed Themselves, and to Make a Conforming Change to the General Statutes." The measure called for a November, 1986, referendum on succession, yet allowed Martin and Lieutenant Governor Jordan to seek reelection in 1988. Legislative supporters of repeal, from both parties, contended that succession had marooned too many gubernatorial aspirants; limiting a governor to one term would once again provide a steady outlet for the state's rising political talent. *N.C. Session Laws, 1985,* c. 61; *News and Observer,* March 25, April 3, 1985.

However, the 1986 referendum was never held. Martin condemned the repeal of succession as an affront to the office of governor, and some Democrats worried that Republicans would use the issue to their advantage in the 1986 legislative elections. Lieutenant Governor Jordan said, "I want to get it off the ballot. If it's out there it will be perceived as a slam against the governor, and that was not the intention." Indeed, there was popular support for succession. Fifty-five percent of the respondents to a 1985 Carolina Poll on the repeal referendum favored allowing governors to serve two consecutive terms, while 33 percent opposed the idea and 11 percent were unsure. The General Assembly ratified "An Act to Repeal the Act Calling for a Referendum on Gubernatorial Succession" on July 15, 1986. *N.C. Session Laws, 1985, Extra and Regular Sessions, 1986,* c. 1010; *News and Observer,* March 28, 1985, June 20, 1986.

PRIVATE INDUSTRY COUNCIL

DURHAM, APRIL 3, 1985

You honor me, today, by your invitation to precede a distinguished panel of corporate speakers at this conference of the Private Industry Council, a joint venture of the Durham and Chapel Hill chambers of commerce. This afternoon, you'll hear some exciting success stories about how business and government can, and should, work together, productively and collectively, to extend a hand, rather than a hand-out, to unemployed and disadvantaged workers in the Durham and Orange County area. You'll want to be involved if you're not already.

At the heart of this area, of course, is North Carolina's crown jewel of high technology, the Research Triangle Park—an industrial dynasty that has gained international recognition and acceptance. Your speakers will represent both the Davids and Goliaths of the business world. They range from Fortune 500 giants to bootstrapping entrepreneurs. What they share is the ability to make the Job Training Partnership Act, JTPA here in Durham and Orange counties, the most effective program in the state and, indications are, among the leading five in the nation.

As you know, the Job Training Partnership Act was signed into law by President Reagan in October, 1982.[1] It was an administration initiative directed at training and employment that enjoyed bipartisan support in the Congress, and one which I favored strongly and was actively involved in promoting as chairman of the House Republican Research Committee.

This legislation was designed to replace CETA, the often controversial jobs training program that focused on public service employment, public sector jobs.[2] The Job Training Partnership Act, on the other hand, targets the private sector for job opportunities through a business-oriented private industry council, of which there are thirteen in North Carolina today.

Here in Durham, the chamber of commerce has supported the Private Industry Council in a variety of ways. The chamber recruited high-tech firms—among them Amphenol, Data General, Northern Telecom, IBM, and Sperry—to design and implement an electronics assembly training program for economically disadvantaged women. The results of this Women in Electronics program have been extraordinary. Eighty-five percent of the trainees, many of whom are former welfare recipients, have gone to work at an average wage of $5.55 an hour. The program has received national attention from such organizations as the National Alliance of Business.

Last July, in response to a chamber proposal, IBM officially opened a word-processing job training center at Durham Technical Institute. IBM donated Displaywriters, Selectric typewriters, and mag-card units to train eligible applicants for jobs in business and industry.

These are examples of how I want to see North Carolina's $70 million share of job-training funds used—effectively and with lasting results; with real jobs. The key to success in employment and training is to link economic development—business—with employment and training—government and community colleges—to produce those results, and that's precisely what the Private Industry Council has accomplished.

Not all of the participants from the private sector have been the flagships of North Carolina industry. For example, MDK, Incorporated, a small entrepreneurship that assembles those famous Lionel trains, has obtained some of its most qualified workers from this program. That's a great way to run a railroad! What more companies need to learn is that it's a valuable asset that can be tailored to the needs of any company, regardless of size, and they need to participate.

Today we must face up to the fact that North Carolina is part of the larger world marketplace. We've been experiencing a new wave of foreign competition in recent years, and unless industry, government, and labor become allies, rather than remaining adversaries, we'll be washed away by that wave. We're beginning to overcome that habit of an adversarial, confrontational relationship, but we need to do much more, and what that requires is quite basic: We need to accept the fact that industrial competitiveness, technological leadership, focused innovation, and entrepreneurship, are fundamental to our economic and social well-being. We must understand that nothing less than a cohesive and comprehensive statewide effort to compete domestically and internationally will suffice in securing our future.

I think it's helpful in this discussion of our economic future to look at our origins as well as destinies. I won't try to perform a historical autopsy here, since even the doctors of economics can't agree, and experience has shown that when two or three economists are gathered together, there are four or five opinions. What I will do is simply state the profoundly obvious: No state is immune to time, and I'm convinced that much of our problem is our failure to remember that.

Had not government, in fact, grown preoccupied with redistributing wealth, rather than creating it—with dividing up the pie, rather than baking a bigger pie, so all could get a bigger slice? And hadn't consumption, not investment, become job number one? President Reagan set out four years ago to try to change that. I worked with him in Congress and will continue, as governor, to encourage our congressional delegation.

My administration is addressing those questions. We've already placed before the North Carolina General Assembly a major tax-relief proposal, one that can be financed entirely by growing surplus revenues. The people don't want us fighting in Raleigh; what you want to see is a lot more cooperation, to compete better as a team, as a united state. So, it's time to stop being a house divided. Let's soften our stance toward each other in our common interest.

I've taken that approach since my first day in office. I've appealed for reason, compromise, and consensus. I held out the olive branch, time and again. That's why I welcome Lieutenant Governor Jordan's invitation to a summit.[3]

The first issue is whether we're going to continue to spend all of the huge surpluses of revenue generated by economic growth, as past administrations have recommended; or are we going to take part of those surpluses, just a fourth of it, and give taxpayers, business and individuals alike, some much-needed relief.

The renewal policy for our state, one that will carry us into the twenty-first century, needs to be dealt with forthrightly, just as you've done with your private industry council. You've faced up to the reality that displaced workers need to be retrained, so as to enhance North Carolina's most valuable resource: its people. We've tried a lot of job programs—Community Action, Model Cities, OIC.[4] We may have to kiss a lot of frogs before we find the one who's the prince, but find him we must, because too much is at stake. [I'm] beginning to believe JTPA [is] the prince.

I believe my tax-cutting proposals can help. They include elimination of the inventory and intangibles taxes, as well as the 3 percent sales tax on food and over-the-counter medicines.[5]

We have the available resources to accomplish these goals and still have adequate revenues to maintain state government's services and provide adequate reserves for contingencies. My budget proposes to increase [the] percentage of General Fund [going to] public schools, [from] 42.6 percent [to] 44.4 percent.

So where does North Carolina, and its people, stand on these matters? If North Carolina is not to become the King Lear of economic development, for traditional industries as well as advanced ones, then we must stand together.

You have many other speakers today, so let me conclude. What this administration is trying to do is nothing less than create a competitive renaissance for North Carolina, a renaissance that will encourage investment, give relief to overburdened individual taxpayers, and enable our traditional industries to weather difficult times and make necessary adjustments; to build a climate where all who provide jobs can be more competitive and more survivable in the marketplace. It's an uphill fight, a struggle to build bipartisan cooperation out of partisan politics; to build a stronger job market by business, and labor, and government singing together in harmony, but I'm convinced it's a challenge we can meet, and must meet, intelligently and wisely. JTPA is using intelligence and wisdom, so be a part of it. Together, as one united state of North Carolina, we will meet the challenge.

---

[1]P.L. 97-300, "Job Training Partnership Act" (short title), *United States Statutes at Large*, Act of October 13, 1982, 96 Stat. 1322-1399.

[2]The Comprehensive Employment and Training Act (CETA) and other federal occupational training efforts created upwards of 750,000 public jobs early in the Carter administration. However, CETA programs were roundly criticized for bringing "little permanent benefit" to trainees, and incidents of administrative waste and fraud were reported nationally. In North Carolina, the Department of Natural Resources and Community Development came under close scrutiny for irregularities in its oversight of CETA funds during the probe of state AFL-CIO president Wilbur Hobby. On December 29, 1981, Hobby was sentenced to eighteen months in prison, five years' probation, and ordered to pay a $40,000 fine for "fraudulently obtaining and misapplying" approximately $130,000 in CETA contracts. The monies ostensibly were awarded to his Durham printing firm, Precision Graphics, to provide the disadvantaged with job skills. A grand jury investigation of Precision Graphics also culminated in the indictment of an NRCD employee and one of Hobby's business associates. "Comprehensive Employment and Training Act of 1973" (short title), P.L. 93-203, *United States Statutes at Large*, Act of December 28, 1973, 87 Stat. 839-883; *Congressional Quartlerly Almanac, 97th Congress, 2nd Session . . . 1982, Volume XXXVIII* (Washington, D.C.: Congressional Quarterly, Inc., 1983), 61, hereinafter cited as *Congressional Quarterly Almanac*, with appropriate year; *Durham Morning Herald*, March 28, 1982; *Greensboro Daily News*, December 30, 1981; *News and Observer*, May 30, 1981, July 3, 1984.

[3]During the first quarter of 1985, relations between the Governor's Office and General Assembly worsened as officials of both parties actively employed the newspapers and airwaves to stake positions in increasingly acrimonious disputes over such matters as the scheduling of the governor's biennial address, his control of the Board of Elections,

and the gubernatorial succession and veto bills. Martin's press release of April 1, 1985 (see pages 61-64, above), in which he called the defeat of the veto proposal an "arrogantly repulsive act apparently . . . engineered by the Senate's increasingly partisan leadership," particularly attracted the lieutenant governor's notice. "I woke up this morning and saw in the paper that I was arrogant; I've never been called arrogant before," Jordan told reporters. He requested an April 3 conference with the governor and Speaker Ramsey that he hoped would "give us a chance to talk about the events of recent days and discuss how we can better communicate directly, without having to talk through the media." *News and Observer*, April 3, 1985.

[4]P.L. 88-452, "The Economic Opportunity Act of 1964" (short title), *United States Statutes at Large*, Act of August 20, 1964, 78 Stat. 508-534, established Community Action programs. The Model Cities program was established under P.L. 89-754, "Demonstration Cities and Metropolitan Development Act of 1966" (short title), *United States Statutes at Large*, Act of November 3, 1966, 89 Stat. 1255-1296; see also Vincent Ostrom and others, *Local Government in the United States* (San Francisco, California: ICS Press, 1988), 54-55. The Opportunities Industrialization Center concept was born in Philadelphia and had spread across the country by the end of the 1960s. Founder Leon Sullivan described the privately established OICs as "masssive, militant, people-centered, people-directed, self-help programs initiated by the black community for the black community." OICs eventually received some federal assistance. Leon H. Sullivan, *Build, Brother, Build* (Philadelphia: Macrae Smith Company, 1969), 94, 110-111.

[5]At this point the governor inserted into his prepared text the note "The first two: strategic. The food tax relief gives perception of fairness."

INAUGURAL CONVOCATION OF DR. WILLIAM H. LIKINS

GREENSBORO, APRIL 11, 1985

As a former mild-mannered chemistry professor in real life, I am deeply honored by your invitation to address this inaugural convocation of Dr. Likins[1] as the sixteenth president of Greensboro College, an institution that is deeply rooted in the history of North Carolina and the United Methodist church. On behalf of the people of North Carolina, Dr. Likins, I extend you a cordial welcome to our state—realizing you've been here long enough to confidently unpack the china—and I wish you every success as you accept the mantle of continuing leadership of a great academic community, one which unites, in a nonsectarian way, Judeo-Christian values and the liberal arts.

Since its founding by the Reverend Peter Doub as a school for girls 152 years ago,[2] Greensboro College has placed strong and rightful emphasis upon acquainting students with our Judeo-Christian religious tradition. At the same time, it has adhered faithfully to a strong basic core curriculum, even in times when such an approach to the liberal arts was not in vogue at more trendy institutions. As your statement of purpose sets forth so eloquently, "The central purpose of the college is the encouragement of the individual to become liberated." That's not a new notion. "Such persons would be freed from ignorance and provincialism and freed for critical thinking and clarity of expression; freed from intolerance and freed for human values. Such persons would possess a sense of history, an understanding of literature and language, a knowledge of mathematics and science, an awareness of political and social realities, and a respect for physical soundness."[3]

In our society today, the subject of values is fraught with emotion and controversy. We live in a time when there is a pervasive sense that values are of little relative consequence, private personal matters arising from individual subjective preferences, or even prejudices, not from widespread agreement on the basic ends and means to be used in the conduct of our life and dealings with others. Perhaps at most, values are often seen as attributes of groups such as churches, families, fraternal organizations, clubs, or ethnic groups.

Our national commitment to pluralism as a fundamental feature of our society tends to reinforce this subjective, relativistic, concept of values, and thus it tends to obscure the possibility that values can unite rather than divide us. That requires commitment, individually and as a society. You've heard the story of the chicken who invited the pig to a breakfast of ham and eggs. The pig demurred: "For you that's a contribution; for me it's total commitment."

In some colleges and universities, the prevailing and dominant concept of education also adds to the confusion about values. In the last fifty years, education has come to mean primarily the acquisition of factual knowledge and the attainment of instrumental skills or competencies. Under the influence of a positive approach, facts and factual knowledge have been conceived as value-free. Indeed, the most rigorous adherents to this attitude proclaim that any vestiges of values distort knowledge of facts. What they ignore, as they reduce reality to the narrow confines of their definition of factual knowledge, is that their very outlook itself expresses a value; as one of their critics pointed out more than seventy years ago, with appropriate irony, "They espouse with fine enthusiasm the cause of not espousing any cause."

This is not the occasion to give an account of twentieth-century intellectual history that would explain why the concept of education had been pared down to mean little more than the transmission of factual knowledge. What I want to do here is to turn our attention to two other matters: First, why is that concept of education inadequate, and second, what can be done to broaden the goals of education once again—as you have demonstrated so successfully on this campus.

Before I proceed, I want to make sure that I am not misunderstood. In deploring that education has been reduced largely to the acquisition of factual knowledge, I am not making light of the importance of such learning, nor of the skills and discipline acquired with it. Before we can read to learn, we first must learn to read.

The transmission of key bodies of knowledge is, and always will be, a major end of education, but that is not enough! Reality is more than the facts which our analytical faculties derive from it. Among other things that make up the reality in which we live, and which affect the way in which we live, are values. They are as essential to our cultural atmosphere, as indispensable to our social life and welfare, as air is to our physical well-being.

We can see evidence of values all around us every day. As we drive on our streets and highways, bumper stickers ask us, "Have you hugged your kid today?"—or your lawyer?—or inform us "I brake for animals"; or prod us to be considerate, by saying, "If you can read this, thank your teacher"; or telling you how to vote! All of these express values.

If reality is not value free, then it follows as naturally as day comes after night that an education, adequate to teach people to cope with reality, cannot be value free or value neutral.

Not only is it important to appreciate the logical or philosophical justification for education to include values in its programs of instruction, it also is prudent to take notice of the public demand for our institutions of learning to give attention to values. *The Connecticut Mutual Life Report on American Values in the '80s* reveals a growing anxiety about the weakening of our hold on the values that are the foundation of our democratic society.[4] Another report argues persuasively that values are "intrinsic to the preservation of a free and democratic society and a civilized life, that they are transitional, that they stand above immediate political issues, and should be a more conscious and specific responsibility of educational institutions than they are at present." Finally, the Gallup Poll has shown that 70 percent of Americans want their educational institutions to provide instruction in values and ethical behavior.[5]

Confronted with such imperatives for providing education in values, we can perhaps gain assurance about the legitimacy of what is needed by rethinking, for our time, the place of education in the American polity. This relationship seems so elementary and self-evident that it should need no special emphasis, yet its original and primary purpose is often neglected, because it has been taken for granted as something given and established for all time, rather than something that each generation must discover for itself, strive to understand, and keep workable for its own needs and purposes.

By the word *polity*, I mean the fundamental principles, both written and unwritten, that are the basis for our free, democratic government and society. Please note that I include society as well as government among organizations created and supported by the fundamental principles that constitute a polity; I do so deliberately because our American polity cannot be confined only to the constitutional and legal principles, as important as they are, that make up our government. For example, justice and respect for the sanctity of individuals have led not only to constitutional safeguards and laws to enforce them, but also an outpouring of voluntary organizations, both to cooperate with government and, in some cases, to serve people in ways that either forestall the need for government action or go beyond the limits of what the law requires.

The fundamental principles that comprise the polity of American society as a whole can be summed up as those that undergird and guarantee the constant observance of respect for human dignity and freedom. They include all those that define the structure and purpose of government and, also, others that are essential in ensuring that civility and justice prevail in all of our dealings with one another. One of the policy papers I referred to earlier supplies a useful catalogue of these principles and values. It reads:

> Integrity and honesty are basic to any civilized society. So are tolerance, objectivity, compassion, and respect for the rights of others. Included as well are humility, sympathy, benevolence, open-mindedness, self-control, reasoned discourse, independent thought, the sense of responsibility, participation in the democratic process, and devotion to the common good.

The place of our educational establishment in a polity founded on these values has seemed to be self-evident, at least since Jefferson drafted the "Bill for the More General Diffusion of Human Knowledge" only two years after he wrote the Declaration of Independence.[6] He knew "of no safe depository of the ultimate powers of society but the people themselves," and he went on to say: "If we think them not enlightened enough to exercise their control with wholesome discretion, the remedy is not to take it from them but to inform their discretion."[7] Our public schools and our institutions of higher learning are the primary places to ensure that citizens have that Jeffersonian ideal of an informed discretion.

Knowledge of values is not enough to ensure good citizenship. Education also must develop an understanding which provides the basis for sound judgment and wise choices among conflicting values and pressures. A mature, democratic society requires citizens with a clear comprehension and firm commitment to the values they have chosen for themselves and their society.

I shall conclude by setting out six responsibilities that I believe educators at all levels must accept if they are to initiate and enhance education in values as a life-long process:

First is to provide a clear, authentic, and faithful exposition of the values of a good society—one that is free, democratic, and respectful of the dignity of each member. Those values also must be practiced in the process of education itself, or they will carry little conviction.

Second is to provide the student, at the appropriate point in one's educational development, with the bases of different value systems, allowing for critical commentary and enhancing the student's capabilities to make his or her own judgments about them and the value system that has been received—not to undermine the values one brings but to foster self-appraisal.

Third is to provoke instruction in a sufficiently wide range of disciplines so that the evaluation of one's own and other belief systems is informed and seriously pursued. Values can and must be evaluated. They must not be trivialized.

So: Fourth is to encourage the student to then evolve a deeper personal framework of values for committed living, to carry them into coherent action, and to resolve conflicts in an orderly and rational way.

Fifth is to inculcate knowledge of the past in terms relevant to the student's present and future. Knowledge of the past is particularly important to understanding and dealing with transitional problems.

Sixth is for educators to reexamine the fundamental assumptions of our profession, or the science of teaching. The role of teaching, indeed, is one which should be optimized. That's why it is so critically important that we build public support for strengthening the teaching profession, to restore its attractiveness to our best and brightest of this next generation.

Years ago, Alfred North Whitehead gave voice to words that have never been more pertinent than they are today. "The future," he said, "is bright with every possibility of achievement and tragedy."[8] There has never been a more crucial time for our citizens, now and in the future, to have a sturdy commitment to those values which underpin our society; achievement or tragedy will depend upon what values they hold and how faithful they are in observing them.

[1]William Henry Likins (1931-   ), born in Louisville, Kentucky; A.B., Asbury College, 1951; M.Div., Emory University, 1954; Th.D., Boston University, 1961; Ph.D., Peabody College of Vanderbilt University, 1979. Minister, Covenant Methodist Church, Worcester, Massachusetts, 1956-1962; senior minister, Fisk Memorial Methodist Church, Natick, Massachusetts, 1962-1967; director, National Division of Higher Education, The United Methodist Church, Nashville, Tennessee, 1967-1976; executive director, Commission on Higher Education, Louisville, Kentucky, 1976-1977; vice-president for development, Adrian College, 1979-1984; president, Greensboro College, since 1984. William Henry Likins to Jan-Michael Poff, July 29, 1988.

[2]Peter Doub (1796-1869), native of Stokes County; died in Greensboro; doctor of divinity degree, Normal (later Trinity) College, 1855. Methodist minister, ordained 1820; circuit rider in North Carolina and Virginia for forty-two years; professor of biblical literature, Trinity College, 1867-1869. Organized Greensboro Methodists in building town's first denominational church, 1830; opened school for members' children, 1832, that eventually became Greensboro Female College (now Greensboro College), chartered by the Methodist Conference in 1838. Powell, *DNCB*, II, 95-96.

[3]"Greensboro College declares as its central purpose the encouragement of individuals to become liberated. Such persons would be freed from ignorance and provincialism and freed for critical thinking and clarity of expression, freed from intolerance and freed for human values. Such persons would possess a sense of history, an understanding of literature and language, a knowledge of mathematics and science, an appreciation of the arts, an awareness of political and social realities, a respect for physical soundness, and familiarity with the Judaeo-Christian religious tradition." *Greensboro College Academic Bulletin, 1984-1985* (Greensboro: Greensboro College, n.d.), 3.

[4]Research and Forecasts, Inc., *The Connecticut Mutual Life Report on American Values in the '80s: The Impact of Belief* (Hartford, Connecticut: Connecticut Mutual Life Insurance Company, 1981).

[5]National Commission on Excellence in Education, *A Nation at Risk: The Imperative for Educational Reform* (Washington, D.C.: U.S. Government Printing Office, [1983]), 16-18, hereinafter cited as *A Nation at Risk*, discussed the findings of the Gallup Poll's *Public's Attitudes Toward the Public Schools* (1982).

[6]For the text of "A Bill for the More General Diffusion of Knowledge," 1779, see Saul K. Padover (ed.), *The Complete Jefferson: Containing His Major Writings, Published and Unpublished, Except His Letters* (New York: Tudor Publishing Company, 1943), 1048-1054.

[7]Excerpt of letter from Thomas Jefferson to William Charles Jarvis, September 28, 1820, quoted in John Bartlett, *Familiar Quotations: A Collection of Passages, Phrases, and Proverbs Traced to Their Sources in Ancient and Modern Literature*, edited by Emily Morison Beck (Boston: Little, Brown and Company, fourteenth edition, revised and enlarged, 1968), 473, hereinafter cited as Bartlett, *Familiar Quotations*.

[8]Alfred North Whitehead (1861-1947), native of Ramsgate, England; B.A., 1884, M.A., 1887, D.Sc., 1905, Trinity College, Cambridge University. Faculty member, mathematician, Trinity College, 1885-1911, and at University College and the Imperial College of Science and Technology, University of London, 1911-1924; philosophy professor, 1924-1936, and professor emeritus, 1936-1947, Harvard University; author. *Who Was Who in America, 1943-1950*, 573.

GOVERNOR'S TASK FORCE ON ALCOHOL AND DRUG ABUSE AMONG YOUTH AND TEENAGERS

RALEIGH, APRIL 16, 1985

[Alcohol and drug use among youth, and the necessity of adult involvement in countering such problems, also were topics of the governor's speech introducing the anti-substance abuse film *Get It Straight*, at its Raleigh premiere, October 1, 1985, at Enloe High School.]

I am always delighted to join with those who share the commitment that Dottie and I have made to combatting the problem of substance abuse among the children and youth of North Carolina.

When you confront abused children, you find abusing children. I addressed that problem, as well as many others affecting our children and youth, in my "State of the State" message to the General Assembly on February 28, and I called upon our legislators to take timely and appropriate action on a number of innovative and effective programs to deal with those problems.

Among the solutions I proposed was the Families and Schools Together program, better known as FAST.[1] This would provide for the establishment of cooperative local task forces, composed of leaders from the private and public sectors, in every school district of the state. The key is to build effective working task forces through which we can turn the tide of abuse and promote a healthier generation of North Carolinians.

The program has three vitally important goals: first, is the promotion of increased awareness, at the community level, of drug and other substance abuse problems; second, is bringing the family together in a program of dialogue and interaction, one which fosters communication and understanding; and, third, is the implementation of what we call Project Alert—the combining of comprehensive education and peer support to identify and target children at the crossroads, the sixth- and seventh-grade levels.

Legislation to establish the FAST program, and to appropriate $800,000 for its implementation, was introduced April 1 in a bill sponsored by Senator Charles Hipps of the Twenty-ninth Senatorial District.[2] But I want to emphasize that its enactment will depend upon you and the citizens of our state as much as it does this administration. If we are to stamp out the drug and other substance abuse epidemic that has decimated many young lives, it will require the strongest support a concerned public can give.

It seems obvious to everyone but the public, as individuals, that our society is disposing of our past rewards at a greater pace than we are replenishing our investment today for future harvesting. Let me cite an example: Among nations, Japan has the lowest infant mortality rate, the highest percentage of literacy, the longest average life span, the highest education level among youth, and it is the lowest in violent crimes of any nation. Overpopulated and under-resourced, Japan still comes on like an undaunted David taking on Goliath.

In fairness to the rest of us in the western world, I must point out that centuries of inbred Japanese culture have had a significant, positive influence on Japan's resilience. The astonishing means by which they outdistance us is through a process referred to as *nemawashi*, wrapping roots of a tree or bush together before moving it; a free translation might be "circular agreement," bringing together people as a group communication device. Ironically, the modern concept was developed by an American, W. Edwards Deming,[3] in 1948. It is the nemawashi style of togetherness that the FAST program will utilize.

As a society today, we protest for individual liberty and social order in the same breath. They conflict, but we achieve a balance of both. We strive for material wealth, and would like spiritual wealth as a by-product. We want more protection from crime, including the abuse of children and abuse by young people, but we demand less interference in our social habits.

But, we can't always have it both ways. If we want results, we must pay the price. I believe—in fact, I am confident—that the majority of North Carolinians are willing to pay the price. That's why Dottie and I are taking the leadership in programs that offer solutions, not promises, to the problems of children and youth in our state. We're saying, "Come on, wake up, North Carolina! Let's hitch up the wagon and move out again."

If God gave us the law of cause and effect so that we could take stock of how we're faring, we can take advantage of it by studying the effect of how our children and youth live. But, the secret lies in changing the cause. The cause of many of our problems affecting children and youth consists of many separate, smaller causes.

I've traveled widely throughout our state in the last year or more, meeting with students at every grade level, teachers, business executives, ministers, parents, politicians, and other citizens. The same message from each group comes through loud and clear: Responsibility needs to be redefined and retaught to this and future generations—responsibility for one's actions, responsibility for one's future, responsibility for one's area.

The record needs no embellishing. As I speak here today, a traffic accident will occur every 15 seconds, involving an intoxicated teenage driver bringing injuries to others. Every 23 minutes, one of our children or youth dies in an automobile accident, and, in most cases, drugs or alcohol is involved. This year, of the several hundred thousand American young people who try to commit suicide, more than 5,000 will carry out the tragic, irreversible act; North Carolina statistics are equally distressing. Some 80 percent of these suicide victims will have made open threats before they follow through.

What is causing this onslaught of violence and tragedy? The culprit is a six-word slogan: "Relief is just a swallow away," only in this case, it's either alcohol or drugs. The single biggest problem affecting our children and youth is the irresponsible obsession with immediate sensual gratification. If it feels good, I'll try it. If I can't be certain to win, then I won't enter. I want the American dream I saw on TV, in the movies, and the one my parents said I'd get because I'm so special, and I want it now. Tomorrow is too late!

In his compelling book, *Me: The Narcissistic American,* psychoanalyst Aaron Stern brilliantly pierces to the heart of the problem. "To attain emotional security," he writes, "each of us must learn to develop two critical capabilities: the ability to live with uncertainty and the ability to delay immediate gratification in favor of long-term goals." Self-discipline. "Adolescence is the time of maximum resistance to further growth. It is a time characterized by the teenager's ingenious efforts to maintain the privileges of childhood, while at the same time, demanding the rights of adulthood. It is a point beyond which most human beings do not pass emotionally. The more we do for our children," even if for the best of motives, "the less they can do for themselves. The dependent child of today is destined to become the dependent parent of tomorrow."[4] Aaron Stern.

The greatest gifts parents can give their children are roots and wings, roots of responsibility and wings of independence. When those roots and wings are missing, the results are very disturbing, even tragic. Today, the average parents spend less than seven minutes each week alone with each child, one on one, at a time when each is receptive. This relationship with young people has been referred to by Denis Waitley, the noted author and lecturer, as the "seven-minutes-per-week syndrome." What children really need, then, are concerned parents, teachers, neighbors, and other adults, to listen; to share their problems; to offer guidance; to teach responsibility; to show that values are important. In other words, they need caring communities, for the community is all that surrounds them.

The Families and Schools Together program seeks to answer that need. It opens the channel of communication, to advise, to counsel, to help, and to teach that independence is won only by responsible living. If we are to achieve a united state, in a real sense, we must first join together as a unifying force. FAST can help us to accomplish this goal. It also will save our future generations.

---

[1]At this point, the governor inserted the following information into his prepared text: "Acronym FAST: to fast, to abstain (obsolete verb), control consumption, diet; by education to avoid experimentation and help/support in removing dependency. FAST. DOPE—supply and demand. DOPE FAST." DOPE stood for Drug Observation, Prevention, and Education; see "State of the State," February 28, 1985, above.

[2]S.B. 166, "A Bill to Appropriate Funds to Establish the Families and Schools Together (FAST) Program and to Combat the Youth Drug Problem in North Carolina," was referred to the Senate Appropriations Committee on April 1, 1985, where it remained through the end of the session. N.C. Senate Journal, 1985, 145.

[3]William Edwards Deming; resident of Washington, D.C.; B.S., University of Wyoming, 1922; M.S., University of Colorado, 1924; Ph.D., Yale University, 1928; honorary degrees. Award-winning consultant; engineering, physics, and statistics educator; mathematical physicist, U.S. Department of Agriculture, 1927-1939; adviser in sampling, U.S. Bureau of Census, 1939-1945; professor of statistics, Graduate School of Business Administration, New York University, since 1946; Union of Japanese Scientists and Engineers honored him by establishing the Deming Prize; author. Who's Who in America, 1986-1987, I, 688.

[4]In quoting from Aaron Stern's book, Me: The Narcissistic American (New York: Ballantine Books, 1979), the governor combines passages from four different pages into one excerpt. "To attain emotional maturity, each of us must learn to develop two critical capacities: the ability to live with uncertainty and the ability to delay immediate gratification in favor of long-range goals" (p. 28). "Adolescence is the time of maximum resistance to further growth. It is a time characterized by the teenager's ingenious efforts to maintain the privileges of childhood while at the same time demanding the rights of adulthood. It is a point beyond which most human beings do not pass emotionally" (p. 55). "The more we do for our children, the less they can do for themselves" (p. 46). "The dependent child of today is destined to become the dependent parent of tomorrow" (p. 51). Except for the material from page 28, the governor quoted Stern accurately.

STATE BOARD OF EDUCATION

RALEIGH, APRIL 17, 1985

I'm delighted to meet with you, today. It's the first opportunity I've had since becoming governor of our state, and I've looked forward to it eagerly. Before I address the subject of public education, I want to welcome my three appointees to the board: Mrs. Cary Owen, Mrs. Mary Morgan, and Mr. Mebane Pritchett.

Mrs. Owen, a Phi Beta Kappa graduate of the University of North Carolina at Chapel Hill, has served with distinction for eight years as a member of the Buncombe County Board of Commissioners. As a former member of the Buncombe County Board of Education, she comes to the board with a wealth of experience, experience from which I believe we can all benefit.[1]

Mrs. Morgan is a graduate of East Carolina University. In addition to serving on the Onslow County Board of Education, she also is a member of the National School Board Association and the National School Volunteer Program. She, too, is an eminent member of this distinguished board, as her credentials reflect.

Mr. Pritchett is the executive director of the John Motley Morehead Foundation in Chapel Hill. A Morehead Scholar graduate of the University of North Carolina at Chapel Hill, he later was graduated from Harvard University School of Law—after which he practiced law in New York City. He is a member of the board of directors of this board, as well as the North Carolina Nature Conservancy. I am pleased that he has accepted reappointment, for I know that you value his service and the many contributions he made during his previous short term.[2]

I don't believe I need to emphasize that these valuable leaders are a true representation of my bipartisan philosophy of placing only the most qualified individuals in positions of great responsibility. Public education is a sector in which we not only need responsible leaders, it is one in which we must demand it.

This year, 1985, has been proclaimed the "Year of the Child" in North Carolina, a year in which we place as our highest priority the needs of our children and youth. It is a year in which North Carolina is turning again to the classroom.

For the first time since Sputnik, public education is at the top of North Carolina's agenda, and I'm extremely proud that our great state is in the forefront of this surge of optimism about the public schools. I am proud that this administration is providing $108 million of new spending for the vital programs that have proved their contributions to improving the quality of education in North Carolina. More than 60 percent of the General Fund proposal that has been submitted by this administration, to the General Assembly, is devoted to education. I'm proud, also, that the proposed budget I have submitted to our legislators provides almost $40 million for a career growth pilot program for the teachers of North Carolina during the biennium.

We want our teachers to be paid adequately. We want to insist upon accountability in our school system; and we want the best teachers to enter our classrooms, or remain there, and be compensated for their excellence. But, we want to develop the best, and the most equitable, method possible to reward excellent teachers before full implementation.

I'm proud of the fact that by the end of the first year of my administration, subject to legislative approval, more than one half billion dollars of new money will have been spent for public education in a consecutive two-year period.

Our citizens have issued a mandate: They do not want our state to throw vast amounts of money at problems in education. They want the most efficient use of their tax dollars, and they want to see results.

I'm proud of North Carolina, most of all, because we believe that public education is the most successful of all the government's efforts to improve the lot of its citizens. Much of government is intended to solve problems—to punish offenders, to alleviate pain, to remedy disasters. Only in education do we systematically set out to prevent problems by shaping the future.

Our system of public education is unlike any other institution anywhere in the world. Our schools have socialized wave after wave of refugees and immigrants. Our schools have integrated the races. Our schools have equalized economic opportunity. Our schools have provided the classic means for upward social mobility. Thomas Jefferson said that, given a choice between government without a free press and a free press without government, he would have no hesitation in choosing the latter.[3] But without free and uniform public schools, we will not long have either a free press, a free government, or a free people, for a free press requires universal literacy.

A free government requires informed citizen participation, and free people require an appreciation of the choices before them if they are to help decide those choices. And in our system of public education, there is one role, one function, one person at the center of the process; one person whose performance determines the performance of the entire system; one caring, dedicated person who can change the world, one student at a time; one lucky person with the most satisfying job in the world—to illuminate minds, shape futures, and build dreams. That person is a teacher, the central focus of the entire educational process.

I think it's time for us to recognize our dedicated teachers for the good job they do and to challenge them for the changing role they will play in the future. I'm proud that in North Carolina, and all across the nation, public education has become priority number one, and the number-one priority of every principal, every superintendent, every school board member should be to support good teachers. To make that support meaningful, I propose the following short agenda:

First, we need to pay teachers adequately. We can't afford to entrust our children to the care of teachers exhausted from working two or three jobs to supplement their income.

Second, we need to show teachers we care about them in indirect ways. Today, if there's a piece of art in a school, it's probably in the principal's office. Our schools require more than a coat of paint, but pleasant surroundings would represent great change in our classrooms.

Third, we must give teachers upward mobility within their profession without abandoning what they do best. I submit that the highest-paid individual in a school system should be the best and most experienced teacher in that system.

Fourth, we must free principals from scheduling buses and filling out forms and get them back in the business of educational leadership. Every school needs an educational leader. Teachers need inspiration, and the principal is the person to provide it.

And finally, we need to give teachers a sense of fellowship within their discipline. A chemistry teacher at a local high school should feel a sense of academic brotherhood or sisterhood with a chemistry professor at the University of North Carolina and with a research chemist at NASA [National Aeronautics and Space Administration] headquarters.

Teachers, too, need to recognize some new realities. To achieve the highest standards, we must demand more training in what they teach—not just how to teach. Teachers must capitalize on the willingness of North Carolina to invest resources while that willingness exists. We know all too well how fragile the public will can be, and teachers must recognize that the public's willingness to support education is tied to results in the classroom. Teachers must recognize that the rewards inherent in the movement toward higher standards depend on performance.

Our state legislators—indeed, all state leaders—must recognize that it is a state responsibilty for preparing North Carolina for the future by educating children today. As governor, I've made education a priority, a personal political priority, and I've invested my own personal political capital in better public schools. Legislators, as well as the governor, must be willing to stand accountable for the performance of students.

When we all stand together, we'll have a better public education system, one which reflects excellence throughout. Our schools do not yet achieve the goal of distributing excellence as widely as we want, but they are North Carolina's greatest success story. Let us join together, with our teachers, in recognizing that our schools are what we make them, nothing more or nothing less.

How we regard our schools has a powerful effect on what happens in our classrooms, and classrooms, in the last analysis, are where our teachers help the great American dream continue to grow. I charge you, today, to join with me in building one united state of education, one in which our children not only learn to read well, but read to learn.

Knowledge is the frontier of tomorrow. Brain is becoming more and more the master of brawn. The prominent Soviet scholar, Ivan Yefremov, has told the Soviet people, "Throughout our lives we use only a fraction of our thinking ability. We could, without any difficulty, learn forty foreign languages, memorize a set of encyclopedias from *a* to *z*, and complete the required courses of a dozen universities."

According to the UCLA Brain Research Institute, the potential of the human brain to create, store, and learn may be virtually unlimited. The human mind is still the best computer in the world. Today, let us embark together upon a course of action to utilize fully the great capacity of our children's minds. We have the ability. Let's put that ability to work.

---

[1]Cary Caperton Owen (1935-   ), born in New York City; resident of Asheville; A.B., University of North Carolina at Chapel Hill, 1956. President, The Greenwood Co.; member, Buncombe County Board of Education, 1969, and Board of Commissioners, 1972-1980; Buncombe County chairwoman, Jim Martin for Governor, 1984; former treasurer, vice-president, Asheville Area Chamber of Commerce; Republican. Cary Caperton Owen to Jan-Michael Poff, September 11, 1989.

[2]Mebane Moore Pritchett (1935-   ), born in Lenoir; A.B., University of North Carolina at Chapel Hill, 1957; J.D., Harvard University, 1963; U.S. Navy, 1957-1960. Attorney in private practice, 1963-1967; associate director, 1967-1972, executive director, 1972-1987, John Motley Morehead Foundation; member, 1983-1987, vice-chairman, 1985-1986, chairman, 1986-1987, State Board of Education; president, Coca-Cola Scholars Foundation, Inc., since 1987; Democrat. Mebane M. Pritchett to Jan-Michael Poff, September 28, 1989; *News and Observer*, February 6, 1986.

[3]"The basis of our government being the opinion of the people, the very first object should be to keep that right; and were it left to me to decide whether we should have a government without newspapers, or newspapers without a government, I should not hesitate a moment to prefer the latter." Letter, Thomas Jefferson to Colonel Edward Carrington, [January 16, 1787], quoted in Bartlett, *Familiar Quotations*, 471.

STATE EMPLOYEES ASSOCIATION OF NORTH CAROLINA

RALEIGH, APRIL 23, 1985

[The governor discussed many of the same topics mentioned below, including health and on-the-job safety, in his speech to the annual convention of the State Employees Association of North Carolina, September 12, 1985. Convention goers learned of the Wellness Improvement for State Employees program, newly created by Executive Order Number 20. WISE was designed to "help each agency develop health-related personal activities for employees" and included "education in health and nutrition (and) opportunities for exercise and for improving your skills to cope with the daily demands of your job." Martin also outlined the State Employees' Workplace Requirements for Safety and Health, a newly operational plan intended to aid all state agencies in establishing and implementing improved safety standards.]

Allow me to express sincere appreciation for your kind invitation to attend this get-acquainted luncheon today. I wasn't brought here to make a speech, but I'll do it anyway. I don't want to neglect the opportunity you have provided to comment on some important matters in which we share a vital interest.

It takes good people, people working together as a team and who take pride in the excellence of their work, to make state government a responsible public entity as well as responsive to the needs of our citizens. As governor, I'm privileged to be a member of our association, the largest independent state employee association in the United States, with more than 47,000 members; and I am pleased that I can count elected Council of State, supreme court, my cabinet secretaries, senior assistants, and a growing number of staff members in the executive branch among this membership. This attests to the fact that we are now one state employee association, which by the uniqueness of its example is representative of North Carolina as one united state.[1]

It is by example that we have the opportunity to bring all of our 6.2 million citizens together as a moving force. It also is a challenging experience, as governor, to join with you in a dedicated effort to make state government, through the efforts of employees, the most efficient and effective of any state in our nation.

Last week, as a result of my initiative, a joint resolution was introduced in the General Assembly directing the State Personnel Commission to conduct a study of the State Personnel Act.[2] The purpose of that study is to correct numerous inadequacies in existing statutes. The commission is directed to design changes to give professional career employees the protection and security from political pressures to which they have, so unjustly, been subjected in the past. The exempt classifications have been used to pressure subordinate employees to feel obligated to make campaign contributions. We must assure them that this pressure will never again be exerted by those who seek only personal political gain.

Another accomplishment we seek to achieve, as a result of this bill, is a reduction in the number of exempt positions in the administration. During the eight years of the previous administration, the number of these positions was doubled, far in excess of the number required by the executive branch for the proper management of its affairs. It's time we controlled this practice.

The joint resolution introduced last week by Senator Redman and his colleagues in the Senate provides for the appointment of a special committee, appointed by the House, Senate, governor, and State Employees Association, to work with the commission in the development of legislation to address these problems.[3]

Another concern I want to share with you, today, is the growing number of accidents involving state employees. Within the last thirty-one months, accidents among state employees have resulted in the loss of 102,000 workdays. The number of accidents during that period approached 12,000, resulting in more than $9 million in medical costs and almost $5 million in workmen's compensation claims. And these figures do not include the cost of the state time taken by employees as sick leave or vacation time associated with recovery from these accidents.

In violation of statutes, many departments have not designed or implemented safety programs to protect their employees. Consequently, I have instructed Dick Lee and the State Personnel Office to consult with the North Carolina Department of Labor and OSHA [Occupational Safety and Health Administration] in the development of appropriate safety programs to ensure that employees will have safe conditions in their respective workplaces. To that end, I solicit your cooperation, assistance, and support.

In addition to these measures, I want this administration to be one in which employees will take pride in their jobs and will seek every opportunity to advance their knowledge and skills. We seek to provide all state employees competitive salaries, not only so we may attract the best and the brightest, but also to retain them and provide them greater opportunities for upward mobility. This includes a wide range of fringe benefits for themselves and their families. I am firmly committed to improve employee incentives as conditions require and as available revenues permit.

We must constantly scrutinize our health insurance plan, for employees and retirees, to ensure its continued vitality. The administration of this plan has come under severe criticism in recent years as it relates to accurate and timely processing and payment of claims. There have been recent improvements in administration, but we must strive for greater efficiency, and I welcome your comments and suggestions in this regard.

All of you are aware that I support the concept of merit pay steps to reward exceptional state employees, and you are aware, also, that I favor systematic cost of living increases based upon inflationary growth rates. I shall work to achieve continuity in these areas and shall seek legislative consensus in an effort to achieve results.

All of us must constantly remind ourselves that we are held accountable by our fellow citizens. We cannot afford to do less than our best in their interest. Today, I ask you to join me in encouraging our more than 47,000 fellow members in a united effort to lift our sights to higher levels of accomplishment. All I ask: Do your job with pride.

---

[1]The North Carolina State Employees Association and the North Carolina State Government Employees Association merged, on July 1, 1984, to form the State Employees Association of North Carolina. *News and Observer*, July 2, 1984.

[2]S.J.R. 329, "A Joint Resolution Directing the State Personnel Commission to Study the State Personnel Act and to Design Changes to Give Professional State Employees the Protection and Security from Political Pressures They Deserve and Establish a Senior Executive Service," was introduced before the upper house on April 16, 1985, and remained in committee through the end of the session. *N.C. Senate Journal, 1985,* 209, 386.

[3]William Walter Redman, Jr. (1933-   ), born in Statesville; resident of Iredell County; B.S., Embry-Riddle Aeronautical University, 1972; N.C. Air National Guard, 1952-1953; N.C. Army National Guard, 1953-1954; U.S. Army, 1954-1974. Real estate broker; elected state senator, 1978, and returned in subsequent elections; former senate minority leader; reelected to Senate, 1986, but resigned March 11, 1987, after appointment to state Utilities Commission was confirmed; Republican. *North Carolina Manual, 1985,* 275, *1987-1988,* 279-280n. Redman was joined by Republican senators Paul Sanders Smith (Rowan), Robert Vance Somers (Rowan), and Julius Arnette Wright (New Hanover) in introducing S.J.R. 329. *N.C. Senate Journal, 1985,* 209.

PRESS RELEASE: GOVERNOR MARTIN'S POSITION PAPER ON DAY-CARE POLICY

RALEIGH, MAY 3, 1985

1. Because they have the primary responsibility for the care and protection of their children, parents should have the right to choose

the type of providers that will furnish day-care services for their children.

2. People differ as to the kind of day-care services they wish for their children. Accordingly, providers of day-care services should be free to offer the type of day-care services that their customers wish, free of interference by the state except to the extent necessary to ensure the basic health and safety of children entrusted to them.

3. Church day-care programs, their curriculum, and their training standards which are now exempted by statute, should remain exempt from government interference.

4. The purchase of day-care services shall be the responsibility of the Department of Human Resources.

   a. The licensing and regulation of day-care services purchased by the Department of Human Resources shall be performed by the Department of Human Resources. Such licensing and regulation shall be done according to the same standards as that of the Department of Administration, except where such standards conflict with federal regulations, in which case the latter shall prevail.

   b. The licensing and regulation of day-care services, other than those purchased by the Department of Human Resources, shall be administered by the Department of Administration.

5. We must ensure that basic health and safety needs of children are met. Child-staff ratios should be both reasonable and affordable.

6. Checks into the backgrounds of persons furnishing day-care services are helpful in assuring protection to children in the care of day-care providers and peace of mind to parents. I have directed my staff to study proposals for legislation that would screen child-care workers for a history of child molestation or other criminal charges.

7. Training of the child-care workers is an important factor in ensuring the quality of child care. The excellent course offerings for child-care workers now available in community colleges and technical institutes across the state should be continued and encouraged.

8. In order for the Day Care Licensing Commission[1] to work effectively with the department secretaries, the members of the commission should be appointees solely of the governor, or as now provided.

---

[1]The Child Day Care Licensing Commission, formerly of the Department of Administration, was renamed the Child Day Care Commission and placed under the Department of Human Resources, effective July 1, 1985. *N.C. Session Laws, 1985*, c. 757, s. 155(a). For changes in state day-care standards, see c. 757, s. 156.

EDUCATION FOR CITIZENSHIP: A COMMENCEMENT SPEECH

WILSON, MAY 5, 1985

[The following address was delivered at Atlantic Christian College. Governor Martin also discussed the civic importance of an educated citizenry in remarks at Polk Central High School, Columbus, on September 23, 1985.]

Today is an important rite of passage for each member of this graduating class. Every society celebrates its own rituals, events involving special kinds of behavior based on old rules, that serve to divide the part of a person's life from old situation to new situation. An academic commencement is one of our happy rituals, an act of achievement and renewal. The ritual is important for those who watch the graduates, as well. In it, we of the audience—family, friends, and teachers—celebrate, through these graduates, our most important national resource: the minds of our young people.

I want to talk to you today about the best use of these minds in the years ahead, the years in which a student develops as a citizen—in which the training for careers and citizenship that has been given here will, in large measure, determine the course of our state of North Carolina and our nation. Before I do that, however, let me look for a moment at this special time of going to school and this special place that has been so important in your lives.

It is special, first, because you have been young here. Youth is a time of particular sensitivity and awareness and discovery. Here you have had special problems, special failures, and, I hope, special kinds of rewards. You may not know for years what actually happened to you at this place, but the forces that formed you here will be present in your lives whether you are conscious of them or not. The problems and rewards that will be yours in the years ahead will be quite different from the ones encountered here, but if your kind of education has been successful, it has provided you well with the special tools you need to deal with new experience. You can use them to make a difference.

Here at Atlantic Christian College, in Wilson, which Josephus Daniels once called the "loveliest village of the plain,"[1] you have received your education within the framework of Christian ideals and principles. Eighty-five years ago, a commencement speaker at a school that was a forerunner of Atlantic Christian said:

In a vision that shall be more than a vision, I see yonder in one of our beautiful North Carolina towns, a Christian College with an able Christian faculty. To our College I see young men and women gathering from all parts of the state and from South Carolina and Georgia, spending years in hallowed association, developing their God-given powers and preparing themselves for life's great work.[2]

In the decades since those words were first said, the good seed that has been sown in Wilson has germinated and grown. Atlantic Christian has become a residential college of quality and has drawn its students, not merely from three states, but from a quarter of the states in the union and from many foreign countries, as well.

It is my opinion that few educational institutions have crafted such a high statement of purpose as the one that appears in your catalogue. At the end of your years at Atlantic Christian, let me remind you again of a few of the words of your purpose, which many might consider a prose poem:

> The purpose of the college is to provide an environment
> In which the heritage of man's past is transmitted
> And in which students and faculty explore and examine critically
> Man's intellectual, religious, and esthetic experience
> In order to realize their obligation to the past, the
> Present and the future
> For the ultimate improvement of the quality of life.[3]

Now let us think about you as one whose education has really begun and yet has attained an important distinction. Your job as a citizen starts with you as an educated human being. It is your first duty as citizen to be the best kind of person you possibly can. I urge you to put the tutored discipline and the self-discipline, that you have learned here, to work every day of your life. I urge you to seek after excellence in the common tasks in your homes and in your jobs. Some of these jobs may be the direct result of your educational training here; others might appear to be totally unrelated to what is, in itself, a public service. If you fail to reach your best potential, you do a disservice not only to yourself but to all of us, to all humankind, and especially to the system of education, government, and society that has produced you at this level. If you become less than you can be, you are shortchanging humanity, because all of society needs you to be prepared, to be willing to work, to do your part, both for yourself and for others.

I urge you, in the years ahead, to be flexible about learning new things. This is a changing world, and you will have many opportunities, even necessities, for changing the direction of your lives. In my own experience, I look back on a working life that began in a chemistry classroom, first as student, then as teacher. But I now realize that I didn't go to college only to study chemistry—I went to college to learn to study.

The habit of study has been with me over the years since I left the classroom. When I served in Washington, my training in chemistry served me well, of all places, [on] the Ways and Means Committee; the Tax-Writing Committee; when we studied the problems of pollution and energy policy; and also in defending saccharin. But even more, I found myself using my habits of study when I needed to learn about basic economic principles; about tax policy, budgets, and accounting; and now, as governor, about management of this great state.

There are other subject areas, nourished first in my school days, that have served me in my leisure hours, that help me try to become a complete person. I have depended a great deal on the fine arts to help me express how I feel about things. I learned to play tuba well enough to serve five years in the Charlotte Symphony. I have depended on the habit of reading for comprehension, that was essential during the years I was in school, to give me much pleasure over the years, quite beyond reading I have done for information. I urge you to use your education systematically in the wide, unpredictable areas for experience and service that will come your way. This is a plea for you to be involved in life-long education, either through formal refresher courses, from time to time, or in using privately the skills and attitudes you have learned in school for learning new things throughout the rest of your life.

One of the best examples we have in American history to demonstrate self-education and life-long education is that of Abraham Lincoln, who had less than a year of formal schooling and never set foot in a classroom after the age of fifteen, and yet, what an example! On one occasion, when he had to fill out a standard government form, he filled in the blank after "Education" with one word: "Defective." You, who can proudly fill the blanks after "Education" with reference to the quality years you have spent here, have a special responsibility for keeping your minds alert, flexible, and well furnished in the years ahead.

Now let us move to the idea of citizen. A citizen is a member of a state or nation, owing allegiance to a government and being entitled to its protection. A North Carolina Congressman, Carlyle, said at a commencement a number of years ago:

> When is a citizen good and useful? When he maintains a decent home for himself and his family; when he is self-supporting and financially independent through conscientious and regular work; when he protects his credit and pays his taxes without default; when he respects and obeys the

law; when he votes his intelligent convictions in all elections and discharges every civic duty; when he puts his roots down where he lives and seeks to help build a stronger and better community.[4]

Let us look at several of his points in greater detail.

A good citizen, I feel, is one who is aware of the mechanics of American government, is aware of the issues—who has thought about the issues from the point of view of the public interest and not only his or his group's interest. At minimum, a good citizen is capable of casting a competent vote on the basis of evaluated issues.

Beyond the minimum, a good citizen is someone who participates in the life of the community and in his government in an active way. While one doesn't have to be a member of a political party, it is best to be a member of a party because our government is based on the theory of competition between responsible, organized, rival political parties. It is important that our parties stand for something and that citizens within them work so their party continues to stand for something. You stand for something, or you fall for something. Many citizens tend to cast their votes on the basis of party; therefore, the decisions made by the party must be meaningful about basic beliefs, about who gets nominated and their commitments. Political parties, acting as a unit, can help make government act more coherently. I urge you to take part in grass-roots politics so you can influence issues. You make your own choice on that, but don't neglect it or leave it to others. The more effective you are in helping a person get elected, the more influential you will be in that person's political and policy decisions.

You owe local and state government a good, critically informed presence. Be an informed and skeptical participant in public processes and debates. Political decisions touch our lives in uncounted ways. Remember that many important decisions are made at the state and local level—so many needs roost there, so much money is spent there. One of my bedrock principles is that things should be solved and public issues should be joined at the lowest feasible level, the level that most immediately engages people and is closest to them. So, I started in local government, and perhaps you will, too. I urge you to be a consciously political person, to know politics as firsthand experience, because the person that you are is so much formed by politics.

Being a good citizen is not only trying to influence your government, it includes whatever is public. This includes many kinds of voluntary associations that contribute to the web of life in our towns and cities. Much that is done for the public good need not be done by the government. In fact, many times the jobs are much better done by people who want them done. Voluntary associations cover the full spectrum of human interests and needs—sponsoring the arts, sheltered workshops. You can find voluntary associations that will use the skills and knowledge you acquired in your school years and translate them into tangible civic good. I urge you to find your place in the world of voluntary associations, civic clubs, churches, to make a contribution there to human and cultural betterment.

There is another aspect to citizenship that is larger than the subjects I have already mentioned. We cannot avoid global responsibilities. To be a good citizen in the twenty-first century is going to demand a high degree of knowledge and awareness of the international sphere. Knowledge is crucial for citizenship and for survival. If the U.S. is going to insist on peaceful relations, we know we must remain militarily strong. In the twenty-first century, we've got to think ahead in terms of international competition in business, banking, manufacturing. To do that, you have to understand this twentieth century—and the nineteenth, and the eighteenth.

America, taken as a whole nation, has been extraordinarily blessed. We have had rich natural resources. We have not had to work too hard to compete in international business. As a result, we don't know very well the languages, cultures, the institutions of those with whom we trade. We haven't had to. For 150 years we enjoyed a privileged position of some isolation; only the last fifty years have taught us that we can't continue to live that way.

The South may well have a special vocation for international understanding, for it has an intuitive grasp of the problems involved in the great north-south division of the globe. Many Latin Americans say that the South is the only part of the United States that they can really identify with, because they understand our traditional kind of society, the family-oriented conservation of an old society mixed with the aspirations of the new.

We in North Carolina will have much to say on the subject of international trade in the future. Foreign investors are already taking an interest in building businesses and jobs in our state; we are interested in marketing our products to the larger world. There is more involved here than just being a part of the Sunbelt phenomenon. It is partly because our educational system has tried to prepare you to become useful citizens in this new North Carolina, with its prospect for economic success and fulfillment. We are moving toward high-technology industries and service industries; well-educated persons are important in this kind of economy.

You are in a favored position compared to young people in many other parts of the world. A new economy is growing up around you. Careers are coming here. The future is coming to North Carolina. You have been prepared, in this unique institution, not only to take part in in this future but to actually help mold it into a style of life we have always treasured in North Carolina.

I would like to leave you on this graduation day with some thoughts of Judge William Gaston, a member of the North Carolina Supreme Court between 1833 and 1844. Judge Gaston had special reason to be interested in full citizenship. He was a Catholic, and at the time he was appointed to the court the state constitution did not allow Catholics to hold public office. Two years later the constitution was altered, largely due to Gaston's efforts toward religious liberty.[5]

Judge Gaston wrote, 140 years ago, words that are fresh for our time:

> Those who engage in public service must be in sympathy with the feelings and wishes of the people whom they serve. Honestly seek to serve our country, for it is glorious to advance the good of your fellow-man. The high road of service is indeed laborious, exposed to the rain and sun, the heat and dust. Children of the same common family, we are bound to help each other in the trials and difficulties of our common pilgrimage. It will be your duty to make and keep the public well enlightened. As your country grows in years, you must also cause it to grow in science, literature, arts.[6]

Judge Gaston speaks to our day; so must you, as today's new leaders.

In my sixth term in Congress, I remember counseling with a group of intense freshmen about a difficult vote they would face—how we needed them on an important issue facing the security of our nation, how they had to expect a backlash against them if they stuck with what they thought was right. One [member from] Arkansas spoke for all the rest: "We came here to make a difference." We came here to make a difference.

Years from here, and now, face your own challenges. Make a difference.

---

[1]Josephus Daniels (1862-1948), born in Washington, North Carolina; died in Raleigh; was educated at Wilson Collegiate Institute; attended University of North Carolina law school, 1885. Editor, publisher, of newspapers in Wilson, Kinston, Raleigh, and Rocky Mount, from 1880; obtained control of Raleigh *News and Observer*, 1895; publicity director for Woodrow Wilson's 1912 presidential campaign; U.S. Navy secretary, 1913-1921; appointed U.S. ambassador to Mexico, 1933; author; Democrat. Powell, *DNCB*, I, 13-14. "To this day I think of Wilson as I knew it when a boy as 'the loveliest village of the plain.'" Quotation from Josephus Daniels, *Tar Heel Editor* (Chapel Hill: University of North Carolina Press, 1939), 144.

[2]Daniel Esten Motley (Ph.D., Johns Hopkins University, 1899; state evangelist, North Carolina Disciples of Chirst, 1900-1901) spoke to the graduating class of 1900 during commencement exercises at Carolina Christian College, a predecessor of Atlantic Christian College, in Ayden. Charles Crossfield Ware, *A History of Atlantic Christian College: Culture in Coastal Carolina* (Wilson, North Carolina: Atlantic Christian College, 1956), 51-52, 61; excerpt from Motley's address, above, reprinted in the *Watch Tower,* June 8, 1900, is quoted in Ware, p. 62.

[3]*Atlantic Christian College, General Catalog, 1984-85* (Wilson: Atlantic Christian College, n.d.), 9.

[4]Frank Ertel Carlyle (1897-1960), native of Lumberton; was educated at University of North Carolina; served in U.S. Navy during World War I. Attorney; elected solicitor, N.C. Ninth Judicial District, 1938, reelected 1942, 1946; member, U.S. House of Representatives, 1949-1957; Democrat. *Biographical Directory of Congress,* 744; Powell, *DNCB,* I, 324.

[5]William Joseph Gaston (1778-1844), born in New Bern; died in Raleigh; was graduated from College of New Jersey (later Princeton University), 1796; honorary degrees. Attorney; North Carolina state senator, 1800, 1812, 1818, 1819; served in state House of Commons, 1807-1809, 1824, 1827-1829, 1831; U.S. congressman, 1813-1817; appointed president, Bank of New Bern, 1828; state supreme court judge, 1833-1844.

Article XXXII of the 1776 state constitution barred non-Protestants from holding public office in North Carolina. However, Gaston was held in such high regard by his legislative colleagues that they elected him to the state supreme court nevertheless. As Craven County representative to the state Constitutional Convention of 1835, the judge tirelessly worked to eliminate all religious qualifications for holding public office. Unable to abolish such requirements completely, his efforts ultimately resulted in broadening them to include all Christians. *Biographical Directory of Congress,* 1048; Constitution of the State of North Carolina, 1776, Article XXXII, as quoted in Clark, *State Records,* XXIII, 983; Powell, *DNCB,* II, 283-285.

[6]Gaston's advice to students as potential public officeholders formed a significant part of a speech he delivered at the University of North Carolina. See "Hon. William Gaston's Address," June, 1832, reprinted in *North Carolina University Magazine,* IV (August and September, 1844), 298-316. Martin's quotation was a composite of brief excerpts plucked from four pages: "Those, too, who engage in public service, are bound to cherish a hearty sympathy with the wants, feelings, comforts, and wishes of the people whose welfare is committed to their charge" (p. 308). "Honestly seek to serve your country, for it is glorious to advance the good of your fellow-men, and thus, as far as feeble mortals may, act up to the great example of Him to whose image and likeness you are made. Seek also, by all honest arts, to win their confidence, but beware how you ever prefer their favor to their service. The high road of service is indeed laborious, exposed to the rain and sun, the heat and dust; while the by-path of favor has, apparently, at first, much the same direction and is bordered with flowers and sheltered by trees. . . ." (p. 309). "Children of the same common family, we are bound to help each other in the trials and difficulties of our common pilgrimage, nor should we ever be too proud to receive from others that assistance, which it is our duty to render to them" (p. 310). "Yours will, indeed, be no sinecure office. As the public will is the operative spring of all public action, it will be your duty to make and to keep the public well enlightened. There will always be some error to dispel, some prejudice to correct, some illusion to guard against, some imposition to detect and expose. In aid of these individual efforts, you must provide, by public institutions, for diffusing among the people, that general information without which they cannot be protected from the machinations of deceivers. As your country grows in years, you must also cause it to grow in science, literature, arts and refinement" (p. 312).

STATEMENT TO U.S. HOUSE COMMITTEE ON
WAYS AND MEANS

WASHINGTON, D.C., JUNE 20, 1985

[A component of the Tax Equity and Fiscal Responsibility Act of 1982 temporarily doubled the federal excise tax on cigarettes from 8 cents to 16 cents per pack. Sought as a means of easing the government's budget deficit, the increase became effective January 1, 1983, and was scheduled to revert to its former level on October 1, 1985. Congress later approved short-term extensions of the higher rate beyond the original deadline, and ultimately passed legislation in 1986 making the 16-cent tax permanent. P.L. 97-248, "An Act to Provide for Tax Equity and Fiscal Responsibility, and for Other Purposes," *United States Statutes at Large*, Act of September 3, 1982, 96 Stat. 568-569; *Congressional Quarterly Almanac, 1985*, 499, 502, 508-509, *1986*, 521, 557, 572-573.

Governor Martin expressed opposition to prolonging the cigarette tax increase in his statement, below, to the U.S. House Committee on Ways and Means and at Old Belt tobacco market opening ceremonies in Mount Airy, Reidsville, and Winston-Salem, August 13, 1985.]

The doubling of the cigarette excise tax in 1983 has had an adverse effect on the economy of North Carolina. Its effects have been well documented as to the loss in sales, jobs, and income of our number-one commodity, tobacco. The temporary increase in the federal cigarette excise tax, scheduled to expire on October 1, 1985, must not be altered.

North Carolina grows on tobacco: These words were the slogan of a public awareness campaign several years ago, and they still stand true today. North Carolina, last year, produced more flue-cured tobacco than any comparable area in the world—522 million pounds. Flue-cured tobacco, also known as bright leaf, is indeed a bright and shining symbol of economic prosperity in North Carolina. Thousands of North Carolinians depend upon tobacco directly or indirectly for their livelihood.

The state grows three types of flue-cured tobacco leaf in the piedmont and coastal regions and also grows burley tobacco in the western mountain counties. The golden leaf is grown on approximately 42,000 farms in North Carolina, and some type of tobacco is grown in 91 of North Carolina's 100 counties. Cash receipts from tobacco amounted to over $1 billion in 1983; 27.4 percent of cash receipts from all crops and all farm commodities came from tobacco.

At the other end of the spectrum, cigarette manufacturers in North Carolina produced over 313 billion cigarettes in 1983. That's about 47 percent of all the cigarettes manufactured in the United States. North Carolina is the largest tobacco-manufacturing state in the nation.

Other sectors of the North Carolina economy also benefit from the strength of the state's tobacco industry. There are tobacco auction markets in more than thirty counties in the state. Tobacco offers a variety of other support industries: the largest cigarette paper factory in the nation; chemical and plastic suppliers; packaging and container suppliers; cigarette filter producers; fertilizer and farm-equipment suppliers; transportation industries; commercial printing; advertising in the media. All these industries produce important revenues for North Carolina and other states.

Every business must earn profit if it is to grow or even survive. *Growth* is another word for *expansion,* and expansion creates the need for new workers, but expansion must be justified and largely financed by the accumulation of earnings beyond the cost of doing business—in other words, profits. If North Carolina's tobacco agriculture is successful it not only benefits the farmer, but everyone; it carries its part of the tax load; it provides more and better jobs. If North Carolina's tobacco agriculture is unsuccessful, it provides fewer and fewer jobs and less opportunities for all.

North Carolina depends heavily on the golden leaf. The thousands of North Carolinians involved with tobacco are sure that the golden leaf will continue to play an important role in the economy of North Carolina and the life of its citizens. As long as the tobacco industry, from grower to consumer, is allowed to continue to grow, North Carolina will grow with it.

The tobacco farmer has not shared in the economic recovery that most of the nation has experienced in the past few years. Beset by many problems, the tobacco grower has been particularly disadvantaged by congressional action to raise the discriminatory tax on the product on which the grower depends for his livelihood. I hope that the tobacco grower will not be forgotten by my former colleagues when they deal with the future of the cigarette excise tax. To continue the temporary 8-cent excise tax [increase], per pack, past the expiration date of October 1, 1985, would be unfair, unreasonable, and unjustified.

PRESS RELEASE: GOVERNOR'S STATEMENT
CONCERNING SPECIAL PROVISIONS

RALEIGH, JUNE 20, 1985

[Special provisions were sections of appropriations bills that "rarely involve the expenditure of money, but directly affect state laws by amending, repealing, or even creating new laws," according to government analyst Jack Betts, writing for the North Carolina Center for Public Policy Research. Ran Coble further explained that there were five categories constituting the "inappropriate" use of such mechanisms: "(1) to amend, repeal, or otherwise change any existing law other than the Executive Budget Act; (2) to establish new agency programs or to alter the powers and duties of existing programs; (3) to establish new boards, commissions, and councils or to alter existing boards' powers; (4) to grant special tax breaks or otherwise change the tax laws; or (5) to authorize new interim studies by the General Assembly or other groups."

Continued Coble, "Some bills which might not pass on their own merits are often inserted into budget bills in the form of special provisions," their surreptitious use circumventing conventional legislative processes and running counter to the public interest by escaping debate, necessary to ensure full review, in the General Assembly. Special provisions also had the potential to subvert the authority of government agencies and impair "relationships between state and local governments and between the executive and legislative branches of government." During its 1985 regular session, the General Assembly included 108 special provisions in three budget bills. Ran Coble, *Special Provisions in Budget Bills: A Pandora's Box for North Carolina Citizens* (Raleigh: North Carolina Center for Public Policy Research, June, 1986), ii-iv.

Although special provisions also were legitimately employed to clarify the use of funds approved under earlier spending bills, it was their inappropriate application that Governor Martin protested in the statement reprinted below.]

In yesterday's action in the Joint Appropriations Committee, a number of special provisions were agreed to which have caught us by surprise in the administration and which would cause us problems. I have contacted Lieutenant Governor Jordan, Speaker Ramsey, and the two co-chairmen, Senator Plyler[1] and Representative Watkins,[2] to request that these matters be held back from Friday's sessions so that I or my assistants could review with them the problems we see in a few particular provisions.

Several items would limit the authority of the governor to administer the state budget. I would be prohibited from making line-item transfers, even if that would lead to efficiencies and improved delivery of authorized programs. Last year, an attempt to impose a 10 percent limit on line-item transfers was withdrawn because of questions about its constitutionality. The same question must be raised now. I share the view that the governor should not reprogram millions of dollars of "unencumbered balances" after the first year of the biennium, as was done last year to fund $15 million in expanded programs. There is another specific provision to halt that, and I support it, but I cannot support a limitation on the details of budget responsibilities which the North Carolina Constitution vests in the governor.

The second major area that causes a problem is a group of special provisions that delegate to the attorney general the final and sole authority over whether I or any department can retain private legal counsel.[3] I hold the view that the executive authority granted to the governor in the constitution would be eroded if I do not defend my authority, as governor, to designate counsel. In general, the attorney general would have the responsibility to serve as legal counsel to the governor and to my administration. But what if the attorney general feels obligated to represent a legal position different from mine? I should then have the right to designate my legal counsel without seeking his approval.

Several cases bring this issue to the fore. The attorney general, the Speaker, the lieutenant governor, the Board of Elections, and the secretary of state are defendants in the case of *Gingles* v. *Thornburg*, [in] which a federal court has decided to require single-member legislative districts in some areas. Some defendants wish to appeal the decision. I support the decision, as does the current Board of Elections. How can the attorney general represent the Board of Elections as defendants if he chooses to represent the appeal? More to the point: He should not control my right to designate counsel to represent the Board of Elections if he is going to be counsel on the opposite side.[4]

The same issue would be raised if the General Assembly is unable to satisfy my objections to what I regard as unconstitutional intrusions against my executive authority in the House version of the Administrative Procedures Act.[5] I would be obliged to defend my office and would assert my authority to choose private counsel if it appeared that the attorney general could not represent me.

These are fundamental constitutional questions and ought not to be taken up in this legislation in a way that would deprive me of my rights as governor of this state. The attorney general and I have a friendly disagreement, and it ought not to be decided by the General Assembly.

For these reasons I have respectfully requested a deferral of these few matters, so that we might present our objections to the committee in hopes that these particular provisions would be deleted.

I find equally serious the provisions transferring to the attorney general a right to veto the use of private investigators by departments.[6] There are occasions when it is desirable for departments to undertake independent investigations, particularly where sensitive political matters are involved. Basically, if the General Assembly were to enact these provisions transferring my authority to the attorney general, it would give him control over my defense of my office even as I challenge the constitutionality of this very legislation. That ain't fair!

---

[1]Aaron W. Plyler (1926-   ), native of Union County; was educated at Benton Heights School and Florida Military Academy. President, owner, Plyler Grading and Paving, Inc.; president, Hill Top Enterprises; member, state House, 1975-1982, and Senate, since 1983; chairman, Senate Appropriations Committee; Democrat. *North Carolina Manual, 1987-1988*, 315.

[2]William Thomas Watkins (1921-1989), native, resident of Granville County; B.S., 1949, LL.B., 1952, Wake Forest College (later University); U.S. Army, 1942-1946. Attorney; member, State House of Representatives, 1968-1989, and chairman, House Appropriations-Expansion Budget Committee; Democrat. *News and Observer*, August 27, 1989; *North Carolina Manual, 1987-1988*, 493.

[3]Provisions limiting the hiring of private counsel by state agencies, boards, and commissions were passed. See *N.C. Session Laws, 1985*, c. 479, secs. 135, 136.

[4]*Gingles* v. *Thornburg* began in 1981 as *Gingles* v. *Edmisten*. Gaston County resident Ralph Gingles and other black voters filed suit against the state, challenging the practice of establishing and maintaining multi-member electoral districts. Such a system, the plaintiffs argued, "diluted black voting strength, contrary to the federal Voting Rights Act." A federal judicial panel decided against the state in 1984, and legislators ultimately were ordered to create twelve single-member legislative districts to prevent "black registered voters being submerged as a voting minority."

North Carolina appealed the judges' ruling to the U.S. Supreme Court; the Reagan administration, represented by the federal Justice Department, joined the case on the state's behalf. Interestingly, the Republican-controlled State Board of Elections, which supported the 1984 ruling, found itself opposing the U.S. president. Attorney General Lacy Thornburg rejected the board's request to abandon the appeal, which put him at odds with Governor Martin. Hiring legal representation of his own, Martin filed a brief stating that the multi-member arrangement was "the remnant of an earlier time when the government of North Carolina was conducted solely by white male Democrats." U.S. Senate Majority Leader Robert J. Dole, a Republican, and Senator Edward M. Kennedy, a Democrat, also filed a Supreme Court brief supporting single-member districts. On June 30, 1986, the justices declared that the earlier judicial panel acted properly. Paul Luebke, in *Tar Heel Politics: Myths and Realities* (Chapel Hill: University of North Carolina Press, 1990), 114-120, hereinafter cited as Luebke, *Tar Heel Politics*, discussed the *Gingles* v. *Edmisten* case and explained the differences between single- and multi-member electoral districts; see also *News and Observer*, April 18, 30, June 3, 13, 14, 20, July 4, 10, August 31, December 5, 1985, January 22, July 1, 1986.

[5]H.B. 52, "A Bill to Be Entitled an Act to Recodify Chapter 150A of the General Statutes, Add a New Article 12 to Chapter 143B of the General Statutes, and Make Other Changes in the Administrative Procedures of Executive Agencies," was introduced February 12, 1985. Championed by Representative Billy Watkins, the much-debated bill was later modified—and was ratified, on July 12, 1985, as c. 746, *N.C. Session Laws, 1985. N.C. House Journal, 1985*, 38, 292, 308, 318, 326, 773, 785, 811, 938, 944, 952, 957;

for a description of the discussion surrounding H.B. 52 and a review of the features of c. 746, see Joyce, *North Carolina Legislation, 1985*, 12-16.

⁶*N.C. Session Laws, 1985*, c. 479, s. 138, enacted such a provision.

STATE GOP CONVENTION

WILMINGTON, JUNE 22, 1985

[The following transcript was supplied by the Governor's Communications Office.]

I'm here today to give you a report from the governor of the state of North Carolina, how about that? First time in eight years. Better get ready for the next eight years. I know some of you are kind of smug; you're saying, "Hey, he's got his arithmetic all wrong, it'll be seven more years." No, I want to be here and welcome and introduce my successor in 1993. We can do it!

You, we, are the GOP: the Grand Old Party, the Good Old Party, Giver of Peace, Government of the People, the party of Growth and Opportunity and Prosperity for everybody. Congratulations! Here we are on the verge of statewide dominance in North Carolina. We rebounded from tragedy in 1974, and we're ahead of where we were in 1972.[1] You heard the record here: We tied the record for the most we've had in the North Carolina General Assembly with fifty, and we want more! That means a lot more of you need to be ready to run in '86, in '88, in '90, and '92, and just right on. You've got to be ready. You've got to help us.

We hold a new record in the United States Congress in this session. How proud we are of them, with our two senators and five of the eleven of the House of Representatives—that gives us seven out of thirteen. That's a majority! We ought to be able to pick up a few more when you see that the president, Senator Helms, and I carried seven out of the eleven congressional districts—all three of us.[2] The president carried them all, so there's no reason why we can't continue to build on what we've been doing—those valiant candidates who went out there and gave it their best this last time.

Do you remember back during the campaign how we talked about those numbers, about the last decade, the last dozen years—the Republican party's candidates for president of the United States, United States senator, and governor—of those three statewide races, that our candidates had won six out of the last ten, three out of the last four? Well, we've got them again: It's nine out of the last fourteen, six out of the last seven, and three of the last three. And we're not through yet. We're going to keep right on going through 1986 and reelect our senator, John East.

Our party is building on victory; our party is building for more victories, you'd better believe that. We're on a roll, and we're not going to stop. We haven't peaked yet. Do you remember how they said maybe we'd peaked too soon, back in October? We haven't peaked yet, friends. We'll continue to grow.

Let's talk about these first six months, a little bit. I want you to know how proud I am of the team that we've begun to assemble, the cabinet secretaries and their assistant secretaries and staff, our senior staff. We've reformed abuses of our state personnel system; we're saying to people whether you're a Republican, Democrat, independent, or whatever: Do your job with pride, that's all we ask of you, do your job with pride.

You remember how we inherited 1,500 exempt positions? Those that [are] controlled by the thumb of the governor, those who are the leaders, the policy makers, the confidential positions—we said then that we thought that was twice as many as we needed; it was twice what Jim Holshouser needed. And we found out that was right: About half of them had been put under those exempt categories so that they could get them under their thumb and put political pressure on them. And we've reformed that, cut that down to 887—those who must respond to help us lead and deliver our programs.

We're stopping the compulsory campaign contributions, too. You've been seeing those stories recently about campaign contributions. The *Charlotte Observer* has had a good series, but what they missed, too, was, and I hope they're going to continue to look. Because you know, it's been the rule in the past administration that state employees had to buy a hundred-dollar ticket every time the candidates came to town. A hundred dollars? Because you don't have to report a hundred-dollar contribution to state races. And if you're going to do business with the state, what you do is get ten or several dozen hundred-dollar tickets, and they tell you to go out and sell them, and you come back and give them the money, and nobody could ask who you sold those tickets to—or if. Our new Republican, Eddie Knox, told me he just about had that system figured out, and he just didn't get around to proving it.[3]

We're not going to use that system. We're not going to use that system of coercing contributions out of people who work for, or with, state government. We beat that system. We beat it with voluntary contributions and that ragtag gang of volunteers from all over this state. We're not going to change in our team that worked, and the system that worked, for the system that we beat, you can believe that. Why copy a losing system when you've got a winner?

Let me talk to you about the legislative scorecard. We've had some winners; we've had some losers. We've had some successes. We can say to you that we're making a stronger counterattack on drugs and drug trafficking in this state. Our child safety program is helping our missing children; it's helping to find help for them and abused children in this state. We are near a victory on the Open Meetings Law, within a few days of getting a vote on that to have a stronger Open Meetings Law, and you know how our legislators have been fighting for that. We didn't take a vote on the Advisory Budget Commission and the Council of State, we just opened that up because it's right. Public business ought to be done in public.

We're near a victory on anti-pornography legislation. You know the state laws in this state are so difficult to enforce. It provides that if you're a law-enforcement officer you cannot obtain evidence by going out and buying or receiving a dirty magazine. They don't want you to see it. And when you do finally get a conviction the penalty is they can't sell that monthly issue any more, and that's several months later. No wonder it's destroyed the law-enforcement officer. So we're near a victory at the present with that.

We want a victory on the abortion issue. We intend to stop the state funding of elective abortions in North Carolina. We're going to win that issue if they ever give us an honest count. You saw what happened after they announced that their side had won. On one close vote they refused to announce what the number result was, because our people were counting that our side had prevailed on a vote of 41 to 45; and then a day or two later, they came up and figured that they'd better announce it, that actually the vote was something like 47-45—they said there were people who didn't hold their hand up, and they voted yes. Can you believe that? They won with their hands down.[4] Well, they know the day of reckoning is coming. There's going to be a record[ed] vote within these next two weeks, and they better be ready for it. We'll see how they count that. If they jam the voting machines, well, we'll have a roll-call vote. We're going to get it counted right this time. No wonder so many legislators are demanding an ethics committee. They ought to have a math committee!

Another area where we're having success is in building public support for public education in this state. We've submitted our proposals for improvements, but you have to recognize you just cannot outspend the Democrats; whatever it is, they're going to try to trump you on that. But we're directing attention to the classroom teacher. We've spent a lot of money on a lot of other things—let's figure out how to strengthen that profession, the classroom teacher, so we can keep our good teachers, hold them accountable, give them an incentive to do well. After four years of declining—31 percent of the state General Fund that went to the public schools—we've proposed in our budget, with the tax cut, we proposed increases up to 44 percent of the General Fund. But it's always been curious to me how you can be an "education governor" if you preside over a declining percentage of the General Fund going for education, and yet they say you're not doing enough if you propose to raise it. You just can't outspend them, there's no way.

Still, we're beginning to focus attention on the real problems. We've had some successes, we've tried to do more, but I'll tell you this: it's awfully tough with that leadership and the way they respond to our initiatives. They're tough to work with. Every time we get close they threaten, "Pork barrel denial, pork barrel denial," and that usually gets most of them in line. There are some on the other side who have the courage to stand with us on the important votes, but there's not enough, and you can do something about that. I'll get back to that in a little bit.

We've tried to do more. Remember that first welcoming insult, when they rejected our date that we had agreed on for the State of the State message—a postponement—and then accused me of postponing it, while they postponed it? I told them you can hide, but you can't escape. Eventually, sooner or later, one way or another, you've got to sit down and listen. I got a [omission] out of them that time, didn't I?

I'll tell you the biggest problem we've run into, and it's the same thing that Jim Holshouser experienced: They'll do anything they can, every idea they can think of, to try and strip the constitutional responsibilities of the governor of this state. Almost every other week there's some new outrage. They started with a legislative appointment of the Board of Elections director, then they reject the Republican Board of Elections' appeal to support the NAACP in their call for single-member election districts. Of course, they say that favors black and Republican candidates, and fair should be fair. The reason it's favorable is because the multi-member districts have been discriminatory and unfavorable, and they know it, and that's why they want to do it that way.

And what's next on the agenda? They want to strip the governor of being able to run for a second term and let the voters have a say on that. I thought they did. We've only had one example of Jim Hunt, and you shouldn't judge the value of two terms by that. The people are against them on this, and they know it. And what's more, they know the people want the governor of this state to have the veto power, just like the other forty-nine. The people want to strengthen the office of their governor, and the people are embarrassed that our state is still backwards on this after 208 years; they're embarrassed that for the last sixty-five years, since 1920, we've been the only state in the union where the people were not able to give their governor the veto power. They say—get this—"We're still afraid of those royal governors." Well, you know who those royal governors are: it's their leadership that dictates to them how to vote. They say they want to strip the governor's office of authority over regulatory agencies with what they call the Administrative Procedures Act. I call it an assault on the constitution of the state of North Carolina. You know their explanation of this is, "Well, you've got to have a little give and take"—that was in yesterday's paper—"You've got to have a little give and take." We give, they take. They're trying to tie us in knots any way that they can—who has been hired, who has been fired, who has been transferred. Their excuse for this is—this is it, a quote—"Jim Hunt abused that system." Hey, we're trying to reform it; don't blame us, and penalize us, for the way they did it in the old days. We're trying to change that.

Now, you know they want to strip the governor of the authority to appoint, fill vacancies in the Council of State. They want to take that authority, provided in the constitution, away from the highest elected official in the state, elected by a majority of the people, and give it to their party leadership to control the access to all of those positions. They want it so that every position elected statewide, except one, will enable them to dominate, to control and capture that office for the future of that term for their party, for their party chairman. And you know what that one is? The office of the governor of North Carolina.

Now you don't think that's [fair], and it's not fair. They want the party of the lieutenant governor to control every angle of access to the office of governor, and I say it's not fair. And I believe the people are going to see through it. You know they stole one election from Billy Hendon, they stole another one from Wayne Spears, stole another one from Liza Graue and Pat Jones. They're not going to steal this one. They can't change that one without a vote of the people, and I believe the people will understand.

You want to hear the latest outrage? No? I kind of thought you might. They've now come up with a grand scheme to change the law

that gives the governor of the state authority to designate legal counsel to represent him in court. They're going to give it now to the
attorney general. They know that he supports them on multi-member
districts. They hope he'll support them on stripping the governor's
office, so they want to let him control whether I can even have a
lawyer in court or by whom. Think about it. If you're going to court,
would you like for your lawyer to be able to confer with the lawyer of
your adversary, whether or not you can even have a lawyer, or have
to stand naked in court? No, because you would want that support,
and what they've proposed is not fair. Even if Jim Hunt did, as they
say, abuse that right to sue [omission], what they're proposing is not
fair.

We're coming to the closing scene in the tax cuts now. In a few
weeks we'll see what they're going to be. I'm pleased that the debate
is no longer on whether to raise taxes, and how much, but rather
whether to lower taxes, and how much. What a change that is in the
last year, thanks to you. I don't see any way this year that we're going
to get the full $435 million tax cut that we proposed. The House of
Representatives dodged my bill entirely when Betsy Cochrane introduced it.[5] They thought they were going to get away with that until
young Jonathan Rhyne finally challenged them out there today, bless
him.[6] But even so, all they've done is pass a fourth of it. All they've
done is passed a fourth of it. Some of Jonathan's friends over there—
you ought to be Jonathan's friends, too, and that whole delegation, I'll
tell you. The Senate passed half of my plan, so they'll probably bargain somewhere in between, but what worries me is now that the
House is delaying going to conference to iron out the differences. I'll
tell you, I'm worried. A reliable source tells me they're trying to find
some way to get out of there, to close down the session in Raleigh
without voting for the tax cut. They say they're not, but that's what
worries me. They say, "We just want to work it out," and then they'll
appoint their conferees. Well what do they need conferees for if
they're going to do it that way? Just let the two people decide it.

They'll have enough to answer for if they only give us half the tax
cut the people asked for, but they better not adjourn, doing nothing.
We remember, and they remember, that we took that issue to the
voters in November, 1984—and remember, the voters said, Cut those
taxes. Didn't they? Didn't you? And if they couldn't hear it in 1984,
we'll go to the people again in 1986 and say, We've got to ask you one
more time: Do you really want us to cut those taxes? And we'll see if
they hear them the second time around. Do you know I thought the
lieutenant governor was probably right on the mark the other day

when he was quoted in the *Observer* newspaper saying, and I quote, "Increased spending is taking priority over tax cuts." They don't want me in there, the Republicans doing their very best to cut taxes and reform the abuses of state government, and give the kind of government that the people want and deserve, the kind of government you can be proud of. The people resent it. They let their hatchet men savage me and my programs on the floor of the House, but you just let one Republican try to say something critical about their side and their behavior. They even resent it [when] I go over to the House chambers just to sit with my wife, Dottie, and watch the carnage. I can't do that.[7]

1986 can change all that. You can change all that. Let's take our case to the people again. Let's go back and let's say, Do you really want those tax cuts? Do you really want good government? Do you really want us to succeed? Then vote Republican!

---

[1]Republican party fortunes rose and fell nationally, and in North Carolina, with those of President Richard M. Nixon in the early 1970s. The president's 1972 landslide reelection over challenger George McGovern helped the Tar Heel State elect its first Republican governor of the twentieth century in Jim Holshouser, while GOP candidates won fifteen of the state Senate's fifty seats and thirty-five out of 120 seats in the state House. Two years later, the Watergate scandal and Nixon's subsequent resignation damaged the credibility of GOP nominees everywhere. The November, 1974, elections resulted in North Carolina Democrats filling all but one state Senate seat, while the Republicans held on to only nine in the House. *North Carolina Manual, 1973,* 470-472, *1975,* 295, 353-355.

[2]North Carolina sent three fewer Republicans to Washington after the 1986 elections. The GOP members of the state's 1985 congressional delegation, to whom Martin referred, were:

James Thomas Broyhill (1927-   ), native of Lenoir; B.S., University of North Carolina at Chapel Hill, 1950; honorary degree. Furniture manufacturer; U.S. House member, Tenth North Carolina Congressional District, 1963-1986, and vice-chairman, Congressional Textile Caucus; appointed by Governor Martin to complete unexpired U.S. Senate term of John P. East, 1986; defeated by Terry Sanford in U.S. Senate race, 1986; appointed chairman, 1986, reappointed 1987, N.C. Economic Development Board; appointed state commerce secretary, 1989; former president, director, Lenoir Chamber of Commerce. Alexander P. Lamis, *The Two-Party South: Expanded Edition* (New York: Oxford University Press, 1988), 286, hereinafter cited as Lamis, *Two-Party South; News and Observer,* January 25, 1989; *North Carolina Manual, 1985,* 235.

William Wilfred Cobey, Jr. (1939-   ), born in Washington, D.C.; resident of Chapel Hill; B.A., Emory University, 1962; M.B.A., University of Pennsylvania, 1964; M.Ed., University of Pittsburgh, 1968. Bank administrative assistant, 1964-1965; chemical salesman, 1965-1966; physical education instructor, 1967-1968, academic counselor and assistant athletic business manager, 1968-1971, assistant athletic director, 1971-1976, athletic director, 1976-1980, University of North Carolina at Chapel Hill; chairman, Taxpayers Educational Coalition, 1980-1982; president, Cobey and Associates, 1982-1984; unsuccessful Republican candidate for lieutenant governor, 1980; unsuccessful Republican candidate for U.S. House, Fourth North Carolina Congressional District, 1982, won the seat in 1984, but was defeated for reelection by Democratic challenger

David E. Price, 1986; appointed deputy state transportation secretary, 1987. *Biographical Directory of Congress*, 799; *News and Observer*, November 5, 6, 1986.

Howard Coble (1931-   ), native of Greensboro; A.B., Guilford College, 1958; J.D., University of North Carolina at Chapel Hill, 1962; U.S. Coast Guard, 1952-1956, 1977-1978, and Reserve, 1960-1982. Automobile insurance field claim representative and superintendent, 1961-1967; member, state House, 1969, 1979-1983; assistant U.S. attorney, Middle District of North Carolina, 1969-1973; secretary, state Revenue Department, 1973-1977; Greensboro attorney, 1979-1984; U.S. House member, Sixth North Carolina Congressional District, since 1985. *Biographical Directory of Congress*, 799.

John Porter East (1931-1986), born in Springfield, Illinois; was buried in Arlington National Cemetery, Arlington, Virginia; was graduated from Earlham College, 1953; J.D., University of Illinois, 1959; M.A., 1962, Ph.D., 1964, University of Florida; U.S. Marine Corps, 1953-1955. Attorney; political science professor, East Carolina University, 1964-1980; elected to U.S. Senate, 1980; announced he would not seek reelection, 1985. *Biographical Directory of Congress*, 948; *News and Observer*, September 18, 1985, June 30, November 5, 6, 1986; *North Carolina Manual, 1985*, 213.

Jesse Helms (1921-   ), born in Monroe; resident of Raleigh; was educated at Wingate (Junior) College and Wake Forest College (later University); honorary degrees; U.S. Naval Reserve, 1942-1945. *Raleigh Times* city editor, 1941-1942; news and program director, WRAL Radio, Raleigh, 1948-1951; administrative assistant to U.S. senators Willis Smith and Alton Lennon, of North Carolina, 1951-1953; executive director, North Carolina Bankers Assn., 1953-1960; Raleigh city councilman, 1957-1961; editorialist, WRAL Television, and past executive vice-president, vice-chairman of the board, and assistant chief executive officer, Capitol Broadcasting Co., 1960-1972; U.S. senator from North Carolina since 1973; former chairman, Senate Agriculture, Nutrition, and Forestry Committee; minority leader, Senate Foreign Relations Committee; Republican. *Biographical Directory of Congress*, 1168; *Who's Who in America, 1988-1989*, II, 1379-1380.

William Martin Hendon (1944-   ), born in Asheville; resident of McLean, Virginia; B.S., M.B.A., University of Tennessee. Businessman, 1970-1980; U.S. House member, North Carolina Eleventh Congressional District, 1981-1983, 1985-1987; defeated for re-election, 1982, 1986, by Democratic challenger James McClure Clark; author. *Biographical Directory of Congress*, 1172; *North Carolina Manual, 1985*, 237, *1987-1988*, 255.

J. Alex McMillan III (1932-   ), native of Charlotte; B.A., University of North Carolina at Chapel Hill, 1954; M.B.A., University of Virginia, 1958; U.S. Army, 1954-1956. Sales, control, Carolina Paper Board Corp., 1958-1960; various positions with Ruddick Corp., 1968-1983; member, Mecklenburg County Board of Commissioners, 1972-1974; member, chairman, Mecklenburg Board of Social Services, 1974-1977; president, Harris-Teeter Super Markets, 1977-1983; chairman, Charlotte-Mecklenburg Broadcasting Authority, 1978-1983; U.S. House member, Ninth North Carolina Congressional District, since 1985. *Biographical Directory of Congress*, 1480; *North Carolina Manual, 1987-1988*, 251.

[3]Hayden Edward Knox (1937-   ), born in Davidson; resident of Charlotte; B.S., North Carolina State College (later University), 1959; LL.B., Wake Forest University, 1963. Attorney; member, state Senate, 1971, 1973; Charlotte mayor, 1979-1983; appointed to Advisory Budget Committee by Governor Hunt, 1977; defeated by Attorney General Rufus Edmisten in Democratic gubernatorial runoff, June, 1984; appointed national cochairman, Democrats for Reagan-Bush, October, 1984, and officially switched to Republican party, May, 1985. *Charlotte Observer*, December 4, 1983, October 9, 1984, July 21, 1985; Luebke, *Tar Heel Politics*, 187; *News and Observer*, October 9, 10, 1984, May 31, 1985; *North Carolina Manual, 1973*, 583-584; William D. Snider, *Helms and Hunt: The North Carolina Senate Race, 1984* (Chapel Hill: University of North Carolina Press, 1985), 132-135.

[4]Controversy surrounded the outcome of the hard-fought vote, in the General Assembly's joint base budget committee, to continue the existing level of state abortion funding for poor women. Disregarding protests from Republicans and reporters, Senator Anthony E. Rand, the committee chairman, initially declined to release the official count, contending that Senate rules did not specify that committee votes be recorded; consequently, no announcement was necessary. I. Beverly Lake, Jr., Martin's chief lobbyist, and Richard E. Hartney, Jr., executive director of North Carolina Right to Life,

witnessed the vote, counting more hands raised in support of abortion restrictions proposed by Senator Ollie Harris than in opposition. Rand, later that same day, disclosed that committee members voted 49-46 to end discussion of Harris's proposals and that the continued funding level was approved by a 49-44 difference. The chairman speculated that the reason Lake and Hartney saw more "'no' votes than 'yes' votes" was because "several legislative leaders who helped him count votes did not raise their hands during the count, even though they voted for the proposal." *News and Observer*, May 29, 30, June 18, 1985.

[5]Betsy Lane Cochrane; born in Asheboro; resident of Davie County; B.A., Meredith College. Teacher; housewife; member, since 1981, minority leader, since 1985, state House of Representatives; vice-chairwoman, Davie County Republican party, and executive committee member, North Carolina Republican party. *North Carolina Manual, 1987-1988,* 379. Representative Cochrane introduced H.B. 520, "A Bill to Be Entitled an Act to Enact 'The Tax Relief Act of 1985,'" on April 15, 1985. It was assigned to the House Finance Committee for study. *N.C. House Journal, 1985,* 201, 664-665.

[6]Johnathan Laban Rhyne, Jr. (1955-   ), born in Charlotte; resident of Lincoln County; B.A., Davidson College, 1977; J.D., Campbell University, 1981. Attorney; elected to state House of Representatives, 1984, and returned in subsequent elections; secretary, Lincoln County Republican party, 1984. *North Carolina Manual, 1987-1988,* 479. Rhyne unsuccessfully attempted, on June 19, 1985, to recall the governor's tax relief bill from the House Finance Committee to the floor for further discussion; committee consideration of H.B. 520 ended with an indefinite postponement report. *N.C. House Journal, 1985,* 664-665, 674, 843; *News and Observer,* June 20, 1985.

[7]Martin was invited to appear, April 18, 1985, before the House Constitutional Amendments Committee to testify in support of a bill that would have permitted a statewide referendum on the gubernatorial veto. Awaiting the opening of the hearing, he walked into the House gallery to witness floor proceedings on the Democratic tax-cut proposal—the governor's brother and adviser, Joseph; R. Jack Hawke, Jr., then his special assistant for policy; and the First Lady were already there. After the bill passed, Martin held an impromptu meeting with reporters who spotted him as he departed the gallery.

Some Democratic legislators were displeased with Martin's unscheduled visit and his talk with the media. The General Assembly observed a long-standing rule that only its members could give press conferences in the Legislative Building. Finally, although the governor had "as much right as anyone" as "a citizen of the state" to sit in the gallery, acknowledged George W. Miller, Jr. (D-Durham), there was also the matter of "protocol." North Carolina's chief executive usually enters the Legislative Building only upon invitation of the General Assembly; Martin had been asked to the committee meeting, not the House tax debate. *News and Observer,* April 19, 1985.

SYMBOLIC LANDING OF FIRST ENGLISH COLONISTS

Roanoke Island, June 26, 1985

[June 26, 1985, marked the 400th anniversary of the arrival of the first English colonists in America, an event celebrated by the reenactment of the landing of the Sir Richard Grenville-Ralph Lane expedition on Roanoke Island. For a description of the commemoration, see "Governor Participates in Fort Raleigh Ceremony," *Carolina Comments*, XXXIII (September, 1985), 122-124. The speech, below, that Martin presented at Fort Raleigh National Historic Site, was similar to one he delivered April 26, 1987, at a marker dedication in Portsmouth, England. The second Roanoke colony, later known as the Lost Colony, departed from Portsmouth on April 26, 1587.]

William Shakespeare was only twenty-four years old, and had not produced his first drama, when the first book about the drama of North Carolina was published in England in 1588. It was an eyewitness account of what the first English colonists had found in the New World, entitled *A briefe and true report of the new found land of Virginia*. The author was Thomas Harriot, the scientist hired by Raleigh to document the 1585 expedition.[1]

The new found land was North Carolina. I must point out that his reference to Virginia did not mean he had misread his road map. They didn't have any road maps—didn't have any roads! The territory was then part of the lands claimed as Virginia.

Harriot praised our land and climate, saying "The air there is so temperate and wholesome, the soil so fertile and yielding such commodities,"[2] statements that are true today, 400 years later.

Harriot's accounts and the maps and drawings of John White,[3] artist for the 1585 voyage, provide the most information about what this first colony found. This spring their work was the centerpiece of the exciting exhibition, "Raleigh and Roanoke," which brought many of White's drawings and other artifacts home to North Carolina.[4] Nearly 100,000 people saw them in the North Carolina Museum of History in Raleigh. Others will see them at the New York Public Library, where the exhibit is now located for the summer months.

In addition to describing the New World, Harriot's account tells us what life in Elizabethan England was like, and how some Englishmen, if not all, yearned for a place to make a new start, a place with more opportunities. As it turned out, Lane's colony returned home after a year.[5] The English, however, did not give up, and in 1587 a second colony, one including women and children, came back to this area; this, of course, was the Lost Colony whose story is so vividly told each summer in the Waterside Theater only a short distance from where we stand.[6]

Although neither of these colonies was permanent, they were the spiritual beginning of English America, and the information obtained from them greatly influenced English and European ideas of America. There are many questions about these colonies, and neither left much evidence of how and where the English lived. White and Harriot tell us a great deal about the Indians, but little about the English themselves.

The earthworks fort in front of us remains as it was reconstructed about thirty years ago, but the dwelling place of the colonists, named then the Cittie of Raleigh, has never been found. Using funds from a grant from the Z. Smith Reynolds Foundation, America's Four Hundredth Anniversary Committee has sponsored extensive archaeological activity. The National Park Service has also funded search work. Even as I speak today, National Park Service archaeologists are excavating a site several hundred feet from here, looking for what they believe may be the remains of another earthworks fort. Later this summer, archaeologists from East Carolina University will begin an underwater search for the Cittie of Raleigh, on the possibility that a storm or two in those first 200 years might have eroded the site.

Today, I am pleased to announce some exciting finds. For the last two years, a search has been under way for the remains of the Algonkian Indian village of Pomeiooc (pronounced Pom eeok), a village which gave Ralph Lane and his party a warm welcome—friendly, that is—when they visited in 1585. Recently, archaeologists from East Carolina University have found remains of what they believe could be this village, the stockaded village painted by John White in 1585. In a cornfield in Hyde County, Paul Green and his assistant, Jay Holley, found more than 100 shards of Indian pottery and twenty pieces of Indian smoking pipes, as well as post moulds of buildings, all dating from the late 1500s.

This is the only place in Hyde County where this type of material has been found. The quantity and type of artifacts suggest that this was a relatively large and permanent site of habitation, possibly a village about the scale of Pomeiooc, as painted by White. The location also corresponds to the site indicated by White in his maps of the area. Much work still needs to be done before we can positively identify the site; however, this is one of the most significant finds that has been made since America's Four Hundredth Anniversary Committee initiated its archaeological program in 1982.

The site was discovered just as this phase of the program and its funding ended. Thus, it was necessary to seek emergency funding to continue this important work. Today, I would like to thank the East Carolina Bank and its board of directors, many of whom are here today, for their generosity in providing a grant to continue the archaeological excavations. Both the East Carolina Bank and the Z. Smith Reynolds Foundation are to be commended for their support of this most important four hundredth anniversary program. I also want to thank the officials and people of Hyde County and the Hyde County Historical Society, which provided the initial funding of the search for Pomeiooc.

Although these two Raleigh colonies were not permanent, they are an important part of our American heritage and laid the groundwork for an English America which took root later at Jamestown and Plymouth.

Four hundred years ago, the world was a troubled place, and the English, like Americans today, felt that their freedom and way of life were threatened. Yet, they were optimistic as they set out for a new land and a new life. With great difficulty, they and their successors of many nationalities helped to create the settlements which would find fullness as the United States of America.

So, today, I unveil this plaque in memory of the first English colonists, who landed somewhere near here 400 years ago today. They brought with them a dream which still affects and inspires us. [Martin unveiled and read plaque.] "The new forte in Virginia," we have to live with that, "built in the summer of 1585 to defend the colony of 108 men under Ralph Lane from a possible Spanish attack, this fort probably commanded a good view and field of fire across nearby Roanoke Sound. Enemy cannon or musket balls would become embedded in the thick earth walls, resulting in little damage to the structure or its occupants. This refuge for the first English colonists in America is reconstructed on its original site."

---

[1]Thomas Harriot (or Hariot, 1560-1621), born in Oxford, England; died in London; was graduated from St. Mary's Hall, Oriel College, 1580. Explorer, astronomer, mathematician, navigator, scientist; member, 1585-1586 expedition to Roanoke Island; author of *A briefe and true report of the new found land of Virginia: of the commodities there found and to be raysed, as well as marchantable, as other for victuall, building and other necessarie vses for those that are and shalbe the planters there; and of the nature and manners of the naturall inhabitants . . .* (1588), the earliest English eyewitness account of the New World and regarded as one of the foremost treatises on the region as viewed by the first English settlers. Powell, *DNCB*, III, 45-47.

[2]"Seeing therefore the ayre there is so temperate and holsome, the soile so fertile, and yeelding such commodities, as I have before mentioned, the voyage also thither to and fro being sufficiently experimented, to be perfourmed twise a yeere with ease, and at any season thereof. . . ." Excerpt from Thomas Harriot, "The Conclusion," *A briefe and true report of the new found land of Virginia. . .* (1588), quoted in David B. Quinn and Alison M. Quinn (eds.), *The First Colonists: Documents on the Planting of the First English Settlements in North America, 1584-1590* (Raleigh: North Carolina Department of Cultural Resources, Division of Archives and History, 1982), 75, hereinafter cited as Quinn, *First Colonists.*

[3]John White (fl. 1577-1593), artist, explorer; governor of the Cittie of Raleigh in Virginia, 1587; grandfather of Virginia Dare. Paul Hulton, *America 1585: The Complete Drawings of John White* (Chapel Hill: University of North Carolina Press, 1984), 7-16.

[4]The governor opened a special preview of the "Raleigh and Roanoke" exhibition at the North Carolina Museum of History on March 6, 1985. The exhibition commemorating the Roanoke voyages was created by the British Library and originally premiered in London on April 30, 1984. It featured 157 artifacts and documents, many of them never before seen outside the United Kingdom, from seventeen repositories. For more information, see *Raleigh & Roanoke, March 8-June 6, 1985, The British Library Exhibit Hosted by the North Carolina Museum of History* (Raleigh: America's Four Hundredth Anniversary Committee, North Carolina Department of Cultural Resources, 1985); see also, "Major

Exhibition Opens at History Museum," *Carolina Comments*, XXXIII (March, 1985), 37-39, and *News and Observer*, March 8, 1985.

[5]Ralph Lane (1530-1603), born in Northamptonshire, England; died in Dublin, Ireland. Appointed sheriff, County Kerry, Ireland, 1583; leader of unsuccessful colony on Roanoke Island, 1585-1586; muster master, West Tilbury military camp, Essex, England, 1588; muster master general of Drake's army against Spain, 1589; muster master general, clerk of check of garrisons in Ireland, 1592; knighted, 1593. *Who Was Who in America, 1607-1896*, 372. Dwindling supplies and a worsening relationship with the Indians persuaded the Lane colony to depart for England with Sir Francis Drake's fleet. Lefler and Newsome, *North Carolina*, 9-10.

[6]The story to which the governor referred, of the ill-fated and now famous second Roanoke colony, is Paul Eliot Green's play, *The Lost Colony; A Symphonic Drama of Man's Faith and Work: In Two Acts with Music, Dance, Pantomime, and Song* (Durham, N.C.: Seeman Printing, Inc., four-hundredth anniversary edition, 1980). Originally published in 1937, *The Lost Colony* was Green's first outdoor symphonic drama, a format he created. The play is performed at Waterside Theater, Manteo. *Durham Morning Herald*, June 5, 1966; Richard Walser and E. T. Malone, Jr., *Literary North Carolina* (Raleigh: Division of Archives and History, North Carolina Department of Cultural Resources, 1986), 54.

PRESS RELEASE: GOVERNOR MARTIN'S STATEMENT CONCERNING JOINT CONFERENCE TAX PROPOSAL

RALEIGH, JULY 3, 1985

The tax package prepared by the joint conference falls short of my proposals. It fails to provide significant relief to the state's business community, therefore hurting North Carolina's chances for stimulating greater economic development and more jobs.

The package provides only about one third of the tax relief I had originally requested. While this proposal provides some tax cuts, it does not go far enough. That just means we will have to come back next year with more proposals for additional tax relief. Sadly, it appears that those individuals who all along did not want tax relief are winning, while those who wanted to give something back to the citizens are losing. This is not what my administration had hoped for.

Some now argue that any greater tax cut would come at the expense of the education program. That is false. The education budget has been spelled out in the appropriations act. The truth is, adoption of the Senate's tax bill might well have prevented spending more money for preferential spending allocations in districts of favored legislators, a practice known as "pork barrel" that is used to discipline legislators to vote with the party leadership in the House. It is sad that this sorry practice takes precedence over tax cuts.

I am disappointed in the way this partial tax relief package was prepared in the General Assembly. Initially the Senate appeared to be more sympathetic to tax relief for North Carolina citizens, but Senate

Democratic leaders didn't stand firm for very long. They let the House leaders bluff them by saying that if Senate Democrats didn't cave in, there would be no tax bill at all. Indeed, in the first year, 1985-1986, the tax package raises taxes on some taxpayers more than it lowers taxes on others, and on balance, therefore, is no tax cut at all until the second year. The people of this state deserve better.

GIFT OF RETIRED SEABOARD SYSTEM RAILROAD BOXCARS

RALEIGH, JULY 8, 1985

I am pleased tonight to acknowledge and accept, on behalf of the state of North Carolina, the largest private contribution ever made to the development of artificial reefs in the coastal waters of our state. The donation of 200 retired railroad boxcars by the Seaboard System is a major step in the continued expansion of new marine-life habitat and the growth of commercial and sports fishing for native residents and visitors alike. This generous gift by the Seaboard System, which represents a value in excess of $250,000, is another example of how public-private partnerships enhance the quality of life for our citizens and visitors.

By establishing artificial reefs for the spawning, feeding, and cover of many fish species, North Carolina has expanded the economic impact of commercial and sports fishing to more than $500 million in slightly more than a decade. Since 1973, when the state first became involved in this effort, thirteen reefs have been created off the North Carolina coast. Three of these reefs, located near Oregon Inlet and Wrightsville and Atlantic beaches, have been built with World War II Liberty ships taken out of storage at Wilmington. At the present time, we're preparing another ship, the *Protector*, which will be sunk near Cape Lookout to establish a fourth haven for fish.

Having traveled the rails of our nation for many years, the boxcars contributed by the Seaboard System Railroad will enable us to expand these reefs, thus increasing fish populations and attracting many new species for recreational enjoyment. Dick Sanborn[1] put it very appropriately when he said that these cars, having transported the goods of a nation over hundreds of thousands of miles of Americana, will now have a second life. Indeed, they will continue to serve a useful purpose by making one of the country's most outstanding sports-fishing states more attractive than ever before.

I want to take this opportunity to express the deep appreciation of the state for this valuable gift and what it represents to the economic life of coastal North Carolina. Since 1840, when Seaboard's predecessor company, the Atlantic Coast Line, opened the world's longest continuous rail line in the world, stretching from Wilmington to Weldon, you have demonstrated the real meaning of corporate citizenship; and although you now have corporate headquarters in Jacksonville, Florida, your roots are still buried deep in North Carolina soil. Tonight's announcement is a strong demonstration that the partnership begun more than 150 years ago is a lasting one [and] that it will continue to grow in the years ahead.

---

[1]Richard Dyer Sanborn (1936-   ), born in Sanbornville, New Hampshire; B.A., University of New Hampshire, 1957; LL.B., Harvard University, 1960. Attorney, Atlantic Coast Line Railroad, 1961-1972; special assistant to the president, Seaboard Coast Line Railroad, 1972-1973; vice-president, assistant to the chairman, Family Lines Rail System, 1973-1980; president, chief executive officer, Seaboard System Railroad, 1982-1986, and of CSX Distribution Services, since 1986. *Who's Who in America, 1986-1987,* II, 2442.

TESTIMONY SUBMITTED TO U.S. SENATE COMMITTEE ON FINANCE, SUBCOMMITTEE ON TRADE

WASHINGTON, D.C., JULY 15, 1985

[The beating that American textile, apparel, and footwear manufacturers were taking from imported goods engendered protectionist sentiment across the country, and Congress responded. H.R. 1562 and its companion proposal, S. 680, if enacted, would have trimmed textile imports from Hong Kong, South Korea, and Taiwan by 30 percent and placed ceilings on other Third World products. Shoe imports also were to have been curbed, and the legislation even called for a global decrease in copper production. The bills were generally popular in the South, and Governor Martin furnished testimony, reprinted below, in support of S. 680.

The final version of H.R. 1562 emerged from Congress on December 3, 1985. Although President Reagan acknowledged "the difficulties of the apparel, textile, copper, and shoe industries," and was "deeply sympathetic about the job layoffs and plant closings that have affected many workers in these industries," he also feared economic retaliation from countries whose exports to the United States would have been affected by such a law. Requiring support from southern Republicans to ensure safe passage of a tax reform package through the House, Reagan waited two weeks before acting on the textile bill. The House approved the tax plan on December 17, and with an hour remaining on the constitutionally mandated limit for issuing a veto, Reagan killed H.R. 1562.

The House unsuccessfully attempted to override Reagan's veto of H.R. 1562 on August 6, 1986. Reminders that a Republican president rejected the textile bill returned to haunt GOP candidates in congressional elections later that year. Democrats won five seats in the House and three in the Senate, all formerly held by southern Republicans, reflecting in part voter dissatisfaction with the fate of H.R. 1562; James T. Broyhill of North Carolina was among the displaced senators. Martin openly supported the override, as well as a later, "more generous" congressional proposal to curb textile imports that the president also opposed. *Congressional Quarterly Almanac, 1985,* 255-259, 480, 40-D, *1986,* 347-348; Lamis, *Two-Party South,* 287; Luebke, *Tar Heel Politics,* 162; *News and Observer,* November 8, 1986; press releases, "Governor Martin's Statement on the Planned August 6 House Override of the Textile Bill Veto," [Raleigh], August 1, 1986, and "Governor Martin's Statement on President Reagan's Veto of 1988 Textile Bill," Raleigh, September 28, 1988, Governors Papers, James G. Martin.]

As governor of North Carolina, I am very concerned about the job losses in the textile and apparel industries—not only in the state of North Carolina, but for the entire nation. North Carolina is the leading apparel and textile state in the nation. Approximately 300,000 of our citizens work directly in the 2,000 textile and apparel firms of our state. These are dedicated and hard-working, tax-paying citizens who are producing quality U.S.-made products. These industries are severely impacted, and these individuals' economic livelihood is being totally disrupted, because of unfair competition which is beyond their control.

As these textile and apparel jobs leave our state and nation for overseas markets, they disrupt the personal lives and the economic well-being of our society. Some 21,042-fewer textile and apparel jobs existed in April, 1985, as compared to April, 1984. For example, the 21,042 job losses within the last year will cut the textile and apparel payrolls by more than $254 million in North Carolina alone. Moreover, the withdrawal of these paychecks from our economy will mean job losses in other sectors, as well. The dry cleaners, the gasoline stations, the grocers, and hundreds of other businesses, large and small, that serve our textile and apparel families will also feel the loss. In the end, we cannot hope to estimate the total economic losses that are occurring daily to the import-related cutbacks in our apparel and textile industries, nor can we accurately assess the tremendous emotional pain and anguish that is now being and will in the future continue to be felt by those unable to meet the daily needs of their families.

As a former member of Congress, I fully understand that this subject of international trade is a very complicated one. However, we must give our textile and apparel industry an opportunity to regain their competitive footing and remain one of our essential U.S. industries. We must act to limit the magnitude of the costs our society incurs from unbounded imports. The Textile and Apparel Enforcement Act of 1985 is desperately needed to help sustain these two basic and vital industries.

TESTIMONY BEFORE U.S. SENATE COMMITTEE ON GOVERNMENTAL AFFAIRS, SUBCOMMITTEE ON CIVIL SERVICE, POST OFFICE, AND GENERAL SERVICES

Washington, D.C., July 25, 1985

Wages and salaries represent an increasing percentage of the cost of operating government and business. As a result, human resource issues have taken on greater and greater importance. An issue that has received much attention recently is comparable worth. This issue would broaden the legal requirement, of equal pay for equal work, to equal pay for similar or comparable work.

Like many artfully phrased titles, "comparable worth" has a superficial attractiveness. It suggests that behind the label there is some foundation of fairness. In fact, however, all it does is repudiate the marketplace, reject the interplay of supply and demand, and replace it with a socialistic allocator whereby some formula or consultant will artificially determine the statutory economic value of each job without regard to its true economic value. It is based on a belief that we can select a formula that will inherently give just the right weight to each factor of a job's description and requirements and qualifications, without regard to whether that job has an oversupply or shortage of workers, and somehow socially engineer a fairer system for all.

The state of North Carolina has recently considered modifying its personnel system for state employees to encompass the comparable worth doctrine, but ultimately decided against this approach. In June of 1984, the North Carolina General Assembly passed legislation directing that a pay-equity study be conducted and authorized $650,000 for this effort.[1] Although named a pay-equity study, the impetus for ratifying this provision came from a June, 1984, report by a state task force on comparable worth.[2] This report recommended the development of an equitable job evaluation and pay system that would establish the comparable worth of state jobs on the basis of a point factor system. The resulting legislation directed that:

—The study encompass all of the state's classified employees who are subject to the State Personnel Act; this totals about 84,000 employees.

—A consulting firm be hired not later than December 15, 1984, to conduct the study—which was done.

—The consultant "study the state personnel system so it can identify wage policies that inhibit pay equity and develop a job evaluation and pay system. . . ."

—The study "include . . . a factor based on supply and demand," with that factor receiving "equal weight."

—A final report be produced by April 1, 1986.

As directed by the legislature, efforts were begun to employ a contractor. The contractor was to:

—Evaluate any policies that would inhibit pay equity.

—Develop a job evaluation system which would define an overall structure to categorize jobs and develop a method of evaluating jobs to place them in that structure.

—Develop a pay system which would survey pay in relevant job markets and relate the results to the job evaluation structure.

—Recommend how to implement these systems, including costs, alternatives, and phasing approaches.

This information was provided to 130 contractors. Eight actually made proposals. One of these, Psychological Services, Incorporated, was selected in December, 1984.

From the beginning, it had been apparent that it would be difficult to successfully complete the study. Problems evolved into two categories: problems with the logistics of the study itself and, more importantly, problems and concerns from a broad range of citizens on the basic comparable worth doctrine.

With regard to the problems of conducting the study, most difficult was the language of the legislation requiring that a factor based on supply and demand be given equal weight. This language attempted to assure that labor market concerns were addressed, but seemed to be contrary to comparable worth ideals which relate one job to another without concern for the market values of those jobs. A second concern was that fairness called for individual evaluation of each of the 84,000 employees; clearly, this was to be a massive undertaking.

As significant as these problems were, however, the broader concerns on comparable worth doctrine and its implications ultimately proved the most convincing. The arguments were spearheaded by our business community. Foremost was the concern that there was no way of accurately estimating what the cost of salary adjustments, if any, might be. And, if the completed study recommended adjustments beyond the ability of the state to pay, then we might have directed ourselves into a situation similar to the state of Washington, where a study was commissioned but the results not acted upon—after which a court of law somehow concluded that the study itself was invested with the power to compel its advice to be implemented.[3]

Second was the concern that comparable worth introduces an artificiality into wages and salaries. This may hold pay for certain jobs below market rates with a shortage of workers, making it difficult to hire and retain employees in these categories which otherwise could respond to the imbalance of supply and demand by the market adjustment of bidding up wages. Conversely, pay in other categories with an oversupply of workers may be pegged above market. Businesses, particularly those in cities where there are large state employee concentrations, were concerned that they would be forced to meet salaries in categories set above market rates.

Finally, there was significant concern by business and industry that the move by the state toward comparable worth signaled an eventual requirement that the doctrine be forced on private enterprise. Their response was decidedly in favor of the present supply-and-demand approach to setting wages.

The result of these concerns was that the General Assembly, upon returning to Raleigh in February of this year, began a reevaluation of the study requirement. In April, 1985, they directed that the study be terminated.[4]

While there is no doubt that we must take all possible steps to pay our employees fairly and equitably, we supported the termination of the study. Instead, we are making what we believe to be better efforts by trying to improve our existing classification system and developing an improved way of providing incentives to those employees who are our better performers. We believe this is the way to provide the opportunities our employees are looking for.

---

[1]*N.C. Session Laws, 1983, Extra and Regular Sessions, 1984*, c. 1034, s. 146, ordered the pay-equity study.

[2]*Pay Equity in North Carolina State Government: A Report to the Governor and the General Assembly* ([Raleigh: North Carolina Council on the Status of Women, Task Force on Comparable Worth], June, 1984).

[3]An independent study requested by the state of Washington disclosed, in 1974, that state jobs for which females were usually hired characteristically paid 20 percent less than those in which men predominated. In 1982, nine state workers, provoked by legislative lethargy on the issue of pay discrimination and backed by Washington's chapter of the American Federation of State, Municipal, and County Employees, forged the report's findings into a lawsuit. Ruling in favor of the plaintiffs, a district court judge ordered the state to reimburse approximately 15,500 affected workers. Faced with an outlay of $1 billion in back pay and the necessity of revising state pension plans and adjusting salary scales, Washington appealed the decision. In September, 1985, three judges of the U.S. Ninth Circuit Court declared that the state's salaries reflected current

market value, and therefore Washington had no cause "to eliminate an economic inequality which it did not create." "A Loss for Comparable Worth," *Newsweek*, September 16, 1985, 36; "Back to the Bargaining Table," *Time*, September 16, 1985, 36; *New York* (New York) *Times*, June 16, 1985, hereinafter cited as *New York Times*.

⁴"An Act to Repeal Section 146 of Chapter 1034 of the 1983 Session (Regular Session, 1984) Relating to the Comparable Worth Study" was ratified April 30, 1985. *N.C. Session Laws, 1985*, c. 142.

TESTIMONY BEFORE U.S. SENATE COMMITTEE ON LABOR AND HUMAN RESOURCES, SUBCOMMITTEE ON LABOR

WASHINGTON, D.C., JULY 25, 1985

[The United States Supreme Court determined, in *Garcia* v. *San Antonio Metropolitan Transit Authority*, that Congress was constitutionally empowered to open the Fair Labor Standards Act to state and local government employees. The justices' decision, announced February 19, 1985, prompted an outcry from public officials consequently facing the effect of new hourly and minimum wage regulations upon their budgets. The prospect of ending the practice of granting compensatory time off as a substitute for overtime pay proved particularly worrisome; the National Association of Counties, National League of Cities, and U.S. Conference of Mayors argued that local governments would have to spend over $1 billion in the coming year to comply.

Although labor leaders initially contended that public employers were wildly overstating the case against overtime pay, both sides reached an accord and persuaded federal legislators to act. Congress, on November 7, passed the Fair Labor Standards Amendments of 1985. Among its provisions, the law authorized granting compensatory time off "at the rate of one and one half hours for each FLSA overtime hour worked." Public safety, emergency response, and seasonal employees were permitted to earn a maximum of 480 hours of comp time, while all others subject to the act could accumulate up to 240 hours; once those limits were reached, cash payment for additional overtime worked was to be made. *Congressional Quarterly Almanac, 1985*, 23, 471-472; *Major Legislation of the Congress, 99th Congress, Issue No. 4, January, 1986* (Washington, D.C.: U.S. Government Printing Office, 1986), MLC-050-051, hereinafter cited as *Major Legislation of Congress*, with appropriate year; see also P.L. 99-150, "Fair Labor Standards Amendments of 1985" (short title), *United States Statutes at Large*, Act of November 14, 1985, 99 Stat. 787-791.

Governor Martin described the potential impact of the *Garcia* judgment upon the Tar Heel State in both his Senate testimony, below, and in his address to the State Employees Association of North Carolina, Winston-Salem, September 12, 1985. His prepared statement and other remarks to the Labor Subcommittee were recorded in Senate Committee on Labor and Human Resources, *Fair Labor Standards Amendments of 1985*, 99th Cong., 1st sess., 1985, S. Hrg. 99-359, 66-73, hereinafter cited as *Fair Labor Standards Amendments*, S. Hrg. 99-359.]

I appreciate the opportunity to appear before this subcommittee to express the serious concerns that we in North Carolina have as a result of the *Garcia* decision.

Garcia v. *San Antonio Metro[politan] Transit Authority* holds that public employees engaged in the performance of "traditional governmental functions" are subject to the provisions of the Fair Labor Standards Act.[1] Its impact upon North Carolina is two-fold: First, it eliminates the flexibility our state and local governments had to provide protection services to our citizens in an economic manner without damage to employee morale; and second, it undermines the sovereignty of the individual states, and, as stated by Justice Powell in his dissent, "reduces the Tenth Amendment of our Constitution to meaningless rhetoric. . . ."[2]

As a result of applying the Fair Labor Standards Act to state and local governments, our state government expects to incur more than $17 million in unavoidable overtime payments in the 1985-1986 fiscal year. The past practice of compensatory time off for law enforcement officers had the dual virtues of improved productive efficiency of their work and a degree of flexibility that was highly popular among their ranks.[3] Our secretary of crime control and public safety[4] estimates that without this we will need 100 additional highway patrolmen just to continue providing the services and protection at their current levels. We also fear that surveillance details by alcohol law enforcement officers will be eliminated because of overtime requirements.

The economic impact on North Carolina's local governments is enormous and perhaps more devastating than on state government. Our larger cities—Charlotte, Greensboro, and Raleigh—project additional expenditures in fiscal 1985-1986 of $500,000, $600,000, and $233,000, respectively. Our smaller towns, which are struggling to provide essential services, will suffer even more. For example, Wendell, North Carolina, with a population of 2,386, has twenty-three employees and anticipates $30,000 in additional costs during the current fiscal year. On a per-capita basis, this added expense represents more than $12.00 per community resident. To comply with the *Garcia* decision, Wendell town officials either must eliminate services to citizens or raise taxes five cents per $100.00 valuation. Beleaguered property owners should not be subjected to these additional taxes. I am submitting for the record, along with my testimony, a chart which provides information on retroactive costs, compliance costs for fiscal 1985-1986, and the comparative effect on current property tax rates for a sample of cities and towns in North Carolina. I commend it for your review.[5]

Let me share other examples of how the *Garcia* decision threatens to extract a human price. The Greensboro, North Carolina, Department of Parks and Recreation has a special program that provides field trips, to such places as Washington, D.C., for the mentally and physically handicapped. The costs of these trips are expected to double, thereby jeopardizing the program.

In summary, the *Garcia* decision adversely affects public employers and citizens alike. It impacts negatively upon budgets, employee relations, and the level of services provided the public, with little apparent benefit to anyone. While we appreciate the assistance of the [Reagan] administration, through the Department of Labor's decision to delay enforcement until October 15, 1985, the moratorium does not protect North Carolina cities, towns, and counties from private lawsuits. State and local governments, particularly law enforcement, fire fighting, and emergency medical personnel, should be exempted from the Fair Labor Standards Act.

The devastating effect of *Garcia* upon the sovereignty of North Carolina and all states must be emphasized. In its decision, the Supreme Court has taken the view that state sovereignty guaranteed by the Tenth Amendment is dependent upon procedural safeguards rather than fundamental rights set forth in the Bill of Rights. This places the protection of state sovereignty in the hands of the legislative branch—and more particularly in the Senate.

It continues to be my opinion that the role of the states in our federal system rests on the United States Constitution and not upon decisions of elected federal officials. Your recognition that states' rights require remedial action will perhaps lead our Supreme Court to reconsider its opinion; and perhaps it will move the court to restore the constitutionally mandated balance of power between the state and federal government, a balance designed by our founding fathers to protect our fundamental liberties. In conclusion, I respectfully urge that the Congress act to correct *Garcia*, not only to avoid the adverse economic impact upon state and local governments, but also to recognize the sovereignty of the states.

---

[1]"Fair Labor Standards Act of 1938" (short title), *United States Statutes at Large*, Chapter 676, Act of June 25, 1938, 52 Stat. 1060-1069; see also *United States Code* (1982 edition), Title 29, Secs. 201 et seq. See *United States Reports, Volume 469*, 82-1913, 528-589, for prevailing and dissenting opinions of the Supreme Court justices on *Garcia* v. *San Antonio Metropolitan Transit Authority.*

[2]Lewis Franklin Powell, Jr. (1907-   ), born in Suffolk, Virginia; B.S., 1929, LL.B., 1931, Washington and Lee University; honorary degrees; U.S. Army Air Force, 1942-1946. Practicing attorney, 1932-1971; associate justice, U.S. Supreme Court, 1972-1987. *Who's Who in America, 1988-1989*, II, 2493. The words correctly attributed to Justice Powell appeared in *United States Reports, Volume 469*, 82-1913, 560.

[3]Compensatory time regulations, as they existed under the Fair Labor Standards Act and were to be enforced as a result of *Garcia*, were impractical—especially for law officers, the governor caustically asserted. "Highway patrolmen are frequently called upon to assist in traffic accidents involving serious injuries which require these officers to work beyond their normal hours," Martin told the Senate Labor Subcommittee on July 25, "but we cannot get motorists to confine their wrecks to the early hours of the shift. The Fair Labor Standards Act's requirement that this [comp] time be taken off during the same pay period is just often not possible, and so the result of that is that while now they may pursue a suspect across the state line, wouldn't it be ironic if they couldn't pursue him across the time line, into the next pay shift." *Fair Labor Standards Amendments*, S. Hrg. 99-359, 67.

[4]Joseph Wayne Dean (1944-   ), born in Nashville, Tennessee; B.A., The Citadel, 1966; J.D., Wake Forest University, 1969; U.S. Army, 1969-1971. Assistant U.S. attorney, 1971-1977; attorney in private practice, 1977-1985; state crime control and public safety secretary, since 1985. *North Carolina Manual, 1987-1988*, 725.

[5]The chart Martin furnished was reprinted in *Fair Labor Standards Amendments*, S. Hrg. 99-359, 70.

GOVERNOR'S CONFERENCE ON "SHARE THE PRIDE"

GREENSBORO, AUGUST 14, 1985

[The following speech is thematically similar to one the governor delivered at a Kannapolis textile rally, August 24, 1985.]

Thank you, Nancy Schrum, for that introduction and for your excellent prelude to this, the first Governor's Conference on "Share the Pride." I can't think of a better way to begin than by quoting that memorable cable sent from London, in 1897, by Mark Twain to the Associated Press. You know what it said. "Reports of my death," he wired, "are greatly exaggerated."[1] North Carolina's traditional industries have been battered in recent years by the growing flood of cheaper foreign imports. We've been dealt some tough blows, but we're far from being beaten.

How often you've heard people, who should know better, saying we should just forget the past, let the old industries go, and work instead to recruit newer industries. But what does that say to new industrial recruits if we neglect employers who are already here? Well, you can count me as a governor who will not be a party to writing the epitaph of our traditional industries. Even as we continue efforts to recruit new industries of higher technology, or lower, I intend for us to make even stronger efforts to help sustain our existing, traditional industries.

When we speak of traditional industries—fibers, textiles, hosiery, apparel, furniture, footwear, and agribusiness—we're really speaking about people, profits, and jobs. Two men, one from the eighteenth century and one from the twentieth, wrote about these crucial components of a thriving, vibrant economy. In 1776, Adam Smith, in his *Wealth of Nations*, wrote, "It is not by gold or silver, but by labour that all of the wealth of the world was purchased."[2] Two hundred years later, in response to those who railed at obscene profits, Winston Churchill said: "Profits aren't obscene—losses are."[3]

Today, we're losing a growing share of jobs and profits to foreign competition. Far too often, in too many North Carolina communities, the familiar hum of textile mills and the whir of apparel assembly lines have been winding down. An increasing number have become silent and idle. Since 1980, imports of textiles and apparel products have increased more than 60 percent.

Voluntary quotas have worked, all right: for them, not us. Last year alone, our nation posted, in textiles alone, a trade deficit of almost $17 billion. Other sectors of our traditional industries have experienced the same effect. This was a major factor in the closings or permanent layoffs at about forty North Carolina plants and meant the loss of more than 10,000 jobs.

Our problem isn't poor management or low productivity. Indeed, productivity is up: Output per worker in the textile industry has increased more than 50 percent since 1968, and the industry has invested more than a half billion dollars in plant modernization. That takes courage, and it takes commitment and dedication to what's best for America. But will it prove a wise investment against such adversity?

The problem is not the loss of productivity or managerial courage. We can compete with anyone in a system of mutual, balanced trade. On the contrary, our traditional industries are too often confronted with unfair competition. Many foreign countries subsidize their manufacturers and producers. The government provides them raw materials or services at deeply cut rates. In addition, less-developed countries still have lower wage rates. For example, one study last year found that the average workers in U.S. labor-intensive industries earned $8.60 per hour, while their counterpart in South Korea averaged $1.30; Hong Kong, $1.65; Taiwan, $1.64; and China, 26 cents.

There are other root causes that are easily identified. Economists are not at a loss for explanations. Their theories, just like the practical experience of plant managers and workers, can readily recognize the impact of an overvalued U.S. dollar, brought on by chronic federal deficits, caused by insatiable spending appetites, brought on by divided political accountability. The large trade deficit and the massive budget deficit are strange, but inevitable, companions. Getting to the core of the problem involves reducing the federal budget deficit, and that can be accomplished primarily by cutting the growth of government spending. Unfortunately, this is an objective that hasn't been achieved in recent years.

There are other factors, too. Trade with our world neighbors isn't all that free. Under the General Agreement on Tariffs and Trade,[4] all nations select key industries for protection. Most, for example, protect important agricultural sectors, as Agriculture Commissioner Jim Graham can attest.

Furthermore, many of our trading partners have developed formidable and ingenious ways to erect nontariff barriers against our goods entering their countries. The barriers continue to grow. In 1982, Canada restricted the imports of leather goods—and now, upholstered furniture. Austria restricted dresses, and France closed the door on electronic products. Japan found all sorts of reasons for keeping out American goods. Why don't we? Because we have clung to a mystical belief in the free-trade myth, even as evidence mounts that ours is one of the very few open markets left.

Now that Japanese prime minister Nakasone[5] is beginning to lead his nation to recognize and correct practices that have closed their markets against us, I believe we should respond positively to his politically courageous decision. It would be easy to just be skeptical and thus rationalize doing nothing; I propose, instead, that when 120 North Carolina business leaders accompany me to Japan in October, we go with the intention of doing business over there—to test their offer to widen the gate to their markets and see if we can sell North Carolina products.[6] Afterwards, we can evaluate whether a future trade mission to showcase our range of products would be useful. But first, let's see what some individual initiative can do.

Yes, I will be scheduled to call on those Japanese firms who have invested in North Carolina, to thank them, of course, for jobs in our state; but I also intend to talk with them about how vitally important it is to both our great nations to support mutual, balanced, trade. In keeping with that, I will promote sales of our goods and services. We've got the salesmen in North Carolina, let's go sell—and your governor intends to be the number-one salesman for North Carolina products. We've got the quality and the value, and I want the world to know it.

There are several other problems we have to address. One is our specific problem with a siege of imports of textiles and apparel. The United States generally has encouraged foreign exporters to restrain their sales voluntarily, under the Multi-Fiber Arrangement,[7] to avoid the imposition of formal quotas, but we are now eliminating the pretense of volunteerism. The truth is, apparel imports have risen dramatically faster than allowed officially by the voluntary quotas. That's because we don't enforce them, but rely on a sort of honor system. Well, we've certainly been "honored," all right. Now the Congress is moving to do something about it.[8]

While we're at it, we must also acknowledge the great extent to which our government has erected obstacles to our own exports. These are self-inflicted wounds. Frankly, that makes us the laughingstock overseas when we urge other countries to lower their barriers to our exports while we make it more difficult for our exporters.

The sad fact is that, in the United States, many laws and regulations limit our exports. For example, the Export Administration Act provides controls on exports of goods and technology to protect national security.[9] That sounds fine; in practice, the law mandates controls over a great variety of products, including domestically produced crude oil, refined petroleum products, red cedar, and, of all things, horses exported by sea. Well, I want our two seaports, Wilmington and Morehead City, to become *ex*ports, not just *im*ports.

Having returned from the national governors' conference last week, I want to assure you that governors in other states are equally concerned with the impact of imports in their own jurisdictions. Together, we will continue to press the administration and the Congress for action. We met with Japanese ambassador Matsunaga.[10] He seems sincere about efforts to open markets for us. We told him we would like to help.

Here in North Carolina, this administration has set its own agenda. I'm pleased to have at this conference, today, Commerce Secretary Howard Haworth[11] and Assistant Commerce Secretary for Traditional Industries White Watkins. I believe their appointments reflect my strong commitment to your sector of the industrial complex of North Carolina. Both of these leaders come from traditional industries and, together, we're working as a team to identify viable initiatives which our state can undertake in response to the plight of your companies.

I'd like to announce, at this conference, that we will be meeting with representatives of the trade associations representing your industries within the next few weeks. The focus of this meeting will be to seek out your proposals of ways in which the state may assist our traditional industries and to forge a strong, public-private partnership to get the job done.

One of the things that I will continue to work for aggressively is the removal of the inventory and intangibles taxes, the strategic anti-jobs taxes that add to the cost of your goods, weaken your competitive endurance, adversely affect the economic growth of our state, and limit the employment opportunities of our citizens. We got a third of the job done, and even that is the largest tax cut in the history of the state! But we still tax inventories and intangibles, and that handicaps North Carolina business.

With your organ[izations], we're also going to create a public awareness of the quality and value of North Carolina products and why we should purchase them. Let me share with you one such exciting story. I have been discussing our efforts to build pride in North Carolina products with Jack Laughery, my appointee to the Advisory Budget Commission and chief executive officer of North Carolina's Hardee's Food Systems.[12] He told me [he] realized customers work for a living! They need paychecks, too, to buy hamburgers with.

With his permission, I'm delighted to inform you that this good corporate citizen has committed to purchase 100,000 new, American-made uniforms, for its employees, at a three-year cost of roughly $15 to $20 million—half that in the first year. And, they are being manufactured mostly by North Carolinians, as well as other American workers, entirely from the original American fabric to the finished American garment. Most of this production will take place in our state.

This sharing of pride will be reflected in 2,400 Hardee's food outlets in forty-two states. The new outfits are already being worn in most North Carolina Hardee's. Well, I believe those uniforms will look extra sharp with a "Crafted with Pride" star on the lapel, don't you?

While we're at it, let's correct one other matter. Contrary to rumor, these shoes I'm wearing are not Italian. They're from an American manufacturer. So there. Real pretty, real comfortable, and long lasting. By the way, I also have to explain to environmentalists they're not alligator; they're Corfam, and that's no endangered species.

It is estimated by our Department of Commerce that this major decision by Hardee's will account for 1 million man-hours of production, representing approximately $6 million in wages for our workers. Other companies throughout North Carolina should emulate this example. Share the pride!

The craftsmanship of North Carolinians, the quality of their work, and the durability of the goods they produce cannot be matched by any trading nation on earth. These characteristics ought to give us pride in our people and pride in our state. So why not share that pride? When my new office chair arrived recently, from a High Point manufacturer, I was pleased to see it had a tag on it signed by Harold Snider, who finished it, to prove his pride in the quality of his craftsmanship. We all should be so proud.

We're here today to emphasize that pride. In 1893, Jacob Battle, a Tar Heel legislator, introduced a bill to add three words to the great seal of North Carolina: *Esse quam videri*.[13] They are Latin words, but they suit us: "To be, rather than to seem." This great motto speaks to that pride and that integrity.

Charles Kuralt, who has spent twenty-eight years as a newsman for CBS, has a unique way of expressing his pride in his native North Carolina. One of his favorite stories is about Washington Duke, who walked 150 miles back to Durham after being mustered out of the Confederate army.[14] There, in the rhythm of the tobacco grinder, he built the American Tobacco Company, Duke University, and the foundation that bears his name. He is but an example of countless others who founded our textile mills, our apparel and hosiery industries, our furniture factories, our footwear plants, and our agribusinesses.

The greatness of our state has been built and sustained by our traditional industries. I want to take this opportunity to thank you, the industrial leaders of North Carolina, and join you in sharing the pride of your accomplishments. North Carolina is a great state because it is built on the principles of self-reliance, opportunity, and innovation. This conference embodies these great qualities, qualities which give North Carolina its strong character and its determination to succeed against great odds.

We've made a great beginning here, today. Let us build upon this sturdy foundation for ourselves and the generations who will follow. I will be proud to share the positive story of this conference at [the] Southern Governors' Association.

While at the national governors' conference, we discussed trade with the premiers of the provinces of Canada. I asked how we could expand mutual, balanced, trade with them if they uniquely imposed a high tariff on our furniture. Replying with his own question, one premier asked why it was that we were still able to sell so much furniture in Canada, even with their tariff and the adverse strength of the U.S. dollar.

My answer was simple enough. I suggested that perhaps that one of the many great strengths of character of the Canadian people was their appreciation for high-quality North Carolina craftsmanship.

I say let's build such confidence into everything we make, and let's go sell it for all it's worth—and truly share the pride!

---

[1]The governor's rendition of the Twain cable agreed with Bartlett, *Familiar Quotations*, 763. However, Twain himself recalled the text of his famous message from London as follows: "James Ross Clemens, a cousin, was seriously ill here two or three weeks ago, but is well now. The report of my illness grew out of his illness; the report of my death was an exaggeration. I have not been ill. Mark Twain." Entry of January 2, 1897, from Mark Twain's notebook, quoted in Paul M. Zall (ed.), *Mark Twain Laughing: Humorous Anecdotes By and About Samuel L. Clemens* (Knoxville: University of Tennessee Press, 1985), 68.

[2]"It was not by gold or silver, but by labour, that all wealth of the world was originally purchased; and its value, to those who possess it, and who want to exchange it for some new productions, is precisely equal to the quantity of labour which it can enable him to purchase or command." Adam Smith, *The Wealth of Nations* [1776], quoted in George Seldes (comp.), *The Great Quotations* (New York: Lyle Stuart, 1960), 641-642.

[3]Suzy Platt (ed.), *Respectfully Quoted: A Dictionary of Quotations Requested from the Congressional Research Service* (Washington: Library of Congress, 1989), 30, hereinafter cited as *Respectfully Quoted*, recorded the comment attributed to Churchill as follows: "The substance of the eminent Socialist gentleman's speech is that making a profit is a sin, but it is my belief that the real sin is taking a loss."

[4]The United States and twenty-two other nations signed the General Agreement on Tariffs and Trade in 1947. The pact had three main objectives: "(1) equal, nondiscriminatory treatment for all trading partners, (2) reduction of tariffs by negotiation, and (3) elimination of import quotas." The impetus for GATT, as it was also known, grew from American desires for less restricted trade following World War II. Douglas Greenwald and others (eds.), *The McGraw-Hill Dictionary of Modern Economics: A Handbook of Terms and Organizations* (New York: McGraw-Hill Book Company, 1983), 200.

[5]Yasuhiro Nakasone (1918-   ), born in Takasaki, Japan; attended University of Tokyo; served in Japanese Navy during World War II. Member, Japan's House of Representatives, 1947-1987; minister of state, director general of science and technology, 1959-1960; minister of transport, 1967-1968; minister of state, director general of defense, 1970-1971; minister of international trade and industry, 1972-1974; prime minister of Japan, 1982-1987. Charles Moritz (ed.), *Current Biography Yearbook, 1983* (New York: The H. W. Wilson Company, 1984), 262-266, hereinafter cited as *Current Biography*, with appropriate year; *New York Times*, October 30, 1987.

[6]The governor arrived in Japan on October 11; his trade mission continued through October 21, 1985. During that time, he also addressed the opening session of the annual Southeast U.S.-Japan Association meeting, Tokyo, on October 14. Untitled press release, Raleigh, October 10, 1985, Governors Papers, James G. Martin.

[7]The Arrangement Regarding International Trade in Textiles was known more popularly as the Multi-Fiber Arrangement. This mechanism outlining conditions for controlling the textile and apparel trade was negotiated in 1973 and became effective on January 1, 1974. William R. Cline, *The Future of World Trade in Textiles and Apparel* (Washington, D.C.: Institute for International Economics, 1987), 149.

[8]See "Testimony Submitted to U.S. Senate Committee on Finance, Subcommittee on Trade," 113-115, above.

[9]P.L. 96-72, "Export Administration Act of 1979" (short title), *United States Statutes at Large*, Act of September 29, 1979, 93 Stat. 503-536; see also *United States Code* (1982 edition), Title 50, Appendix, Secs. 2401 et seq.

[10]Nobuo Matsunaga (1923-   ), born in Tokyo, Japan; LL.B., Tokyo University, 1944. Various positions with Ministry of Foreign Affairs, including Treaties Bureau director-general, 1973, deputy vice-minister, 1976, deputy minister for foreign affairs, 1981, vice-minister for foreign affairs, 1983, and advisor to the ministry, since 1990; appointed ambassador extraordinary and plenipotentiary of Japan to the United States, 1978, reappointed 1985. Information supplied by the Embassy of Japan, Washington, D.C., April 17, 1990.

[11]Howard Haworth (1934-   ), native of Buffalo, New York; resident of Morganton; B.A., Guilford College, 1957; was also educated at Columbia University and Massachu-

setts Institute of Technology. President and chief executive officer, 1972-1984, and board chairman, 1982-1985, Drexel Heritage Furnishings, Inc.; state secretary of commerce, 1985-1987; appointed as member, 1987, elected chairman, 1988, State Board of Education; president, Haworth Group. *News and Observer*, April 21, 1985, January 8, 1988; *North Carolina Manual, 1985*, 683, *1987-1988*, 710.

[12]Jack A. Laughery; born in Guthrie Center, Iowa; resident of Rocky Mount; B.A., University of Iowa; served in U.S. Army. Food service executive; negotiated 1972 merger of Sandy's Food Systems, of which he became president and chief executive officer in 1971, and Hardee's Food Systems; served as executive vice-president, 1972-1973, and was named president and chief operating officer, 1973, president and chief executive officer, 1975, and board chairman, 1980, Hardee's Food Systems, Inc.; past president, Rocky Mount Area Chamber of Commerce; former chairman, Jobs for Progress; member, state Advisory Budget Commission, Business Council of Management and Development, and Governor's Task Force on Abused Children; Republican. Jack A. Laughery to Jan-Michael Poff, November 3, 1989.

[13]Jacob Battle (1852-1916), native of Nash County; died in Rocky Mount; M.A., University of Virginia, 1872. Attorney; elected to state Senate, 1892; appointed superior court judge, 1893; Democrat. Battle introduced the state motto bill on behalf of Judge Walter Clark. Powell, *DNCB*, I, 111.

[14]Washington Duke (1820-1905), native of Orange (later Durham) County; no formal education; an opponent of secession, he nevertheless served with Confederate forces in Charleston, South Carolina, and Richmond, Virginia, 1864-1865. Farmer; philanthropist; smoking tobacco manufacturer, salesman, and cofounder, W. Duke, Sons and Co., 1878. Duke offered Trinity College (later Duke University) $85,000 to move from Randolph County to Durham in 1890; the relocation agreed upon, he then headed the school's building committee and became Trinity's primary benefactor. Powell, *DNCB*, II, 117-118.

MEMORANDUM FROM THE GOVERNOR TO MEMBERS OF THE CABINET AND SENIOR STAFF

Raleigh, August 14, 1985

Recent events prompt me to direct your attention to the accompanying copy of the regulations captioned "Employment of Relatives" set forth in section 2, page 14, of the *Personnel Manual* published by the North Carolina Office of State Personnel.[1] It is the policy of this administration that the regulation shall be adhered to and enforced in spirit as well as in letter. Simply stated, the spirit of the regulation is that persons considered for employment by the state shall be selected on the basis of merit and not on the basis of family influence. I urge you to become familiar with its contents and to encourage your personnel directors to do the same.

As published, the regulation applies to all persons in state government alike. It is my belief that a standard higher than that set forth in the regulation should apply to persons exercising your influence and power. Accordingly, it is my policy that, henceforth, no relatives of members of the cabinet and senior staff members in the Governor's Office shall be hired in any position under the control of the cabinet or in my office. Further, relatives of deputy secretaries, assistant secretaries, and assistants to the secretaries of the cabinet, and principal assistants to senior staff members of the Governor's Office henceforth shall not be hired within the same department or agency.

This policy shall affect all hiring on or after July 26, 1985.

For your reference, "relative" as used herein shall have the same meaning as the words "immediate family member" as defined in the foregoing regulation.

As you know, I recently completed a study of the employment of family members of high-level staff personnel, through the assistant to secretary level, who work for cabinet officials. Although the above-stated policy has generally been followed, there were four cases which I brought to your attention that required movement of a family member to a different agency. This movement was required because one member occupied a position which had influence or supervision over the other.

I request you to conduct a similar review of your agency and report to me within thirty days any conflicts with my stated policy and corrective action you have taken. I will appreciate it if you have copies of this memorandum and accompanying regulation prepared and see that the same is delivered to each of your deputies, assistant secretaries, assistants to secretaries, and personnel directors.

---

[1]The governor accurately cited section and page numbers for the hiring guidelines of March 1, 1980, then in effect. The latest regulations regarding state policy on employment of relatives, effective January 1, 1988, appeared in section 2, pages 3.1-3.2, of the *Personnel Manual* (Raleigh, North Carolina: State of North Carolina, Office of State Personnel, December, 1984).

BUY AMERICAN WEEK: GRANVILLE COUNTY

Oxford, August 28, 1985

Thank you, Mr. (Lott) Rogers, and thank you, Granville County business leaders, for your interest and concern in an issue that not only affects you, but North Carolina and, indeed, the whole nation. I refer, of course, to the problem of foreign imports and the impact they are making on American industry. It is a serious problem, crowded with complexities, and there are no simple, easy answers to its solution.

The figures are grim. Textile imports alone account for 12 percent of a $13 billion trade deficit. June of 1984 was the last time the average textile worker worked a full, 40-hour week. More than 300,000 permanent jobs in that industry alone have been lost in the last four years. In North Carolina, whose industry accounts for one fourth of the total domestic textile production, 20,000 jobs have been lost in the last eighteen months. Statistics, certainly—but those 20,000 lost jobs mean people are out of work, their spending power sharply curtailed or eliminated; their potential wasted; their lives, in many cases, shattered.

Most of you here are active in the Chamber of Commerce. You know that you are not immune. Retail merchants take a drubbing, also, when industry jobs are lost. If unchecked, the results are obvious: a whirlpool into a recession. You don't want that; no one does.

So what can we do, together, as a team, not only to proclaim this "Buy American Week" but to begin now with a course of action? We must work in concert. Teamwork is of the utmost importance. We will not proceed successfully as a scattering of individuals taking our own courses.

With 80 percent of the industries here in Granville County feeling severe pressure from foreign imports, we must start by setting an example ourselves. Buy American. Educate your buying public by special promotions. Realize that every time you sell a foreign product in your retail establishment, the ring of that cash register slices away at an American-made item; it contributes to eliminating another job.

Somehow we must not only "buy" American, we must start "selling" American. Industries realize this. They know that they must aggressively market their goods on an international scale. You can help them on the local level.

It seems to me that one of the ways I can help is to continue my crusade for inventory tax repeal, on the state level, and to use every bit of leverage I can muster to convince the federal government that the best means of aiding traditional and established industries is to provide productivity-enhancing investment incentives through the federal tax system. Rather than outright repeal of the investment tax credit, which has been proposed in the president's tax reform bill, I have suggested that it be phased out gradually over a ten-year period. North Carolina firms are making good use of this credit, and of accelerated depreciation, in an effort to boost their international competitive edge.[1] If these incentives are scrapped, it will hurt.

It appears that we can never match the cheaper labor market and the government subsidies that our foreign competitors have thrown against us, but we can beat them with two factors: better products, and quicker turnaround time between order and delivery.

Industry studies have shown that most customers are not particularly interested in where a product was made; but they are learning, through campaigns such as yours, to look for a "Made in the U.S." label.

But slogans, alone, will not solve the problem. The buying public, your customers, must realize that if they continue to buy products from Taiwan, Hong Kong, or Japan, they are hurting themselves. You can get this message across on the local level. I intend to push it on the state level.

It's obvious: We're in this together, and the meter is running. It is not an issue that is going to go away if we ignore it. It will take creativity, hard work, and some old-fashioned American ingenuity, but we can pull it off. American industry, with its great tradition of dedication and inventiveness, self-reliance, and record of productivity, cannot be counted out. This is one we cannot lose; indeed, we must not.

---

[1]For an overview of President Reagan's fiscal 1986 budget proposal, see *Congressional Quarterly Almanac, 1985,* 427-441. Regular investment tax credits were repealed under P.L. 99-514, "Tax Reform Act of 1986" (short title), *United States Statutes at Large,* Act of October 22, 1986, Title II, Subtitle B, 100 Stat. 2166-2173. Title II, Subtitle A, 100 Stat. 2121-2165, lengthened time periods over which numerous types of business equipment could be depreciated.

PRESS RELEASE: GOVERNOR MARTIN'S STATEMENT FOLLOWING PRESIDENT REAGAN'S VISIT

RALEIGH, SEPTEMBER 5, 1985

[A crowd of approximately 13,000 people, primarily North Carolina State University students, packed Reynolds Coliseum, on September 5, 1985, to cheer President Ronald Reagan, who extolled the benefits of his tax program in a twenty-four-minute speech. Afterward, not everyone expressed satisfaction with the limited content of the president's address. Textile and apparel interests, beleaguered by an onslaught of cheap imports, were disappointed that Reagan failed to mention the problems facing their industries during his appearance at N.C. State, home of the country's largest textile school. *Charlotte Observer,* September 6, 1985; the *News and Observer,* September 6, 1985, printed excerpts from Reagan's speech.]

President Reagan's visit to Raleigh and the North Carolina State University campus gave the president an opportunity to discuss his goals to revise the income tax code. I am proud of the support the president received from the university and the state's citizens.

In the course of the brief trip aboard Marine One from Raleigh-Durham Airport to the landing zone at NCSU, I had an opportunity to speak personally to the president; Donald Regan,[1] his chief of staff; and Dennis Thomas, Regan's deputy. In that discussion, I outlined to President Reagan my concerns about North Carolina's traditional industries. We talked about phasing in the investment tax credits and the accelerated depreciation schedules so our traditional industries will have time to adjust to the changes.[2]

He and his staff listened carefully to our needs. The president, I am confident, understands and sympathizes with our needs in North Carolina. It is my hope that leaders of our traditional industries will have an opportunity in the future to renew these discussions with the White House staff.

---

[1]Donald Thomas Regan (1918-   ), born in Cambridge, Massachusetts; B.A., Harvard University, 1940; honorary degrees; served in U.S. Marine Corps Reserve during World War II. Financier; executive vice-president, 1964-1968, president, 1968-1970, chairman and chief executive officer, 1971-1980, board chairman and chief executive officer, 1973-1981, Merrill Lynch and Co., Inc.; vice-chairman, director, New York Stock Exchange, 1972-1975; U.S. treasury secretary, 1981-1985; White House chief of staff, 1985-1987; lecturer; author, *For the Record* (1988); Republican. *Who's Who in America, 1988-1989*, II, 2561.

[2]For an evaluation of the president's recommended tax revisions, see "Executive Summary of Governor Martin's Position on President Reagan's Proposal for Federal Tax Reform," August 22, 1985, Governors Papers, James G. Martin.

SOUTHERN GOVERNORS' ASSOCIATION

MIAMI, FLORIDA, SEPTEMBER 10, 1985

[The following speech is topically similar to those delivered before the Tryon Rotary Club, Tryon, September 23, and the Durham Rotary and Tobaccoland Kiwanis clubs, Durham, September 30, 1985.]

Thank you, fellow governors and Governor Graham,[1] for the pleasure to speak to you, briefly, as I undertake to follow in some tough footsteps as chairman of the Southern Governors' Association. Governor Graham, I brought the suntan oil and the bathing suit; you promised sunshine and gentle surf, and how wisely you scheduled this meeting after the hurricane had passed this way. On second thought, on looking back at this meeting, perhaps a year from today we will all think of that hurricane as the calm before the storm of challenges and problems we all face.

We're building a new South and a new role for each of us as governors. Today's South is different, more urban, and, in many ways, more endangered. Perhaps the pleasant, happy, and carefree days of my childhood—growing up as the son of a Presbyterian minister, playing the tuba because it was the only instrument a Presbyterian minister's son did not have to buy in order to join the school band—perhaps all of these warm memories of an easier time will give to me, to each of us, the strength to tackle the problems facing us.

Governor Graham, you put our challenge in focus last year when you began your chairmanship. You said, "Our role is not to decide if we want the future to occur . . . our role is to shape the future to our advantage as southern states. . . ." In twelve months since, that concise analysis of our role has not changed; if anything, it looms more critically.

An underlying theme has been woven into the fabric of our discussions here in Miami these past few days. We are looking at a new South, a South which has, during the past twenty-five years, experienced the greatest growth in its history. It is a growth that has been invigorating and energizing. Southern people have enjoyed greater prosperity, better health, and longer life expectancies than their forebears would have dreamed possible.

But change imposes some costs. It is all too easy to move too quickly into the future. It is all too easy to forget our cherished traditions; to ignore our history; to give up our customs, our values, and our heritage; and to take for granted our traditional industries.

The South of today is not the South of ten years ago, or even the South of last summer. While the rest of the nation looks south, awed by our energy, our diversity, our developing resources, we, as leaders of this seventeen-state region, must avoid the temptation to join the onlookers. Our responsibility is not to adapt to the future, but to create it. We must look deeper at our God-given resources, boldly harness the energy of new industry, and offer sustaining support to the industries which created this new South. We must remember that balance is what good growth is all about.

President Franklin D. Roosevelt, in 1934, termed the South as the nation's "economic problem."[2] These were fighting words to proud southerners, who promptly launched a search to turn problems into opportunities. The cornerstone of that search—then, as now—has been a call for balance: a balance of money crops with food crops, of farms with factories, of hard work with thrift and local investment, of wealth with beauty and culture, of economic gains with gains in moral and human values.

Fifty years ago, those balances were addressed primarily to agriculture. Is there much difference in the objectives of the Southern Governors' Association of today? We now face the challenge of adding a postscript to that list penned so long ago: the balance of healthy, traditional industries and business growth through new technology. Vigorous support of that new balance should be a hallmark of this association for the coming year.

Let me reemphasize my support of the high-tech industries coming into the southern states. My state, like your state, is aggressively seeking to recruit high-tech industries to our area. These new and exciting business opportunities will mean a great deal to the southern states in the years to come. But sometimes our industry hunters subtly indicate we should just forget the past, let the old industries go, and work instead to recruit new industries. We are, all of us, actively competing to recruit the new, but what does that say to new industrial recruits if we neglect employers who are here already and who built our region?

There is not a governor here who wants to be a pallbearer at the funeral of the traditional industries in his or her state. When we speak of our traditional industries in the South—fibers, textiles, apparel, hosiery, furniture, agribusiness, tourism, gas and oil, coal, cotton, sugar cane—we are really talking of people, profits, jobs, and pride. We do not have the luxury to ignore their needs, their importance to the vitality that has brought the South to its new position.

In North Carolina, we recently created a new position within our Department of Commerce, that of assistant secretary for traditional industries. It is our way of underscoring our commitment to the men and women who devoted lifetimes to work in our traditional industries—which comprise three fourths of the 860,000 manufacturing jobs in our state. We intend to balance our recruitment efforts for new and high-tech industries with state support and understanding of the role of our traditional industries. We must not neglect, to put it colloquially, "to dance with what brung us to the party in the first place."

Across the South our traditional industries are hurting, battered by the growing flood of cheaper foreign imports and often shunted aside in the limelight of new, sophisticated business. We have all been dealt some tough blows, but we are far from beaten. Each of us can isolate the enemy that faces us: foreign competition. Jobs and profits are lost to foreign competitors who would be in blatant violation of our cherished antimonopoly laws if they were American companies. We have held on to the free-trade myth, and the United States has become the only open market left.

As chambers of commerce eagerly respond to the inquiries of distant industries searching in our backyards for potential sites for relocation or for new plants, and as many of us in this room restructure our tax systems to accommodate this mouth-watering flow of dollars and jobs, let us not lose sight of taking care of what we already have. We must embellish and fine tune a clear sense of responsibility to improve and accommodate our traditional industries. The arithmetic of 40,000 jobs lost by plant closings cannot be offset by the addition of 30,000 new jobs through high-tech industry. That is a good definition of a deficit.

Too often, however, we do not even keep score on jobs lost in our states, because that reflects negatively on what happens when we are not on watch, but we must keep track of it. I, for one, am willing to be remembered and measured by that tougher yardstick of jobs lost, as well as the positive yardstick of jobs won—after all, it is the difference between the two that defines what really happens to our people. It is my hope that, together, we can develop a reliable and honest yardstick so that we measure this dimension, too. If we don't know the problem, we cannot solve it.

The problem is not the loss of productivity or managerial courage. Our nation—indeed, the South—can compete with anyone in a system of mutual, balanced trade. If it were a game of fair competition, that would be another matter. Speaking with representatives of the hard-pressed textile and apparel industry in our state recently, the observation was made that, "At the rate we are going, about the only thing 'Made in America' will be our children." Someone from the audience wisely quipped, "And crafted with pride."

It is just that pride that will launch each of us into a bold program of expanding our markets, of spreading the good news of American productivity to other nations. We must continue to expand our international mentality, to think of Brazil and Spain as markets, as well as Boston and Los Angeles. I like this year's conference theme, "The South Going Global"; perhaps we need to encourage another business mentality—we can call it "Buy Southern." Tennessee needs citrus from Florida, which needs furniture from North Carolina, which needs cotton from Alabama—though we're growing some, too—you get the picture. Working together, sharing our productive capacity and marketing our products among ourselves, can well serve all of us as a buttress against the damages being done by foreign imports.

Our southern products and our traditional southern industries can and will survive this onslaught, perhaps because we have built in our region a reliance on cooperation and community spirit that cannot be matched anywhere in the world. Our traditional industries are bedrocks of family work and ingenuity. The good southern family life we enjoy today was framed by the work ethic, nurtured and challenged by families like the Cannons, the Haneses, and the Reynoldses, who brought jobs and hope with them, meshed their business acumen into the life-style of our people, and helped mold the type of family pride that built the South. To engender support for our traditional industries is as much a theme for all of us this year as it is a challenge. Sons followed the footsteps of fathers, who echoed the work of their grandparents, in our plants, our mills, our factories.

It was, and still is, family. That leads us to another theme on which we, as governors, must focus our energy and dedication: the building of an effective shield of protection for our children, the very lifeblood of our southern families.

Programs are in place and planned to target attacks on a most insidious destroyer of our family structure, the mind-stealing drugs which are fracturing our children's brains. The war against this enemy is on, and action is everywhere: Governor Graham's aggressive campaigns in Florida to slow the influx of drugs from the Caribbean and South America; major budget increases in several southern states to put more law enforcement muscle to stem the flow of grim white powders and colored pills from reaching the main streets and the schoolyards; illegal substance control programs exist at the presidential level; helicopters break the darkness with infrared spotlights; and dope-sniffing dogs roam our wooded areas. Government action against pusher and supplier is at an all-time-high level. We can do no less than applaud these efforts, along with the grieving parents, and push for more activity.

Let us take the initiative in another way. Let us, governments and concerned citizens, counterattack the pushers and suppliers in our own way. Let us push for comprehensive drug and alcohol abuse education programs in every statehouse, in every city hall, in every county courthouse. Let us take the forefront as suppliers of the right information about the dangers of these substances, and let us make sure that information gets to those who need it the most, our children. I am not talking of just the high school student out for a kick by sneaking into the bathroom during recess to smoke pot. Today's world is far more cruel, far more insidious. We're talking about third and fourth graders stopped at the schoolyard sidewalk, offered dope in exchange for lunch money. This rising tide of drug traffic assaults us almost daily, as more and more families find themselves infected by this epidemic. It is widely recognized, today, as nothing less than a terrorist invasion of our very homeland, and it is time for us to declare war on those who seek to destroy us by psychochemical guerrilla warfare.

We talk about the growing problem of missing children. We applaud the efforts of Florida, with the Adam Walsh tragedy,[3] to confront this monstrosity head on. State and local governments are launching programs to locate children taken from homes and playgrounds; pleading faces peek at us from milk cartons; newspapers and television stations haunt us with pleas for [the] return of lost children. The public is aroused, and positive results are slowly trickling in.

In North Carolina, we established our Center for Missing Children, not only to centralize reporting of missing children and to improve communications among law enforcement agencies, but to reduce the number of lost, disappeared, or otherwise-missing children. We must tie that network together throughout the South.

We proclaimed 1985 as the "Year of the Child" in North Carolina. We are dedicating time, energy, and money to combat the abuses which afflict our children.

We know what we are doing in North Carolina; we are also well aware of the need for more. But we need to know what other southern states are doing, what programs are under way, which ones work and which ones don't. That calls for a sharing by all of us, a call for assistance and cooperation which will echo across state borders.

All around us our young people are dying by the thousands, from drug overdoses, from vehicular accidents where alcohol or drugs are the culprit, and from suicides. Their plea for help is directed as much to us here today as to anyone else. We are looking at another kind of missing child today, a child who has slipped outside the boundary of family, of society, whose life is wasted by mind-warping chemicals. Let us be known as a generation of leaders who did all we could to bring them back home.

We must, each of us, be bold in our initiatives to educate our young people about the terrible blight facing them when they drift outside the circle of society, of family life. Our efforts must involve the family. They must encompass the entire education system, from elementary schools to colleges. They must involve the total community. To stamp out the drug epidemic that has decimated so many young lives, to truly build a shield of protection around our children, will require the strongest support a concerned public can give. As an organization of southern leaders, it is up to us to call for, generate, and nurture that support.

Our families have been the core and the fabric of the South. Traditional industries in the South have a strong link with our strong sense of family. Entire families have worked in the textile mills, in the coal-fields, in the oil fields. Our family farms have been handed down from one generation to the next. To offer support to the family is to offer the same to our own traditional industries which forged the new South we enjoy today; in both cases, the initiatives rest with us. Both are under heavy assault. We can see the fabric unraveling—at different speeds in different corners of this region, but unraveling, nonetheless.

It is time for some serious reweaving of that fabric, time to point the energies and the enthusiasm of our resources in a new direction: to bolster the family structure; to combat at every corner the spreading cancer of drug and alcohol abuse through aggressive education; to remold the family that helped build the basic industries which have shouldered the economic pressures of the past, even as we offer a boost for the emerging technologies we are all eager to develop. There is not enough time to ignore the one and focus on the other. The efforts must be uniform and the response aggressive. We are talking about our future—the future not only of our economy, but of our family structure, as well.

If we count no other victories in the coming year than having fought well the battles to support and encourage our traditional industries, to continue to encourage high-tech efforts and growth, and to have brought the power of education and community to the front lines of the war against drugs, then we can recall 1985 with pride. A year from now, when you come to Charlotte, North Carolina, next August, we can gather to determine which way the battle went. We look forward to that opportunity to host this conference, to join you in grappling for viable responses to the problems and the challenges which face us in the South, and, for sure, to spread some of our North Carolina hospitality across your memory. We are now on the doorstep of our future, the future of the new South. Join me in opening that door wide and in welcoming that future with open arms.

---

[1]Daniel Robert Graham (1936-   ), born in Coral Gables, resident of Miami Lakes, Florida; B.A., University of Florida, 1959; LL.B., Harvard Univesity, 1962. Vice-president, Graham Co.; board chairman, Sengra Development Corp.; member, Florida House, 1966-1970, and Senate, 1970-1978; elected governor of Florida, 1978, reelected 1982; elected to U.S. Senate, 1986; Democrat. Michael Barone and Grant Ujifusa, *Almanac of American Politics, 1986* (Washington, D.C.: National Journal, 1985), 276, hereinafter cited as Barone and Ujifusa, *Almanac of American Politics, 1986; Biographical Directory of Congress*, 1082.

[2]"It is my conviction that the South presents right now, in 1938, the Nation's No. 1 economic problem." Franklin Delano Roosevelt, quoted from *Report on Economic Conditions of the South*, 1, in George Brown Tindall, *The Emergence of the New South, 1913-1945* (Baton Rouge: Louisiana State University Press, 1967), 599.

[3]Six-year-old Adam Walsh vanished from a Hollywood, Florida, shopping mall in 1981. Two weeks later, his head was discovered in a canal. Their son's disappearance prompted John and Reve Walsh to mount a crusade on behalf of missing children in their home state and across the country. They established the Adam Walsh Child Resource Center in Fort Lauderdale, and worked successfully for ratification of Florida legislation authorizing a statewide computer network on missing children. John Walsh's testimony before Congress also helped influence passage of the Missing Children's Act of 1982. *Atlanta* (Georgia) *Constitution*, February 19, 1985; *Durham Morning Herald*, March 12, 1985.

AMERICAN ASSOCIATION OF MOTOR VEHICLES ADMINISTRATORS

CHARLOTTE, SEPTEMBER 16, 1985

President Penny,[1] ladies and gentlemen, we are extremely proud that you selected North Carolina for your fifty-third annual meeting. It gives us a special sense of pride that you chose to do so during the service of your president, Bill Penny, our own deputy commissioner of motor vehicles; let me also underscore William Hiatt's[2] welcome to our distinguished guests. When President Reagan greeted a cheering crowd of over 13,000 students at North Carolina State University a few days ago, the first thing he said was, "Nothing can be finer than to be in Carolina."[3] Well, you are here. I hope you, too, will agree that nothing can be finer.

I recognize and appreciate that your primary role at this convention is to collectively address the administrative problems facing motor transportation throughout this country. It is easily one problem we can agree is common to all states. The rapid growth of the means of transportation, both commercial and private, has brought our states closer together. This has had both a positive and negative impact on each of us.

On the positive side, we can translate modern transportation into the practical affairs of everyday life. Many of us can recall the days when we were literally stuck in the mud. Poor roads and almost nonexistent highways formed a barrier to commerce. Towns and villages were isolated, and entire sections of our country were apart from the mainstream of American life.

But our roads and highways have given the American farmer the chance to get out of the mud and into the marketplace. Our highways have opened larger markets for industry, and thus, more jobs for our people. Our highways have provided the vital link between all our citizens, and thus spawned a national sense of community that overcomes provincialism.

So, you see, our good highways and modern means of transportation have become a practical manifestation of the American promise. But, we are not without our problems. Therein lie the negatives with which we must deal.

Interstate commerce, for example, has increased at a pace which has outrun our collective systems for handling it. The variance of regulations and laws from one state to another has resulted in cost inefficiencies and confusions within the commercial transportation industry. This is a problem which is of specific concern of the National Governors' Association. Our concern was heightened by the advent of various federal legislative proposals which threatened to preempt state jurisdictions.

You are all aware of those proposals. Let me assure you, the National Governors' Association strongly opposes federal preemption of vital state procedures to register and tax commercial motor carriers. We must concert the means to bring greater consistency and coordination to state registration, revenue, and administrative procedures for the commercial trucking industry. It is, therefore, incumbent upon us as individual states to jointly formulate a uniform system of regulations and administration.

We can either propose or be imposed upon. We can either seek our own solutions or have decisions made for us. We can either be leaders or reluctant followers.

We do have a choice. I urge you to choose an action that conforms to the needs of the nation and satisfies the individual requirements of your own state. We all know that in the final analysis we are going to put a plan into action. Let's make it a plan that comes from us as individual states working together.

If nothing else should come from this conference, let it be said that you have agreed to establish a national standard rather than having a standard established for you. To that end, let me suggest to you that it is vital that you establish an honest communication link between your administrative bodies and the commercial carriers of your state. Here in North Carolina, Commissioner William Hiatt has established an advisory committee composed of representatives of the commercial transportation industry. A new line of direct communications has been created, and we expect results to be in the mutual interest of the state and industry.

As you ponder solutions to the problem of interstate transportation, let me add one other—one of equal, if not greater, importance to this nation. That is highway safety.

Death and injury on our highways has reached a level that demands our immediate attention. While safety is everybody's business, programs to encourage sensible and safe driving habits are a responsibility of the states. We must jointly and severally find the means to reduce the national tragedy caused by motor vehicle accidents.

States are now being encouraged to enact mandatory seat belt laws. North Carolina is one of the thirteen states which has done so, so far.[4] It is unfortunate that such a law became necessary, and although we will enforce it, we are committed more to a program of convincing motorists to wear seat belts because it will save lives, not because it's a law.

Drivers impaired by drugs and alcohol have become a growing menace on our highways in spite of harsher penalties which have been imposed by most states. Speeding has become a norm rather than an exception in spite of the uniform 55-mile-per-hour limit. Therefore, I suggest to you that the enactment of laws is not the solution. I suggest that strict and constant enforcement of existing laws is the answer.

When it comes to enforcement, we might all claim to be short-handed, but let's never admit to being shortsighted.

I urge you to establish traffic safety as a priority concern. It is of great national importance that you do so.

I sincerely hope that you take from this conference innovative and practical ideas which will serve well to meet both your individual needs and our national needs. The field of motor vehicle administration is progressively growing in importance as more cars, more trucks, and more drivers are on the highways of our states. The responsibility for the safety, regulation, and licensing of vehicles and drivers rests with this distinguished group. I commend you on the theme of your conference, "Networking for Safety and Service"—this says it all!

Again, I wish to assure you of our pleasure to be your hosts and our sincere desire to have you visit other parts of North Carolina while you are here.

---

[1]James M. (Bill) Penny (1924-   ), born in Wake County; resident of Raleigh; B.S., University of North Carolina at Chapel Hill, 1948; served in U.S. Army Air Force during World War II. Cashier and revenue auditor, 1949-1954, assistant accounting director, 1954-1957, North Carolina Revenue Department; accounting director, 1957-1969, deputy commissioner, 1969-1986, state Department (later Division) of Motor Vehicles; retired, 1986. James M. Penny to Jan-Michael Poff, August 26, 1988.

[2]William Seth (Bill) Hiatt (1932-   ), native, resident of Mount Airy; B.S., Brigham Young University, 1953; U.S. Army, 1953-1955. Vocational education teacher, 1964-1984; member, state House, 1973-1974; state commissioner of motor vehicles, since 1985; Republican. William Seth Hiatt to Jan-Michael Poff, August 25, 1988.

[3]Reagan's comment was reported in the *Durham Morning Herald*, September 6, 1985.

"An Act to Make the Use of Seat Belts in Motor Vehicles Mandatory" was ratified May 23, 1985. *N.C. Session Laws, 1985*, c. 222.

SWEARING-IN, GOVERNOR'S SMALL BUSINESS COUNCIL

Raleigh, September 17, 1985

First, let me thank everyone who took time to attend today's forum and present your ideas and concerns on the subject of small business. Your thoughts are important to this council and will go a long way toward ensuring that its future programs and initiatives are truly responsive to your needs. Already, we are aware of several important issues that must be addressed. The need for increased access to capital, reforming taxes, and less cumbersome regulations are at the top of our list; so is the job of making state government purchasing more accessible to small firms. This administration is addressing all four of those issues just as vigorously as we can.

Over the next four weeks, we're going to be conducting nine more forums, like this one, in cities across North Carolina. We expect that those meetings will also give us valuable insights into the problems and opportunities facing small businesses today. Between the last of these forums and late January of 1986, the council and our Small Business Development Division will get to work designing a comprehensive state response to what we learn. On matters which they believe deserve federal attention, they will prepare a package for the 1986 White House Conference on Small Business.[1]

Then, on January 28, I will host a statewide Governor's Conference on Small Business to present the council's plans and proposals to the Tar Heel small business community. This conference will also serve as North Carolina's state-level meeting in preparation for the White House Small Business Conference in August of 1986. But most important, my January conference will give the Small Business Development Council and me an opportunity to discuss, with small business leaders, our findings from the forums and the initiatives we plan in response. By taking public comment both at the beginning and end of our policy-making process, we hope to craft a series of new proposals that will address North Carolina's most important small business needs effectively and with the full support of our state's small business community.

In this critical day and time, with so many of our North Carolina traditional industries—textiles, tobacco—under severe pressure from imports, we face an enormous challenge.

I firmly believe that North Carolina's small businesses, given the proper environment and assistance, can be a vital new source of economic growth and development for our state. As President Reagan said in his speech at North Carolina State University earlier this month, there has never been a better time for starting a small business or joining a new start-up venture with exciting ideas. I want to make North Carolina the premier state in America for pursuing those ambitions. With your help, we can make small business the big business in North Carolina.

A year ago, I was accused of being for business. The customary political response would have been to duck that kind of populist charge and try to prove you're really meaner than [your] opponent. Well, not me. Yes, I'm for business—small business, large business, in between; high tech—data processing; low tech—food processing; in between. I'm still for business. That's where jobs come from.

---

[1]The North Carolina Small Business Council held hearings in September and October, 1985, in Raleigh, Greensboro, High Point, Fayetteville, Elizabeth City, Greenville, Wilmington, Charlotte, Asheville, and North Wilkesboro; for recommendations stemming from those hearings, see *Report to Governor James G. Martin, January 15, 1986* ([Raleigh: North Carolina Small Business Council, Small Business Development Division, Department Commerce], 1986), 2-6. Issues requiring federal action were listed in *The White House Conference on Small Business, August 17-21, 1986* ([Raleigh: Small Business Development Division, Department of Commerce], 1986), 18-19.

TRIANGLE AREA RESEARCH DIRECTORS CLUB

RESEARCH TRIANGLE PARK, SEPTEMBER 17, 1985

It's a great pleasure for me to be with you, this afternoon. As most of you know, as a chemist in real life and by training, in many ways I feel very much at home with you, today. I believe that research and development are also important keys to sustained economic growth. The new discoveries that come out of basic and applied research are the seeds of invention, and invention the source of new products, new profits, and further growth.

There was a time when our country stood the undisputed world leader in research and innovation. Our laboratories were the source of technologies that shrank the world and lifted man beyond the limits of earth and atmosphere. It was American research and development that, in 1947, created the transistor, launching a technological revolution that has since reshaped our entire society. In the 1950s and 60s,

American technology led the way to crucial breakthroughs in numerical control, digital instrumentation, integrated circuits, lasers, industrial robots, pharmaceuticals, growth factors, and other key fields.

These technological breakthroughs, and hundreds of others like them, have fundamentally altered the world we live in. They have made ours a society of desk-top computers and twenty-four-hour banking machines, of supersonic transport and backyard satellite antennas. We're on the verge of computerized home TV news retrieval. We used to let our fingers do the walking through the Yellow Pages; now our fingers are learning to walk a keyboard, and we will pay our bills, balance our bank accounts, and adjust our stock portfolio to the latest fluctuations in the market.

These are remarkable innovations. But the speed and ease of access which they afford us have, in many ways, inflated our expectations of the sciences behind technology. We are tempted to believe that answers are simple, and inspiration commonplace.

Visiting a local company not long ago, I saw a sign on one technician's door that read, "No instant miracles." Those of us who have spent part, or all, of our lives in the research laboratory can identify with that sentiment. We know that progress, no matter how we define it, is a result of trial and error, of setback followed by success, of riddles followed by inspiration.

This gap between the reality of the laboratory and the expectations of our society has levied a cruel penalty against American innovation in the last decade. Because we have taken our inventions for granted, we have undervalued their source. All too often in recent years, pinched corporate profits have meant less money for research and development. In government, where budget cutting has become essential, funds for research have been easy targets.

During the decade of the seventies, United States spending for research and development dropped from 2.5 percent of gross national product to 2.1 percent. By comparison, research and development spending in Japan during the same period rose from 1.5 percent to 2.0 percent of total economic output. Today we are seeing the results of this funding dichotomy. Where we have not sowed, we cannot reap; and across the board, American technological eminence is being seriously challenged. That's why, with Jim Shannon of Massachusetts, I helped draft legislation in Ways and Means to provide today's tax incentives for research and development.[1]

In the field of microelectronics, North Carolina is working closely with many Japanese companies to develop new technological capabilities and to expand upon the rapid investment of foreign capital in new facilities within our own borders. Our negotiations are not limited to high-technology industries. In exchange for the importation of sophisticated textile manufacturing equipment for use by domestic firms, we are urging Japan to adopt a balanced and fair trade relationship which will permit North Carolina, and indeed the nation as a whole, to export more of our value-added merchandise and products to their country. In my forthcoming visit to Japan, in October, I will not only be there to recruit new industry, I also will be there to explore with business leaders their willingness to practice policies more in keeping with our own open-trade borders.[2]

But we also must concentrate on our ability to recover our balance in the pursuit of new technologies. One answer can be a public-private partnership in support of research and development. Here in North Carolina, we are in an ideal position to lead such an effort. To begin with, we are home to the Research Triangle, one of the nation's top three such research centers.[3] In addition, our university system is widely regarded as one of the best in the nation. In the important field of microelectronics, we have established one of America's most flexible and sophisticated research and development facilities. And I could go on and on.

As governor of North Carolina, I am committed to continuing and broadening North Carolina's strong emphasis on technological development. In my budget package to the most recent session of the General Assembly, I recommended more than $23 million be allocated for the operation and further expansion of the Microelectronics Center of North Carolina. That was the largest such supplemental appropriation recommended for the facility since its creation. In addition, I plan to continue North Carolina's efforts to seize the lead in the field of biotechnology.

But I believe it is also important for our state to support the technological development of its more traditional industries. We need, for example, to help our textile manufacturers develop the new products and technologies that will ensure their future competitiveness. Some of these advancements may well come from our efforts in the fields of micro- and biotechnology; others will be unique. To further our efforts in support of textiles, I am looking strongly at the need for a textile manufacturing research center at North Carolina State University.

But by far, the most important step North Carolina can take in support of research and technological development is the enhancement of our state's system of public education. As I have said, North Carolina is already blessed with a strong system of colleges and universities, public and private; these we must preserve and continue to strengthen. There is much more to be done if we are to build in our public schools and community colleges an adequate system for education and training. As governor, my number-one priority will be meeting these challenges in the field of education.

We must, in the next few years, find a way to dramatically improve the quality of North Carolina's primary and secondary schools. The legislature has made some steps in this direction, but in my opinion, their initiatives will require adjustment in order to be truly effective.[4]

We must also work to strengthen the quality of technical training available through our system of community colleges. These schools teach the skills essential to tomorrow's technology. We cannot afford for them to be second best.

The steps I have just outlined, from direct funding for research and development to ensuring quality education, are all specific actions North Carolina can take to directly support and encourage the development of new technologies. Other, more indirect measures are also available to us. For example, one benefit of the tax reductions I proposed to the state legislature earlier this year would have been to accelerate technological development in our state. In the case of the intangibles tax, the repeal I proposed would have eliminated a significant barrier to the formation of venture capital funds in North Carolina, an area in which we are significantly lacking.

The elimination of North Carolina's virtually unique tax on business inventories would also have contributed to North Carolina's technological development. As many of you know, small firms and start-up businesses are frequently our best sources of innovative new ideas and products. North Carolina's inventory tax hits these firms particularly hard because, like larger firms, they frequently must carry significant inventories and other tangible assests. However, unlike their larger counterparts, small innovators often do not have the cash flow to meet heavy tax obligations.

While my administration was able to win significant rollbacks in both our inventory and intangibles taxes, we were not able to convince the General Assembly to eliminate them completely. I plan to continue pushing for repeal in the next session of our legislature and hope you will support me in that effort.

At the national level, I believe President Reagan's tax reform package also represents an important step toward encouraging technological innovation. As most of you know, the president's package would extend the research and development tax incentives presently scheduled to expire at the end of this year; my Ways and Means legacy will last a bit longer.[5] Entrepreneurs and other businesses with innovative new ideas would also stand to benefit under the president's plan to cut back federal capital gains taxes.

During our time together today, I've tried to communicate some of my thoughts and outlooks on the subject of technological development. Without question, North Carolina is home to some of our country's top research and development institutions. Many of these organizations are represented here today.

Taken together, your presence has contributed enormously to our state's growth and development and lent an important element of stability to the North Carolina economy. In the years ahead, I want to work with your organizations and other technology-oriented institutions across North Carolina to build an even stronger research and development community here. I am convinced that such an effort is in the best interest of our state and will lead inevitably to a more vital and prosperous North Carolina.

---

[1]James Michael Shannon (1952-   ), born in Methuen, resident of Lawrence, Massachusetts; B.A., Johns Hopkins University, 1973; J.D., George Washington University, 1975. Attorney; member from Massachusetts, U.S. House of Representatives, 1979-1985; unsuccessful candidate for Democratic U.S. Senate nomination, 1984; elected Massachusetts attorney general, 1986. *Biographical Directory of Congress*, 1795.

[2]The governor inserted into his prepared text, at this point: "Same message for other countries."

[3]Here the governor added: "Two others (Charlotte and Triad)".

[4]At this point, the governor listed aspects of education he felt deserved "Greater emphasis: classroom teacher; incentives and accountability; teaching as a career."

[5]P.L. 99-514, *United States Statutes at Large*, Title II, Subtitle D, 100 Stat. 2173-2180, extended tax credits for research through December 31, 1988.

NORTH CAROLINA TRUCKING ASSOCIATION

ASHEVILLE, SEPTEMBER 24, 1985

[The governor delivered a condensed version of the following remarks at his September 12, 1985, press conference. He also stressed urban highway needs in his speech at the dedication of Interstate 40 in New Hanover County, November 1, 1985.]

I welcome the opportunity to address the North Carolina Trucking Association, first, because it represents a major industry in our state, and second, because of some urgent transportation issues confronting us now and in the years ahead; and I need your help.

Less than two weeks ago, I pointed out at a press conference that the Department of Transportation budget for next year falls approximately $40 million short of what is needed just to match federal funds and $60 to $80 million less than is needed for truly adequate financing—i.e., we've got a flat tire. But we can fix it, because we've got a spare, fiscally speaking.

But there is another flat tire on our highway program, and I want to talk to you about it, because it, too, needs to be fixed. This job of patching will require a great deal [of] public understanding and support—and, more than that, desire—and I regard the trucking industry to be a vital part of this public. The issue about which I'm speaking is the growing crisis North Carolina faces in urban transportation: chronic congestion; wall to wall, four-lane [parking] lots—a problem that will take innovation and imagination to solve.

Frankly, the urban transportation needs of our state are staggering, and when I say urban areas, I'm not talking only of Asheville, Raleigh, Greensboro, Charlotte, and other metropolitan areas. I am speaking of cities with 10,000 people or more, areas such as Wilmington, Lumberton, Reidsville, Shelby, and Boone, and Tarboro. These and other cities are growing rapidly.

Once a predominantly rural state, nearly 50 percent of North Carolina's residents now live in seventeen metropolitan counties. Employment is even more concentrated: 56 percent of our jobs are located in these seventeen counties. Thirty-four other smaller cities, for [a] combined total of fifty-one, have serious needs. No one should know this better than you, the truckers who serve the industries of North Carolina.

North Carolina is on the move. Traditionally, we have used our highway system as a major drawing card for new industry and other development. This tactic has worked. It has worked extremely well. Factories have sprung up in the farm fields of the east and the mountainsides of the west. North Carolina is now one of the largest industrial states. The piedmont crescent is booming from Gastonia to the Research Triangle Park.[1]

Perhaps we've succeeded too well. Because of our growth and economic development, our most rapidly expanding urban areas are nearing a transportation crisis. They have exceeded the capacity of their roads and the limits of their highway construction programs.[2]

A current assessment by the Department of Transportation reveals immediate urban transportation needs totaling $2.7 billion. Let me translate that into a clearer picture:[3] If we continue to fund urban projects as we do today, at roughly the same level, it will take nearly sixty years to construct the projects that are needed now, and the $2.7 billion doesn't include future needs that will be created by continuing growth.[4]

That growth is expected to generate an additional $2.3 billion in urban highway demands by the year 2000. That's a total of $5 billion in current and future needs. All of this comes at a time of rising costs and stagnant revenues for the Highway Fund.

Two conclusions are obvious. One, traditional thinking and funding methods will not solve the problem; and two, this is not a city problem. It is a problem that affects the entire state. Down east, on [U.S.] 74, can't get through Charlotte.

It's a problem that requires immediate attention and urgent action. This is why I have [asked] our secretary of transportation, Jim Harrington, to assemble the Urban Transportation Task Force, a top-level group of knowledgeable citizens. On September 11, in Fayetteville, the task force held its third educational meeting. It received the last of our planned staff briefings. Now the challenge of coming to grips with our urban transportation problems rests with the twenty-one members of that group. During the coming months, they will meet in Asheville, Raleigh, and Charlotte to discuss possible solutions and develop their recommendations.

Fortunately, these meetings come at a time when your association is considering the timely establishment of a policy committee to address transportation problems and needs from your industry's perspective. I urge you to work closely with the task force, to help forge a public-private partnership to resolve this issue as well as concerns that are limited to the trucking industry. You can assist greatly by attending planned meetings and providing responsible guidance and input.

But let me make one more point: Urban areas are not alone in facing this funding crisis. The need versus the fund gap applies to other needs as well, but the approaching crisis requires that we give our urban areas attention now.

However, we will not, and we cannot, turn away from the long-standing effort to improve the economies of our rural counties by improving their transportation system. Meeting the needs of our urban areas must work in tandem with the improvement of our rural areas. After all, rural highways connect cities![5]

I don't want to leave you with the impression that our transportation problems are obstacles we cannot overcome. There are a number of options. It seems that every problem presents us with a new opportunity to build a greater state. We simply have to turn problems into opportunities.

I am aware that you are opposed to and have lobbied successfully against third-structure taxes, or more specifically, local option taxes on gasoline.[6] As a congressman, I remember the imposition of a special tax on gasoline imposed by the District of Columbia. That strategy didn't work. Motorists simply filled up their tanks elsewhere. The idea was self-defeating. It forced D.C. gas stations to close.

I will not, at this time, foreclose any options available to resolve our urban transportation needs. One of those options includes transferring the cost of the Highway Patrol from the Highway Fund to the General Fund. Although trooper strength has not been increased in twelve years, we've added a million vehicles, 10 percent more miles, [and] DUI.[7] Salaries have increased as well as the cost of equipment and operation—competes for paving and maintenance. Transferring these costs to the General Fund would free up substantial money to help us meet this emerging crisis.

In addition, there is the option of increasing the state tax on gasoline.[8] As most of you know, each 1-cent increase in the tax produces approximately $36 million annually. That does not rise with inflation. As automobiles and other vehicles have become more fuel efficient, tax revenues from gasoline have not kept pace with motor vehicle registrations and increased travel.[9]

I cannot predict how we will solve our urban transportation demands. We must await the recommendations of the task force. But your association, and you as individual motor freight carriers, can assist greatly in shaping those recommendations.

Now that we've dealt with the bad news, let's turn our attention to some very good developments. Last Thursday, the U.S. Congress finally approved the Interstate cost estimate for fiscal year 1986, thus making $4.7 billion available nationwide.[10] North Carolina's share of these funds amounts to $50 million for the Interstate system[11] in addition to $60 million in minimum-allocation funds. Minimum-allocation funds are monies which are appropriated for rural primary and urban projects. The allocation of these funds is a matter on which I lobbied among my former colleagues in the Congress for many months, and I welcome their approval.

Among concerns that are limited to the trucking industry is the issue of access to designated routes for twin trailers and 102-inch-wide semi-trailers. Although the federal law limits travel, off designated routes, to three miles, it also provides for flexibility—and we plan to use that flexibility as generously as the law allows. I have been assured by our state Department of Transportation that it is becoming increasingly liberal in granting reasonable access to designated routes, thus saving your trucks unreasonable miles and delivery times.

Another concern of the trucking industry is the enforcement of the highway act of 1980, which provides funds for and requires inspection of trucks for safety violations. At the present time, our Division of Motor Vehicles is conducting approximately 2,000 inspections each month. It is an ongoing program, and the federal funding for the current fiscal year amounts to $681,000 in North Carolina. These are funds appropriated on an 80-to-20 percent matching formula.[12]

This week, an around-the-clock inspection program will be conducted here in Asheville, and I invite any of you to visit the weigh station where this inspection is conducted and observe for yourselves.[13] We are working diligently to develop a systematic program of enforcement, as well as define the most common safety violations. Let me assure you that our Division of Motor Vehicles will keep your association advised on the manner of enforcement and will work closely to help you avoid violations.

The trucking industry is one of the largest sectors of North Carolina's economy. Of the $227 billion that transportation puts into our state's economy, $200 million of that amount comes from motor freight carriers.[14] I'm also aware that the trucking industry pays 44 percent of all fuel taxes collected by the state of North Carolina. Therefore, you are a major source of funds for the continued operation and improvement of state government.

The goal of this administration is to forge an industry-government partnership that will be beneficial to the entire state. There are problems in every sector affecting our economy; as I mentioned earlier, we can turn these problems into opportunities which will enhance North Carolina and its citizens. By working together, we can make the future bright with unlimited possibility. Indeed, only by working together will we bend that future to higher aspirations and greater accomplishment. Together, we can overcome problems and, in many ways, anticipate and avoid them. Let's make it a team effort.

---

[1]Referring to Research Triangle Park, Martin inserted the following note: "'Crown Jewel'; world-famous; half-filled; can't get there."

[2]At this point, Martin inserted into his prepared text: "Differentiate DOT terminology: urban highways—in and adjoining city limits; rural highways—first degree and second degree (2-lane, 4-[lane]) connect[ors]."

[3]Here Martin wrote: "A lot! Billion: $1,000/day [for] almost 3,000 years!"

[4]At this point, Martin inserted the note: "You've seen prediction: N.C. top 5 expected growth."

[5]"Without . . . insulated/isolated," the governor jotted after this sentence.

[6]Martin inserted into his prepared text, at this point: "(Parlance: city gas tax!)"

[7]The governor was referring to enforcement of the state's law against DUI, or driving under the influence. See "An Act to Provide Safe Roads by Requiring Mandatory Jail Terms for Grossly Aggravated Drunken Drivers, Providing an Effective Deterrent to

Reduce the Incidence of Impaired Driving, and Clarifying the Statutes Related to Drinking and Driving," *N.C. Session Laws, 1983,* c. 435.

[8]Here Martin inserted the note: "Not proposing—am looking at it."

[9]At this point, Martin listed "Other alternatives: Bond issue," "city participation (ROW [rights of way]); 'creative financing.'"

[10]P.L. 99-104, "An Act to Approve the Interstate Cost Estimate and Interstate Substitute Cost Estimate," *United States Statutes at Large,* Act of September 30, 1985, 99 Stat.

[11]Martin added to his prepared text, at this point, "I-40 Wilmington schedule and maint[enance]."

[12]The governor was probably referring to P.L. 97-424, "Surface Transportation Act of 1982" (short title), *United States Statutes at Large,* Act of January 6, 1983, 96 Stat. 2097-2200. Grants for state enforcement of federal safety regulations and the 80 percent-20 percent formula were authorized under Title IV, Part A, Secs. 402-404, 96 Stat. 2155-2157.

[13]At this point, Martin inserted the note: "Delay [leads to] safety."

[14]Governor Martin had difficulty accepting these figures. He wrote below them: "[$]227 billion is too large. GSP [gross state product] only $120 billion. $227 million is very small." He also noted that $200 million was "less than 0.1 percent" of $227 billion. The truth must have been somewhere in between.

STATEMENT ON ADMINISTRATIVE REALIGNMENT

RALEIGH, SEPTEMBER 26, 1985

I have several topics to address today, beginning with the announcement of some logistical and administrative realignments within the Governor's Office. I will be moving my office back to the Capitol building within the next two weeks.[1] My two secretaries, Mr. Lofton,[2] and his secretary will accompany me in that move. I originally wanted to be close to my staff in the Administration Building, both to get acquainted with them and to coordinate our activities during the first six months. Now, however, I would like to return to the more traditional office in the Capitol which has been occupied by a great many of our previous governors. Despite this relocation, I will continue to use and maintain my office in the Administration Building, while also continuing to hold meetings and press conferences here as usual.

Other changes include a realignment of some of my executive staff members. Jim Lofton, executive assistant to the governor, will be responsible for coordinating my daily schedule and movements, with primary responsibilities for the administration of the governor's offices. Mr. Lofton will also oversee the offices of Citizen Affairs, Minority Affairs, and Intergovernmental Affairs, which includes the Western Governor's Office, the Washington office, and the Eastern Governor's Office, when it is established.[3]

C. C. Cameron,[4] executive assistant to the governor for budget and management, will continue his responsibilities as supervisor of budget and management. He will also continue to serve as secretary to the cabinet and work with the Executive Cabinet, as a unit, and the Council of State. Mr. Cameron will continue to serve as the governor's liaison to the Advisory Budget Commission.

Jim Trotter's[5] primary responsibilities will be: first, to serve as special legal counsel; second, to serve as a liaison to the cabinet secretaries, continuing in his position as liaison to the Council of State and the judiciary; and third, to supervise political and legislative affairs. Now I would like to move on to my second announcement concerning the Governor's Highway Safety Program, though if you have any questions concerning these realignments I would be more than happy to answer them during the question-and-answer session later in this press conference.

---

[1]The governor began shifting his office from the Administration Building to the Capitol on October 10, 1985. Press release, "Governor Sets Date for Return to Capitol," Raleigh, October 7, 1985, Governors Papers, James G. Martin.

[2]James Shepherd Lofton (1943-   ), native of Charlotte; was educated at Lees-McRae College. Buyer, Belk Bros. Co., 1963-1966; civic affairs manager, Charlotte Chamber of Commerce, 1966-1969; marketing officer, First Union National Bank, 1969-1973; administrative assistant to Congressman James G. Martin, 1973-1985; executive assistant to Governor Martin, 1985-1987; appointed secretary, Department of Administration, 1987; Republican. *North Carolina Manual, 1987-1988,* 677.

[3]The Eastern Governor's Office, New Bern, was formally opened on November 25, 1985. See "Dedication of Eastern Governor's Office," pages 213-217, below.

[4]Charles Clifford (Cliff) Cameron (1923-   ), native of Meridian, Mississippi; resident of Charlotte; B.S., Louisiana State University, 1941; U.S. Army, 1941-1945. Banker; civic leader; chairman, Executive Committee, First Union Corp.; appointed to state Advisory Budget Commission, 1983, by Governor James B. Hunt, Jr.; executive assistant to Governor Martin for budget and management, since 1985; Democrat. Carolyn Hawkins, assistant to C. C. Cameron, to Jan-Michael Poff, August 31, 1988; *News and Observer,* February 17, 1985.

[5]James R. Trotter (1923-   ), born in Salisbury; B.S., 1947, J.D., 1953, University of North Carolina at Chapel Hill; U.S. Army Air Force, 1943-1945. Attorney in private practice, 1953-1958, 1960-1984; Rocky Mount city attorney, 1960-1968; appointed general counsel to Governor Martin, January, 1985. James R. Trotter to Jan-Michael Poff, August 22, 1988.

"SHARE THE PRIDE" CONFERENCE

GREENVILLE, SEPTEMBER 26, 1985

I want to thank all of you who have come here, today, to join me in offering your support in addressing one of the most critical economic problems in the history of our state—indeed, our nation. That problem, today, is the continuing decline of our traditional industries, that great locomotive that has pulled our economic growth along at accelerated speed for more than a century. Each of us can identify the cause that is responsible for this decline: foreign competition. Across our state and nation, we are suffering growing setbacks and are being battered by the increasing tide of cheaper foreign imports.

When we speak of our traditional industries—fibers, textiles, apparel, hosiery, furniture, and agribusiness—we are really talking about people, profits, and jobs, those values from which we derive pride, and satisfaction of hard work and honest labor, as well as our material well-being. Today, jobs and profits are being lost to foreign competitors who would be in blatant violation of our antimonopoly laws if they were American companies. We have held on to the free-trade myth while our foreign trading partners have closed their markets to our products. America is the only open market that remains.

As everyone knows, two deficits, both multibillion dollar in size, cloud the economic horizon this year. One is our staggering federal fiscal budget deficit, which has led to the rise in the value of the American dollar and which has made our products less competitive in the world marketplace. The second is our trade deficit. It is largely the result of the fiscal deficit. That has attracted capital flows, counterbalanced by cash reflow for purchases.

In 1981, our nation's trade deficit was $31 billion. In 1984, using the same statistical measure, the deficit was $111 billion. I want to use this special occasion to expain why I believe our trade deficit is of critical significance, in 1985, and why it may be of even greater significance in 1986 and the years beyond.

In my judgment, trade is to the 1980s what the energy crisis was to the 1970s. In 1984, we experienced the fourth year in which the United States ran a merchandise trade deficit. This year, according to the International Trade Commission, this deficit, the trade deficit, could be even larger, perhaps up to 15 to 20 percent—or $150 billion, roughly [the] same order of magnitude as the fiscal deficit.

Deficits of this magnitude are unprecedented in world economic history. Not only are we running huge merchandise trade deficits with our principal trading partners—Canada, last year, $22 billion; Japan, $33 billion; Mexico, $6.3 billion—but there are large deficits with Western Europe and the newly industrialized countries, too. Last year, for example, our deficit with our four largest European economies—Germany, France, Italy, and Britain, combined—exceeded $17 billion.

Perhaps the most dramatic development is with the newly emerging industrial countries. Last year, with Brazil, Taiwan, Korea, Hong

Kong, and Singapore, the United States ran a $23.8 billion deficit, up $14 billion since 1983. Approximately half of the increase in the overall trade deficit, roughly $50 billion, was with Japan and the newly industrialized countries.

To appreciate fully the underlying trends, we must look at the changing product patterns of trade. Until several years ago, the United States exported manufactured goods and imported raw materials and petroleum. Indeed, from the 1890s to 1971, the United States experienced a string of trade surpluses. This was brought about by exports of manufactured goods.

Our competitive edge in new products stirred concerns in Western Europe that they could not compete. In 1901, for instance, a British writer complained that U.S. industry controlled every new industry created in the previous fifteen years. That was 1901. He wrote: "What are the chief new features in London life. They are, I take it, the telephone, the portable camera, the phonograph, the electric streetcar, the automobile, the typewriter, passenger lifts in houses, and the multiplication of machine tools. In every one of these, save the petroleum automobile, the American maker is supreme; in several, he is monopolist." Had the same account appeared in 1914, undoubtedly his list would have included the Model T automobile.[1]

If an American writer were to make a similar survey in 1985, he would certainly note the supremacy of Japan in cameras, automobiles, typewriters, machine tools, telephones, and many of the products produced by traditional industries in North Carolina. I suspect that, under current trends, it will not take eighty-five years for the new Japans—Korea, Taiwan, China, and Brazil, among others—to replace Japan as the dominant low-cost supplier of standard consumer items.

In fact, it is already happening. Last year, our five leading exports to Japan were yellow corn and soybeans, bituminous coal, wheat, and cotton. To Taiwan, which incidentally replaced Great Britain last year as our fifth leading supplier of goods, our principal exports were yellow corn and soybeans. To Korea, which has moved ahead of France and Italy as our seventh major supplier of imports, we sold cotton, electronic chips, yellow corn, and cattle hides.

As I mentioned earlier, the soaring dollar is an important part of the problem. After all, it has climbed nearly 30 percent in real terms, above the 1980-1982 average, for a basket of trading currencies. But this is not the whole story. The "superdollar" may explain our rising deficits with some countries—e.g., Western Europe, Canada, and Japan—but does not offer a sufficient explanation for the deficits with Korea and Taiwan. Their currencies have fallen less than the Japanese yen, German mark, or French franc in real terms.

The strong dollar accelerates the flood of imports at present, and it may well camouflage another harsh reality: the import challenge would have come anyway. There are also significant structural forces at work, which, over the long term, are working to integrate and internationalize the world economy; the result is to intensify competition in previously sheltered national markets for standard consumer goods and capital goods. One such unifying force has been our gradual decline of tariff barriers since World War II; another has been the general reduction in shipping costs, resulting from supertankers, large bulk carriers, and wide-bodied aircraft.

Finally, I would emphasize how the gradual diffusion of technology and spread of industry to previously underdeveloped countries has intensified competition in world markets. The newly industrialized nations, many of which are along the Pacific Rim, have low labor costs and state-of-the-art technology. These, coupled with social discipline, their import restrictions on American products, and a strong desire to export, have brought on the emergence of a new, world-class competitor. The real problem confronting our traditional industries is having to play the trade game on a steeply tilted field. Given the problems of low labor costs and improved technology, as well as the frustrations of obtaining access to foreign markets, is there any wonder that our traditional industries are on the decline?

Now we are confronted with the compelling need to launch into a new and bold program of expanding our markets, of spreading the good news of North Carolina and American productivity to other nations. We must continue to expand our international mentality, to think of new nations as markets, as well as our domestic customers.

To engender support for our traditional industries is as much a theme for all of us as it is a challenge. Here in North Carolina, under the banner of "Share the Pride," we must unite as one to recapture the competitive edge that was a hallmark of our industries in the 1970s and earlier.

One of the steps we have taken in this administration is the appointment of an assistant secretary of commerce for traditional industries, Mr. White G. Watkins, formerly with Blue Bell Industries. White is with us today, and I'm confident that many of you have met him earlier. Under our combined leadership, nurtured by your support, we will work to define the real problems of our traditional industries, and we will find ways to resolve them successfully.

Our efforts must be uniform and the response aggressive. We are talking about our future, the future of our economy and the future of our people. If we can count no other victories in the coming years other than having fought well the battles to support and sustain our traditional industries, then we can look back upon our efforts with pride and share that pride in North Carolina.

---

[1]In addition to the Michigan-built product, Ford also produced Model T's in its plant at Trafford Park, Manchester, England, from 1911 to 1927. David Culshaw and Peter Horrobin, *The Complete Catalogue of British Cars* (New York: William Morrow and Co., Inc., 1974), 128-129.

ELIZABETH CITY COMMITTEE OF 100

ELIZABETH CITY, SEPTEMBER 27, 1985

It's always a genuine pleasure for me to return to the beautiful Albemarle region of North Carolina. As a sailor, the coastal area of our state holds a special place in my life. But Elizabeth City is more than a vacation center for visitors; it also is a major retail center, serving an area of ten counties and boasting retail sales in excess of $240 million annually. Elizabeth City and Pasquotank County are important locations for development—just a short distance from the thriving Tidewater region of Virginia—and you've been very successful in developing a modern industrial park and attracting five very good industries to this planned development.

We're never satisfied with desirable growth, and we should never be, because satisfaction breeds complacency, the seeds of decline. But growth requires an adequate infrastructure—water supply, wastewater disposal capacity, good transportation, electric power, a clean environment, educational facilities, and community amenities—to accommodate new industries and help existing ones grow and prosper.

Provision of these facilities and attractions requires a strong community-state partnership. No single entity of government can meet these needs alone, and that's what this administration is building upon: a mutually beneficial and responsible partnership. We're currently laying the foundation for this partnership, and we want it to be a successful and lasting unity of effort.

When we consider opportunities for economic growth in Elizabeth City and the Albemarle region, we cannot overlook or neglect the potential of travel and tourism. It's one of the largest sectors of our economy. Money spent by visitors to North Carolina has increased from $1 billion to more than $4 billion in the last decade.

Americans today have more personal income and more leisure time, and they spend more of that time and money on recreation, travel, and tourism.

The natural beauty, the historic attractions, and the opportunities for active recreation in the Albemarle region will make it an ever-growing magnet for vacationers.

We have to make sure that we are doing all that we can to increase the attractiveness and the unique assets that we have in this area.

I cannot find a better example of this kind of asset than the Great Dismal Swamp Canal. This parallel route of the Intracoastal Waterway has attracted a growing number of boaters who want a different kind of experience. Elizabeth City has taken the initiative to increase this interest and to support it with your free docking and your warm welcome to visitors. You have the making here of a major stimulus to the attractiveness and prosperity of this region, but to take advantage of this unique asset we must keep the canal open!

I appreciated the opportunity of meeting with several members of the Committee of 100 recently to discuss your concern about the poor maintenance of the canal and the possibility that the Corps of Engineers might recommend its closure. I have asked the North Carolina Department of Natural Resources and Community Development to give this issue priority and to offer you all the support it has. I am very pleased with the reports I have heard of the public meeting that you held on the canal last week. The strong public interest that was demonstrated certainly will help our cause.

I have taken the additional step of writing to the Corps of Engineers and requesting that the Norfolk District give immediate attention to the removal of snags and shoals from the canal, so that it can be put back into first-class operation when water levels permit.

We are concerned that the Corps of Engineers may use the figures on reduced navigational use, which were caused in part by their deficiencies in maintaining the canal, to argue that the canal is unjustified. We must make sure that the corps puts the canal back in excellent condition and operates it for a minimum of three years under good conditions and schedules before reaching any conclusions.

Let me assure you that I will be following up on my letter to the corps concerning canal maintenance and will be closely monitoring its study of the canal's future. Your continued observations and recommendations will be most appreciated. We want—and we must keep—this valuable economic, recreational, and historic asset.

When I speak of your observations and recommendations, my interest is in knowing your concerns on a wide range of issues affecting this area. This is one of the major reasons for increasing local representation on state boards and commissions. Since January, I have more than doubled that representation over appointments of the previous administration. These appointments have included Mr. Barry McCarty as chairman of the North Carolina Social Services Commission; Mr. Harold Barnes as a member of the state Board of Architecture; Dr. Jack Graham as a member of the Marine Fisheries Commission; Ms. Shirley Mays as a member of the Elizabeth City State University Board of Trustees; and Mr. Porcious Crank, Jr., as a member of the North Carolina Vocational Education Council. We also have filled thirteen vacancies on the Edenton Historical Commission with individuals from this area. More appointments can be anticipated later in view of the fact that the governor appoints members to more than 550 boards and commissions, fifty-eight community colleges, and sixteen universities.

Prior to my assuming the office of governor, this region had representatives on only two state entities, the state Board of Transportation and the North Carolina Board of Economic Development. The goal of this administration is to ensure equitable representation consistent with qualified individuals on all boards and commissions at the state level, and we will see that this goal is met.

Now let me turn your attention to another vital area of interest: transportation. Today, our state is faced with a transportation [crisis], now and in the future, because we do not have adequate monies to match federal highway grant funds. Many of you have read, or heard, my announcement several weeks ago that the Department of Transportation budget falls about $40 million short of what is needed just to match federal funds, and $60 to $80 million less than is needed for truly adequate financing.

We can fix this flat tire in our urban transportation needs because we have a spare, fiscally speaking; but there is another flat tire in our highway program, and it, too, needs to be fixed. The issue that I'm talking about is the growing crisis North Carolina faces in urban transportation. This problem is staggering, and it will require innovation and imagination to solve.

When I speak of urban areas, I'm not talking only of Raleigh, Greensboro, Charlotte, and other metropolitan areas—I am speaking of cities like Elizabeth City, cities with 10,000 people or more.

North Carolina is on the move. Traditionally, we have used our highway system as a major drawing card for new industry and other development. This tactic has worked; in fact, it has worked extremely well. Factories have sprung up in farm fields of the east and the mountainsides of the west. North Carolina is now the largest industrial state, per capita, in the nation.

These transportation problems are the reasons I have asked Transportation Secretary Jim Harrington to appoint an urban transportation task force to study the situation and to develop recommendations. Meanwhile, we will not—we cannot—turn away from the longstanding effort to improve the economies of our rural counties by improving their transportation systems. After all, rural highways connect cities. Without them we would be isolated.

I don't want to leave you with the impression that our transportation problems are obstacles we cannot overcome. There are a number of options available, and we will consider all of them. Problems present us with opportunities to build a greater state. We simply have to turn problems into opportunities.

On October 10, the North Carolina Board of Transportation will meet to approve the annual update of the statewide Transportation Improvement plan, and I believe you will be pleased with the region's projects that are moving ahead. Among projects on the list for approval are the continued four-laning of U.S Highway 17 and the construction of U.S. Highway 64 from Tarboro to Williamston. We are giving the Albemarle region top priority.

In addition to transportation improvements, this administration also is addressing other needs of this area. We have approved almost $800,000 in community development grants in the region for economic development and housing rehabilitation during the current fiscal year. We have made, and we will continue to make, a good-faith effort to assess all regions of North Carolina and meet their needs as resources become available.

As I said at the beginning, we are laying the foundation for a strong and active partnership. Your commitment of effort and money as individuals will help build that partnership. Your committee is to be commended for its continued commitment to supplementing local needs as private citizens and businesses; as long as this commitment remains, the Albemarle region is destined to become one of the major growth centers of North Carolina.

Dedicated people win. Together, we'll win the race for economic development, and we'll someday look back and say it was a piece of cake.

Governor Martin directed the attention of President Ronald Reagan to the noise meter inside Reynolds Coliseum as North Carolina State University students enthusiastically welcomed him to Raleigh in September, 1985. Reagan journeyed to North Carolina's capital to generate support for his tax program. (Photograph by Jerry Huff, Raleigh *News and Observer*)

Top: Explaining the career ladder concept, a proposal to provide "better pay for better teachers," to the Wilmington media. *Bottom*: At home in the classroom, professor-turned-governor Jim Martin.

NORTH CAROLINA HUMAN RELATIONS COUNCIL

Raleigh, October 4, 1985

[Before beginning his speech, the governor commended Dr. Jerry Drayton,[1] the retiring chairman of the state Human Relations Council, "for the superb leadership he has brought to this state." He also recognized the council's new chairman, Dr. Jimmie V. Morris.[2]]

Throughout North Carolina, there are some citizens who believe the struggle for civil rights is an idea whose time has come and gone; that in twenty-one years since the passage of the nation's first comprehensive civil rights bill, discrimination has ended.[3] Well not quite, unfortunately, even though progress has been made. Here are the facts:

—In North Carolina, black unemployment is twice the rate of white unemployment. Black youth unemployment is estimated at a staggering 40 percent.

—On a statewide basis, blacks can expect to earn less and have shorter life-spans than white citizens. Their median income is consistently lower, and their life expectancy is six years shorter than whites.

—Blacks in North Carolina also have a higher infant mortality rate, and a much larger percentage of their population is living in poverty.

—Although great strides have been made in education and employment, blacks still are less likely than whites to finish high school and are greatly underrepresented in professional and managerial occupations.

—Statistics for our native Indians are similar in kind, but are even worse.

—A smaller percentage of blacks than whites are registered to vote in our state; and only 5.5 percent of elected officials are black, despite the fact that about 20 percent of our eligible voters are black.

These are the facts, and it is not the tradition in North Carolina to evade the facts. We have already begun, in this administration, to address these problems, specifically in the areas of equal employment opportunities, minority business goals, police-community relations, and fair housing. Three months ago, I signed an executive order which commits the state to take positive measures to ensure representation of specific groups in all levels of state employment.[4] These groups include women, minorities, the handicapped, and older persons. The State Personnel Commission has developed policies and programs to achieve greater representation by these groups, and the director will report to me annually on the progress of the program.

We have made a major effort to place individuals in positions of high responsibility of a general nature, not just on minority issues: Lee Monroe (all education); Secretary Aaron Johnson (all corrections); Lew Myers (all small business); Ed Garner (all military affairs); Syl Wilkerson (all highways); Deputy Secretary Henry McKoy (all Department of Administration); Jim Ross (all job training).[5]

In addition, the North Carolina Human Relations Council is charged with advising and assisting the administration in implementing the equal employment opportunity program.

This order is directed not just toward hiring, but to all areas of employment activities, including retirement, recruitment, testing, training, transfer, performance appraisal, promotion, and other conditions of employment. This administration and state government are committed to working toward achievement of equal employment opportunities, and this is a process we believe in strongly.

Another step we have taken is to encourage all state agencies to strive toward a goal of placing at least 2 percent of their purchases and contracts with firms owned by minorities, women, and handicapped people. The goals program is a good-faith effort which, if diligently pursued, could improve many smaller businesses. Two percent is a modest goal; but while the previous administration set a higher goal of 5 percent, it had no mechanism for it and only achieved 0.015 percent.

My goals program began July 1 of this year, and after only three months in operation, our goal of 2 percent has been surpassed. We're in the range of 5 to 6 percent, passing even the higher goal of the previous administration. Minority business contracts represented 5.1 percent of state contracts in July and 6 percent in August. This is outstanding evidence of the program's potential, which we hope will continue to grow.

One area in which the Human Relations Council has achieved significant progress is the field of police-community relations. This was a good initiative in the previous administration. Two years ago, before the program began, no law enforcement officers in our state received any formal training in dealing with the special needs of the minority community. Now, after thirty training sessions, 750 law enforcement officers have received two days of instruction in this area, and these officers believe this special training should be a requirement of every recruit before being sworn as an officer. There are about 7,000 law officers in North Carolina. Obviously, we need to increase our efforts to get more officers trained in community relations.

Throughout our state we have made tremendous progress in civil rights, and we see evidence of this progress every day. But we also see areas in which progress has been very slow. Although our children attend integrated schools, and we go to work with people of all races and nationalities, when we come home, most of us come home to segregated neighborhoods.

Whatever gains we have achieved in education and employment, those gains will always be limited if we do not recognize our responsibility to achieve fair and equal housing opportunities. One of the ways we are working to achieve this goal is through the North Carolina Fair Housing Act, adopted in 1983 and enforced by the Human Relations Council.[6] People who believe they have been victims of housing discrimination bring their complaint to the council, which conducts an investigation and then attempts conciliation. The council also is empowered to take complaints to court. This year, there will be a greater effort to make citizens aware of their housing rights and to educate real estate associations about the fair housing law.

North Carolina is extremely fortunate to have been relatively free of activities conducted by extremist groups, but society has never been totally free of those who commit acts of violence against racial and religious groups. During 1984, there were fifty documented incidents—including threats and harassment, rallies, and more serious violence—attributed to extremist groups in North Carolina. It is vital that we continue to speak out when these acts occur. It is vital that we address these acts with the full force of law.

In a report issued by the U.S. Civil Rights Commission in 1983, it was observed nationally that there is an "indispensable need for strong and unambiguous statements from community leaders and elected officials that acts of racial and religious intimidation will not be tolerated." The report added that "members of hate groups . . . view themselves as true patriots who stand as the last defenders of the American way. They must learn from repeated public statements, as well as the determined enforcement of the law, that they are the most anti-American among us." Although the followers of such groups are relatively few in North Carolina, we must keep a constant vigil against social injustice.[7]

In the field of human relations, North Carolina has been an exemplary leader in the nation. We have taken bold new initiatives to bring all citizens together in a bond of social and economic unity and equity. This administration's commitment to lighting a new lamp of human relations is real and sincere. We stand not on words alone. We stand on the basis of our accomplishments, and history will judge us accordingly.

---

[1]Jerry Drayton (1918-   ), born in Savannah, Georgia; B.A., Morehouse College; B.D., Howard University; honorary doctorate; pastor, New Bethel Baptist Church, Winston-Salem. Appointed to North Carolina Human Relations Council, 1977, and served as chairman; his second term on the council was scheduled to expire June 1, 1988. Mitchell, *Addresses of Hunt, 1977-1981*, 163n; Poff and Crow, *Addresses of Hunt, 1981-1985*, 591.

[2]Jimmie Vaughan Morris (1925-   ), born in Carthage, Mississippi; resident of Granville County; A.B., Tougaloo College, 1950; M.S., Indiana University, 1952; Ed.S., North Carolina College at Durham (later North Carolina Central University), 1968; Ed.D., Temple University, 1981; U.S. Marine Corps, 1943-1946. Former elementary and high school principal, 1953-1971; secondary education director, 1971-1976, personnel services and employee relations director, 1976-1978, Wilmington Public School District, Wilmington, Delaware; director, personnel services, New Castle County (Delaware) School District, 1978-1981; chairman, Granville County Republican Party, and of the Board, Central Children's Home of North Carolina, Oxford; author. Jimmie Vaughan Morris to Jan-Michael Poff, May 29, 1989.

[3]See P.L. 88-352, "Civil Rights Act of 1964" (short title), *United States Statutes at Large*, Act of July 2, 1964, 78 Stat. 241-268.

[4]Executive Order Number 18, signed July 1, 1985, established as state policy "equal employment opportunites for all state employees and for all applicants for state employment without regard to race, religion, color, national origin, sex, age, or handicap." *N.C. Session Laws, 1985*, 1467-1470.

[5]Lee Everett Monroe, Jr. (1943-), born in Wilmington; resident of Raleigh; B.A., Shaw University, 1965; M.Ed., University of Cincinnati, 1970; D.Ed., Virginia Polytechnic Institute and State University, 1984. Teacher and coach, 1965-1970, Cincinnati, Ohio, and Robeson County public school systems; regional education specialist, U.S. Department of Justice, 1970-1972; director, ASPO-Ford Foundation Fellowship Program, American Society of Planning Officials, 1972-1974; institutional advancement director, 1974-1979, and executive vice-president, 1982-1985, Shaw University; senior research associate, National Institute of Education, and visiting lecturer, Virginia Polytechnic Institute and State University, 1979-1982; adjunct professor, Graduate School of Education, North Carolina State University, and senior education adviser to Governor Martin, 1985-1990; author. Lee Everett Monroe, Jr., to Jan-Michael Poff, August 30, 1988; press release, "Dr. Lee Monroe Resigns from Governor's Staff to Become President of Florida Memorial College," Raleigh, January 31, 1990, Governors Papers, James G. Martin.

Aaron Johnson (1933-   ), native of Willard; resident of Fayetteville; B.A., 1957, and was graduated from School of Religion, 1960, Shaw University. Pastor, Mount Sinai Baptist Church, Fayetteville; member, since 1979, mayor pro tem, since 1983, Fayetteville City Council; member, North Carolina Minority Committee to Elect Ronald Reagan, 1980; president, Minority Affairs Committee for Jim Martin; appointed secretary of correction, 1985; Republican. *North Carolina Manual, 1987-1988*, 713.

Lewis H. Myers (1946-   ), born in Carlisle, Pennsylvania; resident of Durham; B.A., Franklin and Marshall College, 1968; M.B.A., University of North Carolina at Chapel Hill, 1972. Director, North Carolina Minority Business Development Agency, 1980-1982; assistant secretary, state Department of Commerce, 1982-1988; vice-president, since March, 1988, Construction Control Services Corp. Lewis H. Myers to Jan-Michael Poff, October 17, 1988.

Edward Garner, Jr. (1942-   ), born in Skippers, Virginia; B.S., North Carolina A&T State University, 1967; J.D., University of North Carolina at Chapel Hill, 1975; U.S. Air Force, 1967-1973; N.C. Air National Guard, since 1973. Corporate attorney, Akzo America, Inc., 1976-1985; former chairman, Asheville-Buncombe Community Relations

Council; assistant secretary, Department of Crime Control and Public Safety, since 1985. Edward Garner, Jr., to Jan-Michael Poff, October 10, 1988.

Sylvania Wilkerson, Sr. (1934-   ), born in Elberton, Georgia; resident of Goldsboro; was educated at University of Louisville (Ft. Knox, Kentucky, extension) and at Fayetteville Technical Institute; U.S. Army, 1952-1955, 1958-1975. Owner, operator, B and S Locks and Safes Service, Fayetteville, 1975-1977, and Goldsboro, 1980-1985; athletic supervisor, City of Goldsboro, 1977-1978; security officer, Wachenhut Corp., 1978-1980; locksmith, Missing Link Key Shop, Inc., 1979-1980; assistant secretary for planning and programs, state Department of Transportation, 1985-1987; owner, operator, AIRS Locksmith and Safes Services, since 1987; Republican. Sylvania Wilkerson, Sr., to Jan-Michael Poff, January 9, 1989.

Henry E. McKoy (1946-   ), native of Raeford; resident of Raleigh; B.S., 1968, M.S, 1971, North Carolina A&T State University; U.S. Army, 1969-1971. Assistant director, 1971-1974, executive director, 1974-1978, Greensboro Human Relations Commission; executive director, North Carolina Human Relations Council, 1978-1979; assistant secretary, 1979-1981, deputy secretary for programs, since 1981, Department of Administration. Henry E. McKoy to Jan-Michael Poff, October 11, 1988.

James Lewis Ross II (1934-   ), born in Mecklenburg County; A.B., Johnson C. Smith University, 1965; M.Ed., University of North Carolina at Charlotte, 1978; U.S. Air Force, 1954-1957. Senior consultant, MMH, Inc., 1969-1980; executive director, Cherry Community Assn., 1981-1985; director, Employment and Training Division, Department of Natural Resources and Community Development, 1984-1985; president, James Ross and Associates, 1985-1988; assistant to the commissioner, Division of Motor Vehicles, Department of Transportation, since 1988. James Lewis Ross II to Jan-Michael Poff, October 7, 1988.

[6]"An Act to Prohibit Discrimination in Housing," ratified June 14, 1983, and effective October 1, 1983, established G.S. 41A, the State Fair Housing Act. *N.C. Session Laws, 1983,* c. 522.

[7]The governor quoted from *Intimidation and Violence: Racial and Religious Bigotry in America* ([Washington, D.C.: United States Commission on Civil Rights], Clearinghouse Publication 77, January, 1983), 25. As a component of the vigil against hate groups, Martin established the Governor's Task Force on Racial, Religious, and Ethnic Violence and Intimidation. See Executive Order Number 29, signed October 2, 1986, *N.C. Session Laws, 1987,* II, 2319-2321.

BREAKFAST REMARKS TO BOARD OF TRANSPORTATION

RALEIGH, OCTOBER 10, 1985

I wanted to have you over to our house, this morning, to thank you for working so hard for the state of North Carolina and her transportation needs. I also want to tell you that if any of you ever decide to look for a different kind of work, I would be glad to recommend you to Ringling Brothers-Barnum and Bailey Circus, because the work done on the Transportation Improvement Program [TIP] that will be announced today represents the greatest juggling act I've ever seen.[1]

Through hard work, good judgment, sacrifice, and just plain old intestinal fortitude, you have managed not only to balance the needs of our rural and urban areas, but you have balanced all of those against available revenues, as well. I realize that funding restraints keep us from doing many vital projects, but I think you have done a great job of allocating available revenues wisely and fairly. I am very proud of what you have done and the attitude of teamwork you have displayed during the process.

I very deeply appreciate the fact that you recognized my preferences in some of these hard decisions. I am particularly encouraged that you were able to incorporate more than $30 million in projects over the next four to six years involving local participation. This shows our willingness to cooperate with local governments as we come to terms with our pressing highway funding problems.

You are already aware that we must put forth new initiatives this year. We must adopt nontraditional ways of funding the existing DOT program and the transportation needs that will come with our growth. Some of those methods have already surfaced and are reflected in your TIP; others will have to develop if we are to address our mounting funding problems in the small, medium, and large cities across our state. I know you are working diligently with the secretary and his staff to find ways to improve the financial efficiency of the highway department. We will need your continued support in this effort. We must lead the way in efficiency. We are asking local governments, developers, and other interests to help with our funding problems, and we must be able to assure them that they are getting the most for their money.

This is a bright day for us; having our TIP is important and significant. But today is also touched with regret, because, with regret, I have accepted the resignation of Rusty Goode as a member and vice-chairman of your board.[2] Rusty is resigning because of the pressure of other activities; since some of those are for me, I couldn't find a real good way to say no.

I expect to be naming a new member of the board next month. That appointment will be at-large. I have asked Johnny Harris[3] to accept the duties of the division board member for that area around Charlotte, in Rusty's place. But I believe it is time for the new at-large member to come from outside the Charlotte or piedmont area to fill out the remainder of this two-year term, and, as you may have learned, I am looking for someone from the northeast area, north of the Albemarle Sound. Governor Kenny Roberson will continue to cover that area as its divisional member.

Finally, I recommend to you and would very much appreciate it if you would take action to name Richard Pugh[4] as Rusty's successor as vice-chairman of the board. Richard is my choice. He has a broad knowledge of my goals for North Carolina in regard to transportation and other issues. He will be a great help to Secretary Harrington.

I understand we need to move ahead as quickly as possible so we can convene the meeting of the Board of Transportation in this same spot in a few moments. Therefore, I will thank you again and will turn this breakfast back to Jim Harrington.

---

[1]See *Transportation Improvement Program, 1986-1995* ([Raleigh: North Carolina Department of Transportation], October, 1985). The governor's draft remarks for a press conference, dated October 8, 1985, stated that the 1986-1995 TIP represented a more businesslike approach to transportation financing. "Previously, projects have been programmed into the TIP based on the total amount of highway funds allocated by Congress. Historically . . . fiscal obligational ceilings have been imposed on the highway program that are lower than those allocations." With the new TIP, however, the state "estimated the amount of federal highway funds we will actually be allowed to spend and have based the program's schedules on that estimate. This should mean that when a project is programmed for a particular fiscal year, funds will be available to proceed with it as scheduled."

[2]Seddon (Rusty) Goode, Jr. (1932-   ), born in Clinton; resident of Charlotte; B.S., Davidson College, 1954; M.B.A., University of North Carolina at Chapel Hill, 1957. Vice-president, Southeastern Financial Corp., 1957-1962; president, Mt. Mitchell Broadcasting Corp./WMIT, 1963; vice-president, North Carolina National Bank, 1964-1968; senior vice-president, treasurer, director, Interstate Securities Corp., 1968-1977; chairman, First Charlotte Corp., 1977-1984; president, director, University Research Park, Inc., since 1981; member, 1979-1985, reappointed in 1987, and vice-chairman, 1985, state Board of Transportation; director, Charlotte Chamber of Commerce, since 1979; chairman, Governor James G. Martin Inauguration and Transition Committee, 1984; treasurer, North Carolina State Ports Authority, since 1985; member, state Advisory Budget Commission, since 1986. Seddon Goode, Jr., to Jan-Michael Poff, August 24, 1988.

[3]John William Harris (1947-   ), native, resident of Charlotte; A.B., University of North Carolina at Chapel Hill, 1969; N.C. National Guard, 1969-1976. Executive vice-president, 1970-1985, president, since 1985, the Bissell Companies, Inc. John William Harris to Jan-Michael Poff, November 15, 1989.

[4]Richard K. Pugh (1935-   ) born in Randolph County; resident of Asheboro; A.B., Elon College, 1957. Owner, Pugh Oil Co., Inc., and of Tank and Tummy Stores. Richard K. Pugh to Jan-Michael Poff, August 27, 1988.

OPENING ADDRESS, NORTH CAROLINA GOVERNOR'S CONFERENCE ON COASTAL STATES OCEAN POLICY

RALEIGH, OCTOBER 31, 1985

Earlier this year, the people of North Carolina celebrated the 400th anniversary of the first English settlement in America. The arrival of these pilgrims on Roanoke Island marked the first great step in the colonization of this continent, but these were not the first Europeans to visit our shores. As early as 1524, a Florentine navigator explored the coastal region between Cape Fear and Kitty Hawk.[1] It was from the sea that this land we know as North Carolina first developed.

Even as this New World colony expanded inland, eventually reaching the Appalachian Mountains, North Carolinians maintained a close relationship with the sea. In the four centuries that have followed that first settlement, we have looked to the Atlantic Ocean as a major source of our commerce, culture, and recreation.

As I look in my mind's eye eastward, toward our coast, different images appear. As many of you are aware, I am a sailor. I have a sailboat and enjoy sailing to rid my system of two weeks' tension and poisons.[2] From that perspective, I have gained a love and respect of our coastal waters. You may also be aware of my scientific training.[3] From that perspective, I have an awareness of the vast potential that is in our coastal waters.[4] As one who has also had an active interest in the arts, if you count semi-pro symphonic tuba player as expression for the soul of an artist, I feel the beauty and majesty of the ocean, the Outer Banks, the sounds, and the inlets. As governor of this one united state, I know of the vital, integral role this coastal region plays in North Carolina's economic development. For me, the future of our coastal waters is a very personal concern.

This is an age in which all of us have been made more aware of the fragile nature of our habitat. As we have increased our environmental consciousness, we have also become aware that our stewardship of this land does not end at the high-water mark. Our responsibilities clearly extend into and beneath the ocean. We have a stake in how our ocean resources—seafood, minerals, oil and gas, and recreation and scenic beauty—are developed. Many of the activities we pursue on dry land have a significant impact on our offshore waters. Many questions face us regarding offshore transportation, fisheries, tourism, and cultural resources.

In 1983, President Reagan issued a proclamation entitled "Exclusive Economic Zone of the United States of America."[5] This action followed the president's decision not to sign the International Convention on the Law of the Sea. For policy makers in coastal states such as North Carolina, this proclamation raised many new issues. The New Federalism, with its promise of decreased federal regulation and funding, raised additional questions about where the federal government's responsibilities end and those of the individual states begin.

North Carolinians have long understood their state's close relationship to the sea and the importance of developing a comprehensive approach to ocean policy. Rather than wait for Washington to resolve these ocean policy questions, it was decided that North Carolinians were in the best position to address these matters. Two years ago this month, the North Carolina Marine Science Council appointed an

Ocean Policy Committee to report on the critical issues that are facing us. The result of this effort was a first-of- its-kind report entitled, *North Carolina and the Sea: An Ocean Policy Analysis*.[6] This was the first comprehensive effort directed exclusively at ocean policy issues undertaken by any state government and was coordinated by the Office of Marine Affairs in the Department of Administration.

This report presented a current assessment of, and recommendations about, issues in sixteen different areas of ocean policy concern. Specifically, the report's recommendations included calls for an inventory of this state's offshore natural and cultural resources, policy and regulatory development regarding submerged lands, a cost-benefit analysis of the extension of state jurisdiction, and a more regional approach to dealing with matters relating to the outer continental shelf. The North Carolina Marine Science Council's report should serve as a model for other states wishing to come to grips with these pressing issues.[7]

A follow-up to the groundwork laid in that report is the conference you are attending this morning: The Governor's Conference on Coastal States Ocean Policy was developed with two specific goals in mind. First, this gathering serves as a platform for creating a greater awareness of the role coastal states have in the development of ocean policy. Secondly, the deliberations of the next two days should help educate policy makers, as well as the general public, about those ocean policy issues that are important to North Carolina and other coastal states. This gathering of local, state, and federal officials, industry representatives, and concerned citizens can serve as a catalyst for positive state initiatives in the coming years.

I believe it is vitally important that coastal state governments take a greater role in addressing ocean policy questions. Too often, in the past, there has been a history of state governments reacting to policy initiatives from Washington. But those days are gone. State governments have begun seeking a greater voice in setting the agenda. At the same time, the regulatory climate in Washington has changed to the point of encouraging a greater role for the states. This conference, as well as others that may follow, here or elsewhere, can send a clear message to Washington that the states are ready, willing, and able to shoulder their share of the load. I will be depending on the advice of councils such as the Marine Science Council to help us develop our policies as we in North Carolina take on those additional responsibilities.

Perhaps the most attractive feature of this conference is the opportunity for information sharing that it presents. Although many of you here this morning come from states that are vastly different from North Carolina, I believe you will find that, when it comes to ocean policy questions, there is a great commonality of interest. The sharing of each other's thoughts and concerns can only lead to a better understanding of the task that lies ahead.

To all in attendance, it is my pleasure to welcome you to this conference. I hope you will enjoy your stay in our capital city. It is also my hope that you will leave these proceedings with a better understanding of the issues, a better understanding of each other's perspective on these issues, and a resolve to take concerted action to preserve and protect our valuable offshore resources.

---

[1]Florentine navigator Giovanni da Verrazzano, sailing on behalf of France, is the earliest known European to explore the Atlantic coast north of Cape Fear. His report of July, 1524, to King Francis I describing the area between Cape Fear and Kitty Hawk was published in England in 1582 and is credited as an influence on Walter Raleigh's plans for colonizing the New World. Lefler and Newsome, *North Carolina*, 3.

[2]At this point in his prepared text, the governor inserted, "Often 3-4 days to get the poisons restored."

[3]Here Martin wrote: "Real life: mild-mannered chemistry professor."

[4]The governor inserted, at this point in his prepared text, "As a former county comm. . . . estab. first enforcement of state air & water pollution regulations."

[5]"Exclusive Economic Zone of the United States of America," *United States Statutes at Large*, Proclamation 5030 of March 10, 1983, 97 Stat. 1557-1558.

[6]*North Carolina and the Sea: An Ocean Policy Analysis* ([Raleigh: Ocean Policy Committee, North Carolina Marine Science Council], November, 1984), hereinafter cited as *North Carolina and the Sea*.

[7]See *North Carolina and the Sea*, 43-46, for recommendations. The report was distributed outside the Tar Heel State; see press release, "Governor Martin Sends Ocean Policy Study to Coastal and Great Lakes Governors," Raleigh, April 18, 1985, Governors Papers, James G. Martin.

NORTH CAROLINA ASSOCIATION OF COLLEGES AND UNIVERSITIES

RALEIGH, OCTOBER 31, 1985

Among his many wise observations we are told that Aristotle once remarked that education is "an ornament in prosperity, but a refuge in adversity."[1] That principle seems to apply to education in North Carolina, which is left pretty much to itself when times are good but becomes a major source of concern when things are not going so well.

Consider, for example, the wave of public concern that swept the nation not long ago about the quality—"mediocrity," it was called[2]—the problems, and the role of education and our schools in national life. North Carolina even produced its own study: *Education for Economic Growth: An Action Plan for North Carolina.*

Hard upon the Bell commission's national report[3] came no less than thirty-six others, each with its own version of our problems in education and its own prescription for educational reform. The same reaction attended earlier the heralded "technology gap" after Sputnik.[4]

In a period of extraordinary concern about the quality of education, our colleges and universities have this time, thus far, largely escaped the intense scrutiny to which our elementary and secondary schools have been subjected. This reprieve should not be taken as proof that higher education is without its own shortcomings—and challenges.

We have become so conscious of public dissatisfaction in our elementary and secondary schools, as well as ways to address this concern, we have failed to recognize that there is no invisible shield to prevent developments in the schools from affecting higher education, and vice versa. It is widely accepted that college entrance requirements, for many, constitute de facto high school exit requirements, and that the less the colleges have demanded of those they accept, the fewer tough academic courses have been taken by high school students.

Similarly, the poor intellectual preparedness of too many new schoolteachers can be traced, in part, to the colleges that admitted and graduated them and then purported to provide them with "higher education" in between. Hence, it is reasonable to predict that the educational reform movement may soon lead to a demand for greater accountability on the part of higher education—at least for teacher training programs, but probably not limited to that.

North Carolina has a unique educational heritage. The University of North Carolina, in 1795, became the first public institution of higher learning in the nation to admit students. A couple of others had earlier charters or proposals, but, of course, our motto is *Esse quam videri.* Private higher education had even been established twenty-four years earlier, under religious sponsorship.[5] Today, the state has sixteen public university campuses, thirty independent four-year colleges and universities, eight private junior colleges, and fifty-eight community colleges, of which thirty-four are technical institutes. With that total of 112 post-secondary institutions, North Carolina is outdistanced in the Southeast only by Texas. We are blessed to have some among our most outstanding national institutions.

Determining quality, however, is far more complex than citing national ratings; acknowledgment of this fact is not intended in any pejorative, adversarial way. On the contrary, it simply recognizes that no institution is perfect; that there are concerns which must be addressed; and in order to address them, an independent evaluation of higher education statewide is in order, and it is equally important that the evaluation should be made in an objective and impartial manner.

The evaluation has already begun. Known as the "Third Century Project," the Z. Smith Reynolds Foundation has been working to evaluate North Carolina higher education. This continuing study will be addressed later in this session by the project director, (Dolph) Norton.[6] I look forward to reviewing the results of the foundation's work. Our Efficiency Study Commission independently recommended a similar blue-ribbon evaluation, and I will seek your response as to what kind of follow-up, if any, would best supplement the Reynolds Foundation study. I might add that on all the efficiency recommendations for education, I plan to review the particulars with Superintendent Craig Phillips, Governor Bob Scott,[7] and President Bill Friday in order to determine how best to achieve the objective to deliver on our educational policies with improved cost effectiveness. If you have concerns, rest easier but stay alert. I want those recommendations to stir your imagination with their potential, not to scare your innovation with their boldness.

For today, I want to concentrate on the role of the governor as part of the state's leadership for higher education—its greatest supporter and most effective partner.

A true education governor is one who understands the role of education in relation to the needs of the state as a whole and who recognizes the economic and social diversity of its people. He must believe in education deeply and be willing to make appropriate investment in education as one of the best purposes of government.

Education in North Carolina, especially higher education, needs the support and leadership of the governor, and he needs to share the views of educators. Indeed, the governor and higher education need the creative and positive support of one another. Both contribute to the dreams and aspirations of the people. If our mission is to achieve the optimal quality of life, enhancing the personal and economic well-being of every citizen, then it is a mission we can only achieve together.

To begin, we need to understand that the great system of post-secondary education in North Carolina has been built by a strong partnership between the state and federal governments. This state-federal partnership had been characterized by a significant increase in research activities on our college and university campuses; by greater student financial aid; by affirmative action programs, in the highest sense of the term; and by an extensive commitment of North Carolina public resources exceeded by few states. This period of federal incentives in higher education clearly is facing a realignment. Extension of the Higher Education Act of 1965 must yet be acted upon by the Ninety-ninth Congress.[8] This legislation provides authority for more than forty federally funded, post-secondary education programs. How the Congress views this legislation is extremely important to North Carolina.

Our state institutions which place emphasis on research received almost $250 million in federal research funds in 1982. In terms of research dollars, North Carolina's three major research universities ranked among the nation's top 100 institutions in federal financial support. Duke received more than $50 million, the largest amount, with UNC at Chapel Hill second and N.C. State third—in truth and in jest, truly our "golden triangle." Only four other states—California, Michigan, Texas, and Indiana—had two public universities with a combined effort greater than UNC at Chapel Hill and N.C. State. However, seventeen individual schools across the nation, ten of which were state supported, received more federal funding for research and development than UNC and N.C. State combined.

It has been our great research campuses that have made North Carolina a flagship state in attracting internationally recognized high-technology firms. The Research Triangle Park, our crown jewel of research and development, is an exciting example of how an effective public-private partnership mutually enhances industry and higher education. Another example is University City in Mecklenburg County, a uniquely conceived plan which combines a new city, a research and manufacturing park, and the University of North Carolina at Charlotte. These enterprising ventures, undertaken in a climate of cooperation and communication among public and private participants, are vital to our future.

We pride ourselves in having become a leading high-tech state. Let me tell you we still depend on a lot of low tech, too: data processing to food processing, terminals to turkeys! We embrace the economic progress which accompanies new technology, and we recognize its benefits not only to our state but to the entire world.

All states lay some claim to preeminence in high technology. In Japan we found, over and over again, the ideal they want to copy: RTP. To maintain our leadership, we must continue to utilize our institutions of higher learning to the fullest capacity.

Research and development are essential, also, to the maintenance of our traditional industries and the improvement of their competitiveness, as much so as they are necessary to attract advanced manufacturing enterprises. This administration is supportive of both, realizing that in our advancement into a changing world of work lies the realization of the hopes and promises the future holds for our people. We must prepare for what is just over the horizon. The acid test of our success will be in pursuing the linkage between private enterprise and post-secondary education. I, too, was delighted, at his recent inauguration, to hear Duke President Keith Brodie proclaim a new initiative for educational enterprise in support of private enterprise—and not just the other way around.[9]

Our community colleges and technical institutes will play an increasingly important role in the continuing challenge of retraining workers in new skills, some of which do not exist today. The Hudson Institute, one of the nation's leading research organizations serving the federal and many of our state governments, predicts that 80 percent of the people in today's work force will be employed in the year 2000. It also forecasts, and this may come as a surprise, that it will be difficult to recruit enough workers in the year 2000 to fill the employment vacancies. Well, some would call that a refreshing problem!

This will require many individuals to be retrained in a variety of skills as our economy changes with increasing frequency. The workers who will adjust will be those who have the basic educational qualifications to master new tasks as they develop. We must recognize that this will require better management of our institutions in the community college system.

I recognize that education is crucial—not just important to the future of North Carolina, but crucial. Consequently, our most important task is to define the specific goals and priorities for higher education. To accomplish this task will require an evaluation of where we are and how we plan to approach the future with confidence. We need to determine if the state is supporting higher education adequately and getting the best R.O.I and R.O.E. (return on investment/education) and if not, what needs to be done. Other concerns involve whether or not the institutions are focusing their expenses—that is, not spilling money on unnecessary things—and whether all institutions involved in education beyond the high school are reaching our young people with opportunities suitable to their own needs and abilities. Finally, is the educational mission of each and every institution being achieved?

All of these questions and others must be assessed by you and by the governor through evaluations from outside the system itself, as well as evaluations from within the system. Surely a governor cannot be effectively supportive of higher education unless he knows, for sure, what is needed and unless he has the evidence from an impartial and objective source of those needs.

Outside of budget considerations, every governor must know what our institutions' administrators care about and what they are trying to do for the young people of the state, for the state itself, and for our citizens. We must know what is needed for the economic health of the state in the development of job capacities, intellectual and artistic talents, research and scientific advancements, and for recruiting and keeping qualified faculty for all of these purposes.

As an educational leader of North Carolina, I have a strong commitment to our efforts, kindergarten through post-secondary and remedial education, to improve and enrich the lives of our citizens. This governor is one who cares about the present and future of higher education and how it addresses the needs of our people and our state. The successes of the governor in this field are the successes of the system and the successes of every individual in North Carolina.

Cooperation and communication will be the key attributes of our combined efforts to make post-secondary education in North Carolina continue as an example of what is best for the nation. One of the areas in which improved cooperation is needed is between our public and private institutions. This has been addressed in previous meetings of your association. Among those speaking out on this concern was my former boss, Dr. Samuel R. Spencer, Jr., former president of Davidson College.[10]

He said that the current, "fierce, unbridled, sometimes downright cutthroat competition" between the two sectors is dangerous to our educational system.[11] I agree. Scholastic competition is productive; political muscle is destuctive. This association can and must continue to be the unifying force of post-secondary education. Our public institutions, community colleges, and independent colleges and universities recognize both competition and cooperation as elements of a healthy higher education system. They must not allow the intensity of competition to become a destructive force. There are no winners when the goal of higher education institutions is to "beggar thy neighbors."

We know that the number of college-bound students is declining, and this means that real funding, which is based on full-time equivalent students but adjusted for inflation, will also tend to decline.

One of the most important tasks we face is to find a better method of funding, one that does not reward unjustified expansion and to be able to tell the difference.

The growth of higher education should be spread among our institutions by allowing—indeed, insisting—that separate but appropriate standards be set to maintain the integrity of state purpose [sic] of each individual academic community. Some must have higher standards— some, the highest—if the state is to be well served. Others quite appropriately should have lesser standards, still having academic integrity, in order to open the opportunites of higher education to young people who cannot or have not achieved quite so well; who can benefit from higher education, even if not from the highest and fastest track; who can develop in a serious academic climate that is not impossibly hostile, as Lee Monroe has observed. There always must remain the opportunity, for those with a less-demonstrated capacity, to have the choice of other instutitions, with a chance for those demonstrating a greater potential than originally shown to move on to more selective institutions.

In my inaugural speech, I used the allusion that our education system can be the rising tide that lifts all boats; but that the tide, and boats, will rise higher if there is a strong lunar gravitational pull of programs that are the best for the brightest soaring across our educational firmament. You see, I do have poetic qualities!

The dual system of higher education, both public and private, has been the making of a great system of higher education in North Carolina. We have had the competitive forces, but we have also had the supporting forces. Each has made a distinctive contribution to the other. North Carolina began with private institutions. The state institutions followed gradually, and then suddenly with the advent of land-grant colleges. Higher education still flourishes, but the private campuses are in trouble, threatened by an everwidening gap in tuition rates. We must not disparage that circumstance, or despair of it, but must devise a way to preserve the invaluable dual system that has meant so much to the progress of our state.

We, the governor and each distinctive part of higher education, must build a strong partnership, and I challenge each of you to buy into this principle as a means of providing the citizens of North Carolina the best service available. Our partnership represents the future of our people and the fulfillment of our service as leaders. As this administration continues working to develop policies affecting higher education, as it offers greater leadership and stronger support based upon objective evaluation of post-secondary education, we welcome you to that partnership. If we can pull it together—and pull together, not apart—then this unifying force will enhance higher education and enrich our students, and our state, for years to come.

Dr. Phail Wynn, my friend whose very name conveys the existential grand dilemma of education, put it this way: "We have the capacity in this state," he said, "to build an excellent all-around educational system, and we have the leadership."[12] Now let's prove him right!

---

[1]"These studies are a spur to the young, a delight to the old; an ornament in prosperity, a consoling refuge in adversity; they are a pleasure for us at home, and no burden abroad; they stay up with us at night, they accompany us when we travel, they are with us in our country visits." Marcus Tullius Cicero, *Pro Archia Poeta I*, 2, quoted in John Bartlett, *Familiar Quotations*, 110.

[2]"We report to the American people that while we can take justifiable pride in what our schools and colleges have historically accomplished and contributed to the United States and the well-being of its people, the educational foundations of our society are presently being eroded by a rising tide of mediocrity that threatens our very future as a Nation and a people. What was unimaginable a generation ago has begun to occur—others are matching and surpassing our educational attainments." *A Nation at Risk*, 5.

[3]Terrell Howard Bell (1921-   ), born in Lava Hot Springs, Idaho; B.A., Southern Idaho College of Education, 1946; M.S., University of Idaho, 1953; Ed.D., University of Utah, 1961; U.S. Marine Corps Reserve, 1942-1946. Educator; Utah superintendent of public instruction, 1963-1970, commissioner of higher education, 1976-1981; various positions with Office of Education, U.S. Department of Health, Education, and Welfare, including commissioner of education, 1970-1971, 1974-1976; secretary, U.S. Department of Education, 1981-1985; professor, University of Utah, since 1985; author. Bell established the National Commission on Excellence in Education on August 26, 1981, which produced *A Nation at Risk. A Nation at Risk*, 1; *Who's Who in America, 1988-1989*, I, 214.

[4]Martin inserted into his text at this point: "Then and now, some: 'An overreaction.' Some: 'A necessary overreaction.' A crisis requires critical creativity. 'Business as usual' is not an adequate response."

[5]In 1770, Mecklenburg County Presbyterians convinced Governor Tryon to ask the provincial assembly to approve "a public seminary in some part of the back country of this Colony for the education of youth." Lawmakers responded by passing "An Act for founding establishing and endowing of Queen's College in the Town of Charlotte in Mecklenburg County" on January 15, 1771. Lefler and Newsome, *North Carolina*, 145-146; Saunders, *Colonial Records*, VIII, 486-490.

[6]James A. (Dolph) Norton (1922-   ), born in Haynesville, Louisiana; resident of Charlottesville, Virginia; B.A., 1945, M.A., 1946, Louisiana State University; M.A., 1948, Ph.D., 1949, Harvard University; U.S. Army Air Force, 1942-1943. Director, Cleveland Foundation, 1963-1973; chancellor, Ohio Board of Regents, 1973-1978; professor, University of Virginia, 1981-1988; interim president, Hiram College, 1988-1989; interim chancellor, University of Maryland system, since 1989. James A. Norton to Jan-Michael Poff, November 24, 1989. Norton's "Progress Report of the Third Century Project: Postsecondary Education in North Carolina" was published in *North Carolina Association of Colleges and Universities, Proceedings of the Sixty-fifth Annual Conference, November 1, 1985* ([Raleigh: The Association], 1985), 59-64.

[7]Robert Walter Scott (1929-   ), born in Haw River; B.S., North Carolina State College (later University), 1952; U.S. Army, 1953-1955. President, North Carolina Society of Farm Managers and Appraisers; master, North Carolina State Grange, 1961-1963; lieutenant governor, 1965-1969, and governor, 1969-1973, of North Carolina; vice-chairman, Democratic National Committee, 1971-1972; federal chairman, Appalachian Regional

Commission, 1977-1979; president, Scott Enterprises, Inc., and owner, general manager, Melville Farms, since 1979; president, state Department of Community Colleges, since 1983; consultant; lecturer. *North Carolina Manual, 1987-1988*, 1051.

[8]P.L. 89-329, "Higher Education Act of 1965" (short title), *United States Statutes at Large*, Act of November 8, 1965, 79 Stat. 1219-1270, was revised under P.L. 99-498, "Higher Education Amendments of 1986" (short title), *United States Statutes at Large*, Act of October 17, 1986, 100 Stat. 1268-1612.

[9]Harlow Keith Hammond Brodie (1939-   ), born in Stamford, Connecticut; resident of Durham; A.B., Princeton University, 1961; M.D., Columbia University, 1965; honorary degree. Psychiatrist; professor of psychiatry, department chairman, Duke University Medical School, 1974-1982; psychiatrist in chief, Duke University Medical Center, 1974-1982; James B. Duke Professor of Psychiatry and Law, since 1981; chancellor, 1982-1985, and president, since 1985, Duke University; author; editor. *Who's Who in America, 1988-1989*, I, 376. The complete prepared text of Brodie's inaugural address was reprinted in the September 29, 1985, edition of the *Durham Morning Herald*.

[10]Samuel Reid Spencer, Jr. (1919-   ), born in Rock Hill, South Carolina; resident of Richmond, Virginia; A.B., Davidson College, 1940; M.A., 1947, Ph.D., 1951, Harvard University; honorary degrees; U.S. Army, 1940-1945. Assistant to the president, 1951-1954, president, 1968-1983, president emeritus, since 1983, Davidson College; history professor, dean of students, 1955-1957, president, 1957-1968, Mary Baldwin College; president, Virginia Foundation for Independent Colleges, since 1983; author. *Who's Who in America, 1988-1989*, II, 2932.

[11]Samuel R. Spencer, Jr., "Cooperation in a Common Cause: The Public-Private Balance," *North Carolina Association of Colleges and Universities, Proceedings of the Sixty-fourth Annual Conference, November 1 and 2, 1984* ([Raleigh: The Association], 1984), 76.

[12]Phail Wynn, Jr. (1947-   ), born in Wewoka, Oklahoma; B.S., University of Oklahoma, 1969; M.Ed., 1974, Ed.D., 1977, North Carolina State University; U.S. Army, 1969-1975. Assistant to the president, 1977-1979, vice-president, 1979-1980, and chancellor, since 1980, Durham Technical Community College. *North Carolina Manual, 1987-1988*, 1087.

NORTH CAROLINA-JAPAN TRADE CONFERENCE

Raleigh, November 1, 1985

Having just returned from a most productive ten-day visit to Japan, this is a very appropriate occasion for me to bring you a report on the purpose of that mission and its mutual benefits to the state of North Carolina and its most important foreign partner.

First, I want to welcome the Japanese consul general, Mr. Nonoyama, to North Carolina and recognize the diverse North Carolina and Japanese interests which are represented here today. I believe that understanding this diversity is one of the major challenges we face in resolving any differences, either perceived or real, which exist between our two nations. In that respect, the three North Carolina State University centers which conceived and worked very hard to arrange this conference today are promoting and encouraging this understanding. I am referring specifically to the North Carolina Japan Center, under the direction of Dr. John Sylvester, Jr.;[1] the Center for Economic and Business Studies, headed by Dr. Edward Erickson;[2] and the International Trade Center, which is guided by Mr. Charles Shields.

These centers, two of which report to Dean William Toole[3] of the School of Humanities and Social Sciences, have very different missions, but they complement one another and bring to our state a great resource in dealing with issues involving trade and investment on a global scale. Indeed, they have been a major force in promoting closer ties between North Carolina and Japan, strong ties that have resulted in a greater mutual respect and which have contributed greatly to the development of the Research Triangle Park. And I can assure you that this tremendous asset to our state is recognized by Japanese business and industrial leaders as the genuine crown jewel of high technology.

But the huge investment by Japanese companies in our state is not limited to the Research Triangle Park. Many North Carolina areas have benefitted in terms of economic growth and new jobs. We want to continue this worthwhile effort to share growth throughout our state.

I am pleased that during my visit to Japan I had the opportunity to hold discussions with several companies that have expressed an interest in new plant facilities here. This reverse investment in our country, and particularly our part of the nation, was one of the purposes of our recent trade mission. Incidentally, North Carolina, which is one of the seven states involved in the Southeast U.S.-Japan Association, had the largest representation at our annual conference in Tokyo.

Another purpose of the mission was to concentrate on the issue of opening the Japanese markets to our products. I had the opportunity to meet with Prime Minister Nakasone and to discuss with him the concerns we have, and which he has, about this issue. I came away from that meeting with the strong opinion that he is conscientious and sincere in what he is trying to do, and that he is committed to a concept which he has about the essential, close relationship between the United States and Japan.

Even with the resurgence of business activity there, he recognizes that Japan's future depends on a close, evenhanded, and fair relationship with the United States. When one member of our delegation sought to put the burden of trade imbalance on federal policies here in the United States—and a good argument can be made about the impact of fiscal deficits on trade deficits—Prime Minister Nakasone made a very important commentary that his country, as well as ours, has a deficit. He also pointed out that the Japanese deficit would be much larger if Japan had to carry the cost of much of the security expenses the United States is making for the protection of Japan and other Asian nations. He said that he recognizes and appreciates this and understands that he believes that there is a long-term relationship between our two countries that can only be sustained if Japan is ready to open up markets that in the past have been closed.

That was a very important conference, and we gained some useful insights that will help in resolving our trade differences on a national scale. We also must acknowledge that North Carolina does not have a trade deficit with Japan, unlike many other states, and we also have reaped a lion's share in reverse investment. Today, there are thirty-eight Japanese companies with major facilities in North Carolina, and they are quite diversified, manufacturing such items as precision instruments, bicycle brakes, stereo components, ball bearings, lawn-mowers, plastic pipe, amino acids for pharmaceutical use, fiber-optical equipment, and textile machinery. Representatives of three of those investors are with us here today and participated earlier in a panel discussion. They and other companies from Japan have helped North Carolina build a growing economy, and we are indebted to them for their confidence in our state.

Together, Japan and the United States comprise 7.8 percent of the world's population, but produce one third of the world's goods and services.

The Japanese presence in North Carolina enriches our state both culturally and economically. The Japan Center here at North Carolina State University has been a strong public-relations vehicle for North Carolina in Japan. It also now offers a full curriculum in the Japanese language. The departments of political science, history, and economics and business offer courses related to Japan. Recently, Chancellor Poulton[4] concluded an agreement with Nagoya University, which has a world reputation in science, technology, and agriculture; this exchange program will strengthen even greater the ties between our state and the Japanese people.

In fact, higher education in North Carolina has exerted tremendous influence on our relationship, particularly in the Research Triangle Park area. I believe the successes we have enjoyed here can be replicated in many other areas of North Carolina where there is a strong university or college presence. This is one area in which we need to invest our time and talents.

I mentioned early on that Japan and the United States have a diversity of business interests. We must try to understand the players, both political and economic, in these diverse settings. Undoubtedly, we will spend our lifetime working on the real and perceived problems between our two nations. This is a rapidly changing world. There are no constants. The future, a changing environment, is closer now than ever before.

Certainly, we can take justifiable pride in the strong relationship between North Carolina and Japan. More than many states, we have established a sturdy foundation for mutual understanding. It is a foundation upon which we may build both trade and investment.

Let us approach the building process in a positive manner. We have too much to lose on both sides by not working together, seeking a fair and evenhanded approach to the areas in which disagreement exists. We owe that to our generation and those which will be the beneficiaries of legacy.

---

[1]John Sylvester, Jr. (1930-   ), born in Newport, Rhode Island; B.A., Williams College, 1952; B.S. Georgetown University, 1955; fellow, Woodrow Wilson School of Public and International Affairs, Princeton University, 1972-1973; served in U.S. Army during Korean War. Foreign Service officer, U.S. State Department, holding various posts in Japan, 1955-1965, 1973-1976, Washington, D.C., 1965-1968, 1976-1980, and South Vietnam, 1968-1972; director, North Carolina Japan Center, since 1981. John Sylvester, Jr., to Jan-Michael Poff, February 7, 1985, and September 6, 1988.

[2]Edward W. Erickson (1936-   ), born in Warren, Pennsylvania; resident of Raleigh; B.A., Pennsylvania State University, 1959; Ph.D., Vanderbilt University, 1968. Professor of economics and business, 1965-1988, and director, since 1984, Center for Economic and Business Studies, N.C. State University; adjunct professor of public policy, Duke University, 1975; editor; author. Edward W. Erickson to Jan-Michael Poff, August 24, 1988.

[3]William B. Toole III (1930-   ), born in Augusta, Georgia; B.A., Presbyterian College, 1954; M.A., 1955, Ph.D., 1963, Vanderbilt University; U.S. Army, 1948-1949. Taught English at Presbyterian College, 1955-1958, and at Vanderbilt University, 1960-1963; assistant professor, 1963-1966, asssociate professor, 1966-1971, and professor, since 1971, of English, N.C. State University; assistant dean, 1971-1972, associate dean, 1972-1984, and dean, since 1984, School of Humanities and Social Sciences, N.C. State University; author. William B. Toole III to Jan-Michael Poff, August 25, 1988.

[4]Bruce Robert Poulton (1927-   ), born in Yonkers, New York; resident of Raleigh; B.S., 1950, M.A., 1952, Ph.D., 1956, Rutgers University; U.S. Army, 1944-1946. Chairman, Department of Animal and Veterinary Sciences, 1958-1966, and vice-president, 1971-1975, University of Maine; director, University of Maine at Bangor, 1967-1968; dean, College of Life Sciences and Agriculture, and director, Maine Agricultural and Forestry Experiment Station, 1968-1971; executive assistant to James B. Longley, governor of Maine; chancellor, 1975-1982, University System of New Hampshire, and dean, 1977-1982, of its School of Lifelong Learning; chancellor, North Carolina State University, 1982-1989; author. *News and Observer*, August 22, 1989; *North Carolina Manual, 1987-1988*, 987.

NEWSPAPER COLUMN ON COUNCIL OF
MINORITY EXECUTIVES

RALEIGH, NOVEMBER 6, 1985

[Early in his first term as governor, Martin resumed a practice he had begun while a congressman: submitting a monthly newspaper column wherein he discussed government issues. The new series was aimed at small daily and weekly journals that lacked capital city reporters, and although Martin did not personally write the articles, he determined the contents of each. His initial installment, describing the creation and goals of the Governor's Efficiency Study Commission, was transmitted to 160 newspapers. Martin was probably the first of the state's chief executives to employ such a column. *News and Observer*, March 20, 1985.]

To expand and improve this administration's involvement with North Carolina's minority community, I have created the Council of Minority Executives, a twenty-member group of state government employees from many agencies. The idea for the council, first discussed months ago, has grown and matured into what I believe will become a creative and positive vehicle for producing specific results.

Thomas Stith III, minority affairs adviser, will serve as executive director of the council.[1] By working closely with the council, Mr. Stith will be able to translate their ideas into a minority relations program that is more broad based and, we hope, more effective. His involvement with the council also will broaden his duties as minority affairs adviser.

Dr. Lee Monroe, senior education adviser, will serve as the chairman of the council for the first year. Dr. Monroe's background in higher education already has proved valuable in this administration. I believe his expertise will give the council good direction in its first year of existence. The chairmanship will rotate each year, therefore opening the channels of leadership to new experience and direction.

The Council of Minority Executives has both broad and specific goals. On the broad front, we will work in all areas of state government to increase minority participation at the executive level. Specifically, this group will recommend policies for fair recruitment and placement of minorities in salaried and nonsalaried positions in state government. The council's other duties include:

1. Advising the governor on policies that affect minority interests in North Carolina.

2. Acting as an advocate to the governor for the needs, issues, concerns, and problems facing minority people.

3. Developing and monitoring an effective communication system between the governor and minorities.

4. Preparing recommendations to assist minority communities to become more involved in the growth of the state.

5. Arranging meetings to bring the governor together with individuals and groups to promote better understanding of minority problems and concerns.

Membership on the Council of Minority Executives reflects our broad-based concerns. The twenty members come from all agencies in state government. Most hold executive-level jobs and are therefore able to see where we should work hardest to improve our involvement with minorities.

The word *involvement* is tossed around by many people in a very general way. When I refer to minority involvement in North Carolina, I mean we seek specific ways to spur more minority participation in state purchases and contracts, in placing minorities in top-level positions, and in determining the best way to create direct lines of communication with minority communities throughout the state.

This administration also has set another important goal that parallels our efforts with the Council of Minority Executives. We want to ensure that all minorities, women and the disabled as well as blacks and Indians, participate in our state's purchasing and contracts. Our goal is a realistic one—2 percent—but our accomplishments already have surpassed that goal. While the 2 percent figure is not a quota, each cabinet agency is making an effort, through their purchasing agents, to ensure that at least 2 percent of their expenditures goes to minority businesses.

Since the goals program went into effect in July this year, we have surpassed the goal every month. That first month, for example, 5.1 percent of the expenditures of cabinet agencies went to blacks or Indians, women, or the disabled. In August, the percentage increased to 6 percent. During the last month of the quarter the percentage dipped to 4.5 percent, reflecting the traditional end-of-quarter business slump. Based on that positive beginning, I have high hopes for this program. It's time North Carolina stepped boldly toward a serious commitment to bring all minorities into the business of government.

Finally, I think it is worth the space in this column to mention the names of the people who make up the Council of Minority Executives. The membership includes men and women, new appointees, and people who worked in the previous administration. They are listed, below, with their job titles:

Richard Bishop,[2] field office manager, Natural Resources and Community Development; James Bowden,[3] human relations director, Administration; Margot Flood,[4] scheduling director, Governor's Office; James Forte,[5] deputy director, employment/training, Office of Economic Opportunity, Natural Resources and Community Development; Dottie Fuller,[6] personal secretary to the governor; Ed Garner, assistant secretary, Crime Control and Public Safety; Wanda Garrett,[7] Parole Commission; Henry Hayes,[8] social services, Natural Resources and Community Development; Bruce Jones,[9] Indian affairs, Administration; Lafayette Jones, director, Office of Civil Rights, Transportation.

Lewis Myers, assistant secretary, Commerce; Henry McKoy, assistant secretary, Administration; Suni Miller,[10] planning/evaluation chief, Natural Resources and Community Development; Vicki Ransom,[11] administrative assistant to the secretary, Human Resources; Nellie Riley,[12] personnel, Administration; James Ross, director, Natural Resources and Community Development; Claudia Simpson,[13] administrative assistant, Corrections; Leon Stanback,[14] Parole Commission; Chrystal Stowe,[15] public information officer, Crime Control and Public Safety; and Sylvania Wilkerson, assistant secretary, Transportation.

The talent and experience these professionals bring to the Council of Minority Executives give me confidence that we will find innovative ways for minority involvement. With the very real economic support of our minority goals program, this administration is moving swiftly and strongly toward a mutual investment in the future of minorities in North Carolina.

---

[1]Thomas A. Stith III (1963-   ), native, resident of Durham; B.B.A., 1983, M.B.A., 1988, North Carolina Central University. Special assistant to Governor Martin, 1985; governor's project director, 1986-1987; marketing representative, IBM Corp., since 1987. Thomas A. Stith III to Jan-Michael Poff, October 8, 1988.

[2]Richard Bishop was director of the Fayetteville Regional Office, N.C. Department of Natural Resources and Community Development.

[3]James W. Bowden was replaced by James L. Stowe as director, N.C. Human Relations Council, in September, 1987. Before Governor Hunt appointed him to head the council in 1979, Bowden had served as assistant director of the Charlotte-Mecklenburg Community Relations Committee and as Goldsboro community affairs director. After leaving the Human Relations Council, Bowden became director of the Youth Services Facility, C. A. Dillon School, Butner. *News and Observer*, September 23, 1987.

[4]Margot M. Flood (1943-   ), born in Washington, D.C.; resident of Durham; B.A., University of Pittsburgh, 1980. Congressional caseworker for U.S. representative James G. Martin, 1972-1976; director, informal education, YWCA, Pittsburgh, 1980-1982; office services coordinator, RSI, Inc., Atlanta, 1983-1985; director of scheduling for Governor Martin since 1985. Margot M. Flood to Jan-Michael Poff, October 6, 1988.

[5]James L. Forte (1950-   ), born at Fort Bragg; resident of Raleigh; B.S., Fayetteville State University, 1973. Deputy director, 1985-1986, appointed director, effective August 1, 1986, Division of Economic Opportunity, Department of Natural Resources and Community Development. James L. Forte to Jan-Michael Poff, October 10, 1988.

[6]Doris (Dottie) Fuller (1943-   ), born in Tucson, Arizona; resident of Raleigh; was graduated from Temple School, 1960, and Bell School for Machine Shorthand, 1964. Accounts billing clerk, U.S. Commerce Department, 1960-1961; various secretarial positions, administrative assistant to John Penello, National Labor Relations Board, 1961-1974; tutor, Learning Development Foundation of Charlotte, 1975; congressional caseworker for U.S. representative James G. Martin, 1976-1978; committee clerk, secretary, for state representative Henry E. Frye, 1979; office manager, legal secretary, Thigpen, Blue, and Stephens law firm, Raleigh, 1979-1985; personal secretary to Governor Martin since 1985. Doris Fuller to Jan-Michael Poff, October 11, 1988.

[7]Wanda Jones Garrett; born in Detroit, Michigan; resident of Durham; B.A., University of Arkansas at Pine Bluff, 1953; M.A., University of North Carolina at Chapel Hill, 1977; J.D., North Carolina Central University, 1986. Instructor, Barbour Junior High School, Detroit, 1955-1962, and at Hillside High School, Durham, 1963-1966; instructor, 1967-1969, and visiting lecturer, 1976-1984, N.C. Central University; producer/hostess, "Black Unlimited" television series, WTVD-TV, Durham, 1971-1979; commissioner, state Parole Commission, since 1985. Wanda Jones Garrett to Jan-Michael Poff, February 17, 1989.

[8]Henry Clifton Hayes (1942-   ), born in Bronx, New York; resident of Warrenton; B.A., North Carolina Central University; was also educated at Vance-Granville Community College; U.S. Army, 1964-1967. Caseworker, New York City Department of Public Welfare, 1968-1970; social worker, Durham County Department of Social Services, 1972-1977; director, Durham County Food Stamp Program, 1977-1985; assistant director, Division of Social Services, state Department of Human Resources, 1985-1987; director, Warren County Department of Social Services, since 1987; member, Governor's Council of Minority Executives, 1985-1987. Henry Clifton Hayes to Jan-Michael Poff, October 19, 1988.

[9]A. Bruce Jones (1929-   ), born in Buffalo, New York; resident of Raleigh; B.S., Pembroke State University, 1957; M.A., George Peabody College, 1964; U.S. Army, 1949-1952. Teacher, principal, Robeson County schools, 1957-1965; project field supervisor, 1965-1966, project director, 1966-1968, N.C. Fund Manpower Program; assistant operations director, 1968-1969, operations director, 1969-1973, N.C. Manpower Development Corp.; owner, operator, Western Auto Store, Hillsborough, 1973-1975; executive director, state Commission of Indian Affairs, since 1976. A. Bruce Jones to Jan-Michael Poff, October 11, 1988.

[10]Suni Miller served as research and information supervisor, 1985-1986, with the Division of Economic Opportunity, Department of Natural Resources and Community Development.

[11]Vicki Ransom (1952-   ), born in Fayetteville; resident of Raleigh; B.A., Pembroke State University, 1973. Program analyst, Governor's Committee on Law and Order, 1973-1975; executive director, Keep America Beautiful, Charlotte, 1975-1978; county manager, Agricultural Stabilization and Conservation Service, Montgomery County, 1978-1982; program consultant, Office of Volunteer Services, state Department of Human Resources, since 1986. Vicki Ransom to Jan-Michael Poff, October 18, 1988.

[12]Nellie Jones Riley (1943-   ), born in Guilford County; resident of Durham; B.S., 1966, M.S., 1974, North Carolina A&T State University; M.B.A., Wake Forest University, 1979. Director, Guilford County Neighborhood Youth Corps, 1967-1974; special manpower program director, Employment Security Commission, Greensboro, 1974-1975; Head Start director, N.C. Training Office, University of North Carolina at Greensboro, 1975-1976; volunteer services coordinator, state Economic Opportunity Office, Raleigh, 1977; director, Winston-Salem Human Services Department, 1977-1979; director, Office of Welfare Reform, Department of Natural Resources and Community Development, 1979-1981; state equal employment opportunity/affirmative action director, Office of State Personnel, since 1981. Nellie Jones Riley to Jan-Michael Poff, October 28, 1988.

[13]Claudia T. Simpson (1929-   ), born in Selma; resident of Fayetteville; B.S., North Carolina A&T State University, 1955; teaching certificate from Shaw University, 1959. Business teacher, Robert Smalls High School, Beaufort, South Carolina, 1955-1957; clerical worker, Johnston County Training School, Smithfield, 1957; teacher in Wilson, 1959-1960, Selma, 1960-1965, Princeton, 1965-1966, Smithfield, 1966-1967, and Fayetteville, 1967-1985, elementary schools; administrative assistant, Office of the Secretary, Department of Correction, since February, 1985. Claudia T. Simpson to Jan-Michael Poff, October 19, 1988.

[14]A. Leon Stanback, Jr.; resident of Greensboro; B.S., 1965, J.D., 1968, North Carolina Central University. Attorney in private practice, 1968-1969, and since 1971; Guilford County assistant district attorney, 1969-1971; commissioner, state Parole Commission, since 1985; president, Guilford County Assn. of Black Lawyers; author. A. Leon Stanback, Jr., to Jan-Michael Poff, October 21, 1988.

[15]Chrystal Harris Stowe (1956-   ), born in Greenville, South Carolina; resident of Raleigh; was educated at University of South Carolina, 1974-1977, and at North Carolina State University. Reporter, photographer, WLTX-TV, 1975-1977, and at WIS-TV, 1977-1980, both in Columbia, South Carolina; reporter, morning news anchor, WRAL-TV, Raleigh, 1980-1982; news anchor, reporter, WBTV, Charlotte, 1983-1985; public information director, Department of Crime Control and Public Safety, 1985-1987, and for North Carolina Low-Level Radioactive Waste Management Authority, since 1988; special assistant for policy and planning, Office of the Governor, 1987-1988. Chrystal Harris Stowe to Jan-Michael Poff, October 20, 1988.

SOUTHERN LEGISLATORS' CONFERENCE ON CHILDREN AND YOUTH

ASHEVILLE, NOVEMBER 11, 1985

Southern legislators and leaders, I am pleased that you have afforded me this opportunity to meet with you, today, and share my thoughts about the opportunities southern leaders have for improving the lives of our southern families. As governor of North Carolina, I welcome you, and as co-host of one seventh of this conference, I wish you success this week as you examine ways to enhance your ability to solve many of the problems confronting our children and youth. I want to commend Lieutenant Governor and Mrs. Jordan,[1] Senator Hipps, Secretary Dean, and others who have helped set our sights in serving the needs of children. In North Carolina, in contrast to some natural differences on other issues, this administration and General Assembly have collaborated productively on children's issues. This bipartisan cooperation led to a Missing Children's Center, anti-pornography laws, and initiatives against exploitation, as we made 1985: "Year of the Child"—and [I] was pleased to present [a] proclamation recognizing. . . .[2] Through this conference, we hope to shape next year's efforts.

The South of today is no longer just the "new" South. It is the South of the future, a South teeming with unbridled energy, growing diversity, and bountiful resources. Our task, then, is to shape this future to the hopes and aspirations of our young people and their successor generations. We must also promote and reinforce among them a respect for traditional family values, so that in their generation the normal healthy challenges to those values will not threaten them. The South of the future rests upon our collective and individual abilities to retain our proud heritage and moral strengths and to reinforce them with our own respect for their worth.

Without caring parents and supportive institutions and public officials, our young people would inherit a bleak tomorrow. But this will not be our legacy, for we are pioneers with a strong sense of purpose and direction. We can take comfort, perhaps, in the fact that we are not the first to face the challenge and uncertainty of the future; a good illustration is the Lewis and Clark expedition of 1804 and 1805.

Lewis and Clark were directed by President Thomas Jefferson to explore the almost completely uncharted west of that time, from St. Louis to the Oregon coast. Consider their challenge: some 3,500 miles of raw territory, some never seen by white men, the rest only by a few trappers and traders; a dozen or more large Indian tribes along the way, each with its own culture and language, each with its own attitude toward intruders; climate changes ranged from deserts, to plains, to high mountains—much of it unanticipated, all of it to be traversed. Lewis and Clark were called upon to manage a project whose ingredients, hazards, time frame, and ultimate end were all very uncertain, and, as you recall, they were triumphantly successful—so much so that the men and their mission have become legends in our pioneer culture.

Four major elements contributed to their success: 1) a long-term single-mindedness of purpose, as determined by a wise president; 2) flexibility; 3) a wealth of knowledge and experience to guide them; and 4) strengths they could build upon. We, too, must master these qualities in solving the problems of our children and youth. How often, for example, I have reflected upon the difficulty my older generation has had in trying to cope with problems of our children which we had not experienced in our youth: hard drug problems, for example. And yet, like Lewis and Clark, we must help find a safe passage for them.

While each of us has a role, I still believe that it is within our families that our young people best learn the moral values which are the foundation of a rewarding and useful life. These values must be reinforced by our schools, churches, and other institutions, but the bedrock of the South has been, remains, and always will be the family.

Many of our families are confronted by a crisis today. It is not a crisis that commands front-page attention; it is an insipient, cancerous crisis that gives few danger signals until there is little chance of recovery. You heard about some of these danger signals during this morning's session—the rising tide of alcohol and substance abuse, the feminization of poverty, increasing child abuse and exploitation, and the growing number of single-parent households—the list seems endless. But the dangers to our children and youth are very real; in fact, they are frightening.

This morning's news reports on a NIMH study, finding that in contrast with a 9 percent rise in child abuse overall, nationally, it was seen to be down 41 percent among two-parent families. Generalizing from a survey of 714 couples it estimated "only" 1 million children were kicked, or otherwise seriously abused, versus 1.7 million ten years ago. The experts attributed this to greater public education and awareness. Or was it just that only 2 percent, or fourteen couples out of 714 questioned, would admit to it— perhaps that was the result of public awareness.[3]

I have asked my wife, Dottie, to chair a commission to examine child victimization in our state. Their six hearings, so far, have provided a timely forum for determining the nature and extent of the problem and what might be done about it. It is not a single issue, but diverse. Relying mostly on news and public service announcements, they have repeatedly had overflow crowds. The commission has found an increase in reported cases of child abuse—reported by witnesses, neighbors, teachers, relatives, and victims who have had enough and are responding to the new opportunity to speak up to law officers, the courts, and to caseworkers.

The new 800 number at the Missing Children's Center has already received reports on twenty-eight cases.

They [commission members] heard of experiments in an urban school system to assign a friendly police officer to each high school, with an office, as part of the local beat, which appears to be well received by students tired of being victimized by schoolmates. They repeatedly heard urgent calls for a court procedure that would allow victimized children to be able to offer testimony by videotape, or closed circuit, or some way more suitable to children, so that they not be intimidated by courtroom tactics or victimized again in the one place that should be their sanctuary of the courts. They acknowledge the constitutional right to confront one's accusers, but some way must be found to provide that confrontation without it being so confrontational. Children as victims/witnesses are still children. To require them to be adults in the aftermath of severe abuse by adults is not justice for them. Can our best legal minds not solve this?

In China, the word *crisis* is made from two words, *danger* and *opportunity*. If we only see the danger in crisis, our options for responding in a positive way are limited. We must take the opposite view. We must consider opportunities and respond to each crisis.

As governor, I have asked for and received many letters from schoolchildren and young people, which provide a backdrop for the commission. Let me share some of their thoughts as they have expressed them to me:

—From a classroom of children who have been chronically truant or frequently suspended, I have learned that they want their school to provide "a safe and secure environment," with rules that are clear and fair. In class, these students have developed their own set of classroom rules which they enforce themselves. They see school as a place which should have fair treatment and instruction which is relevant and exciting. By the way, they told me that after an initially negative reaction and ridicule toward a group of retarded youths who meet in the same building, they have quickly developed a sense of responsibility toward those who need their support. Now their own families claim that their behavior at home is more positive, and they've only had five unexcused absences, to date. That's from some previously probable dropouts who had never really dropped in before.

—Then, from a senior-high law and justice classroom, students offer additional thoughts about their educational setting. They are concerned about the trend toward less discipline in our schools. Even as we think we are beginning to increase it, they say their teachers' authority is undermined when it ought to be reinforced.

These students offer insight into the institutions of home and community, as well. They believe that the family structure, which has always been the fountainhead of southern progress, is diminishing, being eroded by a rising divorce rate, conflicts in parental careers, social permissiveness, R-rated television, and the absence of discipline in the home. That is the troubling example our generation has offered to theirs. These young people fear that parents, as well as others, are permitting laws and regulations and services of government to replace the parental judgments and responsibilities which have worked for generations. They also believe that local health services should have the resources for research and prevention of social diseases.

—And then, from a class of seventh-grade students, I discovered that many students basically are happy with their homes, schools, and communities. It is noteworthy that they look upon alcohol and drug abuse as their greatest menace, from their seventh-grade vantage point.

As southern leaders, we face the challenge of heeding this advice, for their concerns are problems about which we already are painfully aware. Resolving these problems will require us to strike a balance among legislation, programming, and support of our children and families, a balance which will equip them with an environment for accomplishment without robbing them of their individual decision-making responsibilities.

As parents, we must encourage success rather than failure. Every child has the right to feel secure at home, in school, and in the community, and our parents must never fear to discipline through love and care for their children.

Our challenge lies in translating concern into action. We must begin with ourselves and with our own families. We must model the behavior we expect of others.

Our approaches and opinions may differ at times, but we must be united in our concern for children and youth and for our investment in their future. All public services must be directed toward providing quality lives for our children and families in need. We must recruit and keep service providers who care deeply about both, and we, too, must be caring and involved leaders.

Resources, both human and financial, are too limited to continue doing business as usual. Evaluating the effectiveness of present delivery systems will help utilize these resources to greater advantage. In order to make appropriate changes, we must know what is working and what is not working. Then, new programs can be established in place of those that show no evidence of working—not just be piled on top of them. The test is not how much money we spend, but how we spend it.

An important partner in serving our southern families is the private sector. Our industries have been major contributors to the South's progress. Too often we fail to acknowledge their contributions and seek their continued support. They, too, are part of our team.

This conference provides an excellent opportunity to examine our effectiveness as regional leaders. Let us take advantage of the ideas that flow from our group discussions. Let us learn from our sister states.

As we talk about opportunities for serving our children and youth, I am reminded of a sign in front of a church. It read, "There is no heavier burden than a great opportunity." My hope for all of us, as southern leaders, is that we will feel this burden so intensely that our resolve to strengthen our families will be consuming. My hope is that we will shoulder the burden and reap the many opportunities we have to work together, with a strong sense of unity, for the day when no child and no family will be in crisis.

At no time in our history have we needed pioneers more desperately—leaders with a vision of the family's role in the fabric of our society, leaders with a sense of direction. We must not doubt our ability to turn crisis into opportunity. We must always remember:

> Doubt sees the obstacles, faith sees the way;
> Doubt sees the dark of night, faith sees the day;
> Doubt fails to take a step, while faith soars on high;
> Doubt questions "Who believes?", faith answers "I."

The future of the South, and the hopes and aspirations of our young people, depend in large measure upon our faith in them and in ourselves.

---

[1]Sarah Cole Jordan; born in Raeford; resident of Mount Gilead; A.B., University of North Carolina at Greensboro. Teacher, Charlotte City and Montgomery County schools; vice-chairwoman, Montgomery County Democratic Party, 1964-1970; member, numerous organizations, boards, and commissions, including Early Childhood Education Legislative Study Commission, Legislative Study Commission on Child Abuse Testimony and Child Protection, and Children's Mental Health Subcommittee of the Mental Health Study Commission; was married to Robert B. Jordan III, 1958. Ed Turlington, executive assistant to Lieutenant Governor Robert B. Jordan III, to Jan-Michael Poff, August 31, 1988; *North Carolina Manual, 1987-1988*, 567.

[2]The governor's notes, beginning with "I want to commend Lieutenant Governor and Mrs. Jordan," and ending with "recognizing," are incomplete. Anti-pornography and anti-exploitation measures the General Assembly adopted in 1985 included "An Act to Amend G.S. 7A-517 to Prohibit Sexual Exploitation of Children," c. 648, ratified July 8, 1985; "An Act to Strengthen the Obscenity Laws of This State and the Enforcement of These Laws, to Protect Minors from Harmful Material that Does Not Rise to the Level of Obscenity, and to Stop the Sexual Exploitation and Prostitution of Minors," c. 703, ratified July 11; and "An Act to Amend Certain Obscenity Statutes," c. 731, ratified July 12, 1985. *N.C. Session Laws, 1985*.

[3]Martin was commenting on a Louis Harris and Associates poll sponsored by the National Institute of Mental Health. *New York Times*, November 11, 1985.

NORTH CAROLINA LEAGUE OF MUNICIPALITIES

Raleigh, November 12, 1985

I am very pleased to join you, today, as you continue your annual convention and the discussion of its theme, "Governing and Managing in Challenging Times." These are, indeed, challenging times for our nation, the South, our state, and our local governments. Well, North Carolinians have faced many a time that was challenging! We have become a great state, and a mighty nation, because of the ability of our people and leaders to accept challenges as windows of opportunity for growth, and progress, and for the betterment of this and future generations.

"The prosperity of our nation and its people depends directly on the energy and intelligence of its leaders." That sentence should sound familiar to everyone in this convention center. The words are not mine; they were spoken by President Theodore Roosevelt at the beginning of this century, and they are equally meaningful in 1985.

Roosevelt, as we all know from our study of history, was a brand new kind of president. He was a doer. He was not afraid to make important decisions, and he also stood up and took full responsibility for each of his decisions. I must tell you I consider this trait the exemplary way for a public official who is elected to serve to fulfill his or her responsibility.

Roosevelt also is known for another quote. This is what he said with respect to the courage of initiative, which is really the most important responsibility of every public servant, whether elected, or appointed, or from whatever discipline. He said, "It is far better to dare mighty things, to win glorious triumphs even though checkered with failures, than to take rank with those spirits who neither enjoy much nor suffer much, for they live in the gray twilight that knows neither victory nor defeat."[1] That is the essence, in my opinion, of the personality as well as the legacy of a great leader.

Much of the leadership in North Carolina has come from the ranks of its municipal officials. Our test at this point in history is to continue to provide a solid base of local leadership in partnership with officials of state government.

After the War between the States, when life was bleak, the future dim, and all things in the South were torn apart, North Carolina was the first to rally its leadership. Governors Russell[2] and Aycock put our faith in education, and it has been there ever since. That faith has been well rewarded, for it enabled North Carolina to build back from the ashes of war to new and greater opportunities.

Never before have our opportunities been as great as they are today. Economic development in North Carolina is continuing at a strong and healthy pace. We are rebuilding our traditional industries at the same time we encourage new investment in high tech, low tech, and everything in between. Thanks to unusually strong expansion as well as new investment, the first six months recorded an exceptionally high level of investment in new jobs, much of it due to expansions of existing businesses. We don't claim all the credit, but we're pleased with the results.

In government, we are in a period of transition. Many years ago, roads in North Carolina were designed, built, and maintained by decisions rendered by county governing bodies. The responsibilities of meeting the needs of our elderly were met by the operation of a county home, or a "poor house," as it was called in many areas. The schools, although they might have received a little encouragement money from state government, were built and the teachers paid by local governments, which also established educational standards. Law enforcement was provided exclusively by cities, counties, and towns—local police and sheriffs.

But that was yesteryear. Now there's a partnership. When Adam and Eve were being banished from the Garden of Eden, Adam turned to Eve and said, "My dear, we are living in a period of transition." And so it is.

Changes, not in government but in conditions, led us into a new era. The need for transportation facilities, the necessity of multi-county planning, and the advent of modern machinery combined to shift many road decisions from courthouses to the state capital, or at least to state divisional offices. The Depression demonstrated that the areas in which people needed financial help most were the areas least able to provide it. This moved other decisions to the statehouse and the nation's capitol. So, change brought change and will continue to bring more change.

There were some valid reasons for shifts toward more centralization and away from local decisions, but years ago, in too many places, it was a matter of abdication. All across our country, as a matter of fact, local leaders got tired of leading. In recent years, however, we have witnessed a reversal of this trend. As the federal government attempts to reduce a growing deficit—which it thus far has failed to do—funds to local and state governments are being reduced and decision-making is being returned to states, counties, and municipalities. Local governments have modernized and welcome the responsibility.

This change demands that we demonstrate our competence and our willingness to handle the legitimate needs of the people. We can demonstrate this competence and willingness only if we recognize that the state and local governments have a shared responsibility. We can't return to the old ways and blame each other when the needs of our citizens are not met. We must work together, closer than ever before; in our discussion of challenges, I believe this is the greatest challenge facing us today. I am pleased that, within the last eleven months, we have taken some significant steps in this direction.

Some of our urban centers have joined the state in meeting the critical need for funding of urban highways, to get the right-of-way early. We need more cities and counties to share in the cost of meeting these needs arising from dynamic growth and economic development. It is because of that growth and development that our urban areas are approaching a transportation crisis. Their highway uses have exceeded the capacity of our construction schedules, because the Highway Fund is flat. It cannot grow when gasoline consumption per mile is declining.

A current assessment by the Department of Transportation reveals immediate urban transportation needs totaling $2.7 billion. All of this comes at a time of rising costs and stagnant revenues from the Highway Fund. At the rate we're going, it will take us sixty years to meet those needs. Two conclusions are obvious: The first is that traditional thinking and funding methods will not keep pace with massive demands; the second is that we must work together to meet these needs.

The point I am making here is that there is necessarily a statewide and a local interest in most of our responsibilities. This makes continuous cooperation necessary and beneficial to both; but to make it successful, cooperation must be given in the spirit of fairness and in an attempt to harmonize the statewide interest with local administration to achieve efficiency.

Another way in which this administration is fostering cooperation between the state and its municipalities is through the Local Government Advocacy Council. As many of you know, the council was incorporated into general law in 1979. Its functions include serving as an advocate of local government and as an adviser to the governor and his cabinet on policies and programs affecting local government. The council also functions as liaison between local governments and state agencies, and it seeks to identify problem areas and recommend policies with respect to state, regional, and local relations.[3]

Recently, I met with the council, which includes representatives of our municipalities, and reaffirmed my commitment to building a stronger relationship between local governments and the state. To demonstrate the sincerity of this commitment, I have appointed my executive assistant and staff director, Jim Lofton, as my liaison to the council. Moreover, I have opened meetings of state agencies to the public, including the Council of State and Advisory Budget Commission, and my cabinet secretaries have been directed to work closely with our cities and counties whenever changes are contemplated which bear directly on local affairs. This is an administration with an open-door policy, and I fully intend to keep it that way.

I believe, further, that it is the governor's responsibility to foster the interests of local governments when these interests serve the people of the state as a whole. You may recall that, last July, I took the lead and testified before the Subcommittee on Labor, of the U.S. Senate Committee on Labor and Human Resources, concerning the Supreme Court's so-called *Garcia* decision. The ruling of the court in this case would have required state and local governments to pay employees for overtime work rather than give compensatory time. I am pleased with the congressional compromise which was reached last Thursday. This compromise stipulates that compensatory time, not exclusively overtime payments, may be used to compensate government employees for overtime hours worked. In addition, the law establishes a formula designed to prevent local governments from allowing employees to build up excessive overtime hours.

The final decision worked out by the House-Senate conference committee will save North Carolina more than $15 million in overtime payments in the current fiscal year. The decision restores the flexibility all units of government need to provide essential public services by allowing state and local governments, once again, to use compensatory time in lieu of overtime payments. This is a decisive victory for North Carolina, and other states, which faced a grave and costly dilemma if it had been given no option but overtime pay. I am pleased to say that the president is expected to sign this legislation tomorrow, and I intend to be there on your behalf and for the National Governors' Association.

As I mentioned earlier, all of you are painfully aware of reductions in federal block grant programs. It is expected that federal revenue sharing will be discontinued after this year.[4] Another major area in which these funds have been reduced is water and waste-water treatment financing. In the 1970s, North Carolina received more than $80 million annually. Now our state receives only $44 million per year, and the 75 percent federal grant has been reduced to 55 percent of the cost of existing needs. A pending amendment could reduce the state's allocation to $38 million annually. The needs survey, which was completed in 1984 by the Department of Natural Resources and Community Development, placed current waste-water treatment needs at $1 billion.[5] By the year 2000, the needs will be even greater.

In addition to federal funding, the General Assembly this year agreed to my recommendation and appropriated $60 million annually, during the biennium, for water and waste-water treatment facilities. The state allocation includes $39 million for waste-water treatment, with the remaining $21 million designated for potable water facilities.[6]

The impact on local governments is tremendous. There currently are 120 communities throughout North Carolina on the moratorium list. This means that unless they improve treatment facilities, these communities cannot permit further growth and development.

We want to, and we must, use these funds wisely. At the present time, the Department of Natural Resources and Community Development is developing a financing system designed to provide equitable long-term funding and cost-sharing arrangements with local governments. Within the near future, representatives of the department will be approaching the league to discuss various funding alternatives. Our goal is to make the best possible use of the funds to provide a sound infrastructure which is so essential to the continued economic growth and development of our municipalities.

Another source of funds for community and economic development is the Community Development Block Grant program. In the past, there have been problems with a fair distribution of these funds. We appointed a community development block grant task force of local officials to study the distribution formula, and it has just recently completed its work.[7]

The task force found that there were biases built into the rating system that caused the distribution of funds to be tilted to certain areas of the state. These biases have been identified and removed, the application has been simplified and streamlined, and an intensive outreach/technical assistance program is planned. These actions will result in equal access to community development funds, as well as provide a more equitable distribution.

Community development block grants are used for neighborhood revitalization and for loans to businesses and industries which create jobs for low-and moderate-income persons. Community revitalization projects are important to municipalities in terms of meeting infrastructure needs. Equally, the economic development projects are vital to businesses and industries which expand employment opportunities for the citizens of our communities.

In terms of local technical assistance, North Carolina is extremely proud of the assistance it provides in land use planning and management—an important tool in preparing for growth. Eighty percent of the municipalities in our state have a population of less than 5,000 citizens; because they are not as large as our cities, they do not have staff and expertise required to prepare studies, plans, ordinances, and other instruments necessary for orderly growth and development. Currently, the state is providing a total of $1.2 million annually to local governments for these purposes.

Another essential economic development program provided by North Carolina is the Main Street program for downtown revitalizations. North Carolina is one of five states chosen for a pilot program in conjunction with the National Trust for Historical Preservation. We now have fifteen cities in this program, and five additional communities will be added in the spring of 1986. The program provides free design work, training, and technical assistance to selected municipalities with a population under 50,000.

I believe responsible municipal government, carried out close to the people served, should be and can be responsive government. It can, and must, be productive, but it can be responsive and productive only when it is exercised in partnership with state government. As the new report by the Local Governmment Advocacy Council points out clearly, we have a shared responsibility.[8] All of us occupy positions of leadership. We were elected to lead, not simply to preside over government, and we must lead together.

The future potential of our state and our municipalities will continue to flourish so long as we remember that progress is built on teamwork. Like a stone wall, built by adding stone on stone, public confidence is won or lost by our commitment to unity.

Progress follows strong leadership. If our mission is vigorously the mission of the people, then we will turn challenges into opportunities, and these opportunities will carry us forward into the future of a stronger and better state built on the foundation of shared responsibility with our cities and towns.

---

[1]"Far better is it to dare mighty things, to win glorious triumphs, even though checkered by failure, than to take rank with those poor spirits who neither enjoy much

nor suffer much, because they live in the gray twilight that knows not victory nor defeat." Theodore Roosevelt, speech before the Hamilton Club, Chicago, April 10, 1899, quoted in Bartlett, *Familiar Quotations*, 847.

[2]Daniel Lindsay Russell, Jr. (1845-1908), native of Brunswick County; was educated at University of North Carolina; served in Confederate army. Attorney; member, state House of Commons, 1864-1866, and of state House of Representatives, 1876-1877; superior court judge, Fourth Judicial Circuit, 1868-1874; Greenbacker member, U.S. House of Representatives, 1879-1881; governor of North Carolina, 1897-1901; Republican. Cheney, *North Carolina Government*, 331, 333, 423, 457; Jeffrey J. Crow and Robert F. Durden, *Maverick Republican in the Old North State: A Political Biography of Daniel L. Russell* (Baton Rouge: Louisiana State University Press, 1977), 2-3, 9, 21, 32, 34-41, 52-74, 187.

[3]Governor Hunt originally established the North Carolina Local Government Advocacy Council under Executive Order Number 22, signed April 21, 1978. *N.C. Session Laws, 1977, Second Session, 1978,* 269-270. "An Act to Establish the North Carolina Balanced Growth Policy," *N.C. Session Laws, 1979,* c. 412, s. 9, ratified April 19, 1979, provided a statutory foundation for the office.

[4]At this point in his text, Martin penned observations on possible state and local responses to cancellation of the federal revenue sharing program: "For you: revenue; for fed[eral government]: debt. Should that happen: 3 options. 1) Halt capital projects (including schools); 2) Raise property taxes; 3) Raise sales tax one half cent, give local option—not 8 cents, just one half cent so you aren't forced to raise property tax." P.L. 99-272, the "Consolidated Omnibus Budget Reconciliation Act of 1985" (short title), repealed federal general revenue sharing. *United States Statutes at Large,* Act of April 7, 1986, 100 Stat. 327-329.

[5]The EPA and all fifty states collaborated on the survey to which the governor referred. See United States Environmental Protection Agency Office of Municipal Pollution Control, and Roy F. Weston, Inc., *1984 Needs Survey Report to Congress: Assessment of Publicly Owned Wastewater Treatment Facilities in the United States* (Washington, D.C.: United States Government Printing Office, 1985), 1. The Department of Natural Resources and Community Development supplied the figures on North Carolina that Martin cited; see page A-7 of the report. Dan Blaisdell, Department of Environement, Health, and Natural Resources, to Jan-Michael Poff, October 23, 1989.

[6]See "An Act to Make Appropriations to Provide Capital Improvements for State Departments, Institutions, and Agencies," *N.C. Session Laws, 1985,* c. 480, secs. 4, 5.12, ratified June 27, effective July 1, 1985.

[7]S. Thomas Rhodes, secretary of natural resources and community development, appointed the fifteen-member Community Development Block Grant Advisory Task Force in July, 1985. For its findings and recommendations, see *North Carolina Small Cities Community Development Block Grants: Advisory Task Force Final Report* ([Raleigh: Division of Community Assistance, Department of Commerce], September, 1985).

[8]The governor likely was referring to the study, *North Carolina Small Cities Community Development Block Grants,* cited above. Sara Y. Stuckey, Office of Intergovernmental Relations, Department of Administration, to Jan-Michael Poff, October 19, 1989.

NORTH CAROLINA SCHOOL BOARDS ASSOCIATION

High Point, November 15, 1985

[The governor's twenty-point plan for improving the state's public education system formed the basis of his address, below, before the state School Boards Association. The program was also discussed in Twenty Proposals Recommended by Governor James G. Martin to the North Carolina School Board Association (n.d.); Governor Martin's Proposed Educational Program for Elementary and Secondary Education, November 15, 1985, prepared by adviser Gene S. Baker; Improving the Teaching Profession, the speaking points and handout for his meeting with State Board of Education members, January 15, 1986; and in remarks before the Shelby Chamber of Commerce, January 23, the North Carolina Association of Educators' Winter Conference, January 24, the Mt. Airy Chamber of Commerce, February 3, and the Joint Meeting of the State Goals and Policy Board and the North Carolina Education Council, February 5, 1986.]

This year, 1985, commemorates 100 years of service by local boards of education to the advancement of North Carolina and to the development of our elementary and secondary school system. I am deeply honored to have this opportunity to address you at this centennial rededication to the excellence of that system.

Just two and a half years ago, the secretary of education's National Commission on Excellence in Education proclaimed that we were "a nation at risk, threatened by the rising tide of mediocrity." Following the Bell commission report came no less than thirty-six others, sponsored by national educational bodies both great and small, each with its own version of problems in public education.

A number of prescriptions have been offered to cure the ills of education since these reports became public. They have included harder course work, better pay for better teachers, more homework, a longer school day, the elimination of frills, and getting back to basics—to mention only a few. In fact, teachers and staff are so overloaded with changes on top of changes right now that no one should lightly pile on more changes. So, I will offer only a few well-chosen emphases and innovations today.

We did begin to get some good news in 1984 and again in 1985: that SAT scores had stopped declining—in fact, they were up slightly— and that high school students were studying more academic courses and doing better in many other ways. Had we indeed turned the corner? Or is this just what educators call cognitive dissonance? It's like the little boy who went to summer camp and after the first week wrote home to say, "The food is awful, and besides, the helpings are too small."

This leads me to three important introductory points:

First, education did then, and does now, need improvement and revitalization in North Carolina if it is to measure up to the needs of our state. However, the turnaround, however slight, has begun—on the intiative of educators who welcome the recent attention given to the need for providing a quality education. The ground is fertile for additional effort, and the prospects for lasting results are good.

Now, on to my second point. The good news, the signs of improvement, must not lull us into a complacency about the issue of educational quality. The reform movement is now at its most critical stage.

And third, private enterprise and the professions have a major stake in the turnaround because it is cheaper to do the job right the first time and because the students involved will become their future employees, customers, and fellow taxpayers. We still have too many dropouts; too many students who are achieving at levels below their capacities for learning; and too many remedial courses in our colleges, and universities, and factories to make up for what students did not learn in our elementary and secondary schools.

Clearly, North Carolina cannot continue on this course. We have made a substantial beginning in educational reform, and we must continue to build on this momentum and commitment to quality. We must also recognize that with so much change crowding on top of change in the system already, overloading teachers and staff trying to cope with all the redirection, no one should casually try to rewrite the whole thing again and pile on dozens of more changes. Leadership does not require that; it does require a clear message on our greatest priorities: where we are and where we must go.

I believe that North Carolina must focus on three major challenges; you will note that I am using groups of threes today—triads:

1. Improving the teaching profession;

2. Improving the curriculum, instruction, and the development of basic skills; and finally

3. Accountability, that important measure by which we judge the success of our schools and the education of our students.

In support of objective number one, that we need to improve the teaching profession, consider the following facts: Interest in the teaching profession as a career is waning. Each year there are fewer college and university graduates majoring in education. In North Carolina, two thirds of the teachers who scored in the top 10 percent of the National Teachers' Exam left teaching within seven years. Our own teachers told an NCAE survey that they, the teachers, are not promoting teaching as a career for others.

We must win back their confidence. We must demand higher standards for our teachers, and we must pay them competitive salaries. Strengthening their professional role and improving their working environment will enable us to attract and keep qualified and competent professionals. We must find out, e.g., who or what is the source of all the clerical paperwork teachers complain about and get some relief for them.

The improvement of teacher training necessarily involves continued support for the Quality Assurance Program, which was implemented in 1978, and which we must continue to improve as conditions require. In addition, we must insist upon increasing the amount of training each teacher receives in his or her subject area of certification. I believe we can get by with less emphasis on style and method in exchange for more emphasis on mastery of subject matter. We pay more for a master's degree in education; why not pay more also for a mastery of what you teach? I was pleased to read this morning's news story that our education departments are considering similar proposals.[1]

It is just as important for teachers to have a thorough understanding of the subject they present as it is to understand how to present it. This cannot be changed overnight, but it must be changed. Further, we must continue our support of the University Board of Governors' task force to study teacher education.[2] With the advancement of knowledge comes the challenge of mastering new skills, skills which future generations will need as we advance toward the twenty-first century.

Promoting teaching as a career is an integral part of improving the teaching profession. We already have a critical shortage of teachers. We must close this gap by attracting the best of the brightest to our schools and classrooms. A recent news story reported that the gap in SAT between average students and those preparing to become teachers was getting closer. That's good news, because the bad news was that those studying to become teachers had the lower scores. I would suggest that we create an office which would be responsible for developing an effective communications program and which would plan a strategy to make teaching attractive to our best students who are entering college. It should be a promotional office within the Department of Public Instruction, and it should confine itself to the opportunities for advancing teaching as a career pursuit.

I propose further that we make a major expansion of special incentive/loan programs for academically talented education majors. It would be designed to attract them into geographic areas—rural, e.g.—as well as subject areas—math, science, e.g.—in which there are severe teacher shortages. The way to do that is to award competitive loans that will qualify for more favorable terms for those who teach. For those who teach a reasonable number of years in shortage areas— geographic or subject area—the loan would be forgiven so much per year. Many school districts simply lack adequate tax base per student. They need help to recruit teachers, and I want them to know help is on the way! In my next budget message I will propose funding of such a program, with a sunset provision after four or five years, to ensure periodic reassessment of the need, the mechanism, and of the success of the program. We must act decisively. We cannot ignore these problems any longer.

As I emphasized at the outset, the recruitment and retention of qualified teachers will depend in large measure on our ability to provide salaries which are competitive with other fields in which their skills are in demand. We should begin, quite properly, by eliminating the first step in the salary schedule for certified, entry-level personnel. That will raise starting pay 5 percent. Currently, North Carolina ranks thirty-second nationally in teacher compensation. It is quite obvious that this average is lowered by our entry-level salary.

In granting salary increases during its recent session, the General Assembly failed to address entry-level salary—although I had proposed across-the-board pay increases. They outbid me for experienced teachers, which I'm willing to applaud, but neglected new teachers' starting pay. The time to correct this oversight is now. Additionally, I still recommend that we provide better pay for better teachers who are already in the system. More on that in fifteen minutes.

We also need to provide a supplemental salary incentive payment to classroom teachers in those systems that are not participating in the career development pilot project. It is estimated that approximately 25 percent of those classroom teachers would be eligible for this incentive which would continue until the career pilot program is expanded statewide.

Improving the teaching profession also requires that we recognize that discipline begins with the family. Schools should not be expected to account for the breakdown of the family and the lack of parental responsibility. Nevertheless, families, schools, and the community must work together to solve this problem. More on that another day.

This brings me to my second set of recommendations for establishing quality in our schools: improving the curriculum, instruction, and the teaching of basics.

In 1980, North Carolina ranked forty-eighth in the nation in the percentage of persons completing at least four years of high school. The average SAT score in our state declined from 847, in 1972, to 825 in 1983. They slipped nationally, too, but we stood near the bottom of any group of states with which we could appropriately be compared.

Our curriculum, textbooks, and the teaching of basics were not meeting the need for quality education. Functional illiteracy continues at a rate of about 25 percent.

Based on 1984 and 1985 SAT scores, it appears that we may be turning the corner, nationally and in North Carolina. Why are these increases so significant? First, because they represent about one third of all high school graduates and two thirds of those who go on to college. Second, and more importantly, they are not the result of quick fixes or short-run changes. The SAT measures student abilities that are developed over years of learning experience, both in and out of the classroom, so 1984 reforms were not as much of a factor as those from 1980 and 1975. In other words, these youngsters are showing the results of real improvement in the instruction they are getting, the motivation they are receiving, and their own efforts—improvement at every stage of their schooling from the time they entered the educational system a dozen years ago. And please remember that scores on the Scholastic Aptitude Test started to decline in 1963 and continued for more than seventeen years without interruption. This decline was among the most often-cited pieces of evidence that something was wrong with our schools.

The 1984 improvement is ever so slight, being slightly better than 1983 but still worse than any other year in the past two decades. We must be doing something wrong. It deserves note only in that we finally saw the end of the seventeen-year collapse. So, we still have a long way to go.

In order to improve the academic performance of students, the public schools must devote more attention to the teaching of basic skills in elementary-grade/foundation studies. The foundation for learning depends upon the student's ability to read and write, learn the English language, and compute and use problem-solving skills. It is very important that the textbooks, curriculum, and the teaching of basics be appropriate and challenging for each grade and subject area.

There are three areas in which we can enhance the curriculum, instruction, and the teaching of basics. First, we need to strengthen the teaching of traditional basics, and this involves encouraging the State Board of Education to ensure that the priorities of the Basic Education plan, especially in the elementary grades, focus their most urgent attention on the teaching of reading, writing, spelling, grammar, arithmetic, history, and science. We must also insist that good citizenship be taught to enhance respect for our traditional values.

Second, we must make the curriculum more appropriate. The General Assembly has mandated that we continue to review course requirements and upgrade content for a rigorous academic study. Third, we must keep course offerings and graduation requirements in line with the student's ability and interests in addition to the demands of colleges and the labor market.

I am very pleased that concerns which I and others had earlier expressed about the curriculum part of the Basic Education Program are being seriously addressed. Those goals and guidelines are being reviewed subject by subject and class by class. This scrutiny is a commendable, positive response by our educational establishment to public input. So, if you have any specific proposals, send them in!

We also must use the findings of the current legislative vocational educational study to update the vocational educational programs. I suggest we look at coupling the junior and senior years in high school with the first two years of community college, using this two-plus-two approach to enhance education rather than provide remedial education. We cannot afford to have all the latest equipment and all the latest skills in every high school. That level of sophistication can be provided at our community colleges, and I believe we would strengthen vocational education at both levels if their offerings were better meshed.

Another point I want to stress is that some of our textbooks must be upgraded to provide appropriately challenging content. We should allow more flexibility in the selection and adoption of textbooks. It seems to me [that] local school boards should have the option of at least one approved text that teaches reading by intensive phonics. The look-say method may be useful for some students, those whose learning progresses from whole images to their parts, but that is a historic disaster for students whose cognitive process is the other way around. I simply say: Local school boards should have the option to use intensive phonics for those teachers and students for whom it is more appropriate. As it is, they have to spend local money because of four reading texts, none offer intensive phonics. This is not a matter for the governor or legislature to decide or dictate, but I do recommend it for the consideration of the State Textbook Commission.

Thirdly, and perhaps the most difficult and yet the most important single issue that we must consider, is that of accountability. The success of educational reform will depend not only on how much we invest in education, but on how wisely this investment is made. Our return on investment—R.O.I.—is our return on education—R.O.E. It will take effort and commitment by state and local leaders, principals, teachers, and parents to ensure that the resources invested in our schools will result in the highest-possible learning gains for the students. We must look at new ways of addressing the issue of accountability.

Let's explore the issue of accountability at different levels. Our first consideration is the accountability of teachers. Already, North Carolina has begun its effort to develop a policy of incentive pay to attract bright young people into teaching careers, and keep them there, by promising that the better you are, the better you'll be paid. We also assure the public of improved accountability.

I'll get back to that in a few minutes; for now, let me raise a new proposal: Educators should be encouraged to use statistical data on students' progress on achievement and competency test scores each year, relative to their academic aptitudes, as a basis for a self-evaluation—academic feedback, if you will. Teachers whose students, over a two- or three-year period, consistently show less progress when compared to similar classes should be evaluated by appropriate tests and interviews to demonstrate their strengths and weaknesses in both subject mastery and teaching mastery. Upon this self-inventory, and with the help of fellow teachers and specialists, a strategy for self-improvement would be developed. Any teacher whose classes regularly do not respond should welcome such an effort by the system to help salvage and rebuild his or her chosen career.

This approach would not be threatening, but saving—or remedial. It would renew the emphasis on career building. To further enhance this teacher development concept, I believe there must be a way to give an entire school, faculty, and administrative staff a vested interest in improving the productivity of each member of the team. I have asked my staff to examine efforts and innovations that seek to develop accountability for an entire school.

We are developing goals for effective teachers and mechanisms for achieving the goals. We must also develop goals for "effective schools" and incentives for extra recognition, rewards, and advantages for schools that can work as a team to achieve remarkable success. This need not be just another competition, since different schools have different raw material to work with. But whatever abilities the student body brings to the school, if the output reaches a notable degree of progress by the end of the year it will be because of an outstanding staff, or an outstanding pattern of teamwork by the staff, or both.

We ought to encourage effective schools. I talked with one elementary principal who had negotiated with his superintendent a set of goals, as in management by objective. One routine goal was that every classroom of students would show progress. One didn't. The result was not to cull out that teacher, but to put together a team of experienced teachers to help him. Next year, that teacher's students were making progress, too, and the whole staff felt like a successful team.

Next is the question of accountability for governance in education. The question, Who is in charge of education? must be resolved by Senate Bill 46, or something like it.[3] Regardless of how we resolve the issue, the governor must maintain responsibility for appointing the great majority of the State Board of Education. Since Governors Russell and Aycock, the people of North Carolina have looked to their governor for educational leadership. That would be undermined by stripping the governor of appointive power over the State Board of Education, but would be strengthened by having the chief administrator of public instruction appointed either by the chief executive or by his board of education. Proposals that the General Assembly are considering include a constitutional amendment, which would have to be ratified by popular vote, providing for an appointed superintendent as well as a legislative change for appointing a commissioner of education. Regardless of the mechanism, the governor must be able to provide educational leadership. Citizens look to the chief executive officer for accountability, and he must have the authority to see that their best interests are being served.

My earlier efforts to redirect attention to teaching careers and basic curriculum as the highest priorities were virtually ignored by many who had already committed themselves to a so-called Basic Education Program that, for all its virtues, did not do much for teachers or basic education in its twenty-three priorities. It rushes us into a faster expansion of teaching positions without regard for the declining supply of teachers. It adds even more noninstructional personnel in positions that would surely be useful, but are not nearly as urgent as is the overdue effort to upgrade the profession of the classroom teacher.

Few of these twenty-three priorities are anywhere nearly as crucial as it is to make teaching more attractive as a career and more attainable as a mission. And yet, all of these twenty-three good ideas, the whole list, are being pressed forward at a cost that is twice what it would take to fund the full career ladder program statewide for all teachers. It is as though we somehow have to get these improvements committed into place, all twenty-three of them, before we start the full statewide career ladder, so that the only possible way then to fund the incentive pay program for better pay for better teachers, which the people strongly support, will require a tax increase. That's backwards in the public's order of priorities.

Let me make it plain again: I believe that teachers, and incentive pay to build accountability into the teaching system, ought to be our number-one priority. A decision to fund twenty-three other things first means that teacher accountability through incentive pay, the career ladder program, is given twenty-fourth priority, not first. We should not put ourselves in the absurd position of having no option but to raise taxes in order to fund our first priority. I propose the radical idea that first priorities ought to come first! We should have room in our budget projections to be sure we can pay for the full career ladder program when the pilot program is completed and it's time to go statewide. Then, if we run out of money before we get to priorities seventeen, eighteen, nineteen, and so on, then is the time to ask if we're willing to raise taxes to do those good but less urgent things. We would not have to raise taxes for our highest priority, teachers, because we would already have funded that first.

Truly a radical idea: first things first! The people support me on that; and yet they can't hold me accountable to get that done when the contrary agenda is already set in concrete, and few of the team that I inherited have any accountability to me and, therefore, any incentive to help me reform the agenda.

While we're on the subject of accountability, we must return to the state and local boards of education the responsibilities that are by tradition their rightful duties. We must make the boards more accountable and let them be responsible for the development of school policy.

Finally, we must utilize the Governor's Business Committee on Education to foster a strong partnership between public and private interests. The history of education is littered with the pages of reports that never bore fruit in the form of true reform. Unless we can maintain concern, support, and action by those outside of education who have an interest, including employers, the momentum for reform can swiftly dissipate, for it is just when the situation is turning around slightly that the risk is the highest.

So it is an ideal time, I believe, for businessmen to put their influence behind some educational reforms which hold promise for long-range payoff in areas not now being addressed adequately. The Governor's Business Committee on Education, chaired by Jere Drummond,[4] has already developed and promoted many exemplary ways for businesses to help schools. They can recognize good students, good teachers, or good schools. They can provide special opportunities for innovative experiences. They can provide leadership.

We are going to have to find ways to enable an ever-growing proportion of all students to progress further in the higher-order mental activities—the knowing, the reasoning, the understanding—that a new era will require of them. In the past it's been all too easy to adopt high standards and blame the students and teachers for their failure. Today, we cannot afford to do that, and this is something in which business, industry, and the professions should have great interest and to which they can contribute much. I am, in short, suggesting a strong new emphasis in their involvement with the schools which focuses on the academic component.

Today, we have high expectations of our students. In many ways, these expectations are what we need to work toward an educational system that has no losers. It is, of course, statistically impossible to put every student in the top half of the class, but we must strive to make sure that those in the bottom half still have what they need to succeed.

It's been said that the trouble today is that the future isn't what it used to be. That may be true, but we can change it. We have the opportunity to educate the ones who will determine the future of North Carolina in the twenty-first century. Thank you for doing your part to make the most of it.

---

[1]The Holmes Group, composed of thirty-nine deans of education from colleges across the country, proposed that all prospective teachers hold bachelor's degrees in credible academic subjects "other than teaching." *News and Observer*, November 15, 1985.

[2]On September 13, 1985, Philip G. Carson, chairman of the University of North Carolina Board of Governors, announced that he had established a 21-member task force to determine methods of improving teacher training at all North Carolina institutions of higher education. *News and Observer*, September 14, 1985.

[3]S.B. 46, "A Bill to Amend the Constitution and General Statutes to Change the Method of Selecting the Members of the State Board of Education and to Make the Office of the Superintendent of Public Instruction Appointive," was introduced before the Senate on February 21, 1985. A committee substitute bill passed its third reading on May 2, and was sent to the House, where it was assigned to the Committee on Constitutional Amendments. Although the committee initially tendered a favorable report, the measure never came to a vote before the House. *N.C. House Journal, 1985*, 334, 467, 481, 533, 617, 642, 675, 687; *N.C. Senate Journal, 1985*, 44, 291.

[4]Jere A. Drummond (1939-   ), born in Rome, Georgia; B.I.E., Georgia Institute of Technology, 1962; M.B.A., Georgia State University, 1968; M.S., Massachusetts Institute of Technology, 1979; U.S. Army, 1963-1965. Various positions with Southern Bell, since 1962; appointed vice-president, Southern Bell in North Carolina, 1982; appointed to State Board of Education by Governor Martin, April, 1986, elected chairman, 1987; announced resignation after five months as Board of Education chairman to become senior vice-president, regulatory and pricing, BellSouth Services, Inc., Atlanta, effective January 1, 1988; chairman, North Carolina Business Committee on Education; director, North Carolina Citizens for Business and Industry; Republican. *News and Observer*, April 2, 1986, June 14, November 25, 1987.

NORTH CAROLINA DEPARTMENT OF COMMERCE
BUYER-SUPPLIER EXCHANGE

GREENVILLE, NOVEMBER 20, 1985

North Carolina's spirit of capitalism, our Tar Heel ingenuity and drive, has been responsible for the remarkable economic growth and vitality of our state, and your enthusiastic presence here today is strong evidence that this spirit is still very much alive. As leaders of emerging companies, both new and established, you represent the entrepreneurial instinct which is the heart of our very heritage. You are a reminder that we have not forgotten our roots; that innovation, energy, commitment, and a steady vision have been, and always will be, indispensable ingredients to building a better future for our people.

In reality, it is the risk takers who epitomize the spirit of people like Washington Duke, Edwin M. Holt,[1] and others who built great companies in our state. You are the pioneers, the risk takers in this century, but entrepreneurs are the same throughout history. It is opportunities which are available to them that change.

This buyer-supplier exchange, one of two which are held annually in the state by the North Carolina Department of Commerce, represents such an opportunity, for it brings people together from small businesses and large corporations that have a shared interest. On the one hand are those companies that are seeking sources of raw materials, fabricated parts, subassemblies, and a wide variety of supplies; on the other are those companies that are seeking buyers for their products. To the degree that this exchange is successful, it continues to contribute to the prosperity of North Carolina as a whole. Business growth is the engine which fuels the economy and creates new jobs for our citizens, and employment opportunities contribute more than any other factor to fulfilling the hopes and aspirations of a fiercely independent people.

We have never lived at a more exciting time in our history. We are poised on the threshold of a dynamic decade. It is estimated that nonfarm employment in North Carolina will increase at the rate of 1.9 percent, between 1985 and 1995, compared to 1.6 percent for the nation as a whole. Moreover, we are expecting personal income to surge ahead 8.3 percent during this same period, compared to 8.1 percent for the United States.

These new jobs and higher incomes translate into new markets and new opportunities to build upon today's strong business foundation.

We must seize these opportunities before they become captive to foreign competitors. We have the technology to accomplish this mission, and we must apply this technology with greater skill as we work to restore the preeminence of our state and nation in the world marketplace.

Today there are more than 114,000 business firms located in North Carolina, 110,000 or 97 percent of which are classified by the Small Business Administration as employing less than 100 persons each. Of this total, 86.1 percent employ fewer than 20 workers each, but they account for 20 percent of the work force. This is the sector in which the greatest expansion will take place in the future. Already, 75 percent of these companies represent commerce and manufacturing, and 30 percent of them are engaged in textiles and apparel manufacturing, among our traditional industries.

One of the first initiatives of this administration was to establish the office of assistant secretary of commerce for traditional industries. White Watkins was selected to fill this position. Currently, he is working with a traditional industries task force to find innovative and effective ways in which state government may assist in sustaining these industries while they retrofit their plants and develop new marketing strategies.

The role of government is, and should be, limited in our free enterprise system, but government does have the ability to bring diverse interests together in a way that helps them identify mutual problems and define new approaches. Another way is to encourage public acceptance of North Carolina's manufactured goods on the basis of competitive quality, rather than price alone. One of the best ways to accomplish this goal is to set a good example, and state government has done just that. Agencies and departments have been encouraged to buy from North Carolina suppliers when they are competitive in all respects, and I am pleased to say that we are fulfilling this chosen obligation. As a second alternative, these agencies and departments are buying from domestic suppliers. We are a viable partner in this venture, and we have a commitment to make a substantial contribution to this effort.

Another initiative of this administration has been the establishment of the office of assistant secretary of commerce for small businesses, which is under the direction of Lewis Myers. This office has been responsible for planning this buyer-supplier exchange here today, and I want to commend the staff for its superb work.

The state's Small Business Assistance Program extends far beyond the single purpose of expanding sales within North Carolina. There are many other services made available by the Department of Commerce, and I hope you will take advantage of today's conference to learn more about them.

Yet another way in which we are pursuing new markets for North Carolina businesses is within the federal government. Last year, eighty-three of the federal government's purchasing contracts of more than $170 billion were with North Carolina firms, and 29 percent of these contracts were with small manufacturers and suppliers. The strong presence of the military in our state provides a fertile market for additional business.

We need to strengthen our position in terms of penetrating this federal market; one way in which this can be accomplished is by active participation in the White House Conference on Small Business, which will be held at the Civic Center in Raleigh on January 28. The White House Conference provides an excellent opportunity for small business companies to participate in shaping federal policies which affect them and, in turn, affect our entire state and nation. It is open to small businesses throughout our state, and your attendance and active participation will contribute much to increasing the voice of small business in Washington, so I encourage each of your companies to be represented.

As I mentioned at the outset, the future growth of North Carolina will not depend upon attracting flagship industries, as important as they are. We are fortunate to have many of these major facilities within our metropolitan and nearby areas, where they can be part of a larger and more supportive environment. The metropolitan areas have better infrastructures and the critical mass of education, science, and technology required by larger firms, but our small business companies, when combined, are the real job creators of the present and the future. These are the companies which, quite appropriately, can be located outside of our predominantly urban areas.

As state government seeks to assist businesses of all sizes, we have a special obligation to work with our universities, chambers of commerce, local development agencies, and others to deliver to the small business person a range of services to make him more competitive and to reduce the attrition rate which puts 80 percent of all new operations out of business within five years. There is no role more important for the state to play than ensuring that its communities are properly organized to deal with their investment opportunities. This can take the form of using the state's leverage to ensure cooperation between all forces within the community which must work together to retain the existing job base and encourage its growth.

Leaders in many local areas of North Carolina, today, are rethinking their economic development policies. Realizing that the migration of larger plants from the Frostbelt to the South has ended, they are beginning to concentrate on small companies that hold the promise of sustained growth over the long term. Many counties have been successful in attracting small companies and encouraging the establishment of new firms from within; among the counties are Mecklenburg, Wake, Guilford, Forsyth, and Buncombe. These five counties account for 30 percent of all small businesses within the state.

Perhaps one of the most important factors to all business firms is the climate for growth in North Carolina. Public policies and decisions have a tremendous effect on shaping the type of environment in which growth is encouraged and success thrives. During the last session of the General Assembly we proposed and worked for tax relief, including elimination of our inventory and intangibles taxes. We achieved about one third of our goal, but we were more than rewarded by the realization that without the efforts of this administration there would have been no tax relief at all on the public agenda.

This administration has a pro-business commitment, and I take pride in the fact that I am a pro-business governor. Ours is the goal of pursuing economic growth aggressively and in all sectors. We will continue the pursuit of this goal to provide a more favorable business climate for North Carolina and contribute to strengthening the free enterprise system. That's the only way to have a strong job market for our people.

Tax relief will remain one of our major objectives, so long as state revenues expand sufficiently to exceed our commitment for providing a continuing high level of public services. Our other objectives include, but are not limited to, greater efficiency in government, improvement in public education, meeting the demands for improved statewide transportation, and building viable partnerships between state and local governments. Yes, these are but a few of our objectives as we attempt to shape the future and fashion it to accommodate the desirable and beneficial growth we anticipate.

As the horizons expand for the Sunbelt, North Carolina will exert its leadership in many new and innovative ways. To lead is part of the North Carolina tradition. I am confident that our rededication to our strong spirit of leadership will set the course for building a North Carolina in which there will be opportunity for all.

---

[1]Edwin Michael Holt (1807-1884), native of Orange (later Alamance) County; established cotton mill on Great Alamance Creek, 1837. Known for its "Alamance Plaids," the

Holt mill was the first to use power looms to weave plaid and colored cotton cloth south of the Potomac. Holt cofounded, with his sons, the Commercial National Bank of Charlotte and was a benefactor, stockholder, and board member of the North Carolina Railroad. Ashe, *Biographical History*, VII, 181-189.

DEDICATION OF EASTERN GOVERNOR'S OFFICE

NEW BERN, NOVEMBER 25, 1985

I very much appreciate the warm welcome you have given me and the members of our Council of State with us today. Standing on the porch of this historic Jones House,[1] sharing this moment with native New Bernians and city and county leaders from across eastern North Carolina, gives me new confidence in our decision to locate our Eastern Governor's Office on the grounds of the beautiful Tryon Palace.

During my campaign for governor, I made a personal promise to have an office of the governor in the east. Today I fulfill that promise, making it a positive accent on the growth and the promise for this portion of our great state. Raleigh can seem like a long, long way from here. I am sure that every governor who has sat in Raleigh since not too long after the Revolution must have felt the weight of that distance, of the need for closer ties with the people living here.

Why New Bern? I imagine Governor Tryon was asked the same question when he decided to govern from this same area. I like his response, as recorded in his letter to the London Board of Trade more than two centuries ago: "The public business of this colony can be carried on nowhere with so much conveniency and advantage for the greatest part of the inhabitants as at New Berne. . . ."[2]

I find that governor's purpose and mine to be the same. In keeping with the monumental restoration of Tryon Palace, this will be the ultimate restoration—restoring governmental function here, as in the days of early statehood when the Council of State met here, and the governor held meetings here. I also find it very fitting, indeed, that today's ceremony opening this office comes almost 219 years after the legislative assembly of those colonial days voted to build a permanent residence for the governor in New Bern. Wednesday of this week marks the anniversary of that turning point, and just next week, December 5, all North Carolinians can mark with pride the 215th anniversary of the formal opening of Tryon Palace.[3] It makes me wonder if some of the organizers of this occasion did not have their history in mind by choosing this day to open our Eastern Governor's Office.

I am standing amidst history, speaking to you from a porch that has withstood the weight of governors and state officials since 1809. Surrounding me is a beautiful fourteen-acre complex of six major buildings which comprise Tryon Palace.

New Bern: birthplace of good government in North Carolina; the first permanent capital of this great state; the place where proud independence gained its foothold. Many of you know the history of this area far better than I do, and you know that there have been other Martins before me. Somewhere near where I stand today, the very popular governor and patriot, Alexander Martin—no relation—was inaugurated in New Bern in 1789. He was the last governor inaugurated here before the capital moved to Raleigh. Most likely, he recalled at that time another Martin before him who had "ruled," as they put it in those colonial days, this vast colony of wilderness and independent souls. That was Governor Josiah Martin—no relation—the last royal governor of the colony. Faced with a people in rebellion, he very unroyally fled on horseback into the night in 1775, made his way to a ship riding off the coast, and tried in vain to rule for his king from that ship for a short while. Naturally, our native forefathers would have none of that. Awakening with the taste of freedom from kingly rule, they ignored their Governor Martin, assigning the old ways and the old powers into the history books forever.

That Governor Martin not only lacked courage, he lacked vision, as well. He could not possibly have foreseen the New Bern of today, nor the eastern North Carolina of today. He could not have foreseen the dynamic energy and opportunity that abounds from Elizabeth City to Long Beach, to Scotland Neck, Greenville, to Kinston, to Laurinburg. Even if he took the time away from curling his royal wig, he surely could not have foreseen the excitement of this New Bern of ours.

He departed with no sense of vision of a New Bern where the waterfront businesses change the pace of commerce; where new hotels are rising to house the growing numbers of tourists; where 75,000 people a year come to enjoy this palace and the history it offers. I understand he did tour his royal land, getting as far as Hillsborough, but did he sense the presence of a future Kinston, or a Wilmington, or a Lumberton, or a dynamic Edenton?[4] Did he sense in this fair land a wakening hunger for the good life, and a determination to work hard for it, that has come to symbolize eastern North Carolina?

Seemingly endless streams of concrete and asphalt have replaced those long-forgotten horse paths. Towns and cities of all sizes spread throughout the once open fields and forests. People are busy at living. Commerce and industry are humming with a new vitality.

The need to know, to understand decisions, moves in step with the growth of this eastern portion of North Carolina. The need of government to serve, my need to know and to respond, grow along with the pace of history. It has been that sincere reaction to the need for open communication that has made our Western Office of the Governor in Asheville such a success story. That same positive, two-way communication will surely develop here in New Bern, at this new office; for, as governor, I cannot function to the best of my ability, or carry out the mandates of all of the people of North Carolina, unless I know what it is the people want, what you need, and how you expect me to go about your business.

In the mountains of North Carolina, the people have the ears and the attention of the governor through that Western Office of the Governor. Our citizens there can get help; they can get my attention; they can turn to my offices for support, for information, and for guidance. Jim Bishop,[5] who runs the Governor's Office in Asheville, is the ombudsman for the governor, giving the people ready access to my offices in Raleigh. It is working there; it will work here in New Bern!

Under the management of Ed Sweeney,[6] this new office will provide the people of eastern North Carolina that same attention, that same ready access. Ed will be my eyes and ears. Through him, your concerns and your advice can be channeled to me. He will be the key to that open door in New Bern, a bridge for the miles between us. Ed will know what is going on with our congressmen, with our senators. He can refer. He can direct your inquiries. He can solve problems and give you quick response. Ed Sweeney, would you stand so all can see you—and take a bow.

This new office will be doing for me what the regional offices of some of our state agencies are doing for them. Scattered across eastern North Carolina are field offices of our Department of Natural Resources and Community Development, our Department of Commerce, and our Department of Transportation. The major work done by these state agencies is done in the field. Concerns of a businessman in Plymouth, or the mayor of Southport, or the housewife in Bladensboro get ready attention through these regional offices—and quick response. That is what we expect of this Eastern Governor's Office: to give you full attention and quick response.

The opening of this office is the beginning of a new commitment to those of you living in the eastern section of our state. It is a reaffirmation of my commitment to unifying North Carolina as one united state![7] It is the right decision, made for the right place and for the right time. It is a beginning. How it develops and how we can improve it will depend on the response by the people living here.

I need your input, your advice, and your support. Through this office, you have the opportunity to "tell it to the governor." Being the hearty, determined Tar Heels I know you to be, I expect you will tell it to the governor! With Ed Sweeney's help and with my own visits to this office, I'll be listening.

---

[1]The Jones House, 231 Eden Street, New Bern, is named for its first owner, turpentine distiller John Jones. The main section of the Federal-style dwelling was completed about 1809, and the west wing was added approximately eleven years later. The Tryon Palace Commission purchased the Jones House in 1963 and converted it into guest quarters. It became the Eastern Governor's Office in November, 1985. Peter B. Sandbeck, *The Historic Architecture of New Bern and Craven County, North Carolina* (New Bern, North Carolina: Tryon Palace Commission, 1988), 421-423.

[2]William Tryon (1729-1788), born at Norbury Park, County Surry, England; died in London. British army officer, commissioned 1751, recommissioned 1772; appointed North Carolina lieutenant governor, 1764; fourth royal governor of North Carolina, 1765-1771; appointed royal governor of New York, 1770, assumed duties, 1771. As governor of North Carolina, Tryon confronted the Stamp Act crisis, 1765-1766, and defeated the Regulators at the Battle of Alamance, May 16, 1771. Also during his administration, the colony's only permanent capitol and governor's residence, known as Tryon's Palace, was constructed at New Bern, 1767-1771; the Cherokee boundary line finally had been concluded, 1767, in accordance with the Royal Proclamation of 1763; and biweekly postal service had been established, 1769.

Tryon recommended the location for the seat of government in his letter to the Board of Trade, Lords Commissioners for Trade and Plantations, April 1, 1765. "I spent two months in a Tour thro' this province & am determined in my Opinion that the public Business of it can be carried on no where with so much Conveniency and Advantage to far the greatest part of the Inhabitants, as at Newberne, a Towne situated on a Neck of Land at the Confluence of the Rivers Neuse & Trent." William S. Powell (ed.), *The Correspondence of William Tryon and Other Selected Papers* (Raleigh: Division of Archives and History, Department of Cultural Resources, 2 volumes, 1980), I, xv-xxxviii, 55, hereinafter cited as Powell, *Tryon Papers*.

[3]"An Act for erecting a Convenient Building within the Town of New Bern, for the residence of the Governor or Commander in Chief for the Time Being," was passed November 24, 1766, and received Governor Tryon's approval on December 1. Saunders, *Colonial Records*, VII, 398, 420; for the text of the act, see Saunders, *Colonial Records*, XXIII, 664-665. Although Governor Tryon moved into the palace in mid 1770, work on the building was not concluded until January, 1771. Powell, *Tryon Papers*, xxi-xxii.

[4]Josiah Martin, royal governor from 1771-1775, toured the colony of North Carolina during the summer of 1772; Salisbury apparently was his westernmost stop, Halifax his farthest official destination to the east. Whether he visited them on his tour or not, the royal governor likely did sense the presence of three of the four towns Martin listed. Edenton was incorporated in 1722; Kinston, originally named Kingston in honor of George III, was incorporated in 1762; and Newton, chartered in 1739/40, eventually was renamed to commemorate Spencer Compton (1673?-1743), earl of Wilmington. Both Wilmington and Edenton were among the largest towns in mid-eighteenth century North Carolina. Lumberton was not incorporated until 1788. Samuel A'Court Ashe, *History of North Carolina* (Greensboro, N.C.: Charles L. Van Noppen, Publisher, 2 volumes, 1925; Spartanburg, South Carolina: The Reprint Company, 1971), I, 402-403; Robert J. Cain (ed.), *Records of the Executive Council, 1735-1754*, Volume VIII of *The Colonial Records of North Carolina [Second Series]* (Raleigh: Division of Archives and History, Department of Cultural Resources, projected multivolume series, 1963-), xxxvii-xxxviii; William S. Powell, *The North Carolina Gazetteer* (Chapel Hill: University of North Carolina Press, 1968), 157-158, 265, 303, 537.

[5]James H. Bishop (1943-   ), born in Cherokee Springs, South Carolina; resident of Rutherford County; B.A., Georgetown College, 1966; U.S. Air Force veteran. Served as teacher, Rutherford County Schools; area manager, E. J. Taylor Corp.; and general manager, WBBO Radio, Forest City, before being appointed director, Western Governor's Office, in 1985; former Rutherford County GOP chairman; president, Isothermal Broadcasting Co. James H. Bishop to Jan-Michael Poff, August 23, 1988.

[6]William Edward Sweeney, Jr. (1938-   ), born in Newport News, Virginia; resident of Jacksonville; was educated at University of Tennessee, Central Piedmont Community College, and Coastal Carolina Community College. Former salesman, sales manager, and theater manager; field underwriter, Mutual Life Insurance Co., 1971-1974; rehabilitation casework technician, 1974-1984, human resource placement specialist, 1984-1985, Division of Vocational Rehabilitation Services, N.C. Department of Human Resources; field coordinator, Eddie Knox gubernatorial campaign, 1983-1984, and for Democrats for Jim Martin, 1984; appointed director, Eastern Governor's Office, 1985. William Edward Sweeney, Jr., to Jan-Michael Poff, August 23, 1988.

[7]Governor Martin inserted this sentence into his address and then penned the following note, at the bottom of the page, to speech writer Vernon Morton: "The 'One United State' theme is a good one but regularly gets neglected. Look for ways to highlight it. See above." Beginning with his inaugural address and continuing throughout 1985, Martin emphasized the idea of a statewide commonality of interest. However, his recurring handwritten references to "One United State" indicated that the topic was not being included in his prepared texts as often as he had wished.

NORTH CAROLINA FOUNDATION FOR RESEARCH AND ECONOMIC EDUCATION

RALEIGH, DECEMBER 3, 1985

I am extremely pleased to have this opportunity to address the members and guests of the North Carolina Foundation for Research and Economic Education. I am pleased, first of all, because it provides a forum for the discussion of state government as it exists today and where it appears to be headed. And second, it affords an examination of critical issues of our time and what effect the outcome of these issues will have on the future of North Carolina.

Winston Churchill once remarked that "Some see private enterprise as a predatory target to be shot, others as a cow to be milked, but few are those who see it as the sturdy horse pulling the wagon."[1] He's right, as usual.

Yet, the wagon moves on, steadily increasing the wealth of our state and contributing to new opportunity for the individual citizen. The ambivalence by some legislators, and editors, and other "reformers" toward this prosperity results, in part, from a continuing struggle to understand the relationship between business and society. Business and society are interesting—indeed vital—subjects to explore, because in America they define each other to a very great extent. Business is not separate from society; it is not an adversary of the common good. Instead, business is a reflection of society; it is the method by which individuals unite to form a network of common interests. It is a major mechanism for the common good, expressing that ideal of private enterprise that even today, 210 years later, is still the best allocator of goods and services in the world.

Public interest is not something private enterprise must violate in order to earn a profit; it is something they must implement in order to prevent chaos. Profits, contrary to the view of some, are not obscene; losses may be, to the extent they cost jobs, but not profits. Profits, rather, are essential, to induce investment of one's accumulated assets at risk of losing it all but in hopes of making a profit and [incomplete].

Let us begin at the level of the individual. A person needs to act upon his environment in order to achieve expression and an improved standard of living. In order to better themselves, productive individuals must form a communion of commerce. It is at this point that we have an economy.

What is the ultimate end of an economy? I'm afraid there's no absolute answer. We do not know the limits of human skill, creativity, or productive capacity. This renders meaningless such abstract goals as happiness; Thomas Jefferson recognized as much [when] he cited the "pursuit of happiness" as one of society's ends.[2]

Economic man must be free to pursue his unknown limits, just as economic society must be open to change and development. Indeed, we may even go so far as to consider whether pursuit is solely in the material world. The thing we are pursuing is the limit of our potential, a distant horizon that we can chase but which continues to move forward with every step we take.

Private enterprise is the act of changing the world to meet the needs and desires of men and women as they explore their potential. But private enterprise is open ended in its view of the future, and since it works best when it is free from the excessive obstruction of opposing interest groups, it does not function well as a social welfare agency. True, private enterprise has a commitment to charity and community involvement which is extensive and important, but the prime purpose of business is material transformation and the creation of wealth and jobs. The distribution of that wealth is a matter for government to ponder, but not to supplant.

Much has been written in recent years about the shift in political thinking in America. The Brookings Institute wonders if the United States is undergoing "a major electoral realignment." *Commentary* magazine ponders a shift in the "balance of political power" in America, and in the *New Republic* we discover there's a resurrection of the "politically undead" at work today. The political air in our nation is thick with talk of a major realignment of popular support for the two principal parties in our country.

Clearly, state government for almost a decade has been traveling on a collision course with the aspirations of the public. We have become a government in which few legislative giants hold sway over decisions of the entire General Assembly, while other representatives reside as pygmies. This has resulted in widespread disenchantment with our governmental process and a demand for more governmental responsiveness and accountability. This trend became apparent in 1984; it was then that many of the fundamental changes that have taken place in the last several years became more understandable.

A more conservative view of government has the following implications:

1. The election of more conservative, business-oriented political leaders at all levels of government.

2. Massive efforts to reduce taxes at the federal, state, and local levels.

3. A backlash on government spending accompanied by efforts to improve governmental productivity and efficiency.

The ultimate consequences of these deep-rooted structural changes are reflected in a back-to-basics philosophy. We can see it in our schools. We can see it in the private sector.

North Carolina may well be undergoing a socioeconomic renaissance. Our ability to move with the times may ultimately be the greatest asset in our economic and political systems. Common sense and old-fashioned rules of behavior also are making more of a mark, these days. It is as if we are reaching out for some of the values which built our great state in the first place.

Powerful legislators resist these changes for fear of losing control over the legislative process. Resistance to change also has produced countermeasures to infringe upon the powers of the executive branch. Let me offer some examples with which many of you are familiar.

Although it was not sought by popular initiative, repeal of gubernatorial succession will be one of the constitutional issues voted upon by the public in 1986. Obviously, this is an attempt by entrenched leaders in the House and Senate to limit the ability of future administrations to function effectively—more simply, to weaken the office of governor relative to the legislature.

Since the United States Constitution was patterned after the best examples of individual state constitutions at the time of its drafting in

1787, this attempt is contrary to the principles endorsed by the founding fathers. The founding fathers knew precisely what they did not want in an executive: neither a despot, nor a figurehead, nor an officer too weak to protect them from the bad laws and schemes of the legislature. "Publius" argued in Federalist Paper 70 that strength did not have to threaten liberty; on the contrary, it was a necessary ingredient of sound republican government. "The true test of good government," Publius wrote, "is its aptitude and tendency to produce good administration."[3] And he went on to say that good administration requires an executive with the power to lead, the tools to manage, and sufficient time in office to become established.

Other states have found that a single four-year term is not sufficient time to become established. North Carolina voters already have approved a limit of two terms. They should not be required to reaffirm that decision, but reaffirm it they will. Although the referendum will have no effect on my option to seek reelection, it is in the interest of future governors, and of the people, that this decision should stand.

We must look upon this assault on the executive branch of government as no less than an attack upon private enterprise. During the last session of the General Assembly, I proposed $443.5 million in tax reductions to stimulate economic development within our state and to assist the most needy of our citizens. This tax-relief package included removal of taxes on business inventories, intangible assets, and foods and prescription medicines. Given the surplus revenues collected by the state, exceeding $600 million, all of these goals were realistic and justified. Especially today, when we are being challenged anew by the rise of foreign competition, the aging of our resources, and the march of advanced technology, private enterprise needs this relief to provide real jobs and new opportunity.

If we are to have sustained growth and high employment, if we are to compete effectively in international markets, and, perhaps more importantly, if we are to provide for the individual needs of individual citizens, then someone in state government has to be pro-business. We must have a governor who believes that the best social program is a good economy. The administration that has consistently supported that view, I am proud to submit, is this administration.

Although the General Assembly granted only one third of the tax relief requested in my "State of the State" address, some $171.5 million, it is the largest tax reduction in North Carolina history. Still, it is not enough to promote the creation of new jobs at the rate existing employees will be displaced by future technology.

In fact, the largest tax reduction—some $52 million—is in individual income tax rates for individuals earning $15,000 or less annually. It amounts to a savings of only $25 each year for those individuals in lieu of sales tax relief. Moreover, the tax package approved by the legislature comes only two years after it approved increased taxes and fees of $220 million. So, if we view the recently adopted tax-relief package in its true perspective, the General Assembly did nothing more than offset most of [the] recent tax increase.

This does not reflect fiscal responsibility in addressing the issues of our time. These issues include smaller and more efficient government, better and more productive management of state resources, fewer and lower taxes, and a more disciplined budget process. I continue to believe the time has come to reassert traditional leadership in state government and to impose long-overdue fiscal discipline in our state capital.

In addition, I believe in strong state and local government. The state, one of the "laboratories of democracy," as Justice Louis Brandeis so eloquently described it early in this century, is where shared responsibilities must begin.[4] There must be greater cooperation and teamwork in addressing the needs of urban transportation, public education, infrastructure needs, and community development, as the federal government continues to abandon programs and reduce funding to restore national fiscal integrity.

Private enterprise also has a role to play by taking a greater interest in governmental affairs. For too long, the business community has focused its attention on Washington. Most of the decisions affecting private enterprise are made today at the state level. You, as corporate leaders, must redirect your attention to the playing field where the real game is being played: in our General Assembly.

Private enterprise must also continue its efforts to prevent the erosion of power within the executive branch of government, and thus ensure a balance in government.

There is one vital issue which must be offered to the public to decide. That proposal, which is supported by some 60 percent of the electorate, is the question of executive veto power.

The executive veto is an example of how the founders sought to separate and check power. Today, North Carolina is the only state in the nation where the governor does not have veto power over acts of the legislature. In fact, there are forty-three states which have given their executives the line-item veto. This means that forty-three governors have the power to approve so much of any measure passing both houses, as his judgment may dictate, without approving the whole. The Federalist Papers explained veto power this way:

The propriety of the thing does not turn upon the supposition of superior wisdom or virtue in the Executive, but upon the supposition that the legislature will not be infallible; that the love of power may sometimes betray it into a disposition to encroach upon the rights of the other members of the government; that a spirit of faction may sometimes pervert its deliberations; that impressions of the moment may sometimes hurry it into measures which itself, on maturer reflection, would condemn. The primary inducement to conferring the power of veto upon the Executive is to enable him to defend himself; the secondary one is to increase the chances in favor of the community against the passing of bad laws, through haste, inadvertence, or design.[5]

Throughout North Carolina history, governors have supported executive veto. All living governors support it. Yet, the General Assembly consistently has refused the electorate an opportunity to decide the issue. North Carolina is the only state where, for 209 years, the people have never been allowed to vote to give their governor the responsibility of the veto. The time has come to allow the public to settle the question. As Publius said in the Federalist Papers, "Executive veto is one of the tools to manage." This is a prerequisite to good administration.

Aside from controlling public consideration of constitutional amendments, the General Assembly also encroaches upon the power of the executive branch by enacting statutes which restrict the governor's ability to manage. These actions do not serve the best interests of the public.

The ability of a few legislative leaders to decide the agenda of a session and to control its outcome is dictated by the power of these leaders to reward loyal followers and to punish those who advocate different views. This power has been perpetuated by the distribution of surplus revenues to pork-barrel projects, thereby to enhance re-election campaigns of favored individual legislators.

The private sector also must share the blame. Fear of reprisals by influential legislators also has a bearing on campaign contributions. The attitude of many in private enterprise too often has been to support one's philosophical enemies as well as one's friends—never mind the fact that this support strengthens the enemy and diminishes friends. It's time for advocates of private enterprise, in both parties, to make a stand on the side of what is right for the common good of North Carolina and its citizens.

Leaders of private enterprise no longer can conclude their responsibilities by writing a check in support of a candidate. They must get involved in the campaigns of those of either party who share the same beliefs and ideals. They must be willing to make sacrifices. They must be committed, even if the candidate of their choice may be someone they believe can't win. It is this commitment, sacrifice, and support that often makes the difference in victory and defeat of worthy aspirants to public office.

I also believe that we must build a strong, competitive, healthier, two-party system in North Carolina, and we must elect candidates to the legislature, of either party, who are willing to stand up for those things in which they believe, regardless of threats or blandishments by a powerful few. If we fail in these responsibilities, we will have failed government, and we will have no one to blame but ourselves.

A political action committee is one bipartisan catalyst around which we may effect change in the affairs of government. It is a vital, modern mechanism, because it focuses resources. But it is not a substitute for personal involvement. It never will be.

It has been said that capitalism makes a virtue out of selfishness. While that is an ironic analysis, I don't believe that is the essential, existential truth. It is up to the capitalist to be aware of his self-interest and to reflect that interest in a network of responsibilities.

Harmony and balance are required if private enterprise is to continue to give value to human effort and bring to life the most creative achievements of human imagination. The greatest obstacle to these accomplishments would be government that is not sensitive to these needs, and it is within your power to help remove and foreclose that obstacle. Thank you for your commitment to trying. Democracy is not a spectator sport.

And now it is my pleasure, on behalf of the foundation, to present a plaque to Roger Gant, Jr., in appreciation for his dedicated service as chairman for the last two years.[6] It is that leadership that has brought North Carolina FREE this far in advancing the cause of promoting better state government through better representation. I challenge each of you to carry on his efforts to strengthen that mission.

---

[1]"Some people regard private enterprise as a predatory tiger to be shot. Others look on it as a cow they can milk. Not enough people see it as a healthy horse pulling a sturdy wagon." Sir Winston Churchill, *Reader's Digest*, April, 1960, quoted in *The Reader's Digest Treasury of Modern Quotations* (New York: Reader's Digest Press/Thomas Y. Crowell Company, 1975), 204, hereinafter cited as *Reader's Digest Treasury of Modern Quotations.*

[2]The pursuit of happiness was one of the "self-evident" truths that Thomas Jefferson listed in the Declaration of Independence. See Declaration of Independence, reprinted in *North Carolina Manual, 1987-1988,* 57.

[3]Alexander Hamilton, James Madison, and John Jay, writing under the pseudonym "Publius," produced a series of eighty-five articles explaining and supporting the ratification of the federal constitution that had been crafted in Philadelphia. Many of the essays first appeared in New York City newspapers between October, 1787, and May, 1788, and were eventually published in hardcover as *The Federalist.* Charles A. Beard

(ed.), *The Enduring Federalist* (New York: Frederick Ungar Publishing Co., 1959), vi-vii; Alexander Hamilton, James Madison, and John Jay, *The Federalist: A Commentary on the Constitution of the United States . . .* (New York: Robert B. Luce, Inc., Bicentennial Edition, 1976), v-xxii, hereinafter cited as *The Federalist*.

"Though we cannot acquiesce in the political heresy of the poet who says: 'For forms of government let fools contest— / That which is best administered is best,'—yet we may safely pronounce, that the true test of a good government is its aptitude and tendency to produce a good administration." The Federalist No. 68, by Alexander Hamilton, from the *New York Packet*, March 14, 1788, quoted in *The Federalist*, 444.

⁴"There must be power in the States and the Nation to remould, through experimentation, our economic practices and institutions to meet social and economic needs. . . . Denial of the right to experiment may be fraught with serious consequences to the Nation. It is one of the happy incidents of the federal system that a single courageous State may, if its citizens choose, serve as a laboratory; and try novel social and economic experiments without risk to the rest of the country." Dissenting opinion of Supreme Court Justice Louis Brandeis, *New State Ice Co.* v. *Liebmann*, 1932, quoted in David E. Osborne, *Laboratories of Democracy* (Boston: Harvard Business School Press, 1988), n.p.

Louis Dembitz Brandeis (1856-1941), born in Louisville, Kentucky; resident of Washington, D.C.; LL.B., Harvard University, 1877; honorary degree. Attorney; chairman, Provisional Committee for General Zionist Affairs, 1914-1916; U.S. Supreme Court associate justice, 1916-1939; author. *Who Was Who in America, 1897-1942*, 131.

⁵The Federalist No. 73, by Alexander Hamilton, from the *New York Packet*, March 21, 1788, quoted in *The Federalist*, 477. Martin's rendition is faithful to the original, with one minor exception: Hamilton wrote, "The primary inducement to conferring the power in question to the Executive is, to enable him to defend himself. . . ."

⁶Roger Gant, Jr. (1924-   ), born in Burlington; B.S., University of North Carolina at Chapel Hill, 1948; U.S. Army, 1943-1946. Served as purchasing agent, treasurer, and division manager, 1948-1972, before becoming president, 1972, of Glen Raven Mills, Inc. Roger Gant, Jr., to Jan-Michael Poff, August 24, 1988.

PRESENTATION OF UNIVERSITY AWARD TO BILL AND IDA FRIDAY

CHAPEL HILL, DECEMBER 4, 1985

[The University of North Carolina Board of Governors presented the first University Award, the system's supreme honor recognizing service to higher education, in 1980. *Chapel Hill Newspaper*, December 5, 1985; *News and Observer*, December 5, 1985. For a diplomatic transcription of the governor's testimonial to William C. and Ida Howell Friday, see Appendix I, pages 1014-1016.]

President and Mrs. Friday,¹ whose careers have outlasted, and outranked, seven governors so far; Governor and Mrs. Moore,² [and Governor and Mrs.] Scott,³ who can so testify; Chairman and Mrs. Carson;⁴ members of the University Board of Governors; officials of the faculties and administration; members of our General Assembly, whose support has been steadfast; and marvelous presenters of tributes; ladies and gentlemen:

Dottie and I are delighted to have the opportunity of sharing, with you, this evening of the University Awards ceremony in honor of our man Friday and our lady Ida, two individuals who have devoted the major part of their lives to this university, to those it has served, and, in the spirit of their enterprise, to those it will continue to serve for many future generations.

North Carolina has a long heritage of educational diversity, as represented by the sixteen campuses of the Greater University, and this tradition has done much to contribute to our state's greatness, a model of excellence and service that never ceases to win deserved recognition. No one has done more to contribute to the perpetuation of this tradition than Bill Friday. Whether as a student in his undergraduate days, or studying for his law degree, or later, as a dean and president of a great institution, Bill Friday has spent a lifetime taking serious ideas seriously. Too soon, he will end an outstanding career as president of the university system, a career which spans almost one third of a century, commemorating the longest tenure ever served by an individual in that position.

Bill, you and your devoted Ida, without whose support and encouragement this distinguished record could not have been achieved, have earned the deep respect and appreciation of all North Carolinians, and we thank you.

You have brought to us an historic challenge. We have the opportunity to prepare North Carolina, not just for the next fifteen years, but for the twenty-first century. It is a challenge to keep North Carolina moving forward toward that first shining vision, a state of unprecedented opportunity where achievement is limited only by how big we dream, how hard we work, and how well we learn. And we know that the path to that vision is through economic growth, and new technologies, and renewed excellence in education, and the cycle in which each supports the other.

Yet, as important as technology and economic growth are to our future, education is more important still. Bill Friday has instilled that lesson, a lesson which began in 1795 when the university opened its doors for the first time as America's first great adventure in public higher education. Bill Friday has helped us understand that, without education, human advancement and individual achievement are limited. And he has made us aware that, without education, we could even lose our fundamental values, our beliefs in freedom, hard work, and personal initiative. Under his leadership, he has created an awareness that if we educate our young people well, grounding them in our values and teaching them the greatness of spirit, the future will be the best that North Carolina has ever seen.

President Reagan has said that education is the architect of the soul. I say that for all its intellectual grandeur, [education] is the expression of the soul. Bill Friday has helped us search the soul of North Carolina, and that search has enabled us to build one of the truly great university systems of our nation.

Bill Friday has brought unmatched experience and wisdom to his current responsibilities. He has served so long and so faithfully that his presence has almost been taken for granted. Tonight we acknowledge, for all American education, that he is indeed an exceptional individual, a great man, and a caring public servant. He has always been immensely dignified, yet never stuffy; always hopeful, and yet ever realistic. We are proud, then, to honor him for what he has done and, even more, for what he is.

Tonight, we also honor Ida Friday. It has been the good fortune of North Carolina to have this great lady as one of the major forces at work to enhance the arts, culture, volunteerism, and the spirit of individualism. She has had a profound influence on our quality of life.

As a part of our team, Ida Friday has been a steady hand guiding her husband in uncertain times, giving reassurance, rearing a family of three daughters—and Betsy, I can tell you that you made a lot of fathers and mothers very happy and proud tonight.[5] Our co-honoree has given of herself, without compromise, to helping young people find direction and purpose in life. She has helped to create choices for those who saw none. She has turned failures into successes. She has brought hope where there was despair, a friend for so many who needed one. Together with Bill Friday, she has helped to add a new dimension to our lives. Bill, you're a great guy, but we know you married above yourself!

Bill and Ida Friday have given us strength through clarity; security through faith in ourselves; and progress through intellect. They have been the innovators who have helped to lead our state forward.

Jonathan Swift once wrote, "Whoe'er excels in what we prize, Appears a hero in our eyes."[6] Well, Bill and Ida Friday are indeed among the real heroes of North Carolina. The University Awards which have been bestowed upon them tonight are but a token of our gratitude. The meaning of that gratitude will remain with us, and, we sincerely hope, with them always. In truth, you both have become the North Carolina University Awards.

---

[1]Ida Howell Friday (1919-   ), born Ida Willa Howell, in Sumter, South Carolina; resident of Chapel Hill; A.B., Meredith College, 1941; M.P.H., University of North Carolina at Chapel Hill, 1948; was married to William C. Friday, May 13, 1942. Home econo-

mist, Raleigh District, Carolina Power and Light Co., 1941-1942; instructor, director of Public Health Education Workshop, School of Public Health, University of North Carolina at Chapel Hill, 1948-1952; member, numerous boards and commissions. Mrs. Friday actively parlayed her role as wife of the university president into years of service as a volunteer in the cause of public higher education, earning her recognition as "the most underpaid administrator in the University of North Carolina" system. Ida Howell Friday to Charles T. Francis, July 12, 1983, hereinafter cited as Friday Correspondence; *News and Observer*, December 5, 1985; *North Carolina Manual, 1985*, 915.

[2]Daniel Killian Moore (1906-1986), born in Asheville; buried in Raleigh; B.S., University of North Carolina at Chapel Hill, 1927; was also educated at University of North Carolina School of Law, 1927-1928; U.S. Army, 1943-1945. Attorney; member, state House, 1941; solicitor, 1946-1948, superior court judge, 1948-1958, Twentieth Judicial District; division counsel, Champion Papers, Inc., Canton, 1958-1965; vice-chairman, state Board of Water Resources, 1959-1964; North Carolina governor, 1965-1969, and supreme court associate justice, 1969-1978; Democrat. *News and Observer*, September 8, 1986; *North Carolina Manual, 1977*, 611.

Jeanelle Coulter Moore (1911-   ), born in Pikeville, Tennessee; resident of Raleigh; B.A., Western Carolina University; was also educated at Milligan College, University of Tennessee; was married to Daniel K. Moore, May 4, 1933. Former schoolteacher, Canton; First Lady of North Carolina, 1965-1969; established Executive Mansion Fine Arts Committee, 1965; cofounder, 1967, chairwoman, Keep North Carolina Clean and Beautiful; active in civic affairs; Democrat. *Journal and Sunday Sentinel* (Winston-Salem), January 30, 1966; Jeanelle Coulter Moore to Jan-Michael Poff, October 7, 1989; *North Carolina Manual, 1977*, 611.

[3]Jessie Rae Osborne Scott; born in Fayetteville, later moved to Swepsonville; B.S., Woman's College of the University of North Carolina (later University of North Carolina at Greensboro); was married to Robert Walter Scott, September 1, 1951. Former mill worker, bookkeeper, secretary, Internal Revenue Service clerk, and high school teacher; First Lady of North Carolina, 1969-1973; candidate in Democratic primary for state labor secretary, 1976; active in civic affairs. *News and Observer*, July 6, 1964, November 10, 1968; *North Carolina Manual, 1987-1988*, 1051; *Pilot* (Southern Pines), April 18, 1976; *Winston-Salem Journal*, April 25, 1976.

[4]Philip G. Carson (1938-   ), born in Gastonia; resident of Asheville; A.B., 1963, J.D., 1967, University of North Carolina at Chapel Hill; U.S. Army, 1958-1960. Attorney; chairman, University of North Carolina Board of Governors, 1984-1988. Philip G. Carson to Jan-Michael Poff, September 26, 1989, hereinafter cited as Carson Correspondence.

Ruth Bowles Carson (1941-   ), born in Richmond, Virginia; resident of Asheville; A.B., University of North Carolina at Chapel Hill, 1963. President, Collector's Carrousel, Inc.; active in civic affairs. Carson Correspondence.

[5]The Fridays' three children were Frances Howell (1951-   ), Mary Howell (1956-   ), and Ida Elizabeth (Betsy, 1958-   ). Betsy, an actress working in New York, delighted her parents with a "personalized" rendition of the song "Everything's Coming Up Roses." Friday Correspondence; *News and Observer*, December 5, 1985.

[6]From Jonathan Swift, *Cadenus and Vanessa*, quoted in Bergen Evans, *Dictionary of Quotations* (New York: Delacorte Press, 1968), 314.

BARCLAYSAMERICAN CHRISTMAS BREAKFAST

CHARLOTTE, DECEMBER 20, 1985

Good morning, and Merry Christmas. It is an honor and a privilege for me to share this Barclays Christmas breakfast occasion with you today, and I want to thank your chairman and chief executive officer,

Graeme Keith, for his thoughtful invitation and kind introduction. The honor, quite appropriately, comes from the knowledge that this podium has been occupied in the past by such distinguished individuals as the Reverend Billy Graham[1] and other great Americans of towering faith, courage, and conviction. The privilege, of course, is derived from the occasion itself: being back home, with the opportunity of sharing the spirit of the season and the fellowship of this moment. Both are very special.

Christmas, the time when we celebrate the birth of the Christ, is the focal point of our calendar and of our culture. It is more than lights and gifts, music and parties. It is those things, and it is more.

Wise old prophets, like Isaiah, saw it happening in their future: "For unto us a Child is born," he wrote, "unto us a Son is given; and the government shall be upon his shoulder. These will be his royal titles: 'Wonderful,' 'Counselor,' 'The Mighty God,' 'The Everlasting Father,' 'The Prince of Peace.'"[2]

Isaiah wrote in the ninth chapter: "His ever-expanding, peaceful government will never end. He will rule with perfect fairness and justice from the throne of his father David. He will bring true justice and peace to all the nations of the world. This is going to happen because the Lord of heaven's armies has dedicated himself to do it!"[3]

And then it happened!

We believe that Jesus, the promised Messiah, was born almost 2,000 years ago. No one knows whether it was really December 25, but we do know that He was born. So, the most historic part of the prophecy has been fulfilled. But the sad thing is that while many call His name Wonderful, Counsellor, The Prince of Peace, if we're honest we have to admit that, too often, these praises ring a little hollow. His government and peace, His order and justice too often seem a little shaky, both in the private lives of many individuals and in the world around us.

The reason is not because the promise wasn't kept. Look back once more at the wonderful promise of Isaiah. Long before the great event took place in history, he claimed: "For unto us a Child is born; unto us a Son is given."

But for whom was the gift intended? It was intended for us—you and me, Isaiah, the person sitting next to you, our children, friends, and loved ones. We are the recipients of this great gift, each individually; each in his or her turn.

Our Lord himself said, "Look! I have been standing at the door and I am constantly knocking. If anyone hears me calling him and opens the door, I will come in and fellowship with him and he with me."[4]

How do we know that it is Christ who is knocking? Perhaps we can discover the answer in a story told by one of America's great poets, Edwin Markham. It's about a cobbler of long ago who dearly loved the Lord.[5]

One night, at the Christmas season, he dreamed that Christ had promised to visit him personally the following day. Recalling that, early the next morning, Conrad, the cobbler, cleaned and decorated his meager shop. He prepared a fine meal for his expected guest and then sat down in great expectation to await His coming.

Three times that day he had visitors, but not the one he waited for. First, it was a beggar seeking warmth, and Conrad, overcoming his impatience, let him in to rest beside his stove. Noticing that his shoes were worn through completely, he gave him a new pair before the old man left.

Then, the cobbler saw an old woman, bent under a load of heavy firewood, struggling up the street, wet, weary, and cold. He brought her, too, into the warmth of his humble shop. And because he had nothing else to give, he shared with her part of the fine meal he had prepared for the Lord.

As darkness fell, the cobbler, now impatiently waiting by his door for his overdue visitor, saw a lost child, frightened and crying bitterly, entering his shop. Poor Conrad was really torn, for, if he guided the child to his home, far on the other side of the city, he might miss the Christ Child. But, he did what he was called to do: He left the shop, led the child home, and hurried back.

Through what remained of the evening, the cobbler worried, first, that he had missed the Lord's visit—or worse, that the Lord had decided not to come. Finally, he cried out, "Why is it, Lord that your feet delay? / Have you forgotten that this was the day?"

And then, in the silence, Conrad heard a soft voice reply:

> Lift up your heart for I have kept my word.
> Three times I came to your friendly door
> Three times my shadow was on your floor.
> I was the beggar with bruised feet.
> I was the woman you gave food to eat.
> I was the child on the homeless street.[6]

Phillips Brooks wrote a Christmas carol once. Overlooking a wooded valley—Hybla Valley, near where we lived for a while in Fairfax County, Virginia—he wrote, "O Little Town of Bethlehem." In it, he gave a clear answer to where the Christ is born today: "Where meek souls receive Him still, / The dear Christ enters in."[7]

Some people live their lives today, unfortunately, without room for others. Yet, their lives are indeed empty and meaningless.

The things I have been talking about are what you would call the deeper things of Christmas, the very solemn, very holy things. They come first, I believe, because they are the real Christmas, the "always" Christmas. This doesn't mean that there isn't a very special place in our lives for the Christmas holiday and all the special symbols, and reminders, and festivities we look forward to each year. In the case of Christmas, we shouldn't lose the trimming and the gaiety. Indeed, if we take the time, our enjoyment of the symbols themselves can lead us through to what the symbols stand for, what is truly behind Santa's beard and what is shining from the star on top of the tree. In this astronomically very special year, when few have set aside the time to search for one unusually rare symbol, or sign, of Halley's comet, will we miss our generation's one chance to wonder at its soft haze of light in the southern evening sky, in rare conjunction with the lights of Christmas?[8]

For, you see, the symbols become even more wonderful as a significant part of our joy of keeping the real Christmas and our responsibility for passing it on. The magic burns brighter as we realize that each year we are hosts and hostesses at His birthday party. Then, the day after Christmas, or the year after next, we all find that as each new generation graduates into the adult realm, it becomes the custodian of Christmas. It becomes the keeper of its traditions and customs, a link in a chain which has been forged generation by generation, for century after century.

Of course, Santa is an important part of Christmas. This wonderful ruddy fellow in red velvet and his remarkable generosity is part of a myth that began long ago, arising in many different nations. In character, he's three parts the Dutch St. Nicholas and one part the British Father Christmas. All of these were blended in the mighty melting pot of America, to recreate him as we know him today.

The history of Santa is the history of a cheerful myth. But out of the myth has come a spirit that has helped many understand the real Christmas, the true story of the greatest gift ever given. Whenever that spirit prompts you to give something of yourself to someone else, in love, unselfishly, then you become the real Santa Claus.

Now, if Santa at times has become too commercial, it's not because he took Christ out of Christmas. If that has happened in a person's life, then that person is responsible. Since it is you and I who reenact the ancient role, it is up to us to make Christ the central figure. Surely, Santa as he should be, as a symbol of love, of generosity and merriment, would have delighted the heart of the Christ Child. "Be of good cheer," Jesus said on several occasions, and certainly the birth of Christ into the world is an occasion of great joy.

The poet Carpini once asked his friend, the composer Haydn, how it happened that his church music was always of a cheerful character. Haydn replied, "I cannot make it otherwise. I write according to the thoughts which I feel. When I think upon God, my heart is so full of joy that the notes dance and leap, as it were, from my pen. And since God has given me such a cheerful heart, it will be easily forgiven me that I serve Him with a cheerful spirit."

Well, what about giving to others at Christmastime? This is very important on Christ's birthday. Didn't He, himself, say, "When you did it to these my brothers you were doing it to me."[9] But he did not say we had to go out and spend a lot of money on expensive gifts, nor did he say, "Go and take what someone else has, to give to the poor!" Give of yourself.

There are things which all of us can do that will be appreciated more than the things money can buy. It's a real challenge to find how many ways there are to give of yourself. Perhaps you know a needy family, or maybe there's an abused child or a troubled young person who needs your guiding help, or a charitable cause you can serve. There are so many needs.

You will begin to be able to answer some of life's big questions: What is life all about? Does it have a meaning and a purpose? What am I supposed to do here? The answers, of course, go back to something I said in my inaugural speech last January. I called upon all North Carolinians to work together to build one united state. Christmas is a good time to recommit ourselves to that process of cooperation and goodwill.

Let us start contributing to life, to enriching the lives of others, to giving all the love we have, all the time we have, all the thoughtfulness and kindness we have to making North Carolina a happier place, because it is where we live. It is our duty and our privilege. A very wise woman once said,

> Christ has no body now on earth but yours,
> No hands but yours, no feet but yours,
> Yours are the eyes through which Christ's compassion
>   is to look out on the world,
> Yours are the feet with which He is to go about doing
>   good,
> And yours are the hands with which He is to bless us
>   now.

Giving of yourself is all that is asked of you, and don't ever think you have nothing to give. Everyone does.

There is a story about a country minister who had no regular congregation, so he earned his living by filling vacancies around the countryside. One Sunday, he was called to preach in a small town church. As he entered the church, he and his little boy passed a box, labeled "For the Poor." Although he was not overburdened with wealth himself, the pastor fished out a quarter and dropped it in.

At the end of the service, he was informed that visiting ministers were paid with the contents of the poor box. When it was opened, out rolled one lone quarter: his own. "Gee, Dad," said his son, "you'd have gotten more out if you'd put more in."

Christmas is a good time to take stock of what we're putting into the lives of others and to measure our balance with the world. God has been good to us. Let us work as one united state to repay part of that kindness during this Christmas season and all through the year. Yes, it can be more than "Season's Greetings," more than "Happy Holidays." It is Merry [Christmas].

---

[1]William Franklin (Billy) Graham (1918-   ), born near Charlotte; resident of Montreat; was graduated from Florida Bible Institute, 1940, and from Wheaton College, 1943; was ordained as Southern Baptist minister. Began career as evangelist in late 1940s; conducted first overseas crusade, England, 1954; founder, Billy Graham Evangelistic Assn.; syndicated newpaper columnist; author. *Charlotte Observer*, February 7, 1977; *Illustrated London News*, February, 1980; see also Marshall Frady, *Billy Graham, A Parable of American Righteousness* (Boston: Little, Brown and Company, 1979); and see John Pollock, *Billy Graham: The Authorized Biography* (Minneapolis: World Wide Publications, updated edition, 1969), and *Billy Graham, Evangelist to the World* (New York: Harper & Row, Publishers, 1979).

[2]Isaiah 9:6. All biblical quotations in this speech are from the Living Bible.

[3]Isaiah 9:7.

[4]Revelation 3:20.

[5]The governor retold "How the Great Guest Came," in *The Shoes of Happiness and Other Poems*, by Edwin Markham (Garden City, New York: Doubleday, Doran & Company, Inc., 1932), 56-60, hereinafter cited as Markham, "How the Great Guest Came."

[6]As published, the final verse of Markham's "How the Great Guest Came," page 60, reads as follows:

> "Why is it, Lord, that your feet delay?
> Did You forget that this was the day?"
> Then soft in the silence a Voice he heard:
> "Lift up your heart, for I kept my word.
> Three times I came to your friendly door;
> Three times my shadow was on your floor.
> I was the beggar with bruised feet;
> I was the woman you gave to eat;
> I was the child on the homeless street!"

[7]"Where meek souls will receive Him still, / The dear Christ enters in." From the third verse of "O Little Town of Bethlehem," by Phillips Brooks, as quoted from *The Free Will Baptist Hymn Book* (Nashville, Tennessee: National Association of Free Will Baptists, 1964), 275.

[8]Scientists correctly predicted that the return of Halley's comet would be nothing like the spectacular 1910 appearance, when the earth nearly passed through its tail. Coming only to within 39 million miles of earth in 1986, the comet seemed nothing more to the unaided eye than a distant, dimly fuzzy spot in the sky. However, while the general public was largely underwhelmed by Halley's visual impact, scientific research benefited enormously. "Halley's Comet '86: Much More than Met the Eye," *National Geographic*, 170 (December, 1986), 758-85; "The Comet that Left Us Comatose," *U.S. News & World Report*, April 28, 1986, 10.

[9]Matthew 25:40.

GASTON COUNTY CHAMBER OF COMMERCE

GASTONIA, JANUARY 8, 1986

[J. A. Dalpiaz introduced the governor to the Gaston County Chamber of Commerce audience. Martin, in thanking Dalpiaz for his opening remarks, called him a "good friend" and expressed gratitude for his serving as chairman of the Small Business Committee, "and before that in helping Secretary Haworth put together (a) strong team at (the) State Ports Authority."]

I am very pleased to acknowledge the presence of one distinguished guest whom the chamber honors today, my former colleague and mentor for twelve years, your United States congressman, Jim Broyhill. You have noted his achievements as the senior Republican on the very powerful House Committee on Energy and Commerce; in case you don't know, that's the committee that decides what you can and can't do on your own. Many will note his leadership as vice-chairman of the Congressional Textile Caucus, as well as the Footwear Caucus. Others will recall the occasions when he has used his office to help them, as when he helped me by engineering my selection to the Ways and Means Committee in 1975. I join you in thanking him for his outstanding service to the people.

I very much appreciate this opportunity to speak to the Gaston County Chamber of Commerce, for the occasion marks almost to the day the anniversary of my inauguration as governor of North Carolina. The year has been one of challenge, accomplishment, and, I believe, significant progress for our citizens and the state of North Carolina.[1] We've gone about our work, in a quiet but productive way, on a broad range of concerns—from awakening the social conscience of our people about the menace of drugs and alcohol, child victimization, and crime in the lives of our young people—to building brighter futures for the families who work in our industrial plants, stores, and on our farms.

Crucial and central to all of the concerns confronting this administration a year ago was then, and remains now, the vitality and durability of our traditional industries, small business firms, and entrepreneurial efforts which are the very heart of our economic system. [I am a] governor for business—well, yes, not exclusively, but yes, inclusively. That's where jobs come from: people investing assets, at risk of losing it, in hopes of profit, thereby creating jobs.

So, I'm for business. We continue to need their contributions in terms of jobs, trade, and investment as a means of building stronger communities and meeting the needs of an ever-growing labor force. This luncheon is testimony to the strong partnership between public and private enterprise in Gaston County; a salute to a strong textile county where [the] job market improved; a constant reminder that we have not forgotten our roots; that energy, commitment, and a steady vision have been, and always will be, indispensable ingredients to building a better future for our people.

At the same time, we must recognize the value of attracting new industry as a vital transfusion to the lifeblood of North Carolina. In preparing for this luncheon, I was informed that several new, planned, industrial areas have been designated in Gaston County, and that local governments have made a strong commitment to providing the necessary resources for future development. I want to commend you on this spirit of enterprise and enduring faith in a future which will require a sharing of responsibilities. In the immediate years ahead, as the federal government seeks to reduce its alarming deficit and curb future spending, this sharing of decision making and funding among our own units of government will increase. We must be willing and prepared to accept this mission and welcome a return to the original concept of government.

During the first year of this administration, a solid foundation has been built upon which we can expect to expand our initiatives in the years ahead. One of the major building blocks in this foundation has been the $171.5 million tax reduction package ratified by the 1985 session of the General Assembly, the largest tax cut in North Carolina history. Although I had asked for total elimination of the business inventory, intangibles, food, and over-the-counter medicine taxes, totaling $443.5 million, the reduction of the past year is substantial and would not have happened had we not joined to challenge the traditional pattern of raising taxes. Especially today, when we are being challenged anew by the rising tide of foreign imports, the aging of our resources, and the advancement of technology, this tax reduction will help generate new jobs and better opportunities for North Carolina citizens. Further elimination of the intangibles tax on stocks will cure a problem that has discouraged investment capital in North Carolina.[2]

Another building block in this foundation has been the Governor's Efficiency Study of state government, an in-depth examination of ways to eliminate duplication and prevent the waste of taxpayer dollars. This study, completed by a commission of voluntary leaders in business, industry, and finance, has proposed 414 cost-saving measures. Through programming and staff changes implemented by the administration in twenty-three targeted state agencies, we have already saved the state $5 million. We fully intend to pursue other viable measures to reduce the cost of government in ways which will not diminish services to the people of our state or adversely affect the operation of government. This commitment is based upon our obligation to be responsible and accountable as stewards of public funds.

Among the other initiatives which we have undertaken in the first year have been efforts to improve our educational system by encouraging the recruitment and retention of our best teachers and to pay them commensurate with their ability to produce quality students. Strategically, the most important deficiency in our education program is that we are not doing the job we need to do to attract and keep the best teachers available. The future of North Carolina will depend upon the ability of students to acquire the educational flexibility to deal with changing occupational roles.

It is estimated that 900,000 new jobs will be created in North Carolina between now and the year 2000. Moreover, eight out of every ten workers employed today will still be employed by the beginning of the twenty-first century. Most of these workers can expect to change skills between six and eight times during their lifetimes. This means that basic education and retraining will be among the dynamics of the future.

It is estimated that nonfarm employment in the state will increase slightly faster, by about 0.3 percent, than the nation through the next ten years. These new jobs translate into a stronger domestic economy and a new chance to regain our international competitiveness and seize new opportunities to expand markets worldwide. We have the technology to accomplish this mission. How well we apply this technology will determine our economic fate in the years ahead.

Although we are blessed with an impressive list of flagship industries, most of our companies, some 97 percent, are small businesses employing less than 100 workers. Of this total, 86.1 percent employ fewer than twenty workers each, but they account for 20 percent of our work force. Increasingly, small firms represent a growing share of our business community.

Seventy-five percent of today's North Carolina companies are engaged in commerce and manufacturing, and about half these commercial and manufacturing firms comprise our traditional industries: textiles and apparel, furniture, cigarettes, food products, lumber, et cetera. Here in Gaston County, where traditional industries have flourished since before the turn of the century, you know the importance of these manufacturing operations. Statewide, our textile and our related fiber, apparel, hosiery, and footwear industries employ more than half of our manufacturing workers. As we diversify our economy, we must not forget the vital importance of production. No new wealth is created unless [we] grow it, mine, manufacture it, or build it.

And state government has a responsibility, although it is necesssarily limited in a free-market system, to bring the diverse interests of these traditional industries together in an effective coalition. Another way is to promote the acceptance of North Carolina manufactured goods on the basis of competitive quality, rather than price alone.

One of the first initiatives of this administration was establishment of the office of assistant secretary of commerce for traditional industries. White Watkins serves in this capacity, and I am pleased that he is with us here today. Under his direction, a traditional industries task force, composed of industry representatives, has been working to find innovative and effective programs to assist the companies that have been hard hit by unfair foreign competition. I am pleased that this task force has completed the first phase of its work, and I am informed that the findings and recommendations of this group will be presented to me within the coming month.

We are all disappointed that President Reagan recently vetoed the Textile and Apparel Trade Enforcement Act of 1985, but we cannot afford to let this action deter our efforts to fight the way foreign nations undercut our industries in ways that would violate our own antimonopoly laws if American competitors tried the same tactics. Within the last few weeks, I have written to many of our traditional industries reaffirming my commitment, as governor, to seeking enforcement of the bilateral agreements reached in 1981 under MFA, the Multi-Fiber Arrangement. These import quotas were entered into voluntarily by our trading partners and remain theoretically in effect, and need to be honored and enforced. I urge your continued support as we work together to sustain our traditional industries and enable them to employ the new technology and marketing strategies so necessary to our economic future.

Since the first days of this administration, we have adopted a policy of purchasing goods and services for state government from North Carolina firms which are competitive. This policy has worked extremely well, and in the public interest, and it has set an example for the private sector to follow. North Carolina businesses need customers, and customers need payrolls, and that means that to buy American is in the self-interest of any business.

Another important economic initiative has been the appointment of an assistant secretary of commerce for small business. I am also pleased that Lew Myers, who accepted this appointment early in the administration, has joined us for this luncheon; it has been under his direction that the Small Business Division of the Department of Commerce has broadened the scope and range of services to aid the development of new business start-ups.

One of our most effective programs has been the sponsorship of two annual buyer-supplier conferences at which North Carolina companies have had an opportunity to expand the markets and sell their products nationwide. Another program has been the sponsorship of educational seminars and the extension of technical assistance to a growing number of entrepreneurs.

Our goal is to reduce the rate of failures, among emerging companies, by extending a helping hand consistent with the role of government and to help new companies grow. Accomplishing this goal depends upon active participation of small business firms in our efforts to define their needs. We must remember that output is consistent with input.

Building an effective partnership is essential to growth. Representatives of small business firms who are here today can begin to build that partnership through participation in the White House Conference on Small Business, which will be held at the Civic Center, in Raleigh, on January 28. On the eve of that conference, I will be receiving the report of the Small Business Committee of our Department of Commerce which, as I said before, is chaired by "Dal" Dalpiaz.[3] Taken together, this report and your suggestions will help our state and federal governments set better policies.

As I mentioned at the outset, the future of North Carolina is not solely dependent upon the flagship industries, as important as they are to our economy. A large part of our future growth will come from new ventures, and we must be ready and receptive. I intend to work for both.

Perhaps one of the most important factors to business in general is North Carolina's climate for growth. Public policies and decisions have a tremendous impact on shaping the environment in which business thrives. As a pro-business governor who recognizes that new jobs are generated by private enterprise, I will continue the pursuit of those goals which will strengthen that system and, in turn, provide new opportunities for all North Carolinians.

Permit me also to thank all of you for the support you have given me as governor. We love North Carolina not just for what it was in the past, although it has always been great; not just for what it is, although we take pride in our generation's accomplishments; but also for what it can become, as one truly united state. Working together, we can keep North Carolina economically alive, dynamic, prosperous, and progressive.

We share a bright vision of North Carolina's future. Whether we shape the future in the image of that vision is ours to determine, by our choices, today. Only if we work to build a state united will we bequeath, to those who will follow us, a land of hope and opportunity and a satisfying quality of life for all our people. Thank you for what you are doing to build that.

---

[1]At this point in his prepared text, the governor jotted notes discussing the effects of congressionally mandated budget cuts upon state hiring. Having begun with "Feel good about management team," Martin then wrote "Just today—announced steps to prepare state government for impact of GRH" [the Gramm-Rudman-Hollings Act]. His options were, as he saw them: "1. Sit tight until April, May: face disruption [then]; 2. Freeze: disruption now. 2. [sic] Slow down new hires. Keep some vacancies in reserve for those whose jobs might be eliminated in April. My plan: fair to current employees; use job attrition between now and April so something to offer: soft landing."

P.L. 99-177, "Balanced Budget and Emergency Deficit Control Act of 1985" (short title), *United States Statutes at Large*, Act of December 12, 1985, 99 Stat. 1037-1101, was more popularly known by the surnames of its three primary sponsors: Senator William Philip Gramm (R-Texas), Senator Warren Bruce Rudman (R-New Hampshire), and Senator Ernest Frederick Hollings (D-South Carolina). The Gramm-Rudman-Hollings Act was designed to bring the federal budget into balance, in the 1991 fiscal year, by establishing a timetable of stepped reductions in the federal deficit beginning in 1986. If Congress failed to meet specific deficit limits as mandated by P.L. 99-177, the law automatically enacted spending reductions in nonexempt programs. Gramm-Rudman-Hollings was expected to cut $12 billion from the federal budget by March, 1986. *Major Legislation of Congress, January, 1986*, MLC-005.

[2]"The tax policies of government should support and encourage the private enterprise system," the governor told a High Point audience on May 20, 1986.

[3]J. A. Dalpiaz; resident of Gastonia; was graduated from Illinois Institute of Technology, 1953; was also educated at University of North Carolina at Chapel Hill. Chief executive officer, cofounder, Manufacturing Services, Inc., Bessemer City; chairman, Crescent Enterprises, Ltd.; state chairman, 1986 White House Conference on Small Business; author; instructor. Active in local, statewide, and regional GOP politics; delegate, Republican National Convention, 1976, 1980, 1988; former chairman, Gaston County and Tenth Congressional District Republican party. J. A. Dalpiaz to Jan-Michael Poff, December 12, 1989.

MAYOR'S PRAYER BREAKFAST

GREENSBORO, JANUARY 13, 1986

Good morning, ladies and gentlemen. I am delighted to join you today for the Eleventh Annual Mayor's Prayer Breakfast, and I want to thank Mayor (John) Forbis[1] for his kind introduction. In the spirit which this meeting place inspires,[2] I want to speak today on the importance which our founding fathers attached to religion in developing our constitutional formula and emphasize its relevance today.

Before I do this, I believe it is appropriate to express my appreciation to the elected officials, both state and local, who have joined with me and my administration to promote unity, trust, and honor in public office. Exemplary moral standards and untarnished ethical behavior are indispensable ingredients of good government—and without them we would have no value compass to guide us in the task of leading and governing—and so, too, is our ability to work together for the greater public good.

I grew up in a Christian home, the son of a minister. My father was executive secretary of the Presbyterian Synod of South Carolina, and he and my mother instilled in me, at an early age, the timeless spiritual principles which have greatly influenced both my public and private life. There was also the closeness of family which inculcated the bond of love and caring for one another, fostered an understanding of right from wrong, and encouraged compassion for one's neighbors and friends. To use today's idiom, I learned how to set priorities.

In today's society, we have been inundated by a wave of accelerating violent crimes, narcotics addiction, alcoholism, high divorce rates, and deteriorating family life. This is why it is especially incumbent upon public officials to serve as an example of honesty, morality, and priceless integrity.

Many people today fail to realize the supreme importance our founding fathers gave to the role of religion in the structure of the unique civilization they hoped would emerge as the first free people in modern times. The founding fathers also believed the role of religion would be as vital in our own day as it was in theirs.

In 1787, the very year the Constitution was drafted and signed by Congress, that same body of Congress passed the famous Northwest Ordinance. In it, they outlawed slavery in the Northwest Territory; they enunciated the basic rights of citizens in language similar to that which later was incorporated into the Bill of Rights; and they emphasized the essential need to teach religion and morality in the schools.

This is the way they put it: "Article 3: Religion, Morality and knowledge being necessary to good government and the happiness of mankind, Schools and the means of education shall forever be encouraged."[3]

The position set forth in the Northwest Ordinance was reemphasized by President George Washington in his "Farewell Address." "Of all the dispositions and habits which lead to political prosperity," he said, "Religion and morality are indispensable supports. . . . And let us with caution indulge the supposition that morality can be maintained without religion. . . . Reason and experience both forbid us to expect that National morality can prevail to the exclusion of religious principle."[4]

Having established that religion is the foundation of morality, and that both are essential to good government and the happiness of mankind, the founders set about to exclude the creeds and biases of individual denominations. Their hope was to make the teaching of religion a universal cultural adhesive, rather than a divisive force.

Several of the founders have left us with a description of their basic religious beliefs. Benjamin Franklin summarized those which he believed were the "fundamental points for all sound religion." Here is the way he said it: "Here is my creed. I believe in one God, the creator of the universe. That he governs it by his providence. That he ought to be worshipped. That the most acceptable service we render to him is in doing good to his other children. That the soul of man is immortal and will be treated with justice in another life respecting its conduct in this. These I take to be the fundamental points in all sound religion."[5]

The five points of fundamental religious belief which are to be found in all principal religions of the world are those expressed or implied by Franklin:

1. Recognition and worship of a creator who made all things.

2. That the creator has revealed a moral code of behavior for happy living which distinguished right from wrong.

3. That the creator holds mankind responsible for the way they treat each other.

4. That all mankind live beyond this life.

5. That in the next life, mankind are judged for their conduct in this one.

Samuel Adams said these basic beliefs which constitute "the religion of America is the religion of all mankind." In other words, these beliefs belong to all world faiths and should, therefore, be taught without being offensive to any "sect or denomination," as indicated in the Virginia bill establishing elementary schools. John Adams called these tenets the "general principles" on which the American civilization had been founded. Thomas Jefferson pointed out that these beliefs are the principles "in which God has united us all."

From these statements, it is obvious how significantly the founders looked upon religion and morality as the cornerstones of a free government. When Alexis de Toqueville, a French author, visited the United States in 1831, he became so impressed with what he saw that he went home and wrote one of the most definitive studies on the American culture and constitutional system ever published. His book was called *Democracy in America*; concerning religion in our country, he wrote: "On my arrival in the United States the religious aspect of the country was the first thing that struck my attention; and the longer I stayed there, the more I perceived the great political consequences resulting from this new state of things."[6]

He continued by describing what he had observed:

> Religion in America takes no direct part in the government of society, but it must be regarded as the first of their political institutions . . . I do not know whether all Americans have a sincere faith in their religion—for who can search the human heart?—but I am certain that they hold it to be indispensable to the maintenance of republican institutions. This opinion is not peculiar to a class of citizens or a party, but it belongs to the whole nation and to every rank of society.[7]

There is no doubt in my mind that the America of today contrasts sharply with the one which so impressed our French visitor of this revolutionary time. We need desperately to return to the foundation principles that made our predecessors a proud, free, and moral people. All of us are children of God, created in his image and wonderously made. We have immense powers of thought and imagination and an astonishing capacity for courageous devotion. As such, it might well be said that our spirit is the candle of the Lord.

However, we cannot stop here in describing ourselves and our nature. This would be an incomplete account of us, for our spirit, granted to be the candle of the Lord, is often a candle wavering and uncertain, forever in need of God's own grace and mercy to add vigor to its flame. Every person has the capacity to be evil, selfish, cruel, proud, greedy, and cynical, as well as good, loving, humble, devoted, and faithful.

In brief, the essence of our freedom is the real opportunity to choose good over evil. If we choose the good, and the commandments of God are followed, we know the fulfillment of life, its elevation and grandeur, and that peace at the center of our being is a jewel without a price. We can discover today, as the disciples deeply discovered before us, that the longer we live with the words and deeds of Jesus, the more valid they become.

One of the results of entering into the abundant life that we are offered in spiritual communion is that our daily tasks take on new meaning and worthfulness. It is appalling how many people find their life work a daily grind and a monotonous repetition. For others, it is just a way to get by, to earn a livelihood.

All of this underscores the importance of a spiritual conception of what we do. William Gladstone is one of history's most outstanding examples of a man who lived to serve his fellow man. Four times he was prime minister of Great Britain, and for sixty-one years he was a member of the British House of Commons. One day, Mrs. Gladstone said to him, "I can't understand how you are able to bear up under the burdens of your office and the savage and cruel attacks that are sometimes made on you by your political opponents." He replied quietly, "It is only because I try to live under the form of eternity!"

In other words, he let something of the light of heaven fall upon his daily tasks. What a transformation would come over our world if the carpenter at his bench, the merchant behind the counter, the banker at his desk, the doctor in his clinic—indeed, everyone—would all pause in the morning, at the threshold of their labors, [and] say, "What I do here today I shall do for the glory of God, and may his blessings rest upon it." Then a radiance would invest all human toil, and we would be lifted to a new meaning of fulfillment.

We have the capacity to restore meaning to our own lives and the lives of others. We must regain the will.

As we think upon the imperfect world in which we live, I am reminded of the stirring words of Daniel Webster when he spoke to the New York Historical Society in 1852. He said,

> Unborn ages of glory crowd upon my soul, the realization of all which, however, is in the good hands and good pleasure of almighty God, but under his divine blessing, it will be dependent on the character and virtues of ourselves and posterity. If we and they shall live always in the fear of God, and shall respect his commandments . . . we may have the highest hopes of the future fortunes of our country. . . . It will have no decline and fall. It will go on prospering. But if we and our posterity reject religious instruction and authority, violate the rules of eternal justice, trifle with the injunctions of morality, and recklessly destroy the political constitution which holds us together, no man can tell how sudden a catastrophe may overwhelm us, that they shall bury our glory in profound obscurity.[8]

And he concluded, "Should that catastrophe happen, let it have no history! Let the horrible narrative never be written!"[9]

We, as a people in this state and nation, must maintain the fundamental values given us by the founding fathers. If we fail, we shall ourselves become the authors of that terrible history.

---

[1]John W. Forbis was mayor of Greensboro since 1981. *Greensboro News and Record,* April 12, 1987.

[2]First Baptist Church, 1000 West Friendly Avenue, Greensboro, was the site of the prayer breakfast. Governor's Schedule for Weeks of January 13-January 26, 1986, Governors Papers, James G. Martin.

[3]This section of "An Ordinance for the government of the territory of the United States North West of the river Ohio," begins "Article the Third." The remainder of the quotation is accurate. See Peter S. Onuf, *Statehood and Union: A History of the Northwest Ordinance* (Bloomington: University of Indiana Press, 1987), 63.

[4]Washington actually said "prevail in exclusion of religious principle." Otherwise, the remainder of the quotation compares accurately with "Farewell Address," September 19, 1796, in John C. Fitzpatrick (ed.), *The Writings of George Washington, from the Original Manuscript Series* (Washington: United States Government Printing Office, 39 volumes, 1931-1944), XXXV, 229.

[5]"Here is my Creed. I believe in one God, Creator of the Universe. That he governs it by his Providence. That he ought to be worshipped. That the most acceptable Service we render to him is doing good to his other Children. That the soul of Man is immortal, and will be treated with Justice in another Life respecting its Conduct in this. These I take to be the fundamental Principles of all sound Religion, and I regard them as you do in whatever Sect I meet with them." Benjamin Franklin to the Reverend Ezra Stiles, March 9, 1790, quoted in Benjamin Franklin, *Writings,* ed. by J. A. Leo Lemay (New York, New York: Library of America/Viking Press, 1987), 1179.

[6]Alexis de Tocqueville, *Democracy in America,* ed. by Phillips Bradley (New York: Vintage Books/Random House, 1961), 319, hereinafter cited as Bradley (ed.), *Democracy in America.* An improved translation of de Tocqueville's classic was published in 1966; compare with Bradley's version the appropriate lines from p. 271, Alexis de Tocqueville, *Democracy in America,* ed. by J. P. Mayer and Max Lerner (New York: Harper and Row, Publishers, 1966), hereinafter cited as Mayer and Lerner (eds.), *Democracy in America.*

[7]Bradley (ed.), *Democracy in America,* 316, reads "or to a party"; for comparison, see Mayer and Lerner (eds.), *Democracy in America,* 269.

[8]Webster read his speech, entitled "The Dignity and Importance of History," to the New York Historical Society on February 23, 1852. At the climax of his presentation, Webster declared:

Unborn ages and visions of glory crowd upon my soul, the realization of all which, however, is in the hands and good pleasure of Almighty God, but, under His divine blessing, it will be dependent on the character and the virtues of ourselves and of our posterity . . . if we and they shall live always in the fear of God, and shall respect His commandments . . . we may have the highest hopes of the future fortunes of our country. . . . It will have no decline and fall. It will go on prospering and to prosper. But if we and our posterity reject religious instruction and authority, violate the rules of eternal justice, trifle with the injunctions of morality, and recklessly destroy the political constitution which holds us together, no man can tell how sudden a catastrophe may overwhelm us that shall bury all our glory in profound obscurity.

Charles M. Wiltse (ed.), *The Papers of Daniel Webster: Speeches and Formal Writings* (Hanover, New Hampshire: University Press of New England, 2 volumes, 1988), II, 658-659, hereinafter cited as Wiltse, *Papers of Daniel Webster.*
⁹Wiltse, *Papers of Daniel Webster*, II, 659.

NORTH CAROLINA ASSOCIATION OF LOCAL HEALTH DIRECTORS

Raleigh, January 24, 1986

[The governor focused on local health issues in the following address and in speeches to the New Hanover County Health Department, Wilmington, April 16, 1987, and at groundbreaking ceremonies for Hoots Memorial Hospital, Yadkinville, March 29, 1988.]

I want to congratulate your new president, Beth Joyner.[1] I understand Beth is director of the Bertie County Health Department. That's a time-consuming job in itself, and I know everyone appreciates her giving time to this new position as well.

I also want to congratulate Howard Campbell, who received the Hamilton Stevens Award yesterday for outstanding contributions to public health.[2] Howard is health director for [the] Pasquotank-Perquimans-Camden-Chowan Health Department. We certainly appreciate all you've done to earn this prestigious award.

And finally, I want to congratulate all the other health directors in our state. Many of you have given long years of service to your communities; some of you have come into this field more recently. But whatever the length of your careers up to now, I want you to know what important contributions you have made to this state. You are responsible for the health and well-being of thousands of citizens. Because of you, babies are born healthier; children grow up with medical care they might otherwise never receive; adults and the elderly have access not only to treatment services, but to educational and preventive services, too.

You care for individuals in clinics and outreach programs. You care for the whole community through environmental programs. In some way, your work touches every citizen in your county. You have a positive impact on the quality of every life. I know your job isn't easy, and I really appreciate your dedication and your long hours of hard work. You may not hear it as often as you should, but believe me, the people in your community are grateful for the care and attention you give them. On behalf of all of them, I want to thank you for all that you do.

One of the most significant recent achievements has been the reduction of the infant mortality rate. You all are to be commended for this outstanding effort. This achievement was the result of intense teamwork throughout the state, and each one of you were vital members of that team. It wouldn't have been possible without your commitment and your active involvement.

We have come a long way, but we still have a long way to go. I want to encourage each of you not to ease up, but continue working as you have, with energy and determination. None of us can stop until every child born in our state has a chance for a healthy, productive life.

As you know, I proclaimed 1985 as the "Year of the Child" so we could focus on this and other issues involving the health and well-being of our children. We made significant progress in many areas. We laid the groundwork for the childhood injury prevention program. We obtained legislative funding to expand perinatal services, adolescent pregnancy programs, metabolic screening, crippled children's services, and more.[3] And there were other important achievements that have an impact on the health of our children, such as the expansion of the child abuse program, community substance abuse programs, and the Missing Children's Center.

We made gains in other important health services, too. We worked for, and received, appropriations to expand the environmental health program, the migrant health program, the sickle cell and nutritional programs. But government can't do the job alone. There must be a public-private partnership that recognizes the value of established programs and works to expand and enhance them. That happened last year when the Kate B. Reynolds Foundation awarded a grant of $198,000 to the Division of Health Services for a dental health education program. That same foundation has just made another award, to the division, of almost $100,000 for an oral survey of North Carolina schoolchildren. This study will be especially valuable because it will help us plan a more efficient, effective system of dental services for our children.

These awards are another result of teamwork. They are due in large part to each one of you, to the standards you maintain, to the quality of your work, to the reputation your services have in the community.

As you probably know by now, I am strongly committed to community services. I believe that the most effective programs are most often provided at the local level, with the support and involvement of the community. This is especially true for health-related services.

I also believe in the need for flexibility at the local level. As a former county commissioner, I understand the challenges you face. I understand the fact that different communities face different challenges and should have the flexibility to meet those challenges in the way that is best for that community.

In the coming months, there are a number of special issues that I want us to work on together. One is the solid and hazardous waste program. I'm concerned about the need for more staff to carry out our responsibilities in evaluating, issuing permits for, monitoring, and inspecting solid and hazardous waste facilities. We'll do our best to convince the General Assembly of the need for additional funds to ensure public safety.[4]

I also want to encourage local health departments to become more involved in hazardous waste management, especially where small generators, such as cleaners and dyers, are concerned.[5] With the increased federal restrictions on small generators, I think it makes more sense to decentralize some of the oversight responsibility rather than create additional state bureaucracy to handle it. I realize this means greater demands on you, and we need to look for the necessary resources to help you. The key is how best to serve the people and these small generators.

Prevention is another priority. We must do more in this area, not only because of the impact on the health of our citizens, but because of the economic impact, as well. It's not easy to get funding for preventive programs. A legislative study commission is working on this issue now, looking for creative, innovative approaches to financing. I'm following the commission's work with great interest, and I hope they'll be able to come up with a feasible plan.

Prevention is only one of the areas that is going to need innovative funding. The Gramm-Rudman-Hollings bill will have an impact on other health services, as well. I support this budget cutting concept because of the overall benefit to our economy. We will lose some jobs, but we're losing textile and furniture jobs now due to [the] deficit. It will just mean we have to work together even more closely in order to make better use of existing resources and develop a stronger public-private partnership.

It will also mean that volunteers will be more important than ever before. I'm convinced that volunteers are our state's greatest resource. In health departments, they not only help you serve more people with more programs, but they are an outreach program in themselves. Their enthusiasm and support for your work kindle enthusiasm and responsiveness throughout the county. They can help to raise public awareness about your department and help citizens to better understand what you do. I want to encourage each of you to make better use of this valuable resource.

In all the challenges before us in the months ahead, there is one key, and that's partnership—a public-private partnership, a state-county partnership, a joint effort of all of us concerned with the health and well-being of our citizens. I've talked a lot in the past year about the spirit of unity that we have in our state, about the importance of strengthening that spirit. We can strengthen it by listening to each other, by sharing ideas and concerns with each other.

You're the people on the front lines. You know the health issues that are most critical in your community. I want to hear about those issues. Phil Kirk and Dr. Levine[6] want to hear them. Only by listening to you, by talking with you and working together with you, can we respond effectively to the needs of our citizens. Only through a shared effort, a spirit of unity, an active partnership, can we bring a better way of life and greater opportunity to all the people of our state.

---

[1]Elizabeth Price Joyner (1946-   ), born in Norfolk, Virginia; resident of New Bern; B.S., Madison College (later James Madison University), 1968; M.P.H., University of North Carolina at Chapel Hill, 1980. Executive director, Dairy Council of the Shenandoah Valley, Staunton, Virginia, 1968-1970; nutritionist, Roanoke Chowan Hospital, Ahoskie, 1974-1980; health director, Bertie County Health Dept., Windsor, 1980-1986; health director, Craven County Health Dept., New Bern, since 1986; president, North Carolina Assn. of Local Health Directors, 1986. Elizabeth Price Joyner to Jan-Michael Poff, February 7, 1990.

[2]Howard B. Campbell (1936-   ), born in Charlestown, West Virginia; B.S., University of West Virginia; M.P.H., University of North Carolina at Chapel Hill. Health director, Pasquotank-Perquimans-Camden-Chowan District Health Department, since 1971; established state's first health department-operated Developmental Evaluation Center, a regional transportation system to get rural residents to health services, a genetic screening and counseling program, a home health/hospice program, and a mobile, comprehensive dental program for schoolchildren. Founding member, past president, North Carolina Assn. of Local Health Directors; public health lobbyist; winner, ENCPHA Hamilton Stevens Award, 1986. Carolyn H. Cartwright, administrative assistant, Pasquotank-Perquimans-Camden-Chowan District Health Department, to Jan-Michael Poff, February 26, 1990; News and Observer, June 7, 1981.

[3]Adolescent pregnancy and prematurity prevention projects were funded under N.C. Session Laws, 1985, c. 479, s. 102; see c. 479, secs. 2, 99, and 100 for maternal and child health care components. Appropriations for metabolic screening and the Crippled Children's Program were provided under N.C. Session Laws, 1985, c. 757, secs. 83 and 88, respectively.

[4]"An Act to Modify the Current Operations and Capital Improvements Appropriations for North Carolina State Government for the 1986-87 Fiscal Year, to Appropriate Funds for Local Needs, and to Make Other Changes in the Budget Operation of the State," N.C. Session Laws, 1985, Extra and Regular Sessions, 1986, c. 1014, was ratified July 15, 1986. Sections 101 and 102 authorized the Solid and Hazardous Waste Branch, Division of Health Services, Department of Human Resources, to hire additional field inspectors and other staff.

[5]Speaking in a similar vein at groundbreaking ceremonies for Hoots Memorial Hospital, Yadkinville, March 29, 1988, the governor asked his audience "to take part in your community through public education efforts. Environmental issues are ones that par-

ticularly need input of health professionals. I urge you to join the environmental debate in your area. It may be about solid waste, or about low-level radioactive and chemical waste facilities. Do you need them? If so, help us to educate the public about the unhealthy consequences of doing nothing, or of blocking such facilities. It is essential that we learn to live with the results of our advanced technology. We want the benefits it has brought us; we must accept the responsibility for its by-products."

[6]Ronald Howard Levine (1935-   ), born in New York City; resident of Raleigh; B.S., Union College, 1955; M.D., State University of New York, Downstate Medical Center, 1959; M.P.H., University of North Carolina at Chapel Hill, 1967. Pediatrician; chief, Communicable Disease Control Section, 1965-1967, assistant director, Local Health Division, 1967, North Carolina State Board of Health; clinical assistant professor of pediatrics, University of North Carolina Medical School, since 1966; Community Health Section chief, 1968-1973, assistant director for state services, 1974-1979, deputy director, 1979-1981, Division of Health Services, state Department of Human Resources; state health director, assistant secretary of health, Department of Human Resources (later Department of Environment, Health and Natural Resources), since 1981; adjunct professor, since 1982, Department of Health Administration, School of Public Health, University of North Carolina at Chapel Hill; author. Ronald Howard Levine to Jan-Michael Poff, February 7, 1990.

REPORT TO THE PEOPLE

Raleigh, January 25, 1986

[Governor Martin delivered a condensed version of the following address to the Fayetteville Chamber of Commerce, March 18, 1986.]

A little more than a year ago, on another Saturday in January, I took the oath of office as your new governor. I was given the duties and responsibilities, symbolized by this historic Capitol building, to serve you as chief executive officer under our state constitution. Tonight I am making my first annual report to the people of North Carolina, beginning with the challenges we have faced during this first year of reorganization. I want to share with you my vision of what North Carolina has become, and can become, as we seek to provide better jobs, better schools, better public facilities and services, in the effort to win a better quality of life for ourselves and our children. I see the mission, of this administration, to put our priorities in order in relation to that vision of the future and to run this government and deliver its services efficiently and fairly, just the way you would want to do if you were here.

1985 was a year of transition, and a year of testing, and a very busy year just getting organized and building a new leadership team for state government. I recruited a topflight group, including some seasoned and successful executives, to serve as cabinet secretaries and in key staff positions. They have brought a real demand for excellence to this administration and a belief that government is here to serve the people—and not the other way around.

By my proclamation, 1985 became the "Year of the Child" as our programs focused on the serious problems and dangers facing today's children.

In 1985 we reformed the state personnel system to free state workers from partisan political pressure so they could do their jobs with pride and be beholden to no one but the people of North Carolina. The number of political appointments was cut by 40 percent, leaving only those needed to really run the government—so I can govern. With the help of seventy-two volunteer business leaders, I commissioned an efficiency study to identify ways to improve the cost effectiveness of government. We are moving to implement these ideas in the realistic hope of saving over $150 million a year; that's $150 million that can be put to better use for you.

In 1985 we set a record for new and expanded business investment in North Carolina, a record $2.5 billion. While the national economy slowed down in 1985, in North Carolina it actually improved, and it improved substantially. We made a special effort to work with communities and businesses across the state, in partnership, and tonight I can report to you that more than $1 billion of that investment was in areas outside the industrial corridor of the piedmont crescent along Interstate 85. That means the economy of the whole state, as well as the industrial piedmont, is strong and growing. We're recruiting a diversity of new industry—high tech, low tech, financial and other services—and for the first time we've established a new program for our traditional industries, such as textiles and apparel, furniture, agriculture, and tourism. I expanded opportunities for minority companies to do business with state government.

With the future uncertain for our tobacco farmers, the healthy success of poultry production is a good sign of agricultural diversification as poultry became the number-one source of farm income for the first time in 1985.

When I took office just a year ago, statewide unemployment was at 7 percent; today it's down under 5 percent. In 1984, there were sixteen counties with unemployment worse than 10 percent; today there are only four. Our total number of jobs climbed above 3 million for the first time ever.

That's a record I'm proud of, a record I intend to continue and expand into other areas of state government.

Working with the General Assembly, we got a strong start on tax reform. We achieved about a third of the strategic tax cuts I asked for.

We got three fourths of the reduction I proposed in state funding for elective abortions. We funded the Missing Children Center and outlawed public exposure of pornographic materials to children. We expanded the state zoo.

There were areas of disagreement with the General Assembly as well, however. I opposed the practice of "pork barrel" appropriations and legislation which would weaken the office of the governor. I proposed allowing the people of North Carolina to decide whether to give veto power and responsibility to our governor, a necessary and essential power granted to every other governor in every other state in the union but North Carolina. North Carolina is the only state where the people have never been allowed to even vote for or against the veto for their own governor. I proposed merit selection and nonpartisan election of judges. The legislature rejected these proposals. While I believe the public's business should be conducted in public, the legislature has yet to strengthen the Open Meetings Law.

But there are some issues that go beyond partisan concern, issues which control the future of our state and our ability to grow and prosper. For me, the most important of these is the issue of education. That is why I had proposed to increase the percentage of the state budget going for schools—including salary improvements, class-size reductions, computer instruction, math, science and vocational equipment, and the Teacher Advancement Center—and I am happy to commend the legislature for going even beyond that. We were together in supporting the teacher career ladder pilot program to develop an incentive pay system to provide better pay for better teachers. They accepted my recommendation not to rush into it on a statewide basis until we're ready. We want to make sure our children get what we pay for, and that we pay teachers what they deserve. I am particularly encouraged by the support I've received for my emphasis on reserving in the budget enough revenue to cover the improved pay for teachers under the career ladder concept when it goes into effect statewide.

But the foundation of education needs to be strengthened in other areas, as well. That's why I've offered several different proposals in support of public education, proposals to encourage young people to enter the teaching profession as a career; proposals to provide a realistic, goal-directed curriculum for our students and a system of accountability that will ensure that our children will be equipped to meet the demands of a new age for North Carolina, an age of growth, diversity, and opportunity.

Looking back over this last year, my first year, I am pleased with the substantial progress we've achieved in molding our government to meet your needs. Perhaps my most significant effort in this past year has been to cut taxes. We only won a third of the tax cuts I asked for, but it's clear that if I hadn't fought hard for that there would have been no tax cuts at all. That money would have been spent, and the budget would have been just as tight as it is now—only there would have been no tax relief. It's a start.

Well, what's next? What is in store for 1986?

As I have traveled across North Carolina, listening to your ideas at town meetings and community festivals, I have gained a better understanding of the potential of our state—our human resources, our natural resources, our public works facilities, and our business climate. We have great potential, but that potential will only be realized through strong and intelligent leadership so that we may improve the quality of life for all our people. I, for one, will not be satisfied until we do provide better education for our children; better jobs for our neighbors and ourselves; more adequate public facilities; and better health, safety, and environmental protection.

That is my vision of what North Carolina can become: a land of hope and opportunity with a better life for all. But how do we get there from here?

In many respects, things are going well for us, but they could be going great. For example, what can we do to achieve better schools? The world is full of good ideas for improving every aspect of education. The usual approach is to insist that we add on every good idea anybody can think of, regardless of the cost.

My approach is different. I believe that some ideas are better than others. I believe that some needs are more urgent than others. I believe that classroom teachers must come first. The most serious problem facing our schools is that we cannot attract enough bright young people into teaching careers, and we cannot hold on to enough of those who become good teachers because they are lured elsewhere. For two decades in America, we have spent more and more on all the other good ideas for schools and less and less for classroom teachers as a percent of the school budget. That's not putting first things first.

If teachers are truly our first priority, then we must strengthen the teaching career program first. That's not a radical idea, and there would be no need to raise taxes for this, truly our first, priority. We must put teachers first.

There are dozens of ideas for improving education, but the most important mission for me as an education governor, as one who really has been an educator, is not to see how many ideas I can come up with. No, my mission is [to] make sure this most important idea becomes a reality, because good teachers will provide our children the education that will help them get a job and establish a productive career and a fuller life.

Just as we must have better schools for our young people, we must also have jobs for them, jobs that will match their talents so that they won't have to leave to find work elsewhere. Most of those new jobs will have to come from new business ventures and expansion.

Our Department of Commerce continues to compete aggressively for that new business and those new jobs. However, we cannot rely on the same old economic development programs of the past and expect to remain competitive in winning the jobs that our people will need. Things are changing. Last year we only began to explore innovative recruiting concepts for new industries. To stay ahead, we are developing a new blueprint for economic development, which I will announce in the spring. It will show a special emphasis on rural development to expand job opportunities in those cities that can serve as regional growth centers in our rural east and west. It will also shape new strategies for sustaining a healthy and continuing job market in the populous piedmont.

We all want better jobs everywhere in North Carolina. We also want a greater variety of jobs so that our economy is no longer vulnerable because of a dependence on just a few dominant industries. Yet, we want those industries also to survive, thrive, and remain competitive so that they, too, can be part of the building blocks of a great economy.

Good schools and attractive communities are major factors when businesses make decisions about where to locate; another is the quality of a state's transportation system. Next to our schools, we've put more public investment into North Carolina's fine highway system than into any other of our assets. Our administration is moving ahead on my pledge to complete the missing link of Interstate 40 to our truck-related seaport at Wilmington because the entire state will benefit from that. We are moving forward with other strategic highway arteries—U.S. 64 and 17 in the east and highways 74 and 421 in the west—as well as other primary improvements.

But we have also identified a problem. A panel of concerned and distinguished citizens has reported to me that our highway construction program is riding along on a flat tire. While our overall economy has expanded, the funds available for highway construction have not kept up with the rising cost of land, labor, and materials. The principal revenue for highways is the motor fuel tax, at a fixed 12.25 cents per gallon. Although the number of cars on our roads has increased by 30 percent over the last fifteen years, improved gas mileage has offset that and kept our gasoline tax revenue about even. So, the buying power of our Highway Fund effectively has been cut in half since 1970.

We are falling behind and can't meet the highway needs we face right now. There is an increasing demand throughout the state for even more new business and industrial park access roads. Our smaller cities need bypass routes; our larger cities have rush-hour traffic jammed in gridlock; our medium-sized cities have both problems. By the time the state has been scheduled to buy rights-of-way for your bypass, it's been covered with development and its price is out of sight. So all that extra, unnecessary traffic is going through your neighborhood instead of around it.

There are several ways to deal with this, including paying for the Highway Patrol in the General Fund, or reallocating existing sales tax revenues from cars into the Highway Fund. We are also considering a possible new bond issue, with a trust fund for loans to meet strategic needs, and even that may not do it. There is a possibility that a tax increase will have to be looked at as a last resort; one idea would be to adjust the gasoline tax just to neutralize the effect of inflation. We are approaching a final decision which may include some or all of these solutions. That choice will not be easy if we are to meet your needs, but I can assure you there is one option we do not have: to do nothing.

In the 1940s and 1950s, Governor Kerr Scott saw the need for farm-to-market paved roads to get our farmers out of the mud.[1] Our challenge is no less noble: to get our people moving who are stuck just as deeply in traffic jams. Our choice will be how best to build the road to our own future.

Roads are not our only construction needs. New schools, water and sewer facilities, as well as prison expansion, present serious choices for all of us. School construction has traditionally been the responsibility of local governments, but periodically, every ten to fifteen years or so, the state has had to help out because many counties with a low tax base per pupil simply can't afford to pay for the schools they need. In addition, if we're going to increase the number of classroom teachers, we will have to build more classrooms.

Water and sewer services are essential for bringing more business and jobs to our communities, but many of them cannot finance such projects. I asked for $60 million a year to help; the legislature insisted that it be distributed evenly, by population, across the state. That means that most of it will go to cities that don't need this modest help, while the towns that are desperate for help aren't going to get enough to do any good. One municipality will get $12.00 from this fund; another will get $44.00. That's not enough to draw a waterline on a planning map, much less to build one. I have asked the Department of Natural Resources and Community Development to prepare new methods for allocating these funds, and I will take those recommendations to the legislature.

We have another decision to make, an immediate one. Our prisons are seriously overcrowded. It's not an issue we can avoid unless we want to have the federal courts running our lives once more. Our Correction Department has developed a ten-year plan to relieve overcrowding, details of which will be presented to you in a few weeks.[2] It includes several ways of reducing the active inmate population by a program of more intensively supervised probation, community-based alternatives, and restitution as sentencing options for nonviolent convicts. Yet, that still will not be enough to meet the guidelines of the federal courts. Just to meet the remaining current needs, we may have to increase our prison capacity by as much as 2,300 spaces over and above the construction we have already scheduled. Part of that can be done through a new and innovative program using private companies to build and operate minimum security facilities at no more than it would cost the state to do it.

All of these capital investments in facilities are essential if we are to foster and continue economic growth, enhance the quality of life, and maintain the safety of our people. Our priorities are before us; we must determine what we need to do first and decide what we can afford to spend to do it—the same way you do with your family budget at home. That's why I wanted you to know the choices facing me, because they are also the choices facing you.

I began this report talking about the accomplishments of the past year and the challenges we faced reorganizing this administration. Then I offered my own vision of what the future holds, where we are, and where we are going—as one united state, full of hope and opportunity, offering a better life for all. To me, that means better jobs, better schools, and better government services. I've shared with you a review of some of the decisions about our facility needs and the financing considerations we will be facing over the next three to four months so that, in turn, I may have the benefit of your input before making those decisions. I ask you to write to me and to take part in the series of hearings we will hold across the state to get your input.

Just as 1985 was the "Year of the Child," I now designate 1986 in a way that will help direct our attention to another related and very special area of concern. We have found there is a great need to expand our efforts to help children who've been abused. The Child Victimization Commission, headed by my wife, Dottie, has identified a wide range of problems, including the horrors of the sexual abuse of young children. The commission will host the first-ever major national conference on the epidemic extent of child abuse. The commission also recommends that the Center for Missing Children be expanded in name and scope to become the Center for Missing and Victimized Children.[3]

With these ongoing concerns, and with our efforts to develop better schools and better jobs for our children and for ourselves, as well as greater security and involvement for the whole family—for all these reasons and more, I have decided to give special attention in 1986 to meeting the needs of the family, as the fundamental unit of our society. We will seek to help to unite and strengthen, to improve communications and to reinforce the basic structure of the ultimate foundation of our society, the family.

Accordingly, with this proclamation, I am pleased to designate the year 1986 as the "Year of the Family" in North Carolina. We hope to honor and help all our families, including the many who have a relative with a mental illness or deficiency, or with a problem with alcohol or drug dependence. All our families will benefit from a stronger economy, better government services, and public facilities as well as improved public schools.

In 1985, we called attention to the special problems faced by young children. In 1986, let us call attention to the problems faced by families—to help them to become strong and secure, so that they can continue to be the guardians of our cultural, religious, and political heritage.

This youthful, Old North State continued to make progress during 1985. Strengthened by its great resources, guided by respect for its traditional values, steadfast to its commitment to economic liberty and human dignity for all, let us go forward in 1986, confident of what we can make of North Carolina: truly one united state.

---

[1]William Kerr Scott (1896-1958), native of Alamance County; B.S., North Carolina State College (later University), 1917; U.S. Army, World War I. Farmer; county agent for Alamance, 1920-1930; state agriculture commissioner, 1937-1948; governor, 1949-1953; U.S. senator, 1953-1958. Over 14,000 miles of secondary roads were paved as a result of Governor Scott's "Go Forward" program. Cheney, *North Carolina Government*, 423, 426, 438n, 726, 727, 749n; David Leroy Corbitt (ed.), *Public Addresses, Letters, and Papers of*

William Kerr Scott, Governor of North Carolina, 1949-1953 (Raleigh: Council of State, State of North Carolina, 1957), ix-xxvi, hereinafter cited as Corbitt, *Addresses of Scott.*

[2]Martin was referring to "Corrections at the Crossroads," identified earlier in this volume.

[3]"An Act to Expand the North Carolina Center for Missing Children to Include Missing Persons," ratified July 12, 1986, established the North Carolina Center for Missing Persons. *N.C. Session Laws, 1985, Extra and Regular Sessions, 1986,* c. 1000.

RESPONSE TO SMALL BUSINESS COUNCIL REPORT

RALEIGH, JANUARY 27, 1986

I am pleased today to meet with you, the members of the North Carolina Small Business Council, for the purpose of responding to your recent report assessing the needs of our state's small business firms. First I want to thank Secretary Haworth for his kind introduction and acknowledge Scott Peace, under whose chairmanship all of you worked so diligently to complete this assignment.

The history of North Carolina is the history of a state at work, a state of farmers, manufacturers, and merchants joining together to build a better society. Ours is a state which has been built on individual initiative, a competitive spirit, and an intense pride in the achievements of the entrepreneur. Today, this enterprising determination to work and to prosper is embodied in more than 118,000 small businesses in North Carolina, which provide the technology to keep our economy growing, the manufacturing and marketing skills to keep our state competitive, and the innovation to guide us into a better future.

After reviewing your report, I was impressed by the opportunities the council has, working with private institutions and public agencies, to accelerate the growth of small businesses in our state. Let me also say that I have given your recommendations careful consideration. Today I want to respond to them in the same sequence they were presented: capital formation, communications, entrepreneurial education and training, regulations, and taxation—to about thirty topics, in all.

On the first topic, access to capital, you recommend that I encourage our financial institutions to become more aggressive in making loans to small business firms through loan guarantees and the pooling of funds. You've also suggested that they provide descriptions of their services and communicate better with small businesses on matters of policy.

Within the coming week, I plan to write to all of the chief executive officers of banks and encourage them to take an even more active role in providing capital to small firms. I also will request them to furnish written descriptions of their programs and services. This information will be valuable as the Small Business Council works to bring these sectors together.

You have recommended that we retain the Business Development Corporation of North Carolina as a legal entity, and I am now directing Secretary Haworth to take appropriate action to extend its existence. In addition, I want the secretary to work toward establishment of a statewide 503, or certified development corporation.

As suggested, I will work with the General Assembly's Legislative Study Commission on Venture Capital and Enterprise Zones, and I will encourage this commission to consider an enabling measure to designate such zones throughout our state. I will work with the study commission to explore the possibility of loan guarantee programs, direct loans in enterprise zones, and subsidized interest on small business loans. Your suggestion of a tax-exempt means of providing small companies with long-term, fixed-rate financing merits further attention.

On the remaining recommendations related to capital formation, I have instructed my staff to seek restoration of funds inadvertently omitted by clerical error in the last session of the General Assembly for the Technological Development Authority. Moreover, I have requested Scott Peace, who is my appointed delegate to the North Carolina White House Conference, to present our concerns over possible elimination of the Small Business Administration Loan Guarantee Program.

On the topic of communications, we are reviewing installation of a toll-free telephone in our Small Business Development Division so that small firms will have greater access to information and assistance. I also am pleased to report that a brochure listing services offered by the division is being developed, and I have taken steps to improve the state's purchasing directory. In this connection, I want to express appreciation to the Purchase and Contract Division for its help in publishing this directory.

Entrepreneurial education and training are vital to the success of many small businesses. Therefore, I am directing the Small Business Development Division to establish an information/referral clearinghouse to alert small businessmen to available education and training opportunities. As the constitutionally designated budget officer of the state, I will seek the Small Business Council's review and recommendations on proposals to establish training, education, and technical assistance programs to small businesses. The participation of the council will be most helpful in developing the 1987 budget.

Your recommendations to schedule community college courses in or near the business community, and to encourage chambers of commerce to develop mentor programs for small business owners through group discussions and individual consultations, are excellent. Earlier, I requested Scott Peace to meet with community college officials to discuss the location of courses at sites convenient to the business community, and I am pleased to report that this meeting already has been held. The community colleges of North Carolina are vital institutions in meeting the training needs of our citizens, and I want to commend them for the good work they do. Scott also has been directed by me to convene a meeting with interested chambers of commerce and to solicit their cooperation in establishing mentor programs.

Let us now turn our attention to recommendations related to regulations affecting small businesses. Your chairman already has started working with our small business centers to develop proposal-writing workshops to help business leaders conform to state and federal regulations. Additionally, I plan to write to the General Assembly's Simplified Business Licensing Study Commission and request consideration of your recommendation to consider license simplification, consolidation, and fee schedules. The commission also will be sent a copy of your report, and I have directed Scott Peace to meet with this body, as appropriate.

Your request to publicize better the rights of employers in cases involving employee dismissals will require the council to develop information on this issue and to communicate findings to chambers of commerce and other organizations. However, I want to call your attention to the workshops now being held on this matter by the Employment Security Commission throughout the state.

I plan in the very near future to discuss with the Economic Development Board your request for support of a subminimum wage for teenagers and the elderly. When a complete analysis of the proposal is completed, and if it supports such a recommendation, it will be included in my 1987 legislative program.

Our legislators have heard from many citizens concerning problems caused by having 1/2-cent tax increments. As you know, many businesses have become dependent on calculators and business machines. However, the North Carolina Department of Revenue has addressed this concern and provides a sales-and-use tax chart which indicates the specific amount of tax to be collected on a specific dollar amount. In view of this easy method, it does not appear that additional legislation is required.

The concern of the Small Business Council on uniform rules governing the sanitation requirements of bed-and-breakfast homes has been passed on to Secretary Kirk in the Department of Human Resources. I have directed Secretary Kirk to investigate this matter and submit his recommended solutions to me.

Imports and fair trade have played an important role in North Carolina's economic prosperity since its beginning. You have asked that a statement be made, at the White House Conference, on imports, exports, and international trade. The International Development Division of our Commerce Department works very hard to recruit foreign firms, but it also has a less visible, but perhaps more important, activity: promoting North Carolina exports.

I have taken a strong stand in opposition to unfair foreign competition which has hurt many of our traditional industries. That opposition will continue. Nevertheless, the White House Conference is a viable platform for addressing the issue further. Today, I want to ask your chairman to meet with Secretary Haworth, Assistant Secretary White Watkins, and International Development Director Jim Hinkle[1] to develop such a statement and to seek the endorsement of the Economic Development Board.

You have addressed two important issues in your final recommendations on regulations. These concern exempting small businesses from liability on prior contracts in which they were in compliance with rules at the time of contract performance, and to cap liability insurance limits for ski resorts, riding stables, and sports facilities. Committees of the General Assembly are working on these issues now, and I will make suggestions as appropriate. The availability and cost of liability insurance is a major concern to small business people.

I commend the council for offering its continuing assistance to the Legislative Study Commission. I expect you to follow the proceedings closely and to contribute suggestions and ideas.

A number of recommendations have been included in your report on the subject of taxation. They include state and federal income simplification, reduction of payroll tax costs, simplification and centralization of tax reporting, and creation of an investment tax credit in our state tax code. Other recommendations include exemption from taxation on the one-time sale of a small business, and a tax investment credit for individuals who invest in the start-up or expansion of a small business. I have taken all of these recommendations under advisement, and I will be examining them further in the months ahead.

All of you are familiar with my position on tax reform and relief. During the first year of my administration I was successful in obtaining tax reductions totaling $171.5 million, the largest tax cut in history. I will continue to advocate complete elimination of the strategic anti-job taxes that so severely impede growth and development of our economy. We must consider a number of impending factors, such as the effects of the Gramm-Rudman budget balancing legislation and the future growth of state revenues. 1986 is probably not a ripe year.

North Carolina also is confronted with some urgent major needs: better rural roads and urban highways; public education; relieving prison overcrowding; the funding of water, sewer, and other facility needs of local governments; and human services.

The report to which I have responded today has set a new course for improvement of the small business climate in North Carolina. Working together, we can achieve our objectives. I have asked Jack Hawke,[2] my chief of policy and planning, and Lew Myers, assistant secretary for small business, to convene a meeting within the next thirty days which will bring together representatives of all state supported small business programs. Assistant Secretary Myers convenes a monthly meeting of some of these agencies, but the purpose of these special sessions will be to invite the policy makers, as well as staff members, to work on a plan to coordinate better all of our programs and to allocate our resources in a responsible manner.

It is the enterprising genius of our small business people that has created most of our new jobs and provided economic opportunities unsurpassed by any state. Our sustained economic growth is encouraging many North Carolinians, young and old alike, to form their own businesses. These aspiring entrepreneurs have always been on the leading edge of our state's progress. The continued efforts of the Small Business Council will encourage and sustain others, and will contribute greatly to building a brighter future for all citizens. Thank you for these efforts, and keep up the good work.

---

[1]James R. Hinkle (1930-   ), born in Salisbury; resident of Raleigh; B.S., North Carolina State College (later University), 1951; M.B.A., University of North Carolina at Chapel Hill, 1954; former major, U.S. Army Corps of Engineers. Group vice-president, Carolina Power and Light Co., 1967-1973; president, Capital Consultants, 1973-1977; director, International Division, state Commerce Department, 1977-1986; president, West Virginia Round Table, Inc., 1986-1987; president, Treyburn, Durham, since 1987. James R. Hinkle to Jan-Michael Poff, January 30, 1990.

[2]R. Jack Hawke, Jr.; native of Pennsylvania; resident of Raleigh; attended Duke University law school. Former businessman; executive director, state Republican party,

1965; managed successful campaign of James Gardner for U.S. House, 1966; GOP candidate for U.S. House, Fourth North Carolina Congressional District, 1970, 1972; assistant transportation secretary during administration of Governor James E. Holshouser, Jr.; ran gubernatorial campaign of James G. Martin, 1984; Governor Martin's special assistant for policy, 1985; director, Division of Policy and Planning, Department of Administration, 1985-1987. Hawke was elected interim state GOP chairman, January 31, 1987, following resignation of Robert W. Bradshaw, Jr.; was elected to two-year term, May 30, 1987, and reelected on May 20, 1989. *News and Observer*, April 7, 1985, January 21, February 1, May 31, 1987, May 21, 1989.

APPALACHIAN SOCIETY, SOCIETY OF AMERICAN FORESTERS

RALEIGH, JANUARY 30, 1986

[The governor discussed the importance of the state's forestry industry, below; in his Arbor Day remarks, Raleigh, March 21, 1986; and in an address to the North Carolina Forestry Association, Asheville, October 6, 1988.]

The theme of your meeting is a critical one. Lieutenant Governor Bob Jordan, as a forester, may have the edge on me when it comes to the forest productivity part of the theme.[1] We are both collaborating to help support our forest industries. As a chemist, I can make a contribution when talking about atmospheric deposition.

Atmospheric deposition is not new. According to some accounts, acid rain was first mentioned in 1848 by a Swedish scientist.[2] French scientists measured quantities of nitric and nitrous acid and nitrogen oxides in Paris rain in 1852, and the occurrence of acid rain was documented in England in 1872. But it was not until the late 1960s that acid rain gained international attention as a serious concern. It has been cussed and discussed, across the country and around the world, ever since.

It is a hard subject to deal with. There's a range of uncertainties. It seems that for every thesis on what causes it, there is an antithesis—where it comes from, and what effects it has, what reaction process or component controls the kinetic rate.

Last week, newspapers reported on a study of a forest at the Oak Ridge National Laboratory. The report said, in part, "forests may satisfy increasing portions of their nutrient requirements by assimilation of airborne material, while simultaneously being exposed to increasing levels of air pollutants." For trees, that's like saying too much of a good thing.

Too much of most anything can be harmful. A little sugar in the coffee, or on cereal, is OK, but too much can cause problems; the same with table salt. Our system has to maintain an electrolyte balance, but excessive salt regularly is damaging to certain heart ailments, and a couple of teaspoons at once can be toxic. That's the nemesis of atmospheric deposition. A little bit of acid rain probably won't do any harm and can be accommodated, be natural basic minerals—carbonates, e.g. But increasing those amounts and the frequency, and everything becomes affected—some bad effects and some good effects.

As foresters, you know better than the rest of us that what we do to our forest has long-term effects, not only on the forest itself, but in many other areas, as well. Our Department of Natural Resources and Community Development [NRCD] has identified a number of major concerns of North Carolina citizens. Forest and forestry are intertwined in nearly all of these concerns.

—Water supply and watershed protection. Since forested watersheds are the best, the connection here is obvious.

—Natural resources allocation. Too much of our precious agricultural and forest land is being lost or drastically altered. In North Carolina many of our woodlands, especially the small woodlots, are growing less than half of their potential. The Governor's Interagency Committee on Small Woodlots is working on this problem and making good progress.

—Waste management and hazardous waste disposal. We generate a lot of waste in our business, industry, and society, and wood-using industries are no exception. Through our Pollution Prevention Pays program within NRCD, we are helping business, industry, and communities find better ways to make their products and dispose of their waste. As is often the case, what is one industry's waste or by-product is another's raw material.

—Coastal water quality is another area of concern. Most people have a hard time associating what happens on our farms and forests, and in our communities, with coastal water quality. But we have not lost sight of the simple fact that water flows downhill. Runoff from farms, forests, and communities eventually reaches our estuaries, bays, and sounds. That runoff, laden with chemical discharges, fertilizers, pollutants, and silt, affects fish nursery areas, and commercial and sport fishing, and shellfish resources.

—Community infrastructure and forestry may not seem to be related in the traditional sense, but the urban forest and the woodlands surrounding our communities are as much a part of the infrastructure as water and sewer lines, electrical power lines, and roads. Try to picture your hometown without the trees which make up the urban forest.

—The recognition that open space is a vital element of our life-style led NRCD to place concern about public land and parks on its list of priorities. Our administration is listening and responding to those concerns. Last summer, the North Carolina legislature appropriated $50 million to purchase lands critical to the completion of our state parks.

The clock is ticking. Park development master plans molded decades ago have laid dormant far too long. When the developer's bulldozer starts carving out homesites, or industrial sites, on land needed to complete a state park, it's a little late to say, "We meant to buy that land earlier, but. . . ."

—Groundwater protection rounds out NRCD's list of critical issues. While I don't know what the figures are for our neighboring states, I do know that 60 percent of North Carolinians depend upon groundwater for their drinking water. We must all constantly work to protect our groundwater from contamination. Just as too much sugar will make the coffee undrinkable, just a few gallons of old motor oil or discarded gasoline dumped on the ground can seep into a community's well and render millions of gallons of groundwater undrinkable.

Everyone in North Carolina, South Carolina, Virginia, and throughout the nation is dependent upon our forests and forest products. Forestry and forest product manufacturing, including large and small businesses, is the second leading industry in North Carolina: more than 136,000 jobs; an annual payroll of $1.4 billion; products valued in excess of $7 billion each year. The three states represented here today —North Carolina, South Carolina, and Virginia—make up approximately 25 percent of the commercial forest land in the twelve southern states, so the importance of forestry is not confined to my home state of North Carolina.

We have a long history and tradition of forestry in North Carolina. Professional forestry in the United States started in North Carolina when Gifford Pinchot arrived at the estate of George Vanderbilt in 1891. The first school of forestry in the United States was started at Biltmore a few years later. So, North Carolina is known as the Cradle of Forestry in the United States.[3]

When dealing with a resource—a crop, if you will—that takes thirty, or fifty, or seventy years to grow to maturity, it is paradoxical that we don't have time to waste. Let us not waste time pointing fingers and making accusations. We need answers. We are beginning to see that atmospheric acid deposition can have an affect on farms and forests, water and wildlife. The question is, let's find out what the real problems are and not neglect or ignore the whole range of effects. I commend you for your program and urge you to keep working to identify the problems caused by atmospheric deposition. We must find the solutions while we still have time to work on them.

---

[1]The theme of the 1986 annual meeting of the Appalachian Society, Society of American Foresters, was "Atmospheric Deposition and Forest Productivity." Lieutenant Governor Jordan was not scheduled to speak, but probably was in attendance. Dianne Parrish, assistant to the director, Division of Forest Resources, Department of Environment, Health, and Natural Resources, to Jan-Michael Poff, January 16, 1990.

[2]At this point in his prepared text, Martin inserted the following notes on the causes of acid rain: "Some natural—fires, lightning, volcanic; some industrial—boilers."

[3]Gifford Pinchot (1865-1946), born in Simsbury, Connecticut; died in Milford, Pennsylvania; A.B., Yale University, 1889; studied forestry in Europe; honorary degrees. First American forester; commenced first organized forest work in U.S. at Vanderbilt estate, Biltmore, 1892; forester, chief of what was to become U.S. Forest Service, 1898-1910; forestry professor, 1903-1936, professor emeritus after 1936, Yale University; president, National Conservation Assn., 1910-1925; commissioner of forestry, 1920-1922, governor, 1923-1927, 1931-1935, of Pennsylvania; author. *Who Was Who in America, 1943-1950*, 425.

PROCLAMATION CALLING EXTRA SESSION OF
GENERAL ASSEMBLY

RALEIGH, FEBRUARY 7, 1986

Information furnished to me by the Honorable James E. Long,[1] commissioner of insurance of North Carolina, indicates that as a consequence of market withdrawals, massive price increases, and, in certain instances, the availability of only "claims made" coverage, there are no longer available to municipalities and the individual and corporate citizenry of North Carolina certain types of reasonably affordable, commercially available casualty insurance furnished by private insurers licensed to do business in North Carolina. Further, the commissioner of insurance has advised me that circumstances have become such that this inability to procure these types of insurance in North Carolina is disruptive to the governmental, social, and commercial life of the state and that legislation to remedy the situation is needed immediately. He has expressed the opinion to me that the state cannot wait for the General Assembly to meet in June to resolve the matter. Accordingly, he has asked that I use the powers granted to me by Article III, Section 5(7), of the Constitution of North Carolina to convene the General Assembly into an extra session to address the matter now.

In addition, editorial and citizen responses to the recent designation by the United States Department of Energy of the Rolesville Pluton and Elk River rock formations as potential sites for further study for suitability as a high-level nuclear waste repository have made it clear to me that many people in North Carolina oppose such a repository being located in the state. The First Amendment to the Constitution of the United States grants to the people of each state the right to petition their government for a redress of their grievances. Submitting the question of whether they favor the location of a high-level nuclear waste repository in the state to the voters of the state in a nonbinding referendum is an effective way of allowing them to exercise their First Amendment rights on this issue in a timely way.

As required by Article III, Section 5(7), of the constitution, I have sought and received the advice of the Council of State concerning the circumstances facing the state and received from them their advice that immediate action by the General Assembly is required and that the General Assembly should be convened into extra session as provided in Article III, Section 5(7), of the constitution. I have also discussed the matter with the lieutenant governor and the Speaker of the North Carolina House of Representatives, and they are of the same view.

ACCORDINGLY, pursuant to the authority granted to me by Article III, Section 5(7) of the Constitution of North Carolina, I find that the circumstances stated above constitute an "extraordinary occasion" within the meaning of Article III, Section 5(7), of the Constitution of North Carolina, and PROCLAIM that the General Assembly is hereby convened in extra session for the purpose of considering legislation (1) to authorize the commissioner of insurance or insurance companies to create risk-sharing plans for unavailable kinds of property and casualty insurance and to designate areas and coverage under the FAIR plan;[2] and (2) to permit the insurance laws study commission, Liability and Property Insurance Markets Study Commission, and Medical Malpractice and Medical Liability Study Commission, established under the authority of Chapter 792, 1985 Session Laws, to report to the 1986 regular session of the 1985 General Assembly;[3] and (3) to place before the voters of the state, by nonbinding referendum at the May 6, 1986, primary election, the question of whether they favor the location in North Carolina of a high-level nuclear waste repository.[4]

This extra session to consider these matters shall begin February 18, 1986, at 10:00 A.M., and shall continue as provided by law and the rules of each house until both houses shall have adjourned *sine die.*
Done in Raleigh, North Carolina, this 7th day of February, 1986.

[Signed] James G. Martin

[state seal]

---

[1]James Eugene Long (1940-   ), born in Burlington; A.B., 1963, J.D., 1966, University of North Carolina at Chapel Hill. Attorney in private practice, 1966-1975, 1976-1984; member, state House of Representatives, 1971-1975; chief deputy commissioner of insurance, 1975-1976; counsel to state House Speaker Liston B. Ramsey, 1980-1984; elected state insurance commissioner, 1984, reelected 1988; Democrat. *North Carolina Manual, 1987-1988,* 667.

[2]"An Act to Authorize the Commissioner of Insurance or Insurance Companies to Create Risk Sharing Plans for Inadequate or Unavailable Kinds of Property and Casualty Insurance; to Expand the FAIR Plan; to Authorize the Commissioner of Insurance to Designate Additional Coverages Under the FAIR and Beach Plans; and to Authorize Insurers to Form Market Assistance Programs" was ratified February 18, 1986. *N.C. Session Laws, 1985, Extra and Regular Sessions, 1986,* c. 7. FAIR stood for Fair Access to Insurance Requirements; see G.S. 46-5.

[3]"An Act to Permit the Insurance Regulation Study Commission, the Liability and Property Insurance Markets Study Commission, and the Medical Malpractice and Medical Liability Study Commission to Submit Reports to the 1985 General Assembly, Regular Session 1986," was ratified February 18, 1986. *N.C. Session Laws, 1985, Extra and Regular Sessions, 1986,* c. 6.

[4]"An Act to Submit to the Voters of North Carolina Whether There Should Be Located Within the State of North Carolina a High-Level Radioactive Waste Repository Site" was ratified on February 18, 1986. *N.C. Session Laws, 1985, Extra and Regular Sessions, 1986,* c. 1.

CONFERENCE ON AMERICANS OUTDOORS

RALEIGH, FEBRBARY 11, 1986

Welcome to the great Americans Outdoors indoor conference! That's not ironic; it's just ecclesiastical that for everything there's a time and place.

One of the pleasures of being governor is to be involved in programs and policies which have the full support of the people of North Carolina. In addressing the need for practical recreation opportunities for future generations, that support is strong and growing. We all need the escape and the invigoration we get from recreation. Whether on a golf course; or working a fishing lure; or aboard my sailboat, reaching down the coast or across the sound, I not only get the satisfaction of what I'm doing, I can also turn loose all the burdens for a while and enjoy what nature has so amply provided in our state: places to unwind. They remind each of us that life is far more than concrete, traffic, and noise.

By the way, that old skipjack sailboat, to which Wes Davis referred, had an outboard hanging over the stern because the inboard had come apart while moving up the Intracoastal Waterway. That engine, of course, proves to those knowledgeable among you that it was neither authentic nor licensed as an oyster dredge. In it, our family began our cruising experience down the Potomac River, including marvelous excursions down to the Potomac Creek tributary where we harvested fossil shark teeth and watched a pair of eagles working a ravine at dusk.

From Manteo to Murphy, millions of North Carolinians take to the outdoors with the same enthusiasm. Their recreation may be hiking along a mountain trail, espying an eagle's nest; visiting our state zoo; boating on Kerr Lake; or riding on the carousel at the city park, all outdoors. It is a life-style we treasure in North Carolina. Will it be the same for our grandchildren? This conference urges us to make sure those opportunities are there when they are needed.

Those who administer and plan for recreation face the challenge of knowing what Americans, and North Carolinians, want in recreation and to ensure that they will have the places and the facilities to enjoy their leisure time—no easy task, one made more difficult by the pressures of population growth, the encroachment of commercial activity just outside park gates, and the seemingly endless stream of concerns about where the money will come from. This is not a challenge unique to the recreation profession; federal, state, and local government officials face it all the time: increasing demands for service in the face of shrinking dollars.

The President's Commission on Americans Outdoors is to be commended on its pragmatic approach in calling for conferences, like this one, all across the land; in pulling together the best information on what is and what needs to be in recreation; in applying the best minds to tackle new problems of space and money. At the first meeting of the commission in September, our friend and neighbor, Governor Lamar Alexander of Tennessee,[1] chairman of the commission, outlined the dual purposes of this effort. He also instilled in the work of the commission an underlying theme: to conserve our natural resources and avoid recreation services that would harm our environment.

Since the commission was created last August by President Reagan, its efforts already have focused on why new approaches to recreation are needed. Those who provide recreation opportunities pretty well know what Americans do outdoors, but far too little is known about what they want to do outdoors. The process of getting down to that is complex and tricky. What motivates the users of our recreation resources? What drives a factory worker to pack up [the] family and drive for two hours to fish for bass at Satterwhite Point?[2] What draws the family from Ohio into North Carolina for a week at Carolina Beach State Park? What motivates a mother to spend an afternoon with her children at the city park? And once they get to these places, what benefits do they carry home with them? This commission will seek to put the puzzle together, [to] know what people do when they go outdoors, what motivates them, what benefits they derive from the experience, and what more do they want to do outdoors.

What we do with all this knowledge is going to be the real test for us. Let us mark this day with hopes that this new presidential commission will carry into history the high marks accorded another, earlier presidential commission that resulted in the 1958 Outdoor Recreation Resources Review Act.[3] That set new standards of national concern for recreation and left us a legacy of programs and approaches still with us today. Some of them are, admittedly, in their waning moments, but their impacts have been felt, from softball fields, to national preserves, to more zoning requirements for open spaces.

For three years the recreation issues of the 1950s were studied and analyzed, and President Kennedy endorsed most of the recommendations of that commission. The proposals were not only influential at the time, but they have been instrumental in guiding national outdoor recreation policy for twenty years. The work of the commission gave birth to the old Bureau of Outdoor Recreation, unique in that it did not manage property, but coordinated recreation policy and planning.

Out of that 1958 act came the Land and Water Conservation Fund, a new system of financing for recreation.[4] It challenged local and state governments to get more involved in recreational facilities and matched their monetary efforts. Secretary Rhodes[5] will give you more detail on the Land and Water Conservation Fund in his remarks later, not only to underscore the benefits it has brought to North Carolina but to soberly remind us that the clock is ticking and that this fund program phases out in 1989.

Still with us, today, are the effects of the 1958 act, in its establishment of a national system of wilderness, rivers, and trails; in the turnover to local governments of more than 100,000 acres of federal surplus property; and its establishment of recreation areas in or near heavily populated urban centers.

Well, I guess any good workshop worth its salt needs a history lesson. The teacher in me won out. You just had yours for today.

I have recalled the work of that commission in order to spur you on in your work with this new commission, just now moving out of the starting gate. There must be something magic about the twenty-year cycles we hear about in government; with conferences like this, a new cycle begins.

In my twelve years in Congress, I was keenly aware of the needs of our recreation system in this country and, especially, for the booming populations I represented in and around Mecklenburg County. My vote was a strong aye of support for the 1983 Wilderness Act, which rescued some 69,000 acres as wilderness areas in eleven states, including North Carolina.[6] I endorsed then, and endorse today, the Parks System Protection Act, which identified threats to our national park system, both from within park boundaries and from outside.[7]

Those were not struggles that would end with the stroke of a president's pen. They were moves to awaken the American people to what is happening to the land and water that we take for granted as our leisure resource. Something had to give then; something has to give now, before it is too late for governments at all levels to carve out prime recreation space, provide the proper facilities, and stake them out for generations yet to come. That fresh approach is going to be needed—bold action grounded in new ideas.

For North Carolinians, Governor Craig in 1915 started us off on the right track when he moved to create our first state park, Mount Mitchell.[8] He did so in disgust at the clear-cutting which was wiping away the beauty of that lofty perch. I suppose each of us has personally benefited from that rescue operation.

He saw the need for that balance we are talking about. Now we are concerned over a new threat of blight to that timber stand, and our foresters are seeking answers to its cause so we can apply the right remedy.[9]

For forty years, North Carolina's system of state and local parks grew quietly, almost unnoticed except among leaders with vision anxious about the recreational welfare of people crowding more and more into towns and cities. They would need somewhere to escape, and providing it was the challenge for this last half of the twentieth century.

Our state parks system, having moved painfully through some lean years you will hear more about later in the day, is now at a new level of urgency. We now number our park visitors in the millions annually, using much the same space and many of the same buildings that were built by crews from the CC [Civilian Conservation Corps] camps of the 1930s. The 1985 General Assembly responded to the urgency by appropriating $25 million for the current biennium to buy critical acres needed just to complete state parks planned years ago, but never fulfilled.[10] It is a beginning.

We believe we must spend that money wisely if we are to justify more later, so we will not rush into bad deals. No, we don't have the money to expand like we must. We don't have enough money to rebuild and fix up other areas like we must—not for highways, or schools, or parklands.

The needs cry out, while the recreation-hungry public keeps coming. New partnerships are needed between businesses which serve the recreation needs of the public and the governments which provide the space. New attitudes towards creative financing must be developed.

In my view, federal budget balancing has been postponed far too long. This new day of Gramm-Rudman-Hollings dictates that all belts be tightened, so even the slim recreation waistline will surely feel the pinch. The flow of dollars into states from the Land and Water Conservation Fund could stop at any time. Operation and maintenance support for the federal parks within our own borders may well be weakened as the balance-the-budget process picks up steam, as necessarily it must. So, we must keep our eyes on these needs and urge that there be balance even in budget balancing. Will there be toll gates replacing welcome signs along the scenic roadways of the Great Smokies National Park? Will federal park facilities become fewer and farther between?

What will a decline in the accessibility of our federal parklands within North Carolina mean to our $5 billion tourist industry, which has doubled in the last six years? How will we weave a new partnership of private and governmental support for recreation that ensures its vitality, that carries out the purposes and hopes set forth by this new commission? How realistic can we be, in North Carolina, in facing the dilemma of a growing population blessed with more leisure time than ever before—and millions of us in a continuing pursuit of recreation?

Do we have enough resources, and are we bold enough to put them into play? This workshop begins the process. From your input, your willingness to give of time and concepts, will come solutions. We will keep North Carolina a great place to play as well as to work. Our future has been, and will continue to be, as big as all outdoors.

[1]Andrew Lamar Alexander (1940-   ), born in Knoxville, Tennessee; B.A., Vanderbilt University, 1962; J.D., New York University, 1965. Newspaper reporter; practicing attorney, 1965, 1971-1978; law clerk, Fifth District, U.S. Circuit Court of Appeals, 1965-1966; campaign coordinator, 1966, legislative assistant, 1967-1969, and special counsel, 1977, to Senator Howard Baker of Tennessee; candidate for Tennessee governor, 1974; Nashville television commentator, 1975-1977; Tennessee governor, 1979-1987; chairman, Appalachian Regional Commission, 1980, President's Commission on Americans Outdoors, 1985-1987, and of Leadership Institute, Belmont College, Nashville, since 1987; Republican. Barone and Ujifusa, *Almanac of American Politics, 1986*, 1251; *Who's Who in America, 1988-1989*, I, 37.

[2]Satterwhite Point Park was located on the south shore of Kerr Reservoir, seven miles north of Henderson. *1982-83 North Carolina Transportation Map and Guide to Points of Interest* (Raleigh: North Carolina Department of Transportation, and Travel and Tourism Section, Department of Commerce, n.d.).

[3]P.L. 85-470, "Outdoor Recreation Resources Review Act" (short title), *United States Statutes at Large*, Act of June 28, 1958, 72 Stat. 238-241.

[4]P.L. 88-578, "Land and Water Conservation Fund Act of 1965," *United States Statutes at Large*, Act of September 3, 1964, 78 Stat. 897-904.

[5]Samuel Thomas Rhodes (1944-   ), born in Wilmington; B.A., University of North Carolina at Chapel Hill, 1966; M.S., Auburn University, 1969. Oceanography and marine biology instructor, Cape Fear Technical Institute, 1969-1980; member, state House of Representatives, 1973-1983; investment adviser, E. F. Hutton and Co., 1980-1984; appointed natural resources and community development secretary, 1985; Republican. *North Carolina Manual, 1987-1988*, 789.

[6]The governor was describing P.L. 98-324, "North Carolina Wilderness Act of 1984," *United States Statutes at Large*, Act of June 19, 1984, 98 Stat. 263-267; for further confirmation, see *Congressional Quarterly Almanac, 1983*, 343, *1984*, 316.

[7]Congressman Martin voted in favor of H.R. 2379, the National Park System Protection Act, on October 4, 1983. *Congressional Quarterly Almanac, 1983*, 106H-107H.

[8]Locke Craig (1860-1924), born in Bertie County; was buried in Asheville; was graduated from University of North Carolina at Chapel Hill. Teacher; attorney; state House member from Buncombe County, 1899-1901; North Carolina governor, 1913-1917; Democrat. During Craig's administration, the state's first highway commission was appointed and 15,000 miles of state-funded roads were constructed, putting North Carolina on the way to becoming the Good Roads State; local taxation to support education was encouraged, and school districts were consolidated. Apart from his interest in Mount Mitchell, Craig, as a member of the Appalachian Park Commission, was also a supporter of Pisgah National Forest. Cheney, *North Carolina Government*, 477, 479; Powell, *DNCB*, I, 452-453.

[9]The National Acid Precipitation Assessment Program released preliminary findings of its acid rain damage survey in December, 1989. The study indicated that acid rain, ozone, drought, and disease and insect infestation were factors in the large-scale decline of red spruce and Fraser fir populations on Mount Mitchell and throughout the southeastern Appalachians. *News and Observer*, December 31, 1989; see also "What's Killing the Trees?" *Business: North Carolina* (July, 1984), 13-16, 18, 20.

[10]See *N.C. Session Laws, 1985*, c. 757, s. 126.

CHAMPION INTERNATIONAL EXPANSION ANNOUNCEMENT

Roanoke Rapids, February 11, 1986

It is indeed a pleasure to join you today. For more than seventy-five years, Champion International Corporation has been one of North Carolina's leading corporate citizens—and North Carolina has long been a leading home for Champion, ranking as the second strongest investment state for the company. In 1907 you constructed what was then one of the largest paper mills in the world at Canton, North Carolina. Later you acquired this plant, which was the first sulfate-kraft paper mill in the United States, built in 1909. As your business grew, you continued to invest in North Carolina. Today, Champion owns three manufacturing facilities in our state and employs more than 3,000 North Carolina workers.

Because of Champion's long partnership with the people of North Carolina, I am particularly pleased to join with this firm, today, as it officially announces a major reengineering of its kraft paper operations here at Roanoke Rapids. As has already been noted, this reengineering project involves more than $30 million in capital investment and will involve improvements in Roanoke's woodyard, pulp mill, and Number Three paper machine. That, and your improvements in the Number Four linerboard machine, make very clear that (a) Champion is in the unbleached kraft paper and board [business] to stay, and (b) Champion recognizes the championship quality of work that our people do here—and your strong work ethic, as President Bob Longbine commented appreciatively, even before I could bring it up, when we met in Champion headquarters in Stamford, Connecticut, in December, on my birthday, which he celebrated by telling me about this $30 million commitment.[1]

While this investment will not by itself add new new jobs here at Roanoke Rapids, it will save what we have. It will allow this Champion plant to produce some of the strongest, most versatile, multiwall stock in the world today. Needless to say, that step will go a long way in protecting jobs, here in Roanoke Rapids, by enhancing this mill's vigorous position in the increasingly competitive world paper market.

In many ways, Champion's work here at Roanoke Rapids is being paralleled by other traditional industries around North Carolina. From textiles and furniture, to agribusiness, and chemicals, and nearly a dozen other long-term North Carolina industries, our companies are moving to improve their competitive position through the development of new products and the installation of more productive manufacturing technologies.

Unfortunately, even aggressive efforts in modernization are sometimes not enough to meet the growing economic and competitive challenges facing our traditional industries. By now, we all know what the real problems are. There's unfair competition from some foreign industries subsidized by their governments and paying wage rates far below those in the United States—and neglecting any comparable environmental protection, such as will require another $6 million, this year, on top of [the] $29 million you have already invested in cleanup facilities.

Then, there's the high value of the dollar, which has been brought on by excessive federal deficits and astronomical real interest rates. And, of course, there's the fact that not all of America's trading partners are really being all that free when it comes to trade in their domestic markets. All these factors, and others, are working against our traditional manufacturers, but I do not believe, and the people of North Carolina do not believe, that our traditional industries should have to meet these challenges alone.

Traditional industries are the bedrock on which our economy is based. For years they have provided the economic energy required to raise our standard of living. Traditional industries' taxes and payrolls have built our schools, paved our roads, provided water and sewer service, and made available a myriad of other government services. Even today, North Carolina's forest resource industries alone—furniture, paper, and lumber—employ some 125,000 North Carolinians, with $1.6 billion in wages; and, together with textiles, apparel, fabric, and fiber manufacturers employ well over half of our state's manufacturing work force. Other traditional manufacturers employ thousands more.

To assist these industries in meeting the challenges before them, one of my first steps as governor was to appoint a secretary of commerce who was formerly the head of one of North Carolina's most successful traditional manufacturers. Secretary Howard Haworth is with us today. There's an important traditional tie to this occasion, in that it was the Champion corporate management that selected Howard Haworth to become president and chief executive officer of Drexel-Heritage Furnishings when that company was a part of Champion; and thus, for their own good purposes at the time, unknowingly prepared him for the leadership he is literally giving our entire state today—for which we are grateful.

Later, as we began to understand the great amount of work that would be necessary to effectively assist our traditional manufacturers, Commerce Secretary Haworth and I appointed a new assistant commerce secretary for traditional industry. The man who fills that post, White Watkins, is also a former traditional industry executive and is in the audience.

Throughout last year, the North Carolina Department of Commerce has worked hard to identify specific measures we North Carolinians can take to strengthen our traditional industries against the rising competition that faces them. We sponsored a statewide Governor's Conference for Traditional Industries and took an aggressive role in lobbying for action in Congress, but I think one of our best decisions was to establish an ongoing Traditional Industries Action Committee to suggest specific steps the state can take on their behalf. Today I am pleased to report to you that the Traditional Industries Action Committee has completed a comprehensive survey of North Carolina's long-term manufacturers; the survey asked leading traditional industries across our state for their best ideas on meeting the import challenge. The committee's report is due later this month, and I am looking forward to reviewing the steps they suggest and beginning an even more aggressive effort on their behalf.

Here in Roanoke Rapids, perhaps better than anywhere in North Carolina, you understand the importance of our traditional industries. A list of your corporate citizens reads like a "Who's Who" of traditional manufacturers—names like Champion International, J.P. Stevens, Georgia Pacific, Perdue Farms, and I could go on and on. My point is, here in Roanoke Rapids, you know how important our traditional industries are. You've seen companies like Champion bring jobs and opportunity to this area. You've seen them work to protect our environment and preserve our natural resources; and you have seen our traditional industries face good times and hard times, but stick with North Carolina nevertheless, because it is a good home. The Champion International modernization we celebrate today is a perfect example of that stick-to-itiveness.

As I conclude today, I hope you will join me in saluting not just Champion, but all of North Carolina's traditional employers. We will do our best, in major ways and marginal ways, to help you to sustain your business so that you will remain competitive—not just to survive, but to thrive in North Carolina, and not just for investors and management, but mainly for those you employ. I've said it often, and I'll say it again, regardless of the critics: Yes! I'm for business—large, and small, and in-between; new and traditional; high tech, and low tech, and in-between. I'm for business, because that's where jobs come from!

---

[1]Governor Martin was born December 11, 1935. *North Carolina Manual, 1987-1988*, 547.

SIGNING OF EXECUTIVE ORDER ON HISTORICALLY BLACK COLLEGES AND UNIVERSITIES

RALEIGH, FEBRUARY 13, 1986

It's my pleasure today to welcome all of you, the presidents, chancellors, and trustees of North Carolina's historically black colleges and universities, to the Executive Mansion. I especially want to acknowledge Dr. (Mel) Bradley, who is here representing President Reagan, and Dr. (Ron) Kimberling, who is attending on behalf of Secretary Bennett.[1]

This is an historic occasion. Never before has a North Carolina governor undertaken a program of this magnitude to bring the resources of the public and private sectors together in support of our traditional black institutions of higher education. The executive order which I will sign in a few moments is a reaffirmation of my commitment to the proposition that keeping historically black colleges and universities as a vibrant force in our state should not be just the goal of black North Carolinians, but of all of us.[2]

As an education governor, one who really has been an educator, my greatest priority is to return opportunity to our young people and restore excellence in our classrooms, from elementary grades to college level. A major part of this task requires strengthening the capacity of historically black colleges and universities to provide quality instruction and to overcome the effects of past discriminatory treatment. My executive order sets us on a sure and steady course of turning this goal into a reality.

In summary, the executive order directs my senior education adviser, Dr. Lee Monroe, to supervise the development of a comprehensive state plan designed to achieve a significant increase in the participation of historically black colleges and universities in state-sponsored programs. This plan also seeks to involve business and industry in providing greater private support to black colleges and universities through endowments, grants, scholarships, research programs, building funds, and other types of assistance.

My executive order directs cabinet secretaries and executive agencies to establish measurable objectives and planned actions to fulfill the requirements I have set forth and to submit completed plans to me on an annual basis. Prior to development of the first annual state plan, Dr. Monroe will supervise a review of all departments and executive agencies to determine the extent to which historically black colleges and universities are provided an opportunity to participate in their programs. This review will examine unintended regulatory barriers, determine how well state program opportunities are communicated to these institutions of higher education, and identify ways of increasing equity and advantage.

I anticipate the first annual state plan for assistance to historically black colleges and universities to be submitted to me by the end of the fiscal year for my approval, in consultation with my cabinet secretaries. Thereafter, annual performance appraisals will be submitted to me, through Dr. Monroe, to ensure that the measurable objectives developed by each department and agency have been accomplished.

Working together, we can make this strategy our most successful effort to ensure that our historically black colleges and universities remain a strong force in contributing to the continued economic and educational development of North Carolina.

Perhaps the greatest challenge facing your institutions today is the recruitment and training of our best and brightest students for careers in the teaching profession. The critical shortage of good teachers in subject areas, as well as our rural school systems, looms as our greatest threat to providing our students a quality education.

As all of you know, there are fewer black students than white aspiring to teaching careers. In addition, more of our good black teachers are leaving the classroom to accept positions in the private sector; others are retiring. A recent study by the North Carolina Association of Educators shows that, at present, there are more than 6,000 teachers who have completed thirty years of service and who could retire, at any time they choose, with maximum retirement benefits. Coupled with increasing enrollments in our public schools, the current shortage of good teachers in North Carolina, which grows more acute annually, places the integrity of our public school system in jeopardy. That's why I've made improving the teaching profession my number-one public education priority.

There are many things we need to do to enhance public education in our state. I have outlined the most urgent of these needs in a twenty-point plan submitted to the State Board of Education and other groups throughout North Carolina, but let's put first things first—and good teachers, adequately compensated, must come first, because they are central to everything we do in education. Just as we join today in implementing a new strategy to strengthen our historically black colleges and universities, I ask you to join me in helping to meet the challenge of resolving our shortage of good teachers.

This great state has been built, and it has endured, in the spirit of unity. We must preserve this spirit of unity, in both public and private education, if we hope to train a generation prepared for the future. And now, I want to invite the presidents and chancellors of our eleven historically black colleges and universities to join me for the ceremony and signing of my executive order to increase the participation of their institutions in state-sponsored programs.

---

[1]Melvin Leroy Bradley (1938-   ), born in Texarkana, Texas; resident of Fort Washington, Maryland; B.S., Pepperdine University, 1973; honorary degrees. Former postal clerk, 1956-1960, real estate broker, 1960-1963, and Los Angeles County deputy sheriff, 1963-1970; assistant to Governor Ronald Reagan of California, 1970-1975; public relations director, Drew Medical School, 1975-1977; assistant to vice-president, United Airlines, 1977-1981; senior policy advisor, appointed special assistant, 1982, to President Reagan. *Who's Who in America, 1988-1989,* I, 345.

Charles Ronald Kimberling (1950-   ), born in Cleveland, Ohio; B.A., 1972, M.A., 1977, California State University at Northridge; A.M., 1974, A.M., 1977, Ph.D., 1981, University of Southern California; honorary degrees. Editor, reporter, 1972-1974; assistant professor of journalism, California State University at Northridge, 1975-1980; deputy assistant for higher education programs, 1982-1985, and assistant secretary for postsecondary education, 1985-1988, U.S. Department of Education; executive director, Ronald Reagan Presidential Foundation, since 1988. *Who's Who in America, 1988-1989,* I, 1687.

William John Bennett (1943-   ), born in Brooklyn, New York; B.A., Williams College, 1963; Ph.D., University of Texas, 1970; J.D., Harvard University, 1971; honorary degrees. Assistant to president, Boston University, 1972-1976; executive director, 1976-1979, president and director, 1979-1981, National Humanities Center; associate professor, 1979-1981, University of North Carolina at Chapel Hill and at N.C. State University; chairman, National Endowment for the Humanities, 1981-1985; secretary, U.S. Department of Education, 1985-1988. *News and Observer,* September 15, 1988; *Who's Who in America, 1988-1989,* I, 226.

[2]See Executive Order Number 24, "Governor's Program to Strengthen Historically Black Colleges," signed February 13, 1986. *N.C. Session Laws, 1985, Extra and Regular Sessions, 1986,* 678-682.

CONCERNED CHARLOTTEANS

CHARLOTTE, FEBRUARY 21, 1986

As many of you know, I took the occasion of my televised "Report to the People" last month to proclaim this year, 1986, as the "Year of the Family" in North Carolina.

Events of our time—epidemic drug and alcohol addiction, victimization and sexual exploitation of our children, and the steady increase in violent crimes—have brought us to a brutal realization that the values which once guided us as a people are being undermined rapidly. Those ideals and values were rooted in the Judeo-Christian concepts which shaped our modern civilization and came into their sharpest focus in the founding of our nation.

Up to and including the early part of this century, the human being was defined according to his or her relationship to God, the community, and to the family. From each of these relationships the individual received strength, and to each one he or she owed obligations: to God; to the community; to one's family. That is an altogether different way of looking at human life from the present widespread, conflicting supposition that each of us is but a forlorn single unit, snatching such pleasures as possible from each brief moment on this earth, with questionable responsibility for the consequences of one's own actions.

We must restore faith in the family as the basic building block of a great state and nation. The loving family is the support and refuge for each of us, and it is the only truly effective training ground for the responsible citizen. Government cannot do this for us. We as a people, working together, must do it for ourselves through our churches and our community institutions, a good example of which is the Concerned Charlotteans.

In today's world, many young people find it extremely difficult to live by principles, but beyond any question or denial, principles are most easily learned in the environment of the loving family. In this environment, the child absorbs and can accept as a pattern of life such principles as duty, humility, sacrifice, kindness, helpfulness, and all of the other components of emotional and social maturity. These are the qualities which lead to a competent, secure, and productive life.

Thus, the family remains and is properly regarded as society's greatest hope. The sacrifices a person invests in maintaining a strong family will provide joys and rewards greater than can be derived from any other effort, for they give enduring meaning and purpose to life.

I have great confidence that we have accepted this challenge. I find this confidence in the many community groups that are organizing, throughout our state, to combat the threats to family life. I see it in our schools, where there is the beginning of renewed emphasis on the inculcation of values among students, and I find it emerging in support from the private business sector. I see it in the legislative majorities that tightened down on pornography and on the funding of elective abortions; and which provided instead more money for prenatal care and perinatal care for those born prematurely.

Tonight, I want to commend the Concerned Charlotteans. Your involvement in programs to find and reunite missing children with their families, to counsel young people on the dangers of drug and alcohol addiction, and to prevent child victimization sets an excellent example for all communities. So long as organizations such as yours exist, there is hope that the North Carolina of the future will be the brightest in our history. As governor, on behalf of all concerned citizens, I express my deepest gratitude for your good work.

PRESS RELEASE: GOVERNOR MARTIN'S STATEMENT
FOLLOWING MEETING WITH PRESIDENT REAGAN

WASHINGTON, D.C., FEBRUARY 24, 1986

As part of the winter meeting of the National Governors' Association, Governor Jim Martin joined the nation's governors for a thirty-five-minute-meeting Monday with President Reagan. Following the meeting with the president, Governor Martin issued the following statement during [a] meeting with Washington-based North Carolina newspaper reporters.

"It was a very interesting meeting in several respects. One is in comparison with the kind of meeting we had a year ago, right after I had become governor. At the time of the last (NGA) winter meeting here in Washington, at least the most outspoken governors were disagreeing vehemently with the president about his proposals for tax reform and budget cuts. Today there wasn't as much discussion about tax reform, because for one thing, the point of view of the critics has been sustained in the House—that is, they are not eliminating the deductibility of state taxes so there was not as much discussion of that. But in regard to the Gramm-Rudman-Hollings budget balancing effort, I had expected there to be more criticism and more argument about that, today, and there really wasn't. There was more of a receptive attitude on the part of governors that we've got some problems to face, but we are going to try to do our part.

"For years the governors have been chiding the federal government because the state governments generally have to balance their budgets, but the federal government does not. Now that the federal government is moving to balance its budget, there are going to be some consequences and people just have to be prepared to meet those consequences. In North Carolina, for example, we've estimated some $35 to $40 million of impacts in the first year. It will get a little larger in the next year and keep going from there, but we are going to do our best to prepare to meet that. We are not going to automatically pick up everything the federal government drops, but by the same token, we are not automatically going to let everything fall, either. We are going to pick and choose as it becomes clear to us which programs are going to be sustained.

"The other point I would make is that the particular programs to be cut are not the only impact of balancing the federal budget. There's another very important impact—that is, the relief from the damage that's been done by chronic federal deficits. Those massive federal deficits have to be financed either by inflation—that is, printing more money—or by borrowing heavily in the credit market, and in the last few years, that's the way it's been done. The result of that is to have the effect of overvaluing the U.S. dollar relative to other currencies; and the result of that is to price our manufactured goods out of the markets here and overseas.

"One of the major reasons we've had severe damage to our textile, footwear, and agricultural industries is because of the over-valued dollar that resulted from financing that massive federal deficit. If there are programs we have to cut, there are, on the other hand, some very severe burdens we've [been] carrying the last several years because of the large deficit."

In response to a question about whether the governor endorsed President Reagan's budget proposal, Governor Martin said: "No one needs to endorse all the particulars of anyone else's budget, because there are some things you like and some things you don't like. What I do say is that it (the president's budget proposals) is an initiative that will get the federal budget into balance. It meets the targets of Gramm-Rudman-Hollings so that that artificial budget balancing device doesn't have to take effect."[1]

---

[1]*Congressional Quarterly Almanac, 1986,* 525-541, provides an overview of President Reagan's 1987 federal budget proposal.

INTRODUCTION OF PRESIDENT GERALD R. FORD

ELON COLLEGE, FEBRUARY 25, 1986

I have been given the honor and privilege of introducing your guest lecturer this evening. But first, I want to take a moment to acknowledge and pay tribute to an outstanding North Carolinian whose record of service to this institution is unparalleled in the annals of Elon College.

The Honorable Thad Eure, our secretary of state for a half century, began his fiftieth year in that office only a few days before I observed that many birthdays.[1] Forty-four of his years have been devoted as a trustee to making Elon one of the finest independent colleges in the United States. For the last thirty-one years, he has served as chairman of the board. Although he is unable to be with us this evening, I want to publicly commend him for his continuing involvement in pursuit of a worthy ideal: the preservation of excellence in higher education. His is an example of selflessness for all of us.

Ladies and gentlemen, twice in the course of American history a president has been called upon to bind up the wounds of our nation. In both crises the responsibility rested with presidents of the same party: the previous Republican president, Gerald Ford, and the first Republican president, Abraham Lincoln. I am proud of both of them. Both were men of vision, courage, and greatness. Had they not possessed these rare qualities, the course of our history might have been altered for all time.

The first event is remembered only as history, reuniting a people just after concluding a great war which had divided them. Brother had been turned against brother in a bitter struggle which theatened the very existence of the Union. Abraham Lincoln rose to his postwar challenge to heal a torn nation, "with malice toward none, with charity for all."[2]

The second event was another time of national testing and trial, both at home and abroad. It was the mid 1970s, after another war which in a different way had divided our nation. Unemployment nationally had soared above 9 percent, housing starts were at an all-time low, and the U.S. economy faltered. Nations were falling to communism. The Middle East remained a tinderbox, and war between Israel and its Arab neighbors was a constant threat. America was just beginning to learn to cope with drug trafficking. America had lost its will and lost its way in foreign policy. A president was being driven from office in one of our great national tragedies.

The new president who emerged in this period was confronted by what seemed to be insurmountable problems. He had never sought the presidency; it had sought him. And yet, only such a man, seasoned by more than a quarter of a century of public service at the national level, with an enormous reservoir of respect for his personal and political integrity, could have restored the confidence of a nation. Tonight's speaker was such a man. He was that man.

In his characteristically steady way, President Ford began to address and manage our problems. During his first year in office, employment grew by more than 2.5 million workers, inflation was eased, and unemployment declined by some two percentage points. A new peace treaty had been negotiated between Israel and its Arab neighbors. Renewed progress was made in a budding policy of détente with the Soviet Union and the People's Republic of China. America had once again become united, and restored, and calmed.

As a strong advocate of conservative spending policies, he exercised some fifty vetoes of big spending measures which would have piled more debt upon deficit—a veto power, incidentally, given also to every other governor in America except the governor of North Carolina. But I was there to help sustain President Ford's vetoes. Of course, he paid a political price for those vetoes, but he did what he had to do. I was proud of him.

Today, our country continues to grow and prosper in a world at peace. It is in large measure the result of his legacy as president that our nation has regained its will not only to endure, but to succeed.

I suppose there will never be a news story about him which will not also remember him for an occasional stray golf shot. You good weekend golfers think about facing a gallery of thousands. I remember how the fun-loving media would lay in wait to caricature him if he stumbled, because he didn't spend a lot of time looking downwards. Big deal. It was an incredible irony because the truth is—you think about it—he was the most athletic, best conditioned, best coordinated human ever to serve as president. More important, he was a good president. He was, before that, a good congressman from Ann Arbor, Michigan; a good party leader; a good teacher and friend to this rookie congressman.

He has always been a good, decent person. As vice-president, he helped reassure the nation. As president, he helped heal the nation. Ladies and gentlemen, it is my high honor and great privilege to present to you, and ask you to welcome back to North Carolina, the thirty-eighth president of the United States, Gerald R. Ford.

[1]Thad Eure (1899-   ), native of Gates County; attended University of North Carolina at Chapel Hill, 1917-1919, and its school of law, 1921-1922; U.S. Army veteran. Lawyer; county attorney, Hertford County, 1923-1931; Winton mayor, 1923-1928; member, 1929, and principal clerk, 1931-1936, state House of Representatives; elected secretary of state, 1936, returned in consecutive elections, and retired from post in 1989; Democrat. *North Carolina Manual, 1987-1988,* 575.

[2]"With malice toward none, with charity for all, with firmness in the right as God gives us to see the right, let us strive on to finish the work we are in, to bind up the nation's wounds, to care for him who shall have borne the battle and for his widow and his orphan, to do all which may achieve and cherish a just and lasting peace among ourselves and with all nations." Abraham Lincoln, "Second Inaugural Address" [March 4, 1865], quoted in Bartlett, *Familiar Quotations,* 640.

LETTER TO NORTH CAROLINA VOTERS

Raleigh, March 1986

[North Carolinians rejected a pair of referendums in the May 7, 1986, primary elections. A proposed constitutional amendment, changing the election of state officials to odd-numbered years, failed by a 58 percent to 42 percent margin. Meanwhile, 92.5 percent of the voters opposed federal plans to locate a high-level radioactive waste dump in North Carolina. *News and Observer,* May 8, 1986. No day was indicated in the date of the following letter outlining the governor's position on the referendums.]

Dear Fellow Citizens:

As the governor of North Carolina, I once again take this opportunity to encourage each of you to vote in the upcoming primary elections. Voting is a right, fought for and obtained by individuals who believed strongly that government must reflect the will of the people. Yet, like any other freedom, the right to vote may be squandered away through apathy and indifference.

This year's primary is of special importance to the people of North Carolina because the ballot includes a referendum on nuclear waste and a proposed constitutional amendment providing for the election of state and county officers in odd-numbered years.[1] I intend to vote *no* on each of these issues.

The nuclear waste referendum provides us with an opportunity to express our views regarding the location of a high-level radioactive waste burial site in North Carolina. This is a nonbinding referendum; we cannot force the United States Department of Energy to withdraw its consideration of our state as a possible waste site. We can, however, strongly state our opinion which I believe will weigh heavily in future considerations by the Department of Energy, Congress, and the president.

I intend to vote against locating a high-level waste site in North Carolina because I am convinced there is no suitable site for such a facility in our state. I urge you to vote against it, also.

You have the opportunity to choose those men and women you want to represent your interests in state and local government in this election. You also have the opportunity to express your opinion on the nuclear waste referendum and proposed constitutional amendment. Your vote does count. It is your right; please exercise it.

Sincerely,
[Signed] Jim Martin
James G. Martin

---

[1]"An Act to Amend the Constitution of North Carolina to Provide for Election of Statewide Officials in the Fall of Odd-Numbered Years" ratified July 15, 1985, authorized the constitutional amendment referendum. Had the referendum passed, state election laws would have been altered as the act directed. *N.C. Session Laws, 1985*, c. 768.

STATE EMPLOYEES ASSOCIATION OF NORTH CAROLINA

RALEIGH, MARCH 4, 1986

I am pleased to join you again, this year, along with my cabinet and senior staff members. I continue to encourage fellow employees to become members of our association.

This occasion, I'm certain, is one that brings us together at a time when there are many concerns about the future of our state employees. Perhaps the most urgent concern is the impact of the Gramm-Rudman-Hollings deficit reduction legislation on the state of North Carolina and, specifically, on state employees. As all of you know, I addressed this concern on January 8, when I signed an executive order to limit hiring in various state departments and institutions.[1] This measure was taken to prepare for substantial reductions in the funding of federal programs at the state level. It was an important first step to protect those already employed by the state.

Under present circumstances, I do not foresee a reduction in force, but I cannot guarantee there will be none. I am doing all I can to minimize the impact on current employees. Ironically, some people interpret my efforts to avoid the impact of RIFs by reserving some unfilled vacancies as the opposite, as evidence that RIFs are intended. No: Our intention is to minimize that, but I see no way to guarantee we will succeed. We'll do our best.

The number of existing vacancies in state government is growing through natural attrition, according to reports I've received, and this result may help us in the long run to maintain some programs that otherwise might be affected adversely. Since the signing of the executive order on January 8, we have established through attrition more than 200 additional vacancies that could be utilized in the event Gramm-Rudman-Hollings would threaten elimination of other existing positions. These were jobs that were useful and productive, but not critical to state government. By not filling these slots, we have built in an added measure of protection for workers.

Slowing down employment in state government is only one measure we have taken to prepare for reductions in federal funding. I am pleased to report that approximately 45 percent of the recommendations presented by the Governor's Efficiency Study Commission have been accepted by state departments and agencies. While many of these improve managerial efficiency and service delivery with improved computer capacity, thus at greater cost, that is more than offset by other savings. As these recommendations are implemented, additional efficiencies in state government will result in further savings, savings that can be applied toward maintaining a high level of service to the public.

Today I want to announce that I have appointed key members of my senior staff to examine ways in which we may establish a career executive program within state government. We want to recruit the best high school and college graduates possible for careers in government, but we need to offer some measure of security to those who want to remain in government and build upon their skills. The career executive program that we are considering will provide that measure of security by providing alternative guarantees against arbitrary dismissal. I will be saying more on this subject when the details have been completed.

There are other matters of concern to you, of course, but it would be premature to address them at this time.

Taken together, our efforts to slow down employment of new personnel in noncritical areas, and the implementation of measures to achieve greater efficiency in government, will go a long way toward protecting the jobs of state employees. Both approaches build up a reserve of jobs and funding. We can later decide whether to transfer into these slots workers whose jobs are defunded, or propose to transfer dollars saved in these slots to replace defunded dollars. Either way, current employees get some protection.

For example, we will not have a reliable estimate of available revenues for the next fiscal year until the end of April or early May. I can only say that I will do my best, as governor, to use those revenues to the greatest advantage and in a manner that will provide the most benefit for the citizens of North Carolina. I have under advisement your association's request for a $2,000 across-the-board pay increase. That alone will cost an extra $347 million, counting a similar increase for school personnel, and that is far more than the expected increase in recurring revenues.[2]

As you will recall, in my fiscal 1985-1987 biennial budget message I had recommended for SPA employees in 1985-1986 an increase of 5 percent across the board, plus an increment for two thirds of state employees.[3] That would average 8 percent. Then for 1986-1987, I proposed a reserve for an additional 7 percent increase in compensation, totaling 15 percent over the biennium—even with the tax cuts I proposed. Instead, you were voted a one-time 10 percent—9.8 percent— increase all in the first year of the biennium. All I can say for now is that I hope to be able to have enough growth in recurring revenues to propose some further improvement.

Last week I returned from a meeting of the National Governors' Association in Washington, a meeting in which governors, for the first time, were unanimous in wanting to work to reduce the federal deficit. Some tried to have it both ways by asking that the cuts be made somewhere else. The adjustment which the states must make will be uncomfortable, but discomfort is a small price to pay for the economic relief from the present situation in which federal debts, financed by borrowing, have overvalued the U.S. dollar and forced many of our manufacturers out of business, costing us thousands of jobs in the private sector.

Let me take this opportunity to call upon our association of state employees to recognize the dynamics of change which governments—federal, state, and local—will experience in the coming years. I hope you will convey this message to the entire membership. I am, and I will remain, a governor with a strong commitment to the welfare of fellow state employees.

Together, let us remind ourselves of our strong commitment, also, to the welfare of those we serve, the citizens of North Carolina. As long as we put service to our fellow citizens above our own personal interests, we in government will be amply rewarded by a growing state with greater resources and greater public support.

[1]See Executive Order Number 22, "To Implement Certain Economies in North Carolina State Government to Respond to Federal Legislation Requiring a Federal Balanced Budget." *N.C. Session Laws, 1985, Regular and Extra Sessions, 1986,* 673-674.

[2]Most state employees were scheduled to receive a $75.00 per month raise, effective July 1, 1986, under *N.C. Session Laws, 1985, Regular and Extra Sessions, 1986,* c. 1014, s. 19(a).

[3]SPA employees held jobs covered by the State Personnel Act.

INDIAN UNITY CONFERENCE

GREENSBORO, MARCH 13, 1986

I'm delighted to be with you again, this year, for the annual Indian Unity Conference during the Spring Festival. Let me thank Lonnie Revels for that introduction.

Although it was a year ago, it seems like only yesterday that I came to your tenth annual conference in Fayetteville and announced Lonnie's appointment as chairman of the North Carolina Commission of Indian Affairs; today, I can announce that he's still it! Today I want to take this opportunity to commend him for his outstanding leadership and deep sense of dedication to improving the lives and well-being of the lineal descendants of North Carolina's original inhabitants, its Indian people. He has brought to the commission a deep appreciation of your proud culture, traditions, and heritage, and has shown a keen understanding of the problems, and needs, and goals of our 65,000 Indians.

The past year—my first year as governor—has been eventful, busy, and productive, and it has been especially successful in terms of achievements on behalf of North Carolina Indians. One of our major accomplishments has been the establishment of the first statewide Indian Housing Authority in North Carolina's history. Organized specifically to meet the acute housing needs of low-income Indian families, the authority holds the promise of new hope for many children and adults who have been forced to live in inadequate surroundings. I am pleased to report that this new organization has received a preliminary loan contract of more than $7 million from the U.S. Department of Housing and Urban Development. These funds will provide for the construction of some 200 subsidized dwelling units in Warren, Cumberland, Hoke, and Robeson counties, areas in which we have substantial Indian populations.

The Commission of Indian Affairs, which is part of our North Carolina Department of Administration, worked extremely hard to make this project a reality, but I also want to acknowledge with appreciation the assistance provided by one of our platform guests. He is Mr. John Meyers, director of the Office of Indian Housing in the Department of Housing and Urban Development. On behalf of North Carolina, Mr. Meyers, I want to thank you for your efforts to address this critical need; by raising the living standards of those families who will benefit, you offer new hope and encouragement for self-improvement. I am also pleased to report that this project will be administered under the direction of Mr. Leon Jacobs, director of the Office of Indian Programs, which is located in Chicago. Mr. Jacobs is a native North Carolinian and a member of the Lumbee Indian tribe.

Improving the housing conditions of needy Indian families has been one of my major objectives since becoming governor. Another important goal has been enhancing the educational standards of Indian youth and adults. Raising the level of education for all of our young people should be our single most important priority, for a good education enables the individual to participate fully in our economic system, to make informed choices, and to contribute the most to society. That means that overall, we must upgrade the talent and performance of our teachers by paying them better for teaching better, and we must insist that our students learn the basic skills of language and math.

We also have programs targeted for special goals:

—Last year, more than $200,000 was spent in North Carolina to enable Indian adults, who had no diploma, to obtain a high school equivalent certificate. Over 80 percent of the individuals who participated in this program were successful in obtaining their diploma.

—The first doctorate scholarship also was provided for an Indian student in a pilot program which I will work toward establishing on a permanent basis. This will permit many deserving young educators to go on and join the faculties of our colleges and universities.

A growing number of North Carolinians have entered such professional fields as law and medicine; many have advanced into positions of prominence in their chosen disciplines. There is, however, a severe shortage of Indians as schoolteachers and university professors. Many of our Indian educators now in the public system are reaching retirement age. We must work to encourage the best and brightest Indian students to pursue careers in teaching and perpetuate the contributions that their predecessors have made to North Carolina education.

Through the North Carolina Department of Human Resources, funds have been made available for some time to support the operation of four day-care centers for Indian children. Secretary Phil Kirk of that department has taken a great interest in providing the highest quality of care for Indian children of working parents, and he'll continue to do so.

I believe the accomplishments I've just reviewed demonstrate that my administration has a strong commitment to serving our Indian citizens. Let me assure you that this commitment continues into the future.

As all of you know, and as heralded by the banner above me, 1986 has been proclaimed by me as the "Year of the Indian." This is an historic event, because North Carolina is the only state in the nation to have set aside a yearlong commemoration. It is a timely part of the 400th anniversary of the Roanoke settlement.

On January 10, I was given the honor of opening the "Carl Woodring Native American Art Exhibit" at the North Carolina Museum of Natural History. This occasion also afforded me the opportunity to present copies of my proclamation to all of our tribal chiefs and to meet the visiting chiefs from Alabama and Nebraska.

The week of January 10 was the Winter Festival of this year's celebration. The week we now observe is the traditional Spring Festival—another step on the commemorative calendar for the "Year of the Indian." The Unity Conference brings you together during this festival to discuss the diverse subjects of economic development, financial management, job training, health care, and leadership development—and what a strong program it is. This agenda reflects a growing awareness that you are at the heart of the problem-solving process and that your future and the future of your children depend, in large measure, on self-intiative and enterprise.

I encourage you to build upon the rich culture, traditions, and heritage of a great and proud people and to make this and future generations worthy of that inheritance. As you continue to make progress, the role of government will decrease—as will your need for assistance to help catch up with society after years of neglect. Then, and only then, the Indian people of North Carolina will have the strongest hand in managing their own affairs.

All of the people of North Carolina face a challenging future: farmers, textile workers, merchants. Our state must find ways to meet the need for an improved and expanded system [of] rural roads and urban highways, to enhance public education, and to solve the problem of our overcrowded prison system. We must work to sustain our traditional industries and make them more competitive with foreign manufacturers who are capturing our markets through unfair trade practices. We must also continue to attract new economic investment.

At the same time, we must make adjustments in state services and delivery systems as the federal government seeks to reduce a staggering deficit through reduced grants and payments to the states.

I do not see these challenges as a bleak picture. On the contrary, our economy remains strong and is growing. It is a matter of redirecting our efforts and funding priorities. As this process develops, there can be temporary discomforts for individuals, groups, and areas. All of us must be willing to accept these adjustments as a very small price to pay for regaining our world leadership and domestic prosperity. My job as governor is to ensure that no group or area is singled out to carry more than its fair share of the cuts.

This conference, and the people, organizations that support it, are dedicated to building unity of unity—unity of effort, and unity of purpose—in one united state. It was this theme which I sounded in my "Inaugural Address" a little more than a year ago. It is a belief founded upon faith. The rewards of unity are immense: better lives for ourselves, a better future for our children, and a sense of satisfaction that we have contributed to the greatness of our state and the fulfillment of our hopes. Thanks to your commitment to those goals for a brighter future, we know we will make it.

CAROLINA SOCIETY OF ASSOCIATION EXECUTIVES

Raleigh, March 14, 1986

[The following address is similar to one delivered before the Fayetteville Chamber of Commerce, March 18, 1986.]

During the past few months, events in Washington have had a dramatic effect on state and local governments, particularly in terms of fiscal responsibility. The Gramm-Rudman-Hollings deficit reduction act recently adopted by the Congress will cut federal funding to North Carolina next year by almost $90 million, and there are more drastic cuts facing us in later years. This comes at a time when North Carolina is confronted by some of the most pressing needs in its history: better schools, improved highways, and expanded prisons. At the community level, there is an urgent need to build water and sewer facilities to accommodate new growth, expanding industries, and all of the other economic activities that provide jobs and greater opportunity for our people.

The dynamics of change, I believe, will be with us until the end of this century, and it is in this context that we must order our lives and drastically change the way in which we conduct the business of government. In my televised "Report to the People" on January 25, I emphasized that the choices before us will not be easy, but I want to assure you that there is one option we cannot afford—and that is to do nothing. At the same time, we must admit that money alone will not solve all of these problems. We must dispel the idea that spending for the sake of spending will cure our ills.

During the six fiscal years ending in 1985, state government experienced an accumulated surplus of almost $3 billion. The surplus of 1984-1985 was the largest, exceeding $700 million. Except for the more than $171 million tax reduction granted by the General Assembly last year, in response to my program for strategic tax reform, all of that money was spent on building a larger state government structure. In fact, using adjusted figures, the growth in the state budget during fiscal 1984 exceeded 16 percent, while the federal budget grew at a rate of less than 4 percent.

In my expansion budget, presented to the legislature shortly after I became governor, I proposed a healthy increase of almost 10 percent in state expenditures for the ensuing fiscal year. Contrary to my budget recommendations, the General Assembly decided 10 percent growth wasn't enough, and enacted a budget which increased spending in state government by more than 16 percent. That, I want to remind you, was the second increase of more than 16 percent in two years.

In the future, starting with the short session of the legislature this summer, we must make the most effective use of our revenue dollars. In addition to addressing the state's current needs, we must also decide which, if any, federal program reductions we can afford to assume with state funds.

Early in 1985, I recognized that the growth of state government had reached such huge proportions that it had become a major concern. As a result, I appointed the Governor's Efficiency Study Commission. This commission had four specific objectives. The first was to identify immediate opportunities for increasing efficiency and reducing costs which could be realized through executive or administrative actions. The second was to evaluate organizational and operational patterns to determine if managerial accountability could be enhanced or administrative control improved. The third objective was to suggest managerial, operating, and organizational improvements with state-wide implications for both short- and long-term savings. Fourth, and finally, the commission sought to identify specific areas where further in-depth evaluations were justified by potential savings.

This commission, composed of some 130 business leaders who volunteered their time and executive talent, presented more than 400 recommendations which, if implemented fully, would account for annual savings of more than $245 million. Today I am pleased to report that, in less than a year, I have implemented more than 50 percent of those ideas which came under executive jurisdiction. Note: That does not reach half the savings. Unfortunately, the recommendations affecting departments outside of executive authority, or requiring action by the General Assembly, have not fared as well. It's time for elected officials to act responsibly on those issues that go far beyond partisan concern, issues which control the future of our state and our ability to grow and prosper.

Other significant steps which I took, last year, included reducing the number of exempt state positions by 40 percent and removing the fear of political reprisal among state employees. I have replaced fewer people in government than any of my predecessors, and just last week, I instructed my senior staff to investigate establishment of a career executive program within government. This would permit career state employees to accept exempt positions in the administration of a governor without fear of dismissal when that governor goes out of office.

Last January, in announcing my priorities for the current year, I also revealed a twenty-point plan for strengthening public education in North Carolina with major emphasis on better pay for better teachers. Last year, I proposed an increase in the share of the state's budget going to education, including salary improvements, class size reductions, computer instruction, and the Teacher Advancement Center. In previous years, it had steadily declined.

I am pleased that the General Assembly was with me on these proposals, as well as supporting the teacher career ladder pilot program. But the Basic Education plan adopted by the legislature in 1985, for all its virtues, poses some serious problems for us. For example, it calls for the addition of more than 10,000 new teachers, and in excess of 15,000 support positions, without reserving in the budget enough revenue to pay for improved pay for existing teachers when the career ladder concept goes into effect statewide in eight years.

[The] simplest way to put it: I want to be sure that we make room in the sequence of the Basic Education plan that we allow room for the career ladder implementation statewide, even if it means some parts of the BEP have to be postponed a year or two. Otherwise, it will require a tax increase. You could justify a tax increase for raising teacher pay with the incentives and accountability of the career ladder. But if that's our highest priority, to strengthen the teaching career, to pay teachers better for teaching well, then we ought to allow for funding that first. Then see if lower priorities justify a tax increase. That's putting first things first. A radical idea?

The personnel expansion mandate also disregards two important factors: our ability to recruit enough qualified teachers to fill these positions and the ability of local governments to build enough new classrooms to provide space for them to teach. The idea of basic education, back to the basics, has widespread popularity; and many people mistakenly think this BEP has something to do with basic education. It doesn't.

During this month and next, the North Carolina Education Council will be holding public hearings throughout the state to seek citizen input into our education planning for the future. Specifically, citizens will have an opportunity to comment on my proposals and to make their own suggestions. During the same two months, the State Goals and Policy Board also will be holding public hearings across the state to solicit public comment on our capital priorities including, but not limited to, highways, prisons, schools, water and sewer facilities, and park and recreational needs.

Just last week, I presented the state's first comprehensive, ten-year plan for dealing with our critical problem of prison overcrowding. During the past ten years, North Carolina's prison population has increased dramatically. It has grown from an average daily population of less than 13,000 to almost 17,500. Last October, for the first time ever, our prison population exceeded 18,000. According to federal court standards mandating fifty square feet per inmate, we've only got room for 13,000. Despite the threat of intervention by the federal courts, we have an opportunity this year to establish a corrections policy that reflects reasonable standards, what should be our own standards, guaranteeing that criminals will not go unpunished, that punishment will fit the crime, and that public safety is enhanced.

Overcrowded prisons are a national concern and a North Carolina problem. Currently, we have lawsuits pending against three of the five geographic regions of the state's prison system. Thirty other states are faced with similar litigation. The issue, then, is whether we will develop our own plan of relief or let federal authorities mandate our policy for us. We cannot afford the latter choice.

At my direction, the Department of Correction has developed, and last week I announced, a ten-year plan that reflects a responsible commitment to a well-managed prison system and uniform corrections policy. The first, three-year, phase of the plan calls for reducing prison overcrowding in two ways: increasing capacity and reducing the population. On the first part, we will expand our existing prisons, construct new prison units, and propose to license several private prison contracts.

Construction, expansion, and privatization represent a good-faith effort to meet federal guidelines. It could all be done by new construction; we believe the mix is the best answer. Moreover, this approach has built-in cost savings, in that it partially uses existing facilities that can be expanded with less overhead cost, and proposes private construction and operation of facilities to meet part of our needs for more space. Such private operations would show us how it works in North Carolina and answer the questions so many seem to have, and it would provide a healthy comparison against traditional patronage operations.[1]

The ten-year plan includes, in addition to construction, a system for probationary sentences with stricter, more intensive supervision. The plan also calls for probation sentencing to be supported through a program of community-based punishments, with restitution to the victims. Such a system underscores the conviction that it must be the offender, not the taxpayer, who can be made to pay.

The plan provides for annual review, so that adjustment can be made in the balance we seek in construction versus probation as the need presents itself.

This strategy, which meets federal requirements, will save North Carolina taxpayers more than $116 million in construction costs and in excess of $27 million in operational expenses over the ten-year period. Alternatives: spend a lot more money; and turn loose more serious offenders.

At this critical junction, when we are facing enormous needs in many areas at the same time that federal funds to the states are being reduced, we must utilize innovative approaches to problem solving. Spending more doesn't mean that we are solving the problem better. Indeed, following old practices of tax and spend will simply take us down the same road, which, for fifty years, led our federal government into its current dilemma.

Having offered programs to strengthen our system of public education and address the need to eliminate prison overcrowding within a budget we can afford, I will now be nearing a decision on how we will meet the demand for improved and expanded highways and rural roads. Working in consultation with Secretary Harrington of the Department of Transportation, we will be formulating recommendations to present to the General Assembly. But first, we want to complete the series of public hearings across North Carolina by the Education Council and the Goals and Policy Board. Only then will we have some concrete proposals which relate needs to priorities and costs to anticipated available revenues. We won't know revenue availability until the end of April or mid-May.

Some of the major programs we have already undertaken have been the appointment of assistant secretaries in the Department of Commerce to enhance our traditional industries and expand assistance to small business firms. Both are crucial to the economy of North Carolina.

Most of you who are here, today, represent associations whose membership is predominately small businesses, traditional industries, or both. There are now more than 110,000 small business firms in our state, and they are increasing at the rate of more than 1,000 per month. Just recently, the North Carolina Small Business Council presented, and I accepted and endorsed, recommendations and proposals designed to improve the business climate for these entrepreneurial enterprises. Before the end of this month, I expect to receive a study from the traditional industries task force which will contain recommendations for sustaining our textile, fiber, apparel, furniture, hosiery, agribusiness, and related industries that have been adversely affected by foreign imports. In the last five years, North Carolina has lost more than 30,000 textile jobs. Fortunately, our state's economy, growing at a rate exceeding the nation's, enabled these displaced workers to find employment in other industries.

As overwhelming as our needs appear, North Carolina is one of the fastest growing states in the nation. We have just completed a record year of industrial investment in new and expanded plants.

Private enterprise is the engine that fuels our economy, generates new jobs, and provides the revenues to operate government. Government, on the other hand, creates no wealth at all. It consumes it in the interest of providing the common needs of our people.

We must continue to impress upon our legislative leaders that the future of private enterprise determines the future of North Carolina. Our state will continue to enjoy the fortunes of prosperity and growth only so long as business itself achieves success and expansion. In providing the public's needs, let us work together in public-private partnership to make informed, responsible choices. Only a viable partnership will ensure that we will make the most of the unprecedented opportunities that lie ahead.

<hr>

¹Martin acknowledged in his press statement of March 6, 1986, that the question of privately built and operated prisons "raises some controversy, because some are timid about innovations. Some argue that licensed private prisons might cut corners to hold down costs; yet that is what the state has done: cutting corners in ways that have created problems we now have to solve. I believe that private construction and operation should be tried, on a limited basis, with safeguards, so we will know how it can work in North Carolina."

TOBACCO ASSOCIATES

RALEIGH, MARCH 20, 1986

I am pleased, today, to join the tobacco growers, warehousemen, processors, and manufacturers from North Carolina and our sister flue-cured tobacco producing states: Virginia, South Carolina, Georgia, and Florida.

It is also my special pleasure to extend a warm welcome to our honored Japanese guests, Mr. Oidaira, senior board member of Japan Tobacco, Incorporated, and vice-president of leaf purchases; Mr. Takahashi, executive director and chief of Japan Tobacco, Incorporated-USA; Mr. Ishikawa, of the Japanese Embassy; and Mr. Ban (prounounced "Bond"), also of Japan Tobacco, Incorporated. Your island nation, gentlemen, is and has been, for many years, the chief export customer for our premium quality tobaccos, the finest that are produced in the world. Indeed, Japanese demand for our flavorful, full-bodied leaf accounted last year for more than $300 million in trade for our nation and, in large measure, helped to sustain the value of our better grades.

In the total world market, however, foreign production of flue-cured tobacco has grown from slightly more than 5 billion pounds, in 1981, to more than 7 billion pounds last season. This represents an increase of 30 percent. Nevertheless, our domestic manufacturers continue to use a larger percentage of American leaf in their products than foreign tobaccos.

Today, the manufacturing industry is stable, rather than continuing on the downside as it did for a number of years. Consequently, our exports are of growing importance to our agricultural economy. The export market will, in fact, continue to make the difference between profit and loss for our flue-cured producers; and this means that Tobacco Associates will remain the most vital organization engaged in promoting the sale and use of our product abroad.

Maintaining a stable tobacco program also is another essential factor in retaining and expanding export trade, for it assures world manufacturers a dependable supply. No less interested in a stable market are our leaf growers, who earlier this week overwhelmingly approved continuation of the support price program. This sends a clear message to our competitors that our tobacco farmers are in business and plan to stay in business.

Tobacco remains an important part of North Carolina's total economy, and our farmers must continue to emphasize quality production, for which there is an increasing demand. Our state is extremely fortunate to have climate, soils, and know-how unequaled in the world. We must make the fullest possible use of these great resources.

As all of you are aware, the Tobacco Improvement Act of 1985, which has been attached to the budget reconciliation bill now before the Congress, has been moving ever so slowly toward a final outcome. This legislation does not satisfy everyone associated with the tobacco industry. However, I want to say that it is a workable program and will lead toward greater stability in the marketplace.

Given the mood of the Congress at the present time, it is the best legislation we can hope to achieve. By setting the price support for 1987 in the range of $1.44 per pound, and providing for an assessment of between 3 and 5 cents—to be shared by the manufacturers—it will set the stage for a buy out of approximately 750 million pounds of surplus stock held by the Stabilization Corporation. The purchases would be made over a five- to eight-year period and would, I believe, dramatically reduce imports of cheaper foreign filler tobaccos. Our congressional delegation is working together for enactment of this legislation, and I have been lending my efforts for some time to resolving this issue.[1]

As governor, I intend to continue working closely with Commissioner Graham, of the North Carolina Department of Agriculture, to sustain tobacco as one of our major crops. In addition, we have recently appointed an agricultural adviser in the North Carolina Department of Commerce to work closely with Secretary Haworth and Assistant Secretary for Traditional Industries White Watkins. No other administration in state history has given more attention to the decline of agriculture, especially the decline of tobacco. We will continue in the future to search for new ways to resolve the problems confronting our growers.

We are all concerned about making American tobacco competitive once again. I believe we are on the right road to achieving this goal. By working together, the goal of returning tobacco to its historically important role can become a reality. As governor, you can count on my continued support and active involvement. Join me in making this a united effort.

---

[1]The day Martin delivered this address to Tobacco Associates, Congress passed P.L. 99-272, the federal deficit reduction package that also contained revisions to the tobacco price-support program. *Congressional Quarterly Almanac, 1986,* 304; for further information, see press release, "Governor Martin's Statement on Tobacco Program Improvement Act," [Raleigh], March 6, 1986, Governors Papers, James G. Martin.

GOVERNOR'S CONFERENCE ON HEALTHY MOTHERS AND BABIES

RALEIGH, MARCH 21, 1986

It has been a very rewarding experience for me and my wife, Dottie, to have taken the initiative in North Carolina's programs to improve the lives of our children. Consequently, this conference has special meaning to us as the state's First Family. I want to thank you, Dr. (Robert) Dillard,[1] for your introduction, and express appreciation to the Perinatal Advisory Council for its invitation to join you this after-noon. Unfortunately, an extremely busy schedule prevents me from remaining as long as I would like, but I want to take this opportunity to express my continuing commitment to the enhancement of child care in North Carolina.

As most of you are aware, North Carolina's infant mortality rate in 1984 was 12.5 percent, the lowest in the history of our state.[2] This represented a decline of some 36 percent in 10 years. While this means that we have made significant progress in preventing infant deaths over the last decade, the percentage remains far too high.

Associated with this unacceptable rate of infant mortality have been the excessive rates of low-weight births and teen births. Additionally, North Carolina in the past has failed to provide an adequate number of neonatal intensive-care nursery beds to care for the number of premature infants born each year.

My "State of the State" message to the General Assembly in 1985, in which I proclaimed the "Year of the Child," sought to refocus the attention of our legislators on these and other problems affecting our children and youth. As a result, an additional $10 million was appropriated for hospital-based, high-risk prenatal care; basic prenatal care; delivery services; and teen pregnancy prevention. These appropriations represent a very broad effort and involve public and private health care providers, schools, social service agencies, and many advocacy and voluntary groups.

Each of your organizations, and each one of you personally, has helped to heighten awareness of our perinatal needs. I commend you for your help and support.

We are making tremendous progress. I am pleased to say that the number of prenatal clinics in our health departments has increased. This, in turn, has improved early access to care for indigent pregnant women and has enabled us to identify mothers at risk and refer them to the appropriate level of care.

Last year, more than 25,000 women were served in health department prenatal clinics. Of this number, some 5,000 were served in a network of high-risk maternity clinics. Since I have become governor, $2.4 million has been appropriated to increase prenatal services in health departments. In addition, the Health Director's Delivery Fund, which is money used at the local level to pay for outpatient and inpatient services for poor pregnant women, has been increased by $1.7 million.

Although services are improving, we realize that North Carolina still has a high prematurity rate. Many of the premature infants are cared for in our eleven regional medical centers. We have now increased the funds to care for these infants and mothers by almost $2 million annually. We also have added another $1 million to provide care for infants transferred to local hospitals; this enables the infant to be closer to the family and allows for better planning in the community for the high-risk infant.

As the commitment of our state to improving the care of poor mothers has increased, we have also increased the number of babies that have survived birth. It is estimated that about 1,900 premature babies have survived infancy, since 1972, that otherwise might not have been saved. I believe we can all take pride in the knowledge that this accomplishment has been due to our ability to work together for better care. There is still much to be done, and we must continue to work in this same climate of cooperation at the state and community levels.

Last year, we made the largest commitment of state resources in history to improving the health of North Carolina's mothers and babies. Let us use these resources wisely and effectively. In the future, I will continue to focus the attention of our legislators and citizens on the needs of our children.

In 1986, the "Year of the Family," and in future years, we want to give every newborn and mother a chance at a healthy and meaningful life. Let each of us accept part of that responsibility. We can afford to do no less.

---

[1]Robert G. Dillard (1942-   ), born in Memphis, Tennessee; resident of Winston-Salem; B.A., University of the South, 1964; M.D., Yale University, 1968; U.S. Army, 1972-1974. Pediatrician; assistant professor of pediatrics, University of North Carolina at Chapel Hill, 1974-1976; assistant professor, 1976-1980, associate professor, since 1980, Department of Pediatrics, Bowman Gray School of Medicine, Wake Forest University; codirector, 1976-1983, director, since 1983, Newborn Intensive Care Unit, medical director, 1987-1988, Neonatal Transport Program, North Carolina Baptist Hospital, Winston-Salem; director, Special Care Nursery, Forsyth Memorial Hospital, since 1983; board member, North Carolina Perinatal Assn.; author. Robert G. Dillard to Jan- Michael Poff, March 1, 1990.

[2]The statewide infant mortality rate dropped to 12 percent in 1985, Martin noted in his April 16, 1987, address at the New Hanover County Health Department.

DELINQUENCY PREVENTION CONFERENCE

RALEIGH, MARCH 26, 1986

It is a special pleasure for me to join you this morning for the Sixth Annual Delinquency Prevention Conference, sponsored by the North Carolina Justice Academy. This year's theme, "We're Building Better Futures," underscores the vital role that families play in raising our children to be responsible, productive citizens. It also recognizes that all of us have a part in helping to strengthen the family unit and making an important contribution to the society which becomes our legacy to future generations.

Let me take this opportunity to commend Attorney General Thornburg, Justice Academy Director (M. A.) Stanford,[1] and Conference Planning Chairman (Bob) Hinkle for arranging the splendid program in which you have participated since Monday. I also want to acknowledge the assistance of the Justice Academy staff and representatives of the state departments of Human Resources, Crime Control, Administration, Correction, and the Administrative Office of the Courts for helping to make this event the most successful in history.

During this year, the citizens of North Carolina are honoring and recognizing the family as our greatest hope for the future. In my televised "Report to the People" on January 25, I announced the issuance of a proclamation commemorating 1986 as the "Year of the Family." This followed almost by a year my 1985 proclamation in observance of the "Year of the Child."

Why so much attention to our children and our families at a time when there are so many pressing problems demanding our attention? The answer is quite simple: Strong families and strong children are the basic building blocks of a strong, free society.

Our own experience teaches us the importance of the family. For most people, the things that give their lives the clearest meaning and the deepest joys are the sacrifices and relationships within the loving family. And isn't the opposite true, as well? Grief in its most penetrating form comes from cruelty inflicted by one family member on the other, or from the family ruptures caused by divorce and death.

Loving family solidarity is the greatest earthly blessing, but it is a blessing earned by a diminishing percentage of people. This conference signals our intention to put family life in North Carolina at the top of our action agenda, and it reinforces the focus of state government on strengthening the bonds of family unity.

Yesterday, you saw the simulation of a troubled family whose difficulties seemed insurmountable. Human service professionals used this drama to make a valuable point. Their task was to convince you that government agencies must work together as a team, not in isolation to one another, to address family problems effectively.

It seems only common sense that children will be less prone to delinquency if they are raised in a stable home environment that provides guidance, love, and support. Let us work together, this year and in the distant future, to prevent juvenile delinquency by adopting this family-centered philosophy.

What else can we do to prevent juvenile delinquency? It has been known for quite some time that a disproportionate number of delinquents come from poor, single-parent homes. In colonial America, families were expected to be self-sufficient. Today we must continue to help our disadvantaged families become economically independent. Our goal must be to continue our efforts to help families get the jobs they need to provide their children the basic necessities of life: food, clothing, shelter, and opportunity.

The chance to work gives needy mothers necessary job skills and a feeling of usefulness and self-respect. More and more North Carolina counties are organizing job-training programs for women who receive public assistance. This, in turn, provides juveniles a new role model to emulate: the productive parent and contributing member to society.

Another step we can take is to strengthen enforcement of our child support laws. In 1718, the Poor Relief Act was passed in England, providing that an absent parent's property could be seized by a church worker or overseer upon a warrant issued by two justices, and that the proceeds of the property could be used to discharge the obligation to that parent's child or children.[2] Yet today, in this country, there are more than 8 million women living with some 14 million children, under the age of 21, whose fathers have deserted the home and family. Among those who are entitled to receive child support payments, only half receive the full amount, one fourth receive part payment, and the remaining one fourth receive nothing.

It's time for us to send a clear message to absent parents. The absence does not absolve that parent of responsibility. Women and children must not be reduced to a life of poverty and despair. I am pleased that the state has made progress in increasing child support collections over the last few years. We intend to do better as we make much-needed changes and begin to enforce child support orders vigorously and consistently.

When families take responsibilty for their own children, the quality of life for an entire generation will be improved. Juveniles, we must remember, can be taught responsibility only by responsible parents who care for their children.

The family has not only been the primary economic unit in our society. The home also has been the place where children learn. Until the middle of the nineteenth century, parents educated their own children. Not only did the parents teach skills, encourage work habits, and instill social and religious values, they also taught the child "book learning."

Since the mid-nineteenth century, public schools have been provided to assume that responsibility. However, parents must continue to regard themselves as the first and foremost teachers of their own children. If parents do not ensure that their children are in school and on time, they can be certain that their children do not learn. If parents permit their children to drink or destroy their minds with drugs, they can be certain that those children will be marked for failure, and perhaps an early death, at a premature age.

We in government must involve the family in our delinquency prevention programs. Without the family's support and commitment, all of our efforts will fail.

As "helping professions," all of you are aware of the important role that informal support networks can play in helping children and youth. Let us work together toward a goal of making families self-sufficient and independent. We cannot rescue all families in trouble, but we can find a source of strength for them in their own relatives, neighbors, and friends.

Finally, I want to speak about the family as the main source of love, comfort, and unqualified commitment to their own children. I know that most families provide this support, but there are many who do not. We live at a time when there is an epidemic of child victimization and abuse.

We cannot, and must not, accept the tragic epidemic of abuse, sexual exploitation, and violence that go unreported and undetected in many families. Again, we as a society must deliver a clear message to abusive parents: We will not tolerate this behavior. Whether perpetrated on a stranger or a family member, crimes against our children will be prosecuted where and when we find it.

In 1986, let us call attention to the opportunities we have for helping the families across our state. Let us help them become strong and secure. Let us celebrate the fact that while families are changing, they are not dissolving.

In support of these efforts, I have set aside the weekend of May 17 as a time for families to spend together, enjoy family activities, and for parents and children to show commitment and love to one another. I want to encourage all of you to join with the various departments of state government in making this event one in which every North Carolina family will participate.[3]

Just as Winston Churchill viewed democracy, the social critics have decided that the family is the worst possible system, except for all others.[4] "There is no better invention than the family, no super-substitute," said a Rutgers sociologist. Our task, then, is not to supplant the family but to support it.

And so it is that the family is the greatest hope of our society. It is the training ground for responsible citizenship. It is the place of refuge and support in times of fear and sorrow. The sacrifices a person invests in maintaining a strong family can provide joys and rewards greater than can be derived from any other effort, for they give enduring meaning and purpose to life. That is an awesome set of claims to make for anything, but I believe it is an understatement of the reality.

In the Bible, the loving family is the centerpiece of life on earth. Human experience tends to tell us the same thing. If wisdom should somehow surface amid the shallow clamors of our day, citizens will roll up their sleeves and labor to rebuild the strong and loving family as our highest social priority. I applaud your efforts and your dedication to that goal. Together, as one united state, let us continue to work toward making this goal a reality.

[1]Martha A. Stanford (1948-   ), born in Asheville; resident of Raleigh; B.A., University of North Carolina at Greensboro, 1970; M.A., Western Carolina University, 1976. Program director, North Carolina Correctional Center for Women, 1976-1978; instructor/coordinator, 1978-1979, training chairperson, 1979-1980, director, since 1985, North Carolina Justice Academy; training manager, 1980-1984, regional administrator, 1984-1985, Virginia Department of Correction. Martha A. Stanford to Jan-Michael Poff, February 5, 1990.

[2]The Poor Relief (Deserted Wives and Children) Act, 1718, 5 Geo. 1, c. 8.

[3]Martin designated May 16, 17, and 18, 1986, as Family Weekend. See "North Carolina Family Weekend, 1986, by the Governor of the State of North Carolina: A Proclamation," April 2, 1986, Governors Papers, James G. Martin.

[4]"Many forms of Government have been tried, and will be tried in this world of sin and woe. No one pretends that democracy is perfect or all-wise. Indeed, it has been said that democracy is the worst form of Government except all those other forms that have been tried from time to time." Winston S. Churchill, Speech to House of Commons, November 11, 1947, quoted in *Respectfully Quoted*, 83.

STATEMENT ON SUPERCONDUCTING SUPER COLLIDER

Raleigh, April 3, 1986

North Carolina is home to some of the finest universities and research facilities in the world. We have attracted some of the brightest scientists and researchers to our state. This movement has also attracted new business and industry to North Carolina and aided in the development of existing commerce. As a result, North Carolinians have seen great improvements in the quality of their lives.

In keeping with this state's commitment to our role as a leader in research and technological development, I am pleased to announce, this morning, the formation of a task force comprised of local and state government officials, educators, and scientific researchers. This fifteen-person panel, which met last month for the first time, has been brought together for the purpose of exploring the feasibility of competing to bring a highly sought-after $6 billion research project to North Carolina.

The project is the superconducting super collider, or SSC, in short. The SSC will be the world's largest and most powerful particle beam accelerator. It will consist of a high-tech tunnel, sixty miles in circumference, and an adjoining complex of research, maintenance, and administrative facilities. Twenty times more powerful than the current state-of-the-art particle beam accelerator located at the Fermilab[1] outside of Chicago, the SSC will allow scientists their greatest opportunity at resolving outstanding theoretical questions about the origins of our universe.

Over the past two years, the United States Department of Energy has invested approximately $40 million in research and development of the SSC. This research and development is being directed and coordinated with the Universities Research Association, a consortium of fifty-six leading research universities; both the University of North Carolina and Duke University are members of this consortium. The progress of this effort has been substantial. Pending congressional funding for the project, a decision on siting the SSC could be made by the president in the spring or summer of 1988.

Site selection for the SSC is a complex process. At last count, twenty-two states were at work on preliminary site assessments in advance of a formal call for proposals from the Department of Energy later this year or early next year. These preliminary studies include a detailed analysis of geological, topographical, and hydrological features of each potential site. They will also include environmental and economic impact statements. Those final proposals will be reviewed by the National Academy of Sciences which will, in turn, make its recommendations to the president.

Last September, I appointed a working group to determine if an appropriate site for the SSC exists in North Carolina. That group, headed by Secretary Grace Rohrer[2] of the Department of Administration, determined that the Granville and Person County area is the most promising. This area appears to best fit the geological siting criteria for the project. It is also in close proximity to major transportation facilities and to major research facilities.

The task force I am introducing today will be working during the next few months on determining the feasibility of North Carolina's pursuit of this project. Task force members will also be meeting with citizens of North Carolina over the next few months to inform them about the SSC project and hear their comments on the matter. Approximately $115,000 has been set aside for this effort, using research funds of the North Carolina Board of Science and Technology.

By June, the task force will report its findings and recommendations to me and the members of the General Assembly. At that time, a decision will have to be made on whether North Carolina is willing to commit the one-half to three-quarters of a million dollars necessary to produce a formal application for the National Academy of Sciences' consideration.[3] Considering the high level of competition for this most prestigious project, there are no guarantees of success.

You might be asking, Why should North Carolina consider investing so much money to attract this project? That is a reasonable
question.

In addition to the benefits that will be reaped by the world of
science, it will be a tremendous boost to the economy of its host state.
The location of the superconducting super collider in North Carolina
will help cement this state's position as a leader in the area of research
and technological development. The SSC will attract the very best
scientists and physicists from around the world to North Carolina.
That, in turn, will enhance those universities and research facilities
already here. If North Carolina is to remain in the upper echelon of
those states hosting scientific inquiry, then an attempt to attract this
prestigious project to our state is a logical step.

The economic impact of the SSC on North Carolina would also be
enormous. Representing an investment of $6 billion, the SSC would
take up to six years to build. During the construction phase of the
project, 7,000 or 8,000 people would be employed. When completed,
3,000 people will be employed at the facility and another 3,000 people
will be engaged in jobs that serve in support of the SSC.[4]

The recruitment of this scientific research project to North Carolina
is very much in line with the plans for economic development I outlined during my "Report to the People" last January. At that time I
spoke of the need for innovative recruiting concepts for new industries. I also spoke of the need for better jobs and for a greater variety of
jobs for North Carolinians. The recruiting of the SSC is consistent
with those goals.

Construction of the superconducting super collider will ensure that
the United States remains the leader in high-energy physics research
well into the next century. It is not surprising, then, that the research
and development effort around this project has been likened to the
effort creating the National Aeronautics and Space Administration in
1957. Should it become a reality, it will have a major impact upon the
world, the nation, and, if it is built here, upon North Carolina.

We are not undertaking this recruitment effort with stars in our
eyes or with visions of sugarplums dancing through our heads. This
has been, and will continue to be, a careful and well-thought-out
process. It may well be that we will find that geological factors prevent North Carolina from presenting an SSC proposal. Hopefully, that
will not be the case, but, if it is, it will be our responsibility to say so
and avoid unnecessary expenditures.

I will be in close touch with the people of this state, local government and business leaders, members of the scientific community, and

members of the General Assembly each and every step of the way. This is a truly bipartisan, or should I say nonpartisan, effort at projecting North Carolina into an international leadership role at the dawn of the twenty-first century.

---

[1]The Fermi National Accelerator Laboratory was known popularly as Fermilab. "Can Scientists Sell Washington on a Dream Machine?" *Business Week*, October 14, 1985, 100.

[2]Grace Jemison Rohrer (1924-   ), born in Chicago; B.A., Western Maryland College, 1946; M.A., Wake Forest University, 1969; Ph.D., University of North Carolina at Chapel Hill. Secretary, departments of Cultural Resources, 1973-1977, and of Administration, 1985-1987; former chairwoman, state Republican party; former director of development and public relations, UNC Center for Public Television. Rohrer was the first woman in North Carolina history to hold a cabinet post. *News and Observer*, January 20, 1985; *North Carolina Manual, 1985*, 659, *1987-1988*, 692.

[3]The task force report of June, 1986, recommended that 1) the General Assembly earmark $750,000 to prepare the state's SSC site proposal; 2) certain academic programs in the state's universities and community colleges be upgraded; and 3) additional means of strengthening the state's SSC site plan should be explored. In summarizing the report before the SSC Advisory Board, June 7, 1988, Martin asserted that "the clear message was that the SSC was a valuable project that would be consistent with North Carolina's concerns for economic growth, educational opportunity, and environmental responsibility." A majority of the members of the General Assembly likely agreed with the governor's assessment of the project and passed "An Act to Provide a Site to the United States Department of Energy for a Superconducting Super Collider" on August 14, 1987. *N.C. Session Laws, 1987*, II, c. 855.

[4]In the autumn of 1988, John Connaughton and Ronald Madsen, of the Center for Business and Economic Research at the University of North Carolina at Charlotte, released an analysis of the economic effects of the supercollider upon North Carolina. Martin summarized their findings in his September 28, 1988, press conference, declaring that the supercollider "will generate an annual average of nearly 10,000 jobs—about 2,500 to 3,000 direct hires" affiliated with the project itself, "and even more for the vendors and others who will serve this growing, exciting community." The Connaughton-Madsen study also forecast that the SSC would generate, over its twenty-five-year lifespan, new tax revenues in excess of $850 million for state and local governments.

However, according to Martin, economic considerations were insufficient in themselves to warrant the state's seeking the supercollider. The governor told the SSC Advisory Board on June 7, 1988: "If we were to spend equal time and effort on industrial recruiting, perhaps we could entice an industrial facility comparable in terms of jobs and payroll to locate in North Carolina. Why then focus so much effort on a project that admittedly is difficult for the public, at large, to understand?

"For me, the answer lies in the profound effect that the SSC would have on education at all levels in our state. It is impossible to assign a dollar value to the influence on young minds of growing up near the world's largest scientific instrument. As a former teacher, I am convinced that the SSC will awaken imaginations, influence lives, and lead directly or indirectly to discoveries that will change the world for the better; and as governor, I am committed to improving the educational infrastructure in North Carolina. The SSC would stimulate and enhance science education in North Carolina from the elementary grades through the graduate level."

U.S. DEPARTMENT OF ENERGY PUBLIC HEARING ON
HIGH-LEVEL NUCLEAR WASTE REPOSITORY

ASHEVILLE, APRIL 4, 1986

Thank you for giving me the opportunity to comment, once again, on the proposal by the U.S. Department of Energy to study two areas in North Carolina as possible candidate sites for a high-level nuclear waste repository. Let me say at the outset that my position on this matter is simple and unequivocal: Having thoroughly reviewed the evidence, I do not believe that any site in North Carolina is technically acceptable for the storage of high-level nuclear waste. Even if the technology you propose works, these old metamorphic rock[s] under extensive water tables won't work.

This position has not been made in haste, nor does it represent an emotional response to the problem of safely disposing of our nation's nuclear waste. I believe, as did a majority of the members of Congress in 1982, that we must find a safe and acceptable method of isolating this highly dangerous material. The intent of the House of Representatives in approving the Nuclear Waste Policy Act was to authorize the Department of Energy to determine whether there were suitable sites for the burial of nuclear waste, but no authority has been given to construct such a repository in any area east of the Mississippi River.[1] This act certainly did not envision consideration of sites in close proximity to major population centers. The Elk River Complex is not isolated—far from it; neither is the Rolesville Pluton near Raleigh. These are dynamic growth areas in terms of both population and economic activity.

The Department of Energy is seeking to determine whether crystalline rock formations in these two areas afford the safest and best long-term storage. The ultimate decision will be based on examinations of hydrology, geology, and population. Unfortunately, the original selection of these twelve candidate sites for further study appears to have been based on only the screening factors, the size and extent of underground rock bodies, and the existence of substantial population at the potential site. Obviously, sites could meet these criteria and yet still be technically incompatible with the concept of permanent vault storage.

The draft area recommendation report says that such large rock formations are found in the Elk River and Rolesville areas, if size and extent are the only factors considered. Yet, that limited factor neglects the water table and the metamorphic character of these rocks, or the proximity of large population. Any one of these factors should rule out North Carolina.

We can, and will, argue this point vigorously, but our concern is not limited just to the composition of the rock formations under consideration. Our larger interest is the future of North Carolina, of our continued success in economic development with maximum safeguards to public health and safety and to our valuable environmental resources. I share these concerns with all North Carolinians, and as a result, I have taken appropriate steps to demonstrate the many reasons why our state is not an acceptable choice.

The results of the full-scale technical and policy review of the draft area recommendation report have confirmed and reaffirmed my initial judgment. Today our secretary of natural resources and community development, Tommy Rhodes, will present in convincing fashion the key points that we will present, on April 15, to show the basis for our conclusion that there is no potentially acceptable site in North Carolina for the storage of high-level nuclear waste.

In conclusion, let me make two important points. First, I want the Department of Energy to reevaluate immediately its siting criteria so as to make population and economic concerns of equal importance to geological and hydrological factors. Certainly they must not be neglected, because that could lead to a false conclusion.

Secondly, we urge you to avoid prolonging unnecessarily the uncertainty as to your final decision. If, at any time, you find that any of the candidate sites possess features to disqualify it, then you should promptly report that finding and withdraw every such site from further consideration. That would treat people fairly and improve public confidence in what you are doing. Don't wait for a complete, edited report. Don't prolong the anxiety of our people. No one gains from that.

I have no doubt that if the factors I have called to your attention today are considered carefully, both North Carolina sites will be eliminated from further consideration.

North Carolina is one united state, united against placing any permanent vault repository in rocks that are not suitable—because of fractures, seismic activity, and overlying water table—or in locations that are not suitable because of proximity to large, growing populations. I hope you will find that we are just as united in our intent to avoid creating hysteria, because we recognize that those who incite panic and fear will only succeed in injuring the tourist and real-estate values, even as you come to the inevitable conclusion that these sites are unsuitable.

As governor, I have established a coordinated response in opposition to these two sites being selected:

1. I have designated a lead agency to handle this matter. It has already used legislative funds to contract with outside experts for independent geological studies and to examine DOE's data base.

2. I have appointed a citizens task force of local citizens and officials, together with technical experts, to help direct maximum attention to this problem;

3. Hired a state coordinator;

4. Prepared a comprehensive, detailed analysis of the DOE criteria as they relate to our two sites, which I will hand deliver to Secretary Herrington on April 15.[2]

5. We are working with neighboring states, like Virginia and South Carolina and Tennessee, to share data and influence at this point;

6. Our members of Congress, who are aggressively lobbying their colleagues to head off any ultimate decision to authorize such a facility in any site that is clearly unsuitable.

I mention this because some[one] just yesterday announced a plan to do these things that are already being done. Since it's such a good idea, I thought everyone should know it's already being done. To set up a rival political front will only confuse.

And, we will have a referendum to express in an orderly and official way the united opposition of our people. This is not because we think such a vote will change the geological and population factors that already exist to disqualify these sites, but because we want all political decision-makers to know that we know these factors should disqualify our areas and that we want no one to consider locating a facility in a site that is not suitable. This will not be a vote on other issues: nuclear power or submarines. Those who would inject these issues will only confuse and cause people to mistakenly vote for those issues.

---

[1]P.L. 97-425, "Nuclear Waste Policy Act of 1982" (short title), *United States Statutes at Large*, Act of January 7, 1983, 96 Stat. 2201-2263.

[2]John Stewart Herrington (1939-   ), born in Los Angeles; A.B., Stanford University, 1961; J.D., University of California at San Francisco, 1964; U.S. Marine Corps. Deputy district attorney, Ventura County, California, 1965-1966; attorney in private practice, 1966-1981; deputy assistant, 1981, assistant, 1983-1985, to President Reagan; assistant navy secretary, 1981-1983; appointed secretary, U.S. Department of Energy, 1985; Republican. *Who's Who in America, 1988-1989*, I, 1399.

WELCOME TO KEIDANREN DELEGATION

CHARLOTTE, APRIL 4, 1986

[Mamoru Sakai, president of the Long-Term Credit Bank of Japan, Ltd., led a twenty-five-member delegation from *Keidanren*, the Japanese Federation of Economic Organizations, on a business development mission to North Carolina on April 4-5, 1986. It was one of three Keidanren study groups dispatched to the United States in March, April, and June to investigate the investment climate in sixteen states. See attachments to Martin's remarks welcoming Keidanren, April 4, 1986, Governors Papers, James G. Martin.]

It is an honor and a great pleasure, President (Mamoru) Sakai, to welcome you and members of your distinguished delegation to North Carolina. *Konnichiwa*.[1] It had earlier been expected that I would be on my way to Europe to recruit the investment of marks, and francs, and pounds sterling to add to your yen, but when I learned that the influential Keidanren would be here in Charlotte, I modified my plans.[2]

Last October I had the privilege of visiting your beautiful country and observing firsthand the tremendous and continuing progress your people are making in the fields of science, technology, and industrialization. Two of my agents, Rusty Goode and Walter Johnson,[3] are even now in Japan, following up on the good contacts we developed there. I even played golf on one of your magnificent courses, Izumi, which means "water hazards!" I played the equivalent of twenty-seven holes. Unfortunately, I took that many strokes on just eighteen holes!

Throughout that visit, during which I met with many of your leaders in business and government, I was pleased [when I] discovered that North Carolina is greatly respected by your people as an international center of high technology and as a welcome place to do business. A recent national survey of business decision-makers found that 100 percent of them agree that, in 1985, we improved the business climate in North Carolina. It was very good; now it's better, say 100 percent of those surveyed. No other state came close to a perfect score.

Further evidence of what we offer can be found in the fact that many major Japanese companies have chosen to build new research laboratories and manufacturing facilities in our Research Triangle Park. This park, anchored by three great research-oriented universities, combines the innovative spirit of private enterprise and the capacity for critical exploration fostered by the academic community.

Now we offer the same opportunity for research investment here in Charlotte at the University Research Park, which you will see.

We in North Carolina understandably take immense pride in our technological leadership, and as governor I have coined the phrase "crown jewel of high technology" to describe our unique position in the world community. North Carolina is known, however, as a highly diversified state—from high tech, to low tech, data processing to food processing. In fact, our state has a larger percentage of its work force engaged in manufacturing than any other state in our nation. Of the thirty-seven Japanese companies which have invested in North Carolina facilities are many engaged solely in manufacturing pursuits— from lawn mowers and power equipment to amino acids, from seafood processing to the production of vitamin B-1—all around our state.

Perhaps the many similarities between our two peoples have accounted for this range of diversity. Both have a strong work ethic, the ability to master new skills, and a strong sense of loyalty to employer. Japanese businesses appreciate that characteristic of North Carolina workers. They work.

Geographically and climatically, our state and your island nation of Japan also have much in common. Like Japan, North Carolina ranges from majestic mountain terrain to crystal coasts, interlaced by clear streams and fertile fields. And, of course, there are the four distinct seasons of the year.

Just as North Carolina's higher education system makes a major contribution to the success of our high-technology community, so too does our system of fifty-eight community colleges all across our state. These institutions are rated among our country's leading centers of training and retraining for the modern world of work. Twenty of them have established small business centers to provide intensive assistance to entrepreneurial enterprises.

During this visit to North Carolina, which is not your first, you will have an opportunity to see the great diversity of our state. Moreover, you will talk to many fellow Japanese business leaders, now living in North Carolina, about their experiences and the business climate in our state. The story you will hear, I believe, will be one of accelerated plans for growth and expansion.

Many of your companies have moved up their planning and construction schedules for larger facilities by as much as five years. Others have expanded markets. Honda, which has a plant in Alamance County, now exports to Canada in addition to serving the

American domestic market for power equipment. Many others are reaching world markets from our ports.

I take much satisfaction and pride, today, in acknowledging the increasing strength and durability of the ties between North Carolinians and the people of Japan. Our state has been enriched beyond its greatest expectation by the proud history, and culture, and organizational ideas which your people have brought from your country to our neighborhoods and communities. Additionally, your generous investment of knowledge and capital in North Carolina has expanded our horizon of economic opportunity. All of this sharing of resources and opportunities has enabled us to build a sturdy bridge of cooperation and mutual benefit between our two lands.

I want to wish you a very pleasant and productive visit to our great state. We trust that this mission will lead to building an even stronger bridge of prosperity and opportunity through continued investment in North Carolina's future. It is a bright future which we may share as partners in progress.

Yoroshiku. I look forward to working with you in the future.[4]

---

[1]*Konnichiwa* is a Japanese greeting that can be translated as "Good morning" or "Good afternoon," depending on the time of day. It also means "Hello" in general. Telephone conversation with Kyoko Mimura, December 18, 1989, hereinafter cited as Mimura conversation.

[2]Governor Martin departed on his European trade mission on April 4 and returned to Raleigh by April 14, 1986. See Governor's Schedule for Weeks of March 31-April 13, 1986, and Governor's Schedule for Weeks of April 7-April 20, 1986, Governors Papers, James G. Martin.

[3]Walter R. Johnson III (1941-   ), born in Winston-Salem; resident of Cary; B.S., 1970, M.A., 1972, Sophia University; U.S. Air Force, 1959-1964. General controller, head of curriculum and instruction, Kanda Institute of Foreign Languages, 1972-1978; director, Japan operations, state Department of Commerce, 1978-1988. *News and Observer*, February 23, April 29, June 28, September 7, 1988; Walter R. Johnson III to Jan-Michael Poff, February 18, 1985.

[4]*Yoroshiku* has many meanings, including "I hope we can work together well." Mimura conversation.

NORTH CAROLINA ASSOCIATION OF EDUCATORS

ASHEVILLE, APRIL 18, 1986

[The following address is similar to those presented to the Wake County Business and Education Conference, Raleigh, April 24, and the Cherokee County Schools Business-Education Partnership Dinner, Murphy, April 29, 1986.]

Increasingly in recent years, teachers have come under attack for the current "crisis" in public education. Yet, we continue to marvel at the wisdom of the younger generation. As the story goes, an elementary teacher, supervising a playground, saw a child fall from a swing. Rushing over, she picked up the child, brushed off her clothing, and said, "Now, now, don't cry—everthing will be all right."

"All right, my foot," the child said without shedding a tear, "I'm going to sue!"

Which brings us to the fact that public education is not the only crisis facing us today.

In this anxious April for North Carolina, however, one priority commands our urgent attention. One need challenges all citizens who are dedicated to building a future for our state that is filled with greater hope and opportunity. That priority, that challenge, that word, is education.

For more than two decades, the quality of education in America, once the envy of the world, has become our nation's number-one shame. The evidence is all around us. Here in North Carolina, more than 1.7 million of our people have never completed high school. It is estimated that more than 875,000 of them are functional illiterates— truck drivers who can't read road signs, parents who are unable to read the caution labels on their children's medicine bottles, and workers who are unable to read instructions dealing with deadly chemicals. The number is growing at the rate of some 20,000 annually. It is extracting an economic and social price the public is no longer willing to bear.

Today the choice, the real choice, lies between education policies that assume responsibility awkwardly and fearfully and policies that accept responsibility with sure purpose and firm will. The choice is between vision and blindness; between doing and apologizing; between planning and improving. The solution to our public education crisis does not lie in quick fixes and Band-Aid treatment. No, the answer rests with shaping a new vision of what education can become, not a return to what it has been. As governor, my vision of education in North Carolina is more than just the transfer of knowledge, although that is vital; it is the architecture of the human soul.

For far too long, government has been the master of education and not its partner. We can no longer hold to the notion that educational excellence can be legislated. It can't be. Excellence begins with the classroom teacher, and what we think of, expect, and require of teachers will, in the end, be a mirror of our own priorities.

Teachers are, day by day, in their own quiet, unsung way, probably more important to the progress and prosperity of North Carolina than any other profession. Good teachers, effective teachers, must be so many different people: our child's third parent and lifelong friend; the person who makes hard things seem easy; who teaches us to think apart, yet act together; and who conveys the meaning of ideas and, through personal example, the nobility of ideals.

In shaping the education policy of this administration, I have made the teacher my highest priority. The status of our teachers, professionally and economically, is inextricably tied to what we as a society think about the importance of raising children. After years of experimentation with new programs and methods, I believe the public—the parents, business leaders, and others of our state—understand and accept that fact.

Today, at a time when North Carolina and other states are poised and ready for educational reform, when public sentiment is on the side of greater support for our teachers, we cannot afford to waste this golden opportunity for constructive change. We must remember just how fragile public sentiment can be. We must also remember how easily that sentiment can be shattered by constant debate of the many wonderful ideas for raising the academic achievement of our children.

Last November, in an address to the North Carolina School Boards Association, I put forth for the first time my vision of a new future for education in our state. It contained twenty priorities, the first of which is teachers, that I believe hold the greatest promise of regaining educational excellence in North Carolina. It was not the first time I had addressed the plight of education in North Carolina: In my 1985 budget message to the General Assembly, I proposed an increase in the share of the state's budget for public schools. Many of you are not aware of that.

For five straight years prior to 1985, that share had continued to decline. So, I proposed a 12 percent increase, including salary improvements for teachers, reduction in class size, and more funds for computer instruction, textbooks, and classroom equipment. Moreover, I also proposed the implementation of the teacher career ladder pilot program. Although there was some disagreement on particulars, I am pleased that the General Assembly joined with me and acted favorably on these measures.

Beyond last year's proposals, the General Assembly also adopted the historic Basic Education plan, which in spite of its virtues, has nothing to do with basic education and, above all, does not even address improvements in the teaching profession. Let me give an example: Although the Basic Education plan establishes the career ladder program, it provides no funds for its implementation when it's time to go statewide.

Fully implemented on a projected timetable of eight years, the Basic Education plan will cost an estimated $691 million; that's today's dollars, without considering inflation. The greatest expense, more than half the total amount, would be spent on hiring over 12,000 additional teachers and some 13,000 new support personnel. All of this comes at a time of critical teacher shortage and a continuing decline in the number of college graduates receiving teaching certificates. In fact, the number of graduates receiving teaching certificates in North Carolina has dropped by more than 50 percent in the last decade. As President Graves[1] has emphasized, the problem is compounded by the fact that 6,000 of today's teachers are eligible for retirement and an additional 2,000 are eligible for early retirement. That's why I've made teachers my first priority. Unless we do, we will never keep enough of our present teachers, who do teach well, or recruit enough of the best and brightest graduates to pursue teaching careers.

For several decades now, we have spent more and more money on all the other good ideas for education, and less and less to improve the pay schedule for teachers. Over the last two decades, the percentage of our school budget going to classroom teachers has dropped from 56 percent to 38 percent. That's not putting first things first! If teachers are to be our first priority, and they must be, then we must budget for the teaching profession first—and that means paying teachers the kind of salaries that make thorough preparation and effective teaching worthwhile.

The Basic Education plan doesn't do this. Just last week, the Public School Forum of North Carolina agreed, calling the General Assembly's disregard for the teaching profession the Achilles' heel of the Basic Education plan. I'm delighted, also, that former governor Hunt, in a speech to the Dilworth Country Club near Charlotte just a few days ago, echoed the same belief. He, too, cites the need for better salaries as our chief priority.

How much should we spend? Consider, if you will, the constant dollar continuation of all existing programs and pay, adjusted for cost of living or Consumer Price Index, plus an extra $500 million. How much of this should go to improving the compensation of classroom teachers and other instructional personnel? Bear in mind that the cost of the career ladder is estimated at $300 million to $400 million. Should we spend all of it? None of it? Should We spend two thirds of it? Assuming two thirds went to salary enhancement, this would result in an increase of 22 percent. Or should we spend it all on the Basic Education plan, adding on more employees?

Clearly, our funding priority over the next three to five years should provide major pay increases for our teachers, structured around the career ladder program. Development of an incentive pay system to provide better pay for better teachers is essential [to] retaining and attracting good teachers. We are not rushing into this concept, for we must allow adequate time for developing a system that works to achieve the desired results; and to succeed, development of this pay system will require teacher input.

I welcome your association's recommendations. Indeed, broad participation is vital in the decision-making process. That's why, for the past three months, the North Carolina Council on Education has been holding a series of public hearings across the state. We have been seeking comment on teacher pay and other concerns. We want to pay our teachers what they deserve, and the public wants to make sure their children get what they pay for. I am pleased with the response to these public hearings, and I am anxious to receive the council's report and recommendations.

Improvement in teacher compensation, as important as it is, will not solve all of our education problems. The proposals I have announced include other steps we must take to strengthen our public schools. Among these steps are incentive scholarships for academically talented education majors to help attract qualified teachers, establishment of a teacher recruitment office, and elimination of the first step in the teacher salary schedule for certified, entry-level instructional personnel. Furthermore, I've proposed giving a supplemental salary incentive payment to classroom teachers in those systems that are not participating in the career ladder pilot project. I've also proposed scholarships for good teachers who want to work toward a master's in their subject area.

All of these proposals will help us build effective teachers and effective schools, and they will help to build confidence and support at the community level. Effective schools are those in which teachers do not work in isolation—[but] where teachers, principals, students, and parents share goals, support each other, and cooperate in a unified set of activities. To achieve effective schools, we must concentrate decision-making authority closer to the classroom, move away from regulatory approaches, and create conditions that encourage local schools to resolve their own improvement problems. In brief, effective schools are those that produce good students; and, as it turns out, among the characteristics of good schools is a willingness to define educational goals, to assess performance in meeting these goals, and to make the results known to the community. More importantly, effective schools start with effective teachers, my first priority.

Years from now, history probably won't care much whether in the last half of the 80s we generated a hundred bright ideas for education. My guess is that we will be remembered for what we do about our best idea: strengthening the teaching profession, both qualitatively and quantitatively. If we don't do that, it won't matter how many dollars we pour into the other good and desirable, but less important, ideas for education.

I am heartened by the growing support for the proposals I announced last November—support from the public, former governors, the Public School Forum of North Carolina, members of the General Assembly, and from you, the classroom teachers of our state. Although it is not perfect, our system of public education is our greatest success story. We can unite to build upon that success and, in so doing, become the model of excellence for our nation. I hope you will join me and help me in fulfilling that vision and that goal.

---

[1]Gladys Fowler Graves (1947-   ), born in Caswell County; resident of Raleigh; B.A., Shaw University, 1969. Schoolteacher in Caswell County, 1970-1971, and Guilford County, 1971-1982, 1983-1984; president, North Carolina Association of Classroom Teachers, 1982-1983, and of North Carolina Association of Educators, 1985-1986, 1987-1988; deputy director, Terry Sanford for U.S. Senate campaign, 1986-1987; director, alumni relations and institutional research, Shaw University, since 1989; consultant. Gladys Fowler Graves to Jan-Michael Poff, April 30, 1990.

LAW ENFORCEMENT OFFICERS APPRECIATION BANQUET

GOLDSBORO, APRIL 18, 1986

[This address is similar to those delivered before the National Governors' Association Committee on Criminal Justice and Public Protection, Washington, D.C., February 24, 1986, and at the swearing-in ceremony of the Governor's Crime Commission, Raleigh, March 14, 1986.]

Since my first days in office, the problem of crime has been a major concern of this administration—even while we had to deal with a number of other compelling legislative issues confronting us during the 1985 session of the General Assembly. Tonight, I want to reassure you that winning the war against crime remains one of our most urgent priorities. It must because, so far, law enforcement is on the losing side. We're losing because government is failing in one of its most legitimate and important functions, particularly in protecting society from those who would prey on the innocent: our children and youth, the elderly, the defenseless.

During the first half of 1985, the latest period for which we have statistics, murder in our state rose by 11 percent, rape by 9 percent, arson by 20 percent, and robbery by 3 percent. In our cities and suburban areas, the rates are even higher. The use of illegal drugs, especially cocaine, has become an epidemic. Marijuana has become one of North Carolina's leading cash crops.

The destruction of young lives through the abusive use of drugs and alcohol has become a tragedy, the proportions of which are difficult to measure. Even among adults, abuse of alcohol and drugs is the major cause of crime. Fully 80 percent of our prison inmates admitted in a survey last year that they were under the influence of drugs or alcohol at the time they committed the crime that sent them to prison.

In the past few years, we've seen the public return to the values that are the basis for a free and just society, the belief that right and wrong matters and that individuals are responsible for their actions. These are the values and beliefs that guided us when I took office, and they are the same values and beliefs that will guide us in the future.

Last year, I launched a major offensive against crime in North Carolina. We achieved some significant goals. These successes included strengthening our obscenity laws, funding the Center for Missing Children, ratification of the boating while impaired law,[1] and establishment and funding of the Alcohol and Drug Offense Program within the Department of Public Instruction.[2] The General Assembly, however, did not act favorably on proposals to increase the number of drug enforcement officers and highway patrolmen. Another bill proposed by the administration, raising the felony classification for certain crimes committed against the elderly, failed to pass the House of Representatives.

Some major accomplishments, however, were made in other ways. In the area of law enforcement, I used my powers as commander in chief of the National Guard to utilize helicopters on routine training missions to locate and report marijuana fields. These missions are conducted in cooperation with local law enforcement agencies and our State Bureau of Investigation. I am pleased to report that during 1985, these missions were responsible for destroying more than 15,000 marijuana plants with a street value in excess of $13 million.

By executive order, I established the Governor's Commission on Child Victimization, which is chaired by my wife, Dottie. This commission has a number of responsibilities, including encouraging private sector involvement in the prevention of child victimization and the coordination of state agencies that deal with children.

The extent of child victimization in North Carolina is not known, but what we do know is that it is one of the most menacing threats to the social fabric of our state. Many children are victims of teenage pregnancy, incest and rape, substance abuse, custody battles, abuse, neglect, exploitation, and abduction. One form of child victimization stands out among all the others: the alarming and distressing issue of child abuse and, more specifically, sexual abuse. The prevalence and severity of this problem has mounted to the point that public caretakers and citizens have been overwhelmed. We must put an end to this needless exploitation of our children.

Problems among our young people also have multiplied in recent years. As I speak tonight, a traffic accident will occur at a national average of every fifteen seconds, bringing injury to others. Every twenty-three minutes, one of our young people dies in an automobile crash, and in most cases, alcohol is involved. This year, several hundred thousand young people will attempt suicide in America. More than 5,000 will succeed.

Nothing shouts louder of our nation's condition than the habits of its youth, and the habits of our youth are nothing more than a direct reflection of how adults handle responsibility. Last February, I announced a new partnership between Athletes Against Crime and North Carolina Amateur Sports. This partnership represents a concerted effort to make young people aware of the consequences of drugs, alcohol, and criminal activities. This state-funded program, developed by the Crime Prevention Division of the North Carolina Department of Crime Control and Public Safety, reaches students through sports clinics. Another program we have launched is the Crime Prevention Awards Project, which seeks to involve young North Carolinians in crime prevention and public safety programs developed by their own student organizations.

One of the most important things we can do in combating crime and preventing alcohol and substance abuse is to increase public awareness of their heavy social and economic costs. Crime costs us a lot, but we get a lot of crime for our money.

This is a task that involves the entire community, every neighborhood, and every family. Government can be a partner in that effort, but there is no substitute for citizen involvement and support. Let's all work together to make that happen.

I'm proud that this administration has led the way in passing new legislation and new programs to strengthen crime prevention and law enforcement; we haven't achieved all that is needed, but we've made an excellent beginning. But most of all, I share the pride of all North Carolinians in honoring you, the men and women of the law enforcement community, who have helped to lead this effort. Each day, you place your lives on the line to protect the citizens of this community and the state. No one could ask more. Through your dedication to protect and defend, you serve as a noble example of law enforcement at its best.

I also want to commend the Civitan Club for honoring you, this evening. This club began this dinner many years ago, and it has since been adopted as a national project by your parent organization. That's a splendid example of how community action can take root and grow.

Let me also commend those of you who will receive special awards this evening. The recognition which this club bestows upon you speaks from the heart of a grateful citizenry. On behalf of the people of North Carolina, I join with them in paying a tribute to you and law enforcement officers throughout our state. We thank all of you for a job well done.

---

[1]"An Act to Establish the Legal Level of Impairment for Boat Operators and to Reduce Litter on the State's Waters," *N.C. Session Laws, 1985*, c. 615, was ratified July 5, 1985, and became effective October 1 of that year.

[2]Chapter 757, s. 79, *N.C. Session Laws, 1985*, established the Alcohol and Drug Defense (ADD) Program in the Department of Public Instruction.

TESTIMONY BEFORE OVERSIGHT HEARING ON CRYSTALLINE REPOSITORY PROJECT, U.S. HOUSE COMMITTEE ON ENERGY AND COMMERCE, SUBCOMMITTEE ON ENERGY CONSERVATION AND POWER

WASHINGTON, D.C., APRIL 23, 1986

[The stagnating nuclear power industry eliminated any need for a high-level radioactive waste repository on the East Coast, according to Energy Secretary John S. Herrington, who announced on May 28, 1986, that his department was going to "postpone indefinitely" its search for a site. "This decision will lift the cloud of anxiety that had hung over North Carolina," Martin said. *News and Observer*, May 29, 1986; Statement on DOE High-Level Waste Announcement, Raleigh, May 28, 1986.]

I appreciate the opportunity to be here, today, to discuss the crystalline repository project for high-level nuclear waste disposal. I would first like to take this opportunity to briefly express my views on the need for a second nuclear waste repository and then relate some of the problems we in North Carolina have had with the siting process to date.

I believe, as did the majority of the members of Congress in 1982, that the nation must find a safe and acceptable method for isolating our highly dangerous nuclear wastes. The original intention of the Nuclear Waste Policy Act was to authorize the Department of Energy to identify a suitable site for the burial of nuclear waste and to construct a geologic repository. Ideally, I envisioned that this facility would be located in a sparsely populated, undeveloped area far removed from major population centers and other areas of intensive human activity. Just as important, I assumed then that rock formations which were unsuitable for this rock-vault technology—because of fractures and overlying water tables—would have been excluded from the study since they could serve no useful purpose.

As you know, we in the Congress in 1982 never fully endorsed the idea of a second repository and never authorized it. The House in particular was opposed to authorizing construction of a second facility, but did agree to a study to determine the best location if it was determined that two repositories were needed. In a fit of bipartisan, east-west, nationwide evenhandedness, we agreed to a study to find whether any eastern sites were suitable for the proposed technology. Now that we know North Carolina's two rock bodies chosen for further study are in fact unsuitable because of geological, hydrological, and demographic factors, we are deeply chagrined that a threat has been created to consider using them anyway!

Unfortunately, the Department of Energy [DOE] has been operating as if the construction of a second repository was a certaintly, but this is not the case; in fact, new evidence suggests that a second repository will not be needed. Estimates of spent nuclear fuel are much lower not than those that were available to the Congress in 1982. No new orders for reactors, combined with extended burn technologies, mean that one repository should be adequate to meet our waste-disposal needs at least until the middle of the next century.

There are other compelling reasons to reexamine the need to look for a second repository site. DOE is concentrating its search, for the second facility, on crystalline rock formations found primarily along the East Coast and in the upper Midwest. While the geology of these regions may or may not be adequate to isolate high-level radioactive waste for thousands of years, other environmental and public safety considerations make the siting of a second repository anywhere in the eastern United States inappropriate. I am particularly concerned that many of the twelve potentially acceptable sites proposed by DOE in the draft area recommendation report [ARR] are in close proximity to population centers. Certainly, this is the case for both areas identified in North Carolina.

Common sense should dictate that it is not sound public policy to even consider the location of a high-level radioactive waste-disposal site near large- or medium-sized cities or anywhere near rapidly growing metropolitan areas. One of our potentially acceptable sites, the Rolesville Pluton, is only nine miles from the city of Raleigh. Our staff has estimated that over 14,000 people live within the area and over 187,000 reside within twelve miles of the area's boundaries. The county in which 57 percent of the Rolesville area is located, Wake County, had a 1985 population of over 340,000 and experienced a 31 percent population increase from 1970 to 1980. All reasonable projections indicate that Wake County will continue to be one of the fastest-growing metropolitan areas in the nation over the next ten years.

The Elk River area in the western part of our state is only about three miles from the Asheville urban area. Over 153,000 persons live within twelve miles of the boundaries of this proposed site. Buncombe County, which contains about half of this 105-square-mile area, had a 1980 population of 161,000, an increase of about 10 percent over 1970. This area is also expected to continue to grow in the foreseeable future, and these figures do not include a substantial influx of summer residents that flock to the resorts and recreation areas in and around Asheville.

I do not believe that Congress envisioned consideration of sites in such close proximity to major population centers.

Aside from questions of proximity to large populations, we believe that both of the proposed potentially acceptable sites in North Carolina are, in fact, unacceptable for a variety of sound scientific and technical reasons involving geological, environmental, and public safety considerations. These scientific deficiencies in DOE's siting process are discussed in detail in our state comments to the department on the draft ARR.

Both rock formations are extensively fractured due to epochs of

geologic stress. That alone should disqualify both. Both North Carolina rock formations lie under extensive and deep underground water
tables which originate much of our groundwater sources and well
water. That alone should disqualify both. It is incredible that DOE
would seriously consider such rock, with known features which make
them technically unsuited for the rock vault disposal method.

I would like to point out for the benefit of the committee members
that consideration of the Elk River area in western North Carolina
poses a special threat to several federally protected lands, including
the Great Smoky Mountains National Park, the Blue Ridge Parkway,
the Shining Rock Wilderness Area, and the Pisgah National Forest. If
the federal government was trying to locate a nuclear waste repository near the maximum number of important public recreational
lands, they could not have picked a more popular location—and, as
most of you probably know, the entire area is now under consideration for a Southern Appalachian Regional Biosphere Reserve under a
United Nations program that is administered in this country by the
State Department.

The Nuclear Waste Policy Act mandates consultation and cooperation with the states in the siting process and requires opportunity for
citizen participation. At the state level, we have had some difficulty
obtaining informational materials from DOE. Our supply of the draft
reports was exhausted after the January 16 announcement, and we
received only a few additional copies despite several calls to the
information staff in the Office of Civilian Radioactive Waste Management. The state has received numerous requests from local residents
and civic and community groups for DOE information reports that we
have been unable to provide.

Communication between the North Carolina Department of Natural Resources and Community Development, the lead state agency for
the crystalline repository project, and the Department of Energy has
often been inconsistent and on occasion has completely broken
down. We have had particular problems with last-minute time
changes for DOE public information meetings and the public hearings. Perfunctory press releases from DOE failed to get the word out
to local people on a timely basis.

The ninety-day period for review and comment was barely enough
time for the state, with its official resources, to prepare a comprehensive response to the DOE draft report. For individual citizens, local
governments, and civic groups, a ninety-day period was an even
more serious constraint, given the lack of resources available to such
groups and individuals. There was little opportunity for public educa-

tion programs, and thus meaningful public participation in the review and comment process was often impossible. DOE's schedule-driven timetable often encouraged an impulsive public response rather than calm and reasoned discussions.

Our state mobilized its resources to see that we provided the most comprehensive response possible to DOE by April 16 [illegible insertion]. We felt it was important for DOE to have this information as quickly as possible. When they evaluate this new documentation and evidence, they should follow a like time frame and eliminate the two sites in North Carolina in ninety days [illegible insertion].

Consultation with the state in the screening process was almost nonexistent. I would like to relate one example that epitomizes the lack of close consultation with the state in this process. The draft report lists the North Carolina Department of Natural Resources and Community Development as the sole source of information on groundwater wells in the Rolesville Pluton candidate area. The source of this information was apparently old, obsolete, written documents. The more recent records on water wells have been maintained by the state on microfiche which was not examined. The outdated reports grossly understated the number of water wells in the area. Had DOE requested that the state gather information on water wells, we would have readily complied, but no such request was made. As a result, vital groundwater information was not considered in the screening process. This omission of crucial data has severely damaged the credibility of the draft report among area residents, and the state has been put in the uncomfortable position of explaining why DOE used inaccurate information and cited the state as its source.

We are also dissatisfied with the statistical methodology employed by DOE's consultants in the screening process. Our objections center on the arbitrary weights assigned to selected variables. While state officials participated in DOE workshops, I am told that their views were given lip service but that the final methodology did not fully reflect state input, particularly with regard to population criteria. States generally asked for population factors to be given much greater weight than geological factors. Instead, they were given much less. This antipopulation bias was compounded by DOE's decision to use only two population factors among the total of twelve on which sites were graded. That alone would almost guarantee that population proximity would not disqualify during the screening stage. That is silly and wasteful of resources.

As the result of the use of arbitrary criteria unrelated to repository safety, the Rolesville candidate area was added late to the list of acceptable sites when earlier statistical analysis indicated that this area did not satisfactorily meet siting criteria. That undermines our confidence.

Due to these inconsistencies, the screening process has failed to adequately take into account population and population growth. DOE stacked the deck in the screening process to emphasize geology—[illegible insertion] the size and extent of the rock mass—while de-emphasizing social and economic considerations. Congress had in mind the selection of sites that would minimize adverse social and economic consequences and pose the least threat to the people. These are the concerns that are of paramount importance to the states. If state government cannot ensure the health and safety of our people, and if we cannot provide an opportunity for our local economies to prosper, then we, the states, become superfluous to the entire process.

To date, DOE has conducted the screening process as if the state of North Carolina were superfluous. While the department may have complied with the procedural requirements of federal laws and regulations, the process has been carried out in a perfunctory manner with little opportunity provided for substantive input from state government—or serious consideration of the input received from us.

My statement represents a somewhat abbreviated review of the problems the state of North Carolina has had in dealing with the Department of Energy. My secretary of natural resources and community development, Thomas Rhodes, will further elaborate our concerns when he testifies later this morning.

It is ironically conceivable that of the twelve sites in the eastern United States, North Carolina's two—unsuitable as they are, with all their faults, fractures, water tables, and nearby population—might just turn out to score highest of the twelve under the arbitrary bias of the weights and formulas used. But, if so, then it would only mean that no suitable sites exist in eastern states. In that case, no radioactive waste repository should be built in the East; even if a second site were needed, it should never be built in an unsuitable rock formation. That is the most important thing I can possibly say to you.

Thank you for inviting me here. I would be happy to answer any questions.

SOCIAL AND ECONOMIC GROWTH THROUGH SCIENCE
AND TECHNOLOGY:
WHITEHEAD LECTURE, UNIVERSITY OF GEORGIA

ATHENS, GEORGIA, APRIL 23, 1986

I am deeply honored by your invitation to deliver the 1986 Whitehead Lecture at this great university—the first public institution of higher education chartered in America, now in its two hundred and second year. The occasion fills me with both pride and pleasure: pride, because I am privileged to have my name associated with an endowed lectureship honoring a man whose contributions to the teaching of analytical chemistry have become a legend on this campus. The late Dr. Thomas Hillyer Whitehead, who served as dean of the Graduate School until his retirement in 1972, was the last of the "forty-year chemists" to serve the University of Georgia.[1] His influence for good has been enduringly imprinted on the life of this university, and the intellectual and moral resources of countless students have been strengthened by his generous benefactions. The pleasure of this occasion derives from a return to the place of my roots, the native soil of Georgia. So, in many respects this visit is a homecoming.

The title of my address, today, is "Social and Economic Growth through Science and Technology," and it deserves a few words of explanation. I chose it, first of all, to underscore the profound importance of the era in which we live, an era of discovery unlike any history has ever witnessed. Sweeping social and economic changes are taking place throughout the world; these changes often are propelled by the discoveries of science and the development of technology. In the Western countries, many speak of our society as "post-industrial," a result of the displacement of traditional smokestack industries by so-called information industries. In the developing Third World, both traditional and information industries are challenging agrarian society. And, in the South, we face a transitional period perhaps more dramatic than industrialization in the period 1877-1913, described by the southern historian C. Vann Woodward as the "origins of the New South."[2] In North Carolina, we are working hard to stay ahead of that change curve.

Many North Carolinians live in three distinct cultures: first, a traditional agrarian life—either farming, full or part time; second, workers in textiles, furniture, and tobacco factories; and third, workers and researchers in high-tech industries and laboratories. As farming and traditional employment decline, North Carolina faces the problem of how to accommodate the transition of relatively low-skilled workers into higher-skilled jobs, and, at the same time, how to continue the development of high-skilled, knowledge-related industry. We have invested in two research parks: at the pacesetting Research Triangle, formed by three universities, and the companion facility at Charlotte. We have built, with state funds, the Microelectronics Center, which is the national laboratory in that field; are developing a biotechnology center; and will build the preeminent textile center for research and engineering.

Integral to this transition are science and technology. Today, I want to explore the general features of science and technology and later show how they pertain to social and economic growth in the South. The general features central to my subject are: I, The Nature of Scientific and Technological Knowledge; II, Science and Technology as Creative Human Enterprises; and III, The Values of Science and Technology.

I. The Nature of Scientific and Technological Knowledge

In our present society, science and technology are intimately related, but they are not the same enterprise—nor is technology merely applied science. Science pursues understanding of nature, while technology designs artifacts for the improvement of human life. Sometimes technology does result from the application of scientific theory, but in many cases technology existed before scientists constructed explanations of how the particular technology operated.

For example, cathedrals and bridges were built long before scientists understood statics and strength of materials. Similarly, the automobile and airplane were developed before the thermodynamics of the gasoline engine or the aerodynamics of a cambered wing were understood. On the other hand, relativity theory preceded the development of nuclear power; more recently, an intimate relationship has developed between the two. Engineers do want to comprehend the theoretical explanations for their machines, and scientists need machinery and instrumentation to investigate the physical aspects of their theoretical predictions.

In particle physics, some observers have wondered whether the indirect evidence confirming the existence of quarks is more the creation of high energy than the discovery of a fundamental phenomenon in nature. Indeed, the border line between science and technology at the frontiers of research often remains difficult to define. In this field, too, North Carolina is preparing to be among the leaders in seeking to be selected for the multi-billion-dollar superconducting super collider.

The basic difference between science and technology still stands: While science pursues knowledge for its own sake, technology engages in development for a purpose. Engineers design structures and machines for a particular purpose—a bridge to improve transportation or a space shuttle to explore outer space. Good design combines attention to economics, aesthetics, ethics, and efficiency, which, at times, conflict. Technologists, therefore, must make a series of trade offs in their design. Machines are constructed for humans, and when the factors of beauty and safety are sacrificed to economics and efficiency, technology often fails.

Scientists also pursue beauty, but the beauty found in science differs greatly from that of the engineer. Where the engineer looks for physical beauty in his design, the scientist looks for beauty in explanation—sometimes a form of mathematical elegance or metaphoric simplicity. Scientific beauty is a much more ethereal and contemplative form.

Critics have blamed scientists for producing knowledge that has resulted in harm. As a scientist, I have often been asked how I can justify the study of nature for its own sake when investigations lead to the production of such things as atomic weapons or poison gas. One line of defense has been that one should blame the users of that knowledge and not the scientists who have discovered it, but such a defense, although partially correct, still leaves the scientist vulnerable.

The more important answer has to do with foreknowledge. Scientists should explore nature for its own sake unless they know in advance that their research will produce unmitigated harm. Humane scientists investigating nature may yield results that can be misused, but no humane scientist intentionally seeks harm.

Scientific and technological knowledge presently pose a rather paradoxical problem. While we welcome the ever-increasing knowledge we have about nature and knowledge we have about how to improve life through the production of mechanical devices, the sheer volume of information produced by these two enterprises poses its own problem. How can we continue to increase scientific and technological knowledge at an almost exponential rate when we find it difficult to comprehend that which we already have?

Ninety percent of all the scientists found in history are alive today; similarly, a very high proportion of history's engineers also are still alive. Why, it's almost as bad as with lawyers! These two facts should produce great hope for the future, but paradoxically, their volume also makes it difficult for the individual researcher to keep up in his field. Like Alice—Alice in Wonderland—who had to run just to stay in place, today's engineer must struggle constantly just to keep abreast of his or her own field. Sometimes, in a larger field, reading *Chemabstracts* or *Physical Abstracts* demands almost full-time attention, leaving little time for reading the pertinent articles abstracted.

And finding the important points and new developments in this vast quantity of information becomes difficult. Computer searches aid the researcher greatly, but they do not eliminate the problem. Since computers can generate so much information, they are used constantly not only to search existing information, but they add their own to the pile. Computer scientists have talked occasionally about "information pollution," meaning by those terms the unnecessary accumulation of information producing waste along with useful knowledge. Determining the difference between necessary and unnecessary information seems almost impossible since discovery in science sometimes results from serendipity—looking for one thing and finding another, instead.

What should we do? Certainly not stop scientific research or technological development, except where they are foreknown to produce harm to humans. We must devise theories of how to handle information that will search for salient features without removing the possibility of suggestion. Scientists could also refrain from adding needless articles through publishing repetitious information. This would happen only if peer review for promotion in universities and industry placed less value on quantities of publication and more upon quality. I'll let you worry about how to grade it, while I [move] on to point number two.

II. Science and Technology as Creative Human Enterprises

In the popular mind, science and technology are seen as absolutely objective and removed from the human condition. Dressed in a white coat, the researcher appears to the public as rational, honest, and dispassionate in his clinical investigations—setting aside, of course, the fictional distortion of the mad scientist. C. P. Snow further popularizes this view in his book, *Two Cultures*, where he claimed that the modern world was divided into the almost exclusive cultures of science and the humanities.[3] Some commentators have observed that the high esteem in which science has come to be held in the modern world verges closely upon being a religion, with scientists as high priests who have been initiated and taken on vows, dedicating them to the pursuit of truth, and the laboratory as a place where rituals are performed.

But is this view of science and technology correct? My own experience and the biographies of many scientists contradict this view. Scientists are very passionate in their pursuit of knowledge, and they are all too human, with obvious failings in their dealings with each other. But, more importantly, they are humanists in the finest sense: Science and technology are human enterprises. Let me provide some evidence in support of this view by briefly showing that scientists are poets and engineers are artists.

Scientists express their theories about nature in languages that are combinations of mathematics and ordinary vernacular language. Although many fervently wish that they could speak in mathematics, algorithms must be related to the physical world in experiments, and, to do that, conceptual bridges must be made from the equations to the experiments. To build these conceptual bridges, scientists often create new language, sometimes poetic in nature.

Newton was faced with exactly this task as he sought to relate his laws of motion, expressed in mathematics, to the ordinary happenings of the everyday world. I don't know if an apple actually fell on his head, but it surely offered an apt illustration. Taking words like *force* and *mass* used earlier by Galileo and others who attempted to explain motion, Newton infused new meaning in these terms by borrowing from theology and alchemy.

Until the last twenty years, textbooks portrayed Newton as the rational, precise scientist. The publication of the nonmathematical Newtonian papers has revealed to us a different Newton, a man who published more on theology and more on alchemy than he did on physics and astronomy.[4] This Newton is revealed in Richard Westfall's massive biography, *Never at Rest*.[5] There we see a passionate Newton seeking to explain the universe in mathematical terms, but in so doing he also borrows from other fields, like theology and alchemy, to give meaning to terms like force and mass.

Some have tried to protect the earlier view of Newton that I and many others have studied in college, of the "objective" scientist, by arguing that Newton kept his science and specializations separate, but his papers reveal that he especially resorted to this borrowing. When attempting to explain action at a distance, Newton speculated that gravity might result from the forces of light, or electrical attraction, or even from ether. He several times identified God with the physical dimensions of space.

We really should not be surprised that scientists borrow language, and sometimes their meanings, from other disciplines. When confronted by a mystery of nature, they require new speculative concepts to express their hypotheses. Like the poet seeking to express new dimensions of human experience, who coins new metaphors and other literary forms, the scientist also stretches language through analogy and metaphor. Murray Gell-Mann invented the scientific term *quark*, about 1964, by taking the word from James Joyce's *Finnegans Wake* and applying it in a completely different sense to represent a new, positive, subatomic particle in physics.[6] That is not unlike the reverse metaphor in which nonscientists often misappropriate *quantum leap* to characterize large changes.

Was Gell-Mann justified? Of course he was, as his scientific poetic license allowed him not only to borrow but to perplex and puzzle the hearer. Of course, quark theory has also developed with a mathematics of its own, but science is not just pure mathematics, and it could not exist without concepts, like that of the quark, that take on not only the character of the mathematics but also experimental aspects. Born as a playful hypothetical label, quark has matured into quarks that are now *colored, charmed, strange,* and *beautiful.*

Another wonderful episode of a famous scientist engaging in poetry can be found in Michael Faraday's naming of the *anode, cathode,* and *ion.*[7] Faraday had already formed the word *electrode* by combining the Greek words for "electricity" and "a way." He also formed *electrolyte,* again by drawing upon the Greek, but this time putting together the Greek words of "electricity" and "I dissolve." Dissolved electricity!

Employing the words *exode* and *eisode,* however, for the electrical poles, left Faraday dissatisfied. The Greek connotations of exode were "to leave," and of eisode the sense of "into" conveying the idea of a process—rather than that of a direction, which Faraday preferred. At the suggestion of a friend, Faraday wrote the to the Reverend William Whewell, a don at Cambridge University.[8] Whewell had become well known for coining new scientific terms, having helped, among others, Charles Lyell by inventing the terms *pliocene, miocene,* and *eocene,* all employed by geology as standard terms for epochs.[9]

Whewell suggested the words *anode,* for eisode, and *cathode,* for exode. At first, Faraday resisted these suggestions, but they grew upon him and he soon admitted them into his experimental usage. He also replaced his word *zetode* by *ion,* which Whewell had also suggested. The poetic aspect of Faraday appears when we find him stating, in a letter to Whewell, that he liked "Anode and Cathode better as to sound. . . ."[10]

Faraday, the scientist-poet, decided upon the choice of which terms to use because of their poetic sound, not upon any compelling experimental evidence. Again, because of theory and experiment, Faraday's terms, born poetically, come to have a life of their own in scientific meaning.

Among contemporary sociologists of science, it has become fashionable to demonstrate the humanity of scientists by showing how their judgments, in situations of peer review for funding and refereeing papers, often become flawed by their divisions into scientific-political parties. Much of their evidence seems correct. All humans in all enterprises have failures.

I prefer, however, to stress the humanity of scientists in their humanistic acts of creating poetry. Newton, Gell-Mann, and Faraday all faced the challenge of suggesting hypotheses about the unknown, and they resorted to stretching language through analogy and metaphor. What are the evolving verbal descriptions of molecular models, and their Tinker Toy versions, but metaphors? The cognitive process of scientific thinking has certain similarities with the work of a poet. Both the scientist and the poet seek to express new insights; both must stretch the language in order to present suggestions about experience and the world that have not been considered before; and both must present their new insights in language that can be understood.

Engineers traditionally have been thought of as men who carry out the designs of architects in the construction of bridges, buildings, and other static structures. In this view, the architect performs the aesthetic function while the engineer plays the role of instrument. But is this view correct? Are engineers mere technicians who leave artistic design to others?

David Billington, a professor of civil engineering at Princeton University, has recently argued cogently that when structural engineers follow engineering principles, they create beautiful, structural, art.[11] Furthermore, Billington claims that when art and engineering are divorced, buildings emerge that seem to be artistic catastrophes. Where Walter Gropius, the architect-founder of the Bauhaus school, argued that form follows function in architecture,[12] Billington's message can be summarized as "form follows structural engineering."

As an art form, structural engineering follows the principles of (1) efficiency, which means, for structural art, the delicate balance between thinness and safety; (2) a principle of economy, not only in construction but also in maintenance; and (3) a partnership with the general public. Billington is convinced that as a good art form, structural engineering must be open to public competitions, thus exhibiting a form of democracy. Examples from the history of architecture abound which fulfill these principles, but one of the foremost contemporary exemplars of structural art was the Swiss bridge engineer, Robert Maillart, who did, indeed, exemplify simplicity and efficiency in his construction of bridges using prestressed concrete; so did John Roebling in his design and construction of the Brooklyn Bridge.[13]

In scientists as poets and engineers as artists, we find expression of science and technology as humanistic disciplines. The sooner we understand science and technology as integral and expressions of what it means to be human, the sooner we will be able to understand, accommodate, and benefit properly from these disciplines. Now to my third point:

III. Values of Science and Technology

The values of both science and technology can be considered in terms of these internal and those external to each enterprise. Both Plato and Aristotle held the exploration of knowledge for its own sake to be an intrinsic value, and modern science since the seventeenth century similarly cherishes this value.

Scientists investigate the physical world primarily to explain it. Scientific explanations are composed of theories, experimental results, and assumptions. All of these combine to produce explanations that are judged to be successful or unsuccessful, by peers, in terms of their confirmation in experiments, their elegance, and their rationality.

Earlier, I argued that structural engineers can be artists. Now I want to claim that, in terms of values internal to science, the scientist expresses the value of beauty. Scientific theories are beautiful in terms of their internal elegance—that is, how the mathematics and theoretical concepts blend together to present a coherent and consistent explanation. Scientific explanations are also beautiful in terms of how they describe the physical world— that is, how the predictions of the theory fit the data found in experiments.

The external values of science are found in how science influences our thinking about the world. To be certain, science does generate practical results, but these values are found in the fruits of technology. As a form of knowledge, science affects how we envision nature and ourselves. The internal values of rationality and beauty find translation into the external demands that we place upon our society, that it be rational in organization and decision making, and that some order and elegance be found in daily life.

Scientists also hope for a comparable degree of dedication to be found in business, industry, and government. To those who claim that science is value free, I respond that not only does science possess the internal values of knowledge, honesty, rationality, beauty, and simplicity, but also that these scientific values could serve as a basis for society's values. Scientists should be proud of their values, for sharing those values can only lead to a better world.

Technology possesses the same internal values as science, plus the added technological values given to it by the purpose of each project. But, unlike science, the internal values of technology depend, in part, upon the external purpose dictated to the enterprise by the engineer— or to him, by the developer. Both scientists and engineers are humanists who want to improve the life of mankind, and reflecting upon the nature of these two fields will allow scientists to be better scientists and engineers to be better engineers.

IV. Social and Economic Growth in North Carolina

Now, what do the subjects I have been reflecting upon have to do with the policies of North Carolina state government seeking to encourage science and technology? How do all of the things in the nature of scientific and technological knowledge, the scientist as poet and the engineer as artist, and the values of both, have to do with public policy? Let me suggest several ways in which my reflections might affect policy.

First, the discovery that science and technology are fundamental knowledge processes—the one more of knowledge for its own sake and the other knowledge to achieve a human goal—suggests that the most important feature of a state seeking to move into the twenty-first century should be to concentrate on education at all levels. Our society has already become a society dominated by knowledge industries. We must provide an education for our citizens not only to participate in these new jobs but also to understand the nature of the scientific theories and technologies impelling this shift in economic growth.

Our responsibility extends beyond those who will fill these high-tech jobs and the researchers who will open up new fields of study not even known today. Our responsibility extends to those low-tech citizens who are presently not equipped to deal with, or even abide, the scientific and technological revolution in which we are now living. Economic growth in North Carolina—indeed, the South—will be possible only as we provide opportunities for our citizens to benefit from an expanding technological society. We must provide, through technology, new opportunities for those who are not currently highly trained. Innovative small industries, which are efficient but simple to operate, may be one possibility. We cannot expect every citizen to be a microelectronics engineer or a computer programmer.

North Carolina expects to continue its leadership in scientific research and high technology, but it also expects to provide, through applications of technology, new opportunities for all of its citizens. This policy of helping all of our citizens through science and technology exemplifies well my second set of reflections that scientists and technologists are basically humanists.

The discovery that scientists are poets and engineers are artists should tell us something about how we should teach science and technology: They should always be taught with the highest expectations for excellence and, also, in the context of the humanities and social scien[ces]. How can a scientist be a good poet, who invents new metaphoric and hypothetical concepts, if he or she does not know how language operates and how it can be beautiful? How can the engineer design beneficial and beautiful structures if he or she knows only statics and strengths of materials? Both scientists and engineers must understand the broader contexts of culture, art, history, and psychology, for example, in order to be better scientists and engineers; perhaps that arises out of my Davidson and Princeton degrees in chemistry, pursued in strong liberal-arts settings.

Creativity arises from scientific and technological rigor set in the cross-fertilization context of deep cultural awareness. Most great creative scientists and engineers not only had depth of understanding, but they also participated vigorously in artistic and cultural endeavors. Newton pursued theology, and Einstein, music.

Finally, my reflections upon values not only stress ethics (honesty) and art (beauty), but also the external impact upon society. As governor, with major responsibilities for economic development and diversification, I am committed to sustaining older, traditional industries and to recruiting new investment—whether high tech, low tech, or any tech in between.

When North Carolina pursues both high tech and low tech simultaneously, we must make sufficient provision for those unintended results, like pollution, that seem almost inevitable. Hence, we must arouse public understanding that the treatment of wastes must be undertaken in the most efficient and humane fashion. Tough choices must be made, but the worst choice is to have no policy for disposal.

We also must enable our citizens to understand the scientific and technological revolution in which they are living, so they can participate in it fully and so they can make informed decisions through the democratic process. Otherwise they fall for phobias, against useful chemicals and nuclear power, foisted on them by those with unknown agendas. The values of science and technology must be well understood if citizens are to have a significant voice in public policy that directly affects their lives.

Science and technology as knowledge processes, as humanistic processes, and as processes which embody internal values and produce external values, all have public policy implications. I am privileged to serve as governor of a state where science and technology are bringing about positive social and economic growth, and where the issues I have discussed today are being vigorously debated. And yet, it is also a state of the arts, where our North Carolina School of the Arts has been just as pioneering as our School of Science and Math.

The essence of our democracy demands informed citizens and debate. Let us all join together in the formulation of a scientific and technological policy, producing social and economic growth, that is honest, humane, and beautiful.

---

[1]Thomas Hillyer Whitehead (1904-1982), born in Maysville, resident of Athens, Georgia; B.S., University of Georgia, 1925; M.A., 1928, Ph.D., 1930, Columbia University. Became University of Georgia faculty member, 1930, chemistry professor, 1946, and served as Graduate School dean, 1968-1972; also with Chemical Warfare Service, 1942-1946, Army Chemical Center, 1951-1952; Atomic Energy Commission consultant; author. *Who Was Who in America, 1982-1985*, 424.

[2]Comer Vann Woodward (1908-   ), born in Vanndale, Arkansas; resident of Hamden, Connecticut; Ph.B., Emory University, 1930; M.A., Columbia University, 1932; Ph.D., University of North Carolina at Chapel Hill, 1937; honorary degrees; U.S. Naval Reserve, 1943-1946. Pulitzer Prize-winning historian; taught at University of Florida, 1937-1938, University of Virginia, 1939-1940, Scripps College, 1940-1943, Johns Hopkins University, 1946-1961; Commonwealth Lecturer, University of London, 1954; Harmsworth Professor of American History, Oxford University, 1954-1955; Sterling Professor of History, 1961-1977, professor emeritus, since 1977, Yale University; editor; author of numerous works on southern history, including *Origins of the New South, 1877-1913* (Baton Rouge: Louisiana State University Press, 1951). *Who's Who in America, 1988-1989*, II, 3366.

[3]Charles Percy Snow, Baron Snow (1905-1980), born in Leicester, England; died in London; M.Sc., Leicester University, 1928; Ph.D., Christ's College, Cambridge University, 1930; knighted, 1957; was made life peer, 1964. Author; publicist; critic; scientific administrator; fellow, Christ's College, 1930-1950; appointed director, technical personnel, Ministry of Labour, 1942; civil service commissioner responsible for recruiting scientists to government service, 1945-1960; member, House of Lords; parliamentary secretary, Ministry of Technology, 1964-1966. Lord Blake and C. S. Nichols (eds.), *Dictionary of National Biography, 1971-1980* (Oxford: Oxford University Press, 1986), 788-789; see also C. P. Snow, *The Two Cultures and the Scientific Revolution* (New York: Cambridge University Press, 1959).

[4]It is possible the governor was referring to Sir Isaac Newton, *Correspondence of Isaac Newton*, ed. by H. W. Turnbull, J. F. Scott and others (New York: Cambridge University Press, multivolume series, 1967—), and *Papers and Letters on Natural Philosophy and Related Documents*, ed. by I. Bernard Cohen (Cambridge: Harvard University Press, 1978).

[5]Richard S. Westfall, *Never at Rest: A Biography of Isaac Newton* (Cambridge: Cambridge University Press, 1980).

[6]Murray Gell-Mann (1929-   ), born in New York, New York; B.S., Yale University, 1948; Ph.D., Massachusetts Institute of Technology, 1951. Physicist; instructor, associate professor, University of Chicago, 1952-1954; was hired by California Institute of Technology, 1954, became R. A. Millikan Professor of Theoretical Physics, 1967; won Nobel Prize in physics, 1969; member, President's Scientific Advisory Committee, 1972-1975. *McGraw-Hill Modern Scientists and Engineers* (New York: McGraw-Hill Book Company, 3 volumes, 1980), I, 425-427. James Joyce used *quark* on p. 383 of *Finnegans Wake* (New York: Viking Press, fifth printing, 1947).

[7]Michael Faraday (1791-1867), born in Newington, Surrey (later part of London), England; died at Hampton Court, Middlesex; little formal education. Major work in analytical, applied, and pure chemistry; physics; discovered electromagnetic induction; created science of electrochemistry; discovered benzene, 1825; scientific career began as assistant to Humphry Davy, Royal Institution laboratory director, 1813; became superintendent, 1821, laboratory director, 1825, and Fullerian Professor of Chemistry, 1833, Royal Institution. Charles Coulston Gillispie and others (eds.), *Dictionary of Scientific Biography* (New York: Charles Scribner's Sons, 16 volumes, 1970-1980), IV, 527-540, hereinafter cited as *Dictionary of Scientific Biography*; see also Leslie Pearce Williams, *Michael Faraday: A Biography* (New York: Basic Books, 1965).

[8]William Whewell (1794-1866), born in Lancaster, England; died in Cambridge; M.A., 1819, D.D., 1844, Trinity College, Cambridge University; was ordained Church of England priest, 1826. Master of Trinity College, 1841-1866; performed major work in science education, architecture, experimental physics, mineralogy, physical astronomy, and the history and philosophy of science; author, translator. *Dictionary of Scientific Biography*, XIV, 292-295.

[9]Sir Charles Lyell (1797-1875), born in Kinnordy, Kirriemuir, Angus, Scotland; died in London; was educated at Oxford University; knighted, 1841; was made baronet, 1864. Established geology as a science; also performed major work in evolutionary biology; practicing barrister, 1825-1827; appointed professor of geology, King's College, London, 1831; author. *Dictionary of Scientific Biography*, VIII, 563-576.

[10]"I like Anode & Cathode better as to sound but all to whom I have shewn them have supposed at first that by *Anode* I meant *No way*." Michael Faraday to William Whewell, May 3, 1834, quoted in Leslie Pearce Williams, *The Selected Correspondence of Michael Faraday* (Cambridge: Cambridge University Press, 2 volumes, 1971), I, 268.

[11]David Perkins Billington (1927-   ), born in Bryn Mawr, Pennsylvania; resident of Princeton, New Jersey; B.S.E., Princeton University, 1950; was also educated at University of Louvain and University of Ghent, Belgium; U.S. Navy, 1945-1946. Registered professional engineer; structural engineer, Roberts & Schaefer Co., New York City, 1952-1960; associate professor, 1960-1964, professor, since 1964, of civil engineering, Princeton University; A. D. White Professor at Large, Cornell University, since 1987; consultant; author. *Who's Who in America, 1988-1989*, I, 264; see also David P. Billington, *The Tower and the Bridge: The New Art of Structural Engineering* (New York: Basic Books, 1983).

[12]Walter Adolf Gropius (1883-1969), born in Berlin, Germany; was educated in Berlin, Munich, and Hannover; honorary degrees; German army officer, 1904-1905, 1914-1918. Award-winning architect; founded Das Staatliches Bauhaus school of design, Weimar, 1919; came to United States, 1937; professor, 1937-1952, department chairman, 1938-1952, Harvard School of Architecture; founder, The Architects Collaborative, 1946; professor emeritus, Harvard Graduate School of Design, 1952-1969; author; editor. Ann Lee Morgan and Colin Naylor, *Contemporary Architects* (Chicago: St. James Press, second edition, 1987), 355; *Who Was Who in America, 1969-1973*, 290; see also Marcel Franciscono, *Walter Gropius and the Creation of the Bauhaus in Weimar: The Ideals and Artistic Theories of its Founding Years* (Urbana: University of Illinois Press, 1971).

[13]Robert Maillart (1872-1940), born in Bern, Switzerland; died in Geneva; was graduated from Federal Polytechnic Institute, Zurich, 1894. Widely influential bridge engi-

neer; pioneer in reinforced concrete; developed three-hinged arch bridge system. His two most celebrated structures were the dramatic Salginatobel Bridge and the curved Schwandbach Bridge, the latter called "an engineering masterpiece"; both were built in Switzerland. *Encyclopedia Americana*, 1984 ed., s.v. "Maillart, Robert"; see also David P. Billington, *Robert Maillart's Bridges* (Princeton, New Jersey: Princeton University Press, 1979).

John Augustus Roebling (1806-1869), born in Mühlhausen, Germany; died in Brooklyn, New York; was educated at Royal Polytechnic Institute, Berlin. Civil engineer specializing in bridges, aqueducts, canals, and dams; became naturalized U.S. citizen, 1837; invented twisted wire rope and equipment to manufacture it, before 1841; built first railroad suspension bridge, 1851-1855, Niagara Falls; author. Chief engineer for the Brooklyn Bridge project, Roebling's plans for the structure were approved in 1869. However, he died before construction began, and the bridge was completed under the supervision of his son, Washington Augustus, in 1883. David McCullough, *The Great Bridge* (New York: Simon and Schuster, 1972), 90-94; *Who Was Who in America, 1607-1896,* 522.

GOVERNOR'S INTERNATIONAL TRADE AWARD PRESENTATION NORTH CAROLINA WORLD TRADE ASSOCIATION

WILMINGTON, MAY 2, 1986

Dottie and I are very pleased to join you, this evening, for the Twenty-second Annual Conference of the North Carolina World Trade Association and for the presentation of the Governor's International Trade Award. Before we get to that important presentation, I want to take a few minutes to commend all of you for enabling North Carolina to end 1985 with an impressive $5.3 billion in export sales. Trade with our foreign neighbors also added 90,000 jobs to our manufacturing sector and meant the difference between success and failure for many [of] our farmers who produce tobacco and other farm commodities.

In many ways, the exporters, shippers, freight forwarders, and industries that aggressively pursue opportunities for trade abroad are among the real heroes of our economic success story. Strengthening this partnership are our international bankers, attorneys, and agents, and our own North Carolina Department of Commerce, which has restructured its Export Marketing Office to enhance assistance to those companies seeking new markets.

During 1985 we also achieved a record $2.7 billion investment in new and expanded industries, accounting directly and indirectly for another 52,000 new jobs. Many of these companies are major exporters.

As governor, I believe my responsibility to promote North Carolina products is just as vital as recruiting new industries and assisting existing ones. During my visit to Japan last year, and again in my recent trip to Europe, I took advantage of every opportunity to seek new trade in addition to new investment.

My vision of North Carolina includes a state in which our industrial genius, productive capacity, and ability to compete on a global scale will fuel our mighty engine of economic growth with new energy. Our successes of the past convince me it is a vision with a future. Tonight, we honor a company which is turning this vision into reality.

With more than 6,000 employees, it represents the second-largest corporate family in the Research Triangle Park and, indeed, one of the largest in North Carolina. As one of our flagship industries, it has been a premier example of growth, inspired by a passion for excellence in technology, manufacturing, marketing, and sales. The DMS Division, which is part of its Integrated Network Systems Group, last year concluded successfully more than three years of negotiations for the sale of approximately $250 million worth of digital telephone central office switching systems, made in North Carolina, to Nippon Telegraph and Telephone Public Corporation of Tokyo. This historic agreement is the first significant penetration of the Japanese telecommunications market by a non-Japanese company.

Opening the Japanese market is not the company's first success in international trade. Switching systems manufactured at its Research Triangle Park facilities have been sold worldwide, including China, the Caribbean, South America, and Europe. Because of this impressive record, the North Carolina World Trade Association has selected the DMS-10 Division of Northern Telecom as the recipient of the 1986 Governor's International Trade Award.

NATIONAL TRANSPORTATION WEEK DINNER

CHARLOTTE, MAY 15, 1986

[Governor Martin introduced his Roads to the Future program to the state's news media on April 17, 1986. The plan was discussed in the press release, "Governor Martin, Secretary Harrington Announce Transportation Program," Raleigh, April 18, 1986; at the dedication of the James E. Holshouser Highway, Boone, April 29, and of the Interstate 77 Welcome Center dedication, Mecklenburg County, May 15, 1986; in his monthly newspaper column of June 3, 1986; before the North Carolina Federation of Business and Professional Women's Clubs, June 13, 1986; and in the following address.]

It seems very appropriate to be in Charlotte, tonight, with such a large group of transportation professionals, for nowhere in North Carolina is there a city more representative of our varying transportation sectors than the Queen City. Tonight, I want to commend all of you who have worked so hard to make this observance a special occasion. I join you in recognizing the importance of transportation to the continued growth and prosperity of our state. Indeed, transportation is vital to our future.

I can assure you that when you sit in the governor's chair, it doesn't take very long to recognize how crucial transportation is to North Carolina—especially when you are confronted with decisions about its future. During the past months, I have spent many hours with Secretary (Jim) Harrington and members of the Transportation Task Force to develop a comprehensive transportation funding program to benefit all North Carolinians, no matter how diverse our interests may be.

When you come to think of it, transportation is about as diverse as the people represented in this room tonight. Some of you are from the trucking industry; others are from the airlines, air freight, and rail industries. Some of you come from state, county, and city offices involved in public transportation, and still others are from steamship lines and corporate transportation. Each of you brings a particular perspective to discussions concerning transportation, its needs, and potential solutions to its problems. Nevertheless, we are all involved in transportation as a total system, and we must all be part of the total solution to meeting its demands.

Recently, I presented my transportation program to the public. It is a program which represents a sincere and conscientious effort to address fairly and equitably the needs of all interests. There has been much discussion about rural needs; about urban requirements; and about eastern, piedmont, and western concerns. All of these are genuine, and all of them must be met. If we want to progress in the populous piedmont, we're going to have to support programs that will benefit the state as a whole. This means that piedmont residents must begin to see their own problems as part of a statewide situation.

Just as many in bigger cities are stuck in the kind of traffic jams their employers came here to escape, so many smaller cities feel neglected because they never got the promised four-lane artery—without which they can't attract industrial jobs. And some are still stuck in the mud decades after Governor Kerr Scott started to get them out. We are known as a "good roads" state. We've got good roads; we just don't have enough good roads with enough lanes where we need them.

I have chosen to call my proposed transportation program "Roads to the Future." However, it is not limited to highways alone. It is a comprehensive program which, when implemented, will meet all of the diverse interests I mentioned a few moments ago.

Highways, of course, attract the most attention because that's where the big dollars are spent, but we do have other needs, too. Let me touch on them briefly before we discuss highways in greater detail.

Since 1977, North Carolina has lost almost 600 miles of rail trackage. We know today of another eighty miles, including the five-mile bridge across the Albemarle Sound, that are threatened with abandonment. Loss of rail service occurs primarily near our smaller towns that have not been able to generate adequate traffic to support its existence. The loss of that trackage will have a continued adverse effect on our ability to serve small manufacturers and agricultural facilities.

Currently, our state is not responding effectively to this problem. We have a budget, adopted one year at a time, of $100,000 for rail transportation. This is no sound financial basis for long-range planning; besides, $100,000 doesn't go very far these days in the rail industry. That's just $1,000 per county! I propose that we dedicate annually the income derived from North Carolina's railroad stock to the rail program of our state. This formula will permit us to plan our spending on a more predictable basis and plan accordingly—and make a difference.

The same principle will work for aviation. The growth of aviation in our state is sort of a hidden asset. We all need to stop and realize that the growth of commercial air traffic in North Carolina is roughly 16 percent annually, and growing 10 percent a year. This growth will continue, and the impact of the "hub" concept on commercial air traffic is going to bring extraordinary pressure on our airport facilities. They will need improved facilities, better runways, improved lighting and navigation aids, and other necessities that foster passenger convenience and safety.

Asheville, Wilmington, Fayetteville, Kinston, Greenville, Rocky Mount-Wilson, New Bern, Jacksonville, and Hickory are particularly in need of improved air transport. These communities are caught between the inability to generate sufficient revenues and the demand for customer service. The state, of course, will need to help with assistance. This is not a big-dollar problem, compared to the hundreds of millions needed for highways, but our current appropriation of $3.5 million just isn't enough to respond to the demands in this area. And worse, we have no long-range plan, because such revenues defy proper planning.

What I propose is to channel aviation revenues into aviation. Isn't that a novel idea? Simply spend aviation revenues on air travel facilities! That's downright radical! If we dedicate to aviation all taxes already related to it, we can solve our two major aviation problems. Now let's turn to our major crisis: highways.

Today North Carolina is locked into a highway funding crisis, one that did not develop overnight. Highways are our routes to the marketplace; the way to research and knowledge; arteries of commerce; strategic job corridors; the call to adventure, and discovery, and access to our variety vacationland; and the measure of civilization. The past leaders of our great state have long shown an appreciation for highways, and they have taken justifiable pride in binding our state together with good roads.

We can do no less than to uphold this proud tradition if we are to be one truly united state, but we've got a problem. Our Highway Fund is running on a set of flat tires. Highway Fund revenues are generated primarily from motor fuel taxes, and they've seen little growth as automobile and truck fuel efficiency continues to improve. Yet, the impact of inflation has been severe.

Even as the economy's overall inflation rate has declined to quite acceptable levels, inflation of highway construction has remained high. In 1985, we experienced cost increases of 18 percent. We have estimated that, since 1975, our Highway Fund has lost more than $3 billion in purchasing power because it was underfunded. In addition, uncertainties over the allocation of federal highway dollars continue to mount. We are bracing for a $30 million shortfall in federal funds this year alone.

The Roads to the Future program which I have proposed will produce more than $200 million annually. This is the minimum amount which a distinguished task force of our state's leaders has said we will need to stimulate development and respond to statewide growth and changing economic conditions. Without it, our current ten-year plan will take us fifteen years to complete; with it, we can get up to speed— and then some.

This money will come from three sources:

1. Savings as a result of implementing cost-effective measures;
2. A 2.75-cent increase in the motor fuel tax; and
3. Expense transfers involving the Highway Patrol and Driver Education program.

The Department of Transportation estimates that it will save up to $40 million annually by using more temporary employees, contracting out for some routine work, using recycled asphalt for resurfacing, and improving efficiency within the department. The 2.75-cent motor fuel tax increase will generate about $100 million a year for new roads and better maintenance. This will cost the average motorist the equivalent of a tank of gas each year. It's a small price to pay for good roads.

The cost of operating the Highway Patrol and the Driver Education program, about $90 million a year, would be transferred, under our plan, from the Highway Fund to the General Fund, where it ought to have been. These two items ought to be in the General Fund, where all the other education and public safety programs are, leaving the Highway Fund to pay for highways. In fact, the General Fund now has a subsidy from highway users: $202 million a year from the sales tax on cars, accessories, tires, parts, and motor oil. I believe that half of that should be used to pay for the Highway Patrol and driver education. We have placed both the expense transfers and a motor fuel tax increase in the Roads to the Future program to add balance. We must have both if the program is expected to work.

Some have said that transferring the patrol and driver education to the General Fund will hurt education. That's silly. In the first place, driver education is education. More importantly, I have no intention of hurting education. I have already taken care of that. No problem. My budget amendments, just submitted for the next fiscal year, incorporate all of my proposals for the highway program. It does not cut one school item. It leaves intact every improvement already approved for 1985-1986 and for 1986-1987; plus, it adds an additional $22 million in improvements for public schools, and it shows revenue growth of $350 million a year, thereafter, for growth in these and other state responsibilities.[1]

The Transportation Task Force which I appointed last year agreed on one thing: Only a combination of funding approaches, coupled with savings, will address our highway crisis. No one solution will do the job, and our recommendations to the General Assembly will reflect this combination approach. Let me point out that the plan includes an increase in spending for secondary roads and the Powell Bill program, the latter of which helps to maintain municipal streets.[2] Both urban and rural citizens will benefit from these changes. They will receive between $7 to $8 million more the first year, and this amount will grow as the state's economy continues to expand.

One of the most important elements of the plan is the transportation trust fund. The trust fund is a new and innovative approach which will help us overhaul our highway funding system. It will provide money for new construction work, and it will save money by permitting us to protect rights-of-way, and acquire it sooner on some projects, before the price goes up with development of surrounding property.

It's a good, balanced, program. All of this will come apart, however, if partisan considerations cause my compromise to be torn apart. Democratic leaders told me that my highway program would pass if I proposed a tax increase (said the spider to the fly) and if I got the majority of the Republicans to vote for it. Now that I have the majority of the Republicans, who insisted on no tax increase, now willing to vote for a $100 million tax increase if the transfers are part of the package, some of the same leadership now want to insist on doing it all with a bigger 5- to 6-cent increase—knowing full well the Republican legislators will not vote a majority for just another tax increase. My plan gives each side half of what it wanted, along with half of what it did not want. That compromise must stand if we are to have a bipartisan bill.

I thought you ought to know what is at stake, and that it will not hurt schools. The Roads to the Future program which I have proposed, and which I will be presenting to the General Assembly, is one of the most important contributions we can make to the quality of life enjoyed by our citizens. With more and better highways, we can win more and better jobs—and thus be able to afford more for better schools. Approval of the Roads to the Future plan requires your support, and I am confident that you will demonstrate this support in ways that will convince our legislators to act expeditiously and correctly.

In my inaugural speech sixteen months ago, I spoke of building one united state. Let us bind this united state together with better roads, truly roads to the future—so that, unlike that tired old joke, we can "get there from here." Highways, better than any other public investment, will generate more economic investment by others and thus generate more taxable activity. If we're going to educate our young people for tomorrow's jobs, we absolutely must bring in the future's jobs for them. We can't do that with congested roads in our bigger cities and too few four-lane highways to smaller cities that could serve as growth centers across our state. I propose to build strategic job corridors to those smaller cities, so we can get the jobs to the people; and more traffic lanes and bypasses to unclog the traffic jams in the larger cities, so we can get the people to the jobs! I propose to replace those flat tires with modern, steel-belted radials.

---

[1]"Nothing does more to strengthen our tax base to support schools than highways," Martin told the North Carolina Federation of Business and Professional Women. His proposed $22 million in additional spending for public education during the 1987-1988 fiscal year included "increasing the starting pay of teachers from $15,680 to $16,915, expanding our career ladder pilot project for better pay for better teachers, and hiring new teachers in order to reduce class size in the ninth grade. It's ironic, or worse, that not a word was said about that by the three education leaders who yesterday claimed these transfers would hurt schools. The truth is, my budget, with the highway program, did not cut schools" and did not affect his recommended spending increases of $32 million for community colleges and $42 million for state universities.

[2]Powell Bill appropriations to local governments for streets and highways are authorized under G.S. 136-41.1 to -41.3.

ACCEPTANCE OF HIGHWAY PATROL MEMORIAL

RALEIGH, MAY 18, 1986

[The monument honoring fallen state troopers was located at the Highway Patrol Training Center, 3318 Old Garner Road, Raleigh.]

On behalf of the grateful citizens of North Carolina, I am honored to accept this monument to the memory of the forty-four gallant troopers who gave their lives in service to our state and our people.

"Memory," Cicero said, "is the treasury and guardian of all things."[1] "Praising what is lost," Shakespeare wrote, "makes the remembrance dear."[2] We meet here today in that spirit. We are gathered to pay tribute to and treasure those who gave their full measure of devotion to duty. We enshrine their names here as a testimonial to their sense of human courage and as an inspiration to all those who wear the badge and bear the duty. Each of these men summed up and perfected the highest virtues of an officer and a citizen.

This gathering also serves to renew our tribute for those whose journey through life safeguarded ours. We are reminded here of noble service by which they, and thousands with the same ideals, made our highways a safer place for travel, and the lives of ourselves and our families more secure.

The history of sacrifice by our troopers in the line of duty is as old as the North Carolina Highway Patrol itself. On July 2, 1929, the second day the patrol was in existence, Patrolman George Thompson was killed in a motorcycle accident near Marion. Since that time, we have witnessed twenty-three years in which one or more troopers have lost their lives in an act of duty—seventeen of those lives as a result of deadly assault. That men and women are so willing to accept the risks that accompany a career in law enforcement is, in itself, a monument to their courage and strength; and it is through their selfless dedication, supported by their families and loved ones, that our Highway Patrol serves so proudly and in the highest tradition of North Carolina.

No more fitting day could we have selected for this memorial dedication. This day joins both this "National Law Enforcement Week" and our "North Carolina Family Weekend." In this one instance, then, we join in honoring not only those who have taken upon themselves the oath, the training, and the calling of upholding the law as the cornerstone of civilization, but also those families who share with them all the dedication, all the risk, all the commitment to duty that goes with the badge—for the whole family wears it, too. With one mind, with one heart, each trooper's family puts on that grey uniform, accepts and understands that authority and duty to make our highways less dangerous, less threatening for the rest of us. And yes, each family accepts and understands that, for that uniform and that authority to protect the rest of us, it must be prepared to take its stand in the way of danger and in the face of hardship and peril. With one heart, with one mind, for each name engraved and memorialized here, a family was bound to that oath, to that duty, to that ultimate sacrifice.

In all walks of life, the support of one's family is an irreplaceable reservoir of strength for facing one's tasks. Especially is that true for law enforcement officers who intervene against those who would violate the order of society and the rights of others. You know the truth and depth of this, and your whole family knows it. For all of you—for the Martin family, too, in our first year, with our personal closeness to the patrol and its members, the loss of Trooper Harmon, Trooper Worley, Trooper Coggins, was a loss in our family.[3]

In closing, I want to express our indebtedness to the Highway Patrol Auxiliary for making this worthy monument possible. Yours has been a labor of love and a beauty to behold. Flanked by the flags which symbolize three rich heritages—of our nation, of our state, and of our North Carolina State Highway Patrol—it will forever remain a treasured gift from you and a treasure of memory for the love which binds your families to such total commitment. No greater sacrifice can be made by one human being for another. Surely, there can be no greater love.

The epitaph of Sir Christopher Wren, at St. Paul's in London, the cathedral he designed, reads, in translation from Latin, "If you would see his monument, look around you."[4] Let me paraphrase that here, today. If you would see the monument to those we honor and memorialize here today, look around. It is in our faces and our hearts.

---

[1]The quotation is from Cicero, *De Oratore*, Book I, sec. 5. Burton Stevenson, *The Home Book of Quotations* (New York: Dodd, Mead and Company, 1967), 1292.

[2]The quotation is from *All's Well That Ends Well*, V, iii, 19, by William Shakespeare. Bartlett, *Familiar Quotations*, 270.

[3]Trooper Giles A. Harmon, of Arden, was shot in April, 1985, as he approached a car parked on the shoulder of Interstate 40 near Tennessee. *News and Observer*, April 11, 12, 13, 14, October 17, 1985.

Five weeks after the death of Trooper Harmon, Raymond Earl Worley, of Northampton County, was killed by the occupants of two vans that he stopped on Interstate 95 in Halifax County. Four men from Washington, D.C., were arrested in connection with his murder. *News and Observer*, May 15, 16, 17, 1985.

Robert Lee Coggins was slain in September, 1985, after having pulled over a pickup truck believed stolen by escapees from an Arkansas jail. *News and Observer*, September 16, 17, 18, 19, 27, 1985, May 22, 1986.

[4]"*Si monumentum requiris circumspice*: If you would see the man's monument, look around." Inscription honoring Sir Christopher Wren (1632-1723) found in St. Paul's Cathedral, London, and composed by his son; quoted in Bartlett, *Familiar Quotations*, 374.

SOUTHEAST INTERSTATE LOW-LEVEL RADIOACTIVE WASTE MANAGEMENT COMPACT

RALEIGH, MAY 27, 1986

[A three-year process to determine the state to succeed South Carolina as host of a regional waste disposal facility ended September 11, 1986, when the Southeast Interstate Low-Level Radioactive Waste Management Compact Commission voted in favor of North Carolina. The commission based its decision on a survey by the New York consulting firm of Dames and Moore, hired to evaluate which of the member states possessed the technical, population, and geological criteria necessary to assume the environmental obligation performed by the landfill at Barnwell, scheduled to close in 1992. North Carolina was chosen despite evidence from state officials indicating that the Dames and Moore study was grounded on incomplete data. "We're disappointed at the outcome," Governor Martin told reporters, "and yet . . . we could not insist that the only solution had to be to pick somebody else or else we would withdraw" from the compact. *News and Observer*, September 12, 1986.]

Good afternoon, and welcome to North Carolina. I am Jim Martin, governor of North Carolina.

North Carolina is pleased to be a member of the Southeast Interstate Low-Level Radioactive Waste Management Compact.[1] As governor, I believe that the regional compact can be a fair and rational way to plan for proper management of low-level radioactive waste. As governor, I also have the responsibility to ensure that North Carolina is treated in an equitable and technologically accurate fashion by the compact in all its processes and deliberations. We will do our part when it is determined, in a fair process, that it is our turn to provide disposal capacity for the states in the compact.

North Carolina is proud of its research, academic, and business communities. Along with creating a favorable climate to nurture these communities, the state recognizes the need for proper management of the wastes generated as by-products. In 1981 the North Carolina General Assembly declared "that the safe management of hazardous wastes and low-level radioactive wastes, and particularly the timely establishment of adequate facilities for the disposal and management of hazardous wastes and low-level radioactive wastes is one of the most urgent problems facing North Carolina." It set out a policy to encourage state-of-the-art management technologies to reduce the amount of waste generated, thus minimizing the amount of waste requiring disposal. The act also promotes full public participation in implementing waste-management policy.[2]

North Carolina has taken its obligation to promote waste reduction very seriously. At the state level, we have a nationally recognized Pollution Prevention Pays program which provides information and technical assistance to businesses, industries, and other institutions. Our citizens have taken on the challenge to reduce waste at the source. One of my privileges, as governor, is presenting each year the Governor's Award for Excellence in Waste Management. This year I recognized Carolina Power and Light Company and Ciba-Geigy Corporation for their low-level radioactive waste reduction programs. In 1984, East Carolina University was honored; earlier, in 1983, Duke Power Company received the Governor's Award for its overall radioactive waste management program, a program that is now considered a model for the industry. Burroughs Wellcome has also been recognized for its achievements.

To accomplish waste reduction, our low-level radioactive waste generators have used such on-site approaches as administration controls, storage for decay, compaction, and I understand that trends in waste-production figures bear this out. We hope you share our view of the importance of waste reduction at the source.

To ensure that by participating in the Southeast Compact, North Carolina does not compromise the policy set forth in our Waste Management Act, our state plan includes several specific provisions:

1. All wastes shall be subjected to state-of-the-art volume reduction, where possible;

2. North Carolina shall retain the right to final determination of the disposal technology of a facility sited in this state;

3. If shallow land burial is the only alternative for land disposal, the design shall at a minimum incorporate engineered barriers to migration of the wastes;

4. In the event of federal regulatory changes that would allow on-site storage at nuclear facilities, the state reserves the right to amend its plan to make maximum use of on-site storage at the point of origin.

The plan also stresses citizen involvement in activities related to waste management. Secretary Kirk, the Radiation Protection Commission, and the Governor's Waste Management Board are developing a plan to expand these opportunities even beyond the current level.

Because we feel that one of the most important criteria is proper site selection, state agencies are also developing siting and location criteria. As stated in our plan, North Carolina will require a full environmental impact analysis of any proposed facility. As you are aware, North Carolina has vigorously opposed the Department of Energy's designation of two sites in North Carolina for a potential high-level radioactive waste repository. We have done so because we believe that the site selection process was flawed and that the two sites are demonstrably unsuitable for such a repository. I have gone to Washington to deliver data documenting the unsuitability of these sites.

We have likewise applied detailed scrutiny to the Dames and Moore study commissioned by the Southeast Compact. We found several places where the authors have used erroneous or outdated information, and we will be providing a detailed report on these to the compact. When all is considered, North Carolina's total unweighted proportional score will drop significantly. This indicates that the entire data base for all the states in the compact must be reevaluated before a final site is selected.

Under the Southeast Compact, I understand that the site selection is up to the host state. If selected, North Carolina will insist on a sound site selection process based on accurate and up-to-date data. We insist that North Carolina be treated fairly by our neighbors, and that means the host state must similarly be selected only on the basis of accurate and up-to-date information.

We recognize the Compact Commission has not had an easy task in analyzing the need for waste management facilities and developing a host-state identification process. We appreciate your coming here, in person, to hear from state officials and the public. Our state agencies and boards have followed your activities closely and will continue to work with you to arrive at an equitable solution to these most important and vexing problems. We believe that we, along with every other compact state, have the obligation to continue a critical analysis of the ranking procedure in assistance to the compact.

North Carolina is not now volunteering to be the next host state. We do stress our intent to honor our commitment to the compact. We joined the compact realizing that the day would come when North Carolina must take its turn to provide for a disposal facility for this regional compact. The question of whether it is indeed our turn must not be reached by a process in which other states gang up on us, but only through a process which is fair and based upon the best evidence available. We expect you to do everything you can to make the selection process a fair and equitable one.

---

[1]The General Assembly ratified "An Act to Approve the Southeast Interstate Low-Level Radioactive Waste Management Compact" on July 11, 1983. Other compact members included Alabama, Florida, Georgia, Mississippi, South Carolina, Tennessee, and Virginia. *N.C. Session Laws, 1983,* c. 714.

[2]The governor quoted from and described "An Act to Provide for the Management of Hazardous and Low-Level Radioactive Waste in North Carolina," also known as the Waste Management Act of 1981. *N.C. Session Laws, 1981,* c. 704.

PRESS RELEASE: GOVERNOR'S STATEMENT REGARDING SHEARON HARRIS PLANT AND CHATHAM COUNTY PARTICIPATION IN EMERGENCY RESPONSE PLAN

RALEIGH, MAY 27, 1986

[Reduced in scope and exceeding original budget projections, Carolina Power and Light Company's Shearon Harris nuclear power facility at New Hill neared completion in 1986. As a prerequisite to full-power testing, the federal Nuclear Regulatory Commission mandated that an emergency notification and evacuation program be in place for inhabitants within a ten-mile radius of the plant. Officials from the affected counties—Chatham, Harnett, Lee, and Wake—accordingly worked out such a plan in conjunction with state agencies.

Despite the existence of an emergency evacuation plan, some area residents continued to question the safety of the $3.6 billion plant. The Chatham County commissioners themselves, disturbed by the program's inadequacies, voted to withdraw their support late in May, 1986. Heartened by the decision, opponents of Shearon Harris hoped other counties would reach the same conclusion, thus blocking its start-up.

Weeks later, the Chatham commissioners reversed themselves without any modification having been made to the evacuation program or to Shearon Harris. Observers attributed the change to three primary factors: irritation at CASH, the Coalition for Alternatives to Shearon Harris, which had been effective in persuading the commissioners to withdraw from the plan initially; a public relations crusade by Carolina Power and Light Company; and the "realization that the withdrawal vote accomplished little or nothing." The utility received a forty-year operating license for Shearon Harris from the Nuclear Regulatory Commission in October, 1986. *Greensboro News and Record,* July 27, 1986; *News and Observer,* July 8, October 25, 1986.]

As we approach the date for the Shearon Harris nuclear power plant to begin generating electricity, there have been many concerns raised by people about the reactor and the emergency preparedness plans for the area around it. This is understandable in the aftermath of the Chernobyl accident in the Soviet Union.

While the many safety features required for a new plant in America go far beyond what was in place at Chernobyl, it is still important to prepare and have in place an emergency response plan. With the cooperation of local governments, the state has developed a good emergency management plan as required by federal law. It includes an evacuation plan for the ten-mile radius around the reactor, with an expedited plan for those within five miles.

The success of this emergency management program depends on the complete cooperation among all local governments. Although we expect no accident at Shearon Harris, it is our duty to be prepared, equipped, and trained to deal with one. Each agency of state and local government within the ten-mile radius would have its responsibility and needs to be able to count on other units to carry out different parts of the plan. Otherwise, there would be chaos.

Accordingly, when I learned from Secretary of Crime Control and Public Safety Joe Dean that the Chatham Board of County Commissioners was considering revoking their agreement to help alert and inform citizens in Chatham County, I immediately contacted Commission Chairman Earl Thompson. I urged him to stay in the program. Chatham County has the equipment and personnel who could get the necessary information to citizens there far faster than the state government is presently equipped to do, because we have been counting on them to do their part. I also offered to try to help if there were any concerns on his part that Chatham County government would not carry out its responsibilities under the state plan.

I also expressed to him my belief that some are trying to get

Chatham County to withdraw its participation in order to halt the completion of the long-delayed power plant. Neither state nor local governments have the responsibility for that decision, which rests with the federal Nuclear Regulatory Commission. Our job is to provide a capability for evacuating those in immediate danger in the unlikely event an accident occurs in the reactor. County governments have to be prepared to help meet that responsibility to their citizens. It is good that people are now beginning to ask questions about what they should do and how they would be advised in the event of an accident. With positive input, I believe we can make a good plan better.

PEOPLE IN HARMONY

CHARLOTTE, MAY 29, 1986

It is with great pride that I join you today in celebrating "People in Harmony," which commemorates the great progress we have made in Charlotte and Mecklenburg County to overcome racial injustice. Indeed, this area was one of our nation's pioneers in setting an example of how individuals can live together in mutual respect and where opportunity is not limited by race or color. This was the idea embraced by the founders of this nation.

They came to these shores and expended blood, sweat, and tears, and under divine guidance set up a system of government based on the concept of the value, the rights, the freedom, and the responsibility of the individual. Our nation was divided by one great war that was fought to ensure that freedom, but it was not until the revolution of the 1960s that the rights which accompany freedom became a reality for all Americans.

In many parts of our nation, this change was difficult and often wrought with extreme violence. This was not the case in Charlotte and Mecklenburg. Perhaps tempers of the extremists flared, but we joined together to drive out hate. I am proud to be among so many of you who worked long and hard over the years to bring about the harmony that brought an end to social injustice, people who had the courage to instill an equality of spirit as well as rights.

We all remember those historic years, for I was here, too. As a member of the Mecklenburg Board of Commissioners, I worked with my friends in city government, with the business community, with the outlying towns, with neighborhoods, and directly with many of you to resolve differences in a spirit of mutual trust and respect. It was not an easy process. However, we believed in the value of the individual, and we devoted ourselves to giving this value meaning. We exercised common sense and took pride in ourselves, our neighbors, and community.

We, above all, demonstrated the quality of leadership that has been a Charlotte-Mecklenburg tradition since before our country won its independence. It was leadership by the business community which recognized that voluntary desegregation of stores, offices, and restaurants held part of the answer. It was also leadership on the part of local government: Charlotte became the first southern city to enact a public accommodations ordinance and fair housing law; Mecklenburg was the first southern county to enact a fair housing law. We watched as the slums of Brooklyn, and Fourth Ward, and Third Ward disappeared in major urban renewal. As people moved into neighborhoods throughout the city, they found they could live together as neighbors and friends.

Yes, we have come a great distance in Charlotte and Mecklenburg County. We can all take pride, not only in our accomplishments, but also in our dignity of effort. We know, too, that by continuing to work in this spirit of harmony we can resolve those problems which remain. All of you deserve the highest commendation for your boldness of thought and your deep compassion.

There are two individuals who I am honored to recognize for their outstanding leadership. One is with us now; the other passed on a few years ago. Stan Brookshire was mayor of Charlotte from 1961 to 1969. Fred Alexander became the first black to serve as a member of the City Council, later becoming mayor pro tem and state senator.[1]

Both men came from different perspectives. They urged moderation; they urged understanding. The never compromised principle. They shared a great love for this community, and they shared a common goal: a community of people living in harmony, with all people treated alike, with respect and dignity.

They did not work alone, but their leadership was a dominant force in those difficult years. Their leadership set the tone of the refreshing harmony only few communities can claim, and it was their leadership which helped to bring about the Community Relations Committee whose twenty-fifth anniversary we celebrate today. I want to ask Mayor Brookshire and Mrs. Theodora Alexander Rousseau[2] to come forward.

[Governor Martin speaks to Mayor Brookshire and Mrs. Rousseau:]
On behalf of your neighbors in Charlotte and Mecklenburg County,

and on behalf of a grateful state, it gives me great pleasure to present each of you this plaque which can only begin to express part of the appreciation for distinguished service.

[Mayor Brookshire and Mrs. Rousseau respond.]

There are two others who were instrumental in making this great Community Relations Committee work. They should also be recognized for their dedication and energy displayed over the years. They have shaped the committee into a positive force. I now want to recognize Dr. Warner L. Hall, former chairman of the committee, and my good friend, Jack L. Bullard, its director.[3] It is also my pleasure to present plaques to these leaders.

---

[1]Stanford Raynold Brookshire (1905-1990), born in Troutman; A.B., Trinity College (later Duke University), 1927; honorary degree. Vice-president, J. C. Brookshire and Sons, Statesville, 1927-1932; became president, Engineering and Sales Co. of Charlotte, Inc., 1932; Charlotte mayor, 1961-1969; won silver medal from National Conference of Christians and Jews, 1964, for efforts to improve race relations. *Charlotte Observer*, May 13, 1969; *News and Observer*, February 17, 1964, October 11, 1990; *Who's Who in the South and Southwest, with Notables of Mexico, 1969-1970* (Chicago: Marquis Who's Who, Inc., 1969), 133.

Frederick Douglas Alexander (1910-1980), native of Charlotte; A.B., Lincoln University, 1931. First black to be elected to Charlotte city council in twentieth century, served 1965-1975; one of first two blacks since Reconstruction to be elected to state Senate, 1976, reelected 1978; Democrat. *Charlotte Observer*, April 15, 1980, February 14, 1982; *North Carolina Manual, 1979*, 291.

[2]Theodora Alexander Rousseau (1946-), native, resident of Charlotte; was educated at Pratt Institute. Homemaker; daughter of Frederick Douglas Alexander. *North Carolina Manual, 1979*, 291; Theodora Alexander Rousseau to Jan-Michael Poff, February 19, 1990.

[3]Warner Leander Hall (1907-), born in Covington, Tennessee; resident of Charlotte; B.A., Southwestern College, 1929; B.D., Presbyterian Theological Seminary, Louisville, Kentucky, 1932; Ph.D., University of Edinburgh, Scotland, 1934. Ordained Presbyterian minister, 1935; pastor of churches in Leland, Mississippi, 1934-1936, Lexington, Kentucky, 1946-1940, and Tuscaloosa, Alabama, 1940-1946; pastor, Second (later Covenant) Presbyterian Church, Charlotte, 1946-1971; chairman, Charlotte Human Relations Committee. *Charlotte Observer*, January 28, 1946, April 12, 1977.

Jack L. Bullard (1930-), born in Greensboro; resident of Charlotte; B.A., Wake Forest University, 1950; M.Div., Crozen Theological Seminary, 1954. Minister, Taylor Memorial Baptist Church, Paulsboro, New Jersey, 1954-1960, and of Millbrook Baptist Church, Raleigh, 1960-1968; director, Charlotte-Mecklenburg Community Relations Committee, since 1968. Jack L. Bullard to Jan-Michael Poff, February 6, 1990.

PRESS RELEASE: GOVERNOR MARTIN ANNOUNCES
JOINT EFFORT WITH NORTH CAROLINA
HOUSING FINANCE AGENCY

RALEIGH, MAY 29, 1986

[The governor discussed state housing programs in his address to the
North Carolina Association of Realtors, Greensboro, May 28, 1987.]

Governor Martin and Gary Paul Kane,[1] executive director of the
North Carolina Housing Finance Agency, announced Thursday a
pilot program that will offer new rent subsidy programs for the
elderly in four geographic areas of North Carolina. The Elderly Rent
Subsidy Program, suggested by Governor Martin, is a cooperative
effort between the Farmers' Home Administration and the North
Carolina Housing Finance Agency that offers 1 percent permanent
financing, and a monthly subsidy of up to $100 per apartment, to
provide affordable housing for low-income senior citizens. The
apartments will be located in counties with a median income of
$20,000 or less.

The program for the elderly is part of several ongoing housing
efforts directed by the North Carolina Housing Finance Agency. The
other efforts include:

—The Single Family Subsidy Program. Started by former governor
Jim Hunt in 1984,[2] the program will be revamped and launched again
in July, 1986. The program helps low-income families buy their first
homes. Initially, the program will assist 110 families earning $20,000 or
less in annual gross income.

—The Multifamily Rental Subsidy Program. Designed to provide
apartment housing for families who cannot otherwise afford it, particularly in rural parts of the state.

—The Home Improvement Loan Subsidy Program. Scheduled to
begin late this year, the program will be financed by a $1.4 million
bond issue that will offer home improvement loans.

"I am pleased to participate in the initiation of new programs and
the continuation of new efforts that are directed at helping solve the
housing needs of North Carolina's elderly and low-income residents,"
Governor Martin said at a press conference Thursday.

---

[1]Gary Paul Kane (1943-   ), born in San Francisco, California; resident of Greensboro; A.B., 1963, J.D., 1966, University of California-Berkeley. Tax counsel, California
Franchise Tax Board, 1966-1970; attorney, Sacramento Redevelopment Agency, 1970-

1973; program director, State HFA Programs, U.S. Department of Housing and Urban Development, 1973-1975; attorney in private practice, 1975-1978; counsel, National Assn. of Homebuilders, 1978-1981; executive director, North Carolina Housing Finance Agency, 1981-1986; chief financial officer, Davidson and Jones, 1986-1988; president, Kane-Weaver Properties Co. Gary Paul Kane to Jan-Michael Poff, January 6, 1989.

[2]The General Assembly approved the creation of the Homeownership Assistance Fund on July 22, 1983. See "An Act for Making Appropriations for Various Local Projects," *N.C. Session Laws, 1983*, c. 923, s. 203. The fund was later transformed into the Single Family Subsidy Program.

PRESS RELEASE: NEW PROGRAM TO HELP PRISONS AND FOREST RESOURCES

Raleigh, June 5, 1986

[BRIDGE, the correctional program described in the following news release, was implemented in Burke County in January, 1987. A component of the plan, recommending that youthful offenders be housed in a permanent forestry camp to be built near the community of Table Rock, aroused local opposition; see "BRIDGE Program," pages 603-604, below. BRIDGE was an acronym for Building, Rehabilitating, Instructing, Developing, Growing, Education.]

A program intended to teach young offenders usable skills, provide the Division of Forest Resources with trained personnel to help with forestry and fire control operations, and relieve overcrowding in the state's correction facilities was announced today by Governor Jim Martin. A joint effort by the Department of Correction's Division of Prisons and the Department of Natural Resouces and Community Development's Division of Forest Resources, the proposed program will allow the first of five, fifty-person forestry camps to be constructed on state-owned land in Burke County. Additional camps are planned for the piedmont and coastal areas. Once the camps are completed, the inmates would live at the forestry camps, yet remain under the custodial supervision of the Division of Prisons.

While building the camps, inmates will learn skills in carpentry, masonry, and electrical wiring under the supervision of Forest Resources personnel. The division will also establish a primary forestry training program and provide inmates with work experience in forest fire control, forest management and timber stand improvement, tree nursery operations, heavy equipment operations, and general mechanics.

Under the proposal, the camps would be constructed by the medium-grade inmates selected for the program. Estimated contract cost for construction of the first camp is $1.1 million. By using future residents of the camps to do the construction, the state will save $500,000 in construction costs at each camp.

NORTH CAROLINA ACADEMY OF TRIAL LAWYERS

Myrtle Beach, South Carolina, June 16, 1986

[Governor Martin delivered an address, nearly identical to the one below, before the North Carolina Bar Association, Myrtle Beach, South Carolina, June 21, 1986.]

I am greatly honored and very pleased today to be the first governor in history who has been invited to address the annual convention of this distinguished body of North Carolina trial lawyers. I want to begin, this morning, by thanking one of my former Davidson chemistry students, Jim Fuller, for that kind introduction. North Carolina is extremely fortunate that, after completing that course, he chose to pursue the practice of law. Someone told me recently, however, that he has improved considerably in football. As the story goes, he participated a few months ago in the varsity alumni game at Davidson, and this time he managed to keep from kicking the football backwards.[1]

North Carolina holds an eminent place in the history of the American legal system. History tells us that the frontier lawyer started with little more than "a horse, a bridle" and saddle, "and a pair of saddlebags as his only possessions, except perhaps for a copy of the *Revised Code of 1835*, a Blackstone *Commentaries*, and a copy of Chitty's *Pleadings*."[2] In his book, *The Rise of the Legal Profession in America*, Anton Herman Chroust describes him in this manner:

> His ambitions and his hopes were the incentives that stimulated his energies and opened upon him a bright future. For a while at least he depended upon his credit, and credit was freely given to anyone with an honest face, a correct deportment, and industrious habits. . . . When a young lawyer swept out his office, chopped his own wood and made his own fires, he was considered worthy of credit, at least of one month's credit.[3]

Thus, the history of the legal profession after the American Revolution is not so much the story of institutions, organizations, or policies as it is the running account of individual lawyers. It was their determination and astounding competence, especially those in North Carolina, which not only shaped the history of American law and American jurisprudence, but also the fate and fortune of the profession itself, and, indeed, of our whole young nation. By common consensus, Thomas Ruffin of North Carolina was considered one of the six outstanding judges of the post-Revolutionary period who influenced the legal profession in the United States.[4] Moreover, it was attorneys from North Carolina who migrated to Tennessee, Kentucky, Missouri, and other states to open the first practices and serve the early settlers moving westward.

Today, the spirit of individualism remains in our legal profession and accounts for the healthy adversarial relationship which has enabled our system of courts to become a model for the world. Lawyers also have played an important, perhaps the most important, role in the development of the laws which govern our state and society. You also have influenced, to a large degree, the specialization which has taken place within your profession. This specialization, however, has increasingly complicated our legal processes, and this complexity of law puts it beyond the comprehension of the general public and contributes to the crisis of confidence in our social order.

What the average citizen expects and asks from the law is usually couched in generalities reiterated so often as to become cliches: "Ours is a government of laws, not men"; "Ignorance of the law is no excuse"; "A government by the consent of the governed"; and "Equal justice under the law."

Implicit in these generalities are some of the basic beliefs about our democracy. Our society places an enormous burden on the law, the legal process, and its institutions. A legal democracy requires an elaborate apparatus for determining and applying majority will and public good.

We are, or should be, constantly engaged in balancing interests—between individuals and groups, between group and group, and between public and private activity. Our greatest task is to balance the scales so delicately that each weight is accorded due measure and no more.

In recent years, this has not been the case in the unmanageable growth of lawsuits, as well as excessive judgments or awards, arising from personal, professional, and product liability claims. This trend has raised a storm of public protest against steep increases in liability insurance premiums, or, in the case of some businesses and professions, the inability to obtain insurance at all.

At the center of this protest is a vast array of conflicting information—and in some cases, the lack of data—provided by representatives of both plaintiffs and defendants related to tort cases.

The problems of obtaining or affording adequate liability insurance coverage, as a result of this confusion, has reached crisis proportions.

The impacts of this crisis have been inflationary pressures on the economy due to high insurance costs; limits on economic growth and innovation as product and technology developers and entrepreneurs shy away from newer and riskier undertakings; and loss of jobs and services in instances where businesses limit or cease operations due to the lack of affordable insurance.

Those affected by this crisis include the public, of course, but more specifically day-care providers, physicians, commercial fishermen, product manufacturers, architects, builders, schools, airports, trucking and bus companies, high-tech industries, environmental risk-management firms, and governmental entities. Many of the specific consumer providers are passing along these increased premiums to the public in the form of higher prices for products and services.

In today's litigious society, there is a widespread need for insurance coverage against the possibility of being sued. According to *Time* magazine, Americans paid $9.1 billion in liability premiums in 1985, 60 percent more than in 1983.[5]

Who's to blame? The answer seems to depend upon whom you ask. Those who claim the judicial system is at fault and needs reform include the insurance industry, major trade associations, local government associations, doctors, and other professional groups. Those who say the insurance industry has created the premium crisis through irrational fears and bad management include the trial lawyers, labor unions, and consumer groups. Both interests, as you are aware, are capable of wielding powerful lobbying efforts and mobilizing members to press for legislative changes. Each side disputes the other's data, and state officials must sort through conflicting or incomplete statistics in an attempt to find answers.

One thing that seems to escape attention is the fact that our tort system needs to be fair to all, and at present it is not perceived to be fair by the public. The time has come for consensus in the public's interest. It's time, indeed, for both sides, the plaintiff's bar and the defendant's bar, to meet and to acknowledge that perhaps the blame for our liability insurance crisis is shared, in one degree or another, by each interest.

As trial lawyers, you are the guardians of tort balance, and I believe it is certainly not too late for you to begin working actively to find a resolution to this growing problem. We must admit, in all candor, that there are some lawyers who pursue frivolous cases, just as there are those businesses and professions whose members, whether intentionally or not, cause injury to others.

The tort system in our nation was designed to treat fairly both the injured party as well as the one at fault. With the insurance industry we now have assuming the risks, society bears the costs, not those who are parties to the litigation.

As governor, I do not believe we should limit the proper rights of citizens to sue for injuries or, for that matter, the use of contingent fees by lawyers as a basis for representing their clients. Most of the plaintiffs are ordinary citizens who work in factories and shops, and, as is most often the case, cannot afford to retain an attorney or a legal firm on a hourly basis. However, I challenge you, as trial lawyers, to make yourselves as accessible to those clients with claims of less than $100,000, for example, as those with claims above that amount. Every client with a justifiable claim is entitled to representation, and you have the obligation to make this representation available.

Thus far, several legislative bills have been introduced in the short session of the General Assembly related to tort reform and insurance industry regulation. I have said previously that I am not comfortable with any of these measures. At present, the absence of comprehensive data inhibits efforts to assess the impact of the current crisis and to analyze the potential effects of the various proposed solutions. Likewise, it prevents my administration from pursuing any sound proposal until further study, and certainly no sooner than the 1987 biennial session of the General Assembly. Let me assure you that the Governor's Office will continue to track proposed legislation, now and in the future, with the intent to ensure that the public's best interests will be served; but at present there appears some element of doubt that any action will be taken by our legislators during the current session.[6]

Another problem I want to bring to your attention today is the long-overdue need in North Carolina to reform the system under which judges are selected and elected. Since constitutional change in 1875, North Carolina judges have been elected on a partisan basis. On occasion, they reach the bench by gubernatorial appointment. Those who are elected, or reelected, usually win their seats in the Democratic primary and almost always run unopposed; superior court judges, who represent specific geographic districts, are on the statewide ballot. This virtually precludes the election of a candidate representing another political party. District court judge vacancies created by death, resignation, or retirement are filled by gubernatorial appointment, but the nominees are selected by the local bar association, and the governor is required to select one from the same party as the judge whose vacancy is to be filled.

The examples I have just cited are legacies of single-party dominance, to some extent institutionalized by law. It is a patronage system cloaked in constitutional respectability. This system denies the citizens of North Carolina any assurance that the best available people will reach the bench, without regard to party connections or political skills.[7]

Although our state has accomplished major court reform with considerable ease, the General Assembly has refused to change the system by which judges are selected and elected. What I want to propose, today, is the establishment of a legitimate, nonpartisan method of electing judges, as well as their appointment on the basis of merit in the event of vacancies.

Thirty-five states now use some form of merit selection. In most of those states, a nonpartisan panel composed of both attorneys and laymen recommends individuals to fill empty judgeships. This frees judges from the conflict inherent in partisan elections. Judges do not represent political parties, they represent the law. Their responsibilities embrace the interpretation and application of laws objectively, and they could do this more easily if they were not forced to run in party primaries.

For many years, governors of North Carolina have favored a merit selection system. The previous administration adopted a modified merit selection process, but it was flawed by the selection of the nominating panel by the governor, who also had the power of appointing judges.[8]

The system I favor, and which is supported by the chief justice, would provide, subject to approval of a constitutional amendment by voters, a nominating panel appointed equally by the governor and chief justice. It would be the responsibility of this panel to recommend to the governor, for appointment to empty judgeships, only those persons who truly merit consideration. Thereafter, judges would seek election or reelection in a nonpartisan race. In the case of superior court judges, only voters from the district in which the judges serve would be eligible to cast ballots; the principle of district voting would then be consistent with election of district court judges. Under this plan, candidates for the court of appeals and the supreme court would continue to be elected statewide, but on a nonpartisan basis which gives all qualified persons who desire to run an equal chance for voter approval.

Merit selection of judges and their subsequent election or reelection on a nonpartisan basis is a system whose time has come in North Carolina. In one form or another, a merit system has widespread support from the North Carolina Bar Association, the Conference of Superior Court Judges, and the North Carolina Courts Commission. Private groups as diverse as the League of Women Voters and the Christian Action League also have worked in the past to bring this constitutional question to a vote by the people of North Carolina. My challenge, today, is for the trial lawyers to join with me, the chief justice, and the support groups I have just mentioned, in North Carolina, to encourage action on this issue by the General Assembly during its 1987 biennial session.

Perhaps the lawyers of no other state, with the exception of Virginia, have influenced equally the development of the legal system in our nation than the attorneys of North Carolina. No other group has displayed a greater interest in public service, and many of our greatest leaders have come from your profession. The North Carolina Trial Lawyers Association is the third largest in our nation, and it is, and should be, a powerful force for constructive change in our systems of law and jurisprudence. I urge you to continue in the same honored tradition of the colonial and frontier lawyers who established your profession as one of the most respected in our society; I challenge you to show the same courage, objectivity, and strength of purpose which is required in our own time to complete the work they began: to build the most perfect legal system in the history of mankind.

Your voluntary efforts to correct the problems affecting our tort system and to help establish an impartial merit selection method for judges, whereby they are later chosen by the people on a nonpartisan basis, can be your greatest legacy to North Carolina and its people. Until these goals are achieved, in the spirit of unity, holding as your highest purpose the public's interest, your work as trial lawyers will remain unfinished. As governor, I'm ready to lead you in that effort. Let's get on with the job.

---

[1]James C. Fuller, Jr. (1942-   ), born in Salisbury; resident of Raleigh; B.A., Davidson College, 1965; J.D., University of North Carolina at Chapel Hill, 1971. Law clerk to Chief Justice Susie M. Sharp, 1971-1972; attorney in private practice in Charlotte, 1972-1983, and Raleigh, since 1984; adjunct professor of law, North Carolina Central University, 1983-1988, University of North Carolina at Chapel Hill, 1984-1990, and at Duke University, 1989-1990; president, North Carolina Academy of Trial Lawyers, 1989-1990.

The errant kick occurred in the 1964 football contest between Catawba College and Davidson at Charlotte Memorial Stadium. With his team "losing one of the few games we had a chance to win" that season, Fuller opted "to punt the ball very high in hopes the Catawba receiver would fumble." As he recalled, "I had never kicked a ball so perfectly or so hard: It spiraled off my foot like a shot from a cannon" and cleared the top of the press box. In fact, it continued to sail upward until, "to the total disbelief of everyone at the game, including me, the point of the football hit a single strand of wire that stretched across the stadium from one pole to the other. The odds of hitting that wire with a football have to be one in a zillion, but hit it I did, in dead center. With an audible 'sproing,' the ball came off the wire back in my direction. By the time it quit rolling, and the other team recovered it, the ball was twenty-seven yards behind me." Said Fuller, "I am told that is the all-time NCAA record for the most negative yardage on an unblocked punt in the history of college football!" James C. Fuller, Jr., to Jan-Michael Poff, June 20, 1990.

[2]The musings of James O. Broadhead, a Missouri lawyer practicing circa 1843, are quoted in Anton Herman Chroust, *The Rise of the Legal Profession in America* (Norman: University of Oklahoma Press, 2 volumes, 1965), II, 118, hereinafter cited as Chroust, *Rise of the Legal Profession in America*.

[3]Broadhead reminiscences, quoted in Chroust, *Rise of the Legal Profession in America*, II, 118-119. The last sentence should read, "[W]hen a young lawyer swept out his office, chopped his own wood and made his fires, he was considered worthy of credit, of one month's credit at least. . . ."

[4]Thomas Ruffin (1787-1870), born in King and Queen County, Virginia; died in Hillsborough; was graduated from College of Princeton (later Princeton University), 1805; honorary degree. Admitted to North Carolina bar, 1808; member, state House of Commons, 1813, 1815, and Speaker, 1816; superior court judge, 1816-1818, 1825-1828; president, Bank of North Carolina, 1829; associate justice, 1829-1833, 1859, chief justice, 1833-1852, state supreme court; delegate, Washington Peace Conference, 1861; delegate, North Carolina Secession Convention, 1861-1862; Democrat. Ashe, *Biographical History*, V, 350-359; Cheney, *North Carolina Government*, 265, 268, 269, 360, 361, 386.

[5]"Sorry, Your Policy is Canceled," *Time*, March 24, 1986, 16-20, 23-26.

[6]Martin told the North Carolina State Bar Association on June 21, 1986: "If the General Assembly responds further so as to place some limit on liability awards, then that certainly should be coupled with a provision to ensure that any reduced costs of claims are reflected in reduced premiums. Otherwise, North Carolinians will continue to pay dearly to defray the premiums in states like California and New York, where awards have escalated more dramatically." He also recommended that, if the General Assembly did not pass tort reform measures and revise insurance industry regulations before the 1987 session, it remained the duty of litigants' legal counsel to "take more active leadership in fostering a consensus which would serve fairly and justly the best interests of all the public. This, I submit, is your responsibility and obligation, and I am confident that you will discharge this in the honored tradition of your profession. If you leave it up to those who, you feel, don't understand, then, you see, you will have been responsible for that, too!"

[7]The governor later couched the existing process of judicial elections and appointments in starker terms. "But do partisan elections of judges serve us well? I say not," declared Martin to the North Carolina Bar Association. "I say it only serves to preserve the partisan advantage of the state's majority party, which is why it's done; and it has effectively denied the state the services of the many well-qualified lawyers who, because of their conservative beliefs, have chosen to register themselves politically as Republicans. Simply stated, this is a perk of partisanship." Shortly thereafter, he asserted that "North Carolina's current system does not ensure the citizens that the best people will become their judges, though we've been blessed with many good jurists. It merely guarantees that whatever your political beliefs, if you want to serve as a judge of our courts, you had better be aligned with the dominant party."

[8]Governor Hunt signed Executive Order Number 12, creating the Judicial Nominating Committee for Superior Court Judges, on July 28, 1977. As originally established, the committee consisted of thirty-four members, thirteen of whom were appointed by the governor, thirteen by the state chief justice, three by the president pro tem of the Senate, and three by the Speaker of the House; two members of the state supreme court also were selected. *N.C. Session Laws, 1977,* 1545-1550. Hunt amended and extended Executive Order Number 12 throughout his two terms in office; see Executive Order Number 24, *N.C. Session Laws, 1977, Second Session, 1978,* 274-275; Executive Order

Number 30, *N.C. Session Laws, 1979,* 1482-1489; Executive Order Number 52, *N.C. Session Laws, 1979, Second Session, 1980,* 310; Executive Order Number 71, *N.C. Session Laws, 1981,* 1779-1786; Executive Order Number 79, *N.C. Session Laws, 1981, Second Session, 1982,* 343-350; and Executive Order Number 108, *N.C. Session Laws, 1983, Second Session, 1984,* 460.

PRESS RELEASE: GOVERNOR, LIEUTENANT GOVERNOR REACH AGREEMENT ON HIGHWAY PLAN

RALEIGH, JUNE 24, 1986

Governor Jim Martin and Lieutenant Governor Bob Jordan announced Wednesday a compromise agreement on North Carolina's long-term transportation needs. After a 45-minute meeting Tuesday afternoon, the governor and lieutenant governor agreed to the following points as a compromise that both believe will carry the state's transportation program into the next decade:[1]

—A 2-cent-per-gallon motor fuels tax that will become effective July 15, 1986;

—A 3 percent state sales tax on motor fuels at the wholesale level, effective July 15, 1986;

—Transfer of the Drivers' Education program to the General Fund, beginning with the 1987-1988 fiscal year. That transfer represents $27.6 million in 1987-1988 and grows to approximately $34.8 million in 1991-1992. The transfer will be initiated on July 1, 1987;

—Initiation of a staggered motor vehicle registration plan on September 1, 1986. Savings from the staggered system will generate $39.8 million in 1986-1987 and $5.5 million in 1987-1988;

—The Department of Transportation will initiate $11.6 million in internal savings during 1986-1987, the first year of a program on continued internal efficiencies.

Governor Martin described the bipartisan agreement as the "Harrington compromise," a reference to Transportation Secretary Jim Harrington, and commended the lieutenant governor for his efforts on the compromise. "This is a good basis for agreement midway between the respective starting positions," Governor Martin said. "Both of us agree to do our best to win support in the General Assembly. This way, we all win. We are demonstrating that we can solve problems where we have differences, and we can govern, so the people win."

Lieutenant Governor Jordan said, "I am very pleased that we can come together, today, and present a bipartisan proposal that will strengthen North Carolina's future and benefit the citizens of this state, who entrusted all of us to represent them."

---

¹The General Assembly legislated the following changes under "An Act to Provide Roads to the Future, and to Classify Household Personal Property and Exclude it from Property Taxes," c. 982, ratified July 11, 1986, and "An Act to Provide Roads to the Future—Part 2," c. 1018, ratified July 15, 1986; see each act for effective dates of components listed. *N.C. Session Laws, 1985, Extra and Regular Sessions, 1986.*

GOVERNOR'S COUNCIL ON ALCOHOL AND DRUG ABUSE AMONG CHILDREN AND YOUTH

Raleigh, June 25, 1986

North Carolina—indeed, our whole society—is confronted today with a chemical dependency problem among children and youth which defies comparison with any previous generation in our history. With the age of alcohol and drug abusers declining steadily, I submit that we now face the most serious challenge of our time: the elimination of alcohol and drug abuse among children and youth. Some have called it a crisis. I suggest it is a threat to our social and economic life and the very defense of our nation, a threat that can be as devastating as the most destructive weapon ever devised.

Alcohol abuse, by far, is our biggest problem, primarily because alcoholic beverages are easily accessible and more acceptable in social circles. Perhaps alcohol is perceived as the least menacing of all substances, a morning-after hangover at worst. Who, we should ask, is to blame?

We live in a society that drinks to drown its problems and celebrate its achievements. What kind of example does that set for our young people?

For just a moment, let me describe how severe this problem has become. A survey published recently by Drug Action of Wake County reveals that more than 20 percent of our youth in grades nine through twelve reported, in 1985, that they had been intoxicated eleven or more times during the year. This same report indicates that some 30 percent of the students who were surveyed in grades nine through twelve were classified as problem drinkers; and, at the rate we [are] going, the percentage within a few years could represent more than half of our younger population.

We all know the effects of alcohol and drug abuse: retarded physical and mental growth, the breakdown of social relationships, the destruction of the family, and even violence and death. Continued abuse carries over into adult life, severely impacting upon friends, neighbors, and employers.

In creating the Governor's Council on Alcohol and Drug Abuse among Children and Youth, I have set out to promote public awareness of youth substance abuse issues and to provide our citizens an opportunity to make recommendations on adolescent services.[1] This morning, I charge you, the members of the council, with the task of reviewing the severity of this problem on a statewide level and presenting recommendations for the coordination of state and local resources to address identified needs. This means that an across-the-board needs assessment will be required to determine the extent of adolescent drug abuse in North Carolina. Communities need to know the extent of the problem, how they can mobilize their resources, and how they can provide needed services, as well as make referrals.

There also exists a need to build a continuum of care, begining with prevention, early identification, and intervention through treatment aftercare. The adult community and the service delivery system, I fear, have not made adequate treatment available to meet the growing needs of young people who have become addicted. Currently, for example, there is no ongoing mechanism to provide inpatient treatment for adolescent substance abusers. We are now contracting for these services from private providers, and we are exploring other ways to implement these services on a much broader basis.

Last year, my proposal to the General Assembly included an appropriation of $2.4 million to address substance abuse service needs. It was my belief then, and it remains my belief now, that these funds are crucial for the development and implementation of necessary program initiatives. However, after much debate, our legislators saw fit to appropriate only one half of my request for fiscal 1985-1986 and 1986-1987.[2] Consequently, it will take more than my efforts, in the future, to sensitize our General Assembly members to the unmet needs of this underserved group: our children and youth.

It is estimated that about one half of the youth currently being treated by the health and human service system are either children of alcohol and/or drug abusing parents, or have moderate to severe alcohol and/or drug problems themselves. Drunk and drugged children cannot learn in the classroom, they cannot acquire the essential social skills to cope with a complex and ever-changing society, and they cannot become good citizens and exemplary parents. That's the tragedy of alcohol and drug addiction. If the abusers of today become the parents of tomorrow, our problem is perpetuated and becomes so deeply rooted it is difficult to overcome.

The majority of the $1.2 million appropriated by the General Assembly last year has already been allocated to area mental health, mental retardation, and substance abuse programs to initiate student assistance programs and outpatient assessment and treatment. In addition, some of these funds will be utilized to conduct a statewide adolescent needs survey and to develop and provide professional interdisciplinary training in youth alcohol and drug abuse intervention and treatment.

The cost of alcohol and drug abuse to society cannot be measured in dollars alone. It takes its greatest toll in human potential, it decreases the quality of family life, and it can destroy the lives of the abusers as well as innocent victims.

This council is faced with an enormous and difficult task, but it is not an insurmountable one. We are extremely fortunate to have among you the best minds in our state. Together, we can—and we will—develop workable approaches to the most sinister problem affecting the future of North Carolina, a future which belongs to the children and youth of today. I join with you in offering leadership and working to make it a future bright with promise and opportunity. And now, it is my pleasure to recognize Associate Justice Rhoda Billings, of the North Carolina Supreme Court, who will administer the oaths of office to the distinguished members of this council.[3]

---

[1]Governor Martin signed Executive Order Number 23, creating the Governor's Council on Alcohol and Drug Abuse among Children and Youth, on January 29, 1986. *N.C. Session Laws, 1985, Extra and Regular Sessions, 1986*, 675-677.

[2]See "An Act to Make Additional Appropriations for Various Statewide Projects and for Other Purposes," *N.C. Session Laws, 1985*, c. 791, s. 17, ratified July 18, 1985.

[3]Rhoda B. Billings (1937-   ), native of Wilkesboro; A.B., Berea College, 1959; J.D., Wake Forest University, 1966. Attorney in private practice, 1966-1968; district court judge, Twenty-first North Carolina Judicial District, 1968-1972; assistant professor, associate professor, and professor, Wake Forest University School of Law, 1973-1984; chairwoman, state Parole Commission, 1985; associate justice, 1985-1986, chief justice, 1986-1987, state supreme court. *News and Observer*, July 31, August 1, 1986; *North Carolina Manual, 1985*, 845, *1987-1988*, 858.

GOODNESS GROWS IN NORTH CAROLINA

RALEIGH, JUNE 30, 1986

I am pleased to join you, today, as North Carolina, "the goodliest land under the cope of heaven,"[1] pays tribute to the goodness of its agricultural harvest. For more than 400 years, we have been a people close to the land and its bountiful resources, a people proud of our rural heritage and passion for excellence. It is this sense of pride that has made North Carolina one of the principal breadbaskets of our nation and the world. No other state outproduces North Carolina in tobacco, sweet potatoes, turkeys, and forest products. We are second in cucumbers and pickles, third in poultry and peanuts, and fourth in commercial broilers. We are gaining recognition rapidly in other commodities, too, including pork, dairy products, eggs, corn, soybeans, and greenhouse and nursery products.

But there is something which is more important than quantity. North Carolina is first in the quality of its farm products. We are a farm state that takes pride in production. The "Goodness Grows in North Carolina" campaign, which has been developed under the guidance of Ms. Hamby[2] and her associates in the Department of Agriculture, seeks to capitalize on this precious asset of quality in the marketplace.

The "Goodness" label is a badge of excellence. It sets apart only those products that are grown, processed, and sold under the highest standards our Department of Agriculture may impose. This label is an assurance, indeed an endorsement, by the Department of Agriculture that the consumer is purchasing a quality product.

Many companies and producers in our state are eligible and qualified to earn this special label, and as governor, I urge them to apply to the Marketing Division of the Department of Agriculture for approval. Thus far, thirteen companies and producers have been certified. They produce and process a wide variety of commodities, including turkeys, eggs, apples, peanuts, pork products, popcorn, milk and dairy products, seafoods, and hydroponic lettuce. It is expected that the number of products marketed under the "Goodness" label will number well into the hundreds by the end of the program's first year.

I want to take the opportunity, today, to commend Commissioner Graham and the staff of the Department of Agriculture for having developed this campaign to promote North Carolina's best agricultural products. The promotion program which has been undertaken in support of this effort will do much to increase our agricultural income.

Early in my administration, I recognized that our traditional industries, including agriculture and agribusiness, represent the very foundation of our state's economy. Yet, they have been adversely affected by foreign imports which, during the month of May, reached the highest level in history. In our abundant state and nation, the center of research and development for all that has made agriculture the pride of the world, we must regain the will and determination to once again become the leader in the global marketplace. The "Goodness Grows in North Carolina" program is an excellent start in making consumers aware that products grown and processed here in our own state are the finest available. Let us all join together, as one united state, in making this campaign an example which other traditional industries may emulate.

Just as our Department of Agriculture is working within its own area of jurisdiction, so, too, is our Department of Commerce seeking to find more effective ways to make our traditional industries more competitive with our foreign trade partners. My appointment of White Watkins as assistant secretary of commerce for traditional industry speaks to my firm commitment to strengthen not only agriculture and its related enterprises, but also to help all of our basic industries thrive and expand.

Within the coming weeks, I will be announcing a new blueprint for economic growth. Under the very able leadership of Commerce Secretary Howard Haworth, our staff of specialists within the Department of Commerce has been working to find ways to assist rural areas in their development efforts. Much of this blueprint is designed to address the problems of family farmers, small businesses, and entrepreneurs. With them rests the true hope of North Carolina in the future. It is their enterprising spirit that has kept North Carolina economically strong, dynamically alive, and on the leading edge of tomorrow's progress.

"Goodness Grows in North Carolina" is a campaign that will fit logically into this new blueprint. It will become a strong thread in the total fabric we weave for development as we approach the twenty-first century. Today I pledge my full support to Commissioner Graham, and the Department of Agriculture, as we work together to keep faith with our farmers and agribusiness firms. As governor, I urge all North Carolinians to lend us their support, for this program, in the truest sense, belongs to all of us.

---

[1]Ralph Lane wrote of North Carolina, ". . . we have discovered the maine to bee the goodliest soile under the cope of heaven. . . ." Letter to Richard Hakluyt, September 3, 1585, as quoted in Quinn, *First Colonists,* 22.

[2]Teresa Hamby (1958-   ), born in Evreaux, France; resident of Fuquay-Varina; B.A., Meredith College, 1980. Marketing home economist, media spokesperson, N.C. Egg Marketing Assn., 1982-1984; marketing home economist, 1984-1985, state Department of

Agriculture, and developer of "Goodness Grows in North Carolina" campaign, and developer, manager of "Flavors of Carolina" program, since 1985. Teresa Hamby to Jan-Michael Poff, August 3, 1989.

COMMUNITY COLLEGES ASSOCIATION ROAST OF LISTON RAMSEY

RALEIGH, JULY 2, 1986

[Governor Martin was introduced on this humorous occasion by former governor Robert Scott, president of the state community college system.]

I am very pleased to join you, tonight, for the rare opportunity to roast our distinguished Speaker of the House. The occasion is made all the more pleasant by the fact that the proceeds of this dinner will benefit the Community College Alumni Scholarship Fund, and thus will enable many deserving young people to pursue an education beyond high school.

Liston Ramsey is many things: a successful businessman, statesman, fiscal expert, and an acrobat. That's right, an acrobat. He can straddle a fence, keep his finger on the public pulse, point with pride, and look to the future, while keeping both ears to the ground and his nose to the grindstone. Try that sometime, and you'll see what I mean.

To say that the Speaker is cagey is putting it mildly. Back in his World War II days, Sergeant Ramsey, a private, and a corporal gathered in their tent one evening to engage in a little sport: poker. The lieutenant became suspicious and double-timed over to the tent to check things out for himself, but Liston and his buddies were too fast for the shavetail. By the time the lieutenant got there, all evidence of a poker game had disappeared.

"Private Jones, were you playing poker?" the lieutenant asked.

"No sir," came the reply, "I wasn't playing poker."

"Corporal Smith, were you playing poker?"

"Absolutely not," the corporal answered, whereupon the officer turned to Liston and asked, "Sergeant Ramsey, were you playing poker?"

Liston simply threw up his hands and answered, "With who?"

I guess it was from such experiences that he learned the political maxim he now lives by: Always play fair when you're holding the winning cards.

I've noticed, since becoming governor, that the Speaker has had a lot to say about those patronage plums I'm supposed to be dispensing to the faithful. There have been more times, however, when he has had a protégé in the Mansion and was in a position to do a little dispensing himself. Once a friend came by to see the Speaker and suggested that another friend would fit nicely into a certain job.

"What can he do?" Liston asked, and the fellow replied, "Well, nothing, to be perfectly frank."

"Good," said Liston. "Then we won't have to break him in."

Well, I once described Liston by saying North Carolina needs more potholes in its highways like Liston Ramsey needs assertiveness training. You may be awed by his power, but you have to respect it.[1]

Liston is the first person since Idi Amin to claim office for life.

You know, I've been thinking through a lot of decisions, lately, and it occurred to me that I could solve a lot of problems with one stroke by appointing Liston Ramsey to the Senate. Think about that for a while. The only catch is, I can't get Lieutenant Governor Jordan to say whether they would accept him over there.

Thank you again for inviting me to this occasion. It's been fun, but now it's someone else's opportunity to turn up the heat.

---

[1]Ramsey's reign as Speaker ended after eight years, his "arbitrary and petty" use of power, in the opinion of one political observer, ultimately proving to be his undoing. In January, 1989, twenty disenchanted House Democrats sided with forty-five Republicans to remove him from the speakership. Luebke, *Tar Heel Politics*, 207.

NORTH CAROLINA LEAGUE OF SAVINGS INSTITUTIONS

HOT SPRINGS, VIRGINIA, JULY 22, 1986

It is a very special pleasure for me to share this occasion today with four of our former governors (Jim Holshouser, Dan Moore, Terry Sanford, and Bob Scott). I am doubly pleased that you have afforded me this opportunity to speak to you briefly about a basic issue we face in North Carolina. It's not a simple issue, but it is basic to our lives and to your vital role as executives of our savings institutions. The issue is housing.

North Carolina always has been, and it remains still, a state of independent, proud, innovative, and productive people. In our state's infancy, their dreams stretched beyond the horizon to the unlimited opportunities that existed for a better life. Here was the one place where an individual could advance as far as their ambitions and abilities could take them [*sic*], a place where the special advantages of noble birth and privilege did not exist to separate them not only from their God-given right to pursue happiness and prosperity, but the opportunity to overtake and enjoy them. If a person was a skilled cabinetmaker, cobbler, farmer, or merchant, and if they put their best into their work, North Carolina represented a place where they could make it. That's what the dream of a new nation was all about. It still is.

From the beginning, some North Carolinians wanted to turn the traditionalist campaign for the rights of Englishmen into a more universal struggle for mankind. To a certain extent, they were successful. The new state constitution put strict limitations on the power of government and gave the vote to taxpayers who did not own property.[1]

Landmarks of the War for Independence survive in every part of North Carolina, but the cultural monuments of independence, although less conspicuous than the battlefields, are even more significant. When the shooting died away, North Carolinians continued to work out the meaning of independence in the fabric of their daily lives and to fulfill the profound opportunities and obligations that liberty brought them. In succeeding decades, a sense of urgency existed as new immigrants cleared forests, built homes, tilled the soil, cultivated crops, and instituted a system of commerce. Fueled by the spirit of enterprise, North Carolina has grown and prospered in a climate deeply rooted in family life and family values.

The family is the most important element in our society—economically, socially, educationally, and culturally. My proclamation commemorating 1986 as the "Year of the Family" should serve to remind us of this. Sometimes, we tend to forget.

Central to the family's ability to function is its living environment, its home, the epitome of the American dream. Sadly, what many of us take for granted—a decent, safe, and sanitary home at an affordable price—is no longer available to many North Carolinians. Housing needs in North Carolina today are critical. Many families live in substandard, deteriorated, or even dilapidated homes and can afford no better; many more are financially and emotionally strained by the cost of housing, whether standard or substandard; and others simply cannot find or afford any housing at all.

These problems affect us all. How can a man and woman living in this environment do their best on the job? How well can their children, our hope for the future, perform in school? What do slum neighborhoods say about our communities? Currently, more than 250,000 North Carolinians live in substandard homes; the problem is appreciably worse in rural areas, where 17 percent of all homes are unfit for occupancy. But perhaps the most shocking fact of all is that, in 1985, 48,000 low-income families in this state could not find a home of their own at an affordable price, regardless of the condition.

Consequently, housing affordability is a growing problem for many of our citizens. Nearly one third of our families are spending more than 25 percent of their incomes on housing. Among low-income families, the number is a staggering 84 percent. Obviously, poor families bear a real housing burden.

These are very real, very basic, problems facing us today. North Carolina will continue to grow—quite rapidly, in fact. We are among the ten fastest-growing states in the nation. This population explosion, coupled with housing market patterns, will make future housing problems acute in North Carolina.

However, as you know so well, we do not have the luxury of addressing these problems under fixed conditions. Significant changes are occurring in the housing market; one of these changes involves accelerated costs. The median price of a new home in the South rose from $20,000, in 1970, to $60,000 in 1980, an increase of almost 300 percent. It is still going up. The North Carolina Association of Realtors estimates that the average home in North Carolina today commands a price tag of $75,000.

New homes are being built at a rapid rate, of course, because of lower interest rates, but these homes are not always in the right places at affordable prices for families that need them most. In addition, the federal government is getting out of the housing business. During the last five years, the Department of Housing and Urban Development's budget authority for public and elderly housing, Section 8 grants, and housing vouchers declined by $17 billion.[2] On a national scale, reservations and starts for public housing projects and Section 8 programs totaled 475,000 in 1982. The projected total for this fiscal year is less than 100,000 units.

The state has an opportunity, and I feel a personal obligation, to help make decent, safe, and affordable housing available to as many of our citizens as possible. But federal government assistance programs have not solved our housing problems; neither will assistance programs undertaken by the state, unless they are pursued in concert with the private sector. Addressing our housing problems will require a strong government and business partnership and a strong commitment to muster the necessary resources.

Government's role in meeting these needs begins by instilling a spirit of confidence and faith in the future and by providing the incentive for individual achievement. It can help, also, by putting its own house in order. Currently, eleven state departments administer a wide array of programs directly affecting housing: building codes, financing of below-market interest rate loans, fair housing assistance and enforcement, subdivision regulation, community development block grants, and even regulation of savings and loan institutions.

In India, one of the poorest nations on earth, the rate of savings exceeds 30 percent. In Japan, it's above 20 percent. Here in the richest society man has ever known, we have an appalling savings rate of approximately 3 percent.

Awakened to the rudeness of this reality, I sense that a new American renaissance is in the making, supported by our own national government's stated commitment to eliminate the staggering deficit that has crippled our competitiveness with foreign nations. We are once again becoming an independent country, led by the determination of our states. Nowhere is this more evident than in our own state.

We began to turn the corner here in North Carolina last year by eliminating intangibles taxes on bank deposits, giving partial tax relief to industry, fostering efficiency in state government, and charting a new course of economic diversification. For the last eighteen months, we've been working to find new and creative ways to help our traditional industries that employ more than half of our labor force. Next month I'll be announcing North Carolina's blueprint for economic growth, which will set forth new strategies for diversifying and expanding development in our rural and urban counties.

We realize and support the necessary investment of public monies to enhance growth and create new opportunities. These expenditures include funds for more and better highways, improvements in our system of public education, solving the problem of prison overcrowding, expanding our research activities, and establishing a public infrastructure in which free enterprise can flourish. State government's proper role is to provide these facilities and services. Its job is not to compete with private enterprise.

The fact is that new and expanding companies, the only real source of new jobs and opportunities for our people, must have a healthy, intelligent work force, and these people must be able to get to work every day. As long as business remains successful, it is an effective counterbalance to the role of government in our lives. When business stops doing its job well, that's the day that government starts doing it for us, and one important freedom, economic freedom, is lost.

I suggest that we must take the same approach to solving our housing problems. The answer does not lie in providing more below-market interest rates for housing loans or increased rental subsidies. Instead, the answer lies in continuing to build a strong and viable economy, characterized by stability, diversity, and growth, that will enable North Carolina's present and future generations to fulfill their needs and aspirations themselves. After all, economic expansion is the rising tide that lifts all boats. The basic things most individuals want are relatively simple: a good job; a decent wage for their labors; a chance to move up the ladder, based on ability and initiative; the opportunity to save part of what they earn; to invest; and most importantly, the freedom to make choices.

One possible way to meet the housing requirements of these needy citizens, as suggested from around the state, is through the establishment of a housing trust fund. The sources of financing for a housing trust fund are limited only by our imagination: General Fund appropriations, real estate transfer taxes, grants from foundations and other private sources, Housing Finance Agency funds, even a combination of these sources. I'm sure that we strongly believe that a housing trust fund could be very beneficial to the very low income families in North Carolina, and we should work together to develop such a fund.[3]

The range of programs a housing trust fund can cover also is unlimited. These programs should address a wide spectrum of our housing needs, including the problems of our rural population, the elderly, homeowners, and renters. The programs should range from self-help housing where the future homeowner participates in the construction of his house, to housing rehabilitation which restores substandard units, to increasing the state's rental housing stock. The trust fund also can support a technical assistance team to help local governments and individuals to take advantage of available housing assistance. Most importantly, these programs would benefit those families with few, if any, options for improving their living environment—North Carolina's low-income families—and they help ensure the health of our housing industry.

There are several other alternatives which deserve mention today. The first is the enactment of legislation which would permit individuals and married couples who have never owned a home to make deposits to a designated tax-exempt account in a bank or savings institution for the purpose of accumulating the down payment for a first home purchase. Such an account would be similar to an individual retirement account and would provide several benefits, including the accelerated formation and recycling of capital by our financial institutions, the promotion of thrift, and the encouragement of self sufficiency. Of course, limits would be placed on maximum annual deposits and total deposits accumulated. This gives working people the chance to help themselves by using part of their income to build a nest egg toward the realization of the American dream, a home of their own. I would even be bold enough to suggest that we return to the old-fashioned idea of issuing a special passbook, something tangible to help reshape our attitude toward thrift as a fundamental principle of independence.

However, there still would remain the truly needy who must be housed adequately and at affordable rents—those who, because of circumstance, do not have the financial resources to purchase a standard dwelling. One possible way to meet the housing requirements of these needy citizens would be through the establishment of a housing trust fund financed from the excess revenues of the North Carolina Housing Finance Agency. These funds could be leveraged against private investment for the purpose of providing low-cost, basic, rental housing which has been constructed at a cost-efficient square-foot allowance approved by the trustees of the fund in advance.

The range of programs which a trust fund can cover is unlimited, and these programs should address a wide spectrum of our housing needs. More importantly, these programs would benefit those families with few, if any, options for improving their living environment: North Carolina's low-income families.

What I have suggested today are several ideas which I believe are worthy of further study and investigation, ideas to foster an even stronger partnership between he public and private sectors. They are ideas that test our ability to shape the future of North Carolina's housing sector.

When we deal with the future, realism warns us that we cannot do everything; common sense tells us that we can do many things. I think we owe it to future generations to come out on the optimistic side of that question. The most creative and forward-moving actions in any society are taken, not by those who doubt, because these people never experience the satisfaction of accomplishment; real futures are created by men and women who have faith in human possibilities. I believe the latter example best describes the people of North Carolina.

---

[1]For provisions on voter eligibility, see Constitution of the State of North Carolina, 1776, Section VIII, reprinted in Clark, *State Records*, XXIII, 981.

[2]A range of federal housing subsidy plans were authorized under Section 8, "United

States Housing Act of 1937" (short title), *United States Statutes at Large*, Act of September 1, 1937, Chapter 896, page 891, as amended. The Housing Voucher Program "assists eligible families to pay rent for decent, safe, and sanitary housing." "Housing Vouchers," *Code of Federal Regulations* (April 1, 1989 ed.), 24 CFR 887.1.

[3]"An Act to Create the North Carolina Housing Trust Fund and to Authorize the Expenditure of Oil Overcharge Funds," was ratified August 14, 1987. *N.C. Session Laws, 1987*, II, c. 841.

NORTH CAROLINA ASSOCIATION OF MINORITY BUSINESSES

RALEIGH, JULY 24, 1986

More than eighteen months ago, when I took the oath of office as governor of North Carolina, I brought to the executive branch a strong and sincere commitment to build a system of government in which all of our citizens could participate openly and fairly. Central to this commitment was the implementation of a program that would enhance the participation of companies owned by minorities, women, and disabled people in state government purchases. Working with my assistant for minority affairs, and with the enthusiastic support of my cabinet, we established a pilot goals program in July of 1985. It was a trial run, so to speak, designed to test our performance, identify strengths and weaknesses, and help us develop a viable purchasing system through which targeted groups would be afforded the maximum opportunity to compete.

Today, I am pleased to report that we have accomplished what we set out to do, and in the process, we have achieved some remarkable results. During the eleven months ending in May of this year, more than 300 contractors have been certified under the pilot project by the nine departments of government within the jurisdiction of the Governor's Office. Of that number, some 225 companies are minority owned. Undoubtedly, there are many other North Carolina companies among targeted groups that offer services and products utilized by the state, and we are working to ensure that all of these firms interested in doing business with state agencies are certified.

Another remarkable accomplishment of the pilot project has been the awarding of contracts exceeding $8 million to companies competing under the certification process. Unfortunately, no records existed in previous administrations for comparative analysis. Therefore, we have no basis of judging performance except to measure results in terms of our established goal of 2 percent of total purchases. In this respect, we equaled or exceeded our mark in seven of the eleven months, and our overall record was precisely what we had set out to achieve. More importantly, the pilot project was a process of discovery; that is, a method of identifying flaws in the system and finding ways to correct them.

Today, I am pleased to announce that I am instructing my legal counsel to prepare an executive order formally establishing the goals program, effective this month, and setting a goal of 4 percent for the current fiscal year. To ensure a continued spirit of cooperation, information, and coordination among departments, I am designating my director of minority affairs, Mr. Emery Rann, to serve as staff coordinator. In support of this action, I am also directing the secretary of administration to provide staff assistance to Mr. Rann on a project basis, thereby ensuring an efficient and effective program.[1]

Moreover, I already have taken steps to bring about greater representation of minorities in purchasing and personnel positions by instructing department secretaries to register all vacancies with the equal opportunity/affirmative action representative in the Office of State Personnel, as well as the director of minority affairs. Currently, we have a vacancy for a purchasing officer and a clerical worker in the Department of Natural Resources and Community Development, and I have notified Secretary (Thomas) Rhodes to set aside these positions for qualified minority applicants. If we hope to meet or exceed our goal for minority contracting, it will be vital to have purchasing officers who understand the minority business community.

From the outset of my administration, I have appointed minorities to key, nontraditional leadership positions. During my first year, we set a new record of appointing or employing minorities in almost 28 percent of all state government job vacancies. Approximately 9 percent of the new minority employees were in official and administrative positions, more than 10 percent were in management-level openings, and over 50 percent were in professional and technical jobs. I believe this represents a good-faith effort by the administration to bring about a favorable impact on purchasing decisions.

No other administration in state government has ever approached the number of minorities appointed to cabinet and subcabinet positions. My appointees have included Aaron Johnson, secretary of correction; Lew Myers, assistant secretary of commerce for small business; Sylvania [Wilkerson], assistant secretary of transportation; Henry McKoy, assistant secretary of administration; Ed Garner, assistant secretary of crime control and public safety; and Brenda McGhee, deputy commissioner of the Employment Security Commission. I could go on, listing dozens of others who are members of my staff or who hold jobs as directors of various divisions within the nine departments under the executive branch. However, I believe that my actions demonstrate a deep personal involvement in minority affairs, something that heretofore has been absent in state government.

All of these appointees are central to the task of shaping a viable program to benefit minorities in general and minority-owned businesses in particular. We are moving rapidly to make necessary adjustments in our minority purchasing program, including upgrading of our computer systems so they can interface with all departments, and consolidation of our purchasing directories to include business listings by product or service codes. These improvements are extremely important.

The first task of meeting and exceeding our minority contracting goal is the identification of companies whose products or services meet our purchasing requirements. Once these firms are identified, we can launch a concerted effort to contact them on an individual basis and make them aware of anticipated purchases. Our Small Business Division and our Minority Business Division, both of which are under the Department of Commerce, are available on a day-to-day basis to provide technical assistance to firms that wish to participate.

All of us should take pride in the increasing number of minority men and women who have conquered seemingly impossible odds to make significant contributions to the economy of North Carolina and their own particular economic sectors. During the past year, black-owned businesses posted a 14.8 percent growth in business on a national basis, compared to a growth rate of only 3.2 percent for the United States as a whole. North Carolina's economy, during the same period, surged ahead even faster. We continue to have unemployment below 5 percent, and for the first time, more than 3 million of our citizens are in the active work force, meaning that they are employed.

As one of the ten fastest-growing states in the nation, North Carolina offers unlimited potential for expansion. Minority business can excel in this business climate. It will require dedication, tenacity, and creativity as their tools of trade, but the opportunities are here for them to carve out a solid place in the bedrock of our mainstream economy.

For decades, minority business enterprise in North Carolina has defied the system in order to realize the dream of business ownership. Today, black entrepreneurs are boldly facing new challenges. We must realize that to achieve a measurable degree of success, these businesses must possess the same level of skills, financial savvy, and technical know-how as their counterparts in majority-run businesses.

More importantly, they must capture the spirit of enterprise, displaying the courage, ingenuity, and determination to succeed, no matter what obstacles lie before them.

State government has, and will continue, to establish a strong public-private partnership, one which fosters economic growth and opportunity for all. Our goal in government is to achieve one united state, a state in which there is success enough for all who have the determination to pursue it. This administration has made a good beginning. It has established a framework for progress. Together, let us build upon this successful beginning.

---

[1]Executive Order Number 34, establishing the Governor's Program to Encourage Business Enterprises Owned by Minority, Women, and Disabled Persons, was signed February 27, 1987. *N.C. Session Laws, 1987*, II, 2330-2333.

NORTH CAROLINA ASSOCIATION OF
COUNTY COMMISSIONERS

Winston-Salem, August 15, 1986

Your invitation to join you again this year pleases me very much, for two reasons. The first reason is that, as a former president of your association, I have a strong attachment to county governments and great faith in the ability of their elected officials to know best how to solve local problems and accommodate the needs of their citizens.[1] And the second reason is that this occasion provides me an opportunity to emphasize again the importance of our continuing effort to build a model partnership between state and local governments.

You will recall that in 1985 I pledged to support the choice of counties to levy a local-option sales tax increase of one half cent to compensate for the anticipated loss of federal revenue sharing funds to our local governments. It is a pledge that I have honored in the interest of keeping our communities and counties fiscally sound and in a viable position to continue a high level of services and provide the resources for future economic growth and development.

Economic development—that is, acquisition of new businesses and the expansion of existing private enterprise—is the real source of jobs in North Carolina and accounts for the creation of the wealth which is taxed to provide for the common good of the public. Here is where state and local governments have a shared responsibility.

There is a clear, but mutually dependent, division between the financial obligations of state and local governments. The state's job is to provide, within its means, those things which local governments individually cannot provide for themselves. The most visible examples include public elementary, secondary, and post-secondary education; an adequate system of highways and roads; courts; and state prisons. These are areas in which much attention has been focused in recent years, and rightly so. But not all examples embrace material things, because the state also furnishes many services, as well; it fosters many worthwhile programs and provides the leadership in countless initiatives.

Local governments, on the other hand, have the responsibility for police and fire protection, water and sewer facilities, school buildings, health-care facilities, and so forth. Like the state, they also have their own sources of revenue, and one of these is the local-option sales tax. The Department of Revenue reports that fifty-one counties already have chosen to implement the additional sales tax authorized by the General Assembly during its 1986 short session.[2] It is anticipated that others represented here, today, will follow their example in the future. With funds generated from this source, counties are positioned to meet the demand for new and expanded public school facilities, which is mandated by the legislation, and to invest more resources in water and sewer systems, and other facilities, to accommodate existing and future growth needs. This is important when we consider that more than 100 communities in our state are under a current moratorium prohibiting adding new customers to their water and sewer systems.

Statewide, the additional local-option sales tax will account for an estimated $182 million in revenues, if implemented by all of our counties. This compares with $120 million now received locally in federal revenue sharing funds. Even when we take into account the General Assembly's revocation of personal property taxes,[3] counties will gain an additional $37 million statewide.

This single legislative measure, however, does not resolve all of the financial problems of local governments. Ahead lies the Gramm-Rudman-Hollings deficit reduction act and even larger cuts in federal program funds to states and localities. How we deal with these reductions will test the commitment of state and local governments to a strong working partnership. It will, in large measure, determine our ability to lead the region and the nation successfully in coping with more change. I believe strongly that we at the state level must work with counties, individually, to determine their priorities and help them achieve local goals.

We also must have the understanding and cooperation of our legislators. In 1985, for example, I proposed the appropriation of $60 million annually to help local governments expand existing water and sewer systems and build new ones, with funds allocated on the basis of need. Instead of following my recommendation fully, the General Assembly appropriated the money on a $7.00 per-capita formula. This means that our rural and smaller units of government, whose local resources are less but whose needs are greater, are receiving little in the way of real financial help from the state.

During my town meetings, this is one of the most frequent complaints voiced by local leaders. In one recent meeting at Albemarle, in Stanly County, a representative of the town of Bolin pointed out that his community is in the lower 25 percent of pending applications for Environmental Protection Agency funds, and that the state's share of money isn't adequate to match the local commitment. As county commissioners, you have both an opportunity and an obligation to help correct this funding inequity by bringing your influence to bear on the General Assembly. Our legislators are responsible for this problem, not the governor.

I must commend the General Assembly, however, on its ability to reach a compromise in funding my Roads to the Future program to improve existing highways and rural roads and undertake desperately needed new construction. North Carolina has the largest and best highway system in the nation. Our highways and rural roads link our farms and markets, our workers and jobs, our children and schools, and our industries and communities. The highway bill approved by the General Assembly did not accomplish everything I wanted, but it was an acceptable compromise—which is a real victory for this administration. During the current year, the measure will produce more than $172 million in new funds, and this amount will accelerate annually into almost $250 [million] annually by 1991-1992.

Earlier this week, the Transportation Board committed itself to transforming plans into pavement. This expeditious step confirms my determination to solve the most pressing of our transportation needs, and I applaud the board's action.

Another major achievement during the last session of the General Assembly was the appropriation of additional education funds to reduce classroom size, establish a teacher recruitment office, and expand teacher effectiveness training. We also obtained funds for tuition grants and loans of $1,000 each, to be forgiven for persons teaching two years in subjects and geographic areas in which there are critical teacher shortages.

Since becoming governor in 1985, I have been a strong supporter of the multiyear pilot program for developing a teacher career ladder program statewide, but I want to make absolutely certain that the funds will be there to implement the program when the pilot program goes statewide. As you expand your educational facilities at the county level, I want to make sure that our classrooms are staffed by the most qualified teachers in the profession. It is often said that the children and youth of our state are our most important resource. Therefore, it should be accepted that our public education system must afford them every opportunity to achieve their maximum potential.

Another obligation we have to our children and youth is our total effort to eliminate illegal drug traffic in North Carolina and to mount an all-out effort to educate them to the menace of alcohol and drug addiction. In the last two years, I have consistently lobbied for additional drug agents and more highway patrolmen. We realized part of this goal in 1985. As part of my Drug Observation, Prevention, and Education program, I called for doubling the number of undercover agents from sixty to 120. Fifteen were granted in 1985, and just this year the legislature authorized twenty-three new SBI drug agents and twelve support personnel.

Through funding of the Missing Children's Center and the establishment of the Governor's Commission on Child Victimization, chaired by my wife, Dottie, we have made substantial progress in involving the private sector in our efforts to make each child's environment safe and wholesome.

I am confident that North Carolina is equal to the challenges of the future, and that through our growing state-local partnership, we are ready to enter into the most dynamic era in our history. What are those challenges? Well, they are many and varied. We need to work together to bring about establishing a system which provides for the nonpartisan election of judges, a system that truly places greater emphasis on judicial merit. I am pleased that retiring supreme court justice Joe Branch has agreed to chair a blue-ribbon committee looking into this need and framing legislative proposals for my consideration.

We also must continue working to eliminate the legislative pork barrel process which undermines our system of representative government. Although much support has been voiced for eliminating special appropriations, more than 2,000 pork barrel measures were enacted in 1985. Some of these nonstate appropriations have great merit and go to legally constituted bodies, but if they are to be made they should go through the appropriate legislative process and not be used by powerful leadership to reward and discipline members of the House and Senate.

Other major goals include allowing the people of North Carolina to vote whether or not their governor should have the veto power. We are the only state in the nation where the General Assembly has refused to call a public referendum on this issue, just as we are the only state in which the governor does not have that power. Surely the citizens of North Carolina should be allowed to make this choice.

North Carolina is a state of good government, but we are challenged to make it the best. We can accomplish this goal and ensure a bright future for our state and local governments by becoming a truly united state.

---

[1]Martin was president of the North Carolina Association of County Commissioners during 1970-1971. *North Carolina Manual, 1987-1988,* 547.

[2]"An Act to Authorize Counties to Levy Additional One-Half Percent Local Sales and Use Taxes" was ratified July 7, 1986. *N.C. Session Laws, 1985, Extra and Regular Sessions, 1986,* c. 906.

[3]See *N.C. Session Laws, 1985, Extra and Regular Sessions, 1986,* c. 982.

PUBLIC SECTOR FORUM, GOVERNOR'S COMMISSION ON CHILD VICTIMIZATION

HIGH POINT, SEPTEMBER 9, 1986

I should explain that Dottie and I were brought here in the helicopter of the Forest Service, the one they use to drop water on forest fires, so you'll notice it's a little wet when you go outside.

I am happy to accept this report,[1] with profound gratitude for your leadership, dedication, and sensitivity to one of the most sinister crimes of our century, child victimization. In all of its immorality, brutality, and hardness of the human heart, this inhumanity to our most defenseless citizens is a blight upon a civilized society. It can no longer be tolerated.

From the very moment of our founding as a state, while we were still groping for direction through a then murky future, one thing was very clear, and is clear for us today: In this land there would be, and will be, freedom from fear and exploitation. We say to ourselves that the protection of our children, and the very creation of a perfect society as our legacy to them, is, and will remain, our foremost responsibility. This elusive goal remains unchanged today, just as it was in our first days.

I am impressed that upon assuming your urgent work as a commission, you embraced a faith that even though the conditions of literally thousands of North Carolina children may be dark and discouraging, you refused to believe that they were hopeless. That faith is stamped indelibly upon this report. This state, nation, and the world will always need people like you: caring and concerned, giving and involved.

Your report echoes the admonition of the great Jewish teacher and philosopher, Martin Buber, when he said, "It is not enough to be concerned with a cause; one must become involved."[2] Today, I want to express my deep and very sincere appreciation to you for having involved yourselves in the task of finding solutions to one of the greatest tragedies of our time. What you have done will make a difference in the lives of every child who has been, or who is at risk of being, victimized by those without conscience or a decent sense of responsibility.

I am pleased to welcome all of you, from the public sector, who have assembled here with the commission for this historic conference, the first ever on this scale in North Carolina. Your very presence is an expression of hope that the work which we have begun, to abolish child victimization in North Carolina, will not end until we have succeeded.

As governor of North Carolina, I have faced no issue that is more troubling or more tragic than the growing problem of child victimization. Reports that cross my desk provide mounting evidence that, every year, 27,000 children in this state will be reported as abused or seriously neglected.

Let's just stop right here and think for a moment: 27,000 children. Let's look at this statistic as one that equals the population of a major urban center, a city of children, hurting children who need your help. Even more frightening is the fact that our best estimates place the number of reported cases of child abuse, in all forms, at one out of every seven actual incidences of victimization; that's like 27,000 reported cases out of 190,000 actual cases. This commission's own report estimates that only 29 percent of sexual abuse cases involving children are ever reported.

That is hard to believe, isn't it? Is it also hard to accept? Over their lifetime, one in four girls and one in seven boys will be sexually abused. And what does it mean to us if 47 percent of the rape victims in North Carolina during 1983 were children?

These figures are staggering and difficult to comprehend, yet they exist behind the facade of peaceful towns and modern cities. Is that just the way the world is today? Do we have to accept it? Is there some higher demand on our time and our attention?

The faces you saw on the videotape, earlier, gave mute evidence to the fact that these crimes, these atrocities, are happening to real children, in real communities. They are children who belong to real families. These faces are not just a statistical nightmare. They belong to children whose lives may be unalterably changed forever.

As a society, we can no longer ignore this problem and wish that it would vanish. As the old Arabic saying goes, "If wishes were horses, beggars would ride." We cannot ride wishes. Wishes will not work. It will take all of us throughout North Carolina, working collectively, to send a loud and clear message that this behavior by the most unsavory of society will not be accepted.

Child victimization is not a new issue for my administration. Shortly after I became governor, in my 1985 "State of the State" message to the General Assembly and citizens of our state, I presented a comprehensive set of measures and budget improvements to address this compelling issue. Building upon many of the ideas and the clear prior commitment of many members of the General Assembly, including the lieutenant governor and leaders of both parties, these measures were designed to build a shield of protection around our most vulnerable citizens: our children. Subsequently, our legislators acted favorably on virtually all of these proposals.

What did we achieve? First, the North Carolina Center for Missing Children was statutorily mandated and adequately funded. Since that time, the center has been enhanced by better reporting methods, more responsive action by law enforcement agencies, and electronic networking with the National Center for Missing and Exploited Children. We will continue our efforts to make the North Carolina Center the best and most effective in the nation, a model for all states. Some critics minimize the dangers facing missing children by citing that most of them are runaways—what's so reassuring about that?— or were abducted by a noncustodial parent—and what's so reassuring about that?

The second achievement was legislative action requiring stiffer penalties for those who abduct and exploit children. From this point forward, those who victimize children are forewarned. Their acts will bring grave consequences for the criminals.[3]

Third, a tough new antipornography law was enacted. This landmark legislation has put an end to the prior adversary hearings that, for many years, had protected purveyors of child pornography and obscene material.

And fourth, additional child protective service workers were employed in local communities to provide early and adequate response to reports of child abuse.

The "Year of the Child" in 1985 was followed by the "Year of the Family" in 1986, and I am pleased that these two proclamations have heightened awareness, in North Carolina, that loving families are the foundation upon which children build futures filled with promise, not heartbreak. Other states have taken notice of our use of these special themes to generate special attention.

The most significant achievement of the year, I believe, was the establishment of the Governor's Commission on Child Victimization. The work in which this commission has been involved is of inestimable value to the state of North Carolina. You, the dedicated members, have listened to the people in communities all across our state. More importantly, you have heard what they have to say. You have researched the issues. You have identified, documented, and applauded innovative programs, already at work at the local level, to build our shield of protection for children. You've raised the real questions and found the right answers.

I believe President Reagan said it best when my wife, Dottie, and I met with him in the Rose Garden at the White House, on April 29, 1985, for the signing of the presidential executive order concerning the Child Safety Partnership. "Even though the abuse and exploitation of children is a big problem," he said, "it is simply no match for the heart and commitment of the American people." You know, he's right.

The report which you have presented me, today, is a work of the human heart—outgoing, feeling, understanding. It is professional and articulate. I assure you that this report will not gather dust on some bureaucratic shelf. You have met your charge, and I intend to do everything within my power, as North Carolina's chief executive, to implement your recommendations with expediency and empathy.

Evidence of this commitment is dramatized, I believe, by some of the steps we have already taken to turn your dreams into realities. As examples, allow me to mention four recommendations that are presented in this report and explain to you what we have already undertaken to do about them, without waiting for the report to be published.

Recommendation Number 6 calls upon my administration to "broaden the charge of the North Carolina Missing Children's Center to include child victimization cases."[4] I am pleased to say that Secretary (Joe) Dean of the Department of Crime Control and Public Safety has already moved us forward to accomplish this task. We have renamed the North Carolina Center for Missing Children the North Carolina Center for Missing Persons, and ha[ve] broadened its strategic functions to include victimized children. Now, I realize that some demean this by claiming that most missing children are runaways. Well, what's so reassuring about that? Aren't runaways more vulnerable to exploitation than if they were safely at home? Is New York City's "Tenderloin District" a gathering of runaways?

Secretary Dean has informed me that North Carolina is among six states in the nation selected to pilot test an interconnected, computerized system to transmit photographs and data concerning missing children and missing family members across state lines. This Lifenet system will enable law enforcement officers to work together more cohesively, and faster, to trace and locate loved ones who have been reported as missing.

Recommendation Number 28 of the commission's report focuses on the development of treatment programs for adolescent sexual offenders.[5] I supported additional funds for this program in my 1986 budget message to the General Assembly, but I didn't get that enacted yet. My pledge to you, today, is that this request will be presented again, in 1987, with the renewed urgency it demands. And with your help, we will succeed.

Another recommendation that has been offered embraces the establishment of local child victimization networks at the various judicial court levels.[6] If this program is to work, and it must, it has to start where the problem exists. This morning, the local coordinators were challenged to complete a local assessment of child victims in their own communities. Now, let me tell you, this is a tough assignment. Admitting that your own community has a problem is the first critical step, the one giant step, in finding out what local needs are and how they can be resolved.

We must take this step together. I have instructed Secretary Dean, Secretary of Human Resources (Phil) Kirk, and Secretary of Administration (Grace) Rohrer to provide staff and technical assistance from their respective departments to help with this effort at local assessment. Above all other missions in which we must be united, this is the one partnership that must be undertaken with a single purpose. We must make that purpose our priority.

There are thirty recommendations in the report which has been handed to me by your chairman, Dottie. So far, I have talked about the progress we have made in three areas of concern. The others are equally important. In fact, they are vital to the success of the total program to abolish child victimization.

Earlier, I told you we've done something about not just three, but four of your recommendations. Well, the final recommendation of the commission proposes establishment of a trust fund, for children and families, to fill the service gaps identified by the judicial coordinating councils.[7] I have done that. By executive order, I have today created this trust fund. I look forward to the generosity of the public and private sectors to finance this fund for needed community services, and we've already got a nice surprise for you. I recently competed in the Crosby golf tournament, in which all winnings go to charity.[8] Coaches Dean Smith[9] and Jim Valvano[10] and I, with one blue sock and one red and white, playing as Team North Carolina, won $6,000, which we are donating to the new North Carolina Fund for Children and Families. An additional $18,000 is being donated by other teams— Don Angell and Senator Jim Broyhill, and Craig Souza[11] and former Virginia governor Chuck Robb.[12]

Good programs, those which achieve success, do not require money alone. The essential element is cooperation and commitment of every group in our society. No single strategy will be sufficient to address the complex and difficult task of eliminating child victimization. Every level of government must be involved. Public-private partnerships must be forged, and new laws must be enacted. You must take the initiative. If you fail, no one else will heed the call.

A great president of these United States spoke of this spirit in 1932, a time of trial for our nation. "In the face of widespread hardship," said Herbert Hoover, "our people have demonstrated daily a magnificent sense of humanity, of individual and community responsibility for the welfare of the less fortunate." I encourage you now, in this moment of compassion and love for our children, to demonstrate anew your magnificent sense of humanity. Our most vulnerable children deserve no less. They ask no more. Thank you for what you are doing to answer their cry for help.

---

[1]*Child Victimization in North Carolina: A Report to the Governor* ([Raleigh]: Governor's Commission on Child Victimization, September 1, 1986), hereinafter cited as *Child Victimization in North Carolina.*

[2]Martin Buber (1878-1965), born in Vienna; was buried in Jerusalem; was educated at universities in Vienna, Leipzig, Zurich, and Berlin; honorary degrees. Philosopher; theologian; Zionist thinker, leader. Professor of religion at University of Frankfurt, 1930-1933; settled in Palestine, 1938; professor of social philosophy, Hebrew University, 1938-1951; author; lecturer. Buber "expounded a personalist philosophy of God, man,

and society that profoundly influenced contemporary thought, including Christianity." *Current Biography, 1965*, 59; see also *Encyclopaedia Judaica*, s.v. "Buber, Martin", and *Who Was Who in America, 1961-1968*, 131.

[3]Laws passed by the 1985 General Assembly bearing on the exploitation of children included c. 509, "An Act Making Technical and Clarifying Amendments Concerning Criminal Law and Procedure, and to Restore the Increased Punishment for Felony Child Abuse that was Inadvertently Repealed by the 1983 General Assembly," ratified July 1; "An Act to Amend G.S. 7A-517 to Prohibit Sexual Exploitation of Children," ratified July 8; and c. 668, "An Act to Strengthen the Felony Child Abuse Law by Prohibiting the Infliction of Any Serious Injury and by Increasing the Punishment," ratified July 10. *N.C. Session Laws, 1985.*

[4]"Broaden the charge of the North Carolina Missing Children's Center to include child victimization cases so that the center may serve as a clearinghouse for child pornography, child prostitution, and child sexual abuse cases." *Child Victimization in North Carolina*, 12.

[5]*Child Victimization in North Carolina*, 24.

[6]Recommendation 29, *Child Victimization in North Carolina*, 24.

[7]Recommendation 30, *Child Victimization in North Carolina*, 24.

[8]Singer-actor Bing Crosby (1904-1977) founded the Crosby National Pro-Am Golf Tournament. Martin announced in New York City, on February 10, 1986, that the event, perennially held in California, was relocating to the Bermuda Run golf course near Winston-Salem. The governor participated in North Carolina's inaugural Crosby during the weekend of June 6-8, 1986. Governor's Schedule for the Weeks of May 26-June 8, 1986, Governors Papers, James G. Martin; *Who Was Who in America, 1977-1981*, 132-133.

[9]Dean Edwards Smith (1931-   ), born in Emporia, Kansas; resident of Chapel Hill; B.S., University of Kansas, 1953; U.S. Air Force, 1954-1958. Assistant basketball coach, golf coach, United States Air Force Academy, 1955-1958; assistant basketball coach, 1958-1961, and head coach, since 1961, University of North Carolina at Chapel Hill; guided 1971 Tar Heels to National Invitation Tournament title; coached U.S. men's basketball team to gold medal, 1976 summer Olympics, Montreal; coached Tar Heels to NCAA national championship, 1982; winner of conference and national coaching awards; has more 25-win seasons than any college basketball coach in history. Art Chansky, with Eddie Fogler, *March to the Top* ([Chapel Hill]: Four Corners Press, 1982), 109-116; prepared biography from Dean Edwards Smith, June 25, 1985; *Who's Who in America, 1988-1989*, II, 2886.

[10]James Thomas Valvano (1946-   ), born in Queens, New York; resident of Cary; B.A., Rutgers University, 1967. Assistant basketball coach, Rutgers, 1968-1969, and at University of Connecticut, 1971-1972; head coach at Johns Hopkins University, 1970, Bucknell University, 1973-1975, Iona College, 1976-1980, and at North Carolina State University, 1980-1990; athletic director, North Carolina State University, 1986-1989; coached North Carolina State Wolfpack basketball team to NCAA national championship, 1983. *News and Observer*, April 5, 1983, August 26, December 13, 1989, April 8, 1990; prepared biography from Department of Athletics, North Carolina State University, July 9, 1985; *Who's Who in America, 1988-1989*, II, 3154.

[11]J. Craig Souza; resident of Raleigh; was graduated from East Carolina University, 1971; chief assistant to the secretary, state Department of Human Resources, prior to 1977; executive vice-president, North Carolina Health Care Facilities Assn., since 1977; president, American Society of Heath Care Assn. Executives, and of Assn. Executives of North Carolina. J. Craig Souza to Jan-Michael Poff, March 23, 1990.

[12]Charles Spittal Robb (1939-   ), born in Phoenix, Arizona; B.B.A., University of Wisconsin, 1961; J.D., University of Virginia, 1973; U.S. Marine Corps, 1961-1970. Attorney in private practice, 1974-1977, 1986-1988; Virginia lieutenant governor, 1978-1982, and governor, 1982-1986; chairman, Education Commission of the States, 1985, and of Democratic Leadership Council, since 1986; elected U.S. senator from Virginia, 1988; married Lynda Bird Johnson, daughter of Lyndon Baines Johnson, thirty-sixth U.S. president, December 9, 1967. Barone and Ujifusa, *Almanac of American Politics, 1986*, 1378-1379; *New York Times*, November 10, 1988; *Who's Who in America, 1988-1989*, II, 2605.

PRIVATE SECTOR FORUM ON CHILD VICTIMIZATION

HIGH POINT, SEPTEMBER 9, 1986

I am very pleased to join my wife, Chairman Dottie, in welcoming you to this Private Sector Forum on Child Victimization. Earlier this afternoon, at the public sector luncheon, I accepted the report from her as chairman of the Governor's Commission on Child Victimization. It is a vital policy report, of course, but it also is a working document, containing specific recommendations that are designed to help us eliminate one of the most serious and tragic problems of our time: child abuse and exploitation.

Many of you may be wondering why I have invited you to join us at this special forum. One of the reasons is that we hope that we can impress upon you the extent of the child abuse problem in our state. The problem is real, not imaginary.

Every year in our state, approximately 27,000 children will be reported as victimized or seriously neglected. But these children are only a fraction of the actual number of cases that actually occur. Best estimates place the number of reported cases at only one out of every seven incidences of victimization. If so, then 27,000 reported cases could represent an actual problem of 190,000 cases. Is that hard to believe? Just so, it's even harder to tolerate!

It is obvious that the problem of child abuse has reached epidemic proportions. Here are a few more numbers to support this conclusion: Over their lifetime, one in four girls and one in seven boys will be sexually abused. In 1983, 47 percent of the rape victims in North Carolina were children. Forty-seven percent! These figures are staggering and difficult to comprehend, yet they exist in the shadow of society.

A year ago, when I established the Governor's Commission on Child Victimization, I appointed members who represented law enforcement, education, human service agencies, and the judicial system; and among my appointees were members from the private sector. I charged the commission with the responsibility of researching and making recommendations on public policy matters; of achieving better collaboration and coordination between and among various state agencies; and also encouraging private sector involvement in our efforts to shield against child victimization as one of the most tragic problems affecting thousands of children throughout North Carolina. Your response has been overwhelming, and I am most grateful to all of you for your participation and help.

As chairman of the Governor's Commission on Child Victimization, our First Lady Dottie issued weekly reports—sometimes nightly!—on the progress of the group's work. She steadily praised the energetic efforts of the commission members. She was troubled by the fears of child abuse and victimization expressed by citizens at public hearings across the state, and she was extremely concerned about the complexity and enormity of the problem.

In January, she invited a small but influential group of foundation and corporate leaders to the Executive Mansion to talk about these issues. Most importantly, we wanted to know what could be done to forge a public-private partnership for victimized children. Partnerships are created every day to address such diverse issues as community revitalization, business recruitment, and economic development matters. So we asked ourselves if a similar joint venture could be formed to make life better and safer for children.

Many of you were at that meeting. Bishop [Kenneth] Goodson represented the Duke Endowment, the largest foundation in the state and one that historically has been sensitive to the needs of orphaned and neglected children. My longtime buddy from Charlotte, Gordon Berg, as director of the Foundation for the Carolinas, was there, too, and contributed to our discussion.[1] Both of them voiced concern that private sector decision makers needed to know more about the epidemic proportion of the child abuse problem. A number of others who joined us that day suggested a conference, tailored to the needs of the philanthropic community. Today's conference within a conference, this private sector forum, is our response to that suggestion.

So far, this conference has concentrated on defining the child victimization issue. Let us now begin to move beyond the problem and find out what we can do about it. Over the next two days, speakers and workshop participants will be talking about some of the creative programs that have proved successful in dealing with children and families. Public and private agency representatives will talk about how they can do a better job of working together; these representatives subsequently will examine the child victimization problem in their own local community and complete a needs assessment to determine what additional programs are needed. They will explore such things as the availability of a crisis center for victimized children, a network of volunteers who can help, and whether or not treatment is available for those who have been victimized. Beyond this conference, beyond the needs assessment of available community services, they will look at what can and must be accomplished at the local level. I want to challenge you, today, to take action, to help mobilize people across the state, and to work together in partnerships to eliminate child victimization.

Some of you have suggested that both public and private sector money to finance new and much needed programs would increase if a state challenge fund was created. Therefore, by executive order, I have created the North Carolina Fund for Children and Families Commission which will take up where the Commission on Child Victimization leaves off. The resources of this fund will be used to stimulate innovative, creative community programs to respond to family violence problems. Grants, gifts, and bequests are a potential source of revenue. Dottie and I are even considering the idea of a telethon to take our appeal to individual citizens. I also am exploring the possibility of a voluntary state income tax check-off as another potential source of revenue;[2] a divorce filing fee surcharge has also been suggested. These last two ideas, of course, will require legislative action, but I am prepared to call upon the General Assembly for its assistance during the 1987 session.

The purpose of the North Carolina Fund for Children and Families is to start up new, community-based programs needed to help support coordinated, comprehensive, and integrated services for child victims. The fund I have described will receive grants from foundations, corporations, the United Way, private nonprofit groups, local governments, and philanthropists. Public and private dollars could be commingled through this arrangement, and thus a new partnership is forged on behalf of children and their families. Let me make one thing clear: The fund is designed to supplement, not displace, existing service dollars.

The executive order which I mentioned creates a board of directors to administer the funds, establish criteria for awards, and make grant decisions. Private sector participation of this board will be vital, so I will appoint members on the basis of their belief in the public-private partnership concept.

I strongly believe that this new mechanism, this North Carolina Fund for Children and Families, will attract interest and support from individuals and groups all across North Carolina. I am confident that you will continue to be sensitive to the needs of our youngest and most vulnerable citizens, our children, and give accordingly. I believe that is why you are here today, and that is why I can count on you tomorrow.

To get the North Carolina Fund for Children and Families off to a good start, Jim Valvano, Dean Smith, and I chose this new children's fund for our winnings, as Team North Carolina, for our participation in the Crosby golf tournament at Bermuda Run. This was the first year that the tournament has been held in North Carolina, and I am delighted that some of the proceeds will benefit victimized children. We won $6,000 with our combination of skill and hand-to-eye coordination—that, and a real friendly handicap/score adjustment! I announced to Kathryn Crosby that our winnings would go to our children's fund.[3] Our three children didn't have a fund and each of them could use one!—no, this was to help start up the North Carolina children's fund.

There's more: At this time, it is my pleasure to present Mr. Don Angell, the developer of Bermuda Run, the new home of the Crosby "Clambake,"[4] who has asked for this opportunity to make a special presentation. Don, we're delighted to have you here today, and we look forward to your comments.

---

[1]Gordon Berg; native of Minnesota; was graduated from University of Minnesota. Former social worker; former director, St. Paul (Minnesota) Day Care Program; executive director, Council of Social Agencies, Norfolk, Virginia, 1945-1950; associate director, Community Chests and Councils of America, 1950-1955; executive director, United Way of Mecklenburg and Union Counties, 1955-1978; various posts with Foundation for the Carolinas, from 1958, including secretary, executive director, 1975-1986, senior consultant, and president emeritus; author. Gordon Berg to Jan-Michael Poff, June 20, 1990.

[2]Senator Robert G. Shaw (R-Guilford) introduced two bills to aid abused children on April 8, 1987, both of them supported by Governor Martin. S.B. 322, "A Bill to Permit the Allocation of Individual Income Tax Refunds to the North Carolina Fund for Children and Families," was ultimately referred to the Children and Youth Committee. S.B. 334, "A Bill to Permit the Allocation of Corporate Income Tax Refunds to the North Carolina Fund for Children and Families," was sent to the Senate Finance Committee and later rereferred to the Children and Youth Committee, which in turn produced a substitute bill that was delivered to the Appropriations Committee for consideration.

Speaking of S.B. 322 and S.B. 334 in his address to the North Carolina Victims Assistance Network Conference, April 30, 1987, Martin said that the revenue generated by both bills would "be distributed by the North Carolina Fund for Children and Families Commission as incentive grants to local communities. There they would be used to fund community-based programs that provide a family-focused, comprehensive, and coordinated approach to dealing with abused children and their families." Unfortunately for the governor, neither measure passed the General Assembly by the end of the 1987 session. N.C. Senate Journal, 1987, 192, 194, 364, 411, 542.

[3]Kathryn Grant (Olive Grandstaff) became the second wife of Bing Crosby on October 24, 1957. Who Was Who in America, 1977-1981, 132-133.

[4]A clambake had been a highlight of Crosby's West Coast golf tournament since the 1930s; the sporting event was popularly known by that name, according to Martin's February 10, 1986, statement in New York City.

STATE EMPLOYEES ASSOCIATION OF NORTH CAROLINA

CHARLOTTE, SEPTEMBER 11, 1986

["This has not been my best day," Governor Martin wrote at the top of his September 11 speech to SEANC members. "The Southeast Regional Compact for Low-Level Radioactive Waste just picked us Number 1. So go easy on me, hunh?"]

Being here with you, today, to participate in your Third Annual Convention is a real pleasure, and I am grateful to your officers and directors for providing me this opportunity to speak again to my fellow state employees. I even remembered to wear my SEANC pin. Of all the rewards that I have received as governor during the last twenty months, none equals the opportunity I have had to work with you as a partner, a friend, and as a fellow state employee, dedicated to the task of broadening the dimensions of human aspiration and achievement for those of us who serve the people of North Carolina. Yes, I like my job, and I hope it's getting so that, more often, you like yours.

We have worked together at a time of great adjustment in the relationships and responsibilities of our federal, state, and local governments. Undoubtedly, this process of change will be with us for some time to come; so will the uncertainty it brings. Yet, I have confidence that we will emerge from these changes a few years hence as a stronger and better state and nation. I have that confidence because I believe the people of North Carolina and the United States will make it so with their dedication, hard work, and commitment to an inspiring purpose.

The future of state government is intricately interwoven into the fabric of our private sector. Business growth means new jobs in the marketplace, jobs that are desperately needed by an expanding labor force in our growing cities and our adjusting rural areas—and more taxable income all around.

New and better jobs fuel the engine of economic growth. Jobs create taxes that finance the services and support the programs government provides. Without business and industry, without private sector jobs, government as we know it would not exist. We couldn't afford it. This means that North Carolina must continue to grow. Its economy must continue to expand if we expect to meet the needs of our citizens, even as the federal government increasingly reduces grants to the states.

Last month, on August 27 to be exact, I announced *North Carolina's Blueprint for Economic Development: A Strategic Business Plan for Quality Growth*. Now you may ask, Did he bring the wrong speech? What does this have to do with state employees? The answer is very simple: Everything!

It's the right speech. For one thing, state government, and state employees, are vital to the success of this plan. All of us share the responsibility of providing the quality public services and delivery systems that will make North Carolina attractive and more competitive in economic development. We share the task of providing these things efficiently and effectively, always striving to increase productivity in a way that reduces the burden of taxation upon the public.

We are the architects and the builders of our state's future, and we will be judged by how we design and shape that destiny. To paraphrase President John F. Kennedy: To meet our urgent responsibilities will take determination, dedication, and hard work, but I believe state employees are more than equal to the task. It will take vision and boldness, but we are a bold people.

There's also the realization that state employment can't thrive unless the North Carolina economy thrives. When it is squeezed by a recession, you get squeezed, too. So you have a stake in a good business-sector climate. In talking with some railroad executives, I appreciated their philosophy that they can make money only if their customers do. The same philosophy is similar for us: Without a strong economy, we face more demands for services and can afford less rewards for service.

I'll give you an example. In 1982, our state and nation were held in the grip of a widening recession. People who had devoted entire lives to building careers in the private sector were jobless for the first time. There was no pay raise for North Carolina state employees that year, but jobs were relatively safe, with few layoffs. That was probably as much as could be expected.

How have you fared since then? Let's look at incomes first. State employees today are earning approximately 25 percent more than they were in 1981, five years ago, in across-the-board salary increases. That's almost 4.5 percentage points better than the average improvement for all Americans, including the private sector, during the same period of time. All right, about half that edge came from the couple percent extra when the legislature outbid my cost-of-living increase of 3.5 percent and gave you a slightly bigger average boost, but paid for it out of nonrecurring, one-shot revenues. Of course, I'll be the one who politically has to figure out how to pay for it next year and thereafter—that's my job, right? Let's agree on this: You don't think my pay proposal was adequate; neither do I. It's just the best I could do with recurring revenues.[1] My point is, you get better when taxable business gets better.

Second, let's examine state government's level of employment—that is, how many people have jobs. Currently the number of permanent, full-time employees subject to the State Personnel Act is well above 66,000, representing the group from which your association has recruited a majority of its members. This accounts for a 4 percent increase in employment since December of 1982. This means that state government employment, which has increased by more than 2,500 people, grew at a faster rate than employment expanded nationwide.

State government employment today stands at an all-time record high, even after a bit of belt tightening. Expecting more federal cuts than we got, I slowed new hirings to fill vacancies. That way, few people lost jobs due to a 2 percent reduction in positions, because they were mostly vacant positions. No, we didn't quite pull it off perfectly; but we did reasonably well, and I would welcome your advice how to do better if it has to happen again.

Not included in the figures I've just used are faculty members of our state-supported institutions of higher learning, community colleges, public school teachers, and exempt state employees. All of these sectors have increased substantially, as well, with the exception of exempt employees. Here there's no valid comparison, because I virtually cut in half this classification by restoring Personnel Act protection to some 700.

My belief, as governor, is that the number of exempt employees in the executive department should be held to a minimum and certainly no more than is needed for the effective management of my administration. I said I would reform that abuse, and I did, and your association has taken notice. Perfect? No, but a vast improvement.

Having spoken about state government employment in broad terms that affect all of you, I want to turn your attention to some specific areas in which we have achieved remarkable results. Many of you in the audience are women and/or minorities. Some of you are single parents. In years past, upward mobility for many of you into administrative and professional positions of management has been difficult, at best. But I have always held the position that opportunity should never be limited except by one's own abilities, education, talents, experience, willingness to accept responsibility, and motivation. This is, and will remain, the policy of my administration.

Since becoming governor, I have undertaken several new programs and adopted aggressive policies to ensure fair and equal treatment for all state employees. By Executive Order 18, issued on July 1, 1985, I established a firm equal employment opportunity program to guarantee the effective use of all of our human resources.[2] This is supported by the Model Cooperative Education Program designed to attract more women and minorities into state government employment, and the New Horizons program which allows them to enhance their skills and advance according to their potential.[3]

This has enabled us to increase the number of women in highly visible, well-paying positions, as administrators, to 20.4 percent of the persons in this category, including a third of my cabinet members. Women also hold 40 percent of all management and related professional positions in state government.[4] Employment and promotions of minorities, as I reported earlier, also are increasing, and opportunities are being opened up in new job classifications.

Working with Dick Lee, our state personnel director, we have developed other new programs. Last year, I reported to you that we had initated a personal safety and health effort for all state employees through Executive Order 6. Since that time, we have published and implemented a model health manual to aid all departments design specific programs for their workers. This year, I am expanding the safety and health program to include monitoring and technical assistance in administering the state's workers' compensation self-insurance plan.

Our Employees' Assistance Program to help employees get professional help for personal problems affecting the quality of their work also has met with success. Participation is voluntary, or it may be encouraged by management if there is a noticeable decline in job performance. However, all assistance is offered in a confidential manner and in a way to protect an individual's sense of dignity. So far, this program already has served over 700 employees, more than 75 percent of whom have returned to equal or better job performance.[5]

There are many other intiatives I could review with you today, but you have been, or will be, informed about them through your individual departments or agencies. The point of my brief review is to show my interest in and concern for all of you.

Expanding the employment opportunities and improving the welfare of state employees and their families, as I said earlier, has been made possible by North Carolina's robust economic growth in the private sector. Some sectors have not fared as well. We have lost some 35,000 textile jobs in the last five years, and as Charles Kuralt said recently on CBS news, "Our farmers have taken all that the market-place and the good Lord could dish out to them." Agricultural employment statewide has declined 48 percent in the last decade, and tobacco manufacturing employment is down 7 percent in the same period. Fortunately, most of these displaced workers have found new employment within the state.

The year 1985 was our best year ever. Statewide unemployment was down to its lowest point in seven years, and it's still holding as the third-lowest and best in America. Since January of this year, total employment in North Carolina has increased by 134,000, a gain of 4.5 percent. Growth is continuing, but in a significantly different way. Most of the new jobs are in government—federal, state, and local; services, retail trade, finance, insurance, and real estate.

There are adjustments we must make in our strategy to help traditional industries, encourage new entrepreneurships, assist small businesses, and recruit new firms. The North Carolina *Blueprint for Economic Development* is a first step toward accomplishing the goal of creating new jobs, stimulating business growth, and increasing the revenue base of the state. Critical elements of this plan expect us to build upon continued educational reform, our Roads to the Future program, eliminating adult illiteracy, expanding job and skill training, and expanding our so-called infrastructure. These are some of our major priorities.

It's a good, solid plan, with no trendy funny business, no pork barrel, and no suggestion for risky investment of your pension fund! My point is that you benefit from a strong economy. State employees are vital partners in the success of this initiative, for the challenge belongs to us as a united people in one united state. If we work together; if we put aside our own self-interest for the welfare of all North Carolinians; if we realize that North Carolina state government won't work if its able-bodied citizens can't all find work—we will achieve an inspiring purpose.

North Carolina is a great and thriving state, in large part, because of the dedication and commitment of our state employees. We have always been the master of change, not its servant. We can always do better. If we set ourselves to this task, we have nothing to fear; we have everything to gain, both for ourselves and our state. That's why I like my job; that's why I hope you like yours.

---

[1]For related press release, see "Governor Responds to State Employees Association," Raleigh, May 8, 1986, Governors Papers, James G. Martin.

[2]See *N.C. Session Laws, 1985*, 1467-1470, for text of Executive Order Number 18.

[3]Martin announced the inauguration of the New Horizons program in his June 13, 1986, address to the North Carolina Federation of Business and Professional Women's Clubs. The program was established to assist women and minority state government employees to "prepare for opportunities to perform at the highest potential, advance according to their ability, and realize their full work potential; provide a pool of quali-fied . . . employees to be recruited for professional, managerial, and technical job open-ings which allow for the effective and efficient delivery of services to the public; and prepare women for employment in traditionally male-dominated occupations."

[4]Speaking to the Federation of Business and Professional Women's Clubs, the gover-nor noted that three women—Grace Rohrer, Administration; Patric Dorsey, Cultural Resources; and Helen Powers, Revenue—had been appointed to cabinet posts, and more were assigned as department-level deputies and assistant secretaries. "Between January 1 and December 31, 1985, more than 28 percent of the new officials and admin-istrators employed by state government were women. In addition, women represented more than 22 percent of all promotions in this category. This record exceeds any previous administration in history.

"Among management-related personnel, the figures are even higher: Women were 49 percent of all new managerial employees and almost 44 percent of all promotions, which exceeds the proportions of the mix from which the promotions were made. The same is true in professional classifications. Seventy percent of all new professional jobs and more than 51 percent of all promotions went to women."

[5]At this point, the governor inserted into his prepared text, "Talk with you [about] drug abuse. Is it a problem? So far, only isolated cases—no pattern; but incidence may not be too different from rest of North Carolina. Ask your help. Have you noticed I've resisted stampede to order mandatory tests. Not confident—don't have answer. [There-fore,] ask you to put together a task force to recommend fair and compassionate response. Cite Kemper: What should we do? Wait on law? Help?"

U.S. 64 BYPASS GROUNDBREAKING CEREMONY

ROCKY MOUNT, SEPTEMBER 12, 1986

We're going to get a lot of mileage out of this!

It is a pleasure to be here, today, for a number of reasons, not the least of which is the fact that this is the first time I've had a chance to speak to this many members of the Board of Transportation in a long time—the first chance we've had to celebrate since the enactment of my Roads to the Future [program]. Since you all usually meet in Raleigh, and I live there for the time being, it seems strange that we should have to travel to Rocky Mount to see one another. It's not strange; rather, it's important to meet out among the people, so they can see what we're building, and I suspect that most of my board members are as comfortable out here on the roadside as they are around the board table in Raleigh.

In a minute or two I'm going to take advantage of the opportunity I have, today, to talk to so many of my Board of Transportation members; and I'm going to preach to the choir a bit. But first, let's talk about the reason that brings us together here this afternoon. You know, a groundbreaking is, by nature, a symbolic gesture. The first shovels of dirt turned here, today, will represent countless cubic yards of soil that will have to be moved as the surface of the ground is reshaped to forge the future.

The humble beginning we strike in a few minutes will set workers and machines in motion. It will initiate construction which will continue until 1990. That construction will produce a four-lane highway from here all the way to Tarboro. Additionally, the four-laning of U.S. 64 between Tarboro and Williamston has been programmed and will become reality along with many other vital projects, and then on down to Plymouth.

Construction, or plans for construction, are in motion on other sections of this highway, like the bypass around Plymouth; and similar work, or planning, is under way on U.S. 17 and U.S. 64. The chart which is in front of this platform illustrates what I'm talking about, and I am proud to say that many of the projects shown on it have been added by my administration.

Yes, today's ceremony is symbolic of the start of another single project, but much more is embodied in this action than just the start of the four-lane highway between Rocky Mount and Tarboro. I promise you that what you will witness is Jim Martin's unbendable commitment to bring modern, four-lane transportation to eastern and northeastern North Carolina. We'll keep the pavers rolling from here to Tarboro, to Williamston, to Plymouth, and other projects to connect us as one united state. There are some gaps remaining in the map, but in my judgment, we are building what will eventually be a connected system. That's my goal.

We can't make every road a four-lane highway, but we can complete some four-lane arteries in each part of our state. It will take time, and it will take money. We will invest both.

I took the steps needed to make such highway plans come true last spring when I proposed the Roads to the Future program. That program, which eventually passed the legislature with bipartisan support, does a number of things; and it makes it possible for us to look forward to a day in the future when Highway 64 and other desperately needed highway projects will be off the drawing board and on the ground.

The Roads to the Future program ensures our ability to match federal funds. It allows us to return maintenance work to acceptable levels, levels high enough to regain some of the ground we've lost to inflation over the years. It allows us to continue the vitally important safety and small urban programs which touch millions of lives every day, and save countless lives every year. It allows for an improved highway resurfacing program which is vital to protect the investment we have in place.

And, for this one year only, the legislature authorized a state supplemental construction program, something we haven't had in North Carolina in a number of years. That's an important part of the Roads to the Future program, because it will allow us to get more bang for the buck, more action for the taxes, more saving for the paving, when it comes to highways. It will mean we can build some projects that will get the job done without some of the extra features often required by the federal construction program. Eventually, the tax and transfer package adopted by the legislature will provide more than $200 million a year for highway work. Believe me, we can use every penny of it.

That leads me to my next point. We still haven't finished the job when it comes to providing you with the most for your highway tax dollars, but then, I'm not finished trying, either. First, let's talk about the legislation needed in 1987. Secretary Harrington has already started working with the legislature.

We need laws that allow local governments to do more to protect future right-of-way from development. Money that we can save, if we don't have to spend it on land acquisition, can be put to work where it really counts: buying pavement. It's estimated that our current practices cause us to spend $20 million to $30 million more than we need to for highways around our larger cities because we don't protect the proposed right-of-way, and smart people build on it. I want to save that—more saving for the paving!

Without getting into the highway building business, local governments need to have the ways and means to become part of the solution; and to help reach better, faster solutions, they need the right to participate financially. They, along with the state DOT, need to be able to work with private developers who are willing to share the load with the taxpayers—at a bargain that can speed up their project if they donate right-of-way. That saves money to spend on other projects, you see—more honey for the money.

Another goal is: We need the state construction funding made permanent, at a higher level. That higher level of funding, incidentally, would not be produced by asking for higher taxes. Roads to the Future revenue will grow automatically next year—when the cost of the Drivers' Education program is transferred to the General Fund, which already pays for all other education costs. And Highway Fund collections will now do a better job of keeping up with inflation because, for the first time, some of our motor fuel taxes will be tied to the price of fuel and not to the number of gallons sold.

We'll need your support to get action, during the next session of the legislature, on the state projects fund and the right-of-way protection act, so we can get the job done. I'm also counting on the people I've brought to Raleigh on the Board of Transportation to continue the money-saving, good-government initiatives they've begun and to find more ways to stretch tax dollars and to provide more efficiency. Here are some specific examples.

I want you to continue and expand the maintenance savings programs you've begun. When fully implemented, our program of contracting many services now performed by state workers will save millions. Millions—millions, every year, and it will be done without painful forced reductions in the work force. Normal turnover will match the pace we can achieve.

I want you to continue the emphasis on resurfacing, proper maintenance, and those vital safety and small improvement projects. And look for more ways you can get a million dollars' worth of benefit for a fraction of that amount of money. I want you to think with imagination at every turn. Remember, for example, the flexibility that exists in such things as the resurfacing program. With some creative thought, that program can produce a lot of widening projects, turn lanes, and the like.

I want you to continue to do what you have done since I appointed you. Put the public good above political gamesmanship. You have created a record to be proud of, and I am proud of you for it.

Lastly, beyond the legislative changes and internal efficiencies, more needs to be done. It is time to bring more dependability to the early years of the Transportation Improvement Program. It is time to make a major change that has been suggested from both sides of the political fence, and as governor, it is my place to step forward as its advocate.

I, today, am proposing that we change the TIP from a single ten-year document to a two-stage plan, one that has a higher degree of reliability to its first half and [a] higher degree of flexibility to respond to changing needs in its "out years." Furthermore, I am requesting that the TIP which comes before the board for consideration and adoption in December fit the new mold. The change is overdue and no benefit will result from further delay.

A number of steps will be necessary. I will not detail all of them at this point, but as guidance to the board, I will mention four specifics.

We should return to a seven-year TIP as established by general statute.[1] That plan would show schedules for such things as planning, engineering, right-of-way acquisition, and construction.

Beyond the seven-year period of the plan, we should consider an additional three to four years of projects for study and right-of-way protection. That additional period will allow for greater right-of-way protection, especially in our urban areas where land costs are skyrocketing, often to as much as 60 percent of a project's cost! Greater right-of-way protection will mean more than savings; it will also mean that we will be able to increase the accuracy of our project cost projections. Most importantly, it will give us a chance to see how well each city responds to protect the right-of-way when a project is designated for such protection, before we decide to commit to put it in the seven-year schedule.

Since the TIP's major funding source is federal aid, the program should match the federal fiscal year. It should, for administrative purposes, begin on October 1 and end on September 30. And finally, I think you should develop and adopt a formula which rates projects based on their benefits. The general statute directs the Board of Transportation to develop priorities.[2] I want you to do that, in part, by utilizing a formula which considers such factors as cost, economic development potential, and environmental impact. Participation by developers and/or local governments which lowers the state cost of a project—right-of-way protection, for example—can thus be reflected in the cost-benefit ratio.

This groundbreaking is a grand occasion. It represents a step towards the future. We must do what needs to be done to ensure that these grand occasions continue. That is why I am proposing change. That is why you should demand it.

---

[1]G.S. 143B-350(f)(4).
[2]G.S. 143B-350(f)(1).

NATIONAL CONFERENCE ON COOPERATIVE EDUCATION

WINSTON-SALEM, SEPTEMBER 23, 1986

[Winston-Salem State University provided the forum for the following address.]

For a number of years, cooperative education has been one of the building blocks of our historically black colleges and universities, providing students both a new perspective of their academic experience and an opportunity to gain an insight into the real world of work. At no time in the history of these institutions is it more important than it is today, when student financial aid is declining; for without an opportunity for full-time students to earn income, many of them would never have the chance to complete their work toward a degree.

Cooperative education was an innovation which emerged from the University of Cincinnati almost sixty-five years ago and involved only twenty-five students. It was called cooperative education because it demanded cooperative arrangements between the university and employers. Because it was a new idea its acceptance was slow, and it was only until after World War II that it began to flourish on campuses across our nation. At this point in the history of higher education, innovation was the wave of the future.

Here in North Carolina the partnership in cooperative education was confined, until recent years, to the private sector. Some of the corporate pioneers are represented at this conference: RJR Nabisco, Hanes Hosiery, IBM, Westinghouse, Wachovia Bank and Trust Company, Burlington Industries, Duke Power, Piedmont Aviation, and Sears, to name only a few. It is because of these pioneers that the diversity of this program has expanded greatly and has been extended to a growing number of black institutions.

But where did state government, until recently, fit into this partnership? Quite frankly, it didn't. When I became governor in 1985, it was evident that many of our state government agencies and departments were experiencing great difficulty in recruiting qualified and experienced minority applicants. So, we set out to do something about it through a new Model Cooperative Education Program administered by the Office of State Personnel. My administration recognized, early on, that cooperative education is a viable system to help meet state government's need for career-oriented minority students who seek opportunities in public service fields. Moreover, we reasoned that this program was an organized approach to correcting the underrepresentation of minorities in management, middle-management, and professional and technical careers.

These are worthy goals, indeed, but cooperative education in and of itself, alone, is not enough. Education is a lifelong process; the world of work is constantly changing, and the need for training and retraining on the job is a fact we must face with new urgency in the years ahead. To address these demands, our Office of State Personnel also developed a companion program, called New Horizons, which permits state government minority employees to enhance their skills at work and to advance according to their own potential. Under the leadership of Dick Lee, the director of state personnel, we are constantly seeking even more innovative approaches to making equal opportunity a living example in state government.

One of the chief benefits of our Model Cooperative Education Program in state government has been our increasing partnership in programs offered by our historically black colleges and universities, as well as our linkage to the institutions themselves. Another benefit has been the remarkable increase we have achieved in the percentage of minorities now holding highly visible, well-paying positions as administrators. Significantly, I have appointed many to broad-gauge leadership positions other than those traditionally reserved for black administrators. Instead of continuing assistant secretaries for minority affairs and minority businesses, I have appointed them assistant secretaries for all small business, for all law enforcement and military affairs; deputy secretary for all programs at the Department of Administration; cabinet secretary for all corrections; my personal secretary; my senior adviser on all higher education.

These results are gratifying, but we still have a long way to go toward helping our historically black colleges and universities and the students who attend them. I'm pleased to say that we've already made a good start in this direction. Last year, working with my senior adviser for higher education, Dr. Lee Monroe, I announced the first Governor's Initiative on Historically Black Colleges and Universities in state history. This initiative seeks to identify and implement programs that will help them achieve greater parity among the institutions of higher learning in North Carolina. Recently the first annual plan, mandated by the executive order creating the initiative, was delivered to my desk. I am pleased to report that it is an articulate, comprehensive plan, and I would like to share with you some of the major recommendations we now have under consideration relating to cooperative education.

There exists a great human potential for conducting research at our historically black colleges and universities. However, in many instances the resources of these institutions are not adequate to support or complement efforts of students to gain firsthand knowledge of the latest technology and disciplinary developments. Our first priority, then, is to expand public and private funding of facilities and equipment. As governor and as the first chief executive of our state to serve as honorary chairman of the United Negro College Fund, I am dedicated to this very important task. Government cannot provide all of the means, of course, but strong public-private partnerships can do much to fill this void.

Our next logical step is to work toward expansion of our Model Cooperative Education Program, thereby continuing to increase the opportunities afforded students to earn and learn the practical aspects of career development simultaneously. We plan to accomplish this expansion by making more information available to students regarding internships and cooperative education experiences through the Department of Administration. Some of these opportunities, as recommended, will include two positions in the International Division of our Department of Commerce and additional experiences for criminal justice majors within our Department of Correction.

The Department of Human Resources, as the largest department of state government, has been one of the major participants in cooperative education. However, our goal is to raise the department's level of participation significantly by providing at least one new, permanent, ongoing position in each of its divisions. We also plan to take the same approach in the Department of Transportation, Department of Revenue, and the Department of Natural Resources and Community Development. Only through the involvement of all departments within the jurisdiction of the executive branch can we expand the breadth of career diversification for minority students.

The Governor's Initiative on Historically Black Colleges and Universities embraces many subjects of mutual interest that time does not permit me to cover in my address today. Let me say, however, that it does not overlook any area of concern which has been identified or expressed to me by the presidents and chancellors of our black institutions. In this respect, it is one of the most complete plans ever to come to my attention, and it has my full support.

If a cooperative education program is to survive in any academic environment, the faculty of each institution must have faith in its value as a part of the student's total education. In this respect, those who lead our historically black colleges and universities must continue to be the principal agents of persuasion. At this point, I also want to emphasize that cooperative education is not an experience confined to our flag-ship business firms. We must constant[ly] seek to expand employer participation, and the greatest opportunity for this expansion is among small businesses.

The secret of successful cooperative education programs rests upon building strong partnerships. Our North Carolina black colleges and universities are fortunate, for we have always been known as a state whose leading position in education has been built on the ability of all sectors to work together. Almost 1,000 institutions of higher learning throughout our nation are participating today in cooperative educa-tion ventures. As this growth continues, black institutions cannot allow themselves to fall behind. The opportunity to become the lode-star of learning in a new dimension of education awaits you. We can achieve this goal only if we continue to work as a united partnership to make this become truly one united state.

DEDICATION OF BOONE VISITORS CENTER

BOONE, SEPTEMBER 25, 1986

Returning to the high country is always a welcomed break from the affairs of state in Raleigh, but the dedication of this visitors center here in the heart of our magnificent mountains affords me a special pleasure this afternoon. Thank you for asking me to share in this celebration.

As I look at this building, which will serve as the center of tourist information for more than 1.5 million visitors to Watauga and sur-rounding counties each year, I am again reminded of what can be accomplished when our public and private sectors work together. Partnerships have always been a vital part of North Carolina's eco-nomic growth and the enhancement of its quality of life, and this facility, headquarters for High Country Host and the Boone Area Chamber of Commerce, represents one of the strongest ones in our state. It was because of partnerships that North Carolina exceeded $4.6 billion in travel revenues in 1985, posting an all-time record for our state.[1] In fact, travel and tourism account for the fastest growing segment of our economy and provide important jobs for more than 200,000 of our fellow citizens.

This growth has been made possible, in large measure, by the com-bining of private and public resources. A good example of this is High Country Host, the tourism and travel promotion arm of Alleghany,

Ashe, Avery, Mitchell, and Watauga counties. A little more than six years ago, a small group of businessmen and developers from these counties met to explore ways of expanding destination travel to this area; High Country Host grew out of that meeting, and today it has more than 225 members who contribute to its support. Since that time, travel and tourism expenditures in each of these counties have doubled, attesting to the value of this strong partnership.

The state of North Carolina has also become an enthusiastic supporter of your efforts, as represented by this remodeled center which was purchased and donated for use by the Department of Transportation. I join you, today, in sharing your pride in this splendid facility.

In addition to this visitors center here in Boone, the state also owns eight welcome centers on the major highways entering North Carolina. The last of these centers, located on I-77 near Charlotte, was dedicated last May 15 and completes the building program which was begun more than a decade ago. This and other centers to provide information and assist travelers are a growing part of our marketing strategy to increase tourism in all parts of North Carolina. The good people of northeastern North Carolina have asked us to talk with them about a similar partnership for a visitors center for tourists on Highway 17.

Last year, the state also increased its advertising budget by more than 50 percent. This has resulted in a substantial increase in out-of-state inquiries about vacation destinations, resorts, and conference facilities. Another factor in our favor has been the decline in gasoline prices, which has encouraged more travel; that also will help us to build more roads to our future. Coupled with a decline in travel abroad due to a rise of other currencies versus the dollar, more Americans are finding interest in their native country.

There are many other ways, of course, in which we promote North Carolina as a tourist attraction. A travel film, *North Carolina: A Special Kind of Splendor*, is sponsored by the Department of Commerce Division of Travel and Tourism. Last year it was viewed by more than 15 million out-of-state residents, bringing its total audience to 40 million people who have seen it.

The state also gives a helping hand to local communities through its matching-fund program to improve tourism marketing strategies. Currently, we are spending $250,000 to provide additional resources to promote our tourism-oriented communities. I am delighted to inform you, also, that today Commerce Secretary Howard Haworth and I are announcing a new regional office for economic development to be located in Lenoir. As part of our *Blueprint for Economic Develop-*

ment, it will serve this nine-county northwestern region with developers who can only be evaluated on how well they serve you—since they can't make their record on Charlotte, Winston-Salem, or Asheville.

All of these state efforts, however, are a supplement and not a substitute for local initiative. State government certainly can do much to help attract visitors to North Carolina, but the job of bringing them to your area rests with you. Travel is a competitive business and demands your best promotion efforts. I am confident that this new center will enhance your work.

There is much reason for optimism in the travel industry. Our economy remains strong, but optimism bears fruit only to the extent that we strengthen the partnership between our communities, private interests, and state government. Dedication of this visitors center is proof that we're working toward that goal. It's a good example of what we can do when we all work together as one united state.

---

[1]Speaking before the Avery County Chamber of Commerce, Banner Elk, September 25, 1985, Martin noted that spending by tourists visiting North Carolina grew from $1 billion to over $4 billion annually during the previous decade. The governor attributed the increase to improved proficiency in promotion and marketing by public and private travel and tourism interests.

LINCOLNTON-LINCOLN COUNTY AIRPORT DEDICATION

LINCOLNTON, OCTOBER, 3, 1986

I am very pleased that you have asked me to be a participant in this historic dedication today. The occasion, indeed, is historic in two respects. First, this ultramodern general aviation facility is the first to have been completed since the adoption, by our General Assembly, of an 80 percent funding formula for airport construction.[1] But the second, and most important, reason for this celebration is that it underscores dramatically the General Assembly's urgent need to get on with the work of establishing a permanent transportation trust fund which is replenished annually from continuing appropriations.

Creation of this trust fund was a critical part of my "Roads to the Future" legislative package which I presented to the General Assembly during its last session. A majority of that package was eventually adopted with bipartisan support. The trust fund, however, was replaced by a one-time supplemental construction program.

For the first time in more than a decade, the accomplishments of the last legislative session offer some light at the end of the tunnel in moving desperately needed highway projects off the drawing board and on the ground. The funding that was provided will enable us to match federal highway dollars, to return maintenance work to acceptable levels, and to move urban and rural projects ahead more rapidly. Eventually, the tax and transfer package adopted by the General Assembly will provide more than $200 million annually for highway work. When we couple this funding with savings which we are achieving as a result of greater efficiencies, the results are compounded.

Highways are important. They link our children to our schools, our workers to jobs, our tourists to vacation destinations, our industries to markets, and our state to the nation. But there are other urgent transportation needs, as well, and air, rail, sea, and public transit—all of which are vital elements of a total transportation system—need our attention, too.

The trust fund which I proposed in the last legislative session addressed these needs. In brief, it would have created separate accounts for highway, air, rail, seaport, and public transit improvements. Continuing appropriations to each account would have been pledged from existing sales and use taxes in each of those areas. For example, funding for airport construction and other air travel improvements would have come from existing sales and use taxes on aircraft, aircraft fuels, lubricants, parts, and avionics.

Today, North Carolina has more than forty airports that are twenty years old and older, and by 1991 we'll add another ten to this growing list. These are, in reality, obsolete airports that are in need of major lighting and paving rehabilitation work. We expect the cost of bringing these existing airports up to acceptable standards to exceed $40 million, and that's in terms of today's dollars, not tomorrow's inflated dollars. In addition, the North Carolina Airport System Plan recommends construction of twenty-four new publicly owned airports—airports like the one we dedicate today—by the year 2000 to provide maximum benefits to all of the state.

Three of these airports currently are under construction and should be open by mid 1987. In fact, we've obligated more than $7 million in airport construction funds since I came into office twenty-one months ago, but that's not enough. Based on the status of current local planning projects, we anticipate having between six and nine new airports ready for funding by 1991, at an estimated cost of about $44 million;

and by the year 2000 there will be another ten to twelve airports awaiting the money to build them.

Public airports, those that serve business, industrial, and private aircraft, represent only one side of the coin. The other side embraces airports that are served by major and commuter passenger airlines. Last year alone, these airports served almost 15 million air passengers —three times the number served a decade ago.[2]

Air passenger service into and out of our two major hubs and twelve feeder airports is literally mushrooming. North Carolina is rapidly becoming a major national and international center of air transportation. In 1980, Piedmont Airlines established its main connecting hub at Charlotte's Douglas International Airport; since then, passenger traffic has increased by almost 400 percent and continues to grow at a rapid pace. In 1987, American Airlines will establish its East Coast hub at the Raleigh-Durham Airport, and a similar growth rate is expected there. By having these two hubs, Piedmont and American can be expected to compete vigorously for feeder traffic from North Carolina's other airports, placing an enormous strain on these facilities. In addition, the growth of allied commuter airline services is expected to add a number of airports to the service list within the next five years.

All of these communities will require extensive financial outlays to rehabilitate runway and taxiway facilities, expand passenger terminal buildings, and provide improved instrument landing devices. Based on present estimates, the state's smaller airports face needs of about $55 million through 1991 to accommodate service demands. We can add to those costs another $4 [million] to enhance our weather reporting capability and $10 million to improve small airport safety by equipping them with instrument landing systems.

These are only some of the reasons, specifically related to air travel, why our General Assembly must begin efforts anew to ensure that North Carolina will have a permanently financed trust fund to meet our total transportation needs, both now and in the future. I worked during the last legislative session to achieve this goal, and I'll renew that effort in 1987, but I need your help. We don't need new taxes to get the job done. We need only the commitment of one united state.

It has taken more than a decade from planning to completion to bring the Lincolnton-Lincoln County Airport into being. I can appreciate your frustrations, your false starts, and the mighty effort that was invested in making this facility a reality. You had your own slogan for it: "We missed the train; let's don't miss the plane." Well,

North Carolina can't afford to miss the train, the bus, the plane, or the boat. Our economic well-being, our jobs for a growing labor force, the creation of new opportunities, and our link to the world, depend upon a modern, comprehensive transportation system.

This system won't fall into place automatically; we must make it happen. For the first time in the history of our state, we have it within our power to become a greater national giant than ever, dwarfing anything we have ever accomplished before. For North Carolinians, destiny is not a matter of chance, it is a matter of choice. There is no better proof of that than the airport we dedicate and celebrate today. So let us not follow where the path may lead us blindly, but go instead where there is no path and blaze new trails across our land. They will be trails of expanded transportation leading to a fuller life for all of our citizens in the future, created from the great dreams and great deeds of a great people.

---

[1]"An Act to Amend the Limitations on State Financial Aid to Aviation," *N.C. Session Laws, 1983*, c. 319, was ratified May 17, 1983.

[2]"We now have seventy-two publicly owned airports serving North Carolina," noted the governor at dedication ceremonies for the Brunswick County Airport, April 11, 1987, "and the number of commercial airlines flying into and out of our major airports has increased from five to nineteen in the last ten years."

STATEMENT ON PUBLIC SCHOOL CONSTRUCTION PROPOSAL

Raleigh, October 9, 1986

[The governor also discussed his school construction proposal before the North Carolina School Boards Association, Winston-Salem, November 13, 1986.]

Good afternoon, distinguished ladies and gentlemen, and thank you for accepting my invitation to attend this special news conference.

Only after providing for the establishment of our three branches of government, assuring their financial stability, allowing for the organization of local governments, and creating a system of free commerce, the framers of the North Carolina Constitution placed education as our state's first priority. "Religion, morality, and knowledge being necessary to good government and the happiness of mankind," they wrote in Article IX, "schools, libraries, and the means of education shall forever be encouraged."[1]

The authors of the constitution knew from experience that the very foundation of good government, and the fulfillment of individual opportunity, rested squarely upon an enlightened public; since the adoption of our first constitution by the Fifth Provincial Congress, in December, 1776, our state has held true to this commitment. North Carolina was the first state in the nation to establish a public university. We have always taken pride in our leadership; to follow is not in the true character of our state. It is our nature to lead, to pioneer the future.

It wasn't very long ago, however, that some of our people wondered if education even had a future. This awareness that something was wrong with our schools has led to healthy debate and change. Call it a rededication, if you will, but there is a new morning for education, not a twilight.

During the last session of the General Assembly, I proposed the largest budget for public education in the history of our state. It contained an increase of more than $40 million to reduce class size, establish a new teacher recruitment office, and expand teacher effectiveness training. We also achieved tuition grants and loans of $1,000 each—to be forgiven for teacher candidates who agree to teach for two years in subjects and geographic areas of acute shortage.

The most important investment our state can make is in its children. When public schools are successful they become a treasure. They can give life to local communities, contributing to their economic growth and social well-being. They can pave the road to employment, greater opportunity, and more productive lives. Our public schools, of course, cannot and should not supplant the family or the community in building character or instilling the values of a free society; nevertheless, all of us have an obligation to provide our children, and our children's children, with the best possible education. We have a responsibility to see that our schools develop the intellectual skills and reinforce the positive attitudes and behavior that will serve our children well.

Improving the professional and economic status of our best teachers is central to the task of making our schools what they should be. This is why I have made the teacher my first priority in terms of state responsibility. This is why I support the pilot teacher career ladder program, insisting that we have the funds available to implement this plan when it is ready to be implemented statewide.

Local school districts also have their responsibilities and priorities, and one of the most important is to provide adequate facilities which enhance the learning experience of our children. Currently there is a shortage of these facilities, estimated in one study published by the

North Carolina Department of Public Instruction, to total $2.2 billion. It is also estimated that about 54 percent of our school buildings are twenty years old or older, rendering them obsolete for today's needs. This situation has been called nothing less than a crisis by many local school officials.

Over the years, the state and federal governments have been sympathetic to this problem, allocating hundreds of millions of dollars for capital outlay purposes; the result has been a strong and viable government partnership. However, the responsibility of each level of government for education is clearly defined and supported by precedents. Capital outlay for school construction is the basic obligation of local government.

With adoption by Congress of the Gramm-Rudman deficit reduction act, and the subsequent decline in federal aid to state and local governments, it is clearly evident that state and local governments must now take their individual financial responsibilities more seriously than ever. Our General Assembly took this into account in 1983, and again in 1986, by restricting part of two one-half-cent local option sales tax increases for public school capital outlay purposes. Some counties have set aside a larger portion of the first tax increase for school construction than was required; some have not. In either case, school officials have complained that construction funds have not been generated rapidly enough to meet local needs. In addition, construction costs have escalated annually, and every year of delay in meeting current capital outlay requirements will cost more of our scarce dollars.

For too many years, the state of North Carolina has attempted to supplement local funding for school construction purposes without succeeding in solving the classroom shortage crisis. It is clearly time for a new approach which will get the job accomplished. I have requested your presence here, today, to announce a new and innovative statewide program which is designed to address, on a local option basis, North Carolina's pressing school construction problem.

What I am proposing, first, is an accurate assessment of school construction needs, in each district, based upon established standards and criteria set by the state. The purpose of this assessment will be to arrive at a reliable estimate of construction needs statewide. Although the figure of $2.2 billion has been suggested by one study, this figure has not been supported in uniform manner or detail.

Second, I am prepared to approach the 1987 session of the General Assembly with sponsorship of legislation requesting a statewide referendum on the question of issuing bonds in an amount sufficient to meet current school construction needs. These bonds, if approved by the voters, would then be issued and loaned on an as-needed basis to individual counties for school capital outlay purposes. Loans made by the state under this plan would be secured by counties with the restricted portion of the two one-half-cent local option sales tax increases, and if necessary, from other sources of unrestricted revenue. Each separate loan for such a purpose would be amortized on a separate repayment schedule. The state, under my proposal, would have statutory authority to intercept tax proceeds in the event a county defaulted in repayment.

Currently, counties are mandated by statute to set aside 25.56 percent of the combined local option sales taxes for school capital outlay expenditures. Based on this percentage of restricted funds, we have determined that almost $1.3 billion in triple-A bonds can be supported at an interest rate of 6.75 percent. If statewide needs should exceed this amount, the state could issue additional bonds based on meeting actual school construction requirements.

There are many advantages to the proposal I have just presented. One of these advantages is that this financing vehicle would be available to all counties on a local option basis. Participation would not be mandatory. For those who did participate, funds would be available to advance construction on a timely basis and as needed. Another advantage is that it would enable counties to obtain loans at a considerable savings in interest, since state bonds could be sold cheaper than local debt obligations. For example, the Office of State Treasurer estimates the savings on a $2.2 billion debt at approximately $100 million.

Further savings would be achieved by eliminating the necessity of separate bond referendums in each of our 100 counties. Moreover, a statewide bond issue would eliminate the uncertainty of voter response at the local level. A recent survey of North Carolinians indicated they are willing to support a tax increase to improve education. Surely it stands to reason they would approve a method to save money and avoid increased taxes for construction purposes.

Although there are no reliable estimates available, the savings in construction costs would be considerable. Construction could be undertaken today, at today's costs—not tomorrow's inflated costs. Finally, counties could leverage restricted sales tax revenues by building today and using sales tax as debt service payments. In effect, this means getting the use of the money before it is collected.

It is estimated that the two local option sales tax increases will generate an average of approximately $240 million annually. As I pointed out earlier, slightly more than 25.5 percent of this amount is restricted for school capital outlay. However, actual sales tax collections have been substantially larger. The one-half-cent tax collected last year, based on quarterly remittances from August 15 to May 15, exceeded $154 million. Therefore, our estimated average is a conservative figure.

The proposal I have presented to you today has been based upon figures provided by the state treasurer. I have discussed this plan with him, and he concurs in its feasibility. Whether or not I present this plan to the General Assembly will depend upon its acceptance by our county boards of commissioners, which are responsible for school construction financing in their individual jurisdictions. Some counties will not need this assistance; others will. Nevertheless, I welcome a response from all of you.

The need for public school construction in North Carolina is sweeping—yet, the extent of this actual need is largely undefined. We have before us, for the first time, a sound plan to determine this need and move forward in meeting it in a timely fashion. I am heartened by the swelling public support for constructive educational change in our state. I hope you will join with me in seizing this opportunity to make our time one of the truly great moments in the history of North Carolina education.

---

[1]Constitution, 1971, Article IX, Section 1, as quoted in *North Carolina Manual, 1987-1988*, 140.

OUTSTANDING VOLUNTEER RECOGNITION CEREMONY

NEW BERN, OCTOBER 10, 1986

[Parts of the following speech are identical to earlier remarks the governor delivered at volunteer recognition ceremonies in Raleigh, September 24, and Asheville, October 3, 1986. However, the final two paragraphs calling for aid to midwestern farmers were written by Martin and are unique to the New Bern address.]

From the colonists of 1710 to the colonial patriots of 1776, the people of eastern North Carolina depended upon one another for survival, first against hostile Indians and later against the repressive crown. Out of this mutual dependence, out of this willingness of neighbor to help neighbor, came the original spirit of volunteerism in

North Carolina. It is in this spirit, handed down from one generation to another, that I am pleased to be here today in this historic setting to honor you for your many selfless acts of commitment to others.[1] Your caring, compassionate ways should remind us all that the greatness and the goodness of North Carolina have always flowed from the heart—the volunteer heart.

The spirit of volunteerism is deeply ingrained in us as a people. From the very time of our settlement as a colony, the one guiding and distinguishing characteristic of North Carolinians has been our ability to join together to help one another. Never was this more important than when our forebears pioneered the building of a new state and nation in the coastal marshes and fertile fields that became the cradle of freedom and liberty; and today, the need for us to act as a community, working with one another, for one another, has never been greater.

In a recent survey, more citizens said that no matter how big government gets and no matter how many services it provides, it can never take the place of free-spirited volunteers. In other words, the people of North Carolina believe there simply isn't any substitute for gifts of service from the heart. As your governor, as a former congressman, and as a fellow citizen, I've always held firm to the idea that the size of government should be limited to those activities which we, as individuals, cannot provide for ourselves. We've learned many times over that our dollars and our energies are better utilized when we manage them ourselves than when we turn them over to government to administer for us.

And as citizens of North Carolina, we hold fast to this spirit of independence. Our state has always been a model for the nation. More than 71 percent, over 4 million individuals throughout North Carolina, perform volunteer work day-in and day-out. That's the best record in the United States.[2]

On this very special occasion we have every reason to feel good about ourselves, because the time we contribute to the welfare of others gives us a satisfaction that simply cannot be measured in material ways. Our gift becomes a personal treasure, to both ourselves and others. As recipients of the Governor's Award for Outstanding Volunteer Service, you represent the best of volunteerism in many fields of activity: schools, hospitals, volunteer fire departments, Community Watch programs, senior centers, Meals on Wheels, and countless other valuable programs. You are the champion givers, all of you—humanitarians who have earned a place in the history of North Carolina.

Our state, our nation, and the world will always need people like you. You reflect best upon the words of the great Jewish philosopher, Martin Buber, when he said, "It is not enough to be concerned with a cause; one must become involved." Today I am pleased, on behalf of the people of North Carolina, to express our deep appreciation to all of you for bestowing the greatest gift of all, your compassion, upon our fellow citizens. What you have done, and what we hope you will continue to do on behalf of others, will give living testimony to the true greatness of North Carolina.

I also have a request. It occurred to me while watching the news accounts of the severe flooding in Missouri, Kansas, and other mid-western states. North Carolina has been blessed by the generous response of farmers and others in those states to our needs caused by a severe and prolonged drought. We have said thank you every way we know how: letters, TV spots for their stations, hosting Ohio farmers at the Charlotte Motor Speedway. Now we have a new and fitting way to say thank you. We can send food, clothing, volunteers, whatever they need—straight from the grateful heart of North Carolina.[3]

Before you leave today, or soon after, let us know what you can do to help. I'll ask Mrs. Pulley[4] to find out what they need most, and then coordinate our volunteer response all across this one great united state. They helped us when we needed it most. Now, it's our turn: the best way to say thanks, America.

---

[1]Martin was speaking in Tryon Palace Auditorium.

[2]North Carolina's volunteers daily provided services valued at an estimated $1.2 million, Martin asserted during a recognition ceremony held in Raleigh, September 17, 1987.

[3]For related press releases, see "Governor Martin Seeks Volunteer Effort to Aid Flood Victims in Midwestern United States," Raleigh, October 10, 1986, and "Governor Martin Urges North Carolinians to Assist Midwest Flood Victims through Local Red Cross Chapters," Raleigh, October 16, 1986, Governors Papers, James G. Martin.

[4]Arlene C. Pulley; native of Raleigh; was graduated from Peace College; appointed administrative aide to state House Speaker James C. Green, 1975; administrative officer for Lieutenant Governor James C. Green, 1977-1984, manager of his 1980 campaign for lieutenant governor and 1984 primary campaign for governor; liaison for Democrats within Governor Martin's transition team; appointed executive director, Governor's Office of Citizen Affairs, 1985; office manager, Office of the Governor, since 1987; coordinator, Governor's Volunteer Program. Laurie Lamm, Office of the Governor, to Jan-Michael Poff, July 27, 1989.

NEWS CONFERENCE FOR AGRICULTURAL MEDIA

RALEIGH, OCTOBER 20, 1986

I am pleased, today, to announce to our farm families and the agribusiness community the appointment of a twelve-member Farm Finance Task Force. Its job will be to undertake, for the first time in history, a massive partnership effort by our three major sources of farm credit to refinance and retire, on a timely basis, the debt of farmers who are threatened with bankruptcy and foreclosure. The participants in this effort will be our commercial banking institutions, the Farm Credit System, and the Farmers Home Administration. Our goal is a simple one: By bringing together our banking community and our farm lending institutions, we will try to halt financial crises at their most personal and painful level, the loss of the family farm.

In recent years, primarily because of declining interest rates, private banks have become the major source of production loans for North Carolina farmers. The Farm Credit System has not been able to match these rates, and the Farmers Home Administration, simultaneously, has reduced funds for direct loans. However, the Congress has increased authorizations for loan guarantees through the Farmers Home Administration, and by using this vehicle to underwrite loans that otherwise would be considered credit risks, refinancing can be arranged with the remaining two sources of available money.

Basically, the three lending sources will work to restructure viable loans and, in addition, offer assistance to farmers in counseling and financial management. In effect, the process will redistribute the debt among three lending agencies rather than a single source, and thereby limit the potential loss to any single one. I believe that by working together on terms and payment schedules of outstanding loans, the three financial groups can help prevent some farm foreclosures and strengthen our agricultural sector.

I am pleased to announce that the Farm Finance Task Force will be chaired by Mr. James B. Powers, chairman and chief executive officer of Planters National Bank and Trust Company.[1] It also includes senior officers of six other private banks; our commissioner of agriculture, Jim Graham; Chief Executive Officer Maxey D. Love, Jr., of the Farm Credit Banks of Columbia;[2] and State Director Larry Godwin, of the Farmers Home Administration.[3] I have made available to you at this news conference a list of the entire membership, as well as a news release setting forth the three goals that the task force will seek to achieve.[4] I will not attempt to review all of the details in that release, but I will be happy to answer your questions at the conclusion of my announcement.

It is estimated that approximately 20 percent of our farmers operate with a dangerous debt-to-asset ratio. If a farmer's debt exceeds 40 percent of his assets, he is considered in a difficult financial situation. Moreover, on July 31, 1986, the Farmers Home Administration's North Carolina office reported that of about 9,000 loans on record, approximately 30 percent had been delinquent for at least seven months. Seven months is the threshold period for delinquency classification. This poses a serious problem to our agricultural economy, and we anticipate that it will get worse because we have just experienced the worst drought in history. The effects of the drought are compounded by depressed commodity prices, increasing production costs, declining agricultural exports, and other critical factors.

This is a bold step, to be sure, but it is also an historic one. It reflects a major shift in the attitudes of our major lenders, who now seem more willing to help us solve our farm credit crisis. The best way to help our farmers is to give them a safety ladder rather than a safety net. This is what the Farm Finance Task Force seeks to do. Its objective is to restore the financial independence of our farm families, bolster our agricultural economy, and lift us to a greater position of leadership in the most productive country on earth.

I want to thank Commissioner Graham for making this facility available to me, today, for this announcement. This is his fair, and I am here at his invitation.[5] In addition, I want to thank him for agreeing to serve on the task force and for supporting the partnership I have just announced.

---

[1]James B. Powers (1924-   ), born in Laurens, South Carolina; resident of Rocky Mount; was graduated from Furman University, University of North Carolina at Chapel Hill, and Louisiana State University; U.S. Navy, 1942-1945, 1950-1952. Accountant, Daniel Construction Co., Greenville, South Carolina, and vice-president, Wachovia Bank and Trust Co., Raleigh, before becoming director and executive committee chairman, Planters Corp. and Planters National Bank, Rocky Mount; vice-chairman, director, Atlantic States Bankcard Assn., Atlantic States Bankcard Properties, and of Atlantic States Bankcard Services Assn. James B. Powers to Jan-Michael Poff, December 1, 1989.

[2]Maxey D. Love, Jr. (1933-   ), born in Trenton, Florida; resident of Columbia, South Carolina; B.S., 1959, M.S., 1961, University of Florida. Various positions, 1962-1976, executive vice-president, 1976-1980, appointed president, 1985, Columbia Bank for Cooperatives; appointed executive vice-president, chief operating officer, 1980, Central Bank for Cooperatives, Denver, Colorado; chief executive officer, Farm Credit Banks of Columbia, 1985-1988; chief executive officer, since 1988, Farm Credit Bank of Columbia. Maxey D. Love, Jr., to Jan-Michael Poff, December 8, 1989.

[3]Larry W. Godwin (1948-   ), native of Dunn; B.S., Campbell College (later University), 1970. President, Godwin Real Estate and Development Co., Inc.; state director,

since 1982, Farmers Home Administration. Larry W. Godwin to Jan-Michael Poff, December 5, 1989.
    [4]Press release, "Governor Martin Announces Creation of Farm Finance Task Force," Raleigh, October 20, 1986, Governors Papers, James G. Martin.
    [5]The governor unveiled his plan for the Farm Finance Task Force during the State Fair, which was organized and operated by the Department of Agriculture. The press conference was held in the Hall of Fame Room, Jim Graham Building, North Carolina State Fairgrounds.

AWARDS PRESENTATION, GOVERNOR'S BUSINESS COMMITTEE FOR EDUCATION

Raleigh, October 23, 1986

We are here, today, for two reasons: first of all, to honor our state's exemplary teachers. They have been selected for special recognition because they, representative of so many others, have given their students the inspiration to excel; and through their efforts, they have given new life to their schools, contributing to the economic growth of their communities and social well-being of their fellow citizens. The second reason we are here is to honor the outstanding business firms and community organizations that have shown extraordinary interest in their local schools and thereby have made them a local treasure. The list of contributions by these companies and organizations is long and impressive. It demonstrates that North Carolina is moving forward rapidly in the formation of stronger business-education partnerships.

Today, on a scale unmatched in our history, educators are going into our business firms to learn more about how our system of private enterprise works. Business men and women are going into our schools to share their knowledge and experience. As business executives and educators, we are keenly aware of education's role in producing informed and productive citizens. We also see increasing evidence that education has a direct impact on employment, productivity and growth, and on the ability of our state and nation to compete in the world economy.

Therefore, we cannot fail to respond to some alarming danger signals that are revealed in recent surveys of our schools. As a state, North Carolina ranks thirty-second in teacher salaries. Educators are abandoning our classrooms in record numbers in favor of better paying jobs in the private sector. Moreover, many of them are taking early retirement, rather than remain in our schools. Our best and brightest college-bound students are not opting for careers as teachers. The Basic Education plan, when fully implemented, will require more than 10,000 additional teachers. When we add all of the hard numbers together, the teacher shortage could approach a crisis.

Throughout my term as governor, I have supported the multiyear pilot program to establish a career ladder for teachers, insisting that we prioritize adequate funds to implement this program when it is ready to go statewide. This past year I proposed, and the General Assembly approved, $5 million for scholarships and loans to attract the best and the brightest of our young people into the teaching profession. This money will provide tuition grants and loans of $1,000 each to be forgiven for persons teaching two years in subject areas and/or geographic areas where acute shortages exist. Part of the additional $40 million included in my budget this year for education also enabled us to establish a teacher recruitment office in the Department of Public Instruction. Taken together, these initiatives will help, but they will not resolve, our teacher concerns.

Nationally, North Carolina is in thirty-seventh place in the number of our citizens who have graduated from high school, and more crucial is the fact that we're forty-eighth among the states in the number of persons in the work force who have received diplomas. Even today, our dropout rate is an alarming and unacceptable 31 percent of all students. With more than 800,000 adult functional illiterates, North Carolina is the state with the third-highest illiteracy rate in America, a situation that compels us to consider a massive rescue program.

Unless we settle these educational problems satisfactorily, unless we develop adequate solutions, the current economic development momentum of our state will fade. Particularly hard hit, if we fail, will be our rural areas. The North Carolina Business Committee for Education is doing much to help us correct this situation, but we must expand this effort to include all educators, businessmen, school board members, local government officials, parents, and civic clubs. When we do, our entire state and our economy will be the better for it.

The companies we honor today have already made major contributions to our primary and secondary school system. Through scholarships, they are helping capable students who might otherwise have difficulty pursuing further education. Their technology is being used in our classrooms, and they're implementing programs to reduce our dropout rate.

More especially, I commend them for their support of school bond issues to provide better facilities. Recently I announced that I will ask the 1987 General Assembly to call a bond referendum for this purpose. Subject to statewide approval by citizens, it would be the largest bond issue in the history of our state—five times the $300 million record approved in 1974.

Bonds sold by the state would be used to establish a low-interest loan program for school construction, passing through the bargain interest rates our state can get with its triple-A bond rating. This method enables counties in North Carolina to leverage the part of their local option half-cent sales tax, dedicated to schools, to build, improve, and expand schools now—and at today's costs, not tomorrow's inflated costs. To help five counties whose half-cent sales tax revenues are less than $2 million annually, I have proposed setting aside $5 million for supplementary grants.

A study by the North Carolina Department of Public Instruction estimates current school construction needs at $2.2 billion. We will survey each county, asking the county commissioners to review their needs with their school boards, and tell us how much they need and are willing to pay for out of sales taxes already available. That will give us a better fix on what we truly need. It's not mandatory, and it will require no new taxes above what is already earmarked for schools; and it will help counties meet their responsibility to build schools without using their limited bond capacity; and it reserves state revenues to pay for teachers and programs, which is the state's historic responsibility. Then, as if that's not amazing enough, bond specialists tell us that it will solidify our triple-A bond rating when we finance strategic needs.

As we think about improving the quality of life and the economy of North Carolina, there are other major goals I would like to see us achieve in the coming years. Our schools and our business leaders must help us provide more highly skilled workers who are able to use the latest technologies. We need this because our economy is changing drastically. We must learn to think and work smarter. We can't do that without language and math.

How can we effectively reduce our dropout rate in North Carolina? For one thing, we can make education a challenge, an adventure for our young people, stimulating their minds and providing them new goals to achieve. The ultimate cost of allowing about 27,000 students to drop out of school each year is too great. Successful reform of education requires a concerted effort to confront the special educational needs of the lowest achieving students, those who are at greatest risk of dropping out or who remain in school without acquiring basic skills. We need to increase our expectations of these students and, with appropriate help, to move them toward the performance standards that ought to be expected of them.

There are many other areas of concern we could address today, but we are here to acknowledge and reward outstanding achievement: twenty-four teachers and seventeen business firms in particular. I also want to commend thousands of teachers and business leaders for your support of the Governor's Business Committee for Education, and especially Jere Drummond, who is completing his superb leadership as chairman. So let us proceed with the importance of the occasion. Chairman Drummond, I am pleased to assist you at this time in presenting the 1986 awards.

DAVIDSON COLLEGE FALL CONVOCATION

Davidson, November 1, 1986

[Davidson College granted Governor Martin an honorary Doctor of Laws degree as a highlight of its 1986 fall convocation; a transcript of the address he delivered on that occasion is reprinted below. Martin received his Bachelor of Science degree at Davidson in 1957, and returned as a member of the chemistry faculty in 1960 after having earned a Ph.D. at Princeton. *The Davidsonian* (Davidson College), November 7, 1986; *North Carolina Manual, 1987-1988*, 547.]

I am delighted to be here; I hope that you are. I have to say to you, I am awash in reflection this morning. I suppose over my career I have sat in some 500, 600 assemblies of this sort, going back to the days when it was required three times a week, and there are so many memories. Will Terry[1] and I were reminiscing this morning about an occasion when there was one of those great flare-ups among the student body, and through my impeccable connections in the underground I had found out that during the assembly, just as he was speaking, the students were going to walk out on him; and we took all the greatest advantage we could of that information, because when the time came, it was too late. He had already walked out on them.

I also have to say to you that I remember one occasion when the Democratic candidate for lieutenant governor of our state, Pat Taylor, was here addressing a convocation.[2] And he spoke to us about the one thing that he thought we needed to know, and one thing that we must never forget, and that was, he said, "The Democratic party runs this state!" I never forgot!

And it is good to be back. I want to pay my respects and express my thanks and appreciation to the faculty for their courtesies, their generosity, their forebearance in making this occasion possible. Apparently, we didn't have to vote on it.

I remember very well that, when we were here, everybody tolerated me. Now, they loved Dottie; they tolerated me. But those of you students who have been taking chemistry courses will have been told already how you are lucky you missed me. I was tough!

It was also interesting to reminisce yesterday evening, as student Leah Howell brought her famous parents, Barbara and Leon, by, and they spent the night with us; but we also reminisced awhile yesterday evening about required vespers and all the mysteries that went on. Reminiscing about the time that I eased Charlie Ratliff's final exam.[3] Don't you forget it, Charlie! You don't want to take credit for my economic, ah, ideas, but I remember that very well. I anticipated seventeen out of twenty questions and faked the other three and came out pretty good.

I also want to say a word on behalf of my successor, Felix Carroll.[4] Felix, are you here? Where? Yeah, here we go, because there is a story that has to be told. Felix is sort of my protégé. You see, when I was first running for Congress in 1972, I worked out a deal with the president and the dean.[5] And the deal was that I needed to be able to take a leave of absence so that I could campaign full time in the fall, and so they said all right, they had a substitute lined up—a whiz kid from Cal Tech, I believe it was—and the deal was that if I lost I would continue away for the rest of the year on my first sabbatical and then come back and get politics out of my system. But, if I won, Felix had a permanent position here on the faculty. So, needless to say, I carried his precinct overwhelmingly—which you call enlightened self-interest.[6]

I have so often had an occasion to tell the story about what it was like running that first year, in 1972, as a member of the faculty. You know, back in those days that was sort of a handicap, because there was a famous southern politician, whose name for obvious reasons will remain "George Wallace," who was going around talking about the "horny-headed intellectuals" that couldn't even open their own briefcase. And I had one of these nice, zipper-topped ones, you know. I thought I could handle it!

And it was kind of tough because, you see, they began this whispering campaign—you know, it often happens in campaigns when things get desperate—and they started this whispering campaign, and they said, "Hey! You can't vote for Martin. He is a college professor!" and the eyebrows would go up.

You know, friends, when they are out there telling lies on you, it is bad enough, but when they are telling the truth, you better—you have to come up with something. So, our folks decided we would fight truth with truth; and whenever we would see two heads close together, the telltale eyebrows rising, our folks would go and they would whisper in the other ear. They knew they had just been saying, "Hey, you can't vote for that Martin, he is a college professor," and our people would go and whisper in the other ear, "Don't you worry about it, he is not a good one!" It worked!

Very similar to the occasion in 1984 when I was running for governor, and here again, things were beginning to get desperate. The polls were showing that we were just like that shark in *Jaws*, were drawing close, so they began to talk about the fact that I wasn't even born in North Carolina. And so we began to run into folks who would come up and they would say, "Martin! They tell me you weren't even born in North Carolina! What is worse, you were born in Savannah! What do you have to say to that?" I said, "I had to be near my mother!" It works!

It worked, and I want to share with you a little bit this morning—that is a great job! I have to confess that to you, and I want you students to pay attention, because if history repeats itself at least two of you are going to be governor of this state, and perhaps some of you others, but think about it. It is not too bad! You got nice cars, a couple of airplanes, a helicopter, a squad of troopers to go before and to go behind, starboard, and port! I remember that Governor Bob Scott said that the toughest thing that he had after losing the office of governor is that he kept running into doors.

You get a nice house, a 100—almost a 100—year-old mansion, with forty-two rooms, twelve bathrooms, chandeliers in most of the bathrooms. It is really something! Comfortable, if you are accustomed to living, as we are, in 18-foot ceilings, plus a mountaintop retreat in Asheville. I hope you like the idea. I want you to try it. It is the best public housing in North Carolina. I don't know how you could take something like that, but, you know, we just decided we were going to relax and enjoy it, what the heck! That is my philosophy!

So, you know, one of the things that I really like about it is that the Mansion is just a few blocks, say five minutes, away from where I work at the office, which is a 150-year-old State Capitol, so that I can get home fairly regularly for lunch—almost as often as when I was working here, which shows that it is almost that good a job. Think about it! So, I get to see Dottie a lot, except when she is out making a speech somewhere, running around heading up a conference or hearing on missing children or drug education, or hustling some donation of furniture or art for the Mansion. She has been pretty busy since she became chairman of the North Carolina Child Victimization Commission. She was appointed by the governor. They are pretty close. In fact, one of the neatest things that he did was to put her picture on the back of the state road map. I hope you get a copy and you enjoy that. Help you get back where you are going.

In case you wondered, no, we would rather not be back in Washington; yes, we like what we are doing! It is not that national issues aren't important and stimulating—war, peace, a little of both in Central America; helping write the biggest tax cut in history, overshooting, and then helping to write the biggest tax increase in history. When you put them both together, it is still the biggest tax cut in history! Bombing the ban on saccharin—you remember that one, Will? It was for Will Terry that I did that. Heady stuff, but it doesn't match the satisfaction of work as chief executive officer of our state.

It is a big state, 6.25 million people! Over 500 miles from Manteo to Murphy, from the mountains to the seashores. Only 24 U.S. corporations have a larger budget or payroll. State government is much closer to the concerns and the problems that people have in their daily lives. We pay for the operation of 141 school systems, 16 universities, 58 community colleges, and that is 70 percent of our budget there, plus we provide tuition grants for North Carolina students attending North Carolina private colleges. We run the prisons, the criminal courts, the mental institutions, museums, the parks—not very well, in that case—a zoo, the North Carolina Symphony Orchestra. By the way, I used to play that tuba back in the olden days. I like the way you handle that [questionable transcription omitted] and one of the best economic development programs in America.

You see, we are out there recruiting high tech and low tech and everything in between—that's from terminals to turkeys, data processing to food processing, and everything in between. I remember during 1984 I was accused of being in favor of business. My answer was to say, Yes! Big business, small business, and anything in between, because that's one of the things that I remember from Ratliff 101. Because that is where jobs come from.

Next year—well, let me tell you that this past year one of the great thrills was to put together a highway program. Our state has built and maintains the largest highway program in America, and last year we won approval of over $200 million [in] improvements in the construction program—$200 million a year in the construction program of our highways. And next year, if I get my way, we are going to pass a $1.5

billion bond issue to build the schools, the public schools that we need in this state and that are overdue; and I will tell you that is five times as large as the next-largest bond issue that this state has ever considered: $300 million during the Holshouser administration.

But the beauty of the proposal that we have come forward with—think about this a little bit, it is a neat lesson—is that it can be done, [a] $1.5 billion bond issue, at no substantial cost to the state. We will borrow the money at our AAA bond rating and then pass through those low-interest loans, to the counties, only as much as they need and are willing to pay for, and it will require no new taxes for the counties over and above the taxes that are already recently dedicated to school construction. So, it just gives an advance on that, and they use the schools while they pay it off over the next twenty years. Beyond that, it saves them a substantial part of their statutorily limited debt capacity that each county is allowed to carry so that they can use that for other requirements, and it is not mandatory. As I said, they can take all that they believe they need and that they are willing to pay for. One of the interesting things is that the editorial consensus is that it is too good to be true!

We have got some serious challenges facing us in this state. One of them is how we rebuild the teaching profession in our public schools; how we rescue that honorable profession and strengthen it; how we get you young people to consider teaching as a career; how we get those established teachers to stay with us. So, we are working on changes in the certification and the training requirements for teachers so that you liberal-arts graduates can teach in our public school classrooms. We are developing a career-ladder pay system, as many other states are working on, to provide incentives with evaluation for competence and effectiveness—accountability. What would you say if we could start you out at $18,000 or $20,000, with the opportunity to grow to $40,000 if you are good. If that doesn't lure them in, we will do better!

We are providing college tuition loans, for those who are willing to prepare for teaching careers, which will convert to scholarships. That is, you don't have to pay them back if you teach in geographic areas or subject areas where we have a shortage.

Another great problem in states all over America is, and we particularly in North Carolina, the problem of dropouts. Thirty percent of our young people do not graduate from high schools. That is the statistics to date. Little consolation in the fact that it was worse 100 years ago. What do you do with those who are therefore functionally illiterate in a high-technology society? Well, we are providing remedial help in our community colleges, and we are going to expand that in our public libraries and in our prisons. We are adopting and developing reforms for elementary and secondary education to see that they drop in instead of drop out.

Let me tell you another troublesome concern that is a consequence of modern society, and that is, what do you do today with the waste generated by society, especially the toxic and radioactive waste? I can give you a neat example of how North Carolina is a part of an eight-state Southeastern Compact for Low-Level [Radio]active Waste—whatever that is—disposal; and our seven fellow states have given us the honor of being the next host state for that facility when they close operations at Barnwell, South Carolina. And you can appreciate the response of the man on the gallows who said if it weren't for the honor of the thing, we had just [as] soon let somebody else take the turn. Well, I am going to be recommending to the legislature that we take our turn for twenty years on two conditions: 1) that the provisions of the compact be amended with Congressional affirmation, so that at the end of that twenty years none of the other states can pull out but will have to take their turn, in order; 2) that we establish a fee structure that is adequate, not only to compensate the community that will be so favored, but more especially so that we can afford to do it right and not put the dangerous stuff in the ground as has been done.

We have a serious problem in this state with a farm credit crisis. It has been building for years. We have been losing on the order of 3,000 farms a year, not just in the last five or six years, but for the last several decades; and I have put forward a fifteen-point plan that we are beginning to implement, beginning with a program involving banks and the Farm Credit System and the Farmers Home Administration to help our farmers to restructure their loans so that they are affordable, so that they can stay in farming. And for those who are not going to be able to do that, to provide a program under the Dislocated Workers' Act for the first time to retrain them for a job in the rest of society; and whatever the consequences, to provide that when they lose the farm because of overindulgence in credit, or the drought, or whatever it might be because of market conditions, that if the farm is lost that at least the homeplace, the homestead, won't be lost.

One of the most serious problems facing society today—not just in North Carolina, all over America, all over the world—is what do we do about drug enforcement and drug education? No one really knows what the answer or answers are going to be, but we realize that we must deal with both the supply and demand side of that equation, too. I would tell you that I am not considering mandatory urine testing, but we do have a problem, and it is not going away, and it is frightfully serious! It would be foolish for us to pretend in any walk of life that any profession or any institution, as a part of society, is somehow immune or insulated from the problem.

We need to develop programs that will help to identify those who have the problem, not just to remove them from society, not just to throw them to their own devices, but rather to identify them so that we can help them—help them with counseling, help them with therapy, help them with rehabilitation, help them with support that they need. We are trying to develop such a program for our state employees. Their first reaction was to say, Well, why are you looking at us? And my answer is that because that is my responsibility right now—you are; and you are part of society, and you are going to have whatever illnesses that are sweeping society today.

And I believe that American colleges need someone to take the lead in dealing with this particular problem. American colleges and universities, collegial society, needs a leader today, and I would express to you my hope and my challenge that my alma mater, Davidson College, will take that lead, and be that example, and find those answers, and share them with society to develop the kinds of programs that would be appropriate for students, and all of the academic community, and the community in which we live. If you will do this, you will be heroes! You will set the example that no one has yet set, and you will deserve all the honor, and accolade, and respect that would come with it. I am convinced that students today really don't want to have to contend with drug pushers and narcotics on campus, and I am convinced that we can do something about it. They want your leadership. They need your leadership, and so I am willing to offer to make another deal with you, today. If you will undertake to pioneer successful programs to help students and each other with drug education and countermeasures, the most compassionate kinds of education and countermeasures, I will help you to raise the money that you need to do it right, and I hope you will take me up on that.

In closing, I do want to tell you that I do have two other objectives in this job. Both are structural, and I think both are historic. One relates to the admittedly partisan remarks that I made at the beginning of my statement to you today. I believe in a healthier, more competitive, two-party system for North Carolina and for the Southeast. I won't belabor it further, but just say to you that I am committed to building that.

Secondly, I believe it is time for the governor of North Carolina to have the veto, just like the president of the United States and the governor of every other state in America. Now, those of you from away in other states may not have known this; you may not have learned it in your government class or your civics class, but there is only one governor in America that doesn't have the veto, and you are listening to him, I hope, right now—the only one who can't use the veto to halt flawed legislation, bring it back for another look; to halt mischievous legislation, bring it back for another vote, even to protect his own office. Our people are embarrassed when they find out about it, because, you see, the governor of South Carolina has a veto. Even in Georgia, they have got the veto! Samoa has the veto, Puerto Rico has the veto, but North Carolina is the only state where, the only state where not once in 210 years of statehood have our people ever been allowed to vote on that question. And so, I intend to fight to get that historic referendum on the ballot.

So you see, there is excitement enough in this job. A governor doesn't have to spread thinly over a thousand or 2,000 different issues. Other folks can plow into those and remedy those and reform them and solve them, but these are ten things which I wanted to share with you, which are high on my agenda and among my priorities; number one among them being to strengthen public schoolteaching, as our school system in this country and in this state desperately needs. I want your help on that, and I hope you can figure out how to do it.

---

[1]William Holt Terry (1932-   ), resident of Davidson; B.S., Davidson College, 1954; B.D., 1958, D.Min., 1985, Union Theological Seminary. Minister, Acme, North Carolina, Presbyterian Church, 1958-1962, and of Davidson College Presbyterian Church, 1966-1971; chaplain, 1962-1966, dean of students, since 1971, Davidson College. William Holt Terry to Jan-Michael Poff, February 13, 1990.

[2]Hoyt Patrick Taylor, Jr. (1924-   ), born in Wadesboro; B.S., 1945, LL.B., 1948, University of North Carolina at Chapel Hill; U.S. Marine Corps, 1945-1946, 1951-1952. Practicing attorney since 1948; member, 1955-1965, Speaker, 1965, state House; elected lieutenant governor, 1968; unsuccessful candidate for Democratic gubernatorial nomination, 1972. North Carolina Manual, 1971, 542; Winston-Salem Journal, October 18, 1981.

[3]Charles Edward Ratliff, Jr. (1926-   ), born in Morven; resident of Davidson; B.S., Davidson College, 1947; A.M., 1951, Ph.D., 1955, Duke University; U.S. Navy, 1944-1946, and Reserve. Davidson College faculty member since 1947: instructor, 1947-1948, assistant professor, 1948-1949, of business and economics; assistant professor, 1951-1954, associate professor, 1954-1960, professor of economics, 1960-1967, and department chairman, 1966-1983; Charles A. Dana Professor of Economics, 1967-1977, William R. Kenan, Jr., Professor of Economics, since 1977. Professor of economics, Forman Christian College, Lahore, Pakistan, 1963-1966, 1969-1970; author; Democrat. Martin was a former

student, and later faculty colleague, of Ratliff. Charles Edward Ratliff, Jr., to Jan-Michael Poff, January 25, 1990.

⁴Felix A. Carroll (1947-   ), born in High Point; resident of Davidson; B.S., University of North Carolina at Chapel Hill, 1969; Ph.D., California Institute of Technology, 1972. Polymer synthesis chemist, Burlington Industries Research Center, 1968-1969; assistant chemistry professor, 1972-1980, associate professor, 1980-1986, and professor, since 1986, Davidson College; author. Felix A. Carroll to Jan-Michael Poff, January 23, 1990.

⁵The president of Davidson College in 1972, Samuel Reid Spencer, Jr., is identified elsewhere in this volume.

⁶Martin won the opportunity to represent the Ninth Congressional District, in a landslide victory over Democrat James Tully Beatty, in the November 7, 1972, general election. Beatty (1934-   ), was born in New York City; resident of Charlotte; A.B., University of North Carolina at Chapel Hill, 1957; U.S. Army, 1957-1958. Vice-president, Harmon Products Co., Gastonia; elected to state House of Representatives, 1966, 1968, 1970; first human to run indoor mile in less than four minutes; winner, Sullivan Award, America's Amateur Athlete of the Year, 1962. *Charlotte Observer*, November 8, 9, 1972; *North Carolina Manual, 1971,* 666-667.

NORTH CAROLINA FOOD PROCESSING CONFERENCE

RALEIGH, NOVEMBER 25, 1986

I am very pleased, today, to join with leaders of North Carolina agriculture to discuss the importance of food processing to our state's economy and the great challenge we now face in expanding this vital industry to capture an increasing share of a growing world market. Those of you who are attending today's session represent research, education, extension, production, processing, supply, and marketing—all of the forces that have made North Carolina one of the largest producers of farm commodities in the most abundant nation on the face of the earth.

Today, 31 cents of every household food dollar goes into the pockets of our producers, and another 31 cents accounts for processing. The remainder includes 6 cents for transportation, 10 cents for wholesaling, and 22 cents for retailing—and this doesn't count the amount we spend on institutional foods: hotels, restaurants, and fast food chains, and the vast military market.

Although the percentage of the consumer dollar spent on food has declined from 22 cents, in 1950, to 15 cents in 1986, it isn't because we're eating less or worse. Both consumption and demand for quality have increased. It's just that we've had a dramatic rise in personal incomes in the last three decades, while commodity prices have remained relatively stable. At the same time, prices of other goods have increased sharply.

North Carolina is, and always has been, a predominantly agrarian state. We're grateful to our farmers and agribusiness people for becoming the best and the most efficient in the world. Yet, agriculture has been through some tough times in this generation—high interest rates, inflation, rising production costs, and more recently, a devastating drought. As Charles Kuralt, a native Tar Heel, said recently on his nationally televised CBS program, "Our farmers have suffered just about all the Good Lord and the marketplace could dish out."

As governor, I've taken some immediate steps to provide vitally needed relief, including obtaining federal designation of North Carolina as an agricultural disaster area, thereby qualifying farmers for financial assistance. Additionally, I have appointed a Farm Finance Task Force to promote coordination and cooperation by private and public financial institutions in the restructuring of viable farm loans, thus averting possible additional foreclosures. Recent changes in federal bankruptcy laws also will help by permitting many farmers to reorganize their operations and obtain additional credit.

Working with the North Carolina Employment Security Commission, I have expanded our assistance programs for dislocated industry workers to include farmers and farm workers. Approximately $1.3 million is currently available in the Dislocated Worker Program to help eligible dislocated farmers and farm workers. These funds can be used for vocational counseling, remedial education, job search assistance, vocational skill training, on-the-job training, intensive job development and placement, and relocation assistance for those who must move more than fifty miles to obtain employment. Our long-term plans of assistance, however, contain fifteen priorities for agriculture prepared by our state's farm organizations, commodity groups, the North Carolina State University Agricultural Extension Service, and the North Carolina Department of Agriculture.

Finding permanent solutions to our problems in agriculture, however, is our ultimate goal. We simply have no other alternative but to get our marginal farmers out of red ink and into the profit column. Food processing holds one of the best promises of helping us do this.

North Carolina is a significant producer of horticultural crops. Vegetables account for almost 200,000 acres of production and about $200 million in farm income. Berries, fruits, greenhouse crops, outdoor flowers, and ornamentals add substantially to this amount, bringing the total farm income for horticulture to nearly $375 million.

In the southeastern region of the state, we have about 240 growing days a year, enough to produce two crops and possibly three, depending upon weather conditions; because of climatic changes, the season shortens to around 90 or 100 days in northwestern North Carolina.

During this growing season, we supply the bulk of selected fresh produce for markets east of the Mississippi. These crops include peppers, eggplant, squash, cucumbers, snap beans, cabbage, carrots, strawberries, tomatoes, watermelons, and both Irish and sweet potatoes. During certain harvest seasons, the North Carolina share of the national market for sweet potatoes, peppers, cucumbers, and early apples ranges from 30 to 50 percent.

Most of our early season opportunities exist in larger, northern cities when local supplies are unavailable and supply quantities from California, Texas, and Florida are seasonally low. The fact that half of the nation's population lives within a radius of 500 miles places us in an enviable position to serve consumers, but distribution patterns are a key factor in serving this enormous market.

Basically, farmers currently have three marketing alternatives: local markets, regional markets, and national markets. Local market options include direct farmer-to-consumer sales, selling to custom fee packers and shippers, and sales to institutional outlets and independent food stores. Regional markets offer services similar to local assembly markets, but the assembly and sales areas are much broader—a good example is cooperative marketing through which smaller farmers can amass volume, share costs, and gain leverage in the marketplace. National markets lend themselves to large farm operations and consist basically of sales to chain stores through agents or brokers.

It appears that a major problem we have in North Carolina is that we are not intervening constructively to expand existing markets and create new ones. Moreover, farmers are not reaping the financial benefits of value-added [products] by adapting to a consumer-driven, market-oriented farm economy. Specialists advise me that we need to undertake a comprehensive investigation of numerous alternatives. Roughly, these alternatives can be divided into six categories: research, quality control, extension education, marketing, finance, and expansion of processing opportunities.

Research would include, but certainly would not be limited to, the improvement of existing varieties of crops grown in North Carolina and the development of new crops currently not being produced but which would be conducive to soil types, climate, and other factors; and it should necessarily concentrate on new processes such as chilling, individual quick freezing, dehydration, and radiation, to mention only a few. Quality control, on the other hand, would involve crop maturity, uniform size and color, elimination of defects, improved grading, and other factors that are considered important characteristics to the consumer. Extension education consists of working with producers to introduce new varieties, adapting to new methods such as removing field heat from produce to extend the cycle of freshness, maximizing output, achieving quality controlled production, and removing defects.

Marketing represents an entirely new world of agricultural processing, including grading, washing, packaging, labeling, promotion, and other value-added factors to attract consumers in the fresh market. It means taking advantage of new opportunities. By extending the process one step further, it could include the production of complete salad mixes for the institutional market. Briefly stated, it represents convenience.

Expansion of processing is probably the most important way we can extend our marketing season and utilize maximum production output. We need more facilities for grading and packing, quick-chill operations, slush freezing to produce concentrates, individual quick freezing and canning for the consumer market, and bulk freezing to serve as ingredients in soups and other quick-preparation, table-ready products for families that are spending less time in the kitchen. Processing expansion can be generated in one of three ways: the attraction of new plants to North Carolina, the establishment of homegrown enterprises, or a combination of both. The latter might include farmer cooperatives, entrepreneurships, and joint or individual operations by established companies.

And finally, we must consider the all-important matter of finance: private, public, or a combination of the two. This is particularly important if our emphasis is going to be on creating an entirely new agribusiness venture which combines all of the ingredients of research, production, education, and marketing.

Earlier this year, Sampson County employed specialists to study the feasibility of establishing a self-contained agricultural park. The results of this study are very promising and deserve further consideration. Preliminary plans for the park include canned food processing, dehydrating facilities, quick freezing, chilling, preparation, grading, packaging, cold storage, shipping, marketing, and even a day-care facility for the children of park employees. It would have its own independent water supply and waste disposal facilities, the latter consisting of land application using rotational plots that also could be used for crop production and experimental purposes. The idea behind this innovative park, in reality, is very simple: to enable farmers to grow, process, package, and put convenience food products on America's dining tables as a result of an integrated operation, providing expanded opportunities for production of value-added products, higher profit margins, and the creation of new jobs.

At the present time, the farmer is the only business person who produces a commodity before he or she knows where it will be sold, or what price it will command in the marketplace, except under subsidized programs; and we've already learned the painful way that subsidies are not the answer to a vibrant, supply-demand, private enterprise system. Let me cite an example. Dairy products, which are subsidized and tightly controlled, are growing in terms of surplus stocks. Just recently, a congressional study revealed that we can't give this surplus away to the poor without compounding the problem. Each time we give away $200 million in free cheese and butter under the food stamp program, there is a 40 percent decline in the retail market. Consequently, the declining private market creates a larger surplus which the federal government must buy and store at ever-mounting costs. It's a no-win situation.

Food processing is a bright horizon filled with opportunities to put North Carolina agriculture back on the road to success and prosperity. We can expand our domestic markets by being innovative, and we can extend our sales of food products to a growing world market. Japan is an excellent prospect, given fair trade arrangements. Less than 15 percent of the land in Japan is tillable, and the Japanese are turning elsewhere for food production. Another important factor in our favor is that we produce many foods that are part of the Japanese diet; sweet potatoes and soybeans are excellent examples. Some of our farmers already are taking advantage of these market opportunities, but we need to expand them to include more producers.

Horticultural crops represent only one component of our agricultural production. Additional opportunities exist for the processing of beef, pork, poultry, lamb, and other livestock. Broiler production in North Carolina was up 4 percent in 1985, setting a record high of 1.97 billion pounds. We became the fourth-largest broiler producer in America, with a total of 447 million birds produced.

Pork production also is up 4 percent, to almost 4 million pigs produced in North Carolina in 1985. Milk production rose 6 percent, and turkey production again placed number one in the nation with a record 31.9 million birds. And cash receipts from cattle and calves totaled $154 million, up almost 50 percent from the previous year as we experienced a 38 percent rise in the number of cattle.

We've accomplished some amazing feats in the marketing of poultry and turkeys. We now sell them precooked, portion packed, in frozen dinners, in select parts, and even the chicken nugget has carved out its own major institutional and household markets.

Food processing research, production, and processing are not confined, however, solely to commodities and livestock grown on the farm. We have an extensive ocean shoreline, and there is a bountiful catch of fish and shellfish to be had from our sea, sounds, wetlands, and rivers. Aquaculture, the artificial breeding of sea and stream life, offers an exciting future for North Carolina. In the west, the Cherokee Indians are experimenting with the production of mountain trout; the Lumbees are doing the same with catfish; and on our coast a whole new field of aquaculture is developing a hybrid fish with unique marketable features.

Mariculture, the growing of aquatic plants and organisms under simulated conditions, is yet another expandable opportunity for the production of food supplements for both animals and humans, as well as the production of vital pharmaceutical ingredients. One company, Maracultra, Incorporated, is working with the University of North Carolina at Wilmington, under the auspices of two grants from the North Carolina Department of Administration, to pioneer in this work.

Outside of Raleigh, in North Carolina's Research Triangle Park, our Biotechnology Center is exploring entire new areas of research in agriculture that will put us years ahead of other states in the development of new food crops, such as vegetables and fruits. Right here at North Carolina State University, one of the nation's most important land-grant institutions, the School of Agriculture and Life Sciences and its Department of Food Science have been working for decades on new varieties, processes, equipment, marketing strategies, and conducting research in water management, irrigation, and wide-scale greenhouse production in the field. All of the emerging developments will lengthen our growing season and our ability to accomplish things we never dreamed could be done. With a staff of thirty-two professors—twenty-two devoted to research, development, applied technology and teaching, and ten engaged in the agricultural extension component—the Department of Food Science is one of our state's most valuable resources.

Food processing may not be the complete answer to all of our agricultural problems, but it is a gigantic step in that direction. As consumer preferences become more sophisticated, as institutional food service expands, and as a health-conscious world becomes more discriminating in the selection of fresh produce, we can—in fact, we must—be ahead of these trends. North Carolina must become the leader, not the follower.

This means that we must expand research, change our methods of production, pool our resources, enhance our marketing techniques, and explore the feasibility of freestanding, integrated agriculture parks—perhaps as many as three strategically situated in the southeast, northeast, and piedmont-west. Achieving this goal will take hard work, diligent study, and strong cooperation. As governor, I'm ready to take on the leadership in this unique effort.

I am pleased today to announce that I am appointing a North Carolina Inter-Agency Food Processing Task Force, with the responsibility of assessing what we must do, how we must do it, and proposed methods of finance to enhance our food production/processing capabilities. It will have the task, in effect, of laying out a new type of blueprint to guide us in the future as we seek to anticipate and become the first state to meet new consumer demands and marketing opportunities. Hopefully, we can identify both short- and long-term advantages that will help us restore agriculture as a profitable, diversified economic venture and offer new hope to our farm families. The membership of this task force will include representatives of all farm organizations, our university community, Extension Service, appropriate state and federal agencies, producers, private industry, and financial institutions. To obtain the best output from this effort, we must make absolutely certain that we have the best input.

During the last six years of our national administration, more federal assistance has been extended to agriculture than the previous five administrations combined. Most of this money, however, has gone into Commodity Credit Corporation support payments. This year alone, $25.6 billion in federal funds will go into farm support programs. I favor spending more of the dollars allocated in the future for research, market development, extension education and demonstration, short- and long-term financing for farmers, and both grants and loans to enable us to undertake innovative programs. I support using whatever state resources we have available to supplement this assistance.

We all agree that recent years have been difficult ones for agriculture, but we didn't get in this fix overnight, or necessarily as the result of any single factor. Agriculture has seen tough times before, but our farmers are tough people. As the world population raises its quality of life and its standards of living, so, too, will North Carolina be ready to seize the opportunities this progress offers.

This is an exciting time in which to live. We've gone from low tech, to mid tech, to high tech. We are bordering on the age of super tech, and North Carolina has staked its claim on this exciting future. We can, and we must, work together as one united state, united as never before to eclipse agriculture's proud heritage.

NORTH CAROLINA FARM BUREAU FEDERATION

WINSTON-SALEM, DECEMBER 9, 1986

I am especially pleased to be here today and address the fifty-first annual convention of North Carolina's largest farm organization, the Farm Bureau Federation. Jim Oliver,[1] my agricultural adviser, tells me that your organization has enjoyed a net increase of more than 13,000 members in 1986 and that you've reached a new record of some 255,000 farmers. At a time when farm families are facing some of their most difficult problems, I don't believe anyone could find a better illustration of how people have come together as one united state.

I am also very pleased, on behalf of the state of North Carolina, to extend a very warm welcome to President Dean Kleckner of the American Farm Bureau.[2] I trust, President Kleckner, that your visit will provide you a broad overview of how the people of our state are working together, in public-private partnership, and how we are putting innovative ideas to work for the benefit of the families who have helped to make our nation the most abundant producer of food and fiber in the world.

Agriculture is continuing to undergo some of the most significant changes in the history of our state and nation, and I welcome this opportunity to speak to you about the challenges and opportunities these changes hold for us in the future. First, allow me to review very briefly how I have responded, with the wise counsel and the strong support of the North Carolina Farm Bureau, Commissioner Jim Graham, the state Department of Agriculture, and other organizations, to our most recent crises.

We've just ended a summer drought that has been the most devastating in our history, and we're still living in its shadow. Rainfall has been above average in two of the last three months, but groundwater aquifers are not being recharged rapidly enough to prevent wells from going dry in the piedmont and west. Surface reservoirs are critically below normal levels in many areas. We are on our way back, but we still have a long way to go.

I don't need to remind you of the historic haylift efforts which were mounted to save our livestock farmers. Indeed, some of you were among those farmers. This spirit of cooperation among countless thousands of caring people has become a point of national pride. It has given us renewed hope; it has restored our faith in the ability of rural America to respond in a positive, constructive way to even the most severe obstacles facing our agricultural sector.

Although monumental in scope, the haylift effort was only a temporary, emergency measure. As a result of my urgent request, Secretary of Agriculture Richard Lyng[3] has designated eighty-one North Carolina counties as agricultural disaster areas. This, I am pleased to report, qualifies approximately 4,400 affected livestock farmers for $9.5 million in financial assistance for the purchase of grain and hay. Currently, Agricultural Conservation and Stabilization Service offices in these counties are expediting applications for certificates of payment, and we are monitoring their progress closely. In addition, I have requested a presidential declaration of disaster as a result of drought which, among other types of assistance, will provide federal grants for well drilling in rural areas.

Adversity, however, is not limited to our livestock producers. Almost all of our farmers have been affected, as well; and Congress, in adopting the 1986-1987 federal budget, recognized this fact by providing an appropriation of $400 million nationally for flood and drought disaster aid under the Consolidated Farm and Rural Development Act.[4] Eligible farmers are those who have sustained a loss of 50 percent or more in the production of commodity program crops such as wheat, feed grains, upland cotton, soybeans, tobacco, and peanuts. The Agricultural Stabilization and Conservation Service also will be administering these payments, which include financial assistance to farmers who sustained losses in non-program crops.

One of my primary concerns has been the timely distribution of these various assistance payments to our farmers; next week, Commissioner Graham and several of my senior advisers will be traveling to Washington with me to discuss this concern, among other vital issues, with Secretary Lyng.

Many other recent problems have plagued North Carolina agriculture. Equally devastating to the rural economy of North Carolina has been the loss of many family farms. Historically, we've been losing between 2,000 and 3,000 farm families annually as a result of mounting financial failures. In 1950, the total farm debt in the United States was around $12 billion. Today, it exceeds $230 billion. Debt-to-asset ratios have reached the highest levels in history.

This national trend, in many respects, mirrors and reflects the critical situation in which some of our farm families find themselves today. Not all of these farmers can be saved, but many of them can. However, in one way or another, we can help them all.

In October, I announced the appointment of North Carolina's first Farm Finance Task Force to identify at-risk farmers who were in need of financial planning assistance before they reached the point of foreclosure. One of the goals of this task force is to bring together government and private lenders in a coordinated effort to restructure viable farm loans. Another goal is to reduce the uncertainty of obtaining production loans from such agencies as the Farmers Home Administration, the Farm Credit System, and others. Decisions by lending institutions on loan applications for harvesting and operating capital must be on a timely basis, and this means that creditors must develop a greater understanding of the problems farmers face and adjust their lending attitudes accordingly.

Many of our best farmers are being squeezed out of business by declining commodity prices and by high interest rates on land and machinery. Most of these farmers are good businessmen who contribute to both the regional economy and the civic leadership of our rural communities. We all have an obligation to help alleviate these pressures whenever possible, if only in the interest of the continued economic growth and the enhancement they provide to our quality of life.

Shortly after appointing this task force, I also expanded the Employment Security Commission's assistance program for dislocated industry workers to include farmers and farm workers. About $1.3 million is available in the Dislocated Worker Program to provide assistance to those who cannot avoid displacement. This money, part of the Job Training Partnership Act, can be used in many ways; some of the uses include vocational counseling, remedial education through community colleges, job search assistance training, vocational and on-the-job training, intensive job development and placement, and relocation assistance. I see this as a helping hand we have extended to our farmers and farm workers in time of great need, and although they are fiercely independent by tradition, I sincerely hope they will take advantage of the assistance we have offered as a way of building a new life.

Disaster assistance, financial planning and loan restructuring, and assistance for dislocated farmers and farm workers, are simply the immediate steps we have taken in concert with the Farm Bureau and other similar organizations, commodity groups, the private sector, and government agencies. Working with these same groups, including your own, we have developed a total of fifteen long-range goals, including assistance in dealing with production, marketing, management, finance, education, laws and regulations, legal advice, and taxes.

But we haven't started addressing these issues only recently. All of our governors in the past have recognized and acknowledged that North Carolina is a predominately agricultural state. However, I am a governor who believes deeply that state government can make a big difference in the vitality of our agricultural economy. One of the first issues I addressed during my initial year in office was the problem of our mounting tobacco surplus, which was rapidly destroying our quota system, price support program, and most important of all, threatening the very existence of our leaf producers.

Tobacco is, and always has been, our leading cash crop. In terms of dollar volume, it is our chief farm export. We would be hard pressed to find a replacement commodity of equal or higher value. Yet, agreement on a solution to our increasing surplus was nowhere to be found among the various interests involved.

The buy out of the Flue-Cured Tobacco Stabilization Corporation's existing stock by our six major domestic manufacturers, which I worked to achieve in a summit meeting of these diverse interests, proves the point that state leadership is not only desirable but absolutely necessary. Results of this accomplishment have been borne out, I believe, in the tobacco marketing season just ended. Producer assessments were substantially lower, demand was strong, prices were higher, and, for the first time in years, very little volume came under the support program. It wasn't the ideal market, but it was the best we've enjoyed in a long time, and I have every reason to believe it's going to continue to improve. Here's why:

Last month, I wrote to the chief executive officers of the six major manufacturers and called their attention [to] a USDA report showing that tobacco imports had increased from 120.1 million pounds, in 1984-1985, to 151 million pounds in 1986. I strongly emphasized that this trend could possibly result in a quota reduction in 1987, thus eroding our farm income and compounding the marginal rural economic conditions of North Carolina. Specifically, I made two requests: (1) their consideration of reducing flue-cured imports, and (2) an expression of their intent to increase domestic purchases in order to increase the 1987 flue-cured quota.

Let me say that I am pleased with the responses I received. One executive pointed out that his company had reduced imports by two thirds this year alone. There were, however, two points on which all companies were in agreement. The first is their desire to maintain a strong market and to ensure the success of our "new" tobacco marketing program. The second point has become almost redundant over the years: We must continue to improve the quality of our leaf, which is the single most important feature in strengthening demand and achieving premium prices.

I believe we can, and must, work together and trust one another in good faith in order to reach our mutually supportive goals. The buy out agreement and the enactment of the new tobacco program which prevented the collapse of the Flue-Cured Tobacco Stabilization Corporation have, in effect, given us a second chance, a new opportunity to avoid past mistakes. We must make the most of this opportunity.

Although domestic consumption of tobacco is remaining flat or declining, the world market is increasing, and we are becoming more competitive as currencies in other nations adjust to higher values. Our tobacco program didn't deteriorate overnight, and we won't get it back to record high levels overnight, either. Our long-term prospects are excellent, however, and we must hold to a steady course of continued improvement.

While soliciting an intent to increase purchases by our major buyers, I also have called upon Secretary Lyng to exercise his discretionary authority to increase flue-cured quotas by 3 percent in 1987. Let me assure you that I will work diligently to that end during my meeting with him next week, and I will welcome your support in this effort.

The initiatives I have just reviewed with you describe some of the steps we have already taken, and are in the process of taking, to restore the vitality of our agricultural economy. Now let me address the challenges and opportunities of the future.

North Carolina has entered into a new age of agriculture. It is a consumer-driven, market-oriented age in which we no longer can produce on the slim chance that we will somehow find a market for our commodities and other products. For the remainder of this century and beyond, we must heed the words of Henry Ford. The secret to success, he said, is to find a need and fill it. And while this advice may sound simple, it is a complex task to which we must devote our full energies, our best research, our most innovative production methods, and our smartest private financing mechanisms. We must rethink our marketing strategies and take advantage of value-added considerations. We must anticipate consumer demands, not respond to them. We must create new markets and improve existing ones, create new images, and sell quality and convenience.

"Until recently, marketing as applied to agriculture was simply what you did to dispose of production," writes William E. Nothdurft, the author of *Going to Market*. "But today, marketing influences what is produced in the first place, how it is produced, and where and when and how it is sold."[5] Let me give you an example, one that lends itself to this special season:

Hal Johnson grows Christmas trees in western North Carolina; in fact, they're quality trees, pruned to perfection, with rich color and superb freshness; but when he first went into business, you wouldn't have guessed it by the price he was getting from the wholesaler. It wasn't any better or worse than his competitors. Then Hal decided to create his own market niche through targeted promotions of the "Booger Mountain Christmas Tree," and soon he was commanding premium prices and customers were asking for his trees by name. Now Hal is getting 10 to 15 percent more for his trees than his competitors, and he sells all that he can produce. Hal Johnson is only one of many examples of strategic marketing at work.

North Carolina is a significant producer of horticultural crops. Vegetables account for about 200,000 acres of farm production and almost $375 million in cash receipts. Berries, fruits, greenhouse crops, outdoor flowers, and ornamentals add substantially to this amount, bringing total farm income from horticulture to nearly $375 million each year. Most of our production goes to fresh markets locally, regionally, and nationally. This means that the marketplace dictates prices because of limited shelf life.

Direct marketing has been part of our farm economy for many years through farmer-to-consumer operations such as tailgate selling, farmers' markets, roadside stands, and "pick-your-own" farms. But we simply must do better, and food processing is one of the answers.

Included in processing are such operations as chilling to remove field heat and extend shelf life, individual quick freezing, dehydration, canning, and radiation—to mention only a few. We must follow Hal Johnson's example and make quality our number-one trademark by producing fruit and vegetables of uniform size and free of defects. We must get into the business of improved grading, washing, packaging, labeling, and promotion. This means that we must take advantage of new opportunities. By extending the process one step further, it could include the preparation of complete salad mixes for the institutional market.

Expansion of food processing is probably the most important way we can utilize expanded production and extend our marketing season. But we need more facilities for grading and packing, quick-chill operations, slush freezing to produce concentrates, and bulk freezing to serve as ingredients in soups and other quick-preparation, table-ready products for families who are spending less time in the home kitchen.

Processing expansion can be generated in one of three ways: the attraction of new plant investment to North Carolina, the establishment of home-grown enterprises, or a combination of both. The latter might include farmer cooperatives, entrepreneurships, and joint or individual operations by established companies. Finally, we must consider the all-important issue of finance—private, public, or a combination of the two. This is extremely important if we expect to create an entirely new agribusiness venture that combines all of the factors of research, production, promotion, and marketing.

Last month, the Sampson County commissioners shared with me a special study investigating the establishment of a self-contained agricultural park in their own region. The results of this study are very promising and deserve further consideration. Preliminary plans for such a park include tailgate retailing, but they also add canned food processing, quick freezing, chilling, preparation, grading, packaging, cold storage, shipping, marketing, and promotion in a vertically integrated environment.

I was so impressed by this study that I am appointing a Food Processing Task Force to look into the possibility of establishing three "ag parks," following the Sampson County concept, to serve the northeast, southeast, and piedmont-west areas of our state. Membership of this task force will include the commissioner of agriculture, representatives of our farm organizations, our research universities, the Extension Service, and other appropriate state and federal agencies. I'll also appoint producers, executives of private industry, and representatives of our financial institutions. Ideally and preferably, these parks should be financed with private capital and should provide a means of access for all of our farm families to reach new markets and share in the expanded opportunities they will offer in terms of added income and maximum utilization of production.

In North Carolina, we need to spend more of our dollars for expanded research, market development, extension education, short and long-term financing for farmers, and both grants and loans to undertake a wide array of innovat[ive] programs. I support the use of whatever state resources we have available to supplement this assistance.

Recent years have been difficult ones for agriculture. Farmers have experienced tough times before, but they are tough people. The future of agriculture is bright with promise. Am I suggesting that we've solved all of our problems? Hardly—but we have reached a critical crossroads, and we are the ones who must choose the direction to a better, more prosperous tomorrow. By working together as one united state, by harnessing high tech, low tech, and everything in between, and shaping them to our advantage, North Carolina can become the agricultural pioneer of the twenty-first century.

---

[1]James R. Oliver (1932-   ), born in Lumberton; resident of Raleigh; was graduated from North Carolina State College (later University), 1954; U.S. Army and Reserve. Farmer; former master, North Carolina State Grange; agribusiness specialist, state Department of Commerce, since February, 1986; appointed agriculture adviser to Governor Martin, March, 1986; author. James R. Oliver to Jan-Michael Poff, November 21, 1989.

[2]Dean R. Kleckner; corn, soybean, and hog farmer from Rudd, Iowa; former president, Floyd County (Iowa) Farm Bureau, and of Iowa Farm Bureau; elected president, 1984, reelected, 1988, American Farm Bureau Federation. Biographical sketch, dated February, 1988, provided by Information and Public Relations Division, American Farm Bureau Federation.

[3]Richard Edmund Lyng (1918-   ), born in San Francisco; Ph.B., University of Notre Dame, 1940; U.S. Army, 1941-1945. President, E. J. Lyng Co., Modesto, California, 1949-1966; director, California Agriculture Dept., 1967-1969; assistant secretary, 1969-1973, deputy secretary, 1981-1985, appointed secretary, 1986, U.S. Department of Agriculture; vice-chairman, Commodity Credit Corp., 1981-1985; president, Lyng and Lesher, Inc., 1985-1986. Who's Who in America, 1988-1989, II, 1943.

[4]For provisions of the Consolidated Farm and Rural Development Act, see United States Code (1988 edition), Title VII, Sections 1921 et seq.

[5]Of the material attributed to William E. Nothdurft, the first sentence is quoted correctly; the second, as written by the author, read: "Marketing is no longer what you do to dispose of production, it is what you do to influence what is produced in the first place, how it is produced, and where and how it is sold." See Going to Market: The New Aggressiveness in State Domestic Agriculture Marketing, by William E. Nothdurft (Washington, D.C.: Council of State Policy and Planning Agencies, October, 1986), 1.

Left: Martin attended tobacco market openings annually. A steadfast supporter of the state's traditional industries such as farming, furniture, and textiles, he was the first governor to designate an assistant secretary of commerce to work on those industries' behalf. Martin also established the position of agriculture adviser within the Commerce Department.

Above: Participants and witnesses joined Governor Martin on the Executive Mansion steps, July 2, 1986, to announce the signing of the biggest business contract in state history: the buy out by major tobacco companies of $1.2 billion in surplus leaf stockpiled in Flue-Cured Tobacco Cooperative Stabilization Corp. warehouses. Row 1 (l-r): N.C. Agriculture Commissioner Jim Graham; U.S. Deputy Agriculture Secretary Peter Myers; U.S. Senator Jesse Helms; Martin; Executive Director Fred G. Bond, Flue-Cured Tobacco Cooperative Stabilization Corp. Row 2: Murray Jones, of Senator Helms's staff; Witcher Dudley, vice-president of leaf, Philip Morris; Congressman Charles Whitley; Congressman Jim Broyhill.

New and expanding businesses announced plans to invest $5.4 billion in the state in 1987, creating upwards of 76,000 jobs. *Top*: Ribbon-cutting for American Airlines' new regional hub at Raleigh-Durham Airport, June 15, 1987 (l-r: Gene Hardin, Wachovia Bank president, RDU Airport Authority board member; Congressman David Price; Martin; Robert C. Crandall, president, chief executive officer, American Airlines; D. P. O'Hare, vice-president, American Airlines' Southeastern Division). *Bottom*: Groundbreaking for Sheller-Globe's Truck and Body Division plant, Grover, August 24, 1987 (l-r: State Senator J. Ollie Harris; Alfred H. Grava, president, chief executive officer, Sheller-Globe; Josh Hinnant, Cleveland County commissioner; Martin).

LOCAL GOVERNMENT ADVOCACY COUNCIL

RALEIGH, DECEMBER 11, 1986

[Speeches the governor delivered to the Greensboro Retail Merchants Association, Greensboro, November 12, and the Northeast North Carolina Legislative Caucus, Elizabeth City, November 24, 1986, were topically similar to the address reprinted below.]

I am very pleased, today, to have the opportunity to meet with the Local Government Advocacy Council, my Council of State colleagues, and members of the cabinet. We all need to find time to meet like this more often. I say this because state and local governments have become the giant locomotives, working in tandem, to move North Carolina forward and into a future where all of our citizens can fulfill their basic aspirations for a challenging job and a satisfying and rewarding life for themselves and their families; and unless we pull the train together, this very promising future will fade dimly into the horizon. State and local governments are no longer busy little switching engines, moving federal funds around from one place to another. We are the ones who now must decide the direction we want to take and provide the fiscal power to get us there on schedule.

Today I want to discuss with you some new ideas—not radically new, because I've talked about them before, and they also aren't radically new in terms of strategic methods of accomplishment. What makes them new is that they challenge old habits, and we all know how difficult it is to change old habits.

North Carolina is approaching a relatively tight budget year, which is another way of saying we will be required to make some intelligent choices. Perhaps *frugal* would be a better substitute for *tight*—that's the proper way to run government in the first place. My administration has been practicing this philosophy since the day we took office, trimming away almost $85 million in costs annually as a result of greater efficiency in governmental operations. Will the General Assembly reexamine the concept of pork barrel and follow our example by getting truly meaningful results? There appears to be a willingness on the part of the leadership. I hope it will.

But frugal management certainly doesn't mean we don't have the minimum financial resources to stay the course and, in time, to accomplish our major budget-related goals, which are:

1. To provide a stronger transportation system that will meet our needs and accommodate the immediate and future growth of our

state and our communities. Good highways and rural roads, better airports, improved public transit, and expanded seaports serve everyone. As a result of bipartisan agreement and support, the 1986 legislature appropriated $220 million on a one-time basis to expand our highway program.

I had proposed a permanent trust fund, as well as legislation to permit municipalities to protect rights-of-way by acquiring them at lower cost prior to development. Both of these measures passed the 1986 Senate. We were halfway there. The permanent trust fund was a new idea. Our task, with your help and support, is to revive this legislation in the 1987 session.

2. To provide the basic facilities for water distribution and waste water collection and disposal. More than ninety North Carolina communities are under federal moratoriums preventing them from serving new homes, business establishments, and industries. Others must expand facilities to accommodate rapid growth. Both of these critical needs must be met.

My Expansion Budget in 1985 requested $120 million during the current biennium to provide water and sewer grants to municipalities on a needs basis. This, too, was a new idea, but the General Assembly chose, instead, to allocate funds on a $7.00-per-capita basis, which gave the least help to those communities whose needs were greatest. Again, with your persistent and determined help, I will try to change this, in 1987, by establishing a program of low-cost loans and grants to be awarded on a needs basis. Will you, as individuals, and collectively as organizations, convince your legislators this idea has merit? I'll have more to say about this program in a few moments. Let's move on to the next two priorities.

3. To provide low-interest loans which will enable our county governments to construct $1.5 billion in new, expanded, and improved school buildings to address current and future needs and help facilitate the orderly implementation of the Basic Education plan with greater local control. As I work during the coming biennium to move toward implementing the first step of the teacher career ladder statewide and maintaining our momentum for funding the Basic Education Program, there will be a desperate need for new facilities to serve our best teachers, smaller classes, and a more productive system of public education—to match classrooms equal to the programs in them.

Most, if not all, of you are familiar with my school construction bond proposal which I announced last October 9. It's a new idea that's quite simple. I will submit legislation in the next session of the

General Assembly which will allow North Carolinians to vote on the issuance of $1.5 billion in bonds for school facility needs. These funds will be used to establish a state loan pool from which counties may borrow, at the low interest rates available to the state, using the dedicated part of two, one-half-cent local sales tax increases as repayment. I'll also have more to say about this proposal, particularly in respect to its unique advantages, but let me at least mention the fourth proposal.

4. To put into effect a workable economic development blueprint which will enhance our recruitment of new business investments while, at the same time, strengthening our 1985 initiative to serve traditional industries, small businesses, and innovative entrepreneurs. Economic development—that is, business and job growth—is the bottom line, the final result of our first three priorities: transportation, public facilities, and education together lead to jobs!

Although business firms differ in many respects, these three requirements are basic to all: transportation, facilities like water-sewer lines, and educated workers. Economic development is the only activity that creates wealth, from which we in turn obtain the revenues to operate government for the general welfare of all citizens.

Since the great migration of industry from the Northeast in the late 1950s and continuing through the early 1980s, North Carolina's impressive record of growth has been built on a strong, local-state, partnership. This partnership must be maintained and refined, and to accomplish this we must first agree on a plan which recognizes (1) that the migration has slowed to a trickle, although there is still evidence of expansion into our region, and (2) that the growth sector has shifted from manufacturing to services oriented.

There are two very similar plans now on the table for consideration, one prepared by our Department of Commerce and the other by the legislature's Commission on Jobs and Economic Growth. At a time when other states have become more competitive, we cannot afford divisiveness at the expense of rural and urban growth. Our plan emphasizes what can be done in the executive branch, like targeting industrial sectors and companies that are ripe for recruiting; and their plan emphasizes legislative initiatives. With a few debatable exceptions, they do not conflict. I would hope, therefore, that these two complementary plans can be brought together; that we can combine the best of both and move forward aggressively for the benefit of the entire state, rural and urban areas alike. To accomplish this goal, I am meeting with Lieutenant Governor Jordan and some of our state's most outstanding business leaders, next week, to seek accord, to find a basis of consensus. This effort also deserves your support.

Now that I have placed our four major legislative goals in proper perspective, I want to share with you my thinking on the two objectives that affect local governments most directly: school facility and water and sewer financing.

Several years ago, the state Department of Public Instruction conducted a survey which placed public school facility needs in North Carolina at $2.2 billion. It may be that this survey gave very little consideration to hard numbers and, in effect, more or less represented a wish list. In addition, several counties have received public approval of local bond issues since the survey was made. Five counties, for example, received approval of school facility bonds in last month's general election.

We now believe that $1.5 billion in financing would address current needs in North Carolina, and based upon that estimate, I will ask the 1987 General Assembly to authorize a statewide bond referendum to establish a loan pool from which counties could borrow. The advantages of using the state's triple-A credit rating to provide loans to counties are significant, and include:

1. State bonds can be sold at a considerably lower interest rate, thereby reducing the debt obligation of individual counties. The savings could amount to as much as $50 million statewide.

2. Funds would be available on an as-needed basis to meet construction schedules in a timely manner. This means that counties no longer would be forced to wait until revenues accumulate from the dedicated part of their local optional sales tax to consider school facility projects.

3. No tax increase would be required for repayment of loans from the state construction pool. In almost all cases, dedicated sales tax revenues are adequate to meet repayment schedules.

4. A statewide bond referendum would eliminate the need for separate referendums in each county, thereby removing the uncertainty of voter response—although the public has shown a willingness to support school needs in recent years—and the cost associated with separate referendums could be avoided. And finally,

5. Counties could take advantage of today's lower construction costs, as opposed to waiting several years during which costs are almost certain to increase as a result of inflation.

By providing a revenue source for school construction through a dedicated one-half percent of two local option sales tax increases, the General Assembly put into motion part of the solution to meeting critical facility needs. With my proposal for establishing a loan pool, it has an opportunity to go full circle in the attainment of this worthwhile goal.

I am delighted with the support this measure has received from the North Carolina School Boards Association, the North Carolina Association of School Administrators, State Treasurer Harlan Boyles, and State Schools Superintendent Craig Phillips, both of whom contributed to the plan. I sincerely hope that our League of Municipalities and the Association of County Commissioners will join this list of active supporters and will work for its enactment.

Equally critical to the progress of our state is the provision of adequate water distribution and waste-water collection and disposal facilities by our municipalities. The Environmental Protection Agency assesses these current needs at $1 billion to build waste-water facilities and an additional $600 million for water supply and distribution works. The enormity of these needs has put many of our communities into a Catch-22 situation. Because the tax base of many communities will not support additional financing, facilities can't be built to accommodate current and future economic growth; and because new and expanding economic activities cannot be served, communities cannot broaden and increase their tax base to expand revenues and justify additional debt capacity.

During the legislative session beginning next February 9, I will go back to the General Assembly once again to plead the case for a needs-based program. However, I will ask the legislature to structure the water and sewer funding program quite differently—in a way that more realistically addresses our revenue picture. The structure I will propose will include a combination of low-interest loans combined with special grants to meet special needs. The loan program will provide a source of continuing financing that only a revolving loan fund would provide. It also would permit municipalities to use the dedicated portion of their local option sales tax revenues to repay borrowed funds. The advantages, of course, would be similar to those gained from the school facility loan pool.

At the same time, we recognize that some communities simply can't make a financing program work solely on a loan basis. Sometimes costs are going to exceed what a municipality can afford to support out of user fees over the long term. Thus, grant assistance would be made available for high-cost waste-water treatment projects in conjunction with loans and would cover these excess costs. Excess costs would be defined as those where the average user fees required to meet debt service, plus operation and maintenance, would exceed a specified percentage of the median household income in the community. This provision recognizes a threshold above which users will not be expected to accept the primary responsibility for financing the construction of facilities required to meet water quality standards.

I also am proposing that grant assistance be made available for special-need water supply and waste-water treatment projects. These grants would provide engineering and construction assistance to address urgent needs of low-income families. Included would be cases where circumstances prevent local governments from meeting these needs through the loan program or a combination of loans and grants.

Since I first proposed this program at the League of Municipalities convention in October, several things have happened to complicate our planning. The first factor involved is the uncertainty of federal funding. The second factor actually was raised at meetings of the Local Government Advocacy Council and embraces funding groundwater protection costs of sanitary landfills to the loan program.

Secretary Rhodes of the Department of Natural Resources and Community Development is here today and will answer any specific questions you may have about what his department is doing in this area. For now, I want to give you an overview of what we are developing for presentation to the 1987 General Assembly. First, we will ask for an appropriation to provide water supply and waste-water treatment loans. This appropriation will be divided into five separate loan accounts, which are:

1. *Waste-water treatment loans* for treatment plants, interceptors, outfalls, and collection systems. This will be a broad-based account;

2. *Water supply loans* to include treatment plants, impoundments, mains, and distribution systems;

3. *Loans for protection costs of sanitary landfills.* These loans will be made for the purpose of groundwater protection measures associated with landfills and will include liners, leachate collection, and leachate treatment;

4. *Set-aside loans for waste-water treatment and water supply for economic development.* These funds will be coupled with existing community development block grant/economic development funds for job creation-retention; and

5. *Set-aside loans for emergency waste-water treatment and water supply.* Eligible projects will include the costs of addressing ruptures in collection or distribution systems, surges in waste-water treatment plants, and other interruptions in water supply and waste-water treatment services.

Grant funds, on the other hand, would be distributed between two separate accounts, including:

1. *Grants for high-cost waste-water treatment projects.* These projects are

defined as those exceeding median household incomes, as I previously explained, and would be made only for the amount of the excess costs; and

2. *Grants for special-need water supply and waste-water treatment projects.* These grants would be made to local governments and local action agencies to address urgent water supply and waste-water treatment needs of low-income families.

This method of financing current and future water supply and waste-water treatment needs also is a new idea and deserves your support. By providing dedicated revenues for repayment of loans, the legislature has met part of its responsibility. It's now time to create a source from which funds can be made immediately available, on a revolving basis, to municipalities at low cost.

All of the goals that I have outlined today—education, highways, school facilities, water and sewer, and economic development—are inseparably linked together, and all of them benefit our local governments. We cannot afford to sacrifice one for another. We must forge ahead on all of these fronts, making whatever progress our resources will allow. Some years will be better than others in terms of revenue growth, permitting us to make greater strides toward meeting these goals. The clarion call now is to continuing working together and to adjust to the realities of our time.

I believe these new ideas I have presented today permit us to do that, but let us remember that new ideas either find a champion or they die. No ordinary involvement with new ideas provides the energy required to cope with indifference and resistance, to change old habits, to perceive change and shape it to our own will. We can all become champions of these new ideas by remaining one united state, by pooling our resources, by working together, and being mutually supportive. Indeed, we can display persistence and courage of a heroic quality and, in so doing, become the rising tide that lifts our boats together and casts us upon a new and exciting wave of progress and prosperity.

SWEARING-IN CEREMONIES FOR CLAUDE POPE

RALEIGH, JANUARY 8, 1987

I am very pleased, this morning, to join the family, friends, former business associates, and fellow state officials who are gathered in these historic chambers to witness administration of the oath of office to North Carolina's fifth secretary of commerce. Claude Pope is a dedicated and talented public servant who, prior to his appointment to this position, served our state with pride, competence, and distinction as chairman of the North Carolina Economic Development Board.[1] In that position he not only earned the respect and admiration of those with whom he shared a deep sense of commitment to the people and state of North Carolina, but also my sincere gratitude, as governor, for having been an able adviser and one of the most effective and articulate architects of economic development policy.

Today, in these grand old House chambers, he becomes the top gun at Commerce, stepping out of his familiar role as architect and assuming the task of leading our state forward into what I believe is the dawn of its most promising future and its most rewarding era for our working men and women. Into his hands we now entrust the responsibility of carrying on the challenging work begun by his predecessor, Howard Haworth, to whom North Carolina owes a debt of gratitude for his skill in fashioning a blueprint for economic development which recognizes the realities of a new age of transition in the business world.

Claude Pope brings a uniquely broad perspective to his cabinet role: that of former executive of a flagship financial institution and, more recently, as president of his own small mortgage banking firm. He knows intimately the promise of high tech and the threat to our traditional industries. He brings to Commerce the boundless energy which is so necessary to nurture each.

Born and raised on a farm in Harnett County, our new commerce secretary shares with our farm community an understanding of rural life and the importance of our agricultural economy. He is sensitive to the compelling need to diversify our farm production, penetrate foreign markets with value-added commodities, and thus preserve the heritage of the family farm as an economic unit.

When our administration came to Raleigh two years ago, we brought with it a commitment to improve the quality of life for all North Carolinians and to make it possible for all citizens to enjoy the fruits of our growth and prosperity. During 1985, my first year in office, unemployment declined to a record 5 percent; and for the first time in history, more than 3 million North Carolinians held jobs. Reported investments in new and expanded business peaked at an all-time high of $2.5 billion. Our commitment has become a promise fulfilled.

Today, I am pleased to report that 1986 has been another successful year, although the national economy has remained flat. We ended the year with the lowest unemployment of any southeastern state. New business investment remains brisk, and our traditional industries such as textiles, apparel, fibers, furniture, and food processing are making a remarkable recovery from the downward trend which we and the remainder of the nation experienced early in the decade.

In new areas of development, North Carolina has emerged as the second-largest moviemaking state in the nation, and tourism remains a major dollar contributor to our economy. Military bases make a major boost to our economy, but we see opportunities to take better advantage. It is appropriate to point out that Claude Pope assumes his new post at a time which is as challenging as it is potentially rewarding.

As we seek to implement a new strategy for business growth, it will require of us a new determination to restore excellence as the mainstay of public education, shine new light into the darkness of illiteracy, shore up our public facilities, build the schools we desperately need, and maintain the best transportation system in the nation. The budget which I will submit to the 1987 biennial session of the General Assembly, the first of my own making, reflects the strongest possible commitment to these urgent tasks. This budget will require your support; indeed, it merits the support of all citizens who realize that North Carolina has just scratched the surface of its great potential. I have an abiding confidence in our ability to shape the years ahead to a new vision of North Carolina, a new and more dynamic North Carolina built on the enlightenment of future generations.

Even as we assemble here, today, for the official swearing-in of Claude Pope as secretary of commerce, I am pleased to announce that, simultaneously, Sheller-Globe Corporation is announcing the selection of the town of Grover, in Cleveland County, as the location of a new, $10 million, state-of-the-art truck cab manufacturing plant to supply Mack Trucks in neighboring South Carolina. This new facility will mean jobs for more than 100 residents initially, with others to come with future expansions. Congratulations, Secretary Pope.

Sheller-Globe is the first new industry to be announced in 1987, and it serves as a good omen on this very special occasion. I have every confidence that under the strong leadership of Claude Pope, our Department of Commerce, working as a partner with communities throughout North Carolina, will sustain our leadership in economic growth and eclipse our past record. I take this opportunity to congratulate you, Claude, and extend to you every good wish for success in your new role as secretary.

¹Claude E. Pope (1934-1989), born in Harnett County; B.S., University of North Carolina at Chapel Hill, 1956; was also educated at Northwestern University Graduate
School of Mortgage Banking. Various positions with Cameron-Brown Co., 1956-1980,
including president and chief executive officer, 1973-1980; president, Mortgage Bankers
Assn. of America, 1978-1979; chairman, General Electric Mortgage Capital Corp., 1980-
1984; chairman, president, Pope Mortgage Co., Raleigh, from 1984; chairman, North
Carolina Board of Economic Development, 1985-1986; secretary of commerce, 1987-1989;
Republican. *News and Observer*, May 5, 1989; *North Carolina Manual, 1987-1988*, 695.

STATEMENT ON RJR NABISCO

RALEIGH, JANUARY 13, 1987

During a time of rumors and news stories regarding the question of
relocation of the RJR Nabisco corporate headquarters to Atlanta,
Georgia, I have been in frequent contact with Mr. F. Ross Johnson,
president and chief executive of the holding company.[1] He has given
me firm personal assurances that any changes which might be under
consideration would not involve the historic connection of the R. J.
Reynolds Tobacco Company in Winston-Salem.

The board of directors, at its meeting on Thursday, will consider a
proposal to move to Atlanta up to 300 positions associated with the
international, financial, and legal management of the holding company. It was indicated that these operations are of a nature that
require proximity to a much larger metropolitan center. The corporate
management of the vast tobacco manufacturing, marketing, technology, and research operations would all remain headquartered in
Winston-Salem, along with the present 14,000 employees. They would
be under the direction of Mr. Edward A. Horrigan, Jr., chairman and
chief executive of R. J. Reynolds Tobacco, Incorporated, and vice-
chairman of the international holding company, along with Mr.
Gerald H. Long, president of R. J. Reynolds Tobacco, who heads its
domestic operations.[2] Both of these executives will remain in
Winston-Salem. Similarly, as part of the decentralized organization of
RJR Nabisco, other operating components will continue to be headquartered in their current home bases: Nabisco Brands, Incorporated,
in East Hanover, New Jersey, and Heublein, in Hartford, Connecticut,
for example.

In my three conversations with Mr. Johnson, I raised every factor
and idea on behalf of North Carolina, and I am satisfied that all were
given full consideration from every angle. While I would, of course, be
extremely happy to have all of these offices, and more, located in

Winston-Salem, I can only accept and respect any decision that may be reached by the board of RJR Nabisco as being in the best interest of the company, especially its ongoing North Carolina operations.

---

[1]F. Ross Johnson and RJR Nabisco put the rumors to rest on January 15, 1987, by announcing that corporate headquarters would relocate from Winston-Salem to Atlanta. However, the Georgia capital did not long enjoy the prestige of calling itself home to the largest company based in the South. After RJR Nabisco agreed to a buy-out offer from the investment firm of Kohlberg Kravis Roberts and Co., in November, 1988—for a record $14.53 billion—speculation surfaced that headquarters operations might return to Winston-Salem. The company disclosed, on April 27, 1989, that corporate headquarters indeed were to be moved: from Atlanta to New York City. Throughout, the long association of R. J. Reynolds Tobacco with its hometown was not threatened. "Gone with the Wind," *Business: North Carolina* (April, 1987), 13-16, 18-20, 76; *News and Observer*, January 20, 1987, December 4, 8, 1988; *Winston-Salem Journal*, January 16, 18, 1987, December 2, 3, 7, 1988, February 10, April 28, 1989; see also Bryan Burrough and John Helyar, *Barbarians at the Gate: The Fall of RJR Nabisco* (New York: Harper & Row Publishers, Inc., 1990).

F. Ross Johnson (1931-   ), born in Winnipeg, Manitoba; resident of Atlanta; B.Comm., University of Manitoba, 1952; M.B.A., University of Toronto, 1956; honorary degrees; served in Ordnance Corps, Royal Canadian Army. Various executive positions with Standard Brands, Ltd., Toronto, and with Standard Brands, Inc., New York City; president, chief operating officer, 1984-1985, vice-chairman, 1985-1986, Nabisco Brands, Inc.; president, chief operating officer, 1985-1987, R. J. Reynolds Industries, Inc. (RJR Nabisco after 1986); president, chief executive officer, RJR Nabisco, Inc., 1987-1989. *News and Observer*, February 10, 14, 1989; *Who's Who in America, 1988-1989*, I, 1577.

[2]Edward A. Horrigan, Jr. (1929-   ), born in New York City; resident of Winston-Salem; B.S., University of Connecticut, 1950; was graduated from Harvard University Advanced Management Program, 1965; U.S. Army, 1950-1954. Board chairman, chief executive officer, R. J. Reynolds Tobacco International, Inc., 1978-1980; board chairman, president, chief executive officer, 1980-1981, chairman and chief executive officer, chairman and chief operating officer, 1987-1989, R. J. Reynolds Tobacco Co.; executive vice-president, 1981-1984, president and chief operating officer, 1984-1985, board vice-chairman, 1985-1989, RJR Nabisco, Inc. *News and Observer*, February 14, 1989; *Who's Who in America, 1988-1989*, I, 1473-1474.

Gerald H. Long (1928-   ), born in Mineola, New York; was graduated from Adelphi University, 1952. Various positions with R. J. Reynolds Tobacco Co., since 1969, including president and chief operating officer, 1981-1984; became chairman, chief executive officer, R. J. Reynolds Tobacco U.S.A., 1984. *Who's Who in America, 1988-1989*, I1, 1914.

NORTH CAROLINA ASSOCIATION OF SOIL AND WATER CONSERVATION DISTRICTS

WINSTON-SALEM, JANUARY 13, 1987

I am very pleased this morning to have the opportunity to address this, the Forty-fourth Annual Meeting of the North Carolina Association of Soil and Water Conservation Districts. The roots of our nation's soil and water conservation movement are anchored deep in the history of North Carolina. It was here, in 1937, that the first conservation district in the United States was chartered in Anson County, the home of Hugh H. Bennett.[1]

Bennett, who was born on the farm just before the turn of the century, marveled at the wonders of the good earth. Yet, as a boy, he was bewildered by the rude violence of nature and the toll it inflicted upon the land. His native Anson was scarred by ruts and gullies as winds swept away precious topsoil, and heavy rains cut gaping swaths through once-fertile fields. He vowed to conquer the consequences of nature's violence, and the vow became his life's mission. Out of this mission, North Carolina emerged as the pioneer of the conservation movement. It has remained a pioneer to this day, and I am determined, as governor, to maintain this position of national leadership.

The North Carolina of 1986 [sic] is vastly different from the state in which Hugh Bennett began his career as a soil surveyor. Our growth in population, the development of our communities, and the expansion of our industrial and agricultural sectors have reached significant levels in recent years. Soil erosion has many implications we've just begun to recognize since the early 1960s.

Central to the development of our state has been the availability of clean water, but we've noticed in recent years that development, which we have sought aggressively, has brought with it some major adverse effects. Several of our state's rivers and lakes have reached critical nutrient levels, caused by excessive nitrogen and phosphorous intakes from municipal waste treatment plants and surface water runoff from cultivated fields, livestock operations, and other farm activities. The results of this pollution have included fish kills, undesirable odors, decreased recreational values of our lakes and streams, and increased treatment costs for municipal water users.

More than two decades ago, the North Carolina Department of Natural Resources and Community Development began to assess this damage. In tandem with this assessment, an agricultural task force composed of environmental and agricultural agencies worked to develop strategies for nonpoint source pollution control. This assessment led to the identification and classification of three areas as nutrient sensitive: the Falls Lake, Jordan Lake, and Chowan River watersheds. These watersheds embraced sixteen counties.

To the extent that nutrient discharges from waste treatment plants were reduced by controls imposed by this designation, we experienced some slight improvement in surface water quality. However, it wasn't until 1984 that the North Carolina General Assembly appropriated slightly more than $2 million to help agricultural land-owners install Best Management Practices on their farms and thus implement a program to reduce nonpoint pollution. As you know, this program provides formula grants for the implementation of approved practices, with the state bearing 75 percent of the costs. In addition, cost sharing funds were provided in designated counties, on a fifty-fifty basis, to employ technical personnel to assist farmers in planning, designing, and installing conservation measures to prevent downstream pollution.

The overwhelming acceptance received from landowners during the first two years speaks for itself. Agreements were signed with 1,300 landowners for the application of Best Management Practices on more than 80,000 acres of agricultural land. I'm told that these prac-tices will save more than 300,000 tons of soil per year for the next ten years.

But what does this mean in terms of water quality? Gradually, these watersheds are being restored in terms of aesthetics and protection of aquatic life, thereby enhancing their value as natural resources. Moreover, the offsite benefits are worth millions of dollars in lower municipal water treatment costs. The Best Management Practices program has, in all respects, exceeded our greatest expectations, and I want to take this occasion to commend all of you, as well as our county commissions, environmental organizations, agricultural groups, and concerned individuals, for having made it a great success. I applaud your efforts and urge your continued support as I work to expand the program on a statewide basis.

Currently, the state's Cost Share Program for Best Management Practices has been extended to cover thirty-three counties. It is my intent, however, to expand its benefits to all 100 counties during the next three fiscal years, including the addition of adequate technical personnel on a matching support basis with our counties.[2] Thus far, we have relied heavily upon the federal Soil Conservation Service for technical support in planning, design, and application, but the con-tinued availability of federal personnel is threatened by the increasing work load which will be imposed by the "sodbuster" and "swamp-buster" provisions of the 1985 Farm Bill.[3]

During the current year, the $3 million appropriated by the General Assembly for Best Management Practices represented only half of the amount requested by agricultural landowners. In fact, it is estimated by the Department of Natural Resources and Community Develop-ment that about $12 million will be needed annually, through 1997, to eliminate nonpoint pollution. Additional money also will be required for planning and technical assistance. The total cost adds up to something like $139 million over the next eleven years.

Unless federal revenue reductions result in major cuts in conservation funds over the next few years, we can expect to receive approximately $4 million annually. Although these funds are used differently than are state funds, they contribute significantly to the improvement of water quality standards and have about the same net effect as our Cost Share Program.

The North Carolina Cost Share Program was created, as all of you know, for nonpoint source pollution control. This is not the purpose of the 1985 Farm Bill, and there undoubtedly will be instances where the different objectives of the two programs also will create gaps in the utilization of technical assistance in the Soil and Water Conservation Service offices. To help rectify this situation, I am submitting to the North Carolina General Assembly, during its biennial session beginning in February, a budget containing substantial increases in funding for the Office of Water Resources, the Water Quality Control Division, Local Planning and Management Division, and the Soil and Water Conservation Division. The increase in funding for fiscal 1987-1989 will exceed $1.5 million and bring the total budget for that year to more than $4.5 million. My budget also provides an additional $2.6 million in funding for fiscal 1988-1989, thereby boosting the budget for that year to some $5.6 million. Program increases which I am recommending will be used for statewide water supply planning, technical assistance to local governments for water supply planning, protection of watersheds, and expansion of the agricultural cost sharing Best Management Practices program for nonpoint source pollution prevention.

Bear in mind that these increases in my budget, the first budget prepared under my direction since assuming office, come at a time in which we will face demands for funding other major programs, such as public education, economic development, water and sewer financing, highway construction, and improvements in our system of corrections. Consider, also, that our revenue growth is expected to fall below previous years. In spite of the tight budget year ahead, my recommendations to the General Assembly will reflect the largest nonpoint pollution prevention program of any governor in history. My budget expansion will increase the Best Management Practices Cost Share Program to $4 million in 1987-1988 and $5 million in 1988-1989. This means that I am almost doubling the funding over a two-year period. When these funds are combined with federal grants for conservation practices, we will be approaching rapidly the estimated

$12 million required annually to restore our watersheds to their previous high quality standards.

Earlier I voiced my commitment to expand the Cost Share Program statewide. Jim Oliver, my agricultural adviser, informs me that last Sunday the Soil and Water Conservation Commission adopted a recommendation of the agricultural task force supporting that measure. Let me assure you that this expansion necessarily must be contingent upon the allocation of adequate funding to carry out this mission. I believe my budget for the next biennium, and my continued commitment to the program beyond that period, demonstrate a strong determination to allocate the necessary funding, subject to availability of revenue. Thus far, we have shown the state and nation that we intend to maintain our leadership in the conservation movement.

The products of our land and water are enjoyed by all consumers who continue to benefit from the fruits of our labors on the farm. The cost of planning and implementing Best Management Practices cannot be recovered fully by our farmers from the sale of their commodities and livestock. We in North Carolina have an opportunity to provide the assistance which will enable our farmers to improve the quality of life for all citizens, rural and urban alike; we must work together, as one united state, in realizing these goals. I am proud of the partnership that has been established between our participating counties and the state, and I am confident that this partnership will grow as we expand our Best Management Practices program statewide.

Those of you who are here today, representing the ninety-four soil and water conservation districts now serving our 100 counties, are to be commended for sharing Hugh H. Bennett's dream of a land restored to its natural beauty and abundant productivity. You have taken that dream one step beyond his mission: the restoration of our lakes and streams. He would have shared my pride in your accomplishment. As North Carolinians united in a common cause, you have made his legacy a reality which benefits all of our citizens. For that and much more, your dedication and sense of purpose, you have my deepest gratitude.

[1]Hugh Hammond Bennett (1881-1960), native of Wadesboro; B.S., University of North Carolina at Chapel Hill, 1903. Soil conservationist; Soil Erosion Service director, U.S. Interior Department, 1933-1935; Soil Conservation Service director, U.S. Agriculture Department, 1935-1951; author. Powell, *DNCB*, I, 137-138.

[2]The 1987 General Assembly expanded the state's Agriculture Cost Share Program for

Nonpoint Source Pollution Control to include twenty-three new counties. See *N.C. Session Laws, 1987*, II, c. 830, secs. 101-103.

[3]P.L. 99-198, "Food Security Act of 1985" (short title), *United States Statutes at Large*, Act of December 23, 1985, 99 Stat. 1354-1660. Under the "sodbuster" program, farmers cultivating crops on "highly erodible" land were to be denied price supports, crop insurance, FmHA loans, and other federal benefits for all crops. The "swampbuster" program penalized those who transformed designated wetlands to agricultural use; see also *Congressional Quarterly Almanac, 1985*, 524-525.

BLACKS UNITED IN STATE GOVERNMENT TRIBUTE TO DR. MARTIN LUTHER KING, JR.

RALEIGH, JANUARY 15, 1987

I am pleased to join my fellow state employees again, this year, as we honor the memory of Dr. Martin Luther King, Jr., whose preaching, whose example, and whose leadership moved us closer than any living soul to the ideals on which America was founded.

Today, we reflect on his words and his works. Dr. King was truly a prophet who reached out over the chasms of hostility, prejudice, ignorance, and fear to touch the conscience of his native land. Yet the heart of Dr. King's legacy was not only in his teachings as a minister of the Gospel, but his influence as the most skilled advocate of human rights in modern history. Dr. King spent his youth in the Deep South, where he felt both anguish and anger at segregation, "partly because the separate was always unequal," he said, "and partly because the idea of separation did something to my dignity and self-respect."[1]

His life might have taken a different turn had it not been for Rosa Parks, who defied racial etiquette in Montgomery, Alabama, by refusing to yield her seat on a bus. Her arrest for that so-called offense galvanized an entire black community into action. Dr. King later wrote that Rosa Parks "had been tracked down by the *Zeitgeist*—the spirit of the time."[2] It was an observation that he also could have applied to his own emergence as the great civil rights leader whose spark touched off a flame of aspiration among others of his race.

Shortly before he died, Dr. King reminded us what is most important, and this is what he said: "When I die," he said, "don't build a monument to me. Don't bestow on me degrees from great universities. Just say I tried to clothe the naked. Say that I tried to house the homeless. Let people say that I tried to feed the hungry."[3] The real lesson of his life and of his sacrifice, Jesse Jackson said after Dr. King's death, is that the best hope for equality is a people who are well fed and well read.[4]

Twenty-four years ago, Dr. King spoke to a quarter of a million Americans gathered near the Lincoln Memorial, in Washington, and to tens of millions more watching on television.[5] It was there that he held up his dream for America as he would a bright banner for the future. When my administration came to Raleigh two years ago, we brought with it a commitment to improve the quality of life for all North Carolinians, regardless of race or creed, and to make it possible for every citizen to enjoy the fruits of our state's growth and prosperity.

In the spirit of Dr. King's legacy, our commitment has become a promise approaching fulfillment. We have opened the doors of state government wide to all who seek to advance according to their potential, and we have extended help through in-service training, enabling minorities to enhance the skills so necessary to career development and upward mobility. Opportunities have been expanded for minority contractors of goods and services to do business with state government. Through our historically black colleges and universities initiative, funds have been appropriated to establish the first Minority Entrepreneurial Institute on the campus of North Carolina A&T University. Additional projects are now being developed, for implementation at other historically black institutions of higher learning, to strengthen their production of public school teachers.

The first Office of Civil Rights was established in the Department of Transportation, with the late Lafayette Jones serving as its director and infusing it with a new sense of purpose. More black executives now hold key administration positions than at any time in North Carolina's history, and we are constantly opening up new opportunities for other qualified minorities.

These are benchmarks of progress achieved. This is the next wave of equal opportunity, but our larger goal is to reach out through an expanded economy and create good jobs for all who seek employment. No one knew better than Dr. King that economic independence is the real key to personal freedom, and that only through excellence in education does independence have breadth and meaning.

In this commemoration of Dr. King's life there is not only cause for celebration, but cause for commitment to his and his country's unfinished tasks. Dr. Martin Luther King, Jr., believed that America, the richest and most powerful of nations, can lead the way to "a revolution of values" that would ensure a decent life for all people. We share that faith, that dream, on this special occasion; and we join together, here today as one united state, in rededicating ourselves to its ultimate fulfillment.

¹"I could never adjust to the separate waiting rooms, separate eating places, separate rest rooms, partly because the separate was always unequal, and partly because the very idea of separation did something to my sense of dignity and self-respect." Martin Luther King, Jr., "Stride Toward Freedom," in James Melvin Washington (ed.), *A Testament of Hope: The Essential Writings of Martin Luther King, Jr.* (San Francisco: Harper & Row, Publishers, 1986), 421, hereinafter cited as Washington, *Testament of Hope.*

²Rosa Parks (1913-   ), born in Tuskegee, Alabama; was educated at Alabama State College; honorary degree. Former clerk, insurance saleswoman, tailor's assistant; former youth adviser, Montgomery NAACP; Southern Christian Leadership Conference activist. Parks's unwillingness to vacate her bus seat for a white passenger instigated a 1955 boycott that led to the end of segregation on Montgomery city buses; it also earned her recognition as the "mother of the modern civil rights movement." Iris Cloyd (ed.), *Who's Who among Black Americans* (Detroit: Gale Research, Inc., sixth edition, 1990), 979. King commented on Parks in "Stride Toward Freedom"; see Washington, *Testament of Hope,* 424.

³The words attributed to King appear to paraphrase the conclusion of his sermon, "The Drum Major Instinct," delivered February 4, 1968, at Ebenezer Baptist Church, Atlanta. Washington, *Testament of Hope,* 266-267.

⁴Jesse Louis Jackson (1941-   ), born in Greenville, South Carolina; B.A., North Carolina A&T State University, 1964; postgraduate study, Chicago Theological Seminary; honorary degrees. Cofounder, 1966, national director, 1967-1971, Operation Breadbasket; ordained Baptist minister, 1968; founder, executive director, since 1971, Operation PUSH (People United to Save Humanity); candidate for Democratic presidential nomination, 1984, 1988; chairman, National Rainbow Coalition. *Who's Who in America, 1988-1989,* I, 1540.

⁵King delivered his famous "I Have a Dream" address on August 28, 1963, as keynote of the civil rights march on Washington, D.C.; see Washington, *Testament of Hope,* 217-220, for the text of the speech.

GOVERNOR'S PROGRAMS OF EXCELLENCE IN EDUCATION

WINSTON-SALEM, JANUARY 19, 1987

It is my pleasure, this evening, to present the governor's awards for excellence in education. These special citations recognize and reward those schools across our state that have developed, and successfully implemented, exemplary programs to arouse and challenge students at all grade levels and, as a result, enhance their academic achievements. Sixteen outstanding school systems have been selected by the Governor's Committee on Excellence in Education to receive the 1987 awards. Those of you who represent these systems have earned our respect and admiration for your professional dedication.[1]

The task of preparing our future generations, of instilling in them the knowledge, and the skills, and the wisdom to fashion a more perfect North Carolina is one of the noblest and highest callings of a civilized society. Minimum standards are not enough. Excellence is our standard! Let us make no mistake about the challenge before us. How successfully we accomplish the task of building excellence in education will determine the ultimate fate of our state and its citizens.

The consequences of this challenge are sobering. Four years ago, a presidential commission identified us as "a nation at risk." It was an indictment that applied no less, or more, to North Carolina than to most other states. Today, we are a nation engaged in reform. States are leading that reform.

But how far have we advanced since 1983? *U.S. News & World Report* recently asked the same question of twenty-two scholars from the United States, Western Europe, and Japan. Their assessment was published just last Tuesday. Rated against fifteen other countries according to how public education is doing its job, the United States came in next to dead last in math and science in comparison [to] Japan, Russia, West Germany, France, and Britain. We fared the worst among all six nations in teaching our own language and only marginally better in foreign language. The only subject area in which we made a decent showing was in social studies, and even then we were behind West Germany.[2]

With a 180-day schedule, the United States is one of the few major countries with classrooms idle more than half the year. American children, on average, spend 15,000 hours, between the ages of six and eighteen, watching television—2,000 more hours than they spend in school. This statistical observation prompted Richard Darman, deputy secretary of the U.S. Treasury, to say: "We are training generations of experts in 'Wheel of Fortune' and 'Miami Vice.'"[3]

So goes the nation, but in what direction is North Carolina headed? Thirty-one percent of our students drop out of high school without graduating, compared to 25 percent nationally. In Japan, it's only 10 percent. I liked what I read about the progress report on Granville County's success at countering "dropitis," and I want to read good stories about what all of you are doing.

North Carolina has the third-highest rate of functional illiteracy in the nation, with some 800,000 adults lacking the ability to read and write adequately. Our problems do not end here. In descending order, we are thirty-seventh among the states in high school graduates, and forty-eighth in the number of workers who have earned diplomas. Those who remain in school continue to score poorly in math and reading. Few of our schools do well at teaching how to write. In short, our report card "needs improvement."

Last August, in announcing my administration's *Blueprint for Economic Development*, I addressed these problems as major obstacles to attracting new business investment and creating additional jobs and better vocational opportunities for the people of our state. I said then, and I repeat now: Overcoming these barriers to a more exciting and rewarding future for North Carolina must be among our highest priorities. We must make that conquest a compelling goal.

When my administration came to Raleigh two years ago, we brought with us a commitment to improve the quality of life for all North Carolinians and to enable all of our citizens to enjoy the fruits of our state's growth and prosperity. The fulfillment of this commitment is within our reach. We have made a beginning.

For twenty-four straight years prior to my election as governor, state appropriations for elementary and secondary education declined steadily as a percentage of the General Fund—except for two years, 1966 and 1984. This indicates, of course, that many other state responsibilities have accumulated and grown during that span. That's true enough. My point is that it does not show a growing commitment to stronger public schools.

During our first six months in office, state appropriations for public schools were increased by more than $187 million over the biennium, plus an additional $35 million for the same period. State support has grown consistently since that time, from $1.8 billion in 1984-1985, to $2.1 billion in 1985-1986, and to $2.3 billion in 1986-1987. It has grown as a percentage of the General Fund, and I will propose that it do so over the coming biennium.

Last year, I proposed and worked successfully to continue the reduction of teacher-student ratios, established a teacher recruitment office within the Department of Public Instruction, and expanded teacher effectiveness training. At my request, the General Assembly funded tuition grants and tuition loans of $1,000 each to be forgiven for instructional personnel teaching a minimum of two years in subject and geographic areas of teacher shortage. These are significant accomplishments that have demonstrated the sincerity of our commitment, but much still remains to be done. Tonight, I want to take the opportunity this occasion affords me to describe briefly my public school priorities for the next two years.

As we approach the 1987-1988 fiscal year, we are confronted with some critical budgeting decisions. In spite of continued economic expansion statewide, revenue growth during the twelve-month period ending next June is not expected to equal the vigor of the most recent previous years. Don't misunderstand—revenue continues to grow, but at a slower pace. At the same time, we are faced with many important needs in addition to education. They include:

1. Continued expansion of our highway system and stepped-up maintenance of existing roads;

2. Additional improvement of community and countywide water and sewer facilities; and

3. Continuation of our aggressive efforts to recruit new business investments and strengthening our 1985 initiative to serve traditional industries and small business firms.

However, public education is fundamental to all of these. We must provide a better, more productive school system with the best teachers we can find, train, and keep. We must pay them commensurate with their qualifications and effectiveness. This means that we must increase our resources for education in the elementary and secondary schools. If we do not provide adequate funds for education, who will? If not now, when? If we fail in our obligation to our children, how will this affect our opportunities for growth and development?

Make no mistake: The budget I will propose for the next biennium will be tough and tight. It also will be a responsible budget in terms of what our state can afford, and a responsible budget for North Carolina public education—for our children, their schools, and their futures. It will be a budget to build excellence into our schools.

The biennial budget which I will submit to our legislature, next month, will include full funding for the third and fourth years of the Basic Education Program, with the exception of approximately $33 million in additional funding for the expanded 1987-1988 remedial summer school program. Deferment of the summer school program to 1988-1989 is unavoidable in view of the fact that the budget won't be adopted by the General Assembly in time to permit school systems to enter into contracts with teachers for next summer. More importantly, in terms of priorities, [it is] better to be a year late with summer school expansion than to skip even one year's progress in reducing class size, missing one crop of college graduates.

We are currently in the second year of implementing the Basic Education Program which, by 1992, will cost an estimated $800 million. That's an increase of 32 percent for Basic Education alone. Our major purpose is to strengthen state support, statewide, so as to overcome the disparities among schools and school districts across the state, and ensure every child the fullest opportunity for education. I am fully committed to this goal. Although I have had the temerity to question certain priorities in the Basic Education Program, I favor and support much stronger financing of expanded educational opportunity along the lines of the plan now in effect—subject, of course, to any improvements we can make.

One of these improvements—giving local school boards more control over how these funds are spent—will be part of my proposal to the General Assembly next month. In recent years, the state has continued to lay down one mandate after another. It has done so in spite of the fact that a substantial body of research indicates that the most effective schools are those where the learning environment inside the school more closely matches and complements the needs, values, goals, and aspirations of the parents and community in which it is located. The state has gone as far as to impose the acreage required for school facilities and the square footage of offices, custodial space, and general storage. It has mandated staffing levels, and in doing so, it has overridden any notion of local initiative.

Even if this highly structured formula for school design and staffing is assumed to have defined the average needs of our average school, does that mean it should be imposed on a typical school that is not average? Not all schools have the average dropout rate. Must we staff all schools as if they do? When we mandate from Raleigh the number of social workers, psychologists, maintenance workers, transportation supervisors, nutrition specialists, and secretaries, we undermine local judgment, and discretion, and needs; and when we do this, we remove control of individual schools from those closest to the scene— from those who know best the specific priorities of the specific school system.

Therefore, I am proposing to the General Assembly that we grant local school boards more flexibility in terms of how money is spent locally for education. I want them to have more initiative for allocating these increased resources, subject to state board approval. The most effective schools are those in which everyone works together to achieve clear and specific objectives; where parents, teachers, and school board members share the credit when a school performs well and share the blame when it does not.

We also must recognize that if we want excellence in the classroom, we must have professionals in the classroom whom we trust to make wise decisions about the education of our children. If we expect teachers to be professionals, we must treat them as such and reward them accordingly. We must provide them with opportunities for career development; for promotions; for opportunities to accept more responsibility and to earn greater financial reward.

The teacher career ladder pilot program now being tested in sixteen systems seeks to accomplish these goals. We must, I believe, increase our commitment to this program for evaluating teachers and rewarding them with promotions in the classroom. If there is any financial possibility of moving all systems statewide to Career Level I during the biennium, that must be done. Otherwise, the remaining 126 systems could fall so far behind the pay levels of the pilot systems as to create serious problems.

My budget recognizes this need and pledges optimum funding, to the extent revenues are available, to go statewide with Career Level I before the end of the next two years. In this way, we would make a clear commitment to prepare teachers for promotion to Career Level I in all remaining schools in 1988-1989, after three years of experience at that level in the sixteen pilot systems. I would, for now, withhold a decision on going to career levels II and III until the pilot systems will have had some experience at those levels, evaluated by research. Hopefully, that would not be delayed long.

Full funding of the Basic Education plan, on schedule, and statewide implementation of the teacher career ladder program are my first two priorities. Equally important, however, is fulfilling a third need: providing low-cost financing to counties for the construction of school facilities. Last October, I announced that I will ask the 1987 session of the General Assembly to authorize a state school bond referendum to finance a loan pool for construction purposes. This would enable counties to borrow low-interest funds, as needed, to build new schools. Each loan would be amortized separately and repaid from the dedicated half cent of local-option sales taxes, already authorized by the legislature, which is collected by the state and distributed to counties on a per-capita basis.

This proposal, I am pleased to say, has bipartisan endorsement by State Superintendent Phillips and State Treasurer Harlan Boyles, both of whom made valuable contributions to its development. Additionally, endorsements have come from the North Carolina School Boards Association, the Association of Public School Administrators, and countless local school boards, as well as University of North Carolina president C. D. Spangler, Jr.[4] My office is now working with the Department of Public Instruction and the State Treasurer's Office in making an inventory of school construction needs. We currently estimate that approximately $1.5 billion will be needed, and if so, it would represent the boldest bond proposal ever submitted by a governor to the legislature—five times larger than the biggest previous issue.

Meeting the school construction needs of our state is an old problem which has been neglected far too long. We must finally put this issue behind us and move on with urgency in elevating our system of public education to a position of national leadership.

The three priorities I have just outlined will move us light years ahead in achieving excellence in education. But I ask you, are we expecting enough for our money? We will be spending approximately $3.6 billion by 1992. Clearly, and this point cannot be lost, the public is willing to invest in education. Our citizens are willing to pay the price for excellence, but they want results. The time has come for us to redefine our three R's—resources, responsibility, and results. Our public schools cannot become quality schools without all three.

I take great pride in the fact that North Carolina public education is primarily a local-state partnership. It requires the involvement of parents, business leaders, industrial executives, teachers, support personnel, school board members, and local and state elected officials. Public education must become the chief concern of every citizen if we are to move, and we must move, to the forefront of the reform movement.

Former U.S. education secretary Terrell Bell sums it up nicely. He said recently, "Nothing short of a creative state-by-state effort to strengthen education at all levels, comparable to the Marshall Plan in scope, cost, and dedication, can insure the preservation of our democratic legacy for the twenty-first century."[5]

How will we measure up by that challenge? Well, first, the public education program initiated by my administration is creative, coordinated, and comprehensive; and second, we have given it scope and are providing the necessary resources on a scale never before attempted. We will continue to monitor our progress in public education and make adjustments when and where they are required in the interest of excellence. One example of this approach is demonstrated by an announcement I made earlier today at a press conference here in Winston-Salem.[6]

The Basic Education Program mandates the strengthening of foreign language instruction in our schools by 1992, yet it disregards the fact that we must first enhance the training of our foreign language teachers. This afternoon, I announced a proposal to establish the Governor's Foreign Language Institutes. This program of providing intensive training of our promising foreign language teachers will begin operationally in 1988, following a one-year planning period beginning next month. Initial planning will be financed by a $25,000 grant made available by the Mary Reynolds Babcock Foundation and $25,000 in state funds.

The institutes, which will be housed in existing facilities strategically located throughout our state, express a profound belief that our ability to compete in an international economic arena relies upon a sound knowledge of the speech, literature, culture, and life of other countries. The program will be administered by the North Carolina Department of Public Instruction and will focus initially on the traditionally taught languages: Spanish, French, and German. There are two reasons for limiting the program to these languages initially. The first is that they already are widely offered in our public schools and the teaching of them will be enhanced. The second reason is that, at the present time, exceptional instructors in these languages are more readily available. An advisory board appointed by the governor will oversee the institutes, and a consultant will be selected to determine the curriculum, sites, and sources of future funding.

Improving the teaching skills of our foreign language teachers is an integral part of an overall effort to enhance teacher effectiveness, expanded funding for which was included in my 1985 budget. Let me assure you that my administration is fully committed to all of the priorities I have set out tonight. We are determined that our public schools will not become an educational wasteland. We will continue to build toward excellence, just as you have done through the exemplary programs for which you have earned and will receive awards this evening.

"North Carolina will march to greatness on the feet of educated citizens . . . or it will not march. This state must build with its teachers and through them . . . or it will not build." These are not my words. They are the words spoken by Governor W. Kerr Scott in 1949. He went on to say, "I do not need to emphasize the wastefulness of permitting our great company of young people to be subjected to the influence of dispirited and distressed teaching forces from whose numbers the strongest members are being driven away."[7]

His speech of 1949 came shortly after the end of World War II. Our schools, even then, were overcrowded, our teachers underpaid, and our children ill-educated, by national standards. We were a state in transition, intoxicated by a war victory over two formidable enemies.

Governor Scott sounded a clarion call for excellence that continues to this day. We have the chance to redeem his dream, and the vision of Governor Charles Brantley Aycock—who founded our public education program a half century earlier—and Governor Daniel Russell before him. State government does have many responsibilities. Let us prove our commitment is to the first priority among them, to public schools, and let us put first things first: much more effective, top quality schools for our children!

---

[1]The sixteen school systems what won the 1986-1987 Governor's Programs of Excellence Award included: Alamance County, Brunswick County, Buncombe County, Burlington City, Gates County, Goldsboro City, Granville County, Haywood County, High Point City, Iredell County, Johnston County, Kinston City, New Hanover County, Perquimans County, Scotland County, and Shelby City. Press release, "Governor Martin Announces Governor's Programs of Excellence in Education Awards," Winston-Salem, January 19, 1987, Governors Papers, James G. Martin. The release also named the specific program commended in each system.

[2]"The Brain Battle," *U.S. News & World Report*, January 19, 1987, 58-65, hereinafter cited as "The Brain Battle."

[3]Richard Gordon Darman (1943-   ), born in Charlotte; B.A., 1964, M.B.A., 1967, Harvard University. Investment banker; business consultant; educator; deputy assistant, U.S. Department of Health, Education, and Welfare, 1971-1972; assistant to secretary, Department of Defense, 1973; principal, director, ICF, Inc., 1975, 1977-1980; assistant secretary, U.S. Commerce Department, 1976-1977; assistant to President Reagan, 1981-1985; deputy secretary, U.S. Treasury Department, 1985-1987; became managing director, Shearson Lehman Brothers, Inc., 1987; author; editor. *Who's Who in America, 1988-1989*, I, 712. Darman's comment on the television viewing habits of American youth was recorded in "The Brain Battle," 60.

[4]Clemmie Dixon Spangler, Jr. (1932-   ), born in Charlotte; resident of Chapel Hill; B.S., University of North Carolina at Chapel Hill, 1954; M.B.A., Harvard University, 1956; U.S. Army, 1956-1958. President, C. D. Spangler Construction Co., 1958-1986, and of Golden Eagle Industries, Inc., 1968-1986; chairman, State Board of Education, 1982-1986; board chairman, Bank of North Carolina, 1982-1986; director, Hammermill Paper Co., from 1982, and of Aeronca, Inc., 1983-1985, and NCNB Corp., 1983-1986; succeeded William C. Friday as University of North Carolina president, 1986. Trudy Atkins, assistant to the president, University of North Carolina, to Jan-Michael Poff, March 7, 1986.

[5]"The Brain Battle," 64.

[6]For related press release, see "Governor Martin Announces Plans for Governor's Language Institutes," Raleigh, January 19, 1987, Governor's Papers, James G. Martin. Martin also presented an overview of his proposal for the Governor's Language Institutes in remarks to the Second Language Conference, Raleigh, March 16, 1987.

[7]"For instance, we cannot withhold a living wage from the 26,000 public school teachers in this state without a great cost in terms that can be measured, as well as in values that cannot be measured. Let us never forget that our richest possession is the great army of children who were born to North Carolinians and who are with us as citizens of the immediate future. North Carolina will march to greatness on their feet or it will not march.

"More than a million of these young people are under the daily inspiration and instruction of these 26,000 teachers. This state must build with them and through them or it will not build. I do not need to emphasize the wastefulness of permitting this great company of young people to be subjected to the influence of dispirited and distressed teaching forces from whose numbers the stronger members are gradually being driven away." Radio address, "School and Road Bond Election," Raleigh, May 10, 1949, quoted in Corbitt, *Addresses of Scott*, 116.

NORTH CAROLINA JOB TRAINING COORDINATING COUNCIL

RALEIGH, JANUARY 22, 1987

I am delighted to be here today and to have the opportunity to address the North Carolina Job Training Coordinating Council, chairmen of the state's Private Industry Council, and local administrators of our Job Training Partnership Act programs. I also want to welcome members of the Council of State, representatives of the cabinet, staff, and guests.

Most recently, the renaissance of American business and industry has been described as the reinvention of the corporation. Just as North Carolina is seeking to define its role in training and retraining our working citizens for jobs of the future, both flagship business firms and entrepreneurial ventures are attempting to delineate their place in an expanding global economy. North Carolina must be especially alert to the consequences that can follow mergers because that can cause our finest, most successful, homegrown businesses to acquire a wider national—even international—set of loyalties, and responsibilities, and markets. Yet, the main thing for us to do about that is to work hard to improve our climate for doing business. Most important to the private sector in its site selection is the part that workers will play in their survival and success.

As we tackle the enormous task of preparing workers for the future, I am comforted, as governor, by the fact that those of you who are here represent a diversified and well-balanced group of public and private interests. I am confident that, together, you possess the ability, the desire, and the expertise to fashion our job training programs in such a way as to utilize our resources wisely and in the best interest of all North Carolinians.

As most of you know, the Job Training Coordinating Council includes business leaders and representatives of labor, local education, and community-based organizations. Similarly, local-level private industry councils draw the majority of their membership from the business community, with other members coming from a variety of local organizations. Each contributes significantly to a truly effective public-private partnership.

Today I want to discuss with you the reason our labor force development is a major challenge, requiring a renewed public-private commitment, and some of the answers to this challenge. Labor force development is a major challenge more so than ever because our economy, and thus, the demands on our workers, are changing rapidly.

North Carolina's economy is diversified. It is based on traditional industries—such as textiles, fiber, apparel, furniture, tobacco and other agricultural products—as well as research, technology, finance, services, information, and communications. However, we no longer can depend solely upon having a hardworking, dependable work force as in the past, when our only concern was domestic competition. Now we must be prepared to compete at all levels in an international economy. This means that we must have a well-trained and trainable work force capable of acquiring new and better skills.

Since labor force development is one of the key elements of economic development and prosperity, as explained in our *Blueprint for Economic Development*, we must anticipate and prepare for radical changes. If we succeed in the challenge of developing our work force to meet the needs of new and expanding businesses, we will indeed prosper as a people. We will prosper because jobs of the future will demand higher technical skills, and, as a result, will pay substantially higher wages.

What will it take to meet this challenge? Trends indicate that a worker no longer can depend upon remaining in the same job, or even the same career, during his or her lifetime. Instead, our workers will change jobs, on average, as many as six or eight times before retirement—I have, four times already.

Experts tell us that 80 percent of the people who are employed today will still be in the work force in the year 2000, and that at least one half of these workers will require retraining by the dawn of the next century. Add to this startling forecast the fact that, nationally, the work force is shrinking. The post-World War II baby boomers have peaked. Birth rates are declining. People are living and remaining active longer. More people will need to work by the year 2000 to keep our economy growing.

The answer to this challenge of developing a viable work force for the future is to make sure that our citizens have the basic skills demanded by a business world in evolution. Let me assure you that I am firmly committed, as governor, to two responsibilities: (1) providing ample opportunities for training and retraining, and (2) enhancing the educational status of every individual who desires to fulfill his or her potential. To support this commitment, I am proposing to the North Carolina General Assembly, as part of my legislative program, the establishment of an independent North Carolina Employment

Security Commission reserve fund.[1] I announced this proposal for the first time last October.

Establishment of this reserve fund will allow the state to reduce federal unemployment insurance taxes approximately 30 percent. This reduction will free by about $50 million the amount employers must pay, thus providing a $50 million tax cut as a shot in the arm for the entire state's economy. The remaining $50 million will be used to create the reserve fund, earning approximately $4 million the first year to be used for retraining programs to help all unemployed workers—including, for the first time, displaced farmers and farm workers—to find jobs and to help train people who are entering the labor market. As the state reserve fund grows, so will interest earnings to finance retraining programs.

The first part of accomplishing this mission, that of placing workers in a position to be retrained, requires a level of literacy in reading, writing, and math skills which many of our workers don't have. They may have managed to get by without these basic skills in their present jobs, but they won't be as fortunate in the future. Consequently, a major challenge we face is adult literacy, and it's going to be a tough challenge. Many people are reluctant to admit they are illiterate and do not seek help. Consider, if you will, that an estimated 800,000 North Carolinians are functionally illiterate. That means their contributions to our state are severely limited.

We need a variety of methods to reach these people, as well as effective programs to correct their educational deficiencies. To help meet this challenge, I plan to request local literacy councils, throughout the state, to play the major role of reaching out to those needing literacy training and to work with our community colleges in teaching them the basic skills. Currently, there are fifty local literacy councils in North Carolina operating under the umbrella of the North Carolina Literacy Association, an agency funded by the North Carolina Department of Cultural Resources. These councils receive grant funds from the state library system, under the Library Services and Construction Act, to establish offices and employ staff personnel.[2]

I also plan to ask the Department of Community Colleges to play the major role of providing literacy programs and to augment their efforts to make training available at convenient locations, including the work site. My request to the Department of Community Colleges will include encouraging it to utilize innovative techniques, such as individual, self-paced literacy training, instruction of small groups, and individual tutors. In short, I propose that we do whatever is necessary to get the job done. We simply cannot afford to waste a resource as great as 800,000 adults.

Now let me turn my attention to another part of this challenge: the task of providing up-to-date labor market information. With the job market changing so rapidly during this transition of our economy, labor market information becomes a critical factor in determining what jobs are available and the requirements they demand. This information needs to be updated and distributed in a timely fashion. The Employment Security Commission has produced a new labor market guide that gives this type of information. I propose that we distribute it widely, especially for use in assisting workers who have lost their jobs in our traditional industries—including farming. I also propose that it be made available to every high school student.

Related to literacy training, one of our state's major concerns must be the growing number of students who drop out of school before graduation. That's the supply source of new illiterates. Many experts think the reason for our high dropout rate lies in the fact that many students consider high school a dead end, that it has no purpose and has no bearing on their getting and keeping a good job. Another reason may be that high school students have so little knowledge about available jobs.

For these reasons and many more, I propose that students in the eighth and twelfth grades be given career guidance testing and counseling, using the General Aptitude Test Battery. The GATB is the method most frequently used by employers to evaluate potential employees. The test results will indicate to the student his or her general aptitude for a variety of careers, as well as potential earning power should the student consider entering the work force at the time the test is given. From test results, a student can choose a career and find out what education and training is needed to obtain a job in that field.

The goal of testing and counseling is to help the student prepare for entry into the work force. These devices are not designed to dictate which courses must be taken. On the contrary, testing and counseling will help prevent the student from dropping out of school by contributing to an understanding of the importance of education in earning a good living, doing satisfying work, and living a rewarding life.

Turning now to the impact of technology on the workplace, we find a compelling need to upgrade our technical skills training programs. No longer can we depend on traditional technical skills training to prepare students for life beyond the classroom. We must offer them more.

It is well known that I favor and support the "two-plus-two" program in which a high school student spends two years acquiring the applied basic foundation for two years of training to learn the more highly technical skills in community college. I understand that this approach is now called Tech Prep. By whatever name it is called, I believe it is important for students to have a firm foundation in the basic skills of reading, writing, and math—taught in such a way that the student can relate this education to a chosen field of work before being offered the technical skills associated with the career. I am told that the Department of Community Colleges and the Department of Public Instruction, the latter through its Vocational Education Program, are moving in this direction, and I am delighted that progress is being achieved. Let's continue to work toward this goal with renewed effort.

So far, I've covered considerable ground—adult literacy, job information for adults and young people, and technical skills training. Now I want to talk about the greatest challenge of all: retraining.

I mentioned earlier that trends indicate that we can expect our workers to change jobs and require retraining perhaps eight times during their working life. A good example of this can be found in our traditional industries. As companies in this sector make changes to become more competitive, they require workers with higher technical skills. Those without these skills are laid off. This means that, for the work force in North Carolina to remain competitive with other states and foreign countries, we must provide our people greater opportunities for retraining.

The focus of retraining should be on retraining and reemploying workers who have lost their jobs in traditional industries, including farming. Therefore, I propose supplementing the Dislocated Workers Program with state funds. At the present time, federal funds are used here to send teams of interagency specialists to sites of plant closings to help retrain and reemploy those workers who have lost their jobs. Our program in this area has been so successful that North Carolina has become a national model. In fact, we're doing such a good job that we are one of the few states that has spent its regular allocation of federal money and has received discretionary funds. I want to say that I'm proud of this success—so proud that I recently made farmers and farm workers eligible for this assistance.

There are many other initiatives that I support. One of them is the continued funding of our program to train individuals for jobs in new and expanding North Carolina industries. Another is the continued funding of the community college program for cooperative skills training to help traditional industries upgrade employees to the point that these industries become more competitive in the world market-place. And, third, I favor and will support the shift of funds to occupational extension courses providing training and retraining that is tailor-made to the specific needs of business and industry. The level of funding now available does not support this most important aspect of retraining. Finally, I plan to promote continued grant diversion in our Aid to Families with Dependent Children program in those cases where the welfare payment reimburses a business for part of on-the-job training given to an employed welfare recipient.

As the job market continues to undergo its metamorphosis from caterpillar to butterfly, our challenge will be to simplify the job training and job search process. One way to do this is to establish one-stop job centers across our state to serve as a starting point for individuals seeking jobs, job training, job information, and referral to employment and training programs. These centers could be, and should be, the one place a citizen could go to obtain whatever assistance is needed to get a job.

Today I have talked about some rather broad and far-reaching ideas for developing North Carolina's labor force. To work out the details of these ideas and to put them to work to enhance our state will take a strong commitment from job training experts in both the public and private sectors. Since the Job Training Coordinating Council embraces the strong partnership necessary to meet these challenges, it is the ideal group to undertake this task. With this in mind, I charge you, the council, with the responsibility of meeting the new challenges of labor force development. Specifically, by executive order, I am expanding the role of the council to oversee all labor force efforts in North Carolina; to recommend how we can best use the interest generated by the Employment Security Commission reserve funds, if enacted; and most importantly, to take the ideas I have presented today and fashion them into a comprehensive and coordinated statewide program. Make it work for me.

I am depending on you, the council members, under the capable leadership of Ron Davis,[3] to accept this challenge and to succeed. I believe that North Carolina is a special place with a special destiny. I believe that North Carolinians are special people, and I believe we are destined to be the beacon of hope in a changing world which calls upon us, above all, to be great. As one united state we can make it so, for this generation and those to follow.

¹"An Act to Reduce the Rates of Unemployment Insurance Contributions and to Establish the Employment Security Commission Reserve Fund" was ratified March 16, 1987. *N.C. Session Laws, 1987,* I, c. 17.

²For provisions of the Public Library Services and Construction Act, see *United States Code* (1988 edition), Title XX, Sections 351 et seq.

³Ronald H. Davis (1932-   ), born in Richmond, Virginia; resident of Greensboro; B.S., University of Richmond, 1953; U.S. Army, 1953-1955. Personnel manager, Plastics Division, Reynolds Metals Co., 1962-1967; employee relations manager, Gilbarco, 1967-1972; vice-president for administration, Carolina Steel Corp., since 1972; chairman, North Carolina Job Training Coordinating Council. Ronald H. Davis to Jan-Michael Poff, September 6, 1988.

NORTH CAROLINA ASSOCIATION OF CHAMBER OF COMMERCE EXECUTIVES

RALEIGH, FEBRUARY 3, 1987

[Martin presented a similar speech to the North Carolina Retail Merchants Association, Pinehurst, February 4, 1987.]

I am very pleased, this afternoon, to have the opportunity to meet with you, our chamber of commerce executives and volunteer leaders from across the state, and to discuss our agenda for the next two years. I'll come back to that agenda in a few minutes. But first, I want to say that your conference comes at a time of unprecedented optimism in North Carolina—optimism about our future, optimism about the direction in which North Carolina is going, and optimism among our citizens about their own lives.

We've just ended 1986 with the lowest unemployment rate in the Southeast: 5.1 percent. Not too shabby; indeed, comfortably lower than the national average. More of our citizens than ever before are working today—well above 3 million—many of them at higher skills and better pay; working to raise our standard of living, to enhance our quality of life, and to strengthen our family values. Jobs in our traditional industries—textiles, apparel, fiber, furniture, food, tobacco, and other agricultural commodities—are rebounding from pre-1985 lay-offs and plant closings.

Our economy is on the move, thanks in part to our programs to help small business firms and to encourage more entrepreneurs. It's on the move because we seized the moment, when it was ripe, to begin to reduce our strategic anti-job taxes, enabling our traditional, homegrown industries to retrofit their plants, improve their manufacturing processes, and become more competitive in world markets.

And we achieved this tax cut, the largest in North Carolina's history, without reducing revenues to our local governments.

When my administration came to Raleigh two years ago, we brought with us a strong commitment to increase North Carolina's investment in public education, better highways and roads, port facilities, community airports, and expanded water and sewer systems— all of the things that are fundamental to economic growth, thriving communities, and financially independent people. Running state government demanded that we do things more efficiently and effectively, and use the savings for extended services; more paving; teachers. Increasing competition by other states in the recruitment of new business investment alerted us to the need for a blueprint for economic development as a more accurate guide to the future growth of our communities and state. We knew that we had to do a better job of domestic marketing and exporting abroad to increase sales of our agricultural products and manufactured goods; and finally, we recognized that we needed to strengthen our state and local partnership, to work together as one united state, to achieve our goals.

We've made a strong beginning toward achieving these goals during the past two years. The time has now come for us to continue building on this record, as true partners in progress.

Last week, I delivered to the Advisory Budget Commission my biennial budget for 1987-1989, seeking to establish bipartisan support as we prepare to convene a new session of the General Assembly. It proposes spending some $19.6 billion over the next two years, slightly more than $4 billion of which will be received in federal funds. That may sound large, but it is a responsible budget in terms of what North Carolina can afford, without increasing taxes or placing an additional burden upon our citizens. Moreover, it is responsible in the way it addresses our agenda, which includes:

1. A quality basic education for every child in our state, taught by effective teachers in schools that truly aspire to excellence;

2. New and better primary and secondary highways and rural roads for a growing state, linking our industries to markets, workers to jobs, farms to cities, and tourists to vacation destinations;

3. Expanded water and sewer facilities to serve our growing urban centers and rural communities and to meet the needs of new and existing businesses and industries; and

4. Innovative, more aggressive approaches to recruiting additional business investment, assisting small business firms, financing new ventures, expanding food processing, and increasing exports, while continuing to strengthen our traditional industries.

There should be no doubt in anyone's mind that we must put education first, or that the place to start is in our elementary and secondary schools. Consider these facts:

—31 percent of our students who start school drop out before graduation, compared to 25 percent nationally. The rate in Japan is only 10 percent.

—North Carolina ranks thirty-seventh among the fifty states in the number of students who actually graduate, and we're almost dead last—in forty-eighth place, to be exact—in the number of adult workers who have received diplomas.

—Our young people continue to score poorly in math, reading, and other skills.

—North Carolina has about 800,000 functional illiterates, people who cannot read, write, and work math problems well enough to hold a job; and

—Approximately 900,000 North Carolinians are employed in jobs below the federal poverty level. Most of them never completed high school.

It is estimated that American industry spends about $25 billion annually to train poorly schooled workers. David Kearns, chairman of Xerox, warns that "We cannot compete successfully (with other nations) unless we have a competitive work force." He says, "Clearly, we have to rethink our education system from the ground up."[1]

We've been doing just that in North Carolina for the last two years. Prior to my becoming governor in 1985, state spending for all public education declined as a percentage of the General Fund in all but two of the preceding twenty-four years, almost a quarter century spanning five certified "education governors." We ended that backward slide during our first six months in office, adding more than $187 million to the education budget during the biennium ending next June. State support has grown consistently since then, from $1.8 billion in 1984-1985, to $2.1 billion in 1985-1986, and to $2.3 billion in 1986-1987.

However, money alone cannot solve all of our problems in education. Our citizens are prepared to support education reform, but they want us to invest wisely and to get results. This is what my budget for 1987-1989 seeks to accomplish. It proposes full funding of the Basic Education Program for the third and fourth years, allocating $112 million to the program in 1987-1988 and $245 million in 1988-1989.

The only departure from the BEP's schedule is the deferment of the remedial summer school program next year at a cost of less than $33 million. Deferment of this program is not a matter of choice, but rather necessity, since the budget won't be adopted by the General Assembly in time for school systems to enter into teacher contracts for next year. There is, however, $14 million left over from this past summer, and I propose that be used for summer school expansion since those commitments can be made now with these carry-over funds.

We currently are in the second year of the Basic Education Program which, by 1992, will cost an estimated $800 million. That's an increase of 32 percent for Basic Education alone. The Basic Education Program's chief virtue and purpose is to equalize the disparities among schools and school districts across our state; to strengthen state support for all our schools, statewide. Although I have questioned some of the priorities of the program, I favor and support much stronger financing and expanded educational opportunity along the lines of the BEP; this, of course, is subject to any future improvements we can make.

One of these improvements is to give local school boards more flexibility, subject to prior approval by the State Board of Education, in how these funds will be spent. Improved local control will ensure we get the most for our money. My goal is not simply basic education; it is quality basic education, resulting from local initiative to match these new resources to local needs. I believe this is what North Carolina really wants to achieve. Indeed, I believe this is what our citizens are demanding of our schools.

In recent years, the state has continued to impose one mandate after another upon our local school systems. It has done so in spite of overwhelming research that the most effective schools are those where the learning environment inside the school more closely matches and complements the needs, values, goals, and aspirations of the parents and the community in which it is located. When these mandates are imposed, local judgment and discretion are undermined. Control of our schools is removed from those closest to the student—from school board members, teachers, and administrators who know best the specific needs which must be met. Therefore, my budget proposes more local control over how Basic Education funds will be spent.

We also must recognize that if we want excellence to become the standard in our schools, we must have professionals in our classrooms whom we trust to make wise decisions about the education of our children. In short, if we expect to get and keep the best teachers available, and if we expect them to be truly professionals, we must treat them as such and pay them accordingly. No resource is as vital to improved schools as a stronger teaching staff.

We must provide them with opportunities for career development, opportunities to accept more responsibility, to enhance the effectiveness of their teaching and, as a result, earn greater financial rewards for doing what they do best: teach. We have never before been able to offer good teachers a promotion in the classroom. The teacher career ladder program, now being tested in sixteen school systems across North Carolina, is designed to accomplish this goal. It is essentially a promotion system. We must, however, increase our commitment to this program to evaluate teachers on the basis of performance, and reward them with better pay for better teachers.

My budget for the biennium asks the General Assembly to speed up implementation of this program by adding approximately twelve new systems in 1987-1988, and to go statewide, just up to Career Level I, by 1988-1989. I believe there is adequate experience with the pilot program to take this step after three years of experimentation. And, I am concerned that if we delay implementation further, we will be creating serious problems. Some of the school systems adjoining those in the pilot program already are having difficulty recruiting and keeping good teachers because of the disparity in salaries. This problem will only get worse the longer we delay statewide implementation.

Ensuring quality basic education for our children and raising the professional and salary levels of our teachers are but two of our immediate objectives in public education. The third is providing low-cost loans to counties for the construction of new facilities to relieve overcrowding and to provide for expansions required in the Basic Education Program. Last October I announced that I would ask the 1987 General Assembly to authorize a state school bond referendum which, if approved by voters statewide, will enable us to use the state's triple-A bond rating to generate a state loan pool. Under this plan, counties could borrow against the dedicated part of local sales tax revenues already set aside for schools to build the facilities they need now. It is estimated that approximately $1.5 billion is required to build the schools we need. The only way to meet this pressing need is to provide a way in which counties can finance construction, thus preserving the historical responsibility of counties for school buildings.

I believe the budget which I have presented to the Advisory Budget Commission establishes education as our first, but certainly not our only, priority. In addition, I am asking for additional funds to provide continued highway construction, water and sewer loans to local governments, and $5.7 million for implementation of the *Blueprint for*

Economic Development. I understand that it is this latter proposal in which our chambers of commerce are particularly interested.

Currently, it is difficult for smaller firms to procure industrial revenue bond financing because of the high transactional costs. By creating a pooled industrial revenue bond mechanism, we can reduce significantly these costs and ensure that small businesses have the same access to this type of financing as larger companies. We also are finalizing plans for two new initiatives in the field of seed venture capital.

Ours is a state and nation founded by venture capitalists. In one way or another, all of our great innovations and inventions have been started or expanded through the effective use of venture capital. In considering this fact, I am recommending, fourthly, with the concurrence of the state treasurer, that state trust funds be authorized to invest in private, investment-quality venture capital funds—not mandated; authorized. This would help send a message to the entrepreneurs of this country that North Carolina appreciates the value of their contribution to our economy, and that we have an environment that encourages innovation and stimulates ideas.

Fifth, we also are working to bring about a private, early venture capital, or seed venture capital fund in North Carolina, which might include tax credits or similar benefits to investors. I have asked Hugh McColl,[2] chairman and chief executive officer of NCNB Corporation, to lead this effort. This fund would be established and replenished from private investments, not [by] infusions of appropriations out of the state budget!

Finally, sixth, the Commerce Department is now engaged in efforts to establish a statewide "504" certified development corporation. Currently, there are fifty-two counties in North Carolina with access to the Small Business Administration's "504" program. This has been accomplished through the establishment of local "504" certified development companies to act as loan originators and facilitators. In order to bring similar services to other areas of the state, we are setting up a state-sponsored "504" development company. Through this program, we will be able to provide the same services to small business firms in the forty-eight counties that are not served now by local programs.

These are six, new, private-sector solutions that avoid the risky alternative of doling out state dollars to favored businesses. Other initiatives planned by the Department of Commerce include the opening of a Pacific Rim office to stimulate more trade with foreign nations in that part of the world and to encourage more reverse investment by foreign companies in North Carolina. Part of the funds

I have proposed for implementing the *Blueprint for Economic Development* will be used to strengthen staffing at our regional offices throughout the state, as well as to open a regional office in the northeastern counties. We currently are in the process of staffing a new office in Lenoir, and this represents our continued effort to increase the department's services to our cities, counties, and towns.

I spoke earlier about the need for training and retraining our current work force as the demands for new skills increase. Time does not permit me to review the entire budget with you today, so I want to describe briefly some of our initiatives in that area of interest.

Last week, Secretary of Commerce Claude Pope announced that he and I are proposing several innovative ways to provide funding for small business firms and entrepreneurships. These would enhance financing of homegrown business in North Carolina, but without establishing a state governmentally funded program that would likely degenerate into pork-barrel-like, political decisions as to who would be favored—who would win and lose.

The first would work to enhance the availability of fixed-rate, long-term financing for small business. This program would embrace a joint effort by the Treasurer's Office and financial institutions throughout the state. Under this plan, the state and other interested institutions would place long-term certificates of deposit at cooperating banks. The funds invested in these certificates would then be committed by these banks for lending to small businesses on a fixed rate, long-term basis at prevailing rates and terms.

The second proposal would provide a secondary market for small business loans guaranteed under various Small Business Administration programs. This would encourage the financial institutions in North Carolina to make more such loans available to small business firms, since they would have a method of selling those loans in a secondary market. Our third proposal in the field of conventional financing involves working to make North Carolina's industrial revenue bond program more widely accessible to small businesses, especially in rural counties that have been left out. We plan to do this through what is commonly known as an "umbrella bond" mechanism.

To support our commitment to meet this need, I am asking the General Assembly to establish an independent North Carolina Employment Security Commission reserve fund. This reserve fund will allow the state to reduce federal unemployment insurance taxes approximately 30 percent. This reduction will cut, by about $50 million, the amount of taxes employers must pay, thus providing a $50 million shot in the arm to the entire state's economy. The remaining $50 million will be used to create the reserve fund, earning about $4 million in interest the first year to be used for retraining unemployed workers—including, for the first time, displaced farmers and farm workers. As the reserve fund grows, so will interest earnings to finance new and expanded training programs.

I have also proposed that, as we amend the state tax code to keep parallel those features that copied the federal law before 1986, if there is expected a substantial revenue gain, greater than $25 million picked up, we should offset that excess with a compensatory tax cut aimed at the same taxpayers to avoid sticking them with a heavy, net tax burden. This may give us just the opportunity we need to relieve the intangibles tax, or at least another part of it.

As chamber of commerce executives and business leaders, you can do much to help North Carolina increase its business growth by supporting the budget that I am asking the General Assembly to approve, and staying alert to these features. We must continue to work as partners, as citizens of one united state, to ensure all of our citizens a future that is filled with opportunity and a higher standard of living. This is the real secret to building better communities for everyone. North Carolina doesn't need to be timid, or attack those who invest in jobs here. North Carolina needs bold leadership. I hope you feel like you've got it!

---

[1]David Todd Kearns (1930-　　), born in Rochester, New York; B.S., University of Rochester, 1952; U.S. Naval Reserve, 1952-1954. Various positions with IBM Corp., 1954-1971; with Xerox Corp., since 1971, chairman and chief executive officer since 1985. *Who's Who in America, 1988-1989*, I, 1646.

[2]Hugh Leon McColl (1935-　　), born in Bennettsville, South Carolina; B.S., University of North Carolina at Chapel Hill, 1957; U.S. Marine Corps Reserve, 1957-1959. Started as trainee, 1959-1961, later served as president, 1974-1983, and board chairman, from 1983, NCNB National Bank; president, 1981-1985, board chairman, from 1983, NCNB Corp.; Democrat. *Who's Who in America, 1988-1989*, II, 2055.

ACCEPTANCE OF CRIME COMMISSION REPORT

RALEIGH, FEBRUARY 6, 1987

[Governor Martin discussed the problem of victims' rights, below, and in his address before the North Carolina Victims Assistance Network Conference, Raleigh, April 30, 1987.]

I am pleased, today, to accept this legislative agenda, *In Pursuit of Justice*, with profound gratitude for the leadership and dedication you have given to the study of North Carolina's major criminal justice issues and concerns.[1] In May of 1985, I directed the Department of Crime Control and Public Safety and the Department of Correction to conduct a comprehensive study of our state's sentencing practices, alternative punishment programs, and prisoner and probationer recidivism—among other matters—and to relate how they impact upon our problem of prison overcrowding. In cooperation with the Governor's Crime Commission, Secretaries Dean and Johnson assumed this urgent and important mission with the determination that our state has the ability to solve this problem without federal intervention. This determination is stamped indelibly upon this report, and this morning I want to commend you for its depth and scope. It reflects the fact that your concern became a matter of collective involvement in seeking to arrive at viable recommendations.

As you know, public confidence in our system of justice is not what it should be. Many North Carolinians are not satisfied with a system they say is out of balance, with the scales tipped in favor of the criminal. They are complaining that, somewhere along the line, the system has lost track of its mission to be fair and to protect those who obey the law, while punishing those who break it.

Citizens are demanding tougher sanctions for criminals and greater sensitivity to victims. This legislative agenda, *In Pursuit of Justice*, embraces these concerns and strives to make better use of our criminal justice resources to protect the public more effectively.

The section of your report dealing with sentencing reform is the culmination of a year-and-a-half-long study of current sentencing practices in North Carolina. It bears out the conclusion that we must restore truth in sentencing. With all of the various provisions for early release, time off for good behavior, and work furloughs, even judges complain about not having any idea how long an offender will spend behind bars. I believe that the sentence imposed should be the sentence served. Therefore, I support your recommendation for extending the time a prisoner serves under correction supervision by eliminating good-time credits.

Our state must continue to sentence its most dangerous criminals to prison. For some, there is simply no alternative. However, to ease our serious prison overcrowding situation, it is imperative that alternatives to incarceration be sought and utilized when appropriate for the crime, and the criminal, and in cases where no threat is posed to society. I agree with the commission's recommendation to limit the number of persons convicted of misdemeanors—that is, lesser offenses—sent to prison. Only those repeat offenders or those on probation should receive an active jail term.

In the budget which I have proposed for 1987-1988, I am asking for $37.7 million to relieve prison overcrowding by reducing case loads for probation officers, implementing a community punishment pilot program, and providing for two privately built and run minimum custody facilities. I also am recommending that $17.5 million be appropriated as soon as possible for the construction of thirty-two, fifty-man satellite jails.[2] I believe these remedies will take us far in relieving the prison overcrowding we now have.

Let me also say that I look with favor upon your idea of adopting an administrative remedy procedure for the Department of Correction. In compliance with federal law, this procedure would reduce the number of inmate lawsuits. Currently, an average of 300 lawsuits are filed each year. An administrative remedy procedure would help to end this drain on the resources of the Department of Correction, Attorney General's Office, and the federal courts.[3]

Many citizens are not satisfied with the quality and level of services provided to victims of crime. An increasing number of victims feel they have been overlooked, their pleas for justice have gone unheeded, and their emotional, personal, and financial wounds have been neglected. All of us in government and the courts must not forget about the victims. Our criminal justice system could not survive without their cooperation and participation. If victims and witnesses are so turned off by the system that they refuse to report and testify about crime, our free society is powerless to hold criminals accountable for their actions. To restore balance to the administration of justice, we must improve services for victims of crime.

You, the members of the Crime Commission, heard victims across the state speak out at public forums which you held last fall. You heard law-abiding citizens speak out against injustices, not only suffered at the hands of criminals, but also at the hands of insensitive attorneys. One woman, who was the victim of rape, complained that no one kept her informed about pretrial release. She thought the man who raped her was still in jail, until he called her at home and threatened her again.

One way to improve services for victims is to provide them with financial compensation for medical expenses resulting from the crime. Many states have passed laws providing financial assistance to victims; North Carolina's Victims Compensation Act has been on the books since 1983. However, the General Assembly has declined to fund it. Without money, this law is meaningless, and victims are no better off today than before the law was passed. I do not believe it is too much to ask that funds be set aside to compensate victims of violent crimes for their uninsured physical losses. As an alternative, perhaps we need to look at the possibility of asking the legislature to increase court costs as a means of providing revenue for this purpose.[4]

Your recommendation involving the privacy of victims is excellent, and I commend you for your compassion and sensitivity to the needs of victims. It should be difficult for defendants to get personal information about crime victims. Addresses and telephone numbers should be omitted from records and testimony, unless the judge needs to know.[5]

Reporting and testifying about crime have become burdensome and inconvenient for many people who otherwise would be willing to come forward. Continuances, delays, and repeated trips to court can result in loss of income and time on the job for some victims and witnesses. In view of this, I am pleased that you recommend that victims' concerns be included in the Speedy Trial Act.[6] I believe that judges should consider the effect that a delay would have on victims when deciding a motion for continuance.

Another recommendation that I welcome is one that suggests that victims be included in the notification of parole eligibility of the prisoner.[7] It is important for the Parole Commission to hear from victims about how the release of a prisoner impacts upon the victim and family.

For far too long, victims have been the silent majority, but they are now demanding to be heard. They want better treatment and a greater role in the court process—the right to be informed about the progress and outcome of their cases, the right to receive financial assistance and compensation, and the right to be heard concerning the impact of the crime.

As I looked over this legislative agenda, one other recommendation caught my attention that I want to mention briefly. It involves the drug menace which threatens our state and nation. I am especially concerned about the abuse of drugs by our young people. In Mecklenburg County, for example, 25 percent of the drug-related calls received by the drug education center during one month involved children between the ages of ten and nineteen. In Wake County, recently, more than ninety high school students were arrested with drugs in their possession following a surprise raid on their schools.

To reduce the incidence of drug use and abuse, we must send a clear message to our youth and adults that drugs are unacceptable and that we will have no tolerance for people who push these drugs on our schools and our communities. I support the get-tough attitude, by the Crime Commission, on drug pushers. Anyone who distributes cocaine, which results in the drug user's death, should be punished to the full extent of the law. The drug dealer should be charged with second-degree murder.[8]

I want to thank Senator Cobb,[9] who chairs the Crime Commission; Attorney General Thornburg; Secretary Dean; Secretary Johnson; and all of the members of the Crime Commission for this excellent and comprehensive report. It is professional and articulate, and I intend to do everything within my power as North Carolina's chief executive to implement many of its recommendations.

---

[1]*Agenda in Pursuit of Justice: 1987 Legislative Program of the Governor's Crime Commission* (Raleigh: North Carolina Department of Crime Control and Public Safety, Feburary 6, 1987).

[2]"An Act to Provide for County Satellite Jail/Work Release Units for Misdemeanants" was ratified May 18, 1987, and became effective on July 1 of that year. Interestingly, Section 4 stated that passage of the act ". . . shall not be construed to obligate the General Assembly to make any appropriation to implement its provisions, nor shall it be construed to obligate the State to make any grant for which no funds have been appropriated by the General Assembly." *N.C. Session Laws, 1987*, I, c. 207.

[3]"An Act to Establish a Corrections Administrative Remedy Procedure" instituted the State Grievance Resolution Board. The legislation was ratified August 7, 1987, and became effective January 1, 1988. *N.C. Session Laws, 1987*, II, c. 746. The federal law to which Martin referred was *United States Code* (1982 edition), Title 42, Section 1997.

[4]"An Act Providing Compensation for Innocent Victims of Crime" was ratified June 20, 1983. *N.C. Session Laws*, 1983, c. 832. According to section 6, the measure was not to become effective without specific appropriations from the state legislature; funds had not been forthcoming for four years, and the law lay dormant. However, on August 7, 1987, the General Assembly approved the transfer of $100,000 from the Assistance Program for Victims of Rape and Sex Offenses, of the Department of Crime Control and Public Safety, to the Crime Victims Compensation Fund, thereby implementing certain provisions of the 1983 law; see *N.C. Session Laws, 1987*, II, c. 738, s. 118. Finally, "An Act to Create the North Carolina Crime Victims Compensation Fund and to Clarify the North Carolina Crime Victims Compensation Act" was ratified on August 13, 1987. *N.C. Session Laws*, 1987, II, c. 819.

[5]H.B. 202, "A Bill to Be Entitled an Act to Omit the Victim's Address and Phone

Number from Criminal Process Upon Request," was introduced on March 11, 1987; amendment of the proposed legislation failed to win approval of the House Judiciary Number 2 Committee, however, and the bill received an unfavorable report. *N.C. House Journal, 1987*, 98, 417, 558.

[6]H.B. 203, "A Bill to Be Entitled an Act to Amend the Speedy Trial Act to Include Consideration of Victims' Rights," was introduced on March 11, 1987, and referred to the House Judiciary Number 2 Committee, where it received an unfavorable report. An attempt to resurrect the measure on May 27, 1987, failed. *N.C. House Journal, 1987*, 98, 821, 850.

[7]H.B. 165, "A Bill Entitled an Act to Require Notification of Victims that a Parole Decision is Pending," was introduced on March 5, 1987; it later received an indefinite postponement report from the House Corrections Committee. *N.C. House Journal, 1987*, 82, 332.

[8]Representative Michael Decker (R-Forsyth) introduced H.B. 424, "A Bill to Be Entitled an Act to Make Distribution of Cocaine Resulting in Death Punishable as Second Degree Murder," on April 3, 1987; the proposal expired in the House Judiciary Number 2 Committee. *N.C. House Journal, 1987*, 196, 593.

[9]Laurence Arthur Cobb (1933-   ), born in Teaneck, New Jersey; resident of Mecklenburg County; B.S., 1955, J.D., 1958, University of North Carolina at Chapel Hill; U.S. Air Force, 1959-1962, and Reserve, since 1962. Attorney; member, 1971-1976, minority leader, state House; elected to state Senate, 1984, and returned in subsequent elections; Senate minority leader; Republican. *North Carolina Manual, 1987-1988*, 289.

"YEAR OF THE BICENTENNIAL" DINNER

Raleigh, February 10, 1987

I am very pleased, this evening, to join my fellow citizens, from all reaches of North Carolina, as we begin the official observance of the U.S. Constitution's bicentennial. As governor, I want to welcome you to a cause which yet may prove to be as much of an experiment in leadership for us as it was for the moral and political philsophers who, 200 years ago, framed the charter of this republic.

I commend the appropriateness of the bicentennial's theme, "One Common Interest," as a means of uniting us as a people, to build upon our strengths as a great state, rather than an effort to divide us by stressing our differences in how we approach the challenges of the future. The 200th anniversary of our nation's Constitution comes at a time in the life of North Carolina when there is abroad in our state some debate on our policies to promote growth and prosperity. Debate is healthy, and we gain much from it in choosing what is right.

But in seeking, on this occasion, to build one united state, we would be well advised to heed the words of the Constitution's elder statesman, Benjamin Franklin. "The opinions I have had of its errors," he said of our Constitution on the final day of the Philadelphia convention, "I sacrifice to the public good. Within these walls they were born, and here they shall die."[1]

And he went on to explain to the delegates: "If every one of us, in returning to our constituents, were to report the objections he has had [to] it and endeavor to gain partisans in support of them, we might prevent its generally being received."[2] He concluded with this admonition: "I cannot help expressing a wish that every member of the convention who may still have objections (to the Constitution) would, with me, on this occasion doubt a little of his own infallibility and, to make manifest our unanimity, put his name to the instrument."[3]

We owe the success of our Constitution to the ability of its framers to put aside personal beliefs to foster one common interest.

Although amended twenty-six times, the United States Constitution has passed the test of time for two centuries, and today it represents the world's oldest written charter. It has been described by many as "the most important document, next to the Holy Bible, ever written for the benefit of mankind."

To us, in this year of 1987, falls the singular opportunity to educate all North Carolinians about the system of government and guarantees of freedom that the Constitution established, as well as its continuing relevance in modern times. If we fail in this enterprise, if we sacrifice the teaching of the root values of our Constitution to the cause of celebration alone, we will have failed in the greatest mission of our time.

It has been said that each new generation must discover the Constitution for itself. Therefore, the real centerpiece of our bicentennial observance must be to perpetuate public understanding of those tenets which guarantee every American liberty, equality, and justice under the law.

Tonight, I want to commend and applaud the people who are responsible for this bicentennial commemoration. Ten years ago, in 1977, the North Carolina Veterans Council, as part of its Heritage Program, began lobbying the Congress of the United States to enact legislation to create a national Bicentennial Commission on the Constitution. The council's efforts succeeded with enactment of Public Law 98-101.[4]

On July 7, 1984, the North Carolina Commission on the Bicentennial of the U.S. Constitution was established by the General Assembly, and it was through this legislation that we became the second state in the nation to give formal recognition to this anniversary year.[5] As governor, I take pride in the fact that it was a member of my staff who drafted and promoted legislation to create the North Carolina commission.

The founders of our nation had a sense of manifest destiny. Perhaps it is summed up best by James Madison. Writing in the Federalist Papers, he observed: "Happily for America, happily we trust for the whole human race, they (the founders) pursued a new and more noble course. They accomplished a revolution which has no parallel in the annals of human society. They reared the fabrics of governments which have no model on the face of the globe. They formed the design of the great Confederacy, which it is incumbent upon their successors to improve and perpetuate."[6]

The United States Constitution melded the Confederation of States into one nation, indivisible. I believe, just as our founders believed, that America has a divine destiny, and that when we work together, truly as one united state, to perform that great service to humanity which they envisioned, I believe that North Carolina will be a happier, more prosperous, and a more peaceful place to live, and that our nation will be stronger because of it. I believe that we will have continued to take the high road of sound principles and moral responsibility on which our nation was founded, and that we will have justified their faith in us.

---

[1]"The opinions I have had of its errors, I sacrifice to the public good. I have never whispered a syllable of them abroad. Within these walls they were born, and here they shall die." Speech by Benjamin Franklin to the Constitutional Convention of 1787, September 17, 1787, quoted in James McClellan and M. E. Bradford (eds.), *Jonathan Elliot's Debates in the Several State Conventions on the Adoption of the Federal Constitition,* Volume III: *Debates in the Federal Convention of 1787 as Reported by James Madison* (Richmond, Virginia: James River Press, 1989), 619, hereinafter cited as Franklin speech, McClellan and Bradford (eds.), *Debates in the Federal Convention of 1787.*

[2]"If every one of us in returning to our Constituents were to report the objections he had had to it, and endeavor to gain partizans in support of them, we might prevent its being generally received, and thereby lose all the salutary effects & great advantages resulting naturally in our favor among foreign Nations as well as among ourselves, from our real or apparent unanimity." Franklin speech, McClellan and Bradford (eds.), *Debates in the Federal Convention of 1787,* 619.

[3]"On the whole, Sir, I cannot help expressing a wish that every member of the Convention who may still have objections to it, would with me, on this occasion doubt a little of his own infallibility, and to make manifest our unanimity, put his name to this instrument." Franklin speech, McClellan and Bradford (eds.), *Debates in the Federal Convention of 1787,* 619.

[4]P.L. 98-101, "To Provide for the Establishment of a Commission on the Bicentennial of the Constitution," *United States Statutes at Large,* Act of September 29, 1983, 97 Stat. 719-723.

[5]*N.C. Session Laws, 1983, Extra and Regular Sessions, 1984,* c. 1116, sec. 47, established the North Carolina Commission on the Bicentennial of the United States Constitution.

[6]The Federalist No. 14, by James Madison, from the *New York Packet,* November 30, 1787, quoted in *The Federalist,* 85.

DELINQUENCY PREVENTION CONFERENCE

RALEIGH, FEBRUARY 18, 1987

I am very pleased today to have the opportunity to address the 1987 Delinquency Prevention Conference, and I want to thank you for inviting me to share some of my thoughts with you concerning alcohol and substance abuse among the children and youth of our state. Later this morning, Mrs. Martin will speak to you about the human dimensions of this growing epidemic in North Carolina. She also will tell you about some of the private initiatives that we believe you can help us encourage among business firms, churches, civic organizations, and other groups. As chairperson of the Governor's Commission on Child Victimization, and as a member of the Governor's Council on Alcohol and Drug Abuse among Children and Youth, she speaks with the experience gained by examining this problem over a two-year period. Much of what she will say relates not only to her concern, but to her continued involvement in finding new and innovative ways to address this crisis.

Although you are involved as professionals with youngsters who end up in our criminal justice system, usually behind bars, I believe you will acknowledge that alcohol and drugs are involved in a high percentage of crimes committed by youths. Consequently, all of us must think increasingly about the interrelationship of crime and the abuse of alcohol and drugs by the younger members of society.

I want to concentrate specifically today on some, but certainly not all, of the measures I have taken as governor to coordinate and increase the effectiveness of our anti-alcohol and substance abuse programs at the state level. In my first "State of the State" message in 1985, I attempted to galvanize the attention of our legislature and the citizens of North Carolina on the problems affecting children and youth. Until I proclaimed the "Year of the Child," many of these problems had received less than the desired level of state recognition.

The "Year of the Child" led to my appointment of the Governor's Commission on Child Victimization and the Governor's Council on Alcohol and Drug Abuse among Children and Youth. As these groups went about their work of developing recommendations for legislative and executive action, my administration moved steadily forward in a broad effort to address some very obvious problems.

For the first time ever, I recommended funding of the North Carolina Center for Missing Children, which has since been renamed the Center for Missing Persons. Since then, we have installed sophisticated electronic equipment to transmit photographs and data about missing persons across state lines. We are one of only six states participating in this federal Lifenet pilot project.[1] The problem of missing children takes on new urgency when we stop and consider the fact that 27,000 youngsters are reported missing each year, and this number represents only a fraction of the actual cases.

We took on the issue of a tough, new antipornography law, and we achieved legislation requiring stiffer penalties for those who abduct and exploit children. And finally, I provided funding to employ additional child protective service workers, thereby providing early and adequate response to child abuse reports.

When I established the Governor's Council on Alcohol and Drug Abuse among Children and Youth, which is chaired by Dr. Jonnie McLeod,[2] I presented four tasks in my charge to its membership:

—First, I instructed the council to coordinate all of the state government activities and efforts related to alcohol and drug abuse among children and youth;

—Second, I charged the council with the task of establishing local citizen task forces in as many communities as possible;

—Third, the council was given the job of examining the statutes and program standards in North Carolina and to advise what changes, if any, we needed to make;

—And fourth, I asked the council to find innovative ways to involve the private sector in seeking effective solutions to the problem of alcohol and drug abuse among children and young people.

I am pleased to report that this group has made remarkable progress in responding to the substance of my charge. Early on, for example, the council accepted the role of serving as the focal point for planning and the enhancement of services rendered by drug abuse professions. This means we can do a better job of referring parents to the proper channels in their efforts to get professional help.

As many of you in the juvenile delinquency profession already know, the council initiated efforts to organize an interdisciplinary planning and working group from all state agencies concerned with abuse. This group already has sponsored a retreat and, out of that meeting, committees have been formed, and are still working, with various task-oriented council committees.

I plan, in the near future, to ask cabinet members and directors of various state departments and agencies to come together and form a working group to communicate at the top level regarding program priorities and decisions. During the next fiscal year, we anticipate that approximately $11 million in federal antidrug funds will be channeled into state government. I have asked Dr. McLeod and her council to review federal regulations related to the use of this money and to help us find ways, under prescribed guidelines, to use it wisely and where it will do the most good.

Now, allow me to talk for a few minutes about what the council has accomplished in terms of organizing community-based task force groups to deal with alcohol and drug abuse among children and youth. Approximately twelve communities already have formed local parent groups throughout the state. More of these groups will be organized in the coming months.

The council's Ecumenical Committee has organized the large religious denominations in the state, with its objective being the training of parents and the fostering of citizen efforts at the local level. In an effort to step up its activities, the Ecumenical Committee will host a statewide conference in Raleigh next month. My wife, Dottie, who serves on the Ecumenical Committee, will tell you more, later this morning, about the problem we face with parents. I believe that when we deal with families, the greatest problem we face is the denial that a problem exists, especially if it affects their child.

Five cities in North Carolina have begun, or soon will begin, special programs to address the increasing number of children who are dropping out of school. This is important because research has found that the same factors which cause children to quit school before graduation are the same as those which cause alcohol and drug abuse. In Charlotte, business firms are becoming involved actively in dropout prevention through a program, known as Cities in Schools, which I mentioned last Monday evening in my "State of the State" message. The council has the goal of increasing substantially the communities and business firms statewide who become involved in this initiative.

The council's work involving an examination of existing statutes and pending legislation is ongoing under the guidance of a legislative committee chaired by Ms. Christine Dean.[3] In addition, new standards for drug abuse prevention programs have been written, and the process of getting them adopted has started. There is no question but that we need to upgrade the standards for treatment programs. Ideally, some of the federal funds we anticipate in the next fiscal year can be used for this purpose, thereby eliminating the resistance of professionals who often complain, and rightfully so, that money isn't available to back up improved standards.

To conclude my review of the council's current activities, I want to discuss briefly what we need to do in order to encourage more private sector involvement in alcohol and drug abuse among our younger generation.

There is a growing need to involve more ministers to counsel families and to know what to do when a young person becomes the victim of abuse. Moreover, we must encourage more corporations to sponsor programs similar to Cities in Schools, or Dropout Prevention. Private firms have a major role to play in helping to fund programs and encourage employees to serve as volunteers to tutor students, make home visits, and provide scholarships for professional counseling, and treatment, and services. The Zale Corporation, in Dallas, Texas, has become a model for the nation, and we have much to learn from its example of exemplary corporate citizenship.

Other steps we might consider taking include the establishment of an institute for drug abuse studies involving the collaboration of our major research-oriented universities. Such an institute could develop and make available short but intensive training courses for professionals who already are working with young victims of alcohol and drug abuse but who want to learn more about addiction and all facets of drug abuse. The council already is working with universities and community colleges, throughout our state, on the expansion of education programs about alcohol and drug abuse, especially fetal alcohol syndrome; but I believe all of us will admit that education is the key to prevention, and we must expand this effort.

As court counselors, community alternative leaders, mental health officials, school counselors, and law enforcement officers, I urge you to join with me to eliminate alcohol and drug abuse as the leading cause of juvenile crime in North Carolina. The future of our state belongs to the next generation, but upon our shoulders rests the task of shaping that generation into responsible and productive citizens. I urge you to join with all of us who are involved, as one united state, to make ourselves worthy of this task.

---

[1]Lifenet was a computer data base that joined North Carolina and five other member states—Colorado, Illinois, Kentucky, New Jersey, and New York—to the National Center for Missing and Exploited Children and to law enforcement agencies. Its purpose, as the governor described, was to transmit quickly a missing child's picture and other information nationwide. *News and Observer*, August 15, 1986.

[2]Jonnie Horn McLeod (1923-   ), born in Lucedale, Mississippi; resident of Mecklenburg County; B.A., 1945, M.D., 1949, Tulane University. Pediatrician, Mecklenburg County Health Department, 1952-1971, and in private practice, 1961-1968; founder, Open House Drug Counseling Service, 1969; founder, 1970, executive director, 1971-1975, Charlotte Drug Education Center; part-time instructor, 1973-1975, associate professor, 1975-1978, College of Human Development and Learning, and professor, since

1978, Department of Human Services, University of North Carolina at Charlotte; appointed chairwoman, 1986, Governor's Advisory Council on Alcohol and Drug Abuse among Children and Youth; chairwoman, Governor's Inter-Agency Advisory Team on Alcohol and Drug Abuse; consultant; author. Jonnie H. McLeod to Jan-Michael Poff, August 26, 1988.

³Christine W. Dean (1947-   ), born in Washington, D.C.; resident of Apex; A.B., Sweet Briar College, 1968; J.D., Duke University, 1971. Associate attorney, Office of the Attorney General, state Justice Department, 1971-1972; assistant U.S. attorney, Eastern District of North Carolina, 1973-1978, and since 1987; attorney in private practice, 1978-1987. Joseph W. Dean to Jan-Michael Poff, March 15, 1990.

NORTH CAROLINA DEPARTMENT OF THE AMERICAN LEGION

Greensboro, February 21, 1987

[The following address is thematically similar to those delivered before the North Carolina Department of the American Legion, Raleigh, June 13, 1986; the Veterans of Foreign Wars' Council of Administration, Raleigh, February 13, 1987; and the North Carolina Disabled American Veterans, Fayetteville, June 5, 1987.]

I am especially pleased to join you here in Greensboro, today, for the Spring Conference of the American Legion and its Women's Auxiliary. Allow me to begin by extending a warm welcome to your national commander, James Dean.

It is always an honor to address the men and women of North Carolina who served our state and nation with fidelity and devotion in times of war and peace. Your devotion to God and country, the Legion's founding principle, has given you a very special appreciation for life and liberty; and I commend you, as governor, for sharing this precious heritage with the youth of our state. We must never allow future generations to forget that the freedoms we enjoy were won, and continue to be protected, by great sacrifice.

Throughout our nation today, the American Legion continues to remain the paragon of veterans organizations. Its more than 16,000 posts serve some 3 million Legionnaires and almost a million Auxiliary members. Now in its sixty-eighth year, its membership includes veterans of four wars.

From Valley Forge, to Vietnam, to lonely outposts throughout the world today, countless brave North Carolinians left their homes to serve in the cause of their country. It has been their willingness to give freely and unselfishly of themselves, even their lives if necessary, that has given America the security we enjoy today. To all of you in the American Legion, who have served our nation with valor, and to those whose hearts went with you to answer the call to duty, I offer the humble tribute of a grateful state.

To be the governor of North Carolina is to be reminded constantly of the many gallant North Carolinians who have brought honor to our state. The reminders are never far away. Just outside my window at the Capitol stands the statue of Henry Lawson Wyatt, our first native son to fall in the War Between the States; and just beyond is another memorial, this one to Ensign Worth Bagley, who was mortally wounded by enemy gunfire as his ship, the USS *Winslow*, launched its attack at Cardenas Bay, Cuba, during the Spanish-American War. There's also a monument honoring the men of "Old Hickory," the U.S. Army's Thirtieth Division, who broke through the Hindenburg Line in World War I and sent the kaiser's troops in retreat. Nearby is another honoring the men of the Eighty-first "Wildcat" Division, who fought to turn the tide in the Meuse-Argonne offensive in France. Soon there will be a new memorial, this one paying tribute to the men of the Vietnam era, who gave their lives as America debated the efficacy of the battle.

They are reminders of friends, neighbors, and relatives—ordinary North Carolinians of extraordinary devotion and courage. Governors cannot escape these reminders, nor should they try, for these heroes call forth the memory of the faithful among us. These faithful include more than 600,000 living North Carolina veterans, among them some 3,000 survivors of World War I and approximately 240,000 veterans of World War II, the wars to end all wars. They include you, our Legionnaires.

To all of these men and women, to you of the American Legion, in gratitude for your service, North Carolina owes more than a simple debt of gratitude. It owes you and them a promise, a promise that we will not forget your service to God and country and that we will always be there with a helping hand when you're in need. I am one governor who intends to keep that promise.

During the next fiscal year, beginning in July, North Carolina will spend almost $3 million in support of its Division of Veterans Affairs. The service officers of this division are there, whenever they're needed, to provide assistance to veterans and their dependents in obtaining Veterans Administration [VA] benefits. That's a pretty tall order when we consider that veterans and their dependents comprise almost one third of North Carolina's total population.

During the last calendar year, the division responded to almost 200,000 requests for help. Types of assistance provided ranged from helping veterans obtain hospitalization at one of our four VA medical centers[1] to filing [for] death and disability benefits. The total amount of these benefits, some $800 million, has a tremendous impact upon North Carolina's economy and the well-being of our people. Death and disability benefits alone represented $461 million, or approximately 60 percent of the federal funds received by our state's veterans and their dependents.

In addition, the division awarded state scholarships totaling more than $2.5 million to the children of POW-MIAs and disabled and deceased veterans. Each year since the scholarship fund was established in 1945, an average of 1,600 young men and women have received financial help to attend 118 colleges and universities. I'm quite proud of this record, and I intend to continue the strong support of these scholarships in my budget, ensuring that the money will be there to serve the children of our Vietnam veterans as they approach college age.

Last year, I added a full-time chairman of the Governor's Jobs for Veterans Committee, Charles Harris,[2] and I am pleased to report that he is working effectively with the public and private sectors, as well as our veterans organizations, to find jobs for veterans who have experienced difficulty entering our work force. On this note, I want to commend the North Carolina Employment Security Commission for its special outreach program to serve our veterans. During the last biennium, the ESC placed more than 45,000 veterans in jobs, and this was accomplished in spite of a 20 percent reduction in U.S. Department of Labor funds to help place veterans in nonsubsidized employment.

Yet, there are some concerns that have been brought to my attention by the North Carolina Veterans Council, and I want to take the opportunity today to discuss what I have done about them. The first concern I want to address is the matter of veterans preference: giving preference to veterans for employment in state government.

The Veterans Council reported to me that the Office of State Personnel, over the years, had not revised or amended adequately our state personnel policies consistent with the older state statute or as personnel practices have changed. Very few jobs are offered on the basis of competitive exam anymore, so what good does it do to get veterans preference on an examination if you don't take an exam?

Let me say that this is not the intent of my administration. I have already taken steps to give veterans preference in the employment of applicants to fill vacancies in state government. I have notified the Office of State Personnel that, effective immediately, recognition will be given for related work experience to qualify eligible veterans for jobs, so that the time that they spend in the service, in work that is related to the job, would not be overlooked in meeting the basic qualifications of the job. In addition, it is my intent that the time spent in the service, even in work that was not related to the job that you're applying for, will also be taken into account—not to qualify for the job, but will be taken into account so that if two candidates are of equal qualifications, and both are qualified for the job, and all other things being equal, then the one with service to our nation would get the edge in that job.[3]

I won't always be there to look and check to see that all things are being equal, and that is subject to interpretation. In talking with the Veterans Council, there's a recognition of that because there are so many factors that need to be taken into account. My feeling is that if there are so many factors that are to be taken into account, your service to your nation ought to be among them. That's going to be our policy.

In summary, this means that we're going to give credit to qualify veterans, to make them eligible for jobs, on the basis of related military work experience. Beyond that, we'll take all of your career as a member of the armed services into account as among those factors that we are going to consider. We owe that much to our veterans, and as governor, I intend to see that we provide that.

The second concern that was brought to my attention by the Veterans Council during our meeting last month relates to benefits that are availble to veterans, and which are administered by the state, under the Job Training Partnership Act (JTPA).

During the current fiscal year, $177,000 has been allocated by the federal government to provide professional assistance to veterans in obtaining access to JTPA programs. These funds have been used to employ seven veterans service officers who are assigned strategically throughout the state to respond to veterans' needs. They not only respond, they also carry on an aggressive outreach program to locate veterans and make them aware of training programs that are available.

I fully intend to see that our veterans get their fair share of Job Training Partnership Act funds, and in keeping with this commitment, I have instructed Secretary Thomas Rhodes, of the Department of Natural Resources and Community Development, to continue requiring that special emphasis be placed upon veterans' training needs. This requirement has been written into our policy regulating the twenty-six private industry councils in North Carolina, and I assure you that it will be enforced by order of the governor. Furthermore, we anticipate that $180,000 in federal funds will be available to provide JTPA assistance for veterans in the next fiscal year, and I am proposing, for the first time since this program was established, to expand services to veterans by a state match of these federal benefits.

In addition to the JTPA programs to help veterans, I also have proposed a bold, innovative, and new approach to expanding our job training and retraining services. I am asking the General Assembly, during its current session, to pass legislation establishing an independent North Carolina Employment Security Commission reserve fund. We have already shared a copy of this legislation with your commander and adjutant.[4]

The purpose of this independent reserve fund is threefold: (1) to generate a special fund for job training and retraining programs; (2) to accompany a tax reduction, approximately 30 percent, for North Carolina employers and to eliminate the escalator tax provisions; and (3) to generate necessary funds for Employment Security Commission administrative costs, which are being cut by the federal government.

The employer tax reduction will cut by about $50 million the amount of taxes that employers must now pay, thus providing a $50 million shot in the arm to the entire state's economy. That will help to create thousands of new jobs. The remaining $50 million will be used to create the reserve fund, earning about $2 million in interest the first year for retraining displaced workers. As the reserve fund grows, so will the interest earnings to finance new and expanded training programs for unemployed veterans and other unemployed workers in North Carolina.

I want to point out that this independent reserve fund will not jeopardize the solvency of our current Federal Unemployment Insurance Trust Fund, which is used to pay unemployment benefits. The current balance in our Federal U. I. Trust Fund is in excess of $1 billion, and it is projected to grow to $1.8 billion by 1991. We have determined that $1.4 billion will be a sufficiently solvent trust fund level, by 1991, to protect the benefits for our unemployed workers. As a result, we are in a position to cut unemployment insurance taxes paid by employers and, at the same time, build up a $200 million independent reserve fund by 1991.

I am pleased to report that House Bill 22, authorizing establishment of the independent reserve fund, has been introduced by Representative Jeff Enloe, and that the first hearings on the bill were held last Wednesday.[5] However, I have been informed that some veterans have expressed concern that the bill does not set aside a specific percentage of interest earnings from the proposed fund for veterans training. I had not thought that necessary, in the legislation, since we intended to emphasize training for veterans anyway. Nevertheless, if you would feel better having it spelled out, I would ask our veterans organizations to take their concern, if it is sufficiently strong, to our legislators. The only risk in doing that is that any delays will allow others to propose competing set-asides.

The final matter I want to discuss with you, today, addresses the approaching inadequacy of our four national veterans cemeteries in North Carolina. It is estimated that, unless additional land is acquired, these cemeteries will reach capacity by 1992.

I am both sympathetic and concerned with this situation. During the past year, a legislative study commission looked into this matter and reported its findings without recommendation. It considered, among other remedies, the possibility of acquiring and maintaining three state veterans cemeteries located in the east, piedmont, and west regions of the state.[6] The Veterans Council estimates that there are approximately 37,000 remaining World War I and World War II veterans who may wish to have a final resting place in a national or state cemetery reserved for them and their dependent spouses and children. Moreover, the council has suggested that a feasibility study should be conducted into the possibility [of] establishing three state cemeteries.

I have no objection to such a study and would give it my support if appropriate legislation were introduced and passed by the General Assembly. If you feel strongly about this concern, it would not be inappropriate for the American Legion and other veterans organizations to take the lead in requesting action by the General Assembly. Certainly, this matter deserves serious consideration.

Although you have completed your military obligation, you have never wavered in recognizing that peace is a very fragile thing that requires constant vigil. We rely upon our active-duty military personnel to maintain that vigil, and they rely upon our support. We must continue to urge our young citizens, if need be, to stand ready to defend this peace and to discourage our adversaries wherever they may be.

I must express to you, though, the concern I have that 30 percent of North Carolina's youth fail to learn their basic educational skills, drop out without graduating, and are thereafter unqualified for service in today's armed forces. I want you to help us do something about it. I call on you, individually, to speak up in support of our efforts, including my school bond proposal, to strengthen public schools in North Carolina to become the equal of any in America.

I commend the American Legion for the exemplary work which is carried on through your Americanism Program,[7] and I would ask the American Legion to find ways, in its patriotic programs, to promote our literacy campaign as a vital objective for our security. It is through such efforts that the patriotism and love of country among future generations will be nurtured and sustained. I want it taught in modern, well-equipped classrooms, by enthusiastic, well-motivated teachers.

In closing, as North Carolina's commander in chief, I have always supported a strong Army and Air National Guard—well equipped, well trained, and always combat ready. I am proud of these men and women who have volunteered themselves in service to our state and nation. They demonstrate daily, as do our active duty forces, that our commitment to peace is in strong and capable hands.

The Guard is now part of America's first line of defense, ready to deploy as part of the first team. I am so very proud that, unlike other states, North Carolina's National Guard has not asked to be excused from hazardous voluntary duty in Central America, the Philippines, or anywhere else.[8] I'll be willing for other governors to judge whether their troops are better suited to serve just as a home guard, equipped with a helmet, a flashlight, and a bucket of sand. As for the North Carolina National Guard, I am proud to report to you that they are combat ready and have earned the right to have the most modern equipment, including the Cobra and Apache helicopters, the Bradley vehicle, and Abrams tank, and any weapon system reserved only for the best and for those who are part of America's first team.

It is important for me to report to you that the entire range of regular and reserve forces in North Carolina are true to the standards and commitment that you exemplified. To you, our Legionnaires, who have served so valiantly, and to those who are prepared to follow in your footsteps whenever our nation is threatened, the people of North Carolina will always be indebted. Your governor and your state will never forget what you have done, for God, and country, and for all mankind. You made history and have inspired others to keep it alive.

---

[1]Veterans Administration hospitals were located in Asheville, Durham, Fayetteville, and Salisbury, according to Martin's speech to the North Carolina Disabled American Veterans, June 5, 1987.

[2]Charles M. Harris, Sr. (1918-   ), born in Augusta County, Virginia; resident of Charlotte; was educated in Augusta County public schools; U.S. Army, 1941-1945. Founder, Harris Office Supply and Equipment Co., 1956; commander, Disabled American Veterans, 1968-1969, 1971-1972; former veterans representative, CETA program,

Charlotte-Mecklenburg County; chairman, Governor's Jobs for Veterans Committee, since June 1, 1986. Charles M. Harris, Sr., to Jan-Michael Poff, June 19, 1989.

[3]Martin told members of the North Carolina Department of the American Legion, June 13, 1986, that he had instructed State Personnel Director Dick Lee to draft legislation that "will make preference for veterans in state employment a reality." The General Assembly, on August 14, 1987, permitted an investigation of the "advisability" of bolstering the policy of granting veterans priority when state agencies assess competing job applicants. See *N.C. Session Laws, 1987*, II, c. 873, s. 2.3; see also *News and Observer*, July 9, 1987, *N.C. House Journal, 1987*, 451, 668, 868, 897, and *N.C. Senate Journal, 1987*, 588, 833, 840.

[4]Jerry L. Hedrick, of Lexington, was state commander of the North Carolina Department of the American Legion. Information from North Carolina Department of the American Legion, July 2, 1990.

C. Keith Sink (1928-   ), born in Lexington; resident of Raleigh; B.S., Davidson College, 1949; B.D., Lancaster Theological Seminary, 1952; U.S. Army chaplain, 1952-1955, 1959-1976. Pastor, Emanuel Evangelical and Reformed Church, Thomasville, 1955-1959; adjutant, North Carolina Department of the American Legion. C. Keith Sink to Jan-Michael Poff, July 22, 1990.

[5]H.B. 22 was ratified as c. 17, *N.C. Session Laws, 1987*, I. Its chief sponsor was Jeff Hailen Enloe, Jr. (1914-   ), born in Franklin; resident of Macon County; B.S., North Carolina State College (later University), 1938; U.S. Navy, 1943-1946. Retired after thirty-four years with U.S. Department of Agriculture; elected to state House, 1974, and returned in subsequent elections; chairman, House Employment Security Committee; Democrat. *North Carolina Manual, 1987-1988*, 418.

[6]See *Veterans Cemetery: Report to the 1987 General Assembly* (Raleigh: Legislative Research Commission, December 12, 1986). The Third, Seventh, and Eleventh Congressional Districts, areas with large populations of former servicemen and women, were recommended as locations for future veterans cemeteries under *N.C. Session Laws, 1987*, I, c. 183, ratified May 14, 1987. Later that year, the Division of Veterans Affairs applied for $1.35 million in federal funds to develop three state veterans cemeteries: two were proposed for the Fort Bragg and Camp LeJeune vicinities, while forty-two acres near Black Mountain were reserved for the third. Untitled press release, Raleigh, October 15, 1987, Governors Papers, James G. Martin.

[7]The primary goal of the Americanism Program was to "emphasize the significance of the American tradition" by infusing "a sense of personal obligation to accept an active part in the duties and responsibilities of American citizenship." Through community service, recreation and safety activites, education and flag education, contests, patriotic holiday observances, and other means, the program sought to recognize "the ideal of human values, and the dignity and worth of the individual." *Americanism Manual* (Indianapolis, Indiana: National Americanism Commission, American Legion, February, 1989), 3, 5-6.

[8]Traditional understanding of federal law did not require state compliance, "in the absence of a national emergency," with any Pentagon call for mobilization of National Guard contingents. Some governors, protesting United States policy in Central America, cited that legal interpretation to justify their withholding Guardsmen from training maneuvers in Honduras. In response, Congressman G. V. "Sonny" Montgomery (D-Mississippi) attached an amendment to H.R. 4428 that prohibited any state chief executive from preventing Guard units from participating "in a Pentagon-sponsored training exercise because of the location or purpose of the exercise." Governors Michael S. Dukakis of Massachusetts and Rudy Perpich of Minnesota contested the law, but the U.S. Supreme Court affirmed the constitutionality of the Montgomery amendment in 1990. *Congressional Quarterly Almanac, 1986*, 481; *News and Observer*, April 3, November 9, 1986, June 12, 1990; P.L. 99-661, "National Defense Authorization Act for Fiscal Year 1987" (short title), *United States Statutes at Large*, Act of November 14, 1986, Title V, Section 522, 100 Stat. 3871.

NORTH CAROLINA TRUCKING ASSOCIATION

RALEIGH, FEBRUARY 25, 1987

For the benefit of those who were not taking notes when I delivered my "State of the State" message a little over a week ago, I've decided tonight to read it again—just in case any of you missed a few points. And now that I have your attention, let me say that I am very pleased, again this year, to attend the legislative dinner of the North Carolina Trucking Association.

With more than 200,000 direct employees, the trucking industry represents one of our state's largest economic sectors. Hardly anything that we consume or use comes to us without the involvement of one or more of the 22,000 motor freight carriers that are licensed to do business in North Carolina. So important is the industry, in fact, that last month, for the first time ever, I appointed a sixteen-member Motor Carriers Advisory Committee to the governor.

This committee, comprised of trucking company executives and representatives of North Carolina's taxing and regulatory agencies, held its first meeting day before yesterday. One of its first tasks will be to deal with the complex interstate administrative procedures required by the various states for trucks that travel long distances. Consider, for a moment, that a trucker desiring to operate an eighteen-wheeler in our forty-eight contiguous states must:

1. Purchase as many as four separate license plates;

2. Buy thirty-two fuel use decals to stick on the outside of his cab;

3. Acquire thirty-five cab cards for mileage-based fuel taxes and other highway-use taxes;

4. Purchase what truckers call a "bingo card" that carries thirty separate stamps which allow the operation of the vehicle across state lines; and

5. File about 200 different fuel reports annually, representing a stack of paperwork more than two inches thick.

If all the permits, stickers, stamps, and licenses were spread out on the floor, they would cover an area ten feet long and three feet wide— and that's for just one truck! Imagine the problem this causes for a company operating 500 to 1,000 vehicles.

These examples illustrate the complexity of highway-use taxation procedures that individual states use to regulate interstate motor carriers. "Eb" Peters, executive vice-president of your association, tells me that it's impossible to drive a truck from North Carolina to California without violating one or more regulations.[1] Making regulations simpler would increase compliance, reduce administrative costs, and as a result, boost state revenues. Another equally important consideration is that by streamlining regulatory procedures, we could help lower transportation costs for the consumer.

As governor, I have been concerned for some time about the regulatory nightmare faced by our motor carriers, as well as the adverse effects it has on building a stronger state economy; and I've asked the governor's committee to come up with recommendations for implementing simplified, one-stop regulating in North Carolina, similar to the one-stop permitting I proposed for small business firms in my "State of the State" address. Establishment of a single office for obtaining the credentials needed and paying the taxes required could save millions of dollars and greatly improve revenue collections for our own state, as well as participating sister states. I am pleased that other governors, throughout the nation, are joining with me to implement the consensus report prepared by the Working Group on State Motor Carriers Procedures of the National Governors' Association.

North Carolina, in 1977, joined thirty-three other states to establish an International Registration Plan under which a single license plate and cab card are issued by the base state, or home state. Under this plan, a single registration fee is paid based on the percentage of fleet miles traveled in each member state the previous year, and distributed accordingly. However, we can do much to expand this plan to include fuel use decals and other permits which still must be obtained from a variety of agencies in other states.

The committee also will take a look at the possibility of North Carolina's participation in a base state fuel tax agreement. Called the North American Fuel Tax Agreement, it would be patterned after the International Registration Plan.

It's time for government to find ways to make it easier for companies to do business in North Carolina, not more difficult, and I am one governor who remains dedicated to accomplishing this goal. Working with me on North Carolina's transportation agenda are two very capable and dedicated leaders, Transportation Secretary Jim Harrington and Commissioner of Motor Vehicles Bill Hiatt. Ken Younger, one of my appointees to the Board of Transportation, is a past president of your association, and he brings a special understanding of motor carrier problems to our task of improving your operating procedures in North Carolina.

I want to take this opportunity to commend the work of the Division of Motor Vehicles, particularly in regard to enforcement of motor carrier safety regulations. This program has been greatly expanded, and we have applied for a federal grant of $1.39 million next year to enhance out exemplary safety record, the best in the nation. Very few people understand the enormous job the division performs. Last year alone, more than 8 million trucks were weighed at that state's twenty-two truck weigh stations, and the number is growing annually.

As we continue to build upon our reputation as the Good Roads State, we will need the help of our General Assembly to establish a permanent state highway construction fund. We also need authorization for local governments to set aside, zone, and acquire rights-of-way which can be contributed and dedicated to future highway and road use. We have the means provided by a prosperous state to meet these responsibilities to our citizens. I ask those of you who serve in our General Assembly to supply the will and the way to get the job done.

North Carolina can, and must, meet our expanding transportation needs while also moving forward on our Basic Education Program, teacher career ladder, and providing a bond referendum which, subject to voter approval, will provide a bold and imaginative step to build the new schools we need. The 1987 session of the General Assembly is an historic one. I ask you to join with me in making us worthy of the public trust we have been given to accomplish these noble deeds.

---

[1]Elbert L. (Eb) Peters (1928-   ), born in Reidsville; resident of Raleigh; B.A., Elon College, 1952; U.S. Marine Corps, 1952-1955, and Reserve, 1952-1976. Various positions, including personnel director and director, driver education and accident records, state Division of Motor Vehicles, 1957-1965; district director, National Safety Council, 1965-1967; coordinator, Governor's Highway Safety Program, 1967-1973; various positions with state Department of Labor and U.S. Department of Transportation, 1973-1975; commissioner, state Division of Motor Vehicles, 1977-1981; president, N.C. Trucking Assn., since 1981. Elbert L. Peters to Jan-Michael Poff, December 15, 1989.

PRESS RELEASE: GOVERNOR MARTIN'S STATEMENT ON
STAFF REASSIGNMENTS

Raleigh, February 25, 1987

Governor Jim Martin, Wednesday, announced executive and cabinet staff reassignments designed to streamline Governor's Office operations. The governor issued the following statement:

"Beginning tomorrow, I shall be assisted in the performance of my constitutional, statutory, and political responsibilities as governor by an executive staff composed of a chief of staff, a budget director, and a general counsel. Each member of the executive staff will report directly to me and will serve as members of my cabinet and Executive Cabinet.

"My chief of staff will be Secretary of the Department of Human Resources Phillip J. Kirk, Jr. In his new role as chief of staff, he will be responsible for the administration of the Governor's Office and will act as my liaison with state agencies administered by my cabinet secretaries. Most functions in the Governor's Office will be directed by my chief of staff.

"My executive assistant and special counsel, James R. Trotter, will become my general counsel. He will be responsible for legal and research offices within the Governor's Office and for the legal affairs of state agencies administered by my cabinet. He also serves as a member of my cabinet and Executive Cabinet.

"My director of the budget, C. C. Cameron, will continue in that role and will serve as my fiscal adviser and oversee the implementation of the state's capital projects. He also serves as a member of my cabinet and Executive Cabinet.

"My executive assistant, James S. Lofton, will become secretary of administration. This move will expand his administrative responsibilities in my administration. Lofton will continue to serve as a member of my cabinet and Executive Cabinet.

"Secretary of Administration Grace J. Rohrer will serve as my special assistant and director of policy and planning and will report directly to me. She will continue to serve as a member of my cabinet and Executive Cabinet. In addition, she will be my adviser on women's issues and will be responsible for the state's Women in Economic Development program and the Council on the Status of Women.

"My legislative liaison, J. Ward Purrington, will become my special assistant and director of legislative relations.[1] In his new role, Purrington will become a member of my cabinet and Executive Cabinet. Dr. Paul T. Kayye, director of the Division of Mental Health, Mental Retardation, and Substance Abuse Services, will serve as interim secretary of the Department of Human Resources pending the appointment of a replacement for Secretary Kirk."[2]

---

[1]John Ward Purrington (1940-   ), native of Raleigh; A.B., 1962, J.D., 1967, University of North Carolina at Chapel Hill; U.S. Naval Reserve, 1962-1964. Attorney in private practice, 1968-1975, 1977-1983; member, state House, 1972-1974, state Transportation Board, 1973-1974, and of state Utilities Commission, 1975-1977; chairman, Governor's

Advisory Council on Drug Abuse Prevention, 1973-1974; deputy revenue secretary, 1985; governor's legislative counsel, director of legislative relations, 1986-1990. John Ward Purrington to Jan-Michael Poff, December 22, 1989; press release, "Governor's Legislative Counsel Returns to Private Practice," Raleigh, February 28, 1990, Governor's Papers, James G. Martin.

²Paul T. Kayye (1937-   ), born in Baltimore, Maryland; resident of Angier; M.D., University of Miami, 1962; U.S. Navy, 1962-1967, and Reserve, since 1967. Director, Medical and Psychiatric Services, Youthful Offenders, Department of Correction, 1971-1980; director, Child and Youth Services, Cherry Hospital, 1981-1985; director, Division of Mental Health, Mental Retardation, and Substance Abuse Services, 1985-1989, interim department secretary, February-April, 1987, and assistant secretary, Office for Children and the Family, since 1989, Department of Human Resources; psychiatry professor, University of North Carolina School of Medicine. Paul T. Kayye to Jan-Michael Poff, December 29, 1989. Governor Martin appointed David T. Flaherty to succeed Kirk as human resources secretary on April 8, 1987. *North Carolina Manual, 1987-1988,* 787.

DISTINGUISHED WOMAN OF NORTH CAROLINA AWARDS

RALEIGH, MARCH 4, 1987

Dottie and I are very pleased to join all of you for this happy occasion, tonight. How gratifying and appropriate it is for me to have a part in presenting the awards to the 1987 outstanding women of North Carolina. This endeavor by the Council on the Status of Women is to be highly commended.[1]

If our state is to continue as a bastion of enterprise and opportunity for people everywhere, attracting the best and the brightest entrepreneurs and humanitarians from throughout the world, then it will be owed in no small part to women like the five recipients we honor tonight.[2] Each of them has brought distinction to North Carolina, in a very special way, through their contributions to business, politics, public service, art, literature, education, and the humanities. They have lived inspiring lives, and by their example, they have inspired others to greater achievement.

During the past two years, North Carolina women have established an outstanding record of accomplishment through bold and imaginative programs supported by state government. In June of 1986, our state took the lead role in a national Women in Health Care Services trade mission to Japan. As a result of that mission, a group of eleven Japanese business leaders, men and women representing a coalition of 600 small to medium-size Japanese firms, visited North Carolina last October.

This buying mission to North Carolina, hosted by the Office of State Development-Women and the Economy, has already led to several overseas contracts for small business firms in our state that are owned by minorities and women. One minority businesswoman in Raleigh, for example, is brokering the shipment of more than five tons of frozen vegetables each month to a leading chain of Japanese department stores. Another firm, located in Wilmington, is shipping several tons of tuna to the same Japanese firm each month. I am told that negotiations are now under way which may result in a contract to supply a chain of some 100 Japanese sauna/health spas with more than 1,000 high-quality terry cloth robes and towels each month. Again, this is a result of aggressive marketing by North Carolina business firms owned by minorities and women.

There are many other initiatives that the Office of State Development is pursuing, including participation by North Carolina businesswomen in the first trade and investment seminar sponsored by the Council of Eastern Caribbean Manufacturers. This seminar, which will be held in the West Indies, will target new opportunities for women in health care, education and training services, agricultural products, and specialized joint ventures in the textile field.

As we continue to seek out opportunities for business firms owned by women and minorities in the private sector, we are expanding our program to involve them in purchases made by state government. I am pleased to report that the Office of State Development has published a catalog of North Carolina firms owned by women, minorities, handicapped persons, and Native Americans who want to do business with the state of North Carolina.[3] This catalog, the first ever published by state government, will contribute greatly to our efforts to exceed the goals we have set for minority contracting.

There are numerous innovative programs involving women and minorities throughout North Carolina. The New Horizons program, which provides in-service training and assistance to help women and minorities elevate themselves to higher-level jobs, is opening new avenues for professional growth in state government. I am indeed proud of this program and the fact that it was our administration that made it a reality.

With that observation, I believe I have intruded too long on the time allocated to our guest speaker, a distinguished woman herself. In 1986, she made history by becoming the first woman ever elected governor of the state of Nebraska, and the first Republican woman governor elected in the United States. That might have been unusual, but pioneering roles are not new to Governor Kay A. Orr. In 1982, she became the first woman ever elected by Nebraska voters to a statewide constitutional office, that of state treasurer; and in 1984, she became the first person, male or female, other than a member of the Congress or a state governor, to serve as a cochairman of the Republican National Convention's Platform Committee.[4]

For twenty-one years, Governor Orr has been an active leader in local, state, and national Republican party affairs. Beginning with her election as cochairman of the Lancaster County Young Republicans in 1967, she has since been honored with many party positions, including election as delegate to the national conventions of 1976, 1980, and 1984. She cochaired former governor Charles Thone's successful campaign in 1978, and then served as the governor's executive assistant until June of 1981, when he appointed her state treasurer. She was elected to that office by a wide margin the following year, completing a four-year term on the same day that she took the oath of office as governor. It is an honor and distinct pleasure for me to present an extraordinary woman, the Honorable Kay A. Orr, governor of the state of Nebraska.

---

[1]In remarks delivered at the Distinguished Woman of North Carolina Awards presentation ceremony, March 30, 1988, Governor Martin recounted the founding, in 1963, and purpose of the Council on the Status of Women.

[2]Each of the five honorees was recognized as a Distinguished Woman of North Carolina: Mary Ulmer Chiltoskey, preserver of Cherokee Indian heritage; Bonnie Ethel Cone, higher education advocate; Alice Priscilla Stateman Hannibal, humanitarian, volunteer leader; Helen Rhyne Marvin, state senator; and Helen Ann Powers, North Carolina's first female revenue secretary. Peggy O'Brien, Council on the Status of Women, to Jan-Michael Poff, May 7, 1990.

[3]"North Carolina Special Interest Directory: Minority, Handicapped, & Women-Oriented Directory" ([Raleigh]: North Carolina Division of Purchase and Contract, [1986]); see also press release, "Minority, Disabled and Women-Oriented Businesses Listed in New State Government Purchase Directory," Raleigh, January 7, 1987, Governors Papers, James G. Martin.

[4]Kay A. Orr (1939-   ), born in Burlington, Iowa; resident of Lincoln, Nebraska; was educated at University of Iowa, 1956-1957. Elected governor of Nebraska, 1986. *Who's Who in America, 1988-1989*, II, 2350.

AGRICULTURAL STABILIZATION AND CONSERVATION CONFERENCE

GREENSBORO, MARCH 10, 1987

I am both pleased and honored, this morning, to participate in this forward-looking conference: pleased by the challenge of sharing some of my thoughts about the forces of change that are reshaping agriculture in North Carolina and the nation; honored by the opportunity to address a group whose contributions I recognize as having been important factors in the progress that has given us the greatest agricultural system in the world. Before going on, let me extend a warm welcome to Mr. Verne Nepple, associate administrator of the Agricultural Stabilization and Conservation Service [ASCS], U.S. Department of Agriculture. We're delighted, Mr. Nepple, to have you in a state that is on the go—and where agriculture is on the grow.

Our farmers have experienced some very difficult recent years. On top of falling commodity prices and higher production costs, we in North Carolina have experienced a record drought—all this coming at a time we're saddled with excessive debt. This combination of factors has caused some of our family farms to falter or fail. Yet, many more have survived, in large part because of the excellent work you have done to distribute payments under the 1986 disaster law. I'm told that, so far in North Carolina, this year a total of $14 million has been paid out in the form of commodity certificates, $15 million under the Emergency Feed Program, and about $1 million in payments for conservation practices. Moreover, these payments were made in a timely and efficient manner. I know that many of your people worked excessively long hours, sometimes fourteen to sixteen hours a day when you were paid for only eight, to ensure that these benefit checks went out on time. We sincerely thank you, for this reflects a true sense of dedication to our farmers.

I'm aware, also, of the many ways in which ASCS offices and your employees cooperated with the joint effort by the state—our North Carolina Department of Agriculture, under Commissioner Jim Graham, as well as with my office—and the private sector, to distribute the free hay donated to our farmers by growers in other states. Without this spirit of working together, many of our livestock farmers would have been devastated. It was a remarkable example of neighbor helping neighbor.

Undeniably in other ways, North Carolina agriculture has been undergoing some unsettling and dramatic changes in the past several years, changes which are likely to continue and which will affect its future for decades to come. Later this week, I will be announcing the appointment of a new committee or task force, chaired by former lieutenant governor Jimmy Green, to make a comprehensive study of these changes and to recommend ways to address them. I have every confidence that we can make the future work for us, not against us.

While change is inevitable and certainly not new to agriculture, the rapidity with which it is occurring and the complexity of its nature is startling, to say the least. Indeed, agriculture is at a crossroad. Which way we go from here will depend on how we respond; on how and what we decide about our future course. One thing is certain: We do have a choice. We can either retreat from the impending changes, or we can take the lead in controlling and directing them for the benefit not only of agriculture and our economy, but of all humanity.

Over the past two years, North Carolina has shown that, given active and positive leadership, our state can resolve many of its own problems. One of the best examples of this is the buy out of our Flue-Cured Tobacco Stabilization Corporation's surplus tobacco and the subsequent influence we exerted on our major buying companies to purchase increasing amounts of domestic leaf. When I came into office in 1985, our tobacco program was at the most critical point in its history. It was virtually ready to collapse. Through a series of summit meetings at the Executive Mansion, I brought four of our major manufacturing and buying companies together for the negotiated purchase of surplus stocks totaling 584 million pounds, as permitted under Senator Helms's landmark legislation. It was the largest single business contract ever negotiated in North Carolina history, a total of $1.2 billion.

The results have justified our expectations. In 1986, the poundage assessment paid by growers was lowered from a projected 32 cents to only 2.5 cents. In addition, the major manufacturers participating in the agreement last year purchased almost 40 percent of the existing surplus, although they agreed to take only 12.5 percent annually over the eight-year buy out. Continued reduction of our huge tobacco surplus, reduction of the financial burden which was placed on our growers by an increasing assessment, and the achievement of new and better tobacco legislation will combine, I believe, to help us stop the precipitous decline in tobacco production.

I am also pleased that our combined efforts encouraging our major tobacco manufacturing companies to increase their purchases of domestic leaf next season have achieved some success. Philip Morris already has announced that, upon honoring existing contracts for foreign tobaccos, it will buy only domestic leaf for use in cigarettes sold in the United States. R. J. Reynolds Tobacco Company has indicated it will take the same position, provided that the Congress does not increase the excise tax on cigarettes.

The buy out of Stabilization's surplus stock, and the encouraging results it brought about, clearly demonstrates that states can be an important part of American agricultural reform. We can make a difference. That's a contradiction of the earlier belief that agricultural problems could be addressed only at the federal level.

The problems of our tobacco farmers are only a few of the challenges to agriculture which we have been addressing. For more than a decade, some 3,000 farmers have been forced out of business annually by excessive debt, high interest rates, and increasing competition by foreign nations which have captured a growing share of our markets. Not long after the tobacco buy out, I called another series of summit meetings, involving a wide range of agricultural interests, to address other key elements of our farm economy. The participants in these summit meetings included commodity organizations, the state Department of Agriculture, Agricultural Extension Service, farm researchers and educators, and leaders from our financial institutions, both public and private.

One of the results of these meetings was my appointment, last fall, of a special Farm Finance Task Force to help our family farmers restructure viable farm loans. This task force, which continues in operation, brings together, for the first time, all three major farm lending institutions: private banks, the Farm Credit System, and the Farmers Home Administration. The major task of this group is to link our financial institutions to farmers who need more time to retire major debts or who need financial counseling. By opening new avenues of communication and exploring innovative new financing arrangements, this task force is helping to ease our farm financial crisis at the most personal and painful level. The work of the task force already has attracted national attention, and South Carolina legislators recently expressed interest in emulating our plan.

Over time, the Farm Finance Task Force will help salvage many of our farm operators. But during the past year, I was challenged to take some emergency steps to help those farmers who, in spite of their best efforts, were forced to leave their traditional livelihood and their love of the land. One of the first steps I took to help these families was to expand North Carolina's Dislocated Worker Program, designed for dislocated factory workers, to include farmers and farm workers for the first time. Under this program, farmers and farm workers are now eligible for such services as remedial and vocational education through the state's community colleges, job search assistance training, intensive job placement, and relocation assistance through the North Carolina Employment Security Commission.

Steps already have been taken, and legislation has been introduced, to establish an independent Employment Security Commission reserve fund, the interest from which will be used to initiate new job training programs and expand existing ones. What this reserve fund will do is cut by almost $50 million the amount of taxes employers currently pay, thus providing a $50 million shot in the arm to the state's economy and help create thousands of new jobs for those who have been displaced in farming. The remaining $50 million will go into creating the reserve fund, earning about $4 million in interest the first year for retraining displaced workers, including farmers and farm workers. As the reserve fund grows, so will the interest earnings to finance new and expanded training programs, for the unemployed, and other benefits.

Increasing markets for our farmers is a matter of urgent priority. I started out my administration by placing emphasis on improving the condition of our traditional industries, including agriculture and food products, by appointing the first assistant secretary of commerce for traditional industry. We also set out to pursue food processing firms more aggressively and effectively. I am pleased to report that both programs have met with great success.

Since becoming governor, food processing companies have invested more than $100 million in North Carolina in new and expanded facilities. While these operations do not always purchase North Carolina commodities immediately, they do provide increased long-term opportunity for North Carolina farmers. Moreover, they have a stabilizing effect on overall agricultural markets and prices.

To take additional advantage of our efforts to expand food processing throughout the state, I appointed a Food Processing Task Force last October to investigate the feasibility of establishing three agricultural parks in North Carolina. These parks, for which there is $4.4 million available for the next biennium, will enable us to lease space for business investments in equipment for quick chilling, processing, grading, packaging, canning, and freezing of fruits and vegetables. By providing single, integrated facilities for food processing operations, these parks not only could help us expand our markets, but could also improve profit margins and expand job creation in our agricultural sectors and our rural communities.

Under my administration, we have established a new direction for agriculture in North Carolina. We're going to go forward in the future. Too often in the past, we have tended to add to, rather than modify, structures that no longer serve us.

It has taken a 150-year evolution to bring agriculture to its present position of importance to the national and world economy. Our abundant land, capital, and human resources, coupled with our excellent climate in North Carolina, have combined to ensure this success. We will continue to make additional gains. No doubt this will surpass anything we have seen thus far, creating excitement and hope on one hand, and the responsibility for assessing potentially negative effects on the environment on the other.

To help us manage our environment better on a statewide basis, I have proposed that North Carolina expand its cost-sharing program for Best Management Practices to all 100 counties during the next three fiscal years. During the current fiscal year, the $3 million appropriated by the General Assembly for Best Management Practices represented only half of the amount requested by farm landowners. In fact, it is estimated by the North Carolina Department of Natural Resources and Community Development that about $12 million will be needed annually, through 1997, to provide adequate funding on a statewide basis. This includes money which will be required for planning and technical assistance. The total cost of the needs adds up to something like $139 million over the next eleven years.

To help rectify this situation, I have submitted to the General Assembly a budget containing substantial increases for funding the Division of Water Resources, the Water Quality Section, Local Planning and Management Division, and the Soil and Water Conservation Division of NRCD. The increase in funding for fiscal 1987-1988 will exceed $1.5 million and bring the total budget for that period to more than $4.5 million. The budget also provides an additional $1.1 million in the second year of the biennium, thereby increasing the budget for that year to $5.6 million. Program increases which I am recommending will be used for water supply planning, technical assistance to local governments for water supply planning, protection of watersheds, and extension of the agricultural cost-share program for Best Management Practices to reduce and prevent non-point-source pollution.

We're told that in the future, bioengineering research is expected to yield even more profound alterations in the production of food and fiber. The possibility of enhancing photosynthesis efficiency will multiply crop growing seasons and usable acreage. The advent of self-fertilizing plants will lead to the substitution of biochemicals for petrochemicals. The ability to stimulate and regulate growth, to create more nutritious hybrids, to engineer and blend nutrients and flavorings, will speed the maturing processes and compound enormously the variety and nutritional value of agricultural products. Rubber and oil may one day come from plants, and much of our energy needs may be supplied by biomass. Aquaculture and ocean farming, better known as mariculture, are opening up a vast array of food and energy potentials.

Continued North Carolina leadership and strength in agriculture may be tied to our remaining in the forefront of new research. But if this is the case, the future of agriculture will continue to be tied to the education of our farmers and their willingness to anticipate change, to adapt to new ways, and to shape the future to their resolve. I believe strongly that we are moving progressively to an agriculture that rewards the efficient producer of food and fiber, contributes to the growth of our rural communities, and enables worthy people to stay on the land.

North Carolina can benefit from a diversified economy, but that diversification can eclipse our greatest dream if it includes low tech, high tech, and everything in between—from microchips to potato chips; from terminals to turkeys; from data processing to food processing; and from soup to nuts. North Carolina must be all of these, working and prospering together as one united state; building tomorrow's future, today, on yesterday's heritage. That's agriculture; that's North Carolina.

FARM ECONOMY TASK FORCE

RALEIGH, MARCH 12, 1987

[Martin promulgated the signing of Executive Order Number 36, establishing the Governor's Task Force on the Farm Economy in North Carolina and the Governor's Advisory Committee on Agricultural Parks, at a news conference on March 12, 1987. The announcement is reprinted, below; Executive Order Number 36 was reproduced in *N.C. Session Laws, 1987*, II, 2337-2340.]

North Carolinians have always taken great pride in our agricultural heritage, and we have remained steadfastly committed to preserving the future of our agriculture industry in this state. Our farmers have experienced difficult times in recent years, times brought about by a combination of falling commodity prices, higher production costs, and a record drought.

My administration has taken a number of steps designed to strengthen the agriculture industry. You will remember our summit meeting, resulting in the buy out of Flue-Cured Tobacco Stabilization stocks; my creation of the Farm Finance Task Force and the Food Processing Task Force; expansion of the Employment Security Commission assistance program to include farmers and farm workers; and a variety of other efforts. We have recognized that changes are taking place in the marketplace—changes which must be met—and we are dedicated to meeting these changes head-on to preserve and strengthen the future of our farm families. Today I am announcing the signing of Executive Order Number 36, which creates the Governor's Task Force on the Farm Economy in North Carolina and the Governor's Advisory Committee on Agricultural Parks. Both these groups will study problems currently facing our North Carolina farmers and develop effective, productive methods for meeting and alleviating those problems.

The Governor's Task Force on the Farm Economy in North Carolina consists of thirty members from various areas of North Carolina to ensure that all rural regions of the state are represented. That membership includes farmers, food processors, wholesale and retail food vendors, bankers, and college and university representatives. Ex-officio members include representatives of the departments of Commerce, Transportation, Natural Resources and Community Development, State Budget Office, and Employment Security Commission. All members, including the chairman, are appointed by the governor. You should have a complete list of this distinguished membership in front of you. Former lieutenant governor Jimmy Green has kindly agreed to oversee the functions of this task force as its chairman.

Members of the task force will work to assess immediate problems facing the farm economy in North Carolina, develop proposals for immediate action, and recommend methods to coordinate state agencies' activities with local rural leaders. After consulting the Governor's Advisory Committee on Agricultural Parks, the task force will also make recommendations to the governor concerning development of agricultural parks in all sections of North Carolina. In addition, the task force will define a comprehensive strategy to further the development of food processing in North Carolina.

The second organization created by my executive order, the Governor's Advisory Committee on Agricultural Parks, will study the feasibility of developing agricultural parks in all sections of North Carolina and report their findings to the Governor's Task Force on the Farm Economy. All seven members and the chairman are appointed to the committee by the governor. Mr. Worth Gurkin, chairman of the Sampson County Agriculture Extension Service, will serve as chair of the committee.[1] I again refer you to your press packet for a complete membership list.

I firmly believe creation of the Governor's Task Force on the Farm Economy and the Governor's Advisory Committee on Agricultural Parks are two more steps forward in our aggressive efforts to shape the future of our agricultural economy. We are confronted by the challenges of change. It is our responsibility to anticipate those changes, adapt to new ways, and shape the future to our benefit. Through these efforts, we are moving progressively onward to a new agricultural heritage that rewards the efficient producer of food and fiber, contributes to the growth of our rural communities, and enables our farmers to stay on the land.

I would like to thank [Lieutenant] Governor Jimmy Green, Worth Gurkin, Jim Oliver, my agricultural adviser, and the distinguished members of the Governor's Task Force on the Farm Economy in North Carolina and the Governor's Advisory Committee on Agricultural Parks for being present here today. I commend each of you for your willingness to offer your time and talents on behalf of our North Carolina citizens, and I look forward to working with you. At this time, I would like to ask [Lieutenant] Governor Green to step forward and give us his comments concerning the task force.

---

[1]Worth Wicker Gurkin (1934-1989), born in Beaufort; resided in Clinton; B.S., 1956, M.S., 1970, North Carolina State University. Vocational agriculture teacher, Whiteville school system, 1956-1957; Sampson County agricultural extension agent, 1957-1964, and county extension director, 1964-1988. George Upton, Sampson County extension director, to Jan-Michael Poff, November 29, 1989.

YOUTH LEGISLATIVE ASSEMBLY

RALEIGH, MARCH 13, 1987

I am very pleased, today, to have this opportunity to speak to you, the members of the North Carolina Youth Legislative Assembly. In the spirit of the remarks I will make, welcome to your capital city. Raleigh is one of those truly unique places where the focus of daily life is bringing the perspectives of our citizens to bear on governance— self-governance. That's what I want to talk to you about today.

The writers of the United States Constitution, which is 200 years old this year, were deeply concerned with limiting the authority of government. They were concerned with what was described in the Declaration of Independence as the tyranny of a monarchy ruling its colonies from great distance without concern for the good of the people. Consequently, the founders created a nation and governance which sought to prevent the tyranny of a central government and preserve individual freedom. What developed subsequently, through conscious design and tradition, was the establishment of three independent branches of government.

The North Carolina Constitution of 1776 bore no resemblance to our form of national government, which first was organized under the Articles of Confederation. At first, all public officials were appointed by the legislature, including the governor. This practice continued until 1835, when the state constitution was amended to provide for the governor's election by the people.

However, major differences still exist in the two documents. North Carolina remains the only state in our country where citizens have not been allowed to decide whether or not their governor should have the power of veto, and this is in spite of the fact [that] the North Carolina Constitution has been completely rewritten twice, first in 1868 and again in 1971. It's interesting to note that the Consitution of 1868, including its amendments, totaled more than 100 typeset pages. The much shorter 1971 version was an attempt to bring it more in line with our national charter.

But there is one thing that both documents, the U.S. Constitution and the state constitution, provide, and that is for the establishment of three independent branches of government. This separation of powers provided in the North Carolina Constitution allows for the so-called balance of powers and encourages cooperation and accommodation. It encourages conflict, as well; and when these inevitable conflicts arise, negotiations, bargaining, and compromise are tools of resolution, the tools of consensus building.

The process of passage or defeat of a particular legislative proposal is a good example of the interactions between branches of the government and the public. We encourage participation in government by calling it a right and making it one of our fundamental responsibilities. As students, you have been taught about state and national affairs and the participatory process of governance. You also have been taught to practice participatory skills through the Youth Legislative Assembly. But to participate effectively in the public policy arena, an individual citizen needs two things: (1) an agenda; and (2) the practical skills to address that agenda with policy makers.

Through this process, the agenda moves from the self-interest of the individual to the point of reaching the best in self-governance, which we as citizens try so hard to achieve and work so fiercely to protect.

The skills to address that agenda are numerous. Let me outline some of them for you. The first is *presence*. Decisions are made every day in government. They are made whether or not you or your interest is there. To be absent is to abdicate your rights—and your responsibilities, as well.

Second is *accessibility*. The making of a law can often move as slow as a turtle, or it can race with the wind. Your views are critical during this process, and you must be accessible to present them.

The third skill is *constructive and realistic suggestion*. The issues which are addressed in any session of our legislature are many, and the need for suggestions is great. Simply identifying problems does not advance the search for consensus. Moreover, you must realize that there are competing demands for resources, and that in attempting to achieve what you want, you will not always win—either the battles or the wars.

Fourth and finally, there is the all-important matter of *credibility*. As you place yourself in the public policy arena as a participant, your knowledge and integrity must never be in question. As a participant in shaping public policy, whether as a public official or not, you are subject to the scrutiny of the public and will be held accountable for misadventures and violations of the public's trust.

I'm confident that you have learned all of these valuable lessons as members of the Youth Legislative Assembly. You have also learned that our system of government allows for the participation of citizens and demands accountability of policy makers. In our pluralistic society, both the citizen and the policy maker have the responsibility to participate, to play fair and by the rules of the process as it has become so well defined and ingrained in our state and national lives.

This process was won at great cost to the leaders of a young nation. The fifty-six men who signed the Declaration of Independence pledged "their lives, their fortunes, and their sacred honor" in support of that declaration.[1] What burden did they bear? What sacrifice was paid for liberty and independence? The following passage is from the concluding summary of a book entitled *Greatness to Spare*, by T. R. Fehrenback:

Nine signers of the Declaration of Independence died of wounds or hardships during the Revolutionary War. Five were captured or imprisoned, in some cases with brutal treatment. The wives, sons, and daughters of others were killed, jailed, mistreated, persecuted, or left penniless. One was driven from his wife's deathbed and lost all of his children. The homes of twelve signers were burned to the ground. Seventeen lost everything they owned. Most were offered immunity, freedom, rewards, their property, or the lives and release of loved ones if they would break their pledge word or take the King's protection. Their fortunes were forfeit, but their honor was not. No signer defected or changed his stand throughout the darkest hour.[2]

As you continue to participate in Youth Legislative affairs, strengthening your skills and becoming more involved, remember that the right and responsibility for participation in governance were received from the great leaders who came before us. It is a heritage we must defend and pass on to generations to come.

---

[1]"And for the support of this Declaration, with a firm reliance on the protection of Divine Providence, we mutually pledge to each other our Lives, our Fortunes, and our sacred Honor." Declaration of Independence, as quoted in *North Carolina Manual, 1987-1988*, 59.

[2]See T. R. Fehrenback, *Greatness to Spare: The Heroic Sacrifices of the Men Who Signed the Declaration of Independence* (Princeton, New Jersey: D. Van Nostrand Company, Inc., 1968), 247:

Nine Signers died of wounds or hardships during the Revolutionary War.

Five were captured or imprisoned, in some cases with brutal treatment.

The wives, sons, and daughters of others were killed, jailed, mistreated, persecuted, or left penniless. One was driven from his wife's deathbed and lost all his children.

The houses of twelve Signers were burned to the ground. Seventeen lost everything they owned.

Every Signer was proscribed as a traitor; every one was hunted. Most were driven into flight; most were at one time or another barred from their families or homes.

Most were offered immunity, freedom, rewards, their property, or the lives and release of loved ones to break their pledged word or to take the King's protection. Their fortunes were forfeit, but their honor was not. No Signer defected, or changed his stand, throughout the darkest hours. Their honor, like the nation, remained intact.

PRESS RELEASE: STATEMENT ON FEDERAL-AID HIGHWAY BILL

RALEIGH, MARCH 18, 1987

For some time now, highway projects in a number of states, including North Carolina, have been put on hold while Congress struggled to pass a federal-aid highway bill. However, Congress now appears to be on the verge of making a terrible mistake by approving a bill that would require substantial cuts in North Carolina's highway construction program during the next five years. Furthermore, this legislation will set a dangerous and harmful precedent by denying states the ability to set highway construction priorities and schedules, and instead vest that authority with a few powerful members of Congress and a handful of congressional staffers.

While the public's attention has been focused on one particular aspect of the bill, the question of raising the speed limit on rural interstate highways, the rest of this disastrous legislation has gone virtually unnoticed. Only a limited examination of the highway bill is possible at this time, because its details have just been released to the public. But based on the information currently available, plus additional analysis provided by the U.S. Department of Transportation, we have enough data to conclude that North Carolina will be particularly hard hit if this bill becomes law.

The heart of the problem with this proposal is the creation of a new form of federal pork barrel. That pork barrel takes the form of so-called demonstration projects which will cost nearly a billion dollars over the life of the bill, money that could otherwise be used by the states for crucial highway construction work that has already been planned. As a direct result of these demonstration projects, federal highway apportionments for North Carolina and other states will be dramatically reduced.

When the effects of the new proposal on North Carolina are compared with the highway bill passed earlier by the U.S. Senate, a grave disparity is evident. According to Department of Transportation estimates, our state would lose over $32 million per year—more than $160 million over the five-year life of the bill. And that total is in addition to the continuing major loss of North Carolina gas taxes to big-city transit programs.

The cost alone is sufficient reason to oppose the proposal now before Congress, but the precedent it establishes—the policy of having Congress designate highway construction priorities for the states—will, I believe, be more harmful over time. This precedent destroys the relationship that has been the cornerstone of the state-federal highway partnership for decades. Historically, Congress has developed funding formulas and approved appropriations. The states, rightly, have always decided how, when, and where to use the money, based on their own particular needs.

My twelve years of experience in Congress tell me that once this dangerous precedent is established, it will grow and, in time, will completely eliminate the states' ability to control their destiny. For the reasons I have stated, I strongly oppose the conference committee's highway proposal. I urge the North Carolina congressional delegation to take whatever action is necessary to ensure the passage of a bill that better serves the needs of the citizens of North Carolina.

PRESS RELEASE: GOVERNOR MARTIN CONTACTS U.S. NAVY OFFICIALS TO DISCUSS EXPANSION OF MILITARY OPERATING AREAS

RALEIGH, MARCH 25, 1987

[The United States Navy proposed establishing two low-level aerial training sites, called Cherry I and Core, to adjoin the existing Cherry Point Marine Corps Air Station bombing range. Cherry One would have occupied a 25-by-30 mile zone covering parts of Beaufort, Craven, Hyde, Pamlico, and Washington counties. Core consisted of a 4-by-30 mile area of Cape Lookout National Seashore and extended into the Atlantic. Many local residents opposed the idea of jet aircraft howling overhead at altitudes of 500 feet; the issue was not resolved by the end of the first Martin administration. *News and Observer*, February 27, April 1, May 15, 1988.]

Governor Jim Martin has directed the North Carolina Department of Administration to coordinate an in-depth review of a U.S. Navy request to expand military operation areas over eastern North Carolina. In addition, the governor has written the U.S. Navy to express the state's concerns regarding the expansion proposals known as Cherry I and Core. The Department of Administration has been coordinating a comprehensive, in-depth review of the draft environmental impact statement concerning these expansion proposals. The Departments of Transportation, Justice, Natural Resources and Community Development, and Agriculture have also worked together to review the project.

"I understand the U.S. Navy's needs, and I certainly believe in a strong military," Governor Martin said. "But my point of view focuses on the welfare and safety of our citizens, and that is why I have asked for a detailed analysis of this issue." Environmental concerns surrounding the expansion of military operations include the noise effects on citizens and wildlife and the disturbance of the character of the Cape Lookout National Seashore. Potential economic effects on commercial fishing operations, tourism, and agricultural operations utilizing aerial spraying are also being studied.

"The cumulative impact of future proposals is also of tremendous concern to us," Governor Martin said. "I will continue to work with the navy and the North Carolina congressional delegation to ensure that the concerns and rights of our citizens are fully addressed and protected." Governor Martin shared these concerns with the navy and also asked that they be adequately addressed in the preparation of the final environmental impact statement.

NORTH CAROLINA NATIONAL GUARD ASSOCIATION

ASHEVILLE, MARCH 27, 1987

I am very pleased to be here today and to have the opportunity to speak to all of you, citizen-soldiers and families alike, on the occasion of the North Carolina National Guard Association's Twenty-seventh Annual Convention. The city of Asheville, nestled here in the Great Smoky Mountains, is one of North Carolina's most beautiful convention cities, especially in the spring, and I hope that each of you will enjoy this visit to the Land of the Sky, as it's so often called. This is where the Western Governor's Residence is located, as many of you know, and it's also where we maintain the Governor's Western Office under the supervision of Jim Bishop. Although I'm not here nearly as often as I'd like, I want you to know that your governor and commander in chief is well represented. Jim has done an outstanding job for the citizens of this region, and I am delighted today to recognize and commend him for his exemplary performance.

Over the last two years I've also depended upon all of you— twenty-two times in the last year, to be exact—to respond to emergencies which have threatened the lives and property of fellow North Carolinians. You've been indispensable in responding to forest fires, floods, tornadoes, hurricanes, and the capture of dangerous fugitives. You've put your lives on the line without question many times, and I want to express my deepest personal appreciation for your being there when it counted. It has been an honor to serve with you.

The primary mission of the National Guard, however, is to serve as a combat-ready element of America's fighting force. Nationwide, the Army National Guard comprises 37 percent of the army's entire support structure and 44 percent of its combat units; of the twenty-five divisions in the army's force structure, nine of them are National Guard. Here in North Carolina, the National Guard consists of more than 13,000 citizen-soldiers assigned to 135 army units in 101 different towns and cities. The Air National Guard has units located in Charlotte and Badin and performs critical airlift missions for our ground forces.

Although the North Carolina Air National Guard is not quite at full strength, it is growing. I am very pleased that I will soon be announcing the formation of a new Air Guard unit and the construction of new facilities to serve in support of that group.[1] The fact that we currently are in the process of organization of new units attests to our commitment to bring the Air Guard up to, and over, its authorized strength. I am also pleased to announce that the Air Guard has been allocated three additional C-130 aircraft by the Defense Department, with the potential for several additional planes during the current year. This "robusting" of our Air Guard equipment, as the Defense Department calls it, now gives North Carolina a total of twelve C-130s in service.

In spite of this enhancement of our Air Guard, North Carolina remains the only state on the East Coast that does not have a tactical fighter wing. With many young retired pilots choosing to make their home in our state, and with the excellent support facilities we have at Seymour Johnson and Pope air force bases, North Carolina is a logical choice for such a unit. It just makes good sense. Consequently, I am working with our congressional delegation in an attempt to strengthen the Air Guard by adding a fighter wing, appropriately equipped with the A-10 fighter aircraft, to our defense capabilities. This is an effort in which I welcome and encourage the support of your association.

The Army National Guard, which comprises the majority of North Carolina's personnel, is one of the best-equipped and best-trained military forces in the world. Because of your outstanding performance in missions both at home and abroad, we have received the most modern equipment in the army's arsenal. This includes the M-1 Abrams tank, the M-2 Bradley infantry fighting vehicle, and the M60-A3 main battle tank. Recently, we received the UH-60 Black Hawk helicopter, and later this year we are scheduled to receive eighteen AH-64 Apache attack helicopters.[2]

I believe this investment expresses better than words the pride and confidence our nation places in the North Carolina Guard. No commander in chief commands a more exemplary and dedicated group of men and women than does the governor of this state, and I want you to know that I am no less dedicated and committed to each of you.

There was once a time when enlistment in the Guard required the commitment of one weekend a month and two weeks of summer training. This is no longer the case, as you and your families have come to realize. Last year, North Carolina National Guard units served in eight foreign countries: Turkey, the Philippines, Honduras, Egypt, Germany, Norway, Panama, and Italy. The frequency of these missions has increased, as well as the potential dangers, but they remain vital in the event you are someday called upon to serve in hostile regions of the world.

You have taken your duty seriously because you know the truth of the words which were spoken by President Theodore Roosevelt. He said, "If we are to be a really great people, we must strive in good faith to play a great part in the world. We cannot avoid meeting great issues." This is even more true of us today.

You served voluntarily in 1986 where some others failed to go. As commander in chief, I have always supported these missions and have upheld our responsibility for our readiness to help maintain peace throughout the world. We know that some governors have not, and in one state, federal authority has been appealed to the courts. My view is that those reluctant governors know better than I do if their Guard units are not combat ready or lack the motivation and dedication. So let them demonstrate that theirs are qualified only for a flashlight, helmet, and sand bucket like the old Home Guard. Our units are ready to serve in America's first team, and that's why we are getting the best equipment.

General Douglas MacArthur, one of the great military leaders of World War II, is said to have written that no man is entitled to the blessings of freedom unless he is vigilant in its preservation and vigorous in its defense. For 350 years, the National Guard has kept faith with the noble ideals that brought it into existence: America's freedom and independence. In North Carolina, we will continue to preserve this proud heritage for those who came before us and those who will follow.

Even as we rededicate ourselves to our country, I share with you some of the concerns about current federal budget constraints. Nationwide, we have a backlog of more than $2 billion in Army National Guard construction, and the needs of the Air Guard are estimated at $857 million. Here in North Carolina, we have a current need for at least ten new armories or replacements; only one will be completed this year. In the last two years alone, North Carolina has spent almost $2 million for roof replacements on twenty-four facilities. But we, too, are entering an era of major commitments to our public schools, highways, and other public facilities. These are long-standing needs which we absolutely must provide for in order to remain a growing, prospering state. The major financial burden for construction of additional armories falls in the area of federal responsibility. Accordingly, it is important for us to continue impressing upon our congressional delegation the need for an aggressive construction program.

In addition to these needs, General Scott[3] and his staff have identified nine counties where demographics could support the establishment of new Guard units. Discussions already are under way in three of these counties to determine the extent of local commitment to meeting the facility requirements there. If all of these new units could be organized, it is quite possible that we could recruit additional personnel to the extent of reaching 125 percent of authorized strength.

In terms of Air Guard needs, the National Guard Bureau has approved more than $4 million in new construction, and completion of these projects is anticipated within the next five years. Included in this list is the expansion of the aviation flight facility at Salisbury and the construction of a new aviation flight facility at Morrisville.[4]

I have been told that during this convention your association will address several of the army's procurement decisions, each of which could affect the allocation of additional equipment to our Guard units. The first decision relates to the army's plans to halt production of the AH-64 Apache helicopter after 1988, awaiting development of the new LHX experimental helicopter. This would leave the total army with less than half of the 1,200 Apache helicopters that were originally anticipated. Moreover, there would be a six-year time lag between the halt in production and the development and manufacture of the new LHX. Another concern affects the announced halt in production of the Bradley fighting vehicle, which would leave the National Guard with a 35 percent shortage of armored personnel carriers. I share these concerns, and I want to assure you that I will work with our congressional delegation in opposing these actions. North Carolina men and women have always made a strong commitment to the National Guard, and certainly the Congress ought to match that commitment.

Today, the North Carolina Army National Guard is at 103 percent of authorized strength, which attests to our heritage as citizens who are willing and ready to serve and to take the risks necessary to protect and defend the principles upon which our nation was founded. The National Guard, which began as a militia, is as old as our state. North Carolinians were among the first troops to reinforce the Continental line during the Revolutionary War. They were among General George Washington's command and suffered a bitter winter at Valley Forge— tired, hungry, and tattered, but never defeated. And, on the last day of battle, North Carolinians were there when Cornwallis surrendered his sword at Yorktown on October 19, 1781.

Now, as in the infancy of America, North Carolinians have served our state and nation—not because they have to, but because they want to. Like your active-duty counterparts you excel in your chosen mission, providing for the common defense. The Army and Air Guard are no longer just forces in reserve, they are fully capable partners with the active forces. On behalf of all North Carolinians, I commend and applaud your proud record. You will always have the commitment of a grateful state.

-----

[1]The governor stated officially, on April 23, 1987, that the 449th Aviation Group, Army National Guard, would locate its new headquarters in Kinston. A $1.1 million armory was planned.

[2]The North Carolina National Guard received nine of its eighteen Apache AH-64 helicopters in ceremonies held November 9, 1987, at Raleigh-Durham Airport, making it the first of only three Guard units in the country to be equipped with the armor-destroying aircraft. In a symbolic gesture, Governor Martin accepted the keys to the lead helicopter from its pilot, Lieutenant Colonel Duncan M. Stephens, commander, First Battalion, 130th Aviation Division, North Carolina National Guard. Martin quipped, "I'm not going to try to drive it." News and Observer, November 10, 1987.

During the ceremony, the governor said the Apache was so sophisticated that "We must, therefore, be ever mindful of the educational backgrounds of the designers, the builders, and the pilots, and resolve to keep America's military capability strong by keeping America's education system strong. North Carolina is surely doing its part." Having been entrusted with such equipment, Martin suggested, "says everything that needs to be said about our Guard's work and reputation. I don't mind telling you that every other governor in the United States would love to be standing here, today, as the commander in chief of the North Carolina National Guard. I am proud to be the one who is standing here." Apache Helicopter Ceremony, Raleigh, November 9, 1987.

[3]Charles Edward Scott (1932-   ), born in Apex; resident of Cary; B.S., University of the State of New York, Regents College; military education courses, 1959-1983. Enlisted in N.C. National Guard, 1949; former platoon leader, intelligence officer, communications officer, and company, battalion, and group commander; appointed deputy adjutant general, Headquarters, State Area Command, N.C. National Guard, May 1, 1985; appointed adjutant general, N.C. National Guard, October 1, 1985, and retired in March, 1989; promotion to major general confirmed by U.S. Senate, September 18, 1986. Prior to appointment as adjutant general, Scott served as field office support manager for Carolina Power and Light Co.; returned to CP&L after retirement as director of information architecture. News and Observer, December 29, 1988; Charles Edward Scott to Jan-Michael Poff, May 23, 1989.

[4]The U.S. Defense Department's proposed budget for fiscal 1986 recommended $1.8 million for National Guard projects in Jefferson, Murphy, and Salisbury; see News and Observer, February 6, 1985. Martin participated in groundbreaking ceremonies, on June 9, 1987, for new National Guard facilities to be located at Raleigh-Durham Airport. Seven of the site's thirty-five acres were slated for a $3 million, 400-man armory; the remaining land was reserved for Flight Facility Number One, a $4 million terminal supporting the Guard's Apache and Black Hawk helicopters.

PRESS AVAILABILITY, HALIFAX COMMUNITY COLLEGE

WELDON, APRIL 1, 1987

I am very pleased to be here, today, and to commend the leaders of Halifax County and the towns of Weldon and Enfield on the occasion of their most recent economic development successes. Many of these leaders are with us today, and I want to take this opportunity to recognize and ask each of them to stand as I introduce them.[1]

This is the first time since I became governor, twenty-seven months ago, that I have had the honor of participating in ribbon-cutting ceremonies for three new industries in the same county in the same day.[2] Nowhere in our state could we find a better example of rural growth through strong local initiative than right here in Halifax County. I commend and applaud your efforts. At the same time, I want to welcome these new companies to Halifax County and North Carolina, and to thank their owners for the confidence they have expressed in us by their decisions to invest in this area.

Let me also take a moment to recognize and ask the officials of these companies to stand as I introduce them.[3] I am delighted, ladies and gentlemen, that you could join us today for this press conference. I am confident that I speak for both state and local leaders in pledging our commitment to the enhancement of the investments that your companies have made in North Carolina, and we will continue to be supportive of your growth and success.

I am also pleased to be meeting with you, today, on the campus of Halifax Community College, one of fifty-eight such institutions in our state which help us meet the growing need for the training and retraining of our citizens for better jobs in new and expanding industries, in addition to providing special education courses and an associate degree program for thousands of our citizens each year. The new Technology Development Center, in which we are meeting today, provides facilities for the Department of Continuing Education, the Cooperative Skills Center, the Halifax Economic Development Commission, and the Small Business Center. In addition, it offers classroom space, shops, and labs for instruction in a variety of skills. In fact, Action Sportswear, the company where we will cut the first ribbon immediately after this press conference, currently has a training program being conducted for new employees here in this very building. This training project represents only one example, although an important example, of the many services that combine to help us remain a growing and prosperous state while strengthening our attractiveness as an excellent location for operating a business.

There are some leaders in North Carolina who, for reasons of their own, are currently debating whether we are, indeed, a growing and prospering state. They point to the piedmont Triad's loss of approximately 300 jobs in the relocation of RJR Nabisco's headquarters to Atlanta, for example, and ignore the creation of 2,000 new jobs in the same area by the new American Express Regional Operations Center. Bad news is all that some people want to talk about. They talk about layoffs as a result of Blue Bell's merger,[4] but they fail to mention the 1,000 new jobs and $80 million investment announced by five new major industries in January of this year, alone, or the fact that we had a net gain of 5,000 textile and apparel jobs.

The reality is that North Carolina has just experienced two of its most successful back-to-back years in history, 1985 and 1986. We ended both years with a record of more than 3 million North Carolinians holding full-time jobs. Statewide unemployment in 1986 dropped to 5.3 percent, the lowest in seven years. It was only slightly higher in 1985, averaging 5.4 percent for the year. The fact is that North Carolina has enjoyed four years, back to back, of strong and growing investment in new and expanding business and industrial ventures; and that, of course, translates into a major net gain in new jobs for our people, many of which are in our rural areas.

Some critics emphasize that North Carolina lost 16,000 jobs in 1986. The truth of the matter is that we did, but at the same time, we created 139,000 new jobs, giving us a net gain of 123,000 new opportunities for our citizens. Why should we feel negative about that? Companies have been opening and closing plants, transferring operations, and changing their corporate compositions since the industrial revolution. They always will. The important thing for us to concentrate on is staying substantially ahead in our strategic efforts to create new and better opportunities for our citizens, and we are doing that!

Two weeks ago, a so-called study supported by sponsors who were dominated by labor unions gave North Carolina Ds and Fs on its economic development report card.[5] Other right-to-work states also came in with poor showings. States dominated by big labor scored As and Bs, as expected. What this shows is that organized labor isn't interested in anything that builds a stronger economy outside of their domain, so they ignored the important factors that make North Carolina an attractive place in which to invest and do business.

In contrast to this unfavorable report, a study which was announced yesterday by *Manufacturing Week*, one of the most respected publications in the industrial real estate field, names North Carolina as the most attractive location for new industry in the continental United States. The survey was conducted among 132 corporate real estate managers. Of that number, 22.7 percent chose North Carolina above all other states, with California and Texas running a tie for second place. Other states that ranked high were Georgia, Arizona, and Illinois. [Governor shows card.]

This shows that North Carolina is rated first or second among corporate executives as America's most attractive location for manufacturing facilities. That's the opinion of the people who make the decisions. We ranked first in a survey by *Business Week* in 1984,[6] and second in a survey by *Fortune* in 1982—now first again, in '87—and we'll still be on top in the twenty-first century. Why should we continue to listen to the negatives? Why should we continue to heed leaders whom I call the "bad news bearers?"[7]

At the very moment that North Carolina is strong and healthy, relative to the nation, and growing even more so each day, week, and month, our reputation can be undermined by leaders who dwell on our few negatives; who overlook the tremendous progress we are making and all that we have to be thankful for; who sweep the good news under the rug. We could lose the confidence of business decision makers, like the ones we have with us today, if all they hear is a repetition of the few items of bad news. North Carolina can't afford negative leaders. They offer nothing for the future.

North Carolinians must build on its [sic] achievements, which are many and significant. In 1985 we won the largest tax cut in history. A few weeks ago, we achieved another $50 million cut in unemployment taxes on employers and established an independent Employment Security Commission Reserve Fund, the interest on which will help us finance the training and retraining needs of our workers for future jobs, not doles.

In 1985 and 1986, we worked together to take some bold initiatives to strengthen our public schools, to expand and improve our highways and rural roads, and to meet our needs for community facilities such as water and sewer facilities. Before I accept questions from the media, I want to take a few minutes to review what we propose doing to continue these bold initiatives in the next two years, with particular emphasis on public schools. [The governor spoke extemporaneously and then concluded:]

If we focus our attention on what is best for our people, rural and urban alike, we can continue to build for them a brighter future, with better jobs, in growing, prospering communities, with better public schools, in a cleaner, safer world. That's really what we want for ourselves and our children. That's what we want for our state. Together, as one united state, let us continue to work to achieve these noble goals.

---

¹Governor Martin introduced State Representative Thomas Hardaway, of Enfield; Mayor Sam Oakley, of Weldon; Mayor Lloyd Andrews, of Roanoke Rapids; Mayor Ronnie Tripp, of Halifax; county commissioners William Massey, of Roanoke Rapids, Quinton Qualls, of Littleton, Dock Brown, of Weldon, and David Allsbrook, of Scotland Neck; Dr. Phillip Taylor, president, Halifax Community College; and Jack Bishop, state highway commissioner.

²The governor participated in ribbon-cutting ceremonies for Action Sportswear, Weldon, and Seaboard Box Co. and Tillery Manufacturing, both in Enfield.

³At this point, Martin introduced Henry Gurganus of Wake Forest and Ed Monroe of Greensboro, owners of Action Sportswear, Weldon, and Tillery Manufacturing, Enfield; Roy Williams, Enfield plant manager; George Wade, of Martinsville, Virginia, president, Pluma Corp.; and George Rabinoff, board chairman, Allen Rabinoff, president, and Dora Rabinoff, Maurice Snyder, Harold Rice, Elaine Marks, and Pete and Barbara Boudreau, representing Seaboard Folding Box Co.

⁴Pennsylvania-based VF Corp. purchased Blue Bell, the Wrangler jeans manufacturer headquartered in Greensboro, in November, 1986. Two months later, the buyers announced that seven of thirteen Wrangler plants in North Carolina were to be closed, laying off approximately 900 workers and raising to 1,500 the number of employees idled since the takeover. *Greensboro News and Record*, July 28, 29, November 19, 1986, January 14, 1987.

⁵North Carolina received *D*s in economic performance, economic capacity, and policy strength, and an *F* for business vitality, according to a report produced by the Corporation for Enterprise Development. *News and Observer*, March 19, 1987.

⁶*Plant Site Selection: A Survey of Management Subscribers in Industry* ([New York: *Business Week*, 1984]), 4, 14.

⁷Martin adapted the title of a 1976 movie about Little League baseball, *The Bad News Bears*, to describe detractors of the state's economy. Jay Robert Nash and Stanley Ralph Ross, *The Motion Picture Guide* (Chicago: Cinebooks, Inc., projected multivolume series, 1985—), I, 127, hereinafter cited as Nash and Ross, *Motion Picture Guide*.

SITE LOCATION CONSULTANTS' SEMINAR

WINSTON-SALEM, APRIL 6, 1987

[The following speech is similar to those delivered before the Independent Grocers Association, Kenansville, April 7, and at the American Express Regional Operations Center dedication, Greensboro, April 9, 1987.]

I am very pleased, this morning, to extend to all of you a warm welcome to North Carolina and to thank you for attending this seminar. For many of you who have been involved in the location of manufacturing plants in North Carolina, this seminar commemorates a long-standing relationship with our state. For others, it is an introduction, an opportunity for you to get to know us and North Carolina better—and for us to get to know you better. But for all of you, we trust that the program we have arranged will help you focus on an increasingly important element of North Carolina's economy: the nonmanufacturing, or service sector, a sector which is playing a vital and expanding role in our robust growth as a highly diversified state.

Before I address some of the factors that uniquely qualify us for consideration as a location for nonmanufacturing companies, I want to review very briefly our strong record of manufacturing growth. During the last two years, North Carolina has enjoyed a total of around $5 billion in manufacturing investment. Today, more than half of the Fortune 500 companies have at least one plant in our state, and a growing number of international conglomerates have chosen North Carolina as the headquarters for their operations in North America. This has enabled us to become a state of more than 830,000 manufacturing workers, the largest per-capita manufacturing work force in the country.

Indeed, we have experienced increased employment in all areas of the economy, ending both 1985 and 1986 with more than 3 million North Carolinians holding full-time jobs. Because of our highly favorable manufacturing climate, North Carolina has now surpassed pre-recession manufacturing employment levels to achieve a record number of manufacturing jobs. During the same period, our nation has gained back only two thirds of the manufacturing jobs lost during the recession.

North Carolina's continued attractiveness as a manufacturing center was confirmed just a few days ago. *Manufacturing Week,* one of the most prestigious publications in the nation, reported that North Carolina was chosen by more industrial real estate managers than any other state as the most favorable location in the continental United States for a manufacturing facility. Of the real estate managers surveyed, 22.7 percent named North Carolina number one, beating Texas and California, both of which tied for second place. We are quite proud of that distinction, of course, but I would hasten to add that we have worked very hard as a state to strengthen the quality of life and the infrastructure that has made our leadership possible.

Today a new age is dawning in North Carolina, an era that I will choose to call the "Age of the Service Industry." We quite naturally intend to build on this strong manufacturing base, increasing our aggressiveness in that field, but we also have broadened our developments to include recruitment and development of nonmanufacturing operations.

We have already experienced some remarkable successes in this area of development; American Express is an excellent example. On Thursday of this week, I will be participating in that company's dedication of a new, 370,000-square-foot Regional Operations Center. When fully staffed by the end of the current year, it will have more than 2,000 employees, only 160 of which have been transferred into our state from other locations.

American Express Travel-Related Services is only one example; Royal Insurance Company is another. Just prior to the end of last year, Royal relocated its national headquarters to Charlotte from New York City, where it had been located since 1851. This move has provided employment for some 1,200 Charlotte-area residents. Later in this seminar, both American Express and Royal Insurance officials will be making presentations to you on why North Carolina was selected as a new location.

I have chosen these two companies simply as an illustration of the many nonmanufacturing firms that invested more than $1.5 million in North Carolina during 1985. Secretary Pope informs me that the 1986 figure, which his department is still compiling, will likely exceed $1.8 billion. Both of these totals may not reflect the true growth of the nonmanufacturing sector because North Carolina has just installed a system of reporting investments.

There are many good reasons for this record growth. One of them is North Carolina's strong position in the travel industry. Investment in our three major airports has been expanded considerably in the last three years. Piedmont Airlines' hub at Charlotte now offers 197 departures daily to fifty-four cities. At Raleigh-Durham Airport, which serves our internationally acclaimed Research Triangle Park, American Airlines is building a new national hub which will be opened later this summer, offering 185 flights to fifty-five cities by 1989.

The second reason for North Carolina's nonmanufacturing growth has been its world-class telecommunications and utilities systems. With the increasing use of fiber optics in telecommunications, North Carolina has worldwide, state-of-the-art service. In fact, one of the largest telecommunciations equipment producers in the world, Northern Telecom, has major operations in Research Triangle Park. Last year, it negotiated the largest contract in North Carolina's private industry history, consummating an agreement to supply its new DMS-10 telecommunications switching system to Nippon Telegraph and Telephone Company of Japan. The first shipment of equipment under this agreement, a multiyear contract, will take place at Northern Telecom's plant on Wednesday.

In addition to excellence in telecommunications, North Carolina has a highly reliable electric power supply, with two major companies, Duke Power and Carolina Power and Light, offering excess capacity.

The third factor favoring North Carolina, the one in which we take immense pride, is our system of public education. The University of North Carolina, the first public institution of higher learning in America, has a system of sixteen campuses, many of them doing the most advanced research in the world in collaboration with private enterprise. Among the strong business schools in the state are the Fuqua Business School, at Duke University, and the Babcock School of Business at Wake Forest University; both Duke and Wake Forest are among the thirty-eight independent colleges and universities in North Carolina.

Augmenting our public and private colleges and universities are fifty-eight community colleges, one of the largest systems in the United States. It is in our community college system that North Carolina offers a wide range of training in skills for manufacturing and service industries, including computer data entry, programming, and maintenance; clerical skills; and other special courses. As an added service to new companies, we also offer training tailored to their specific needs.

Our system of public schools is the foundation upon which we have built our extensive higher education establishment. During the next two years, I have committed $357 million to the expansion of our Basic Education Program in our public schools, and additional funds have been budgeted to implement Teacher Career Level I statewide, providing better pay and greater professional recognition for better teachers. Of all the obligations North Carolina has to its citizens and prospective business firms, nothing has a higher priority than education. As governor, I am committed to the preparation of all North Carolinians to take advantage of tomorrow's opportunities.

There are two other factors I want to mention in conclusion which favor our state for nonmanufacturing, as well as manufacturing, industries. With five interstate highways, we offer access to the entire continent. Interstate Highway I-40 to Wilmington, now under construction, will provide a fast and direct link to one of the finest ports on the East Coast; another port, located at Morehead City, is undergoing extensive expansion. An I-40 bypass around Winston-Salem is now in the planning stage, and we have committed funds to similar projects elsewhere.

With more than 78,000 miles of highways and roads linking our metropolitan areas to our urban centers and rural communities, North Carolina rightfully claims the reputation of having the largest state-maintained system in the nation. As a result of our Roads to the Future program, we are constantly expanding and improving this system for the twenty-first century.

The last point I want to make is by no means the least important. North Carolina, with our country's first state-supported symphony orchestra and the first museum of art, takes great pride in its quality of life. Our metropolitan areas are of manageable size, and they are surrounded by many smaller cities that offer a comfortable life-style. You might add to this a moderate climate that favors golfing, skiing, racing—and indoor facilities for Atlantic Coast Conference basketball. If I had to describe North Carolina's quality of life in one sentence, it would be that we nurture the human spirit.

All of the factors I have listed for you, today, combine to give North Carolina its excellent climate for service industry growth. I hope that you will take the time, during this visit, to explore more of our state and to experience this spirit of renewal firsthand.

North Carolina's nonmanufacturing business climate has fostered the creation of some 400,000 nonmanufacing jobs since 1980. This sector of our economy now provides employment for a total of 1.9 million of our citizens. As we continue to seek growth in all areas of our economy, our Department of Commerce remains at your service, and you may be assured that you will always have an open door to the governor. This is not simply a promise, it is a commitment.

America was discovered on the shores of North Carolina more than 400 years ago. It is here that our bountiful resources spawned the most revolutionary wave of industrialization in a nation reunited after a great war, and it is here that we are creating the state of the future. Let me wish you an enjoyable and productive seminar here at Grayland[1] and a relaxing and rewarding visit to North Carolina. We sincerely hope you will visit with our state often, on business as well as pleasure. North Carolina is excellent for both.

---

[1]The site consultants' seminar was held at Grayland Conference Center.

STATE EMPLOYEES ASSOCIATION MEMBERSHIP KICKOFF

RALEIGH, APRIL 7, 1987

It's a real pleasure for me to be here, today, with Lieutenant Governor Jordan, Chief Justice Exum,[1] members of the Council of State and Executive Cabinet, and leaders of the State Employees Association of North Carolina. I am also pleased to lend my support to the association's annual membership drive, an effort which I am told has a goal of 3,000 new members by October. With 50,000 members already enrolled, the association represents the largest nonunion organization of state employees in the nation. This is a record in which we may all take pride, but I am confident that under the leadership of your 1987 membership chairman, Kay Goins of Spruce Pine, the association will reach out and touch even more employees this year. You have my best wishes for a successful campaign.

The State Employees Association of North Carolina is, and always has been, dedicated to improving the working conditions and representing the best interests of the more than 191,700 individuals who are employed by our state government. Your goals are no less the goals which I, as both governor and a member of your association, also am working to achieve. During the twenty-seven months that I have been in office, we have enjoyed an open and free exchange of ideas; we have shared problems; and we have worked together to find solutions that are for the benefit of our state employees and their families.

An excellent example of this cooperative spirit is the association's Task Force on Substance Abuse among State Employees, which was appointed at my request last September. I am told that the task force will be meeting tomorrow, and that its report and recommendations to me will be completed within the coming month. Allow me to commend and applaud your efforts to approach this task in a timely, yet comprehensive, manner. If substance abuse indeed is a serious problem, and we won't know if we ignore it, then we want to do everything possible to help employees who are affected and, more importantly, to place greater emphasis on prevention. Therefore, I look forward to receiving your report and taking the recommendations of the task force under consideration.

There are any number of problems that can affect an employee's performance. In recognition of this fact we have had in place, for several years now, an Employee Assistance Program which provides confidential help to those employees who need professional guidance. It is a program founded on understanding and compassion, rather than indifference to employee needs. Accordingly, we have worked to strengthen related services, and I have recommended appropriating an additional $187,000 during the next biennium to establish four regionally based Employee Assistance Program offices, expanding its services to every region of North Carolina.

Occasionally, there are problems affecting a number of employees over which they have no control. One of these problems concerns the compensation of state employees who have been injured on the job. As your association is aware, the Industrial Commission has ruled that state employees no longer can take sick leave in lieu of workers' compensation payments. Often, this leaves an employee receiving an amount which is less than his or her regular salary.

I am pleased to report to you, today, that the Office of State Personnel has developed a new program which will permit state employees who have been injured on the job to use part of their annual sick leave benefits to make up the differential which might result in their receiving workers' compensation below their regular salaries. This new policy is now being circulated for review and comment, and I plan to recommend its approval to the State Personnel Commission.

Pay, and performance pay, are issues that have always dominated the concerns of state employees. I have always been mindful of the need to provide salary enhancement in keeping with cost of living increases. Such a policy is necessary, I believe, if we expect to remain reasonably competitive with the private sector. We want to keep good, career-oriented employees who are dedicated to their work.

Therefore, I have recommended a 4.2 percent salary increase for all state employees in each of the next two years. I believe strongly that part of this increase should be in the form of performance pay to reward those state employees who do exemplary work. In the final analysis, it will be the General Assembly which decides on how this increase will be applied in terms of across-the-board raises and so-called merit increases. I trust that whatever is ratified in the budget process will be no less than what I have recommended.

Recently, the task force which was appointed to prepare a concept report on a new pay and performance pay plan for state employees has submitted its findings. I believe that those of you who have reviewed this report will agree that it is a concept worthy of consideration, but that the development of the final pay plan will require considerable work. The best way to arrive at a plan which reflects the best thinking of state employees, the executive department, and the General Assembly, is for all [of] us to work together to ensure that it is administered properly. I sincerely hope that we can accomplish this in the spirit of developing a system that truly rewards outstanding performance.

The health and welfare of state employees and their families are among my highest priorities as governor; indeed, they are among the greatest responsibilities conferred upon any governor. I assure you that I accept these responsibilities very seriously. In recent months there has been some concern among state employees, a concern which both Insurance Commissioner (Jim) Long and I share, about the deficit which has developed in the Teachers' and State Employees' Health Benefit Plan. The administration of this plan has been a matter of controversy for years, and this latest development does nothing to enhance the confidence of our teachers, state employees, and their families in one of their most important benefits.

I trust that the General Assembly, which has taken the sole responsibility for overseeing the plan from its board of trustees, will resolve these concerns quickly and in a manner that will not result in the further erosion of benefits or an excessive increase in premiums for dependent coverage—or reduce your pay increase! The Teachers' and State Employees' Health Benefit Plan was established as one of the most outstanding benefit programs of its type in the nation. Our General Assembly has a responsibility to maintain the integrity of this program, and I am more than willing to work with our legislators in the best interest of our teachers and state employees.

I should mention that, as you are already aware, I have had state personnel officer Dick Lee circulate letters to state agencies for employees to indicate their preference for a holiday to be eliminated under the law creating a new holiday in honor of Reverend Martin Luther King, Jr., in January. That tough choice had been sidestepped by the General Assembly, leaving. . . . [incomplete].[2]

In the executive branch, there are many innovative ideas we are putting into practice to make employment for the state a continuing experience of positive career development and advancement. I want to thank the State Employees Association of North Carolina for its strong support as we continue to work together to accomplish our mutual goal of remaining the leader among all of our sister states.

---

[1]James Gooden Exum, Jr. (1935-   ), native of Snow Hill; A.B., University of North Carolina at Chapel Hill, 1957; LL.B., New York University, 1960; U.S. Army Reserve, 1961-1967. Practicing attorney, 1961-1967; member, state House, 1967; resident superior court judge, North Carolina's Eighteenth Judicial District, 1967-1974; associate justice, 1975-1986, elected chief justice, 1986, state supreme court; visiting lecturer, University

of North Carolina School of Law, 1978-1985; Democrat. *North Carolina Manual, 1987-1988,* 845.
[2]The governor inserted this partial paragraph into his prepared text.

TESTIMONY BEFORE U.S. HOUSE COMMITTEE ON SCIENCE, SPACE, AND TECHNOLOGY

WASHINGTON, D.C., APRIL 8, 1987

Introduction

I am Jim Martin, governor of North Carolina, and I want to express my thoughts on the superconducting super collider. I will address the importance of the SSC for maintaining the traditional preeminence of the United States in experimental high-energy physics; the importance of the SSC as an instrument for fundamental research, in physics, about the most basic aspects of nature; and the importance of North Carolina as an ideal site for the SSC.

Before proceeding to these points, however, let me share some personal thoughts with you. I am by training an organic chemist, and before entering the exhilaration of politics I have experienced the exhilaration of uncovering nature's secrets. In my investigations, I sought fundamental explanations of the structure of organic molecules.

Why do scientists pursue the unknown? Humans express their fundamental natures not only through their emotions in poetry but also in the rational poetry of mathematics. Science exists as a fully human, cultural activity. Scientists pursue knowledge for its own sake, to express their humanity, and only when the pursuit is foreknown to produce destructive results should they refrain from the pursuit. More often, scientists investigate the unkown to understand, hoping that the fruits of this research will contribute to the betterment of mankind.

Honesty forms the centerpiece of science; the scientist commits him- or herself to the pursuit of truth, fully knowing the evasive nature of hard facts. In searching for scientific facts, the scientist necessarily must depend upon instruments, those extensions of his own perceptual system; to penetrate deeply into nature, extremely complicated instruments are required. Reconstructed computer images from satellite probes provide modern data which are further analyzed by mathematical tools like cluster analysis. If one investigates the tiniest particles of nature, the instrumentation becomes even more complicated and sophisticated. Paradoxically, to look at the smallest objects in nature, we require some of the largest and most powerful instruments, and the SSC is just such an instrument—the most powerful and largest accelerator ever conceived.

Importance of the SSC

Since the Second World War, the United States has maintained world leadership in the field of high-energy physics. We have built accelerators, trained scientists, postulated theories, and tested these theories in those same accelerators.

Quarks, through "strong force" interactions, compose a set of larger particles, called *hadrons*, that include the proton and neutron. Another set of particles, called *leptons*, are believed to be elementary or fundamental. Leptons, however, experience only the "weak force" and electromagnetic interactions. In offering theories of how quarks operate, scientists have resorted to both the poetry of words—as in colored quarks, strange quarks, and charmed quarks—and in the poetry of mathematics, as in gauge theories.

Beyond the poetry of theories, we find the empirical necessity of testing these theories in instruments, the accelerators. The SSC offers physicists the opportunity of looking into the most fundamental aspects of nature and testing the validity of that poetry.

Science cannot exist without technology. Building the SSC will not only ensure continued world leadership in high-energy physics, but will also contribute to restoring America's status in technology. We have lost our technological leadership in so many areas, and the technology associated with the SSC will be extremely specialized and advanced. Not to go ahead with the SSC would prevent the United States from pursuing the technology necessary to make the giant accelerator work, a technology in superconduction which undoubtedly will have numerous applications in the creation of new commercial products. If we do not construct the SSC, the United States will once again abandon its scientific and technological leadership to other countries. We have the imagination and the creativity to formulate new theories and test them; what we need now is the political courage to translate these bold ideas into a reality.

North Carolina as a Site for the SSC

North Carolina has been active in assessing its suitability as a site for the SSC for more than two years. I, as governor, have organized a task force and directed that a feasibility study be conducted. That study, which was completed in June of 1986, indicated that North Carolina does, indeed, have a site that is geologically favorable, is proximal to population centers that offer a high quality of life, is well served by air and ground transportation, is close to three major universities and several smaller colleges and community and technical schools, and is environmentally suitable.[1]

SSC Project Management

We have recently reorganized our SSC project staff and we have awarded, or are in the process of awarding, several contracts for specific studies that are necessary for us to adequately evaluate our site and prepare our proposal in response to the recently released Invitation for Site Proposals. The attached project organizational chart shows that our SSC project is being administered through the North Carolina Board of Science and Technology and the Department of Administration.[2] We have hired a project director, Dr. Paul H. Frampton, and a project manager, Dr. William L. Dunn.[3] These two individuals will be responsible for organizing and directing our site proposal preparation, working through and with my science adviser, Dr. Earl Mac Cormac.[4] Dr. Frampton is a theoretical, high-energy physicist and a professor of physics at the University of North Carolina in Chapel Hill. He has B.S. and D.Phil. degrees from Oxford University, as well as an honorary D.Sc. degree, also from Oxford. Dr. Dunn has a B.S. degree in electrical engineering and M.S. and Ph.D. degrees in nuclear engineering; he has been working for the last eight years in contract research. In addition, various committees, subcommittees, and contractors are already hard at work, helping to prepare North Carolina's bid.

North Carolina's Infrastructure

The beauty of our proposed SSC site rests not only in the ideal geology, which I shall describe below, but also in the fact that the laboratory would be fifteen miles from Research Triangle Park. SSC scientists would have the best university-industry research park in the world available to them, as well as three of the most distinguished universities in the world. Both the University of North Carolina at Chapel Hill and Duke University are world renowned in arts, sciences, and medicine, while North Carolina State University has achieved world-class status in engineering and biotechnology.

In Research Triangle Park, North Carolina has developed one of the finest series of research facilities in the world. More than 20,000 research workers pursue scientific and technological research in such facilities as the research laboratories of Burroughs Wellcome, Glaxo, IBM, EPA, NIEHS, Ciba-Geigy, General Electric, and a host of others. The state of North Carolina has invested more than $82 million in the construction and operation of the Microelectronics Center of North Carolina. We have also founded the North Carolina Biotechnology Center, with an annual budget of almost $6 million.[5] The creation of the North Carolina School of Science and Mathematics, a residential school for high school juniors and seniors, has served as a national model; Illinois and New York have explicitly copied this model, and other states have expressed interest in founding similar institutions.

In the late 1950s, leaders in North Carolina, including Governor Luther Hodges,[6] dreamed of forming a research park founded upon the strengths of the University of North Carolina, in Chapel Hill; Duke University, in Durham; and North Carolina State University, in Raleigh. These three universities and cities form the "triangle" of Research Triangle Park. One of their first acts in forming the Triangle was the creation of Research Triangle Institute, a research organization designed not only to assist these universities but also other laboratories in the park. Now an institution with more than 1,000 researchers and an annual budget of $56 million, Research Triangle Institute is ready to serve the SSC. Plans are also under way to develop a supercomputing facility in the park, and this, too, would be available to the SSC laboratory.

Located at the edge of Research Triangle Park, and also fifteen miles of interstate and four-lane state highways from the proposed North Carolina SSC site, is Raleigh-Durham (RDU) Airport. This facility will become, on June 15, 1987, the eastern hub for American Airlines. The opening of the American Airlines hub will occur when $60 million of airport construction [is] completed. Plans are also under way for the establishment of international service from Raleigh-Durham to Europe. The RDU Airport now offers easy access to major cities and other scientific communities in the U.S., which will be enhanced by [the] opening of the American Airlines hub.

Along with the Research Triangle Park and the three major universities, North Carolina has an extensive system of fifty-eight community and technical colleges, several of which are located in the vicinity of our proposed SSC site. These technical training facilities have played a major role in attracting research laboratories to the Triangle by training laboratory technicians, and they could play the same role in training highly skilled technicians for the SSC.

North Carolina's Site and Geology

Introduction

The proposed North Carolina SSC site is located in eastern Person, western Granville, and northern Durham counties, in the northeastern corner of the piedmont physiographic province of North Carolina. The climate of the area is humid subtropical with an average temperature of 60 degrees Fahrenheit. The average temperature ranges from about 42 degrees Fahrenheit, in December and January, to 79 degrees Fahrenheit in July. The topography forms a gently rolling terrain typical of the North Carolina piedmont. Surface elevations along the proposed collider orientation range from a low of 360 feet at Knap of Reeds Creek, in northern Durham County, to a maximum of 740 feet near the town of Roxboro, in Person County.

SSC Orientation and Tilt

The preliminary orientation for the collider places the injector and campus in the northern corner of the Camp Butner property, which is federally owned property currently being used by the National Guard. The long axis—17.43 miles—of the SSC ring is oriented in the northwest-southeast direction and is located between the towns of Roxboro and Oxford, North Carolina. In this orientation, portions of the ring would be within fifteen miles of the Virginia border. The preliminary SSC orientation relative to a horizontal planar surface below the ground surface is tilted approximately 0.1 degree along a northeast-southwest trending axis oriented at 45 degrees to the major and minor axes of the SSC configuration. The highest point of the tilted tunnel is located in the northwest quadrant, southeast of the town of Roxboro, North Carolina; the lowest point is located in the southeast quadrant, between the Tar River and the Camp Butner property.

The depth below the ground surface ranges between fifty feet at the Flat River in the southwest quadrant and 285 feet southwest of the town of Allensville in the northwest quadrant. The injector complex is at an average depth of 160 feet below the surface. The tunnel crosses the Tar River in the southeastern quadrant at a depth of sixty-three feet below the stream bed and crosses Mayo Creek in the northwestern quadrant at a depth of fifty feet below the stream bed. The exact orientation and tilt will be optimized after examination of drill core and other subsurface geotechnical data. An engineering firm is presently under contract to the state to perform geophysical studies, take core borings, and prepare a geotechnical characterization study of the site area.

Hydrogeology Characterizations of the SSC Site

The southern part of the SSC site is located just north of Lake Michie, in northern Durham County, and Lake Butner, in southern Granville County. The Tar River drainage flows from northwest to southeast through the upper one half of the proposed SSC site. The site also contains the drainage divide between the Tar River and the Flat River, both of which have their headwaters in Person County.

The Flat River, at Bahama, North Carolina, in northern Durham County, drains an area of 150 square miles and has an average measured flow of 143 cubic feet per second. The measured flow of this stream mirrors the normal flow of the other major streams within the area and is indicative of a relatively low surface flow in comparison with similar piedmont drainage areas in other parts of North Carolina. The stream beds of all major drainages within the site area occur at or near the contact between the residuum and bedrock.

Stream flow during periods of slight rainfall is maintained by groundwater discharge. The low measured surface flow along this reach of Flat River, coupled with water well data verified in the field, suggest that groundwater capacity in the SSC area is less than average when compared with adjacent areas of the North Carolina piedmont. The porosity of the intrusive and metamorphic rock types in the SSC site is controlled by joints, fractures, and bedding planes within these rocks. Groundwater moves down through the overlying saprolite to either discharge into local streams or to move into the available openings in the bedrock.

Other than the general characteristics noted above, the hydrogeologic charateristics of the rock units in the study area appear to be relatively similar. Long-term average groundwater yields in this area can be expected to range from 200,000 to 300,000 gallons per day, per square mile, from the bedrock aquifers. Groundwater discharge from the saprolite might be slightly higher than the bedrock yields. The depth to the water table generally ranges from ten to thirty-five feet below land surface, depending on topographic location. Annual seasonal groundwater variations are usually less than ten feet.

Groundwater quality is somewhat variable in the bedrock aquifers of the piedmont area of North Carolina, but the available data in the site area show that it is generally suitable as a source of drinking water with a pH that ranges from 6 to almost 8, but usually ranges from slightly more than 7 to slightly acidic.

The proposed North Carolina site is shown in Figure 1. The rock types found at that site are characterized in the Appendix.[7] The basic conclusion that can be drawn from the information available to date is that North Carolina has a geologically suitable and stable site, located in an area with a preponderance of granite and felsic volcanic rock types.

Land Use Characteristics within the SSC Site

In spite of its proximity to the major urban complex of Raleigh, Durham, Chapel Hill, and the Research Triangle, the SSC study area is surprisingly rural in nature. By initial survey of Person, Granville, Orange, and Durham counties, it was determined that the study area ranged from 93 percent to 99 percent rural, with two thirds of this land being forested. The SSC ring as currently oriented would not pass under any significant population centers (see Figure 1). The site would be well served by existing highways; in particular, Interstate 85 would pass near, but not over, the collider ring.

Conclusions

Preliminary geological, structural, and hydrological studies for siting the SSC in the area previously described have provided sufficient data to make the following conclusions relative to geology, hydrology, and engineering of the site:

1. Surface analysis of rock types within the area reveals no adverse compositional or structural characteristics that would prohibit the location of the SSC within the area. Based on the available data, the proposed location and orientation appear to be in an area of good rock quality with low differential *in situ* stress. Occasional occurrences of discontinuities remain to be established during the geotechnical characterization program and will affect the cost estimate for design, construction, and operation.

2. Major rock deformation within the site area is associated with ancient tectonic events that occurred approximately 600 million years

ago. No recent rock deformational event of 10,000 years or younger is known. Therefore, the site area can be considered seismically stable.

3. Hydrologic data indicate that surface flow and groundwater yields are less than average for similar areas within the North Carolina piedmont. This further reinforces the preliminary conclusion that the proposed site has no major adverse groundwater conditions. On the other hand, there are several reservoirs near the site area that could be used to help satisfy site requirements for industrial water.

4. The SSC site was chosen to avoid local seismic vibrations resulting from railroads, interstate highways, et cetera, and to provide the optimum topographic orientation.

5. Based on the data available at this time, it appears to the geologists and engineers of the task force that North Carolina offers an excellent site for the SSC. More detailed testing of the site is currently in progress.

The Schedule for the SSC Proposal

North Carolina can meet, with special efforts, the deadline of August 3, 1987, for the submission of our proposal. If we had not spent a year doing a preliminary study, the results of which were published in a two-volume report in June, 1986, we would not now be in the position of beginning a more detailed and careful geophysical study to provide the data necessary to establish the relative merits of our site. Establishing a deadline of December 31, 1987, however, would have made our task easier and less costly. A four-month time frame for the submission of a proposal of this magnitude does not allow us much time for the normal process of peer review of our proposal, a process which I, as both governor and as a scientist, advocate as essential for the development of good research and site proposals.

Conclusion

I will present a proposal for the location of the site of the SSC in North Carolina, confident that a decision to locate it in the Old North State will continue the innovative research tradition already established in Research Triangle Park. The park is also viewed as an international center, with companies from England, Japan, Canada, and Germany forming some of the largest research laboratories. Researchers from all parts of the United States and colleagues from other nations have come to North Carolina not only because we have a critical mass of scientists and engineers engaged in fundamental research, but also because of the natural, friendly ambience of North Carolina. Native North Carolinians and those new citizens arriving in North Carolina to work, live, and do research all want to stay in North Carolina. It is an honor and a pleasure to be governor of a state whose natives and newcomers love the beauty of their mountains, plateaus, and coast and who enjoy the friendships of each other.

---

[1]*The Superconducting Super Collider in North Carolina: A Feasibility Study. Report of the Governor's Task Force on the Superconducting Super Collider* ([Raleigh]: North Carolina Board of Science and Technology, June 1, 1986).

[2]See "Superconducting Super Collider Project Organizational Chart," Testimony before U.S. House Committee on Science, Space, and Technology, April 8, 1987, page 10, Governors Papers, James G. Martin.

[3]Paul Howard Frampton (1943-   ), born in Kidderminster, England; B.A., 1965, M.A., 1968, D.Phil., 1968, D.Sc., 1984, Oxford University. Fellow, European Organization for Nuclear Research (CERN), 1970-1972; visiting associate professor, Syracuse University, 1972-1975, University of California at Los Angeles, 1975-1977, Ohio State University, 1977-1978, Harvard University, 1978-1981; faculty member, since 1981, professor of physics, since 1985, University of North Carolina at Chapel Hill; author. Paul Howard Frampton to Jan-Michael Poff, October 10, 1988. Frampton "originated" to Martin "the idea of locating the SSC in North Carolina," according to the governor's September 3, 1987, remarks on the state's super collider site proposal.

William L. Dunn; resident of Durham; B.S., University of Notre Dame, 1968; M.S., 1970, Ph.D., 1974, North Carolina State University. Project engineer, Carolina Power and Light Co., Raleigh, 1973-1977; reactor applications engineer, Technical Services Group chief, Department of Nuclear Engineering, North Carolina State University, 1977-1979; senior research engineer, Research Triangle Institute, 1979-1982; principal engineer, Nuclear and Mechanical Engineering Group manager, Applied Research Associates, Inc., Raleigh, 1982-1988; appointed project director, North Carolina superconducting super collider project, 1986; president, Quantum Research Services, Inc., Durham, since 1988; author. William L. Dunn to Jan-Michael Poff, October 3, 1988.

[4]Earl R. Mac Cormac (1935-   ), born in New York; resident of Raleigh; B.E., 1955, B.D., 1958, M.A., 1959, Ph.D., 1961, Yale University; U.S. Naval Reserve, 1956-1965. Appointed to faculty, 1961, philosophy professor, 1972-1981, department chairman, 1976-1985, Charles A. Dana Professor of Philosophy, 1981-1986, Davidson College; Fulbright Lecturer, University of Madras, 1985-1986; science adviser to the governor and executive director, North Carolina Board of Science and Technology, since 1986; adjunct professor of industrial engineering, North Carolina State University; author. Ann Cooper, North Carolina Board of Science and Technology, to Jan-Michael Poff, August 17, 1988.

[5]The North Carolina Biotechnology Center was established in 1981. Poff and Crow, *Addresses of Hunt, 1981-1985,* 170-171.

[6]Luther Hartwell Hodges (1898-1974), born in Cascade, Virginia; buried in Eden, North Carolina; was graduated from University of North Carolina at Chapel Hill, 1919. Various positions with Marshall Field mills, including general manager and vice-president, through 1950; served as textile division price administrator, U.S. Office of Price Administration, consultant to U.S. agriculture secretary, and textile consultant to U.S. Army in Germany during and after World War II; hired as industry division chief, Economic Cooperation Administration, 1950; U.S. State Department consultant for International Management Conference, 1951; elected lieutenant governor, 1952; became governor upon death of William B. Umstead, 1954; elected governor, 1956; U.S. commerce secretary during Kennedy and Johnson administrations; president, Rotary Inter-

national, 1967; author; lecturer; Democrat. Apart from conceiving Research Triangle Park, Governor Hodges was known throughout the South for his industrialization program; he also backed North Carolina's first minimum wage law. Powell, *DNCB*, III, 156.

[7]See "Appendix: Major Rock Types Typical of the North Carolina Site," Testimony before U.S. House Committee on Science, Space, and Technology, April 8, 1987, pages 11-13, Governors Papers, James G. Martin.

NORTH CAROLINA CHAPTER, SPECIAL LIBRARIES ASSOCIATION

Greensboro, April 9, 1987

I am very pleased today to have the opportunity to address the opening session of your annual conference, which has as its theme, "Information for Progress: A Southeastern Approach."

Howard McGinn,[1] assistant state librarian for North Carolina, has described information as the most plentiful, yet least valued, export produced in the United States. He is correct, of course, on a number of counts. We have spent billions of dollars in America to build the most modern transportation system in the world, to develop a defense system that is rivaled only by the Soviet Union, and to establish systems of finance, services, manufacturing, and commerce. Our accomplishments as a nation and as a people reflect the genius that has belonged to us almost exclusively for more than 200 years. However, while federal, state, and local governments have taken direct and creative steps to enhance their physical infrastructures, very little has been accomplished in terms of organizing information in a way that is useful for economic development, in spite of the fact that our economy is well into the information age.

In North Carolina, we are attempting to correct this misuse, and in many cases, lack of use, of the vital resource which information has become. Last October I joined Secretary of Cultural Resources Patric Dorsey in announcing the establishment of the North Carolina Information Network, a computerized system to access data quickly and efficiently.[2] The purpose of this network is to build an information infrastructure for our state based on the vast resources which are already in place in North Carolina's public and private academic libraries. In addition, it incorporates other information bases, such as community college, federal, corporate, health science, and public libraries.

To give you an idea of the network's scope, allow me to point out that it includes more than 2,600 public and private libraries in our state, with more than 40 million volumes, 6 million of which are already in the network's on-line computer data base. It is an understatement to say that the infrastructure, which is being formed by the network, holds the promise of significant educational and economic development benefits. Indeed, the network will increasingly become one of our most valuable assets.

One of the reasons we have been able to make notable progress in the start-up of the network in just a few short months is the fact that it involved only a small infusion of tax dollars. It builds on the investment which has been made for over two centuries in our public and private institutions of library resources. Dependence on commercial contractors for its technical functioning has eliminated the need for major, duplicative expenditures for hardware, software, and data base construction.

With this brief explanation of what the North Carolina Information Network represents, allow me to address the more practical aspects of its uses. The services offered by the network are fourfold. Through the use of the Online Union Catalog and the Online Union List of Serials, an individual anywhere in North Carolina can locate and borrow, electronically, the more than 6 million volumes now in the data base. Located in Ohio, these data bases are maintained by the Online Computer Library Center, Incorporated. Through two other programs provided through Western Union's Easylink System, it is now possible for the first time ever, in North Carolina, to provide electronic mail and bulletin board services.

Electronic bulletin boards, in particular, provide a tremendous advantage in the distribution of public information. For example, these scrolling electronic newsletters allow for easy creation and distribution of text information files, such as job openings, contract opportunities with state government, new tax and other regulations, and consumer-oriented materials. These services are particularly valuable to those of you in such specialized areas as the arts, communications, business, industry, research, the biomedical sciences, and geosciences, just to mention a few. And what's more, your governor is on line, both at the office and with my own computer at home, both with modem and 30 megabyte hard drive.

The heart of the North Carolina Information Network is the microcomputer, the use of which allows access to hundreds of electronic information services. Because of this universal access, the development and use of the network are being deliberately geared up toward economic development, and rural economic development in particular. This could very well put us light-years ahead of other southeastern states in strengthening our economic development efforts.

Information access is a constant in economic development. It can be used by industrial- and service-sector recruiters, on a local and statewide basis, as a powerful tool to attract new plants to rural and urban areas. Many of you have heard economic recruitment referred to as the "great buffalo hunt"; more recently, you've probably heard that the hunt is almost over because of the diminishing herd. We certainly hope our sister states believe this, for this gives us an even greater advantage as we pioneer the use of the Information Network to find the few buffalo that are still left.

But even as the number of new industrial plant locations diminish[es], the products of the network can be used to assist existing business firms by providing the intellectual and data capital needed to fuel new small businesses and entrepreneurships. Additionally, information serves the needs of traditional manufacturing companies, as well as the growing high-technology and nonmanufacturing sectors.

Because of the inexpensive ease of access to information, no matter where you are, in all geographic areas of North Carolina, entrepreneurs are given greater latitude in the choice of areas for their investment dollars. This means that they are afforded an advantage which heretofore has been available only to the flagship corporations and in large urban areas. The North Carolina Information Network will never bring an end to the careless use of information, but it does represent a bold and innovative step in the efforts of North Carolina state government to use the great abundance of its data resources to generate future growth, especially in our rural areas.

Getting the network started has been a comparatively easy job when we consider the effort we must put forth to help local governments and business firms apply this new and instant gold mine of data. We are now taking steps to coordinate the network's development and marketing programs with the work of existing educational and economic development institutions. These include our Community College Small Business Development Centers, the UNC Small Business and Technology Development Center, our own Department of Commerce's Small Business Development Division, and our local public library systems.

North Carolina knows that the use of information can produce positive economic results. The world-acclaimed North Carolina Research Triangle Park, nestled among Raleigh, Durham, and Chapel Hill, was founded on the human and material resources of the area's three great universities: Duke, UNC, and N.C. State. The North Carolina Information Network is a logical extension of this very successful effort. The network will seek to bring about the same economic magic in rural North Carolina, while remaining one of the most valuable development tools for our urban centers. The network will truly achieve its goal, however, only when it realizes peer status with the physical infrastructure. As governor I invite you, as an association and as individual custodians of the specialized knowledge of the ages, to join with me in making the North Carolina Information Network our greatest resource for progress.

We are also developing plans for special library services to help functionally illiterate adults become readers in this, the "Year of the Reader."

The Special Libraries Association, now in its seventy-ninth year, came into being to fill a special need: the need to bring together librarians in specialized fields. That effort accomplished much more— it created a new kind of librarianship, that of library service geared to meet the needs of specialized situations. With your help, and the same kind of determination which brought your organization into existence, we can build upon the start we have made in the North Carolina Information Network and develop it into the asset it is intended to be for all of our citizens.

---

[1]Howard F. McGinn (1943-　　　), born in Pittsburgh; resident of Sanford; B.A., Villanova University, 1966; M.S.L.S., Drexel University, 1970; M.B.A., Campbell University, 1984. Assistant director of libraries, St. Charles Seminary, Philadelphia, 1968-1969; library director, Chestnut Hill (Pennsylvania) College, 1969-1972; English teacher, Ursuline Academy, Wilmington, Delaware, 1972-1973; audiovisual media marketing coordinator, 1973-1976, audiovisual sales manager, 1976-1978, Division of Higher Education, J.B. Lippincott Publishing Co.; managing editor, 1978-1983, general manager, 1983-1984, New York Times Co./Microfilming Corp. of America; consultant, New York Times Co., 1984-1986; owner, Carolina Business Archives, Inc., 1984-1985; network development director, 1985-1986, assistant state librarian, 1986-1989, state librarian, since 1989, Division of State Library, North Carolina Department of Cultural Resources; author; editor. Howard F. McGinn to Jan-Michael Poff, September 27, 1988; *News and Observer*, November 25, 1988.

[2]Governor Martin and Secretary Dorsey made the announcement launching the North Carolina Information Network at a news conference held October 2, 1986. Patric Griffee Dorsey (1924-　　　), born in Reno, Oklahoma; attended Wayne State University, 1943-1946, University of Southern California, 1953-1955, and University of Maryland, 1960. Owner, manager, Whitford Galleries, Mulberry Boutique, Mulberry Antiques; chairwoman, Craven County Industrial Development Commission, 1975-1985, and of Craven County Reagan for President Committee, 1976; delegate, Republican National Convention, 1976, 1980; Craven County campaign manager, Helms for Senate, 1978; Republican candidate for state house, 1980, and secretary of state, 1984; vice-chairwoman, 1981-1983, chairwoman, 1983-1985, GOP First Congressional District; chairwoman, 1985 Gubernatorial Inaugural Committee; state secretary of cultural resources, since 1985. *North Carolina Manual, 1987-1988,* 743.

GOVERNOR'S COMMISSION FOR THE FAMILY

RALEIGH, APRIL 23, 1987

Thank you for coming today for an announcement that can have a major impact in the lives of North Carolinians. No one disputes the challenges families face today, when both parents hold jobs; when latch-key children come home alone after school; when some of our senior citizens find themselves alone and out of touch; and when so many pressures—drug and alcohol abuse, divorce, the breakdown of parent-child relationships—threaten our families, which remain the foundation of our society.

Last month I signed an executive order creating the Governor's Commission for the Family.[1] The creation of the commission represents one more step in my continuing efforts to develop a comprehensive government effort aimed at providing assistance to families and children. We should never overlook the very people whose lives and work in North Carolina give our state the character so admired by visitors.

It's time to look seriously for answers to some of the pressing problems facing our families. That is the charge of this commission. The twenty-six members of this commission provide a diverse cross section of the talent pool available in this state, from law enforcement, from the judicial system, from leaders of our communities, and from the invaluable volunteers that serve in many varied capacities in cities and towns across North Carolina. Among this group, you'll find a sprinkling of business, of cabinet secretaries, and of people who have dedicated their lives to the public good. We have sought out and gotten commitments from an impressive group.

Just like the Governor's Commission on Child Victimization and the more recently created North Carolina Fund for Children and Families, this new commission will bring its talents and resources to bear on the immediate problems of our families and our children. There is much to be done. Through the work of this commission, we hope to not only heighten public awareness of the need to strengthen our families, but work to find ways to reduce the factors that place undue stress on so many of our families.

The Commission for the Family will need to look at our current laws to see if they are adequately addressing the needs of our families. The commission will need to look at community-based services that can assist us in addressing this problem. Finally, this group will need to take a hard look at asking families to help themselves, with our assistance. Looking at the membership gathered here this morning, I know that this Commission for the Family will not be just another commission. I know that you are dedicated professionals from business, from government, and from all walks of life who share one common goal: Seek out the forces that disrupt our families, and find ways to quell those forces.

Now let me introduce my wife, Dottie, who will serve as chairman of this commission. You already know of her work in this area. I know that she is eager to begin this new task.

---

[1]Executive Order Number 40, establishing the Governor's Commission for the Family, was signed March 16, 1987. *N.C. Session Laws, 1987*, II, 2349-2353.

ASSOCIATION OF UNIVERSITY RELATED RESEARCH PARKS

RESEARCH TRIANGLE PARK, APRIL 23, 1987

[This address is nearly identical to one Martin delivered at the Professional Engineers of North Carolina-Governor's New Product Awards ceremony, Raleigh, February 6, 1987.]

I am very pleased to welcome the Association of University Related [Research] Parks to North Carolina, and more especially to North Carolina's internationally acclaimed Research Triangle Park—at 6,500 acres, the largest planned research park in America. Indeed, we're fortunate to have two research parks in North Carolina: RTP and University Research Park, of Charlotte. Built with an investment of $50,000 twenty-two years ago, University Research Park has 2,800 acres and a market value of $22 million. These research parks build upon a commitment to excellence in research and service, a commitment for which our state has become internationally acclaimed—not just for acres of ground, but for innovation and jobs.

As we all know, there was a special time in our history, a window of time, when the idea of the research park was born. The three research universities—UNC, N.C. State, and Duke—anchoring the Triangle at Raleigh, Durham, and Chapel Hill, were on the leading edge of this development; and out of the dream, a reality was born. There have been many imitations since that time; we do not take offense to that, but we acknowledge that imitation is the sincerest form of flattery. Consequently, it pleases me very much to be here in the flagship of all research parks to recognize and applaud your accomplishments.

Historically, North Carolina's economic growth, its rise as an industrial giant among states, and its record level of employment—now in excess of 3 million workers—have been tied inextricably to innovation within our homegrown industries. But as companies continue to merge, and consolidate, and become more international in scope, we are beginning to see a gigantic change in this trend. State leaders, indeed national leaders, are now placing technology at the top of their checklist of strategies for economic growth.

The result is that technology has become an industry of its own. In the United States, in Japan, and throughout the industrialized world, spending on research and development is increasing. For the past several years, U.S. industry has averaged an increase in research and development spending of at least 5 percent, adjusted for inflation. I want to emphasize that this is spending by private industry. In fact, private sector support of research and development in the last several years has surpassed that of the federal government.

The global economic order of the 1980s is far removed from the predictable conditions of just two decades ago. In the mid-1960s, more than 75 percent of the world's technology was generated in the United States. Today, only about 50 percent of all new technology is American, and that level is predicted to fall to 35 percent by 1995. This trend is characterized by several key elements:

—First, there is a rapid and diverse transfer of technology among nations. Leaders in business and industry are concerned about the viability and durability of the technology base upon which their companies are built. Product and process changes are coming at a more rapid pace, and competition comes from the most unlikely places.

—The second characteristic of our time is the movement of people with technical expertise within companies and from one company to another. These are the change makers, and in many areas of specialization they are in short supply.

—Finally, the third characteristic is the ability to bring products from the laboratory to the marketplace more rapidly. The goal of research and development is not only to create new or improved products, but to shorten the time required to get them on the market. For example, the introduction of electrophotography, the photocopier, in the 1950s required twenty-two years, compared to the introduction in the 1980s of the videotape recorder, which took only six years.

These are some of the forces that are shaping the way leaders in business and industry think. In many respects, what we see is a new management philosophy. Much greater value is now devoted to new product development than in the past. One reason is that business leaders see new products as the key to diversification, a way of avoiding being overrun suddenly by a new technology—to keep from ending up with a company that has neither markets nor products for the future. Another reason has to do with finding specialty products, as opposed to commodities and products available from several sources.

At the same time, there has been a major change of attitude among industrial leaders in their approach to the *acquisition* of new technology—and acquisition is a good word for describing what is happening today. Only a few years ago, the management of many companies, particularly the larger ones, never considered looking outside their own organizations for new technology. There was the sense of self-sufficiency. Some companies backed away from new ideas and concepts that required risk and long-term payoff. The orientation was on the bottom line: the quarterly report.

This attitude applied to companies throughout the industrialized world. The major exception was Japan, which has done a remarkable job of moving around the world, acquiring technology, and applying it successfully to its own needs. What we are seeing, as a result of Japan's success, is that companies everywhere, no matter how large, are finding that they cannot rely solely on their own internal resources to stay competitive. The world of technology is simply moving too swiftly.

Leaders today are utilizing all kinds of imaginative approaches to reach outside for new technology and innovation. The "not invented here" syndrome, which for many years was prevalent in America, no longer exists. Some large companies are, for example, becoming limited partners in venture capital partnerships with smaller new and existing firms that are technically oriented. Prospects for capital gains no longer are as important as having a window on new research. Joint ventures and joint projects appear to offer even more possibilities; we now see joint ventures announced frequently, and many of them are international in character.

In addition to this trend of joint ventures, we are witnessing another strategy, one involving cooperation among companies on a much larger scale and involving the huge reservoir of research and scientific talent in our universities. North Carolina's Research Triangle Park, pivoting on UNC at Chapel Hill, NCSU in Raleigh, and Duke University at Durham, is an excellent example of this cooperative effort; another is University Research Park, oriented to the University of North Carolina at Charlotte.

Many of these cooperative programs can be called "precompetitive," as opposed to "noncompetitive," which means that the technical base required to stay competitive is beyond the capability of any single company to develop or sustain. But even in cases where companies do not go beyond their own organization for research and development, there are some significant events taking place to generate technology and to do it more quickly. Some of our flagship industries have set up mechanisms within their own organizations to encourage employees with an entrepreneuring spirit.

The point of all this is that technology is a very dynamic business, and I expect it to remain so in the future.

Over the years, North Carolina has earned an enviable reputation as the "State of Science and Technology," and building on this solid reputation has become one of my chief priorities as governor. I announced just last month that I am intensifying North Carolina's efforts, in cooperation with our state's scientific community, to obtain the superconducting super collider, a $6 billion federal project which, upon completion, would represent the world's largest and most powerful particle beam accelerator. The benefits of this project to our state would be staggering. More than 6,000 workers would be involved in its construction, and upon completion, it would employ approximately 3,000 people, with another 3,000 in supporting jobs.

If for no reasons other than economic, the superconducting super collider would be a tremendous boost to North Carolina, but our main consideration is more far-reaching: It would take us to the twenty-first century as the premier national leader of scientific discovery. The superconducting super collider is a huge, underground, mega-machine consisting of a circular tunnel sixty miles in circumference. The tunnel would serve as a racetrack for beams of subatomic particles, traveling at fantastic speeds, that would be smashed together to mimic conditions at the earliest moments of the universe. This experiment would enable physicists to probe fundamental mysteries about the origin of matter and energy. The knowledge gained from this research would help scientists achieve a long-sought goal: to weave the four known forces of nature—electromagnetism; gravity; the weak force, responsible for radioactive decay; and the strong force, which holds atomic nuclei together—into a single, elegant, unified theory.

Last April, I announced the appointment of a special, fifteen-member task force to explore the possibility of bringing the superconducting super collider to North Carolina. However, my staff of advisers and I began work even earlier, in September, 1985, under a $750,000 appropriation granted at my request by the General Assembly. Based on geological and logical criteria, we have identified a prospective site in Granville and Person counties as the most suitable location in North Carolina; and with the recent announcement by President Reagan that he will seek funds from Congress for construction, I am confident that this early effort will put us ahead in the competition among other states.

At a recent congressional hearing, I was asked how such expensive science could be justified when compared with other demands for funding for established technologies. My answer was that tomorrow's technology grows out of today's science. Ignore the science and someone else will control the technology.

In addition to the superconducting super collider, we have been doing some other exciting things in the past year to expand North Carolina's technology base. We are developing an engineering research center for the School of Textiles at North Carolina State University. This center will involve research in three areas: (1) product design, (2) product formation, and (3) process integration. This is extremely important. Succcess in building this center would enable North Carolina to accomplish advanced research in a traditional industry that has been under extreme pressure from foreign competition in recent years. Textiles and apparel, when combined, represent the largest share of our state's current manufacturing work force, some 36 percent, or 302,000 people. Research and technology are the keys to sustaining these jobs in North Carolina, creating new employment, and maintaining the viability of our existing companies.

Moreover, the School of Textiles at N.C. State is a logical choice for this center. It is the largest school in the free world, graduating more than half of all undergraduate and master's candidates, and approximately 75 percent of all doctoral candidates, in the textile field. Therefore, the siting of a center on the North Carolina State University campus would have national, as well as state, impact.

We have also built here the Microelectronics Center of North Carolina, the national laboratory where industry can interact with university research to produce a marriage of economic benefit. Like the proposal for the engineering research center in the School of Textiles, this would enhance our ability to compete with anyone in the semiconductor field.

I believe that in the future, more companies will become better organized and more adept in acquiring technology they can use in a profitable way. North Carolina must be prepared to supply this technology in an ever-increasing complex age. Probably the best news is that there's no shortage of ideas in North Carolina. They are in good supply. We have one of the largest university-based and private industry scientific communities in the United States, but selecting the right ideas and developing them into new products are difficult tasks—and we must be patient.

Some technology development may represent short-term investment, but much more of it is a long-term investment requiring as many as ten years for a return. With a new openness by business and industry toward technology acquisition and utilization, we in North Carolina have the opportunity to become the best organized technological megamarket of the future. We must continue to build on our strengths in the field of high-tech, utilizing to the fullest the capabilities of our scientific community, our institutions, and our state government.

In the technological race, North Carolina remains one of the most capable runners. This has made it possible for us to almost double our standard of living every forty years. Technology and innovation cannot take all the credit, but they have made a crucial difference.

I am confident North Carolina will continue to enjoy this success. That's because we have the will and the enthusiasm to embrace technological changes, and because we have the government-business climate that encourages innovation. Our people and our institutions continually respond to the need for doing things better, for making the world a better place, and it is this positive attitude that allows technical innovation to flourish. As you hold your meetings throughout the remainder of the week, remember that innovation and research are the keys to a better future for all of us. They are the keys to tomorrow.

NATIONAL WORKSHOP ON FEMALE OFFENDERS

RALEIGH, APRIL 28, 1987

I am very pleased, on behalf of the state of North Carolina, to welcome you to this Second Annual Workshop on Female Offenders. I have been told that there are delegates here today from some forty-two states and from the countries of Australia, and Canada, and China. In our audience are five commissioners of corrections and a number of federal officials who oversee our nation's prisons. Accordingly, we have brought together for this conference a unique group of specialists to address the difficult and critical issues facing all of us in the correctional field. Let us use this great wealth of experience wisely and effectively in developing solutions to our common problems.

Managing and controlling criminal law violators is a major local, state, and national responsibility. It is also a challenge, especially in view of the growing number of inmate-initiated lawsuits related to how we operate our prisons.

Despite the massive efforts of the criminal justice system, crime has remained on the increase for more than a decade. Increasing numbers of offenders are being sentenced to prison and, in many instances, for longer terms. Over the years, this has placed an unusual strain on our existing prison facilities. Our options for dealing with this situation are varied, but we must be careful about how we select from among them in order to minimize the possible risks to society and the safety of the public.

Undeniably, today's problems in our prison systems exist because of past failures to act appropriately and decisively in the ways we have dealt with them. Too often we view the threat of federal court intervention as a primary reason for correctional change. Although the courts have been instrumental in increasing public awareness of the need for change, we must not allow judges to establish an arbitrary agenda for us. It is in gatherings such as this one that we have the opportunity to take the first giant step in setting our own agenda which fits our local, state, and national priorities.

Correctional officials, law enforcement leaders, jail and detention officials, jurists, legislators, and volunteers all have their own special expertise and experience to contribute to this agenda. Nothing is more crucial to our democracy than for us to decide the future course of events in public settings where the forum is open to all who are concerned with corrections. Otherwise, we will continue to be handed down edict after edict by the federal courts. Today I want to emphasize that I believe strongly in safeguarding correction's freedom to develop appropriate and constitutional methods of managing offenders once they are placed in the custody of that system.

During my administration, we have examined carefully the past failures of our state to deal effectively with its prison problems. We have asked some hard and difficult questions about which direction our corrections system should, and must, take. As a result of this process, we developed, in March of 1985, a comprehensive corrections system plan titled "Corrections at the Crossroads: Plan for the Future."[1] This is a ten-year plan with both short- and long-range goals and objectives.

In terms of addressing the needs of offenders who absolutely must be imprisoned, the plan called for three specific steps: (1) expansion and improvement of our existing prisons; (2) construction of new prisons to provide additional facilities; and (3) an innovative and cost-effective private prison contract. We also recognized that imprisonment is not the only means of punishment and rehabilitation and sought to strengthen community-based programs for probationary offenders.

I am pleased to report today that North Carolina takes the business of corrections seriously. My administration has persuaded the General Assembly, working together, to provide some $52 million for the purpose of making major improvements in our prison system. A total of $12 million was appropriated in 1985 to bring prison facilities in one area, the South Piedmont area of the state, into compliance with a court-mandated consent decree. This step has been very significant. It has demonstrated to the court our good faith in acting expeditiously in dealing with the problems of that area. Just a few weeks ago, U.S. Fourth District Court Judge James B. McMillan wrote of North Carolina's efforts that "the defendants have made commendable progress towards accomplishing the goals of the consent decree."[2] I believe this recognition of our progress by the courts far outweighs the voices of the few critics who complain that we are not moving along responsibly in bringing our prison system into compliance with recognized standards and objectives. In spite of what we do, there will always be a few critics among our leaders.

I am also pleased to report that, this year, more than $29 million in additional funds have been appropriated by the General Assembly to add to and/or modify sixteen of our prison facilities throughout the state. At the same time, we have strengthened our probation and parole services with the addition of eighty-four probation-parole officers, fifty intensive supervision probation-parole teams, and the development of two new pilot programs. The first pilot program involves enhanced house arrest using electronic surveillance equipment. The second is a pilot model community-based punishment, treatment, and restitution program.

When we add all of these improvements together, a total of almost $53 million has been committed over the last two years, in North Carolina, to enhance our correctional programs. Coupled with an annual operating budget of some $255 million, correction resources represent a major investment in preserving the high standards of North Carolina and in enhancing its public safety.

As governor, I have emphasized that responsibility for improving our system of corrections goes hand in hand with better schools, better roads, better community facilities, and better human resources.

All of these goals are necessary to continue our strong record of economic growth and the creation of new jobs for our citizens. The best answer to crime is a growing state with increasing opportunity for all of its people. Last year, more than 350,000 arrests were made in North Carolina. Probation case loads soared to 61,000, and prison population edged above 18,000 inmates. I cannot avoid the notion that our state can address these problems best through continued economic development.

Each year since I took office, twenty-eight months ago, I have identified an area for special emphasis by my administration. Our 1985 focus was on the "Year of the Child," followed in 1986 by the "Year of the Family." These companion issues have helped us to focus on the need to address child victimization, alcohol and drug abuse among our youth, family values, and domestic violence. This year, I have proclaimed 1987 as the "Year of the Reader," and we have begun to implement plans and programs to reach the more than 800,000 adult functional illiterate people among our population. The purpose of this initiative is to teach them the basic skills they need to become self-sufficient citizens.

As part of this year's effort to reach North Carolinians who are functionally illiterate, our Department of Correction has implemented an innovative remedial program for female offenders. This program, appropriately, is called Motheread. It is a program which will allow mothers who are incarcerated to visit with and read to their children outside the prison environment during weekends. We believe this initiative will present a powerful motivational force for wanting to learn to read, for both mothers and their children.

As a means of preventing illiteracy, sixty literacy councils have been organized throughout the state to assist in stemming the tide of high school dropouts, many of whom fall through the cracks of our education system and wind up on the wrong side of the law, and ultimately, on the wrong side of the prison bars. Because some of these young people who go astray are females, let me turn my attention more specifically to the topic of this workshop, the female offender.

During calendar year 1985, the state's Uniform Annual Crime Report listed more than 70,000 females who were arrested for various crimes. In that year, women represented 19 percent of all arrests in North Carolina. The crime of fraud led the list of offenses with more than 18,000 arrests. Other crimes included larceny, approximately 8,000; driving under the influence, almost 7,000; and simple assault, in excess of 5,000. The more serious crimes were also represented:

murder, manslaughter by negligence, aggravated assault, and burglary. Usually these offenders, on average, are thirty years of age, have not finshed high school, and are either single or the resident of a single-parent household. They have a high rate of alcohol and drug abuse, are unskilled and unemployed, and have a prior record of juvenile delinquency. Experts will say there is a correlation between these crimes and the environments from which these women come.

Traditionally, North Carolina had confined its female offenders to one central facility. The North Carolina Correctional Facility for Women, located here in Raleigh, was constructed in the 1930s, and for some fifty years it remained the only prison facility for women in the state. Since that time, we have provided two additional facilities.[3]

In 1977, a legislative research commission undertook a comprehensive study of the needs of women who were confined in our state.[4] The recommendations which came out of this study were as wide-ranging as they were numerous. It will suffice to say that these recommendations have led to many improvements in the conditions which affect female offenders, but that study is now a decade old, and it is time for us to lay the groundwork for even greater achievements in the years ahead.

Today's female offender management system must go beyond correctional facilities. It must have an all-encompassing view, beginning at the local level and following through to the state's Female Offender Plan. Some of the elements which should be considered in the local plan include the following:

1. Pretrial release for carefully screened, nonviolent offenders;

2. Presentence investigations to assist the courts in making appropriate sentencing decisions. These investigations should take into account community programs that can meet the treatment, education, and training needs of the offender. Sentences should include payment of restitution and the performance of community service work; and finally,

3. The plan should provide local facilities for the secure and non-secure confinement of women and their children during periods when controlled supervision is required as an interim measure to imprisonment in state facilities.

A state plan must have two components: first, probation and parole supervision; and second, program planning for female offender confinement in a state facility. Expanded use of probation for female offenders is both desirable and cost effective. However, expansion of probation cannot take place in isolation to all other considerations. When we place unskilled or drug-dependent female offenders on probation, we simply frustrate the offender, as well as probation officials and community leaders.

One of the ways to solve these problems is to contract for the special services which probationers and parolees require, the very services which will increase their chances for rehabilitation and return to society. Substance abuse treatment, coupled with continued employment and training and child care, appear to allow the most productive use of limited state resources to manage probationers and parolees with special needs.

Intensive probation-parole supervision also will allow larger numbers of female offenders to remain in their communities. House arrest, using electronic surveillance, offers a vital application of technology in managing offenders willing to accept the strict requirements imposed by this program.

When we consider the planning and construction of new and/or improved prison facilities for women, we must give more attention to services and facilities which help build upon the strengths of each female offender. Upon initial confinement, inmate orientation should concentrate on helping the offender make the best use of the time to be served. Innovative programs must challenge the majority of inmates to modify actively those conditions which led to their criminal acts. Private industry programs offer excellent opportunities for female offenders to work at meaningful jobs while incarcerated. Job skills and work attitudes can, indeed, be transferred from private enterprise to the prison environment. This transfer also should be accompanied by an assurance of employment beyond prison.

We must also expand and improve conditions that promote good physical and mental health among inmates. These services are crucial to maintaining a healthy environment for human restoration. With these ideas in mind, North Carolina is planning to build a well-designed mental health facility and infirmary at the North Carolina Correctional Center for Women in the near future. We also plan to establish effective liaisons with local mental health and substance abuse programs to ensure that treatment continues after release from prison.

The Motheread program I mentioned earlier also will have a tremendous impact beyond promoting increased literacy. It also will aid in strengthening family ties and promoting loving mother-child relationships. Recently, the North Carolina Department of Correction developed an inmate maternity leave policy which will allow selected inmates to be placed on maternity leave to manage the affairs of child care while the mother completes an active prison sentence. At the same time, we are making a sincere effort to improve the decision-making process as it affects mothers confronted with family-life problems. This kind of planning takes on a new sense of urgency when we consider that one of our female offenders now in prison has eleven children. We want to make sure that these children do not perpetuate the cycle of crime of the mother.

Today, I have had the opportunity to discuss a number of unique ideas with you affecting female offenders, in particular, and our corrections system, in general. These ideas are not all new, of course; many of you already have some of them in place and working well. What is significant about these ideas is that where they exist there is evidence of strong correctional leadership. Your responsibility as individual correction professionals is to replicate those ideas that will improve your female offender programs and services.

I commend you on the exemplary achievements you have made in your own jurisdictions. I encourage each of you to continue on this course of progress to the end that we all succeed. Surely, here in North Carolina, we will do our best to carry out our responsibilities to protect society from lawbreakers, but do so in a way that will be worthy of the name "Corrections."

---

[1]Martin announced this plan in March, 1986. See "State of the State," February 16, 1987, footnote 25, page 42, above.

[2]James Bryan McMillan (1916-   ), born in Goldsboro; A.A., Presbyterian Junior College (later St. Andrews), 1934; M.A., University of North Carolina at Chapel Hill, 1937; J.D., Harvard University, 1940; U.S. Navy, 1942-1945. Appointed judge, U.S. District Court, Western District, June 24, 1968. Cheney, *North Carolina Government*, 753; *North Carolina Manual, 1987-1988*, 269.

[3]Women prisoners were incarcerated in four state facilities: the North Carolina Correctional Center for Women, Raleigh; Fountain Correctional Center, Rocky Mount; Black Mountain Advancement Center; and Wilmington Treatment Facility. *News and Observer*, August 16, 1987.

[4]*Report to the 1977 General Assembly of North Carolina: Females in the Department of Correction* (Raleigh: North Carolina General Assembly, Legislative Research Commission Committee on Females in the Department of Correction, 1977).

GENERAL ASSEMBLY BICENTENNIAL SESSION

Tarboro, April 29, 1987

[State lawmakers gathered in Tarboro, April 29 and 30, 1987, to observe the 200th anniversary of the historic meeting that set North Carolina on the road to ratification of the United States Constitution. The commemoration was described in the *N.C. House Journal, 1987,* 417-419, *N.C. Senate Journal, 1987,* 315-319, and the *News and Observer,* May 1, 1987.]

Dottie and I are very pleased, this evening, to be here in historic Tarboro, whose settlement predates America's War of Independence and the ratification of the constitutions that govern the affairs of our state and nation. I am especially pleased to have the opportunity to share this proud occasion with the distinguished members of our General Assembly, for it was here, two centuries ago this year, that their predecessors, deeply divided by political controversy over a national government, began the process which two years later, in 1789, would add the twelfth star to the American flag.

Only two months earlier, in Independence Hall at Philadelphia, the United States Constitution had been adopted, with three of North Carolina's six delegates signing the finished document. Therefore, when the assembly met in Tarboro it was expected, as the *State Gazette of North Carolina* editorialized in October, 1787, that "the Federal Constitution seemed to meet with an almost universal approbation."[1]

This did not prove to be the case. When the subject of ratification came before the state Senate on December 5, 1787, Thomas Person blocked all attempts to debate ratification.[2] The following day, the matter was referred to a constitutional convention to be held at Hillsborough on July 21, 1788.

Elisha Battle, one of Edgecombe County's native sons, chaired the committee of the whole which fashioned the compromise to hold the convention a year later. It was his statesmanship, perhaps most of all, that speeded the United States Constitution along to its ultimate ratification by North Carolina without further dividing the assembly.[3]

There was also another contentious matter which came before the assembly when it met in Tarboro: the selection of the site of North Carolina's permanent state capital. When the representatives of North Carolina's fifty-eight counties met here in 1787, the people of Tarboro took them into their homes, lavished them with food and drink, and generally extended to them the superb hospitality of the town. Today that's called lobbying.

Obviously, this didn't work. The assembly postponed until the

Hillsborough convention the decision to locate the capital within ten miles of Isaac Hunter's plantation in Wake County. This, too, was not a popular decision with many legislators, for 119 of them voted against the Wake County location—remembering, no doubt, Tarboro's generous hospitality during the previous year's session.

This evening, the people of Tarboro and Edgecombe have joined together to demonstrate to the 1987 General Assembly that the spirit of hospitality lives on 200 years later in this cradle of history; that the past error of selecting Raleigh as the state capital is forgiven; and that it is here, once again, where the dream of one united state is born anew.

There is much history to relive this evening. The General Assembly of 1787 met in Tarboro from November 19 until December 22, barely more than a month. In that short period, it ratified fifty-six laws, argued the merits of a federal government, established the framework of a constitutional convention, deferred selection of the site of a permanent state capital, and elected Samuel Johnston as the new governor.[4]

This was also the year, for the first time in history under American constitutional government, that a law previously passed by the General Assembly was ruled unconstitutional by the courts. That law, the Confiscation Acts of 1777 and 1779, gave the state the power to confiscate and sell the property of former tories. Moreover, the legislature of 1785 passed a law prohibiting the courts from "entertaining suits for the recovery of property" taken under the acts.[5]

The courts refused to abide by the 1785 law, citing it unconstitutional and upheld a plaintiff's right to a jury trial under the Bill of Rights. Subsequently, a jury ruled against the state in a case brought by a Mrs. Bayard to eject a buyer of the property left to her in the estate of her tory father. The courts also dismissed all cases pending at that time under the Confiscation Acts. Chief Justice John Marshall, of the United States Supreme Court, applied the principle of the North Carolina case to support one of the high court's rulings in 1801, thus making it one of the fundamental principles of American law.[6]

We are reminded, again today, that we are a land of laws, and not men; that "We, the People" rule in the affairs of government and not the other way around. This was the spirit of North Carolina in 1787. It remains today the spirit of a state which is now more than 6.3 million people strong. This is the spirit we must bequeath to our children, the new generations who will continue to proclaim themselves, "We, the People of One United North Carolina."

¹North Carolina's five delegates to the Constitutional Convention of 1787 in Philadelphia were William Blount, William R. Davie, Alexander Martin, Richard Dobbs Spaight, and Hugh Williamson. Davie and Martin were not in attendance at the signing on September 17, 1787. Lefler and Newsome, *North Carolina*, 279-280. The quotation attributed to the New Bern *State Gazette of North Carolina* could not be verified.

²Thomas Person (1733-1800), resident of Granville County; was buried in Warren County. Surveyor; landowner; Regulator; militia general; represented Granville County in colonial assembly, 1764, 1768, 1769, 1771, 1773, 1774, 1775, provincial conventions, 1774, 1775, and provincial congresses, 1775, 1776; member, provincial council, 1775-1776, and council of safety, 1776; elected to Council of State, 1776; member, state House of Commons, 1777-1785, 1788-1790, 1793-1795, 1797, and Senate, 1787, 1791-1792; elected to Continental Congress, 1784; Antifederalist delegate to state ratification conventions of 1788, 1789. Ashe, *Biographical History*, VII, 380-398; Stephen E. Massengill, *North Carolina Votes on the Constitution: A Roster of Delegates to the State Ratification Conventions of 1788 and 1789* ([Raleigh]: Division of Archives and History, Department of Cultural Resources, 1988), 47, hereinafter cited as Massengill, *North Carolina Votes on the Constitution*.

³Elisha Battle (1723-1799), born in Nansemond County, Virginia; resident of Edgecombe County. Planter; landowner; Edgecombe justice of the peace, ca. 1756-1795; county court judge; cofounder of Tarboro, 1760; chairman, Edgecombe committee of safety, 1774-1775; represented Edgecombe in colonial assembly, 1773, provincial congresses, 1776, and state Senate, 1777-1781, 1783, 1785-1787; Antifederalist delegate to state ratification convention, 1788. Massengill, *North Carolina Votes on the Constitution*, 4; Powell, *DNCB*, I, 109-110.

⁴Samuel Johnston (1733-1816), born in Dundee, Scotland; was buried at Hayes Plantation, Edenton; was educated at Yale. Attorney; planter; member, provincial assembly, 1759-1775; represented Chowan County in provincial conventions, 1774, 1775, provincial congresses, 1775-1776, and state Senate, 1779, 1783-1784; member, Continental Congress, 1780-1781; governor of North Carolina, 1787-1789; elected state's first Masonic grand master, 1787; Federalist delegate to, and president of, state ratification conventions, 1788, 1789; cofounder, 1789, first trustee, University of North Carolina; state's first U.S. senator, elected 1789; superior court judge, 1800-1803. Massengill, *North Carolina Votes on the Constitution*, 32; Powell, *DNCB*, III, 306-308.

⁵The quotation appears in Lefler and Newsome, *North Carolina*, 258. Texts of the Confiscation Acts, and the law of 1785 that the governor also mentioned, were reprinted in Clark, *State Records*, XXIV: see "An Act, for confiscating the Property of all such Persons as are inimical to the United States, and of such persons as shall not, within a certain Time therein mentioned appear and submit to the State whether they shall be received as Citizens thereof, and of such Persons as shall so appear and shall not be admitted as Citizens, and for other Purposes therein mentioned," Laws of North Carolina, 1777, Chapter XVII, 123-124; "An Act to carry into effect an Act passed at New Bern in November, in the year one thousand seven hundred and seventy-seven, intituled, An Act for confiscating the property of all such persons as are inimical to this or the United States, and of such persons as shall not within a certain time therein mentioned appear and submit to the State whether they shall be received as citizens thereof, and of such persons who shall so appear and shall not be admitted as citizens, and for other purposes therein mentioned," Laws of North Carolina, 1779, Chapter II, 263-268; and "An Act to Secure and Quiet in Their Possessions all Such Persons, Their Heirs and Assigns who Have Purchased, or May Hereafter Purchase Lands Tenements, Goods and Chattels, Which Have Been Sold, or May Hereafter Be Sold By Commissioners of Forfeited Estates, Legally Appointed for That Purpose," Laws of North Carolina, 1785, Chapter VII, 730-731.

⁶The significance of *Bayard* v. *Singleton* (1786-1787), the case to which Martin referred, was felt far beyond North Carolina. When the superior court hearing Bayard declared the Confiscation Acts unconstitutional, it established the concept of judicial review. Chief Justice Marshall drew on that precedent in his *Marbury* v. *Madison* decision of 1803. Lefler and Newsome, *North Carolina*, 258; George Brown Tindall, *America: A Narrative History* (New York: W. W. Norton & Co., 2 volumes, 1984), I, 325-326.

NORTH CAROLINA WORLD TRADE ASSOCIATION

RESEARCH TRIANGLE PARK, APRIL 30, 1987

I am very pleased that you have invited me back again, this year, to participate in the Twenty-second Annual Meeting of the North Carolina World Trade Association. Indeed, we in North Carolina, by tradition and enterprise, have always been a vital part of the world community, and I think it's time for optimism.[1]

It was only three days ago, at this same hour, that I was aboard a return flight from London, where my wife, Dottie, and a delegation of leaders from our state had participated in ceremonies at Portsmouth, England, commemorating the departure of the first trade mission: Sir Walter Raleigh's second group of colonists to America in 1587.[2] That group mysteriously disappeared and has become known as the Lost Colony, but the dream of opening a new continent from the Outer Banks of North Carolina lived on and gave birth to the industrial genius of a new nation, the United States of America. As a result of that pioneering adventure, North Carolina became a state of farmers and craftsmen, merchants and traders. Import and export became our link to existence. Fleets of sailing vessels plied the Atlantic, shipping raw materials to England and returning with finished goods.

Flying at jet speed high above the Atlantic last Monday, as my "jets unlagged," there was a brief period to contemplate how time has condensed the globe from its once awesome scale to a tiny speck in the universe.

Independence in 1776 brought us new freedom, and the industrial revolution which followed the turn of the century gave freedom the power to turn genius into greatness and wealth. America literally became an industrial giant among nations. But all of that has changed; we are now a giant among many giants.

The truth of that statement lies at the very heart of your conference theme, "International Competitiveness: the Challenge for America." Somehow it implies that we have lost the fire that once ignited the engine of a mighty economy. Today, I want to suggest that the fire burns more intense than ever before, and it would be difficult to find a more impressive example than right here in North Carolina.

One of the best examples I can cite is North Carolina's record of attracting foreign investments. They provide jobs here, and compete on the same end of the playing field. Our latest figures for 1986 show that reverse investment by foreign companies in North Carolina is well in excess of $200 million, and when fully tabulated may well exceed the previous record of $258 million set in 1983. The same factors which made 1986 such a good year still exist, and if we capitalize on them—and I assure you that we will—1987 will be our best year ever. Currently we have plans to locate a new office in the Pacific Rim, followed by one foreign trade mission to the Far East, in October, 1987, and two missions to Europe.[3] The opening of the Pacific Rim office and our missions to other nations provide an excellent opportunity to promote North Carolina quality products and, at the same time, tell the exciting story of a business climate in which new enterprises can flourish.

Attracting reverse investment is only one of our aims to expand our growing list of exports. North Carolina already is the leading exporter of manufactured goods in the Southeast, and we now rank tenth in the nation. Export production represents 9 percent of our gross state product and accounts for approximately 90,000 North Carolina jobs. Our two seaports provide two-way trade: exports and imports.

We can add to this glowing report a promising outlook for the future. On the international level, the value of the dollar is shrinking against major foreign currencies, moderating one of the major reasons for our huge trade deficit in recent years. Data Resources, Incorporated, a nationally respected econometrics consultant, is predicting that exports will play an important role in future U.S. economic growth. In fact, their analysis predicts a 43 percent increase in American exports over the next three years, rising from $373 billion, in 1986, to more than $534 billion in 1989. That won't happen if we don't make it happen.

North Carolina is well positioned to capture a significant share of this growth. The wide diversity of our state's products and services, particularly in selected high-technology industries, gives us the competitive edge against other competing states. But to capitalize on this opportunity, we need an increasingly strong effort on the part of North Carolina companies to engage in export trade, advancing the work that members of this association have been doing for many years.

Our *Blueprint for Economic Development* recognizes this need and commits the resources to get this job done through expanded state services which support international trade and development. Not long ago, the North Carolina Department of Commerce, under the direction of Secretary Claude Pope, prepared an aggressive export development program for 1987 and the years beyond. Time does not permit me to review the entire plan with you today, but I want to touch on a few points.

First, we are excited about our computerized trade leads program. This system involves computer matching of trade leads gathered by our staff to trade interests in North Carolina who have expressed an interest in exporting. Other components of our export trade program include strengthening the counseling services provided to exporters by our Department of Commerce; an export mentor program; and a more aggressive program of seminars and other educational efforts. We'll also be expanding our excellent relationship with the U.S. Department of Commerce, which has been extremely helpful and cooperative in all of our undertakings.

Of course, even with all of these programs and activities, the ability of state government to reach every potential exporter within our state is limited. This is why we are extremely grateful for the strong partnership we have with your association and its members. Through our joint efforts, we have an effective coalition working for North Carolina.

In today's global economy, no nation, no state, no company can afford to neglect its international trade potential. It is critical for all of us to carry this message to North Carolina's growing business community, and in particular our small business community. I commend and applaud the companies represented here today, and I express my sincere gratitude to the North Carolina World Trade Association for its many contributions to building a stronger and more viable state economy. You have opened the doors of the world to North Carolina commerce and trade. By sharing good ideas and attitudes, we can all take advantage of this opportunity to build upon a successful beginning in a new world of competition.

---

[1]The governor inserted into his prepared text, at this point: "Pessimist forecasts flood; optimist builds ark."

[2]Governor and Mrs. Martin departed for England on April 24 and returned to North Carolina on April 27, 1987. Governor's Schedule for Weeks of April 20-May 3, 1987, Governors Papers, James G. Martin.

[3]Martin conducted two overseas trade missions in 1987. He visited Japan, South Korea, and the Peoples Republic of China, October 1-17, as well as France, England, the Netherlands, and West Germany, November 14-21. Commerce Secretary Pope headed a state trade delegation to France, Italy, and West Germany in May, 1987. Press release, "Governor to Lead Economic Development Mission to Europe," Raleigh, November 9, 1987; see also Governor's Schedule for Weeks of September 28-October 11, October 3-October 18, November 9-November 22, November 16-November 29, 1987, Governors Papers, James G. Martin.

PUBLIC HEARING ON H.B. 589, SENATE JUDICIARY IV
COMMITTEE, N.C. GENERAL ASSEMBLY

Raleigh, May 5, 1987

Mr. Chairman,[1] members of the committee, I am appearing before you pursuant to Article III, Section 5(2), of the state's constitution, which provides that the "Governor shall from time to time give the General Assembly information of the affairs of the state and recommend to their consideration such measures as he shall deem expedient."

I am pleased that you are holding this public hearing to consider views on H.B. 589, which proposes to alter the election of superior court judges in North Carolina.[2] As I said in my "State of the State" address, it is time to reform the way we choose our judges in North Carolina. No aspect of that system needs immediate reform more than the way in which we elect superior court judges.

At present, our superior court judges are nominated in primaries in their judicial districts but elected in statewide partisan elections. This is not a good system. While the voters in the nominating primaries may know the candidates for whom they are voting, the same is not true in the general election. There the voters choose candidates about whom they know little or nothing, and their votes are meaningless.

The system of electing superior court judges in statewide elections began with Reconstruction. Its effect in this century has been to keep blacks and Republicans from being elected as superior court judges. Because of its discriminatory effect on racial minorities, the system is under attack in the federal courts—as well it should be. More importantly, it denies to all people of North Carolina the right to cast meaningful votes in the selection of their superior court judges.

I applaud the fact that your committee and this legislature are finally addressing some of the century-old inequities in the present system, but H.B. 589 has several faults:

1. The bill retains partisan, statewide election of superior court judges rather than reforming the system with nonpartisan, district elections.

2. I am advised that, if the bill is enacted, it will not resolve the federal lawsuit challenging the discriminatory manner in which our superior court judges are elected.

3. The bill abolishes the office of special superior court judge, an office that is essential to the efficient functioning of the administration of justice in the state.

The people of North Carolina have made it clear that they want three things in the selection of their superior court judges: (1) They want them to be elected, (2) they want the elections to be meaningful, and (3) they want the elections to be nonpartisan. Trial judges are the judges before whom the people appear and whom the people know. They are the judges that have the power to take or preserve their property, their liberty, and in extreme instances, their lives. It is important to the people that their trial judges remain directly accountable to them. Any change in the current system must ensure this direct accountability.

It is also clear that the people of this state want the election of their judges to be meaningful. They want to know who they are voting for, but they do not know in statewide judicial elections. They cannot know. The voter only knows the candidates from his or her own district, if that. He does not know the other candidates on the ballot from other parts of the state. The effect is that the votes of the least knowledgeable electors can offset the votes of the most knowledgeable electors. For example, voters in Senator Kaplan's district, Forsyth County, have as much or more to say about who will be the resident superior court judge in Senator Soles's judicial district than the people who live in Senator Soles's district.[3]

Imagine what would happen if other local law enforcement officers were elected the same way. Would anyone favor electing sheriffs in statewide elections? Would the people of Bladen, Brunswick, and Columbus counties stand for having their sheriffs elected by the voters from the other ninety-seven counties? The answer to both is, clearly, no. Is a superior court judge any less important to the people than a sheriff? Again, the answer is no.

The people also want partisan politics out of the judicial system. They want judges to be impartial, not partisan. How else can judges do justice? Partisanship calls into question the integrity of the whole judicial system. It should be removed.

You have in your committee S.B. 214, which was introduced by Senator Cobb over two months ago. Senator Cobb's bill establishes a new system which corrects the flaws of the archaic statewide superior court judge election system that has been with us since 1868. It provides for nonpartisan elections of superior court judges by district, without staggered terms or numbered seats. I urge you to bring this bill forward and enact it into law. It will cure the present evils of our judicial election system. It will end the pending federal litigation and preempt the lawsuits that are sure to continue until the people of this state are given a fair and meaningful vote in the choosing of their superior court judges. Senator Cobb's bill also affords minorities equal opportunity to use their voting power in whatever manner they feel would be most successful in electing the judges of their choice, be they black or white.

Finally, I urge you to keep our special superior court judges, as presently authorized, and not abolish them as is provided in H.B. 589. The importance of special superior court judges to the efficient operation of the superior court system cannot be overstated. They provide flexibility in the administration of our trial courts. Among other things, special superior court judges:

1. Fill in when resident superior court judges can't hold court due to illness;

2. Serve as supplementary judges when unusually heavy case loads clog dockets;

3. Try complex or lengthy cases that would otherwise take up all of a court's time.

Special superior court judges were created to solve the problem of inflexibility in our judicial system and have done so for seventy years. They stand ready and capable of going anywhere in the state where the chief justice decides they are most needed. I believe that most resident superior court judges would agree with me when I say that such flexibility is vital to our court system.

In my "State of the State" address, I said that the time is ripe to act on judicial reform and that all but the most partisan among us would see the virtue of that reform. We are but thirteen years from the year 2000. It's time to do something about the status quo of the past 120 years. Let's fix what is fundamentally wrong with our system of electing superior court judges instead of tinkering at the edges of the system in response to a federal lawsuit. Let's put partisanship aside and work to bring into being a system for administering justice in North Carolina that is suitable for these times.

---

[1]Robert Charles Soles, Jr. (1934-   ), native of Tabor City; B.S., Wake Forest University, 1956; J.D., University of North Carolina at Chapel Hill, 1959; U.S. Army, 1957-1967. Attorney; member, state House, 1969-1976; elected to state Senate, 1976, and returned in subsequent elections; chairman, Senate Judiciary IV Committee; Democrat. *North Carolina Manual, 1987-1988*, 325.

[2]"An Act to Provide for Continued Compliance with the Voting Rights Act and to Improve the Administration of Justice by Providing for the Elimination of Staggered Terms for Superior Court Judges, Creating More Superior Court Judicial Districts, Eliminating the Office of Special Superior Court Judge, and Making Conforming Changes" was ratified June 29, 1987. *N.C. Session Laws, 1987*, I, c. 509.

[3]Ian Theodore Kaplan (1946-   ), born in Greensboro; resident of Forsyth County; was educated at Guilford College; U.S. Navy, 1969-1971, and Reserve, 1968-1969. Presi-

dent, Kaplan Press; member, state House, 1977-1982; elected to state Senate, 1982, reelected 1986; chairman, Senate Committee on Election Laws; Democrat. *North Carolina Manual, 1987-1988,* 308.

GOVERNOR'S CONFERENCE ON TRAVEL AND TOURISM

HIGH POINT, MAY 11, 1987

[Governor Martin delivered a condensed version of this address at a press conference, May 11, 1987, in High Point.]

This is certainly a distinguished group of travel professionals, elected officials, and celebrities. Let me start by thanking all of you gathered here, tonight, to celebrate one of our most dynamic and exciting industries. It is largely the result of your dedication and hard work that tourism has become one of the leading sources of jobs and revenue in North Carolina today. I look forward to working with you to ensure the continued development and growth of the tourism industry to which North Carolinians owe so much.

It is a particular pleasure to discuss with you our tourism successes in 1986. You, the people who make this industry what it is, deserve the credit for an outstanding year. Even if you have heard the official figures, they're worth repeating. I think you'll enjoy another chorus.

Let's start with the best news. As I announced two weeks ago, travel expenditures totaled nearly $5.1 billion last year. Want to hear that again? More than $5 billion. That is a lovely, nice, round number for an industry that is so clean and trouble free. Of those total expenditures, North Carolina residents spent $1.4 billion traveling within our borders, but the bulk of those dollars came from people you attracted to our state from other states and around the world. Those out-of-state travelers spent $3.7 billion in North Carolina.

The travel industry in this state paid more than $1.8 billion in wages and salaries and accounted for more than 215,000 jobs, nearly 8 percent of our private-sector work force. In addition, the travel industry paid nearly $175 million in taxes. All these figures represent an increase of about 10 percent over 1985.

There's more good news. More than 50 million visitors came to North Carolina, during 1986, to visit our state and spend their money. The goods and services they consume provide an ever-expanding source of jobs and income as we move toward the twenty-first century.

North Carolina tourism has become our fastest-growing industry.

Again, we can look to 1986 for examples. Nearly 87 million nights were spent in North Carolina hotels and motels. Nearly 689 million meals were served in North Carolina restaurants. Attractions across the state reported record attendance: Biltmore House and Gardens, in Asheville, entertained 618,000 visitors; the USS *North Carolina* thrilled more than a quarter-million sightseers; and Carowinds enjoyed its best year since 1973, opening its doors to 1.2 million fun seekers. I could go on and on with individual examples, but when attractions as diverse as those do so well in one year, you can sense the success story that builds with each passing tourist season.

This administration is committed to continuing the success story of North Carolina's travel industry. The Department of Commerce's Travel and Tourism Division coordinates several aggressive programs to boost our efforts through nationwide publicity and promotional efforts with state, regional, and local tourism organizations. One special element of our efforts is the division's award-winning advertising program that last year generated nearly 420,000 requests for travel information.

In support of these important efforts, I have requested that the General Assembly appropriate funds that would enable us to substantially upgrade our ability to respond to the ever-increasing number of requests for travel information through our "800" telephone system. This system is our front line in presenting a positive, wholesome, inviting image of our state. It is of critical importance in influencing travelers to visit North Carolina.

I have also asked for additional funding for travel trade missions to midwestern states. As you know, these trade missions have proved an extremely effective and efficient means of selling our state through travel agents and media in our most productive target markets. In North Carolina, natural blessings are so bountiful that our promotions spark very positive responses when we get them out there for people to see, and read, and think about. We want people planning their vacations in North Carolina. In just a minute, I will describe why the summer of 1987 is going to be one of the best seasons yet.

Another important area addressed in my budget is the upgrading of the computer system in the Division of Travel and Tourism. Improvement in the capacity and response time of this vital communications link will greatly enhance the division's ability to respond to travel information requests, as well as to the growing needs of the tourism industry.

If these funding needs can be met, and I think the General Assembly will agree with the need for these requests, we believe that these crucial steps will position us to move forward more aggressively, with even better results. In the long run, these steps move us toward our greater goal: strengthening the state's economy and providing more and better jobs for North Carolinians.

Already we are recognized across the country as one of the leaders in economic development. Just last week, the Southern Industrial Development Council reported that North Carolina led the Southeast in job creation from announced manufacturing investments in 1986. I'm proud of that record. We worked hard to get there and to keep the momentum of industrial development moving forward.

Your industry plays a critical role in our overall success, and certainly the two successful records for manufacturing investment and tourism in 1986 are no coincidence. The theme for your program here in High Point, "Futurescope: North Carolina Travel 2000," reflects your commitment to the next century. I believe we can keep our entire economy moving toward, and preparing for, that new century.

Just as 1986 set new records for the tourism industry, I believe this year will prove equally successful.[1] Our goal is to make each year bigger and better for the tourism industry. To accomplish that, we have to set higher goals and plan for bigger events; 1987 gives us perfect opportunities, stretching from the Outer Banks, to the piedmont, to the Blue Ridge Mountains.

America's premier outdoor drama, *The Lost Colony*, celebrates its fiftieth anniversary with a very special birthday party on July 4. Set in Manteo on our beautiful Outer Banks, *The Lost Colony* is the oldest outdoor drama in the nation and has served as a model for many of America's finest outdoor theater programs.

We will reach another milestone in September, this year, when we dedicate the final, seven-and-one-half-mile section of the 470-mile Blue Ridge Parkway. The highlight of that final section, of course, will be the magnificent Linn Cove Viaduct, which already has become a major attraction even before it is opened to traffic. Many North Carolinians probably do not realize that the Blue Ridge Mountains are [the] nation's most popular national park area. When we open the final section on September 11, the Blue Ridge Parkway finally fulfills its original promise of an uninterrupted drive along the continent's oldest mountain range.

In the piedmont section of the state, this year we will play host to the U.S. Olympic Sports Festival to be held in mid-July in Raleigh, Durham, Cary, Chapel Hill, and Greensboro; you'll hear more tomorrow from Hill Carrow.[2] More than 6,000 of America's top amateur athletes, coaches, and media representatives will descend on the Triangle and Triad areas of our state. The financial impact will top $9 million, but the real value is that opportunity to showcase North Carolina in yet another way. The Sports Festival offers a terrific travel opportunity for all North Carolinians, and it will bring literally tens of thousands of out-of-state visitors to our state; and while they're here, of course, we want to get them to the mountains or the coast to take advantage of all of our natural resources.

We will seize the moment while the festival unfolds, in North Carolina, with two very creative initiatives. First, the Division of Travel and Tourism will operate portable welcome centers at four key sites for the festival: the Raleigh Civic Center; the Dean Smith Center, in Chapel Hill; the Greensboro Coliseum; and at Duke University, at Durham. These centers will distribute brochures, maps, and other materials, as well as assist festival visitors in making room reservations and travel plans across the state.

We'll also promote the centers as official gathering points for the exchange of lapel pins. As you know, the lapel pin exchange has become an important element of past Olympic events. To kick off this pin exchange, each athlete will receive, upon his or her arrival in North Carolina, one of our state's "Variety Vacationland" lapel pins and a letter from me inviting them to participate in the exchange process. I have asked travel leaders and chambers of commerce across the state to develop lapel pins to represent their attractions and areas. These pins will also be distributed at our welcome centers, free of charge, to the 6,000 festival participants so that we, as a state, can share the spirit of the games and the gesture of goodwill that the lapel pins represent.

Because we want you to share in our spirit of success, you'll find a special pin in front of you at your tables tonight. Accept it as a small token of North Carolina's appreciation for what you have been doing. It is one small way of saying thanks, to you, for all you have done to keep our travel and tourism on the move each year. Thanks to your everyday efforts, the future of tourism looks extremely bright. If we could reach the $5.1 billion revenue level in 1986, let's shoot for cresting the $6 billion mark this year.

I want to take this opportunity to thank Jan Howard, who was recently appointed to chair the Governor's Advisory Committee on Travel and Tourism, and Frank Freeman,[3] president of the North Carolina Travel Council. Both of you play major roles in keeping this industry as vibrant and healthy as it is today. I'm sure your leadership will carry us to that $6 billion mark—and well beyond.

We've come now to a special part of this program in which I am honored to present the first annual Bill Sharpe Award, established by the Travel Council of North Carolina. The late Bill Sharpe, one of the first travel directors for the state and the editor of *State* magazine, became legendary for promoting and publicizing North Carolina and our many attractions.[4] I have asked Hugh Morton,[5] the elder, who worked closely with Bill Sharpe, to come up here and tell you about him. Hugh?

[Hugh Morton speaks.]

Thank you, Hugh. This award will be presented annually to honor an individual in public employment, or someone residing outside the state, who has rendered outstanding service to the state's travel industry. It is appropriate, I think, that this first award should go to a man who is, himself, something of a modern-day tourism legend.

All of you know Charles Heatherly, the former director of travel and tourism.[6] If you don't know him, you haven't been in the travel business, and you're not even here tonight! Since he started in that position in 1981, he has been deeply involved in the remarkable growth of your industry. Under his watchful tenure, travel expenditures have doubled to $5 billion. The development of welcome centers is now complete across the state. He has been a major participant in our aggressive recruitment of more and bigger conventions. In sum, I think it is best to say that he is a deserving recipient of this very first Bill Sharpe Award, which will now be unveiled: an appropriate collector's print of "Cardinal and Dogwood," by well-known wildlife artist Ray Harm.

---

[1]Travel expenditures in North Carolina amounted to $5.7 billion in 1987, the largest total in state history, Martin announced in Greenville on April 11, 1988.

[2]The U.S. Olympic Sports Festival, comprised of thirty-four sporting events planned to prepare American athletes for the 1988 summer games in Seoul, South Korea, was held in North Carolina from July 13 through 26, 1987. Organized by North Carolina Amateur Sports, the festival drew 460,884 spectators and produced a record-breaking $1.55 million profit. *News and Observer*, July 18, 27, December 3, 1987.

H. Hill Carrow, Jr. (1955-   ), native of Kinston; A.B., University of North Carolina at Chapel Hill, 1977; J.D., Columbia University, 1980. Attorney in private practice, 1980-1982, and for Carolina Power and Light Co., 1982-1985; executive director, N.C. Amateur Sports, since 1985, and chief organizer, 1987 U.S Olympic Festival. *News and Observer*, August 2, 1987.

[3]Frank Marshall Freeman, Jr. (1939-   ), born in Columbus, Ohio; resident of Greensboro; B.B.A., University of Mississippi, 1961; U.S. Navy, 1961-1964. Area manager, Dobbs House, Inc., 1964-1971; president, Freeway Foods, Inc., since 1971. Frank Marshall Freeman, Jr., to Jan-Michael Poff, September 7, 1988.

[4]William Pleasant Sharpe (1903-1970), born in Spartanburg, South Carolina; died in Raleigh; was graduated from Winston-Salem High School, 1921. Journalist; various positions with *Winston-Salem Journal*, Selma *Johnstonian*, *New Orleans Times-Picayune*, and *Twin-City Sentinel*, Winston-Salem; organizer, initial director, North Carolina Advertis-

ing Division, appointed 1937; initial director, state Office of War Information, appointed 1942; war-time public relations director, Fairchild Aircraft, Burlington, 1943-1944; returned to state Advertising Division, 1944, and served until 1949; publicity manager, Carolina Power and Light Co., 1949-1951; owner, editor, *The State*, 1951-1970; author. *News and Observer*, January 7, 1970; William S. Powell, *North Carolina Lives: The Tar Heel Who's Who* (Hopkinsville, Kentucky: Historical Record Association, 1962), 1093-1094.

[5]Hugh MacRae Morton (1921-   ), born in Wilmington; was educated at University of North Carolina at Chapel Hill; honorary degrees; U.S. Army, 1942-1945. President, Grandfather Mountain, Inc.; founder, Azalea Festival, Wilmington; member, state Board of Conservation and Development, 1951-1961; sound and light show creator for USS *North Carolina* historic site, and chairman, 1961-1965, USS *North Carolina* Battleship Commission; chairman, Governor's Advisory Committee on Travel and Tourism during Hunt administration; appointed by Governor Martin to Blue Ridge Advisory Committee and Western Carolina Environmental Council. "Businessman in the News: Hugh Morton of Grandfather Mountain," *North Carolina* (May, 1990), 8, 10-12; Mitchell, *Addresses of Hunt,* I, 735n; Hugh MacRae Morton to Jan-Michael Poff, May 28, 1990.

[6]Charles Heatherly (1942-   ), born in Haywood County; resident of Cary; A.B., University of North Carolina at Chapel Hill, 1964; N.C. National Guard, since 1965; U.S. Army Reserve. Journalist, 1964-1969; various positions with state Department of Commerce, including publications editor, Division of Travel and Tourism, 1969-1975, and division director, 1981-1986; Communications Section chief, Department of Natural and Economic Resources, 1975-1977; consultant, 1986-1988; vice-president, Pennington Heatherly Brewer, since 1988. Charles Heatherly to Jan-Michael Poff, May 25, 1990.

COMES THE MILLENNIUM

WINSTON-SALEM, MAY 18, 1987

[This address was presented at Wake Forest University's spring commencement exercises.]

Some thirty-odd years after his graduation, Adlai Stevenson, a great but luckless politician, returned to his alma mater, Princeton, to deliver the commencement address. He arrived the evening before the scheduled exercises. Here are his reflections:

"I came here last night in darkness, with an old friend, a classmate. We drove a little through the campus, after dusk. Sentimental? Yes. Nostalgic? Perhaps. Yet beautiful, too. Your days are short here," he said. "This is the last of your springs. And now, in the serenity and quiet of this place, touch the depths of truth—and feel the hem of heaven."[1]

It is a story that suggests that nothing is so hard for us in America to manage, it seems, as recollection and perspective—those exercises that are the first to go when a nation that once knew its limitations has forgotten them in the intoxication of imperium. You ought to think of this when you are setting your priorities. The meaning matters very much. What are you going to do with all these things? What is to be the end for which these four years will be the means? Is economic, social, and technological progress all that counts—if the way to get there is to narrow choice, to forego generosity, to demean idealism, to put a price on everything? That may be one way of constructing priorities, but it will not guarantee a future; nor will science, for all its wonders, do that, if the conscience and the search for meaning are left out.

This great university, which honors you today for your achievement, stands for survival, for beliefs and traditions that have passed through the fire many times over and have come through intact. It is this university, among the great institutions of learning in America, that keeps the lamps of Western civilization from going out. And without lamps, however low they flicker, we can't distinguish light from darkness; nor achievement from failure; nor what has been preserved, or should be, from what has not; nor good from evil.

It is especially important on this day to remember the words of Adlai Stevenson: "This is the last of your springs." Now comes the millennium! You are the pioneers, the navigators, setting your compasses by the known fixed star of enduring values while reaching out to the unknown. What will be your mission in the new era beyond the year 2000? What are your priorities? I would suggest to you, today, that the most important mission we, your predecessors, leave to you, is to study, preserve, and yes, defend Western civilization.

Why? First, we must study the West because it is ours. It is the culture in which we live and in which most of us will continue to live. It is the water, and we are the fish.

We live in a society governed by laws that are products of Western civilization and that bear witness to its moral development. The institutions that inform our conduct as a people—our schools and universities, our churches and synagogues, our communities and governments, and even our notions of friendship and family—acquired their shape through the course of Western history. The ideas and beliefs that bind us as a people, our belief in human rights, the dignity of man, the inviolability of conscience, have also gained life at particular times in Western history. To understand our society, our institutions, our ways, and our contemporary controversies, we need to understand our political, social, and intellectual history. We need to know the story of Western civilization, for that is where our institutions and society were made.

Western civilization is strong, in part, because it has learned to be open, to study and learn from others. But even those who are interested in studying other cultures are best advised to begin with a thorough knowledge of their own. Knowledge of one's own civilization provides a platform from which to view others. In the words of Arthur E. Murphy, "We do not understand the ideals of other cultures better by misunderstanding our own, or adequately enrich an intercultural synthesis by offering to it anything less than the best that we have."[2]

This, then, is the first reason why we should study the West: It is ours. It is where we live—culturally, economically, socially, morally, and legally. It tells us where we have been and suggests possibilities for where we might want to go in the next millennium. The second reason we must study, nurture, and defend Western civilization is because it is good.

It is not all good. There are certainly great blots on our record. In the story of the West, there are injustices, massive ones, and catalogs of sins and errors. Nevertheless, the West has produced the world's most just and effective system of government, the system of representative democracy.

In the story of inhumanity and misery that is history, in the totality of its acts, the Western achievement stands the highest on the face of the globe. The story of the West is the most hopeful story, for, as Allan Bloom has written in his new book, "Our story is the majestic and triumphant march of two principles: freedom and equality."[3]

These are not principles shared the world over. Whole nations and whole political systems exist under which they are systematically denied. Indeed, though these principles represent the best of the West, the culmination of the West, there are parts of the West in which they are not respected.

George Orwell once said that, at times, the first duty of responsible people is the restatement of the obvious, to say that which goes without saying. So allow me to emphasize the obvious: Not all systems of government are equal. Some forms of government are better than others; some are more just, less oppressive, more open, less resistant to reform. And first among these forms of government is the pluralistic, competitive democracy of the West. The founders knew this. Lincoln knew it. Martin Luther King, Jr., knew it. Many of our enemies know it. Democracy is at once the world's greatest form of government and among the greatest products of Western thought and effort—painstaking, at times bloody, effort.

From the western face of the Berlin wall, westward around to the westernmost shores of Japan, democracy has been virtually synonymous with and tantamount to improvement in the standard of living and the quality of human life. From Poland, to El Salvador, to the Philippines, what Lord Bryce observed 100 years ago is even clearer today: "The institutions of the United States . . . are believed to disclose and display the type of institutions towards which, as by a law of fate, the rest of civilized mankind are forced to move, some with swifter, others with slower, but all with unresting feet."[4] And the brightest beacon to that way of life has been the United States and its Constitution, the most enduring and the most imitated political document in the world.

There is a second way in which Western civilization is good. It offers an unsurpassed record of serious discussion, by serious men and women, of questions like: What can I know? What is good? For every person who seeks serious answers to these questions, indeed to the very question, How should I live? there is no better place to look for guidance than the great books, and deeds, of the Western tradition. Otherwise, we answer these questions in ignorance of many of the most thoughtful presentations of the most fundamental alternatives. There is no need to impoverish ourselves in this way.

The Western tradition is an unparalleled resource from which we can all learn and profit in the way we lead our lives. Therefore, the second way in which Western civilization is good is that it provides the most serious guidance to us in our fundamental choices. Yet, while we turn to great books to ask fundamental questions, the answers they provide are unpredictable. The great books are, in fact, a great conversation in which the conclusions are not fixed beforehand.

Consider the great range of alternatives. On the merits of religious life, whom do we follow, Aquinas or Voltaire? On the nobility of warfare: Homer or Erasmus? Or Kissinger? On the worth of sexual fidelity: Tolstoy or James Joyce? Or someone contemporary? On the place of virtue in politics: Aristotle or Machiavelli? Or Abraham Lincoln?

The case for the study of the liberal arts is not, then, a case for ideology. It is a case for philosophy and for thoughtfulness. Those who take such studies seriously live very different lives and come to very different conclusions, among themselves, about particulars. So, another virtue of Western civilization is that it fosters a tradition of discussion, dissent, and correction as much as one of affirmation and agreement. There is no greater example of this discussion, dissent, and correction than this country itself.

This is a country that declared itself independent from England so that a new political order might be established. No one asserted independence sooner than a bunch of backwoods farmers, and merchants, and preachers in Charlotte, North Carolina, in 1775. That new American political order was one arrived at by reason and examination, after centuries of discussion and debate, and it was one that dissented from an age-old political tradition which is still embodied in some European states.

When it was formed under the Constitution, this new nation was designed specifically to accommodate, indeed encourage, tensions between divergent political beliefs. John Adams called the Constitutional Convention itself "the greatest single effort of national deliberation the world has ever seen," and in our 200 years under that Constitution, deliberation has been a central characteristic of our government. It was open deliberation and dissent that enabled Abraham Lincoln to convince the nation that slavery must be overcome. In our own state of North Carolina, and in our own time, it is dissent that has set one political party against the other in an effort vying to see which one can and will do the most to strengthen our public schools. In this respect, dissent, and debate, and robust rivalry often provoke progress.

Again, the reason that we should study, nurture, and defend Western civilization is because it is good. It has not always been good. It is not now all good. But, as Leszek Kolakowski said in his Jefferson Lecture last year,

> However distasteful our civilization might be in some of its vulgar aspects, however enfeebled by its hedonistic indifference, greed, and the decline of civic virtues; however torn by struggles and teeming with social ills, the most powerful reason for its unconditional defense is provided by its alternative. It faces a new totalitarian civilization, and what is at stake is not only the destiny of one particular form of culture, but of humanity as we have known it.[5]

This brings me to the third reason that I believe that we must study, nurture, and defend Western civilization and its tradition of discussion and dissent: We must do so because the West is under attack. It is under attack, first, from those who declare themselves hostile to Western progress, Western principles, and in some cases, Western religions. This attack comes from without, of course, but it also comes from within. Theirs is not an America which, despite its imperfections, its weaknesses, and its sins, has served as a beacon to the world. Theirs is an America which they see as corrupt with racism, elitism, and imperialism. We most certainly do have a degree of that. However, nowhere else in the world are the rights of our citizens more secure.

It has been said that the rights of man were the rights of Englishmen first. In a sense, that is true. The rights and truths that we consider self-evident today were not always so evident. They were not always acknowledged.

They were first expressed by the British and first secured by Americans. Today these rights are enjoyed by women as well as men, and if it can be said that today there is one objective to which all men and all women—all Americans—should adhere, I believe it is the defense of Western civilization. To those of you who are most concerned with justice, equality, and the dignity of life, there can be no greater cause than the defense of the West and the extension of its principles.

In a little more than a decade, America will reach the twenty-first century, the millennium; another thousand years begins. Closer to [the] human scale: Your little niece starting kindergarten will just be graduating from high school—into what? Into what career? Into what civilization? Is that your responsibility now? Will these ideas, these Western ideas, remain the last, best hope on earth? Think it over, especially a few days from now when the aura of this celebration, your graduation, clothes itself in memories. "This is the last of your springs," Adlai Stevenson said. Now comes the millennium; now the future.

Satchel Paige once said, "You can't steal second if you keep your foot on first base."[6] As a nation, as a civilization worth preserving, protecting, and defending, we've kept our foot on first base too long. The time has come for you to make the dash. Just don't get picked off.

In many ways, my message to you today could be restated, in condensed form, as a pledge of allegiance—not just to the flag of the United States of America, but to the republic for which it stands, and with full respect for Western civilization out of which it grew, one nation, under God, indivisible, with liberty and justice for all.

---

[1]Adlai Ewing Stevenson (1900-1965), born in Los Angeles; died in Bloomington, Illinois; A.B., Princeton University, 1922; J.D., Northwestern University, 1926; honorary degrees; U.S. Naval Reserve, 1918. Attorney; assistant to U.S. Navy secretary, 1941-1944; chief, U.S. Economic Mission to Italy, 1943, and of War Department Mission to Europe, 1944; assistant to U.S. secretary of state, 1945, 1957; U.S. United Nations delegate, 1946-1947, and representative, 1961-1965; Illinois governor, 1949-1953; Democratic presidential candidate, 1952, 1956; author. *Who Was Who in America, 1961-1968*, 904.

Martin quoted from "The Educated Citizen," an address Stevenson delivered at the Princeton University senior class banquet on March 22, 1954. According to *The Papers of Adlai E. Stevenson*, ed. by Walter Johnson and others (Boston: Little, Brown and Company, 8 volumes, 1972-1979), IV, 344-345, the former Illinois governor actually said: "I came here last night in darkness, after an absence of four or five years. I came with an old friend, an old classmate." After having introduced and read an excerpt from a poem, written about Princeton by Alfred Noyes, Stevenson continued: "Sentimental? Yes. Nostalgic? Perhaps. Yet beautiful, true. Your days are short here; this is the last of your springs. And now in the serenity and quiet of his lovely place, touch the depths of truth, feel the hem of Heaven."

[2]Arthur Edward Murphy (1901-1962), born in Ithaca, New York; was buried in Austin, Texas; B.A., 1923, Ph.D., 1925, University of California. Philosopher; taught at University of California, 1926-1927, University of Chicago, 1927-1928, 1929-1931, Cornell University, 1928-1929, 1945-1953, and Brown University, 1931-1939; professor, department head, University of Illinois, 1939-1945, University of Washington, 1953-1958, and at University of Texas, from 1958; author; editor; Democrat. *Who Was Who in America, 1961-1968*, 689-690.

[3]Allan Bloom (1930-   ), born in Indianapolis; resident of Chicago; A.B., 1949, A.M., 1953, Ph.D., 1953-1955, University of Chicago. Assistant professor, later associate professor of government, Cornell University, 1963-1970; political science professor, University of Toronto, 1970-1979; professor, Committee on Social Thought and the College, University of Chicago, since 1979; author. *Who's Who in America, 1988-1989*, I, 292. Martin likely quoted from Bloom's *The Closing of the American Mind* (New York: Simon and Schuster, 1987).

[4]James Bryce, First Viscount Bryce (1838-1922), of Dechmont, Lanarkshire, Scotland; B.A., Trinity College, Oxford University, 1862; honorary degrees. Barrister, until 1882; Regius Professor of Civil Law, Oxford University, 1870-1893; member of Parliament for Tower Hamlets, 1880, and Aberdeen, 1885-1907; foreign affairs undersecretary, 1886; Board of Trade president, 1894; chairman, Royal Commission on Secondary Education, 1894; chief secretary for Ireland, 1905-1907; British ambassador to the U.S., 1907-1913; author. *Who Was Who, 1916-1928* (London: Adam & Charles Black, third edition, 1962), 141-142. The quotation came from Bryce, *The American Commonwealth* (New York: The Macmillan Company, new edition, 2 volumes, 1918), I, 1.

[5]Leszek Kolakowski (1927-   ), Ph.D., Warsaw University, 1953; honorary degrees. Award-winning philosopher; assistant philosophy professor, Lodz University, 1947-1949; Warsaw University faculty member, from 1950, served as professor and chairman, Section of History and Philosophy, 1959-1968, before expulsion "for political reasons"; research fellow, All Souls College, Oxford University, since 1970; winner, Jefferson Award, 1986; author. *Who's Who 1990* (New York: St. Martin's Press, 1990), 1032.

[6]Leroy Robert (Satchel) Paige (1906-1982), born in Mobile, Alabama. Legendary baseball pitcher, 3.29 ERA; played first in Negro leagues, 1925-1947, and later with Cleveland Indians, 1948-1949, St. Louis Browns, 1951-1953, and Kansas City Athletics, 1965; coach, Atlanta Braves, 1968; named to Baseball Hall of Fame, 1971; author. Gene Karst and Martin J. Jones, Jr., *Who's Who in Professional Baseball* (New Rochelle, New York: Arlington House, 1973), 738-740; *Who Was Who in America, 1982-1985*, 311.

NORTH CAROLINA VIETNAM MEMORIAL DEDICATION

RALEIGH, MAY 23, 1987

[Martin spoke at other military memorial dedication ceremonies during his first term, including the unveiling of the Beirut Memorial, Jacksonville, October 23, 1986; the Vietnam Highway Memorial, I-85 between Lexington and Thomasville, November 11, 1986; and the Medal of Honor Grove, Valley Forge, Pennsylvania, October 22, 1987.]

With an almost irresistible force, we yearn today to begin this dedication, as one would begin a book, with a disclaimer: "All of the events and characters herein portrayed are fictitious." But the war in

Vietnam was horribly real, and it cannot be washed away by tears of regret. The long days of remembrance remain with us, not as a dream, but as a reality to haunt us forever.

The Vietnam War was a tragic war; and there is implicit in all human tragedy, especially in war, a waste, a pointlessness lost in battle. Tragedy unobserved is even more pointless, but tragedy unremembered surely must rank with profound sin.

The chronicle of the Vietnam War is written with a bold flourish across the pages of American history, not to revive shock and tears, but to remember. Thus, in this dedication ceremony, we seek to honor those men and women who served in that war, only to return to a hostile nation; and we also seek to honor those who gave their lives, those who survived unbearable torture, and those whose fates remain unknown, lost somewhere in the rice paddies and jungles of Asia.

Yet, there is another message in this dedication, a message that must not be lost on future generations. We pray that those who come after our Vietnam veterans will find an insight and a wisdom and an unforgettable moral in the events which, so far, elude those who continue to live them. Therefore, this dedication is as much for those of the future as it is for those of the present.

Twelve years ago, as an era of unrest and intolerance came to an end in this country, the last known living American military forces returned from the shores of a distant country. In that country, Vietnam, these men and women had fought a difficult war in a strange and unfamiliar land. They did not come home as Americans of other wars had come home, with red, white, and blue banners; with parades; with homecoming crowds and celebrations. Those lucky enough to come home came back alone. They carried a great weight on their shoulders, a weight of unsettled memories, of friends lost in fire fights, of uncertain support from their countrymen. They had been called to do what generations before them had been called to do—and they did, with unfailing courage.

These American heroes in Vietnam played their part in history, like those before them, with dignity, with honor, with valor, and of course, with sacrifice and the uncompromising sense of duty as God had given them the power to see that duty. They are, as the great poet, Tennyson, wrote, men and women who exhibited

> Some sense of duty, something of a faith,
> Some reverence for the laws we ourselves have made . . .
> Some civic manhood firm against the crowd.[1]

They are men and women who gave themselves in service to this great land we call America, founded upon the ideals that have been the most imitated, but never fully duplicated, on the face of this earth.

Take time to ponder this word: *service*. In its broadest sense, it means contributing to the defense and the perpetuation of our proud national values on whatever soil they are threatened. Our forefathers, men like George Washington and James Madison, understood just how important service was to our new republic. Aware that our fledgling government did not have the strength to defend its people against foreign aggression, they called for a constitutional convention, in 1787, to forge a new nation together in the fire of commitment.

This year, our nation prepares to celebrate and commemorate the bicentennial of that bold new Constitution written in Philadelphia that summer. As we do, we should not forget that among its most prominent stated purposes was to "secure and defend the blessings of liberty for ourselves and our posterity."[2] Yet, in its deepest meaning, it stood for something more: It represented our chosen responsibility—indeed, our duty—to defend the principles of freedom throughout the world. The freedom of other people to elect their own governments. The freedom of other people to voice political opinions without fear of reprisal. The freedom to worship in whatever way one chooses. Those who went to Vietnam answered freedom's call to duty, to service, and to sacrifice self for those who hungered to share the blessings which we ourselves take so naturally for granted.

President Theodore Roosevelt once said that "the first requisite of a good citizen in this republic of ours is that he shall be willing to pull his own weight."[3] Our heroes of Vietnam, in Teddy Roosevelt's terms, are good citizens several times over.

During the longest conflict in our history, North Carolina soldiers, marines, airmen, sailors, men and women alike, served with heroism and determination. However, controversy over that conflict has delayed proper recognition from being given by our citizens to the many who served and sacrificed. With this life-size sculpture of two Vietnam heroes carrying a wounded comrade to safety, now given its rightful place on the grounds of the North Carolina State Capitol, we give recognition to the tragic events they lived and to which many gave their lives—their devotion to their state, their country, and their commitment to duty, which is burned indelibly in their memory by the reality of it all. And it is our way of saying we remember, too.

High above us on the Capitol, unfurled in the breeze, is another reminder: the POW-MIA flag. It is, and will remain, a constant reminder of those whose fates remain unaccounted for, of relatives with empty hearts, who still hope and pray and seek answers to the unknown. Today we join them in hope and prayer that these loved ones who are still missing, or possibly may still remain captive, in Vietnam, will someday be accounted for. We beseech our heavenly Father to give their families peace in the knowledge that they did not serve in vain, that they are with us in spirit, and that someday, if not in this life, they will be reunited with us in His house.

For our living veterans of Vietnam, for those who gave their lives in that struggle, and for those who remain missing, we reserve for them a special place in our hearts, a place reserved for the few in every generation called upon to sacrifice themselves so that a great nation's ideals of liberty, justice, freedom, and peace may live and prosper and endure.

When the Vietnam Memorial in Washington was completed in 1984, one of the dedication speakers was Everett Alvarez, himself one of the longest held prisoners of war in Vietnam. His words on that day still ring true: "There was a time, long past, when words would have mattered more," he said, "but at this place, for all time, it is our hearts that speak." And so it is that we speak with our hearts today; and we speak of a time to heal, to put aside the bitter memories that divided our nation, and to remember the sacrifices which hold us together as a people and as the United States of America.

One of the most remarkable aspects of the Vietnam Memorial in our nation's capital has been the tradition in which flowers and flags and other offerings of love are left by friends and family. This year, the custodians of the memorial found something which seemed to typify this silent communion of remembrance. Attached to a single dollar bill left beneath the name of a young man who never came home was a note, saying, "I've owed you this for a long time." Today, as we dedicate the North Carolina Vietnam Memorial, we can only say humbly, gratefully, and in the spirit of that note: We've owed you this for a long time.

---

[1]Alfred, Lord Tennyson, wrote:

> Some sense of duty, something of a faith,
> Some reverence for the laws ourselves have made,
> Some patient force to change them when we will,
> Some civic manhood firm against the crowd.

See *The Princess: Conclusion,* quoted in Bartlett, *Familiar Quotations,* 649.

[2]"We, the people of the United States, in order to form a more perfect Union, establish justice, insure domestic tranquility, provide for the common defense, promote the general welfare, and secure the blessings of liberty to ourselves and our posterity, do

ordain and establish this Constitution for the United States of America." Constitution of the United States, Preamble, as quoted in *North Carolina Manual, 1987-1988*, 195.

[3]"The first requisite of a good citizen in this Republic of ours is that he shall be able and willing to pull his weight." From a speech by Theodore Roosevelt, delivered in New York, November 11, 1902, quoted in Bartlett, *Familiar Quotations*, 847.

CHALLENGE '87 ANNOUNCEMENT

RALEIGH, MAY 28, 1987

[The following announcement to the press provided the basis for a similar, more condensed speech that Martin delivered at the opening of the Challenge '87 Conference, September 28, 1987.]

I am very pleased today to welcome all of you to Challenge '87, our state's initiative to address a subject of increasing concern to all North Carolinians: drug and substance abuse. I am especially grateful to the private sector leaders and bipartisan officials of state government who have taken time from their busy schedules to participate in our discussion of what is considered the greatest threat facing our state today.

Last year, almost $400 million in illegal drugs were seized by law enforcement officers in North Carolina, twice as much as was seized in 1985. Arrests for drug violations increased by some 11 percent, yet most of the drug traffic still escaped detection. In view of these facts, it should be quite evident to all of us that our state must unite, as never before, in the fight against drugs.

Drug and alcohol abuse have become a major problem in North Carolina, touching the lives of almost everyone. Cocaine and crack have taken the dominant lead as drugs of choice, invading our homes, neighborhoods, schools, and communities. Marijuana, once considered the leading threat to our society, has become North Carolina's number-one domestic commodity.

Last year, the State Bureau of Investigation, in cooperation with state and local law enforcement agencies, destroyed more than 150,000 marijuana plants, an increase of 50 percent over 1985. Once an importer of this deadly plant, our state has become one of the nation's leading exporters. Even so, marijuana pales by comparison to alcohol.

Clearly, alcohol has become our most abused substance. Two thirds of our adult population use alcoholic beverages, and more than 10 percent of them have become problem drinkers or alcoholics. We cannot begin to estimate the expense of these problem drinkers to our state in terms of lost production, personal and property damage, health and medical costs, deaths on our highways, and violent crimes.

The problem of drug and alcohol abuse is gigantic in North Carolina, and it is getting progressively worse. This situation has been a matter of concern to me for some time; and today it has become a matter of concern to our citizens, many of whom are directly affected by the toll it takes in human misery. But this problem is not new; it is an old menace revisited upon a new generation of North Carolinians, our children and youth.

Almost two and a half years ago, I appointed the Governor's Council on Drug and Alcohol Abuse among Children and Youth in an effort to measure the extent of this problem and to seek community-based solutions. During the past year, this council, chaired by Dr. Jonnie McLeod of Charlotte, completed a series of ten public hearings throughout our state. At the same time, our General Assembly, under the leadership of Lieutenant Governor Robert Jordan, has held four legislative hearings to explore such areas of concern as education, law enforcement, abuse prevention and intervention, and treatment of victims.

I am pleased to report that a bipartisan coalition has grown out of these hearings, a coalition that is committed to creating a state without drugs. I am confident that if we can set aside partisan considerations in favor of this noble goal, we can also build community coalitions that can be effective and efficient in our approach to eliminating the greatest menace our state has ever faced.

This is where the battle against alcohol and drug abuse must begin: in our business firms, homes, schools, churches, neighborhoods, and communities. The disease, and it is a disease, is one which defies a solution imposed by state government. Yet, we can do much more at the state level to coordinate the services of our many agencies and departments of government; to establish new programs to fill unmet needs; and to take bold and new approaches to the growing problem of alcohol and drug abuse.

When it became clear that many agencies were launching off on separate uncoordinated efforts, with some thirty-three separate programs identified in the press kit (yellow cover), several months ago I organized an inter-agency team to foster the coordination of services and programs at the state level. The leaders of this inter-agency team are here today to share with us what they are doing, and what they plan to do in the future, to mount a cooperative, full-scale assault on this problem. Already they have found ways to help each other, with shared money and ideas, in a truly incredible, unprecedented example of working together without regard to politics, turf, or personality.

Before I call upon them, I want to emphasize that our foremost responsibilty as a society is to nurture and protect our children. This is a difficult job when their health and well-being is threatened by drug and alcohol abuse. This challenge has called forth the best in us.

This is the challenge we face in North Carolina today, and appropriately "Challenge '87" has been adopted by state government's inter-agency team as its slogan for the year ahead. We will plan to build upon the work of this team in determining how to use our resources, both state and federal, to combat drug and alcohol abuse in ways that will be more successful. In addition, I want to announce today that we will hold our first statewide conference of alcohol and drug abuse beginning September 28, and we are inviting mayors, county commission chairman, heads of local law enforcement agencies and mental health organizations, educators, business leaders, and concerned citizens to come to Raleigh and participate actively in this effort to build local coalitions.

Beginning in the next fiscal year, some $12.2 million in federal funds will be available to North Carolina to fight alcohol and drug abuse. The budget which I sent to the General Assembly allocates additional resources to supplement these funds. This money will be used for drug education, prevention, intervention, treatment, and law enforcement—the whole range of response. In the supplemental budget amendments recently sent to the General Assembly, I have proposed that $1.4 million be spent for intensive, twenty-four-hour residential treatment for youthful drug abusers.

Some of these funds will be available to local coalitions, and some leaders are insisting that in no instance should they be granted to communities in which there has not been established a coordinated approach to solving drug and alcohol abuse problems. Just as we have done at the state level, we must have a team approach to drug and alcohol abuse in our communities. Nothing less than total community involvement will work. Agencies and organizations must put aside turf in the larger interest of doing a job, and doing it well. Only as teams can we win this deadly challenge.

Now it is my pleasure to introduce those who have joined us, today, for this special press conference. Our first speaker who will present brief comments is the lieutenant governor of North Carolina, the Honorable Robert Jordan.

(Lieutenant Governor Jordan speaks.)

Thank you, Bob, for the initiatives you have taken. I now have the pleasure of presenting the chairman of the Governor's Council on

Alcohol and Drug Abuse among Children and Youth, Dr. Jonnie McLeod. Before you begin, I want to publicly commend and thank you for once again agreeing to lead a difficult challenge—and for your determination to push all of us to set aside our separate strategies and objectives and to work together. You have been an inspiration to all of this team, and we applaud you for it.

(Dr. McLeod speaks.)

Thank you, Dr. McLeod. We also have with us, today, the attorney general of North Carolina, the Honorable Lacy Thornburg, who will address the programs directed by the Department of Justice. Judge Thornburg, your department has a major leadership role, and I want to commend Charles Dunn.[1]

(Attorney General Thornburg speaks.)

Thank you, Lacy. Education is one of the most important tools in preventing alcohol and drug abuse, and equally important is having schools that are drug free. Here with us to discuss the drug prevention programs in our public schools is State Superintendent Craig Phillips.

(Superintendent Phillips speaks.)

Thank you, Craig. Four of my cabinet secretaries have joined us today, as they and their departments. . . . [incomplete]. They are Secretary Dave Flaherty,[2] of the Department of Human Resources; Secretary Joe Dean, of the Department of Crime Control and Public Safety; Secretary Jim Lofton, of the Department of Administration; and Secretary Aaron Johnson of the Department of Correction. I now want to ask each of them to speak in the order that I have introduced them.[3]

You have heard described a large array of programs to deal with drug abuse in a coordinated way. I want to thank all of the state officials who have joined us today and who have participated in launching Challenge '87. As we have heard, alcohol and drug abuse has an impact upon the life of every citizen, directly or indirectly. Local agencies are actively involved; they, too, must develop a coordinated team approach.

The statewide alcohol and drug abuse conference which I have scheduled on September 28 will provide us an opportunity to take the next step in making this commitment. As members of the news media, you have the means by which to raise the awareness of all North Carolinians to the menace that alcohol and drug abuse has become. I want to commend those news organizations who have helped to alert us and inform us, and I call upon each of you to get this message across to every home and every family in our state.

At this time, in the few remaining minutes, I believe any of the panel members would be glad to entertain questions from the audience. I would ask that questions be limited to this topic. If you have other questions on other topics, we would be glad to answer them at a separate time.

---

[1]Charles J. Dunn (1934-   ), resident of Raleigh; A.B., University of North Carolina at Chapel Hill, 1956; U.S. Army. Administrative aide to Congressman Horace Kornegay, 1963-1965; administrative assistant to Governor Dan K. Moore, 1965-1969; director, 1969-1975, deputy director, since 1986, State Bureau of Investigation; executive vice-president, N.C. Textile Manufacturers Assn., 1978-1986. Charles J. Dunn to Jan-Michael Poff, March 15, 1990.

[2]David Thomas Flaherty (1928-   ), born in Boston, Massachusetts; B.A., Boston University, 1955; U.S. Army, 1949-1952. Various positions with Broyhill Industries, including national advertising manager, and manager, Plastics Division; elected to North Carolina Senate from Caldwell County, 1968, reelected 1972; secretary, state Department of Human Resources, 1973-1976, reappointed in 1987; Republican gubernatorial candidate, 1976; chairman, state Republican party, 1981-1983; chairman, state Employment Security Commission, 1985-1987. *North Carolina Manual, 1969*, 585, *1988-1989*, 765, 787.

[3]The governor briefly introduced, and then thanked, secretaries Flaherty, Dean, Lofton, and Johnson. For his introduction of Johnson, the governor jotted, "When all else fails, they end up with your department. You have to bat as a clean-up hitter in a game where. . . ." [incomplete].

STATEMENT ON PUBLIC SCHOOL CONSTRUCTION

RALEIGH, JUNE 10, 1987

[Governor Martin advocated his school construction bond proposal in addresses to the Catawba County State Legislative Issues Forum, Raleigh, May 14; the North Carolina Association of Realtors, Greensboro, May 28; the Southern Textile Association, Asheville, June 11; the North Carolina School Food Service Association, Raleigh, June 18; and in his newspaper column of November 13, 1987. He also compared his financing plan to legislative alternatives in his press conference of June 10. A transcript of that statement to the media, reprinted below, was furnished by the Governor's Office.]

I want to thank all of you for being here, since we're not able to have a news conference tomorrow. I don't have any announcements to present to you today, but I do want to open a discussion as to how we can get serious about school construction.

As you know, over the last several months the stage was being set for a showdown as to what would be the best way to finance a long overdue major construction program to build the schools that we need in every community—so that every county, every community in

North Carolina would have schools that they could point to with pride.

There are some in the House of Representatives—the Democratic party members, for example—who are on record as saying they favor an increase in a sales tax just as was done in 1983 and, again, in 1986. There are others of us who believe that it would be better to follow the proposal, that I put forward, of an innovative bond issue that would require no new taxes but rather would make better use of the taxes we've already got.

So, the stage was being set for that decision to be made for a showdown. So much was at issue; so much was at stake, and it seemed to me that the time had come for a rallying of public support to let the legislature know that the time had come for a choice to be made. And no one was coming out against school construction—just a question of what is the best way to do it. And here you had the lieutenant governor and I on one side, with the bipartisan Senate leadership, favoring the bond referendum of the Royall bill[1] which I am sure you have noted is not unlike the proposal that I proposed and put forward last year. Then there were House Democrats on record on the other side for the third sales tax hike in five years.[2]

Then a strange thing happened. Last week, Lieutenant Governor Jordan pulled a plug on that. He bailed out. Quit. He surrendered without the vote being cast on this question.[3]

It was pressure time, I thought. Time to let legislators know that it's time to get the process to work, to let that internal pressure build as it ought to do in a legislative session so that the process could work the way it is intended to do.

But Lieutenant Governor Jordan just bowed to what he refers to as reality and gave up. It was like the second down and long yardage and his proposal was, "Let's punt." But even worse than that, I suggest that he messed it up for those of us who are serious about building schools and who are willing to fight for school construction.

His plan that he has put forward is not a policy, it's a charade. If I can describe it this way, it would be a pretty accurate and complete representation of it. First, he says you add up all the money that's already available for school construction and then take credit for that. Second, you redefine what the counties can do with some of it and then you promise—the third step—you promise that future legislatures will somehow vote for more than he's willing for this legislature to vote for. And then fourth, you pretend that is a compromise.

I say, "What compromise?"

He's described his proposal as having no new taxes and no new borrowing. I suggest to you that's not quite true. But to the extent that it's a proclamation of his proposal, he could say "No new taxes, no new borrowing, little new money, few new schools," because that's the impact of the proposal that he's offered and called it compromising. It will provide practically no additional strength in school construction.

If it's a compromise, with whom is he compromising? Not with me. He hasn't discussed it with me. Apparently it is not a compromise with Representative Billy Watkins, whose mere hint that he might run for governor has created more panic on the other side than on ours. I would say that I, as you know, disagree with Billy Watkins about the need for another tax hike. He's entitled to his view, and I'm entitled to mine. We're in disagreement on that, but at least I know where he stands. We've discussed it. On a recent occasion we had a chance to talk about it a little bit, so I could hear how he feels about it, and I can say that he speaks with great conviction about his belief in favor of an increase in the sales tax. He believes deeply and sincerely in what he stands for, and he stands for what he believes. You won't see Billy Watkins indecisive; you won't see him cut and run or pretend that he's come up with a compromise [when] it's not. He may be wrong— he's never in doubt and you got to give him credit for that.

You might want to consider that there is an element of "The Twilight Zone" in all of this. The Senate had just passed S. 205— remember, that was the bill that endorsed, once again, that long-honored tradition that counties would be expected to build the schools while the state would pay for the operation expenses.[4] Well, that didn't last very long.

As an afterthought, it does appear that Lieutenant Governor Jordan continues to favor a bond issue for infrastructure, though not for schools. Well, I would suggest that's the wrong priority. We ought to be putting schools first, and if he's not going to fight for his bill—if he's not going to fight for the bill that Senator Royall introduced and which I was supportive in hopes that we could get that through—if he's not going to fight for that then I think I'll go back to the bill that was my original proposal, the bill introduced by Senator Paul Smith[5]—the one that State Treasurer Harlan Boyles and I put together, the one that the school part of Senator Royall's bill was based on. The one that Senator Hardison[6] was about to introduce until party leaders ordered him not to introduce a major initiative on behalf of a Republican governor—you remember that episode.

I say to you, let's stop fooling around.

So I asked the lieutenant governor to call up the Smith bill in the

Senate and let the senators vote on it, and I asked Speaker Ramsey to call it up in the House; and I asked the people of this state, who care deeply about public education and who care deeply about schools, to call it up with their legislators and let them know that you are for it. Let them know that you want to see something done in this session. Demand that the General Assembly take a stand, for schools' sake. Let's get it back on track. There is so much at stake.

Now, I know we're in a position where it looks like we've reached a stalemate, but it doesn't have to be one. I've got a suggestion that I made privately to several legislators and the leadership, and I'm willing to suggest again, and that is if we're at a point where the House refuses to go along with a bond issue and the Senate refuses to go along with a tax increase—if, in short, the General Assembly refuses to make a decision—then let's let the people decide. Sure, just put both questions in referendums on the ballot and let the people decide.[7]

They elected the legislature to make the tough decisions, but if it's too tough then let the people make those choices. They can vote on both as separate issues, and there are different combinations of how that might turn out. Just briefly, I could point out that it could be that they would defeat both of them if the public really doesn't want to rush into replacement of old firetrap schools that we've got. Or, they might approve one proposal and not the other if there is a strong consensus in favor of one approach and not the other, and I happen to believe that that's what the outcome would be.

There is another possibility, and that is they could end up passing both, and that would happen if the public wants to see schools built no matter how we go about doing it. There are some people who feel that's what the outcome would be. I don't. I think the public would support the bond issue and not the tax increase, but we can resolve that by putting both questions on the ballot in November. And we ought to anticipate that there is a chance that both could be passed, and therefore the authorizing legislation ought to spell out what the precedence would be. Do you try to build schools with both, or if both pass, do you follow one course and not the other. But at least, let's build the schools that we need, and let's build with bricks and mortar—and not with smoke and mirrors. That concludes my initial statement on that subject, and I'll be glad to respond to questions.

---

[1]Martin was referring to S.B. 236, "A Bill to Create a North Carolina Local Government Finance Authority, to Authorize the Issuance of Not to Exceed One Billion Dollars in

General Obligation Bonds to Provide Funds for School Facilities, to Authorize the Issuance of Not to Exceed One Billion Dollars in General Obligation Bonds to Provide Funds for Infrastructure Improvements, and to Create and Appropriate Funds for the North Carolina Clean Water Loan Subsidy and Grant Program." Introduced by Senator Kenneth C. Royall, Jr., on March 31, 1987, the bill did not pass the upper house. *N.C. Senate Journal, 1987,* 169, 451, 653, 796.

Kenneth Claiborne Royall, Jr. (1918-   ), born in Warsaw, Duplin County; resident of Durham County; A.B., University of North Carolina at Chapel Hill, 1940; attended University of Virginia and Wake Forest College (later University) law schools; honorary degree; U.S. Marine Corps, 1942-1945. Furniture retailer and owner, Style Craft Interiors; member, state House, 1967-1971, and Senate, since 1973; Senate majority leader, 1973-1974, 1977-1978; chairman, Advisory Budget Commission, since 1981, and of Senate Ways and Means Committee; Democrat. *North Carolina Manual, 1987-1988,* 318.

²Representative Billy Watkins (D-Granville) and three colleagues introduced H.B. 307, "A Bill to Be Entitled an Act to Increase State Sales and Use Taxes by One Percent and to Earmark the Full Proceeds for Public School Buildings," on March 24, 1987. It passed the House on May 13 and was sent to the Senate, where it remained in the Finance Committee through the end of the session. *N.C. House Journal, 1987,* 150, 557, 566, 581; *N.C. Senate Journal, 1987,* 462. "Under the Watkins bill," the governor told a Greensboro audience on May 28, "an additional penny would be added to the sales tax to fund public school construction. Collections of the tax would be monitored annually to determine when sufficient funds have been raised to meet school construction needs, but there is no assurance—absolutely none—that once levied this regressive tax would ever be removed." He concluded that "any suggestion that a new tax is necessary is ridiculous. We need only to make better use of the sales taxes increased in 1983 and 1986. We don't need another in 1987."

³The escalating intraparty struggle between House and Senate Democrats over competing school construction bills persuaded Lieutenant Governor Jordan of the necessity of a deadlock-breaking alternative. Withdrawing his endorsement of the the Royall bill, which he concluded would not pass the House, the lieutenant governor offered a different funding plan on June 4. His willingness to compromise with House leaders led to the ratification, on July 16, of chapter 622, *N.C. Session Laws, 1987,* identified earlier in this volume. *News and Observer,* June 5, 8, 9, 11, 19, July 16, 17, 1987.

⁴S.B. 205, "A Bill to Establish State and Local Funding Responsibilities for the Uniform System of Free Public Schools and to Establish a Special Fund to Meet Critical School Facility Needs," was introduced on March 23, 1987. A Senate Education Committee substitute, also designated S.B. 205, passed its third reading on May 14, and was sent to the House. There it was supplanted by yet another substitute bill, which remained in committee through the end of the session. *N.C. House Journal, 1987,* 631, 961, 995; *N.C. Senate Journal, 1987,* 129, 395, 419.

⁵Martin's initial school construction funding plan, S.B. 434, was identified earlier in this volume. Paul Sanders Smith (1927-   ), born in Salisbury; resident of Rowan County; was educated at Catawba College and University of North Carolina at Chapel Hill; U.S. Navy, 1943-1945. Executive vice-president, marketing and operations, Holding Brothers, Inc.; chairman, Rowan County Board of Commissioners, 1978-1979; member, state Senate, since 1981, minority whip, 1985, and vice-chairman, Commerce Committee; Republican. *North Carolina Manual, 1987-1988,* 324.

⁶Harold Woodrow Hardison (1923-   ), native of Deep Run; was educated at Atlantic Christian College; U.S. Army Air Force, 1942-1946. President, Eastern United Tires, Inc.; member, state House, 1971, and Senate, 1973-1988; chairman, Senate Commerce Committee; defeated by Senator Anthony E. Rand in Democratic primary for lieutenant governor, 1988. Hardison was listed as cosponsor of S.B. 205, identified above. *N.C. Senate Journal, 1987,* 129; *News and Observer,* July 14, 1988; *North Carolina Manual, 1987-1988,* 301.

[7]Because the General Assembly never backed the idea of a school bond referendum, Martin suggested that readers of his November 13, 1987, newspaper column press their county commissioners to include the issue on local ballots for the March 8, 1988, presidential primary.

BRIDGE PROGRAM

MORGANTON, JUNE 11, 1987

In recent months there has been considerable public attention given the BRIDGE program, most of it centered on the location of a proposed permanent campsite. While the location of the camp has been in dispute, the value of the program, many believe, has merit.

My administration believes in listening to the citizens of this state, engaging in a free exchange of ideas and opinions. We are also mindful of our obligation to explore meaningful opportunities for rehabilitation of young offenders. After reviewing the comments made at a May 13 public meeting here in Morganton, and having met with representatives from Burke County as well as the two responsible state agencies, I have decided that the BRIDGE program does not require the construction of a residential facility in the Table Rock community of Burke County, and therefore, I have asked the departments to withdraw that proposal. The program will continue to operate from the Burke Youth Center until a suitable permanent site elsewhere can be identified.[1]

Applicants will continue to be screened by both the Division of Prisons and the Division of Forest Resources. Custodial care will be provided by the Division of Prisons, and the program participants will be housed at the Burke Youth Center. The crew members will continue to work under the direct supervision of the Division of Forest Resources, just as they have since the program became operational in January of this year.

During the first four months of this year, BRIDGE crew members spent more than 1,700 hours in classroom training for forest fire control and forest management operations. These young men put in 440 hours of practical fieldwork and more than 3,800 hours of fire control work, either in fire suppression, on standby, or on controlled burning operations. These men also put in nearly 600 man-hours working on the trails at South Mountain State Park, and on the Mountain-to-Sea Trail, and another 500 hours working in two of our educational state forests. In March and April, these men spent more than 800 hours repairing ice damage on the Blue Ridge Parkway and access roads to our fire towers.

Of the thirty-three inmates who have taken part in this program since it began in January, fifteen have completed their court-imposed sentences and have been released. I understand that, as a direct result of this program, at least one of these young men has applied to a community college to study forestry.

For those of you who are wondering, BRIDGE stands for Building, Rehabilitating, Instructing, Developing, Growing, Educating. My thanks to all of the citizens of Burke County for their interest in participatory government. As we listened to your concerns on retaining the School for the Deaf in this county, we have listened again on this issue.[2] We will continue to listen in the future. You may not always agree with our decisions in the future, but at least you know you can be heard and your questions will be answered.

---

[1]"The BRIDGE program resident camp is currently being built in Avery County, with the construction work being done by the participants themselves," Martin told the North Carolina Forestry Association on October 6, 1988.

[2]A Department of Human Resources task force recommended, on January 19, 1987, that secondary education programs at the state's eastern and western schools for the deaf, located in Wilson and Morganton respectively, be consolidated in Greensboro. The plan was unpopular among those whom the schools served as well as their parents. The governor, considering "the students' personal needs against [the state's] economic needs," also rejected the idea. *News and Observer*, January 20, 21, February 6, 1987.

AMERICAN LEGION AUXILIARY GIRLS' STATE

Greensboro, June 12, 1987

[This address is nearly identical to the one Governor Martin delivered to the Boys' State assembly, Wake Forest University, June 12, 1987.]

I am both pleased and honored by your invitation to address the Forty-eighth Annual Tar Heel Girls' State, the oldest continuously held Girls' State in America. This year, our state and nation are observing the bicentennial of the United States Constitution, and it is in the spirit of this celebration and commemoration, the very theme of Girls' State, that I want to speak to you today.

What is it that has made our Constitution the envy of the world? There was hardly a single idea which the American founding fathers put into their formula that someone hadn't thought of before. However, the singularity of it all was the fact that, in 1787, when the Constitution was being written, none of these ideas was being substantially practiced anywhere in the world.

It was here in America that the founding fathers assembled all of the fundamental principles, that dynamic success formula, which have proved to be a blessing to modern civilization. Today, many of these precious principles are fading into oblivion, and scores of unnecessary problems have arisen to plague humanity. Is it not fitting, then, that in this 200th year of our Constitution, it should be here in America that we once again raise the banner of human hope?

When the founding fathers met in Philadelphia in the summer of 1787, they knew that no single delegate to the convention could arrive at a constitutional formula by himself. At that very moment, the states were bitterly divided. The Continental dollar was inflated almost out of existence. The economy was deeply depressed, and rioting had broken out. New England had threatened to secede, and both England and France were standing by, ready to snatch up the dis-United States at the first opportunity.

Writing a constitution under these circumstances was a frightening experience. None of the delegates had expected the convention to require four months. In fact, within a few weeks many of the delegates, including James Madison, were living on borrowed funds.

From the opening day of the convention, it was known that the brainstorming discussions would require frequent shifting of positions and changing of minds. For this reason, the convention debates were held in secret to avoid public embarrassment as the delegates made concessions, reversed earlier positions, and moved generally toward some kind of agreement. The relative uniformity of thought shared by these men included strong and unusually well-defined convictions concerning religious principles, political precepts, economic fundamentals, and long-range social goals. They quarreled on particulars, of course, but when discussing fundamental precepts and ultimate objectives, they were practically unanimous. The founding fathers had strong criticism of one another as individual personalities, yet admired each other as laborers in a common cause.

Most historians agree that the single most important feature of the settlers who came to America was their overwhelming sense of mission, a conviction that they were taking part in the unfolding of a manifest destiny of divine design which would bless all mankind. This sense of manifest destiny has continued from that day to this. It is reflected in almost all of the inaugural speeches given by the presidents of the United States. As John Adams wrote, "I always consider the settlement of America with reverence and wonder, as the opening of a grand scene and the design of Providence for the illumination of the ignorant, and the emancipation of the slavish part of mankind all over the earth."

Thomas Jefferson looked upon the development of freedom under the Constitution as "the world's best hope," and wrote to John Dickinson in 1801 that what had been accomplished in the United States "will be a standing monument and example for the aim and imitation of the people of other countries. . . ."[1] Alexander Hamilton expressed this same point as the Constitution was presented to the states for ratification. He wrote: "It has been frequently remarked that it seems to have been reserved to the people of this country, by their conduct and example, to decide the important question, whether societies of men are really capable or not of establishing good government from reflection and choice, or whether they are forever destined to depend . . . on accident and force." He went on to say that if the people of the United States failed in this mission, it would operate "to the general misfortune of mankind."[2] John Adams later said that if the people abandoned the freedom gained by the adoption of the Constitution, it would be "treason against the hopes of the world."

When the Constitution was written, the founders embraced a unique idea. Nothing like it had ever been done before. The power of the idea was in the recognition that people's rights are granted by the Creator, not the state, and that the people then, and only then, grant rights to the government. This was the statement of guiding principle for the new nation and, as such, had to be translated into a concrete charter for government. The United States Constitution became that charter.

During the past week, you have been afforded the opportunity by the American Legion Auxiliary to learn how democracy works in our state. By establishing your own two-party system, selecting candidates for office, and participating in a free election, Girls' State has enabled you to gain valuable practical experience and develop a sense of responsibility as political citizens. This brings me, quite naturally, to the point of emphasizing the importance of strong political parties to the success of our system of government.

Those of you who are here, today, do not remember the party reforms of the sixties and seventies. Those were the days when reformers welcomed the demise of our parties and did what they could to hurry it along. They craved greater outside participation in the presidential nominating process and lobbied to change rules in ways that would allow candidates to build their own independent organizations and political bases.

They pointed out time and again that the founding fathers did not provide for political parties in our Constitution, and that George Washington despised the very idea of parties—or factions, as they were called in his day. Yet, what is a political party but men and women with common views and interests who decide to pool their talents, energies, and resources to affect public policy and place their own people in leadership roles. In a democracy, such combinations are inevitable and desirable. Without strong political parties, democracy becomes a sham. They guarantee the lively debate and choices which make democracy work.

Thus, almost from the beginning of American history, political parties have played an important role in our system of government. James Madison was a principal organizer of one of the two great national parties. Some of our greatest presidents, including Andrew Jackson, Abraham Lincoln, Woodrow Wilson, and Franklin Roosevelt were party men.

Through most of our history, parties and party workers have been the chief means by which state and national leaders organized their campaigns and kept in touch with what voters were thinking. Usually, one party or the other was clearly in charge of the national government and clearly accountable for what came out of it.

In the sixty years from 1896 to 1957, the White House and both houses of the Congress were under unified party control for all but eight years. Here in North Carolina, a single party has been in control for more than a century. In the last thirty years, this situation has changed greatly. About one third of the voters in America now tell pollsters they consider themselves members of no political party. Many voters split their tickets when voting for state and national leaders.

Many people who study and write about politics say that we are entering a period of de-alignment, in which political parties will have less and less effect on government. I, for one, do not see that happening in North Carolina. On the contrary, I see the emergence of two strong, competitive parties.

But, let's ask ourselves for a minute whether it would make any real difference if the parties died. First, let me acknowledge that party competition can be carried too far. Particularly in dealing with education, highways, health and human resources, and a score of issues affecting a majority of citizens, a state is the strongest when the two parties stand together and support the legitimate policies of the administration in office. In addition, strong party organizations provide a means for political leaders to stay in touch with the people. Pollsters and consultants can be useful, but neither can reach into the living rooms or workplaces of most North Carolinians. A strong party organization, built from the bottom up, can serve as an early warning system to political leaders when public dissatisfaction begins to develop. A good party organization also works in the other direction: It gives leaders a way of getting their message out to the people without dependence on other sources.

Finally, political parties are an excellent means of recruiting future government leaders. There is an important place in government for some administrators and some policy makers whose primary background is outside politics. But government that comes close to excluding politicians is bound to sacrifice the unique values and practical advantages of a democracy.

A strong, two-party system is vital to good government. But this will not come about until thousands of citizens recognize that they can accomplish more by working together within a party framework than they can by themselves. Indeed, if our political parties ever disappeared, we would be forced to reinvent them.

Throughout the four months during which the Constitution was being drafted in Philadelphia, the founding fathers emphasized the need for moral and virtuous citizens. As James Madison said, "Is there no virtue among us? If there be not, we are in a wretched situation. No theoretical checks—no form of government, can render us secure. To suppose that any form of government will secure liberty or happiness without any virtue in the people, is a chimerical idea."[3]

He went on to say: "If there be sufficient virtue and intelligence in the community, it will be exercised in the selection of these men; so that we do not depend upon their virtue, or put confidence in our leaders, but in the people who are to choose them."[4] Samuel Adams said the same of our leaders when he wrote: "He therefore is the truest friend to the liberty of his country who tries most to promote its virtue, and who, so far as his power and influence extend, will not suffer a man to be chosen into any office or power of trust who is not a wise and virtuous man."

Through your week-long experience at Girls' State, you have gained a greater appreciation of the American precepts and principles for which the leaders of our nation mutually pledged their lives, their fortunes, and their sacred honor. The history of Girls' State dates back to the American Legion caucus at St. Louis, in May, 1919. Out of that caucus grew a commitment by the Legion to preserve the ideals of Americanism through education. At the charter convention in Minneapolis that same year, the National Americanism Commission was established by the Legion, and, in 1935, Girls' State became a national movement. As participants in Tar Heel Girls' State, you represent North Carolina's future leadership, its hopes, and its dreams. I urge you to continue to develop and nurture that leadership. It is our most precious resource.

---

[1]Thomas Jefferson to John Dickinson, March 6, 1801, quoted in Paul Leicester Ford (ed.), *The Writings of Thomas Jefferson* (New York: G. P. Putnam's Sons, 10 volumes, 1892-1899), VIII, 8.

[2]The quotations attributed to Hamilton are from Federalist No. 1; see *The Federalist*, 3.

[3]James Madison, speaking June 20, 1788, in Richmond, at the Virginia debates on the ratification of the U.S. Constitution, quoted in Jonathan Elliot (ed.), *The Debates in the Several State Conventions on the Adoption of the Federal Constitution, As Recommended by the General Convention at Philadelphia in 1787* . . . (Washington: Printed by and for the Editor, 5 volumes, 1836), III, 489, hereinafter cited as Elliot, *Debates*.

[4]"If there be sufficient virtue and intelligence in the community, it will be exercised in the selection of these men. So that we do not depend on their virtue, or put confidence in our rulers, but in the people who are to choose them." James Madison, June 20, 1788, quoted in Elliot, *Debates*, III, 489.

INAUGURATION OF PIEDMONT AIRLINES' SERVICE TO LONDON

CHARLOTTE, JUNE 15, 1987

I'm delighted to have the opportunity to join all of you, today, as we celebrate Piedmont Airlines' inaugural flight from Charlotte to London, England. This is indeed an important day for all of North Carolina, for it establishes the first direct, nonstop travel link by air between our state and an international destination. Significantly, this flight, and the others that will follow on a daily basis, commemorates the close ties between North Carolina and the country from which the first settlers came to our shores more than 400 years ago. That migration later turned into a wave of new citizens who have enriched us both culturally and economically.

North Carolina, in the last decade, has become an economically diverse state, and this new air service will do much to broaden and strengthen that diversification. Piedmont's daily flight from Charlotte to Gatwick Airport, the third largest in the world in terms of international passengers, provides a direct connection to more than twenty cities throughout Europe. This means, of course, that many foreign companies that have an interest in investing in new facilities in the United States will now have a convenient means of access to North Carolina. This access also will expand our tourism and travel industry and make North Carolina a more attractive destination for foreign vacationers. I am honored to be among the many to commend Piedmont Airlines for providing this service to London, and I look forward to the addition of other international flights from North Carolina in the future. [After having cut the ribbon, the governor announced:]

Ladies and gentlemen, Piedmont Flight 160 from Charlotte to London, England, is now ready for boarding.

RESPONSE TO PROGRESS REPORT ON
EDUCATIONAL IMPROVEMENTS
SOUTHERN REGIONAL EDUCATION BOARD

Atlanta, Georgia, June 20, 1987

[The governor was elected, in June, 1987, to a one-year term as chairman of the Southern Regional Education Board. *News and Observer*, June 21, 1987.]

I appreciate very much the opportunity which the board has given me, today, to respond to the progress report on educational improvements in our southern states. First, and most appropriately, I want to commend and applaud the Commission for Educational Quality, chaired by former governor (Richard W.) Riley of South Carolina, for having prepared such an excellent and comprehensive presentation. He had some nice things to say about us—and some bold challenges. This report provides all of us with a unique overview of our regional accomplishments, and our persistent problems, and offers us some commonsense recommendations to address the additional steps that are required of us if we're going to sustain a long-term public commitment to quality education.[1]

For most of this century, the South has lagged behind the national commitment to public education. It was as if we had no intention that "the South rise again!" We excused it, and rationalized it, that we could not be expected to match the national average investment in schools. Our per-capita income was below the national average. We were poor.

Well, it was a poor excuse, and we're not hiding behind it anymore.

We are rebuilding public education in the South. We intend to have schools as fine as anywhere. It's our future.

There can be no argument that the high rate of students who are dropping out of school—now in excess of the 29 percent national average in two-thirds of the southern states, including North Carolina—is unacceptable and poses one of the most insidious obstacles to our continued economic growth and social well-being. Today's dropouts represent tomorrow's generation of functionally illiterate adults, and unless we cope with this problem effectively, and do it now, our failure to meet this single challenge will become a contradiction of all the good things we do to strengthen our public schools. We simply cannot afford to allow almost one third of our future citizens to continue entering the work force unprepared to deal with the technological changes that are being forced upon us by an increasingly competitive global economy.

One of the chief virtues of the Basic Education Program, which was introduced in North Carolina in 1985-1986, is that it allocates a greater share of our state's financial resources to remedy the conditions that contribute to our disturbing rate of high school dropouts. By 1992, the year in which we will complete the implementation of this program, North Carolina will have employed some 10,000 additional teachers, thereby reducing student-teacher ratios at all grade levels. This means that our teachers will have a greater opportunity, as a result of smaller class sizes, to give more individual attention to at-risk students.

Moreover, the Basic Education Program also provides for staffing our schools with additional social workers, psychologists, guidance counselors, and other support personnel, specialists whose professional skills address an ever-widening range of conditions that contribute to our high dropout rate. Coupled with other improvements, the Basic Education Program commits North Carolina to almost $1 billion in additional funding for public schools over an eight-year period—a one-third increase over and above inflation.

Another serious problem affecting North Carolina and other southern states is the large number of functionally illiterate adults who are already in the workplace, or who are unable to find work and make a contribution to society because they lack the basic skills to compete. North Carolina has more than 825,000 adults who cannot read, write, and work math problems well enough to function independently. Nothing less than our total commitment to conquer illiteracy will enable our region to realize its full economic and social potential.

Earlier this year, I created the Governor's Commission on Literacy in North Carolina, chaired by former president William Friday of the University of North Carolina; and we hired recently retired community college president Dick Hagemeyer as executive [director].[2] This commission is charged with the task of developing a comprehensive strategy to reach these adults through a community-based, coordinated, public-private partnership and to bring them into the social and economic mainstream of our state. Our system of fifty-eight community colleges has accomplished some very promising work in the field of literacy, yet it is reaching only a small fraction of those who need help. However, by involving the efforts of our entire system of state government, and by actively enlisting the help of private industry and thousands of volunteers, we now believe we can solve this problem; there's no practical reason why we can't, once we decide to do something about it.

Now let me turn my attention to the subject of quality teachers in the southern states. Of all the things we do to strengthen our public schools, nothing has a more profound effect than our efforts to improve the quality and effectiveness of our teachers. Providing quality teachers involves a two-step process. First, we must recruit and train the brightest and most talented of our high school graduates to pursue careers in teaching; and second, we must take the appropriate and necessary steps that are required to retain and reward the good teachers we already have.

One of our chief concerns in recent years has been the recruitment of enough good teachers to fill our classrooms. After a decade of erosion, North Carolina has recently become extremely fortunate in this respect. Enrollments in undergraduate teacher education programs in our fifteen-campus system of state-supported universities have increased between 10 to 30 percent in the last two years, and application rates are even higher: between 30 and 50 percent. Our largest increases have occurred at East Carolina University and Appalachian State University, which together account for fully 70 percent of all new teachers who are graduated from our state system.

The first reason for this increase in enrollments and applications has been the establishment of a teacher recruitment office within the North Carolina Department of Education, which I proposed in 1985. The second factor which accounts for this increase has been the growth in scholarships and loan programs, as well as the generous funding which has been committed to them. This year, for the first time, some 400 annual teaching fellowships of $5,000 each are being offered through the North Carolina Public School Forum to qualifying high school seniors throughout our state. I am pleased to report that the 400 high school seniors who have been identified for these fellowships have an average SAT score of 1,050, which is approximately 150 SAT points higher than for students entering teacher education programs in the previous year. Of that number, more than 100 have chosen to attend North Carolina State University, at Raleigh, indicating they will pursue courses of study in those subjects where we have our most critical shortages: math, science, and technology.

In addition to the teaching fellowships that are offered to our brightest high school seniors, 400 annual scholarships of $2,000 each are offered annually in North Carolina to college juniors and seniors who have chosen teaching as a career pursuit. Supplementing these 800 fellowships and scholarships are loans that are forgiven for graduates who agree to teach in areas of the state where we have shortages; I'm talking about geographic and subject areas.

There is, of course, a third factor that has contributed to the growing interest of our current college generation in the teaching profession. This has been the teacher career ladder pilot program which was implemented in sixteen local school systems, in 1985-1986, and which provides better pay for better teachers. With all of its anxieties and [incomplete] it has generated excitement about the profession because, for the first time, it allows us to give teachers promotions in the classroom.

During the first year of this program, we experienced a high degree of success in helping teachers improve their skills and their effectiveness in the classroom. Yet, the first year did not meet all of our goals. Some teachers complained that there was too much paperwork and described the evaluation methods as unfair. As a former teacher, I remember that my students used to moan about how difficult my evaluation methods were.

There were problems in those schools that were new to the evaluation methods. In spite of this, 90 percent of them passed, and more importantly, quality education improved. It is important to remember that any time we try a new idea, a better idea, we will experience some problems. Especially in a pilot program, more excessive paperwork and control is necessary for research purposes. But it appears that these difficulties will be overcome with practice, and familiarity, and flexibility. By the end of the 1988-1989 school year, North Carolina will have had three full years of experience with the crucial first year of preparation. This will provide a solid foundation upon which we can continue to build for the future.

As the progress report on educational improvement in the southern states emphasizes so well, we must continue to insist on making education our number-one budget priority. Polls show generally that there's widespread support for raising taxes if that's what it takes to improve the quality of public education. Well, I propose a radical idea for any state expecting any normal increase in revenue. If our public schools are given the first priority in budgeting, there will be no need for us to raise taxes for education. That's radical! Put schools first, and second, and third; then turn to lower priorities, improving number four, five, six, on to ten, twenty—for when the money runs out somewhere at the twenty-second or twenty-third priority on the public agenda, our schools will have already been strengthened, and we will have fulfilled the most solemn of all our pledges: our pledge to educational excellence. No polls show support for raising taxes for the sixteenth or twenty-fifth priorities, and there's no need to raise taxes for our first priority if we budget for that first. Put first things first! See how radical that is.

I again want to thank the board for allowing me to respond to the report we have received today, and to relate its findings to North Carolina's continuing efforts to strengthen its public schools.

---

[1]See Commission for Educational Quality, *A Progress Report and Recommendations on Educational Improvements in the SREB States* (Atlanta, Georgia: Southern Regional Education Board, 1987). The commission's chairman was Richard Wilson Riley (1932-   ), native of Greenville, South Carolina; resident of Columbia; B.A., Furman University, 1954; LL.B., University of South Carolina, 1960; U.S. Naval Reserve, 1954-1956. Attorney, 1959-1978; member, South Carolina House, 1963-1967, and Senate, 1967-1977; was elected governor of South Carolina, 1978, and reelected in 1982; Democrat. Barone and Ujifusa, *Almanac of American Politics, 1986,* 1218.

[2]Richard H. Hagemeyer; B.S., Bowling Green State University; M.S., University of Michigan; Ph.D., Wayne State University. Administrative staff member, Henry Ford Community College, Dearborn, Michigan, 1952-1962; founding president, Central Piedmont Community College, 1963; president, Southern Assn. of Community and Junior Colleges, 1973-1974, and of League for Innovation in the Community College, 1977-1978; director, 1974-1977, chairman, 1976-1977, American Assn. of Community and Junior Colleges; consultant; author. *North Carolina Manual, 1985,* 1055.

NORTH CAROLINA INDUSTRIAL DEVELOPERS ASSOCIATION

WRIGHTSVILLE BEACH, JUNE 23, 1987

[Martin's address to the North Carolina Industrial Developers Association was almost identical to his speech to the Southport-Oak Island Chamber of Commerce, Southport, June 26, 1987.]

Someone once described Raleigh, the center of our state government, as a capital city completely surrounded by reality. To the majority of our citizens who live elsewhere in North Carolina, it often seems that some of our political leaders are provincial and are frequently unable to reach decisions on the major issues that are of concern to the rest of our state and, indeed, are of greater consequence to its future prosperity and growth. Today, here in the region which the first settlers described as "the goodliest land under the cope of heaven," I am fully aware that I am in reality country, the mainstream of North Carolina; and in the spirit of this realism, I want to speak to you about the rising tide of economic activity that continues to lift North Carolina to new heights of national and international leadership.

No single group in North Carolina is more aware of our state's human, economic, and technical assets than this association. Indeed, no single group is more conscious of how these assets, strengthened by the expanded and continuing commitment of my administration over the last two and a half years, have enabled us to attract record investments by new and expanding businesses and to create hundreds of thousands of new jobs. You are the key players who have put together the local teams of business leaders, one of whom we will honor today. This local partnership has become a great advantage.

Although our record of accomplishment has been distorted and our assets have been debased in recent months by a vocal group of "bad news bearers," the economic heart of North Carolina remains strong, beating to the rhythm of new activity. Yet, there are those few individuals who try to compare us to selected data for the years immediately prior to 1985, and who claim falsely that we are not on target with our strategy for economic growth. Frankly, for political reasons, I'm glad they are drawing attention to what we are doing.

This reminds me of the story about the young man who enlisted in the army and whose first assignment, of course, was to a basic training camp. There, for eight weeks, he underwent a rigorous course of military discipline, physical fitness, and weapons training. By the time graduation arrived, he had earned a badge in marksmanship, which he decided to wear proudly on his uniform when he returned home on his first leave.

On his second day at home, he passed a meadow where a young boy, about ten years old, was doing some target practice with his rifle. The first thing he noticed was that the boy had scored a perfect bull's-eye on every target.

"Tell me," he asked the boy in astonishment, "How do you manage to hit the bull's-eye with every shot?"

"That's easy," the boy replied. "First, I take very careful aim and squeeze the trigger gently until I run out of ammunition. Then I walk down to the target and draw a circle around the holes."

In essence, that's what our critics have been doing with pre-1985 economic development statistics. They've been firing off a volley of shots and then circling them with a magic marker to resemble facts.

The truth is, these critics are distorting the facts. Admittedly, North Carolina has had a few disappointments, just as in previous years, but we've had an overwhelming number of incredible successes. It's when our leaders concentrate on our disappointments, to the exclusion of our successes, that they paint a false picture of North Carolina as a state that does not have an excellent business climate. This attitude could drive away new business investment and discourages the expansion of existing firms, the very opposite of what you, and I, and our state economic developers are working so hard to continue to attract. These leaders do North Carolina and its citizens a disservice.

The true facts are quite simple. Between January, 1985, and January, 1987, North Carolina added more than 268,000 new jobs, or an increase of almost 10 percent in two years, the third fastest growth rate in America. Our state ended both years, 1985 and 1986, with more than 3 million North Carolinians holding full-time jobs, the highest number of working citizens in our history. We averaged over 3 million in '86.

Unemployment in 1986 also continued to decline to an annual average of 5.3 percent, the lowest in the Southeast and the third lowest of the eleven largest states in the nation. This year it's below 5 percent. Are we doing something wrong? Last year, the total investment in North Carolina, by manufacturing and nonmanufacturing companies, totaled $5.2 billion and resulted in a total employment increase in excess of 85,000 new jobs. If, for political motives, they want to point out that I can do that "sitting down," while fighting off my adversaries with one arm tied behind my back by unfriendly legislative leaders, well, that's all right by me.[1]

Of course, the truth is, no one person can take credit for what in reality is a team effort, and I'm proud to be part of the development team, working with you. I can promise you I am working long hours, as hard as I can, to continue recruiting more jobs to North Carolina. Ask Alvah Ward,[2] or anyone else, off the record or on, and they'll tell you I spend more time on more recruiting calls than any recent predecessor. And the results are good.

Just last week, *Business Week* magazine announced that in a poll of 440 corporate executives, the fourth such poll conducted since 1976, North Carolina was rated first above all other states as the leading choice of locations for new manufacturing facilities. The survey, which is conducted by McGraw-Hill Research at the request of *Business Week*, gave North Carolina preference over such states as California, Texas, and Colorado. Of the last four surveys conducted by McGraw-Hill, this is the fourth consecutive time that North Carolina has placed number one as the best place in America to locate a new industry.

However, the latest survey has shown that North Carolina's 1986 position has gained considerably over 1976, with 21 percent of all executives favoring our state, compared to 15 percent twelve years ago. In fact, between 1980 and 1984, North Carolina actually lost seven percentage points in the ratings, although still maintaining first place. Maybe I'm lucky my term didn't begin in 1984: They would be all over me. I'm proud to say that we've gained those points back in three years.

Inc. magazine, one of the nation's most respected business publications, also has given North Carolina high marks. In 1986, the magazine placed North Carolina in fifteenth position nationally in an entrepreneurial business climate survey. Incidentally, again the bad news bearers just drew a phony bull's-eye away from that ranking to claim we had strayed, to imply that we were down from first place to fifteenth. The truth is, we've never been in first place in that survey. In fact, fifteenth rank was an improvement, compared to twenty-eighth place in a similar 1984 survey—a gain of thirteen places in three years. In fact, the Research Triangle area, for the first time ever, was voted the seventh-fastest growing entrepreneurial and small business center in the nation.

These reports follow many other surveys of executives that show that North Carolina is the leading choice among all states for new manufacturing investment—such as *Manufacturing Week*, recently. So, I say, keep talking about it, fellows. Or, as Br'er Rabbit would say, "Please keep throwing me in the briar patch."

This brings us to where we are, but I now want to outline for you where we are planning to go in the future. In my biennial budget for 1987-1989, I have asked the General Assembly to approve an additional $500,000 annually to expand the number of regional offices in North Carolina, from six to seven, and to strengthen the staffing by allocating two development specialists and a secretary to each office—all the better to serve you. These offices will provide stronger support for our existing industries, our traditional manufacturers, and also will allow us to give more concentrated effort to assisting community development in rural areas, with timely help in getting permits completed and approved. In addition, these offices can be expected to support the efforts of a proposed rural development center by providing information and technical assistance to the center itself, as well as to coordinate its pilot projects.

I have also proposed spending an additional $1 million for business and industry development advertising, presently funded at only $510,000. Together with other funding to support trade missions and to enhance our research capabilities, my total requests amount to an extra $1.5 million in 1987-1988 and $1.3 million in 1988-1989.

International development, the attraction of reverse investments to North Carolina and the expansion of our exports of quality North Carolina products to other nations—that is among our chief priorities. Perhaps our single most important opportunity lies in the Pacific Rim. Accordingly, I have requsted funds to establish a foreign investment office in Tokyo and to locate two Far East trade offices, one each in Hong Kong and South Korea. The efforts of these offices will be supplemented by adding more than $650,000 to our budget over the next two years to expand our Raleigh-based export marketing program. This, of course, brings me to the theme of your annual meeting, our North Carolina state ports and how they can benefit local communities in their efforts to expand industrial investment throughout our state.

Total capital investment in our two ports at Wilmington and Morehead City has totaled only $57 million since their establishment thirty-five years ago. Yet, the revenue from the operation of our ports last year alone totaled $23 million, an increase of 14 percent over the previous year. Profits exceeded $2.6 million, or a 7 percent increase over 1985. When we examine the ports in this perspective, they represent North Carolina's best, though underfunded, investment. As a result, I have proposed a major capital improvement program, exceeding $36 million, at these two facilities over the next two years— the largest in history, with more in the next two years.

This investment, I believe, is vital if we expect to expand our exporting capabilities to other countries. Last year, Morehead City contributed one third of all revenue produced by our two ports, and fully one third of the profit, yet it is our most underdeveloped ocean gateway to the world. General cargo was up at the port by 13 percent, and ship calls increased 10 percent. The high generating cargoes, such as tobacco, logs, linerboard, and hardboard began moving across the Morehead City docks again in sufficient quantities to produce the desired income results. Already this year, we have developed some general cargo movements at Morehead City, particularly in steel and lumber. This expanded business will contribute significantly to the economic benefit of companies in our state over the next twelve months.

We had a close call this past winter. I got word that a small berth had collapsed, sand was flowing out undermining a group of fuel storage tanks, and a major disaster was in the making. I didn't wait to place a phone call. I flew to Morehead City, reviewed the damage assessment, and authorized an immediate repair job that night. The entire estuary was in danger. Fast action saved it.[3]

At the Port of Wilmington, revenue for the past year was $12 million, or 12 percent higher than in 1985. Of that amount, approximately $1.6 million represented net profit. Containerized cargo represented the greatest share of the imports and exports handled at the Port of Wilmington. The total shipments accommodated at the port amounted to more than 650,000 tons, a 36 percent increase over 1985. However, total volume of all trade exceeded 2.6 million tons. Much of this increase has resulted from the growth in rail traffic from the intermodal terminal at Charlotte, which now has some 500 companies shipping through its inland facilities. The satellite terminal at Greensboro, which offers service to the Port of Wilmington by motor freight only, has attracted some fifty new companies in the past year.

It will become even more attractive to ship through Wilmington when I-40, my only highway campaign promise, is completed. As promised, the last segment will be under contract next year. Next, we will build the Smith Creek connector to route the port traffic around the local and downtown streets. You've seen a lot of local stories about that because we're trying to be careful not to cause more problems than we solve. Understandably, folks get nervous when we ask questions.

The main point I'm making is that our ports have matured into two of our most important assets. Combined with expanded air passenger travel and cargo delivery, via Piedmont and American Airlines, and with major improvements in our major highways, transportation facilities have become a vital force in moving our state ahead in the future. We must continue to expand and improve these facilities, even as we work to strengthen our public schools and community facilities.

A major challenge faces us today, one of self-determination and the growth it will bring to North Carolina, and unless we meet this challenge, we may not get another opportunity again for more than half a decade. Last year, the focus was on highways, and we succeeded. This year, it is on new schools. We must succeed again.

Schools play an important part in reassuring industry and business that we are serious about competing in a world economy. I want every community in North Carolina to have schools we can point to with pride. When prospective industries and service-related companies see inadequate schools and the lack of evidence of commitment to quality education as our foremost priority, they will become discouraged and look elsewhere, hopefully in North Carolina, for a more suitable location in which to locate or expand.

How often have you helped a rural city prepare to show an attractive site to a business team? They often have to figure how to get them from the landing strip to the plant site without going by the run-down, old, three-story firetrap of a school—because that doesn't say what we want to say about our commitment to schools. I had asked the North Carolina General Assembly to do something big for schools, but I can tell you we're in danger of adjourning without doing anything much for new schools. If you agree it's important, you need to speak up.

Together, as one united state, we must make a long-term commitment of our energies and resources to the growth of North Carolina. We must overcome the obstacles that impede progress and move forward, with renewed confidence, toward the next century. It is this commitment that will ensure the success of the present generation of our citizens and guarantee the future of those who will follow in our footsteps. May God grant us the wisdom and the courage to fulfill this commitment.

---

[1]Kenneth L. Eudy, Jr., state Democratic party executive director, often referred to Martin as "the sitting governor," criticizing him for his administration's perceived "inaction on education and economic issues." Martin, acquainted with the former WBTV and *Charlotte Observer* reporter, returned the favor, derisively referring to Eudy as "a media star." *News and Observer*, June 17, December 18, 24, 1987.

[2]Alvah H. Ward, Jr. (1929-   ), born in Wanchese; resident of Knightdale; B.S., The Citadel, 1951; M.B.A., University of North Carolina at Chapel Hill, 1954; U.S. Army, 1951-1954. Manteo businessman, 1954-1969; seafood-marine industries consultant and

seafood marketing program chief, state Department of Natural and Economic Resources (later Commerce Department), 1969-1974; industrial development representative, 1974-1980, Industrial Development Division director, since 1980, state Commerce Department (later Department of Economic and Community Development). Alvah H. Ward, Jr., to Jan-Michael Poff, June 13, 1990.

[3]Captain D. H. Whitten, federal on-scene coordinator and commanding officer of the United States Coast Guard's Marine Safety Office, in Wilmington, officially commended Governor Martin in February for "taking decisive executive action on Friday, January 16, 1987, to prevent a major oil spill at the State Ports Authority, Morehead City, North Carolina." Whitten praised Martin's visit to the scene of impending disaster and his consequent order to obtain rock fill to avert a spill and for waiving road weight limits so that the fill could be transported over state highways, decisions the captain termed "the most significant, positive action taken in preventing a major catastrophe." Press release, "U.S. Coast Guard Honors Governor Martin for Action Preventing a Major Oil Spill at Morehead City," Raleigh, February 12, 1987, Governors Papers, James G. Martin.

NORTH CAROLINA COMMITTEE ON MANAGEMENT

RALEIGH, JUNE 25, 1987

Today is a significant time for me to present you a status report on our legislative program. First, today marked the ninety-eighth day of the 1987 biennial session of the General Assembly; if tradition prevails, only a month—more or less—remains before adjournment. Second, the Joint Appropriations Committee this morning convened its first meeting, which begins the process of deciding the fate of many pending bills with fiscal implications.

School Bond Referendum

In spite of approaching adjournment by the House and Senate, many issues remain unresolved. Chief among these issues is action on my proposal to authorize a $1.5 billion statewide school bond referendum to provide loans to counties for public school construction. This measure, developed with the assistance and support of State Treasurer Harlan Boyles, was introduced in the Senate on April 15, by Senator Paul Smith, and subsequently it was referred to the Finance Committee.

You will recall that I made this proposal last October at a statewide meeting of school superintendents. Since that time, it has gained the overwhelming support of educational groups, county commissioners, and citizens throughout North Carolina. Yet, the Senate Finance Committee prevails in holding it hostage. There has been some speculation that if the General Assembly fails to resolve what is obviously an escalating shortage of school facilities in many of our counties, we may not get another oppportunity to seek a legislative remedy for another five years or more.

I, for one, do not believe this battle has been lost in this session. I believe public sentiment is on the side of strengthening our schools, both qualitatively and quantitatively. Therefore, our task—and it is no less an urgent one—is to bring the pressure of this sentiment to bear on the conscience of our legislators, compelling them to act before going home. This will require the efforts of our best leaders in business and education. All of us must speak up on behalf of education.

We must impress upon our lawmakers that we cannot afford to lose the momentum that has been gained for the benefit of our public schools in the last two and a half years. Already, North Carolina has completed the second year of implementing the Basic Education Program, for which I have proposed full funding of $357 million during the next biennium. By 1992, the last year of implementation, more than 15,000 additional employees will have been added to our state school system under this program, including teachers and support personnel. Together with curriculum improvements, we will have spent almost $1 billion in additional funds by that time to provide our children quality schools they so rightfully deserve.

In addition, I have proposed spending $95.5 million during the next two years for expansion of the teacher career ladder pilot plan, which provides better pay for better teachers. These funds will allow us to add twelve new systems to the teacher career development program in 1987-1988 and to go statewide with Career Level I in the remaining 127 local systems by 1988-1989. I have proposed that we go only that far during the biennium, reserving until the next budget cycle any decision on further expansion of the Career Development Program.

The General Assembly and I worked together in 1985 to get these programs off the ground, and I am confident that my 1987-1989 budget recommendations to strengthen them substantially will be approved. However, it is imperative for us to provide quality facilities to match quality public school programs. Traditionally, our counties have been responsible for providing public school facilities, reserving to the state the responsibility for instructional costs. Only recently this tradition was reaffirmed in legislation ratified by the General Assembly.

Until recent years, with the exception of two modest state bond issues, counties have financed public school construction solely through property tax revenues. In some counties, these revenues have been sufficient to build adequate, safe, and functional school facilities; in many others the revenue has not been enough to meet current needs.

In 1984, and again in 1986, the General Assembly authorized a one-half-cent local option sales tax to help counties finance school construction. All 100 counties have now exercised this option. Unfortunately, this tax does not generate funds rapidly enough to keep up with school construction needs. Many of our counties, some with our worst school facilities, are forced to wait years before enough money has been accumulated to plan for and begin school construction.

The bond referendum that I have proposed to finance a state school facility loan fund eliminates this problem by allowing counties to borrow from the state the money now for the schools they need now, and to pledge future sales tax revenues toward repayment. Thus, it avoids a tax increase and gives us a way to use better the taxes we already have.

Moreover, this plan is abundant with other advantages. First, counties would have the benefit of borrowing money at the low interest rate afforded by the state's triple-A bond rating. Second, repayment of loans could be made on a long-term basis. Third, it is an optional plan that does not require, but does permit, every county to participate. Fourth, it results in more schools for less money by avoiding future building cost increases. Fifth, and finally, no county would be obligated for a debt incurred by another county.

I have described the proposal as bold and innovative, yet nothing less than a bold and innovative approach will help us avert a pending school facility crisis, and that crisis will come as surely as tomorrow unless the General Assembly intervenes. Our legislators simply cannot afford to wait any longer to face this problem.

Thus far in the current legislative session, I have made every effort to work with the General Assembly's leadership to resolve the school facility needs of our counties. Last month, I reached a compromise with Lieutenant Governor (Robert) Jordan to support an alternate bill introduced by Senator Kenneth Royall.

Under Senator Royall's measure, a $2 billion bond referendum—$1 billion for school facilities and $1 billion for other local construction needs—would have been submitted to the public. Although this proposal was $500 million less than we needed for school construction, I agreed to support it because it offered us a better chance for bipartisan legislative approval.

However, the lieutenant governor withdrew his support of Senator Royall's bill three weeks ago to advance his own financing plan, using a dubious combination of revenue sources over a ten-year period. I believe it's fair to say that this plan has little endorsement.

Subsequent to Lieutenant Governor Jordan's withdrawal of support for the Royall bill, the Senate killed yet a third proposal offered by Representative Billy Watkins and approved by the House to raise the state sales tax one cent over a four-year period to finance public school construction. We had opposed the Watkins bill from the beginning on the valid grounds that no tax increase was needed.

With my proposal remaining in the Senate Finance Committee, and with little support seen for the lieutenant governor's plan—at least in the House—it appears that we have now reached a critical crossroad on the issue of school facility planning. It is at this crossroad that our business and educational leaders—indeed, all North Carolinians—must unite to help us forge a workable agreement.

As governor, I'm willing to try again with our legislative leadership to find a basis of agreement that will start us moving forward, just as we have done on the Basic Education and teacher career ladder programs, to strengthen our public schools with facilities in which we can all take pride. I have personally conveyed this positive approach to the lieutenant governor, the Speaker, Senator Royall, and Representative Watkins.

As to the merits of the proposals that have already been offered, I'm willing to trust the judgment of our citizens to make an informed decision. Notwithstanding my concerns about the plans that have been put forward as alternatives to my own, when it comes down to the finish line I believe the people of North Carolina will make the right choice.

What I oppose, and oppose strongly, is the withholding of that constitutional right from the people of North Carolina by the General Assembly's leadership. I do not believe this is what a majority of our legislators desire. Most of our legislators want to do what is in the best interest of North Carolina and its people. It's only when partisan considerations get in the way of decision making that we find ourselves unable to resolve pressing issues.

Today, I want to ask each of you to again bring your considerable influence to bear upon the members of the legislature to put this matter to a public referendum and to urge your friends and associates in business and industry to do the same. Our arrival at this critical crossroad in education's history presents us with one of the greatest opportunities ever granted to the leadership of North Carolina, perhaps the greatest opportunity since the turn of this century.

There is precious little time remaining, but there is still enough time if we work hard, to emerge before adjournment of this session with a victory for our future generations—those generations of North Carolinians that will be called upon to preserve the proud heritage of our state. We owe these generations this legacy.

Thus far, I've concentrated on a single issue that remains to be resolved, and which I hope and trust will be resolved successfully within the coming weeks. I now want to turn my attention to some other major areas of legislation in which we have been quite successful.

Emergency Prison Facility Legislation

For more than a decade prior to 1985, North Carolina had been moving toward a crisis in prison facilities and the threatened takeover of our corrections system by the federal government. It was a crisis that had been building for the lack of attention and adequate capital funding. This no longer is the case.

In March of 1985 we developed a comprehensive plan, titled, "Corrections at the Crossroads: Plan for the Future." This was a ten-year plan with both short-and long-term goals and objectives. First, the plan set out the ABCs of what we needed to address: (a) the expansion of existing prisons, (b) construction of new prisons, and (c) a private prison contract designed to help us operate more prisons more efficiently and effectively. Second, it recognized that imprisonment is not the only form of punishment and sought to strengthen community-based punishment for probation offenders.

Early on in the administration, the General Assembly joined with me to appropriate some $52 million for prison improvements. At the same time, our legislators also placed some major obstacles in the way of using these funds to achieve timely and appropriate construction. Of that amount, a total of $12 million was appropriated to bring one area, the South Piedmont area, of prisons into compliance with a federal court consent decree. Since that time, we have been commended by the Fourth Circuit Court "for commendable progress towards accomplishing the goals of the consent decree."

In addition, the General Assembly last year appropriated an additional $29.6 million to add to or modify sixteen facilities across the state. Legislation also was enacted to provide eighty-four additional probation-parole officers, fifty intensive supervision probation-parole teams, and the establishment of two new pilot programs: (1) enhanced house arrest using electronic surveillance, and (2) a pilot community-based punishment, treatment, and restitution program.

This year, the General Assembly ratified legislation creating an Emergency Prison Facilities Development Program to be administered by the Office of State Budget and Management with the assistance of outside professional consultants. The purpose of this program is to expedite construction of prison facilities. With the enactment of this legislation, the administration scored a major victory. Together with the transfer of $14.2 million of the 1986 appropriation to the Emergency Prison Facilities plan, the General Assembly also ratified my request for an additional $15.1 million of new construction money.[1]

The second integral part of this emergency legislation was the enactment of House Bill 48, which places a cap on our prison population. Again, this bill represented a cooperative effort by my office, the attorney general, the secretary of correction, and the General Assembly. Ratified in March, this legislation mandates that when the prison population remains above 97 percent of 18,000 inmates (17,460) for fifteen consecutive days, the secretary of correction must notify me, and, in turn, I must notify the Parole Commission. At this point of notification, the Parole Commission must parole enough prisoners to reduce the number of inmates to 96 percent of 18,000 (17,240) within sixty days. From the date of notification until the prison population is reduced to achieve the cap at 17,240 inmates, the secretary of correction also is prevented from accepting misdemeanants serving sentences from 30 to 180 days, and he is given the authority to return prisoners serving these short sentences to local confinement facilities.[2]

Unemployment Insurance Reserve Fund

Another success that we have achieved during the current session is the adoption of legislation permitting the state to establish, for the first time ever, an independent state unemployment insurance reserve fund. In effect, this legislation reduces by $50 million annually the amount of unemployment insurance taxes paid by employers and, as a result, gives North Carolina's economy an immediate $50 [million] shot in the arm.

Five years ago, this tax was increased by the General Assembly to add more money to a federal unemployment reserve account that had, during the recession, declined to approximately $300 million. In the intervening years, the fund had recovered to a healthy $1.1 billion, and the federal government was getting the benefit of interest earned on that balance. By creating the independent state unemployment reserve fund, this interest will now accrue to the benefit of the state and will help provide additional funding of training and retraining programs for displaced workers, including those who are displaced in our agricultural sector. As the fund grows in future years, by the infusion of new money, North Carolina will be able to expand these programs to meet the emerging needs of business and industry for higher-order skills. I suggest that this training and retraining is vital to preserving our competitive edge in a world market and will enable us to continue our impressive record of economic growth.

Defeat of Comparative Fault Legislation

I am pleased to report that the members of the General Assembly, at the urging of myself and others, closed ranks to defeat legislation that would have established a comparative fault liability system in North Carolina, incorporating among its provisions joint and several liability. Under this principle, a victim of injury would be allowed to collect all court-awarded damages from a single defendant, although others also were at fault.

Comparative fault, without joint and several liability, apportions damages among defendants according to the extent that each defendant contributes to the injury. Enacted in that form, the legislation would have been fair to both plaintiffs and defendants.

The Senate version of the bill, amended to eliminate joint and several liability, was approved in March by a vote of 37-10. However, the House later stripped away the amendment. As a result, the House version would not only have increased the number of liability suits brought in our state, but also have increased liability insurance rates by allowing defendants to collect damages from the best-insured defendant.

In recent years, liability insurance rates have become burdensome, and often unbearable, as a result of excessive litigation. Granted that our current system of contributory negligence may need reform, the House bill was not the way to bring it about responsibly and fairly. On that basis, I opposed and worked against its enactment.[3]

Funding of State Construction[4]

North Carolina's state building program is big business. Our state currently owns more than 10,000 buildings, embracing more than 71 million square feet of floor space. These buildings represent an investment in excess of $5 billion. Yet, many of our buildings need to be replaced.

To meet this need, my budget for the next biennium recommends the expenditure of $436 million for capital improvements. These projects include, but are not limited to, a new $6 million Museum of Natural Science, an $8 million Museum of History, and replacement of our Revenue Building at a cost of $20.3 million. Also incorporated into this budget recommendation is a $45 million judicial complex, $6.3 million for renovation of the Education Building, and approximately $36 million in improvements to our state ports. This is only a partial listing.[5] I have already reviewed for you separately our needs in the Department of Correction.

We now have in place a basically sound system of administering and managing these construction funds. But although it is a sound system in most respects, it still has some faults. Perhaps its biggest fault lies in its inability to function expediently. In order to correct this problem, I created by executive order last March a State Building Commission, under the jurisdiction of the Department of Administration, and composed of twelve professionals representing the various disciplines, professions, industries, and agencies involved in state construction.[6]

This step was certainly not all that we needed to do to speed up our construction program, but it was a major accomplishment over what had been done by previous administrations. It may have followed many years of too little improvement, but it also represented a commitment to do more than had ever been done before by any governor. Regretfully, I must report to you that my executive order of March has been nullified by legislation that creates a State Building Commission which further erodes the executive branch of government of its constitutional authority to operate state government and vests in the legislative branch majority control over its appointees.[7]

Curbing Abuses of Legislative Power

This brings me to two remaining constitutional questions: veto power for the governor and governance of our state education system.

We were defeated again this year, for the second time, in our efforts to place executive veto power before the people by referendum. For 211 consecutive years, the General Assembly of this state has refused to allow the people to decide whether our governor should have the same power that is granted to all of the governors in our remaining forty-nine states and which the founding fathers placed in the United

States Constitution to strike a balance between our national executive and legislative branches of government.

At issue is not whether the governor should have this authority, but whether the people should have the right to decide the issue by public vote. There exists in North Carolina at the present time overwhelming editorial and public opinion on the side of the people. Ignoring this widespread support, the General Assembly continues to let North Carolina remain the only state in America where the people have not been given the opportunity to speak on the issue. We must continue to work to bring this question to a referendum, not just for this governor but for all future governors of North Carolina.

Also defeated this year was a proposal which would have allowed the people of North Carolina to decide, by referendum, whether the superintendent of public instruction should become an appointed, rather than elected, official and would have vested in the State Board of Education the power of appointment. Contributing to this defeat, of course, was the opposition presented by the Council of State, which favored the present method of public election.

There was strong editorial support of this measure, and it also was endorsed by the lieutenant governor and passed in the state Senate. It also had my support, provided that the governor's power to appoint a majority of the Board of Education was not weakened. However, it was defeated by the House, thus continuing the practice of withholding from the public its right to amend their constitution.[8]

Economic Development Issues

Shortly after my appointment of Claude Pope as secretary of commerce to replace Howard Haworth, I proposed a number of initiatives to broaden and strengthen the financial mechanisms available to business and industry, particularly to small business firms and entrepreneurs. These proposals sought to avoid picking winners by doling our public dollars to finance new and expanded economic growth. Several of these mechanisms requiring legislative approval have already been ratified by the General Assembly.

I am pleased that the House and Senate have already approved measures to create a State Certified Development Corporation, extending SBA financing to all of our 100 counties, and that legislation has been enacted that will permit the pooling of industrial revenue bonds. At the same time, we are forging ahead with steps to increase the availability of venture capital. We believe these and other steps we are taking will encourage more entrepreneurial effort and small business growth throughout the state, especially in rural areas.

Last year, North Carolina continued to enjoy dynamic economic growth. We ended 1987 with $5.2 [b]illion of investment in new and expanded facilities, creating 85,000 new jobs. For the second straight year more than 3 million North Carolinians held full-time jobs. Unemployment continued to decline to an annual average of 5.3 percent, the lowest in the Southeast and the third lowest among the eleven largest states in the nation.

Growth was robust in both the manufacturing and nonmanufacturing sectors of the economy in 1987, and we believe my recommendations to strengthen our programs in the Department of Commerce will enable this robust growth to continue in the year ahead. I have proposed funding of a reverse foreign investment office in Tokyo and the establishment of foreign trade offices in Hong Kong and South Korea.

Here in North Carolina, I have recommended increasing the number of Commerce Department regional offices from six to seven, with a new office in northeastern North Carolina. Funding also has been recommended to strengthen the staffing of each office with two development specialists and a secretary in each.

In 1985 we accomplished the largest tax cut in North Carolina's history, reducing both inventory and intangibles taxes. We did not get all of the tax relief we asked for, but our accomplishments were historic and significant. In my supplementary budget request, which has been submitted to the current session of the General Assembly, I have requested that the intangibles tax be reduced further by some $40 million. It appears that revenue growth will permit us to make this additional cut without affecting adversely my budget requests for the next biennium.

Some of you may remember that my 1985 tax-relief proposal—the elimination of inventory and intangibles taxes altogether—was received by the General Assembly with predictions that cutting taxes would weaken the state's fiscal posture. However, since 1985, tax collections have grown by almost $1 billion. This should prove that the elimination of strategic anti-job taxes, both of which place us at a competitive disadvantage in attracting new business investment, benefits both the state and its overall economy.

Miscellaneous Legislation

We are continuing to work to strengthen funding for new and better highways and roads, and to get the enactment of legislation that will allow local governments to protect rights of way for future arterial highways. With more than 78,000 milles of state-maintained roads and highways, North Carolina has the largest and best system in America. My intentions are to maintain this proud reputation.

Additional budget requests made to the General Assembly include $40 million annual[ly] for the next biennium to build new and improved water and sewer facilities. Federal funding will supplement this money to the extent that $60 million annually will be available to establish a revolving loan fund from which cities and counties can borrow to meet their water and sewer needs.

Still pending in the General Assembly are some proposals to strengthen the state's DWI laws; a request for 100 additional Highway Patrolmen; and a measure which would strengthen funding for high-technology research at our major research-oriented universities.

Time does not permit me to review these and other measures now awaiting action by the General Assembly. This overview has touched on only some of the major issues and to provide a status report on them. If there are any questions, I will be happy to answer them.

---

[1]"An Act to Create an Emergency Prison Facilities Development Program and an Emergency Prison Facilities Fund to Pay for the Same" was ratified March 6, 1987. *N.C. Session Laws, 1987*, I, c. 3.

[2]"An Act to Provide for the Stabilization of the Prison Population" was ratified March 11, 1987. *N.C. Session Laws, 1987*, I, c. 7.

[3]S.B. 65, "A Bill to Adopt a Comparative Fault System and Make it Inapplicable to State Torts and to Abolish Joint and Several Liability," passed the Senate on March 25, 1987, and was sent to the House. The House Judiciary Committee rejected the Senate-approved bill, replacing it with a substitute measure that did not survive a second reading. *N.C. House Journal, 1987*, 161, 941, 958; *N.C. Senate Journal, 1987*, 48, 74, 134, 137, 142.

[4]Much of the information contained in this section appeared in the speech Martin delivered to the State Building Construction Conference, Raleigh, March 23, 1987.

[5]Governor Martin suggested spending $435.6 million on capital improvements for the 1987-1989 period. The figure given in the speech for the Museum of Natural Science probably was a typographical error; he actually recommended spending $14.6 million on the project over the coming biennium. Martin's capital improvements proposals were described briefly in *North Carolina State Budget, 1987-89: Summary of Recommendations*, 75-80. For a list of the $413 million in capital improvements approved by the General Assembly, see *Post-Legislative Budget Summary, 1987-1989*, 159-177.

[6]Executive Order Number 42, establishing the State Building Commission, was signed March 23, 1987. *N.C. Session Laws, 1987*, II, 2357-2361.

[7]"An Act to Create the State Building Commission," ratified April 14, 1987, abolished the entity of the same name that Martin organized under Executive Order Number 42. *N.C. Session Laws, 1987*, I, c. 71.

[8]Martin was referring to S.B. 149, previously identified in "State of the State," February 16, 1987, footnote 23, page 41.

INTERSTATE 40 RIBBON-CUTTING

DURHAM COUNTY, JULY 1, 1987

[Speaking of Interstate 40 at a Winston-Salem press conference, November 9, 1987, Martin called the completion of the thoroughfare "the state's number-one highway priority. It is on schedule, and we will keep it on schedule—the first major highway project in North Carolina to be built from start to finish without interruption." He also reminded listeners that "I-40 was the only highway commitment" he made "during the 1984 campaign, but it is not the only strategic corridor we need; and it has not been my only highway priority as governor."
The following remarks were delivered at the opening of the 7.7-mile segment of Interstate 40 that connected N.C. 55 with U.S. 15-501.]

It is indeed a pleasure, a special and significant pleasure, to be here with you today. As I stand here, this evening, it is difficult in some respects to decide what should be said. There are so many things that can be, and should be, mentioned about this road.

But, it's not hard to know where to begin. The first thing we must do is remember and recognize those people who, through dedication, perseverance, and perspiration, made it possible for us to be here today.

Many of you know this project was originally not scheduled to be completed before December of this year. Then we learned that the U.S. Olympic Festival was coming to North Carolina. Everyone who travels Highway 54 can tell you that the additional traffic generated by the festival would have done nothing but turn a bad dream into a genuine nightmare. So, in effect, the Olympic Festival was the straw that broke the camel's back. Something had to be done. That something was the completion of Interstate 40, and we said we would do it.

The fact that we are here, today, to open this road and dedicate it to public use, offers a textbook example of what can happen when people determine that they are going to succeed. And, of course, it offers hard-to-dispute evidence of two things: the existence of good luck and the power of prayer. But more than anything else, the fact that we are gathered here, today, is a testimonial to those who labored to bring us to this point. I would like to ask that everyone who worked on this project please stand, and allow us to thank you for a job well done. [Governor leads applause.]

The 7.7-mile section of Interstate 40 that we are opening, today, will mean many things to many people. Obviously, starting tomorrow morning, it will begin to benefit the commuters who travel to and from Chapel Hill everyday. Later this month, it will make a world of difference to the U.S. Olympic Festival. In the near future, it will do much to allow Durham and Orange counties to grow and prosper; and it will truly unite the Triangle.

History will look back on today and call it a turning point. The significance of this project begins with the road itself, but it certainly doesn't end there. Beyond the era of convenience ushered in by this highway, there will be continuing contributions in the form of increased prosperity and progress.

This section of Interstate 40 has a significance that extends in other directions. It stands for something bigger than itself. Obviously, it represents our commitment—my commitment—to the completion of I-40. We are going to build this road, and the work is under way to prove it. Interstate 40 is now under construction all the way to Wilmington. A new segment of it is being built around Winston-Salem. And, you will notice that construction continues where this project ends: We will make another ceremonial appearance down the road next year, when I-40 and I-85 are tied together at Hillsborough.

But the section of road that is being opened today is representative of more than Interstate 40. It is part of our broad and deep commitment to improving North Carolina transportation. Beyond the Interstate system, we have work under way on a number of arterial routes. Highways such as U.S. 17, 25, 70, 64, 264, 74, 321, 421—are vitally important; and major improvement projects are under way on all those roads, along with work on many other highways. Also, construction is in progress on major urban projects across the state.

The Transportation Improvement Program has two coequal goals: to ease traffic congestion where we are being overwhelmed by growth, and to build roads where they are needed to pull development into an area. We are also building more than roads; we are building public confidence through a Transportation Improvement Program that keeps its promises.

One of the things that makes Interstate 40 special is the fact that it speaks to a number of the things that are important to us. It represents a promise kept. It represents traffic congestion relief here in the Triangle and in other urban areas, and it represents the hope for economic growth in many rural areas across North Carolina. Those are the things that make this ceremony important. Those are the reasons that I'm proud to be here.

We are witness to one of the most significant highway openings to occur in a long time. This is something the Triangle and the rest of our state will remember, but it won't be remembered for what we said; it will be remembered for what this project did, and that is as it should be. Thank you very much for being here on this special evening in July. I hope you will join me in the motorcade that opens this valuable road to public use.

TESTIMONY BEFORE U.S. HOUSE COMMITTEE ON WAYS AND MEANS

WASHINGTON, D.C., JULY 15, 1987

[Working to draft a budget bill in 1987, members of Congress investigated various revenue-generating mechanisms to reduce the federal deficit. Some lawmakers advocated doubling the excise tax on cigarettes as a partial remedy for the nation's fiscal ills; an increase to 32 cents per pack, they asserted, would produce at least $3 billion annually. However, as the year closed and the Omnibus Budget Reconciliation Act became law, the 16-cent-per-pack rate remained unchanged. Occupational taxes on tobacco product manufacturers went up. *Congressional Quarterly Almanac, 1987,* 619; *News and Observer,* November 13, 1987; P.L. 100-203, "Omnibus Budget Reconciliation Act of 1987" (short title), *United States Statutes at Large,* Act of December 22, 1987, 101 Stat. 1330-449 to 1330-450.]

The doubling of the cigarette excise tax in 1983 has had an adverse effect on the economy of North Carolina. Its effects have been well documented as to the loss in sales, jobs, and income of our historically number-one commodity: tobacco. The proposed doubling, again in 1987, of the excise tax from 16 cents to 32 cents would have a devastating economic effect. It is anticipated, based on previous experience, that North Carolina would lose 3,614 jobs and over $95.6 million in income and benefits in the tobacco industry. In addition, North Carolina would lose some $7.1 million in state and local tax revenues. North Carolina cannot afford to lose these jobs as the source of income during these days of severe economic stress in agriculture.

North Carolina last year produced over two thirds of the flue-cured tobacco grown in the United States—over 430 million pounds. Thousands of North Carolinians depend on tobacco directly or indirectly for their livelihood. The state grows flue-cured tobacco leaf in the piedmont and coastal regions and also grows burley tobacco in the western mountain counties. The golden leaf is grown on approximately 21,000 farms in North Carolina and in 91 of North Carolina's 100 counties. Cash receipts from tobacco amounted to over $681 million in 1986. Slightly over 20 percent of cash receipts from all crops and all farm commodities came from tobacco.

At the other end of the spectrum, cigarette manufacturers in North

Carolina produced over 18.872 billion packs of cigarettes in 1986. That's about 57.4 percent of all the cigarettes manufactured in the United States. North Carolina is the largest tobacco manufacturing state in the nation.

Other sectors of the North Carolina economy also benefit from the strength of the state's tobacco industry. There are tobacco auction markets in more than thirty counties in the state. Tobacco offers a variety of other support industries: the largest cigarette paper factory in the nation, chemical and plastic suppliers, packaging and container suppliers, cigarette filter producers, fertilizer and farm equipment suppliers, transportation industries, commercial printing, and advertising in the media. All these industries produce important revenues for North Carolina and other states. Every business must earn a profit if it is to grow or even survive. If North Carolina's tobacco agriculture is successful, it not only benefits the farmer but everyone. It carries its part of the tax load; it provides more and better jobs. If North Carolina's tobacco agriculture is unsuccessful, it provides fewer and fewer jobs and less opportunities for all.

The tobacco farmer has not shared in the economic recovery that most of the nation has experienced in the past few years. Not only has he faced increased foreign competition, but also a decline in domestic consumption due, in part, to the doubling of the excise tax in 1982. The entire tobacco program was in jeopardy of collapse prior to the approval, by Congress, of the Tobacco Reform Act of 1985.[1] These changes, as explained to you by Mr. Fred Bond,[2] managing director of the Flue-Cured Cooperative Stabilization Corporation, earlier in these hearings, brought some degree of stability to the program and allowed many of our tobacco farmers to realize a profit for the first time in several years. Doubling the excise tax, with the resulting reduction in consumption, could very well cause many of our tobacco farmers to go out of business.

A staff working paper published by the Congressional Budget Office in January, 1987, stated that "an increase in the excise tax on tobacco would be the most regressive of all the tax measures considered."[3] As a percent of income, the tobacco excise tax is twenty-seven times higher for low-income (under $10,000) families than for high-income (over $200,000) families.

The tobacco grower would be unfairly disadvantaged by congressional action to raise the discriminatory tax on the product on which the grower depends for his livelihood. In 1984, the Tobacco Institute reported that cigarette taxes collected at federal, state, and local levels of government amounted to $9.3 billion, while U.S. tobacco farmers who produced the domestic leaf for these cigarettes received only $1.45 billion. In other words, cigarette excise taxes are already more than six times the farm value of domestic tobacco used in cigarettes. This makes cigarettes the most heavily taxed consumer commodity in the United States today.

I hope that the tobacco grower will not be forgotten by my former colleagues when they deal with the future of the cigarette excise tax. To increase the cigarette excise tax above the current 16 cents per pack would be unfair, unreasonable, and unjustified.

---

[1]The governor probably was referring to P.L. 99-272, Title I, Subtitle B, *United States Statutes at Large*, 100 Stat. 83-100; see also *Congressional Quarterly Almanac, 1985,* 539, *1986,* 304-305.

[2]Fred G. Bond (1929-   ), born in Elbert County, Georgia; resident of Cary; B.S., University of Georgia, 1949. Formerly employed by Georgia Agricultural Extension Service; became affiliated with Flue-Cured Tobacco Cooperative Stabilization Corp., 1952, served as general manager/secretary-treasurer, 1968-1987, and chief executive officer/secretary-treasurer, since 1987; former town councilman, mayor, of Cary. Lisa J. Eddington, assistant to Fred G. Bond, to Jan-Michael Poff, September 8, 1988.

[3]"Distributional Effects of an Increase in Selected Federal Excise Taxes: Staff Working Paper" ([Washington, D.C.]: Congress of the United States, Congressional Budget Office, January, 1987), 2; the report used the phrase "tax increases considered" rather than "tax measures considered."

BIOTECHNOLOGY TEACHERS' PROGRAM

RESEARCH TRIANGLE PARK, JULY 21, 1987

Our mutual honor, this morning, is to be in the company of thirty-one distinguished high school teachers who, in a short time, will become our resident teaching experts in one of the most advanced disciplines in the entire realm of high technology. You have to understand how difficult it is for a former chemistry professor to grant that accolade to biology [instructors].

They will also become our best hope in the ongoing challenge to master and teach our schoolchildren the global and strategic importance of biotechnology. It is my pleasure to be able to recognize your past accomplishments and to challenge you for the three years of work that lie ahead.

The Secondary Education Project represents the very best of North Carolina education in the 1980s. I'm sure that just as your work in the past brought you this recognition—indeed, this opportunity—you teachers will become future experts on recombinant DNA research. It is our hope that, in turn, you will help North Carolina's students develop the skills and know-how so critical to keeping up with this ever-expanding realm of science.

This project reflects positively on North Carolina, mirroring our progressive approach to education. The commitment to this project from the North Carolina Biotechnology Center gives me another opportunity to salute the center's tradition of excellence. The Burroughs Wellcome Fund, as the primary benefactor, deserves sincere thanks for supporting this state and its future through this major commitment. To the officials of Carolina Biological Supply, a longtime partner in the business partnership of biology and schools: Thank you for sponsoring this recognition luncheon. These teachers deserve it. Most especially, [I want to] thank Cold Spring Harbor Laboratory for conducting the laboratory workshop.

The strength of this program rests in its design. By starting with a core group of the state's best and brightest teachers, we send out ripples that, in the next three years, will touch 900 teachers and 40,000 students. Certainly, as the people here at the Biotechnology Center know, the timing of this effort is critical. We simply cannot afford to slip behind in this effort to prepare our best minds. My challenge to you, the participants, is to keep forever in mind the importance of the tremendous influence you will have at public schools across North Carolina.

And what a group of teachers we have! From east to west, from north to south, from rural to metropolitan, this group of educators touches almost every geographic region of this united state. The potential for success is built in. But, as you teachers know, that has not always been the case for teachers in the scientific disciplines.

Most high school biology teachers received their education before major advances in the field reached college classrooms. An obvious example is the first recombinant DNA pharmaceutical product, human insulin. It was not approved for use until 1982. The first plant gene expression in a plant of a different species was not achieved until 1983.

These remarkable advances have unfolded within a very short time frame, but it is disturbing when we look at how far behind we lag in teaching the importance of these developments to our students. A research director at a medical diagnostics company here in the Research Triangle Park estimates that 80 percent of all references cited in the scientific literature are less than seven years old. Half of those references are less than three years old. Now ask yourself: Would that research show up, even as a passing reference, in even the most current editions of a high school biology textbook?

As teachers in this discipline, you know personally how frustrating these problems can be. What about lesson plans or the basic skills needed to tackle a subject such as genetic engineering? Unfortunately, the truth is, we have not been able to prepare for these classroom challenges.

We all know the result. When we cannot challenge our students with interesting, current information, we lose the attention of our most gifted. Then the ripple effect goes the other way. They do not become the scientists, researchers, and medical pioneers we so desperately need. This innovative Secondary Education Project offers us a rare opportunity to combat those problems and to build and develop the talent that is among us.

The success of this project, however, depends on the commitment of you, the teachers. When you begin to acquire a mastery of the complexities of gene-splicing research, remember that your ultimate goal will be to develop skills to pass your knowledge on to other teachers. The fact that you are here, of course, reflects an intelligence and an energy that sets you apart from your colleagues. But remember that the overall success of this program depends on how well your colleagues benefit from your efforts. In many respects, it all hinges on your willingness to work hard and bring those results back to the public schools in North Carolina.

I like to think of it this way: The excitement of the technical experience you are about to absorb, coupled with your own experience and talent as our best teachers, should provide this state with a force every bit as dramatic as the gene-splicing experiments you will be witnessing. This is a giant first step in our ongoing efforts to strengthen our public schools by constantly reevaluating and improving curricula. Think of the impact you will have had by 1990, a scant three years away, when the training and materials you help develop will have reached 1,200 high school biology teachers.

The key, I think, is the shared effect of what you pass on. You can touch the minds of many future scientists now attending our public schools. Your opportunity is as great as your challenge.

TALKING POINTS FOR NORTH CAROLINA WILDLIFE
FEDERATION BOARD OF DIRECTORS MEETING

RALEIGH, JULY 25, 1987

—Oregon Inlet and the access it provides to the ocean and sounds is a matter of environmental, recreational, economic, and social importance to the people of North Carolina.

—If the Army Corps of Engineers' cost-benefit analysis is favorable, the state of North Carolina is committed to the Oregon Inlet stabilization project. The project has the backing of the administration and the legislative leadership. Interior Secretary Hodel[1] has been told that North Carolina is prepared to pick up $20 to $30 million in costs related to the project.

—The project has the commitment from the Oregon Inlet Waterway Commission, which has hired former congressman Bill Carney to lobby in Washington on their behalf.[2]

—The construction of jetties will preserve a number of recreational and commercial areas that are currently at risk. This includes the Cape Hatteras National Seashore Park and Wildlife Refuge.

—Dredging has proven to be ineffective and may add to the erosion problem.

—The stabilization of the Oregon Inlet could have an annual impact of $150 million on North Carolina's economy. Without it, the commercial fleet has dwindled to a fraction of what it once was. Stabilization would also allow North Carolina recreational and commercial fishermen to reap the benefits currently enjoyed by foreign factory ships working off our coast.

—By stabilizing the inlet, the federal government would be living up to its promise to preserve the lifestyles of the region—promises that were made when the state worked with the federal government toward the establishment of the national seashore. Nine people have lost their lives due to conditions at the inlet since this project was first authorized by Congress in 1970.

—The state is asking the support of the North Carolina Wildlife Federation for this project which would so greatly benefit the state, its people, and its environment.

---

[1]Donald Paul Hodel (1935-   ), born in Portland, Oregon; B.A., Harvard University, 1957; J.D., University of Oregon, 1960. Attorney; chairman, Oregon Republican State Central Committee, 1966-1967; deputy administrator, 1969-1972, administrator, 1972-1977, Bonneville Power Administration; president, National Electric Reliability Council,

1978-1980, and of Hodel Associates, Inc., 1978-1981; undersecretary, 1981-1982, appointed secretary, 1985, U.S. Department of Interior; secretary, U.S. Department of Energy, 1982-1985. *Who's Who in America, 1986-1987,* I, 1301.

²William Carney (1942-   ), born in Brooklyn; resident of Hauppauge, New York; attended Florida State University; U.S. Army, 1961-1964. Heavy equipment salesman, 1972-1976; member, Suffolk County, N.Y., legislature, 1976-1979; member, U.S. House of Representatives, 1979-1987; Republican. *Biographical Directory of Congress,* 745; *New York Times,* May 23, June 1, 1986.

VIRGINIA DARE BIRTHDAY CELEBRATION— QUADRICENTENNIAL FINALE

Manteo, August 18, 1987

It is indeed a high honor to have the opportunity to speak on the occasion of Virginia Dare's 400th birthday. What other governor has ever helped celebrate the 400th anniversary of the birth of the first child born to English parents, in the New World, and the anniversary of the beginning of our nation?

We have just heard President Reagan remind us of the spirit of adventure that brought these colonists to Roanoke Island 400 years ago.[1] It is to that indomitable spirit we pay homage today.

This observance of Virginia Dare's birthday marks the end of a three-year observance of our quadricentennial, an extraordinary undertaking by any measure. Secretary (Patric) Dorsey, Mr. (Lindsay) Warren,[2] and Mr. (John) Neville,[3] I want to take this opportunity to thank you, America's Four Hundredth Anniversary Committee, and the hundreds of staff and volunteers who helped put this incredibly complex enterprise together. We are all grateful, I am sure, for your making it possible for us to witness, however distantly in time, such an important part [of] the state's and the nation's history.

We in North Carolina are blessed with a rich and unique history, which had its start with the first English attempt to colonize the New World, on Roanoke Island, in 1585. Our forebears were men and women of adventure and daring, looking to invent a new future out of harsh conditions and great uncertainty. They epitomize the straining reach of humanity to better itself.

Here is what President Franklin Delano Roosevelt said, on Roanoke Island, fifty years ago: "We do not know the fate of Virginia Dare or the Lost Colony. We do know, however, that the story of America is largely a record of adventure. . . . These people who landed on your island had the courage to do what their countrymen had not done before. Our heritage is the fruition of their brave endeavor."[4]

In a few minutes we will unveil a plaque that reads: "Virginia Dare—An infant born August 18, 1587, at Roanoke Island, was the first English child born in the New World. The following Sunday, 'because this child was the first Christian born in Virginia, she was named Virginia.'"[5]

It is entirely fitting that we look back not only with gratitude and admiration on this occasion, the celebration of our 400th anniversary, but that we use this occasion as an historic milestone from which to consider what better futures we might invent for present and future generations of North Carolinians; that we carry on in the adventure-some spirit of those who first settled this land. In this period of rapid change and increased economic competition, we dare not do less. With all our natural competitive rivalries, we must remind each other that there is no limit to what we can achieve if we have the courage of these early settlers and work together as one united state. We can cause North Carolina to be first in so many good ways, if only we will put North Carolina first.

Although much is shrouded in mystery, many lessons can be learned from the Lost Colony; and the most important lesson is that a nation's greatest strength is in its people—and the wisest investment any state can make is in its people. As we build toward the future in North Carolina, this must be an article not only of faith, it must be our sacred pledge. What better place to rededicate ourselves than here at this shrine of hope and courage, at this glorious monument to visions of a better, more fulfilling life? On what better note can we possibly conclude America's 400th anniversary celebration?

Have courage. Work together in unity. Keep faith in the future.

---

[1]Reagan sent a videotaped message. *News and Observer*, August 19, 1987.

[2]Lindsay Carter Warren, Jr., (1924-   ), born in Washington, North Carolina; B.S., 1948, J.D., 1951, University of North Carolina at Chapel Hill; U.S. Coast Guard, 1943-1946. Attorney in Goldsboro; state Senate member, 1963-1969, chairman, Courts and Judicial Districts Committee, 1965-1968, and of Appropriations Committee, 1969; member, chairman, North Carolina Courts Commission, 1963-1969, and of America's Four Hundredth Anniversary Committee, 1980-1987; president, North Carolina Bar Assn., 1969-1970; Democrat. Lindsay Carter Warren, Jr., to Jan-Michael Poff, June 21, 1990.

[3]John Davenport Neville (1942-   ), born in Nash County; resident of Richmond, Virginia; A.B., 1964, M.A., 1967, University of North Carolina at Chapel Hill; Ph.D., Vanderbilt University, 1976; M.S.L.S. candidate, Catholic University of America. History instructor, East Carolina University, 1967-1969; editor, Virginia Colonial Records Project, Virginia State Library and Archives, 1973-1979; executive director, America's Four Hundredth Anniversary Committee, North Carolina Department of Cultural Resources, 1979-1988; director, Tercentenary Observance, College of William and Mary, 1988-1990. John Davenport Neville to Jan-Michael Poff, May 22, 1990.

[4]"We do not know the fate of Virginia Dare or the First Colony. We do know, however, that the story of America is largely a record of that spirit of adventure. . . . These people who landed on your island had courage to do what their countrymen had not done before. Our heritage is the fruition of their brave endeavor." Franklin Delano Roosevelt, quoted in *The Lost Colony Souvenir and Program, 350th Anniversary Celebration, 1587-1937* (Manteo: Roanoke Island Historical Association, Inc., [1937]), 6.

Martin's speechwriter might have changed Roosevelt's "First Colony" to "Lost Colony" for purposes of historical accuracy. The expedition establishing the first Roanoke colony, known also as the Ralph Lane colony, reached the island on August 17, 1585. The entire settlement departed for England in 1586. Lefler and Newsome, *North Carolina*, 7-10.

[5]The part of the quotation explaining the rationale behind the naming of Virginia Dare is from "John White's Narrative of the 1587 Virginia Voyage," in Quinn, *First Colonists*, 102. White was Dare's grandfather and governor of the colony.

TOLL FELLOWSHIP CONFERENCE KEYNOTE ADDRESS

LEXINGTON, KENTUCKY, AUGUST 30, 1987

Let's start with an overriding truth: Because the federal government is withdrawing from, or cutting back on, its involvement in many program areas, state governments are taking on increased responsibilities. Thus the management of state government and the necessity for leadership looms much larger than ever before. It is essential that we get more for our money—more results, more cost-effective services—but how?

You will recall it was Archimedes who claimed that if you gave him a lever and a place to stand, he could by himself move the world. He was also the one who was seen running naked down the streets of Athens, yelling "Eureka." He had just found how to measure the volume of the king's crown—thus its density, and thence the purity of its gold—while sitting in his tub displacing his bath water.[1]

Well, old Archimedes was much on my mind when thinking about what I might say to you about the management of enterprises such as state governments and your role as leaders. A question that emerged was: Are there any levers, a vital few things, that could move organizations and individuals toward much more innovation and greater performance? The answer is, yes, there are indeed a vital few ideas or practices that can make an enormous difference in the performance of state government in particular and public service institutions in general. Let's try one.

The idea I wish to offer for your consideration might be called "state entrepreneurship." If we, in state government, are to keep pace with the incredible pace of change, we will have to be much more innovative than we are. And to achieve greater innovation will require the careful nurturing of entrepreneurial people.

Entrepreneurship in the state bureaucracy! Many say it can't be done. As the great Italian writer and educator, Giuseppe Borgese, noted about another mission, "It is necessary; therefore, it can be done."[2] Indeed, entrepreneurship, and innovations it generates, may be the only solution to our emerging out of a number of crushing emergencies.

Let's look a moment at the obstacles against entrepreneurship in public service institutions; and here I turn to no less an authority than Peter F. Drucker—*Innovation and Entrepreneurship*—who cites three reasons why it is difficult to have entrepreneurship in public service institutions. "First," says Drucker, "the public-service institution is based on a 'budget' rather than being paid out of results." And Drucker goes on to say "'success' in the public-service institutions is defined" more surely "by getting a larger budget than" by "obtaining results." Thus, innovation becomes very difficult in such a setting. And then Drucker puts his finger on the heart of the matter: "Any attempts to slough off activities or efforts thereby diminishes the public-service institution. (The activities and efforts) cause it to lose status and prestige. Failure cannot be acknowledged. Worse still, the fact that an objective has been attained cannot be admitted."[3]

I don't know about your state, but in North Carolina we have policies that actually lead to the throttling of innovation. One example that comes quickly to mind is paying people on the basis of the number of people they supervise. This one policy alone contributes to the building of empires and the reluctance to streamline operations. It takes little imagination to see what will happen when some bright eyed, bushy-tailed person comes up with an idea for reducing staff— and thereby making the operation more efficient and effective.

"Second," according to Drucker, "the service institution is dependent on a multitude of constituents. . . . A public-service institution has to satisfy everybody; certainly it cannot afford to alienate anyone." He goes on to say: "The moment a service institution starts an activity, it acquires a 'constituency,' which then refuses to have the program abolished or significantly modified. But anything new is controversial. This means that it is opposed without having formed, as yet, a constituency of its own to support it."[4]

All this suggests new approaches to the art of constituency building—or, maybe, rising above constituencies. We had inherited a problem of severely overcrowded prisons. Who is the constituency there? The federal district court, that's who! Yet, we found that four to five years was our normal prison construction time frame. Innovation: We asked the private contractor to oversee all the work.

The third and most important reason Drucker offers for why it is so difficult to have entrepreneurship and innovation in service or budget-based institutions is "that public-service institutions exist . . . to 'do good'. . . ." Well, "if one is 'doing good,' there can be no 'better.' Indeed, failure to attain objectives in the quest for a 'good' only means that efforts need to be redoubled."[5]

Because Drucker's next comment is so cogent, I want to underline it: "This means that (public-service institutions) tend to see their mission as a moral absolute rather than as economic and subject to a cost-benefit calculus."[6] Perhaps that is because constituencies see their needs as moral absolutes.

Nowhere are the words of Drucker more prophetic than in our attempts to deal with the problem of adult literacy. With considerable passion, we say we are going to completely eliminate [il]literacy from the face of the state. Seldom do you hear that this year we are going to help x percent of adults read up to a certain level, or, we are going to help x number of adults get their GED diplomas. I recently met Y. C. James Yen, now 92, who in 1923, six years out of Yale, began a project that soon taught 60 million Chinese coolies to read and write. I asked how he did it, and he said: fifty at a time.[7]

You know, we all get so caught up in the passion of doing something about a terrible problem that we become downright improvident when it comes to allocating money to combat the problem. Let me cite one example of what I'm talking about. I had appointed a distinguished panel to evaluate illiteracy. One of my proposals was that no additional funds be appropriated for Adult Basic Education programs in our community colleges, which covers much more than literacy, until we could get a better picture of what the precise needs are. Naturally, I was severely criticized in a number of editorials for this recommendation. Providence intervened on my behalf, however. Not only did the ABE program not spend all the money allocated to it by the state legislature, ABE monies were actually misspent on other programs. And after all this, guess what? The state agency responsible for the ABE program asked the legislature to give it more money!

But what is most disturbing about the literacy initiative in North Carolina is that we are taking far too little initiative in pushing for innovation in adult literacy programs. At this point, I want to share these thoughts of Drucker: "There is only one way to make innovation attractive to managers: a systematic policy of abandoning whatever is outworn, obsolete, no longer productive, as well as the mistakes and misdirections of effort. Every three years or so, the enterprise must put every product, process, technology . . . , not to mention every internal staff activity, on trial for its life." And continues Drucker, if the response to these examinations is, "Let's make another study," we should ask, "What do we have to do to stop wasting resources on this product, staff activity," et cetera?[8]

Three widely acclaimed literacy programs in our state—the wide use of microcomputers in the PLATO program; the new and extremely effective Adult Basic Literacy Education program; and most recently, the Motheread program, designed to help imprisoned mothers read to their children—were started by outside groups and not by the state agency having the largest literacy program, our public schools.

One of the reasons I created the Governor's Commission on Literacy was to foster a better climate for innovation in adult literacy programs. But after reading Drucker, you know this does not go far enough. At any rate, if we are ever to achieve a significantly higher level of literacy in North Carolina and other states, our programs must be significantly different. Pumping more and more money into failed strategies is not an acceptable approach to the problem.

In approaching the subject of achieving more innovative organizations, Drucker notes that we start with the wrong question. We ask, "How can we overcome the resistance to innovation in the existing organization?" The answer is, we never will because resistance to innovation is endemic to the existing organization itself.

The appropriate question is, "How can we make the organization receptive to innovation, want innovation, reach for it, work for it?" This question I leave with you—repeat—how can we make the organization receptive to innovation, want innovation, reach for it, work for it?

As you engage in your studies and deliberations in the coming days, I ask that you keep in mind this simple principle: The shape of any liquid container determines the shape of the contents in it. Any other conclusion is absurd. Until we are willing to change the shape of our organizations, it logically follows, the behavior in our organizations will be shaped by their containing structures. Innovation will take place at a petty pace, if at all.

The traditional approach to achieving better results is to invest in staff development. Last year in North Carolina, we had seventy-five people graduate from a two-and-a-half-year program to improve their managerial skills. Then many went back into a structure that actively or passively resists their newly acquired skills. These graduates have two choices: They can become dysfunctional in terms of the ways of the organization, or they can just hunker down and quit trying to do anything differently.

I submit it makes little sense to have staff development that aims at changing the ways things are done, without changing things like policies, procedures, and organizational structure. We need an ecological approach to changing people and organizations. To paraphrase Winston Churchill, "We shape our organizations and afterwards they shape us."[9]

Looking at the ecology of the workplace means that we have to look at all the things that impact on innovativeness. We need, for example, to look closely at how performance is evaluated and how people are rewarded. We need to use performance appraisal for, among other things, evaluating managers on knowing and using sound managerial practices—not on managerial practices that serve merely to maintain and perpetuate the status quo and to consolidate empires, but on practices that lead to greater effectiveness and economy.

Michael Le Bouef recently wrote a book called *The Greatest Management Principle in the World*.[10] You know what the greatest management principle in the world is? The answer: that people are motivated by and respond to what they are rewarded for. The painful truth is that, far too often, our bureaucracies not only do not reward innovative and entrepreneurial behavior, they punish it. You want more home-ownership, give it a tax break. If you want to raise the effectiveness of teachers, offer better pay for better teachers. You want to eliminate waste and inefficiency? Offer a bounty and a promotion to those who find it—unless they also created it!

A Latin poet described human beings as having *rerum novarum cupidus*—love for new things. Just as we are moved to protect neglected species among lower animal forms, we need to protect and honor those of the human species who have this love for new things, the innovators and creators among us. We must see to the care and feeding of the entrepreneurial spirits among us.

Let us conclude with these words by John Diebold: "Unless we succeed in making our institutions work, we need not worry about a grand and sweeping vision."[11] That's something to think about for another day!

---

[1]"Give me where to stand, and I will move the earth," attributed to Archimedes by Pappus of Alexandria, *Collectio*, bk. VIII, prop. 10, sec. 11, quoted in Bartlett, *Familiar Quotations*. Archimedes cried "Eureka, I have found it!" as he discovered the principle of

specific gravity; attributed by Vitruvius Pollio, *De Architectura*, bk. IX, 215, quoted in Bartlett, *Familiar Quotations*, 105.

[2]Giuseppe Antonio Borgese (1882-1952), born in Polizzi Generoso, Sicily; Ph.D., University of Florence, 1903. Educator; author; taught literature, aesthetics, history of criticism at University of Rome, 1910-1917, and University of Milan, 1917-1931; literary and foreign editor, *Corriere della sera*, 1912-1931; chief, Italian Press and Propaganda Bureau, 1917-1918; came to United States, 1931, was naturalized, 1938; instructor at University of California, 1931, New School for Social Research, 1932, Smith College, 1932-1935, and University of Chicago, 1936-1948; cofounder, secretary, Committee to Frame a World Constitution, 1946, and became editor of its publication, *Common Cause*, 1947; returned to Italy, reinstated at University of Milan, 1948. *Current Biography, 1947*, 53-55, *1953*, 84; *Who Was Who in America, 1951-1960*, 91.

[3]The governor quoted from *Innovation and Entrepreneurship* accurately, with the exception of the following passage. Drucker wrote: "And 'success' in the public-service institution is defined by getting a larger budget rather than obtaining results. Any attempt to slough off activities and efforts therefore diminishes the public-service institution. It causes it to lose stature and prestige." Peter F. Drucker, *Innovation and Entrepreneurship: Practice and Principles* (New York: Harper & Row, Publishers, 1985), 179, hereinafter cited as Drucker, *Innovation and Entrepreneurship*.

Peter Ferdinand Drucker (1909-   ), born in Vienna, Austria; resident of California; LL.D., University of Frankfurt, 1931; honorary degrees. Award-winning management expert; economist, London Banking House, 1933-1937; American adviser to British banks, correspondent for British newspapers, 1937-1942; consultant to major U.S. corporations, since 1940; philosophy professor, Bennington College, 1942-1949; professor of management, 1950-1972, management area chairman, 1957-1962, distinguished lecturer, since 1970, New York University; Clarke Professor of Social Sciences, Claremont Graduate School, since 1971; art professor, Pomona College, 1979-1985; author; movie producer. *Who's Who in America, 1988-1989*, I, 827.

[4]"Second, a service institution is dependent on a multitude of constituents. . . . A public-service institution has to satisfy everyone; certainly it cannot afford to alienate anyone.

"The moment a service institution starts an activity, it acquires a 'constituency,' which then refuses to have the program abolished or even significantly modified. But anything new is always controversial. This means that it is opposed by existing constituencies without having formed, as yet, a constituency of its own to support it." Drucker, *Innovation and Entrepreneurship*, 179.

[5]"3. The most important reason, however, is that public-service institutions exist after all to 'do good.' This means that they tend to see their mission as a moral absolute rather than as economic and subject to a cost/benefit calculus. Economics always seek a different allocation of the same resources to obtain a higher yield. Everything economic is therefore relative. In the public-service institution, there is no such thing as a higher yield. If one is 'doing good,' then there is no 'better.' Indeed, failure to attain objectives in the quest for a 'good' only means that efforts need to be redoubled." Drucker, *Innovation and Entrepreneurship*, 179-180.

[6]See footnote 5, above.

[7]Yang-Ch'u James Yen (1894-   ), native of Szechuan province, China; A.B., Yale University, 1918; M.A., Princeton University, 1920; honorary degree. Educator; became executive director, National Association for the Advancement of Mass Education, China, 1924; vice-president, Szechuan Province Planning Commission, 1936-1938; member, 1938, People's Political Council, China's wartime parliament; adviser to Chiang Kai-shek. Yen developed the "Thousand Character" system of learning Chinese, teaching millions of illiterate peasants in his native land to read and write. He and his coworkers subsequently directed their newly educated countrymen in a massive rural rehabilitation campaign against what Yen perceived as China's principal problems: ignorance, poverty, disease, and misgovernment. *Current Biography, 1946*, 670-672.

[8]"1. There is only one way to make innovation attractive to managers: a systematic policy of abandoning whatever is outworn, obsolete, no longer productive, as well as the mistakes, failures, and misdirections of effort. Every three years or so, the enterprise must put every single product, process, technology, market, distributive channel, not to mention every single internal staff activity, on trial for its life. It must ask: Would we *now* go into this product, this market, this distributive channel, this technology *today*? If the answer is 'No,' one does not respond with 'Let's make another study.' One asks, 'What do we have to do to stop wasting resources on this product, this market, this distributive channel, this staff activity?'" Drucker, *Innovation and Entrepreneurship*, 151.

[9]"We shape our buildings; thereafter they shape us." Winston Churchill, *Time* magazine, August 8, 1954, quoted in *Reader's Digest Treasury of Modern Quotations*, 767.

[10]Michael LeBouef, *The Greatest Management Principle in the World* (New York: G. P. Putnam's Sons, 1985).

[11]John Theurer Diebold (1926-   ), born in Weehawken, New Jersey; B.S., United States Merchant Marine Academy, 1946; B.A., Swarthmore College, 1949; M.B.A., Harvard University, 1951; honorary degrees; served in U.S. Naval Reserve during World War II. Management consultant; known as "the elder statesman of automation"; founder, 1954, president, board chairman, Diebold Group, Inc.; founder, 1967, chairman, John Diebold, Inc.; author. *Current Biography, 1967,* 95-97; *Who's Who in America, 1988-1989,* I, 781.

EMPLOYMENT SECURITY COMMISSION
FIRST ANNUAL JOB SERVICE EMPLOYER AWARDS

RALEIGH, SEPTEMBER 2, 1987

There are at least two sets of winners here today: the recipients of the first Job Service Employer Awards and the people who benefit from the presence of the recipient companies in their communities. They are big winners! Either way, we're all winners.

That reminds me of my neighbor, whose dog had been acting poorly, so he took him over to the vet. He said it surprised him to see the sign that said "Veterinarian/Taxidermist." That's a new one! Veterinarian/taxidermist. In smaller letters, it said: "Either way, you get your dog back."

It is also an extraordinary pleasure to greet you, hail you, and salute you, the recipient companies, because you are a state treasure, vital to our economy and quality of life. You, the recipients of the very first Job Service Employer Awards, have clearly made positive contributions to the North Carolina economy. You have brought your businesses to the Tar Heel state. You have been the acknowledged leaders in economic and community affairs.

Talk about economy—consider the economy of effort. I get to talk to seventy-two representatives of companies, whose names read like a corporate "Who's Who" and all in one place as a captive audience, not being able to leave until they get their "just awards." Talk about a politician's dream! Seriously, though, we very much appreciate all the recipients coming and honoring us with their presence.

You know, ideas like this Job Service Employer Awards recognition ceremony didn't come full blown from the head of Zeus. They come from the creative minds of caring, involved people. But an idea, however sound, is one thing; putting it into action is something else. It all started with several discussions among Employment Security Commission [ESC] chairman [sic] (Betsy Y.) Justus;[1] labor market information director Mr. (Greg) Sampson; employment services deputy director Mr. (Lee Roy) Singleton;[2] employment services director Mr. (Manfred) Emmrich[3]—to see if the idea would fly in North Carolina. Job Service Employer coordinator Mr. (John) Bridges, the chair of the JSEC committee, along with his hard-working committee, fine tuned the idea, culminating in this splendid event.[4] I want to recognize particularly Mr. (Bob) Scruggs, chairman of the statewide Job Service Employer Committee for his role in making this event possible. Would all of you stand so we can see who you are.

I, too, want to salute Ms. (Betsy Y.) Justus as the first woman to serve as an ESC chairman in North Carolina, and one of the few ever to serve in the United States—and I appointed her. She does justice to her job.

This awards luncheon may also be seen as an occasion to express formally our appreciation to all of our business and corporate friends in the state—and to tell you that you are loved and wanted. You should know that approximately 140 employers were nominated for Job Service Employer Awards from among the state's employers by local Job Center offices of the ESC and local Job Service Employer committees. You will be pleased to hear that the competition was fierce.

It was not easy to choose the best of the best, and as Mr. (Manfred) Emmrich so well put it, there were really no losers. Indeed, all North Carolinians are winners. But make no mistake, you have won the gold, and we want you and the world to know.

Many of you, I am sure, have read the book, *In Search of Excellence*, and seen the TV programs on corporate excellence by Tom Peters.[5] One of the pervasive messages that Tom Peters communicates is that celebrating excellence is important to fostering excellence in the workplace. This luncheon is a celebration of your accomplishments—indeed, a celebration and recognition of the contributions that you and other companies have made to the economy and quality of life in our state.

It is interesting to note that the seventy-two companies represented here, today, account for 60,000 jobs in North Carolina! Note-worthy, also, is the fact that the companies you represent are responsible for adding 9,846 jobs to the employment rolls in North Carolina last year. In fact, in large measure, you and others in the corporate and business community have helped create what some would call a veritable windfall: North Carolina finds itself in an enviable condition.

Before telling you what our happy condition is, and to add just a dollop of suspense to these proceedings, I'd like to delay giving you the best news by providing some necessary background information. As you well know, every employer in North Carolina pays unemployment insurance taxes on employees. Every dollar received for the payment of this tax goes to Washington—D.C., not Washington, North Carolina. Here it is held in trust and may be used only for the payment of benefits of unemployed workers.

In 1983, as all of you no doubt know, a severe recession hit North Carolina and the nation. With the consequent high unemployment, our federal trust fund was in danger of bankruptcy. Acting on the counsel of the Employment Security Commission, the General Assembly responded by increasing taxes on employers through the following means: one, imposing an escalator tax; and two, raising the tax base on which taxes are charged.

To make a long story short, since 1983 our economy has enjoyed an incredible recovery. Indeed, no one really expected such a vigorous and quick turnaround. With the improved economy, and some aggressive recruiting for new industries and expansion of existing industries by our Department of Commerce, the trust fund in Washington swelled to unprecedented levels. In research by our Employment Security Commission, it was determined that with the trust fund standing at close to $1.1 billion—and that $1.4 billion was all that was required to maintain the solvency of the fund—we were faced with continuing to pay into the federal trust fund an amount greater than that required to keep the fund solvent. In point of fact, if the rate of payments into the fund, and interest generated, continue at the present rate, the federal trust fund is projected to grow to a level of $1.8 billion, an amount far in excess of the $1.4 billion required to keep the fund solvent. I think you can understand why I have an extraordinary case of the "prouds."

As a result of my proposal, and the action of the General Assembly, North Carolina is the first state ever to have a state controlled unemployment trust fund—and North Carolina will be able to administer this fund and use earned interest, subject to the approval of the General Assembly. Actually, the General Assembly established not one, but two, trust funds: the Employment Security Commission Reserve Fund, which is projected to have in it a total of $200 million by 1991, and the Worker Training Trust Fund.

The Worker Training Trust Fund will be used for three purposes: (1) worker enhancement activities; (2) to provide funds to keep local ESC offices open; and (3) to provide refunds for employers. This fund is subject to the appropriations process of the General Assembly. In case any of you out there are wondering what worker enhancement activities are, let me emphatically state, particularly for members of the media: This provision in the trust fund is not to provide happy hours for workers. It is a humane provision designed to support activities such as job counseling and training—in fact, to support a wide range of activities designed to help unemployed workers get jobs.

A word about ESC and Job Service offices is essential at this point. Interest from the trust fund will help compensate for over $4 million in cuts for 1987. Since 1984, the ESC work force has been reduced by 20 percent through attrition alone. Among other cuts, to try to keep operations afloat, was a 30 percent cut in travel funds. Other economy measures could be cited. ESC is still in danger of experiencing further cuts in federal funding.

Now with the alternative source of funding the Worker Training Trust Fund provides, the unhappy possibility of having to close local ESC offices has been lessened considerably. Currently fourteen, and possibly as many as twenty-seven, state employment security agencies across the nation received money from state legislatures to support their operations. We in North Carolina are now in a unique position to help fund the operation of ESC offices through our own trust fund. A happy prospect is that, should we have a serious downturn in the economy sometime in the future, we will not be faced with the necessity of having to close ESC offices or curtail their activities when they are most needed, as we were forced to do in the last recession. And, because we have our trust funds in place, we lessen considerably having to impose increased unemployment taxes on businesses—and at a time when they can least afford to pay additional taxes.

In regard to the third purpose of the Worker Training Trust Fund, the intent is to allow the granting of rebates to employers in the event the federal trust fund reaches an acceptable level of solvency. But of more immediate interest to employers is this: Before the enactment of House Bill 22, introduced at my request by Representative Jeff Enloe, a Democrat from Macon County, North Carolina had the unhappy distinction of having the highest taxable wage base in the Southeast.

Now, because of our trust funds and our low rate of unemployment, total unemployment taxes paid through 1991 will be reduced an estimated $278 million, with $108 million being saved in 1987. Incidentally, House Bill 22 is retroactively effective to January 1, 1987.

I have seen win-win legislation in my time, but surely House Bill 22 has to be put in place with highest honors. Particularly gratifying is what can happen when we put aside party differences and work for the good of all North Carolinians. House Bill 22 is a monument to the power of bipartisan politics and therefore redounds to the credit of both parties.

There is a cloud, presently no bigger than a man's hand, on the horizon, which if ignored could add to your unemployment taxes. It is a proposal being considered by the House Ways and Means Committee to extend the present temporary tax under the Federal Unemployment Tax Act for another three years. Having served in the U.S. Congress, I know something about the rationale that is used in extending legislation that has already served its purpose. It goes something like this: The federal unemployment tax is scheduled to expire, by law, this year. It's been around for eleven years. They'll say employers are used to paying for it. They're looking for ways to raise money. Eureka! Look what they found. The extension of the 0.2 percent FUTA, they will say, is a natural. After all, it would neither be a new tax nor an increase in taxes. That's what they will say to rationalize it.[6]

You can call it anything you like, but any way you cut it, bend it, twist it—an extension of FUTA will be a new tax. Indeed, voting to extend this tax on business is a breach of promise. I am opposed to it on economic grounds because it hurts business, and I am opposed to it on moral and ethical grounds because it breaks a promise made to business when the tax was imposed eleven years ago. I felt so strongly about the imposition of this new tax on business, and what I saw as reneging on a promise by Congress, that on July 23, 1987, I wrote a letter to House Ways and Means chairman Dan Rostenkowski.[7] Let me share parts of three paragraphs of that letter:

> The legislation provided that the 0.2 percent tax would automatically expire January 1 of the year following the year the debt is paid. This year the debt was retired and the tax should expire January 1, 1988. The tax is still in effect for the remainder of 1987 and will result in a surplus in the EUCA[8] of over a billion dollars.
>
> Since this debt has been paid, it is time for Congress to remove this unnecessary tax. The savings to North Carolina employers will be more than $35 million.

I urge you and your colleagues on the Ways and Means Committee to keep the intent of the 1976 legislation that the tax would expire when the debt was repaid.

Some of these temporary taxes are a good deal like the temporary buildings constructed around Washington during World War I and II. After decades, these "tempos" were still around.

All this business about taxes and trust funds can sound pretty complicated, and besides, I bow to a well-known physiological fact: After eating, blood that normally would serve your brain goes to your stomach. Realizing that your brain may not be running on all cylinders, we will be making available to employers, in the simplest English possible, printed information about how these state trust funds will work and how they will benefit you. It's the least we can do. You made it all possible.

Ashley Montagu says that "dependency and interdependency are the indispensible conditions of life."[9] He was speaking as an anthropologist. He could just as well have spoken as an economist.

Dependency, interdependency, and trust: These are the DNA, the basic building blocks, of economic development in any state. The state depends upon the entrepreneurship and the capital generated at risk, by business, to support desired services for, and the quality of life of, its citizens. Business depends upon the good will, skills, expertise, and quality of workmanship by the state's work force to grow and prosper; and business depends upon the government of the state to create and maintain the conditions that allow business to be profitable, thereby redounding to the benefit of citizens. In chemistry, we call this *synergy*; in biology, *symbiosis*. Whatever the term one may prefer, the inescapable truth is, for any of us to be successful in economic development, we must all work together, with proper regard for dependency, interdependency, and trust.

We have come together on this special day to break bread with you—with you whose companies have made it possible for many of our citizens to break bread with pride and dignity. This is really an occasion for thanksgiving. On behalf of the people of North Carolina, I wish to say to you, one and all, as simply and as profoundly as possible, thank you!

---

[1]Betsy Y. Justus (1946-   ), born in Aulander; resident of Cary; was educated at East Carolina University. Various positions, including branch manager, North Carolina National Bank, Hickory, 1972-1979; membership and finance manager, Catawba County Chamber of Commerce, 1980-1983; corporate relocation director, Coldwell Banker/Boyd

and Hassell Realtors, Inc., Hickory, 1983-1984; chairwoman, administrator, North Carolina Employment Security Commission, 1985-1990; active volunteer. Betsy Y. Justus to Jan-Michael Poff, January 8, 1990; press release, "Governor Appoints Betsy Justus as Revenue Secretary," Raleigh, March 27, 1990, Governors Papers, James G. Martin.

[2]Lee Roy Singleton (1932-   ), born in Washington, North Carolina; resident of Raleigh; B.S., East Carolina University, 1959; U.S. Navy, 1951-1955. Various positions with Employment Security Commission of North Carolina, since 1960, including Raleigh local ESC office manager, 1967-1971, local office coordinator, 1971-1983, and deputy employment service director, since 1983. Lee Roy Singleton to Jan-Michael Poff, January 5, 1990.

[3]Manfred Emmrich; resident of Durham; B.A., Davidson College, 1959; U.S. Army and Reserve. Various positions with Macke Co., 1959-1973; state Employment Security Commission chairman, 1973-1978, Employment Service Division director, since 1985; president, Interstate Conference of Employment Security Agencies, Inc., 1977-1978; senior associate, MDC, Inc., 1978-1985. Manfred Emmrich to Jan-Michael Poff, April 19, 1990.

[4]John W. Bridges (1938-   ), born in Sanford; resident of Raleigh; B.A., Wake Forest University, 1960. Various positions with Employment Security Commission of North Carolina, since 1961, including occupational analyst, 1967-1971, state employer relations supervisor, 1971-1984, and state Job Service Employer Committee coordinator, since 1984. John W. Bridges to Jan-Michael Poff, January 8, 1990.

[5]Thomas J. Peters and Robert H. Waterman, Jr., *In Search of Excellence: Lessons from America's Best-Run Companies* (New York: Harper & Row, 1982).

[6]Congress did indeed extend FUTA for an additional three years. See P.L. 100-203, "Omnibus Reconciliation Act of 1987" (short title), *United States Statutes at Large*, Act of December 22, 1987, 101 Stat. 1330-326, which amended the Federal Unemployment Tax Act, *United States Code* (1988 edition), Title 26, Section 3301, paragraphs 1 and 2.

[7]Daniel David Rostenkowski (1928-   ), native of Chicago; was educated at Loyola University; U.S. Army, 1946-1948. Member, Illinois House, 1952, and Senate, 1954-1956; elected to U.S. House of Representatives, 1958, and returned in subsequent elections; chairman, House Committee on Ways and Means, since 1981; Democrat. *Biographical Directory of Congress*, 1745.

[8]The Extended Unemployment Compensation Act was established under sec. 9905(a) of the Social Security Act. See *United States Code* (1988 edition), Title 26, Section 3301.

[9]Montague Francis Ashley Montagu (1905-   ), born in London, England; resident of Princeton, New Jersey; Ph.D., Columbia University, 1937; honorary degrees; served in Welsh Guards. Anthropologist; social biologist; assistant professor of anatomy, New York University, 1931-1938; associate professor of anatomy, Hahnemann Medical College and Hospital, 1938-1949; naturalized U.S. citizen, 1940; helped draft federal National Science Foundation bill, 1946-1947; drafted UNESCO statement on race, 1949-1950; Anthropology Department chairman, Rutgers University, 1949-1955; author; lecturer. *Current Biography, 1967*, 294-297; *Who's Who in America, 1988-1989*, II, 2188.

STATE EMPLOYEES ASSOCIATION OF NORTH CAROLINA

WINSTON-SALEM, SEPTEMBER 11, 1987

Bobby[1] has impressed upon me what a tight schedule you're working under and told me that I can only have about twenty minutes. I'll talk as fast as I can, and if you will listen faster, I think we can get this speech down to less than that.

Aren't you proud of this association and how far we've come?

There are two obvious things about this audience: One, you are here because you were elected to this deliberative body by your colleagues—you have their confidence; two, you are career state employees. Thus, by definition, you are a dedicated, caring group of people. You have a responsibility, both to your profession or craft, and to your district constituents—those who sent you to act on their behalf—and my observation is that you exercise your responsibilities with considerable vigor. I will testify to that.

There are two other factors that make me more than a little prejudiced toward your goal to improve the lot of state employees: One, I, too, am a state employee; and two, I work closely with, and rely upon the services of, state employees every day, including weekends. Therefore, I am able to see firsthand your dedication and commitment to excellence. In a word, I admit to a strong bias in regard to state employees. You work hard, and that makes me look good.

Furthermore, I am grateful to state employees. An indisputable truth is that except for the support and vote of many of you, someone else would be talking to you tonight. Being governor is a great job, and being able to serve the people of North Carolina in such a position is extremely gratifying.

So, I've come here tonight to address some of your concerns and aspirations, but first I want to say thank you to each one of you. As you know, I've proclaimed this as State Employee Appreciation Week, and I must add that I have enjoyed eating ice cream with you, then burning off those calories by leading the WISE walk twice around the state Capitol, hosting the breakfast for you this morning, and having the opportunity to visit informally with many of you.[2] We should express our appreciation to you daily because your contributions are beneficial to so many of our state's citizens.

I specifically want to thank you for your outstanding and enthusiastic response to several of our initiatives during the past year. Your giving blood to the American Red Cross in record numbers has benefited many grateful people. An official of the Red Cross told me just this Wednesday that 4 percent of the general population donate blood, while 20 percent of the state employees in the Raleigh area responded to my call for greater participation. Now that is a great testimony to your care and love for North Carolina.

I am also grateful for your response to our initiatives for better health promotion and disease prevention among state employees. I dedicated the Wellness Trail at Broughton Hospital last year, and I have seen other examples of your interest as I have visited the institutions and state departments and agencies across our state.

You have also helped to prove that executive orders issued by governors are more than words on a fancy sheet of paper. I specifically refer to our efforts to improve safety for staff and clients, patients, and residents. We are making progress in this area, thanks to your leadership and support.

So, thanks—let's keep it up. More remains to be done in these and other areas, such as the State Employees Combined Campaign which is now under way. I'm sure you'll help surpass the various goals which have been established.

From looking over your platform and the 1987 amendments, I'm aware that you have dreams of creating better working conditions and a more fulfilling quality of life for state employees. In the time I have, I would like to address six of those dreams and pledge to you that I will make them part of my legislative and personal agenda.

First, I unqualifiedly state that I do not believe state employees should be treated as second-class citizens when it comes to pay and benefits. I will actively seek to create parity for state employees.

As you know, the governor of North Carolina has to exercise the art of politics differently from any other governor in the country. In our state, politics is truly the art of the possible; this is why a North Carolina governor has to play the game in a different way, particularly if the legislature is controlled by the opposition. I was pleased that they enacted 85 percent of my budget improvements, but they sure strained at it. They figured if they passed my programs, I might get some credit for it, and if they refused good proposals to deny me any credit, then that would give me a hot political issue—like their refusal to toughen the drunk-driving laws! Either way they lose. It's sort of like when I took my dog for his shots, and the sign over the door said "Dr. Smith, Veterinarian/Taxidermist." Wow! Veterinarian/taxidermist. Under that it said: "Either way you get your dog back."

You know, we got some things passed, but we couldn't get them to adjourn. [There] was a collision between House and Senate leadership. When they clashed, it did [give] us a chance to test our proposal for the supercollider—not a wiggle on the seismograph. Finally, I decided to take a vacation and make them mad at me instead of each other. Four days after I returned, they finally quit.[3]

Strange things happen. One example was in the last legislative session. In budget making, especially with salary increases, there is always a bidding game between governors and legislatures, and they get to see my bid. You'll remember how legislative leaders predicted at first that two percent was all that could be afforded in the face of other needs. I proposed a four and a half percent raise, each year, on average, while asking the legislature to increase that if revenue growth would allow it. They did outbid me, with just a half percent. I'm pleased they did. In fact, I wish, and you wish, they could have done better—but another half percent, and they would have no pork barrel. Unfortunately, they only appropriated enough for one 5 percent increase over two years, which is not as good as two consecutive raises totaling 9 percent, which I proposed, so I'll have to see that gets corrected in my 1988 budget amendment.

I had the pleasure to present eight state employees with the Governor's Award for Excellence this past Tuesday. We all say we're for excellence, but the one way we can foster more excellence among state employees is to reward their good work by promoting them from within, and I don't believe that, in the event an employee gets a promotion, he or she should get less money for the same job than a person would if he came from outside. Nothing undermines loyalty or the striving for excellence as much as passing over qualified state employees to bring in an outside person. We believe in a proper balance—not firing people merely to make room for our supporters, but giving them an equal chance to be hired when vacancies occur. I see nothing wrong with integrating my party into state government jobs from which they've been segregated most of this century, but only when there are vacancies. We have not driven off career employees because of their registration, nor pressured them to change parties. We beat that system. Why copy it! A proper mix of promotions from within, combined with recruiting new, enthusiastic, loyal talent and experience from outside—that has been, and will continue to be, our policy.

I was very pleased to see among Corrections promotions this past week were two former district supervisors who earlier had been demoted, who have persevered, and proven themselves, and earned their way back. Agency heads have to make tough decisions. I demand that they be fair. And when we have to eliminate certain positions for efficiency, we get new jobs for those RIF'ed, which means our eager supporters are the ones who have to wait. But that's fair.

I know that state employees are paying more and getting less health protection—that indeed, much of the gain you make by way of salary increases is eroded by inflation and increased insurance costs. That's where your second-year pay hike went, by the way. Frankly, I don't know what can be done to control the costs of medical insurance. HMOs [health maintenance organizations] are certainly one way, and we support maintaining this option, but they may not be for everyone. They leave out some. You do have my pledge that afford-able, quality medical insurance will be at the very top of my program agenda this next year. Regretfully, the legislature has taken this pro-gram away from the executive branch, and we have had little to do with it. As you know, it is actually run by the appropriations chair-man. No one else has a say. I don't. You don't.

Fourth, I will continue my efforts to depoliticize and professionalize employment in state government. This conforms with my belief in state employment as a career. Just as I don't believe a worker in a nonexempt position should be rewarded for having certain political or partisan views, neither should they be punished for their views, either—or squeezed to make political contributions. If we are to con-tinue to provide a high quality of service to the citizens of North Carolina, we must be able to attract and hold competent employees—and one way to achieve this goal is to protect state employees against any form of reprisals for their views. And I will repeat that I don't want anybody pressuring subordinate employees to make campaign donations. You have a right to, but if anyone coerces you, you're not in trouble—they are. We've already removed some who abused this, and it takes evidence. This morning, at breakfast, I was told of a new case. When I get the details, I'll personally look into it.

Fifth, I commend you on your interest in the special challenges which the AIDS virus syndrome brings to us as a society and to us as a state employees. Former secretary of human resources Phil Kirk had named an AIDS task force more than a year ago to give guidance and recommendations as we tackle this difficult public health problem, and specifically, to increase education and awareness. I have pro-claimed November 8-14, 1987, as AIDS Awareness Week in North Carolina, and I would encourage you to take advantage of that time to learn more about AIDS and help others to understand.[4] We can rightly fear what we know to be fearful; we should not fear the unknown.

I have directed my chief of staff to work with state officials having employees who may be exposed to communicable diseases and would ask that you select a representative of your association to participate in this effort. Several departments have already written suggested guidelines for handling patients. Working together on addressing this critical issue will be beneficial to all concerned. Just as we worked together on getting my budget request adopted to expand our valuable Employees' Assistance Program to respond appropriately to employee problems, we can be successful with this new issue and concern.

Family issues are important to all of us. It is clearly documented that employees who are experiencing problems in providing for their families are less efficient and less productive in the workplace. So, in addition to our moral and ethical obligation to address the needs of families, it is to the benefit of the state as an employer to do so. I have created the Governor's Commission for the Family, and I have appointed my wife, Dottie, to lead this effort. Several state employees serve on the commission.

We know that one of the major problems working families face today is the availability of quality child care. I have asked Secretary Dave Flaherty and Dr. Nancy H. Brown, chief of child day care in the Department of Human Resources, to prepare a proposal to address the child day-care needs of state employees. I have suggested that she explore the availability of space in state-owned buildings which could be used for child care. I understand that space on the Dorothea Dix campus has been identified which would require only minimal renovation and offers excellent possibilities for a pilot project for employees located in Raleigh. This center could also serve as a way to provide hands-on training for our day-care consultants who visit the state's 2,500 day-care centers and more than 6,000 day-care homes. Another possibility could be the old Murphy School right in the governmental center. We have discussed in the State Capitol Planning Commission how this would be a convenient site for many state employees with young children. The legislators from Wake County have already shown a good response to this.

Dr. Brown recommends that child day-care facilities located in state-owned buildings be operated as parent-owned cooperatives so that, after initial start-up costs, the program would be self-supporting, based on fees charged to parents. She once started the day care program for the United States Senate and operated it before we recruited her back to her home state, so she knows how to get this accomplished. The General Assembly will be requested to appropriate monies for start-up costs and to pass legislation so that space in other buildings could be identified to meet the needs of employees located in other areas of the state.

In a word, I share with you the desire to make state government the best it can be. The number of competent employees leaving state government for other opportunities is unacceptably high. We simply must be able to attract and hold competent employees.

In conclusion, I share your dream to create the best possible conditions for state employees and their families. I stand ready to work with you, to use whatever energy and influence I have, to ensure that state government employment is career employment, treated with fairness and the dignity it deserves and rewarded as career employment should be, so that you, in turn, can continue to do your job, to serve our people, with pride.

It's really been great being with you today. I wish I could stay and dance with all the ladies. I'd love it, but we've got to drive home tonight. So I'll count on all the guys to stand in for me and dance with all the ladies. I'll be thinking about you. Good night.[5]

---

[1]Bobby L. Reardon (1936-   ), born in Buies Creek; resident of Raleigh; associate's degree in business administration, Kings College, 1976; U.S. Army, 1960-1963. Various positions with state Department of Correction, since 1963, including correctional administrative services manager, since 1981; first president of State Employees Association of North Carolina to succeed himself in office, 1985-1986, 1986-1987; Republican candidate for state Senate, 1990. Bobby L. Reardon to Jan-Michael Poff, March 27, 1990; telephone conversation, April 5, 1990.

[2]"State Employee Appreciation Week and State Employee Appreciation Day, 1987, By the Governor of the State of North Carolina: A Proclamation," signed June 23, 1987, Governors Papers, James G. Martin, designated September 7-11 as State Employee Appreciation Week and September 8 as State Employee Appreciation Day.

[3]The General Assembly convened on February 9, 1987, for what transpired as the third-longest legislative session in North Carolina history. Wrangling between Lieutenant Governor Jordan and the House leadership over the state budget stretched the session weeks beyond the July 4 adjournment date envisioned months earlier. Indeed, lawmakers did not officially conclude business until August 14.

As the session seemed to grind on interminably, Martin kept to his long-arranged vacation plans and departed August 1 for a two-week sailing trip in the Virgin Islands with his family. Promising to return to the capital "if some problem comes loose," the governor explained that he was unable to delay his plans because other family members had already arranged to be away from work; furthermore, his youngest son, Benson, would have to be in Raleigh for the beginning of school later in the month.

Martin maintained daily telephone contact with his office while on vacation and cut short his trip by four days as the General Assembly moved more speedily toward adjournment. Nevertheless, Democrats criticized his decision to leave town so near the end of the session, political scientists and editorialists also questioned the move, and even some Republican legislators would have preferred that the governor remain in Raleigh. Phillip Kirk, Martin's executive assistant, said that the governor and his staff thought they had brought all the influence to bear that they could on the state budget. Even so, said Kirk of Martin's vacation timing, "It's not the ideal situation," and added, "It was unusual and it wasn't planned that way." News and Observer, February 10, August 1, 7, 11, 12, 14, 16, 20, 30, 1987.

[4]"AIDS Awareness Week in North Carolina, 1987, By the Governor of North Carolina: A Proclamation," was signed August 25, 1987. Governors Papers, James G. Martin.

[5]The governor commented on the theme of the evening's festivities in notes he wrote at the beginning of this speech: "Don't ya'll look pretty. This was a good idea—Prom '87. I don't know how we're all going to get on that little dance floor."

ANNOUNCEMENT ON ACQUISITION OF PERMUDA ISLAND

PERMUDA ISLAND, SEPTEMBER 14, 1987

[Situated in Stump Sound, Permuda Island lay in one of North Carolina's most bountiful shellfishing areas. Plans by Lumberton developer J. Hal Kinlaw, Jr., to build a condominium and marina project on the fifty-acre island ignited the passions of local fishermen and conservationists who viewed the complex as a potential environmental disaster. Regional opposition, led largely by Mrs. Lena S. Ritter, succeeded in convincing state officials to deny Kinlaw a permit for the project in 1986. A year later the state, assisted by the North Carolina Nature Conservancy, acquired Permuda from Kinlaw for $1.7 million. *News and Observer*, February 21, 1988; press release, "State Completes Purchase of Permuda Island," Raleigh, September 14, 1987, Governors Papers, James G. Martin.]

I'm pleased to be here to accept the key, symbolically, to the Permuda Island gate on behalf of all North Carolinians. This is a special place; generations of fishermen and farmers—and Indians, long before them—who have made their lives here, have known just how special. In Raleigh, not being able to see the water and marshes here, it was possible to think that development regulations alone would protect Permuda Island and its outstanding shellfishing waters and archaeological sites. It took the strong, unceasing voice of Lena Ritter[1] and others to make us see that rules simply weren't enough.

This area is too vulnerable to allow development. To truly protect Permuda Island, we would have to preserve it. I am pleased that we listened to Mrs. Ritter and were able to purchase the island and add it to the North Carolina estuarine sanctuary system. Shellfishing and farming will continue along Stump Sound, and students, researchers, and the public will have a valuable outdoor laboratory where they can come to learn more about the coast.

I am especially glad to be here because this occasion gives me a chance to recognize not only the importance of protecting Permuda Island, but the importance of individual effort. The Department of Natural Resources and Community Development, local governments, and environmental and civic groups can be very effective in protecting coastal resources, but ultimately, the choice to maintain the quality of these lands and waters is up to each person who lives and visits here. Mrs. Ritter showed us just how much one person can accomplish, and I hope her work will inspire others throughout the coastal area and the state.

I am happy to tell you that in recognition of her willingness to take responsibility, I am appointing Mrs. Ritter to the Marine Fisheries

Commission, representing commercial fishermen; and next week, she will receive the 1987 Eure-Gardner Award from the Coastal Resources Commission for her work here. By the way, on the occasion of her recognition by the Z. Smith Reynolds [Foundation], she boldly and publicly prevailed on me to reappoint Duke professor (Richard T.) Barbour to the Environmental Management Commission, because of his effective role in helping to save Permuda. I boldly and publicly agreed, recognizing *vox populi* whenever I hear it. I reappointed Dr. Barbour only to receive his reply that he was moving to a new job out west.

There are many other individuals who helped to protect Permuda Island: Katherine Skinner of the Nature Conservancy, Hal Kinlaw, Senator A. D. Guy,[2] Representatives Robert Grady[3] and Bruce Ethridge,[4] Secretary Tommy Rhodes, Dave Owens[5]—I thank you all.

As some of you know, I have been working on a plan to stimulate environmentally compatible development of recreational resources and facilities around the communities on the Pamlico and Albemarle sounds and tributaries and along the Intracoastal Waterway. The plan is to be unveiled on October 22 at a public meeting in New Bern. With the response we receive to that, I hope we can perfect a concept that will help to protect the pristine treasure of the rich marshes, and wetlands, and harbors that are now undeveloped, while encouraging marine recreational investments in existing villages which presently have little economic strength. Permuda Island is just such a pristine sanctuary, which enhances the value of the development and water resources of which it is an integral part.

There is no doubt that preserving Permuda Island is an important accomplishment, but we all will continue to face tough development decisions. It is quite a balancing act, managing quality growth in this sensitive natural environment. Let us hope that, as those future decisions are being made, we will remember Permuda Island; and how people have lived at the coast since North Carolina was first settled; and how preservation and development must be mutually compatible and supportive. While change is inevitable, we do not want to lose the resources, nor the way of life, that brought people here in the first place.

---

[1]Lena Sanders Ritter (1935-   ), native of Holly Ridge; was educated at Dixon High School, Holly Ridge. Commercial fisherman; conservationist; president, N.C. Coastal Federation, since 1987; received Z. Smith Reynolds Foundation's Nancy Susan Reynolds Award, "honoring unheralded people who contribute to their communities," for her tireless efforts to preserve the ecology of Stump Sound, 1986; member, state

Marine Fisheries Commission, 1987-1988. *News and Observer*, November 29, 1986, January 12, February 21, 1988.

[2]Alexander Duke Guy (1918-   ), born in Calypso; resident of Onlsow County; was educated at North Carolina State College (later University) and University of North Carolina at Chapel Hill. Insurance, real estate executive; member, Onslow County Board of Commissioners, 1969-1970, and of Jacksonville City Council; mayor pro tem, mayor of Jacksonville; member, state House, 1979-1982, and of state Senate, since 1983; chairman, Senate Committee on State Government; Democrat. *North Carolina Manual, 1987-1988*, 300.

[3]Robert Grady (1950-   ), born in Jacksonville; was educated at University of North Carolina at Chapel Hill. Businessman; member, Jacksonville City Council, 1981-1987; Jacksonville mayor pro tem, 1983-1986; elected to state House of Representatives, 1986; Republican. *North Carolina Manual, 1987-1988*, 430.

[4]Wilbur Bruce Ethridge (1938-   ), born in Rocky Mount; resident of Carteret County; was educated at North Carolina State University and Fayetteville Technical Institute. Owner, operator, Beaufort Inn; Carolina Telephone and Telegraph engineer; elected to state House of Representatives, 1978, and returned in subsequent elections; Democrat. *North Carolina Manual, 1987-1988*, 422.

[5]David W. Owens; resident of Raleigh; A.B., 1972, Master of Regional Planning, 1974, J.D., 1975, University of North Carolina at Chapel Hill; was also educated at Oxford University. Attorney, planning analyst, Office of State Planning and Energy, Wisconsin Department of Administration, 1975-1978; chief, Planning, Policy, and Technical Services Section, 1978-1980, acting chief, Implementation and Enforcement Section, 1980, 1981-1982, and assistant director, 1980-1983, Office of Coastal Management, North Carolina Department of Natural Resources and Community Development; director, Division of Coastal Management, state Department of Natural Resources and Community Development, 1984-1989; author; lecturer; visiting professor. David W. Owens to Jan-Michael Poff, January 9, 1989; *News and Observer*, January 11, 1989.

AMERICAN FISHERIES SOCIETY AND INTERNATIONAL ASSOCIATION OF FISH AND WILDLIFE AGENCIES

WINSTON-SALEM, SEPTEMBER 16, 1987

Visitors to our state, fellow North Carolinians, it is a distinct pleasure to welcome you to North Carolina and the beautiful city of Winston-Salem. Particularly exciting is the opportunity to meet with so many of you for the first time at this joint conference of the American Fisheries Society and the American Association of Fish and Wildlife Agencies. We are honored that such distinguished groups as the two you represent have chosen to meet in our state. It is particularly gratifying that as many as 1,000 or more have come to participate in this conference and that you have come from all over North America, Europe, and other parts of the globe.

You have an understanding of the state of health of our fish and wildlife. You understand, as few others do, the responsibilities for stewardship of our natural resources. You, more than perhaps any group, are painfully aware of the terrible ransom that we are paying for our disregard, and disrespect, for what biologists call our ecosystem. We are one planet, and the wilderness, streams, and waterways in your states, regions, or countries are an integral part of the whole earth; and to paraphrase John Donne, no place on earth can be an island unto itself.[1]

In a wonderful and beautiful book, *Chop Wood, Carry Water*, I chanced upon these words that express well the philosophy that most of you espouse: "At its base, ecological awareness is spiritual; it is a return to the simple, profound respect for and responsibility to the earth that our ancestors knew and practiced. Ecological philosphy," it continues to say, "like spiritual philosophy, teaches that we are all one, all united. No matter how deeply we look into the fabric of material being—the biological level, chemical level, subatomic level—we see that life forms are interdependent. . . ."[2]

In a word, your work is vital because of your stewardship and your activities in research, management, public education, and enforcement. I say this knowing well that your fine work may not always be understood fully or appreciated adequately by some.

I would like to take a few moments to tell you briefly about a few projects here in North Carolina that are of particular interest to me. They are certainly related to your interests, and indeed, some of you here are involved in them.

North Carolina has one of the most extensive estuarine areas in the world, particularly in the Albemarle and Pamlico sounds. This vast resource has been giving us clear signals that we must act to protect precious life in these waters. Nutrient loads are growing beyond the sounds' ability to assimilate it. Already we are acting to help. For example, our Environmental Management Commission has moved to require municipal sewer plants in nutrient-sensitive watersheds to discharge no more than two parts per million of phosphate. Our General Assembly also has enacted a statewide ban on phosphate detergents, but that won't improve the effluent, since it merely reduces the inflowing phosphate from sixty parts per million to forty-five parts per million.[3] We're going to require them to take it down to two parts per million, regardless of the intake level.

Of even greater concern is agricultural fertilizer runoff. We have begun a major program to teach and encourage farmers to use no-till planting and other techniques that minimize the amount of fertilizer while also reducing soil erosion. We are pushing to expand these Best Management Practices to all areas of North Carolina.

We have also adopted storm-water runoff controls for developers.

We have recently begun a five-year, $5 million study of this estuarine system to be certain we aren't missing anything. Through this cooperative state and federal study, we hope to learn what we need to know to improve water quality, reduce nutrient levels, and restore these vast estuaries that are so important to us in economic, recreational, and aesthetic terms. Special emphasis will be placed on the dwindling striped bass population, and of course we will be looking, also, at virtually every aspect of this area's natural resources.

Another related effort has been undertaken to head off a potentially damaging pipeline that has been proposed to remove water from Lake Gaston and pipe it to the rapidly growing tidewater Virginia area.[4] We are greatly concerned that this pipeline, if operational, will affect fisheries—especially striped bass—in the lake and result in low flows in the Roanoke River and downstream. The Roanoke flows into the Albemarle Sound and is the prime nursery stream for "stripers" in this estuary.

No small matters are at stake here. In the words of the Oriental philosopher, Lao Tsu, "The highest good is like water. Water gives life to the ten thousand things and does not strive."[5] But we will have to strive to keep the waters. You can certainly appreciate how interrelated things are.

One project I am particularly proud to be a part of is a cooperative venture among southeastern states to find solutions to the region's declining populations of small game. In fact, last year I wrote to the governors of the southeastern states to invite them to participate with us in a regional study of small-game populations. I am pleased to report that all governors responded favorably to this initiative. A preliminary meeting was held, followed by a small-game workshop this past August, which we hosted. Initially, our efforts will be concentrated on quail and rabbits, because these are two popular species that are in trouble in the Southeast.

The decline of small game has been going on for some time. While we don't anticipate any miracles or quick solutions, we are, nonetheless, hopeful that this workshop and resulting cooperative studies will lead us to solutions that will help restore our small-game populations to an acceptable level. Naturally, what we learn will be freely shared with others outside the region.

Although there are other projects under way—more than I have time to mention—there are two more I think will prove particularly interesting to you.

Many states now have expanding nongame programs, and we are vastly proud of the success that North Carolina is having with its overall effort. Since 1983, taxpayers filing state income taxes have been able to designate a part or all of their refund to be used especially for nongame programs.[6] The public response to this option is growing each year. As a consequence of this tax provision, many nongame species are being helped and more will doubtlessly be in future years. Already, we are seeing astounding results: For the first time in many years, eagles are nesting in North Carolina, and our peregrine falcon restoration project has also resulted in the first active nesting.

North Carolina, I am proud to say, has been among the first to find successful alternative means of funding our overall wildlife program. Indeed, I hope you do not think I am being chauvinistic when I say we have the most successful of all such programs, and we invite you to look into it, take it home with you, and implement any version of it you like. Incidentally, this year I proposed a similar tax refund designation to fund programs to help abused children. Our legislators didn't take to that as well as they have to nongame wildlife, so I guess you can have mixed feelings about that.

In 1981, the North Carolina Wildlife Resources Commission began a program that offered lifetime hunting and fishing licenses and lifetime subscriptions to the agency's monthly magazine, *Wildlife in North Carolina*. Operating as the Wildlife Endowment Fund, the money from this program is invested by the state treasurer at low risk, with the highest rate of return possible.[7] Only the interest generated may be used to support wildlife programs. As you may guess, this has proven to be an immensely popular and successful program. The principal in this wildlife fund now stands at $12 million. It has been predicted that, eventually, income generated by this fund will provide much of the financial support of the agency. It goes without saying this is an innovative concept, uniquely adaptable to wildlife agencies because of our strong support constituencies.

While we are on the fascinating subject of money: On behalf of our Wildlife Resources Commission, I'd like to thank you for the key role you played in the U.S. Congress supporting the Wallop-Breaux legislation that has given North Carolina expanded funding for aquatic resource programs.[8] This legislation has already had a very favorable impact on the overall program. I'm certain that other states are enjoying the same results.

Shortly I hope to announce that, as a result of studies done by one of our task forces, a plan of action will be implemented to clean up and restore a number of contaminated beds in our waterways. Of course, such corrective action will require time before we have discernible results.

Finally, let me close with one other observation: This is, in some measure, a dangerous world we live in—dangerous because with such rapid change, we do not always take the time to consider the consequences these changes may have on our environment. The challenge is to act responsibly and profitably, with proper regard for the quality of life and quality of the environment, not only for ourselves but for our children and their children.

Robert Hunter, in *O Seasons, O Castles*, expresses an attitude all of us could adopt. Here is what he says:

> In nature, there is no such thing as a clash of colors. The more carefully you look, the deeper the subtleties of harmony. It is not so much that things flow into each other or around each other like perfect jigsaw pieces; rather it is that there is only One Thing out there. And somehow, it is not really "out there." Somehow it is "in here" too. Inside. At the furthest wavelength of thought, the sea and the wind and the trees and the sand are . . . me.[9]

Again, let me welcome you to North Carolina, a friendly state where hospitality has traditionally been one of our most important commodities. I hope you enjoy your visit and come back many more times. In sharing is strength, and we've got a lot to share with you. We will continue to strive to make certain that our little part of the globe will be an inviting place to visit and live.

---

[1]"No man is an island, entire of itself; every man is a piece of the continent, a part of the main; if a clod be washed away by the sea, Europe is the less, as well as if a promontory were, as well as if a manor of thy friends or of thine own were; any man's death diminishes me, because I am involved in mankind; and therefore never send to know for whom the bell tolls; it tolls for thee." John Donne, *Devotions XVII* [1623], quoted in Bartlett, *Familiar Quotations*, 308.

[2]Rick Fields and others, *Chop Wood, Carry Water: A Guide to Finding Spiritual Fulfillment in Everyday Life* (Los Angeles: Jeremy P. Tarcher, Inc., 1984), 219, hereinafter cited as Fields, *Chop Wood, Carry Water*.

[3]"An Act to Provide for the Sale of Clean Detergents in North Carolina" was ratified April 19, 1987, and became effective January 1, 1988. *N.C. Session Laws, 1987*, I, c. 111.

[4]North Carolina's six-year-long attempt to prevent construction of the Lake Gaston-Virginia Beach pipeline received a setback in February, 1990, when the federal District Court upheld the Army Corps of Engineers permit for the project. The state, convinced of the environmental hazard posed by the pipeline, planned to appeal Judge W. Earl Britt's ruling. *News and Observer*, February 3, 16, March 6, 1990.

[5]Lao Tsu was quoted in Fields, *Chop Wood, Carry Water*, 220.

[6]"An Act to Establish the North Carolina Income Tax Refund Checkoff Program for the Management of Nongame and Endangered Species" was ratified July 20, 1983. *N.C. Session Laws, 1983*, c. 865.

[7]"An Act to Provide Lifetime Licenses for Hunting and Fishing and to Create and Maintain a Wildlife Endowment Fund with the Proceeds" was ratified May 29, 1981. *N.C. Session Laws, 1981*, c. 482.

[8]Malcolm Wallop (1933-   ), born in New York, New York; was graduated from Yale University, 1954; U.S. Army, 1955-1957. Businessman; cattle rancher; member, Wyoming state House, 1969-1972, and Senate, 1973-1976; elected to U.S. Senate, 1976, reelected 1982, from Wyoming; Republican. *Biographical Directory of Congress*, 2000.

John Berlinger Breaux (1944-   ), born in Crowley, Louisiana; was graduated from University of Southwestern Louisiana, 1965, and Louisiana State University School of Law, 1967. Attorney; U.S. Representative, 1972-1987, elected to U.S. Senate, 1986, from Louisiana; Democrat. *Biographical Directory of Congress*, 662.

[9]See Fields, *Chop Wood, Carry Water*, 220.

GOVERNOR'S HIGHWAY SAFETY COMMISSION

RALEIGH, SEPTEMBER 29, 1987

[The following remarks were similar to those presented at a public meeting of the Governor's Highway Safety Commission, Greensboro, February 4, 1988.]

It is good to see each of you this morning. As you know, one of the top priorities of my administration is highway safety. We have a tremendous responsibility to make all our roads safe for all our citizens and the motoring public. I appreciate all the work the members of the Governor's Highway Safety Commission have done over the past two years. Chairman Joe Biesecker has done an outstanding job in leading this group in studying issues such as school bus safety, truck safety, and driving while impaired [DWI].[1] Your advice and counsel are greatly appreciated by me and members of my staff.

My purpose in addressing you, this morning, is to focus on our state's serious driving-while-impaired problem. Public concern over this problem has resulted in additional and renewed efforts to crack down on drunken drivers. State, county, and local law enforcement agencies report that, in 1986, in North Carolina, 77,020 people were arrested for DWI, an 11 percent increase over 1985. Unfortunately, the UNC Highway Safety Research Center estimates we are only apprehending one out of every one thousand impaired drivers on our roadways. Statistics show our courts are convicting 91 percent of those DWI offenders who register a .10 blood alcohol content level or higher, and while only a few receive the maximum sentences allowed under the Safe Roads Act of 1983, the penalties are much more severe and consistent than in prior years.

We have made some progress in the fight against drunken driving. Last year the Governor's Highway Safety Program launched a comprehensive statewide public awareness multimedia advertising campaign against drunk driving, with the donated services of Raleigh-based advertising agency McKinney and Silver. The campaign focuses on the serious personal consequences of driving while impaired in North Carolina. We have received excellent support from the state's radio and television stations and outdoor advertising companies. We need more support, however, from newspapers around the state. Our plan is to produce a second series of PSAs [public service announcements] next spring.

Through the Governor's Highway Safety Program, we have also established youth traffic safety councils in high schools across the state, with cooperation from the Department of Public Instruction. These councils will examine traffic safety problems, such as DWI, from the youth perspective, and establish drug- and alcohol-free "Project: Graduation" parties across the state this spring.

My administration also proposed a comprehensive package of anti-DWI legislation this past session. These bills targeted the multiple repeat DWI offenders and made the penalties more severe for driving while impaired at all levels. Unfortunately, the legislature chose to pass only three of these bills, with the remainder of the bills dying in committees without a clear and proper study.[2] Fortunately, the cause was salvaged by creating a legislative study commission on the subject, which will make legislation eligible for consideration in the short session. I will continue to press forward and push for a bipartisan effort between the executive and the legislative branches of our government to ensure that this much-needed anti-DWI legislation is addressed.

Much more needs to be done if drunk driving is ever to become socially unacceptable in this state. Last year, in North Carolina, 707 people were killed and 19,242 people were seriously injured in DWI-related traffic crashes. These figures represent a 10 percent increase over 1985. These increases have occurred during a period of increased vehicle miles traveled and increased numbers of registered vehicles and licensed drivers in our state. Even though these numbers continued to increase, our highway patrol manpower level remains the same as it did in the mid-1970s. As you know, I requested 100 additional troopers for the next two years. The General Assembly approved twenty for each year during the biennium. That's not a serious response.

It is obvious there is a real need to continue stepped-up enforcement activities against those driving while impaired at all levels across the state. At the same time, we must realize the need to toughen penalties for the offense of DWI by enacting laws that address the seriousness of the multiple repeat offenders who continue to drive drunk in this state.

We must also take a close look at the provisions of the Safe Roads Act of 1983 to determine if there are areas in the law that need updating, based on our experiences of the past four years. Swift, sure, and severe punishment must be handed out to all those who continue to drive while impaired in this state.

We must reach out and educate the public about the serious personal consequences of DWI in North Carolina. We also must reach out to medically diagnose and treat those who have a substance abuse problem and who continue to drive while impaired.

Many of these solutions come at a high cost. Our current enforcement effort statewide, per trooper, is among the highest in the country. To increase this effort will definitely require a substantial increase in the number of on-the-road troopers. We believe our enforcement people are doing a good job in apprehending DWI offenders; however, once these offenders are apprehended, we must take the proper steps to ensure that these people do not continue to drive while impaired. When the DWI problem is examined in its entirety, it seems there is a never-ending circle that begs for a solution.

To summarize: Our enforcement agencies are arresting DWI offenders in record numbers, statewide. Our courts are logjammed with DWI cases. Our jails are approaching an overcrowded status. Our community service programs are operating at a full capacity. Our medical assessment and treatment personnel are handling maximum caseloads. Our alcohol and drug education schools are booked to capacity. And yet, the DWI problem continues to increase.

I commend efforts by Mothers against Drunk Drivers (MADD) and Students against Driving Drunk (SADD). We've got MADD and SADD, maybe we need GLADD—Government and Legislators against Drugs and Driving Drunk!

I sincerely believe now is the time for action. We must direct the forces of state government to attack this serious problem. I would like the Governor's Highway Safety Commission to make the driving-while-impaired problem its top priority. I would like the commission to hold a series of public hearings around the state after the first of the year to study the DWI problem, in depth, and report back to me with recommendations for the June, 1988, legislative session. I believe this will assist my administration in moving in the right direction to attack this problem. Hopefully, we will be able to help prevent the senseless tragedies associated with driving while impaired in North Carolina.

¹Joe E. Biesecker (1937-   ), native, resident of Lexington; A.B., Catawba College, 1965; J.D., Wake Forest University, 1968; U.S. Navy, 1957-1961. Attorney; member, North Carolina Railroad Board of Directors; appointed chairman, Governor's Highway Safety Commission, 1986. Joe E. Biesecker to Jan-Michael Poff, September 12, 1988.

²Martin summarized the features of his 1987 legislative package against drunken driving in a speech to the Governor's Highway Safety Commission, February 4, 1988. "The proposals attempted to expand the current law by reducing the legal level of impairment for operators of commercial vehicles; increasing the civil license revocation for certain persons charged with DWI from ten days to thirty days; requiring permanent revocation of a driver license in the case of murder in the first or second degree resulting from motor vehicle operation; and establishing the period of license revocation for provisional licensees convicted of driving after drinking," explained the governor. "In addition, the proposals called for mandated revocation of any limited driving privilege when charged with DWI; clarification that juveniles are included within the class of persons subject to the DWI laws; and my proposals called for an increase in the penalty for felony death by vehicle to that of second-degree murder."

Three of the DWI bills the Martin administration brought forth were passed. Chapter 352 (S.B. 700), "An Act to Permit the Department of Human Resources to Enter into Interstate Reciprocal Agreements for the Transfer of Driving Under the Influence Offenders," was ratified June 12, 1987; c. 658 (S.B. 597), "An Act to Expand the Definition of Offenses Involving Impaired Driving," ratified July 23, became effective October 1, 1987; and c. 797 (S.B. 508), "An Act to Amend the Assessment Procedures for Defendants Sentenced for Driving While Impaired and to Establish Pilot Programs," ratified August 12, became effective October 1, 1987. *N.C. Session Laws, 1987,* I, II.

BIOTECHNOLOGICAL IMAGES AND PUBLIC POLICY

YOKOHAMA, JAPAN, OCTOBER 3, 1987

[Governor Martin led a state trade and economic development mission, October 1-18, 1987, to Japan, South Korea, and the People's Republic of China. While in Japan, Martin presented the following speech before a meeting of scientists and corporate managers at Yokohama City University; in so doing, he became the first governor from the United States to address members of Japan's scientific community formally. Press release, "Martin Delivers Scientific Paper at Yokohama City University," Yokohama, Japan, October 3, 1987, Governors Papers, James G. Martin.

Although the governor greeted his audience in Japanese, he delivered his remarks in English.]

Introduction

Three revolutions—the development of the digital computer, the application of the digital computer to automated equipment to form robots, and the development of genetic engineering—are sweeping society at the end of the twentieth century. Each of these revolutions has its own origin in the wellspring of human invention, but perhaps more importantly, each is also the result of human cooperation and the interweaving of many patterns of research and development. Together, the changes these technological revolutions have brought about are reshaping the societies in which we live. Each has been a tremendous positive force in improving the quality of life of millions of people the world over.

Yet, the technological innovations of recent years can only be the beginning of even greater strides. With the growth of human knowledge in the fields of computers, robotics, and biotechnology, we undoubtedly beget still greater technological accomplishments in the years to come. As scientists and leaders of our communities, each of us has an obligation to foster further innovation and to direct the benefits of scientific advancement toward the improvement of the overall human condition. Today, I would like to discuss with you the essential elements of the recent innovations I have just named—to extrapolate from these some possibilities of future innovation and, most importantly, explore means by which governments can foster the interweaving of new scientific discoveries to promote future technological advancement and social improvement. Let me begin with computers and the prospects for artificial intelligence.

Artificial Intelligence

The first major modern computer, Eniac, developed at the end of the Second World War, was a slow, cumbersome device of vacuum tubes and relatively simple circuits and was used to perform straightforward mathematical calculations. The invention of the transistor, and then its development in the form of a miniaturized silicon chip, allowed the production of microcomputers. These microcomputers can be networked with each other and with a supercomputer capable of incredibly fast calculations of algorithms. Extremely complex mathematical models of weather systems are now possible.

Along with the development of enormous calculating power has come dazzling reduction in cost. Microcomputers that now sell for a few thousand dollars just twenty years ago would have had costs of hundreds of thousands, if not millions, of dollars. One might argue that the digital computer represents nothing revolutionary at all, but rather an extension of the degree of computing power that can be traced from the abacus, to the slide rule, to the hand-held calculator, to the Eniac, to the supercomputer. But such an argument fails to note a number of qualitative differences between the microcomputer, or supercomputer, and the abacus.

The rise of artificial intelligence suggests the strong possibility that computers can be designed to think. The advent of expert systems allows microcomputers to make decisions formerly made only by humans. Many of the early debates about whether computers could think hinged upon issues of whether computers could learn and be creative. In their ability to recognize adaptive patterns, computers proved long ago that they could learn in a genuine sense of "learning"; and they have been employed to generate poetry—some of it very bad, but after all, humans do not always reach the heights of Dylan Thomas or T. S. Eliot—and to write plays. Most critics acknowledge that computers can be creative even if their creativity is limited.

Expert systems of the fifth generation, in which the Japanese have pioneered, seek to develop computers capable of programming themselves. Such an achievement would transcend the limitation now recognized that computers can think only to the degree to which they are programmed to think. Artificial intelligence of the fifth generation would come much closer to our notions of what constitutes the full range of human intelligence, and the achievement of this fifth generation of computers, as I shall suggest in a major portion of this paper, may be dependent upon utilization of the biotechnological revolution. Now let me speak about robotics.

Robotics

The combination of digital computers with machines has produced robots able to produce manufactured goods with greater precision and reliability, and faster than humans engaged in the same task. Japanese automobile companies have led the world in manufacturing productivity through the use of robots. Behind the automated production lines linking computers and machines lies a mathematical concept of queuing theory, integrating parts, manufacturing processes, and human beings into an efficient system of production.

The synergism of computers, machines, and humans, however, will probably not result in the development of artificial intelligence capable of wise technological decisions. Finite deterministic algorithms that operate the queuing process are not capable of enough flexibility to allow for creative decisions which humans achieve by such personality traits as feeling and intuition. It remains a given that present digital computers cannot defeat grand masters in chess largely because, while the computer resorts to the crunch power of trying all possible combinations, the chess master sees pattèrns and follows a heuristic procedure of recognizing a pattern and applying his intuitions to that pattern to infer future moves. This does not mean that computers will not be developed that can defeat chess masters, but given the present strategies of trying all possible combinations for a move and then optimizing that particular move, they will not. Parallel processing offers more flexibility to this problem, but it may not be sufficient to produce a potent enough artificial intelligence to solve these kinds of decision problems. Let me turn briefly to biotechnology.

Biotechnology

The revolution generated by the new biotechnology offers a new horizon for possible solution of how to achieve a flexible artificial intelligence required for the fifth generation of computers. Biotechnology has existed for centuries in the form of bioprocesses such as fermentation and the use of live organisms to produce drugs. The newness of new biotechnology arises from the discovery of how to clone genes. The discovery of the structure of DNA has led to the ability to recombine genetic structure. Techniques of recombinant DNA have been applied to the commercial produce of monoclonal antibodies.

In higher animals, an immune response to disease often occurs through a complex series of events in which specialized cells called B-lymphocytes recognize antigens and respond by producing antibodies that specifically recognize and bind to those antigens. The traditional method of producing antibodies was to inject antigens into animals and then collect the antiserum—blood serum containing antibodies—from the animal for diagnostic, therapeutic, and investigational purposes. The discovery of how to make monoclonal antibodies occurred in the following, almost accidental, manner:

> By what Cesar Milstein calls a "lucky circumstance," he and Georges Köhler began experimenting with the well-established technique of cell fusion in myeloma (antibody-producing tumor) cells . . . with antibody-producing . . . B lymphocytes from mice that had been immunized with sheep red blood cells (SRBCs), and they found that some of the resulting hybrid cells, called hybridomas secreted large amounts of homogenous (monoclonal) antibodies directed against SRBCs. The myeloma parent cell conferred on the hybridoma the ability to grow permanently in cell culture and thus to support almost unlimited antibody production, while the B lymphocyte parent contributed the genes coding for the specific antibody against an SRBC antigen.[1]

The application of recombinant DNA techniques to the production of monoclonal antibodies can improve the quality, purity, and specificity of the yield. These new biotechnological methods allow for the production of portions of antibody molecules. This latter alteration of molecules by techniques of genetic engineering offers fantastic opportunities not only in combating disease, but also in solving certain problems in artificial intelligence.

In the immune response of an organism, the formation of a molecular antibody occurs in recognition of the presence of an antigen. The development of biosensors, enzymes attached to semiconductors, depends upon the ability of one molecule —in the biochip, assisted by a tiny electronic circuit rather than the neural circuit of the body—to recognize and bind to another molecule. Biosensors have been developed to measure urea, insulin, et cetera. Japanese engineers in companies like NEC have successfully constructed these biosensors and are presently selling them in the world market.

So biotechnology, robotics, and computers have each progressed in recent years from infant technologies to powerful forces in science and society. Furthermore, the development of each of these technologies has often benefited greatly from cooperative research and interweaving of independent scientific findings, sometimes in unrelated fields.

Today, we stand at a threshold where a new process of development, involving components of each of the three technologies I have already discussed, offers great promise for still newer leaps of innovation. Specifically, the recognition of molecular chemical structures by biological organisms offers the possibility of building a bioelectronic computer that can solve at least one major, almost insurmountable, problem for the traditional digital computer, even in its supercomputer incarnation: that of recognizing patterns. I have already noted this problem by citing the difficulty that the digital computer has in combating the master in a game of chess.

A computer based upon the principles of biological molecules, like those found in the immune response, could recognize various patterns through a biochemical process rather than through a traditional algorithmic computation. Recognizing this possibility, Japan has wisely devoted a portion of its program of developing a fifth generation of computers, that can partially program themselves, to bioelectronics.

A computer based upon biochemical principles that could recognize patterns would operate at electronic speeds much slower than digital computers, but paradoxically might solve problems of recognizing patterns faster. Such a biocomputer could also model those neural networks that are so elusive to digital computers designed with parallel processes. And if one combined a parallel digital computer with a biocomputer, one might have the best of both worlds—a device in its digital aspects, which can perform enormous numbers of algorithmic calculations at lightning speed, and in its bioelectronic aspects, which could recognize patterns and intuitional paths leading to fruitful and perhaps creative decisions.

Public Policy Issues

As governor of North Carolina, a state with a strong commitment to research on both microelectronics and biotechnology, I am concerned with the formation of public policies that will aid in the development of advanced biocomputers fulfilling the possibility which I have just suggested. I believe that the role of government should be that of a catalyst, or facilitator, rather than a doer or manufacturer. In a system of private enterprise, which I strongly espouse, the government does not do the research, but rather encourages it.

Scientific and technological research in the United States takes place in industries, universities, and federal, national, laboratories. A look at the total U.S. research and development budget of $118 billion for 1986 shows that the federal government contributes $55.25 billion; industry, $59.5 billion; colleges and universities, $2.5 billion; and nonprofit institutions, $1.2 billion. States do not even appear as a separate category, although much of the $2.5 billion for colleges and universities comes from appropriations to state-supported institutions. Of the $55.25 billion appropriated by the federal government, approximately $37 billion goes for research in defense.

Industrial research rarely funds either pure scientific or pure technological research and worries little about economic development at a regional or national scale; industry invests in research to produce goods and services that will make a profit. Government funding for research has shifted, during the past several years, from basic nonmilitary research to research in defense. A sizable portion of federal monies supports basic research in science and engineering, especially through the National Science Foundation and the National Institutes of Health. But although Congress funds basic nondefense research to ensure a stronger national economy, usually these are general aims and do not focus upon a particular area of the country. Moreover, economic development is not a major purpose in most college and university research.

Given this situation, states and prefectures can play the role of imaginative coordinators and facilitators attempting to combine the research sectors within their borders into institutional networks that produce economic growth. Participants in this alliance are primarily universities and industries. Drawing upon the differing research skills and orientations of both groups, states can create interdisciplinary consortia which integrate the long-range, fundamental research of the university with the mission-oriented research of the company.

Why will this work and why may it stimulate economic growth? First, university researchers have tended to view all industrial research as applied and not fundamental, committing the error of viewing all technology as applied science. Second, industrial researchers have too often viewed scientists as impractical and unconcerned with technology, forgetting that especially in instrumentation, scientists are necessarily concerned with technology. By combining these two research orientations, innovations can be developed that will yield new products and new industrial processes. Instead of attempting to conduct research in state-sponsored laboratories, the state can coordinate its existing research in universities with private industries. University researchers will force industrial researchers to take a longer and broader view of their investigations, while university scientists and engineers in turn will often be exposed to the superior instrumentation and organization that companies can afford but few universities can match.

North Carolina's Experience

A number of North Carolina's public and private leaders foresaw, in the late 1950s, that the state would have to change its economic base because of shifting national and world market conditions. They envisioned a centrally located research park that would provide economic development through research in science and technology. Acquiring land that was largely composed of scrub pine trees, but centrally located among three universities—the University of North Carolina at Chapel Hill, Duke University at Durham, and North Carolina State University at Raleigh, forming a triangle—they began to encourage firms to locate their industrial research laboratories in what was named "Research Triangle Park."

To aid efforts to improve research in North Carolina, the state founded the Board of Science and Technology, in 1963. Composed of fifteen representatives from universities, industry, and government, and chaired by the governor, the board operates as (1) a miniature version [of the] National Science Foundation, by making grants for research in science and technology with full peer review, and (2), as a think tank which plans and initiates new institutions for economic development through research in science and technology. Since 1964, the board has made grants of more than $5 million, which have been matched by more than $100 million of external monies.[2]

The board's planning efforts have resulted in the founding of the North Carolina School of Science and Mathematics in Durham, a statewide facility attended by exceptional high school juniors and seniors; the Microelectronics Center of North Carolina; the North Carolina Biotechnology Center; and the Technological Development Authority, which oversees the operation of incubators and makes equity investments in small, start-up companies. Although the seeds for these enterprises were planted by the Board of Science and Technology, all now operate autonomously.

The success of the Research Triangle Park can be measured by the major corporate research and development facilities it has been able to attract: the Environmental Protection Agency's air pollution laboratory, Burroughs Wellcome, Sumitomo, Glaxo, IBM, and Ciba-Geigy. Mitsubishi operates a semiconductor plant at nearby Durham. University Research Park, located adjacent to the University of North Carolina at Charlotte, has successfully followed the pattern of the original Research Triangle Park. The major research universities of the state have also thrived in this positive climate for research.

One of the brightest stars in the Research Triangle Park, and certainly the one of most interest to this forum, is the Biotechnology Center of North Carolina. The center was established in 1981 as one of America's first major state biotechnology initiatives. It was already clear at that time that North Carolina could benefit from biotechnology and could quite particularly contribute to it, given the close match between our state's economic strengths and the areas for which biotechnology has application: plant and animal agriculture, forestry, marine resources, biomedicine, pharmaceuticals, and research. It was also clear that a number of strong resources already in place—the universities, Research Triangle Park, and appropriate industries—could be drawn together in a thoughtful, long-term effort.

As a private, nonprofit corporation, the center can more effectively and innovatively aid, draw on, and bring together researchers, universities, companies of varying size and stage of development, venture capitalists, government, and other interested parties. No research is undertaken at the center, since research would narrow the center's statewide intent and potentially limit the capabilities of universities and companies. The more useful course, by far, is to build on, rather than duplicate, existing academic and commercial strengths. Six years of activity and presence have proven this approach to be sound; as measured by both academic capabilities and a growing cadre of companies, biotechnology is maturing visibly in North Carolina.

The center remains distinctive in America as the only statewide endeavor directed solely to this technology and involved at all points in the movement from basic research to economic development. The state's commitment is strong and long-term. The center has been appropriated $6.49 million yearly from 1985 through 1989. Individual programs and research projects are also funded by various government and industry sources.

The mission of the center is to ensure that North Carolina benefits economically, over time, from research and commercial development in biotechnology. To meet this mission, to chart development of a new technology in a new way, the center operates under four mandates:

—Foster industrial growth through expansion of existing companies, relocation of biotechnology firms to the state, and development of new biotechnology and biotechnology-related companies throughout the state;

—Strengthen North Carolina's research foundation by enhancing the capabilities, resources, and personnel of its universities;

—Facilitate mutually beneficial partnerships and collaborations among universities, government, and industry;

—Provide public education about biotechnology to ensure citizens are informed about the importance of this technology to their personal, social, and economic futures.

To implement these mandates the center funds, initiates, aids, and sponsors research, university development, meetings, collaborative programs, educational activities, and economic development. The center encourages research and activities that are multidisciplinary and multiuniversity; that create useful interaction among, and technology transfer between, universities and industries; and that will likely lead to commercially sound products applicable to development within the state. Funding from the center supports basic research, both academic and industrial; recruiting and equipping exceptional scientists at North Carolina universities; improved or new research facilities; meetings, conferences, workshops; educational projects; and certain components of new business development.

Perhaps of greatest interest to this forum, the North Carolina Biotechnology Center has formed a committee of academic and industrial researchers on bioelectronics and has been promoting research in this area through grants and conferences. In the fall of 1986 at such a conference, technical papers on bioelectronics were presented, including several dealing with the development of biocomputers and one paper reviewing Japanese efforts to advance fifth-generation computers through molecular computing. The concept of a biotechnological image forming the organizing principle for an intelligent computer will be investigated further by both Japanese and North Carolina scientists and engineers.

Cooperation between North Carolina and Japan

A great deal of discussion takes place today, in both Japan and the United States, about the trade imbalance between the two countries. I believe that free and fair trade can occur between the two countries and that the best of relations will depend upon mutual cultural understanding and collaborative, rather than exclusive, research efforts. Each country must complement the strengths of the other. Each can learn from the other. Japanese excellence in manufacturing serves as a model for the United States, but we must come up to Japanese standards by developing an industrial organization compatible with our culture. Japanese cultural homogeneity allows for harmonious labor relations, while American individuality poses a different problem for production—but a tremendous advantage for creative discovery in science and technology.

Japan has recognized biotechnology as one of the most important fields for development in the future. Traditionally, Japan has been a world leader in bioprocess engineering. A conscious decision has been made to extend this traditional biotechnology into the new biotechnology, which features techniques like those of recombinant DNA. Accordingly, the Ministry of International Trade and Industry, the Science and Technology Agency, the Ministry of Agriculture, Forestry, and Fisheries, and the Ministry of Health and Welfare, have all established grant programs to sponsor mostly applied research in various areas of new biotechnology. In addition to these independent research efforts, many Japanese biotechnology companies have entered into joint ventures with companies in the United States.

North Carolina has a long-standing tradition of cooperation with Japan in economic development and a growing collaboration in research. Approximately forty-seven Japanese companies are located in North Carolina, including Sumitomo, fiber optics; Mitsubishi, semiconductors; Ajinomoto, amino acids; Takeda, vitamins; and Honda, lawn mowers. Konishiroku is now building a major manufacturing facility in North Carolina.[3] North Carolina also maintains an office in Tokyo to further relations between itself and Japan. As an organic chemist and governor, I look forward to increasing the connections between Japan and North Carolina, not only in economic development, but especially in collaborative research efforts that will lead to exciting new discoveries like the possibility of a biocomputer and other biotechnological advancements.

[1]*Commercial Biotechnology: An International Analysis* (Washington, D.C.: U.S. Congress, Office of Technology and Assessment, OTA-BA-218, January, 1984; Research Triangle Park, N.C.: North Carolina Biotechnology Center, June, 1987), 39.

[2]See *North Carolina's Commitment to Research: Excellence through Science and Technology* (Raleigh, North Carolina: North Carolina Board of Science and Technology, 1986).

[3]The governor was referring to the Konica Manufacturing USA, Inc., plant in Guilford County. Konica's parent company was Konishiroku Photo Industry, Ltd. "Guilford Park Lands 'The Kodak of Japan,'" *Business: North Carolina* (December, 1986), 25-30.

OPENING CEREMONIES
SOUTHEAST UNITED STATES-KOREA ASSOCIATION

SEOUL, SOUTH KOREA, OCTOBER 12, 1987

[Martin delivered a thematically similar address at opening ceremonies for the Southeast United States-Korea Association conference, November 14, 1988, in Williamsburg, Virginia.]

Fellow delegates, it is indeed a great pleasure and honor to be a part of this second joint meeting of our two associations. On behalf of the entire North Carolina delegation, I express our sincere appreciation for the great courtesy and gracious hospitality you and your fellow delegates have afforded us on our arrival here in the Republic of Korea. Already we have had the pleasure of seeing much of your country and your people, and we are entranced. Upon arrival during your Thanksgiving holidays, my first meeting was with soldiers from North Carolina, to bring them news from home and to thank them for their commitment to [the] defense of freedom. We have also met with several of your leading corporations—and by them we have been impressed—and we are optimistic about future business ties. In the days ahead, we look forward to exploring still further the great culture your country embodies as well as the great economic opportunities our two peoples now share.

I am pleased to report to you that North Carolina has recently taken a major step toward solidifying and strengthening the business ties that are already growing between our two countries. Earlier this summer, our state established a new ports office here in Seoul which will work to ensure smooth transportation and trade between North Carolina and the corporations of your country. This new office is staffed by one of your people, Captain Kwang Sun Rim, who is president of Korea Maritime International, Incorporated, and whose long experience in shipping will help us steer our course.[1] Captain Rim's office is [in] the Mediterranean Building in Choong-ku, and we genuinely hope that those of you with interest in North Carolina will find time to visit in the near future.

North Carolina has established this office here in Seoul because we are sincerely interested in furthering trade relations between the businesses of our state and the Republic of Korea. Already, your companies have been highly successful in our marketplace. Indeed, Korean business [has] found success worldwide. Your industriousness and determination have made South Korea's economy one of the fastest growing in the world today. In North Carolina, we appreciate the importance of your success and seek to solidify business relations through stronger trade with the consumers of your country. Free trade can thrive best as two-way trade, so we commend you and your government for your commitment to opening your markets.[2]

Our North Carolina Ports Authority operates two deepwater ports, one at Wilmington and the other at Morehead City, North Carolina. Both have just received funding from our state legislature for a major expansion and modernization plan. Our ports look forward to the opportunity to serve you.

Also, North Carolina hopes that as your economy grows, Korean companies with interest in overseas manufacturing operations will look favorably on North Carolina and take advantage of our strong business climate, rated number one for investment by surveys of American business leaders and equally attractive to investment by international businesses.

But North Carolina's interest in this conference goes far beyond simple business ties. We also seek stronger social and cultural understandings. As a people, we have found that through exploration of other cultures and other heritages, we come to more fully understand and appreciate [our] own. To this end, we offer not only the hand of business partnership, but of friendship and understanding as well.

North Carolina recently hosted the U.S. Olympic Festival to prepare our athletes for the Olympic Games in Seoul next year; as relations between our two countries grow, so, too, should our commitment to social, cultural, and educational exchange.

These are the hopes and aspirations of North Carolina's delegation to this conference: for strong bonds of trade and even greater bonds of friendship. Again, we express our deep appreciation for the warm and gracious welcome we have received in your country.

---

[1]Kwang Sun Rim (1929-   ), native, resident of Seoul, Korea; B.S., Korea Maritime University, 1949; was also educated at Korea University, 1961-1962. Maritime consultant and president, Korea Maritime International, Inc.; former managing director, FEMTCO Shipping Co., former president, Venus Trading Co., and former chairman, Hanjoo Shipping Co.; became Korean representative for North Carolina State Ports Authority, June 30, 1987, and for state Commerce Department, March 1, 1988. Kwang Sun Rim to Jan-Michael Poff, March 22, 1990.

[2]The governor told delegates to the Southeast United States-Korea Association meeting, November 14, 1988, that "In North Carolina, we appreciate not only the importance of your investment potential, but also your growing consumer market. As your workers win higher wages, that strengthens the buying power of your consumers, as does the recent appreciation of the wan. We have also noted your government's commitment to reduce tariffs on consumer goods. For these reasons, we hope to increase sales of our goods to your markets, and thereby improve the balance of trade between exports and imports. Surely, balanced two-way trade will add great strength to our political and military alliance."

A STATE PREPARED: 1987 CRIME AND JUSTICE CONFERENCE

RESEARCH TRIANGLE PARK, OCTOBER 30, 1987

[Events during 1987 at which Martin discussed the state's staggering illiteracy problem included his press conference on the Governor's Literacy Council, Raleigh, April 3; Motheread program press conference, Raleigh, August 25; the Plus II Breakfast, Raleigh, October 21; Catawba College Founders Day, Salisbury, October 21; the meeting of the North Carolina Association of Certified Public Accountants, Winston-Salem, October 27; and before the Crime and Justice Conference, reprinted below.]

I want to commend you for an outstanding conference and for the foresight in your selection of the theme, "A State Prepared: Pursuit of Justice in the Twenty-first Century." You have given me an awesome task: to speak, today, to how North Carolina prepares for the future.

Perhaps, before I speak to the future, I should call on a philosopher of the past for guidance. From the seventeenth century, Pascal reminds us that "the present is never our goal: the past and present are our means: the future alone is our goal."[1] Today, we have serious responsibilities: to play well the hand we've been dealt. Our goal, however, is to prepare for the future.

What, then, is our goal for the twenty-first century? This conference has given us three potential goals to explore: 1) to be prepared for crime; 2) to provide justice; 3) to provide opportunities.

If we choose as our goal the first alternative, to be prepared for crime, then we must focus on the vignettes into the future that we have been exposed to earlier this week: the pictures of crime in North Carolina in the year 2001. Those snapshots have included familiar crimes—the crimes against people and their properties—and proliferating high-technology crimes, including such different venues as computer embezzlement and drugs that will destroy minds and bodies; as well as the low-tech crimes of prostitution and pornography that place only a commercial value on life; and George Orwellian, *Nineteen Eighty-Four*, thought-control crimes.[2]

With a goal of being prepared for the crimes of the future, many of our current tasks must continue. We must continue to wage our war on drug trafficking. We must continue to intervene in crimes against persons and property. We must continue to intercept gambling, prostitution, and other vices. We must embark on fairly new tasks: We must become experts in how illegal drugs are produced and how to uncover home laboratories. We must become experts in computer programming to prevent the tremendous potential for sabotage. We must rethink our concepts of time and space to accommodate telecommunications links to criminal activities.

If we choose the second alternative, justice, as our goal, then we must focus on the issues raised in workshops this morning and yesterday afternoon—the issues of balance: balancing society's values of order and individual rights, restoring balance to the victims without denying defendants' rights, achieving a carrot-stick balance between incarceration and rehabilitation, and using three constitutionally separate powers to provide a balance in criminal justice clients' needs. With this goal, a just society, our task becomes that of becoming experts in constitutional law—or at least respecting those who are. We must provide the child victim the security of not being further traumatized by having to repeat painful accounts of the victimization in the presence of the alleged offender, while, at the same time, ensuring the defendant the right to confront the accuser without letting that confrontation be too intimidating. Balancing the rights of the accuser and the accused demands our best thinking on constitutional law.

Protecting society without eroding the very basic rights, the rights of the individual, on which so much of our society is founded, becomes an increasing challenge as our technology allows the potential for more and more intrusiveness. And understanding and appreciating the empowerment of each branch of government becomes crucial in achieving justice.

There is yet another goal on which we must place our focus and energies, the goal of opportunity. Yesterday we learned about choices, but our choices are limited only by opportunities. What did Pogo, the Okefenokee marsupial philosopher say? "Our greatest challenge is insurmountable opportunity."[3]

We were also reminded that today's children may be either productive citizens in the twenty-first century, or they will surely be the criminals we prepare for. I doubt that any of us have been surprised when we look at the contributors to delinquency and criminal behaviors, for they have been with us a long, long, time: inadequate education and training, illiteracy, unemployment and underemployment, poverty, physical and mental health problems, nonsupportive families, cultures of violence, abuse of children, and substance abuse.

But lest we doubt these contributors, let me briefly profile some of the information on the 23,000-plus men and women incarcerated last year in our prisons. In a self-report, almost two thirds said that they either never use, or only occasionally use, alcohol or drugs. In actuality, however, only one third of them were sober at the time of their offense. Educationally, while half of the inmates report finishing tenth grade or better, the reality is that only one sixth are functioning at, or above, the tenth-grade level in reading, while almost half are functioning at, or below, the sixth-grade level—and almost one third score at the third-grade level or below. I believe we have here what is known as a correlation!

Occupationally, only one eighth had been unemployed at the time of incarceration, but two thirds were employed in jobs calling only for low-level skills. Other demographics reveal that just over one fourth of the inmates had immediate family members with felony and/or misdemeanor records, which is probably not a strong correlation, while two thirds existed at or below a subsistence level—definitely a correlation.

In my "State of the State" address, I announced that I was creating a Governor's Commission on Literacy and was declaring 1987 the "Year of the Reader." To head this important commission, I appointed the very best person I could find: Bill Friday, president emeritus of the University of North Carolina. As executive director, I appointed Dr.

Richard Hagemeyer, who established himself as a national leader in literacy training for adults while serving as president of Central Piedmont Community College in Charlotte.

Why would I bring up the matter of a literacy commission in a crime and justice conference? The answer should be obvious, to anyone who looks at our prison population, that if [we] do not solve the problem of adult illiteracy in our state, we cannot hope to solve the problem of prison overcrowding. Currently, we are serving only 6 percent of those who need literacy training, and the growth in the number of illiterates added to our rolls each year is far in excess of the number we are able to bring up to an acceptable level through various training programs. And the evidence is indisputable: [Il]literacy has the face of crime and poverty. I think there can be little doubt that the exponential growth of illiteracy among our adult population, with its attendant ills, will result in a corresponding growth in unemployment, welfare dependency, and prison population.

Our literacy programs, in spite of millions in investments and great dedication of those who are working in literacy programs, are not good enough. As I stated in a recent speech given at Catawba College, "If we expect to get significantly better results in our literacy programs, we simply must do something significantly different from what we are now doing." In short, we have got to be a lot more innovative than we now are. This should not be taken as criticism of all those who are working so hard to deal with the problem of adult illiteracy. What it does mean is that we must adopt a different mind-set.

Part of a needed mind-set is that just spending more money on what we have always been doing will not get the job done. Here is how I stated it in the Catawba College speech: "I would like to offer what I hope will become a credo or law for our literacy programs: Investing more and more money in failed strategies will serve only to consolidate and institutionalize those strategies, thereby hindering adoption of promising strategies more capable of raising the level of literacy in North Carolina." Another way of saying this is that what we too often see, in programs where innovation is a dire necessity, is a form of Gresham's law: Bad, unproductive programs drive out the good, potentially productive programs by absorbing all the energy and funding resources.[4]

Clearly, all that we are doing is not enough. If our goal is opportunity, it is incumbent upon us to reframe the contributors to criminal behaviors to become opportunities for change, to provide choice for positive change. Our strategies, then, must focus on equipping today's children for success. Our future, our children, must provide enlarged opportunites through their support systems—the family, the school, the community—in order that they may experience success rather than failure. Children must be provided with the essentials of nurturance, guidance, education, assistance, unconditional love, control, structure, and appropriate discipline. Our government's contribution to the formula for success lies in enabling the family, the school, and the community to provide sufficient opportunites for success for each and every child, in North Carolina, and to give them a sense of self-worth and power to shape their own destinies.

How does the government of North Carolina enable the family, the school, and the community to provide supportive opportunities? Assistance is offered through our laws, our services, and our courts. We have a rich history, in North Carolina, of providing services of quality to, and for, the vast majority of children. This is achieved through legislation and appropriations, through the courts' protection and guidance, and through services as varied as recruitment of industries to financial assistance.

But for our most at-risk children and families, we must do better. We can do better. As your governor, I am calling upon your voice, the criminal justice system's voice, to join with mine in ensuring that we have the resources, the resourcefulness, and the will to end the scourge of illiteracy at all age levels.

How can we expect our next generation to be prepared to assume their responsibilities when they and the parents who help them with their homework cannot read? There is an exponential growth in the rate of adult illiteracy. Adult illiteracy is far outstripping our present best efforts to bring it under control.

How can we expect the children to learn to read when, for many at-risk children, schools are no longer havens of curiosity but "jails" to be escaped? And how can we expect parents to support our efforts with the schools when they, too, experienced failure there over and over again? No amount of opportunities in other areas of peoples' lives can compensate for both the lack of skills and the poor self-concept that this lack engenders.

We must also break the vicious cycle of poverty that claims too many of our children and their families. While it is critical to feed our hungry children now, it is even more crucial that we provide them and their families with the skills and work opportunities that enable them to feed themselves. Our future cannot tolerate a system of support that encourages workers, whose families depend on both their wages and financial assistance, to work only four or five days because they would lose their benefits otherwise. I am not saying that those who work and also receive our assistance should be denied our assistance; rather, I am saying that we need to provide the necessary training, child care, medical benefits, and transportation that allow these workers to earn an income sufficient to support their families. We must turn the disincentives of today into incentives for the future.

We can no longer tolerate absent parents' abandonment of their children. There can never be adequate supervision of children if the parent they are living with is not at home because they are forced to work two or more jobs to provide for their families.

North Carolina must ensure the health of its children and their families. Malnourished children suffer not only from physical problems, but also demonstrate diminished abilities to concentrate on intellectual tasks. Their future, and ours, requires the brightest minds of all our children.

Their future, and ours, requires them to have the protection of childhood. For each child that has a child, two children have been robbed of the glory and the protection of childhood, and our future has been diminished. For each child that survives the brutality of sexual victimization in the remaining years of this century, the potential for seventy children to be brutalized in the twenty-first century increases. Each child battered, or witnessing the battering of other family members, carries into the twenty-first century this battering model as parenthood is assumed.

The goal of opportunity requires all of us—businesses, churches, the legislature, law enforcement, human services, schools, the courts, advocacy groups, private citizens—to join our resources of time, talents, finances, and priority together. We have long since passed the time of simple solutions, for the barriers to opportunity are complex and varied.

When our goal for the twenty-first century is opportunity, the greater becoming of children, we achieve also the first two goals. Our goal of being prepared for the crimes of the twenty-first century should result in reduced crime. Our goal of a just society will also be met, for there will be fewer crimes and fewer victims. Isn't that the ideal of justice?

Many of you may remember my theme of "One United State" from my inaugural address in 1985. I implore you to use this conference, "A State Prepared: Pursuit of Justice in the Twenty-First Century," to be united by directing resources to meet children's and their families' needs, thus diminishing the potential for crime. An investment of half our criminal justice resources in prevention, and half our resources to those presently involved in the criminal justice system, will produce benefits in the twenty-first century that we can only begin to envision. To do less is to make us robbers of the twenty-first century, thieves of greater possibility.

Let me conclude by calling on another philosopher, a future twenty-first century philosopher—an anonymous young man of eight years of age. He shares with us what makes America special:

> America to me means love and freedom. America means duty to God and all children. America means growing up to be whatever I want to be, a policeman, a fireman, an engineer, or a scientist.
>
> America means building and living anywhere you want to live or to go anywhere you want to go.
>
> America is to change things to make them good for everyone in the world. America to me means to feed the poor and to give homes to the people who live in the streets. So what makes America special is caring for one another and helping each other because we are a big family. We are the same and are blessed by God.

Please join me in helping to provide these opportunities to all North Carolina's children. Don't let the words of another twenty-first century philosopher, a young lady sixteen years old, haunt us: "Tell me you love me now. Don't carve it in stone."

Only now can we work toward a future when we can claim, "North Carolina prepared." Let us work, as one united state, to reach this honorable goal.

---

[1]"The present is never our end. The past and the present are our means; the future alone is our end. So we never live, but we hope to live; and, as we are always preparing to be happy, it is inevitable that we should never be so." Blaise Pascal (1632-1662), as quoted in Rudolf Flesch, *The Book of Unusual Quotations* (New York: Harper & Brothers, Publishers, 1957), 225.

[2]George Orwell's novel, *Nineteen Eighty-Four* (New York: Harcourt, Brace, 1949), is a grim tale of one man's unsuccessful struggle against totalitarian society. Margaret Drabble (ed.), *The Oxford Companion to English Literature* (Oxford: Oxford University Press, 1985), 701.

[3]Award-winning cartoonist Walter Crawford (Walt) Kelly created the syndicated comic strip, *Pogo*, in 1948. It was named for its main character, "an amiable opossum" who, with his fellow denizens of the Okefenokee Swamp, took satirical notice of contemporary politics and the world about them. An estimated 20 million newspaper readers followed Pogo's daily adventures. *Current Biography, 1956*, 332-334, *1973*, 456; *Who Was Who in America, 1974-1976*, 222.

[4]The economic principle known as Gresham's law states that "when two or more kinds of money of unequal exchange value are in concurrent circulation, each being available for payments, the one of inferior value tends to drive the one of higher value out of circulation." David F. Tver (comp.), *The Gulf Publishing Company Dictionary of Business and Science* (Houston, Texas: Gulf Publishing Company Book Division, 1974), 229.

PRESS RELEASE: GOVERNOR TO DISCUSS COASTAL
INITIATIVE PROPOSAL

RALEIGH, NOVEMBER 19, 1987

[Nearly identical drafts of speeches on the Coastal Initiative plan, dated September 2, 1988, were prepared for delivery in Columbia, Edenton, Plymouth, and Swansboro, during a planned visit to eastern communities. In remarks presented at a stop in his northeastern tour, September 19, 1988, the governor mentioned the participation of Plymouth in one of five pilot programs launched under the initiative.]

Governor Jim Martin will visit New Bern, Tuesday, November 24, to present his proposal to enhance North Carolina's untapped coastal resources. Recognizing that it is North Carolina's pristine image that draws people to the coast, Governor Martin's plan seeks greater protection in specifically designated waters while focusing growth in key areas with less sensitive profiles. "I believe that by working together, we can find new ways to make coastal havens like the Albemarle and Pamlico sounds more attractive to economic opportunities while establishing stronger environmental safeguards in our most sensitive and productive waters," he said. "I don't see any reason we cannot create a plan that will satisfy the needs of tourism, development, and ecology alike."

Governor Martin has invited coastal residents, city and county officials, local legislators, environmentalists, fishermen, and other concerned citizens from the twenty county coastal area to attend the meeting scheduled to begin at 3:00 P.M. in the Tryon Palace Auditorium.[1]

Under the Coastal Initiative concept, communities that elect to participate in the program would receive priority status for state-issued grants, loans, and permits. In addition, the coastal region will benefit from improved waterways, navigation aids, and environmental designations. "I want to make it clear that local governments will retain control of their zoning and growth regulations," Governor Martin said. "Only those communities that wish to participate will be included. However, once all the details are explained, I think everyone will be very interested in the opportunities that can be created through this innovative program."

Members of [the] Coastal Initiative's Blue Ribbon Commission and administrative group also will be on hand to discuss various aspects of the governor's proposal.[2]

North Carolina Coastal Initiative [Attached]

Purpose: To create a framework to ensure the protection of water
    quality, fisheries habitats, and preserve outstanding natural
    coastal features and to encourage harmonious waterfront devel-
    opment in local communities.

North Carolina's coastline possesses unique natural beauty. The
sounds and coastal waterways attract recreational boaters, sports
fishermen, and vacationers. Many coastal areas have lagged behind
the regional average for economic development and need a local
growth plan for commercial and residential expansion. Beneath the
coastal waters, however, are fragile resources such as marine habitats,
nursery areas, and shellfish beds. These resources need extra protection against degradation.

To provide this delicate balance between coastal development,
tourism, and the marine environment, Governor Martin has established the Coastal Initiative Blue Ribbon Commission. Chaired by
former lieutenant governor Jimmy Green, the commission is comprised of state and local officials, [and] coastal, environmental, and
business leaders. The fifteen-member commission serves as a policy
board, giving leadership and direction to the working body, the
administrative group. The group consists of senior management staff
from each of the participating state departments and divisions.
Members of the administrative group will formulate proposals for
achieving the following objectives:

—Increase protection of ecologically fragile and environmentally
significant areas;

—Create a marine waterways system;

—Stimulate shoreline commercial development and waterfront
investment.

Increased Environmental Protection

Protection of water quality is vital to the coastal economy and is
necessary to protect marine resources. Certain of our coastal waters
require special attention and protection over and beyond our normal
environmental regulations to remain viable. Examples include highly
productive shellfish areas, primary nursery areas, unique natural
areas, wildlife habitats, and other exceptional ecosystems. These areas

should be identified using the Natural Heritage Program, the Marine and Estuarine Sanctuaries Program, primary nursery area maps, shellfish maps, and the North Carolina Nature Conservancy.

Once identified, the most appropriate protection measures will be employed to ensure that each is protected from development and remains in a natural state. Protection measures include:

—*Outstanding Resource Waters Designation.* This designation by the Environmental Management Commission requires special, tailor-made protection from development to be applied. To qualify, an area must be unique or ecologically significant or in exceptional condition. Once approved for nomination and detailed study, the area immediately is protected from both point and nonpoint sources of pollution.

—*Natural Heritage Program.* In this program, environmentally significant areas are identified through an inventory. Owners are contacted and encouraged to register, donate, or otherwise protect the property. Efforts in the coastal area will be increased by giving this area priority in updating inventories, conducting inventories in new areas, and contacting landowners about protection measures.

—*Acquisition of Environmentally Significant Areas.* Acquisition can be used in cases in which other measures do not adequately or appropriately protect an environmentally significant area. For example, acquisition was used successfully in the case of Permuda Island and is now being used to protect Buxton Woods.[3] This approach requires funds and the continued cooperation of the North Carolina Nature Conservancy. Since funds are so limited, alternative funding sources will be explored.

Shoreline Commercial Development

Many towns and communities on the coast are ideally situated to take advantage of an increased emphasis on recreational boating. For whatever reason, these communities, especially ones in which the economy has changed dramatically over the years, have not capitalized on their geographic location.

The concept is to focus specific state efforts on selected communities which demonstrate the local initiative and commitment necessary to succeed. Economic potential and feasibility will be key criteria. Incentives such as concentrated technical assistance and priority for grants and loans, permits, and other programs will be given to the selected communities. The factors used to select the communities will include:

—*Local Initiative*. The community must demonstrate that their leaders, both private and governmental, are committed to improving the economy. The local leaders must show that they will take the lead in this project with the help of the state.

—*Potential*. The community must demonstrate that it has the potential to succeed. These include such factors as the suitability of the waterfront for development; public access by land, sea, or air; navigability of the harbor; and presence of local points of interest, attractions, and amenities for boaters.

—*Need*. The community must demonstrate that it needs the concerted efforts of the state to help it improve its economy. Priority will be given to communities that have continually lagged behind the average in economic development.

Marine Waterways System

Boating on North Carolina's lakes and rivers has long been recognized as an important tourist attraction, and in recent years, recreational boating in coastal waters has increased its appeal among boaters and marine-related businesses alike. A marine waterways system will serve the navigational needs of the recreational boating public by:

—Providing a navigational system of linkages, anchorages, and channels similar to the highway system;

—Preparing maps and guides suitable as navigational aids;

—Identifying needed waterway improvements including dredging, channel marking, and access.

---

[1]Counties initially invited to participate in the Coastal Initiative program included Beaufort, Bertie, Brunswick, Camden, Carteret, Chowan, Craven, Currituck, Dare, Gates, Hertford, Hyde, New Hanover, Onslow, Pamlico, Pasquotank, Pender, Perquimans, Tyrrell, and Washington. Attachment to press release, "Governor to Discuss Coastal Initiative Proposal," Raleigh, November 19, 1987, Governors Papers, James G. Martin; for other related press releases, see "Coastal Initiative Group to Meet in Edenton," Raleigh, March 4, 1988; "Coastal Initiative Moves Forward," Raleigh, March 31, 1988; and "Coastal Initiative Workshops to Be Held in April in 20 Counties," Raleigh, April 19, 1988.

[2]Executive Order Number 57, signed November 23, 1987, established the Governor's Blue Ribbon Commission on Coastal Initiatives and its Administrative Working Group. *N.C. Session Laws, 1987, Regular Session, 1988,* III, 931-935.

[3]For related press release, see "Governor Announces Acquisition Initiative for Buxton Woods," Raleigh, October 23, 1987, Governors Papers, James G. Martin.

ALBEMARLE AREA DEVELOPMENT ASSOCIATION

ELIZABETH CITY, DECEMBER 3, 1987

[The following address is similar to one delivered at du Pont's Fayetteville works, December 1, 1987.]

What a great pleasure it is to be with people, like you, who are making such a difference in the economic and social life of northeastern North Carolina; and what an honor it is to be here on the occasion of the twenty-fifth anniversary of the Albemarle Area Develoment Association. My congratulations, and may you have many more productive years.

Before getting to the heart of my remarks, I think it's important to review my charge. Bill Meekins[1] told me that it would be appropriate to give you a thorough review of economic development in North Carolina and the northeastern area—a kind of "State of the Economy" address. And then Bill gave me the punch line: "You have a whole fifteen minutes to do it."

I don't want to appear to be picking on Bill. Believe me, I'm not. It's just that I'm getting a little sensitive about a growing trend: people telling me, over and over, "Keep it short." Things really came to a head in a speech about two weeks ago. I started my speech with "In the beginning"; with this utterance, the emcee jumped up and said, "Thank you, governor, for those inspiring words."

I promise to keep my remarks as brief as possible, no matter how long it takes. When Pharaoh Ramses was mummified, they said he was strapped for time. So in conclusion—but seriously, it is no exaggeration to say that all of you, who are a part of this ten-county consortium, are partners in an economic miracle that has taken place in North Carolina over a period of almost three years.

Whenever I talk about economic development, I'm reminded of a story that Dottie told me about a first-grader. It seems his teacher had asked all the children to bring something in on Monday for "Show and Tell." Little Johnny piped up and said, "Shucks, teacher, mine's not 'Show and Tell,' it's 'Bring and Brag.'"

I find that people like you here in the northeast, and other parts of the state, are giving me a lot to brag about. We in North Carolina have every right to be proud. Consider this: *Business Week* magazine found that more business leaders across America consider North Carolina the most attractive location for new plant sites than any other state in the union. *Manufacturing* magazine found the same degree of confidence in North Carolina's pro-business climate by chief executive officers of American companies. This confidence in North Carolina is only partially reflected by the fact that, in the first six months of 1987, manufacturing companies announced an average of more than two new plants a week, with more than one plant a week valued at over $5 million.

This extraordinary vote of confidence by business in North Carolina is perhaps stated most convincingly by the fact that our state had its best business recruitment ever in the week of July 13 through 19, 1987, when five new and expanding businesses announced plans to create more than 3,000 jobs. And the truly historic part of that is that, for the first time in many decades, we had more investment in more jobs in rural centers outside the piedmont corridor than in the big cities of the piedmont—by a factor of three times as much. That's not because the piedmont cities stopped scoring. It's because we've learned how to score in rural areas with the kind of teamwork that you display here in the northeastern part of our state.

The upbeat goes on. New and expanding manufacturing and service-related industries invested a total of $5.2 billion in North Carolina facilities, in 1986, and announced plans to create an estimated 55,000 jobs. But hold it: Commerce Secretary Pope has just informed me that this is a gross underestimate of the net increase in jobs in 1986—that the actual increase was about 80,000 jobs, which includes all jobs created in 1986, minus all jobs lost.

As good as 1986 was, 1987 is shaping up as even better. New manufacturing industries alone, in the first three quarters, announced investments of $776 million, with 11,000 jobs. These statistics, I should add, do not include any numbers on existing industry or service industry investment; and if the pace continues in the fourth quarter, 1987 could well be the best year ever for business investment in North Carolina.

There is more good news. Manufacturing companies invested $2.7 billion in new and expanded North Carolina operations in 1986—the second highest level yet, next to 1985's record year of $2.8 billion. Not so coincidentally, the 1986 investments are expected to create 23,000 jobs in our state.

Results like these, and the return to work of laid-off workers, gave North Carolina a net gain of 268,000 jobs in 1985-1986. Our critics like to say that we lost 19,000 jobs. That's not even half the truth. They neglect the larger part of the truth, which is that even if we lose 32,000 jobs and add 300,000 jobs, you have a net improvement of 268,000 jobs over a two-year period.

But in spite of all the glowing testimonials to North Carolina, there are still those who would have you believe we are losing our appeal. Well, I believe that we must all be willing to bear the truth about our state, no matter how pleasant it is. Here is another truth that I will try to help my critics bear: Since becoming governor, total personal income in North Carolina has risen to more than $77.5 billion, a gain of over 13.6 percent. I ought to take full credit for this remarkable achievement since I would be blamed if things weren't so good.

Good things just don't happen, however. They happen as a result of our actions, yours and ours. There is great truth in the biblical saying, "As ye sow, so shall ye reap."[2]

Let me tell you about one very fruitful harvest. Although we have made impressive gains in reducing strategic anti-job taxes in North Carolina, starting with the largest tax cut in history in 1985, fiscal-year tax revenues have risen by almost $1 billion. So much for the doom-sayers who warned that by cutting anti-job taxes we would have resulting cuts in essential human services such as education.

I don't know why, but this story comes to mind: Three men came out of a building and found they had locked themselves out of their car. One of them said, "Get me a wire coat hanger, and I can straighten it out and figure how to trip the car handle with it."

And the second man said, "You can't do that. Someone will see us and think you're stealing the car."

The third man said, "Well, we better do something quick, because it's starting to rain and the top's down."

We are not like these three "dimboes" who were looking for the wrong solution when the solution was obvious.

You know, when it comes to how far we can go in economic development, nobody knows where top performance is in North Carolina. We can reach the top, working together as one united state, today and tomorrow. A degree of humility is in order, though. I like to remind our administration that we didn't earn our merit badges all by ourselves. Statewide teamwork does it. People in Raleigh; people like you, here in the northeast; people all over the state share in the glory. It just shows what can be done when we work together as one united state—where we work together, east and west, and piedmont, and sandhills—to build a brighter future with better jobs, better roads, and better schools. And it is impossible to overemphasize: You are an essential part of our march toward progress.

Commerce Secretary Claude E. Pope has provided me with a thumbnail historical sketch of economic development in our state. As early as the 1930s, we were working to diversify our economy. Governor Luther Hodges began today's modern era of development strategy with Research Triangle Park and aggressive trade promotion programs. The 1980s have brought about levels of economic growth envied by other states.

Under my administration, we have continued what has become accelerated economic growth in this state, with a far greater balance of industries and far greater geographical balance of businesses than had previously been realized. As a result, today North Carolina has a broad range of development programs, from travel and tourism, to film development, to high tech, to agribusiness, to our traditional industries.

All this notwithstanding, we have seen economic development become dramatically more competitive. There are, for example, now 10,000 development organizations in America pursuing roughly 1,400 projects a year. It is not surprising, then, that the business of recruiting business has become a major business of state government. This is why, as governor, I take every opportunity to seek opportunities, in this country and abroad, for economic development and job creation. Business recruiting is a contact sport. It cannot, as some of the newspapers would have you believe, be done with me sitting in Raleigh. "Jobs to our people" is not just a motto for the administration; it is a passionate commitment.

Up to this point, I have spoken about what has happened with economic development and job creation in the state as a whole. It goes without saying: You, here in the northeast, are an important part of our success story. But now I'd like to spend the remainder of the time telling you about some of the things that have happened, and are expected to happen, in this part of the state.

Overall, we can be proud with the strong levels of job creation in smaller communities. In fact, so far this year, 70 percent of new jobs have gone to communities of 10,000 people or less. We have been able to announce more than $121 million in investment by new industries in twenty-one counties served by the state Commerce Department's Northeast Regional Office. We had the highest level of investment this decade, and the figures we have only cover the first three quarters of 1987. For example, we had Fruit of the Loom, in Williamston, with an investment of $40 million and 300 jobs; Pharmafair, in Martin County, with an investment of $2 million and 100 jobs; Weyerhaeuser, in Ayden (lumber mill) with 140 jobs; Stanadyne, in Kinston, with an investment of $2 million and 75 jobs, initially; then there is Davis Yachts, here in Elizabeth City.

Let me take just a moment to say something that I think is of extreme importance to the future economic development of this area. As I have tried to emphasize, my administration is putting a strong emphasis on economic development in rural areas, and we have had some proud achievements, but I know that resources and manpower are stretched thin. This is why I proposed spending about $500,000 to expand the Commerce Department's network of regional offices. Here in the northeast, my plan was to add an entirely new office. This addition would have meant that instead of having our staff in Williamston serve twenty-one counties, we would have divided this region in two and posted a total of four developers right here in Elizabeth City.

Unfortunately, the legislature denied funding for this expansion proposal. The result of that inaction is that we are still working out of one office here in the northeast. What the majority of legislators failed to see, apparently, is that these regional offices are an investment, not an expense. They will more than pay for themselves. Who was it who said that there is nothing so powerful as an idea whose time has come? We intend to propose our expansion plan for [a] regional center again in next year's short session of the General Assembly. With your help, we fervently hope we can get this proposal funded.

Meanwhile, we must all continue working as hard as we can with what we've got. Even working under handicapping conditions, according to research done by our Commerce Department, as of September of this year, we've had more new industry development here in northeastern North Carolina, in 1987, than during any other year this decade. In fact, we may even be on the way to our best year ever for industrial investment in the northeast. In fact, in the first nine months of this year, new manufacturing operations announced plans to invest more than $121 million in the twenty-one counties served by the Commerce Department's Northeast Regional Office. The bottom line is that this performance is greater than the previously best record of 1983, when announcements totaled only $100 million for the entire year.

There is more good news. On my recent trip to Europe, I took the opportunity to meet with officials of Airship Industries, which earlier this year won a $168 million contract to develop a new prototype surveillance blimp for the U.S. Navy. I know a lot of rumors have been flying around concerning Airship's plans for locating here in North Carolina. Airship's president has laid these rumors to rest. He assured me that a large portion of the new development work at Airship Industries will be conducted in Weeksville.

In a very real sense, this is an occasion for thanksgiving and celebration—a time for giving thanks to you for all you have done, and are doing, to help North Carolina keep its date with destiny and a time for celebrating our incredible accomplishments. You know, one of the most important things I do, as governor, is to honor excellence throughout the state. In this role, I have had the honor to recognize outstanding teachers, farmers, business people, state employees, and programs. Now it is my privilege to honor you for the outstanding job you are doing in economic development and job creation. One aspect of peak performers such as you is that you are always trying to do better. We can bask in the warmth of our achievements, but there is always the feeling with those committed to excellence that they can do better, and we will do better.

Several years ago, I chanced upon an interesting anecdote. It seems that back in the fifteenth century, before Columbus discovered the New World, all Spanish coins bore the inscription *Ne plus ultra*, "No more beyond." After Columbus's voyages, all coins were changed to read *Plus ultra*, "More beyond." You, as exemplars of excellence, are changing perceptions of the possible. You have, by your accomplishments, written large for all to see, *Plus ultra*, more beyond.

---

[1]Elizabeth City resident William C. Meekins, Jr., began an eight-year term on the State Board of Education effective April 28, 1987. Letter of appointment to William C. Meekins, Jr., May 7, 1987, Governors Papers, James G. Martin.

[2]"Be not deceived; God is not mocked: for whatsoever a man soweth, that shall he also reap." Galatians 6:7.

SCIENCE AND PUBLIC POLICY: THE ROLE OF THE STATES

DENVER, COLORADO, DECEMBER 4, 1987

[The National Superconducting Super Collider Symposium provided the forum for the following address. Martin was joined on the occasion by Governor Richard Celeste, of Ohio, who spoke on the "Outlook for the SSC among the States." Press release, "Governor Martin Presents Paper on the Superconducting Super Collider," Raleigh, December 4, 1987, Governors Papers, James G. Martin.]

Introduction

I am delighted to be here at this important meeting discussing various aspects of the superconducting super collider. Preparing our proposal to the Department of Energy for the SSC has been one of the most exciting experiences for many North Carolina civil servants.[1] Under the overall direction of my science adviser, Dr. Earl Mac Cormac, and directed by Dr. Paul Frampton and managed by Dr. Bill Dunn, when we came to the final few days of preparation almost 100 state employees worked voluntarily, for four days and nights, without sleep and without overtime pay, to complete the proposal. Several told Dr. Mac Cormac that this was the most exciting project that they had ever worked on, and that their commitment arose from the very scientific nature of the project as well as their sincere dedication to preparing the best proposal that they could for North Carolina.

I want to spend a few minutes sharing with you this excitement about the fundamental nature of science. I began my career as a scientist, an organic chemist; and before I was lured into politics by the prospect of endless free dinners, a vast mansion with twelve bathrooms, and long vacations, I labored not only in the classroom but also in the laboratory, attempting to understand the complex nature of organic molecules.

Motivation for science arises from a passionate human desire to know. Researchers strive to understand the most fundamental aspects of nature. To achieve this understanding, they stretch their imaginations, producing beautiful mathematical theories which they confirm or disconfirm in ingeniously conceived experiments measured in elaborate and complex instruments. I want to reflect, for a few moments, on several famous critical experiments in the history of science by examining their instrumentation. Then, I will proceed to consider some of the implications for public policy of the largest and perhaps most expensive purely scientific instrument ever proposed, the superconducting super collider.

Two Famous Experiments

A. The 1919 Eclipse Test of General Relativity[2]

On Friday, November 7, 1919, the *Times* of London featured the headlines: "Revolution in Science/New Theory of the Universe/Newtonian Ideas Overthrown." Below the headlines appeared a story reporting the extraordinary joint meeting of the Royal Society of London and the Royal Astronomical Society, on the day before, where the results of the total solar eclipse of May 29, 1919, were announced. These observations confirmed predictions from Einstein's General Theory of Relativity that rays of light passing near the sun would be bent; Newton's gravitational theory also predicted that light passing near the sun would be displaced, but far less. The Newtonian law of gravitation would cause the image of a star with a position on the limb of the sun to appear to be displaced 0.87 inches from the sun. Einstein's theory postulated a gravitational mass of E/c^2 and predicted a displacement of 1.75 inches.

So familiar are we with relativity that we tend to forget that when Einstein first proposed his theory, many scientists believed it to be nothing more than an interesting mathematical conjecture. Accustomed to think in Newtonian terms, conjectures like that of the speed of light as a constant seemed absurd and unjustified. T. J. J. See, the American antirelativist, warned in a letter to the *Observatory* that the new theory should not be taken seriously, because "the whole doctrine of relativity rests on a false basis and will someday be cited as an illustration of foundations laid in quicksand."[3]

George Mathews, however, suggested that if Einstein's mathematics could be tested experimentally, then his conjectures might represent a legitimate scientific theory:

This is a matter of mathematics merely; the most striking fact, from a physical point of view, is that Einstein has used these formulas successfully to account for the secular motion of the perihelion of Mercury. . . . The more predictions the new theory can give us, which are verified by experiment, the more we shall be inclined to trust it and this is quite independent of what we call the "true meaning" of the symbols involved.[4]

And physicists like Arthur Stanley Eddington,[5] who had learned of the General Theory of Relativity during the First World War through a Dutch scientist who was in contact with both Eddington and Einstein, sought ways to test the theory. The astronomer royal, Frank Watson Dyson,[6] suggested that the total eclipse of May 29, 1919, would provide an opportunity to test the predicted results from both Newton's and Einstein's theories. Under the auspices of the Joint Permanent Eclipse Committee of the Royal Society and the Royal Astronomical Society, two expeditions were dispatched with the one sent to the island of Principe led by Eddington. The other, to Sobral in northern Brazil, was led by A. C. D. Crommelin, who clearly stated the resulting possibilities for this crucial observation:

There are thus three possibilities: no shift, the half shift, or the full Einstein shift. The definite establishment of any one of the three as the truth would be an important addition to our knowledge of physics. Should the decision be in favor of the Einstein shift, it would, in combination with the success of the latter in explaining the motion of the perihelion of Mercury, suffice to lead to its acceptance as the actual system of the Universe. Its definite disproof would also be of service, since it would avoid the dissipation of further energy in its elaboration.[7]

The instruments for these two expeditions consisted principally of astrographic lenses, mirrors, and photographic plates. Both expeditions did obtain photographic plates of the eclipse, but Crommelin's expedition experienced difficulties because the sun caused their mirrors to expand unevenly and distort the images. Because of clouds, Eddington got fewer plates and less data to check for random errors. Instrumental flaws in both expeditions led to careful evaluation of the data, in England, before the results were released.

During the summer of 1919, when preliminary conclusions had been reached, this news leaked to the continent. On September 27, 1919, Einstein wrote to his mother: "Dear Mother, Good news today. H. A. Lorentz has wired me that the British expeditions have actually proved the light deflection near the sun."[8] Few in England, however, learned of the results until the November 6, 1919, meeting of the Royal Society which Alfred North Whitehead, the mathematician and philosopher, has vividly described in his *Science and the Modern World*, as follows:

> It was my good fortune to be present at the meeting of the Royal Society in London when the astronomer royal for England announced that the photographic plates of the famous eclipse, as measured by his colleagues in Greenwich Observatory, had verified the prediction of Einstein that rays of light are bent as they pass in the neighbourhood of the sun. The whole atmosphere of tense interest was exactly that of the Greek drama: we were the chorus commenting on the decree of destiny as disclosed in the development of a supreme incident. There was dramatic quality in the very staging: the traditional ceremonial, and in the background the picture of Newton to remind us that the greatest of scientific generalisations was now, after more than two centuries, to receive its first modification. Nor was the personal interest wanting: a great adventure in thought had at length come safe to shore.[9]

B. The Discovery of the Positron[10]

The interrelationship between theory and experiment is also vividly demonstrated by the discovery of the positron. Although in 1931 Dirac had predicted an electronic particle with positive charge, and had decided that the proton would not do since its mass was too large, when Carl Anderson first experimentally identified a positive electron on August 2, 1932, he was unable to show that this was the particle predicted by Dirac.[11] Anderson, under the direction of his professor, Robert Millikan,[12] constructed a cloud chamber employing a powerful water-cooled electromagnet ten times more powerful than any previous cloud chamber's. Anderson, however, was unfamiliar with Dirac's work and, when confronted with a strange new particle track, he was unable to explain its presence. While identifying it as a positive electronic particle, Anderson was puzzled as to how it could occur and why other researchers had not also found it. Only shortly thereafter, when Blackett and Occhialini had developed a new technique for photographing particle tracks, were they able to equate the particle found by Anderson with that theoretically predicted by Dirac.[13] In this observation, the experimental results and theoretical prediction were welded into one particle, the positron.

In Dirac's theory, a few of the quantum states of negative kinetic energy are unoccupied by electrons and, instead, are filled with particles of positive charge, namely, positrons. When showers of these positrons occur, they quickly disappear as they react with readily available negative electrons to form two or more quanta of energy. This latter fact explains why so few early experimenters had encountered positrons. Probably, as scrutiny of earlier photographic plates seems to indicate, some researchers did record tracks of particles that we now know as positrons, but they did not "observe" positrons in the sense of knowing what they were seeing. In order to do that, they would have had to know what to expect, and this could only have been provided by a theoretical prediction.

It is significant that in the discovery of the positron we have clear-cut evidence of a theoretical term becoming an observation term. What was predicted by Dirac was discovered by Blackett and Occhialini. Anderson had merely found evidence of an unusual, positively charged particle, but he really did not know what he had uncovered. Like the observations of the 1919 eclipse, the discovery of the positron depends upon adequate instrumentation—but the degree of sophistication has increased.

The Superconducting Super Collider: The Largest of Them All

I could have continued my narrative of the history of scientific instrumentation, which would show not only a growth of more complex and precise instruments, but also a growth in size and cost. Ironically, as we seek to understand the fundamental nature of the smallest particles, we require the largest instruments. We stand today in a situation not dissimilar from that of the 1919 eclipse: We have a new and only partially tested subatomic theory. The proposed standard model, or Grand Unified Theory as it is sometimes called, postulates three fundamental particles: quarks, leptons, and gauge bosons. Six leptons seem to be accompanied by six quarks occurring in three separate generations: the up and down quarks, with the electron and its neutrino; the charm and strange quarks, with the muon and its neutrino; and the top and bottom quarks, with the tau and its neutrino.

These three generations exist at very different levels of energy. Only the first generation can survive at the energy level of the universe, today. The gauge bosons are forces that include the photons which impart the electromagnetic force, the weak force that gives rise to radioactivity; and a very strong force, expressed in gluons, which hold quarks together within the protons and neutrons and also holds the atomic nucleus together. Construction of the SSC will allow us to explore this theory more fully, at energy levels more than twenty times greater than existing accelerators. That was what Anderson required: an instrument—cloud chamber—with greater power to discover those strange positive particles that Dirac had predicted and Blackett and Occhialini recognized as positrons.

Public Policy Issues: The States

The major issue about the SSC is how it will be funded, and to answer that question, we must consider two issues: (1) the development of a comprehensive public policy in science, and (2) fairness. I served in Congress for twelve years and had membership on the committee now named the Science, Space, and Technology Committee, and the Ways and Means Committee, and I have observed the difficulty of funding large scientific projects—which seems to grow ever larger and more complex. And this is not the result of the avariciousness of scientists, but the result of the increasing depth of understanding of science and the increasing complexity and sophistication of instruments.

I have always believed that instrumentation was crucial to both science and technology, and as a congressman voted to appropriate funds for scientific instrumentation. As governor, I have also supported requests from the executive director of the Board of Science and Technology for appropriations for instrumentation for scientists and engineers in North Carolina. If we fail to provide scientists and engineers with adequate instruments, we will fall behind in our economic competitiveness. Indeed, our relative decline in economic competitiveness may have resulted, in part, from our failures to provide adequate instrumentation for basic research in science and basic research in technology.

Now is the time for us to devise a national policy for funding instrumentation in an orderly and rational manner. One way might be to establish a permanent revolving fund for scientific and technological instrumentation. Many states, including North Carolina, have done this for water and sewer funds, providing an ongoing appropriation which can be used for a series of projects with the sequence determined on a priority basis. Perhaps the federal government could pursue such a course to fund the SSC and other worthwhile projects in science and engineering requiring large expenditures for instrumentation.

The SSC is an instrument for scientists, not only in one state but in all the states, and even in other countries, and as such, is a national scientific instrument. Fairness, therefore, dictates that no one state should be allowed to purchase a share of this instrument solely for their own benefit. I supported, and still support, the Domenici amendment for the selection of the site for the SSC on the grounds that encouraging contributions from states, for construction or operation, might mean that the site was chosen on the basis of largess, rather than upon the basis of which state had the site best suited for the scientific characteristics of the instrument: geology, available power and water, supporting academic institutions, transportation, et cetera.[14] This does not mean that states should not provide the land and infrastructure like roads, water, and sewer. If the scientific benefit of this instrument is primarily for one state, then that state, or even group of states, should bear the full costs. If the SSC is a national instrument, as I believe it should be, then all of the states should bear the cost through a federal appropriation.

Similarly, the economic benefits of the SSC will enrich the entire nation. I do not mean to hide the fact that the state chosen for the site will not have relatively more direct benefits in the form of construction jobs and permanent jobs manning the facility, but all the hype about the SSC misses the scientific significance of this project and its benefit to the entire nation. Dr. Mac Cormac, my science adviser who has full responsibility for our bid, told me that after our press conference releasing our proposal to the public the day after we had submitted it to DOE, in Washington, a science reporter from one of our leading state newspapers came up to him and said, with apology: "We, the press, have trivialized this project by treating it as a gigantic, high-tech windfall. In all the glitter of the SSC project, the excitement about the science of this project has been lost; we have failed to communicate the scientific importance of this project to the public."

Obviously, I hope and want North Carolina to win this project, but whichever state wins should win fairly and because that site is the best location, chosen in a fair competition with full peer review. And let us not lose sight of the wonder and awe in nature that this instrument will allow us both to conceive, in theory, and perceive, in detectors. The educational benefit, like the economic benefit, may be relatively more for the state and region receiving it, but let us be clear that with quick air travel and computer networking, scientists throughout the United States and countries all over the world will have access to and benefit from the SSC.

Let us be like the Royal Society, in 1919, which appropriated £1,000 for two astronomical expeditions to confirm or disconfirm Einstein's General Theory of Relativity. Let us band together, as states, to join with the federal government to forge a science policy with adequate appropriations for scientific instruments like the SSC. With the SSC, we will be able not to watch an eclipse of the sun which changed fundamentally how we understand and live in our world, but explore a new and exciting theory about how the forces inside the nucleus operate, and what is the nature of those quarks held together by gluons inside protons. And most of all, let us not forget the exhilaration and beauty in scientific discovery. Aristotle described knowledge as an intrinsic virtue,[15] and dedicated scientists continue to pursue that virtue with dedication and honesty.

---

[1]*Site Proposal for the Superconducting Super Collider* (Raleigh, N.C.: Office of the Governor, State of North Carolina, 9 volumes, [1987]).

[2]This section of the speech is derived from Donald Franklin Moyer, "Revolution in Science: The 1919 Eclipse Test of General Relativity," in Arnold Perlmutter and Linda F. Scott (eds.), *On the Path of Albert Einstein* (New York: Plenum Press, 1979), 55-101, hereinafter cited as Moyer, "Revolution in Science."

[3]T. J. J. See, *Observatory*, 39 (1916), 511-512, quoted in Moyer, "Revolution in Science," 61.

Thomas Jefferson Jackson See (1866-1962), born near Montgomery City, Missouri; resident of Vallejo, California; was graduated from University of Missouri, 1889; A.M., Ph.D., University of Berlin, 1892. Astronomer; geometer; organized, headed astronomy department, cofounder Yerkes Observatory, University of Chicago, 1893-1896; work as astronomer in charge of southern heavens survey, Lowell Observatory, 1896-1898, led to discovery and measurement of 600 new double stars; served with U.S. Naval Observatory, 1899-1902; mathematics professor, U.S. Naval Academy, 1902-1903; director, Naval Observatory, Mare Island, California, 1903-1930. *Dictionary of Scientific Biography,* XII, 280; *Who Was Who in America, 1961-1968*, 845.

[4]George Mathews, "The New Physics," *Nature*, 100 (1917-1918), 155, quoted in Moyer, "Revolution in Science," 62-63. Mathews used the word *formulae* instead of *formulas;* otherwise, the excerpt is textually accurate.

George Ballard Mathews (1861-1922), born in London, died in Liverpool, England; was educated at University College, London, and at St. John's College, Cambridge University. Mathematician, specialist in classical theory of numbers; held mathematics chair, University College of North Wales, 1884-1896, returned in 1911 as special lecturer; mathematics lecturer, Cambridge University, 1896-1911; author. *Dictionary of Scientific Biography*, IX, 173.

[5]Arthur Stanley Eddington (1882-1944), born in Kendal, died in Cambridge, England; was educated at Trinity College, Cambridge University. Major work in astronomy, relativity; chief assistant, Royal Observatory, Greenwich, 1906-1913; Plumian Professor of Astronomy, Cambridge University, 1913-1944; president, Royal Astronomical Society, 1921-1923, and of International Astronomical Union, 1938. *Dictionary of Scientific Biography*, IV, 277-282.

[6]Sir Frank Watson Dyson (1868-1939), born in Measham, England; died aboard ship returning from Australia; was educated at Trinity College, Cambridge University; honorary degrees; knighted, 1915, K.B.E., 1926. Award-winning astronomer; chief assistant, 1894-1906, astronomer royal, 1910-1933, Royal Observatory, Greenwich; astronomer royal for Scotland, 1906-1910; president, Royal Astronomical Society, 1911-1913; vice-president, Royal Society, 1913-1914; president, British Astronomical Assn., 1916-1918; president, International Astronomical Union, 1928-1932. *Dictionary of Scientific Biography*, IV, 269-270.

[7]A. C. D. Crommelin, "The Eclipse of the Sun on May 29," *Nature*, 102 (1918-1919), 444-446, quoted in Moyer, "Revolution in Science," 71.

Andrew Claude de la Cherois Crommelin (1865-1939), born in Cushendun, Northern Ireland; died in London, England; was graduated from Trinity College, Cambridge University, 1886; honorary degrees. Astronomer noted for work involving comets and minor planets; additional assistant, Royal Observatory, Greenwich, 1891-1927; president, British Astronomical Assn., 1904-1906, and of its Comet Section, 1897-1901, 1907-1939; president, Royal Astronomical Society, 1929-1931, and of the Subcommission of Periodic Comets, International Astronomical Union, 1935-1939; author. *Dictionary of Scientific Biography*, III, 472.

[8]Banesh Hoffman, *Albert Einstein* (New York: New American Library, 1973), 131, quoted in Moyer, "Revolution in Science," 78.

Hendrik Antoon Lorentz (1853-1928), born in Arnhem, died in Haarlem, the Netherlands; earned doctorate from University of Leiden, 1875. First professor of theoretical physics, University of Leiden, 1877-1912; won Nobel Prize in physics, 1902; president, Solvay Congresses for physics, 1911-1927; member, Dutch government board of education, 1919-1926, and president, department of higher education, from 1921; author. Lorentz's work in theoretical physics influenced Europe's younger generation of scientists, among whom was Einstein, exploring that area of research. *Dictionary of Scientific Biography*, VIII, 487-500.

[9]Alfred North Whitehead, *Science and the Modern World: Lowell Lectures, 1925* (New York: The Macmillan Company, 1947), 15.

[10]Much of this section of the speech was taken directly from Earl R. Mac Cormac, *Metaphor and Myth in Science and Religion* (Durham, North Carolina: Duke University Press, 1976), 31-32.

[11]Paul Adrien Maurice Dirac (1902-   ), born in Bristol, England; B.Sc., Bristol University, 1921; Ph.D., Cambridge University, 1926. Award-winning physicist; fellow, St. John's College, since 1927, and Lucasian Professor of Mathematics, since 1932, Cambridge University; awarded Nobel Prize for physics, 1933; author. Allen G. Debus and others (eds.), *World Who's Who in Science* (Chicago: Marquis Who's Who, Incorporated, 1968), 463, hereinafter cited as *World Who's Who in Science*.

Carl David Anderson (1905-   ), born in New York City; B.S., 1927, Ph.D., 1930, California Institute of Technology; honorary degrees. Award-winning physicist; assistant professor, 1933-1937, associate professor, 1937-1939, professor of physics, 1939-1976, chairman, Division of Physics, Mathematics, and Astronomy, 1962-1970, professor emeritus since 1976, California Institute of Technology. *Who's Who in America, 1988-1989,* I, 65.

[12]Robert Andrews Millikan (1868-1953), born in Morrison, Illinois; resident of San Marino, California; A.B., 1891, A.M., 1893, Oberlin College; Ph.D., Columbia University, 1895; honorary degrees; U.S. Army, 1918. Award-winning physicist; physics faculty member, University of Chicago, 1896-1921; director, Norman Bridge Laboratory of Physics, and executive council chairman, 1921-1946, later professor emeritus, California Institute of Technology; won Nobel Prize in physics, 1923; author. *Dictionary of Scientific Biography,* IX, 395-400; *Who Was Who in America, 1951-1960,* 602.

[13]Patrick Maynard Stuart Blackett (1897-1974), born in London; M.A., Magdalene College, Cambridge University. Award-winning nuclear physicist; physics professor, Birkbeck College, 1933-1937, and at University of Manchester, 1937-1953; professor, 1953-1965, professor emeritus and senior research fellow, from 1965, Imperial College of Science and Technology; won Nobel Prize for physics, 1948. *Current Biography, 1974,* 455; *World Who's Who in Science,* 184. Blackett's partner in confirming the existence of the positron was Giuseppe P. S. Occhialini. *Dictionary of Scientific Biography,* XII, 33, XV, 26.

[14]The Domenici amendment was named for sponsor Pete Vichi Domenici (1932-   ), born in Albuquerque, New Mexico; was graduated from University of New Mexico, 1954, and Denver University Law School, 1958. Attorney; elected to Albuquerque City Commission, 1966, served as chairman, 1967; elected to U.S. Senate, 1972, reelected 1978, 1984; Republican. *Biographical Directory of Congress,* 919.

[15]"All men by nature desire knowledge." Aristotle, *Metaphysics,* book I, chapter 1, quoted in Bartlett, *Familiar Quotations,* 97.

NORTH CAROLINA FARM BUREAU FEDERATION

ASHEVILLE, DECEMBER 7, 1987

It is always a special pleasure to address a group that is so important to the life and progress of our state. As I move about the state, one thing impresses me more than almost anything else: the people's hunger for brevity in speech making. Over and over I'm told, "Keep it short, but don't leave anything important out."

When Bob Jenkins was telling me about expectations for this speech, he said, "Make it something like a state-of-agriculture-in-North Carolina speech, but for heaven's sake, our members' endurance is not over ten minutes."[1] I promise to be brief, no matter how long it takes.

This is truly an occasion for thanksgiving and for celebration: thanksgiving for all that you have and are contributing to the economy and quality of life in our state; celebration of your extraordinary accomplishments over the years. Your federation has demonstrated its importance and its relevance most eloquently by the fact that your membership is currently in excess [of] 270,000, a gain of 16 to 17,000 over last year.

You are demonstrating that you are a force with a vision. For example, I know you have worked diligently to achieve consolidation of migrant housing laws—that is, to simplify the procedures for the state's farmers by making one agency responsible. You have repeatedly sent representatives to testify before the Governor's Task Force on the Farm Economy in North Carolina, addressing such issues as Immigration and Naturalization Service rules and regulations; migrant farm labor; labeling of imported fruit juice concentrate to reflect the actual point of origin. You have helped develop legislation that was needed to continue the viability of the Farm Credit System; and you performed a service of inestimable importance to our state when you moved forcefully to head off an international panic concerning the dicamba contamination of North Carolina tobacco—you did this by taking the initiative of assembling a "tobacco family" composed of growers, buyers, warehousemen, North Carolina State University experts, and others.

You have indeed proved that you are a force with a vision, and you have gone a long way toward [re]pealing Olmstead's law, which states, "After all is said and done, a hell of a lot more is said than done." You match your actions to your rhetoric. You are living proof of what can be done when we work together, as one united state— where we work together, east and west, and piedmont, and sandhills—to build a brighter future with better jobs, better roads, and better schools.

When I cite my administration's accomplishments over what is now almost three years, I am always mindful that all that we have been able to do is the result of team effort, and you have been an important part of that team. This, too, is cause for thanksgiving. Let me sketch, somewhat briefly, what teamwork has accomplished in our state.

Item: North Carolina agriculture did not suffer nearly as much as our midwestern and far western farmers did in the recent economic downturn. As a whole, our farmers have done fairly well except for corn, soybeans, and small grain.

Item: The tobacco farmer, in 1987, enjoyed his most profitable year in the last several years. The outlook for the future is bright. Information I have received indicates that our domestic companies intend to increase their purchases considerably, in 1988, and reduce their foreign purchases. Recent entry into the Japanese and other foreign markets with American cigarettes is one of the reasons for increased purchases. Also, it is anticipated that there may be a slight increase in the quota for 1988.

All this is no accident. Who better than the farmer knows the truth of the biblical saying, "As ye sow, so shall ye reap." For example, increase in foreign trade and investment in industrial facilities in North Carolina is the result of aggressive campaigning and marketing. Industrial recruiting and increasing foreign trade is a contact sport, not something that can only be done by having the governor sit at his desk in Raleigh, as some newspapers would have you believe; and these visits to Pacific Rim and European nations is [sic] paying off, as I will illustrate later with some more specific examples.

Item: While North Carolina agriculture is highly diversified, as a whole, our individual farmers have understandably had a tendency to specialize. We must change this tendency, and many of our farmers [have] taken the lead in diversifying their operations. They now raise poultry, or hogs, or catfish, and produce, along with their tobacco.

Item: Marketing has become an increasingly important concept in agriculture. Our efforts must be to provide markets for all products produced by our farmers. We are attempting this much-needed service through a series of agricultural parks, which will offer grading, packaging, and quick chilling—in some cases quick freezing—of fruits and produce.

Item: With the assistance of the Farm Bureau Federation, we hope to obtain additional funds to expand our marketing in Europe and the Far East. With these funds, we will be able to provide office space and administrative support for personnel from the Department of Agriculture, and the Division of Forestry in the Department of Natural Resources and Community Development, in order to promote the sale of agriculture, seafood, and forestry products.

Item: In exploring additional crops for North Carolina farmers, we are investigating the possibility of growing fresh- and saltwater shrimp, crayfish, mushrooms, kiwi fruit, lambs, and kenaf—a tree-like plant that grows rapidly from a seedling to a nine-foot plant capable of being used for the production of newsprint.

The upbeat goes on. New and expanding industries invested a total of $5.2 billion in North Carolina facilities in 1986 and announced plans to create an estimated 55,000 jobs. But hold it: Commerce Secretary Pope has just informed me that this is a gross underestimate of the net increase of jobs in 1986—that the actual increase was about 80,000 jobs, which includes all the jobs created in 1986 minus all jobs lost.

As good as 1986 was, 1987 is shaping up as even better. New industries alone, in the first three quarters, announced investments of $776 million, with 11,000 jobs. These statistics, I should add, do not include any numbers on existing industry or service industry investment; and if this pace continues in the fourth quarter, 1987 could well be the best year ever for business investment in North Carolina.

Since becoming governor, total personal income in North Carolina has risen to more than $77.7 billion, a gain of over 13.6 percent. I ought to take full credit for this remarkable achievement, since I would be blamed if things weren't so good.

It is important that farmers share fully in our expanding economy. This is why our administration is putting such a strong emphasis on rural economic development.

Item: Concerning rural economic development during the past year, over 70 percent of the new industries coming into North Carolina have gone to those towns and communities with fewer than 10,000 residents. Additionally, members of my staff have been named to the USDA's Rural Enterprise Team. This team brings together state, federal, and local efforts for rural development.

We are truly making history in rural economic development. Consider that, for the first time in many decades, we have more investment in more jobs in rural centers outside the piedmont corridor than in the big cities of the piedmont—by a factor of three times as much— and that's not because the piedmont has stopped scoring, either. It's because we've learned how to score, in rural areas, with the kind of teamwork that you display in your organization and in your relationship with other partners devoted to enhancing and improving agriculture in our state.

Let me take just a moment to say something that I think is of extreme importance, if we are to continue our momentum of achieving greater geographic balance in industrial and business development in our state. As I have stated, my administration is putting a high priority on economic development in rural areas, and as the record shows, we are achieving substantial successes in [attaining] our goal. But I know that resources and manpower are stretched thin. This is why I proposed spending about $500,000 to expand the Commerce Department's network of regional offices. This addition would mean that we can do an even better job of industrial recruiting for rural areas in our state than we are presently doing.

Unfortunately, the legislature denied funding for this expansion proposal. What the majority of legislators failed to see, apparently, is that these regional offices are an investment, not an expense. In time, they will more than pay for themselves.

Who was it that said there is nothing so powerful as an idea whose time has come? I think this is an idea whose time has come, but I'm not willing to wait around for the forces of fate to take effect. We intend to propose, in our expansion plan, regional centers in next year's short session of the General Assembly. With your help, we can make sure that a good idea's time for realization is 1988!

There is more on the agenda of accomplishments I would like to share with you.

Item: A new and exciting development that is being pursued by our Department of Commerce and members of my staff is an ethanol plant for North Carolina. This facility will utilize not only corn, a product abundant worldwide and especially in the United States, but will furnish a by-product, DDGS—dried distilled grain soluble—used for livestock and poultry feed.

North Carolina agriculture, like that of the rest of the nation, as all of you know, is in a period of extraordinary change. The lesson that is becoming clearer and clearer is that, if North Carolina is to continue as one of the great agricultural states, we will have to change from a production-driven agriculture to a consumer-driven, market-oriented agriculture. I believe North Carolina is taking a leadership role in accomplishing this new approach to agriculture, that we are on the leading edge of a new era in agriculture. We do have, however, some areas of deep concern, but working together, as we have done in the past, we will overcome the remaining obstacles and return a greater profit to our farming industry.

You know, in practically all the books and articles on entrepreneurship that I have read, nobody mentions the farmer. This is truly surprising, since the farmer is and has always been the foremost example of the entrepreneur. The difference now is that the farmer must begin to think of himself and herself as an entrepreneur—and just as importantly—as an entrepreneur, [*sic*] if he or she is to be truly successful in one of the most important enterprises in our state and nation.

One aspect of entrepreneurship is risk taking, and no one lays it on the line any more than the farmer, year after year. Certainly, as you know, a sad chapter in our state's and nation's history has been the steady erosion of small family farms. No group in [our] economy has felt so keenly the twin effects of depressed farm prices and high operating costs.

I know that some of you here have heard this, but it bears repeating. To confront this problem, I have taken several intiatives. To help farmers, and to curb the tide of farm foreclosures, I convened a meeting at the Executive Mansion of members of the banking community and farm organizations. The result is that bankers are now restructuring loans in far more instances, rather than foreclosing. Hundreds of

North Carolina farmers have thus been able to restructure their loans instead of having to leave the farms.

I want to pay high tribute to those who have served on the Governor's Farm Finance Task Force, ably chaired by Jim Powers, executive officer of Planters National Bank in Rocky Mount. Working with bankers, we have been able to shorten the time that farmers have had to wait for a loan. This has meant that many farmers could survive or expand who may not otherwise be able to do so.

Unfortunately, some farmers went into bankruptcy or had to leave their farms because their operations were marginal. To respond to this situation, my administration put together the Dislocated Workers Program for Farmers, administered by the Employment Security Commission. Under this program, dislocated farmers can now apply for job training, and after being trained, if they have to relocate, they can receive relocation expenses for themselves and their families. But that's not all: With the cooperation of commercial banks to use Farmers Home Administration guaranteed-loan programs, we had, last year, an 1100 percent increase in the number of loans granted farmers last year.

But some of you may be thinking, "What's the bottom line?" How's this for a bottom line: For eleven or twelve years prior to 1986, 3,000 families had to leave their farms in North Carolina. In 1986, the number was down to 1,000, and with the kind of help and advice you have given over the past three, we will improve on that record.

Here's some more good news that teamwork brought about. I know that most of you are familiar with how the tobacco buy out program helped take a lot of tobacco farmers off the economic ropes. The buy out is now over 60 percent; in 1988, we expect it to be 100 percent.

Even with all these outstanding accomplishments, I know we can do better. With your help, we will do better. I always talk about what we have been able to accomplish, with a sense of gratitude and humility. I like to remind our administration that we didn't earn our merit badges all by ourselves—state teamwork does it. People in Raleigh; people like you, here; people all over the state share in the glory of what is coming to be seen as an economic miracle in North Carolina. You have our administration's pledge that every effort will be made to see that farmers share fully in the economic resurgence in our state. You have been a wonderful audience, and as always, it is a special pleasure to meet with one of our most important partners in our march toward progress.

<hr>

[1]W. B. (Bob) Jenkins (1932-   ), born in Franklinton; B.S., North Carolina State College (later University), 1954; U.S. Army, 1954-1956. Assistant county agricultural extension agent, 1956-1961; field representative, 1961-1962, 1964-1972, field services director, 1972-1975, assistant to president, 1975-1985, president, since 1985, North Carolina Farm Bureau Federation; postmaster, Hookerton, 1962-1963. W. B. Jenkins to Jan-Michael Poff, January 15, 1990.

RED TIDE PUBLIC MEETING

MOREHEAD CITY, DECEMBER 10, 1987

[For press releases about the red tide crisis, see "Governor Martin Visits Wilmington, Sneads Ferry, to Calm Red Tide Concerns about N.C.'s Finned Fish Products," Raleigh, November 20, 1987; "Martin Alerts Counties to Red Tide Assistance," Raleigh, November 25, 1987; "Red Tide Meeting in Morehead City," Raleigh, December 4, 1987; "Fish Fry Set to Benefit Red Tide Victims," Raleigh, December 15, 1987; "Department of Corrections Purchases 10.5 Tons of North Carolina Fish as Part of Effort to Bolster Coastal Seafood Industry," Raleigh, December 18, 1987; "Small Business Administration Low-Interest Loans Will Be Available to Coastal Fishermen, Businesses," Raleigh, December 23, 1987; "Disaster Assistance Centers Continue Operation Despite Snow," Raleigh, January 8, 1988; "North Carolina Celebrities Promote Seafood as Healthy, Delicious," Raleigh, January 11, 1988; "Council of State Approves Governor Martin's Request for Emergency Funds for 'Operation: Red Tide,'" Raleigh, February 2, 1988; "Emergency Management to Open Red Tide Application Centers as Part of 'Operation: Red Tide,'" Raleigh, February 2, 1988; and "'Operation: Red Tide' Provides More Than $1.6 Million in Financial Aid for Coastal Residents," Raleigh, June 9, 1988, Governors Papers, James G. Martin.]

First, I would like to thank all of you for gathering here in Morehead City, today, to discuss the red tide situation with local and state officials, private business leaders, and various representatives from the public sector. I also would like to thank Senator Harold Hardison, and Representative Robert Grady, and local resident Mike Bell for separately suggesting that we all get together to discuss this issue. I agreed that it was a good idea and asked my staff to set up this meeting—so, here we are.

Many of our state leaders are here: Lieutenant Governor Jordan, Agriculture Commissioner Graham, Secretary of Natural Resources and Community Development Rhodes, and many members of our General Assembly: Senator Rand, Representative Bruce Ethridge. I might also point out that Warren Hepler, from Representative Martin Lancaster's office,[1] [and] Les Roark, representing Senator Terry Sanford,[2] have joined us today to make sure our officials in Washington,

D.C., know about your problems and concerns. Senator Helms's local staff are attending the funeral of the mother of Frances Jones, who runs the Raleigh office, but Senator Helms assured me by phone of his support for what we're doing. He said he would eat twice as much fish as usual when they get home next week.

We all know that mild weather in the fall and early winter is what traditionally brings fishermen to the North Carolina coast. Their coming represents the fuel that powers much of the sports and commercial fishing industry that has become so famous throughout the country. This year we need a quick dose of cold weather. Why?

You can color the reason red—as in "red tide." This algae nightmare has been devastating, coming at the worst possible time, and now it just sits off our coast, and on it, lingering. The experts tell us that the only two things that can make this new bane to North Carolina waters go away is a storm strong enough to displace Gulf Stream currents, and cold weather; or, to put it another way, the water temperature needs to drop to 50 degrees Fahrenheit and below.

Toxic saltwater algae, *Ptychodiscus brevis*, first appeared along our coast October 30 in the Emerald Isle-Indian Beach area. The alarm was duly sounded, and all of us hoped it would be an isolated incident. Then the red tide spread north, in stages, to Avon, on the Outer Banks, and south to Carolina Beach, a span of about 170 miles. Our environmental officials had no choice but to close the affected area to shellfishing. The potential for human danger was too great not to act.

Thousands of acres of prime shellfish beds were closed. With the toxin in their system, oysters and clams immediately became inedible, until a couple weeks after the algae disappear so they can purge themselves. Scallops have since been ruled out of bounds for human consumption, pending further tests of toxicity levels. Even with oysters, clams, and scallops, we need to remember that beds outside the restricted zone, including the inland side of the sounds, are not affected—so that oysters and clams from these areas are perfectly healthy and, if offered at a grocery or restaurant, can be enjoyed as usual.

Finfish, shrimp, and crabs, however, remain edible, even if exposed to the algae. To prove that point, I came to the coast a few weeks ago, and again today, to eat finfish caught in red-tide waters. There may be a few people around who are saddened by the fact that I have not suffered any ill effects from this feast, but I am glad to report to you today, however, that I am still alive, and well, and having a great time. It is my sincere hope that these little demonstrations will encourage other people to put fresh, North Carolina fish back on their shopping lists, and when they get to the fish market and notice the shellfish that have been harvested from noninfested coastal waters, I hope they will decide to buy those, too.

As I have spoken to the Gastonia and Charlotte chambers of commerce, the Farm Bureau state convention in Asheville, and last night in my message as we turned on the downtown Raleigh Christmas lights, I have put a special emphasis on encouraging people to enjoy North Carolina seafood—and for them to make a special place for seafood in their diet out of concern and support for our coastal neighbors. What better religious symbol could we have at Christmas than the sign of the fish, North Carolina fish, on our tables. You will hear many ideas today for ways to help, but none can do as much as if we rally as one truly united state to restore and boost the market by putting wholesome North Carolina seafood on our tables.

I don't have to tell the shellfishermen of Sneads Ferry, or Cedar Island, or Swansboro, or Avon that the damage has been widespread. Our fishing experts predict a loss to coastal fishermen in excess of $3 million through the end of this year. Other coastal businesses—the motels which house the winter sports fishermen, the restaurants that feed them, the tackle shops that supply them, the fishing piers and the charter boats—have all suffered heavily. Our latest estimates indicate those businesses are losing anywhere from $10,000 to $100,000 each week. Our commercial fishermen and those people who depend upon the sports fishing industry have just about reached the end of their ropes. They have now reached the point where they are fighting for their survival. They need our help.

As is the North Carolina tradition, neighbors and friends of the coast have rallied to support the fishermen who are suffering. From town to town, money has been raised to offset the economic hardships they face.

In some areas, things are looking up, but algae counts have ranged to highs of 20 million per liter, offshore, and 2.2 million per liter in close to shore. When you consider the fact that 5,000 counts per liter is the maximum acceptable level, those are high numbers, but they don't come near that high in our inlets and marshes. That proves the problem came not from the sounds, but from offshore. Even better news is that the algae count in the northern and southern areas has been dropping the past few days; in many cases they are below the closure level, and some areas may be close to reopening. Samples taken from Masonboro Inlet south have been running at zero, but they are still 10,000 counts per liter at the West Onslow Beach bridge. On the northern border of the closure area, Ocracoke Island waters have returned algae counts of 5,800 per liter, and at Hatteras Inlet it has been recorded at 12,000 per liter, rising again after a recent drop. The Cedar Island area has been at zero count for about two weeks now, a hopeful sign indeed. But until we can reopen closed areas, we can still enjoy oysters and clams from the unaffected areas, and shrimp, crabs, and fish from anywhere.

Believe me, we in state government are just as frustrated as you are. I assure you, if we could shoot it or sweep it away, we would have done that long ago. We have, however, left no stone unturned in our search to find ways to help those who have been most affected by this problem. While our elected officials in Washington are still working hard to make low-interest-rate loans available through the Small Business Administration, we have continued to seek help through other avenues.[3] Each of the counties that have been affected by the red tide have state-funded assistance programs provided to people in need due to a crisis. One such program is the Crisis Intervention Program, and you will be hearing more about that from the Department of Social Services in a few minutes.

I also hope to have good news for our shellfishermen, soon. Last Friday, I asked Secretary Tommy Rhodes at the Department of Natural Resources and Community Development to request a $275,000 grant from the National Marine Fisheries Service that would be used to increase future stocks of oysters and clams. Although this would not provide any immediate relief, it would bolster restoration of our shellfish production by planting 100,000 bushels of shell clutch for two years in Core and Bogue sounds. The estimated benefits of such a project would be $3.9 to $4.4 million.

Commissioner Graham has another idea to share with you, as do others, but what we really need now is two things: one is an extended period of cold weather to bring the temperature down below 50 degrees. At those levels, the algae should not be able to survive. Meanwhile, the best thing we can do is to unite as one united state and reassure our customers that any seafood they can buy is as good as ever, because it is!

This is just a quick overview of the situation and the basics of what we are trying to do [to] help our coastal industries. I have several professionals with me, today, to expound on the various aspects and effects of the red tide upon North Carolina's coastal waters. First, I would like to introduce Dr. William T. Hogarth, director of the Division of Marine Fisheries in the Department of Natural Resources and Community Development.

[Following Dr. Hogarth's remarks, Governor Martin introduced Dr. Thad Wester, assistant state health director for the Division of Health Services, Department of Human Resources; Jerry Schill, director of the North Carolina Fisheries Association; and Rick Hamrick, executive director of the Carteret County Chamber of Commerce, who, in turn, also addressed the gathering.]

These four speakers have presented the impact of the problem. We also have several people with us, today, to discuss the various types of assistance that are available to businesses, families, and individuals affected by the red tide. First, I would like to introduce James Graham, commissioner of the North Carolina Department of Agriculture.

[Mark Aydlette, Region Four income maintenance supervisor of the Division of Social Services, North Carolina Department of Human Resources; David Allen, Carteret County office manager for the Employment Security Commission, North Carolina Department of Commerce; James Painter, Carolina Division director of the Salvation Army; Gary Keel, Small Business Administration district director; and members of congressional delegations were recognized by the governor and offered remarks.]

Some of these programs are of a type that many fishing families would not have wanted to have to depend on. Don't be proud. It's one way we can help. Let us help.[4]

I would like to thank all of you for being here today. I realize that you have already put a lot of effort into providing help and information for our coastal residents and that there is still a long way to go, yet. We appreciate your continued efforts. At this time I would like to open the meeting to hear questions and comments from the public. We would all appreciate it if you would step up to a microphone so everyone can hear your comments. Lieutenant Governor Jordan has indicated that he would prefer to speak after hearing from the people.

[Public question and answer period.]

Before we break this off, I would like to acknowledge Senator Hardison and Representative Grady, who may have comments they would like to make at this time.

Many of the questions that you have asked have already been addressed by the various state agencies and private groups that spoke earlier. To help answer any other questions you may have, or to assist you with seeking aid from some of the sources that were mentioned earlier, the state agencies have set up an assistance and information area here at the civic center. Those tables will be attended by individuals who can help answer specific questions after the meeting today.

Before you go, I want to reassure everyone that we will continue to seek solutions and assistance for those people who have been hurt by the red tide, and I want to thank you all for taking time to come and address this very important issue. And please, put seafood in your Christmas, so thousands of coastal families can have a Christmas, too.[5]

---

[1]H. Martin Lancaster (1943-   ), born in Patetown; A.B., 1965, J.D., 1967, University of North Carolina at Chapel Hill; U.S. Navy, 1967-1970, and Reserve, since 1982; U.S. Air Force Reserve, 1971-1982. Attorney; member, state House, 1979-1986; elected to U.S. House from Third North Carolina Congressional District, 1986, reelected in 1988; Democrat. *North Carolina Manual, 1987-1988*, 239.

[2]Terry Sanford (1917-   ), born in Laurinburg; A.B., 1939, J.D., 1946, University of North Carolina at Chapel Hill; U.S. Army, 1942-1946, and Reserve, 1948-1960; N.C. National Guard, 1948-1960. Attorney; FBI special agent, 1941-1942; member, state Senate, 1953-1955; North Carolina governor, 1961-1965; president, 1969-1985, president emeritus, since 1985, Duke University; U.S. senator, since 1986; Democrat. *North Carolina Manual, 1987-1988*, 231-232.

[3]P.L. 100-220 authorized the Small Business Administration to declare the red tide contamination an economic disaster, thus making affected North Carolinians eligible for federal assistance. See "United States-Japan Fishery Agreement Approval Act of 1987" (short title), *United States Statutes at Large*, Act of December 29, 1987, Title V, Secs. 5001-5002, 101 Stat. 1480-1481.

[4]The governor inserted, "May need extra staff locally."

[5]Martin added the following notes at the end of his speech: "1, use part of advertising budget/Commerce and Ag. Marketing advertising; 2, Hold hearings on coast (concentrate resources where they are needed); 3, Ask private corporations, meet on coast; 4, Fish for inmates—schools. Purchase more seafood."

HOLLYWOOD TRIP ANNOUNCEMENT: SUCCESS OF 1987 FILM INDUSTRY

Raleigh, January 13, 1988

[Martin reviewed the health of the state's film industry in remarks he made in Wilmington, June 14, 1986, before conferring "Honorary Tar Heel" status upon motion picture producer and DEG Studios owner Dino DeLaurentiis. On that occasion, the governor asserted that "since the establishment of the North Carolina Film Office in 1980, more than seventy theatrical motion pictures and literally hundreds of national television commercials" had been filmed in North Carolina. "This activity has contributed more than $655 million to the state's economy in the last six years," he added.]

As I begin to prepare for a very brief trade mission to Hollywood later this month, I wanted to take this opportunity to proclaim another record-setting year for the North Carolina film industry. Last year, the booming new movie industry shattered all previous records and generated an estimated $384.1 million impact on the state's economy. That's nearly $400 million! But that's all estimated, based on assumptions about secondary stimulus effects.

In 1987, thirty-five productions—sixteen theatrical features, six made-for-TV features, and thirteen short subjects or specialty projects—accounted for the majority of North Carolina activity. It's easy to sit up here and toss out numbers on total new investment, but to give you some measure of what this means to counties, and cities, and towns around North Carolina, just look at the list of locations in the back of your press release.[1] You'll see how dramatically this business touches the lives of North Carolinians.

When Hollywood moviemakers first started coming here, they brought everything and everybody with them. They had to. But in the past three or four years, we've had a significant increase in the number of homegrown jobs. We now have 9,200 jobs directly related to this industry: 600 technical jobs, 600 acting jobs, and 8,000 extras jobs each year. The great news is that this is only the beginning.

This North Carolina success story did not just happen. It did not magically snowball into a major industry. We had to work on it, and work diligently, to make it grow. A lot of credit goes to Commerce Secretary Claude Pope, and Film Office Director Bill Arnold,[2] and Paula Wyrick. I believe our teamwork approach has paid dividends in many areas. Our success in this still-developing arena is a shining example.

I'm proud of my role in our efforts to develop and strengthen this new industry. Bill Arnold, who has been involved in this business long before me, will tell you that my trip to Los Angeles in 1986 helped directly influence fourteen of the thirty-five productions wooed to this state last year. Some of my Raleigh critics talked long and loudly about that 1986 trip; I believe these numbers from last year should quiet the criticism. At least I hope they will see the tremendous benefit this industry is bringing to North Carolina. If I don't go out and help bring it back, who is going to do it?

You can't enjoy the kind of success in the movie recruitment business that North Carolina has experienced in the past without being there. You have to go into the offices of movie people and show your interest in their business; that is true in all industrial recruiting. In short, that is why I am leaving on Sunday, January 24, to visit some of these executives and tell them of the successful environment we can offer in North Carolina. This will be a quick trip—I'm there for only two full days—but I'm sure this will open new doors for North Carolina.[3]

---

[1]The press release dated January 13, 1988, "Governor Reports Record Year for North Carolina Moviemaking," indicated that the thirty-two counties that served as filming locations in 1987 saw $87 million pumped directly into their economies. Filmmakers also compensated the state's 9,200 actors, extras, and technicians with an $8.9 million annual payroll. In total, the record $384.1 million generated by the motion picture industry in 1987, in North Carolina, exceeded the 1986 level by $117 million. Governors Papers, James G. Martin.

[2]Bill Arnold (1936-   ), born in Greenville; resident of Raleigh; B.A., East Carolina University, 1959; U.S. Army, 1959-1961. Newspaper reporter, editor, in North Carolina and Virginia, 1961-1965; assistant commissioner, Virginia State Travel Service, 1965-1975; director, North Carolina Division of Travel and Tourism, 1975-1980; director, since 1980, North Carolina Film Office. Bill Arnold to Jan-Michael Poff, July 11, 1989.

[3]Martin returned from his film industry trade mission on January 27, 1988. Governor's Schedule for Weeks of January 25-February 27, 1988, Governors Papers, James G. Martin.

"CHAMPION NEEDS A CHAMPION":
HEARING OF THE U.S. ENVIRONMENTAL PROTECTION AGENCY

CANTON, JANUARY 14, 1988

[The waste water discharged from Champion International Corporation's Canton paper mill stained the Pigeon River coffee brown as it flowed for thirty-eight miles to the Tennessee line and Douglas Lake beyond. The color of the river had long been an environmental concern of eastern Tennesseans, and in 1983, state officials in Nashville initiated lawsuits seeking Champion's adherence to federal clean water standards. The corporation countered that the cost of meeting those criteria would force the plant to close, a circumstance threatening dire economic consequences for the region.

In March, 1988, the Environmental Protection Agency offered a compromise, proposing to relax the color standard for the river to 85 units, the hue of ginger ale—providing North Carolina and Tennessee approved water-quality variances. North Carolina gave its consent in July, but in the Volunteer State, the Dead River Pigeon Council stiffly resisted any limit higher than the 50-unit level originally demanded by the EPA. Governor Ned R. McWherter agreed and, refusing to waive his state's water standards, denied the corporation a variance in December, 1988. Ken Renner, speaking for Governor McWherter, said, "Champion will be required under Tennessee law to meet the same standards of water quality that apply to other corporations in Tennessee. It is the governor's personal opinion that Tennesseans have the right to expect water in their river below the mill to be as clean as the water that citizens of North Carolina enjoy above the mill." The water in the Pigeon River above the Canton plant varied in color from 10 to 20 units; below the plant it fluctuated between 200 and 600 units.

Champion indicated in January, 1989, that McWherter's refusal to grant a waiver would either necessitate cutting back production at the Canton plant, at the cost of 1,000 employees, or closing the facility entirely. The EPA eventually issued the corporation a waste-water permit in September, 1989, that gave it three years to meet Tennessee's water color standards and regulated dioxin contamination and whole effluent toxicity. When the paper manufacturer announced a modernization program in March, 1990, intended to protect jobs and the Pigeon River, the news pleased Governor Martin: "Throughout my administration, I've supported the company's efforts to keep pace with increasingly stringent environmental standards while protecting the livelihood of Champion employees." *News and Observer*, January 26, March 10, July 14, 24, August 19, October 24, December 24, 1988, January 14, 26, September 26, 1989, March 28, 1990; press release, "Statement by Governor Jim Martin Concerning Champion Announcement," Raleigh, March 27, 1990, Governors Papers, James G. Martin; *The Wire: The Monthly Newspaper of the Champion Community*, January, 1990.]

I am here today to speak on behalf of the people of western North Carolina, and all of North Carolina, in support of a reasonable decision as to the kind of permit terms to be imposed on Champion International. As governor of North Carolina, I have been urging all the agencies that are involved in the EPA-NPDES [National Pollution Discharge Elimination System] permit for the Champion mill at Canton to resolve this issue with a reasonable balance that fits the needs of all parties. This issue is of profound importance to the people of western North Carolina and eastern Tennessee. It is time to get it settled!

Champion needs a champion. So, I want to make it very clear that I am firmly opposed to the 50-color-unit requirements of EPA's draft permit, which I and our environmental experts in the North Carolina Department of Natural Resources and Community Development regard as arbitrary, excessive, unduly harsh, and unattainable, and, therefore, unjustified. Neither we nor Tennessee have ever adopted such a standard. We take the position that North Carolina should have been allowed to issue a permit, without interference from either the EPA or the state of Tennessee.

North Carolina has a well-deserved reputation as a national leader in environmental protection. We are deeply committed to protecting and improving the environment. We have the same commitment to maintaining and improving the economic strength of this mountain region.

Two years ago, North Carolina was working with Champion to achieve a color reduction of 50 percent below current levels. Champion was planning a $200 million investment to modernize this 80-

year-old mill, which would reduce the effluent color generated by an improved process and make the facility more competitive. That would have guaranteed a prolonged future economic boost to this region, while improving the appearance of the Pigeon River. Now, two years later, we have 1) lost that expected $200 million investment, 2) the future of this plant is in jeopardy, and 3) even the intended color reduction has been indefinitely postponed until Champion can get some kind of reliable decision about its permit; and the best that can be done to reduce the color going into the Pigeon River is still 50 percent—not 50 color units, or even 85 color units, but a 50 percent reduction—exactly the same as it was two years ago, before the EPA and Tennessee intervened and injured North Carolina. Nothing has been gained; too much has been lost. Our ox has been gored!

It's not as if Champion has had a poor environmental record; quite the contrary. Over the past thirty years, Champion Paper Company has already invested more than $70 million installing the best air and waste-water treatment facilities to protect the Pigeon River area. Champion is regarded as a leader in pollution abatement in its industry and is now achieving 96 percent or better removal of all contaminants that could pose a real threat to the environment. It is remarkable that a mill built in 1907 could have been retrofitted to be one of the best in the world in pollution technology! It is more remarkable that anyone would want to shut it down, by insisting on a color standard of arbitrary origin which cannot be met and which is not imposed on all other rivers or businesses in Tennessee and North Carolina.

Mr. Hearing Officer, let me tell you what Champion's Canton plant means to this area. This mill employs about 2,200 workers, with an annual payroll of $100 million. Another 8,000 or so jobs are generated by the economic stimulus and direct business activity of the Champion mill. Each year, it purchases goods and services worth $35 million, including 2,500 cords of wood a day. It might be worth noting that of that $35 million in yearly purchases, over 40 percent—$15 million—of that comes from vendors, merchants, woodlot owners, and others in Tennessee! Champion's total economic contribution to this area, in 1985, was more than $160 million, all from just this one mill. Folks, that is a whole lot of food on the table, clothes to wear to school, and tax money to build those schools in both states. We must not forget that this region has a relatively less capitalized economy and that these proud mountain people would be in serious financial difficulty if you force Champion to close. The economic factor must not be overlooked or minimized.

Much has been said about the domino effect. Consider this: The entire work force of Haywood County is about 22,200. If you shut down these 2,200 Champion jobs and the estimated 8,000 dependent jobs, it would be the equivalent of suddenly causing unemployment in Haywood County to surge from a currently healthy 5.7 percent to a disastrous 52 percent unemployment. There is little consolation in noting that not all those jobs are in Canton, for that simply recognizes that the calamity would be widespread. Who wants that?

We must realize that a healthy environment and a healthy economy are mutually interdependent, not exclusive. It would be tragic to close these 2,200 jobs all because someone regards a 50 percent improvement in color as aesthetically unacceptable and insists on an unattainable color standard, but that's what it all comes down to. North Carolina has already lost one of the largest expansion investments in our history, all because of the opposition that has been aroused against a reasonable permit and a responsible company. How much more must we lose?

There is a solution to this, if neighbors will just be neighborly. Champion International has stated that, if given sufficient time, they could reduce the color that discharges out of their pipe into the Pigeon River by 50 percent from what they are now currently doing. North Carolina Environmental Management is prepared to issue a permit to Champion, based upon the strictest achievable color standard, which will require that 50 percent reduction in color. That's the best anyone can do. By this approach, Champion will be able to meet the 50 color-unit level 60 percent of the time and the 85 color-unit level 90 percent of the time.

I would hope that our neighbors in Tennessee would recognize that this will achieve all that they want most of the time, and the best that can be done all of the time, without putting thousands out of work on both sides of the state line. It is not technically possible for Champion or anyone to reach either of those goals 100 percent of the time without closing down the mill entirely. Since our plan is the best that can be done, I ask you to let North Carolina proceed to approve a waiver under our laws and procedures, and let us issue the permit based on the best available technology.

Since EPA has no authority to grant a variance, but the states do, we ask EPA and Tennessee to accept and accommodate a variance granted by North Carolina. In this way, we can move forward to improve the appearance of the Pigeon River substantially, without immediately having to close 2,200 jobs or suddenly losing this major source of economic strength.

This controversy has gone on long enough. North Carolina and Tennessee are neighbors. We share a common state line. We share these very mountains and rivers. We share a long history of family, business, educational, and recreational ties. We share the same environment. We also share the economics of tourism, trade, and manufacturing which our shared natural resources provide.

Today, we share the responsibility of providing a reasonable settlement that assures our mutual future, with an improved environment, but without sacrificing our ability to afford an improved quality of life. Mr. Hearing Officer, thank you for this opportunity to present the best compromise, one that is the only fair solution. Help us to get this done. Help us to do the reasonable thing, the fair thing, the right thing. We've lost too much already. Let's settle this before we lose much more.

I came here this morning, by car, from Cherokee. As we drove by Canton, I looked over and saw that Champion was hard at work, with its big white plume—of condensed water vapor. I couldn't help but think how that plume represents 99.6 percent removal of air pollution and how proud we should be of a company that does all that it can do; and I couldn't help but think how strange it is that anyone would shut them down because they can clean up to this color, but not this.

MARTIN LUTHER KING, JR., BIRTHDAY OBSERVANCE

RALEIGH, JANUARY 18, 1988

I am here today, as in past years, to take part in these ceremonies, ceremonies to honor a great American and humanitarian, Dr. Martin Luther King, Jr., and celebrate his life and work. In honoring Dr. King, we pay homage not only to an extraordinary human being, but we honor the best in ourselves.

Let me thank all who have made this event possible: Mrs. Coretta King,[1] who continues her husband's passionate pursuit of the dream, for her suggestion to create a state commission to commemorate the life of Martin Luther King; Mr. (Bruce) Lightner and the Wake County Martin Luther King Commission; the Reverend J. B. Humphrey[2] and Ms. Elreta Alexander Ralston,[3] co-chairs of the Martin Luther King, Jr., state commission, and all the commission members; Jim Polk,[4] the governor's special assistant for minority affairs; Jim Stowe,[5] executive director of the North Carolina Human Relations Council, and his staff; and Ms. Barbara Fellers,[6] staff liaison to the Martin Luther King state commission. You have performed a wonderful service in bringing this special occasion to fruition.

We are here to honor a man and his dreams of equality and justice. We are here to bear witness to his goodness and to his love of all mankind. The world is a lot better place because Martin Luther King, Jr., lived.

Because he lived, we are here today to celebrate the theme, "Living the Dream—Let Freedom Ring through Serving Others." Without his example, far fewer of us would be sitting down at the table of brotherhood. Because he lived, our state and nation are ideologically richer, spiritually more fulfilled. Because he lived, more and more blacks are included in the educational, social, and economic mainstream—yet not perfectly, for there is still a long way we need to go. Perhaps most importantly, because he lived, we have his luminous dream, his most powerful legacy.

Dr. King is still a force with a vision, and the vision lives on in the hearts and minds of people of goodwill, of all races and creeds. His dream now becomes ours. His dream now becomes our responsibility. It is for us to continue to fulfill the dream through serving others—not in the abstract sense, but through action. It is for that reason that this administration has pioneered a new horizon of opportunity for black men and women to share the fullest responsibilities for leadership—not alone in the stewardship of minority affairs offices, though we still need such guides and interpreters, but also in the highest levels of leadership to serve all people of all races.

The truth is, Dr. King's dream is a work in progress; all great dreams are. We, here, must continue to work the dream. We start with the dream; we end with the dream. That is Martin Luther King's rich gift to us.

The American poet, T. S. Eliot, could well have been addressing Dr. King's dream when he wrote:

> What we call the beginning is often the end
> And to make our end is to make a beginning.
> The end is where we start from.[7]

The dream is where we start from. Amen—and amen!

---

[1]Coretta Scott King (1927-   ), born in Marion, Alabama; A.B., Antioch College, 1951; Mus.B., 1954, Mus.D., 1971, New England Conservatory of Music; honorary degrees. Human and civil rights activist; lecturer; author; former concert singer; married Martin Luther King, Jr., June 18, 1953; voice instructor, Morris Brown College, 1962; commenta-

tor, Cable News Network, since 1980; president, Martin Luther King, Jr., Center for Nonviolent Social Change. *Who's Who in America, 1988-1989*, I, 1690.

[2] J. B. Humphrey II; born in Lumberton; resident of Charlotte; A.B., M.Div., Shaw University; honorary degree. Pastor, First Baptist Church-West, Charlotte, since 1947; president, General Baptist State Convention of North Carolina; active in civic and religious affairs. J. B. Humphrey II to Jan-Michael Poff, January 9, 1990.

[3] Elreta Alexander Ralston (1919-   ), born in Smithfield; B.S., North Carolina A&T State University, 1937; LL.B., Columbia University, 1945, first black female graduate. Attorney in private practice; established state's first integrated law firm, Greensboro, 1965; district court judge, 1968-1981, first black woman elected to North Carolina bench; author. Elreta Alexander Ralston to Jan-Michael Poff, December 12, 1989.

[4] James K. Polk (1926-   ), born in Charlotte; resident of Raleigh; was educated at Johnson C. Smith University and at Temple University. President, 1960-1965, Grier Funeral Services, Inc., Charlotte; executive director, Community Comprehensive Manpower Program, 1965-1968; marketing director, Success Motivation Institute, Inc., Waco, Texas, 1968-1969; president, Management Manpower and Associates, Charlotte, 1969-1987; special assistant for minority affairs, Office of the Governor, since 1987. James K. Polk to Jan-Michael Poff, June 22, 1989.

[5] Jim Stowe (1956-   ), born in Belmont; resident of Raleigh; B.A., North Carolina State University, 1978. Section manager, Data General Corp., 1979-1985; assistant football coach, N.C. State University, 1985-1986; chief, Division Personnel Services, Personnel Management Services Division, state Department of Human Resources, 1986-1987; executive director, North Carolina Human Relations Council, since August, 1987. Jim Stowe to Jan-Michael Poff, June 22, 1989.

[6] Barbara Cooper Fellers Robinson (1948-   ), born in Durham; resident of Clinton; B.S., 1970, M.B.A., 1979, North Carolina Central University. Trainer, 1973-1975, customer service representative, 1975-1979, credit-collection representative, 1979-1981, test group member, 1981-1984, Amoco Oil Co., Raleigh; field service representative, Norrell, Inc., 1984, Greensboro; economics instructor, Wake Technical College, 1985; human relations specialist I, North Carolina Human Relations Council, since August, 1985. Barbara Cooper Fellers Robinson to Jan-Michael Poff, June 30, 1989.

[7] T. S. Eliot, "Little Gidding," Part V, *The Complete T. S. Eliot* (New York: Harcourt, Brace and Company, 1952), 144. The second line should read: "And to make an end is to make a beginning." The remainder of the passage was quoted correctly.

SOUTHEASTERN REGIONAL RURAL DEVELOPMENT ROUNDTABLE

RESEARCH TRIANGLE PARK, JANUARY 22, 1988

[The following speech is similar to remarks delivered to the Wallace Chamber of Commerce, Wallace, January 18; the Farm Credit Luncheon, Cooperative Council of North Carolina, Greensboro, February 18; and the North Carolina Association of Electric Cooperatives, Raleigh, March 10, 1988.]

What a timely and important conference, the Southeastern Rural Development Roundtable, with its theme, "Access '88—The Secret to Rural Development." First, I want to express appreciation for the opportunity to address an area of overriding importance to North Carolina's rural economic development and job creation, and I am

delighted to have this chance to tell you that we, joined in a partnership for progress, are turning rural economic development around in
North Carolina.

Indeed, in the last three years, we have made history in economic
development. Since becoming governor, I have had the pleasure to
see total personal income for North Carolinians rise to more than
$77.5 billion, a gain of 13.7 percent! There are many reasons for this,
and none of them is accidental. Statewide teamwork is what did it.

Statewide teamwork is what has helped us achieve $15 billion in
investments by industry over the past three years. Teamwork and
vision is what has given us a net gain of roughly 303,000 jobs since
taking office in January, 1985; teamwork and vision is what is helping
us move toward a more balanced and diverse economy in North
Carolina. This is true in terms of diversity in the kinds of industries we
have been able to attract in North Carolina, and it is true in terms of
the geographic distribution of plant locations.

In a reprint of a *Wall Street Journal* article just this past Sunday, it was
pointed out that while states in the Sunbelt have made great progress
in attracting industry, the benefits have not been enjoyed in rural
areas.[1] North Carolina can take pride in the fact that our rurai areas
have shared fully in our economic miracle. Consider: In the first three
quarters of 1987, nearly 70 percent of all new jobs announced by
manufacturing businesses in the first three quarters of 1987 occurred
in communities of 10,000 or less. This is not because we stoped scoring
in the piedmont; it's because we have also learned how to attract
industry to our more rural areas. This has meant that fewer of our
young people have found it necessary to move away to large cities in
our state for jobs or to move out of state entirely.

Our achievements in rural development provide forceful testimony
to our administration's efforts to achieve balanced economic development. In fact, in both 1986 and 1987, we had more new job
announcements outside the piedmont tha[n at] any time in this
decade. This is not a fluke, it's a trend; it's not luck either, unless you
accept the definition of luck as when preparation meets opportunity.
We have been ready for opportunity, and we have seized the historical moment. The results speak for themselves. Gary Player said it well:
"The harder you work, the luckier you get."[2]

Now, all this good news can be unsettling to some people, but you
know, one of my responsibilities as governor is to try to help some
people bear the truth no matter how pleasant it is. The "bad news
bearers" are determined to tell one and all that the many initiatives in
economic development and job creation we have taken have sacri-

ficed rural development to more urban parts of the state. When it is pointed out that most of our economic development and jobs have gone to rural areas, the response is, "Yes, but we can do better."

Do you know how the bad news bearers would do better? They would dismantle the main mechanism for our march toward economic progress, the state Department of Commerce. When the lieutenant governor announced his plan to push the destruct button on the Department of Commerce, I was quite temperate in my remarks. I said the idea was "incredibly dumb." It is more than that—it is downright reckless and could wipe out all the gains we have made toward a balanced and diverse economy.

You know, it's the old NIH syndrome all over again. You all have had experiences with the NIH—not invented here—syndrome. In this case, it goes something like this: If it works, change it; if it works exceptionally well, scrap it.

You know, one of the most important things about leadership is knowing when to have your hands on and when to keep your hands off; it's know[ing] when to let the magic of people's dedication, imagination, and energy work. Leadership is also knowing when to sit, when to stand, and what to stand for; when to walk, when to run, and yes, when to keep your mouth shut. No one has improved on President Eisenhower's definition of leadership: achieving results through others. This is what our private-public partnerships have been all about.

Leadership at its best is faith in the power of others to help solve problems. If you want to see the best example of hands-on leadership, go to the Soviet Union with its controlled, centralized economy. Centralized planning and decision-making are not working in the communist countries, and they will not work here in North Carolina.

An area of vital importance is what is called our traditional industries. The argument has been put forth, in our zeal to attract new industries, [that] we have neglected our traditional industries—those businesses already in our state. What is conveniently forgotten is that, in 1985, we established the first program ever for assisting North Carolina's traditional industries. Part of this initiative was a request from the state Department of Commerce to improve assistance to existing [industries] through its regional office system. That proposal would have expanded a pilot program that has already reached hundreds of businesses in western North Carolina and saved at least three western industries that might have otherwise closed. Expanding that highly successful program would have cost only $500,000 and would have targeted those very companies the lieutenant governor suggests we help.

Instead of funding this proven program, the General Assembly poured more than $2 million into the lieutenant governor's think tank for rural development. Why spend $500,000 to address a problem when you can spend $2 million to study it, right? What is obviously not sufficiently appreciated is, the money for expanding our regional centers is not an expense, it is an investment that will return dividends many times over.

Let me make one thing clear: Recruiting for new industries and serving the interests of existing industries are not mutually exclusive interests, as some would have you believe. It is a curious irony that, at a time when North Carolina is the envy of the nation for its success in recruiting industries, the lieutenant governor is saying that industrial recruiting is no longer a viable economic development strategy. As he puts it, "The buffalo hunt is over." I don't know about the lieutenant governor, but the state Commerce Department is not hunting buffalo, we are hunting jobs—and 303,000 net jobs over the past three years is quite a bag.

Agriculture is still the centerpiece of our rural economy. Successful agriculture and successful rural development are inseparable. Because of this fact, we have put a high priority on agriculture; to this end, I have appointed an agricultural adviser, Jim Oliver, who is also the agribusiness specialist with the state Department of Commerce.

This is a new position whose purpose is to coordinate economic development efforts in Commerce with agriculture, and the closer relationship of overall economic development is paying off. For example, with North Carolina producing two thirds of the nation's flue-cured tobacco, it was imperative that the tobacco program remain a viable industry for our farmers. Mission accomplished: As many of you know, in 1985 the whole system was on the verge of collapse. The Stabilization Corporation held tremendous surpluses, and farmers were paying the cost. In an example of hands-on, hands-joined-together leadership, I brought together at the Governor's Mansion the four major tobacco manufacturing and buying companies with the farm organizations and Stabilization respresentatives. As a result of these meetings, contracts were negotiated, enabling the four firms to purchase surplus tobacco stock from the cooperative. The contract, signed at the Governor's Mansion, was the largest single contract ever negotiated in North Carolina: a total of $1.2 billion! The bottom line of this collaboration was, in 1986, farmers paid a poundage assessment of only 2.5 cents instead of the 32 cents a pound they were expecting to pay.

The outlook for tobacco's future is bright. In 1987, the tobacco farmer enjoyed his most profitable year in many years. Information I have received indicates that our domestic companies intend to increase their purchases considerably in 1988 and reduce their foreign purchases. Recent entries into the Japanese and other foreign markets with American cigarettes is one of the reasons for increased purchases.

All this is no accident. Who better than the farmer knows the truth of the biblical saying, "As ye sow, so shall ye reap?" For example increases in foreign trade and investment in industrial facilities is the result of aggressive campaigning and marketing. The trade missions are paying off. We have worked for greater diversification in agriculture; as a result, farmers now raise poultry, or hogs, or catfish, or produce along with their tobacco. With the help of the Farm Bureau Federation, we hope to obtain additional funds to expand our marketing in Europe and the Far East. In exploring additional crops for North Carolina farmers, we are investigating the possibility of growing fresh- and saltwater shrimp, crayfish, mushrooms, kiwi fruit, lambs, and kenaf: a tree-like plant that grows rapidly from a seedling to a nine-foot plant capable of being used for the production of newsprint.

As you know, all over the nation we have witnessed a reduction of farms. In 1987, we lost only 1,000 farms. Over the previous eleven years, 3,000 families a year left their farms. What explains this dramatic turnaround? To reduce farm foreclosures and the necessity for farmers to move off their land, I convened a meeting of representatives of the banking industry and farm groups. The result was that many farmers were able to have their loans restructured in such a way that their farms were saved. Dramatic evidence of just how effective this effort was, for farmers, is that there was a 1,100 percent increase in the use of the Guaranteed Loan Program.

Unfortunately, some farmers went into bankruptcy or had to leave their farms because their operations were marginal. To respond to this we put together the Dislocated Workers Program for Farmers, administered by the Employment Security Commission. Under this program, dislocated farmers can now apply for job training and, after being trained, if they have to relocate they can receive relocation expenses for themselves and their families.

Another exciting development is what we are doing in the area of agriculture parks. Much credit for this idea and the development of the specifics of the program go to a special committee of the Governor's Task Force on the Farm Economy. To give you a shorthand version of what these parks are, they would be state-sponsored, free-standing facilities, housing privately operated grading, packaging, quick chilling, cold storage, and other food-processing operations. These parks would be tied together through a statewide computer network.

The agriculture parks will provide our producers with the processing facilities long needed to improve the quality of our fruits and vegetables and, in the long run, allow for expansion of production of these products. Agriculture parks can be an economic boon in our rural area[s].

Let me sum up a very complex subject this way:

1. Rural development is, by its very nature, a difficult task. If it were easy, it would have been done by now.

2. The reason it is not easy is that rural development runs against some of the most basic forces of economics: the tendency of goods and services to gravitate to markets, the tendency of production to gravitate to infrastructure, and the tendency of capital to gravitate to labor.

3. Therefore, it takes a special effort to achieve rural development.

4. We are making that effort, and we are succeeding. We are succeeding because of our public-private partnerships.

I'll look forward to other ideas as I serve on the Committee on Agriculture and Rural Development, a new committee of the National Governors' Association. Governor Terry E. Branstad of Iowa has asked me to serve.[3] I believe our success in North Carolina, as well as the challenges for our future, will serve the greater good of North Carolina and the entire country.

No discussion of rural development is complete without attention to transportation. Intricately bound up with economic development is transportation; indeed, an immediate correlation can be made between transportation and the economic well-being of our citizens. To grow, to prosper, it is necessary to get the jobs to the people and the people to the jobs.

This administration's efforts to improve the highway program in our state actually began on the 1984 campaign trail when I called for integrity in our programs. I took the unheard-of step of not promising road improvements all over the state, promises that could not possibly be kept. I didn't come into office carrying excess baggage of more commitments to our citizens than could actually be delivered. I am determined now, as I was then, not to make promises I can't keep, that indeed all the facts show cannot be kept. Indeed, a belief of our administration is, "promises made, promises kept." I don't count on voters' loss of memory over what was promised; I do count on integrity in government, and I believe the voters appreciate this honesty and that they will continue to do so.

Several points illustrate this honesty in government, this belief that promises made should be promises kept. In 1985, we began to make the highway program more credible by beginning to balance accurate, not pie-in-the-sky, estimates of project costs. This was a seemingly simple and sensible step, yet one that had never been taken.

In 1986, we studied highway needs and developed the Roads to the Future program. This plan did more than raise revenues for roads, it also produced efficiency and contained provisions designed to put the lid on runaway right-of-way costs. Again, more innovation. With the help of the legislature, most of the plan has become law and is working for the citizens of North Carolina. It is working for economic development.

The product of tough decisions, innovation, and bullet biting, led by the hands-on, hands-off governor and Board of Transportation, brought us into 1988 with a better, more equitable highway program. As we begin to consider program additions, the principles of integrity and credibility were foremost. What we did was to take a lot of sleaze out of our highway program, and my goal is to achieve a sleaze-free highway program; and as additions were made in our highway program, they reflected a third important element: purpose combined with vision. Indeed, our transportation program, like our whole economic development program, has proven to be a force with a vision.

The highway program should be going somewhere, and it should be going where it will do the most good. The idea of regionally important, strategic highways has been part of this administration's approach since the very beginning; it started with a commitment to Interstate 40. This strategic highway network represents the roads important to North Carolina's intrastate system. As usual, we don't have enough money to build everything all at once, but because of our success at eliminating the sleaze—empty promises and favoritism— we are going a long way toward meeting our major priorities.

Currently, more than 90 percent of North Carolina's population, and a vast majority of our towns with over 5,000 population, are within 10 miles of a strategic corridor. It should not be lost on us that this transportation strategy is vital to the continued economic development in rural areas of our state. By development of this system, and development of connectors to it, we can build a highway system that works hand in hand with our efforts to provide for more balanced economic growth, for continuing the momentum we have in tourism—which, incidentally, is our fastest-growing industry.

Good things just don't happen, they happen as a result of our actions—all of us, in North Carolina, working together. We have put up successful partnerships with local, civic, political, business, and spiritual leadership, together with our state departments of Commerce, Agriculture, Transportation, and Natural Resources. We're not just talking about partnerships and integrity in government, we're doing it! We're not just putting up little green signs saying, "Governor's Community of Excellence"—remember those signs?[4] Now we have more tangible signs of economic progress; we're putting up and expanding jobs at unprecedented levels, especially in the rural areas of our state. Promises made, promises kept. The numbers tell the story.

Yogi Berra put it well: "You can observe a lot just by watching";[5] so did another of our great American philosophers, Pogo, that quintessential sage of the Okefenokee Swamp, who observed that "Our greatest problem is insurmountable opportunity."

For eleven years, we have had a Balanced Growth Policy.[6] Well, now we finally are having balanced growth, and following a policy of participative government, of both hands-on and hands-off ways of conducting business, we will reach new heights of achievement and excellence.

Some years ago, I ran across an anecdote that has always stuck with me. It seems that back in the fifteenth century, before Columbus discovered the New World, all coins in Spain were inscribed with the Latin motto, *Ne plus ultra*: No more beyond. That was Spain's way of saying, "We're number one!" After the voyages of Columbus, all coins were changed to read *Plus ultra*: More beyond. There is much more beyond our horizon, thanks to the power of the people of North Carolina. Let *Plus ultra* be our motto as we continue to build a better future for all North Carolinians.

---

[1]See *News and Observer*, January 17, 1988.

[2]Gary Jim Player (1935-   ), born in Johannesburg, South Africa; was educated at King Edward School, Johannesburg. Professional golfer since 1953; joined Professional Golfers Assn., 1957; winner of numerous tournaments, including British Open, 1959, 1968, 1974, U.S. Masters, 1961, 1974, 1978, and U.S. Open, 1965; inducted into World Golf Hall of Fame. *Who's Who in America, 1988-1989*, II, 2469.

[3]Terry E. Branstad (1946-   ), born in Leland, Iowa; B.A., University of Iowa, 1969; J.D., Drake University, 1974; U.S. Army, 1969-1971. Attorney; farmer; member, Iowa House of Representatives, 1973-1979; elected lieutenant governor, 1978, and governor, 1982, of Iowa, reelected 1986; Republican. Barone and Ujifusa, *Almanac of American Politics, 1986*, 482; *New York Times*, November 6, 1986.

[4]When smaller towns met certain criteria deemed effective for attracting economic development, they qualified as "Communities of Excellence" under a program established by Governor Hunt. Roadside signs proclaiming the honor were placed at town limits across the state during his administration. Hunt credited the program with attracting over $3.8 billion in industrial investment and 28,000 jobs in those communities between 1977 and 1984. Mitchell, *Addresses of Hunt, 1977-1981*, xxix, 656-657, 788-789; *News and Observer*, July 29, 1986; Poff and Crow, *Addresses of Hunt, 1981-1985*, 510-511; see also *The Governor's Community of Excellence Program* (Raleigh: North Carolina Department of Commerce, Small Community Economic Development [1981]).

[5]Lawrence Peter (Yogi) Berra (1925-   ), born in St. Louis; U.S. Naval Reserve, 1943-1946. Professional baseball player; catcher, outfielder, 1946-1963, manager, 1964, 1984-1985, coach, 1975-1984, New York Yankees; coach, 1965-1972, manager, 1972-1975, New York Mets; named coach, 1986, Houston Astros; winner, American League Most Valuable Player award, 1951, 1954, 1955; holds American League record for most home runs hit by a catcher; elected to Baseball Hall of Fame, 1972; vice-president, Yoo-Hoo Chocolate Beverage Co; author. *Who's Who in America, 1988-1989*, I, 248.

The Yankees announced their selection of Berra as manager at an October 24, 1963, press conference. Responding to a reporter's question, "How have you prepared yourself for this job?" the team's new leader commented, "You observe a lot by watching." Phil Pepe, *The Wit and Wisdom of Yogi Berra* (Westport: Meckler Books, revised second edition, 1988), 64.

[6]See *N.C. Session Laws, 1979*, c. 412.

STATEMENT ON DRIVER LICENSE SYSTEM

RALEIGH, FEBRUARY 4, 1988

I am today announcing the creation of the Governor's Task Force on the North Carolina Driver License System, and I will predict that this group will affect our citizens as few groups have ever done.[1] The North Carolina driver license system has been in place since 1935, and to give you an idea of how we have grown since then, I will tell you that in 1935 we had less than 500,000 drivers in this state. Today there are almost 4.5 million. That is a tremendous numerical difference, but it is representative of changes in our society that are even broader than those sheer numbers indicate.

Driving an automobile today is a vitally important part of life. We are truly a mobile society. In most cases, you can't make a living if you can't drive to work.

Since 1935, the driver license system has undergone countless statutory and administrative changes, including a number of significant changes recently—like computers tied to a central record mainframe. Yet since it was formed there has been no comprehensive study of the licensing process. That is what I am announcing today.

The Driver License System Task Force will undertake a comprehensive review of licensing policies, services, and processes. It will review the business of driver licensing and what it is, a public service function of state government. From that perspective [it] will make suggestions on how services to North Carolina's 4.5 million drivers can be improved.

I want the task force to make suggestions concerning ways to streamline and simplify the business of getting and renewing licenses. In some ways, I expect the task force will find North Carolina's situation to be unique and will recommend changes tailor-made for our system and our citizens. In other cases, perhaps we can learn from the experience of other states.

The task force study will include the operation of driver license stations. It should evaluate the renewal process, and that review should include an evaluation of such innovative ideas as license renewal by mail for drivers with clean records and the possibility of longer license validation periods. I believe those deserve consideration and am proposing them for review by the task force, in hopes they will find them to be pure benefits.

Also while the task force is studying the public aspect of driver licensing, I am directing that it take a look behind the scenes. If there are ways that our procedures can be improved, I will expect the task force to make recommendations in these areas, also. The Division of Motor Vehicles' Driver License Section has many hard-working, dedicated employees. Those workers have been responsible for making our system work, despite the fact that demand has grown at a rate much greater than their numbers and their available resources. The task force includes DMV employees among its members; I am sure they will be able to provide valuable insight and ideas.

The task force will be under the leadership of Mr. Kermit Edney, of Hendersonville, who will serve as its chairman.[2] Former lieutenant governor Jimmy Green will be vice-chairman. Both of these men are with us today, and I would like to ask them to stand and be recognized.

In most cases, a new resident's first contact with the state of North Carolina is the DMV. The services that are provided and the impression that is left have a lot to say about North Carolina. Perhaps more citizens have yearly contact with the Division of Motor Vehicles than any other state agency. Too often the process has involved long waits, though that is improved. New residents or old, most people have a need to drive, and they have a right to expect the state to have a streamlined, efficient system in place to meet that need.

I believe that the task force I am announcing today will be a big step in the right direction. I believe it is time to look at the possibility of change, because I think we have outgrown the capacity of our present system. Consider, for instance, that last year the number of driver licenses issued was 164,000 more than the number issued in 1986. Growth like that must be addressed.

The task force begins its meetings next Friday. The executive order that creates it calls for a final report by September 1. I look forward to reviewing that report, and I am confident that the process will be followed closely by my fellow drivers in North Carolina.[3]

---

[1]Executive Order Number 60, signed December 11, 1987, established the Governor's Task Force on the North Carolina Driver License System. *N.C. Session Laws, 1987, Regular Session, 1988,* III, 939-942.

[2]Kermit Edney, native of Hendersonville; was educated at University of North Carolina at Chapel Hill, Valparaiso Technical Institute, Sacramento Junior College, and Texas A&M University; served in U.S. Army during World War II. Began radio broadcasting career in 1947; president, Radio Hendersonville; past president, Hendersonville Chamber of Commerce; served as chairman, WNC Regional Planning Commission and of Upper French Broad Economic and Development Agency; appointed chairman, Governor's Task Force on the North Carolina Driver License System, 1988; author. Kermit Edney to Jan-Michael Poff, September 16, 1988.

[3]The governor penned these notes on the last page of his speech: "Hearings in May and June. We won't halt improvements in good government just because there's an election. We have had higher priorities (schools, roads, jobs, prisons, personnel reforms) that got tended to first. This is next."

CONFERENCE ON SUBSTANCE ABUSE IN THE WORKPLACE

DURHAM, FEBRUARY 8, 1988

Let me take a moment to welcome each of you to this important Conference on Substance Abuse in the Workplace. This morning you heard representatives of government and business outline the severity of this problem in our society, as well as share various possible approaches and solutions to the problem.

Let me ask you this: What will it take to make North Carolina a drug-free state, and do we have what it takes? Certainly it will take stronger enforcement and penalties against drug traffickers. It will also take more effective education, treatment, and intervention to help the victims. Today's conference has been addressing that human dimension in the workplace.

We in North Carolina have developed a strong tradition of partnership and cooperation, between government and business, in economic development and in the field of education. Now it is time to approach the human suffering and financial loss brought about by substance abuse in that same spirit of cooperation. Let me tell you what we've done, in state government, as the single largest employer in North Carolina.

We have been both an innovator and a copier of good ideas. Along with a number of businesses and private organizations throughout North Carolina, state government has already developed a program to address substance abuse in our workplace. Since 1982, the State Employees' Assistance Program has been implemented in nearly every department and university in state government. Through confidential consultation, and assessment, and referral, the State EAP assists in identifying and confronting employees who may have work performance problems and then provides an organized approach toward a solution.

Whether the problem is alcoholism, drug abuse, emotional disorders, family problems, marital discord, or legal and financial difficulties, the State EAP helps to return employees to full work capacity at satisfactory job-performance levels. For example, over 1,300 individuals have been assisted through the State Employees' Assistance Program. A confidential, statistical evaluation of the first 300 referrals indicates that 73 percent of those employees using this service have returned to satisfactory job performance. That's good!

To further assist in coordinating efforts against substance abuse on the state government level, I appointed the Governor's Inter-Agency Advisory Team on Alcohol and Other Drug Abuse in July, 1987.[1] Composed of leading government officials, this bipartisan group has built cooperation between state agencies, thereby eliminating program duplication and maximizing the efficient use of resources—even sharing financing with agencies with components that had no source of funding.

The practical implication of these and other such efforts can be seen in our Department of Correction, which inaugurated a comprehensive Substance Abuse Program last fall by an act of the General Assembly.[2] The department will implement offender treatment programs, an offender substance abuse tracking system and data base, and a substance abuse enforcement and control program. In addition to inmates, this Substance Abuse Program is geared toward probationers and parolees. The department is also using the Employees' Assistance Program in providing aid to troubled state employees.

Earlier, to help expand our fight against substance abuse statewide, I established the Governor's Council on Alcohol and Drug Abuse among Children and Youth, by executive order, on January 29, 1986.

The council supports education, prevention, and treatment programs to reduce alcohol and drug abuse problems among children and youth and helps develop legislative programs and public policy on this issue. As part of this latter effort, the Governor's Council established and oversees the ongoing efforts of Challenge '87, a community-based planning process for developing local responses to alcohol and drug problems. The Governor's Council and Challenge '87 staff provide technical assistance to those counties seeking to form their own coalitions for attacking the problem in their own community.

Public hearings held across the state by the Governor's Council on Alcohol and Drug Abuse among Children and Youth have given us a clear understanding of the problem we face. Our experience with the success of the State Employees' Assistance Program has given us some knowledge about how to approach and overcome that problem in the workplace. Our efforts to establish local coalitions in all 100 counties in the state have taught us practical methods of implementation.

Until now, these and other similar efforts have been isolated, existing within the internal organization of government, business, and civic organizations. I propose that we pool our knowledge and resources, share our experiences, and develop a statewide, comprehensive strategy to eradicate substance abuse in both the public and private sector. This approach could especially benefit our small businesses across the state. An employer with ten or twenty employees is not likely to have the resources to establish an employee assistance program within his own organization; but that employer could join with ten or so other small businesses, and together they could provide their employees with all the guidance and assistance they might need to alleviate problems in the workplace.

There are many things we're doing: law enforcement, education, Challenge '87—and today's emphasis on sharing workplace solutions.

To paraphrase a biblical proverb, "Where there is no vision, the people perish."[3] Nowhere does this proverb apply more than in the case of substance abuse in the workplace. We must not let our people perish for lack of creative vision. As one united state, we will do all we can to become a drug-free state.

---

[1]Martin signed Executive Order Number 53, creating the Governor's Inter-Agency Advisory Team on Alcohol and Other Drug Abuse, on July 30, 1987. *N.C. Session Laws, 1987*, II, 2393-2396.

[2]The Department of Correction established its Substance Abuse Program under c. 738, s. 111, *N.C. Session Laws, 1987*, II; for amendments, see c. 830, s. 13, and "An Act to Make Miscellaneous Changes to the State Budget for the 1987-89 Fiscal Biennium," *N.C. Session Laws, 1987*, II, c. 876, s. 7.
[3]Proverbs 29:18.

NORTH CAROLINA AND THE SSC: U.S. DEPARTMENT OF ENERGY SCOPING SESSION

BUTNER, FEBRUARY 9, 1988

I am delighted to welcome you to North Carolina. We are proud to be one of seven states being considered to serve as the site of the superconducting super collider.[1] As a scientist in real life, I strongly support the construction of the SSC to enable high-energy physicists to investigate the fundamental nature of the smallest particles in nature. Ironically, to study the smallest known particles we require the largest instrument ever conceived, which will operate at extremely high energies. I believe not only that this instrument should be built, but that it can be built safely, without harm to humans or to the environment, and with great benefits to the people of this area.

My responsibilities as governor begin with the protection of the health and safety of the people of North Carolina, protection of the environment, and expansion of educational and economic opportunity. In accordance with these goals, I am glad that you are here today, beginning the process of conducting an environmental impact study; from today's input, you will determine the scope of this environmental impact study. I pledge to the Department of Energy [DOE] the full support of my administration to provide you with whatever data you need, and full access to our facilities' personnel, to accomplish this task; and I pledge to the people of North Carolina that not only will we attempt to reduce any adverse environmental impact of this facility, should it come to North Carolina, but also we will take positive steps to enhance the environment.

I have directed my staff to advise me on ways that the state can act to ensure that this project will represent an environmental benefit to the citizens of this state. Such measures might include designating the SSC site as a watershed protection area and establishing a state park nearby, if there is support for such measures.

Obviously, I hope that North Carolina will be the eventual winner, but this is neither the time nor place to debate the merits of our proposal relative to other states. You are here to hear the concerns of our citizens. As both governor and as a citizen, let me share with you my environmental concerns.

First, as to Growth:

I began my political career as a county commissioner who established the first air- and water-pollution enforcement program in North Carolina and the first countywide zoning. I am well aware that any large project like the SSC raises the issue of growth. What will the impact be of the SSC project? How will Durham, Granville, and Person counties assimilate not only the tunnel itself, and experimental areas, but how will they accommodate the additional houses and businesses, with their requisite water and sewer lines necessary to support the additional 3,000 workers for the SSC, as well as the merchants and professionals who will serve them?

Debates about this issue often become needlessly polarized at extremes. On the one hand, some want a perfect plan of how to make this accommodation before the project begins. They believe that no project such as the SSC should be undertaken until we have provided for every contingency. To accept that standard would be to halt all growth. Indeed, some would oppose all growth on the grounds that we must keep the environment "pure," forgetting that man is indeed part of the animal kingdom and, as such, a natural rather than an unnatural participant in the environment. Most of us agree that we must not spoil our habitat by letting uncontrolled growth get away from us.

At the other extreme, we find those who desire rapid growth at all costs because it provides additional wealth and income. They might advocate the SSC or any major project as a growth fetish, regardless of whether it brings genuine benefit to the state or if it endangers public health or places an undue strain upon the natural environment. Extremists from both groups may resort to hyperbole and name-calling, providing the media with exciting headlines and confrontational TV images, but this is not the responsible way to proceed.

What should be done? We must debate this issue openly, without name-calling and hostility, and with as much honest attention to the facts as possible. We want to promote scientific investigation and to provide economic benefit for the communities in which the SSC will be located, and we intend to do this without harm to public health and with as little disruption of the environment as possible. Many of us believe that the super collider can be beneficial to its surroundings and bring great improvement to the quality of life of most neighbors.

Should the decision be made to locate the SSC in North Carolina, I
believe that very careful planning must be undertaken to accommodate growth so that we will neither destroy our way of life, nor destroy our environment.

The actual planning is the responsibility of local governments. I
pledge the state of North Carolina to provide our technical resources
to cooperate with and advise the three county commissions in planning for the growth of this project. With the concurrence of the leadership of the North Carolina House and Senate, we have offered in
our proposal at least $15 million of impact monies for the local
governments to provide infrastructure to meet anticipated growth:
water, sewer, and schools. We can do more as the need is shown.
Certainly, we will meet our highway responsibilities, as I will describe
in a moment. The point here is that we will work with our local
governments to ensure orderly, high-quality growth of which the
entire area will be proud.

Secondly, as to Watershed:

We recognize that the SSC will be located in a major watershed area
and that its impact must be very carefully considered in this respect.
This is not only an environmental issue, but has recently become a
political issue of jurisdictions among local governments. It seems that
everybody's growth is in somebody else's watershed, so we must be
thoughtful and responsive to our neighbors' needs.

Our proposal provides a great deal of data on the watershed, but
more will be required, and careful environmental analysis must be
undertaken. We have already expanded our environmental subcommittee of the SSC Technical Advisory Committee and are commissioning a detailed study of the watershed. We want to be sure that the
SSC does not have an adverse effect upon either surface or ground-
waters. We strongly believe that the SSC can be located in North
Carolina without detriment to the watershed. Just as you cannot
allow water to seep into the apparatus, we don't want anything to
seep out into the water; that should be a compatibility of interest.

Now, Let's Talk about Roads:

Of the $137 million of new roads described in our SSC proposal,
most of them are already in the Transportation Improvement plan as
part of our responsibility to the needs of this area. The location of the
SSC in North Carolina would accelerate their construction, by moving

them to the top of the priority list in order to meet the SSC schedule, if we are selected. These roads, however, and those that would only be constructed because of the SSC, must be carefully assessed in terms of their effects upon the environment. When one concentrates this much construction of roads for a single project, special and careful assessment must be made; because they will be in a watershed area, the impact of the roads must be included in our study of the watershed.

Fourthly, as to Waste:

During most of my administration, waste issues have been hotly debated, especially radioactive wastes, because of our designation as the host state for the Southeast Low-Level Radioactive Waste Compact. Many citizens have been unable to understand why I have been consistently opposed to locating high-level radioactive wastes in North Carolina, but willing to accept a low-level radioactive waste site. Many citizens fail to distinguish between low-level and high-level radioactivity and are not aware that they receive exposure to low-level radioactivity from such natural sources as soil, water, and sun, as well as normal building materials.

The fact that the SSC will produce low-level radioactive materials has been used to scare ordinary citizens who do not understand radioactivity; they are frightened into believing that all such radioactivity is extremely dangerous. We will need assistance from this environmental impact study to put the radioactivity produced by the SSC into its proper context. DOE has estimated that the volume of waste that the SSC will generate will be about 8,000 cubic feet, which is approximately equal to that produced by the Duke University Medical Center; yet, who would oppose such a medical research complex, even if it produced the same amount of radioactive waste, the same number of jobs, the same acreage requirements? Some would.

Conclusion:

With more time I could elaborate additional issues that I, as both governor and a concerned citizen, would like this environmental impact study to address; but I will leave that to others. We are pleased that you are here; we look forward to cooperating with you in this important task of assessing how we can protect our environment.

On a related issue, I want to assure you all that the state is genuinely concerned about those North Carolina citizens who will have to be relocated if the SSC is sited here. A fair and careful process will be undertaken which ensures that those whose land must be acquired will be paid top dollar for their land, including existing improvements. It is unfortunate that anyone must be displaced, but there is no location that has our advantages that would displace fewer, and the SSC will benefit the local communities as well as the state.

In recognition of that benefit, those who must be displaced must also be fairly compensated. North Carolina has a well-earned reputation for being fair to its citizens when land acquisitions are necessary. We have shown this, for example, with many highway projects which were necessary but required relocation of many more households and businesses than the SSC.

One last word: From my experience as a county commissioner, I know that one of the first questions that local citizens raise about something from the outside, about which they know little and perhaps may be uncertain, is, as a public official, would you be willing to live next to this, or in this case, on top of the tunnel? My answer is, unequivocally, yes.

I would like to point out that at Fermilab, in Illinois, many scientists do just that. They live above the tunnel. Indeed, not only does farming continue above and around Fermilab, but a wildlife preserve exists on the site, with buffalo roaming above while protons and antiprotons collide below.

People are entitled to ask what it will do to their land. First of all, it will do no harm. Property owners will be fairly compensated for their land in sectors where buildings, labs, and transformers need to go, and for their mineral rights in other areas where they will have to give up their rights to drill wells or dig mines.

What about the rest of the land they own? In all likelihood, its value will be greatly increased by the economic boost this project will bring to the area. Understandably, some will not want that if it means having to sell part of the land they love. The best we can do as a state is to ensure that you get treated fairly. Your counties can receive a great stimulus if this project comes to North Carolina, provided local governments work diligently to provide orderly growth controls—with state assistance and support.

The SSC may go somewhere else, in which case all of us in North Carolina will miss being part of this exciting development. Our choice is whether to build orderly growth or block it. North Carolina chooses to build.

---

[1]The Department of Energy received formal site proposals for the superconducting super collider from twenty-five states, each of them determined to win the prestigious project and the employment bonanza that proponents said it would generate. Federal officials revealed the seven finalists on January 16, 1988: Arizona, Colorado, Illinois, Michigan, Tennessee, Texas, and North Carolina. *Congressional Quarterly Almanac, 1988,* 640; for related press releases, see "North Carolina Makes DOE Short List for Superconducting Super Collider Project, Statement by Governor Jim Martin," Raleigh, January 19, 1988, and "Governor to Speak at DOE Meeting for Superconducting Super Collider," Raleigh, February 5, 1988, Governors Papers, James G. Martin.

TRANSPORTATION 2020 FORUM

RALEIGH, FEBRUARY 15, 1988

It is a pleasure to be here, today, and an honor to speak to you concerning one of the most important issues facing our state and the nation: transportation. "2020" is a forum about our vision for the future of surface transportation, in America, thirty-two years from now. Indeed, if we can show true 20-20 vision, our future will be clear and bright.

After listening to the information we just heard, about what North Carolina is likely to be like in the twenty-first century, it is obvious that there is plenty to talk about—and just as obvious that, between now and then, we are going to have to do a lot more than talk. Our overall transportation commitment must also include waterway and airport improvements, but this national forum looks at the next three decades of land-surface transportation.

As we take this first step, we are reminded that the forum that brings us together today is part of a national process, and we must remember that the leaders of other states are beginning to come to grips with these same issues. I wish them well, but at the same time I want us to do a better job of facing the future than anybody else. Because North Carolina never gets our fair share of federal highway money, we have to do better than other states. If we do our best, North Carolina will more than maintain the competitive advantages it now has; it will become stronger. The fine quality of life we now enjoy will improve, and our citizens will be able to harvest the rewards of our foresight.

That is what we all want. Now, how do we get there? The first step we must take is the purpose of this meeting, the purpose of the entire 2020 process. We must come to understand what our society can be in the future, and from that projection, we must determine what our needs will be. Understanding those needs will allow 2020 to take its next step: the development of the federal transportation laws that must be considered, by the Congress, by 1991; and we must understand that the enactment of a well-conceived, much more fair, and dependable program is the first thing this state needs and expects from the federal government. On that point, we can and must agree.

As I said before, since 1955 North Carolina has been shortchanged on federal highway funds. For every federal fuel-tax dollar collected in this state over the last thirty-three years, only 83 cents has been returned. We fare even worse in the 1-cent transit tax, and steps taken last year threaten to worsen that trend for the next thirty-two years unless we find some way to correct it.

North Carolina must [protest] the practice of diverting highway funds to other purposes, which has expanded and is undermining our ability to provide the return that citizens have a right to expect from their highway trust-fund tax contributions. First of all, highway funds are now heavily committed to such uses as mass-transit services in other states—and committed in such a way that the vast majority of American motorists stand no chance of realizing any benefit from them or getting any fair return on their taxes.

One thing North Carolina must do is to begin now to analyze and plan for our railroad needs into the next century, especially rail passenger service linking our largest cities.

The second problem is that highway funds are being further diverted from their legitimate programming through a growing number of so-called demonstration projects that are nothing more than gigantic pork-barrel appropriations. Such pet projects are increasingly being funded by the Congress in total disregard for state priorities. Why not allocate each state its full formula share and let each battle internally over its own share, not raking off another's share? And if that situation isn't bad enough, now there is talk of raising federal highway fund taxes and using the resulting revenue—not for transportation, but to fund nonhighway programs as a means of reducing the deficit.

All such diversions are bad public policy. Even more bad policy is made through the highway program when strings are attached that are completely unrelated to highways. The program has been used to do everything from reduce the drinking age to control outdoor advertising.[1]

North Carolina and the nation need a highway program that builds and maintains highways with a fairer allocation of funds. We need a program that is enacted on time and isn't subject to repeated funding fluctuations, and we need a program that isn't hamstrung by either excessive design standards or over-detailed categorical allocations. Given a just and practical program, we can put it to work for the best interests of our citizens.

Every corner of North Carolina has unmet highway needs, and we have a desire to build a balanced improvement program that gives everyone something for their highway tax investment. The citizens in our rural areas have needs that can be met through an appropriately structured federal program. We have a host of arterial highways—the most vital of which have been identified through the Strategic Corridor Highway Network—that are top-priority candidates for construction funding. As time passes, it becomes ever more apparent that we must build a system of high-quality roads linking our regions to each other. Such a system will promote balanced growth and development, and adequate funding of it will allow us to channel more of our state resources into other areas—such as increased emphasis on secondary road paving, which is badly needed. And we must be in a better position to preserve abandoned rail rights-of-way to serve rural freight needs.

And the citizens that live near urban areas, or commute to our cities, are facing needs just as great as their rural-dwelling counterparts. Our cities have grown because they are attractive, yet that growth, and the economic health it brings, will be severely restricted unless we can cope with the traffic congestion that is present and getting worse. That is why, again, I propose that we give special attention to our future needs and potential justification for rail passenger service.

Through stock in the North Carolina Railroad, the state owns majority interest in the rights-of-way joining the major cities of the piedmont urban corridor from Raleigh to Charlotte. While recent experience with rail passenger service proved not to be economical without a heavy subsidy, that was largely because we had to carry the cost from Richmond to Raleigh—which had few riders.[2] Amtrak is now reported to be considering a new route, from Raleigh to Greensboro to Charlotte, among several alternatives. If they choose that route, it could involve a major improvement in the railbed between Raleigh and Greensboro to allow high-speed trains. Such an improvement could make attractive not only the service contemplated by Amtrak, but also daytime commuter service—whether by an existing company or by some future short-line company, public or private.

As the North Carolina Railroad prepares to renegotiate its lease with Norfolk Southern, consideration should be given to preservation of future options for interurban transit by a carrier able to offer afford-able, reliable passenger service and whether a part of our related income should be allocated to its costs. To prepare for those decisions, I propose a rail passenger service task force which I will appoint from recommendations submitted by the secretary of transportation and the president of the North Carolina Railroad and from other inter-ested parties.[3] This task force will be charged with studying the pres-ent, near future, and more distant future needs for rail transit service connecting our major cities, as well as the potential for providing affordable service; I will ask the General Assembly to continue its independent study committee on this subject, so that we can coordi-nate the submission of timely and appropriate legislation to the 1989 session.

After years of on-again, off-again passenger trains, North Carolina is fast approaching the day when daily commuter service will be fea-sible, especially between our larger cities. Their intracity congestion can be relieved by intercity alternatives. Their growth is rapid and will require it. The time has come for us to get ready—and get our commitments on track.

In short, North Carolina's needs are many and varied. Even the best of federal programs will fall short of meeting them all. We realize that, and realize that the state will probably have to shoulder a larger role. We are willing to examine that probability; at least North Carolina gets its fair share of its own funds, and I have great confidence that we can forge an approach that will be acceptable to all of us, an approach that will work for North Carolina. To do so, we must be willing to look at new approaches and review all the options. The federal program should undergo the same type of review, and if a fair and appropriate program is adopted in a timely fashion, it can count on my support.

In closing, I would like to sincerely thank all of you who have devoted energy to this meeting. Carlton Robinson and the other staff members of the Highway Users Federation, and Secretary Harrington and the DOT, have worked hard to produce the well-structured forum that will be held today. Senator Goldston,[4] Representatives Hunter,[5] Bumgardner,[6] and Nesbitt,[7] Rusty Goode, and all of the other members of the Highway Study Commission are working hard to develop answers to our state highway funding questions. I appreciate their participation in the 2020 process, along with their labors. I'd like to thank those of you who have agreed to serve on today's panel—and all of you who have come here to testify. All of you are serving your state, and that service will be reflected through a better future. Thank you for helping us build a better future for North Carolina.

[1]States that failed to enact legislation *raising* the minimum drinking age to twenty-one risked losing federal highway funds under P.L. 98-363, "An Act to Amend the Surface Transportation Act of 1982 to Require States to Use at Least 8 Percent of their Highway Safety Apportionment for Developing and Implementing Comprehensive Programs Concerning the Use of Child Restraint Systems in Motor Vehicles and for Other Purposes," *United States Statutes at Large*, Act of July 17, 1984, 98 Stat. 437-439.

[2]In October, 1984, Amtrak began what was envisioned as a one-year trial run of its daily Carolinian passenger train from Raleigh to Charlotte, with a connection to Richmond. Revenue shortfalls pulled the train from service after September 2, 1985, despite the governor's efforts to persuade Amtrak officials to keep it rolling beyond Labor Day. Nearly five years later, Amtrak launched round-trip service between Rocky Mount and Charlotte on a resurrected Carolinian. *News and Observer*, April 13, August 16, 30, 31, September 3, 1985, May 12, 1990.

[3]Executive Order Number 71, signed March 11, 1988, established the Governor's Task Force on Rail Passenger Service. *N.C. Session Laws, 1987, Regular Session, 1988*, III, 973-976.

[4]William David Goldston, Jr. (1925-   ), resident of Rockingham County; B.S., High Point College, 1947; U.S. Army Air Force, 1944-1945; N.C. National Guard, 1947-1950. Retired business executive; president, Goldston, Inc., 1952-1983; elected to state Senate, 1984, reelected 1986; member, Senate Transportation Committee; Democrat. *North Carolina Manual, 1987-1988*, 299.

[5]Robert Carl Hunter (1944-   ), resident of McDowell County; A.B., 1966, J.D., 1969, University of North Carolina at Chapel Hill. Attorney; former district attorney, North Carolina Twenty-ninth Judicial District; elected to state House, 1980, and returned in subsequent elections; chairman, House Appropriations Expansion Budget Committee on General Government, and member, House Transportation Committee; Democrat. *North Carolina Manual, 1987-1988*, 446.

[6]David Webster Bumgardner, Jr. (1921-   ), resident of Gaston County; was educated at Belmont Abbey College, 1938-1940, and Jones College of Mortuary Science; U.S. Army, 1942-1945, and Reserve, 1949-1955; N.C. National Guard, 1955-1974. Mortician; president, McLean-Bumgardner, Inc.; elected to state House, 1966, and returned in subsequent elections; chairman, House Public Utilities Committee, and vice-chairman, House Transportation Committee; Democrat. *North Carolina Manual, 1987-1988*, 399.

[7]Martin L. Nesbitt, Jr. (1946-   ), resident of Buncombe County; A.B., 1970, J.D., 1973, University of North Carolina at Chapel Hill. Attorney; appointed to state House, 1979, to complete unexpired term of Mary C. Nesbitt; elected to state House, 1980, and returned in subsequent elections; chairman, House Committee on Appropriations Expansion Budget-Education; Democrat. *North Carolina Manual, 1987-1988*, 470.

TESTIMONY BEFORE CONSOLIDATION OF ENVIRONMENTAL REGULATORY AGENCIES STUDY COMMISSION, N.C. GENERAL ASSEMBLY

RALEIGH, FEBRUARY 17, 1988

I have come today to present for your consideration a plan for reorganization of environmental regulation functions within state government. The essential features of this plan are:

1. The establishment of a new department of health and environment.

2. The combination within that department of one consolidated division of environmental management, mostly from NRCD [Department of Natural Resources and Community Development] and partly from DHR [Department of Human Resources]; one division of health services, taken from DHR; and one division of natural resources, mostly from NRCD, along with a management division; each of which division would be headed by an assistant secretary.

3. The remaining Community Development and Community Assistance grant programs would be transferred to Commerce and DHR, respectively; and other functions of NRCD would be realigned with Commerce or Administration, as appropriate, thus discontinuing the Department of Natural Resources and Community Development, as such.

Before presenting more detail of this plan, let me comment upon its history and upon its proposed future. As you know, there developed considerable interest, back in 1980, in consolidating environmental regulation functions which had been scattered over numerous uncoordinated departments. That early impetus also focused upon separating this from economic development grant functions, which then environmental leaders asserted belonged more appropriately in Commerce, as I propose. Nothing happened.

Business leaders also expressed support for consolidation, because of unsatisfactory experience with a maze of uncoordinated regulators and general confusion over how and where to go for permits or what it took to set up a business in compliance with conflicting mandates. In subsequent years, you and other legislators began to seek alternative ways to achieve the desired consolidation, only to find resistance to change within existing departmental alignments and turf. The same interagency rivalries that generated confusion and failure to cooperate across departmental lines, creating the need for reorganization in the first place, were quite naturally arrayed against its success.

In 1985, my Efficiency Study Commission weighed in with a call for reorganization of many of these functions in the interest of more logical and clearly accountable lines of authority. Quite frankly, our administration recognized the inherent difficulties that had stymied the previous administration and focused on other objectives which seemed more urgent and/or more attainable.

The problem, of course, would not go away. We made some headway getting environmental regulators under DHR Secretary Flaherty and NRCD Secretary Rhodes to collaborate more productively, while building a more cooperative link between Commerce developers and

NRCD's grant administrators. Still, we continued to hear of complaints and frustration inside and outside government. The time was ripening. If ever there were to be a reorganization, the time seemed to be right.

Your earlier hearings helped greatly to set the stage for action as you effectively pressed us to develop a plan. Your message was heard by me. In preliminary discussions with my staff and cabinet leaders, I insisted that we answer your call. Many advisers felt that an election year was no time to risk stirring up those opposed to change, but I argued that government innovation must not grind to a halt in election years.

Immediately, we encountered the expected resistance. No one in one department would readily accept the uncertainty of being transferred to another. With persistence, the holdouts began to come around. Today, I am pleased to say, I have every affected cabinet secretary here in support of this plan.

Some are skeptical that it can be approved and even advised me not to propose it as legislation for fear it would be shot down in the June "short" session. Again, my answer was that if it would be defeated in '88 then holding it back for '89 would merely reschedule the defeat. Furthermore, I felt that the fortuitous timing of support expressed simultaneously by Lieutenant Governor Jordan could help us to avoid any apparent partisan advantage and thus maximize our bipartisan support for it. I also have had the benefit of very positive, constructive conversations with both Representative Hackney[1] and Senator Walker,[2] which convinced me of your sincerity in wanting to succeed. You did not have to commit yourselves before seeing the plan, and you cannot commit all your colleagues, but your interest was genuine, so I have offered to proceed via the legislative route.

The biggest encouragement came on February 4, at a public meeting to receive reports from an interdepartmental task force and to hear comments from various associations who had shown interest for or against such a change. Staff presented a thorough analysis of five different options, plus the Maryland plan, as alternatives to the present misalignment. Several minor variations were mentioned. It looked strongly like an academic exercise going nowhere slowly.

Then, when the outside advocates began to speak, I saw that there was the beginning of a consensus forming. First, the public health directors represented that their two associations were indeed in favor of consolidation of environmental regulation, as long as it was not separated from Health Services because of their relationships to both areas. When an environmental advocate of consolidation spoke, he dropped his earlier insistence on separating Environmental Management and Health Services—as I'm told he had also earlier testified to your committee. His only reservation now was that Environmental Management must remain wedded to the Natural Resources programs, like forestry, parks, marine fisheries, the state zoo, and soil and water conservation programs. This would retain the advantage of tying together the regulatory and promotional elements of environmental concerns—the head and the heart, respectively—and no one strongly objected to that. It's great when a plan comes together!

It then occurred to me that not one of the options prepared by staff could meet both these qualifications unless Natural Resources and Environmental Management were submerged within DHR and its $2.2 billion budget and more than 17,000 employees of its own. That led me to ask that a sixth option be prepared: a new department combining Environmental Management with both Health Services and Natural Resources and not much else. The result is before you.

As you will quickly see, after you get past that strategic choice, there are many remaining choices that could be argued either way. For example, I propose to leave Pesticides in the Agriculture Department so that our farmers would only have to deal with one agency, as now. Similarly, Radiation Protection should be left in DHR since it presently is heavily oriented with its duties for permits for hospitals and other medical facilities. In both cases, you or any others might opt to amend this plan so as to move these offices into the new agency, but you will find that the advantages of consolidating them with one set of functions would be offset by the disadvantages of separating them from equally logical functions in their present departments.

My staff associates are here prepared to respond to your questions and suggestions about specific details of the plan. Should you decide to hold meetings to receive public comment, which I would welcome, any ideas for improving upon this organization plan could then be incorporated before you, or we, together, submit it to the General Assembly in June. Most of the proposed changes could be in the form of budget amendments which I could include in my 1988 budget message, requiring only a simple majority for enactment. Some changes in specific authority and realignment of certain boards and commissions would require legislation needing a two-thirds majority to suspend the rules. If the consensus holds up, that should be no problem—nor should it delay the General Assembly from adjournment.

It is always possible for it to come unraveled. I acknowledge that. Yet, if we don't try, it most probably will unravel. If we fail to seize the best circumstances yet for making these much needed changes, there is no reason to believe that we will ever have as good a chance again.

Today, major players are willing to support a major reorganization and redistribution of turf. That hasn't happened before and might not again. This plan may not be exactly the way anyone wants some of its details; after all, there are some tough choices. That doesn't have to derail our progress. Either you can amend the plan, or rewrite it some other way, or take it much as it is; but either way, you can always come back later, after seeing how it works out, or doesn't, and make needed adjustments then.

Today we present you with a plan that will work, in response to your request. All of us are ready to work with you to refine it, and build support for it, and make it work. Thank you, very much.

---

[1]John Joseph (Joe) Hackney (1945-   ), born in Siler City; resident of Orange County; A.B., 1967, J.D., 1970, University of North Carolina at Chapel Hill. Attorney; assistant district attorney, Fifteenth Judicial District, 1971-1974; elected to state House of Representatives, 1980, and returned in subsequent elections; chairman, House Finance Committee; Democrat. *North Carolina Manual, 1987-1988,* 433; *UNC Alumni Directory,* 460.

[2]Russell Grady Walker (1918-   ), born in Conetoe; resident of Randolph County; was educated at High Point High School; U.S. Army Air Force, 1941-1946, and Reserve, 1947-1955. Retired supermarket executive; member, Asheboro City Council, 1961-1965; elected to state Senate, 1974, and returned in subsequent elections; chairman, Senate Committee on Appropriations-Human Resources; chairman, state Democratic party, 1979-1983. *North Carolina Manual, 1987-1988,* 333.

GOVERNOR'S NEW PRODUCT AWARDS PRESENTATION PROFESSIONAL ENGINEERS OF NORTH CAROLINA

GREENSBORO, FEBRUARY 18, 1988

[In addition to the following speech, the governor also stressed the relationship between literacy and economic development in addresses to the Greensboro Jaycees, January 20; North Carolina Council of Engineers, Charlotte, March 23; combined Rotary Clubs, High Point, April 21; and the Rotary District Governors Conference, Lake Junaluska, May 14, 1988.]

What a great honor and pleasure it is for me, once again, to address a group of such importance to our state's continued growth and prosperity.

Over the past three years, North Carolina has had one of the greatest upsurges in plant investment and job creation in our history.

During this same period, personal income has risen to more than $77.5 billion, an increase of 13.5 percent. Over the same three-year period, we have averaged $5 billion in new and expanded plant investment for a total of $15 billion. Since January, 1985, we have added more than 300,000 new jobs in our state. This 300,000 figure represents the difference between all jobs gained, less all jobs lost, in a three-year period.

For years, we have had a Balanced Growth Policy in North Carolina. Now we have balanced growth. Instead of putting up little green signs that say "Governor's Community of Excellence," we are putting jobs in communities.

We have made giant strides toward a better geographic distribution of jobs. In fact, in 1986 and 1987, we had more job announcements in the rural areas of our state than in our more populated areas—60 percent in 1987. This is not because we have lessened our effort, or been less successful, in our job creation efforts for urban areas; it's because we have learned, also, how to attract industry to our less populated areas.

In this three-year time frame, our state has experienced tremendous movement toward fuller participation in high technology and our information-intensive age. Indeed, we have positioned North Carolina as preeminent in what Alvin Toffler calls the "third wave."[1] Part of this positioning results from our efforts to have North Carolina declared the site for the super collider and Sematech. Although Sematech went to Texas, things look promising for our getting a part of this lucrative, high-tech contract.[2]

We are still very much in the running for the super collider. Whether we win or lose this $4.4 billion scientific contract, North Carolina will be a winner. This is because we will have positioned ourselves even more strongly as a leader in science and high technology.

There are yet other indicators showing the high regard held by business. Consider: *Business Week* magazine, in a survey of top CEOs across the country, reports that CEOs would rather invest in new plants in North Carolina than in any other state. The same high regard for our state was reported in *Manufacturing Week* magazine. It should be noted these are not isolated examples.

What we are seeing is a growing consensus that the Tar Heel State is the place to do business. For example, in a just-published report, "'North Carolina FREE' Senior Manager Management: Executive Summary," top business executives gave an overwhelming vote of confidence to both the Governor's Office and the state Department of Commerce for being positive influences on business. The Governor's

Office received an 86.7 percent favorable response; 2.9 percent were unfavorable. The only factor more positive was our university system. The Department of Commerce got an 84.1 percent favorable rating, and 2.5 percent were unfavorable.[3] Apparently our business leaders don't want us to abolish the Commerce Department.

As survey after survey shows, the bottom line is that business, both domestic and foreign, likes North Carolina. The truth is, we are on an economic roll; and when you're number one, you've got to try harder. Teamwork and vision are what has brought about this tremendous resurgence in economic development and job creation in our state. Now we must call upon the same teamwork and vision, the same kind of imagination and passion for excellence that drives engineers to create new solutions, to help us through a grave crisis confronting our state.

The city of Charlotte calls this crisis an "economic time bomb," and it threatens to undo the momentum we have managed to create in economic development over the past three years. If you haven't guessed what this time bomb is, it's illiteracy. As the "Music Man" would say, it starts with an *i* and it spells trouble, trouble right here in North Carolina.[4]

Now back to those questions: Are we a state at risk, and are we living on borrowed time? After I have given you some facts, these are questions you will have to answer.

Recently, David T. Kearns, chairman and CEO of Xerox, noted that "the American work force is running out of qualified people," and warns that "if current demographic and economic trends continue, American business will have to hire a million new workers a year who can't read, write, or count." In fact, currently American industry is having to shell out $25 billion a year to provide literacy skills to their workers.

We can take little comfort in the statistics coming out on the state of illiteracy in North Carolina. While precise figures on the scope of adult illiteracy are hard to come by, it is becoming increasingly clear that if we continue to do business as usual, even our most conservative figures are of such magnitude that all the money in our treasury will not correct the problem. We do know, with a high degree of precision, that the amount of money we are spending on our state literacy programs has mushroomed from just over $3.5 million, in 1983-1984, to a budgeted amount of more than $11 million in 1987-1988. If you add federal monies for literacy allocated for our state, the overall figure jumps from close to $6.5 million to nearly $14.5 million in five years.

We know, also, that this money is paid on the basis of seat time, not actual results. In fact, under the present funding arrangement for our literacy programs, the more efficient a program is in providing literacy skills, the less money it will receive. In other words, the more inefficient you are, the more money you will get. Seat time, not results, is the criterion.

Michael LeBouef wrote a book called *The Greatest Management Principle in the World*, and do you know what he says the greatest management principle in the world is? It's this: Reward people for the right behavior and you get the right results. Fail to reward the right behavior and you will likely get the wrong results. Adherence to this overriding principle is what has prompted me to advocate a career ladder for teachers, to ensure that teaching excellence is rewarded and encouraged, with promotions for teachers.

Results coming in from our pilot programs across the state show that the system of rewarding excellence is working. Oddly enough, the NEA [National Education Association] teachers union is opposed to promotions for teachers. They're trying to sabotage it.

The power of the management principle of rewards is illustrated by the story of a weekend fisherman. He was out on a lake casting his line, when he saw a snake swim by the boat with a frog in its mouth. Feeling sorry for the frog, he reached down and released it. Then he got to feeling bad about the snake and looked down around his boat for some food to give it. All he could find was a flask of bourbon, so he gave the snake a shot. The snake swam away, and the fisherman went back to his fishing. About ten minutes later, he heard this thump on the side of his boat. He looked down, and there was the same snake—this time with two frogs in its mouth.

Few groups operate so much by the greatest management principle as do engineers. You are a results-oriented profession.

We do know that we cannot continue to reward inefficiency. No one knows this better than engineers.

We do know, according to the 1980 U.S. census, that more than 835,000 North Carolinians over the age of twenty-four have not completed eighth grade. We do know that almost 27,000 students, or almost a third, dropped out of our high schools last year.

We do know we cannot continue to prosper as a state when a third of our young are undereducated. We have learned from the U.S. Department of Labor that in two years—hold that thought—in two years, three fourths of the jobs will require some education and technical training beyond high school.

You know that we actually have a condition in our society called math anxiety. It's apparently so widespread that many books have been written, and workshops given, on how to get rid of it. Not so parenthetically, females are those mostly afflicted by math anxiety. I really don't understand why. Many teachers, also, suffer from this affliction.

It's encouraging that more women are going into the sciences and fields like engineering, but we must do more to encourage women to take subjects such as mathematics and physics. The same may be said of certain minorities who, for a variety of reasons, are excluded or exclude themselves from entry into fields like engineering.

As honorary chairman of MATHCOUNTS, I am aware of the efforts of the engineering profession to improve math literacy.[5] I want you to know how proud I am that our MATHCOUNTS team finished eighth out of fifty-four at the national MATHCOUNTS competition in 1987, and that North Carolina is one of only two states that have placed in the top ten every year since the program began in [1983]. Unfortunately, these fine young people are the exception, not the rule.

It is obvious we must do much more. What we are seeing is an upping of the literacy stakes in math, reading, and English, so that what is good today will not be adequate for tomorrow's needs—and for all practical purposes, tomorrow is less than two years away. A recent study by the Remediation and Training Institute in Washington reveals that one third of all graduating seniors test below ninth-grade norms; and even among high school graduates who go on to college, one third must take remedial courses. Indeed, just the other day, C. D. Spangler, president of the University of North Carolina, announced that over 30 percent of all students entering the university system required remedial work in math and English. In other words, they must take remedial-level courses at the university.

We take pride in our nation as a leader in science and technology, but the facts are that we are losing our competitive edge to nations that have no illusions [about] what it takes to develop a technologically literate society. Nowhere is this reality more telling than in the marketplace. Over the years we have ceded to other nations leadership in a whole array of high-tech industries.

Here's some arithmetic that should interest you: In spite of a budgeted amount of almost $14.5 million in state and federal monies in the current fiscal year for our state literacy program, we still are reaching only about 6 percent of the adults needing literacy services. If we were to serve all those in our state with literacy needs, at the present level of expenditures it would cost more than $235 million a year.

In my "State of the State" address to the General Assembly in January, 1987, I announced the establishment of a Governor's Commission on Literacy, to be chaired by Bill Friday, president emeritus of the University of North Carolina. For executive director of this commission, I was fortunate to secure the services of an outstanding adult educator, Dr. Richard Hagemeyer, president emeritus of Central Piedmont Community College, in Charlotte—and nationally recognized for his innovative approaches to literacy training for adults. The Governor's Commission has been hard at work, and as a result, we have a much clearer understanding of the nature and extent of the problem and the directions we need to take.

Several clear findings have emerged. One, we cannot afford to continue funding procedures for literacy programs that actually penalize efficiency and innovation—that indeed reward low productivity. Two, we must have greater accountability in our literacy programs. Three, people requiring literacy skills must have access to a variety of programs in literacy training, not just one; people with literacy needs ought to have second chances with variety. Four, there has to be better coordination of literacy programs throughout the state. Five, preventive programs are better and less expensive than remedial programs; we must slow the flood of illiterate students coming out of our schools.

Four [sic], and an overall conclusion is, if we are to get significantly better results in our literacy programs, we must be significantly different. Also, I would like to offer what I hope will be a credo for all publicly funded literacy programs: Investing more and more money in failed strategies will serve only to consolidate and institutionalize those strategies, thereby hindering adoption of promising strategies more capable of raising the level of literacy in North Carolina.

Assuming we have the will and vision to make the necessary changes in our literacy programs, we can, in spite of the gloomy picture I have painted, emerge out of our emergency. Literacy, it must be emphasized, is not a partisan issue, it is a human issue touching us all.

The Governor's Commission on Literacy is very involved in seeking answers to the problems I have outlined above. It is encouraging that the commission is being supported by private-sector groups such as the Jaycees. A collaborative alliance of public and private sectors will be required if we are to make the kind of headway that is required.

The time for action is now. One million babies born in this country last year will not complete school. Unless we do something significantly different and significantly better, this rate will continue to grow, damaging individuals, and families, and derailing our efforts toward greater prosperity for all North Carolinians.

The economic time bomb called illiteracy continues to tick away its deadly seconds. We must have the will and vision to defuse it. I'm optimistic that we can. I'm optimistic because, given the opportunity, the imagination and will of people like you and others in our state will pull us through. You can help. Push locally for better schools, for higher literacy levels, better pay for better teachers. Get yourself involved. North Carolina will be glad you did.

---

[1]Alvin Toffler, *The Third Wave* (New York: William Morrow and Company, Inc., 1980).

[2]The Sematech research consortium was established in March, 1987, to create advanced manufacturing processes that would end Japanese domination of the semiconductor industry. Research Triangle Park was one of twelve finalists in the site-selection competition and appeared to have the best chance of landing the project, expected to produce an estimated 800 jobs. But Tar Heel hopes came to naught after intensive lobbying by Texas officials persuaded the Sematech board to decide in favor of Austin. *News and Observer*, January 5, 6, 7, 1988.

[3]Verne R. Kennedy, *Executive Summary* [Prepared for North Carolina Foundation for Research and Economic Education] (Jackson, Mississippi: Marketing Research Institute, September, 1987), 5.

[4]"Professor" Harold Hill, also known as the "Music Man," was the central character in the play *The Music Man* that opened December 19, 1957, at the Majestic Theatre in New York City; five years later, Warner Brothers released a motion picture version of the musical comedy. A con artist who "could not tell a bass clef from a bass fish," Hill arrived in River City, Iowa, to sell its citizens band instruments. He initiated his sneaky commercial overture in the song "Trouble," warning of the evil that a soon-to-open pool hall would instill in the local youth while touting the benefits of music lessons as a preventative of dissipation:

> Ya got
> Trouble (Oh we've got
> Trouble) Right here in River
> City! (Right here in River
> City) With a capital
> T and that rhymes with
> P and that stands for
> Pool. (That stands for
> Pool!)

Nash and Ross, *Motion Picture Guide*, V, 2062-2063; *The Music Man: Book, Music, and Lyrics*, by Meredith Willson (New York: G. P. Putnam's Sons, 1958), 9, 37.

[5]The MATHCOUNTS national mathematics contest, open to seventh and eighth graders, was begun in 1983 by the National Society of Professional Engineers and the CNA Insurance Companies. The Professional Engineers of North Carolina sponsored the state competition. Information courtesy of Suzanne Letchworth, Cary High School mathematics teacher, July 18, 1990, and the Professional Engineers of North Carolina, July 26, 1990.

SOUTHERN REGIONAL EDUCATION BOARD, SOUTHERN GOVERNORS' ASSOCIATION WINTER MEETING

Washington, D.C., February 22, 1988

I am pleased to report to you this morning, in my capacity as chairman of the Southern Regional Education Board, on two counts: first, that states in the SREB region remain out front in the push for educational reform, and second, that SREB continues to play an important role in this regional leadership. Let me illustrate by referring to two developments, one having to do with assessment of student progress, the other with illiteracy.

The three-year pilot program, developed by SREB and the National Assessment of Educational Progress (NAEP) to demonstrate the feasibility of providing state-by-state comparisons of the achievement of secondary students, has concluded. In the third year of the pilot, about 16,000 eleventh-grade students, from 700 public schools in eight SREB states, were tested in mathematics and United States history. A report showing the state-by-state results and outlining their implications was released by SREB in October.[1] The pilot project has stimulated and become the model for a new, nationwide student assessment program being developed by the Council of Chief State School Officers.

The SREB states that have participated in this pilot testing program have learned a lot about the performance of their secondary students, much of it highly encouraging. They have also demonstrated leadership of a high order, and when we soon have the first nationwide testing program with truly comparable results among our states, we can thank this regional pilot program. I am glad that North Carolina has participated in this pilot for the past three years; we learned much about ourselves and we will be using that knowledge in the future.

The second development I want to mention is a new effort to promote family literacy. Funded by the William R. Kenan, Jr., Charitable Trust and administered by SREB, this project will develop model programs in which at-risk preschool children and their undereducated parents will go to school together. A child's success in school, and consequently successful employment in later life, is closely tied to the educational attainment and positive support of the parent. The two problems, youngsters who are in danger of being left behind even before they reach school age and their undereducated parents, are interrelated and should be attacked systematically.

In the Kenan/SREB Family Literacy Project, children will be taught the basic kindergarten readiness skills that can establish a pattern for success at each level of schooling. Parents will be instructed in the basic academic skills needed for high school equivalency certification, instruction that can open up opportunities in the job market and for further vocational training. A vital part of the program will be strengthening the relationship between parent and child through instruction in life skills and parenting techniques. The expectation is, that as parents and children work together, both can recognize more clearly the value of education.

The Kenan/SREB Family Literacy Project, based on Kentucky's Parent and Child Education (PACE) Program, will establish new sites in Kentucky, later North Carolina, and hopefully other states. This project can create a productive environment in which schools, higher education, states, the federal government, and the private sector can come together to consider and develop new approaches to help young children and illiterate adults. As Secretary of Education William J. Bennett often has asserted, parents are their children's first and most influential teachers, and increased parental involvement in children's education will support educational reform.

These examples of leadership in the South, for education reform, and I could have cited others, should be encouraging to us all. Later this year, SREB will publish a statement of specific, measurable goals for educational improvement that states should pursue over the next decade—still another example of how we can learn from each other as well as gain added confidence in our respective efforts to achieve outstanding schools and colleges.[2]

---

[1]*Measuring Student Achievement: Comparable Test Results for Participating SREB States and the Nation* (Atlanta, Georgia: Southern Regional Education Board, 1987).

[2]*Goals for Education: Challenge 2000* (Atlanta, Georgia: Southern Regional Education Board, 1988).

STATEMENT ON SUPERCONDUCTING SUPER COLLIDER TO DURHAM COUNTY COMMISSIONERS

DURHAM, FEBRUARY 23, 1988

It has been some time since I have had the pleasure of sitting at and speaking from a county commissioners' dais, and it feels good. I appreciate very much your gracious invitation to be here to discuss North Carolina's superconducting super collider project. The participation of Durham County has been, and continues to be, very important in our efforts to secure the SSC for North Carolina. Since the Department of Energy announced the list of best-qualified sites, our proposal has received a great deal of attention, both locally and nationally. I welcome this opportunity to let you know, firsthand, the status of the project, and I will address three specific issues that have been publicized recently: the safety of the SSC, the effect on property owners, and the likely regional impact.

First, as to the safety of the SSC: The superconducting super collider will be the world's largest scientific instrument and most powerful particle accelerator, so it is quite natural for people to ask how such a large project would affect them, and their families, and their environment. Certainly, anyone outside this area would share the concerns of citizens here for their safety and well-being.

To understand the safety issues associated with the super collider, it is important to understand the nature of the facility. The SSC's purpose is to make protons collide with other protons at very high speeds, extremely high energies, so that scientists can study the fragments produced by those collisions. These experiments will provide the scientists with insight into the fundamental nature of matter and the universe.

The SSC is not a nuclear reactor. A reactor works by splitting large, complex, unstable atoms into smaller atoms, many of which are radioactive, and it gives off an enormous amount of energy. In contrast, the SSC works by splitting protons, which are smaller than the simplest atoms and which are not unstable. The fragments produced in proton collisions are themselves smaller than atoms and thus cannot be radioactive; they cannot decompose or decay by any radioactive process. A small amount of low-level radioactivity would be expected to be produced as a by-product of some SSC operations— by proton interactions with other materials, such as some of the surrounding materials—but not in the proton-proton collisions that are the main business of the SSC. In the process of splitting atoms, nuclear reactors produce vast amounts of energy. In contrast, the super collider will be a net user of energy; it will require a large amount of energy to make it work. It will not give off energy, it will use energy; thus, it cannot experience a meltdown or any such uncontrolled release of large amounts of energy. We need to understand that, because if we don't understand it, there will be some who will try to generate fears that that might be the case.

We can understand a great deal about the safety of the super collider from the experience that has been gained at other particle accelerators which have been operated for years. The operating histories of Fermilab, near Chicago; the Stanford Linear Accelerator, in Palo Alto; CERN,[1] near Geneva, Switzerland; and Brookhaven National Laboratory, on Long Island, provide a convincing precedent for the safe operation of this type of instrument.

Last week, a group from North Carolina toured Fermilab, which is today the largest operating accelerator in the world. The accelerator at Fermilab is a collider, as the SSC will be, and it has recently been upgraded to use superconducting magnets to make it more powerful. It was operating while our group was there. Our visiting team from North Carolina was free to move about the premises, as the general public is able to do, and they drove over the accelerator tunnel, which is about thirty feet underground. They saw there a wildlife preserve on the Fermilab property and saw that farming goes on over and within the ring. The staff of Fermilab, local residents, and visitors flock to the on-site recreational ponds on weekends.

Fermilab's insurance premiums are in the lowest category: that established for businesses with primarily office staff. The most common accidents experienced there are back injuries and cars backing into other cars in the parking lots, not accidents associated with high-energy technology. The chief safety officer at Fermilab stated that there have been no measurable releases of accelerator-produced radioactive materials into the soil or the groundwater since the facility began operation over fifteen years ago. The waste the SSC would produce is similar in extent to that produced by a small industry, or a medical center, and can be handled and disposed of by standard procedures. One of the members of the group that visited Fermilab last week was Dr. Fearghus O'Foghludha, professor emeritus of radiation physics at Duke University, who will be speaking this evening to provide further information on the low-level radioactive waste issue.[2]

I have spoken to environmental issues, including growth, watersheds, and roads, in my remarks to the Department of Energy at the Environmental Impact Statement Public Scoping Meeting, on February 9, in Butner. On that occasion, I affirmed my belief that careful planning will enable us to accommodate the growth and development that this project will stimulate, while preserving—and even enhancing—the desirable features of our environment and our way of life. I pledged that the state would cooperate with and advise Durham, Person, and Granville counties, which would have the principal responsibilities for planning for the growth associated with this project. I stressed the importance of protecting the watersheds in the project area from any adverse effects, including the effects of our proposed road improvements, and I assured the citizens of North Carolina that the state will follow a fair and careful process in compensating those who must be displaced if the SSC comes to North Carolina. Tonight, let me discuss further the issue of property purchases in a bit more detail.

It is unfortunate that anyone must ever be displaced from their home or land to make way for any public improvements. However, as we have seen from time to time, the public good occasionally requires individuals and businesses to be relocated—for instance, to make room for highways and other transportation improvements, for utilities, for recreational projects, for educational facilities, and for government buildings. In those cases it is only proper for the society that benefits from such projects to ensure, through its governments, that the affected property owners are fairly compensated. You will hear later this evening from Mr. Charles Holliday,[3] director of the State Property Office, who will discuss in more detail the state's procedures for property purchases and relocations.

In our proposal to the Department of Energy, we were required to propose a specific location for the SSC—to draw it on a map and show where it would be—and also to discuss the flexibility that our site would allow in the final, precise placement of the facilities. We discussed in our proposal what has been referred to as an "envelope" of flexibility—that is, certain limits within which the SSC could be placed. This envelope stretches 2,000 feet in all horizontal directions and allows for small rotations from a base position that was specified in our proposal.

I make that comment because it would help us to begin to develop a response to a question that was raised in a conversation that I had with Chairman Bell[4] at the Governor's Mansion, a question that was raised particularly because of the concerns of a larger number of people than we had thought would be affected in the Rougemont area of northern Durham County. I want to be very careful, in speaking to you, not to make any definitive commitment until we have seen what the alternatives would be. I can at least indicate to you that, so far as we understand from the Department of Energy, it is possible to make a slight lateral movement of the entire project within the 2,000-foot envelope, or rotate it a few degrees about a central vertical axis, and we would consider the consequences of doing that. For example, if that would enable us to move the facility so that it would not affect as many neighbors in one area, we would then have to see how many people might be affected in another area. I can assure you that we will try our best, working with the Department of Energy, to see if there is any movement of that sort which would minimize the impact of the project. It is a good suggestion and one that ought to be worked out.

After the DOE has chosen its preferred SSC site from among the seven finalists, that agency will prepare a final site-specific design for the super collider, taking into account the data in the site proposal and the additional, more detailed environmental data that is now being provided for the seven best-qualified sites. It is the policy of the state of North Carolina and Department of Energy to minimize the impact of the SSC on the existing land uses in the area of the SSC site. If the DOE chooses North Carolina as its preferred site, the final site-specific design process would allow adjustments that incorporate the most current land-use information. The exact location of the SSC land areas at our site would then be finalized.

It would be premature for us to identify any property owner as definitely being affected by the SSC, yet we have notified the property owners who are most likely to be affected. We are conducting six property information sessions so that we can give these potentially affected property owners a chance to discuss their concerns, one on one, with personnel from the State Property Office who are skilled and experienced with these kinds of discussions, as well as with the staff of the SSC projects. The first of these meetings was held last night in Roxboro, and the rest will be held this week and next week.

Some have expressed apprehension about the effect of the SSC on developments, neighborhoods, and land values. That kind of apprehension can be allayed by looking at the local effects of other large accelerator facilities. As at Fermilab, roads passing through SSC property would be open to the public. Development on the SSC property would be of low density, so there would be built-in protection for adjoining property holders. At Fermilab, much of the land has been leased back to farmers for agricultural use, and the property is an aesthetic and environmental asset to the area. Surrounding property values have not been adversely affected there, and they might be considerably enhanced around the SSC site, particularly if the communities organize for orderly use of the land around the site.

The state and Department of Energy will try to minimize any adverse effects of the SSC on property owners. Nevertheless, if the SSC comes to North Carolina, some property owners inevitably would be affected. I pledge to you that the state will adequately and fairly compensate them to the degree and extent that we are allowed to do so by law, and in the way in which we have done in other property transactions in the past, so that they would be compensated for all aspects of the land acquisition process for those areas where the land would be needed for buildings and other improvements related to the collider—including relocation.

Now let me talk about the wider impact of the super collider on the entire community. In North Carolina, the SSC tunnel would be about 170 to 175 feet underground, on average, and would be essentially unnoticed. Many of the world's largest cities have underground tunnels that are used for subways. Those tunnels are relatively shallow, but have little effect on life on the surface. The CERN accelerator tunnel passes under a suburb of the city of Geneva, Switzerland. If the SSC tunnel were located directly beneath this building, and if the collider were operating right now, we would be totally unaware of it.

The SSC, with its $250 million annual operating budget, will definitely boost the local and state economies. The 3,000 jobs at the SSC are modest in comparison with the more than 30,000 jobs at the Research Triangle Park and in the context of the region's growing economy, but it is fair to anticipate that those 3,000 jobs will lead to other jobs for merchants and professionals who will move to the area to be of service to them. Although the SSC would attract some of the world's top physicists, most of the jobs at the SSC would go to technical, professional, and clerical staff, many of whom would be hired from the local labor pool. For example, fewer than 20 percent of the jobs at Fermilab are in high-energy physics, just as only about 10 percent of the jobs at Duke Medical Center are for M.D.'s. In addition, many jobs would be created in the surrounding communities in businesses providing services to the SSC.

The impact of the SSC on North Carolina would be profound. No other site under consideration would provide as much for the super collider or benefit as much from it. The SSC matches the intellectual and research strengths and resources of this area—the universities of the Triangle area, the Research Triangle Park, the medical centers—in a unique way. Dr. Leon Lederman,[5] the director of Fermilab, is quick to point out the medical spin-offs of the accelerator technology at Fermilab, such as magnetic resonance imaging and positron emission tomography.[6]

Think of the potential for even more dramatic medical spin-offs if the world's largest particle accelerator were located only ten miles from the "City of Medicine." Think of the benefit to the students of the North Carolina School of Science and Mathematics, and in the region's public schools, if they could talk directly with the world's best minds in physics and mathematics. Think of the impact that the addition of sixty new positions in science and technology at the local universities could have, as well as another ninety positions in high-energy physics to which our neighboring southeastern states would commit themselves so that they could share in the benefits of this great project, not to mention the millions of dollars in federal research grants that these people would generate. Think of the opportunity for coordinated regional planning to control growth and protect our watersheds that a regional project such as this would have to stimulate. In sum, it is difficult to envision any $4 billion project that would be less intrusive on the environment, and more easily incorporated into the countryside of North Carolina's piedmont, while providing such enormous environmental, educational, and economic benefits for so many of our citizens.

Mr. Chairman, commissioners, and especially the people of Durham and neighboring communities: The state of North Carolina needs and asks for your support and cooperation for this project. We are in the finals of the competition to host the largest and most expensive scientific apparatus in the history of the world. Just as today it can be estimated that more than 40 percent of today's gross national product is based upon what we learned about the electronic and nuclear structure of atoms in the early twentieth century, this scientific research, when completed in the early twenty-first century, will undergird the technologies of the next 50 to 100 years. I want that to be North Carolina's story.

More immediately, just as the engineering of the National Aeronautics and Space Administration has led to many marvels benefiting medicine, therapy, communications, computers, weather forecasting, and agriculture, similarly the engineering and technology needed to make the collider work—quite apart from any scientific discoveries about the nature of matter—will surely give us faster, more reliable electrical controls, detector and monitoring technology that would not otherwise be available, new materials, and probably a profound improvement in electricity transmission capacity through superconductors. I want that to be North Carolina's story.

---

[1]CERN is an acronym for *Centre Européen de Recherche Nucléaire* (European Organization for Nuclear Research). See Bryan Bunch (ed.), *The Science Almanac, 1985-1986 Edition* (Garden City, New York: Anchor Press/Doubleday, 1984), 517, 532.

[2]Fearghus Tadhg O'Foghludha (1927-   ), born in Dublin, Ireland; B.Sc., 1948, M.Sc., 1949, Ph.D., 1961, National University of Ireland. Senior physicist, St. Luke's Hospital, Dublin, 1954-1963; various positions, Medical College of Virginia, 1963-1970, including professor of radiation physics and division chairman; professor of radiation physics, division director, 1970-1988, professor emeritus since 1988, Duke University Medical Center; editor; president, American Assn. of Physicists in Medicine, 1971-1972. *Who's Who in America, 1988-1989*, II, 2327.

[3]Charles L. Holliday (1939-   ), born in Jamesville; resident of Fuquay-Varina; bachelor's degree in business administration, East Carolina University. Director, State Property Office, Department of Administration. Charles L. Holliday to Jan-Michael Poff, September 13, 1988.

[4]William Vaughn Bell (1941-   ), born in Washington, D.C.; resident of Durham; B.S., Howard University, 1961; M.S., New York University, 1968; U.S. Army, 1961-1963. Senior engineer, IBM Corp.; elected to Durham County Board of Commissioners, 1972, and returned in subsequent elections; chairman, Durham County Board of Commissioners, since 1982. Garry E. Umstead, clerk to the Durham County Board of Commissioners, to Jan-Michael Poff, September 13, 1988.

[5]Leon Max Lederman (1922-   ), born in New York City; B.S., College of the City of New York, 1943; A.M., 1948, Ph.D., 1951, Columbia University; U.S. Army, 1943-1946. Prize-winning physicist; assistant professor, 1952-1954, associate professor, 1954-1958, and professor, since 1958, of physics, Columbia University; director, Nevis Laboratories, 1960-1967, and since 1969; consultant, CERN accelerator laboratory, since 1970; director, Fermi National Accelerator Laboratory, since 1972. Who's Who in America, 1986-1987, II, 1650.

[6]Martin also touted the potential health-care benefits of the supercollider in his June 7, 1988, remarks to the state SSC Advisory Board. Duke Medical Center physicians, he asserted, "have already expressed great interest in using protons from the SSC for medical research purposes. In particular, new cancer therapies could be investigated using the unique source of high-energy protons provided by the SSC." Beyond magnetic resonance imaging, the superconducting magnet technology required to operate the SSC might lead to major discoveries "in the search for more powerful and sophisticated diagnostic techniques."

NORTH CAROLINA ASSOCIATION OF SCHOOL ADMINISTRATORS

WINSTON-SALEM, MARCH 9, 1988

I very much appreciate this opportunity to speak to you on one of the most important issues confronting our state, the governor's role in educational leadership. On a particularly pressing matter, that of student bus drivers, let me say that I have today asked our attorney general to seek a restraining order against the sudden and unreasonable decision of the U.S. Labor Department. The department is attempting to force us to change, without valid reason, our state's long-standing practice and asking us to change that practice practically overnight—and today has rejected our appeal for reason.[1]

As we pursue our legal options, we will continue our efforts to negotiate an agreement with the Department of Labor that would allow us to use seventeen-year-old drivers through the end of this school year. Also, we will continue to support legislation introduced by Congressman Rose[2] and supported by other members of our delegation. Hopefully, one of these options will prove successful. If that is the case, it will be incumbent upon the state, and particularly incumbent on you, to ensure that we strictly comply with the terms of our understanding.

As we work for administrative and legal developments, we are proceeding, as best we can, to meet the challenges that may confront us. I have directed the Division of Motor Vehicles to assign the highest priority to the training of new drivers. Of course, I understand that driver training is the second step in the process; the first step is the recruitment of driver candidates. I know that will present many of you with a difficult dilemma. Furthermore, as many of you probably know, the State Board of Education has voted to request additional funding for driver salaries; accordingly, the budget that I submit for the June short session will include full funding for raising bus drivers to $6.10 an hour, with benefits.[3] The lieutenant governor and Speaker Ramsey agree that it's time to get this behind us and move on to more constructive issues.

It is an honor, indeed, to be able to share ideas with you. In some areas, the leadership role of a governor is obvious. He or she is elected to office by the will of a voting majority, representing all the citizens of our state. The governor has responsibility for the overall administration of the state's affairs in such diverse areas as transportation, job and wealth creation, correction, environment, health and welfare, tax collection, public safety, unemployment compensation and services, and so on. But educational issues are prominent in the election campaign, so a governor has to have a clear commitment for education.

But all of you certainly know, in North Carolina, responsibilities for education can become blurred, because we have a state superintendent elected separately by the people and a state board whose members are appointed by the governor and the legislature. It's so diffuse, with no authoritative leadership position, that the Public School Forum was created to bring all the disparate groups together; but often it just energizes a different agenda from any of them. In other words, there is a problem of accountability. To what extent is the state superintendent accountable to the board, which sets educational policy? He's not. To whom are the members of the board accountable? Currently, the bare majority were appointed by me, but for most of my term the majority were appointed by my predecessor!

Your speech request asked that I address three specific areas: values development in the public schools, professional autonomy, and personnel issues. Given this focus, I will attempt to define a governor's leadership role.

There are few who would argue the social importance of values. Values constitute a kind of gyroscope to guide all our actions and to sustain us in times of crisis. Values provide cultural stability and continuity.

But two compelling questions arise when considering the teaching of values in our schools: What values, whose values, should we seek to affirm? Those of the majority? Yes, if you're talking about a historically established majority. And what must be done to ensure that the rights of others are respected in our pluralistic society? These are tough questions.

I do believe, however, that there are what may be called sovereign values, some of which derive from the U.S. Constitution and our Bill of Rights. Certainly, the value of security, of one's person, and of one's possessions, and of one's privacy, must be respected and maintained in the schools. The same may be said for respecting the freedom to hold unpopular beliefs.

Let's accept, then, that values in a democratic society are often in conflict—far more so than in a totalitarian society. There can be no more instructive way to teach the value of opposing viewpoints, and of the supremacy of the majority, than to look at the creation of our nation. Our country was born out of differences of opinion, differences that yielded to a higher purpose.

Clearly, the values of democracy, individual responsibility, and initiative should be an integral part of schooling. So, too, should the idea that each child is a creation of incalculable value and that our bodies should be treated with reverence and not defiled by abuse of drugs or sex.

One additional point on values should be made. We are a capitalist nation, rising to greatness in large measure through the enormous vitality of entrepreneurship and our free-enterprise system. I believe our schools need to teach the value of that system, as well as the practicality of how it works. The essential value is that this system is based on the freedom to invest one's wealth in a business, at the risk of losing it all, but in hopes of a favorable return from market acceptance, and thereby providing jobs for hundreds of others. That deserves to be respected and taught in our schools.

This entrepreneurial theme brings us nicely to the next issue, that to professional autonomy. Peter Drucker, in his book *Innovation and Entrepreneurship*, shows the importance of professional autonomy in the management of our schools. He notes that "schools . . . need to be entrepreneurial and innovative fully as much as any business does. Indeed, they may need it more. The rapid changes in our society, technology, and economy are simultaneously an even greater threat to them and an even greater opportunity."[4] Schools need to be entrepreneurial? He means: willing to take risks—and free to do so.

Overly centralized planning has proved not to be very efficient anywhere it has been tried, but somehow it takes hold in education. If we want our educational system to be significantly better, we must be willing to do a number of things that are significantly different. An important part of such a thrust is the freedom to have greater decision making at the local level—the freedom to experiment, to take risks in order to find a better way.

We must be willing to put decision-making power where the action is: in the schools. I believe that. Lockstep central control won't solve the problem. That's what caused the problem. I believe that schools and school systems should be rewarded for good performance. Individual principals and teachers should be rewarded for exemplary performance.

In much the same sense that we have developed a program to make venture capital available to business entrepreneurs, we must provide "venture capital" to schools so they can install programs and practices that are more cost-effective. It is imperative that we build a collaborative alliance between education, government, and business. And clearly, a leadership role of the governor is to help in the creation of such alliances. This is precisely what we are doing with the Governor's Business Committee for Education, Incorporated: building partnerships between education and business throughout the state, businesses that adopt schools and promote schools. It had been chaired by Jere Drummond and Howard Haworth, each of whom went on to chair the State Board of Education, and now has an equally able new chairman in Graeme Keith. I hope you will avail yourselves of the opportunities offered by the committee.

Nothing is so essential to the quality of our schools as the quality of educational professionals. This is why I have made the career ladder for teachers and administrators a top priority. Stated simply, this program means the opportunity for classroom promotions to keep outstanding teachers in our classrooms where they belong, to keep them from having to consider career pursuits outside the classroom. I call it better pay for better teachers.

Now in its third year as a pilot program, evaluations show that the career ladder is working. Morale is up; actual learning results are improving. More class time is spent on task. There is a much stronger sense of professionalism among those participating in the program.

In the upcoming short session of the General Assembly, I intend to ask for money to expand our pilot program by adding eight systems to our present sixteen pilot sites. These additional sites would allow us to put into practice some of the things we've learned from the sixteen original pilot projects. After all the controversy in the first year, these new eight will demonstrate how to train, evaluate, and promote teachers to Career Level I, without all the paperwork and with more flexibility. Without this, we'll finish the four years of the first sixteen pilots with only one year of experience at Career Level I. We will be better served by making sure that this program for the professionalization of teaching is the best it can be.

As we strive to improve teaching as [a] career, we must also remember that there are other factors important to a quality education. Educational leadership is certainly one of these. We must be willing to pay competitive salaries to administrators and supervisory staff. Further, we must develop more effective mechanisms for helping school superintendents and other administrative staff to upgrade their skills and keep abreast of emerging developments in education.

The Basic Education plan, passed by the legislature and supported by me, has imposed considerable administrative burdens on some of the smaller school districts. I would welcome the opportunity to work with you on ways to alleviate this situation.

On another topic: Not all the learning that needs to take place has happened. We still lose almost 30 percent of each class before graduation. For that reason, the Governor's Commission on Literacy was created to improve literacy and reduce dropout rates. This commission is chaired by Bill Friday, president emeritus of the North Carolina university system. As a result of the commission's work, we have a much better understanding of the nature and scope of illiteracy in our state and what we need to do about it. A report, along with recommendations, will be issued shortly.

It is obvious that illiteracy poses a threat to our future prosperity. Consider this: It is estimated that close to 1 million adults in North Carolina are functionally illiterate. That's like a fourth of our work force. These people are falling further and further behind. It is forecast that, by 1990, three out of four jobs will require some education or technical training beyond high school. That's another measure of literacy, and we are not meeting that requirement.

All this lends an urgency to what direction we take over the next several years. Those who work in our schools, and those who attend them, have every right to expect modern and safe facilities. It is inconceivable that we can work toward improving the quality of education without serious attention to this area. This is why I proposed, in 1986, that the legislature authorize a statewide bond referendum for school construction. Our plan would have raised $1.5 billion.

A very important aspect of this construction financing plan is that it would have provided substantial funds for school construction now, instead of having to space it over a period of years at what will surely be increased construction costs. This plan for the creative financing of school construction, at no additional cost to taxpayers, died without a vote of either the legislature or the public. It had the support of the state superintendent and the treasurer, as well as county commissioners, school boards, editors—but it lost the support of legislative leaders, and they never let it come to a vote. It is the duty of this governor, as education leader, to remind them and pin that tail on the donkey!

Discussion of the role of the governor in educational leadership cannot be complete without bringing up the matter of the veto. As all of you know, North Carolina is unique in being the only state in the union in which the governor does not have a veto. That is taught in our schools, and it is embarrassing. North Carolina also has the distinction of being the only state that has refused to let the people decide whether it wants the governor to have veto power.

The balance of powers was an important concept to our founding fathers. The truth is, the veto will bring better, more responsible governance to our state. No single action will do more to enhance the leadership role of the governor in education than the power of the veto. It will assert the governor's leadership in an arena where legislative leaders have demonstrated disrespect for the office of governor for fifteen years—for the last four terms of three governors.

For that, and other valid reasons, I will seek in the upcoming short session to place the veto on the legislative agenda. It is an historic issue. It is a good government issue, and it will never be put on the ballot unless and until someone fights for it. My friend, Lieutenant Governor Jordan, says he's for it—now. I say, let's put it before the legislature and see who has more influence.

I'd like to take this opportunity to thank all of you here for working with us to improve the quality of education in our state. If we continue to build strong partnerships in education, as we have done in economic development, I am confident we can make extraordinary progress in education in the coming years—even to the point of making our state a role model for the nation. Much of our success will depend on your energy and imagination, which will be possible through providing greater professional autonomy to local school systems. Together, we can create a new dawning for education in our state.

---

[1]Someone once lampooned the South's priorities by observing that it was the only region of the country where adults delivered newspapers and youngsters drove school buses. In reality, while other states such as Iowa, Nebraska, and Wyoming also employed youthful bus drivers, the practice of hiring students to ferry other students to and from school in North Carolina ground to a halt in 1988.

As signed into law, the federal Fair Labor Standards Act prohibited employing school bus drivers younger than age eighteen. However, a 1968 amendment allowed the use of sixteen- and seventeen-year-old operators with the consent of the secretary of labor. Both North and South Carolina were granted a waiver, valid for the first eight months of 1988, permitting them to use seventeen-year-olds as long as they had clean driving records.

On February 25, 1988, the United States Department of Labor ordered that North and South Carolina end the practice of allowing seventeen-year-olds to drive school buses by April 1. The decision followed an investigation of randomly selected school districts in both states that revealed eighty cases of noncompliance with the conditions of the waiver in North Carolina and 200 violations by its southern neighbor. The review was initiated after a school bus, operated by a seventeen-year-old with two infractions on his driving record, ran over a 4-year-old South Carolina kindergarten pupil on January 8, 1988.

State officials protested the Labor Department ruling, arguing that it would be impossible to hire and train enough adults to replace the approximately 2,100 seventeen-year-old bus drivers in North Carolina in time to meet the federally mandated deadline. Many schools would have to park some buses and vastly reconfigure the remaining routes as a consequence. Poorer rural districts, unable to afford salaries commanded by adult bus drivers, were expected to be particularly hard hit by the ban on youthful operators; for example, 80 percent of Duplin County's school bus drivers were seventeen years of age in the autumn of 1987.

Legislative and diplomatic means were attempted to force a change in the federal decision. U.S. Representative Charles G. Rose III introduced a bill, that passed the house on March 3, to permit seventeen-year-olds to continue to operate school buses through June 15, 1988. Although delegations from the Carolinas failed, on March 9, to convince federal officials to reinstate the department's waiver, six days later the two states reached a compromise with the Department of Labor that allowed the use of seventeen-year-old drivers through June 15. After that date, all school bus operators were to be at least eighteen years of age. In the end, Martin persuaded federal negotiators "that it would be safer to continue using 17-year-old drivers who could not be replaced by April 1 than to operate with fewer buses and longer routes." *News and Observer*, January 31, February 5, 8, 26, 27, 29, March 2, 3, 4, 10, 11, 16, 30, 1988.

[2]Charles Grandison Rose III (1939-   ), native, resident of Fayetteville; B.A., Davidson College, 1961; LL.B., University of North Carolina, 1964. Attorney; chief district court prosecutor, Twelfth Judicial District, 1967-1970; elected to U.S. House of Representatives from North Carolina's Seventh Congressional District, 1972, and returned in subsequent elections; Democrat. *Biographical Directory of Congress*, 1742.

[3]In an attempt to attract more adult job seekers, lawmakers raised school bus driver wages and improved benefits during the 1988 legislative session. The average hourly rate at which the state reimbursed school systems increased from $4.91 to $6.10 per driver. *News and Observer*, July 11, 1988.

[4]"Public service institutions such as government agencies, labor unions, churches, universities, and schools, hospitals, community and charitable organizations, professional and trade associations and the like, need to be entrepreneurial and innovative fully as much as any business does." The remainder of the excerpt was quoted accurately. Drucker, *Innovation and Entrepreneurship*, 177.

The North Carolina National Guard received nine Apache AH-64 attack helicopters on November 9, 1987, becoming the first of only three Guard units in the country to be entrusted with the advanced aircraft. Martin, who received the keys to the lead helicopter in ceremonies held at Raleigh-Durham Airport, is shown seated in an Apache cockpit.

The demands of the state's highest public office did not abate when the governor left the Capitol at the close of the day. Returning to the Executive Mansion, Martin often worked into the night.

JAPANESE KIMONO EXHIBITION OPENING
"ROBES OF ELEGANCE"

Raleigh, March 10, 1988

What a grand evening for North Carolina! Tonight we celebrate the opening of a very significant, very unique exhibition at the North Carolina Museum of Art. For the first time ever in the American South—and only the second time in the United States—our museum will exhibit, for three months, ninety magnificent Japanese kimonos: robes of excellence!

This exhibition is scheduled exclusively at the North Carolina Museum of Art. Many of the kimonos we will see have never before been outside Japan.

The Japanese kimono is a traditional form of clothing, as well as an exquisite art form. The ninety kimonos that our museum will show trace the development of this historic garment over the past 400 years. There will be three, four-week installations at the museum. I invite each of you, and all the citizens of North Carolina, to visit the museum several times during this period to get a broad understanding of the kimono and its evolution.

Last October, Seretary Dorsey and I traveled to Japan to encourage stronger trade relations with that dynamic Asian country. One of the products of that mission was the establishment of productive cultural relations between North Carolina and Japan. Secretary Dorsey and Museum Director Dr. Richard Schneiderman[1] have collaborated closely with officials of the National Museum of Japanese History to secure this exhibit. I want to congratulate both of them and their staffs. We can all be proud of the work they have accomplished.

For a number of years, Japan and North Carolina have been economic partners. We are privileged to have a number of Japanese companies located here in North Carolina. Two of these companies, Mitsubishi Semiconductor and Takeda Chemical, have joined the Hudson-Belk Company and Broyhill Industries Foundation to help sponsor this exhibit. I want to thank all our corporate sponsors, as well as the North Carolina Museum of Art Foundation, for making this unique showing possible.

And finally, I want to extend my special thanks, and the thanks of the state of North Carolina, to Tsuchida Naoshige, the director general of the National Museum of Japanese History, in Sakura, Japan.[2] Tsuchida-san and the staff of the National Museum of Japanese History have cooperated to make this exhibition a significant cultural event in the history of our countries. I would like to ask Tsuchida-san to come forward to receive a special honor. [Tsuchida comes forward.]

As governor of North Carolina, it is my great pleasure to name Tsuchida Naoshige, director general of the National Museum of Japanese History, an Honorary Tar Heel—an honorary citizen of North Carolina—and I extend to you the sincere thanks of the people of this state. Congratulations! *Domo arigato gozaimasu.*[3]

---

[1]Richard S. Schneiderman (1948-   ), born in New Jersey; resident of Raleigh; B.A., Hartwick College, 1970; M.A., University of Cincinnati, 1973; Ph.D., State University of New York at Binghamton, 1976. Curator, prints and drawings, 1976-1986, acting director, 1980-1981, and director, 1981-1986, Georgia Museum of Art; director, North Carolina Museum of Art, since 1986; author. Richard S. Schneiderman to Jan-Michael Poff, December 5, 1989.

[2]Naoshige Tsuchida (1924-   ); resident of Narashino City, Japan; was graduated from Imperial University, Tokyo, 1949; honorary degree. Various positions with University of Tokyo since 1949, including: professor, since 1971, head, 1975-1977, Historiographical Institute; literature professor, since 1974; professor emeritus, since 1985. Commissioner, Council for the Protection of Cultural Properties, 1982-1988; director, National Museum of Japanese History, since 1983; author. Chihiro Nanbu, secretary to Director General Naoshige Tsuchida, to Jan-Michael Poff, February 19, 1990; telephone conversation with Kyoko Mimura, April 19, 1990.

[3]*Domo arigato gozaimasu* translates as "Thank you, very much." Mimura conversation.

NORTH CAROLINA ASSOCIATION OF EDUCATORS

Winston-Salem, March 18, 1988

[The following address is similar to one delivered to the Scotland County Literacy Council, Laurinburg, March 22, 1988.]

It is a great privilege to meet with a group whose members are such a vital force in the future of our state. Basically, what I want to talk about, today, is how we can bring about a greater professionalization of teaching and a higher degree of autonomy for those who work most closely with our children. I was going to discuss the career ladder, again, and the positive reinforcement it can give to teaching as a professional career, with opportunities for promotions for teachers without having to leave the classroom—as I did. I was going to talk about school construction and school management, too, and the need for innovation—nothing really new there. But on the way to my earlier speech, and on the way back, I decided to share with you instead a discussion of the next issue to put on our agenda—with some ideas I have been discussing with State School Board Chairman Howard Haworth.

Let's talk about the next single area of greatest concern that has arisen in the last couple of years: illiteracy and the dropout problem. Surely, no one can accept the fact that a fourth of our adult population is functionally ill-equipped to handle the more technically demanding jobs of today and tomorrow, or that over a fourth of our students drop out of school without graduating. To focus attention on this problem, I proclaimed 1987 the "Year of the Reader" and appointed Bill Friday to chair the Governor's Commission on Literacy, with former CPCC president Dick Hagemeyer as his executive.

They have studied the extent of the problem and have identified many resources being used to improve literacy: community colleges lead the way with ABLE, their Adult Basic Literacy Education, using interactive computers to teach reading in one fifth the time. Churches, libraries, the prison system, employers, and many volunteers are making valuable contributions. We will continue to expand these efforts, which currently reach only 7 to 8 percent of those needing it. To show a better example to other employers, I have asked each cabinet secretary to develop a departmental program to identify employees who need help and encourage them to use the resources available to improve their language skills.

Now it's time to solve the root problem of "dropitis," to make a major crusade to dramatically reduce the dropout rate. Surely we cannot prepare North Carolina for the future if we lose illiterate youth faster than we save newly literate adults. The State Board of Education has been examining this problem, as has the Literacy Commission. The understanding is growing that the dropout problem does not suddenly occur in the ninth, tenth, eleventh grades when they may legally drop out. No, the problem comes in the primary grades when they never really drop in!

When third graders realize they are not comprehending the written words, when fifth graders give up on lessons that they really can't read, it is then that they lose interest and begin to acquire protective coloration—to appear competent to their peers while only they and their teachers know the anguish that failure has gripped them. Then it may well be too late. The loss, you see, had actually been complete for many of them before they reached school or kindergarten. Those three- and four-year-olds who had no one to read to them, to point out words to match pictures, and who grew up in broken homes, with family, poverty, or alcoholism, or abuse of spouse or child—those children never had a real opportunity to get ready for language skills.

Brad Butler,[1] former chairman of Proctor and Gamble, spoke to the North Carolina Citizens for Business and Industry, Wednesday, on the correlation between poverty and illiteracy. We've found that illiteracy causes poverty, and poverty causes illiteracy. So what are we going to do about it?

I will ask the State Board of Education, at its April meeting, to begin a state-sponsored study to evaluate what's working, to identify programs that are succeeding here and across the nation. In North Carolina we have three state-funded pilot programs to identify four-year-olds who are at risk, based on multiple factors that can be observed and scored, and seventy-nine other systems are doing similar things with local money. Some of those at risk are already being helped. Head Start works!

The stage is being prepared for a major public commitment. How major? I would estimate that the most urgent need will cost out at $100 [million] to $200 million. Yes, we could spend a lot more: prekindergarten for all three- and four-year-olds, which could soak up $800 million a year—as much as the entire Basic Education plan. That would block out our ability to do anything else.

But is that urgent, to spend $800 million on all three- and four-year-olds whether they need it or not? I think not. Most youngsters get the benefits of lap-reading and mental stimulus at home. Private day-care services are available for their needs. We don't need to replace all that at such expense. We do need to focus on the real [problem], the crucial unmet needs, and fix that.

If a fourth of the youngsters are at risk, then that will take a fourth of $800 million, or $200 million, to cover those 200,000 three- and four-year-olds. If we start with the four-year-olds as a first stage, it cuts that in half. During the next four years, we have major fiscal commitments to the BEP and the career ladder which should not be deferred. That means that it will be difficult to suddenly move full scale, all at once, for these at-risk children, but we must make a start. We could begin with those four-year-olds for whom we can identify multiple factors of poverty, child abuse, paternal alcohol or drug abuse, et cetera, with two or more factors.

To prepare us for that giant step, I will ask our State Board [of Education] to undertake an intensive study to show us what is the most productive use of our money. I want them to look at the pilot programs in North Carolina, look at what's being done in other states, and report back in time for the 1989-1991 biennial budget so that we can begin to build public and legislative support for the next great stride for better schools, and better jobs, and a better quality of life in

North Carolina for future millions that otherwise would be left out and behind. If illiteracy and poverty are the fundamental cause and effect of each other in a never-ending cycle of frustration—we must break that cycle.

I have presented to you my ideas about literacy and what we need to do about it, especially early childhood readiness. I began by telling you what I was going to tell you; then I told you; now I have told you what I told you. Along the way I read all this so as to demonstrate what it's like to be able to read and write. You see, I've almost covered all the elements of the six-point lesson plan for effective teaching. All that's left is to generate some classroom discussion, or feedback, or an exam to see if you're with me on this—or, more likely, way ahead of me.

So, if this program will allow, I would welcome any questions or discussion from you on today's topic. Can we do it? Is it worth the cost, such as the cost in deferred or displaced alternative priorities? Will it work? What do you want to see happen? What do you think? Be specific. Be thorough. Use complete sentences. You have five minutes.

---

[1]Owen Bradford Butler (1923-   ), born in Lynchburg, Virginia; U.S. Naval Reserve, 1941-1945, 1950-1951. Various positions with Proctor and Gamble, 1945-1986, including board chairman, 1981-1986; senior adviser, Daiwa Securities America, since 1986; Republican. *Who's Who in America, 1988-1989,* I, 488.

INDIAN UNITY CONFERENCE

RALEIGH, MARCH 18, 1988

It is a great honor to be with you, this afternoon; it always has been. The Indian Unity Conference presents a unique opportunity for the Native Americans of this state to come together in a spirit of cooperation. While many of the issues you face as individual tribes and organizations are as diverse as the people you represent, this conference brings you all together to find solutions to the many challenges you have in common. Thank you for inviting me.

I feel that this year's conference represents a critical turning point for North Carolina's Indian population. The events of the past few months have refocused everyone's attention on a legacy of discrimination and inequality that has plagued the Indian community for generations. While most of the recent attention and publicity has focused on Robeson County, the solutions to these problems apply to all Indians. The problems are themes that inspired and are so well portrayed in *Strike at the Wind* and *Unto These Hills*, our two outstanding outdoor dramas, both of which you have shared with me. I am here, today, to tell you that I am committed to helping find solutions to improve the lives of all Indian people.

This is not a time for rhetoric. It is time for hard work and action, action by state, county, and community leaders. It is that partnership for change that I want [to] talk about today.

At the state level, we are moving ahead to work with you on [a] number of different fronts: education, economic development, and equal justice for all Indians.

Education

According to a recent status report on the North Carolina Indian population, of persons age twenty-five and over, a far smaller percentage of Indians have completed high school than blacks or whites. An Indian education policy statement by the North Carolina Commission of Indian Affairs was issued last October, recommending ways we could begin to improve this situation. The State Board of Education has taken those recommendations seriously.

On February 4, the State Board of Education adopted a landmark policy statement, adopting many of the commission's recommendations, underscoring a commitment to ensuring that Indian students receive meaningful and quality education. The policy statement re-affirms the board's responsibility to see that each student attending North Carolina public schools has an equal educational opportunity. It recognizes that, historically, Indian students have been unable to enjoy the full benefits of public education. If I may read directly from the policy's mission statement: "This policy has as its goal meaningful and quality education for all Indian students and suggests a process for ensuring that aspirations and expectations of Indian parents for educational excellence are attained by their children."[1]

How? First, the State Board of Education and I will be seeking legislative authority to establish a state advisory council on Indian education.[2] A fifteen-member council made up of Indian parents, educators, and leaders from all the tribal and Indian organizations will advise the board on ways to more effectively meet the needs of Indian students. So, you can help.

The council will also advocate meaningful programs to attack the low achievement and high dropout rates among American Indian students. Illiteracy and dropouts is the major challenge facing us, and the Board of Education and I intend to get help for those who have a special need for early childhood readiness—which I have discussed at greater length with the North Carolina Association of Educators this morning.

The policy statement also calls for continuing efforts to expand and strengthen the Division of Indian Education in the Department of Public Instruction, encourages periodic reviews of curriculum materials, and, where appropriate, adds information on the history and culture of Indians to the standard course of study. Perhaps most important of all, the policy stresses the need for more Indian involvement in public education—selection of Indians to participate on committees and councils appointed on local boards of education, employment of Indians by local boards, and selection and appointment of Indians to boards and committees appointed by the State Board of Education.

Economic Development

Economic self-sufficiency is a major goal of the Indian community in the state. Reaching this goal is directly related to the continuation of the strong economic development successes we have had in North Carolina in the past three years. During 1987 alone, businesses announced plans to invest more than $873 million in new manufacturing facilities in North Carolina, more than any other state. These investments are expected to create more than 13,500 new jobs.

The economic growth is particularly good news for rural areas of the state. Rural investment is at its strongest level this decade. Over two thirds, 68 percent, of all new jobs announced by manufacturing industries [in] 1987 went to communities of 10,000 or less. We're not just talking about rural economic development; we've been doing it for two solid years, with greater success than ever in history.

The majority of North Carolina's Indian population—77.9 percent—are located in rural areas, some of which have been the direct beneficiaries of this industrial growth and expansion. In the past two years, three companies have announced new or expanded facilities in Robeson County. Campbell Soup announced a $20 million upgrade of its Maxton manufacturing facilities. That's good news! Haleyville Drapery opened a bedspread and drapery manufacturing plant in Parkton—more good news—and, as I announced at a news conference last year in St. Paul's, Rocco, Inc., is building a $12-to-$15 million turkey-processing plant near St. Paul's. This plant is expected to employ up to 600 workers. We almost lost it across the line to South Carolina, but extra effort saved the day, and we've got more in the works—if we can lay out the welcome mat and put our best face forward.

I don't want to imply that the economic news is good for everyone. There are areas of the state, and individuals, who have not been able to benefit from the growth I described. I also know that the Indian labor force is overwhelmingly employed in traditionally lower-paying jobs. The best cure for that is to attract more investment. The Department of Commerce is working to assist every corner of the state [to] take advantage of North Carolina's reputation with America's business leaders as companies expand and relocate here. No one person can do it. The governor, alone, cannot. State government, alone, cannot. Together, as partners, we can. Education is again the key to unlocking better employment opportunity.

There are other opportunities out there, as well. I would encourage the tribal and Indian organizations to designate a liaison to the film industry office in the Commerce Department. I know many of you were involved in the historic 400th Anniversary production of the television documentary, "Roanoak." North Carolina's film industry is booming; for the fourth consecutive year the industry has shattered previous records. In 1987, the film industry spent more than $128 million in the state, a 44 percent increase over 1986. Find out how you can get involved, because I intend to get more films made in North Carolina.

Another big business in North Carolina is travel and tourism. Travelers spent more than $5.1 billion—I said, billion—in North Carolina in 1986, the highest level ever. We'll probably have exceeded that in 1987, when the numbers are all in. The North Carolina Indian cultural center is going to be able to take advantage of this growing industry. Market surveys indicate that center will be not only an outstanding educational, cultural, and recreational center, but a successful tourist attraction. I understand an architect will be selected in April to start a site development plan. I look forward to participating in the ribbon cutting of this new facility.

Equal Justice

In February, 1987, my Commission of Indian Affairs appointed an ad-hoc committee to review the treatment of Indians within the criminal justice system in North Carolina. The committee's charge was to examine the treatment of North Carolina Indians throughout the entire law enforcement process, including the courts. Following a six-month review, the committee issued its findings and recommendations to the commission.[3] This report took on new significance following the hostage incident in Robeson County, but it's very important to note that it preceded the *Robesonian* hostages by almost a year.[4]

Department of Administration Deputy Secretary Henry McKoy, who chaired the ad-hoc committee, has already discussed the committee's review process with you, this morning, but I want to let you know what specific actions I am taking on the recommendations. I fully support all these recommendations and have directed my staff to develop an implementation strategy to put them into effect immediately. That strategy has now been worked out.

The successful implementation of these recommendations is going to have to be a team effort. Some of the recommendations are clearly within my power to take the lead on; others will require local or state judicial initiative, while others fall directly on the shoulders of community leaders, tribal, and Indian organizations for full implementation.

Recommendation 1 calls for the establishment of a public defender office in North Carolina's Sixth, Sixteenth, and Thirtieth judicial districts, those with the largest Indian populations.[5] I will be convening a meeting of the legislators to discuss the possibility of introducing legislation to establish public defenders' offices in the Sixth, Sixteenth, and Thirtieth judicial districts.[6] My budget office will be reviewing the cost of establishing these offices and what we can include in my upcoming budget recommendations. It may even save money; if not, it may take a couple of budgets to complete, in which case I would assume you would recommend we start with the Sixteenth District, serving Robeson County, but we'll ask you to advise on that if we can't do it all at once.

Recommendation 4 establishes mandatory training for law enforcement officers, in the Twelfth, Sixteenth, and Thirtieth judicial districts, in dispute resolution, race relations, crisis intervention, psychology, conciliation techniques, and nonviolent confrontation techniques.[7] I will be offering, to local law enforcement officials, access to the human relations training course being taken by members of the state Highway Patrol. As you know, this training grew out of a recommendation of a special committee that explored ways to improve the relationship between Indians and the Highway Patrol in the early 1980s. If necessary, I will supplement this training by offering the services of the police-community training offered by the North Carolina Human Relations Council.

Recommendation 7 calls for the establishment of special recruitment efforts to enhance Indian participation, in all phases of the criminal justice system, in an effort to significantly increase Indian representation.[8] I have directed the North Carolina Human Relations Council to work with the Robeson County commissioners in establishing a triracial human relations commission to promote good relations among all races in Robeson County. I will also ask the North Carolina Commission of Indian Affairs and the North Carolina Human Relations Council to meet with each criminal justice official to seek ways to recruit, hire, and maintain positions within each of those respective levels of the criminal justice system. I will also ask the commission and the council to work with state agencies that assign law enforcement officials within Robeson County—the Highway Patrol and Probation and Parole, for example—to improve opportunities for Indians and blacks.

Recommendation 10 would involve the cooperation of the chief justice of the North Carolina Supreme Court in appointing a special task force to conduct systematic and periodic reviews of judicial districts in the state and make recommendations to him and other appropriate individuals and organizations to remedy disparities.[9] The recommendation also calls on the chief justice to establish an ombudsman in the appropriate office to receive and investigate complaints alleging that criminal justice officials have engaged in actions resulting in patterns of discrimination. I plan to ask Chief Justice Exum to discuss with me, in the near future, the implementation of these recommendations and how we can work together on these topics. We will also ask the chief justice to take the initiative in exploring ways to implement this recommendation.

Six other recommendations remain. I am looking to your tribal and local community organizations to take the lead on these, but I will support them, every one.

I recently wrote a letter to Lonnie Revels, chairman of the North Carolina Commission of Indian Affairs. In that letter, I offered my own, and my administration's, support and assistance to find solutions to the challenges you and I face. I think I have demonstrated that we take that responsibility seriously, but serious change, however, is going to take a change within people.

That's where you must again take the lead. These other recommendations will require meetings with local judicial officials; developing community awareness, interest, and participation in the electoral process; and organizing people to monitor day-to-day court proceedings. The recent vote on the merger of the schools in Robeson County is a concrete example of what can happen when you take the lead.[10] The ability to affect change is within you.

On one final matter, many of you have expressed public concern about illegal drugs in Robeson County or elsewhere. On Monday of this week, I met with newly appointed U.S. Attorney Margaret Currin[11] regarding cooperation between state and federal authorities—particularly in Robeson County. I shared with her the concern of many that potential witnesses might be brought forward to testify to crimes of drug marketing and any other illegal activities in and around Robeson County, but that some would only testify against more serious crimes if given immunity not to be prosecuted for lesser crimes that might be revealed in their testimony. For example, someone who comes forward to testify against drug dealers would not want to then be prosecuted for buying the illegal drugs.

You must understand that has precedent for drug prosecution, if negotiated properly in advance, but it is not likely the drug dealer could get immunity by agreeing to testify against the customers' lesser crimes. You must also understand that the governor of this state has no authority to grant immunity or negotiate it. I and my task force would refer anyone seeking immunity to discuss this with the U.S Attorney's Office, preferably through your attorney so that your rights can be protected. During our meeting, U.S. Attorney Currin assured me that this was the correct procedure so that anyone with evidence may be able to present it to the FBI, or the Drug Enforcement Agency, while avoiding self-incrimination. You have indicated that some are interested in some kind of protest, tomorrow, on this subject; my recommendation is that you make it a positive statement in support of courageous neighbors who might come forward as witnesses, rather than a negative statement against someone whose help you are seeking.

Let's strive, together, to improve the lives of all people. It's going to take teamwork, a partnership working toward common goals. I want to be a member of that team. Teamwork, not hostility; understanding, not undermining; brotherly love, not hatred. And determination.

Years ago, and years after his triumphs as prime minister during the World War II Battle of Britain, Sir Winston Churchill, well past his eightieth birthday, was introduced to address a convocation at Oxford University. His message was powerful. He began by looking out over the audience for several silent minutes. The place was either about to explode or collapse when he finally began one of his shortest and greatest speeches. He said, "Never give up! Never, never, never give up!"[12]

Let that be your determination as you face obstacles, handicaps, injustice, or frustration: Never, never give up. Remember also the words of the Master: "Do unto others as you would have them do unto you."

---

[1]"State Board Policy on Indian Education" (February 4, 1988 [typescript]), furnished by Carolyn B. Honeycutt, Department of Public Instruction.

[2]"An Act to Establish the State Advisory Council on Indian Education" was ratified July 8, 1988. *N.C. Session Laws, 1987, Regular Session, 1988,* III, c. 1084.

[3]Ad-Hoc Committee on Indians and the Criminal Justice System, "A Report on the Treatment of Indians by the Criminal Justice System" ([Raleigh]: North Carolina Commission of Indian Affairs, October, 1987), hereinafter cited as "Report on the Treatment of Indians by the Criminal Justice System."

[4]Eddie Hatcher and Timothy Bryan Jacobs, of Pembroke, claimed to have proof of the willful mistreatment of minorities and of drug trafficking by Robeson County law enforcement and government officials. Stymied by a system of local authority that they felt was arrayed against the county's substantial Native American and black populations, the pair of Tuscarora Indians was determined that the governor hear their evidence. To gain their audience, Hatcher and Jacobs entered the office of the Lumberton *Robesonian* on the morning of February 1, 1988; brandishing sawed-off shotguns and a pistol, they demanded to speak with Martin and took as many as seventeen of the newspaper's staffers hostage.

The governor, convinced the situation would be best resolved if he avoided direct contact with Hatcher and Jacobs, supported Phil Kirk, his chief of staff, in negotiations leading to the four-point agreement that brought the ten-hour hostage crisis to an end. One of the terms of the accord called for an investigation of the Robeson County sheriff's department and district attorney's office, as well as local and district SBI offices. However, the state government task force subsequently appointed was unable to verify allegations of wrongdoing.

Acquitted of federal hostage-taking charges in October, 1988, the duo later was indicted by a state grand jury on fourteen counts of second-degree kidnapping. Jacobs and Hatcher both fled North Carolina; the former was captured in New York state, while the latter was extradited from San Francisco after an attempt at seeking asylum from Soviet diplomats. Jacobs pleaded guilty and, on May 4, 1989, was given a six-year prison term. Hatcher also pleaded guilty; on February 14, 1990, he was sentenced to eighteen years in Central Prison. *News and Observer,* February 2, 3, 1988, March 11, July 1, 2, 1989, February 15, 1990; see also "Statement of Agreement on Behalf of Governor James G. Martin," Raleigh, February 1, 1988, Governors Papers, James G. Martin.

[5]See "Report on the Treatment of Indians and the Criminal Justice System," 45-46. According to the *Directory of the State and County Officials of North Carolina, 1987* (Raleigh: Department of the Secretary of State, n.d.), 71, hereinafter cited as *Directory of State and County Officials of North Carolina, 1987,* the Sixth Judicial District consisted of Bertie, Halifax, Hertford, and Northampton counties, while Robeson and Scotland comprised the Sixteenth. Cherokee, Clay, Graham, Haywood, Jackson, Macon, and Swain counties formed the Thirtieth Judicial District.

[6]New public defender divisions established by the 1988 General Assembly included districts Sixteen A (Scotland, Hoke) and Sixteen B (Robeson); see *N.C. Session Laws, 1987, Regular Session, 1988,* III, c. 1056, s. 8(a).

[7]"Report on the Treatment of Indians by the Criminal Justice System," 47-48. Cumberland and Hoke counties made up the Twelfth Judicial District. *Directory of State and County Officials of North Carolina, 1987*, 71.

[8]"Report on the Treatment of Indians by the Criminal Justice System," 49.

[9]"Report on the Treatment of Indians by the Criminal Justice System," 51-52.

[10]Robeson voters narrowly approved consolidating the county's five school systems in a referendum held March 8, 1988. *News and Observer*, March 10, 1988.

[11]Margaret Person Currin (1950-   ), born in Oxford; A.B., Meredith College, 1972; J.D., Campbell University, 1979. Legislative assistant, 1979-1981, legislative director, 1981, to U.S. Senator John Tower, of Texas; assistant dean, associate professor, Campbell University law school, 1981-1988; U.S. Attorney for the Eastern District of North Carolina, since March, 1988. Margaret Person Currin to Jan-Michael Poff, August 20, 1990.

[12]An alumnus of Harrow, Churchill spoke at his alma mater on October 29, 1941. Midway though a brief speech entitled "These are Great Days," the British prime minister said: "But for everyone, surely, what we have gone through in this period—I am addressing myself to the School—surely from this period of ten months this is the lesson: never give in, never give in, *never, never, never, never*—in nothing, great or small, large or petty—never give in except to convictions of honour and good sense." Robert Rhodes James (ed.), *Winston S. Churchill: His Complete Speeches, 1897-1963* (New York: Chelsea House Publishers/R. R. Bowker Company, 8 volumes, 1974), VI, 6499.

CONCERNED CHARLOTTEANS

CHARLOTTE, MARCH 21, 1988

You have truly blessed and upheld our state and nation. Each year, your concern for the family and for family values has grown. Each year, your numbers have grown. Each year, your influence and example have multiplied and magnified. Thank you for your concern and all that you give.

Last year at your second banquet, we studied together and committed ourselves to help save and protect abused children. I am pleased to tell you that the Governor's Commission on Child Victimization, chaired by our First Lady, Dottie, has seen many of its recommendations enacted by our General Assembly. That has now grown to a new Governor's Commission on Children and the Family, also chaired by my wife Dottie. Sounds like she must have a very strong relationship with your governor!

During this past year, we have called together a bipartisan force against drug abuse. The attorney general, the lieutenant governor, the state superintendent of public instruction, as well as my cabinet appointees—the secretary of crime control and public safety, the secretary of human resources, and the secretary of correction—have all united forces with me to share our resources to combat drug abuse through drug education, treatment, and law enforcement to crack down against drug traffickers. Through Challenge '87, we began a movement to spread this bipartisan cooperation to the local level, so that each local community could begin to unite with us against drugs. But it is only a beginning.

We are encouraged by the response of our schools and especially of our young people. Learning more about the wonderful potential of their young minds, and bodies, and spirits, and about the potential for destruction posed by dangerous narcotics, is helping many to have the strength to say no and to be a strong example to each other. Yet, as we intercept $5 million worth of cocaine being transported into North Carolina, there is another hundred million that gets through. As we seek and destroy an acre of marijuana grown in our woods, many more acres elude us. Yes, we are making progress, but so are the drug traffickers.

It is time for us to get tougher. We need more undercover agents with more "buy money" to gather the evidence against drug dealers. We need to be able to confiscate their property acquired with their evil earnings, and we need much longer sentences for those who deliver this deadly commodity into our communities and who make millions by organizing these deadly markets and supply lines to bring dope into America, and cut it, and sell it to our addicted neighbors. If a man is convicted of masterminding the heroin or cocaine trade in our state, he should never get out of jail.

This is not a nonviolent crime, to get rich off of drug trafficking—it is the deadliest crime against the people. It should be punished as such. For such a monstrous crime, or for repeat conviction for selling drugs, the penalty should be long, mandatory sentences with no parole, with no reduction for time served. Drug traffickers should serve every day the sentence they are given. Our prisons are over-crowded, yes, but surely we can build enough to remove such criminals from society. Any lesser sentence, a few years served, whatever the fine, is to them just a minor inconvenience or just a tax on their enormous profits. Make the punishment finally fit the crime.

Our great state is surely facing many challenges. We are working together to build better schools, better roads, and better jobs for all our people. Surely these efforts will unite us, bring us together as one united state. We are one of the fifty United States of America, yes; but I want us to grow together as one truly united state of North Carolina: east, west, and piedmont, and sandhills, and all the people of all the sections of North Carolina sharing one another's joys and sorrows.

When our farmers faced the 1986 drought, churches, schools, clubs—individuals from all over—came to their aid. When our fishermen faced the red tide, they didn't face it alone. When jobs were lost, we united to help, just as we united to attract many thousands of new jobs for our people. Now let us unite to oppose the pestilence of drugs. Let us come together, as one united state, so that our schools will be drug-free schools, our state will be a drug-free state, and our people will be drug-free people.

ROXBORO CHAMBER OF COMMERCE

ROXBORO, MARCH 23, 1988

What a pleasure it is to meet with all of you on this, the fourth day of spring. We are in the spring of development in the Tar Heel State; things are breaking out all over, in more and better jobs, more and better roads, and better schools. I want to share some of the wonderful things that have happened in North Carolina since January, 1985.

A lot of good things have happened since I talked to the Roxboro Chamber of Commerce during the campaign back in '84. What has happened over the past three years is this: We have had one of the greatest economic upsurges in our state's history. In new and expanded investments by business in manufacturing and nonmanufacturing plants, we witnessed a record three-year total of $15 billion. In fact, we ranked first in the nation, in 1987, for new plant announcements by U.S. industries. This information comes not from state government but from a national trade journal, *Site Selection and Industrial Development Handbook*—so, it must be true.[1] Its survey showed that we had 113 new manufacturing plants in North Carolina, more than in [any] other state in the union. During this same 1987 calendar year, sixty-four plant expansions were announced, placing us fourth behind more populous California, New York, and Texas.

A lot of you will remember all the little green signs all around North Carolina proclaiming, "Governor's Community of Excellence." Instead of putting these little green signs out in the community, we are putting jobs out in the communities. In fact, since January, 1985, we have had a net gain of roughly 300,000 new jobs.

Before I came into office, most of the jobs that came to our state went to our more populated areas; less than one fourth went to towns of under 10,000. We turned this around in the last three years. Nearly

70 percent of all new jobs announced by manufacturing industries in the first three quarters of 1987 actually went to communities of 10,000 or less. Over half, roughly 60 percent, of new plant investments by manufacturing companies went to counties outside the piedmont. This doesn't mean that we haven't continued to do well in more populated areas; it's just that we have learned how to attract businesses to the rural areas of our state.

Can we do better? Yes. Have we done as well in Roxboro and Person County as we would like? No, we haven't. Person County could, however, be at the very threshold of unprecedented economic development. This is why we have worked so hard to win the superconducting super collider project. If we win, this single $4.4 billion project will catapult this whole region into one of the prime research and development areas in the entire nation, resulting in truly breathtaking economic development.[2]

I would like to take this opportunity to thank many of you here for your support of this project. The SSC has been a true bipartisan effort. It shows what we can do when we put aside our partisan differences and put North Carolina first; and when we put North Carolina first, North Carolina will be first.

I want to thank Mike Wilkins and many of the Person County commissioners for their encouragement and support. I know there have been honest concerns about this project; anything as big as SSC is bound to raise some anxieties. The way to deal with these is to respect honest differences and to behave in a spirit of openness; this we have tried to do.

The potential economic impact of this project is truly mindboggling. In construction alone, 4,000 jobs will be generated. At the facility itself, it is estimated there will be 2,500 permanent staff and 500 visiting scientists. A lot of people think that most of the jobs will go to scientists—not so. If employment in a similar high-tech facility, the Fermilab in Illinois, can be used as a guide, the vast majority of jobs at SSC will be nonscientific. At the Fermilab facility, only 19 percent of those employed are scientists; the remaining 81 percent consist of clerical, trades, technicians, maintenance, and so on.

I mentioned technicians. Our research shows that the two community colleges in the area, Piedmont Tech and Vance-Granville, already have in place many of the courses necessary to prepare people in the SSC area for these well-paying jobs. Think for a moment what this project will mean to these two community colleges, how they will be thrust into the forefront of technical training.

In addition, it is estimated that 3,000 jobs will be created in the community. These will provide services to SSC and its employees. Certainly we are talking about significant growth, but it is small in comparison with recent growth in the Triangle area. Actually, we expect growth to be distributed throughout the region, not just concentrated in the immediate area of the SSC facility.

This notwithstanding, the state values the importance of sound planning and growth. For this reason, we stand ready to assist the affected counties in preparing land-use plans and constructive zoning ordinances. Also, the state proposes to provide direct financial support, of at least $15 million, to Granville, Person, and Durham counties—this in order to assist these counties in providing the necessary county services.

There has been an understandable concern among some of the citizens in the region over the environmental impact of the SSC project. I have asked my staff to come up with recommendations on how to minimize the effect of the SSC not only on watersheds but to develop long-range plans for protecting the environment from harmful development. Indeed, the SSC staff has put into its budget request a line item for environmental initiatives. This will be submitted to the General Assembly in its next session.

Naturally, improved highway arteries are an essential part of any undertaking on the scale of the SSC. We have developed several alternative plans to provide access from RDU [Raleigh-Durham Airport] to the proposed SSC campus. All these, it should be noted, are consistent with current long-range regional transportation plans. The road improvements in the plan minimize both environmental effects and state expenditures. All the specific road improvements outlined in the SSC proposal represent one approach, not a final commitment. Now that we are on the SSC best-qualified list, we will undertake more detailed studies to determine the least environmentally disruptive approach to road construction.

Many of you here have heard previous presentations on SSC, so I will keep my remarks brief to allow for more discussion during the question and answer period following. But I would like to address the concern about radioactive waste generated by the SSC. First, let me emphasize: The SSC will produce low-level waste, within the tunnel itself and not in the rock around it. The U.S. Department of Energy estimates that the SSC will dispose of only 8,000 cubic feet of low-level radioactive waste a year. This amount could, in turn, be reduced 20 times through the use of technology developed by Fermilab, bringing the total activity of this waste to 8 curies. This is less than the activity of waste typically shipped each year from a major research university with a large medical component, and no one, to my knowledge, is suggesting that Duke or UNC do away with its medical component; yet the waste that will be generated at the SSC facility is less and poses no hazard to the health and safety of our citizens.

Then there is the rumor that after the SSC project is over, twenty-five years from now, the underground tunnel will be a target for the storage of radioactive waste. This fear is completely unfounded, the reason being that by then the area encompassed by the project will be considerably more populated, thereby precluding radioactive storage under federal guidelines. So, it would help to lay that particular rumor to rest.

We have come a long way in three years, and much of the credit must go to our private-public partnerships all over the state—and the skill and imagination of our state Department of Commerce in the area of job and wealth creation. With our efforts to eliminate or reduce and hold down anti-job taxes, we have created a business climate in our state that has made us the number-one choice of business as the place they would like to set up operations. I will propose that the legislature restore most of the 3 percent merchants' discount that was abolished last year to help pay for the school construction program—[a] program that was substituted for my plan, which would have established a $1.5 billion loan fund, from which school districts would be able to borrow money on a long-term basis to meet immediate school construction needs. The beauty of this creative construction financing plan was that it would require no additional taxes. This plan had widespread support. What North Carolina wound up with was a school construction program that cost more and offered less.

As I said before, we are in the spring season of new and promising developments for our state. Teamwork and vision is what has gotten us here. Together, we can go much further.

---

[1]See *Site Selection and Industrial Development Handbook* (February, 1988).

[2]Secretary of Energy John S. Herrington announced on November 10, 1988, that the superconducting super collider was to be located in Waxahachie, Texas, twenty-five miles south of Dallas. Ideal geology and the lack of local opposition to the project swayed the decision in favor of the site, according to Herrington. Some observers questioned whether political considerations might have played a larger role in the selection process than objective criteria, noting that George Bush, the president-elect, Lloyd Bentsen, the Senate Finance Committee chairman, and James C. Wright, the Speaker of the U.S. House, were Texans. The Lone Star State also offered a billion-dollar subsidy and a free, 200-square-mile tract of land as incentives.

North Carolina promised $537 million in support funding and spent more than $1.9 million in state appropriations to attract the super collider. However, some residents of

Durham, Granville, and Person counties, concerned about potential environmental damage from the SSC and outraged over the number of families that the project's land requirements would displace, organized their opposition. Citizens Against the Collider Here—CATCH—fought the project for ten months, and their activities proved a factor in influencing the final site determination. *Congressional Quarterly Almanac, 1988,* 640; *News and Observer,* September 2, 1987, November 11, 15, December 4, 1988.

STATEMENT ON RED TIDE

MOREHEAD CITY, MARCH 24, 1988

When I think about the red tide, I'm always reminded of that phrase from the movie, *Jaws*: "Just when you thought it was safe to go back into the water. . . ." Well, last fall, just as our shellfishermen were all set to go back in the water and make a living, here came the most unwelcome visitor to our shores since the days of Blackbeard the pirate. We couldn't shoot it; we couldn't clean it up. We just had to wait it out, and it hasn't been easy on you—that we all know—and this administration did not take the matter lightly. We responded, and we responded quickly.

The economic impact on our commercial fishermen was widespread and severe.[1] Unable to harvest oysters and clams, many fishermen were faced with the very real possibility of not being able to pay the mortgage on their homes or their boats, the very thing they needed to earn a living; many others were faced with the choice [of] paying utility bills or buying food for their families. Government agencies responded by coordinating relief efforts, providing food stamps, and working with the utilities and lending institutions to modify the fishermen's payment schedule. Even Congress got into the act by passing legislation which allowed fishermen to apply for, and receive, low-interest loans from the Small Business Administration.

The economic effect was not confined to the commercial fishermen. The ripple effect of fishermen not being able to practice their trade was felt by nearly all businesses along our coast. Retail sales dropped off, hotels and motels reported fewer guests using their facilities, and restaurants, particularly those specializing in seafood, often found themselves with more staff than customers.[2]

As word of the red tide spread across the country, summertime tourists from other states began calling, wanting to know if it would be safe to plan their annual trip to our beaches. Several coastal-area chambers of commerce have undertaken promotional campaigns to let visitors know that, yes, it is safe to plan your annual vacation to

North Carolina's coast. The North Carolina Department of Commerce instituted the "North Carolina, First in Fish" campaign, for our finfish have always provided good eat'n.

If there is one positive aspect of the red tide, I believe it is the oyster relaying program conducted by our Division of Marine Fisheries. Because of this program, more than 380,000 bushels of oysters were harvested from contaminated waters and placed in waters where the oysters will be able to cleanse themselves. We should have a bumper crop of oysters next year, and hopefully, for years to come.

The people of North Carolina admire your fortitude and courage in the face of economic hardship. We admire your hard work on the successful shellfish relay program. If we have one wish for you, who live and work on the coast, it's this: May the red tide stay in the Gulf Stream and never visit us again.

---

[1]The toxic red tide caused the state to close 200 miles of coastline to shellfishing in October, 1987, and subsequently cost commercial fishermen $5.5 million. *News and Observer*, March 25, 1988.

[2]North Carolina's coastal economy lost an estimated $25 million because of the red tide. *News and Observer*, March 25, 1988.

NORTH CAROLINA WILDLIFE FEDERATION

RALEIGH, MARCH 26, 1988

It's a real pleasure once again to participate in this important event, the presentation of the Governor's Awards for Conservationists of the Year. Over the past three years, it has been my pleasure to recognize and celebrate excellence in a wide area of human endeavor: farming, environment, scholars, scientists, Congressional Medal of Honor recipients, government workers, teachers, bravery and heroism, artists, the list goes on. What better thing to do than to celebrate the excellence of our citizens! It is therefore entirely fitting that we honor those who exhibit uncommon caring for a great and, to a large extent, irreplaceable resource, the wildlife of our state.

You know, the Bible says that man shall have dominion over the earth.[1] With dominion comes responsibility. The North Carolina Wildlife Federation has assumed and channeled that responsibility. In assuming its responsibility, the Wildlife Federation has become an outstanding steward of the ecology in our state, for which we can all be grateful. But more than that, in your quest to conserve our wildlife, you are a bearer of gifts to future generations of North Carolinians, who, but for your and other conservationists' efforts, might not see the majesty of a bald eagle or the grace of a deer in their natural habitat. So, in addition to presenting conservation awards this evening to outstanding stewards of our sacred trust as human beings, this is a time to give thanks for [the] federation's service to North Carolina. Because of you, our state is a much better place to live in.

I know and share your concern for the quality of our air, water, and soil. This evening, I want to share information about one of our important undertakings to protect and enhance our environment, what we call the "Coastal Initiative." This program is designed to help citizens and communities in eastern North Carolina, who have the will and the desire, to make changes to improve their environment and their economy. A basic undergirding belief of the Coastal Initiative is that it's possible, with sound planning and sensitivity to environmental needs, for environmental and economic development interests to coexist. Indeed, good environmental planning is good business.

Let me emphasize, at this point, the most important aspect of this program is to establish stronger safeguards for any and all waters already considered productive, sensitive, or protected in any way. The heart and soul of this program is protecting the environment. This is the foundation upon which any new industry and prosperity will be built.

We are currently working on proposals with the following objectives in mind:

—Increase protection of ecologically fragile and environmentally significant areas;

—Create a marine waterways system;

—Stimulate shoreline commercial development and waterfront investment in the existing towns where the shellfish beds are already closed permanently.

Three broad protection measures are part of the plan. The first measure, called [the] "Outstanding Resource Waters Designation," is designed to protect areas that are ecologically significant or in exceptional condition. Once approved for nomination and detailed study, the area is protected immediately from point and nonpoint source[s] of pollution.

The second measure comes under the heading of "Natural Heritage Program." Under this program, environmentally significant areas are identified through an inventory. Subsequently, owners are contacted and encouraged to register, donate, or otherwise protect the property. Efforts in our coastal areas will be increased by giving this area priority in updating inventories, conducting inventories in new areas, and contacting landowners about protection measures.

The third measure is "Acquisition of Environmentally Significant Areas." Under this measure, acquisition can be used in cases in which other measures do not adequately or appropriately protect an environmentally significant area. For example, acquisition was used successfully in the case of Permuda Island and is now being used to protect Buxton Woods. This approach to conservation requires funds and continued cooperation with the North Carolina Nature Conservancy, which serves as our advance acquisition team. Since funds from this source are so limited, alternative funding sources should be explored.

I've given you, this evening, a crash course on our Coastal Initiative. I would welcome the opportunity to discuss it with you more fully in the future. It is a far-reaching plan. There are some who want the development aspects in place first, and the environmental provisions can follow. Others want to implement the environmental aspects first, with the development part to follow; that's partly because they see that as a way to change the rules on someone who already has a project ready to go even if it meets all laws and rules in effect now. My hope and intention is to be able to bring the package together in a historic combination, so that we can say to developers before they invest in land: Put your marina or waterfront restaurant in these small towns that need it and where you won't harm our estuarine resource. We'll help you. Don't try it in pristine waters and marshes. We'll have to fight you.

If only something like this had been done ten to fifteen years ago! As it is, there's still time, for most of our shellfish beds are open. If we bog down because of frustration over the limitations of existing laws, then existing laws are all we will have to work with.

North Carolina has been recognized as having one of the strongest environmental programs in the nation. In fact, when it comes to surface water protection, we have the best record for protecting this vital resource of any state in the country, in 1987.[2]

We have been making great progress in economic development, education, and conservation through use of a powerful formula: p to the third power—private-public partnerships. Together with groups like the Wildlife Federation, industry, and departments of state government such as Agriculture and Natural Resources and Community Development, we are creating a better environment, both for our wildlife and for all North Carolinians. Working as one united state, east and west and sandhills and piedmont, there is nothing we can't achieve.

---

[1]"Be fruitful, and multiply, and replenish the earth, and subdue it: and have dominion over the fish of the sea, and over the fowl of the air, and over every living thing that moveth upon the earth." Genesis 1:28.

[2]The Fund for Renewable Energy and the Environment recognized North Carolina, in 1988, for its surface water protection program and policies. Martin accepted the organization's second annual "State of the States" award on February 23 in Washington, D.C. Press release, "North Carolina Receives Top Environmental Award," Washington, D.C., February 23, 1988, Governors Papers, James G. Martin.

CAREER LADDER FORUM

Raleigh, April 8, 1988

I very much appreciate this opportunity to be with you this afternoon. I appreciate your candor, your openness, in sharing with me reactions to experiences you and your colleagues have had in regard to the career ladder program. Your recommendations are of vital importance in improving the career ladder program.

Thank you for coming to Raleigh to give us your point of view. Being on the front line, your views will receive serious consideration, you can be sure. I do want to make one point in particular. What all of you are involved in are pilots; so in a large sense, you, as professional teachers, are taking a journey into the unknown. But isn't this really what a lot of good education is all about, expanding our frontiers of learning? Indeed, if teachers and administrators have an attitude of openness, the career ladder pilots can be a real learning experience.

Thus, in a very real way, you are trailblazers. It follows, then, that whenever anybody tries something new, there'll be surprises—some good, some not so good. On the other hand, in a sense, all experiences are good ones, if we learn from them. In the end, the great thing about a pilot is that you have the chance to experiment and to make adjustments as you move along. Nothing should be fashioned in concrete.

Speaking as a chemistry professor, I am committed to honest and open inquiry. It is part of my training as a scientist. I understand, too, the danger of bias in experimental undertakings. So, as we move along, let's all keep an open mind. Let's have the pilots run their course, and let the chips fall where they may. It's possible that career ladder is not the very best way to go toward the professionalization of teachers; it's possible there's something better. The important thing is to be open to all promising possibilities. But, if there were no career ladder, no incentive for teachers to reach higher levels of excellence, we would still be left with a problem that is not going away: how to attract and retain the brightest and best teachers in our North Carolina schools. This is the challenge the career ladder addresses.

Quality education is a much-used term, but quality education without quality teachers is a profound contradiction. So, fellow scientists, I look forward to your continued participation in the career ladder program. You have been invited to Raleigh because you are the experts. In fact, you may well be among the foremost authorities on career ladder in the nation. So, thank you for coming and for sharing your knowledge with me.

ADOPT-A-HIGHWAY ANNOUNCEMENT

Raleigh, April 14, 1988

[The progress of the Adopt-A-Highway program in Gaston County was the primary topic of the governor's address in Belmont, October 8, 1988.]

Many citizens have been voicing their disgust with the way North Carolina's roadsides look, these days. I know the complaints are legitimate, because I've seen a lot of trashy highways myself. In an attempt to attack the problem, I am happy to announce a new, statewide program called Adopt-A-Highway. It will be carried out under the direction of the Department of Transportation and Keep North Carolina Clean and Beautiful.

Adopt-A-Highway is designed to generate more public awareness of the littering problem, to teach people to dispose of their garbage properly, and to renew a sense of pride in public lands. Volunteer organizations and businesses can join the Adopt-A-Highway program by contacting their local Department of Transportation office and agreeing to keep a two-mile section of roadway clean for one year. In return for this commitment, the Department of Transportation will provide trash bags and bag pickup, orange safety vests, safety training, and signs recognizing the participating groups.

I mentioned Keep North Carolina Clean and Beautiful, which always brings to mind its founder, Mrs. Dan K. Moore. I have asked Jeanelle to join me this morning because she symbolizes beautification in North Carolina. We all know this great lady has worked hard for the last twenty-plus years to improve the appearance of our state, and she's still going strong. In fact, exactly one year ago, Jeanelle and my wife Dottie flew across North Carolina, stopping six places to speak out against litter. Dottie wanted to be with us, but she chairs the Commission for the Family and that group is meeting today. Jeanelle, we're glad you're here. Would you like to say a few words?

[Jeanelle Moore speaks.]

Thank you for sharing that with us, Jeanelle. We commend Keep North Carolina Clean and Beautiful for the role it's played in the "Take Pride" campaign and especially for its awards. All these activities help to reduce our litter problem.

We must keep in mind, though, that litter is only the symptom of the problem. The real problem is littering, or people who litter; to solve it, we must change people's attitudes about how they handle their trash. Right now, littering is an acceptable attitude. We need to educate our citizens, young and old, that littering is no longer acceptable. We believe the Adopt-A-Highway program will help this educational process.

Already we have experienced success with a pilot Adopt-A-Highway program this past fall and winter. About twenty organizations and businesses were hand picked to test the program. They included: Carolina Telephone and Telegraph employees of Kinston; the Rocky Mount Evening Rotary Club; Ditch Witch of Raleigh; Fayetteville Coca-Cola Bottling Company; Telephone Pioneers of America, in Winston-Salem; For a Cleaner Environment (FACE) of Highlands; and a number of community clubs of the Western North Carolina Development Association, headquartered in Asheville. I might add here that quite a number of these community development clubs instituted their own "adopt-a-highway" programs and have been operating them for years; one club reports thirty-six years, and many report twenty-five and twenty years!

All the pilots for our statewide Adopt-A-Highway have been pleased with cleaner roads, and the Department of Transportation has been delighted with the extra and free help in roadside maintenance. We anticipate more of the same positive response with our expanded Adopt-A-Highway program. Volunteer organizations and businesses are already calling in to join. Jeanelle mentioned the effort in Texas; after two years and 2,600 organizations participating, Texans boast, as usual, of cleaner roads, taxpayer savings, and overwhelming pride.[1] Since we intend to tell the same story in a couple of years, we encourage organizations and businesses to start signing those adoption papers!

---

[1]North Carolina's Adopt-A-Highway program was modeled on the one begun in Texas. *News and Observer*, September 22, 1988.

NORTH CAROLINA INDUSTRIAL DEVELOPERS ASSOCIATION

RALEIGH, APRIL 19, 1988

[The following address is similar to one the governor presented to the North Carolina Economic Development Board, Hickory, May 20, 1988.]

It's a pleasure to join you and North Carolina's economic development team here in Raleigh, today. How do you like this banner? North Carolina—number one in the nation in new plant announcements in 1987! We didn't say that; *Site Selection Handbook* did. According to their survey, North Carolina had more new manufacturing plant announcements than any other state in the nation last year. That was 113 that met *Site Selection*'s criteria. Texas had 112, and no other state had as many as 100. If the great buffalo hunt is over, they didn't tell the buffalo!

Say it with me: number one in new plants. Sounds good, doesn't it. I don't know about you, but I think it's kind of silly for anyone to propose abolishing the North Carolina Department of Commerce at the peak of its success and number one in the country. You can see why Secretary Claude Pope has a worried look.

Other Number Ones

But North Carolina wasn't just number one in new plant announcements last year, we were number one in some other important rankings, too. Last spring, a survey by *Business Week* magazine found that North Carolina has the best reputation for business growth, as well. In that survey, more corporate executives named North Carolina as their first choice for new plant sites than any other state in the nation. A similar study by *Manufacturing Week* magazine found the same thing.

It's hard to see how North Carolina could be much better off—with corporate executives all over the nation not only thinking about our state, but putting their investments and jobs here, as well. Kentucky didn't believe it, so they did their own survey, asking business leaders to rank the states on seven different categories. To our delight, North Carolina scored number one in five of the seven categories!

Successes

So what has North Carolina's positive reputation brought us? Well, last year it brought us one of our strongest years ever in overall economic development. The annual report you received this morning shows that clearly. Let me run it down for you.

Well, let me restate that. My political opponents don't like all this success, so they're "running it down!" What I'll do is review it for you!

New and expanding businesses announced plans to invest $5.4 billion in North Carolina, in 1987, and create more than 76,600 new jobs. Here are a few highlights:

—Companies building new plants announced plans for $893 million in investment and 13,600 new jobs, an increase of roughly half again over 1986. Manufacturing expansions were off a bit from '85, the record year, and '86, second best, but outdid every other year except 1984, the third best.

—International investment set a new record: $639 million in new plants and 4,200 new jobs announced.

—Travel and tourism spending set a new record: $5.7 billion and 227,900 jobs.

—Film industry spending set a new record: $128 million in direct spending, with $384 million in economic impact. Only California and New York did better.

Jobs

And what do those accomplishments add up to? Jobs. Look at the numbers: Total employment in North Carolina reached an average 3,130,000 in 1987, the highest level in our history. In nonagricultural wage and salary employment, we added 124,500 new jobs, the largest gain in more than a decade. Manufacturing employment rose by 23,400—nonmanufacturing by 101,000, second best ever.

Rural Development

And some of the best news of the year is where those new jobs went. Over two thirds—68 percent—of the new jobs announced by manufacturing industries in 1987 went to communities of 10,000 or less. More than 60 percent of new investment went outside the piedmont. Those numbers are so high, not because our urban areas have stopped scoring—they did as well as in 1986—but because our rural areas are finally starting to get their fair share of new economic growth.

Your Work

Who's responsible for all this success? Well, in large measure it's you, the people in this room. You are the people who make economic development happen in North Carolina. Our state Commerce Department does a lot of work, but they know, and Secretary Pope and I know, that without your help we'd never be able to achieve the kind of overall performance that North Carolina deserves. You are part of our team.

Cooperation

This workshop is recognition of that fact. It's designed to improve communications between our agencies and yours. It's designed to tell you what we in state government are doing and how we are doing it. Perhaps most importantly, this workshop is also about where we are going. 1987 was a great year, but there is still room to improve. We can't rest on our laurels. The competition from other states is too tough.

Budget

For that reason, Secretary Pope and I will be going to the state legislature this year to ask for additional funding for North Carolina economic development programs. The details of our request are outlined in the packets you have received today. A number of specific funding increases are requested, but the two most important, and the two we will be pushing hardest for, will be business-industry development and export marketing. Let me highlight those requests for you.

Business-Industry

In business-industry, we want to do three things. First, we want to expand our regional office network to provide better service to you and our state's existing industries. We've been experimenting with such a program in western North Carolina for about eighteen months now. That program has been so successful that it has saved at least three companies from closing and helped hundreds more take better advantage of existing assistance services.

When the program started, we were amazed to find that many companies don't know about some of our most important business assistance programs. They don't know about things like free customized skills training offered through our community colleges, or about export assistance from our state Commerce Department, or about access roads, or other expansion assistance. We want to tell them. For about $600,000 we can promote that program statewide and, through it, really get going on growth from within.

Second, we want to do more business development advertising and marketing for North Carolina. Under our present budget, we are spending about $500,000 a year for business-climate advertising. This year's budget request would increase that to $740,000 a year. These added funds would be used for audio-visual presentations, brochures, direct mail, and industry ads as a part of our targeted industry marketing program.

Finally, we'll also be asking for funds to expand the analytical staff that supports our state business development effort. These are the people who write the promotional materials and come up with the facts and figures that support you and other developers.

Export

The second major element of our budget request will be for exporting. The falling value of the dollar has created tremendous opportunity for American businesses willing to explore new markets overseas. We want to help North Carolina firms tap those markets.

The budget we're sending to the legislature will request about $865,000 to establish new North Carolina trade offices in Hong Kong and Korea, and to strengthen our existing efforts in Japan and Europe. While the dominant emphasis will be on trade, these expansions will also help us market North Carolina as the place for foreign investment in new plants and jobs. We only got half [of] what we asked for last year, and we don't want North Carolina to miss this golden opportunity, so export promotion will become a major crusade for us.

Other

While business development and exporting will comprise the lion's share of our expansion request, we'll be seeking smaller funds for other programs. We'll ask for about $500,000 to expand our Travel and Tourism Division's marketing efforts; $50,000 more for our Small Business Development Division; $100,000 for our emerging industries and women's economic development programs; and about $120,000 for a new sports development office to recruit sports activities and events to our state. All together, our expansion request will total about $2.8 million.

Your Help

That's where you come in. You may remember that the Commerce Department made some similar budget requests last year, requests that really didn't fare very well in the General Assembly. In fact, last year's legislature actually cut the budgets of many of our economic development divisions.

To help make our case this year, we'd like to ask for your support. Many of the requests we're making will help not only our Commerce Department, but your local agencies as well. The legislature needs to see that we can't play political football with North Carolina's economic development budget and still be competitive in today's business world. In our presentations to you today, we've tried to go over each of the items in this year's request and to explain how they will work to your benefit and ours. The details are also presented in the packets you received this morning. We'll be thankful for whatever help you can lend us.

Conclusion

Let me conclude by thanking you for coming to Raleigh, today. As I said earlier, you are the people that really make economic development work in our state. The support of your agencies has been North Carolina's longtime secret weapon in the competition for new jobs and investment. Last year, your efforts helped make North Carolina number one in the country. Let's go do it again this year.

GOVERNOR'S BUSINESS COUNCIL ON THE
ARTS AND HUMANITIES

RALEIGH, APRIL 19, 1988

[Martin addressed the Governor's Business Council on the Arts and Humanities annually during his first term. On each occasion, he emphasized the relationship between North Carolina's cultural and business climates. In his April 16, 1987, speech, the governor also told listeners that the state increased the budget of the North Carolina Arts Council by $1 million, provided $250,000 for the art museum's outreach program, and furnished $100,000 to match a federal grant awarded to the American Dance Festival.]

It is always a pleasure for me to attend these meetings of the Governor's Business Council on the Arts and Humanities. The work you do is so very important in encouraging a creative and productive partnership between business and the arts here in North Carolina. Tonight I want to discuss with you, for a few minutes, North Carolina as the "State of the Arts," as we like to say, and the role our business community plays in making this a reality.

State of the art is a phrase we hear a lot these days. A stereophonic music system can be state of the art, or so can your computer; a new home can have state-of-the-art conveniences. Very simply, it means the best and the most up-to-date available, especially in electronics and technology.

Well, for many reasons, you really can't talk about state of the art without talking about North Carolina, because our state is a leader in high-tech research and industry. The Research Triangle area, for example, has more Ph.D.s in science, per capita, than anywhere else in the world—so, for that matter, does our Governor's Mansion!

But North Carolina is more than just state of the art in modern technology. In North Carolina the arts, too, are a big part of the state. Our cultural institutions, such as the new Museum of Art, are signs of the strength of our state economy, but they're something more: I venture to predict that institutions like our Museum of Art will help keep our economy strong, as well.

Let me explain. Attendance data show that, throughout the United States, more people visit art galleries, museums, attend ballet, theater, opera, and symphony concerts in a year than go to all the major professional sports events combined. In North Carolina, the private sector understands this. Private corporations and individuals, for instance, have endowed seventeen principal chairs in our state symphony, contributing over $2.5 million. They understand the importance of the symphony to our state's well-being, and they've done the same for other orchestras. The Charlotte Symphony, for example, has an endowed tuba chair in my name. When you consider that every appropriated dollar for the arts in North Carolina is parlayed into $10.00 of actual spending by arts organizations, and that every arts-related job creates a total of 1.72 jobs in the total job market, that's good box office. It's good business, and it's good for business!

A study supported by the Governor's Business Council reveals just how significant the arts are in the economic life of North Carolina. In 1984 alone, the arts pumped nearly $300 million into our state's economy; 11 million citizens attended events and productions sponsored by North Carolina arts organizations. During the last three years, those figures have risen impressively. Attendance at events supported by the Department of Cultural Resources has increased, overall, by nearly 40 percent. At the state Museum of Art alone, attendance has gone up a dramatic 153 percent, over 2 1/2 times what it was three years ago. Add to these statistics the fact that North Carolina's booming film industry shattered all previous records in 1987, for the fourth consecutive year, generating approximately $384 million in economic activity, and you begin to realize the impact the arts, including cinema, have on North Carolina!

The arts are not only the heritage we leave our children, the arts have helped the economic revival in this state and in other states throughout the nation. Like great sports events, vital arts help companies attract, stimulate, and keep forward-looking people in North Carolina. The arts stimulate construction, real estate, transportation, hotels, downtown shopping, and tourism.

The arts make our environment agreeable. For example, you can see the healthy connections between the arts and commerce in downtown Winston-Salem, at Winston Square and the Sawtooth Center. In Charlotte, the Spirit Square Arts Center and the Mint Museum of Art are both sparking cultural and financial growth. We have marveled at the handsomely restored school in Hickory that now serves as the Catawba County Art Center and Museum. Other activities, such as the highly successful and significant "Raleigh and Roanoke" exhibit at the state Museum of History and the recently opened kimono exhibit[1] at the Museum of Art, bring in visitors and strengthen our state's reputation for excellence while providing opportunities for our citizens to experience the best in art and culture.

Historically, North Carolina has been in the forefront of supporting the arts. The birth of American craft art occurred, before the Revolutionary War, in places like North Carolina's Jugtown area. More recently, North Carolina was the first state to set aside a special fund for buying art. We were the first in the nation to have a cabinet-level agency for the arts, a state-supported symphony, and a state-supported School of the Arts. The first of the 3,000 arts councils that are now thriving in the United States was founded here in the Tar Heel State. In short, we have a marvelous history and tradition of support for the arts, and in it all, our state's industries are involved.

When business and the arts collaborate, it makes sense for society, and it makes even more sense for business. No wonder surveys rank our cities among the best places to live anywhere in the country. There's a rich quality of life here that business finds most appealing.

As many of you know, one of my goals as governor is a close working relationship between business, government, and the arts. North Carolina's business and civic leaders have exerted enormous influence to bring to North Carolina better companies and industries. What impresses business leaders is that state officials are concerned about more than new plants; we care about a whole social fabric, about how people work and live together, about the quality of life of our citizens.

I link the state of the arts with the state of the economy because the way business and the arts strengthen each other shows just what North Carolina, and all North Carolinians, can achieve working together; but there are still some companies that are not exercising their potential. Too many businesses don't understand the reasons why they should take more responsibility for the well-being of society. The marketplace is not an isolated sector of the community, but in the middle of it. Strong business support of the arts is in the corporate community's best self-interest. It aids the community and, in turn, makes the community more attractive to better industries and companies.

It's no secret that, in times of limited budgets, arts organizations must look increasingly to private resources. It may seem difficult at times, but it can be done. During fiscal year 1984-1985, the North Carolina Symphony received 61 percent of its total budget through state appropriations; by the 1986-1987 fiscal year, this dependence had been reduced to only 32 percent. Conversely, earned receipts and private contributions, which made up only 39 percent of the symphony's revenues in 1985, now provide over 68 percent. As a former Charlotte Symphony member, I know that this is quite an achievement, and it has been possible because individuals and farsighted members of the corporate community recognize the importance and value of the symphony!

Let me encourage you to continue the work the Governor's Business Council has begun, and let me challenge you to redouble your support of the arts and humanities in North Carolina. The success and flowering of the arts here in North Carolina means success for us all and a better North Carolina. Again, thank you for the opportunity to be here, tonight, to share in this occasion.

---

[1]Governor Martin officially opened the "Robes of Elegance" exhibit of Japanese kimonos, on March 10, 1988, at the North Carolina Museum of Art; see pages 775-776.

CHARLOTTE HAWKINS BROWN MEMORIAL HIGHWAY DEDICATION

Sedalia, April 22, 1988

I imagine today is something of a second homecoming for those of you who attended Palmer Institute or have maintained an interest in its place in the history of our state. Dr. Charlotte Brown, or "Lottie," as she was known by friends and relatives, founded the Alice Freeman Palmer Institute in 1902. Born in Henderson, North Carolina, in 1882, Dr. Brown moved to Cambridge, Massachusetts. At the age of eighteen she was offered a teaching position at Bethany Institute, a small mission school in Sedalia, North Carolina. Her salary of $30.00 a month went largely to buy clothing for her students; that's the kind of teacher and the kind of person she was. Because of financial problems, the school closed only a year after Dr. Brown began teaching there.

Dr. Brown returned to Massachusetts just long enough to raise the money needed to open her own school right here in Sedalia. Twenty students filled an old blacksmith shop in the first classes held at her school, the Alice Freeman Palmer Memorial Institute, named in honor of the first woman president of Wellesley College.[1] By 1908, Palmer Institute had three buildings and five teachers; the school sat on a 220-acre campus that also included a farm. Incidentally, some of Dr. Brown's students paid their tuition with food they grew at home.

Palmer grew to become one of the nation's leading preparatory schools for blacks. As the fame of Charlotte Hawkins Brown and Palmer Institute spread, she became nationally known not only as an educator, but also as a lecturer, social worker, and religious leader. Dr. Brown's associates included Mary McLeod Bethune,[2] Nannie Burroughs,[3] Eleanor Roosevelt, and Booker T. Washington.

During the fifty years that she was president of Palmer, Dr. Brown was active in many civic and professional organizations. From 1935 to 1937 she served as president of the North Carolina Teachers' Association. She was president of the North Carolina Federation of Women's Clubs, founder of the National Association of Colored Women, and a member of the Federal Council of Churches, Urban League, Southern Interracial Council, and the National YMCA Board.

When Dr. Brown retired as president of the school in 1952, Palmer had graduated more than 2,000 young people and its buildings were valued at about $1 million. Dr. Brown died in 1961 and is buried just behind us, appropriately on her beloved Palmer campus. Ten years after Brown's death, the Alice F. Palmer Building, the academic center of the campus containing the library, auditorium, and classrooms, was devastated by fire. Shortly after this, the school closed its doors.

Fortunately, the final chapter in the history of this school has not been written. Once again, what could have been a hopeless situation became a hopeful one. On November 7, 1987, ceremonies officially opened the former school to the public as a state historic site. The Alice Freeman Palmer Memorial Institute became the Charlotte Hawkins Brown Memorial State Historic Site, the first in the state to honor a black person and the first to honor a woman.

We, in our day, must continue to meet our challenges in the spirit of Dr. Brown's hard work and dedication. This is best summarized in her epitaph:

> Leader of women in their quest for finer and more productive living—mentor, by her writings, of those seeking to live more graciously—by her eloquence, inspired youth to nobler achievements; by her vigor of mind and force of character, championed for a disadvantaged race in its striving for human rights and adult responsibilities. She gave 58 years completely of her unique energies and talents in an old blacksmith shop. Her vision, dedication, singleness of purpose, and undaunted faith made this school possible in her native state—North Carolina. May her memory in turn lend inspiration always to this place and its people.

Leader. Champion of the disadvantaged. Mentor. Inspirer of youth. Visionary. A woman of undaunted faith. Indeed, it is fitting and proper that this section of U.S. 70, from Birch Creek Road to N.C. 100, now be named the Charlotte Hawkins Brown Memorial Highway, and it is also fitting that the state of North Carolina and this administration support the ongoing efforts by so many of you to preserve Dr. Brown's legacy.

In the budget I will present to the short session of the General Assembly this summer, there will be a capital improvement fund request, through the Department of Administration, for $482,110 to restore three historic buildings at this important site. This appropriation, if approved by the General Assembly—and I'm sure you'll be heard on that—will go for roof repairs [and] interior and exterior renovation for Canary Cottage, Kimball Hall, and Stouffer Hall.[4]

Dr. Brown's efforts deserve no less, and I am proud to be a part of this ongoing tribute to her memory. This highway will serve the people of North Carolina, just as the intellectual roads Dr. Brown built will live on in the achievements of her students and their descendants. I am honored to be a part of this special day as we say thank you, Dr. Brown—thank you, for the children.

---

[1]Alice Freeman Palmer (1855-1902), born in Colesville, New York; resident of Cambridge, Massachusetts; was graduated, 1876, Ph.D., 1881, University of Michigan; honorary degrees. Educator in Lake Geneva, Wisconsin, 1876-1877, and in Saginaw, Michigan, 1877-1879; history professor, 1879-1881, president, 1881-1887, Wellesley College; dean, Women's Department, University of Chicago, 1892-1895; president, Women's Education Assn. *Who Was Who in America, 1897-1942*, 930.

[2]Mary McLeod Bethune (d. 1955), born in Mayesville, South Carolina; was buried in Daytona Beach, Florida; was graduated from Scotia Seminary, Concord, North Carolina, 1893; was also educated at Moody Bible Institute, Chicago, 1893-1895; honorary degrees. Award-winning educator, humanitarian; founder, 1904, president, 1904-1942, and president emeritus, from 1942, Daytona Normal and Industrial School for Negro Girls (later Bethune-Cookman College); founder, past president, Central Life Insurance Co.; Negro Affairs director, National Youth Administration, 1936-1944; special advisor on minority affairs to President Franklin D. Roosevelt, 1936-1944; author; Democrat. *Who Was Who in America, 1951-1960*, 72.

[3]Nannie Helen Burroughs (1878?-1961), born in Orange, Virginia; died in Washington, D.C.; was graduated, with honors, from M Street High School, Washington, D.C., 1896. Educator; secretary, 1900-1948, president, from 1948, Baptist Woman's Convention; founder, National Training School for Women and Girls (later National Trade and Professional School for Women and Girls, ultimately renamed Nannie Burroughs School, 1964), Washington, D.C., opened 1909; author. Barbara Sicherman and others (eds.), *Notable American Women, The Modern Period: A Biographical Dictionary* (Cambridge, Massachusetts: Belknap Press/Harvard University Press, 1980), 125-127.

[4]The General Assembly earmarked $50,000, for the 1988-1989 fiscal year, to fund renovations at the Charlotte Hawkins Brown State Historic Site. *Post-Legislative Budget Summary, 1988-89*, 87.

MOLECULAR MODELING LABORATORY DEDICATION

Chapel Hill, April 26, 1988

What a great day this is for this ceremony to dedicate this molecular modeling laboratory here at UNC. You know, even on a cloudy day you can see part of the twenty-first century from here. It is clear that, with the building of this facility, the School of Pharmacy will be on the leading frontier of developments in the area of drug creation for many years to come.

Naturally, as a chemist, I'm excited about what you are doing here. Molecular modeling is the use of metaphor at its most sophisticated. As my former protégé and second cousin, Dr. Robert Morrison,[1] can attest, even in a strictly undergraduate institution I was pleased to get some students active in research both in synthetic reactions of small-ring organic compounds and also in some early molecular modeling of steric effects using a first-generation computer having less power than my wife's PC. It was not a Univac—even a Ray-O-Vac—but we were excited to be able to make it work. At the time, I think I was pleased that after iterative churning, and blinking, and whirring all night, our computer printed out geometric coordinates for the same most stable conformation that we had predicted more intuitively using ball-and-stick models and Dr. Eliel's excellent text.[2] In retrospect, I wonder if that was the result of being mathematically captive to that more rudimentary model.

So much has happened since I left the classroom. It reminds me of the story about the prospective new faculty member who was visiting a chemistry lab at a university. It wasn't in North Carolina.

As the chairman led him on a facility tour, in one room there was a witch stirring a large caldron. The chairman explained, "She's from the old school."

Well, it's clear from what you are accomplishing here, you have moved to the cutting edge in chemistry, biology, and computer technology; but I trust there will always be a well-found section of labs for the "old school" of "wet chemistry and biology" and some traditional work with mortar and pestle.

I was particularly impressed with information from Dr. (J. Phillip) Bowen, director of the laboratory.[3] He said that for every drug that gets to the market, there might be 10,000 compounds that have been extracted or synthesized, then purified and tested, by a pharmaceutical company. And then Dr. Bowen went on to provide the hopeful view that the process of molecular modeling techniques may reduce targeted potential drug candidates by half—to 5,000 tested compounds. Of course, 5,000 may still sound like a lot, but such a reduction would be a major breakthrough, resulting in a significant reduction in the cost of creating new drugs.

Computer-assisted drug design. Wow! It doesn't take much imagination to see that what you are pioneering here will serve as a powerful attraction to scholars and drug manufacturers, alike.

Something else that is so exciting is the partnership you have forged with business in the creation of this exciting laboratory. I would like to add my thanks to yours for the support of Tripos Associates, Evans and Sutherland, Tektronix, Polygen, and Silicon Graphics. These companies donated the computer hardware and software. Then there is the support, being provided by Burroughs Wellcome and Glaxo, through research grants, donations, and lecture participation. [The governor presented certificates of appreciation to representatives of the aforementioned organizations.]

Now I would like to present the Order of the Long Leaf Pine to the individual who spearheaded this project. Would Dr. Bowen please come forward. [The governor then presented the award to Dr. Bowen.]

Thank you for inviting me to be a part of this important event. I hope you will let me come back at a later time and try some of your exciting technology. Best wishes for continued success.

---

[1]Robert W. Morrison, Jr. (1938-   ), born in Columbia, South Carolina; resident of Raleigh; B.S., Davidson College, 1960; M.A., 1962, Ph.D., 1964, Princeton University. Research chemist, Chemstrand Research Center, 1964-1968; visiting assistant professor, 1968-1969, adjunct associate professor, 1969-1971, North Carolina State University; with Burroughs Wellcome Co. since 1969, director, Division of Organic Chemistry, since 1988. Robert W. Morrison, Jr., to Jan-Michael Poff, June 6, 1990.

[2]Ernest Ludwig Eliel (1921-   ), born in Cologne, Germany; resident of Chapel Hill; D.Phys.-Chem. Sci., University of Havana, 1946; Ph.D., University of Illinois, 1948; honorary degree; became naturalized U.S. citizen, 1951. Award-winning chemist; faculty member, 1948-1972, chemistry professor, 1960-1972, department head, 1964-1966, University of Notre Dame; William Rand Kenan, Jr., Professor of Chemistry, University of North Carolina at Chapel Hill, since 1972; author; editor. *Who's Who in America, 1988-1989*, I, 885. His "excellent text" was *Conformational Analysis* (Washington, D.C.: American Chemical Society, 1965).

[3]Joel Phillip Bowen (1956-   ), born in Toccoa, Georgia; B.S., Piedmont College, 1979; Ph.D., Emory University, 1984. Assistant professor, School of Pharmacy, since 1986, and director, Laboratory for Molecular Modeling, University of North Carolina at Chapel Hill. Joel Phillip Bowen to Jan-Michael Poff, September 5, 1990.

NORTH CAROLINA MEDICAL SOCIETY

PINEHURST, MAY 5, 1988

[Delayed in Raleigh, the governor arrived late for his engagement with the North Carolina Medical Society. Martin humorously prefaced his remarks by instructing his audience: "First, let me ask everybody to set your watches to 10 o'clock, because that was the time I was supposed to be here. We're running on governor's time."

The following speech includes topics that also were addressed in the governor's aging plan announcement, Raleigh, March 24; remarks at dedication ceremonies for senior centers in Boonville, March 29, and Coats, May 9; and in messages to the North Carolina Hospital Association, Raleigh, June 9, and the North Carolina Public Health Association, Winston-Salem, September 28, 1988.]

When Mr. (George) Moore[1] and Dr. (John) Fagg invited me here to speak to your membership, I thought once again about today's challenges facing the medical profession, including so many of my former student protégés: challenges of professional liability, quality care, indigent care, care for the elderly, and a host of other serious concerns. I thought, too, of the many frustrations inherent in facing those challenges, frustrations which can eventually make even the most dedicated individual simply want to toss those concerns out the window and forget about them—and go fishing, or something else with immediate positive feedback.

I am reminded of a story about four men riding on a train together: a Russian commissar, a Cuban officer, a doctor, and a lawyer. The Russian had a bottle of vodka with him which he pulled out of his luggage and shared with his companions. After filling their glasses he still had half a bottle of vodka remaining, but he opened the window of the train and threw the bottle away.

When they saw this, the other travelers complained: "Why did you throw away a perfectly good supply of vodka?"

The Russian replied, "In my country, we have plenty of vodka. We have so much vodka that we cannot drink it all. In a hundred years we could never drink all the vodka we have in Russia. I can get vodka any time I want. Russia is a great country."

At this point, the Cuban remembered he had a box of choice Havana cigars with him, which he opened and also shared with the others. He still had half a box of cigars remaining when he, too, threw the remaining cigars out the train window.

The other travelers asked the Cuban, "Why did you throw away a perfectly good box of cigars?"

The Cuban replied, "Same reason. In my country, we have plenty of cigars. We have so many cigars we cannot smoke them all. Never in a hundred years could we smoke all the cigars we have in Cuba. I can get cigars any time I want. Cuba is a great country."

The doctor sat for a moment, drinking his vodka and smoking his cigar, thinking about what had just happened. Then, all of a sudden, he stood up and threw the lawyer out of the window.[2]

"America is truly a great country!"

You know the problems facing the medical profession better than anyone. You know the cost of escalating professional liability rates, both to the practice of medicine and the quality of patient care. Some blame the doctors, some blame the lawyers, some blame the insurance companies, and some blame the patients, but in the end, we all pay the price.

There are no easy solutions. You all know that, too. But we can't just toss our responsibilities out the window. When you took the Hippocratic Oath, you swore to provide quality medical care to your patients. That care should be available to all our citizens, regardless of their race, creed, color, or level of income.

Yet, just as all doctors have a responsibility to care for individuals and families, those of us in government have a responsibility to care for society as a whole. It is our challenge to provide for those members of our society who cannot provide for themselves, but within the limits of our available resources. Former governor Charles B. Aycock perhaps expressed this sentiment best when he said, "It undoubtedly appears cheaper to neglect the aged, the feeble, the infirm, the defective, to forget the children of this generation, but the man who does it is cursed by God, and the state that permits it is certain of destruction"[3]

I do not believe, however, that the state can or should assume full responsibility for the cost and provision of all medical care, first dollar to last dollar, cradle to grave. Nor do I believe that the private sector can or should shoulder that responsibility on its own. The only possibility is a mutual coordination of efforts, a two-pronged approach which leverages the cost of private care while making sure that government targets specific areas of need and delivers those services as efficiently and effectively as possible.

Environmental Consolidation

In an effort to restructure state agencies to simplify accessibility to services for our citizens, I have submitted a proposal to the North

Carolina General Assembly for consolidating the health, environmental protection, and natural resource functions of state agencies into a separate Department of Health and Environment. The need for such consolidation is obvious: twenty-eight related environmental programs alone are currently spread over six separate departments in state government. It is also obvious that actions impacting the environment also impact both the state's natural resources and the health of the people living in that environment. My plan for the consolidation of services emphasizes this organic interrelationship between health and the environment while also maintaining the link between environmental protection and natural resource management.

The organizational chart for this new department includes the appointment of a deputy secretary for health. George Moore has expressed to me the concerns of this organization that at least one of the major policy-making positions in the new department be filled by a medical doctor. I believe this recommendation has substantial merit; however, I cannot determine any personnel appointments until after the General Assembly votes to accept or reject my proposal.

Unfortunately, it now seems that the General Assembly is attempting to stall any vote on this issue until after the general election. I have been notified that the study commission considering this question has decided not to meet until after the session adjourns, thereby killing any chance for a commission recommendation to the short session of the legislature. I have, however, anticipated that they would do that, so I have included the consolidation as a part of my budget package, so they will have to vote for or against consolidation when voting for or against my budget appropriations. All this controversy has erupted over a plan that has received widespread support from environmentalists, business leaders, and state and local government officials; that support includes the endorsement of your president, Dr. Carr, speaking on behalf of your executive council.

Nurse Shortage

But environmental reorganization isn't our only initiative. One serious problem affecting the quality of health care is the critical shortage of nurses in our state. On February 18 of this year, I signed Executive Order Number 67, creating the Governor's Task Force on the Shortage of Nurses in North Carolina. This panel is charged with studying this important issue and preparing a report which will examine the causes of the shortage, clearly set forth its implications, and recommend possible solutions that can be implemented by both the public and private sectors.[4]

Drug Abuse

We are also working to combat one of the most serious long-term threats to the general health of our population by establishing a number of programs geared to the eradication of substance abuse in our society. Challenge '87, now known as Challenge '88, provides technical assistance, consultation, and resource materials to counties wishing to establish local coalitions for combating substance abuse on the local level. Another administration initiative—the Governor's Inter-Agency Advisory Team, created in 1987—oversees federal substance abuse funding and coordinates existing state alcohol and drug abuse programs and services.

WISE

We have also helped to coordinate a variety of prevention efforts which will hopefully reduce the need for costly health care in the future. I have initiated a personnel program for Wellness in State Government, which is WISE, to increase the physical fitness of state employees and reduce the risk of serious illness. Another prevention measure geared toward older citizens, the Adult Health Screening Program, provides Medicaid funding for annual adult physicals in an attempt to diagnose and treat diseases at an early stage before they become a serious problem.

Our commitment to alleviating the AIDS crisis also continues. As you know, I supported the AIDS Education Program developed by the State Board of Education which requires AIDS education classes to be taught statewide from the seventh through twelfth grades. This program includes provisions for parental involvement and allows for flexibility in adaptation at the local level. While outlining the pros and cons of condom use, the program also emphasizes the importance of traditional family values and states clearly that the only safe sex is abstinence. It acknowledges that, for the sexually promiscuous, some safeguards are relatively safer than no safeguards, but that even with condoms there are risks which must not be ignored, for that creates a false sense of security, and therefore, increases the risks.

I am asking the legislature to establish four new AIDS control positions in the Division of Health Services to assist in administering AIDS education and services for the state. AIDS kills. Our children's lives hang in the balance, and at this point, education is our only effective weapon in the fight against the disease.

In addition to treatment and prevention programs, state government has been moving forward in its attempts to increase the availability of health care to all our citizens. Medicaid's Baby Love program was funded by the legislature in 1987 and increased the number of children and pregnant women assisted to 100 percent of those with incomes below the federal poverty level.[5] It is my understanding that the Indigent Care Study Commission is currently studying a recommendation to increase that level even higher: to 185 percent of the federal poverty level.

Our older adults also need assistance, and I have developed a $48 million package, to be implemented over three years, which would address a variety of needs. The first $5 million installment of that plan has been included in my budget proposal for the short session of the General Assembly and specifically includes $857,000 for in-home services to allow older adults to remain in their homes rather than moving to rest homes or nursing homes; $600,000 in health promotion monies for local health departments to conduct health promotion and disease prevention programs for older adults; and nearly $46,000 to start a foster family care service which would provide an alternative to group care for older people needing a supervised living arrangement. Another proposal in my aging policy plan would appropriate more than $1.4 million, to be matched locally, to develop senior centers, in the nineteen counties lacking one, which could serve as focal points for aging services. These centers would not oversee or replace existing services; rather, they would provide a central coordination point for all information concerning services available to older adults in that area.

In response to my proposal, the Legislative Study Commission on Aging has developed its own recommendations for a total of $5.6 million, the bulk of which is provided for transportation, support for family care-givers, and in-home services. However, the study commission's proposal provides no funding for health promotion, foster family care, monitoring of rest homes and nursing homes, incentive grants to counties, or focal points for aging services, all of which are included in my budget and are needed. Either way, we will make a start and expand it next year.

Funding from the legislative commission's proposals would be allocated to the eighteen area agencies on aging, to be contracted out, while funds under my proposal would be distributed to several agencies in the Department of Human Resources that plan and provide care and services to older people and their families. This would include county health departments and county social service agencies in addition to the area agencies on aging.

Then there is the issue of who pays for these programs and services. One way or another, we all do. My proposed budget includes a request for $4.5 million to adjust for changes in the federal matching rates for the Medicaid program. The federal matching rate will decline from 68.68 percent in October, 1988, to 68.01 percent, making this request mandatory. I am also requesting $4.6 million for increased Medicare "Part B" premiums.[6] These rates were increased by 28 percent, effective January 1, 1988, and another large increase is expected next year. As the federal government reduces its funding of these programs, the states are required to pour more of their limited resources into picking up the slack, thereby decreasing the amount of money available for expansion or new programs.

And then there is the rising cost of liability insurance. The problem is so great that twenty-one of our counties currently have no prenatal obstetrical services. Over half the residents in twenty North Carolina counties must go to other counties for their deliveries. This situation increases the potential for worsening our infant mortality and morbidity rates.

You all know that in 1986 I called the special, one-day session of the General Assembly to address the problem of insurance availability and give the insurance commissioner initial powers to obtain information and evaluate the cost problem. Tort reform issues were the subject of extensive debate in the 1986 short session, and further legislative study followed.

In 1987, having reviewed the reports of the Property Insurance Markets Commission and the Medical Malpractice Study Commission, I advocated action on the following issues to restructure the tort system: 1) the proposal for the $250,000 cap on noneconomic losses needed to be enacted; 2) joint and several liability should be abolished—that may not be a professional concern, but it's a personal one if you or your property were involved in an accident; 3) punitive damages should be limited to the results of intentional, willful, or wanton acts while requiring that a portion of punitive damage awards, above a certain amount, go to the state General Fund to discourage exorbitant awards; 4) the "collateral source" rule should be modified to make full information available concerning payments from collateral sources, such as duplicate insurance.

Although the 1987 General Assembly did attempt to address tort reform by passing limited legislation, many of the important proposed changes made little progress. Late this past year, my State Goals and Policy Board unanimously agreed to address the question of tort reform and initiated a detailed study in hopes of developing some workable solutions which I can present to the 1989 General Assembly. These recommendations will undoubtedly call for tort reform, changes in malpractice litigation procedures, and ultimate changes in the North Carolina statutes in this area. Such reforms, along with stricter monitoring by our insurance commissioner, should help alleviate liability coverage problems in all areas and especially in those rural areas that have suffered diminished health care.

I will continue to support the right of an injured person to seek to recover actual damages, medical expenses, and lost wages, but recognize that the abuses of these rights have proved costly to everyone in our economy. State government should help to protect consumers from unwarranted increases in health-care costs, but should not impose costly regulations that discourage free-market competition from providing quality health care at the lowest possible cost. My role as governor has been, and should be, to foster cooperation between the state government, private business, and North Carolina hospitals to provide voluntary agreements on new hospital construction and hospital service rates; to encourage statewide health-care planning to avoid costly duplication of services; and to urge the state medical community to adopt, when appropriate, voluntary cost-containment practices regarding fees for services. Neither government nor the private sector can provide necessary services and funding alone. We must work together to develop solutions to our problems that will benefit both the medical profession, the private sector, government, and the citizens of North Carolina. We can't throw our resources and challenges out the window. Like the four men on the train, we must overcome our differences and share our resources, because our job is to keep the train on track. We can't afford to do otherwise.

---

[1]George E. Moore; resident of Raleigh; A.B., University of North Carolina at Chapel Hill, 1962; served in U.S. Marine Corps. Director, Junior Science and Humanities Program, Duke University, 1962-1966; federal programs director, Roanoke, Virginia, 1966-1968; director of development, Hollins College, 1968-1980; associate vice-chancellor, North Carolina State University, 1980-1983; executive vice-president, North Carolina Medical Society, since 1983. George E. Moore to Jan-Michael Poff, September 2, 1988.

[2]At this point in his prepared text, the governor instructed himself to "[Pause . . . pause]".

[3]Aycock used the phrase "cursed of God," rather than "cursed by God," in his address to the 1904 state Democratic convention from which this excerpt was taken. R. D. W. Connor and Clarence Poe, *The Life and Speeches of Charles Brantley Aycock* (Garden City, New York: Doubleday, Page and Company, 1912), 127.

[4]For the text of Executive Order Number 67, establishing the Governor's Task Force on the Shortage of Nurses in North Carolina, see *N.C. Session Laws, 1987, Regular Session, 1988,* III, 958-961.

[5]The General Assembly authorized funding of the program under *N.C. Session Laws, 1987,* II, c. 738, s. 70.

[6]"Part B" premiums cover Medicare recipients' major medical expenses. *Recommended Changes to the 1988-89 State Budget,* 28.

NATIONAL GOVERNORS' ASSOCIATION RURAL DEVELOPMENT TASK FORCE

RALEIGH, MAY 11, 1988

It is my pleasure, as chair of this panel on "Local Community and Government Leadership," to welcome you to share in our proceedings. Before hearing from our distinguished panelists, I would like to share a few thoughts.

First, as governor, I want to say how pleased we are that Governor Branstad and the National Governors' Association Rural Development Task Force chose to hold its hearing in Raleigh. This hearing is focusing on ways rural communities can adapt to rapidly changing economic realities—and on how state governments can help them. This is a timely and critically important undertaking, and I am very pleased and honored to be part of it. I also think it especially appropriate that this hearing is held in North Carolina, because we have a success story to tell.

A great deal of attention is being focused on the economic decline of many rural communities and the small towns that are their business centers. The loss of jobs in rural areas and the loss of future leaders is one result of this urban-rural imbalance. In North Carolina, we feel that we have learned how to turn this around.

For several decades, our larger cities—in the 50,000 to 400,000 range—have been very active and very successful in promoting industrial development by creating energetic, cooperative partnerships between leaders in business, government, and education. The state has enjoyed a degree of prosperity, overall, because of it.

In 1985, we decided to try the same kind of creative, energetic partnerships with our smaller towns. We found that with teamwork, state agencies, local government, business leaders, education leaders, spiritual leaders, can promote the virtues of small-town locations and get the resources together very well. While no one directs a business to invest in a particular community, and no one can wield central power to send jobs to a deserving town, we've found that we can roll out the red carpet, make business feel welcome, and attract the investment.

In 1987, over two thirds of the jobs from new manufacturing announcements went to towns with less than 10,000 population. That's great news, especially since the larger cities did about as well as in 1986. Not every town scored, but towns in every section of North Carolina scored.

For rural economic development to be successful, there is the need to address such matters as infrastructure, land availability—maybe a recently vacated building—quality of life, human resources, financial resources, and education and training. But how do you do that? Cooperative alliances between local leaders and the state made it possible to deal effectively with these concerns. Let me cite some examples to illustrate how this partnership is working in North Carolina.

In Hendersonville, population 8,436, the Apple Growers Association and the Agricultural Extension Service were the catalyst that brought together the essential elements for a collaborative alliance to develop an agricultural park. This coalition was one of bankers, businesses, the chamber of commerce, county commissioners, county developers, and our regional developers. Because of a cooperative relationship, the park is becoming a reality. When completed, it will include processing facilities, not only for apples but also for other fruits and vegetables produced in that area. Food processing operations are, I believe, one of the most promising rural development ideas.

Sometimes it's important for a community to take an honest inventory of its resources. Once that is accomplished, it might be determined that it's time to invest in the future. To do this, a cooperative effort is required.

Valdese, population 4,098, represents an illustration of a community which was losing jobs and population in the earlier part of this decade. A combination of factors turned things around in this rural community of 4,000 population. Six million dollars in investment in infrastructure for water and waste water treatment, a revitalized downtown, and industrial marketing were important factors in this community's economic resurgence, but at the heart of Valdese's economic rise was the strong and stable leadership that has worked closely with state agencies. Last year, new locations and expansions in Valdese resulted in 530 jobs.

Much can hinge on the availability of water supply and land for waste water in certain industries. Rocco Poultry, in St. Pauls, population 1,891, is a good example.

Sometimes a community inventory will focus on available assets, instead of needs. Standard Packaging, Incorporated, in very rural Rowan County, found an appealing location with the existence of two buildings which formerly had housed a mobile home factory. The one drawback was that there were no extensions for providing adequate sewage. County commissioners and developers worked together to provide the necessary service—result: fifty jobs. Again, notice that the heart of the solution involved local leadership and cooperation.

I've heard it said that creative human imagination is the highest form of technology. Certainly, in Kinston, population 25,718, this was the case. Stanadyne, Incorporated, whose major products are plumbing supplies and equipment, wanted to build a 75,000-square-foot distribution center. Kinston was a latecomer in consideration as a site, but the local Committee of 100 happened to own a property in an industrial park close to the airport, and existing industries became important partners in negotiating a deal with Stanadyne.

Still, there was a remaining hurdle: Stanadyne had a leasing agreement with Ryder Trucks, and Ryder had no terminal near Kinston. Teamwork won the day. Successful negotiations were concluded with Ryder to locate a terminal nearby. Henry Kaiser put it well when he said, "I always view problems as opportunities in work clothes."[1]

Then, I could mention Sara Lee as another example. Here our strategic corridor plan in the state, with the completion of the Tarboro—population 11,109—U.S. 64 Bypass, was a major factor in Sara Lee's decision to locate here. Inasmuch as we have Tarboro's mayor, Dr. M. A. Ray,[2] on our panel, we'll leave it to him to tell the rest of the story.

Our secret to success is really not a secret, but just plain horse sense. When you have a strong network of local and common developers and local leaders who know the assets their community has to offer, know who owns land, and know how to sell what their community has to offer—the state can help, but it starts with the local community. They have to want it.

Of course, we have one other excellent tool in our community college system of fifty-eight institutions, which, with programs provided free of charge to new and expanding industries, is the best industrial training program in the country.

In 1987, we were number one in the nation in new plant announcements by businesses. We were fourth in plant expansions, behind the more populous states of California, New York, and Texas, but what we are most proud of is that, in 1987, 68 percent of 23,400 new jobs announced by manufacturing industries went to communities of 10,000 people or less. Indeed, we have been so successful in the dispersal of industries in our state that John Herbers, a *New York Times* reporter, wrote in his book, *The New Heartland*, that the way North Carolina has managed geographically to spread its industries makes it the prototype for America's future.[3]

Nationally, more rural counties are manufacturing dependent than are agriculture dependent, but in our quest to improve our rural economy, we realize that agriculture is still the centerpiece of our rural economy. In other words, successful agriculture and successful rural develoment are inseparable. Recognition of this truth has led us to work toward further expansion in our European and Far East marketing. It has driven us to explore additional crops, such as mushrooms, kiwi fruit, lambs, and kenaf: a tree-like plant that grows rapidly from a seedling to a nine-foot plant capable of being used for the production of newsprint. Tobacco is still strong, but poultry has grown dramatically to become the number-one source of farm income.

On another front, I have just appointed a Task Force on Aquaculture to explore possibilities in this area and to identify barriers to expanding this important industry.[4] Among the aquatic crops we are exploring are catfish, trout, crayfish, and saltwater shrimp.

But profound change is taking place. An example is the move to a market-driven agriculture where all aspects of a farming economy are considered, from marketing, to growing, to processing, to distribution. Indeed, every reasonable opportunity is grist for our economic-development mill, from fish to film, from trees to turkeys, to tourism, to terminals, to tobacco, to textiles—from high tech, to low tech, and every tech between.

Our local officials are working with us, and within their own communities, to promote growth that is consistent with our rural values and heritage. They are relying on, and supporting, their traditional industries, they are encouraging entrepreneurs, and they are the reason our intergovernmental partnership for rural development is succeeding. I believe our rural areas are themselves a precious resource, whose characteristics, and life-styles they engender, will prove an increasingly strong attraction to industry. They key word, however, is *balance*: balance in the kind and location of industries, balance between interests of economic development and environment, and balance between the interests of our citizens and greater economic opportunities.

---

[1]Henry John Kaiser (1882-1967), born in Sprout Hook, New York; U.S. industrialist, founder of over 100 companies; dam, levee, and highway builder, 1913-1930; organized construction companies to build Hoover, Bonneville, and Grand Coulee dams, 1931-1945; built West Coast's only integrated format steel mill, 1941-1942; introduced assembly-line construction methods to shipbuilding during World War II and established country's first health maintenance organization, 1942, for his shipyard workers; established Kaiser Gypsum, 1944; cofounder, with Joseph W. Frazer, of Kaiser-Frazer Corp. automobile manufacturers, 1946. *Encyclopaedia Britannica*, 15th ed., s.v. "Kaiser, Henry J(ohn)"; *World Book Encyclopedia*, 1982 ed., s.v. "Kaiser, Henry John."

[2]Moses A. Ray (1920-   ), born in Clinton; resident of Tarboro; B.S., Shaw University, 1941; D.D.S., Howard University, 1945; U.S. Air Force, 1951-1953. Dentist; Tarboro town councilman, 1965, precinct chairman, 1980, and mayor, 1988; appointed to state Board of Transportation, 1970; member, Triangle East Board of Directors, 1988. Moses A. Ray to Jan-Michael Poff, September 15, 1988.

[3]John Herbers, *The New Heartland: America's Flight Beyond the Suburbs and How it is Changing Our Future* (New York: Times Books/Random House, Inc., 1986), 29-38, 51.

[4]Martin signed Executive Order Number 69, establishing the Governor's Task Force on Aquaculture in North Carolina, on March 11, 1988. *N.C. Session Laws, 1987, Regular Session, 1988*, III, 967-969.

OPENING CEREMONIES, VENTURE '88 VENTURE CAPITAL FAIR COUNCIL FOR ENTREPRENEURIAL DEVELOPMENT

DURHAM, MAY 12, 1988

[Venture '88 was held at the Fuqua School of Business, Duke University.]

It is a very distinct pleasure for me to welcome all of you, this morning, to what is undoubtedly one of North Carolina's most impressive business success stories of the 1980s. I am so very proud and excited about what you have done, on your own, to capitalize on the intellectual resources of the entire Research Triangle.

Fruits of Labor

You are fulfilling the idea that the private sector could consciously work to help itself, that businesses throughout the Triangle area could come together in support of entrepreneurial growth and development. I suppose that when the Council for Entrepreneurial Development [CED] was formed in 1983, there may have been a lot of skeptics, but that didn't stop men like Bert Amdahl, and Horace Johnson, and Dennis Dougherty, Bob Gress, Dave Rodger, Fred Hutchison, and the council's other cofounders.[1] They knew they had a good idea, and they worked for it. They sponsored seminars and began regular meetings. They made it possible for small and emerging companies to share ideas and experience, and to find expert assistance when they needed it most.

Venture Fair

In 1984, the council sponsored its first Venture Fair, like this one, and you've been learning and improving ever since. This year you've had help from your sister councils, which are following in your footsteps across the state. More than 200 investors are attending the venture portion of the conference. As a group, you are more diverse, both in terms of geography and market, than ever before.

Thirty-five up-and-coming companies are here, seeking venture investment in the marketplace you have created. These firms, too, are more diverse than in previous years. They are also more polished. They've learned a lot already from a team of CED specialists who've helped to make their presentations clearer and more precise. This year's conference also includes another new and exciting idea: an entrepreneurial greenhouse program that showcases companies in their earliest stages of development. These embryonic firms have unique business ideas in need of seed capital for further development.

A New Wave

The most important thing about this conference is not so much who's here, but what you're doing—and that is building a future of growth for the Research Triangle, and North Carolina, and even our nation as a whole. The investments that are born here will help launch the growth industries of tomorrow.

Government

As governor, I want to take this opportunity to thank and commend the council, and all those here today, for the work you have done in strengthening North Carolina's entrepreneurial infrastructure. I also want you to know that you are not alone. Over the last three years, we've worked hard in state government to do our part in encouraging new start-ups and business growth.

We've cut taxes. After two years of hard discussions with the legislature, [the] inventory tax was repealed. We reduced unemployment insurance costs, and we've cut our state intangibles tax by $24 million a year. Hopefully, in the next four years we can eliminate the intangibles tax altogether, for that would really stimulate a surge of investment from within our state!

We've also worked hard to improve small business and start-up access to North Carolina capital assets. We've implemented a new system of pooled industrial revenue bonds that gives small companies new access to that form of financing. With the support of the state treasurer, we've made more than $30 million in state reserve funds available for investment in venture capital companies. We've also set up a new, statewide, certified development company and launched a financing program of long-term, fixed-rate loans for small and mid-sized businesses.

A Climate for Growth

But perhaps most importantly, we've tried to preserve and build on North Carolina's positive climate for growth. We're expanding funding for public education. We're improving our highways, ports, and airports. We're broadening state assistance for exporting. We're expanding and strengthening a strong network of business assistance agencies, not only through our state Commerce Department, but in our universities and community colleges, as well. We're providing seed-capital funding through our state Technological Development Authority, and we're establishing business incubators to foster small business start-ups throughout our state. We're working to assist our existing industries so they can devote more resources to "intrapreneurship"—the homegrown development of new ideas and new products in established companies.

Positive Signs

The results of these efforts are encouraging. Earlier this year, *Inc.* magazine, one of America's preeminent authorities on high-growth companies, listed the Research Triangle area as one of America's most favorable locations for new business start-ups. In fact, *Inc.* has been so impressed by what is going on here that it will hold its 1989 national small business conference in Raleigh, bringing more than 500 of America's fastest-growing companies for a firsthand look at this area. I want every local chamber of commerce in North Carolina to be here with a hospitality suite or booth, not just to learn from them, but to recruit those who are looking for a place to expand.

I think North Carolina's future is bright. We're learning how to solve so many problems, especially for rural areas that are now sharing in balanced growth, and especially in raising capital and access to it.

A recent survey by Intersouth Partners, here in Research Triangle, found that the amount of venture capital under management in North Carolina has increased by 750 percent in the last five years. That same survey estimates that by the end of this year, capital under management by venture firms in our state will reach $180 million, a 1,200 percent increase over 1982. Intersouth found that in the last fifteen months, at least twenty-five Research Triangle-area companies have received nearly $42 million from thirty different venture capital funds and other private and corporate investors.

We've still got a long way to go to reach our potential, but that is where we're going. Government has a role, but must be careful not to think it can do your job. I mentioned the SBA and bond financing improvements we've made. We want to put some of our reserves into venture capital, but I believe it would be a serious blunder for government to try to pick the winners, because that would quickly degenerate into political choices and pork-barrel favors. Any use of our reserves must be through existing financial institutions and firms already set up to evaluate investments on the basis of business principles and profit motive. I hope you will help us develop this mechanism, before somebody cooks up another way for government to lose money by the fiscal equivalent of shoveling it out of airplanes!

As we begin today's work, let us not forget the commitment and imagination that have made North Carolina's entrepreneurial growth possible. Indeed, let us remember that it was in this fashion that our forefathers built this country and, through their enterprising spirit, made our nation great. Here is the essence of it: that in America, people are allowed and willing to invest their resources, at the risk of losing it all, but in the hope of a favorable return; thereby providing jobs for dozens, and hundreds, and collectively for millions of their neighbors. Today North Carolina welcomes investors, from throughout America, to take part in our entrepreneurial community. We regard your wisdom, experience, and resources as valuable assets and look forward to your decision to join in our growth.

¹B. J. (Bert) Amdahl (1934-   ), born in Rural Ossian, Iowa; resident of Cary; B.B.A., 1958, executive program graduate, 1971, University of Minnesota; U.S. Army, 1954-1956. Certified public accountant; various positions with Ernst & Ernst, 1958-1964, and Cornelius Co., 1964-1974, Minneapolis; executive vice-president, Medtronic, Inc., Minneapolis, 1974-1982; president, chairman and chief executive officer, Bionexus, Inc., Raleigh, 1982-1987; vice-president, secretary and treasurer, 1987-1988, executive vice-president and area director, since 1988, Glaxo (Latin America), Inc., Research Triangle Park; chief operating officer, Orthomet, Inc. B. J. Amdahl to Jan-Michael Poff, March 17, 1990.

R. Horace Johnson (1944-   ), born in Roanoke Rapids; resident of Raleigh; B.S., University of North Carolina at Chapel Hill. Certified public accountant; consultant; managing partner, Raleigh and Durham offices, Ernst & Young; president, 1986-1987, founding treasurer, Council for Entrepreneurial Development; treasurer, board member, Greater Raleigh Chamber of Commerce, and of Business Innovation and Technology Development Center. R. Horace Johnson to Jan-Michael Poff, March 21, 1990.

Dennis Dougherty; B.S., Oklahoma City University, 1970; was also educated at Duke University; served in U.S. Army prior to 1972. Accounting and finance specialist; joined UNOCAL as sales representative, 1972; former partner, Touche Ross & Co.; founder, 1985, general partner, Intersouth Partners, Research Triangle Park. Dennis Dougherty to Jan-Michael Poff, April 17, 1990.

Robert W. Gress (1934-   ), born in Donora, Pennsylvania; B.S.M.E., Indiana Institute of Technology, 1959; U.S. Army, 1952-1955. Various positions with Corning Glass Works, Corning, New York, 1959-1987, including worldwide business manager/resistors, 1984-1986, business development and planning manager, 1986-1987, and director, U.S.I. Taiwan, 1985-1987; president, NUVO, Inc., Cary, since 1987; president, board chairman, Greater Raleigh Chamber of Commerce; founded concept and team that became Council for Entrepreneurial Development. Robert W. Gress to Jan-Michael Poff, April 4, 1990.

David E. Rodger (1932-   ), born in Chicago; resident of Raleigh; B.S., University of Cincinnati, 1958; U.S. Army, 1954-1956. President, American Data processing, 1964-1968; vice-president, eastern regional manager, University Computing Co., 1968-1971; president, Rodger Enterprises, 1971-1976; president, since 1976, chairman and chief executive officer, Infocel. David E. Rodger to Jan-Michael Poff, March 12, 1990.

Fred D. Hutchison (1949-   ), born in Maryville, Tennessee; resident of Raleigh; B.S., University of North Carolina at Chapel Hill, 1971; J.D., University of Virginia, 1975. Attorney; president, 1984-1985, Council for Entrepreneurial Development; appointed to Governor's Task Force on Development of Private Seed Venture Capital Sources, 1987. Fred D. Hutchison to Jan-Michael Poff, March 12, 1990.

DISMAL SWAMP-U.S. 17 VISITORS CENTER GROUNDBREAKING

Camden County, May 13, 1988

It is great to be in northeastern North Carolina this afternoon and to be a part of this important event for this great region of our state. Today is a day of celebration as we break ground for the Dismal Swamp-U.S. 17 Visitors Center. Groundbreakings of this kind symbolize hope for the future and a commitment to the ongoing progress of an area. The center, when completed by December of this year, will welcome tourists and help them find their way to the many wonders we have been blessed with in northeastern North Carolina.

With its 740-square-foot information center and 820-square-foot rest area, the visitors center will serve as the gateway to expanded tourism in this region; but in a real sense, with the building and operation of this center, we will also have a monument to what a private-public partnership can achieve. The Albemarle Commission is setting a fine example of the good things that can happen when government and the citizens of a region work together to make their area a better place to live.

The Albemarle Commission has been contracted by the Department of Transportation to staff and operate the visitor information portion of the facility. As most of you know, the commission is the regional council of governments to oversee programs in this region concerning economic development, aging, job training, and tourism—to name a few.

This center is significant not only because of this cooperative effort, but also because it will be the first of its kind to have a boat-docking facility. To be constructed behind the rest area portion, the 150-foot dock will allow the people traveling on the canal through the Dismal Swamp area to stop at this facility. I think this is a marvelous dual use of this property, and I congratulate Senator Basnight for suggesting to me such an idea.[1]

People who travel by boat through the canal will also see a new "Welcome to North Carolina" sign. The Department of Transportation will erect a larger version of this sign, which I'd like to show you at this time. [Martin was instructed to hold up small replica of sign.] This sign, the first of its kind, will be placed at the Virginia line and at other strategic points, in North Carolina waters, to welcome out-of-state boaters—similar to Welcome to North Carolina signs posted on the highway at our state lines.

The signs are a part of our Coastal Initiative plan announced this past November in New Bern, which will provide coastal and boater guides and related information later this year. We can do a better job of marking shoals and other hazards and improving the water approaches to our towns.

This Coastal Initiative plan, simply put, will help balance between (a) the need to protect the environment, and (b) the demand to develop some of the coastal area. Protecting the environment is the heart and soul of this plan. It is the foundation upon which new industry and prosperity will be built. The key to it is to help attract the marinas, restaurants, shops, and museums into the existing towns. That way we could bring jobs and income to these towns while keeping the rest of the waters unspoiled. "Sounds" like a wonderful idea.

We have reason to be proud in North Carolina because this facility will help not only boaters, but motorists as well who will stop to rest, relax, or to get information about our state; and it gives us a chance to spread the glory a little bit about northeastern North Carolina and all the natural and historic treasures that abound here, treasures that natives of this area have cherished for years. In many ways, this center represents something even larger: an opportunity for expanded economic growth.

As we all know, economic growth goes hand in hand with a good roads system. Roads are important because they enhance our lives. Good transportation services are magnets for good jobs. They provide a stimulus for travel and tourism. They increase motoring safety.

Since the late 1950s, North Carolina and Virginia have recognized how important the U.S. 17 corridor between Elizabeth City and Norfolk is to the economic growth and transportation needs of the region. Over the years, the need to upgrade U.S. 17 from a two-lane road to a four-lane highway has become more and more apparent. Officials from both states have written letters, forwarded construction plans, and exchanged speeches urging each other to widen their respective portions of the highway.

North Carolina was the first to take action by spending more than $40 million to four-lane U.S. 17 between Elizabeth City and Virginia. Last November, another step was taken to show the importance of this highway to the region. The Board of Transportation designated U.S. 17 and U.S. 64 as a strategic corridor in the Transportation Improvement Program, in response to your multicounty consensus.

This strategic highway network contains the roads most important to North Carolina's "intrastate" system. Highways were selected by the people of each multicounty region as strategic corridors, for their primary importance to a region and for their significance to the entire state. They are routes that combine high traffic volumes and great economic potential. Some are interstate highways, some are U.S. primary highways, and some carry North Carolina designations, but whatever their name and number, these routes have a common purpose: They are the routes that can keep North Carolina moving and tie our state together as one united state.

Our current Transportation Improvement Program contains additional commitments to the strategic corridor system, and future updates of the TIP will contain more improvements. We don't want to add too many projects, though, for [the] ultimate goal is to bring the entire system to the highest standard—to give North Carolina the best highway network it can have. If we can complete this system, and the important local connectors to it, we can build a highway system that works hand in hand with our developmental efforts.

Meeting the strategic highway needs won't build all the roads that North Carolina needs, but it will keep our priorities in order. U.S. 17 was selected as a strategic corridor because it is North Carolina's major north-south route east of Interstate 95. Along with U.S. 64, it will serve the entire northeast region of the state and connect piedmont North Carolina to tidewater Virginia.

I know how important the four-laning of U.S. 64 and U.S. 17 from Rocky Mount to Elizabeth City is to northeastern North Carolina. Our Transportation Improvement Program includes almost $150 million to improve this U.S. 17-U.S. 64 corridor. As a matter of fact, our Board of Transportation this morning in Morehead City approved a $7.5 million project to complete U.S. 64, from Rocky Mount to Tarboro, and a $9.7 million contract to replace the U.S. 17 Roanoke River bridge at Williamston.

As we make improvements along this U.S. 17 corridor, we also must not neglect the section south of Wilmington to the South Carolina line. More than thirty miles of highway, from the South Carolina line to just south of Wilmington, is being widened to four lanes. Some projects already are under construction, with the remaining portions to be let to construction during the next 3½ years at a cost of $55 million.

We also are well aware that Department of Transportation officials in Virginia have expressed an interest in our four-laning N.C. 168 south of the Virginia line, and we have designated this section of N.C. 168 and part of U.S. 158 south of Barco as a strategic corridor. We realize the need to four-lane N.C. 168, but we feel that the four-laning of U.S. 17 in Virginia is an equally important project.

We in North Carolina realize, as you in Virginia do, that funding highway construction is a complicated task, but we feel that the U.S. 17 project in Virginia and the N.C. 168 project in North Carolina are two critically important road projects that should proceed together, not separately. To our friends from Virginia, we know we've been beating you over the head with this issue, but as you can see, there is method, and importance, to the madness. We know that Virginia's highway program update is currently in process. We are hopeful that we will see some signs of progress on U.S. 17 within the next few weeks, but we don't want everyone to get their hopes too high, because Virginia is suffering from the same sort of highway funding dilemma that we are facing in North Carolina. We do feel Virginia is working hard within their system resources to hear us on this critical issue.

By the year 2000, traffic counts on both U.S. 17 and N.C. 168 are expected to increase dramatically. With increased traffic comes the increased probability of traffic accidents. A four-lane highway will help reduce the possibility of such accidents. Working together, we will be able to provide the best possible transportation system for all our citizens.

Speaking of the best possible transportation system ever, let me take this opportunity to express my appreciation for the diligent work of the Highway Study Commission, of which Senator Basnight is a member. The commission is steadfastly working for a bigger and better program to keep North Carolina rolling to the twenty-first century. We are working with the commission to deal with our current $11 billion in highway construction needs, many of which are more than evident right here in northeastern North Carolina.

I find it very exciting to be involved in helping to form this area's future in such an important way, and I look forward to the opening of the Dismal Swamp-U.S. 17 Visitors Center and North Carolina's opportunity to welcome visitors to this beautiful area of the state. You know, there is a partnership that exists between Virginia and North Carolinians in this area of the state, and that makes it important for us to cooperate and compromise on highways, the environment, recreation, tourism, and other critical areas, but there is one thing on which we won't compromise: The good citizens of northeastern North Carolina may be a long way from their capital, in miles, but they're not far away in priority. This welcome center, U.S. 17 and U.S. 64, Oregon Inlet, and other important initiatives for this area indicate our commitment to this region and its progress. We strongly hold claim to this area as Tar Heels only, and we're willing to keep putting our money where our mouth is to see that northeastern North Carolina fulfills its greatest potential—according to our state motto, "To be, rather than to seem." Now, on with the show.

---

¹Marc Basnight (1947-   ), born in Manteo; was educated at Manteo High School. Construction business; member, state Senate, since 1985, and chairman, Appropriations Committee-Natural and Economic Resources; Democrat. *North Carolina Manual, 1987-1988*, 293.

GOVERNOR'S CONFERENCE ON AGING

RALEIGH, MAY 25, 1988

This is truly one subject that everybody shares. If anything is a fact of life, growing older is a fact of life! Of course, we joke about it, as President Reagan did in his debate with that young fellow, Mondale.[1] Sometimes we keep our age a closely guarded secret, but despite our efforts, the gray appears, the eyes need help focusing, and the number of candles on our birthday cake continues to grow.

We can't change the fact of growing older, but we can change the way we look at the process of aging. We should begin to celebrate our lifetimes; celebrate the increased knowledge and experience we have gained, and share that knowledge and experience with younger people who, in their turn, are gaining the wisdom of age. It is time to recognize that aging is a process of growing in knowledge, in wisdom, and in experience. These are not commodities that can be bought; they are truly gifts of life, developed through years of caring, hard work, and sacrifice. Our laugh wrinkles and silver hair should be medals of maturity, accepted with pride as a tribute to a lifetime of truly living.

You know, several former governors—Hunt, Holshouser, Scott, Sanford—were celebrated for being such young men when they took office. So, I celebrate the fact that of my five predecessors whose portraits hang in the Mansion foyer, only one, Dan K. Moore, was inaugurated at an older age than I, and he only by a year or so. The others were at least ten years younger.

During 1988, which I have especially designated the "Year of the Older Adult" in North Carolina,[2] we want to adopt the theme of this conference and begin celebrating our lifetimes while aging together in North Carolina. As you well know, our state population, like that of the nation, is growing older. An American born in 1900 could expect to live to the ripe old age of 47. Today, the average lifespan has increased to age 71 for men and 74 for women. The average lifespan will continue to lengthen as we benefit from further advancements in health care and disease prevention.

We are also experiencing a surge in the number of older adults as a higher percentage of our total population. At the turn of the century, 63,000 of our North Carolina citizens, or 3.2 percent of the population, were aged 65 and older. In just 80 years, those numbers have grown to 603,000, or 10 percent of the population. By the year 2000, over 1 million North Carolina citizens will be aged 65 and older. Those statistics may seem a bit unreal until you realize that 1 million of our 6.5 million North Carolinians are already aged 60 and over. That is just about equal to the total population of Raleigh, Charlotte, Greensboro, Winston-Salem, and Durham put together.

This rapidly expanding group provides our state with a valuable natural resource. Older citizens bring to their communities a wide variety of knowledge, talents, and skills derived from a lifetime of experiences. While strengthening the volunteer services provided by civic and religious organizations in the community, these older adults improve their own quality of life through active involvement in the lives of others. Older adults, particularly retirees, also enhance the economic growth of the state, both as consumers of commercial goods and service providers to government and business. It is time to recognize these contributions and to encourage our older adults to continue sharing their expertise within our local communities, both as volunteers, as civic leaders, as investors, and always as good neighbors.

Knowing that we can look forward to living longer, healthier lives should be good news to most of us, but in this case, even good news raises questions which must be answered at some point: Number one, how do we identify the needs of this growing population, and number two, how do we plan to meet those needs? Well, it is time to answer those questions. It is time to take a hard look at where we are and what remains to be done as we approach the twenty-first century.

The time to plan for our future needs is now, not twenty years down the road when the problems have grown so large they can't be managed. A wise investment in our future will certainly help our current population aged 60 and over, but that same investment will reap dividends for younger citizens who also hope to enjoy growing older in North Carolina. By age 50 or 55, they—we—should have begun to make plans—serious, realistic plans—about our retirement: timing, income, letting go some responsibilities, volunteering for others.

There will be many, of course, who will need some help from society. We have been meeting many existing needs, expanding existing programs, and developing new initiatives within our resource capacity to assist the growing population of older adults. Many of these programs have been successful and can provide us with models for even better program development in the future. We have, for example, worked extensively with the private sector to develop employment opportunities for the older worker, through such companies as McDonald's Corporation, Hardee's, Rose's, Harris-Teeter, and others. Sears recently announced a new catalog service by telephone, in which most employees will work only part time with unusual flexibility for long, irregular vacations. Ideal for Sears, whose calls come in mostly at peak hours! Ideal, too, for many retirees. Older Worker programs in a variety of local agencies have provided training, work experience, and job placement services to economically disadvantaged persons over age fifty-five.[3]

In addition to helping find employment, we are also working to preserve the health of older adults so they retain the freedom and mobility to live life as they choose. The Add Health to Our Years, or AHOY program, helps local communities establish physical fitness programs for older persons. The Walk for Life program also promotes wellness activities by helping developing walking programs on the local level. The North Carolina Dental Society, the Podiatry Association, and the Ophthalmologist Association are working with the Department of Human Resources to expand voluntary health screenings at senior centers across the state. Some critics discount these programs because these don't spend a lot of tax dollars, but it's a virtue, in my book, to help inform and educate people how to take greater responsibility for our own health.

For those who need more intensive care, we have already expanded the Adult Day Care Program and increased the number of nursing home beds available, which had been frozen in recent years. We have contracted with the Duke University Center for the Study of Aging to provide training for local agencies and family members concerning how to work with Alzheimer's patients and how to cope with the stress of caring for that person. The Respite Care Program, begun in 1986, provides some relief for the family caregivers of homebound older adults.

These are only a few of the programs offered through state agencies which benefit our older citizens. We have been working, and we will continue to work, to provide opportunity for those who want it and assistance for those who need it. Yet, though they serve our older adults well, these programs cannot hope to meet the overwhelming demands which we will face in the next ten to twenty years.

At a two-day retreat of cabinet secretaries and other top staff last October at Peace College, we reviewed the many needs and opportunities associated with growing older. We discussed this with folks from the Center for Creative Retirement at UNC-Asheville and decided to make this subject a major priority.

Our single greatest mistake in this effort would be to assume that all older adults are the same and therefore have the same needs. As young people, we discovered different talents and different physical capabilities. As we grew and matured, we chose different careers and developed different interests. As we raised our families, we followed different life-styles. Why should this pattern change just because we turn sixty or sixty-five?

North Carolina's older citizens are a diverse group, varying in life-style, health conditions, income, employment status, housing arrangements, family size and involvement, and use of leisure time, health care, and social services. In planning for our older population, we must realize that not all older people are alike and that a variety of needs exists now and will exist for the future. We had been studying these future needs, both before and since that cabinet retreat, and have developed a comprehensive aging policy plan through the Department of Human Resources.

This plan discusses ten major areas of concern, areas which correspond to the ten issue forums in which you will take part over the next two days. The plan is a beginning which can, and will, be added to and refined over time. It represents the efforts and input of many different groups, both public and private, who have a common goal: to ensure a future of dignity, independence, and well-being for our state's older citizens.

Out of this plan we developed a $48 million budget package to assist in meeting the current needs of older adults in North Carolina. The first $5 million installment of that proposal has already been submitted to the North Carolina General Assembly for consideration in the short session this June. Some of you have quickly and rightly claimed that $5 million is not nearly enough. It's not. But it is a start, in the second year of a two-year budget, in which only 3 to 4 percent more money can be added, and most of that must go for pay increases which got left out by the legislature last year. We will start, and the remaining $43 million will be included in my 1989-1990 biennial budget for the further expansion of these services.

Specific items in this budget request include:

—$1.2 million for incentive grants to counties to develop aging programs;

—$200,000 for the growing Respite Care Program;

—$675,000 for increased Chore Services;

—$182,000 for increased Homemaker Services;

—$350,000 for Adult Day Care Services; and

—$292,000 for additional monitoring of care provided in rest homes and nursing homes. I am also requesting $45,000 to develop a new foster family care service which will provide an alternative to group care for older persons needing a supervised living arrangement. An additional $1.4 million will allow us to fund senior centers in the remaining 19 counties currently without them; these centers could then serve as focal points for aging services statewide, offering information and referral as well as direct services to older adults and their families. Some say they aren't needed! That's because their counties have already gotten theirs.

Finally, I will be presenting legislation making it easier for county governments to use property and equipment purchased with state and federal monies to meet the needs of older adults. I hope this legislation will allow counties to match those needs with the resources they have available. I am also supporting passage of Senate Bill 58, which would provide $2 million in additional transportation assistance for older people.[4]

In addition to the first installment, $5 million budget package, I will be encouraging expansion of the Gatekeeper Program, operated by our utilities' meter readers, and the creation of a special housing unit in the Department of Natural Resources and Community Development to devise a state housing plan and methods to increase existing state housing programs using available resources. I will also establish two special task forces: The first will examine methods of public and private financing for long-term care services; the second will determine options for better utilizing resources to expand Medicaid eligibility for providing a prescription drug assistance program for older adults.

These initiatives will address some of the most pressing concerns of our older adults in North Carolina, but will in no way provide full and complete funding for all the services necessary. Government cannot, and should not, provide or pay for all of them. Government does, however, have a major responsibility to help identify the needs and give leadership in planning how to meet them. That is why we are all here today.

We are here to share our ideas, to learn what is already being done, and to determine how to adapt successful existing programs to other areas of the state. You know what the needs are; you may also have better ideas how we can better use our resources to meet those needs or how we can best initiate and expand aging services on the local level. I would encourage you to listen well and to take an active part in the forum discussions. We are here to share our ideas and to work together to build a more secure and rewarding future for older adults in North Carolina. If each of us has an idea, kept to ourselves, then each of us has an idea. If we share our ideas, then each of us will have hundreds of ideas, and some of them will be great.

We have a challenge before us in this "Year of the Older Adult," a challenge and an opportunity. It is our challenge to provide assistance to those who need it, not only for older adults, but through older adults. Meeting this challenge provides us with the opportunity to work together, to coordinate our ideas and our efforts to developing a course of action that will provide security and assistance for our older adults, both now and in the years to come. By enhancing opportunities for the active involvement of our older adults, North Carolina can become first in the nation in enhancing the quality of life for all our citizens; then we will truly become one united state.

---

¹Walter Frederick (Fritz) Mondale (1928-   ), born in Ceylon, Minnesota; B.A., 1951, LL.B., 1956, University of Minnesota; U.S. Army, 1951-1953. Attorney in private practice, 1956-1960; Minnesota attorney general, 1960-1964; U.S. senator from Minnesota, 1964-1977; U.S. vice-president, 1977-1981; defeated by incumbent Ronald Reagan in 1984 presidential election; Democrat. *Who's Who in America, 1986-1987,* II, 1969.

²"Year of the Older Adult, 1988, By the Governor of the State of North Carolina: A Proclamation," February 12, 1988, Governors Papers, James G. Martin.

³In his editorial of March 6, 1987, marking "Employ the Older Worker Week," the governor recommended "the benefits of hiring wisdom, experience, and maturity" that senior citizens characteristically possessed.

⁴S.B. 58, "A Bill to Provide for an Elderly and Handicapped Transportation Assistance Program to be Administered by the Department of Transportation," was introduced February 23, 1987. Initially assigned to the Veterans Affairs and Senior Citizens Committee, the bill was amended and rereferred to the Senate Appropriations Committee on March 17, where it remained through the end of the session. *N.C. Senate Journal, 1987,* 45, 100. H.B. 222, the House companion to the original Senate bill, led a longer life. It stayed alive in the Committee on Aging from March, 1987, until receiving an indefinite postponement report in July, 1988. *N.C. House Journal, 1987,* 109; *N.C. House Journal, 1987, Second Session, 1988,* 305.

FAMILY ISSUES RALLY

RALEIGH, JUNE 9, 1988

It's a great pleasure for me to share in celebrating with you, today, the importance of the family! We are expressing our concern not only for the future of our own families, but for the future of all North Carolina's families.

Without doubt or question, there are many intrusions into today's family, and as you know, the family must be protected and preserved.

It is not only the most basic unit of governance in society, it is the very basis for that concept of home rule—home rule in your own home, the very concept our nation was founded upon. But the family is more: It is a haven; the place of love, learning, and growth.

Unfortunately, there are those today who are infringing upon the traditional role of the family in society, intrusion by those who mean well! Why? Perhaps we've lost our focus as to what the role of the family should be.

Many of you were here in 1985, fighting for parental consent for a minor's abortions. This is not some new, 1988 issue. It makes good family sense for minor, pregnant girls to turn to their parents when seeking abortions. That's home rule, folks! If you must get permission to attend a school field trip or to get your ears pierced, surely it is not unreasonable to require, by law, that minors seek parental consent for an operation involving greater health hazards than going on a field trip or getting one's ears pierced. The bill does allow a girl who has a serious problem seeking parental consent to ask judicial permission, instead. That allows an alternative and assumes that a minor who maintains she is mature enough to seek an abortion should have no problem making an abortion request before a judge.[1]

Tax-funded abortion on demand is still with us! It's not an election-year issue, either. Many of you have been fighting since abortion on demand was funded in North Carolina on July 1, 1978. You have questioned, too, the wisdom of school-based clinics and other abortion-counseling and contraceptive-related issues.

Just a couple of days ago, we had to announce that our revenue estimates for May were a little low.[2] That's not to say that we are going to end up with a deficit for this year. We won't. It means that we will end up with a $175 million revenue surplus, instead of a $220 million revenue surplus—not as much as we thought. It will be a revenue surplus, whatever it is. But as we look for things to trim back on and to accommodate for, I am going to suggest that we also look at the abortion funding which I believe can be reduced even further. As I proposed in previous years, it's a good time to bring that issue up.

As you know, I introduced some strong DWI measures aimed at getting drunken, dangerous drivers off North Carolina roads, stiffening penalties for those who drink and drive. Many of those bills were held up and assigned to be "studied." Once again, North Carolina was put last. Strong DWI legislation has been a major thrust of my administration and of other North Carolina leaders and lawmakers. Election-year politics has nothing to do with it. Representative Coy

Privette, whom most of you know, has offered some excellent DWI legislation.[3]

Drugs are one of our families' deadliest enemies. I've declared war on drug trafficking in North Carolina. I propose that we make the pushers pay—that they serve full sentences with no time off for good behavior, no gain time, no parole. Know, also, that I agree with you that new revenue sources should also be based on what's best for North Carolina. Pari-mutuel betting preys on the weak. It has no place in our quest for greater revenue sources.

North Carolina has the largest women's work force in the nation. Day care is here to stay. The question now, however, is what kind of day care will we have. I propose balanced growth in the realm of day care, supported by parental choice, as to whether it be public or private, church related, home care, Head Start, corporate day care, or other viable day-care options. Parental choice would also include reasonable corporal punishment upon parental request.

We do not need a statewide day-care program for three- and four-year-old children, as some have proposed. Most children get the nurturing they need at home. We need, instead, only to reach out to those disadvantaged, at-risk children who receive too little care, too little opportunities, too little family nurturing.

Finally, our families must be strengthened because stronger families make stronger individuals, and stronger individuals produce a brighter and better world for all of us to live in.

---

[1]H.B. 1068, "A Bill to be Entitled an Act to Require Parental or Judicial Consent for Unemancipated Minor's Abortion," passed the state House on May 28, 1987, and was sent to the Senate, where it remained in the Judiciary I Committee through the end of the session. *N.C. House Jornal, 1987*, 428, 663, 746, 862, 885; *N.C. Senate Journal, 1987*, 580.

[2]See press release, "Statement from the Governor's Office on Tax Revenue Collections," Raleigh, June 7, 1988; other press releases germane to the state budget include "Governor Martin's Response to Proposed Changes in the General Fund Operating Budget for 1988-89," Raleigh, June 9, 1988, and "Governor Martin Responds to Misunderstanding about the N.C. General Fund Credit Balance," Raleigh, June 14, 1988, Governors Papers, James G. Martin.

[3]Coy Clarence Privette (1933-   ), born in Statesville; resident of Cabarrus County; B.A., Wake Forest University, 1955; M.Div., Southeastern Baptist Theological Seminary, 1958; U.S. Army Reserve, since 1953. Pastor, North Kannapolis Baptist Church, 1962-1976; president, Kannapolis Ministerial Assn., 1965; president, 1975-1977, Baptist State Convention; editor, *Tomorrow*; executive director, Christian Action League of North Carolina, Inc.; elected to state House of Representatives, 1984, reelected in 1986; Republican. *North Carolina Manual, 1987-1988*, 475.

MUSEUM OF HISTORY GROUNDBREAKING

RALEIGH, JUNE 14, 1988

This ceremonial groundbreaking is a significant event for all North Carolinians. In three short years, North Carolina will have a magnificent new Museum of History. Our museum programs, which reach hundreds of thousands of citizens each year, will be greatly enhanced and strengthened. These are exciting prospects, prospects that should make us all proud of what has [been] and is being accomplished.

The success of this project is the result of a total team effort. I want to pay special tribute to Cultural Resources Secretary Patric Dorsey, who has provided outstanding leadership, and I know you will all be pleased to know that she has been recovering nicely, thank you, and will be going home on Thursday.[1]

Our General Assembly has provided strong and steadfast support. The North Carolina Museum of History Associates also have worked diligently to encourage enthusiastic private-sector involvement. To date, $25 million, in all, has been appropriated, contributed, or pledged for the new museum. Together with the support of North Carolinians from every corner of our state, this commitment enables us to construct a truly unique history museum dedicated to educating our citizens about their heritage.

For ninety years North Carolina has attempted, through selective collecting and exhibiting, to preserve the artifacts of its history for a grateful posterity. Since [the] days of Colonel Fred Olds at the turn of the century, our museum of history has had four separate homes.[2] Cramped quarters, limited exhibition space, and restricted storage have been perennial problems. Yet, last year, 180,000 schoolchildren and adults learned about our state's social, economic, and political history when they visited the present museum on Jones Street. But because of crowded conditions, guided tours had to be suspended during heavy visitation periods. One third of requests for hands-on children's history programs had to be refused because of inadequate classroom space.

The lack of space has also posed problems in presenting the museum's outstanding collection of 300,000 historical artifacts. There is only enough room to display 10 percent of the objects at any given time. The remaining 90 percent are stored in such overcrowded conditions that secure preservation of many of the artifacts is endangered. In this new facility, exhibition space will be nearly three and a half times that of the present museum: 50,000 square feet versus 14,500 square feet. A much larger portion of the museum's collection of artifacts, one third rather than one tenth, will be on display.

As Governor Hunt has noted, when the Art Museum moved to its fine new quarters on Blue Ridge Road in 1983, it was determined that its former building on Morgan Street would become the new home for the Museum of History, after renovation and the addition of a new wing.[3] That, however, still would have required continued use of the present Archives and History Building for many office needs. Meanwhile, the Department of Transportation presented its expansion needs, for which the former Art Museum on Morgan Street was both adequate and contiguous, and therefore ideal. So it was that in 1985 our plans were recast, with the strong commitment of our General Assembly, to take advantage of the availability of this space on Bicentennial Plaza for a magnificent, new, North Carolina Museum of History, which we initiate today.

When the exterior design was presented to the Capital Planning Commission, the handsome colonnade on the west front offered a proper and dignified appearance for the main entrance facing the Agriculture Building. Suggestions that the southern side be enhanced with an additional entrance and other suitable architectural features to improve stylistic consistency with surrounding structures were readily incorporated into the design. Exterior use of limestone and two shades of granite are specified to further harmonize with neighboring buildings, especially including our state Capitol building, as will the blending of distinctively modern features with neoclassic styling elements.

Upon entering, you will find permanent exhibits to interpret the chronological history of our state. There will be a North Carolina folk art and crafts gallery, plus a permanent home for the North Carolina Sports Hall of Fame. Increased gallery space will accommodate more changing exhibitions as well as the loan of important exhibits from other museums. Our first changing exhibit to be scheduled will be "North Carolina Women: Private Lives and Public Roles." This is certain to be an important and popular exhibition.

A 300-seat auditorium, six classrooms, and a modern research library will serve the museum's growing educational activities. The main entrance to the museum, located on Bicentennial Plaza, will permit visitors to view handicraft demonstrations from the mall. Conservation laboratories, a design studio, and 17,000 square feet for collection storage will greatly enhance the technical assistance the museum can provide. Centrally located across from the Capitol and the state Legislative Building, the new museum will become a center-piece in downtown Raleigh and a source of pride for all our citizens; underground parking for 650 cars and handsome restaurant facilities will add to its attractiveness.

I am excited about our new Museum of History. When completed, it will be able to reach more people with better services. Special education programs for schoolchildren will be quadrupled. Majestic, modern, and handsome, the new North Carolina Museum of History will illustrate our commitment to our heritage as well as demonstrate that, in North Carolina, we are resolved to build a future for our past.

---

[1]Secretary Dorsey fractured her clavicle and seven ribs in a motor accident in the vicinity of Raleigh-Durham International Airport on May 27, 1988. *News and Observer*, May 28, 1988.

[2]Fred A. Olds (1853-1935), probably born in Pitt County; was buried in Oakwood Cemetery, Raleigh. An amateur state historian, Olds amassed a private collection of 30,000 historical artifacts that ultimately formed the basis of the North Carolina Museum of History. William Burlie Brown, "The State Literary and Historical Association, 1900-1950," *North Carolina Historical Review*, XXVIII (April, 1951), 169-170; *Durham Sun*, June 15, 1977; Frontis W. Johnston, "The North Carolina Literary and Historical Association, 1900-1975," *North Carolina Historical Review*, LIII (April, 1976), 157.

[3]Former governor Hunt and Lieutenant Governor Jordan joined Martin in making remarks at the History Museum groundbreaking. *News and Observer*, June 15, 1988.

NORTH STATE LAW ENFORCEMENT OFFICERS ASSOCIATION

ROCKY MOUNT, JUNE 16, 1988

Thank you for this opportunity to meet with you, today, to discuss some very important matters that are of our mutual concern. The North State Law Enforcement Officers Association has a long and distinguished history of leadership on criminal justice matters in North Carolina. This Thirty-sixth Annual Retraining Conference is an example of this organization's ongoing commitment to professional excellence.

In the years since the founding of your organization, the face of law enforcement has changed in North Carolina. More and more, our law enforcement agencies are reflecting the makeup of our state's population. Women, blacks, and other minorities are not only patrolling our streets and highways in greater numbers, they are also involved in setting policy more than at any other time in the past. We have not reached perfection or the ideal of proportionate participation, but we're moving toward it.

Much has been done to increase opportunities in law enforcement in North Carolina. However, much more needs to be done. Secretary Joe Dean of the Department of Crime Control and Public Safety has informed me that the number of black state highway patrolmen has doubled in the last three years. The same has happened with the A.L.E., the Alcohol Law Enforcement agency: We've more than doubled the number of minority officers. We're not up to where we should be, but nobody has done more at the state level.

We have aggressively recruited new troopers from the minority community. We have also made a concerted effort to move minority troopers up the ranks by promoting from within. In addition to the hiring of new troopers and A.L.E. agents, we have actively sought the advice and counsel from organizations such as yours on matters of public policy. Recently, you made it known that you wanted to have more input into the deliberations of the Governor's Crime Commission. Acting on your recommendation, last month I appointed Felicia Redmond, a Raleigh student from a law enforcement family, as a member of the commission, based on recommendations from some of your leaders; and we will continue to explore ways to make your voice heard in the state capital.

An important aspect of the quality of life here in North Carolina is the ability to pursue our goals without the fear of being victimized by criminals. To preserve and enhance that lifestyle, we have established laws that respect the rights of individuals and protect the common good. How we enforce our law is as important as the law itself. It takes a special kind of dedication to do the job that needs to be done.

Contemporary novelist Tom Wolfe wrote a novel, *The Right Stuff*, about the skills, courage, and personal lives of early astronauts and test pilots.[1] You, the law enforcement officers of our state, are the ones with the right stuff to do this job. On behalf of all of the people of North Carolina, thank you for your willingness to put it on the line each and every day so all of us can live safely and without fear.

As law enforcement officers, you look to elected officials such as me to give you the moral support and resources with which to do this all-important job. For our part, we have to work to create an environment which discourages criminal activity and encourages appropriate social behavior. To that end, state government has undertaken a number of crime prevention initiatives:

—Through a program of both education and enforcement, we have tackled the hideous crime of child abuse.

—We have aggressively promoted crime prevention within public housing.

—We have called attention to the plight of the victims of crime.

—We have enlisted the public's help in the war against crime through programs such as Community Watch and Crimestoppers.

—To provide our children with better role models, we have created an advisory board of Athletes Against Crime.[2]

—Through the Students Against Driving Drunk, S.A.D.D., and Mothers Against Drunk Driving, M.A.D.D., programs, we have enlisted public support in our crusade to make our highways safer.

—And through "Operation Eagle" and "Wolfpack," we have taken that crusade to the streets through strict enforcement of our state's DWI laws.

Perhaps our most significant efforts at crime prevention lie in the area of public education; by providing the people of our state with quality educational opportunities, we are enhancing their chances for success. To give you a better feel for the importance of education as a deterrent to crime, I would like to cite some startling statistics from the North Carolina Department of Correction. Ninety-five percent of the inmates currently in state prisons have tested at a level less than that of a high school graduate, and more than half have tested at an educational level of sixth grade or less. That's a strong correlation. With those figures in mind, is it really a surprise that some of our people turn to a life of crime?

Although it is the individual who is ultimately responsible for his or her own actions, it is our responsibility, as a society, to make certain that each citizen has access to a quality education. In the budget I submitted to the General Assembly last month, I earmarked funds for a number of educational programs that could play a major role in the fight against crime. I am seeking more than $3.5 million for eight pilot preschool programs to target four-year-olds who run a high risk of later becoming high school dropouts. Another $700,000 is set aside for the expansion of the Communities in Schools program, such as they've developed here at Rocky Mount, and Guilford County, and earlier, at Charlotte. I have asked the General Assembly for $214,000 for a new Office of Literacy; this agency would establish a statewide literacy referral system and would develop a comprehensive plan to coordinate literacy activities.

I would like to have been able to report to you, today, that these programs had been warmly received by state lawmakers. However, for reasons of their own, these and other worthy programs were cut from my budget by the Joint Appropriations Committee after less than one hour of deliberations. The legislative leadership has claimed that my budget overestimates revenues. However, their budget changes reflect about the same monies for revenues as my budget. That leaves me to believe that there is some other reason, a hidden agenda, behind these budget cuts.

Some have made headlines saying we have run a deficit, but that's false. The truth is, we will end this fiscal year with a $400 million surplus—the largest in history. It is my hope that the legislature will restore these and other worthy programs to the budget. These programs are just too important to be frivolously tossed aside.

The promotion of crime prevention programs is surely an important element in the battle against crime; we need more of it, but it is not the only element. We must also have an aggressive program of law enforcement. To accomplish this, state and local governments need to give people like you the resources you need to do your very best out in the field. For that very reason, I have submitted a number of significant proposals to the General Assembly.

I don't have to tell you that North Carolina is in the deadly grip of drug abuse. The Governor's Crime Commission has estimated that more than 30,000 drug-related crimes are committed within our borders each year. Property losses from those crimes have been estimated at more than $100 million.

Although North Carolina has in place some of the toughest drug trafficking laws in the land, they have been watered down by other sentencing laws that allow many pushers to become eligible for parole after having served only one eighth of their sentences. When one considers the human misery these criminals have brought to our people, I can't help but question the wisdom of laws that give these people a break that for good behavior in prison to speed back to their bad behavior selling dangerous drugs. For that reason, I have proposed legislation that eliminates parole and good-time and gain-time credits for convicted drug traffickers. They should know that if they are convicted of trafficking drugs in North Carolina, they will serve out their time with no hope of parole or early release.

I have also proposed an amendment to the state's continuing criminal enterprise statute that would provide for mandatory life sentences for drug kingpins convicted under this law, and again, without benefit of parole or good- and gain-time credits. It should be real life.

I have often been asked what effect will these proposals have on the prison overcrowding problem. Let me tell you how Correction Secretary Aaron Johnson answers that question. He says, "If these are not the kind of people that prisons were meant for, then why have any prisons at all?"

The war against drugs is not a political issue; it is a people issue. That's why I am throwing the full support of my office behind worthy anti-drug proposals of both Democratic and Republican legislators:

—I have asked the General Assembly to permanently enact a law that allows a district attorney to convene a special investigative grand jury for the purpose of probing drug trafficking. Otherwise, the law will expire on October 1.[3]

—I support Representative Charles Cromer's bill which designates drug trafficking as one of the aggravating circumstances that can be considered in the imposition of the death penalty in first-degree murder cases.[4]

—I also support Senator Harold Hardison's bill that would make it a felony to possess any amount of cocaine. Cocaine represents a unique threat to our society and is extremely addictive. This legislation is especially needed now since crack is so readily available in small, inexpensive amounts. The Governor's Crime Commission also supports this measure.[5]

Another serious problem that is being addressed by state government is drunken driving. Nearly half of the people that die each year on our state's highways are killed in DWI-related crashes. Many of those killed are the drunk drivers. Too often, those killed are innocent victims whose only fault was to be driving along without knowing a drunk driver was nearby. It is a senseless slaughter that must be stopped.

During this short session of the General Assembly, I am supporting a package of DWI laws that was introduced last year but left in legislative limbo. This package includes an immediate thirty-day license revocation for DWI offenders. It would also lower from .10 percent to .04 percent the presumptive blood alcohol level for commercial drivers—trucks and buses. It is a package that has the support of the people of North Carolina. It deserves the support of the General Assembly.

In an effort to promote highway safety and the safety of the general public, I am asking state lawmakers for sixty additional highway patrolmen. It should be noted that while this administration has sought an additional 175 troopers to patrol our highways, the legislature has only granted about half of those requests. I'm trying for another sixty right now. Don't hold your breath.

When we talk about toughening our laws, it is important to remember that one cannot expect to make changes at one end of the criminal justice system without having an impact at the other end of the system. However, that's exactly what this state has been doing for years, and that is why it has become necessary to upgrade our state's correctional system.

The state is currently engaged in the largest prison construction program in its history. This is necessary if we are to convince the courts that North Carolina can operate a prison system that is constitutionally defensible. Failure to do so would mean that we, the people of this state, could lose the right to determine how to operate our prisons. The federal courts could take over our prisons and run them at the expense of other worthy programs. You need only to ask the people of Texas to discover that that is something we don't want to happen here.

When this administration came in, we inherited a badly overcrowded prison system with no existing plan to solve it. We have come up with a plan, and we're meeting the problem head on. We are building new prisons, and we also are looking at alternatives to incarceration for those persons who can pay their debt to society, for nonviolent crimes, and make restitution to their victims without going to prison. It is a concept that I proposed two years ago and only now is beginning to gain some acceptance within the General Assembly. By the way, in my book, "nonviolent crimes" do not include drug trafficking. That is as violent as any other terrorist assault.

We must ensure that those persons that are on probation or parole are under adequate supervision. My budget recommendations include proposals designed to beef up the Division of Adult Probation and Parole.[6] Unfortunately, those proposals were among those that were cut by the Joint Appropriations Committee last week. In the interest of public safety, they need to be restored to the budget.

A lot has been done to create the crime-free environment of which I spoke earlier. We are moving closer, every day, to a public consensus on a broad range of criminal justice issues. In public gatherings and private meetings, the people of North Carolina have made their wishes known. They want to be safe—in their homes, at their jobs, and on the highways. They want an end to illegal drug trafficking. They want an end to the abuse of children, senior citizens, and the defenseless. They want to get drunk drivers off our streets and highways. They want a strong system of public education that promotes economic growth and reduces the temptations of crime. They want a prison system that preserves public safety and serves the cause of justice.

State government, working closely with the people of this state and with law enforcement groups such as yours, can see to it that these wishes are fulfilled. It requires hard work, some sacrifice, and a willingness on the part of the general public to give law enforcement officers such as yourselves the support and resources necessary to get the job done. I know you will join me in this effort—after all, you're the ones out on the front lines.

You are the defensive line. I hope you appreciate having our support, so you can face your responsibilities with the confidence that we're behind you, doing our best to make your arrests count. Good luck out there. We depend on you, and thank you.

---

[1]Tom Wolfe, *The Right Stuff* (New York: Farrar, Straus, and Giroux, 1979).

[2]Executive Order Number 56 established the Governor's Advisory Board on Athletes Against Crime. *N.C. Session Laws, 1987, Regular Session, 1988,* III, 927-930.

[3]"An Act to Extend an Act Permitting Grand Juries to Investigate Drug Trafficking and Concerning Criminal Contempt and Immunity" was ratified July 5, 1988. *N.C. Session Laws, 1987, Regular Session, 1988,* III, c. 1040.

[4]Representative Charles Cromer introduced H.B. 755, "A Bill to Be Entitled an Act to Add Murder Committed while Engaged in Drug Trafficking as an Aggravating Circumstance in Determining Whether to Impose the Death Sentence on a Convicted Defendant," on April 17, 1987. The Judiciary Committee No. 4 approved a substitute bill that passed the House on May 28. Once delivered to the Senate, the measure remained in committee through the end of the session. *N.C. House Journal, 1987,* 304, 717, 833, 865, 885; *N.C. Senate Journal, 1987,* 594, 606.

Charles Lemuel Cromer (1939-   ), born in High Point; resident of Davidson County; B.A., University of North Carolina at Chapel Hill, 1972; J.D., Wake Forest University, 1975; U.S. Army, 1962-1965. Insurance adjustor, 1967-1971; attorney, since 1975, and law teacher, 1975-1982, Davidson Community College; member, state House of Representatives, since 1985; Republican. *North Carolina Manual, 1987-1988,* 409.

[5]The committee substitute for S.B. 213, "A Bill to Make the Possession of Any Quantity of Cocaine a Felony," passed the Senate on May 19, 1987. It did not clear the House, however, where it remained in the Judiciary No. 2 Committee through the end of the session. *N.C. House Journal, 1987,* 661; *N.C. Senate Journal, 1987,* 136, 431, 449.

[6]The governor requested additional intensive probation-parole teams, parole officers, and supervisory, support, and clerical personnel, in his *Recommended Changes to the 1988-89 State Budget,* 38-39.

OPENING REMARKS, 1988 SOUTHERN REGIONAL EDUCATION BOARD ANNUAL MEETING AND LEGISLATIVE WORK CONFERENCE

NASHVILLE, TENNESSEE, JUNE 20, 1988

It is an honor to open this combined annual meeting of the Southern Regional Education Board and Legislative Work Conference observing SREB's fortieth anniversary. Occasions such as this recall our roots and our historic development. This occasion is not just important for the board, but it also commemorates the SREB Legislative Work Conference which first met in this city in 1952. I invite you, today, to travel quickly with me through four decades of SREB history.

At the close of the Second World War, it seemed that the South, after all, might not rise again. Frankly, we lived in a depressed region that languished in an antiquated agricultural economy. Many native southerners were fleeing to the North and West for the promise of greater opportunity. Too many of those who remained bore the twin burdens of poverty and illiteracy, and, except for a few pockets of excellence, the South was looked down upon as a backwater of American education.

Now, four decades later, the picture is startlingly different. The region's economy is diversified and modernized, boasting urban areas that are hubs of transportation, manufacturing, and service industries. The brain drain has reversed, as the South is keeping more of its "best and brightest" and is attracting a steady influx of new, highly educated residents from other regions. Furthermore, education has advanced dramatically through new initiatives to improve public schools and additional university programs of excellence.

In the mid-1940s, no one had even imagined a Research Triangle Park in North Carolina. Where once there were only pine trees, there are now 30,000 talented men and women working at the frontiers of high technology. Such dramatic developments are being repeated elsewhere in our region. For example, Austin, Texas, boasts two new major national facilities in microelectronics and in semiconductor research, and Texas's chief competitors for these national centers were other SREB states.

Four decades ago, who would have dreamed that the South would have nearly half of the finalists for a major scientific installation, the so-called super collider. In the late 1940s, who would have guessed that in the 1980s the nation's three newest and most advanced automobile factories would be located in southern states? Who would have envisioned that our nation's "space research triangle" would be anchored by Cape Canaveral, Huntsville, and Houston? And today, we have not even begun to imagine what it will mean for the South to be America's spaceport as space activities become one of the key industrial sectors in the twenty-first century.

Forty years ago, if someone had said a southern state would set out to create $1 million endowed chairs to attract some of the nation's most outstanding faculty and, in less than ten years, establish more than 100 of these million-dollar endowments, we would have thought the person was crazy. If that prognosticator had predicted that half of the southern states would start similar programs, and that by the year 2000 there could be several hundred of these endowed chairs at universities in the South, we would have been convinced that the person was mad. In short, who would have foreseen, forty years ago, the South as the nation's premier force in a campaign for educational reform and quest for quality in our schools and in higher education?

Perhaps very few persons held such a vision. Just maybe it was some of these persons with that vision who had a hand in creating the Southern Regional Education Board. Admittedly, there are shadows that still cross this encouraging canvas; we cannot deny that, but few would deny the conclusion that the South has risen. How did we do it?

To make these great strides, it took leadership, and vision, and a sense of regional cooperation unlike that seen anywhere else in the nation. The idea of regionalism took root and flowered in southern soil. In fact, I am proud to say that the vision of interstate cooperation was shaped and adapted by southerners, such as North Carolina's Howard Odum.[1]

We had witnessed the early successes of the Tennessee Valley Authority in producing power and managing resources. The hour had come to attempt an interstate partnership to address our states' mutual problems in education; and, in 1948, the postwar generation of southern governers met in Wakulla Springs, Florida, and called for creation of an interstate compact. The Southern Regional Education Board was born.

Looking back over the forty years, we can now see that SREB was bound to succeed. As a former college science professor, I can observe that the chemistry for regional cooperation was mixed and ready. Southern political and educational leaders already shared a sense of region and common dreams. They all faced the reality factor of extremely scarce fiscal and human resources. They all were seeking new ways to solve lingering problems.

The immediate challenge in 1948 was to address the region's critical shortage of physicians, veterinarians, and dentists, and SREB responded with practical steps that have been the hallmark of its problem-solving initiatives over the past four decades. These realistic solutions are the products of the continuing forum SREB provides, for political leaders in the executive and legislative branches, and educational leaders in state agencies and on campuses, to keep talking with each other forthrightly.

Over the years, SREB has earned the reputation as a reliable source for comparative, usable information, for states, on emerging issues. SREB has helped states to anticipate trends and move with the times with collective will and optimism.

Any overview of the board's impressive history would recognize the past importance of two key developments in the fifties, namely the heightened involvement of state legislators in charting the board's directions and the concerted drive to develop a comprehensive program of higher education research.

From this solid base of sustained involvement of legislators as well as governors and educators in board planning, and with the data that could be trusted, the South entered the sixties as a new era was dawning in economic development, race relations, and education. SREB responded, in 1961, with a goals commission of distinguished lay leaders, who enunciated five broad, long-term goals crucial to the development of higher education and southern society. The commission underscored its optimism by calling its report *Within Our Reach*.[2] This blue-ribbon panel sounded a call that was startling for that era: It challenged the South to measure its progress against national benchmarks of excellence.

Planning and quality are still watchwords of SREB. Today, SREB and state agencies cooperate in a regional network for the exchange and analysis of data on public colleges and universities. Thus, the board is able to provide up-to-the-minute information to educational and governmental leaders faced with immediate policy choices. The drive toward greater quality in education impels SREB to continually emphasize the school-college link and insist on one simple fact: Our colleges can only be as good as our schools.

Before our states had the luxury of an undivided focus on quality, we had to catch up with access, and in the sixties, southern states moved together to expand higher education. In particular, SREB states turned to SREB to help improve postsecondary educational opportunities for black students in both predominantly black and predominantly white institutions. Over the years, North Carolina's William R. Kenan Charitable Trust provided nearly $13 million in targeted funding for a broad-based program to accomplish real opportunity for our black youth.

In the seventies, SREB widened its program of regional sharing of scarce education resources from professional schools to uncommon graduate and undergraduate programs. Through SREB's Academic Common Market, some 1,000 programs at 128 senior colleges and universities in the South are now available at in-state tuition rates, yielding savings to students, institutions, and states. SREB's *Priorities* statement rallied the region to sustain the vitality of higher education in the fact of stable enrollments and increasingly scarce resources as the economy fluctuated.[3]

In 1981, SREB commanded the national spotlight with its report, *The Need for Quality*, which advanced the country's first proposals for educational reform through higher standards in teaching, and learning, and through closer ties between schools and colleges.[4] SREB's recommendations preceded by two years the first of many similar nationwide reports. Furthermore, SREB's analysis undergirded unrivaled action in SREB states, firmly establishing the South as the nation's leader in educational reform. This region has moved from last place in innovation to the vanguard of educational leadership in less than two-score years, and SREB has helped us greatly to achieve this status.

Our region has taken the lead nationally in developing innovative programs to raise the professional standing of public schoolteachers through career ladder programs. While varying in some particulars, the essential feature of these efforts is to evaluate the competence and effectiveness of teachers as a basis for promotions without having to leave the classroom. This new reform will provide better pay for better teachers and will earn the support of all other taxpayers as a means of lifting our SREB states to the front rank in pay for teachers.

Throughout the eighties, the board has relentlessly followed through on these recommendations for quality improvement on several educational fronts, including strengthening teacher education, improving quality in undergraduate education, and bolstering the basic educational tools in vocational training. Last year, SREB conducted a review of state initiatives to improve educational quality. The board acknowledged substantial progress but stressed that long-term public support requires some results from quality-improvement initiatives. In an effort to measure the pace of quality advancements, SREB and the National Assessment of Educational Progress [have] piloted the nation's first program to test student achievement in such a way that the results can be compared across the board.

Thus, the stage is now set for long-lived educational improvements. We know what we want, and we have ways to see if we are getting results, but will the region stay the course? Will we manifest the collective will to make the commitments of efforts and dollars to achieve these goals?

I think we will. We must. The key reason is that, again and again, our citizens rank education as their number-one priority. They want access to quality education. With the cooperative spirit and frank exchange available through the Southern Regional Education Board, we can, together, give our youth the gift of a quality education.

The number forty will be used many times during this anniversary meeting, but let me more modestly suggest four areas where we must keep pushing ahead:

1. We must do what any good team does that excels—that is, it executes its game plan well. We have to successfully implement the many educational reform plans we now have under way. To do this, to keep the public's support for the long term, I believe we have to set educational goals to which we and our citizens can aspire. Those goals can help drive the support for long-term educational improvement. You will be hearing more about this in a few minutes from Dick Riley.

2. We simply must find ways to help students be more successful in secondary education and increase the numbers that graduate from high school. I believe nearly everyone is now agreed our school drop-out problem is a national tragedy, and I believe we have the resolve to do something about it. It is high time we did.

3. One of the most important ways we can help the potential high school graduates of the early twenty-first century is to help them today, when they are four years old. We know today that students don't suddenly become school dropouts at age sixteen or seventeen. The problems that lead to school dropouts may have roots that go back sixteen or seventeen years. The only reason they drop out in high school is because they could not legally do so any earlier. The problem arises because so many were never ready to drop in in the first, second, and third grades; 10 to 25 percent did not get the nurturing benefit of sitting on the knee of someone who cared to read to them at an early age.

We need to do a lot more to nip these problems in the bud. That is why I have recommended in North Carolina a preschool program for four-year-olds that will pay long-term benefits. The early childhood development programs have been the missing piece in our reform efforts. I believe we can make early childhood readiness training the foundation of our reform programs, and it's time to do so.

4. We are doing a better job at it, but I think government and education [are] still missing opportunities to bring business and corporate leaders into partnerships in building quality in our schools and colleges. In many of our states, we would not have the educational reform efforts today without the active support of business and corporate leaders in passing those reforms. Their support is as crucial, or more so, in implementing the reforms. I don't believe that we are

making the most of these opportunities. I urge SREB, perhaps through the board's support of goals for educational improvement, to work with business and corporate leaders on a specific agenda of cooperation to advance educational quality.

I can't think of a better example of the importance of corporate leadership, and the difference it can make in improving education, than embodied in the actions of the chairman and chief executive officer of the Duke Power Company, Mr. William States Lee.[5] I am extremely pleased to have Bill Lee here today. It is appropriate that he is here today, with governors of North Carolina and South Carolina, for his company is a major influence in both states—not only for the electric power it provides, but also for the power it gives in support of education.

William Lee, chairman and chief executive officer of Duke Power Company, is a native of Charlotte, North Carolina, and is grandson of the company's first chief engineer. A civil engineer who graduated Phi Beta Kappa and *magna cum laude* from Princeton University, he joined Duke Power's engineering department as a junior designer in 1955, became executive vice-president in 1976, president and chief operating officer in 1982, and assumed his present position in 1987. He is chairman of the board of trustees of Queens College, in Charlotte, and is also a trustee for the University of North Carolina at Charlotte Foundation. Mr. Lee is a member of many and varied industry, professional, and civil organizations and has received numerous awards; I'm going to mention only two of the latter. He received Duke Power's Robinson Award for outstanding service in the educational community and, just a few weeks ago, was awarded an honorary degree by the University of North Carolina at Charlotte.

Before we hear from Mr. Lee, I would like to say a word about Duke Power and its commitment to improving education—particularly for citizens of North Carolina and South Carolina. The company has a program known as PIE, for Power in Education, that is active in every community with a Duke Power plant. How the organization feels about the link between education and industry is, perhaps, best illustrated by the fact that not only is an individual at each plant designated to be responsible for the local Power in Education efforts, in most cases, that person is the plant manager.

Duke Power is deeply involved in literacy training for its employees, for those whose basic skills are inadequate and to encourage those employees who have the basic skills to improve them. The company supports literacy programs at eighteen adult education centers in North Carolina and sixteen centers in South Carolina. I'm sure we will be hearing about literacy training, as well as other aspects of Duke's Power in Education program, as Mr. Lee presents his views on education and the future economy of the South. I am pleased to present a personal friend, and a friend of education, Bill Lee.

---

[1]Howard Washington Odum (1884-1954), born in Bethlehem, Georgia; was buried in Chapel Hill; A.B., Emory College (later University), 1904; A.M., University of Mississippi, 1906; Ph.D., Clark University, 1909; Ph.D., Columbia University, 1910; honorary degrees. Sociologist; dean, School of Liberal Arts, Emory University, 1919-1920; Kenan Professor of Sociology, 1920-1954, School of Public Welfare director, 1920-1932, Institute for Research in Social Science director, 1924-1944, University of North Carolina at Chapel Hill; chairman, North Carolina Civil Works Administration, 1933-1934, North Carolina Commission on Interracial Cooperation, 1933-1935, and of North Carolina Emergency Relief Administration, 1933-1935; author; Democrat. *Who Was Who in America, 1951-1960*, 650.

[2]Commission on Goals for Higher Education in the South, *Within Our Reach* ([Atlanta: Southern Regional Education Board, 1961]).

[3]*Priorities for Postsecondary Education in the South: A Position Statement* (Atlanta: Southern Regional Education Board, 1976).

[4]*The Need for Quality: A Report to the Southern Regional Education Board by its Task Force on Higher Education and the Schools, June, 1981* (Atlanta: Southern Regional Education Board, 1981).

[5]William States Lee (1929-   ), native, resident of Charlotte; B.S., Princeton University, 1951; U.S. Naval Reserve, 1951-1954. Registered professional engineer; various positions with Duke Power Co. since 1955, including vice-president of engineering, 1965-1971, senior vice-president, 1971-1975, executive vice-president, 1976-1977, president-chief operating officer, 1978-1982, and chairman-chief executive officer, since 1982. *Who's Who in America, 1988-1989*, II, 1834.

VETERANS OF FOREIGN WARS

Winston-Salem, June 24, 1988

[The governor closed the following address by presenting a certificate of appreciation to Carroll Smith, state commander of the Veterans of Foreign Wars.[1]]

Thank you [for] giving me this opportunity to address you, this evening. To begin, I would first like to recognize Colonel Billy Summerlin.[2] Colonel Summerlin is the provost marshal at Camp LeJeune. He also happens to be the Law Enforcement Officer of the Year, chosen by the Veterans of Foreign Wars from many applications. Congratulations, Colonel Summerlin.

And how about Patrick Jordan? He won the state VFW Voice of Democracy contest and placed third in the national contest, for which he received a $6,000 scholarship.[3] Talk about being proud: Tim Pittman, a former winner, is on my staff. Tim's mother is here, and she's very proud of him.[4]

I can't help remembering the story about a professor from UNC who received an invitation to make the Memorial Day address to a local post of the American Legion. Looking at the invitation, he found himself in somewhat of a dilemma. It read: "You are invited to be one of our speakers at our Memorial Day meeting. The program includes the mayor, recitation of Lincoln's Gettysburg Address by a high school boy, your address, and then the firing squad."

Seriously, I can never address a veterans' group without a sense of deep reverence and gratitude. It is a time for revisitation of the sacred values you have exemplified in your service to your country—values of duty, honor, and country. Thus it is mandatory that every speech, to a group such as the Veterans of Foreign Wars, be a celebration to our beloved nation and of thanksgiving for what you have given and continue to give. I say that with great humility because no words can possibly repay you for your service and sacrifice.

As I stand here this evening, I cannot help but recall one of the truly moving experiences of my life. It was a crisp, bright morning on last October 22, at Valley Forge, Pennsylvania. We had flown there, by C-130, to dedicate the North Carolina Medal of Honor Grove, a place of honor for North Carolinians who have displayed extraordinary acts of valor in all wars. You and all North Carolinians can be proud that we now have our special place at Valley Forge.

Today, we have in North Carolina 683,000 living veterans. These veterans, and their dependents, and the dependents of deceased veterans, make up approximately 35 percent of our population. To put it mildly, veterans constitute a powerful constituency in our state.

To help us keep in touch with your needs and concerns, we have the Division of Veterans Affairs to assist veterans in North Carolina, along with their dependents and the dependents of deceased veterans, in obtaining the benefits to which they are entitled. This agency also serves as an advocate for veterans.

When the Division of Veterans Affairs talks, I listen. They told me the old law for veterans preference in state government didn't work anymore. I listened—and got it fixed.[5]

Our state and nation have a debt of gratitude to the men and women who have served in our armed forces—and to those who have fought on foreign soils to ensure and protect our liberties—from Valley Forge, to the beaches of Normandy, to the islands of the Pacific, to Korea, to Vietnam. It is a debt that never can be fully repaid.

To change the mood a bit, here's a question: Why did the chicken walk down the middle of the road? Answer: So it could lay it on the line.

Well, you and other veterans have laid a lot on the line; we in government must also lay it on the line by being as responsive as possible to the needs of veterans. Compassion and fairness require no less of us, and I am not talking about handouts. I'm talking about hand-ups. I'm talking about our putting our hands and heads together to form an ongoing partnership to resolve some chronic problems relating to the welfare of veterans.

Last year the division field offices responded to more than 198,000 requests for assistance. In fiscal year 1987, federal expenditures for veterans in our state totaled more than $732 million, including $507 million in direct payments to veterans.

The division also administers one of the largest and most generous state scholarship programs in the country for the children of deceased, or disabled, veterans and POWs or MIAs. Since 1945, more than 13,000 scholarships have been awarded under this program. I know of no better way for a grateful state to honor its veterans than by providing scholarship opportunities for their children, and the need is even greater now with the federal cuts in scholarship and loan programs.

As many of you know, two years ago I appointed Charles Harris as full-time chairman of the Governor's Jobs for Veterans Committee. There are a number of concerns that are being addressed; one of these concerns is veterans preference, giving preference to veterans for employment in state government, as I said earlier.

Our veterans preference policy was adopted October 1, 1987, by my executive order. This policy is bearing fruit as evidenced by the following numbers: During fiscal year 1987-1988, 1,448 veterans were newly hired into state government—342 more than in 1986-1987. In the three-year period, we have seen the percentage of new hires increase from 9.7 to 11.4 percent. This is a 14.7 percent increase in veterans hiring over 1986-1987, when 1,157 veterans were hired. In fact, 643 vets were promoted during 1987-1988.

Can we do better? We think we can. We are doing better all the time; that is our goal. I am happy to report that with the coordinated efforts of the Employment Security Commission and the Governor's Office on Jobs for Veterans, placement of veterans has been outstanding.

One of the main efforts of the Governor's Jobs for Veterans Office is to bring together veterans' representatives, in a given area, with veterans who are looking for jobs, on a one-on-one basis. This approach has been highly productive, as many of you here know. Just how effective this public-private, essentially grass-roots effort has been can be seen in the following statistics: In the last eleven months, we have placed a total of 20,700 veterans in jobs. Of this total, 8,478 have been Vietnam-era veterans. The disabled veteran job placement stands at 1,486.

What we are seeing, in this program and in veteran preference practices in state government, is implementation of the governor's policy relating to employment preference for veterans, which states: "It shall be the policy of the state of North Carolina that, in appreciation for their service to this state and this country in time of war, and in recognition of the time and advantage lost toward the pursuit of a civilian career, veterans shall be granted preference in employment with every state department, agency, and university." This isn't just rhetoric. We are actually carrying out our commitment.

The Employment Security Commission [ESC] is operating a program to find, identify, and provide technical advisory assistance to over 1,800 Federal Contract Joint Leadership employers to enhance their compliance with affirmative action and recruitment obligations with respect to veterans, to increase listings of job openings with local job offices, and thus, to increase the job placement opportunities for disabled, Vietnam-era, and recently separated veterans with FCJL employers. With the information we have gained, we estimate that there are now over 10,000 FCJL employers located within the five service delivery areas of our state. To maintain the momentum we have created in job placements for veterans through this program, I asked the General Assembly to appropriate $185,000 in additional matching funds for the Veterans' Title IV-C program, of which the FCJL program is a part.[6]

Because this $185,000 would be matched with federal funds, we are actually talking about $370,000 for veterans jobs programs. This money would provide for five additional employment and training assistants in the five service areas. It is estimated that these additional funds would result in placement of approximately 1,325 targeted veterans into unsubsidized jobs and training programs in the five service areas. My request was turned down by the General Assembly.

This money is urgently needed to address serious problems related to veteran unemployment. While we have seen a growth of 300,000 jobs; and investments in new and expanded facilities of $15 billion by businesses in the past three years; and are enjoying a 3.5 percent statewide unemployment rate, the lowest unemployment rate since

ESC began keeping records, Vietnam veterans in North Carolina are experiencing an unemployment rate of 9.8 percent. This is clearly unacceptable.

This high unemployment rate is said to be due in considerable measure to many Vietnam vets having work histories below average by company standards. Many veterans, in addition to having never worked in private industry before entering military service, received little or no transferable skills training while in the military. Thus, vets often find themselves not just in a double bind, but in a triple bind: few transferable skills; limited experience in industry, because, at a time they might be gaining such experience, they were in the service; bind number three is that they most often fall victim to first-in, first-out personnel policies and therefore are the first to be laid off in event of cutbacks.

The estimated unemployment rate of disabled veterans is less encouraging, standing at 17.2 percent. Like other handicapped individuals, disabled veterans have difficulty securing employment due to negative employer attitudes.

While we have good reason to be proud of what we have accomplished in veterans employment, both within state government and the private sector, it is clear we have much more to do. To continue the momentum we have created together, we've got to maintain a full-court press on the problem of veterans unemployment. Veterans have every reason to share in the unprecedented prosperity we have enjoyed over the past three years; more than that, veterans represent a valuable state resource. A veteran's human potential is a terrible thing to waste. This is not a partisan issue, it is a human issue.

Matters of conscience dictate that we redress the problem of high unemployment among Vietnam-era veterans with all the determination we can muster. All of us—veterans' groups, the Office of the Governor, the General Assembly, employers, our fifty-eight community colleges with their training capability, the federal government—all of us, working together, can do, in partial measure, for veterans and their dependents what they have done for us. Monuments to veterans are important, but monuments of action are equally important. I am aware of your organization's untiring efforts to preserve the benefits bestowed upon you by a grateful nation. Working together, we can achieve our mutual goal of equitable treatment of our veterans.

Again the words from the Valley Forge Medal of Honor Grove dedication echo, as across the plains of eternity. They are the words I quoted from General Douglas MacArthur: "Duty, honor, country: These three hallowed words reverently dictate what you ought to be, what you can be, what you will be. They will be the rallying point to build courage when courage seems to fail, to regain faith when there seems little cause for faith, to create hope when hope becomes forlorn."[7]

Duty and honor: We have asked these of you, and you have responded to the call. Duty and honor: Can we in government afford to ask less of ourselves?

---

[1]Carroll Smith (1931-   ), native of Davidson County; was graduated from Linwood High School, 1950; was also educated at U.S. Army Leadership School, Japan, and at Davidson Community College; U.S. Army, 1951-1954. Part owner, 1962-1984, Smith Brothers Super Market, Inc.; later employed at Sherwin-Williams Paint Store and at Davidson Office Equipment; junior vice-commander, 1985-1986, senior vice-commander, 1986-1987, commander, 1987-1988, N.C. Department, Veterans of Foreign Wars; was recognized as All-American Department Commander. Carroll Smith to Jan-Michael Poff, May 25, 1989.

[2]Billy M. Summerlin (1933-   ), born in Duplin County; resident of Jacksonville; B.S., Wake Forest College (later University), 1956; M.S., American University, 1971. Retired as colonel, December 1, 1988, after having served in U.S. Marine Corps for thirty-one years. Billy M. Summerlin to Jan-Michael Poff, July 10, 1989.

[3]Patrick Brooks Jordan (1970-   ), born in Goldsboro; resident of Smithfield; was graduated from Smithfield-Selma Senior High School, 1988; entered Duke University, 1988. Patrick Brooks Jordan to Jan-Michael Poff, May 23, 1989.

The national Voice of Democracy contest, sponsored by the Veterans of Foreign Wars and its Ladies Auxiliary, was a scriptwriting program open to tenth-, eleventh-, and twelfth-grade students. The competition gave entrants an opportunity to broadcast, across the country, their views of their civic responsibilities as United States citizens. Information supplied by Robin Pendleton, Veterans of Foreign Wars State Headquarters, Raleigh, May 18, 1989.

[4]Golda Ralph Pittman (1926-   ), born in Boone Hill Township, Johnston County; resident of Smithfield; was graduated from Princeton High School; was also educated at Hardbarger Business College. Served for thirty-two years as secretary, officer of FICA tax department, First Citizens Bank & Trust Co., Smithfield; state chairwoman, Veterans of Foreign Wars National Buddy Poppy Program, since 1980; secretary, hostess, McLaurin Funeral Home, Clayton, since 1983. Timothy Ralph Pittman to Jan-Michael Poff, August 10, 1990.

[5]Almost two weeks after Martin spoke to the VFW convention, the General Assembly ratified "An Act to Strengthen the Preference to Be Accorded Veterans for State Employment." *N.C. Session Laws, 1987, Regular Session, 1988,* III, c. 1064, was ratified July 7, 1988.

[6]See P.L. 97-300, "Job Training Partnership Act," *United States Statutes at Large,* Title IV-C, 96 Stat. 1380-1381; see also *United States Code* (1988 edition), Title 29, Sec. 1721.

[7]In his address at West Point, New York, May 12, 1962, General MacArthur is recorded as having said "your rallying point," rather than "the rallying point." Otherwise, the excerpt was quoted accurately. See *Reader's Digest Treasury of Modern Quotations,* 728.

RIBBON-CUTTING FOR BOONE PULL-OFF LANE

WATAUGA COUNTY, JULY 1, 1988

It is indeed a pleasure to visit your beautiful section of the state once again, and this clear mountain air is a welcome relief from some of the hot air we've had to deal with from the General Assembly, lately.

We're here, today, to dedicate a pull-off lane that we think will make driving safer and more efficient for motorists who live here as well as tourists who have come to visit a spell. It's part of an experiment in how to solve the problem of traffic congestion. It's an experiment that has been tried and proven effective elsewhere, particularly in the state of Washington, and we are confident it will work here.

To give you a bit of the history of this venture, the idea of a pull-off lane was first offered a while back by Hugh Morton, Sr., and the folks at the AAA Motor Club. They saw the need for a lane into which slower-moving drivers could pull so that faster traffic could pass. That lane would ease congestion that can build up on these roads and ease the tempers of the traveling public that such congestion can cause. It also would reduce the possibility of an impatient driver taking a gamble that might lead to injuries or fatalities.

Hugh Morton and the motor club caught the attention of our state Board of Transportation, and in October of 1987, the funds were found in our Spot Safety Program to build two of these pull-off lanes: the one here on U.S. 421 and [the] other one on N.C. 107 in Jackson County. The Jackson County lane was completed recently and has been well received. Everybody seems to like it.

One of the key factors in taking this approach to traffic safety, and safety is and always will be the primary goal of this administration when it comes to our state's roads, is the relatively minor cost involved. You can imagine the expense in time, money, and inconvenience that widening a road such as this would involve, but this improvement was accomplished, the traffic people tell me, for about $24,000. We think we got a bargain.

As I said, we will carefully evaluate the effectiveness of this lane and the one in Jackson County. We think they will prove to be useful techniques in reducing traffic congestion, and we think they will prove to be popular with the motoring public, but we'll let you be the ones to judge that. If we are right, and if the funds are available, what we have begun here and in Jackson County may be forerunners of a series of similar lanes in areas where we can use them to promote safe and efficient travel—but that's down the road. Right now we've got a pleasant task before us, so let's cut this ribbon and get the show on the road.

STATEMENT UPON ADJOURNMENT, *SINE DIE,* OF THE NORTH CAROLINA GENERAL ASSEMBLY

RALEIGH, JULY 13, 1988

["I want to read this statement," the governor said at his July 13, 1988, news conference. "It's got some good, quotable material." He had been up until at least 3 A.M. that morning, composing on his personal computer the following critique of the short session of the General Assembly. Legislators commenced the session on June 2 and concluded business on July 12. *News and Observer,* July 14, 1988.

Apart from his discussion of fiscal matters, below, Martin also devoted much of his July 29, 1988, press conference to the recently adopted state budget.]

The General Assembly has finally adjourned; a session in which the promise of a three-week schedule was offered as an excuse for not considering important legislation stretched out to nearly twice that long. Yet, even without that excuse, most of the creative proposals of this administration were neglected while the House and Senate leadership haggled over numerous pet bills that had nothing to do with the budget. They did less over a longer period of time than they had said they could not do in a shorter period of time.

Any legislative session is a mixture of successes, and setbacks, and disappointments. This certainly was. There were a lot of disappointments. Let me begin with a review of some of the good news, from the point of view of the legislative agenda I had submitted with my Supplemental Budget for 1988-1989:

TABLE I.   **Supplemental Requests and Appropriations, 1988-1989**

Status[1]		Operating	Salary	Expansion	Capital	Total General Fund	Highway
A.	Request	$324.4M	$210.6M	$113.8M	$239.9M	$564.3M	$29.5M
B.	Granted	292.1M	210.6M	81.5M	69.6M	361.7M	24.9M
C.	(B/A)%	90%	100%	72%	29%	64%	84%
D.	Added	41.4M	0	41.4M	48.9M	90.3M	2.6M
E.	Total	333.5M	210.6M	122.9M	118.5M	452.0M	27.5M
F.	(B/E)%	88%	100%	66%	59%	80%	91%

Of 183 items requested by me in the Supplemental Budget, 101, or 55 percent, were agreed to. In dollar terms, of the $324.4 million requested for General Fund operations, $292 million, 90 percent, was approved. The General Assembly added $41.4 million at its own initiative, for a total appropriation of $333.5 million, 88 percent of which was requested in my Budget Supplement. Some of the more important provisions requested and agreed to are shown in the attached budget summary, prepared by the State Office of Budget and Management. They are, in millions of dollars:

Focused Industrial Training	$ 0.5
Adult School Bus Drivers	18.8
Academically Gifted Students	3.0
University Enrollment Growth	7.9
Low-Level Radioactive Waste	0.5
Super Collider	0.34
Domestic Violence/Rape Crisis	0.37
Division of Aging	3.7
Workfare Expansion	0.14
Catastrophic Illness Match	4.9
Corrections Programs	11.8
Public Defender, Robeson County	0.39
Compensation Increase	210.6
Drought Fund	1.0
Prison Construction	17.4

Equally noteworthy are some important items which were not funded [in millions of dollars]:

Early Childhood Readiness	$ 3.5
Communities in Schools	0.7
Office of Literacy	0.2
Veterans Training	0.18
Highway Patrol (60 troopers)	2.7
Commerce Department	3.6
State Parks	1.4
Expand "Best Management" Farming	1.0
Coastal Studies	0.58
Railroad Fund	1.0
Masonboro Island Acquisition	1.0
	($0.1 received)

Asbestos Removal	1.0
Toxic Waste Cleanup	1.0
Solid Waste Grant Fund	12.0

The greatest disappointments for the program proposals of this administration, however, were some important nonbudget items which could have received attention, but didn't. My proposal for $450 million in highway bonds was ignored. This would have enabled us to make major progress toward accelerating the construction of $1.5 billion in projects under the strategic corridor intrastate system, by the year 2000, without a tax increase. The Senate leadership said, "Not now."

A lot of hard work went into a proposal to consolidate various environmental regulatory functions into a new department of health and environment. Despite widespread support for this long-overdue merger, the Senate leadership said, "Not now."

Only one of the four major recommendations for tougher law enforcement against drug dealers was enacted, and that was merely an extension of an existing provision. Of two major recommendations for toughening enforcement against drunk drivers, one would provide thirty-day revocation of one's driving privilege upon charges of drunk driving. It was bottled up in a Senate committee, as last year. The other was passed in a nonsensical form: The blood-alcohol limit of 0.04 percent for bus and truck drivers was passed, but not to take effect until near the end of the 1989 session on next June 1, then to terminate a month later on June 30. The only excuse for such an absurd result is for the General Assembly to appear to be doing something about this important matter while actually doing next to nothing, impugning our state motto, "To be rather than to seem." For the most part, they just said, "Not now." Put them on notice, here and now, that everywhere I go, I'm going to call them to task for trifling with this serious issue.

In yet another lampoon of our state motto, the legislature toyed with the important issue of the executive veto. The good news is that, for the first time since 1939, a bipartisan majority of the North Carolina Senate actually appeared to take a stand in favor of procedures leading to a popular referendum on the veto amendment. Yet, once again, the General Assembly managed to get through its 212th year without ever once having trusted the people of North Carolina to vote on this historic issue.

Nevertheless, the maneuvering of the legislative leaders to stage a procedural vote, even though no result actually came of it, clearly demonstrates that the political pressure of popular support for the veto can and does cause former opponents to modify their stance—or at least appear to do so. That leads to the hope that, in the next session, the people ultimately will be heard, and the people ultimately will be trusted to make this fundamental decision for good government in North Carolina. But for this session, "Not now."

While repeatedly proclaiming, "We cannot be content with the status quo," the legislative leadership reinforced that status quo at every opportunity. They protested that there was not enough time in this short session to deal with any proposal other than their own, yet they wasted more than enough time in which some of these measures could have been enacted. While two or six of the "Super Subcommittee" were busy making decisions about the pork barrel, special provisions, and undermining the authority of the University Board of Governors, most of the other 165 members were idle. Their committees did not meet; their opinions were not sought; many good minds were wasted. It is no wonder that $30,000 to $60,000 was offered to each of these good but underutilized members as a form of victims' compensation for their constituents.

There was plenty of time for several weeks of standoff between the House and Senate leadership. There was plenty of time for posturing about openness in government, pretending that the legislative decision-making was more open to view, while in truth the same old secrecy was cloaked in new forms of obscurity. If the so-called Super Subcommittee didn't meet, it was because only two members showed up to do the work. Those with political ambitions avoided getting close to the action for fear they would be accused of having something to do with it.

Perhaps in a vain attempt to divert attention from their laggardship, several of the Senate chiefs tried to blame me for the lengthy, unproductive session. That won't work, because there's no truth to it. In the first place, the Advisory Budget Committee rarely has been used to assist any governor with his supplemental budget in any short session since they were initiated in 1974. The Budget Office tells me that Governor Holshouser never used the A.B.C. in his two short sessions. Governor Hunt did use them in 1978 and 1980, but not in 1982 or 1984. I did not use then in 1986 or 1988. Their record of usefulness is limited to two out of eight years. So the fact that I followed the historic precedent of not using the A.B.C. had absolutely nothing to do with the length of this or any other session.

In the second place, my Supplemental Budget was submitted in proper form and on time. As requested,

—It was presented to the General Assembly ahead of time on May 5;

—The appropriations hearings began on May 15;

—The General Assembly convened, on June 2, for organizational work;

—Legislative fiscal staff submitted its revenue picture on June 6;

—My budget balancing revisions were presented on June 8, on their second day of any scheduled work on the budget. From then on, it was just a matter of choosing which items to put in, and which to cut out of the budget, and what to bid on one of the several (bridge) card games in progress while awaiting the outcome of the budget.

No, the real reason for the delay was the disagreements between the House and Senate leadership and the fact that the House leadership was stronger, better organized, and knew how to get its way, while the Senate leadership admitted it was at the mercy of the House. The Senate said, "Open up the process!" The House leadership said, "Not now."

The fact that May revenues were less than predicted did not prolong the session, because I promptly recommended the $60 million worth of capital projects that could be deferred. As shown in Table I, that is in fact where the legislative decisions concurred, in cutting back capital projects rather than cutting back recurring expense increases. It's simply a matter that the 1988 legislature did less over a longer period of time than they said they could not do in a shorter period of time.

---

[1]The governor calculated the percentages in Line C by dividing the value of Line B by Line A. Likewise, he arrived at the figures in Line F by dividing the value of Line B by Line E. Governor James G. Martin to Jan-Michael Poff, October 16, 1990.

NORTH CAROLINA ASSOCIATION OF
COUNTY COMMISSIONERS

GREENSBORO, JULY 15, 1988

It is really great being with you, this morning, at this, your eighty-first annual meeting. This is another way of saying congratulations to your association on being such a force for good government in North Carolina for the better part of a century. In fact, as a former county commissioner myself, and a former president of this fine organization, this is really like old home week.

You know, one term we're hearing a lot these days is *infrastructure*. We all know that infrastructure refers to underlying foundations that help our communities run, such as roads, schools, water and sewage, communications, electricity, and the like. Today, I would like to suggest the use of infrastructure in other ways.

First, we need to recognize that an important part of the infrastructure, the underlying foundation, of representative government is county commissioners throughout North Carolina. Being so closely involved in government at the grass-roots level, you, as much as any governmental officials, are acutely sensitive to the concerns and aspirations of citizens throughout our state. As a former commissioner and chairman of the Mecklenburg County Board of Commissioners, I know you are on the front lines, working to make a better life for your communities. Indeed, individually and collectively—because you are so sensitive to, and must be responsive to, the pulse of our citizens—you are invaluable sources of information for us in state government; information which, if used wisely, can bring enormous benefits [to] the citizens of our state. When you talk, we in state government should listen.

You can be sure that when you talk, our administration listens. On February 10 of this year, for the first time ever, I called a meeting of the Executive Cabinet to hear from your president, and your executive director, and from their counterparts at the League [of Municipalities] about your concerns and views. Of course, you know that Tommie and Ron represented you very well, and they educated several of the state officials who attended—in a nice way, of course.[1] This experiment in participative government was so well received, I hope to plan another get-together next year.

Tommie and Ron, along with Jack Dossenbach, Wayne Hooper, Darryl Frye, Virginia Oliver, and Buster Robertson have also been very vocal—in a nice way, of course—[in voicing] your interests and local governments' views through the Local Government Advocacy Council.[2] Tommie has been a strong chairman of our LGAC this year, and I want to thank him personally for his outstanding leadership of that body.

I want to take this opportunity to thank your association for being, over the past three and a half years, partners in our attempt to bring good things to the life of our state: better schools, better roads, more and better jobs, and a better quality of life for our citizens. You have been leaders in many areas, most recently in organizing our state's overwhelming response to the sale of Farmers Home Administration assets. I know you are proud, and have good cause to be proud, that your hard work and perseverance saved our citizens millions of dollars and preserved local control of our local infrastructure.

Has it really been over three years since I was sworn in as governor? Time really flies when you're having fun. One frog put it a little differently to another frog when he said, "Time's really fun when you're having flies."

Let me say that, as a former county commissioner, I know you have deep concerns about how to provide services to those you represent.

Still another kind of infrastructure can be called our corporate family, which is growing quite rapidly and is the basis for wealth and job creation in our state, and which in a large measure provides money for what we conventionally refer to as our infrastructure: schools, roads, water, sewer, and so on. This morning, I would like to share with you how our improving economic infrastructure is enhancing the quality of life and quality of services for North Carolinians. Because it represents a kind of bottom line in our wealth and job creation program, the first thing I want to share with you is the expansion of our overall revenue base at the state level.

In the fiscal year just ended, we enjoyed the largest General Fund credit balance in our state's history. This means that, with attention to what our priorities are, we are now in a much better position to provide support for much-needed services in our communities across the state. A simple, but not always adequately appreciated, economic fact is that if we wish to provide essential services at an appropriate level, we must have a program to expand continually our wealth and job creation. In a word, economic development is what makes so many good things possible for our people.

This is one reason why we have put together a statewide network of private-public partnerships. You know about these economic development partnerships because many of you here have been an important part of these partnerships, and they have been so successful [that] North Carolina has become the envy of the nation. Let's briefly sketch just how successful our wealth and job creation programs have been.

Since January, 1985, we have seen a robust net gain of well over 300,000 jobs and a steadily falling unemployment rate, which dropped to 3.2 percent in June, the lowest unemployment percentage on record since the state Employment Security Commission started keeping records. Over a three-year period, we have averaged $5 billion each year in new and expanded business investments, manufacturing and nonmanufacturing combined. Not only that, the economic upbeat goes on: In 1987, new and expanded businesses announced plans to invest $5.4 billion in North Carolina. During this same period, we had a net gain of 124,500 jobs, with average employment soaring to an all-time high of 3,130,000. At the same time, we had the highest gain in nonmanufacturing wages and salaried jobs in more than a decade.

I realize that numbers are sometimes difficult to follow in a speech. For this reason, allow me to cite several examples to give additional support to how well we have done in wealth and job creation. In 1987, we were number one in the entire nation in the number of new plant announcements by American industry. We had 113. Texas was second with 112. The score was close, but we're the national champions. We were fourth in the country in expansion of manufacturing facilities, behind three population giants: New York, California, and Texas.

We have also become a national leader in foreign trade. In fact, according to a study conducted by North Carolina State University, if all the other forty-nine states had done as well as North Carolina in foreign trade in the fourth quarter of 1987, the United States would have seen its trade deficit shrink by over 87 percent. But the first quarter of this year was dramatically better, with a $160 million trade surplus of North Carolina exports over imports. This upsurge in exports more than made up for the slight trade deficit for the prior nine months, so that for the year ending March, 1988, North Carolina's foreign trade experienced a twelve-month surplus. We in North Carolina are trying to do our share to reduce our nation's negative balance of payments in international trade.

All this economic development activity, foreign and domestic, contributes to our economic health, with more and better jobs. For example, since January, 1985, North Carolina has enjoyed a net gain of 334,000 jobs in three and a half years. Friends, that means if you look around at all the jobs in North Carolina, one out of nine of them wasn't available three and a half years ago.

Some critics like to moan that some of those jobs aren't high-paying jobs. That's always been true. I would like for these "bad news bearers" to tell us which of those jobs they would want us to eliminate and do without. A young person with limited academic skills may not qualify, right at first, for a high-paying executive job or to be an assembly-line supervisor; but with greater opportunities to enter the job market, he or she can aspire to climb the job ladder as far as possible. Should we cut off the bottom rung so our young people and the unemployed will have no job at all, with little chance to share in the American dream?

With all our economic achievements over the past three years, we have done what few states have been able to do. Consider this: For the first time in 1987, over two thirds, or nearly 68 percent, of all new factory jobs announced in North Carolina went to communities of 10,000 or less. More than 60 percent of new manufacturing investment was announced outside the piedmont. This doesn't mean we've stopped scoring in the big cities in the piedmont; they did as well as the previous year. It's just that we've learned a lot more about how to sell industry on the advantages of locating in our less-populated areas. At a a time when the *Wall Street Journal* is writing how job-starved conditions are in the rural areas of the Sunbelt, we are reversing that trend. We're not just reading about the urban-rural economic imbalance; we're not just talking about it; we're doing something about it.

But our economic balance is not just geographic. It is balance in the kinds of industries we have been able to attract and hold on to, from tobacco, to timber, to tourism, to turkeys, to terminals, from high tech, to low tech, and everywhere in between. For years, North Carolina has had a Balanced Growth Policy but little balanced growth. For many years, there were those little green signs put up all over the state, saying, "Governor's Community of Excellence." Remember those little green signs? Now we're putting jobs in communities—not just in our more populated areas, but all over the state—and who better than you knows this, because you have been an important partner in this growth.

The unvarnished truth is, we're on an economic roll in North Carolina. Consider this illustration: In 1987 the gross national product grew by 2.9 percent. The fact is that our nation is now entering the sixth consecutive year of steady growth, sixty-seven months, with the longest sustained national growth cycle in this century. And here's the rest of the story: North Carolina's GSP, gross state product, grew 5.1 percent in 1987, half-again faster than the GNP!

Some people say we're just lucky. If, by luck, they mean when hard work meets opportunity, they're right. That great little golf player, Gary Player, put it as well as anyone: "The harder I work, the luckier I get." What it comes down to is this: Our hardworking team is a championship team, no two ways about it.

Naturally, I could go on. I could tell you that *Business Week* and *Manufacturing Week* magazines found in their surveys of top business leaders across the nation that North Carolina was preferred by more corporate executives over all other states as the place they would most likely locate new plant facilities. I could also tell you that the state of Kentucky contracted with a national polling firm to find out what state was most highly regarded by top CEOs all over the country. The results of this survey? North Carolina scored first on five of seven categories. Is there any wonder why I am so proud of our economic team, our championship economic team, of our state Department of Commerce working with local leaders in partnerships all over the state? We're winning economic championships, and it's showing up in numbers all over the place.

NC FREE, the nonpartisan business association, polled North Carolina's business leaders recently. Among other things, they were asked to identify factors that had the most positive impact on a favorable business climate in our state. Needless to say, I was extremely pleased that they ranked the governor and the Department of Commerce very favorably, second only to our colleges and universities.

As a result of our incredible economic successes over the past three and a half years, our state finds itself in a far better financial position to attack problems—or better yet, to seize opportunities—in a variety of areas, such as schools, environmental concerns, drugs, and our elderly population.

In the time remaining, I would like to discuss two other infrastructures, one human, the other, physical. People, it goes without saying, are the most important resource in our state. While we in North Carolina have been blessed by providence with the "goodliest land under the cope of heaven," as Ralph Lane wrote in his famous letter in 1585, it is really what we make of our blessings that counts.

This morning, I want to talk about the opportunities we have to strengthen a fundamental, underlying, foundation of our state and its communities. I speak of human relations, a term that communicates a deep human desire to achieve harmony and a community of purpose with our fellow men; and to help you achieve this end, we have a wonderful resource at your disposal. I refer to the North Carolina Human Relations Council and how it can assist you in strengthening your community relations.

A splendid example of the use of the council's services may be found in Robeson County. Here the commissioners of Robeson County, and so many people there of goodwill, deserve our accolades. The county commissioners, in particular, should be singled out for praise for their leadership in seeking to strengthen human relations in Robeson County.

To achieve this goal, people in the community, working with the state Human Relations Council, created the Robeson County Unity Commission, which was approved by the Board of Commissioners. The establishment of this commission represents a fine example of a local-state partnership. In Robeson County, the very composition of this commission tells a lot of the story. It consists of twenty-one members—seven white[s], seven blacks, and seven Indians—under the able leadership of one of the county's most distinguished citizens, Mr. Hector MacLean, chairman of the board of Southern National Bank.[3]

The state council works by invitation, in terms of local needs, and stands ready to provide support, technical assistance, and advice to local human relations commissions or councils; for those counties that do not have a human relations commission, I encourage you to organize one. To give you some idea of the scope of the state council's activities, in 1987 the council's staff served 8,077 individuals. They conducted thirty-one human relations workshops and trained 200 law officers in police-community relations.

Our strength in North Carolina, it should be noted, and indeed the strength of any democratic society, lies as much in our differences as our likenesses. The same principles of brotherhood that have made us a great state and nation are the very principles we must reaffirm from time to time. An effective human relations council can help not only to reaffirm these principles, but help us build better communities. We at the state level stand ready to help; please feel free to call on us. I think you'll be glad you did. We've come so far in human relations in our state, but as Robert Frost said, we've got "more miles to go before we sleep."[4]

The next infrastructure I would like to discuss concerns a matter vital to our health and well-being. I refer to the treatment and disposal of hazardous wastes. To be sure, this is not a pleasant subject, but no one better than you know that it is a problem that cannot be wished away, nor can it be legislated away.

One thing must be made clear, up front: We can no longer expect producers of hazardous waste and low-level waste to dispose of these wastes themselves. Some will argue that since 97 percent of the recorded hazardous wastes produced in North Carolina is treated on site, we must require the other 3 percent to do likewise. This 3 percent translates into literally thousands of small mom-and-pop operators who produce hazardous wastes, like gasoline stations, dry cleaners, and painting contractors who cannot afford to construct their own treatment facilities. At the present time, they do not have a facility to which they can take their wastes for safe treatment. What happens to these substances? Inevitably, they make their way into the environment, either through covert dumping or, more often, by concealed placement in the county landfill. You all remember the PCB dumping along our roads several years ago.[5]

I began my political career as a county commissioner, and I know just how difficult it is to site a landfill. As governor, I am discovering just how difficult it is to site a hazardous-waste treatment facility and a low-level radioactive waste disposal site. As a former county commissioner, I know, however, that if you do not want garbage and trash to pile up in backyards and in the streets, you have got to provide for disposal in an incinerator and/or landfill.

I want you to know I was greatly disappointed that the General Assembly chose not to respond, this session, to our request to provide financial assistance to you in managing our solid waste. As you know, I had proposed creating a $10 million revolving loan fund, coupled with a $2 million research and technical assistance effort. You and your association worked very hard to get the legislature's attention, but we all came up disappointed. You have my pledge that we will keep working to educate—in a nice way, of course—our legislators so that they will recognize the extent and cost of the problems we face and the predictable consequences of neglecting to address this problem.

Knowing the situation in your county, you may empathize with the situation I face as governor. I know that if we do not want hazardous waste and low-level waste to pile up in small businesses and hospitals, then we will have to provide treatment and disposal facilities. The alternative, the only real-life alternative, is for producers to dump it into streams, gullies, trenches, et cetera, when nobody is looking. The reason that is the only alternative is because the self-appointed environmental activists refuse to accept any facility, anywhere. They pretend there's an alternative. There is: It's called illegal dumping.

I don't want to get too technical, but there are vastly different problems related to disposal of solid and liquid hazardous wastes. For example, neither the Barnwell, South Carolina; Beatty, Nevada; nor the Hanford, Washington, waste disposal facilities will accept radioactive liquids produced by hospitals across the state. Several hospitals have incinerators for converting liquid wastes into solids; many throughout the state do not. What will happen to these wastes?

Fortunately, the solution is obvious—and presently, it is the only feasible solution to a growing problem, a problem that is certain to grow with our expanding wealth and job creation. What it all comes down to, is, we must have one central facility, rather than scattered, loosely regulated, decentralized facilities. The truth is that we can have one central disposal site with sufficient funds to ensure safety at a level even better than that of Barnwell, which has had no accidents or contamination in more than fifteen years of operation.

This approach is clearly better than 200 or more small producers struggling with the question of what to do with these wastes. No great imagination is required to see what will happen if we fail to take decisive action on the only sound solution to waste disposal. We need only look at what has happened, and what is certainly happening, in the matter of disposal of hazardous materials.

For example, one of our universities was faced with the challenge of what to do with chemical and low-level radioactive wastes. They had no access to a hazardous-waste treatment facility, nor could they dispose of low-level radioactive liquids. The solution, not wanting to dispose of these materials in their county landfill: They disposed of them in trenches on their own land. The rest of the story is that their disposal site, which was in operation until 1980, is now a candidate for one of the North Carolina EPA Superfund clean-up sites.

The hour is late. Ask not for whom the bell tolls, it is tolling for all of us. As stewards of our environment, as partners in economic development, as trustees for future generations of North Carolinians, we must be willing to take responsible, intelligent action.

I would indeed be remiss if I failed to mention the courageous, pioneering efforts of the Edgecombe County commissioners. Aside from finding that the facility at Barnwell posed little threat to the health and safety of surrounding areas, they saw such a facility as a real economic opportunity. The city and county of Barnwell derive almost $800,000 a year, and the state of South Carolina an additional $5 million annually, from the operation. We, on the other hand, have said that all of this compensation, almost $6 million, would go to the county willing to host the facility, for education, sewers, water, fire protection, streets, and industrial development.

As governor, I must face the responsibility of providing maximum protection for all our citizens and our environment. Naturally, the involvement and support of county commissioners is crucial in this effort. It is obvious that we have a job on our hands to dispel a good deal of false information about the problem of hazardous-waste disposal. Also, the public, with the help of the media, must come to see just how hazardous our present situation is. Indeed, if we do not take decisive action, we will be placing not only our citizens and environment but our economic development at risk.

In summary, we have made tremendous progress over the past three and a half years. We are truly on a roll, and if we are creative and courageous in our actions, there is every reason to believe we will continue to move along the road to greater progress. When we work together as one united state, not just one of the fifty United States— we are that, too, and proud of it—but North Carolina as one united state, east and west, mountains and coast, piedmont and sandhills, men and women, business people, Democrats, and Republicans, and independents, together we can create miracles. What we have managed to accomplish together proves that when we put aside our differences and put North Carolina first, North Carolina will be first.

---

[1]Thomas B. (Tommie) Gray, of Buxton, was serving as president, North Carolina Assn. of County Commissioners. Information from North Carolina Assn. of County Commissioners, May 22, 1990, hereinafter cited as N.C. Assn. County Commissioners information.

C. Ronald Aycock (1940-   ), born in Wilson County; resident of Raleigh; B.S., 1963, J.D., 1966, University of North Carolina at Chapel Hill. Attorney; executive director, Region L Council of Governments, 1971-1973; counsel for intergovernmental relations, 1973-1977, executive director, since 1977, North Carolina Assn. of County Commissioners; president, National Council County/State Assn. Executive Directors, 1985-1986. C. Ronald Aycock to Jan-Michael Poff, May 30, 1990.

[2]Jack Dossenbach, Jr. (1939-   ), born in Durham; resident of Sanford; was educated at Campbell College (later University); served in U.S. Army. Sanford city alderman, 1976-1977; Lee County commissioner, 1982-1990; president, North Carolina Assn. of County Commissioners, 1989. Jack Dossenbach, Jr., to Jan-Michael Poff, May 26, 1990.

Wayne Hooper (1929-   ), born in Cullowhee; resident of Sylva; B.S., Western Carolina College (later University), 1958; U.S. Army, 1951-1952. Former schoolteacher, design technician; Cullowhee postmaster, 1961-1973; convenience store owner-operator, 1974; Jackson County manager and County Commission chairman, since 1978; president, N.C. Assn. of County Commissioners, since 1989. Wayne Hooper to Jan-Michael Poff, May 30, 1990.

Darryl L. Frye, of Trinity; Virginia Oliver, of Fayetteville; and Robert "Buster" Robertson, of King, were members of the Randolph, Cumberland, and Stokes county boards of commissioners, respectively. N.C. Assn. County Commissioners information.

[3]Hector MacLean (1920-   ), son of Angus W. MacLean, North Carolina governor, 1925-1929; born in Baltimore, Maryland; resident of Lumberton; B.S., Davidson College, 1941; J.D., University of North Carolina at Chapel Hill, 1948; honorary degrees; veteran of World War II. Attorney in private practice, 1948-1952; Lumberton mayor, 1949-1953; assistant to president, 1952-1955, president, board chairman, 1955-1976, chairman, chief executive officer, since 1976, Southern National Bank of North Carolina; president, board chairman, 1969-1976, chairman, chief executive officer, since 1976, Southern National Corp.; member, state Senate, 1961-1971; farmer. Hector MacLean to Jan-Michael Poff, July 11, 1990.

[4]Robert Frost wrote:

The woods are lovely, dark and deep.
But I have promises to keep,
And miles to go before I sleep.

From "Stopping by Woods on a Snowy Evening" (1923), stanza 4, quoted in Bartlett, *Familiar Quotations*, 927.

[5]Thousands of gallons of toxic PCB-tainted oil, used as coolant in electrical transformers, had been discharged illegally along 243 miles of rural North Carolina roads during the summer of 1978. As a consequence of their role in the dumping, Robert E. "Buck" Ward, president of Ward Transformer Co. of Raleigh, and three New York residents were convicted of violating environmental regulations. PCB, or polychlorinated biphenyl, was a carcinogen; federal authorities outlawed its production in 1979. Mitchell, *Addresses of Hunt*, I, 348-351; Poff and Crow, *Addresses of Hunt*, II, 306-308.

SAM ERVIN HIGHWAY DEDICATION

MORGANTON, JULY 18, 1988

Just a Country Lawyer: That was the title of the book by Paul Clancy about the life of Sam J. Ervin, Jr., the man we are honoring here today.[1] In one way, the title is ironic. How can you call Sam Ervin "just a country lawyer," as he called himself? He was, after all, one of the giants of our time. A hundred years from now, no historian worth his salt will be able to discuss twentieth-century America without Sam Ervin, Jr.'s name looming large.

But in another way, being just a country lawyer was the most fitting accolade you could bestow on Sam Ervin. It was the epithet he himself favored, and took whimsical delight. And if we examine his life, we will find there's more to the phrase, "just a country lawyer," than an ironic twist.

Sam Ervin, Jr.'s life spanned the greater part of the twentieth century. He was born on September 27, 1896, and he died on April 23, 1985. Throughout his long, fruitful career, there is one theme that ran through his days like a clear mountain stream running through the mountains that Sam Ervin loved so much. That theme is an abiding love for the law. Those historians who fail to grasp this aspect of Sam Ervin's life will never understand the crucial role he played in American politics or how he came to play it.

Young Sam Ervin, Jr., began his love affair with the law during warm summer days at his father's law offices in Morganton. His fascination with the law stayed with him during his undergraduate days at the University of North Carolina and followed him to France, where he was wounded in the Battle of Soissons during the First World War and was awarded the Distinguished Service Cross.

Returning to his home state after the war, there was no doubt what career Sam Ervin, Jr., would choose. He studied law at UNC and was licensed by the Supreme Court of North Carolina in 1919. He then obtained a bachelor of law degree from Harvard University in 1922. That same year, Sam Ervin, Jr., began the practice of law with his father in Morganton. For the next fifteen years, that law practice would shape Sam Ervin, Jr.'s legal philosophy.

In his home county of Burke, and in important trials in Caldwell, Catawba, McDowell, Avery, Mitchell, Yancey, Rutherford, Cleveland, Lincoln, Watauga, Ashe, and Alleghany counties, Sam Ervin, Jr., appeared with and against the region's greatest trial lawyers— lawyers who were wise in the ways of the law and seasoned in the rough-and-tumble ways of courtrooms in county courthouses. These courtrooms were classrooms for Sam Ervin, Jr., and he was an honor student. He competed successfully against the best lawyers of that time, and as his knowledge and ability gained renown, he was retained as counsel in many of the serious and important lawsuits in the region.

Sam Ervin, Jr.'s reputation as a highly skilled, knowledgeable, per- suasive lawyer soon outgrew its regional bounds. He attracted the attention of the state's leaders, who recognized that this was a man of rare ability, ability that could be used in public service for the better- ment of the entire state. And so, during the ensuing years, Governor Hoey appointed Sam Ervin, Jr., to a superior court judgeship; then Governor Cherry appointed Sam Ervin, Jr., as a justice of the North Carolina Supreme Court; then Governor Umstead appointed Sam Ervin, Jr., as a U.S. senator.[2]

Each appointment was a new challenge, and Sam Ervin, Jr., met each challenge with vigor, and confidence, and the vast intellectual gifts that were his. The opinions he wrote as a justice of the North Carolina Supreme Court bear witness to his knowledge and under- standing—and his ability to write clearly, logically, and lucidly, and above all else, with his reasoning grounded soundly in the law.

But it was in the U.S. Senate that Sam Ervin, Jr., made his national mark, a mark that will stand as long as men and women everywhere value freedom; as long as this remains a nation of laws and not men. Amid a galaxy of national political figures and media stars, the coun- try lawyer from Morganton increasingly became the person an anxious American people turned to for strength and courage during a time of national turmoil. With compassion and good humor; with reference to literature, poetry, and the Bible; but most of all with an honesty that would brook no dishonesty; with a wisdom that saw through evasions and specious arguments, Sam Ervin, Jr., helped to communicate and to reaffirm to the American people that everyone, even the president of the United States, and you and I, must obey the law.

Through the smoke and mirrors of questionable actions that the Watergate hearings revealed, Sam Ervin, Jr.'s genial countenance, his steadfast resolve, his keen intelligence, and his unswerving adherence and devotion to the U.S. Constitution gave America a singular hero around whom to rally in its time of need. He was truly the man of the hour, and America was fortunate Sam Ervin, Jr., was there when it needed him.

Looking back on that life, and looking back on that epithet, just a country lawyer, we can see how it helps put Sam Ervin, Jr.'s life in perspective. He was a lawyer, a lawyer's lawyer, whose very life left his profession a legacy of proven precepts: that a lawyer should practice law with unquestioned honesty and integrity; that a lawyer should deal with friends and adversaries in a fair manner; that a lawyer should represent his clients to the best of his ability, but never surrender his conscience; and that a lawyer should serve his country when his country needs him. This is the mark of the legal profession at its best, and Sam Ervin, Jr., was at the top of that profession.

If that is what the word *lawyer* means in the phrase, we need next to turn our attention to the word *country*. It means this wonderful region of the state where Sam Ervin, Jr., toiled so many years to uphold the legal rights of his clients. That's one of the reasons we are so proud to have this important, twenty-three-mile country road here to dedicate today. But it also means this entire country, the United States of America, our nation, the country whose constitution Sam Ervin, Jr., dedicated his life to serving—on the battlefields of France, in the county courthouses of his region, and in the Senate chambers of the U.S. Congress. Sam Ervin, Jr., was a man of the people—of all the people, who value that most precious document, the U.S. Constitution, and its guarantees that each person has the right to search for the truth according to the dictates of his or her conscience, unhindered by government. Yes, he was a country lawyer—or more aptly, a lawyer for his country—and our children, and our children's children, and all generations to come need to hear and heed the message of Sam Ervin, Jr., about liberty and how we must defend it.

To say he was just a country lawyer is, of course, Sam Ervin's humble way of handling a fame he richly deserved, but never sought. That humility casts yet another light on Sam Ervin, Jr., the man. Sam Ervin, Jr., believed in serving his profession, his family, his country, and his God with all his heart and all his might. When he retired, he asked to be thought of as "one of the people of America." He saw nothing special in that. He thought we all should do the same. He was right. We should; and with his legacy to guide us, we see the paths we should walk to ensure, to paraphrase William Faulkner, that liberty does not merely endure, but that liberty prevails.[3]

As future motorists drive on N.C. 18 in Burke County, I hope they will reflect a bit on who Sam Ervin, Jr., was, and what he stood for, and what he did. I hope they will realize how fortunate we were to have him when we needed him and what a debt this country owes him. If they do so, I think they will be thankful that we were able, through the naming of this road, in some small way to pay homage to a man who was just a country lawyer—and a giant among men.

---

[1]Paul R. Clancy, *Just a Country Lawyer: A Biography of Senator Sam Ervin* (Bloomington: Indiana University Press, 1974).

[2]Ervin served as a superior court judge, 1937-1943, an associate justice of the state supreme court, 1948-1954, and in the U.S. Senate, 1954-1974. *Biographical Directory of Congress*, 970-971.

Clyde Roark Hoey (1877-1954), born, was buried in Shelby; studied law in Shelby and at University of North Carolina at Chapel Hill; honorary degrees. Owner, editor, publisher, *Cleveland* (N.C.) *Star*; attorney; member, state House, 1898-1902, and Senate, 1902-1904; assistant U.S. attorney for western North Carolina, 1913-1919; member, U.S. House, 1919-1921; governor of North Carolina, 1937-1941; member, U.S. Senate, 1945-1954; Democrat. The Hoey administration began distributing free textbooks to elementary school pupils and established the State Bureau of Investigation as well as North Carolina's first advertising program for tourism and industry. Powell, *DNCB*, III, 158-159.

Robert Gregg Cherry (1891-1957), born near York, South Carolina; died in Gastonia; was graduated from Trinity College (later Duke University), 1912, where he earned a law degree, 1914; World War I veteran. Elected mayor of Gastonia, 1919, reelected 1921; member, N.C. House, 1931-1939, and Senate, 1941-1943; Democrat. As governor of North Carolina, 1945-1949, he improved mental health care, increased public school-teachers' salaries by 83 percent, and lowered teacher-student ratios. Powell, *DNCB*, I, 361-362.

William Bradley Umstead (1895-1954), born in Mangum Township, Durham County; died in Durham; was graduated from University of North Carolina at Chapel Hill, 1916; studied law at Trinity College (later Duke University), 1919-1921; U.S. Army, 1917-1919. Kinston schoolteacher, 1916-1917; attorney; solicitor, Tenth Judicial District, 1927-1933; member, U.S. House, 1933-1939, and Senate, 1946-1948; governor of North Carolina, 1953-1954; Democrat. *Biographical Directory of Congress*, 1966.

[3]"I believe that man will not merely endure: He will prevail." William Faulkner, from his speech upon receiving the Nobel prize, December 10, 1950, as quoted in Bartlett, *Familiar Quotations*, 1039.

TEXASGULF NPDES PERMIT BRIEFING

RALEIGH, JULY 21, 1988

The state of North Carolina, Texasgulf, Incorporated, and several North Carolina environmental groups have made some history, the kind of history we like to make in North Carolina. Texasgulf has been operating a phosphate mining and agricultural product manufacturing facility off the Pamlico River, in Beaufort County, since the early 1960s; the company has been an important economic force in that part of our state ever since. Their massive operation, which produces more than 12 million tons of phosphate ore per year, employs 1,200 of our citizens and has an annual payroll of almost $50 million per year. In addition, Texasgulf purchases more than $100 million in goods and services in our state each year. That means there are a lot of small businesses in northeastern North Carolina that depend on this large business.

Over the past year and a half, the Department of Natural Resources and Community Development, through its Division of Environmental Management, has labored long and hard with the company and a variety of environmental organizations to come up with a new system which will reduce Texasgulf's discharge of phosphorus by 90 percent and fluorides by 75 percent. At present, the company discharges approximately 3,100 pounds of phosphorus and 2,165 pounds of fluorides per day. We expect the phosphorus discharge to be steadily reduced over the four-year construction period. I would like to point out that, all along, the levels of the discharges of these chemicals were within the limits of the company's original NPDES [National Pollution Discharge Elimination System] permit. However, new knowledge indicates to us that those levels are too high and could have an adverse impact upon the aquatic life in a delicate and valuable North Carolina resource: our estuarine waters, which not only serve as primary nursery areas for important East Coast fish and shellfish but also provide a livelihood for our commercial fishermen.

I want first to give credit to some of my own folks, Division of Environmental Management director Paul Wilms[1] and both his permitting staff and his personnel in the Washington Regional Office. They have all worked tirelessly to come up with a permit that is both fair to Texasgulf and its employees and protective of our environment. I also want to recognize some of the environmental groups who have helped create the climate for this kind of action: the Environmental Defense Fund, the Pamlico-Tar River Association, the North

Carolina Coastal Federation, and the North Carolina Wildlife Federation.

Yes, we have some dedicated, constructive, and intelligent environmentalists in our state, and a lot of them are state employees; and a lot of them, today, are industrial managers, like those here, today, who have led Texasgulf to its major commitment to clean up its discharge into the Pamlico River. I want to say that I have been very favorably impressed with the positive attitude shown by the leadership at Texasgulf and by their new, highly respected, French parent firm, Elf Aquitaine. When I met with their executives in Paris, recently, they made it very clear that while they intended to have a successful business mining phosphate, they were absolutely committed to doing it in a way that they, their customers, and their neighbors would be proud. Their dedication to good environmental stewardship is a tribute to their proper sense of responsibility.

I am convinced that, together, we have set a new tone for the relationship between the regulators and those they regulate. I am certain it was not an easy decision on management's part to spend the $20 million this new closed-loop recycling system is estimated to cost. I am very pleased that this issue was worked out. In fact, I am so pleased that I asked to be able to deliver the new permit to the company personally. We have with us, today, Mr. Michel Schneider-Maunoury, chairman of the of the Board of Directors of Texasgulf, Incorporated, and its parent company, Elf Aquitaine, Incorporated, of France.[2] I would ask him and Mr. Tom Wright, president of Texasgulf, to join me for this presentation, and I will ask Mr. Wright to make any remarks he thinks appropriate.[3]

---

[1]Richard Paul Wilms (1948-   ), born in LeMars, Iowa; resident of Cary; B.A., University of Northern Iowa, 1971; M.S., University of Alabama, 1973; honorably discharged from U.S. Marine Corps, 1976. Water quality engineer, 1976-1978, air planning and environmental standards supervisor, 1978-1981, assistant director for programs, 1981-1985, appointed director, 1985, Division of Environmental Management, state Department of Natural Resources and Community Development. Richard Paul Wilms to Jan-Michael Poff, January 30, 1989.

[2]Michel Schneider-Maunoury (1931-   ), born in Vert-le-Petit, France; was educated at Ecole Polytechnique de Paris, 1950-1952, Ecole Nationale Superieure des Mines de Paris, 1953-1954, and Ecole Nationale Superieure de Petrole, 1954-1955; French army, 1952-1953. State mining engineer, Lyon region, 1955-1957; geophysicist, 1958-1960, various executive positions, 1962-1972, Entreprise de Recherches et d'Activites Petrolieres; assistant to president, Societe d'Exploitation et de Recherche de Petroleum en Tunisie, Tunisia, 1960-1962; senior vice-president for oil trading and strategic planning, 1973-1979, and for chemical and industrial development, 1980-1982, SNEA; chairman, president, chief executive officer, Elf Aquitaine, Inc., since 1982; president, since 1982, chief

executive officer, since 1988, Texasgulf, Inc. Priscilla Littlefield, secretary to Michel Schneider-Maunoury, to Jan-Michael Poff, March 13, 1990.

[3]Thomas J. Wright (1932-   ), born in Livingston, Montana; B.S., Montana School of Mines, 1959; U.S. Army, 1954-1956. Engineering and managerial positions with Texasgulf, Inc., 1964-1973, and since 1975, before becoming president, 1981, and chief operating officer, 1988; plant manager, Agrico Chemical Co., 1973-1975. Thomas J. Wright to Jan-Michael Poff, March 28, 1990.

LITERACY COMMISSION PRESS CONFERENCE

RALEIGH, JULY 21, 1988

[The following transcript was provided by the Governor's Office.]

GOVERNOR MARTIN: I want to present to you now one of the most important educational reports in North Carolina in many decades.[1] That is a study that will show us what we need to do to improve literacy in North Carolina. We've been talking so much about the number of jobs available in North Carolina, and the growth in those jobs, and yet there's that lingering concern that many of our workers are still in low-paying jobs. There's also the recognition that it's no wonder that many of them are in low-paying jobs when 25 percent lack basic literacy skills.

Well, one way to improve the pay level of our people is to recruit more jobs and that way the tight labor market would serve to bid up the pay of our workers; and indeed, since January, 1985, we've seen a net gain of 334,000 jobs right here in North Carolina. The report that is going to be presented to you on behalf of the Governor's Commission on Literacy predicts that, by the year 2000, we're going to add another half million jobs here in North Carolina. And yet, I wonder if we will be able to actually do that and fulfill that prediction if one fourth of our work force continues to lack basic literacy skills, and if our dropout rate of high school dropouts continues at about 26 percent.

It was in recognition of that that in 1987 I declared that to be the "Year of the Reader," to get special emphasis, and attention, and study of this particular concern that we have. That led to the establishment of the Governor's Commission on Literacy, chaired by former president William Friday of the University of North Carolina. And this report will share with you six goals that the commission has developed, along with forty specific, excellent recommendations for achieving those goals, as well as twenty-two organizational objectives. I would suggest, as well, in presenting President Friday to you to bring that report here today, that there are what I would call several overarching goals that should be ours, here in the state of North Carolina, as we look toward the future—the goals by which we should be measured as to our progress in reaching them.

First of all I would say that, by the year 1992, we should have in place efforts to double our present programs for adult literacy—to double our programs for dealing with adult illiteracy. We estimate that we currently reach perhaps 6 percent of those who need this additional help, and some of them drop out again. But it would seem to me that a reasonable goal would be to strengthen our program so that we can reach at least 12 percent a year and, in that way, would expect within the eight years remaining after 1992, should be able to deal substantially with that circumstance by the turn of the century and the year 2000.

Secondly, as I have previously indicated, I believe that it should be the goal for the state of North Carolina, as recommended for all southeastern states by the Southern Regional Education Board, which I recently served as chairman, to cut our high school dropout rate in half by the turn of the century. That would be a major goal, and I would say we should, in fact, set our goal slightly better than that, to cut it more than half by the turn of the century. The reason I say that is because the present level is [a] 26 percent dropout rate, and half of that, 13 percent, is an unlucky number, and so we'll shoot for something a little better and go for twelve years. But that's a goal that has been identified by all states, and I want North Carolina to be the first to make a commitment to that objective for the turn of the century.

Thirdly, I want to, working with our industries in North Carolina, to develop innovative, specific, industry-specific literacy programs and materials. We've already seen some pioneering work done by our community colleges, working particularly with the Broyhill Industries, to develop furniture manufacturing-specific literacy programs, and Burlington Industries, developing textile-specific programs; and I think we can do the same with so many other industries, which they would participate along with our community college specialists, developing computer-assisted, interactive, computer-assisted programs for people to improve their literacy for the kinds of jobs that they'll have. I also want us to develop job incentives for people who need that extra attraction to get them to do the things they need to do to learn to read. I'm pleased that one of the recommendations for [a] "North Carolina Compact" that is included in the report that we'll receive.[2] I also believe that it's important to have an office that will serve as a coordinating office for all of the many various agencies, and private organizations, and volunteer organizations who will be a part of it so that we can get the maximum effort out of every one of our assets here in North Carolina.

And so, I'm very pleased to present to you, for a discussion of the commission, and its work, and its findings, and its recommendation, the former president of [the] University of North Carolina, Bill Friday, who has served as chairman. Bill?

PRESIDENT FRIDAY: Thank you very much, Governor Martin, and good morning, friends. First, may I officially hand you the copy of the commission's report, sir.

GOVERNOR: Well, thank you, sir.

FRIDAY: We'll give you a printed version later—

GOVERNOR: I have an addressed copy, and I've looked at it very carefully. Thank you.

FRIDAY: We're an economy operation. You can see we used the mimeograph machine.

Ah, friends, on March 12th, a year ago, Governor Martin assembled this commission at the Mansion and invited all of us to engage in this study. Many of you were there and heard what he had to say about the six assigned responsibilities he gave us.[3] And over these sixteen months, I can speak for myself. I have had a very interesting experience, because I thought I knew something about some of the major problems of the state, but I found out I didn't know all that I thought I knew about this issue and how fundamental it is to the future of the state. So I thank you for the experience you've given me, and I'm sure all the other members of the commission would do likewise.

And let me say, Secretary Dorsey and Secretary Rhodes were members of this commission, and there are other members who are here. Will you raise your hand? I can't see you all, so—Mr. Lee Monroe is here, Ed Wilson[4] from the community college system, and others all of whom worked very hard during these deliberations, and there are many people here who will be available to you to answer questions, because this is not a simple problem. It is a very complicated problem.

We should, governor, thank Dr. Monroe, and Sheron Morgan[5] and Arlene Fingeret,[6] and other members of the organization, here, who did so much work to help us understand what this problem really is.

We're talking, here, about 8[00,000] to 900,000 people in our state, and particularly are we concerned about the more than 300,000 young people who are involved in this problem, the youth of the country, the state—and you just heard the governor refer to the fact that we have 23,000 young people who drop out annually from the educational process.

Now this commission says, in its documentation here—and I hope you'll take the time to read at least the first twenty-three pages of this report, because it's very instructive. What we're talking about, here, are skills that move from the basic reading skill to include the complex communication, analytical, and quantitative skills that are required, today, to get along in industry, and commerce, and in agriculture in our state. Five hundred thousand new jobs: I think that's a conservative prediction. But against that, you have got to understand that the requirements for getting involved, here, are now more than thirteen years of educational experience if you're going to be a part of this kind of industrial development in our state at the year 2000. That means you finish high school and then go beyond it if you're going to be, really going to be qualified to take part. And, like Governor Martin, I salute the industrial leadership of our state, because here is where some of the most creative, interesting, and innovative ideas are at work. He mentioned several of the companies—Duke Power is another, Borden Manufacturing in Goldsboro, the Statesville Stamping Company, others who are doing things to stimulate their employees and their colleagues in the work force, today—to go on and get their high school credibility: the diploma.

We're talking about a problem that affects adults, children, both races, both sexes, all regions of North Carolina. And what this report seeks to do is, first, create a new awareness in the state of what this problem really turns out to be. How pervasive is it? It says it gives the statistical evidence to back that up. It assesses what we're doing currently—that is, who is doing what. That is one of the assignments given to us by Governor Martin. And we found some very interesting things here, like the literacy council programs, the work of the community colleges, the work of the industries of the state, the schools, and the universities and colleges.

We then turn to what we can do to better solve, better work out the resolution to what we're trying to do here. Obviously, one immediate step is more communication within and among these various groups that are working on the problem—greater coordination, here, greater efforts to get to the people, because dealing in this literacy field is not a very simple problem; because you're dealing with human beings who sometimes don't want to tell you they can't read, or write, or do not possess the skills, and we have to be very sensitive to an understanding of these human factors that are involved.

A third element is continuity, here. This is not going to be a problem we can solve overnight. You heard Governor Martin say the Southern Regional Education Board says by x number of years let's cut it in half. But we want to do better than that in our state, and we can do better than that in our state. And what's going to overflow from this discussion, I hope, I mean the work that can come in the General Assembly when it comes in, under all of our concerns about this, will accelerate North Carolina's effort. This is a bipartisan property. Everybody is involved in this, and everybody will—your future in it—each of you is involved here, just as much of mine is, in resolving what we're going to do to help this group of citizens who constitute one sixth of our population.

If you really want to understand this as news media people, if I may address you directly, go to an adult education class, as some of us have done, and see what happens there. You can see men and women, forty, fifty years of age, learning to do these basic, fundamental things, like writing, reading, words, translating what they see and hear on paper. Let's go out to one of these classes at N.C. State, or the Wake Community College, and sit quietly in the back and see what you'll learn. And if you want to see the other side of it, go to the shelter over here, too, and eat supper one night in one of these food kitchens. Some of us did that, too. And you'll see that there is a large segment of society out here that we've all lost touch with, that we've got to do something about, and we're going to do something about it in our state because this is, first, a severe economic loss to North Carolina not to have this work force operating at its proper capacity.

You can see what a difference it will make when these individuals get these skills and can be gainfully employed. But one of the things I learned about this, personally, is how important it is to give these individual citizens the self-respect, the sense of personal dignity, the sense of personal identity, that possessing these skills would give. The absence of them is devastating, and if you don't believe it, go look for yourself.

The really fundamental question here, is, what is our state going to do about its human capital and getting it qualified to be actively involved in the work force of the state. We're talking about people already born; people already here; people who will be their work force, and every other industry's work force, as we turn into the new century. That's why this document takes the form and advocates the approach that it does, because these are things that can be done now. We can make some of these moves, and be aggressive about it, and get on with doing what the state, in my view, has a moral obligation to do. Thank you, sir.

GOVERNOR: Thank you, Bill Friday. Perhaps you would stay here a moment, and I'm confident there will be some questions from reporters. Yes?

REPORTER: Mr. Friday, I know this is not the direct purpose of this report, but has there been any thought given as to what it might take in terms of money to address this problem?

FRIDAY: No, we did not cost it out. We really didn't have the time to do a lot of that. But much of this does not require additional money. It requires people sitting down together, talking about what we're doing, sharing experiences, and really redirecting our work effort. But I'm sorry I can't be more specific.

REPORTER: I was wondering if—you've been in education a long time— I wonder if you found out the problem is even worse than even you imagined.

FRIDAY: Quantitatively, yes; much larger in the sense of more people involved than I expected. I found out that it's in every region of the state, it's in every city of the state. It's in the farm community, it's in the urban areas. One of the reasons the William Kenan Trust, that I'm associated with, right now has put a huge grant into this area of activity [is] because we want to pursue the notion that maybe, within the family, where mother and child both go to school since the parent does not have a high school diploma, that this is a way to get inside the family where the basic decision of respecting education, respecting learning, has to take place anyway.

GOVERNOR: Tell them a little about that—what you found in Kentucky, Bill, and what you're proposing here in North Carolina.

FRIDAY: Some us went to a little place called Taylorsville, Kentucky, where we heard about this schoolteacher who had come upon the idea that where in a family neither of the parents had a high school diploma and there were little children from the age of three, four, and five years. And she persuaded the state to invest at least enough money so that, every day, mother gets on the school bus with this three and four year-old child, and they both go to school. And they sit in the classroom, and the child gets the kindergarten-type instruction and the mother is getting what she needs in math, and English, and social studies to get the high school equivalency.

I spent a day just wandering through all these classes, watching. Here were twelve women, two of whom had been abandoned by their husbands and had three children each. None of them had completed the twelfth grade. All of them were living in circumstances that we would define as poverty, and you wondered why this would work at all.

There was great laughter and enjoyment. You could see something was happening in the chemistry of this class. So I turned to the superintendent, and I said, "Why is this so?" He said, "Well, you forgot how important it is to learn to read, and write, and communicate." And the whole purpose of this is thereby to get into the General Electric plant, in Louisville, where the job would make the difference. Four of these twelve people lived in homes with no indoor plumbing, and you can imagine that that goes on.

You look around in our state, and you can find some instances; and we're going to begin now with four model schools in North Carolina that you've read about in your papers this past week. Dr. Sharon Darling,[7] who is the person involved here, is now associated with the Kenan Trust through the Southern Regional Education Board, and this was worked out when Governor Martin was chairman. And now we're on the way, and Mrs. Fingeret and others in North Carolina are doing things equally exciting and interesting. The point is, we want everybody to appreciate it, and here is a large segment of our population who deserves a second chance; and we've got to find a way to make them productive citizens and give them the kind of self-respect and decent life that they're entitled to have. So that's why we're putting so much effort into this, so much energy into it; why Governor Martin singled it out as his primary objective during the year 1987.

I think this report, given all of the involvement that we came upon—all of the people who have been at work and put their lives into this for so many years and not received any attention or recognition as we should have been given as citizens. Nevertheless, we've resolved the differences that were there. We now know what the common objectives should be, and it's a matter now that turns to the chief executive and to the legislative leadership. But it's just as certain, in my mind, as I'm standing here, that unless and until we get at this problem and get this work force group up to where they deserve to be, the state will not progress at the rate it should. And this has been true in many states around the union.

REPORTER: You said something about the chief executive and the legislature as to the funding and the implementation.

FRIDAY: Well, there are coordination proposals here, there are advocacy positions, things—there's also an appendix here that has the youth at risk.[8] You'll want to pay particular attention to this, and because I think we've got to attack the problem in five or six directions at once: adult education, the dropout issue, the family issue. If we're really going to get it out of the way and get on with it, it's going to take this kind of coordinated effort; that can only come, the direction for that, can only come from the chief executive of the state. But you've got to involve the legislative leadership, because they, of course, create the financing. But they are, I have found equally interesting—we had members of that group working with us also.

REPORTER: (Largely inaudible on tape)—two or three others . . . recommendations to create an office of literacy . . . Department of Administration . . . describe . . . duplicate a lot of work that's already being done.

GOVERNOR: That apparently was someone who had not read the report, because the report does not propose an agency that would deliver services in competition with someone else. Rather, it would be a small, lean staff office that would have the responsibility to coordinate all of the existing agencies and any additional agencies, as well as the private businesses and volunteers who would be involved in our total literacy program. There was one suggestion that was incorrect, that the literacy office would be providing literacy training. No, that's not necessary and not intended at all, and that's not recommended, as you'll see. We already have the North Carolina Department of Community Colleges, with a strong program which they believe can be strengthened even more, and the concept would be to rely on them to continue to build their programs and their techniques, because they've pioneered this as well as anybody in America.

Our North Carolina community college system has pioneered the Adult Basic Literacy Education. The acronym for that is ABLE: A-B-L-E. And they have taken the PLATO [Programmed Logic for Automatic-Teaching Operation] system and have developed that to a way it works very well for people. We don't intend to duplicate that. We want to be able to strengthen it.

But not all the effort would be in the community colleges. For example, a large part of the recommendations have to do not with those who are already categorized as adult illiterates, but with those who could become illiterate adults if they drop out of school—and if they don't drop in [in] the first, second, or third grades. And so that means that the Department of Public Instruction and our 140 school systems all over North Carolina are going to have a very important part to play. We're not going to duplicate that by any means. All we want is someone to help them coordinate these programs in the community colleges and public schools with programs in private industry.

We found so many employers that have found, that have decided, that if no one else is going to solve the problem of their employe[es] who can't read, that they're going to do it. I'm proud of the fact that the state of North Carolina is one of those exemplary employers, because many of our departments have already put in place pro-grams, that I asked all of them to do, that would help to identify employees who need help with both English language and mathe-matics skills—those basic literacy skills of that sort—and to help them to get the help that they need, encourage them, work with them, not in a punitive way but in a, you know, family approach to encourage them to get what they need. At the same time, our public libraries have a very important part to play for promoting literacy and seeing that there are the kinds of materials that are available for people who are just beginning to learn to read.

Our prison system has launched a program, and they'll be develop-ing additional ideas because of the very high correlation we found between the inmate population and illiteracy. It's much higher than any other correlation that you'd find. That doesn't mean that anyone who's illiterate turns to crime. No, it just means that most of those who turn to crime are illiterate. And we believe if we can solve that, we can have a big impact on that area, as well.

FRIDAY: There was one additional reason behind this, governor.

GOVERNOR: For the office of literacy?

FRIDAY: Yeah. That is, with all that we've done, and all that is being done by all of the agencies that are identified, we still have 900,000 people who are suffering from this disability. Although we figure, and very strongly believe, that when you get these groups together through this mechanism, we will exchange ideas, get on with what we need to do, and get it moving so much more expeditiously. This is what was behind the reasoning. Thank you, very much.

GOVERNOR: And as a matter of fact, we've talked with President Scott of the community college system, and he's indicated that he endorses this approach. That doesn't mean that everybody likes every idea that anybody comes up with—you know how that is—but I think that criticism, while everyone is entitled to their views, that was probably misplaced in this instance because the report is just now being presented. We've had people who have worked with it, and those who have worked with us on it have had a lot of input into the design. I think the community college people will be very pleased at the emphasis in here on establishing a new mechanism for funding, instead of the full-time equivalent program concept that's been used which makes it very difficult for them to get the kind of resources they need for the particular approach for adult literacy education. This will help them to become more efficient to deliver [a] successful conclusion for those students that they do get, and it will help them be able to attract more. And so there are so many [different] people involved and that's why it was felt by the commission that a separate, small, distinct coordinating office was needed.

---

[1]*Literacy for the 21st Century: Recommendations of the Governor's Commission on Literacy* ([Raleigh]: Office of Policy and Planning, North Carolina Department of Administration, July, 1988), hereinafter cited as *Literacy for the 21st Century*.

[2]Based on the Boston Compact, the proposed North Carolina Compact was envisioned as a means of promoting "the participation of business and industry in making entry-level jobs available to persons improving their basic skills." *Literacy for the 21st Century*, 13.

[3]The Literacy Commission's six primary duties were listed in Executive Order Number 32, *N.C. Session Laws, 1987*, II, 2327.

[4]Edward H. Wilson, Jr. (1944-   ), born at Fort Benning, Georgia; resident of Cary; A.B., 1967, M.A., 1969, University of North Carolina at Chapel Hill; Ed.D., North Carolina State University, 1973. Principal, Apex High School, 1969-1972; education development officer, 1973-1978, associate vice-president for instructional services, 1978-1980, Wayne Community College; president, Roanoke-Chowan Technical College, 1981-1983; executive vice-president, state Department of Community Colleges, since 1983. Edward H. Wilson, Jr., to Jan-Michael Poff, June 29, 1990.

[5]Sheron Keiser Morgan (1942-   ), born in Temple, Texas; resident of Clayton; B.A., Mount Holyoke College, 1964; Ph.D., University of North Carolina at Chapel Hill, 1973. Assistant political science professor, director, Community Development Institute, Mars Hill College, 1969-1973; project officer, Office of Economic Opportunity, Department of Human Resources, 1973; policy analyst, Office of Governor James E. Holshouser, Jr., 1973-1974; local and regional affairs chief, Office of Intergovernmental Relations, 1974-

1975; policy analyst, 1977-1979, Policy Section chief, 1979-1985, deputy director, 1985-1988, and director, since 1988, Office of Policy and Planning, Department of Administration. Sheron Keiser Morgan to Jan-Michael Poff, July 12, 1990.

[6]Arlene Fingeret, associate professor of adult and community college education, North Carolina State University; B.S., Massachusetts Institute of Technology; M.S., Ph.D., Syracuse University. *North Carolina State University Bulletin, Undergraduate Catalog, 1989-1991* ([Raleigh: North Carolina State University], December, 1988), 494.

[7]Sharon K. Darling (1944-   ), born in Louisville, Kentucky; B.S., University of Louisville; M.A., Western Kentucky University. Adult basic education teacher, Louisville, 1970-1975; supervisor, Jefferson County (Kentucky) Public Schools, 1975-1978; project director, Jefferson County Adult Reading Program, 1978-1982; director, National Dissemination Project, U.S. Department of Education, 1982-1984; director, Adult Community Education Division, Kentucky Department of Education, 1984-1987; executive director, Literacy Concepts, Inc., 1987-1988; director, Kenan Trust Family Literacy Project, since 1988; president, National Center for Family Literacy, Inc., since 1989; consultant; author. Sharon K. Darling to Jan-Michael Poff, July 6, 1990.

[8]Appendix A, "Report of the Governor's Task Force on Youth at Risk," *Literacy for the 21st Century*, 18-22.

1988 BOARD OF EDUCATION LEADERSHIP CONFERENCE

CHARLOTTE, JULY 23, 1988

I am particularly pleased to be a part of this conference on educational leadership for our state, because I've got some major, specific proposals that I want your help to thin[k] through. It is especially pleasing, for Craig Phillips's valedictory conference as state superintendent, that we be meeting in Charlotte.

Where We've Been

It was here that he and I worked together, in 1967-1968, to reverse a pattern of neglect for our local schools by a previous county commission that had put schools last in priority and bragged about it. It was here that we persuaded this community to pass a major bond issue that was needed for school construction and renovation to modernize the Charlotte-Mecklenburg facilities. It was here that, working with the local school board and its chairman, Bill Poe,[1] we led this community to maintain and build local support for our local schools, even as many parents and students were distracted by issues arising out of court-ordered busing and pupil assignments based on race. And it is here that we have come today to continue our efforts to build schools, to strengthen instructional programs in our schools, and to lift up the occupation of public schoolteacher as not only one of the noblest and most satisfying professions, but also one in which good teachers can find professional advancement and better pay; we're doing that through the Career Development Program first pioneered right here in this Charlotte-Mecklenburg system.[2]

For nearly four years now in our present positions, Craig and I have worked to build the state's financial support for public schools by putting schools first in our order of priorities. After the previous twenty-four years in which schools' percentage share of the state General Fund for Operations went down almost every year (see Chart A), I have proposed budgets for every year in which our schools' share increased. After a twenty-three-year erosion of schools' share from 64.3 percent to 42.5 percent of the General Fund, we have sustained a steady, five-year, uninterrupted improvement to 46.4 percent; and we intend to continue that progress, because there's so much to be done.

We are halfway along, and right on schedule, with the General Assembly's Basic Education plan, designed even before I became governor. It's true the legislature appropriated more than I proposed in my first two years, but they appropriated less than I proposed these last two years. And Craig and I have pushed the General Assembly to assist the counties in their responsibility to build schools. While my proposal to finance 10,000 new classrooms in four years, with a $1.5 billion bond issue, requiring no tax increase, was never voted on or formally debated, it did inspire the legislature to enact instead a tax increase to build half that many classrooms in ten years. At least we can agree that some new schools are better than no new schools. Yet, many counties find that they must now resort to bond financing anyway, at higher local interest rates, to build the additional classrooms needed. Still, some progress is better than no progress.

Where We're Going

And I am very excited that we are on the eve of extending the career ladder and its opportunities for promotions to teachers and other instructional personnel statewide. After one more year of experience with the sixteen pilot systems, if you will continue to push firmly for this, we will finally be able to offer better pay for better teachers in every school in North Carolina. I, for one, am strongly convinced, as a former teacher, that this will be the reform with the greatest potential for strengthening the quality of our public schools of any change we've ever implemented.

While this vital reform had to face intensive criticism and efforts to block it, during the last two years it has won a high degree of support from participating teachers. They have seen firsthand that, through the career ladder, there has been greater opportunity for professional growth; improvement in the quality of classroom instruction; more time on task in the classroom; and enhancement of the status of teaching as a profession. Had we gone forward statewide, this year, as I had recommended in my 1987 budget, teachers in every school would have the satisfaction of knowing that they would be eligible for raises and promotions to Career Level I and that 90 percent would make it, or more. Instead, this was deferred to await two more years of trial in the sixteen pilots, even though those two more years would deal almost exclusively with Career Levels II and III, with no significant further experience with Career Level I. So, two more years were wasted unnecessarily.

Proposed Teachers' Pay

I mention this also because it allows me to disprove the false claim that my proposals for teachers' pay have been less than the General Assembly has enacted. My worthy political opponent has charged that my budget proposals for pay increases for teachers had been only 13.2 percent and offered less than the General Assembly had enacted. That turns out to be incorrect, because his analysis of my proposal conveniently neglects to count all the money I proposed. He disregards a unique and very substantial part of my proposal, namely, the career ladder. That's more teacher pay on average, friends. He also failed to count general pay increases which I had included in my biennial budgets for the second year of each biennium. He only counts a part of my proposal if it passed in its original form.

I am pleased to tell you what the truth is: that if my proposals had all been enacted, average teachers' pay through this fiscal year would be greater than was actually enacted, and our teachers would have the confidence of knowing that we had committed for much larger incentive increments for them as they advanced up that ladder. Specifically, the combined increases in compensation adopted by the legislature these last four sessions have added 33.5 percent to average pay for teachers. Had my proposals all been adopted, without change, the average pay commitment for teachers would have grown by 34.7 percent, just over one percentage point better than the legislature enacted (see Chart B)—and that's if you give me credit only for the freestanding percentage increase of each year and compound them.

My proposal comes out slightly better, but if you take my 1987-1989 budget, and adopt it, the average teacher pay would have risen to

$28,045, much closer to the national average—$1,626 closer! We would only be 5 percent behind the national average had my biennial budget priorities been followed, but the money was spent on other things, and we'll end up 10 percent behind! I thought you might want to know that.

That shows you how very important career ladder promotions can be to provide better pay for better teachers, and what's more, we would be within a year or two of substantially bigger incentive raises for those who qualify for Career II and III promotions in all our schools, not just the sixteen pilots. Instead, we must tell them to wait patiently another year or two.

Even so, I have set a goal for North Carolina to raise teacher pay to the national average or above, via the career ladder and scale increases, by 1992. We can do it if we make that our top priority, and that will be my top priority. We cannot do it if we keep stalling. Even if you want to do some more work on Career Level II or III, there's no good reason to continue delaying Career Level I.

Illiteracy

Recent years have seen a growing concern about the extent of adult illiteracy, in North Carolina and across our nation, and about the high school dropout rate that stands at 26 percent. For that reason I designated 1987 as the "Year of the Reader" and appointed the Governor's Commission on Literacy, headed by former UNC president Bill Friday, to map out the extent of the problem and to propose remedies to get us where we need to be.

This past Thursday, President Friday presented their report. They set forth six general goals and forty specific recommendations to get us there, along with twenty-two procedural proposals to make it happen. Some items can be carried out administratively, some will require legislation, and some will be done by business and volunteers at no public cost.

All deserve our support. They would strengthen our programs dealing with all levels of the problem: adult literacy training at our community colleges, literacy incentives in our businesses and our prisons, high school dropout prevention, and early childhood readiness training. The General Assembly did not fund the early readiness programs I requested, but they did leave us some room to make progress if we could find a way to do it without any additional money, and we're thankful for that. In a few weeks, I hope to be able to announce a new alternative, workable plan to improve public-funded day-care services so as to incorporate more readiness experiences for eligible four-year-olds at risk of becoming dropouts. Stay tuned.

We are determined to deal with the problems of illiteracy and dropouts. To this end, I have set a goal for North Carolina to cut the dropout rate in half by the year 2000, as recommended by the Southern Regional Education Board while I was chairman, and I want North Carolina to be the first state to commit to that objective. Another major goal of this administration is to have operational, by 1990, a preschool readiness program for all those four-year-old children at risk of becoming high school dropouts.

Foreign Language

Meanwhile, another innovative proposal I put forward last year has already moved into operation. I am speaking of the summer foreign language institutes, which have started up this year with a French program, for teachers, at the University of North Carolina at Greensboro, and a Spanish program at East Carolina University. Surely there are more good ideas being worked on to improve public education in North Carolina than at any time in recent history. Yet, there are so many other initiatives that need to be taken. We must not accept the status quo or rest on our laurels.

Career Education

Several months ago, I began to discuss with my brother Joe, a new school board member in Mecklenburg County, our concerns about the high school dropouts and the tragic consequences for these young people who are not ready for the demands of today's workplace. Their communications skills are not adequate. They lack the trainability needed for so many technically demanding jobs. They just aren't prepared for a good job.

One of [the] ideas that arose out of those discussions was the concept of a much stronger high school program emphasizing career education. Either as a separate, free-standing career education high school or as a magnet program within a comprehensive high school, there would be a new commitment to job readiness as an educational objective of our schools. Our students would be ready for college or ready for a job. We would not intend these to be dead-end programs for potential dropouts, but they would attract and meet the needs of academically gifted and not so gifted, for high-tech trades and not so high tech, with the more technical courses being provided by or at the community college. We would provide a solid grounding in basic literacy and arithmetic skills with remedial courses for those who need them. Upon graduation, every student would be guaranteed a job by supporting businesses in the area, and every student would be guaranteed admission to the two-year junior college program at the community college.

Our goal is to have improved and expanded centers, with academic track options, in sixteen communities by 1992. Each would be under the jurisdiction of the local school board. This goal recognizes that we presently have eight career education centers in our state: in Burlington [sic], Ashe, Forsyth, Wilkes, and Union counties; and Lincolnton, Burlington, Winston-Salem, and Greensboro city schools. We are fortunate to be able to build on what these school systems have done, and are doing, in vocational education.

Our goal for expanded career education is based, in large measure, on the knowledge that about 60 percent of North Carolina high school students do not go on to a four-year college; they enter the job market, or a community college program, or both. This 60 percent of our students constitute a neglected majority we must do something about.

Finally, I propose—in conjunction with the improvement and expansion of career centers within the public school structure and their eventual expansion throughout the public school system—the development of a North Carolina School of Technology, similar to the North Carolina School of Science and Mathematics. This school could be built on the N.C. State Centennial Campus, or at North Carolina A&T, or some other campus, or some existing appropriate structure could be modified for use. That would be decided by the Board of Governors. As a demonstration site, the institution would have a modern facility, the latest equipment, up-to-date teaching techniques, and a place to train and retrain vocational teachers for secondary schools and community colleges.

One other thing I want to talk to you about is:

Local Control: Flexibility

In recent years, the legislature has tied resources for schools to an intricate and precise set of minimum requirements, specifying in substantial detail how each school district should spend state funds. For example, it has specified student-teacher ratios, the number of counselors in the schools, the length of the school day, a standard curriculum, and even the means through which a child can be promoted from grade to grade. As well-intentioned as some of these regulations are, they may serve as a serious impediment to innovation.

Do you remember that, in 1984, the School Finance Committee Pilot Project was instituted in order to provide school districts with a small measure of flexibility? Eight local education agencies were given very limited spending discretion in the use of state funds, which superintendents could use for local projects. From all indications, this project has been highly successful.

Local flexibility has provided school systems greater freedom and opportunity to make decisions and judgments that have enabled them to address local needs much better, rather than trying to run a school by a cookbook. Superintendents have asked for more flexibility in areas such as funding, staffing, certification, and facilities. I believe you should have the necessary flexibility to make needed changes in your schools. Centralized planning to such detail at the state level is not the best way to do this.

I didn't just start talking about flexibility today, after the superintendents' meeting yesterday. I started urging that in 1985. In fact, the only criticisms I had for the BEP was (1) to put teacher pay as first priority, and (2) to allow more flexibility. Last year we attempted to give a measure of flexibility to local school districts through legislation, Senate Bill 259, introduced by Senator Daniel Simpson of Morganton.[3] This bill would have allowed educators in the local units a degree of flexibility to vary, somewhat, from the strict mandates of the Basic Education plan when they believed such action could better serve the students.

It must be obvious that we will never achieve the degree of educational innovation the times require until we provide greater autonomy to our local units. Peter Drucker, in his excellent book *Innovation and Entrepreneurship*, emphasizes the importance of professional autonomy in the management of our schools. He says that "Schools . . . need to be entrepreneurial and innovative fully as much as business does. Indeed, they need it more."

When Drucker says that schools need to be entrepreneurial, he is really saying that they must be able and willing to take risks and free to do so. You may be sure I shall continue to press for legislation to provide more autonomy to local units. No issue is any more essential to educational quality than this: that those on the front line have greater authority to fashion programs to increase educational results.

Conclusion

With all the developments in technology and the growing knowledge about human learning, and how to bring it about at a higher level and in a shorter time, there is every reason to believe that we are standing at the threshold of a new age in education. At no time have we had available to us any greater opportunities for exciting breakthroughs in human learning. At no time have we had a greater degree of commitment. I think it's great that we now have two strong political parties vying to see who can do the most for public schools. That's great! We never had that before, and it shows!

I firmly believe that we will see breakthroughs to help us with problems of illiteracy, school failure, and dropouts on a scale every bit as dramatic as we have seen in computer science, the physical sciences, or biology, if only we are ready to respond to them and allow the local flexibility to be able to do so. We can be the Columbus ushering in a new era of education, if—if we can find better ways to work together, as one united state, for education—educators and business people, and Republicans and Democrats, setting aside partisan differences for the greater good of all.

Before Columbus discovered the New World, all Spanish coins bore the inscription *Ne plus ultra*, "No more beyond." That was sort of their way of boasting, "We're number one!" It was also a way of accepting the conventional wisdom about limits. No more beyond: *Ne plus ultra*.

After the opening of the New World, the Spanish, who had thought that they had reached the apex where no greater achievement was possible, because their vision of the world and possibilities had been enlarged by Columbus, changed all coins to read *Plus ultra*: "More beyond." There is more beyond in education, and together we will find it and make it our new world.

---

[1]William E. Poe (1923-   ), born in South Hill, Virginia; B.S., Wake Forest University, 1947; J.D., Harvard University, 1950; U.S. Army Air Force, 1943-1946. Assistant director, Institute of Government, University of North Carolina at Chapel Hill, 1950-1952; Mecklenburg County tax attorney, 1952-1956; member, chairman, Charlotte-Mecklenburg Board of Education, 1964-1976; president, North Carolina Baptist Men, 1982-1985; second vice-president, 1983-1985, president, since 1985, North Carolina Baptist State Convention. *News and Observer*, January 19, 1986.

[2]The Charlotte-Mecklenburg Schools Career Development Program was implemented in August, 1984. The goal was to produce experienced, successful educators who also could be rewarded financially for their accomplishments. Jay M. Robinson, superintendent of Charlotte-Mecklenburg Public Schools, 1977-1986, to Jan-Michael Poff, April 4, 1986.

[3]Daniel Reid Simpson (1927-   ), born in Morganton; B.S., 1949, LL.B., 1951, Wake Forest University; U.S. Army, 1945-1946. Attorney; former criminal court judge; former attorney, councilman, and mayor, town of Glen Alpine; member, state House, 1957-1963, and Senate, since 1985; former chairman, Burke County Republican Executive Committee. *North Carolina Manual, 1987-1988,* 323.

Simpson and Donald R. Kincaid (R-Caldwell) jointly introduced S.B. 259, "A Bill Providing For Variances from the Basic Education Program in Local School Districts," on April 2, 1987. The bill was assigned to the Senate Education Committee, where it remained through the end of the session. *N.C. Senate Journal, 1987,* 173.

NORTH CAROLINA SHERIFFS ASSOCIATION

KILL DEVIL HILLS, AUGUST 1, 1988

[The following address is nearly identical to the governor's remarks to the North Carolina Law Enforcement Officers Association, Asheville, August 4, and similar to his speech at the opening of the Durham Council on Alcoholism's Alcohol and Drug Resource Center, Durham, August 11, 1988.]

The North Carolina Sheriffs Association has a long and distinguished history of leadership on criminal justice matters in North Carolina. This Sixty-sixth Annual Meeting and Retraining Conference is an example of this organization's ongoing commitment to professional excellence.

Contemporary novelist Tom Wolfe wrote a novel, *The Right Stuff,* about the skills, courage, and personal lives of early astronauts and test pilots. The "right stuff" that Wolfe refers to is that intangible quality that made those pilots the right people at the right time to do a critically important job. You, the sheriffs of our state, are the ones with the right stuff to do the difficult job of preserving domestic order.

Law enforcement is a job that brings with it great responsibility, danger, and stress. We recently received a tragic reminder of this cruel reality with the death of Trooper Michael Martin, who died in the line of duty July 22.[1] According to the state Justice Department's 1987 Uniform Crime Report, twenty-one law enforcement officers have died in the line of duty during the last ten years. That report goes on to say that, on the average, a law enforcement officer is assaulted in North Carolina once every four hours. As one sheriff said, "I guess if it wasn't dangerous, they wouldn't need us!"

As law enforcement officers, you look to elected officials to give you the moral support and resources with which to do this all-important job. I believe it is important that we work together as full partners in the fight against crime. Some of you may recall that it was for this reason, back in 1984, that I campaigned in support of restoring retirement benefits for all law enforcement officers, as you had asked me. It brought me great personal satisfaction when retirement benefits were extended, once again, to all law enforcement officers last year.

It is also in that spirit that Crime Control and Public Safety Secretary Joe Dean has repeatedly shared the resources of his department to aid you in your public safety efforts. He has given his promise to you that the Highway Patrol's helicopter will be at your disposal when needed to aid you in any investigation; just two weeks ago, Madison sheriff's deputies and A.L.E. agents joined forces and destroyed almost $11 million in marijuana plants that were spotted from that helicopter. The National Guard provided four-wheel-drive vehicles last winter to help the Johnston County Sheriff's Department respond to a snow emergency.

When many of you expressed concerns last year over proposed new jail standards, I didn't think it was right to require higher standards for your jails than for state prisons. I instructed that a new task force be appointed to rewrite those regulations and to incorporate your ideas into the new version. That task force includes two members of your association.

The Division of Emergency Management stands ready to aid you and coordinate the state's response to any natural or man-made emergency; and, upon its completion, the Highway Patrol's precision driving course near Garner will be available to you, too, as a training resource for your people.

As helpful as it is, I also know that providing funds and sharing resources is not enough to stem the tide of crime. Government also has to work to create an environment which discourages criminal activity and encourages appropriate social behavior. To that end, we have undertaken a number of crime-prevention initiatives.

—Through a program of both education and enforcement, we have tackled the hideous crime of child abuse.

—We have aggressively promoted crime prevention within public housing.

—We have called attention to the plight of the victims of crime.

—We have enlisted the public's help in the war against crime through programs such as Community Watch and Crimestoppers.

—To provide our children with better role models, we have continued an advisory board of Athletes Against Crime, started in the previous administration.

—Through the Students Against Drunk Driving program, we have enlisted public support in our crusade to make our highways safer.

Now we've got MADD, SADD, and GLADD: Government Leaders Against Drunk Driving;

—And through "Operation Eagle," we have taken that crusade to the streets through strict enforcement of our state's DWI laws.

—Perhaps our most significant efforts at crime prevention lie in the area of public education, getting our young people trained and trainable for a productive, law-abiding life.

The promotion of crime-prevention programs is an important element in the battle against crime, but it is not the only element. We must also have an aggressive program of law enforcement. To accomplish this, state government needs to give people like you the resources you need to do your very best out in the field. For that very reason, last spring I submitted a number of significant proposals to the General Assembly.

I don't have to tell you that our nation is in the deadly grip of drug abuse. Although North Carolina has in place some of the toughest drug trafficking laws in the land, they have been watered down by other laws that allow many pushers to become eligible for parole after having served only one eighth of their sentences. When one considers the human misery these criminals have brought to our people, I can't help but question the wisdom of laws that give these people a break that they do not deserve. For that reason, I proposed legislation that abolishes parole and good- and gain-time credits for convicted drug traffickers. They should know that if they are convicted of trafficking drugs in North Carolina, they will have no hope of parole or early release. Unfortunately, the legislative leadership said, "Not now."

I also proposed an amendment to the state's continuing criminal enterprise statute that would provide for mandatory life sentences, without benefit of parole or good- and gain-time credits, for drug kingpins. Now that's what I call real life. Forget rehabilitation for the kingpins—all they want is to get back into the flow of their terrorist war against our people. But again I was told, "Not now."[2]

The war against drugs is not a political issue, it is a people issue. That's why the Governor's Crime Commission has earmarked more than a million dollars in drug grants during this biennium to the SBI. This must be a nonpartisan campaign. That's also why I threw the full support of my office behind worthy anti-drug proposals of both Democrat and Republican legislators.

I asked the General Assembly to continue and extend a law that allows a district attorney to convene a special investigative grand jury for the purpose of probing drug trafficking. Otherwise, the law would have expired on October 1. In this case, the legislature did act positively, and I commend them for it.

I also supported Representative Charles Cromer's bill which designates drug trafficking as one of the aggravating circumstances that can be considered in the imposition of the death penalty in first-degree murder cases. But I was told by the legislative leadership, "Not now."

I also supported Senator Harold Hardison's bill that would make it a felony to possess any amount of cocaine. This legislation is needed because of the introduction of crack, a deadly substance even when trafficked in small amounts. Again I was told, "Not now."

Another serious problem that is being addressed by state government is drunken driving. Nearly half of the people that die each year on our state's highways are killed in DWI-related crashes. Many of those killed are the drunk drivers themselves. Too often, those killed are innocent victims.

During the short session of the General Assembly, I supported a package of DWI laws that was introduced last year but left in legislative limbo. This package included an immediate thirty-day license revocation for DWI offenders. This has the support of the people of North Carolina. It deserves the support of the General Assembly, but again the legislative leadership said, "Not now."

The lawmakers did vote to lower, from 0.10 percent to 0.04 percent, the presumptive blood alcohol level for commercial drivers of trucks and buses.[3] The truck and bus companies were for it. The strange thing is, however, it doesn't go into effect until next June 1, and it sunsets on June 30. It'll be gone before we can get the first case to trial! The only excuse for such an absurd result is for the General Assembly to appear to be doing something about this important matter, while actually doing next to nothing. I can't understand why anyone would choose to trifle with such a serious issue.

In an effort to promote highway safety and the safety of the general public, I asked state lawmakers for sixty additional highway patrolmen. We did not get any. We were told, "Not now." Well, we'll just keep trying.

North Carolina is currently engaged in the largest prison construction program in its history. This is necessary to relieve overcrowding if we are to convince the federal courts that North Carolina can operate a prison system that is constitutionally defensible. Failure to do so would mean that the federal courts could take over our prisons and run them without regard for the expense, or that it would deny funds for other worthy programs. Meanwhile, you and your jails have had to carry part of the burden of accommodating our transition every time we bump the limit of 18,000. At least let me thank you for your patience and spirit of teamwork.

At the same time we are building new prisons, we also need to look to alternatives to incarceration for those persons, convicted of nonviolent crimes, who can pay their debt to society and make restitution to their victims without going to prison. It is a concept that I proposed two years ago and only now, thanks to the work of people like Senator David Parnell,[4] is beginning to gain the acceptance of the legislative leadership.

We also must ensure that those who are on probation or parole are under adequate supervision. My budget recommendations included proposals designed to beef up the Division of Adult Probation and Parole. The legislative leadership said, "OK, but not now." They tagged on a provision that prevents us from hiring any new officers until next February. Now why would they do a thing like that?

Again and again, we are told by the leaders of the General Assembly, "Not now." If this must be the case, then let me ask them this question: If not now, when?

One explanation they give is that, because it's an election year, we shouldn't do things that need doing! Why not? What kind of a deal is that? The people's needs do not stop during an election year; neither should their leaders.

A lot has been done to create a crime-free environment in North Carolina. We are moving closer, every day, toward a public consensus on a broad range of criminal justice issues. In public gatherings and in private conversations, the people of North Carolina have made their wishes known. They want to be safe in their homes, at their jobs, and on the highways. They want an end to illegal drug trafficking. They want an end to the abuse of children, senior citizens, and the defenseless. They want to get drunk drivers off our streets and highways. They want a strong system of public education that promotes economic growth and reduces the temptations of crime. They want a prison system that preserves public safety and serves the cause of justice.

State government, working closely with the people of this state and law enforcement groups such as yours, can see to it that these wishes are fulfilled. It requires hard work, some sacrifice, and a willingness on the part of the general public to give law enforcement officers such as yourselves the support and resources necessary to get the job done. It also requires a political leadership that is willing to put aside partisan differences and that is willing to work together for the common good.

Whenever we put aside our differences, and put North Carolina first, North Carolina's going to be first.

---

[1]Michael Louis Martin was pursuing a speeding motorcyclist, traveling in excess of 100 miles per hour down a two-lane Rockingham County road, when his patrol car slid into a furniture truck. The trooper died of severe head injuries received in the accident. *News and Observer,* July 25, 1988.

[2]The governor also spoke of the General Assembly's reluctance to amend the continuing criminal enterprise statute in his address at the opening of the Durham Council on Alcoholism Drug Resource Center. On that occasion, he added, "If a full life sentence without parole isn't good enough for these kingpins who line their pockets through the suffering of others, then I say let's provide the death penalty for them. That will tell these drug terrorists in a loud and clear voice that we don't want them operating in North Carolina."

[3]Martin was referring to c. 1112, *N.C. Session Laws, 1987, Regular Session, 1988,* III, identified earlier in this volume.

[4]David Russell Parnell (1925-   ), born in Parkton; resident of Robeson County; B.S., Wake Forest University, 1949; U.S. Army, 1945-1946. Merchant; farmer; Parkton mayor, 1964-1969; member, state House, 1975-1982, and Senate, since 1983; chairman, Senate Insurance Committee, and vice-chairman, Senate Appropriations-Justice and Public Safety Committee; Democrat. *North Carolina Manual, 1987-1988,* 314.

NATIONAL FOOTBALL LEAGUE EXPANSION COMMITTEE ANNOUNCEMENT

CAROWINDS, AUGUST 2, 1988

It is indeed both a pleasure and an honor to participate in making this historic announcement. Never before have two states joined forces towards a common goal the way we are joining forces today. I think our unity is going to be the key to success in this effort.

Carroll[1] has given you some vitally important facts and figures. He has presented the very strong case that Carolina has for selection by the NFL. He has, in effect, told you what's in it for the league. It's a winner!

I'd like to take a few minutes to tell you about the other side of the coin. I'd like to talk about what's in it for us, the citizens of Carolina: that stands for North and South Carolina as partners.

We all need to understand the significance of this undertaking. First of all, it's NFL football, our own team. I've just come from the opening of the Border Belt tobacco market, and they told me to get Carolina an NFL franchise—our own team! Yet, the importance of what we are doing goes far beyond the great game of football. It is one of the most important economic development challenges ever pursued in the Carolinas.

The economic effects of having an NFL team will include many things we're accustomed to seeing as a result of ordinary development. Construction of a stadium will produce work for hundreds of people. That stadium will need people to maintain it and a security staff. There will be people hired to work during games—ticket takers, vendors, and concessions operators; many of them will be selling products produced locally. Games will mean fans staying in the area overnight; eating at restaurants here and along the way; enjoying the entertainment found around here. In turn, this will boost those attractions to grow. The direct economic effects of having our own team will quickly move into the upper stages of the economic stratosphere, literally hundreds of millions of dollars.

Can any of us really imagine or calculate the advertising and promotion effects of having an NFL team here in Carolina? Even the experience of other areas wouldn't offer a true comparison, because few other areas have had the advantage of beginning with all the things going for them that we have going for us. Time after time, various parts of the Carolinas have won national attention by winning top ranking and recognition as a place to locate, invest, live, or develop. Now, add an NFL team to our track record, and what do you suppose will happen?

We already have strong state and local advertising efforts under way, aimed at increasing our chances with business prospects. Can we even begin to imagine the way those efforts would be reinforced by weekly exposure as an NFL area? The same goes for our combined $10-billion-a-year travel and tourism industry.

NFL expansion to Carolina will add to our revenues and our attractiveness to industry—and to ourselves! However, let us not forget the famous words of Andy Griffith: "What it was, was football."[2] All the rest I described is in addition to the game of football, but having our own team is why we're here.

Football, and all sports, are a way of life in Carolina. This is a region where the eyes of our business people are glued to a television screen instead of marketing charts or progress reports on football weekends as well as during the ACC [Atlantic Coast Conference basketball] Tournament every year; where record-smashing thousands gathered last summer to watch the most successful U.S. Olympic Festival ever held; where collegiate teams have brought home NCAA championships in basketball, lacrosse, soccer, and football. An NFL franchise will provide another outlet, and I mean a dominant one, for the interest of our great Carolina sports fans. This team has the potential to create enthusiasm as well as additional revenues for our area. It's a matter of pride: Carolina pride.

This is a fine project in many ways. Just being a part of it is exciting. It's a chance to be a part of a very historic undertaking that's bigger than all of us, and you don't get that many chances to be associated with such things. If we're going to be successful, we'll have to be more united—and we'll probably have to work harder than ever before. But this one's worth it. This will be our own team!

---

¹Carroll Ashmore Campbell, Jr. (1940-   ), born in Greenville, South Carolina; was educated at University of South Carolina; M.A., American University; honorary degree. President, Handy Park Co., 1960-1978; member, South Carolina House, 1970-1974, and Senate, 1976; member, U.S. House from South Carolina's Fourth Congressional District, 1979-1986; elected governor of South Carolina, 1986; Republican. *Who's Who in America, 1988-1989,* I, 469.

²Andrew Samuel Griffith (1926-   ), born in Mt. Airy; A.B., University of North Carolina at Chapel Hill, 1949. Stage, motion picture, and television actor; star of "Andy Griffith Show," 1960-1968, "Headmaster," 1970-1971, and "Matlock," since 1986. His humorous monologue, "What it Was, Was Football," 1953, gained Griffith national attention. *UNC Alumni Directory,* 450; "What it Was, Was Football," *Just For Laughs: The Rich and Unique Humor of Andy Griffith* [sound recording], by Andy Griffith (Capitol Records T-962, [n.d.]); *Who's Who in America, 1988-1989,* I, 1231.

PRESS RELEASE: GOVERNOR MARTIN'S STATEMENT ON WILDLIFE RESOURCES COMMISSION PERSONNEL MATTER

RALEIGH, AUGUST 5, 1988

The Wildlife Resources Commission at its last meeting took an unusual step of voting, 5-4, to remove one individual, Sergeant Terry Waterfield, from consideration for promotion to fill a vacancy at the rank of lieutenant. That was contrary to my expressed intention that the commission should stick to policy matters and select the executive director, but otherwise allow him to handle other personnel decisions. Upon inquiry, it has been learned that the Institute of Government had earlier advised the Wildlife Resources Commission that it had the right of approval of specific personnel changes under the law. In order to clarify this issue and prevent a recurrence of specific personnel action by the commission, I am preparing an executive order to make it plain that the commission has the responsibility to hire the executive director and to approve the plan of organization, but that the commission does not have authority to approve specific hirings and promotions, which shall be the responsibility of the executive director.[1]

Subsequent to the meeting described, the executive director, Charles Fullwood,[2] promoted David Hardy from sergeant to lieutenant. Since the decision has been made by Mr. Fullwood, who has the sole authority to make it, any further interference from others would be in further violation of my policy. Therefore, the appointment of Lieutenant Hardy will stand. It has been indicated that Sergeant Waterfield may file an objection, which he has a right to do, and it will be considered on its merits by the Personnel Commission under due process.

---

[1]Executive Order Number 75, "Concerning the Responsibilities of the Members and Personnel of the North Carolina Wildlife Resources Commission," was signed August 12, 1988. *N.C. Session Laws, 1989,* II, 3071-3076.

[2]Charles Fullwood, a Jacksonville native and seventeen-year veteran of the North Carolina Wildlife Resources Commission, was appointed executive director in February, 1986. He had served previously as field operations chief and became the commission's acting director in September, 1985. *News and Observer,* February 25, 1986.

STATE EMPLOYEES ASSOCIATION OF NORTH CAROLINA

WINSTON-SALEM, SEPTEMBER 2, 1988

It's always a great honor and pleasure to speak to a group that is so important to the continuing progress of our state and the welfare of its citizens. One great thing about being here, tonight, is that it gives me an opportunity to thank you, and those you represent, for your part in raising North Carolina to unprecedented heights. We're on the move. Together, we can keep a good thing going.

Just how good have things been? Consider this: In three and a half years, we have seen a net gain of 387,000 jobs, the highest level of employment in our state's history. In July, 1988, we had an incredible jobless rate of 2.9 percent. Estimated statewide employment in this same period stood at a record high of 3.235 million. And in 1987, our gross state product grew by a healthy 5.6 percent, compared to 2.9 percent growth in the gross national product.

Thanks to you and thousands of others throughout North Carolina—men and women, people of all races and religious persuasions, business and professional people, Democrats, and Republicans, and independents—we're on an economic roll. North Carolina is on the move. We've got a real thing going.

In spite of a fiscal fitness that has made North Carolina the envy of the entire nation, there are still the "bad news bearers" who will tell you at every opportunity that we are looking down into a fiscal abyss. To paraphrase Mark Twain, stories about impending fiscal disaster have been grossly exaggerated. The actual, unassailable facts are that we have had back-to-back budget surpluses every year since I took office; and in the 1987-1988 fiscal year, we had a budget surplus of $392 million, the largest surplus in the history of the state of North Carolina.

In spite of this incredible budget carry-over, some in the General Assembly said we were facing a deficit; that the governor had presented an unbalanced budget. First, let me say there are a lot of governors who would like to have this kind of surplus we have enjoyed over the past three years in North Carolina. These surpluses have made it possible to increase salaries and benefits of state employees. And if we can, working together [to] keep a good thing going, state employees will continue to benefit from our growing good fortune. I just wish the General Assembly had not spent the salary reserves I sent forward in the 1985-1987 and 1987-1989 biennium budgets.

Facts are stubborn things. Some, in order to convince the public that their governor is fiscally irresponsible, have charged that I submitted an unbalanced budget. Let me say as forcefully and unequivocally as possible: I have never submitted an out-of-balance budget, period, over, and out. In actual fact, in the short session of the General Assembly, I submitted a budget balanced to the very best revenue projections possible. This is common practice at the federal level, at the state level, and in business.

As you well know, revenue forecasts are far from being an exact science. No one can claim infallibility in this area. I relied on our good, conscientious career employees in the State Budget Office, in March, to estimate revenues for April, May, and June to finish out the fiscal year. They projected a $445 million balance to carry forward. When it was discovered, in June, that revenue as projected would not materialize, due primarily to an unpredictable revenue shortfall, I immediately sent a second amended budget balanced to new, projected revenues. That's not an unbalanced budget; that's *two* balanced budgets.

You don't have to be an economist to appreciate what continuing prosperity means to state workers; what it means to all our citizens in terms of better schools, better roads, more and better jobs, and a better quality of life. As participating partners in our economic progress, it is only fair that you should share in the fruits of our labors. Let's look for a moment at what our unprecedented economic performance over the past three and a half years has meant to you.

From 1977 through 1984, state employees saw a steady erosion of their wages in real purchasing power, which reached a low point in 1982. In other words, by 1982, state employees had seen their incomes eroded by more than 20 percent in terms of actual purchasing power. And when you asked that something be done, you got the 1982 version of "Not now!" Yes, facts are stubborn things.

Another way to state it is that during this eight-year period before I took office, in real dollars, state employees actually got increases that were less than the rate of inflation. These are unassailable facts. But even with these gains, we've got our work cut out for us. We still need to restore merit pay for state employees, as I proposed in my budget in 1987-1988 and again this year.

We've got to maintain a full-court press to get merit pay back into our state salary schedule, and we need to establish and maintain procedures to ensure that excellence is truly rewarded. We are doing this with the career ladder for teachers; we can do it for the rest of state employees, as well. The truth is, we have had consistent employee compensation increases over the past three years. I have not waited until an election year to make promises about what I will do for you if I'm elected. What I promise, I try to deliver. I am proud that, in all my actions, I have been guided by the twin doctrine of fairness and openness: no hidden agendas, no closed doors, no secret covenants.

When I assumed the office of governor, some people told me I couldn't trust state employees. They said I should be partisan and throw out employees of the opposing party, but I chose not to do business the usual way. I opted for fairness. Wherever possible, if a person was competent, and doing his or her job, and willing to work with me, I kept them on in my administration. The facts speak for themselves. Facts are, indeed, stubborn things.

Do you know how many Republicans there were in key administrative positions when I came into office? Exactly one. Well, that isn't exactly true. One Democrat, probably fearing that I would be like my predecessor, changed his registration to Republican about a month before I took my oath of office.

How many Democrats are in exempt positions in my administration? The irony is, I really don't know precisely how many. Party affiliation is not a requirement for a top administrative job; competence is—and a positive, constructive attitude is.

Last fall, you will recall I said that I did not think state employees should be treated as second-class citizens. Well, tonight I repeat that conviction, with this addition: I don't think excellence should be treated in the same way average performance is treated. Here's a story to illustrate my point:

This man was fishing in a lake. He really wasn't all that interested in catching anything, he was just enjoying the day. He looked down beside his boat and saw this snake with a frog in its mouth. He got to feeling sorry for the frog, so he reached down, grabbed the snake, took the frog out, and threw it on the bottom of his boat. Then he began to feel sorry for the snake, because he had deprived him of a meal. He looked around his boat for something to give to the snake. All he could find was a half-empty flask of bourbon. So, he took a snort, then reached down and grabbed the snake, gave it a belt, and let it go. He went back to his fishing and, about fifteen minutes later, the snake was back—this time, with two frogs.

This story illustrates what one writer calls the "greatest management principle in the world." If you want excellence, you've got to reward excellence. Otherwise, you're mandating mediocrity. State employees are a valuable state resource. Their creativity is beyond calculation. We need all their creativity to help solve a host of problems.

I know that all of you are concerned about what is happening to the cost of health care. You have seen costs go up at an alarming rate and the amount of benefits go down. Something must be done. No one has been successful in dealing with this problem, but I believe that putting our heads together, we can come up with some creative solutions. You and your family deserve the very best possible in health care, and I welcome the opportunity to work with you to see that you and yours get it. The biggest problem is that the legislature took this responsibility away from the governor, during the previous administration, and has not been inclined to give it back.

You know, of course, that last year I established a task force under the chairmanship of my chief of staff, Phil Kirk. The purpose of this task force was to study your policy platform and to figure out, together, how we could achieve implementation of your goals. This group proved so successful in creating a spirit of collaboration and give-and-take, and in helping our administration become sensitive to your needs and concerns, that I think we should continue to work together, in an established way, on problems of overriding concern to your members.

One effect of our collaboration was to show that when we work together, we can arrive at better solutions than when we work separately. Another outcome of our partnership was to let you know that when you talk, we listen. We respond.

One of our responses has been to your interest in having more flexible benefits, the kind of benefit plan that will allow each state employee to choose a combination of benefits most appropriate to his or her needs. What we now have is a Procrustean benefit plan. You may remember the story of ol' Procrustes, who would seize travelers, tie them to a bedstead, and either stretch them or cut their legs off to make them fit the bed. We have stretched or cut employees to fit the benefit plan, rather than cut the plan to fit the employees. This is what we are working to change.

I'm also pleased to report that we have expanded the Employees' Assistance Program, which was started in 1982. It's a well-known fact that employees often bring their problems with them to the workplace. While the EAP deals with a variety of employee concerns, last year the most prevalent related to emotional, and marital, and family problems. A total of 611 employees sought help from our Raleigh office, but Raleigh is not readily accessible to all state employees who might need help. I'm pleased to announce that this year we will have, in addition to our Raleigh office, four field offices—in Fayetteville, Morganton, Greenville, and Greensboro—to help with our Employees' Assistance Program.

I know that many of you are concerned about day care for your children. As you know, the Department of Human Resources developed a plan to establish a day-care center on the campus of Dorothea Dix Hospital. One good thing about our plan was that the center would be run by state employees themselves. In the short session, I submitted a request to the General Assembly for $363,000 to make the necessary alterations on the Broughton Building and $45,000 as start-up money to get the program under way.[1] No money was appropriated for this important undertaking at Dix. Seven million dollars, though, was added to the Education Building, which nobody wanted. Lesson: Never spend $363,000 to solve a problem when you've got $7 million to throw at it. It makes you wonder who has real concern for state employees. Action, not words, is what counts.

On another matter, I'm glad that I signed an emancipation proclamation for state employees in 1985. I know this isn't what it was called, but that's what it was. It was in the form of a letter reaffirming your right to "work for, support, and vote for the candidates of your choice, free of concern of any retaliation because your candidates may not be the same candidates as those who are supported by others." I am grateful for SEANC's help in ensuring the rights of state employees, which are expressly stated in state law.

It's human nature that we concentrate on the present and make plans for the future, but I would ask you to think back to this time four years ago—particularly as it relates to political pressure. I want to remind you of the horror stories state employees told me when I ran for governor in 1984. State employees told me: I want to help with your campaign, but I'm afraid for my job. State employees told me: I would like to come to your rally, but I hear they are taking pictures. State employees told me: Those who give and those who spy get raises and promotions.

Well, this is not happening in this administration. If any of you hear of any political coercion from anyone, let me know; I'll take appropriate action. No democracy can afford to degrade employees or the political process by these kinds of actions. Isn't it great to know that now, even in the height of an election year, you can concentrate on doing your job without being harassed, pressured, or obligated to support a political candidate? At the same time, isn't it great to know that state employees can support the candidates of their choice, on their own time, whether it's Jim Martin or Bob Jordan, without fear or favor? Isn't it great that state employees are being treated as American citizens for a change? Why would anyone want to go back to the "good ol' boy" days?

Often we in public life and public service, focus, in a meeting like this, strictly on matters related to employment, pay, benefits, and working conditions—and these are vitally important. But I would suggest that equally important are job security and integrity. I would ask that each of us pause and reflect on our great, shining mission, our great responsibility, our great opportunity as public servants.

There is within all of us an understandable, natural desire to advance our own interests and, at the same time, a parallel desire to serve others; to do our jobs with pride and satisfaction. As free men and women, we have been brought up to exercise individual initiative and advancement—and to learn that, ideally, we are responsible for our own condition and advancement. But as public employees, we have a special trust. Our fellow citizens have conferred upon us some of the most fundamental responsibilities—quality education, a healthy and safe environment, equal justice under law, public welfare, and public safety—and the record shows that most of you have exercised these responsibilities faithfully and with distinction. It has been my great pleasure, as governor and a fellow state employee, to be associated with other state employees who have such a high standard of professionalism and dedication.

You have reason to be proud, but we must be ever diligent to ensure that politics, as an instrument for the possible, is our servant, not our master. We would all do well to attend to the words of Cesar Saerchinger, the European director of CBS in the frightful days between 1930 and 1937.[2] Mr. Saerchinger said, "At its worst, politics is a device for keeping people—and peoples—apart. At its best, politics is a means of bringing them together."

We've seen the parallel to that so often in North Carolina, when politics has been squandered to play off one section of our state against another. University, community college, and highway projects have been cut in one area so that others could be accelerated. Regional rivalries have been inflamed.

My goal is to use politics to unite North Carolina. This we have tried to do; this we have managed to do, through integrity in government and a reaching out to those we serve. To be sure, we have not been perfect in our pursuit to bring peoples together, but our purpose is unassailable and our results proof of the rightness of our approach to building collaborative alliances. You are helping us prove that when we stand together, with a shared vision—when we put North Carolina first, North Carolina will be first, and we will reach higher and higher levels of achievement. State employees are a source of great pride. You are an important part of a team, statewide, whose straining reach and tireless energy have helped us reach new heights in public service.

I have tried to keep this from degenerating into a partisan speech, even though you know I am a candidate for reelection. I do want to ask you to think again about the frog story, where I told you about the world's greatest management principle. If you like the way you've been treated, maybe not ever to perfection, but better and with more respect than before; and if you want to see more of that positive, respectful attitude, rather than go back to a hard-line patronage system, perhaps you will find a way to offer encouragement.

Some will want to return to the old way, in hopes they can get ahead through politics. I hope that most of you will want to go forward. Think of it this way: You don't have to take my word for it, you've got your own experience. Now, it's your choice. We have shown over the past three years that when we work together as one united state, not just one of fifty states, but one united state—east, and west, and piedmont, and sandhills—we can become number one in so many ways. I ask you, do you want to keep a real thing going?

[1]"I am pleased to tell you that plans are well under way to have a day-care facility on the grounds of the Dorothea Dix complex," the governor informed SEANC members on March 1, 1988. "Although the state will provide the facility at the Broughton Building, the cost of operation of the center is proposed to be the responsibility of state employees who keep their children there. Since considerable renovation of the Broughton Building will be required before it is suitable for children," Martin vowed to obtain funds from the General Assembly "to put the building in operational condition. . . . Meanwhile, we are proceeding with architectural plans for the center's design."

[2]Cesar Saerchinger (1884-1971), born in Aachen, Germany; resident of Bedford Village, New York; was educated in Halle, Germany, and New York City. Musician; author; editor; contributor to music magazines since 1912; cofounder, Modern Music Society of New York, 1913; foreign correspondent, *New York Evening Post*, Berlin, 1919-1924, *Philadelphia Ledger*, London, 1925-1926, and Curtis-Mason Newspapers, London, 1926-1930; European editor, *Musical Courier*, 1920-1930; European director, Columbia Broadcasting System, 1930-1937, organized first regular transatlantic service; broadcast "The Story Behind the Headlines," National Broadcasting Company, 1938-1948. *Who Was Who in America, 1969-1973*, 760.

GOVERNOR'S WORKING GROUP ON MOBIL OIL OFFSHORE DRILLING

RALEIGH, SEPTEMBER 8, 1988

[Encouraged by geological surveys indicating a one in ten chance of finding a massive, 5 trillion-cubic-foot natural gas field off the North Carolina coast, Mobil Oil Corporation officials declared plans to drill an exploratory well forty-seven miles northeast of Cape Hatteras. The company's September 2, 1988, announcement anticipated that offshore operations would commence in the spring of 1989. However, technical factors forced a year-long postponement of the initial drilling date; later, requests for further information on the project from federal and state investigators delayed exploration until May, 1991. *News and Observer*, September 3, October 9, 26, 1988, July 2, 1989, February 10, 1990; press release, "Statement by Governor James G. Martin on Mobil Exploration Plan Delay," Raleigh, October 25, 1988; see also untitled press release with attached letter from the governor to Ralph Ainger, acting regional manager, Minerals Management Service, U.S. Interior Department, concerning Mobil's plans, Raleigh, October 6, 1988, Governors Papers, James G. Martin.

Governor Martin delivered the following statement at his 10 A.M. news conference.]

I would like to make an important announcement this morning. As most of you know, Mobil Oil Corporation has announced its intention to submit an exploration plan to the U.S. Department of the Interior to drill off the coast of North Carolina. Most of your organizations have carried stories pointing out my strong reservations to this plan.

The events of the last year have served as timely reminders of the fragile resources we have on the North Carolina coast and the necessity to take every precaution to prevent potential threats to those resources.[1] I believe the Mobil plan presents that type of potential threat. As I advised the attorney general last week, I believe the risks of drilling off the coast of North Carolina are substantial.

While details of Mobil's plan are not yet clearly defined, today I am announcing the appointment of a twenty-two-member working group which will examine the exploration plan and make recommendations to me. I have asked Donna Moffitt, assistant director of the Department of Administration's Office of Marine Affairs, to chair the working group.[2] I have also asked Department of Administration Secretary Jim Lofton and Secretary of the Department of Natural Resources and Community Development Tommy Rhodes to serve on the group. You should have a complete list of the working group before you, many of whom are here this morning. [Governor Martin introduced working-group members in attendance.]

This group represents a broad spectrum of expertise and knowledge about the issues surrounding the Mobil proposal. As we move ahead, we are prepared to add additional people as needed. This working group's input is critical as we study how the proposal will affect our coastline.

When the exploration plan comes in, the state has a twenty-day window to review it and to submit comments to the Department of the Interior. We have already determined that twenty days is much too short, and we are appealing to Interior this week for an extension to at least sixty days. Whether we have twenty days or sixty days, there is a great deal of work to do in a very short period of time.[3] I appreciate the willingness of those who have agreed to serve.

In conclusion, my responsibility as governor is to protect our coastal resources. As I have said, if either Mobil's exploration or production will threaten our coast, I am prepared to take legal action to prevent it.

---

[1]During 1988, North Carolina's coastal communities faced the twin problems of the red tide and the shore-bound medical waste discarded from U.S. Navy vessels; on the latter topic, see press releases, "Statement by Governor James G. Martin Regarding Navy Dumping," Raleigh, August 29, 1988, and "Statement by Governor James G. Martin Concerning Recent Discussions with the U.S. Navy," Raleigh, October 6, 1988, Governors Papers, James G. Martin.

[2]Donna D. Moffitt (1947-   ), native, resident of Raleigh; Bachelor of Environmental Design, 1974, Master of Landscape Architecture, 1976, North Carolina State University; J.D., University of North Carolina at Chapel Hill, 1983. Senior river basin planner, state Office of Water Resources, and community development planner, Division of Environmental Management, 1979-1981; assistant director, Office of Marine Affairs, and staff attorney, North Carolina Aquariums, 1984-1988; director, Outer Continental Shelf

Office, Department of Administration, since 1988. Donna D. Moffitt to Jan-Michael Poff, July 25, 1989.
    ³Early in 1989, Mobil agreed to give the state six months to study the company's exploratory drilling plan. *News and Observer*, February 3, 1989.

BEACH SWEEP '88

RALEIGH, SEPTEMBER 8, 1988

A great deal has been said and written the past few years about the condition of our beaches, especially the amount of trash and debris left by visitors and the tide. Last year, with the help of more than a thousand volunteers, we did something about the problem. On a single weekend, fourteen tons of trash was collected from our beaches—everything from the six-pack holders which cause so much harm to wildlife, to old tires. Known as Beach Sweep '87, the event was so successful that it received a national Take Pride in America award from President Reagan.

I am pleased to announce that Beach Sweep '88 will take place on Saturday, September 24, from 9 A.M. until 1 P.M. With me today are Kathryn O'Hara, marine biologist with the Center for Environmental Education, in Washington, D.C., and Lundie Spence, education specialist with the UNC Sea Grant Program.[1] They will be available after the news conference to answer your questions about this program.

Over the past few weeks a lot of attention has been focused on the medical waste which washed up on our beaches. The intent of Beach Sweep '88 is to remove the tons of debris which is both unsightly and dangerous to wildlife, not to search for medical waste. However, should participants in Beach Sweep '88 find any medical debris, they are instructed not to touch the items but mark the location and notify their zone captain. The zone captains will arrange for the items to be picked up by local police. Individuals not involved with Beach Sweep '88 but who find medical waste are asked to mark the location and notify the local law enforcement agency.

Efforts such as Beach Sweep '88 will clean up the beaches for a while, but it will take the cooperation of all our citizens to keep them that way.

    ¹Kathryn Jean O'Hara (1960-   ), born in Rockville Centre, New York; resident of Hampton, Virginia; B.S., Duke University, 1982; M.S., College of Charleston, 1985. Award-winning marine biologist; staff member, since 1985, director, since 1988, Pollution Prevention Program, Center for Marine Conservation (formerly Center for Environ-

mental Education), Washington, D.C.; author. Kathryn Jean O'Hara to Jan-Michael Poff, July 26, 1990.

Lundie Spence (1946-   ), born in Richmond, Virginia; resident of Raleigh; B.S., Mary Baldwin College, 1968; M.S., Florida State University, 1971; was completing Ph.D., North Carolina State University, 1990. Marine science teacher, Carrabelle High School, Florida, 1971-1973; biology teacher, Douglas County High School, Georgia, 1973-1977; marine science studies instructor, University of North Carolina at Chapel Hill, 1977-1978; marine education specialist, UNC Sea Grant College Program, and adjunct professor of university studies, North Carolina State University, 1978-1990. Lundie Spence to Jan-Michael Poff, June 29, 1990.

NORTH CAROLINA TRUCKING ASSOCIATION

PINEHURST, SEPTEMBER 12, 1988

It's a pleasure to be able to stand before you, today, and report that North Carolina's economy is on a roll—and that a major player in our state's economic growth has been you, the leaders of our trucking industry. Many factories and distribution centers gave us favorable consideration because of our trucking strength.

I hope all of you have heard the good news by now: that our average annual unemployment rate for all of 1987 was 4.5 percent, the lowest in nine years; that our gross state product grew an estimated 5.6 percent in 1987, compared to a GNP growth of 2.9 percent; that our state has gained roughly 387,000 jobs from January of 1985 until this July. My administration is proud of what we, as a state-local, public-private partnership, accomplished in building a stronger economy in North Carolina, just as you in the trucking industry can be proud of what you've accomplished since the Federal Motor Carrier Act of 1980 led to the restructuring of your industry and the resulting boom in highway freight movement.

While we can point with pride to what we, and you, have accomplished, we both have unfinished business ahead of us. Much of that business will require a vigorous, cooperative effort by the trucking industry and state government if you are to realize your goals of keeping your industry strong and productive, and we in state government are to continue our economic expansion and realize our goal of building the safest, most efficient transportation system we can build.

It's important for us to look today at what we, and you, have accomplished, and some of the challenges that remain. I want to focus on what we in state government, and you in the trucking industry, must accomplish together, not only in North Carolina, but nationally.

If there's one thing truckers know about, it's crossing state lines, and in today's economy, those state lines are virtually disappearing as we reach for a slice of the national, and global, economic pie.

A recent report from the Advisory Committee on Highway Policy of the 2020 Transportation Program says that the U.S. trucking industry accounts for 77 percent of all freight transportation revenues in this country. Underscoring the importance of trucking, the report notes that trucks are involved in the delivery of almost all consumer goods, in some point in the journey of those goods, from producer to consumer.

One reason why trucks are so heavily and effectively involved in this delivery system has been the building of the U.S. Interstate Highway System, a job that has almost been completed.[1] That system allows trucks to travel long distances quickly and to meet consumer demands efficiently. The speed with which trucks can get goods to market has led to the growing trend of just-in-time delivery of parts and materials. This has cut the cost of storing large inventories, thereby increasing productivity, and has turned trucks into rolling warehouses that must meet precise schedules. These and other trends have increased the importance of trucking to economic growth and have, in turn, sparked an increase in the trucking industry. In fact, the experts say, commercial trucking is going to grow twice as fast as personal vehicle travel in the immediate future.

Trucking has long been a major industry in North Carolina, and North Carolina has long enjoyed a tremendous economic advantage in trucking—not only because we have superb trucking companies but because of our state's geographic location, as well. Positioned as we are at the center point of the East Coast, our state offers companies easy access to two of the most important markets in the United States: the traditional metropolitan areas of the Northeast and the new-growth economies of the Sun Belt. Companies in North Carolina are within overnight delivery of more than 60 percent of the U.S. market, and they are within 700 miles of more than 150 million U.S. and Canadian customers and 63 of the nation's major metropolitan areas. This unique aspect of our geography has made North Carolina home to more long-range trucking organizations than any other state in the nation. Your trucking firms use our five interstate highways and thousands of miles of roads that are part of the largest state-maintained highway system in the country. You use our two deepwater ports, their intermodal terminals, and other surface transportation, facilities, all of which enhance North Carolina's appeal as a manufacturing and distributing center for North American industries.

Yes, North Carolina has a strategic advantage of geographic location and an exceptionally strong surface transportation system, and these have given our state a competitive edge in the pursuit of new jobs and new industries as well as playing an important role in the strong and continuing growth of North Carolina's existing industries. And, as I said before, our state's private trucking firms have played a major part in the record of success that has translated into a better quality of life for so many of our people during recent years. But surface transportation, like so many other facets of our business and private lives, has been—and will continue to be, for the foreseeable future—affected by innovations in technology, innovations that make life and business more productive and more enjoyable, but always seem to precipitate concomitant challenges in their wake. It's futile to complain about these changes and perilous to ignore them. If North Carolina, for example, is to continue to enjoy the advantages of its geographic location, it must effectively and prudently accommodate technological changes under way in the surface transportation industry.

An example of what I am talking about is the current effort by a committee of the North Carolina Board of Transportation, for over a year now, to try to resolve the problems of defining *reasonable access* and *terminals* in regard to twin trailers. This has become an emotional issue, often fraught with misinformation in some quarters, and the task of resolving this issue is a task we in state government didn't ask for, but one we are going to do and do correctly. Twin trailers, by government mandate, are here to stay. That's a given, but it's also a given that safety is this administration's top priority when it comes to our streets and highways. That's why we are committed, as I know you are, to resolving this issue in a fair way that will keep North Carolina's trucking industry competitive without sacrificing one iota our goal of safe highways for all of North Carolina's citizens. I believe that in addition to the routes used since 1983, the DOT staff recommendation on additional interim access approval based on specific requests and evaluations is a prudent [course], and I hope that you will support that. This will put us in a better position to know what's going on in relation to safety standards on specific routes. . . . [illegible][2]

As you know, we've been working with industry officials at the state and the national level to find solutions to a lot of common problems. One excellent example of this type of cooperative effort has been the National Governors' Association's Working Group on State Motor Carrier Procedures, which is a project the NGA has undertaken to seek administrative uniformity of state motor vehicle procedures. In February of 1986, that working group of state officials and motor carrier advisers adopted a consensus agenda of eight items it felt would improve state motor carrier taxation and regulation procedures. Of those eight items—in fact, the number-one priority—was for the states to establish state motor carrier advisory committees. Two years ago, when I spoke to you in Asheville, I said I would appoint such a committee. I kept my promise, and I'm happy to report that North Carolina has a well-organized, functioning committee that includes an excellent cross section of representatives from industry and regulatory agencies that meets on a quarterly basis and has done much good work.

We've accomplished a lot, but not all we need to accomplish, in regards to the other seven consensus agenda items. North Carolina, for example, has been a leader in the International Registration Plan. We have not yet entered into the Base State Fuel Use Tax Agreement. However, representatives from the Department of Revenue and the Division of Motor Vehicles are working to overcome our major problem in this area: developing an alternative to a decal fee. Such a plan would require legislative approval, as would joining any base state fuel tax compact. The group that is dealing with this challenge has set a meeting for next month to continue its efforts.

Another federal challenge facing us is compliance with the Commercial Motor Vehicle Safety Act of 1986.[3] As you know, all states must comply with minimum uniform standards in such areas as written and driving tests for licenses, fitness requirements, and classes of licenses, among others. If a state fails to comply, it loses federal aid highway construction funds. In North Carolina, the responsibility for motor carrier safety was transferred, in 1986, from the North Carolina Utilities Commission to the Division of Motor Vehicles.[4] DMV's performance in this area, according to the National Highway Traffic Safety Administration, rates as the best in the nation. That's not just among the best; that's *the* best.

When you look at what DMV has been doing in regards to motor carrier safety, it's easy to see why we're number one. Let me give you some examples:

—Motor carrier safety inspections have been expanded from approximately 4,500, in 1984, in the previous administration, to more than 64,000 in 1987, a 1,300 percent increase! If that had been the other way around, you would be reading editorials about it every day!

—Since beginning the state's first terminal audit program in November of 1987, the division has conducted more than 600 safety reviews to help companies comply with federal motor carrier safety regulations.

—North Carolina is one of the first states to equip its motor vehicle enforcement officers with alcohol sensors, set up at truck-weighing stations, to screen truck drivers for alcohol while on duty. Drivers who have a blood-alcohol content of .04 percent are taken off the roads for twenty-four hours. Also, we're organizing a special team to conduct in-depth investigations of truck accidents that involve fatalities and serious injuries.

I said we were serious about highway safety in this administration, and I mean it—and so do you. On every one of these safety initiatives we have had your strong support.

Yes, we're moving ahead, and the trucking industry and government are continuing to develop a public-private partnership toward problem-solving that augurs well for the future. But if, as I said before, that technological innovation often leads to further technological challenge, then it is also true that life often gives us some bad news along with the good—and we've got some bad news in North Carolina's surface transportation system, namely a $12 billion backlog in unmet highway construction needs. Many of you have heard this litany before, but it bears repeating because it's a problem that has to be resolved. It isn't going to go away because we wish it away.

We are, to a great extent, the victims of our own successes. The economic engine of growth in our state has outstripped our ability to keep pace with the demand for safe, efficient roads. In fact, we have many roads that carry traffic beyond their ability to do so safely or efficiently.

A key factor in this problem has been the Federal Highway Fund, which consistently has shortchanged North Carolina since its inception. For every federal fuel tax dollar collected in this state during the past thirty-three years, only 83 cents has been returned. It would have been worse, except for the secretary's discretionary funds that helped supplement our unfairly low allocation. So we averaged 83 cents on the dollar.

For 1987, that figure was less than 68 cents on the dollar. For the next fiscal year, it is anticipated we will get less than 66 cents per federal fuel tax dollar. As you know, that's largely because the 1987 Federal Highway Act, barely passed over President Reagan's veto, took away the discretionary supplements that could have made up our losses and sent it to other states for pork barrel. It was a tragic day for North Carolina when that veto was overridden. Meanwhile, our state's population trends are increasing the demands on our highway system, and the number of motor vehicles on the road is increasing faster than the population in general. And, as I said earlier, the truck census on our highways is increasing at an even faster rate.

This combination of more cars, more trucks, and unmet highway needs has led to expressions of concern in some quarters, as you might imagine, about how safe our highways are going to be in the near future. In its most recent newsletter, the UNC Highway Safety Research Center predicts that more and bigger trucks will lead to more accidents, in part because of inadequate design and maintenance limits on the roadways where these trucks will be operating.[5] It worries me, too.

The answer is to give truckers and all motorists the kind of highway system that sparks economic expansion without sacrificing safety. We tried to take another small but significant step toward dealing with our highway construction needs during this summer's short session of the General Assembly, but we were told, in effect, that the time for our $450 million bond issue had not come—or not now, you might say. Well, we stand ready to work with the legislature, through its Highway Study Commission, to find solutions to this complex highway backlog problem. We won't be able to resolve a problem of this magnitude overnight, and whatever proposals we arrive at are going to take a united effort to implement. We hope we will have organizations such as yours behind us in this endeavor.

A safe, efficient highway system, a North Carolina where the "Good Roads State" continues to be a reality as well as a motto, is what we all, whether commercial trucker or private motorist, desire for ourselves and our posterity. Working together, we can achieve that goal. Our roads will be as safe as we can make them. Our roads will operate efficiently and continue to help attract new industries and expand existing businesses, and North Carolina can "keep on truckin'" down the road to a brighter future.

---

[1] The governor inserted into his text, at this point, "I-40 to Wilmington."

[2] The editor transcribed the handwritten text added to this paragraph, beginning with the words "I believe," from two copies of the September 12, 1988, address to the North Carolina Trucking Association. The comments were incomplete on one copy of the speech and partially illegible on the other. About those handwritten comments, the governor wrote at the top of the first page of his text of the speech that "this position is the same as the Raleigh *News and Observer* editorial favoring the staff recommendation and opposing open season that other states allow." The *News and Observer* discussed the twin-trailer access issue in editorials appearing in its May 22 and July 11, 1988, editions.

[3] See P.L. 99-570, "Anti-Drug Abuse Act of 1986" (short title), *U.S. Statutes at Large*, Act of October 27, 1986, Title XII, "Commercial Motor Vehicle Safety Act of 1986," 100 Stat. 3207-170 to 3207-189.

[4]See "An Act to Add a New Article 17 to Chapter 20 of the General Statutes and Make Other Necessary Changes in Chapter 20 and Chapter 62," ratified June 24, 1985. *N.C. Session Laws, 1985,* c. 454.

[5]University of North Carolina Highway Safety Research Center, *Highway Safety Directions,* I (Summer, 1988), 9.

TRIANGLE AREA WORLD TRADE ASSOCIATION

RALEIGH, SEPTEMBER 12, 1988

[The governor expounded on the importance of foreign business relationships to the state economy in his talking points on "International Challenges Facing the South," Chapel Hill, April 13; the "Export Now" press conference, Raleigh, May 23, 1988; and in his address, below, to the Triangle World Trade Association.]

This is an exciting time in the trade history of North Carolina, and you, as members of the North Carolina World Trade Association, are right in the middle of it. We've come a long way from the years of the early 1980s when the high value of the dollar made exporting very tough for American companies. Today, with the value of the dollar at more favorable exchange rates, and our federal government pushing for equitable trade arrangements with foreign countries around the world, the time has never been better for exporting. And North Carolina is leading the way.

Our new North Carolina World Trade Index, which is inspired by and sponsored jointly with your association, shows North Carolina running a net positive balance of trade for the first half of this year. According to the index's latest summary, North Carolina ran a combined trade surplus of more than $95 million over the first two quarters of 1988. That makes us one of the few states in the nation which is exporting more than it imports.

The trade index estimates that North Carolina exports account for more than 40,000 manufacturing jobs in our state. I want to help make that component of our economy even stronger.

Reasons

There are good reasons for North Carolina's export success, too. Our East Coast location and strong manufacturing sector give us natural advantages in the pursuit of overseas markets. We are also blessed with two excellent deepwater ports at Wilmington and Morehead City, but our advantages are not entirely geographical.

Our large and diverse base of manufacturing industries gives North Carolina a strong array of value-added products to market overseas. The exceptional productivity of our work force makes North Carolina products competitive where others are not.

Perhaps most importantly, our state has a long history and strong reputation for marketing its products overseas. We started under Governor Luther Hodges, who led some of the first state-level international trade development missions in the history of our country. Through the 1960s and 1970s we continued to expand our international development programs, mainly emphasizing investment here by foreign firms.

Recent Years

Today I am proud to say that my administration has continued North Carolina's strong, successful emphasis on international trade development, but with a new emphasis on exports. One of our most important initiatives has been the expansion of our state export assistance programs. In the last two years we've doubled the size of our state export development staff. We now have trade specialists for Europe, Latin America, Asia, Canada, and Africa, and we have three more specialists working intensively with our traditional industries: textiles, furniture, and forest products. We've also added a full-time trade specialist to our European office to track down trade leads and help North Carolina businesses link up with European distributors and importers.

Trade Days

We're also working with our state community college system in a new program, called Trade Days. Once a quarter, on the same day at the same time, our fifty-eight community college campuses offer special seminars on exporting. The programs are designed to help small and mid-sized firms that have good export potential, but no export expertise. After attending the seminars, a businessman can get preliminary assistance from his local community college staff, and then from our state export office. A recent survey shows that there are literally hundreds of small and mid-sized firms in North Carolina with strong potential for export, but who are not yet taking advantage of trade opportunities. The Trade Days program is designed to reach those companies and tap their trade potential.

Ports

Another important trade-related activity of my administration has been the funding of badly needed capital improvements at our state ports. Until we took action in 1987, North Carolina's state ports were literally being starved out of business. While their competitor ports at Charleston and Norfolk were receiving hundreds of millions for capital improvements, our terminals at Wilmington and Morehead could barely carry out a modest maintenance program.

At my request, the 1987 General Assembly approved $36 million for improvement of our state port terminals at Wilmington and Morehead City. We are now under way with construction of a new 900-foot container berth at Wilmington, as well as additional warehouse space at both ports. We're also reconstructing Berth One at Morehead City, which some of you may remember literally fell into the harbor in January of 1987. Had I not been on the scene and ordered an immediate emergency contract to halt the erosion, a fuel and petrochemical storage area would have been undermined, causing vast environmental damage to our fragile coastal resources.

Other Developments

Ports expansion, outreach programs, a beefed-up export staff—these are only a few of the positive steps North Carolina has taken in the last three years to strengthen its position in world markets. We've also added international air service at Charlotte and Raleigh-Durham. We've expanded our foreign trade zones and enacted foreign sales company tax breaks to parallel federal legislation. We've led export development missions overseas.

Keep Moving

Still, we need to keep moving. I was proud, earlier this year, to propose an innovative new export financing assistance office for our state Department of Commerce. As some of you may recall, that new office was to provide one-on-one assistance to North Carolina companies seeking export finance credit and related credit insurance. Through blanket contracts with the national Foreign Credit Insurance Agency and the United States Ex[port]-Im[port] Bank, the office would have arranged private-sector credit insurance for qualifying North Carolina exporters.

During his visit to North Carolina this summer, U.S. commerce secretary William Verity[1] called that new program one of the most innovative he'd seen, and one that he would like to hold up as a national model for other states. Unfortunately, the legislature refused to grant our state Commerce Department the $106,000 in funding that it would have taken to start that program this year. That means that other states will be able to compete against us, using our idea that the legislature won't let us use.

Foreign Offices

The Commerce Department also asked this year's legislature to fund new North Carolina trade and reverse investment offices in Japan and other Pacific Rim countries. As many of you know, Japan, Korea, Taiwan, and other Far Eastern countries represent some of the most lucrative trading markets in the world today. The offices proposed in our budget this year would have helped North Carolina firms tap those markets.

Unfortunately, these proposals also were turned down by the legislature. Only $60,000 was approved for new North Carolina trade offices overseas, barely enough to lease space for a single office in Japan—with no funds left over to expand full-time staffing, utilities, and other unavoidable costs. So, we had to reduce trade missions to Europe and Asia, and we should not have to make that choice.

Future

These new trade programs—export financing and overseas representation for our state—are logically the next major steps for North Carolina's export development effort. In today's positive export environment, they are the kind of programs that could more than pay for themselves in new jobs and economic opportunity for North Carolina, if only we could take advantage of them. If reelected, I expect to propose funding for them again next year and, with your support, win that budget fight on our third try.

Conclusion

North Carolina is on a roll, economically. Our unemployment is at the lowest levels ever. Business spending in our state is at record levels. Our economy continues to grow at a rate far in excess of the national average.

Exports have been, and continue to be, a leading contributor to North Carolina's economic success. Groups like yours, the North Carolina World Trade Association, have worked hard for many years preparing our state for this time of opportunity. Exporting hasn't always been easy, and the time will come when international economic pressures once again turn against American manufacturers. No one has repealed the ups and downs of the business cycle, even after sixty-six consecutive months of uninterrupted growth. But thanks to the efforts of groups like yours, North Carolina is well ahead of the pack in this year's race to capitalize on export opportunity.

In state government, we've also made substantial contributions to North Carolina's world trade performance. Now is the time to keep building. Today's export successes can be only the first wave of North Carolina products overseas, but we can continue to expand our international markets only through effort; through outreach and assistance programs now under way in our state Commerce Department; through self-help and promotional efforts like those sponsored by the North Carolina World Trade Association. I'm looking forward to working with each of you in those efforts and to keeping North Carolina a national leader in world trade.

---

[1]C. William Verity, Jr. (1917-   ), born in Middletown, Ohio; B.A., Yale University, 1939; U.S. Navy, 1942-1946. President, chief executive officer, Armco, Inc., 1965-1971, 1972-1982; cochairman, U.S.-U.S.S.R. Trade and Economic Council, 1977-1984; chairman, U.S. Chamber of Commerce, 1980-1981, and of Presidential Task Force on Private Initiatives, 1981-1983; appointed U.S. commerce secretary, 1987. *Who's Who in America, 1988-1989*, II, 3173.

PRESS RELEASE: STATEMENT ON OREGON INLET

RALEIGH, SEPTEMBER 12, 1988

Governor James G. Martin made the following statement in response to today's announcement by the White House that the Oregon Inlet stabilization project has been disapproved:

"I have been notified that the president has disapproved the state's request that the U.S. Department of the Interior permit temporary use of land required for construction of the Oregon Inlet stabilization project. The president's action is disappointing but not surprising in light of Interior's unyielding opposition to the project and the unfavorable attitude of the Office of Management and Budget regarding federal funding. Presumably, the president's disapproval was based on advice from the secretary of the interior and the director of the Office of Management and Budget.[1] I believe he was ill-advised.

"I am calling for a feasibility study of developing a stabilization project that can be implemented without permits from the U.S. Department of the Interior, and do it within the amount that the state legislative leadership and I have agreed to appropriate for North Carolina's share of the federal project. Stabilization of the Oregon Inlet, together with full development of the Wanchese Seafood Industrial Park, will produce major economic benefits of regional and national importance. The stabilization project developed by the U.S. Army Corps of Engineers, which the U.S. Congress approved for construction in December of 1970, is economically feasible and environmentally safe. I remain fully committed to the goal of stabilizing the Oregon Inlet."

---

[1]James Clifford Miller III (1942-   ), born in Atlanta; B.B.A., University of Georgia, 1964; Ph.D., University of Virginia, 1969. Economist; administrator, Office of Information and Regulatory Affairs, Office of Management and Budget, and executive director, President's Task Force on Regulatory Relief, 1981-1985; chairman, Federal Trade Commission, 1981-1985; appointed director, Office of Management and Budget, 1985; author; Republican. *Who's Who in America, 1988-1989*, II, 2154.

WHITE CONSOLIDATED INDUSTRIES ANNOUNCEMENT

KINSTON, SEPTEMBER 14, 1988

As governor of the great people of North Carolina, it is indeed a pleasure to officially welcome White Consolidated Industries' Major Appliance Group to the All-America City, Kinston, North Carolina. I'll be back to celebrate that distinction on October 16![1]

You know what a great feeling it is to introduce one of your good friends and associates to another good friend and associate, and they hit it off, and you become friends and associates together? That's what happened when we had the opportunity to introduce WCI to Kinston and eastern North Carolina. We North Carolinians take pride in our southern hospitality. Here in eastern North Carolina, there's southern hospitality plus eastern hospitality; you can't get too much of a good thing like that, can you? It just comes naturally in Lenoir County, don't you think?

White Consolidated Industries is already a strong corporate citizen of the Tar Heel State and aware of our strengths. This expansion clearly states that WCI knows Lenoir County is a great place to do business. Today we celebrate the growing partnership between our people and your company.

We are mutually very committed to the success of WCI's forthcoming $75 million appliance manufacturing facility in Kinston. The 850 citizens of the greater Lenoir County area who will fill the new jobs at this plant will have greater economic opportunity for themselves and for their families. To ensure the training and skills they will need, our community college will train them, your way, at our expense! WCI's operation here will directly create 850 jobs, but [just] as important, this new plant creates potential business opportunity for other North Carolina companies, and our eastern North Carolina citizens and communities are forward sighted [sic] for desirable growth and the betterment of public services and needs, such as schools and roads.

Jack Pleininger, to you and your executive team at WCI, we want you to know that you've made the right decision to call Kinston and Lenoir County home for WCI's major new manufacturing operation. About the only thing we like as well as a homegrown company is a company that discovers the great life and business climate in North Carolina, locates here, and then expands here, growing in its new home. Let me tell you that three years ago, I started a new emphasis to help existing employers through a new office of traditional industries. By elimination of the inventory tax, and cutting the unemployment insurance tax, and expanding our community colleges' services to them, too, we are working to help them to thrive competitively, just as hard as we work to recruit new industry—and last year we recruited more than any other state. That's good news for White Consolidated and other new investments, because you only have to be here twenty-four hours and you become a "traditional industry!"

This has been a beautiful courtship! Our state Commerce Department team began working with your site search team in the middle of 1986; that was over two years ago, and look how much WCI has liked what North Carolina has to offer! I fully appreciated the opportunity to meet with Jack Pleininger, Chairman Don Blasius,[2] and other WCI officials in the Columbus, Ohio, headquarters early in 1987. State Commerce Secretary Claude Pope, and I, and our economic development team made every effort to show you the exciting advantages of doing business in North Carolina.

Almost a year and a half ago, in March of 1987, WCI announced, after an extensive site search in our state and in other states—which shall remain nameless—that western North Carolina and Buncombe County was to be the site for the company's $15 million appliance parts distribution center, which is creating 200 new jobs near the Asheville airport on highway I-26. That was a great start, and we're glad WCI continued to consider our state for other projects.

A great many people have worked hard to make this project a reality for eastern North Carolina and Kinston. I especially want to commend Lenoir County, the city of Kinston, the Lenoir County Development Commission, the Lenoir Committee of 100, and especially Senator Hardison and the Lenoir County legislators for their support of this project. Once again we have shown that, by working effectively with local economic development agencies, we can bring new jobs and economic opportunity to rural areas of our state.

As I conclude, let me once again thank you, Jack Pleininger and Bruce Cowgill. We applaud the selection, by WCI Major Appliance Group, of Kinston as the site for this new venture in our state. Tom Smith, to you and your project management team here, we pledge our continued support and assistance. Let us know how we can help you make this plant the best that it can be.

---

[1]See *News and Observer*, July 31, 1988, for article on Kinston's "All-America effort."

[2]Donald C. Blasius (1929-), born in Oak Park, Illinois; resident of Westlake, Ohio; B.S., Northwestern University, 1951; U.S. Army, 1951-1953. Various positions with McCulloch Corp., 1953-1968, including vice-president and general manager; various positions with J. I. Case Co., 1968-1974, including senior vice-president and general manager; executive vice-president, chief operating officer, 1974-1975, president, chief executive officer, 1975-1983, chairman, chief exeuctive officer, 1984-1986, The Tappan Co.; chairman, chief executive officer, 1986-1988, WCI Home Products Group; president, White Consolidated Industries, since 1989. Donald C. Blasius to Jan-Michael Poff, March 9, 1990.

GOVERNOR'S COMMISSION FOR THE FAMILY

HIGH, POINT, SEPTEMBER 16, 1988

[The following address is similar to one delivered at North Carolina Voice for Child Care, Research Triangle Park, October 22, 1988.]

Thank all of you for coming to this conference to listen, learn, and participate in what Dottie and I both believe is an issue of critical importance to the future of our state. This commission grew from our commitment of 1986 as the "Year of the Family."

You have all heard the phrase, *Our families are our future*, many times—a number of them here at this conference. But as often as we repeat it, the truth remains the same: Our families are our future. It's the only way you can get there from here!

Think about it again, for a moment. Think back to when you were a child. Think about what your family meant to you growing up. For those of us fortunate enough to be raised in a loving home, family meant someone to comfort us when the night was too dark and the nightmares were too real—or unreal! Family meant having someone to soothe the hurt when we fell and skinned our knees. Family meant someone to share our latest finger painting or to play catch with in the backyard on long, summer evenings. Family meant warmth, security, and love. Family also meant discipline, learning to share with brothers and sisters, taking responsibility for one's own actions, and respecting the rights of others.

Yet for all too many children, the memories we hold of a strong, loving family are little more than a mystery. Substance abuse destroys the innocence of youth and launches our children into a world of confusion, violence, deceit, and death. That's why we started 1985 as the "Year of the Child." Child abuse destroys their identity and teaches them patterns of behavior that many are destined to repeat with their own children. Delinquency and illiteracy limit their chances of building a future for themselves, forcing them into a world of poverty and unhappiness—and the problems are growing.

More children are affected more deeply, and at a younger age, than ever before in history. More single parents are attempting to raise their children alone and depend on day care and the public school system to provide their children with education and training. Many older adults are living longer, healthier lives, but cannot find sufficient employment after retirement to support themselves. Well, maybe those problems can become each other's mutual answer.

It would be easy to say that's too bad, then go on with our lives and ignore the problems, but we can't do that. We can't do that because the problems are no longer somebody else's problems. The problems affect all of us, in our own homes, in the homes of those we love, and in the communities in which we live. When a teenager takes his or her life, we all suffer. When a child dies from abuse or a drug overdose, a piece of us dies with him. When a parent loses a job because of a lack of sufficient skills and can no longer support their family, we all share some responsibility.

For these reasons, family issues transcend the boundaries that sometimes divide us into opposing camps. I do not consider the needs of our families to be a political football to be kicked back and forth between opposing teams and beaten flat in the process. No, the issue here is not politics. The issue is the stability of our families and the future of our state, nothing less.

We cannot succeed in strengthening our families if we split our efforts. If we insist on fighting over who has ownership rights of the issue on the political playground, we might find in the meantime that the ball has rolled out into the street and been flattened in heavy traffic. We must work together to strengthen our families, all of us, whatever our sex, race, creed, social status, or politics.

So what can we do? We can put North Carolina first! Many of you have already begun the effort and have come together here to share your experiences of challenge and success. Hopefully, what you have learned will help us to develop and expand programs assisting families on both the state and local level. Your efforts and the efforts of such organizations as the Governor's Commission for the Family provide us with a strong base upon which to build our defenses.

We in state government have also begun taking intiatives to strengthen our families. Combating substance abuse is one of our primary concerns, and we are working hard to help our citizens say no to drugs and alcohol. The Governor's Council on Alcohol and Drug Abuse among Children and Youth, begun in 1986 and chaired by Dr. Jonnie McLeod, studied this issue and found that a number of outstanding programs existed across our state, but these programs lacked coordination and sufficient resources. Our response to that shortcoming was to initiate Challenge '87, now known as Challenge '88.

Just as Challenge '87 coordinated substance abuse programs on the state level, Challenge '88 does the same for the local level, allowing communities to develop their own comprehensive response to alcohol and drug abuse problems through a network of local coalitions. The Challenge '88 staff can provide technical consultation and resource materials to counties wishing to develop these coalitions and have achieved a high measure of success for their efforts.

We have also recognized the need to coordinate valuable substance abuse treatment and prevention resources through state government. As a part of Challenge '87, I created the Governor's Inter-Agency Advisory Team, in 1987, to oversee federal substance abuse funding and provide the necessary coordination of services. Together with the Employee Assistance Program, the advisory team seeks to identify the problem of substance abuse in state government, eliminate program duplication, and maximize the efficient use of resources.

The PRIDE [Parents' Resource Institute for Drug Education] program is one I'm especially proud to recognize. You've heard a good deal about PRIDE and the Parent-to-Parent program from Bill Oliver here at this conference, and I'll bet Dottie has had a lot to say about it, too! I'm proud that Dottie has taken such an active role in this outstanding effort. As Bill Oliver has said, the war against drugs will be won on the home front; therefore, we need such programs to educate and train parents how to be more effective in helping our children by knowing the signs of substance abuse, how to deal with the problem, and where to go for help.

But prevention and treatment are not the only means of attacking the substance abuse problem. Tough antidrug laws can play an important role, and we have worked to put them on the books. We need tough laws to deal with drug traffickers. I submitted to the legislature a package of bills designed to strengthen our criminal justice response to drug-dealing terrorists who are destroying our society. Unfortunately, the legislative leadership failed to give these measures the priority they deserve, but I promise you that they will see these proposals again.

We are addressing another serious problem that kills and injures thousands of innocent family members every year: the problem of driving while impaired. Nearly half of the people who die each year on our state highways are killed in DWI-related crashes. Many of those killed are innocent victims. We developed a strong package of DWI laws that was introduced to the General Assembly, last year, but never voted on. Just like the antidrug proposals, these measures deserve better treatment than that. That's why I want next year, 1989, to become the "Year of the Last Drug Trafficker."

Stronger literacy skills pose another goal for families in North Carolina. All our citizens need to have the basic skills they need to get a job and provide for their families. In 1987, as part of the "Year of the Reader," I asked former UNC president Bill Friday to chair the Governor's Commission on Literacy and asked the commission to examine the problem and propose some comprehensive remedies.

The commission has reported its findings. I have endorsed them. Some of the commission's recommendations can be carried out administratively, some will require legislation, and some can be adopted through private business and volunteers at no public cost. All of them deserve our support.

We've seen that literacy programs can work in North Carolina. You've had an opportunity to learn about the Motheread program which helps women inmates improve their reading skills so they can in turn read to their children. We instituted this program at the Women's Correctional Center in 1987 and have experienced great success.

Another program presented here, Time to Read, sponsored by Time, Incorporated, has received enthusiastic response nationwide. It trains employees to teach other employees to read. Our state Department of Human Resources has begun implementing this program statewide for its own employees this year. North Carolina State University has its own program. Other literacy efforts are slated for other departments, and I am committed to making state government a model for literacy improvement efforts.

I am also supporting and promoting the Cities in Schools program which seeks to lessen the dropout rate in North Carolina by identifying and assisting potential dropouts. Right here in High Point, Greensboro, and Guilford County schools have joined Charlotte-Mecklenburg and Rocky Mount in this exciting effort, in which businesses are the driving force. I have asked the North Carolina State Board of Education to work to cut the dropout rate in half, by the year 2000, and hope to have operational by 1990 a preschool readiness program for four-year-old children we can identify as having a high risk of eventually becoming high school dropouts. It is clear that we must reach children when they are young, reach them before school problems develop.

We have to begin early if we want to help our children, and for many single and working parents, that means ensuring that their children can be placed in quality day-care facilities. I have proposed balanced growth in the realm of day care, and I support the idea that parents should have a choice as to whether it be public or private, church related, home care, Head Start, corporate day care, or other viable options. I do not believe we need a statewide compulsory day-care program for all three- and four-year-old children. That would cost a billion dollars that we don't have.

Most children, after all, get the nurturing they need at home. We do need, however, to reach out to those disadvantaged, educationally stymied children who receive too little care, too few opportunities, and too little family nurturing. In this vein, I today announce to you that we are starting a new pilot program to help these children, through a joint effort of the Department of Human Resources and the Department of Natural Resources and Community Development, through the Job Training Partnership Act.

At the present time, approximately 3,600 four-year-olds are in day-care spaces subsidized in whole or part by state funds. We estimate that approximately 2,250 other four-year-olds are eligible and are on waiting lists for state day-care subsidy. The proposal I'm announcing to you will begin to address the very heart of this problem.

One limitation in the law is that in order for Job Training Partnership Act funds to be used for child day care, parents must be enrolled in the JTPA program, such as on-the-job-training or career education advancement. But that matches exactly what we're trying to do: to get families into jobs and self-sufficiency. The very criteria for JTPA participation will ensure that we reach the children who need it the most.

This new program is designed to be an enhanced day-care program. The enhancement will come in the form of preschool readiness and other important developmental lessons. Our start-up program is designed to reach students through the existing day-care structure and designed to reach an initial total of 160 children.

One key feature of my plan is to enlist volunteers—retired teachers and librarians, surrogate grandparents, students after school—to come to the day-care center once a week to read to these four-year-olds; to sit beside them and read to them; to point to the picture of the bird and the word *bird*; to awaken in them the excitement of the English language and their own human potential. The program will provide participation opportunities for parents, trained volunteers, preschool day-care providers, professional day-care organizations, educators, state and local social services offices, and private industry councils.

This demonstration proposal, frankly, is a small step where large ones are needed. Unfortunately, adequate attention and commitment to the problems faced by disadvantaged young children did not appeal to the last session of the General Assembly. A more comprehensive proposal I submitted to the legislature was ignored. I wish we could do more, and I intend to do just that. In the meantime, we must take the steps that can be taken. Hopefully, this pilot project and other useful programs will begin to address a very real problem, but we must do more to meet the challenges before us in this area. We cannot ignore the needs any longer. If we do, we will only face greater problems in the future.

The success of our worker training and retraining programs through JTPA have proven that we can educate and retrain our citizens so they can find jobs and provide for their families. Our outstanding success in economic recruitment has resulted in 3 percent unemployment, the lowest rate in eleven of our nation's largest states; only New Hampshire, Hawaii, Vermont, and Delaware are lower. We have also added a little less than 10,000 jobs per month over the last three years, totaling more than 387,000 new jobs in three and a half years—not bad for a state with a total work force of about 3,400,000.

The primary benefit of such a strong economic climate to the stability of the family is obvious: Our people are working and are therefore better able to provide for their families. Such a strong economic climate also attracts more companies to our state, increasing competition and bidding up wages. This gives our citizens the opportunity to seek new jobs and better jobs.

No wise person would prohibit entry-level jobs, but the jobs we actively recruit are high-paying jobs. Just this morning, we cut the ribbon on another plant in Asheboro: Knorr Foods. In a county with less than 2 percent unemployment, they got 5,000 applicants for 100 jobs. If we can sustain a tight job market throughout North Carolina, it will continue to bid up family income. At the rate we're climbing, North Carolina can catch the national average in seven more years; by 1995, that should be our goal.

The word *family* denotes a lifetime of experiences. For that reason, our approach to family issues is tailored to meet a wide range of needs. Our efforts are not only tied to children, adolescents, working parents, and older adults. Older adults have a wealth of experience earned over a lifetime which they can use to benefit their communities. We hope to encourage their involvement and, at the same time, provide them with the assistance they need to maintain their independence. So, this year became the "Year of the Older Adult."

I submitted the first year of a three-year action plan for older adults to the latest session of the General Assembly. The first $5 million of this $48 million package was designed to initiate and expand services and opportunities offered to our older adults. Much of this plan received bipartisan support and passed in the legislature. With continued cooperation, I plan to implement the remaining $43 million of the plan in the next two years.

Through these and other efforts, we are already working to support our state's families. In doing so, we are also working to support the future of our state. We want to give the innocence and purity of childhood back to our children. We want to provide for them childhood memories of warmth, happiness, and love, memories to last a lifetime.

Our families are our future. By working to strengthen them, you are building a better future for North Carolina. This is why Dottie and I established the Commission for the Family: to help prepare a better future for all. Thank you for all you've done. I look forward to receiving your report.

NORTH CAROLINA LEAGUE OF MUNICIPALITIES

ASHEVILLE, OCTOBER 4, 1988

It is a high honor, privilege, and pleasure to have this opportunity to speak to you, this afternoon—to you who are such an important force for North Carolina's continuing progress. It goes without saying that you are an essential part of a partnership that has helped us reach new heights of achievement over the past three and three-quarter years. So, in addition to having the opportunity to address some of your overriding issues and priorities, I would like to use this occasion to thank all of you for all the help and support you have given our administration since January, 1985.

I very much valued your advice and counsel during this period. You have helped prove that, when we put aside our differences and put North Carolina first, North Carolina will be first. Today, because of our partnership, we are first in new manufacturing; and first in protection of our vital surface waters; and first in the miles of state-maintained roads; and first in pioneering an exciting new educational management principle of better pay for better teachers—as we build on the goals of this administration: better schools, better roads, better jobs, and better environmental protection, for a better quality of life for our people.

As a former county commissioner in Mecklenburg County, I am acutely aware of the problems you face daily with education, transportation, affordable housing, economic development and job creation; water, sewage, and the disposal of solid wastes; and sources of revenue. Without a strong local-state partnership, there is no way any state can resolve the array of problems and challenges we face in our state and in our communities.

You know, over the last several years, *infrastructure* has almost become a buzzword. According to the dictionary definition, infrastructure refers to an underlying foundation, the basic installations and facilities, on which the continuance and growth of a community and state depend. Before addressing your concerns, I want to share with you one additional infrastructure that is critical to our continued success in North Carolina: you, the leaders in our communities and municipalities, and the thousands of North Carolinians involved in private-public partnerships and local-state cooperation and collaboration throughout the state. You are our "extra-structure."

Because our unprecedented economic development has made it possible to do much more for better schools, better roads, and better stewardship, along with more and better jobs, I would like to start my presentation by giving you an overflight report on the state of the economy. Here are some highlights:

—In 1987, American firms announced plans to build more manufacturing plants in North Carolina than in any other state. We were ahead of states twice our size. In all, last year, we attracted 113 new manufacturing plants to our state. Texas, which is slightly larger than North Carolina, followed in distant second place, with 112 to our 113. No other state had more than 100 plant announcements. Massachusetts had four: some miracle![1]

—Since January, 1985, new and expanded business investment has soared to nearly $20 billion.

—Naturally, all this is reflected in our employment figures. Our latest figures show that in June, 1988, we had the highest estimated employment on record: 3,235,000, with a net gain of roughly 387,000 jobs added since January, 1985. That means one in nine jobs today was not available three and a half years ago. Our unemployment rate has also been taking a nose dive during this period. Unemployment in August was 3.1 percent, the lowest of the eleven largest states—lower than all but four small states—and a full two and a half points below the national unemployment rate of 5.6 percent.

—One of the things I am proudest of, is this: In 1987, rural economic development reached its strongest level this decade. Over two thirds, nearly 68 percent, of the jobs in new factories announced in 1987 went to communities of 10,000 or less. What the 68 percent comes down to are many success stories throughout the state, too many to mention. One fine example of rural development is Valdese, which was selected to be featured at the community revitalization conference in Atlanta, this past August, for its outstanding accomplishment in creating more jobs and improving the quality of life for its citizens.

Naturally, a lot of states are asking us how we are doing so well in rural economic development. The answer can be given in one word: partnerships. Our private-public partnerships, engineered by our Department of Commerce, are the secret of our success. When analyzed, we find that our success depends largely on you leaders at the local level, because without your continued, active involvement, our economic engine will stall.

Suggestions have come from some quarters—you've heard them—that we need to do away with the state Department of Commerce, our point guard for economic development. Because this suggestion met with less than an overwhelming response, it was changed. Now they are saying, "Let's restructure it." Well, I've already done that twice, but I will not abolish the number-one economic development team in America at the peak of its success. We've got it fixed. Don't break it.

Now I would like to share with you, what is for you and for me, the most important issue we face as communities, as a state, and as a nation: the quality of education. Without a significant investment in education, or in what some refer to as human capital, we cannot hope to sustain our economic progress and quality of life. This is why I have recommended a number of initiatives for raising the level of education and literacy in our state, always bearing in mind that educational improvement can only take place at the local level.

We face some truly formidable problems in education—among them an annual high school dropout rate of roughly 26 percent, an estimated 40 percent of our adult population who are functionally illiterate, and recent SAT scores that show we are still second from the bottom, nationally. One thing has become crystal clear: If we are going to change things for the better in education, we don't need status-quoticians in charge of bringing about needed reforms. We need people with imagination and the resolve to get significantly better educational performance.

The truth is, if we are to get significantly better results in our schools, we will have to do things that are significantly different from what we are doing now. The way to undertake needed change is to adopt the same practice used by science and our leading growth companies: Create pilot programs in order that we can make sure that we develop programs and demonstrate they have the desired level of quality before installing them on a broad basis.

A good example of the pilot approach to educational reform is our Career Development Plan—sometimes called the career ladder program. This program I consider to be the very centerpiece for significant and lasting educational improvement in North Carolina. Its goal is straightforward: Promote outstanding teachers in the classroom and expand teaching excellence in our schools. To achieve this goal, three objectives are being implemented in the sixteen pilots across the state. The three objectives are: one, identify what constitutes good, effective teaching; two, reward good teaching by giving higher pay for better teaching performance; and three, provide adequate training and support in order to expand teaching excellence in our schools.

Actually, the Career Development Plan is based on what is called the greatest management principle in the world. Let me tell you a story to illustrate this principle.

This fellow was out on a lake, fishing. It was a gorgeous summer day, and he really didn't care if he caught anything or not. He looked down in the water and saw this snake swim up to his boat with a frog in its mouth. He felt sorry for the frog, so he reached down, grabbed the snake, released the frog, and threw it on the bottom of his boat.

Then, he got to feeling sorry for the snake, because he had deprived it of his lunch. So, he looked around the boat for something to give the snake. All he could find was a half-empty flask of bourbon. He took a snort, then opened the snake's mouth, poured a belt down its throat, and let it go.

He went back to fishing. After about fifteen minutes, he looked down beside the boat, and there was the snake—this time, with two frogs in its mouth! The moral of this story stands as a beacon for educational reform: Reward people for the right behavior, and you get the right results. Fail to reward the right behavior, and you will likely get the wrong results.

In September, the Personnel Committee for the State Board of Education held a public hearing to get the views of teachers, principals, superintendents, and other educators on how they felt about the program. There had been early opposition, [but] 90 percent of participating teachers got promoted, with more pay. Of fifty-five educators who testified, only one teacher expressed strong opposition to the program.

A teacher from the Burlington city school system probably best summed up how those participating in the program felt. She told the State Board of Education that the four-year pilot is, quote, "the best thing to come along for students since the invention of chalk." I think this is a highly significant statement for another reason: It stresses the program's importance to students as well as teachers. Our overall findings show that when this program is implemented by teachers, students learn more, because more time is spent on the subject.

The upshot is, we are now moving toward the operational phase of the program. The state board will request in its 1989-1991 expansion budget $38 million for the 1989-1990 school year, and $97 million for 1990-1991, to initiate statewide implementation of the Career Development program. Nothing is more important than strengthening the quality of teaching; and if the General Assembly, in 1987, had adopted my proposed statewide career ladder opportunities, by the end of this school year, our teachers' pay would be within 5 percent of the national average. Instead, we'll end up over 10 percent short.

It is false to advertise that I recommended lower teacher pay than my worthy opponent, when, counting everything, I recommended higher teacher pay—with better pay for better teachers.

Improve the quality of teaching, professionalize teaching, and you will improve the quality and quantity of learning. It's that simple. One way is to adopt the goal I have set to raise teachers' pay to the national average by 1992.

Our basic strategy in education has been to identify what factors will help us best leverage the educational system in order to achieve the maximum results for our educational dollars. Our Career Development program, developed by the 1984 General Assembly, is one such lever. Another lever is my 1987 proposal to cope with the cycle of illiteracy and the poverty it engenders. I refer to my early childhood education pilot program for at-risk four-year-olds. By "at-risk" children is meant those children who stand as high as a five-times greater chance than other children of dropping out of school later and becoming illiterate adults. What the Governor's Commission on Literacy found, in its year of study into the nature and extent of illiteracy in North Carolina, was that we have an iron cycle of illiteracy that passes from one generation to the next.

To make a long, sad story short, the General Assembly turned down my request for $3.5 million to fund pilot early childhood education programs. Well, I didn't give up because of that setback. Using $350,000 from funds allotted to North Carolina from the federal Job Training Partnership Act will enable us to start a pilot program on a limited basis.

How many of you know the curious habit of the cowbird? The cowbird lays its eggs in another bird's nest so the other bird winds up hatching and caring for the uninvited guests. I really didn't set out to lay eggs in the General Assembly's nest, but it seems that I did, and now those squatting on them can't wait for them to hatch. One such example of a fertile egg, it turns out, is our early childhood education proposal. Now everybody's for it! Another is our proposed highway construction bond program. Now everybody wants to hatch it. The list could go on.

Now the lieutenant governor says he plans to recommend that the 1989 General Assembly provide funds for a preschool program for economically disadvantaged four-year-olds. Of course, if he wins, I'll be very pleased if he hatches that one for me. That will atone for his failure to help, this year.

Contrary to some political TV ads you may have seen, we have made substantial progress since January, 1985, in the amount of state money allocated for education. The indisputable fact is that, after a twenty-three-year erosion of the schools' share from 64.3 percent to 42.5 percent of the General Fund, we have been successful in sustaining a steady, five-year, uninterrupted improvement back up to 46.4 percent.

Let me take just a moment to discuss an issue of extreme importance to those of you in local government: the need to upgrade a deteriorating school plant. In late 1986, I submitted a proposal to finance 10,000 new classrooms in five years, with no necessity to increase taxes—a clear instance of win-win legislation. Now that's what some people call creative financing! My proposal was never voted on or even formally debated. In other words, the people were not given the chance to decide the issue. Nevertheless, this school bond proposal did prod the legislature to enact a tax increase on business to build half as many classrooms in ten years.

Meanwhile, the need for school construction did not go away. Many counties, to meet the shortfall in classrooms, are having to resort to bond financing at higher, local rates. We know that, from January '87 through September '88, seventeen counties have had bond elections. Of those, thirteen were approved for a total of $101,790,000. Currently, we know that seven other referenda are scheduled, seeking approval of a total of $63,800,000.

We have instituted a full-court press to bring the high school dropout rate down. I have set a goal to cut the dropout rate in half by the year 2000. While we have a long way to go, we're making progress. Through the Governor's Business-Education Committee, educators and business people are now working together to reduce the number of dropouts. I wish I had time to tell you about other educational initiatives we have taken, things like our Communities in Schools program, with pilots in Charlotte, Greensboro, High Point, and Rocky Mount. I requested $700,000 from the legislature to expand this dropout prevention program, by the way, and it was turned down.

Then there is our proposed state office of literacy. This office will seek to provide better coordination of literacy programs across the state and closer cooperation between the various literacy service providers. That got turned down, too.

Let me wrap up this discussion of education by saying that there can be no doubt that education is the linchpin of economic and social progress in our society.

As a former county commissioner, I keenly empathize with your concern about maintaining the integrity of local revenue sources. My position on this is a matter of public record. I have consistently fought for full reimbursement to local governments for any and all revenue losses incurred through state action.

Most of you are aware that in 1984, as part of my tax package, I proposed the elimination of all inventory and intangibles taxes, with clear provision that local governments should be fully reimbursed, such reimbursement to be on a point-of-origin basis. I even allowed for an inflation factor, based on personal income or retail sales. Unfortunately, the General Assembly took another approach, devising a complicated formula which it is still trying to iron out.

I realize that water and sewage are a growing concern of local governments. Sixty million dollars was requested from the General Assembly, in 1987-1988, for the revolving loan fund. The legislative response: $5.4 million in 1987-1988 and $15.8 million in 1988-1989, a shortfall of almost $99 million.

One example might suffice to illustrate just how important water and sewage are to economic development and jobs—and why our local-state partnerships have paid off in both our rural and urban areas. Post-Software International, Incorporated, wanted to expand its operation near [Louisburg], in Franklin County, but could not because of the lack of adequate water and sewage services to their plant. Through a grant from the state Department of Commerce's Industrial Renovation Fund, water and sewage lines were built. As a result, Post-Software was able to add 30,500 square feet to its plant, with an increase in jobs from 60 to 285. This proves that water and sewage services are not an expense but an investment.

And, as our state becomes more industrialized and populated, the challenges to our ingenuity in dealing with environmental concerns increase. We now have the most stringent surface water regulations in the nation. Since assuming office, water supply classifications have been established for the very first time to protect watersheds from nonpoint sources of pollution. We must continue to work together to maintain our standards of quality.

Disposal of solid wastes continues to be a formidable problem. This is why I have implemented a plan to reduce landfilling by 90 percent by the year 2000. Because the cost of lined landfills and waste incinerators is prohibitively high, the state must assume a much more active role in our partnership to cope with this problem. In addition to long-range strategic planning, we need to provide assistance to local governments, so I proposed a solid waste fund to help.

A concern very much in the public mind is affordable housing. This concern is much on the minds of officials in our less-populated areas as in our urban areas. As I have stated before, as long as the state can afford it, I would support state-financed housing. A superb example of investing the earnings of a state agency in housing is the pilot program I proposed in May of 1986. This proposal makes housing more affordable for low-income elderly people in southeastern North Carolina and other rural areas. Financed by the North Carolina Housing Finance Agency and the Farmers Home Administration, this program offers a combination of rent subsidies and building loans to attract builders for twenty-unit apartment complexes.

The best government is government that is closest to the people. This is why we have adhered to the principle that local citizens' representatives should be more involved in decision making that will affect their communities' welfare. One example of our attempt to a greater stake in decision making is our strategic corridor highway plan, to bring a continuous, unbroken network of four-lane highways within ten miles of over 90 percent of our people.

We have profoundly changed the way of doing business in highway construction. We have gone from a piecemeal system of promising roads to everybody, promises that could not be kept, to a concept [of] an integrated highway system. Instead of unpaved promises of the past, we've had unpromised paving.

I am happy to report that, thanks to the cooperation of the General Assembly in 1986, that our highway fund is healthy and has a sound revenue stream for the next five years. But it's not going to be enough. As you all know, I have responded to the obvious emergency in our roads program by proposing a three-year, $450 million bond issue to the short session of the legislature in June. Transportation Secretary Harrington has pointed out that we now have an $11 billion backlog of highway improvement and construction projects over the next two decades. If we are ever to deal with this backlog, we must start somewhere, sometime. I'm pleased that legislative leaders are now coming to see the merits of my highway bond program.

When we think of transportation, we are conditioned to think of roads. We're working with you to change this. We obviously must have a balance of all modes of transportation: air, rail, and highways. This is why I issued Executive Order Number 71, on March 11 of this year, establishing the Governor's Task Force on Rail Passenger Service. This task force will submit to the governor its report by January 15, 1989. I think rail has tremendous possibilities for increasing mobility between urban centers. I have charged the task force to conduct a study of the present, near term, and future needs for rail transit service connecting major cities of North Carolina, with emphasis on the potential for providing affordable service.

Railroad needs are not just restricted to the corridors between our larger cities. Preservation of railroads is critical in our less-populated areas. Take the example of what happened in the western part of our state with the Dillsboro to Murphy rail line that Norfolk-Southern planned to abandon. I arranged for the state to buy it to save much-needed freight service through a new short line, the Great Smoky Mountains Railway, which will also provide dinner-excursion service to travelers to experience some of the most breathtaking scenery in the state, beginning Sunday after next, October 16.

I could go on. The point is, we can, working together, bring rail transportation back to its rightful position in the total transportation mix. Together, we can move toward greater balance of transportation.

Some of you have expressed concern over my proposal to merge functions scattered in several state agencies into a separate agency: the department of health and environment. This has meant several management changes, namely: the Division of Marine Fisheries was moved from the Natural Resources grouping to the Environmental Protection grouping; another change is that we will have two deputies, one for the environment and one for health. This change was made to address the concerns of both environmental/natural resources groups and health groups.

A particularly important change for you in the Governor's Consolidation Plan is that you will now have a clearly visible focal point for housing and community development matters. Instead of being split between the departments of Commerce and Administration, the Division of Community Assistance is to be transferred to the Department of Commerce to form the nucleus of a housing and community development cluster under the new deputy secretary for housing and community development. The net effect of these changes will be that you, at the local level, will receive better and more timely services from state agencies in areas of critical importance to you.

The sheer range of issues I have tried to share with you, this afternoon, underscores as well as anything else the complexity of your jobs in our municipalities and the necessity for a strong local-state partnership. While we may disagree from time to time on means, we are in total accord on what our priorities must be. Our strength lies in our unity of purpose. Standing together, all opposition to our achieving our goals must yield. When we are united, when we are one united state—east and west, north and south, from the coast, to the piedmont, to the sandhills—we can continue to achieve great things.

---

[1]In his 1988 campaign for United States president as the Democratic candidate, Governor Michael S. Dukakis often described the rapid economic gains made in his state during his administration as "the Massachusetts miracle." Martin referred favorably to Dukakis's tax-cutting and employment-boosting programs when introducing him at the Emerging Issues Forum, in Raleigh, February 11, 1987. But the miracle had faded by late 1989, when the Bay State's fiscal woes prompted Moody's Investors Service, Inc., to downgrade Massachusetts's bond rating to one of the two worst in the country. *City and State*, November 20, 1989.

DIVISION OF MOTOR VEHICLES EXPRESS OFFICE OPENING

Asheville, October 4, 1988

[Delivered at Westgate Shopping Center, the following address is almost identical to those prepared for Division of Motor Vehicles driver license express office openings at Midtown Square Shopping Center, Charlotte, October 10, and The Market Place, Winston-Salem, October 13, 1988. Speaking in Charlotte, Martin announced that the Queen City was to become home to a 10,000-square-foot office building that would house driver license and vehicle registration services as well as the truckers' International Registration Plan. "Upon completion," the governor said, "it will be the largest DMV facility outside of Raleigh."]

Some of you have probably heard me talk about how we're building more good roads; that we're creating more good jobs; that our good schools are getting better; and that our state's economy is continuing to run on a full head of steam. That's not just talk, that's fact! Last year's statewide unemployment rate, 4.5 percent, was the lowest in nine years. Employment is up. North Carolina has gained roughly 387,000 new jobs from January of 1985 through June of this year.

In the first three and a half years of my administration, we've widened and improved more than 5,000 miles of highways and built over 200 miles of four-lane freeways, primarily on our Interstate system—freeways that will soon link the geographic extremes of our state together, from north to south and east to west, bringing new waves of commerce, tourism, and economic expansion to our cities, towns, and countryside. During this same period of time, we've awarded contracts for roads, highways, bridges, and safety improvements totaling $1.4 billion—that's billion with a capital *B*.

Today, we have cause to celebrate yet another good thing that's taking place in North Carolina: the opening of the first driver license renewal express office in our state, right here in Asheville. I'm delighted that all of you have turned out to share in, and to help us celebrate, this important step in providing you, our citizens, with the kind of progressive and modern motor vehicle services that our times demand. This project is the result of planning and hard work on the part of many people: the members of the Governor's Task Force on the North Carolina Driver License System, who conceived the idea, and the dedicated employees of the Division of Motor Vehicles, who had the responsibility of turning the concept into a reality. North Carolina's first DMV express office is a perfect example of the kind of teamwork—indeed, the kind of partnership—that sets North Carolina apart from other states and makes it unique.

The idea of express service is only one of many good proposals that originated with the task force, which I appointed last December, to find ways of cutting red tape and streamlining the operation of our driver license offices. Kermit Edney, who chaired this task force, is with us today, and I want to take this opportunity to commend him and his group publicly for the thorough and credible report which they have prepared. Citizens all across our state are beginning to reap the benefits of their recommendations. Express lanes to handle renewals for safe drivers have been established at several existing, full-service license offices, and more will be added soon.

The Division of Motor Vehicles has also increased efficiency through the extensive use of computers, revision of testing procedures, and shoring up our staff of license examiners in the field. Express offices in shopping centers and malls in major cities represents [sic] the first attempt ever to bring service to the people, rather than requiring them to come to us. Now, safe drivers in Asheville, and soon elsewhere in North Carolina, can do their shopping and renew their driver licenses at the same time. How's that for convenience?

As Commissioner Hiatt has pointed out, express service is a way of rewarding drivers who do not have points against their driving records and thus do not require retesting, except for vision. It does this, among other things, by providing extended hours of operation. For example, this new express office in Westgate Mall will remain open from 10 in the morning until 7 in the evening, two hours beyond the 5 p.m. closing time of DMV's full-service office on Tunnel Road. No longer will safe drivers be forced to take time off from work in order to renew their license. Other drivers may also use express services to replace a lost or stolen license, change their name or address, and purchase a nondriver photo identification card. Yet, this office also will serve a valuable highway safety need: It will help reduce the overwhelming demand placed upon our full-service offices by a growing number of clients and permit our license examiners to devote more time to assisting problem drivers.

It might surprise you to learn that the Division of Motor Vehicles, which is responsible for issuing driver licenses, handles more than 25 million motor vehicle transactions annually. Last year alone, it licensed about 165,000 more drivers than the year before. That means the DMV's Driver License Section has more direct contact with the people of North Carolina than any other state agency. About 10,000 individuals a day visit the state's 180 driver license offices, and another 2,000 a day telephone the Raleigh headquarters to obtain information and assistance.

During the last fifty years, North Carolina has grown from a state of less than 500,000 licensed drivers to one of 4.5 million. In the last six years, there has been a larger percentage growth in licensed drivers than in population. Since 1984, this growth has been accommodated by the Division of Motor Vehicles without any increase in examining personnel, although we have asked the General Assembly for additional resources. One of the most appropriate things we can do, today, is to applaud the Division of Motor Vehicles, and the Driver License Section in particular, for the splendid manner in which they have served the public and promoted highway safety through their efforts to keep problem drivers off our highways.

At this point, I believe it is important to mention that the Division of Motor Vehicles does far more than issue driver licenses. It also enforces state and federal truck safety regulations, a responsibility that was transferred from the North Carolina Utilities Commission in 1986. DMV's performance in this area, according to the National Highway Safety Administration, is rated as the best in the nation. That's not just among the best, that's *the* best; and when you look at what DMV has been doing to improve truck safety, it's easy to see why we're number one. Let me give you a few brief examples:

—Commercial truck safety inspections have been increased from 4,500, in 1984, to more than 64,000 in 1987. In one single year, DMV safety officers inspected more trucks than were checked in all of the four preceding years combined!

—DMV is currently organizing a special team of enforcement officers to conduct in-depth investigations of truck accidents that involve fatalities and serious injuries, thereby expanding our knowledge and helping us find ways of preventing them.

In other areas of motor vehicle enforcement, DMV is at work around the clock protecting consumers from odometer fraud, administering North Carolina's vehicle inspection program, weighing trucks for overload violations, and recovering stolen vehicles. Since 1984, DMV arrests for motor vehicle violations have increased 67 percent.

Our stolen vehicle recovery rate now totals 79 percent, 17 percent higher than the national rate; and last year, our truck weighing stations stopped and weighed 9.3 million commercial vehicles, an increase of 3.25 million over 1984.

DMV's Vehicle Registration Section last year processed 7.5 million title transactions, and for the first time in history, the state's 128 license plate agencies were linked to Raleigh by state-of-the-art computer equipment. The waiting time to obtain a vehicle title has been reduced from fourteen weeks to approximately ten days. And, finally, DMV last year did an incredible job of training and certifying adult school bus drivers in time for the 1988-1989 school term, as mandated by the U.S. Department of Labor.

Often the good work of the Division of Motor Vehicles goes unnoticed, but because of this good work, in part, North Carolina's accident fatality rate last year was reduced by 2.7 percent. I think that deserves our thanks.

The primary reason for issuing driver licenses is to foster highway safety and to ensure that only qualified motorists get behind the wheel. It may not sound like a tough job, but it is. At the same time, citizens are entitled to convenience, courtesy, efficient services, and good facilities to meet their needs.

Since 1985, the Division of Motor Vehicles has made service to the people of our state its most important priority, consistent with promoting highway safety. The opening of this express office, today, underscores our continuing commitment to this priority. Within the coming weeks, six additional DMV express offices will be established and opened in malls and shopping centers across our state. The goal of DMV, given the resources, is to extend this service to all counties with 100,000 or more licensed drivers.

Express service is only one of the many improvements we plan to make in the future. Not all of them can be accomplished administratively. Some will require legislative approval and the support of the citizens of North Carolina. Given this partnership, we can make North Carolina an even better and safer state for all of its citizens.

PINNING CEREMONY, BRIGADIER GENERAL GLENN N. SLOAN

RALEIGH, OCTOBER 11, 1988

If you note an extra twinkle in my eye, today, as we gather here to make public General Sloan's promotion to brigadier general, there is good reason.[1] General Sloan works for du Pont, which has a connection to the world of chemistry; you may recall I, too, have such a connection. General Sloan is also an active member and an elder in the Presbyterian church; you may recall I, too, have a similar connection. General Sloan has spent the better part of his adult life in service to his state and country; I have spent the better part of my adult life in similar pursuit. General Sloan has indicated he wants to continue in that service, as brigadier general; you may recall I, too, have indicated I want to continue in my present form of public service, as commander in chief. We have a lot in common!

There is an old military adage which seeks to determine whether someone is fit for battle. Is he someone you would want to crawl into a foxhole with? the question goes. I am told that General Sloan is such a man.

Glenn Sloan is a native of Duplin County and began his career in the army, in 1953, as a private. He graduated from the North Carolina Military Academy in 1959 and was commissioned as a second lieutenant. He has attended numerous military courses, including the command and general staff college, and he holds a bachelor of science degree in liberal arts. In his new position, he will command a group of 4,000 men and women who specialize in medical, maintenance, field artillery, quartermaster, and combat aviation. Glenn Sloan is one of the reasons North Carolina's National Guard is among the best in America.

Our North Carolina National Guard has earned its reputation through the kind of hard work and dedication exemplified by Glenn Sloan. With his commitment, and the commitment of others like him, I am sure our Guard will be ready should we ever need them.

There seems to be a preconceived notion in some quarters that the National Guard troops cannot be called to federal service without permission from the governor. That is certainly not my position, and it never will be. The army's "total force concept" is vital to our nation's security, because about half of the conventional forces in America's army comes from the National Guard.

Just recently, a contingent of North Carolina guardsmen trained for twenty-one days in Italy. They were there to train with Italian troops who may have to defend that country's border between Italy and Yugoslavia. I received a report last week at the conclusion of that exercise.

It is very clear that if our troops were called to service without benefit of training with Italian troops, on Italian terrain, we might not be able to meet our obligations. There are no Alpine mountain ranges at Fort Bragg to use to practice artillery. There are no rock-infested riverbeds to use for armored tank maneuvers. Learning to deal with even the simplest complications, such as language barriers, cannot be achieved without conducting exercises in locations where conflicts might occur.

Granted, there is no ongoing debate about American foreign policy in Italy. There is nothing controversial about training near communist borders. But it is dangerous, in my opinion, to withhold National Guard troops from training exercises as a means of trying to manipulate America's foreign policy initiatives. So if the president calls *this* governor, and asks to use our National Guard in defense of America, or the Pentagon calls and says we must begin training in a new location so we can be prepared to meet a new mission, I'll forward the call to General Scott—with orders to move out.

If you ask General Glenn Sloan how he feels, I am sure he will tell you he awaits the call to move out. That's just the kind of soldier he is. That is why, in three consecutive years as a battalion commander, General Sloan's unit was chosen "Best in the State" and then honored as "Best in the Nation." That is just the kind of soldier we want leading our North Carolina National Guard, whatever or wherever the mission. General Sloan, on behalf of the people of this great state, I salute you and the members of your command. We're counting on you!

---

[1]Glenn Needham Sloan (1935-   ), born in Duplin County; resident of Mount Olive; B.S., State University of New York, Regents College; military education courses. Enlisted in North Carolina Army National Guard, 1953, and later served as company, battalion, and group commander; promoted to colonel, 1985; transferred to deputy STARC commander, Headquarters, State Area Command, North Carolina Army National Guard, 1988; promoted on state orders to brigadier general, May, 1988, rank federally confirmed, August, 1988; specialist, Maintenance Foreign Technology Group, E. I. du Pont de Nemours Co., Inc., Kinston. Glenn Needham Sloan to Jan- Michael Poff, June 4, 1989.

SUPERCOMPUTING CENTER SITE DEDICATION

RESEARCH TRIANGLE PARK, NOVEMBER 30, 1988

What a great pleasure and high honor it is to participate in this historic event, this site dedication ceremony for the North Carolina Supercomputing Center here in Research Triangle Park; for in this ritual, we are declaring to the world our commitment to be in the forefront of science and technology and our continuing resolve to maintain our momentum in science-based economic development and leading-edge research. What better way to make a statement than with the purchase and installation of an incredible supercomputer which will spur research beyond human imagination. What more forceful way to declare that we intend to be full partners in the age of information.

This is also an occasion to give recognition where recognition is due. Plato talked about being a midwife of ideas.[1] I'm not sure who brought forth the original idea for a supercomputer, the gargantuan baby that will do much to enhance and expand the private-public partnership between our fine research universities and industry and serve as a powerful impetus for basic research, but there can be little doubt about who the lead midwife was for this supercomputer enterprise. I refer, of course, to Senator Kenneth Royall.

It was Ken Royall who spanked the gargantuan baby into life. It was through his leadership and the collective wisdom of the General Assembly that $18 million was appropriated to fund the first phase of this project.[2] He was kind enough to offer me some fatherly advice from time to time. Some midwife.

By almost any measure this is a daring enterprise, one that will provide North Carolina with the most powerful computer in the Southeast. To give you some idea of the power of the Cray supercomputer, it is 27,000 times more powerful than the personal computers. Our supercomputer will be from 100 to 1,000 times faster than conventional computers. In terms of storage, our supercomputer will have 32 million words of memory and be capable of processing more than 1 billion floating-point operations per second. Do you understand what I'm saying?

Well, if Senator Royall is the midwife of this enterprise, then we would have to give much credit for the nurturing of this prodigy to the Microelectronics Center of North Carolina. But what we will have is not just a powerful computer. Through the orchestration of MCNC and the North Carolina Computer Commission—and the active involvement of universities, the Research Triangle Institute, and supportive businesses, and the microwave, high-quality, statewide network in place at MCNC—we have in place a powerful infrastructure of private-public partnerships that will assuredly serve as a potent catalyst for economic development throughout North Carolina.

You know, other states talk about private-public partnerships, but in North Carolina, we're doing them. We are in the forefront. North Carolina has made the practice of private-public collaboration an art form that is the envy of the nation and the world, and it's not something that just happened yesterday. Private-public partnerships have a long tradition in North Carolina, and one of the most dramatic examples of this kind of partnership can be seen in the neighborhood where we are standing today, right here in Research Triangle Park. Research Triangle Park is eloquent testimony to what can happen when we work together with a shared vision of greater possibilities. If we did not have this fine research park, we would not be building a facility anywhere to house our supercomputer.

Thus, this is an occasion to engage in an appreciation of our historical roots, to celebrate those who helped make this event possible. From the recent efforts of George Hitchings and Gertrude Elion,[3] from the administrations of Hodges to Sanford, to Moore, to Scott, to Holshouser, to Hunt, to et cetera—that's me—we have been gripped by a magnificent obsession to advance our state scientifically and technologically. If it had not been for contributions by industry to the Supercomputing Center, what we can now do would be greatly diminished. For example, consider the contribution of Cray Research, Incorporated, alone: It gave $3.4 million to the project.

We have shown that when we work together as one united state, that with a collaborative alliance of legislators, and business, and universities, and mayors, and county commissioners, and departments of state government, there is little we can't achieve. We're on a roll in North Carolina, and working together, we can keep a good thing going.

Let us not forget, also, that when all is said and done, the people of North Carolina have made all this possible; it is to the aspirations of all North Carolinians and their straining reach for better things for future generations that we pay special tribute. This is a site dedication for all North Carolinians, born and unborn.

When I see the passion and vision, the hard work that went into a project like this, I'm reminded of the saying that was inscribed, in 1730, on a church in Sussex, England: "A vision without a task is but a dream; a task without a vision is drudgery; a vision and a task are the hope of the world."[4] It must be clear to all, as we meet here today, that our luminous vision is joined to make a better life for all North Carolinians.

---

[1]"Well, my art of midwifery is in most respects like theirs; but differs, in that I attend men and not women, and I look after their souls when they are in labor, and not after their bodies: and the triumph of my art is in thoroughly examining whether the

thought which the mind of the young man brings forth is a false idol or a noble and true birth." Plato, *Dialogues, Theaetetus 150*, quoted in Bartlett, *Familiar Quotations*, 95.

²N.C. *Session Laws, 1987, Regular Session, 1988*, III, c. 1086, s. 36, authorized appropriations for the supercomputer.

³George Herbert Hitchings, Jr., and Gertrude Belle Elion, two scientists at Burroughs Wellcome Co. in Research Triangle Park, won the 1988 Nobel Prize for medicine. They were recognized for discovering drugs to combat gout, herpes, leukemia, and the rejection of transplanted organs. *News and Observer*, October 18, 1988.

George Herbert Hitchings, Jr. (1905-   ), born in Hoquiam, Washington; resident of Durham; B.S., 1927, M.S., 1928, University of Washington; Ph.D., 1933, Harvard University. Instructor at Harvard and at Case Western Reserve University, 1936-1942; biochemist, 1942-1946, chief biochemist, 1946-1952, associate research director, 1955-1963, chemotherapy research director, 1963-1967, vice-president for research, 1967-1975, board of directors member, 1968-1984, consultant and scientist emeritus, since 1975, Burroughs Wellcome Co.; professor, Brown University, 1968-1980; adjunct professor at Duke University, since 1970, and at University of North Carolina at Chapel Hill, since 1972; visiting professor, 1974-1977, Chuang-Ang University, Seoul, South Korea, 1974-1977. *News and Observer*, October 23, 1988.

Gertrude Belle Elion (1918-   ), born in New York City; resident of Chapel Hill; A.B., Hunter College, 1937; M.S., New York University, 1941. Research assistant, Denver Chemical Manufacturing Co., 1938-1939, and at Johnson & Johnson, 1943-1944; teacher, New York City schools, 1940-1942; food analyst, Quaker Maid Co., 1942-1943; biochemist, 1944-1950, senior research chemist, 1950-1955, assistant to associate research director, 1955-1963, assistant to chemotherapy research director, 1963-1967, experimental therapy department chief, 1967-1983, and scientist emeritus, since 1983, Burroughs Wellcome Co.; president, American Association for Cancer Research, 1983-1984; adjunct professor, 1970-1983, research professor, since 1983, Duke University; adjunct professor, University of North Carolina at Chapel Hill, since 1973. *News and Observer*, October 23, 1988.

⁴Governor Martin penned a warning, adjacent to this quotation on page 4 of his prepared text, to his speechwriter: "When the same quotation is used over and over, it does preempt inclusion in a later volume of speeches." [Editor's Note: The governor's awareness of and interest in this documentary project were indeed gratifying. However, no address or other public paper will go unpublished because some of the material found therein has been repeated elsewhere. Recurring quotations have not prevented noteworthy documents from being included among the governor's published papers.]

PLENARY II: COUNCIL OF STATE GOVERNMENTS' REPORT TO THE PRESIDENT-ELECT ON THE STATE OF THE STATES

KANSAS CITY, MISSOURI, DECEMBER 5, 1988

[Martin was elected vice-president of the Council of State Governments in 1986 and served as the organization's president during 1988; see *News and Observer*, December 11, 1986, and December 3, 1988. Most of the following address is identical to *A Message to the 41st President on the State of the States, 1988* ([Lexington, Kentucky]: Division of Policy Analysis Services, Council of State Governments, 1988).]

Today I am pleased to present the Council of State Governments' report to the president-elect on the state of the states. It is an attempt to describe and provide insight to our forty-first president, George Bush, into some of the biggest challenges confronting the states and the issue areas about which state officials are most concerned. I am very confident that it will receive the attention of the new administration. Our report focuses on seven critical areas, including education, economic development, human services, health care, corrections, environment, and infrastructure needs. It also incorporates an assessment of the state of the states based on the experiences and expertise of state officials from across the country.

The overall message is mixed. It is one of innovation, pride, and satisfaction for what states have been able to accomplish. But this pride and satisfaction [are] coupled with an understanding that more should and must be done to tackle problem areas in the states, and that the "more" must be weighed against the reality of limited fiscal resources.

A recent national survey shows that our people have a pretty good idea about what's going well in government and what needs more attention. When given the opportunity to create hypothetical budgets for their states and chart the programs for which they would increase or decrease funding, the respondents made some interesting choices. Apart from making a not-too-surprising call for an increase in funding for educational improvements, the respondents did not focus on increases in other traditional state service areas such as highways and transportation, corrections and prisons, or state parks and tourism. Instead, they targeted funding increases for programs related to child day care, drug abuse prevention, illiteracy, senior citizen programs, infant health care, environmental protection, and low-income housing.

The Council of State Governments surveyed governors, state senate and house leadership and rank-and-file members, state treasurers, comptrollers, secretaries of state—a cross section of state officials, a cross section of the states—to find out about the ways their states remedied problems, what they thought their states' greatest challenges would be over the next few years. The state officials identified what they believed were the top issues on their states' agendas. There were only a few surprises.

Education, and the elements of reform, restructuring, and funding, received the most votes as the top priority area of concern across their states. Nearly 40 million children are enrolled in public schools at an estimated cost of over $80 billion to the fifty states. Our economy is threatened by foreign competition and increasingly reliant on complex technologies that require a higher level of education than ever before, and the states recognize that an educated population is linked to economic success.

We know that an uneducated population also results in higher welfare and social service costs and increases the possibility of criminal behavior. Clearly, quality education is an investment the states want to make. Between 1981 and 1986, per-capita state spending for elementary and secondary education increased nationally by more than 40 percent, and now education is the single largest budget item in all but two states.

Gains have been made, but all is not well. Test scores have stalled for the last three years. As many as one million students drop out of high school every year, and rates in some inner-city schools are approaching 50 percent. Even more alarming is that as many as one quarter of the students who do graduate are functionally illiterate and ill equipped for the work force. Moreover, surveys indicate that teachers feel constrained by red tape and political intervention, and morale is reported to be at an all-time low.

There is growing concern throughout the states that students at the greatest risk of failure—low-income, inner-city, minority children—may have been bypassed by the reform movement. Appropriately, states are taking preventive measures by focusing on early childhood readiness. Supporters say that early educational readiness programs advance student achievement and are a cost-effective investment for society. At least thirty-five states have implemented such programs targeted at disadvantaged children, from infants to third graders. Drop-out prevention is getting a great deal of attention at the high school level, but many of us believe the problem was created when they weren't ready to drop in as five-year-olds.

We are beginning to restructure the management and organization of our schools. Centralized, top-down management, coupled with rigid bureaucratic regulation, are now viewed as stumbling blocks to teacher innovation. Authority for day-to-day operations is being decentralized. In exchange for increased autonomy, schools are being asked to accept a greater degree of accountability. School districts and individual schools are being held responsible for their progress. Now states are beginning to evaluate schools by their outputs, rather than inputs, such as class size and per-capita funding; test scores, student attendance, and graduation rates are the new measures being used to rate the schools.

The challenge for the states in education is enormous; a second area of great concern to the states is employment. Despite the recent economic recovery, most surveys indicate that jobs remain the number-one issue for most American families. States are in the vanguard in developing comprehensive economic development strategies to compete in the world economy, but the heart of the employment problem for states is not merely business attraction and job expansion. Rather, it focuses on developing a work force trained, or trainable, to handle these new jobs which are technologically more demanding, both in manufacturing and nonmanufacturing. We are working to bring better jobs to our workers; we must also bring better-educated workers to these jobs.

Employment trends suggest that states will have to become even more flexible and adaptable. The majority of jobs are created by expansion of existing companies, many of which are small. As a result, states will have to promote the development of these businesses.

Another trend, however, indicates that minorities, including new immigrants from Asia and Latin America, many of whom have very little education, will make up a large portion of the future work force. Already, the states are finding that these individuals not only need to be reeducated to face the realities of the marketplace, but also need to find work immediately so they can become productive members of the economy.

Finally, with women entering the work force at an ever-increasing rate, the nature of economic opportunities available and the types of goods and services state governments will be expected to provide will be changing drastically. Already, states are involved in employees' family issues, such as parental leave and child day care, to ensure that they will be in step with the changing economic marketplace.

The third critical area of concern to the states is that of human services. In 1988, a series of family-relevant issues—child day care, child support, child and spouse abuse, disintegrating families, adoption needs—moved into the national spotlight and succeeded in grabbing the attention of the American public and officials across the states.

Since the 1950s, the number of working women with preschool children has more than quadrupled. Now approximately 66 percent of mothers aged eighteen to forty-four work, including an estimated 50 percent of those with children less than one year old. As a result, child care has become much more than a family issue; it is now an economic, and work force-related, issue. In recent years, forty-eight states have enacted nearly 350 laws to try and meet the needs of two-earner and single-parent families. In 1988, parental leave for the birth, adoption, or serious illness of a child has grown as a subject of active interest.

The fourth area of concern discussed in the report is health care. Long-term care for the elderly and disabled, AIDS, delivery of health-care services to the indigent, the impending shortage of nursing services, the growing number of the uninsured and underinsured, the rising costs of care—these are frustrating health concerns facing the states today. They are all part of the struggle to provide our citizens with access to adequate and affordable health-care services.

I have developed a general formula for this, called QUACK—Q.A.=C.K.: Quality times Access is proportional to Cost. What that says is that any increase in access to health care, or anything else, will be accompanied by a corresponding increase in cost, or a decrease in quality, of care. The corollary today is that improvements in quality and access have caused a dramatic rise in cost, regardless of cost containment exercises. One consequence is that this cost sector has become a wedge to displace other competing social goals.

The fifth area of concern identified by the survey of state officials is crime and corrections. A big part of that concern is over the use of illegal drugs. The secondary drug link to criminal activity to finance the habit is creating severe enforcement problems for the states, and forcing us to come up with new approaches, using limited resources. On the one hand, we want to take harsh action against the illicit drug industry, like denying parole to drug dealers so they can serve their full sentences. At the same time, our prisons are overcrowded, at least by standards being imposed by federal courts. In more than thirty states, correctional facilities are under court order to alleviate overcrowding, and the costs associated with incarceration are forcing many states to look at alternative punishments for those convicted of crimes not involving assault or drugs.

The environment is the sixth critical concern of the states. Over the years, the states have had to tackle a variety of environmental challenges, from abandoned hazardous waste dumps, to toxic air emissions, and now medical wastes on our beaches. According to a Council of State Governments' survey, eleven states already have new or amended infectious wastes statutes or have promulgated regulations since 1986; in addition, twenty-five have initiated processes that would change their requirements for infectious waste. Meanwhile, ordinary solid waste is threatening the states and localities by its sheer volume and the difficulty of avoiding hazardous contaminants. It is estimated that, by 1995, about half of America's landfills will be closed. Any long-term alternatives, such as recycling and waste-to-energy plants, still have not been widely accepted.

Finally, we come to the seventh issue of infrastructure. Our nation's infrastructure is eroding. America's capital facilities are wearing out. As one example, 42 percent of our bridges are either structurally deficient or functionally obsolete. Most of the nation's mass transit and hazardous waste treatment facilities are dangerously near collapse. The U.S. Department of Commerce recently estimated that infrastructure needs to serve industry will increase by 30 percent in the next decade.

Faced with declining federal funding, states have had to shoulder more of the responsibility for infrastructure development. Indeed, many states feel so unfairly shortchanged by federal highway formulas that some of us would prefer to cut back the federal motor fuels tax so that states can pick it up directly and get more paving for our money. Meanwhile, we all face major construction needs.

In this message to the next president, we have taken a look at the problems facing the states today and what state officials think will be their greatest challenges over the next few years. The list of needs and concerns is long and well documented, but in this message to the new president, we as state officials want to express pride and optimism in our capacity to find creative solutions to often perplexing problems. But we will only be successful in meeting the needs with the support, cooperation, and flexibility provided through a partnership with the federal administration. President-elect Bush has made clear that he wants a working partnership with us. This is our way of saying we want that, too. And thank you, Mr. President.

GOVERNING BOARD, COUNCIL OF STATE GOVERNMENTS

KANSAS CITY, MISSOURI, DECEMBER 7, 1988

I would like to welcome my fellow board members from states across the nation who are devoted to the cause of improving state government and promoting the role of states in the federal system. Thanks for giving your time and expertise to make the Council of State Governments what it is today. You are proof that by working together, we as states really can make a difference in our own governments and in the country as a whole.

The council is unique in that, as an organization of states, it encompasses all three branches of government. The council's umbrella allows executive, legislative, and judicial officials to share their experiences and to address common concerns. This opportunity to work with those from other branches has broadened my own appreciation of the founders' wisdom in creating separate-but-equal branches.

The council's geographic diversity, as witnessed by the state policy makers here today, is another real strength. In meeting with state leaders from across the nation, I have gained an appreciation of the varied regions of the country and the common problems facing us. As a governor who has become involved in CSG, I feel privileged to have met so many outstanding and talented legislators, administrators, and other state leaders from across the country. It is an experience that even more governors should strive to become a part of and one which I deeply appreciate.

As state policy makers, we benefit in many ways from participating in the council's forums—professionally and personally. We are able to learn about the best programs each state has to offer through the council's regional and national meetings, and its research and publications. The council builds partnerships within and across state governments so necessary to resolving the common challenges facing us. As politicians, we talk a lot about values, and the sessions on strengthening the family have provided me with some good ideas on ways to approach these difficult problems facing our society.

This year, the council has moved forward on several fronts that are of real benefit to us as state officials. One of these is the progress made by the newly established Policy Analysis Division at CSG headquarters.[1] Among its many accomplishments in 1988, the policy analysis staff prepared the outstanding message to President-elect Bush on vital state issues for the opening plenary session. It was a message that I was pleased to present. In addition, the staff has worked throughout the year to prepare reports on three significant issues facing state officials: civil rights, business tax and financial incentives, and homelessness. These studies have been used as the basis for articles by the staff in the council's monthly magazine, *State Government News,* and will be released in detailed reports, as well.

Another major accomplishment has been the implementation of the council's State Policy Development Fund. The fund was created in 1987 to conduct research and policy analysis on issues of urgent concern to states and the private sector. Initially, the fund will focus on public-private partnerships in the areas of biotechnology, solid waste, and child care. The fund will help us consider how to develop strong public and private partnerships to deliver public services efficiently and effectively.

The council continues to forge ahead with forums designed to help state officials develop and hone their leadership skills. Among them is the Toll Fellowship Program, an annual, intensive, week-long seminar for thirty-two state officials competitively selected from across the country. This year's program, focusing on emerging state issues and planning for the furture, was one of the most successful to date. Here in Kansas City, CSG held a special program for newly elected state constitutional officers to assist them in developing their skills and making a smooth transition to elective office.

"State to State" is an exciting new program which is close to my own heart, originating as it does in North Carolina. The council has joined with the North Carolina Agency for Public Telecommunications in promoting a series of television programs focusing on state governments. The programs cover issues of interest to public officials and the public nationwide. It airs live, every Thursday from 9 to 10 P.M., Eastern time. Each program consists of a panel of three state government experts on a particular topic, such as hazardous waste, day care, or transportation. The three experts usually represent different states. Viewers from across the nation can call in by telephone and ask questions. A potential audience of more than 40 million viewers in all states can view "State to State." States are invited to join in by calling Executive Producer Lee Wing at the North Carolina Agency for Public [Telecommunications.][2]

In another major media project, the council is part of a nationwide public service advertising campaign aimed at school dropout prevention. The campaign became possible through a joint venture of CSG, Ashland Oil, Incorporated, and the AdCouncil. This fall, the AdCouncil distributed thousands of packets to television and radio stations, magazines, and newspapers across the country to combat school dropouts. The ads were developed from a successful campaign by Ashland Oil, Incorporated, in Kentucky and West Virginia, and funded by Ashland. One out of five students are nationwide dropouts before graduation, and the rate in some cities is half or more. The ads, run as PSAs [public service announcements] nationally, mention the council and the AdCouncil.

Finally, our thanks go to Speaker Bob F. Griffin for being such a genial host and for showing us his state's hospitality.[3] I also want to say what a pleasure it has been to work with Senator Mary McClure, this year, as we conferred on council business.[4] It also has been a pleasure to work with the council's staff, especially Carl Stenberg[5] and Fran Berry, who have worked with the rest of the staff at headquarters, the regions, and D.C. to ensure a successful conference.

[1]The governor was referring to the Division of Policy Analysis Services. The Council of State Governments was based in Lexington, Kentucky.

[2]Lucie Lee Wing (1926-   ), born in New Orleans; resident of Durham; B.A., Newcomb College; M.S., Tulane University. Research associate to academic vice-president, Tulane University, 1948-1962; Marshall Scholarship Selection Committee member, 1966-1976; founder, president, Friends of University Network Television, 1972-1979; policy adviser, telecommunications and the arts, Department of Administration, 1977-1979; staff director, North Carolina Task Force on Public Telecommunications, 1978-1979; executive director, North Carolina Agency for Public Telecommunications, since 1979; author; composer-lyricist. Lucie Lee Wing to Jan-Michael Poff, July 10, 1990.

[3]Bob F. Griffin (1935-   ), born in Braymer, resident of Cameron, Missouri; B.S., 1957, J.D., 1959, University of Missouri at Columbia; U.S. Air Force, 1959-1962. Attorney; Clinton County prosecutor, 1963-1971; member, since 1971, Speaker pro tem, 1977-1981, and Speaker, since 1981, Missouri House of Representatives; Democrat. Griffin was the first person in the history of the Missouri legislature to serve five terms as Speaker. Bob F. Griffin to Jan-Michael Poff, August 6, 1990.

[4]Mary A. McClure (1939-   ), born in Milbank, South Dakota; B.S., University of South Dakota, 1961; M.P.A., Syracuse University, 1980. English and Spanish teacher, Redfield (South Dakota) High School, 1965-1988; elected to South Dakota Senate, 1974, and became first female president pro tem; first national chairwoman, Council of State Governments; special assistant to President Bush for intergovernmental affairs, since 1989. Mary A. McClure to Jan-Michael Poff, July 26, 1990.

[5]Carl Waldamer Stenberg III (1943-   ), born in Pittsburgh; resident of Alexandria, Virginia; B.S., Allegheny College, 1965; M.P.A., 1966, Ph.D., 1970, State University of New York-Albany. Analyst, later senior analyst, 1968-1977, assistant director for policy implementation, 1977-1983, acting executive director, 1982, U.S. Advisory Commission on Intergovernmental Relations; executive director, Council of State Governments, since 1983; former feature editor, managing editor. Who's Who in America, 1988-1989, II, 2970.

CAPITOL CHRISTMAS TREE LIGHTING CEREMONY

RALEIGH, DECEMBER 8, 1988

It is in the spirit of Christmas that Dottie and I are gathered here on historic Capitol Square for this tree-lighting ceremony, a ceremony that officially opens this holiday season in downtown Raleigh and North Carolina. As is the case of all special occasions such as this, there is cause for thanksgiving, a time to thank those who have given so generously of their time, energies, and talents to bring joy to others.

Also, many of you will have the opportunity to see, this evening, the newly located statue of Sir Walter Raleigh on the first block of Fayetteville Street Mall. It is noteworthy that the member of the commission to come up with a name for our capital city was a man from Stokes County, by the name of James Martin, who happened to be the brother of Governor Alexander Martin—no kin, alas. And what better name than Raleigh, after Sir Walter Raleigh, the man who shaped so much of North Carolina's history. Mayor Upchurch,[1] we are delighted that the statue honoring this great man now stands at the center of festivities in downtown Raleigh. I'm sure his lordship would appreciate the honor.[2]

Peace on earth, goodwill toward men, are not just words for one season; they are words for all seasons. They are words for every day of the year. What better example of this than what we have witnessed over the past two weeks: the incredible outpouring of compassion, goodwill, and giving—of giving by North Carolinians of their time, labor, and treasure to those who felt the wrath of what is one of the most destructive tornadoes in North Carolina, on record, on the morning of Monday, November 28.[3]

Who can fail to be touched by the many acts of kindness we have witnessed since that night of terror for so many? In great crisis, the true character of people will emerge. Once again, we have witnessed compassion and charity that North Carolinians have for their neighbors in need.

The acts of charity are many, such as the opening of homes to those who, within a matter of seconds, had no homes; the generous outpouring of money, food, and clothing; the heroic efforts by scores of volunteers to help clean up the debris; and the informative and unifying work of radio and television stations, who showed just why they are such an important part of the community. All these acts stir the human heart and prove the power of our humane spirit, but something that must have touched many of us deeply this Christmas season is the story about volunteers who fanned out from the tornado disaster areas with food, calling the names of lost pets. Many of these frightened, helpless creatures were returned to their grateful owners.

Yes, North Carolinians are very special people; we have a way of proving this over and over again. It was just a year ago, in fact, that many of us stood here to remember North Carolina fishermen who were suffering from the economic effects of the red tide. North Carolinians responded then to make Christmas a more joyous occasion for the fishermen and their families. Is it any wonder that North Carolina has earned the title of "State of the Hearts."

This is a time, also, to remember the four people, including two children, who lost their lives on that terrifying morning in November and to convey our heartfelt sympathy to their grieving families. Let us not fail to remember them in our prayers.

Ironically, this is an occasion for thanksgiving, because it was a miracle that so many of those in the path of the tornado survived.

Experts on such natural disasters continue to be amazed that the toll in life from a tornado with such awesome power was not in the scores or even in the hundreds.

As you may recall from school days, the original day of Christmas was on the first day of winter, the winter solstice—that time of year when darkness and light are balanced, a time of year promising that each coming day will be longer and more fulfilling. Thus is Christmas a season of hope.

A child once asked, "Why can't Christmas come every day?" Why not, indeed. As governor of North Carolina, with the lighting of this tree, I fervently hope that the spirit of Christmas shall remain in effect for 365 days of the year. And from my family to yours, a merry Christmas to you all, and may you be touched with the special grace of charity, kindness, brotherhood, and goodwill toward all humankind.

---

[1]Avery C. Upchurch (1928-   ), native of Wake County; was graduated from Needham B. Broughton High School, Raleigh; honorary degree; U.S. Army Reserve, 1951-1957. Past president, North Carolina League of Municipalities, Raleigh Merchants Bureau, and of Raleigh Tourist Convention Assn.; past chairman, Triangle J Council of Governments; elected 1979, reelected 1981, to Raleigh City Council; elected mayor of Raleigh, 1983, and returned in subsequent elections. Gail L. Crisp, administrative assistant to Mayor Avery C. Upchurch, to Jan-Michael Poff, July 13, 1990.

[2]Governor Martin then thanked participants in and sponsors of the tree-lighting celebration: Wesley Williams and the Raleigh Merchants Bureau; the Downtown Development Corp. and volunteers; Mr. Fuller Stone, who donated the Christmas tree; Landscape Services, Auxiliary Services Division, Department of Administration; Raleigh Garden Club; state Capitol volunteers; Raleigh Junior Woman's Club; the Reverend Dr. George Ballentine, pastor, Hayes Barton Baptist Church; Choral Director Floyd Lowman and the Sanderson High School Women's Chorale; the Raleigh Concert Band; Jan Anderson; the Raleigh Breakfast Optimist Club, Inc., for its $2,000 contribution toward constructing a permanent display apparatus for the annual Christmas tree; "and to all of you who came out this evening for this festive occasion."

[3]Tornadoes struck nine North Carolina counties on November 28, 1988. Preliminary estimates valued storm-related damage at $77.2 million; of that total, the level of destruction amounted to nearly $61 million in Wake County alone. North Raleigh was particularly hard hit. *News and Observer*, November 28, 29, 30, December 5, 1988.

CAROLINA'S PRIDE SEAFOOD, INCORPORATED, DEDICATION

PLYMOUTH, DECEMBER 22, 1988

This is truly an historic event, a milestone in economic development in our state. With the dedication of this new plant and the cryogenic freezing machine, we are entering a new era which holds great promise for the rural areas of our state particularly.

Traditionally, we have sent the majority of North Carolina's harvest out of state to be processed. Now, we have in place a concerted effort on the part of industry, the state universities, the state Department of Commerce, and our Department of Agriculture to ensure that more of our natural resources are processed, packaged, and marketed in the great state of North Carolina, not in other states. This dividend of our private-public partnership will mean more profits for North Carolinians and improved quality control for our products. In effect, we will be producing, processing, packaging, and marketing our high-quality North Carolina products to consumers with the resultant added-value income remaining in North Carolina instead of going to other states.

Another word for it is greater self-sufficiency. In economic terms, the definition of a colony is being in a position of producing or harvesting raw materials and then sending them somewhere else to be processed and marketed. We have historically been one of the richest seafood suppliers to the nation and to the world. With the dedication of Carolina's Pride Seafood, we are taking yet another step away from economic colonialism to greater economic independence, autonomy, and profitability. The result is increased prospects for additional income and jobs in one of our important industries.

Yes, this is a red-letter day, and its significance cannot be over-emphasized. We can gain an additional insight into the importance of this facility by realizing that it is currently shipping fresh seafood to Japan, an increasingly important trading partner for North Carolina products. With cryogenic freezing, we should greatly expand our markets, throughout the nation and the world, for fresh and fresh-frozen North Carolina products.

You know, we must all be stewards of our wonderful environment. We are indeed blessed with a goodly land. In this vein, I want to emphasize that we will do everything in our power to safeguard the water quality of our rivers and sounds as we seek to increase the production of high-quality seafood products. This joint industry-university demonstration project is an important step in this direction.

We would especially like to thank Liquid Air Corporation and Mr. Case Elenbaas for their willingness to participate in this project, as well as the foresight of innovative processors. We would be remiss if we failed to thank Andy Allen[1] and his associates for initiating efforts that will place us at the leading edge of an important aspect of rural economic development. And let's be sure to acknowledge the technical support provided to the project by David Green and Dr. Frank

Thomas of the North Carolina Agricultural Extension Service and the UNC Sea Grant Marine Advisory Service.[2] Someone has said that inspired human imagination is our highest form of technology. What we see here is living proof of that statement.

This processing facility will become a vital part of our growing aquaculture industry. Incidentally, agreement has been reached between Andy Allen and Rob Mayo,[3] of Carolina Classics catfish farm, to process catfish in the cryogenic tunnel. There has been interest shown, also, by several of our produce farmers for using this machine, individually, to quick-freeze produce. This capability will truly move us to an exciting frontier in rural economic development. It is you who have been involved in this project who have helped establish the momentum. Just between us, with the kinds of private-public partnerships we are building in North Carolina, we are going on to even greater things.

This dedication is an historic moment in rural economic development, and I want once more to thank all those involved in this very successful project, as it demonstrates once again that private-public partnerships can help us blaze new trails in economic development, making North Carolina one of the great leaders in the nation. As the great sage of Okefenokee Swamp, Pogo, was heard to observe, "Our biggest problem is insurmountable opportunity." Well, the opportunities are out there in aquaculture, and with the help of people like you, we intend to surmount them for the greater good of the citizens of North Carolina. Now, would Andy Allen, Case Elenbaas, David Green, and Dr. Frank Thomas please come forward to be recognized for your extraordinary partnership. [Governor Martin presents certificates of appreciation.]

---

[1]Andy Allen was president of Carolina's Pride Seafood, Inc. Press release, "Dedication Ceremony for Seafood Processing Facility and New Technology for Eastern North Carolina Industries Introduced," Plymouth, December 22, 1988, Governors Papers, James G. Martin.

[2]David Patrick Green (1954-   ), born in Pittsburgh; resident of Morehead City; B.S., Davidson College, 1976; M.S., East Carolina University, 1980; Ph.D., North Carolina State University, 1989. Extension specialist, North Carolina State University Seafood Laboratory, since 1986. David Patrick Green to Jan-Michael Poff, May 31, 1990.

Frank B. Thomas (1922-   ), born in Camden, Delaware; resident of Raleigh; B.S., University of Delaware, 1948; M.S., 1949, Ph.D., 1955, Pennsylvania State University; U.S. Army Air Force, 1942-1946, U.S. Air Force Reserve. Seafood extension service pioneer; Pennsylvania State University horticulture instructor, 1949-1955, assistant professor, 1955-1958; food processing specialist, Horticulture Department, 1958-1961, became seafood extension specialist, 1961, professor, 1966-1988, and professor emeritus, since 1988, Department of Food Science, North Carolina State University; food technology consultant; member, since 1988, Governor's Task Force on the Farm Economy. *Coastwatch* (April, 1989), 1-3; Frank B. Thomas to Jan-Michael Poff, June 11, 1990.

[3]Robert A. Mayo (1960-   ), born in Norfolk, Virginia; resident of Greenville; B.S., Virginia Polytechnic Institute and State University, 1982; M.B.A., University of Texas, 1984. Consultant, Pace Consultants, Inc., Houston, 1984-1985; founder, 1985, chief executive officer, Carolina Classics Catfish, Inc., Ayden. Robert A. Mayo to Jan-Michael Poff, June 1, 1990.

STATE BOARD OF EDUCATION

RALEIGH, JANUARY 4, 1989

I appreciate this opportunity to address two of the major issues in education facing our state, namely (1) providing fair compensation for the personnel in our schools, and (2) implementing a performance-based salary system.

It goes without saying that our human capital, comprised of our teachers and administrators, is our single most important asset in our pursuit of educational excellence. Indeed, this belief has provided, and continues to provide, the principal energy for our Career Development program, which is now in the fourth year of our pilot effort. There is little need to tell you how important it is to maintain the momentum generated by our pilot effort, but unfortunately, as you are well aware, budgetary realities dictate that we reassess our strategies for full implementation of the Career Development program at this time—this in spite of widespread professional and public support for the program.

Our current fiscal situation, involving the prospect of substantial revenue shortfalls for the 1989-1991 biennium, is all the more reason for us to continue to state our unyielding commitment to full implementation of the Career Development program as soon as possible. While it may be necessary for us to retrench from time to time, we can ill afford to lose sight of our sovereign goal: that of adding value to our students, most notably academic and vocational value. Results, after all, are what count, and the greater professionalization of teaching should be a giant step in that direction.

Integrally related to our Career Development program is the problem of our basic salary schedule for teachers. This was pointed out quite persuasively by the Evaluation, Salary, and Incentives Subcommittee of the Forum Study Group. In effect, what the subcommittee proposed was the necessity to view salaries in terms of a total system of compensation, pointing out correctly that "where employees are already disgruntled because of uncompetitive salaries, merit pay plans intensify employee disgruntlement."[1] Thus, we are faced with the challenge of making the basic salary schedule competitive while at the same time ensuring that educational excellence is amply rewarded.

Equity must be a key word in our consideration of compensation for teachers. Rather than subscribing to what is largely a homogeneous salary schedule, we should seek to implement a differentiated salary schedule for teachers. Equity requires that we reward excellence. We would do well to remember an old saying: "There is nothing quite so unequal as the equal treatment of unequals."[2]

The four guiding principles of the subcommittee certainly deserve serious consideration. In addition to making "teaching more competitive with other white collar jobs in North Carolina," and eliminating "existing inequities in the State's salary schedule," one other far-reaching principle deserves serious study: namely, reducing "the current reliance on years of experience and earned degrees for salary advancement by combining modest annual longevity increments."[3]

While being committed to the subcommittee's fourth guiding principle, that student perfomance is the *sine qua non* of educational excellence, we must be careful that the progress we have made on our Career Development program not be sidetracked. To be sure, the Forum's recommendations regarding student performance are to be applauded; it should be noted that the Career Development program is based on improving teaching practices in the classroom as a forerunner of increased student or school performance. Indeed, it is a little-known fact that the Career Development Plan actually utilizes an important principle of our state's current teacher evaluation system: that teachers, like other professionals such as doctors, lawyers, accountants, and even plumbers, should be evaluated on knowing and using good practice. Thus, promoting good practice, or what experience and research have demonstrated to work, is a centerpiece of the Career Development Plan; the Career Development program, in addition to being a plan to reward teaching excellence, is committed to the development of human capital. The Career Development Plan is a giant step toward improving the profession of teaching.

---

[1]Forum Study Group, *Thinking for a Living: A Blueprint for Educational Growth; A New North Carolina Compact for Better Schools* (Raleigh: Public School Forum of North Carolina, December, 1988), 19, hereinafter cited as Forum Study Group, *Thinking for a Living.*

[2]"It is a wise man who said that there is no greater inequality than the equal treatment of unequals." Justice Felix Frankfuter in dissenting opinion, *Dennis v. United States,* 339 U.S. 184 (1949), quoted in *Respectfully Quoted,* 108.

[3]Forum Study Group, *Thinking for a Living,* 19.

OMITTED SPEECHES AND STATEMENTS

[Speeches and official papers not reprinted in this volume are cataloged, by title, below. Those excerpted or otherwise mentioned in annotations accompanying Martin's published remarks are denoted by an asterisk. Speaking engagements indicated on the governor's weekly agenda, but for which no prepared text was provided, have been incorporated into the following list and are marked by a dagger. Existing copies of Governor Martin's addresses and other public papers are housed at the Division of Archives and History, Department of Cultural Resources, Raleigh.]

1985

January 15, North Carolina Association of Chamber of Commerce Executives, Raleigh
January 28, Sandhills Chamber of Commerce, Pinehurst†
January 31, Statement at Press Conference, Raleigh†
February 7, Statement at Press Conference, Raleigh†
February 11, "Pride in Patriotism," Highland Junior High School, Gastonia
February 12, Sir Walter Cabinet, Raleigh†
February 14, Statement at Press Conference, Raleigh†
February 14, Legislators' Appreciation Dinner, North Carolina Motor Carriers Association, Raleigh
February 16, Presentation of Governor's Conservation Achievement Awards, North Carolina Wildlife Federation, Greenville
February 21, Statement at Press Conference, Raleigh†
February 21, Presentation to IBM, Governor's Award for Excellence in Waste Management, Raleigh
February 21, Presentation of Governor's Award to Rick Ferrell, Hot Stove League Banquet, Raleigh
February 27, Welcome to AME Zion Church Bishops, Raleigh
February 28, Statement at Press Conference, Raleigh†
March 4, Budget Briefing for Press, Raleigh†
March 4, Expansion Budget Presentation, Raleigh†
March 6, "Raleigh and Roanoke" Exhibit Opening, Introduction of British Consul General Trevor Gatty, North Carolina Museum of History, Raleigh
March 7, Statement at Press Conference, Raleigh†
March 13, North Carolina Citizens for Business and Industry, Raleigh
March 18, Budget Briefing, Asheville†
March 18, Budget Briefing, Charlotte†
March 19, Town Meeting, New Bern†

March 21, Statement at Press Conference, Raleigh†
March 21, Letter on U.S. Customs Service Operations in North Carolina to Treasury Secretary James Baker, Raleigh
March 28, Wilmington Chamber of Commerce, Wilmington
April 1, Reception Honoring North Carolina State Ports Authority Chairman Jim Berry, Charlotte
April 2, Western Carolina Industries, Raleigh†
April 3, Town Meeting, Fayetteville†
April 4, Statement at Press Conference, Raleigh†
April 4, Greet Kannapolis Chamber of Commerce, Raleigh†
April 5, Dialogue with North Carolina Student Government Leaders, Raleigh†
April 9, Home Builders Association of Raleigh and Wake County, Raleigh
April 11, Statement at Press Conference, Raleigh†
April 12, Sumitomo Electric Research Triangle, Inc., Dedication, Research Triangle Park
April 12, Speech at St. Andrews College, Laurinburg†
April 16, Town Meeting, Wingate†
April 17, Governor's Business Council Awards in Arts and Humanities, Greensboro
April 18, Statement at Press Conference, Raleigh†
April 18, Presentation of Holocaust Proclamation, Raleigh†
April 22, Swearing-in of State Wildlife Commission, Raleigh†
April 22, Statement at Press Conference, Asheville†
April 22, Statement at Press Conference, Charlotte†
April 22, Statement at Press Conference, Burlington†
April 22, Statement at Press Conference, Fayetteville†
April 22, Statement at Press Conference, Raleigh-Durham Airport, Wake County†
April 23, Town Meeting for State Employees, Raleigh†
April 24, Textile Research Institute, Charlotte
April 24, Statement at Press Conference, Charlotte†
April 24, Mercy Hospital Groundbreaking, Charlotte
April 24, Asheville Manufacturers' Executives Association, Asheville
April 25, Statement at Press Conference, Raleigh†
April 26, Live on Open-Net [no place]†
April 27, Dedication of Walter Royal Davis Library, University of North Carolina at Chapel Hill
April 27, North Carolina Editorial Page Writers, Chapel Hill†
April 29, Governor's Conference on Travel and Tourism, Raleigh
May 2, Statement at Press Conference, Raleigh†

May 3, Fellowship of Christian Athletes, Raleigh†
May 3, North Carolina Strawberry Festival, Chadbourn
May 3, North Carolina Federation of Republican Women,
   Winston-Salem†
May 6, Carolina Turkeys Groundbreaking, Duplin County
May 8, Community College Trustees, Raleigh†
May 9, Statement at Press Conference, Raleigh†
May 10, Flora MacDonald Historic Site Dedication, Red Springs
May 10, Raeford Chamber of Commerce, Raeford†
May 13, American Legislative Exchange Council, Raleigh†
May 14, Town Meeting, Sylva†
May 15, Speech at Masonic Temple, Charlotte†
May 16, Retired Federal Employees Association, Fayetteville†
May 16, Education Public Meeting, Jacksonville†
May 16, Duplin County Municipal Association, Rose Hill†
May 17, Albemarle-Chowan 400th Anniversary Committee, Ahoskie†
May 21, Swearing-in of State Banking Commission, Raleigh†
May 22, Emergency Management Workshop, Apex†
May 23, Statement at Press Conference, Raleigh†
May 23, Council on Physical Fitness, Raleigh†
May 23, Town Meeting, Burlington†
May 24, Black Council on the Aged, Raleigh†
May 28, Onslow County School System Academic Awards Banquet,
   Jacksonville†
May 29, Governor's Crime and Justice Conference, Raleigh†
May 30, Statement at Press Conference, Raleigh†
May 31, Flue-Cured Tobacco Meeting, Raleigh†
June 4, Speech at Enloe High School, Raleigh†
June 5, Governor's Newspaper Column on Proposed University
   System Tuition Increase, Raleigh
June 6, Statement at Press Conference, Raleigh†
June 6, Driver of the Year Award Presentation, Raleigh†
June 7, Commencement Address, West Charlotte High School,
   Charlotte†
June 7, North Carolina Black Republican Conference,
   Winston-Salem†
June 13, Statement at Press Conference, Raleigh†
June 13, Girls' State, University of North Carolina at Greensboro†
June 13, Boys' State, Wake Forest University, Winston-Salem†
June 17, Order of the Eastern Star, Raleigh†
June 20, Statement at Press Conference, Raleigh†
June 21, Air Force Sergeants Association, Raleigh†

June 27, Statement at Press Conference, Raleigh†
June 27, Central Carolina Bank $1 Billion Celebration, Raleigh†
July 2, Press Conferences on Tax Cut Proposals: Air Wilmington, Wilmington; Raleigh-Durham Airport, Wake County; Greensboro-High Point Airport, Guilford County; Thurston Aviation, Charlotte; A&H Flying Services, Asheville; Pitt-Greenville Airport, Pitt County†
July 5, Opening Ceremony, 1985 Tar Heel State Games, Charlotte
July 11, Statement at Press Conference, Raleigh†
July 15, Swearing-in of New Members, North Carolina Wildlife Resources Commission, Raleigh
July 15, Presentation of Plaque to James Sheldon for Purchase of Lifetime Sportsman's License, North Carolina Wildlife Resources Commission, Raleigh
July 16, William Johnson Day Proclamation Presentation, Rocky Mount†
July 16, Town Meeting, Lillington†
July 18, Statement on ECOFLO [Greensboro] Hazardous Waste Treatment Facility License, Raleigh
July 18, Announcement on Governor's Commission on Child Victimization, Raleigh
July 22, Arrowood Technologies Symbolic Groundbreaking, Roxboro
July 23, North Carolina Association of ABC Boards, Asheville
July 23, Speech at Flat Rock Playhouse, Flat Rock†
July 24, Northern Telecom Plaza Dedication, Research Triangle Park
July 24, Welcoming Ceremony, Marine Corps Air Station, Cherry Point
July 24, Havelock Chamber of Commerce, Cherry Point
July 26, Minority Caucus Task Force, Raleigh†
July 26, Operation Switch, Elizabeth City†
July 27, Leath Memorial Library Dedication, Rockingham
July 29, North Carolina Black Republicans, Raleigh†
August 8, Child Victimization Commission, Raleigh
August 10, Fifty Years of Ruritan in North Carolina, Raleigh
August 13, Opening of Old Belt Tobacco Markets: Growers Warehouse, Cooks Warehouse, Winston-Salem; Gold Leaf Tobacco Warehouse, Mt. Airy; North State Farmers, Reidsville*
August 14, Governor's Conference on "Share the Pride," Greensboro [dated August 13; version not used]
August 14, Statement at Press Conference, Greensboro†
August 15, Statement at Press Conference, Raleigh†
August 15, Model Cooperative Education Program, Raleigh

August 15, Town Meeting, Reidsville†

August 16, North Carolina Poultry Federation, Raleigh

August 17, Community Centennial Celebration, Whittier

August 20, Oakwood Homes Industrial Announcement, Pinebluff

August 22, Executive Summary, Governor Martin's Position on
President Reagan's Proposal for Federal Tax Reform, Raleigh*

August 24, Textile Workers Convocation, Kannapolis*

August 28, Cotton Field Day Opening, Sam Edwards Gin Co.,
Scotland Neck†

August 29, Statement at Press Conference, Raleigh†

August 29, Unveiling, Portrait of Governor James B. Hunt, Jr.,
Raleigh†

August 30, Myrtle Desk Co. Dedication, Chadbourn [dated August
23]

August 30, Men of the Church, New Bern†

September 4, United Way-State Employees Combined Campaign
Kickoff, Raleigh

September 4, Governor's Meeting, United Way-State Employees
Combined Campaign, Raleigh

September 10, "Creating the Future of the New South" [condensed
version; acceptance of Southern Governors' Association
chairmanship], Miami, Florida

September 11, American Express Groundbreaking, Greensboro

September 11, Blue Ridge Parkway Fiftieth Anniversary,
Cumberland Knob Recreation Area, Surry County

September 12, Statement on Transportation Needs [revised draft],
Raleigh*

September 12, State Employees Association of North Carolina,
Winston-Salem*

September 13, Historic Morganton Festival, Morganton

September 17, Presentation of National Endowment Conservation
Award, Farm Family of the Year, Thad Sharp Farm, Sims

September 20, North Carolina Chapter, American Ex-Prisoners of
War, Fort Bragg

September 20, North Carolina Chapter, American Ex-Prisoners of
War [revised], Fort Bragg

September 20, Bermuda Village Dedication, Bermuda Run, Forsyth
County

September 20, Convention and Visitors Bureau Dedication,
Greensboro

September 21, Town Hall Dedication [draft], Emerald Isle

September 23, Eastern Secondary Mortgage Market Conference, Raleigh

September 23, Tryon Rotary Club, Tryon

September 23, Polk Central High School, Columbus*

September 24, Press Availability, Asheville†

September 24, Town Meeting, Mars Hill†

September 25, Interstate Mining Compact Commission, Asheville

September 25, Avery County Chamber of Commerce, Banner Elk*

September 27, Visit to Elizabeth City State University

September 28, Inauguration of H. Keith H. Brodie as President of Duke University, Durham.

September 28, Inauguration of H. Keith H. Brodie as President of Duke University [revised], Durham

September 30, Durham Rotary and Tobaccoland Kiwanis Clubs, Durham

September 30, Meeting of Manufacturing Association Executives, Raleigh

September 30, "North Carolina Waterfowl: In the Wood and In the Wild" Exhibit Opening, North Carolina Museum of History, Raleigh

October 1, Proposed Statement for Seat Belt Demonstration, Raleigh

October 1, Premiere Showing of *Get it Straight*, Enloe High School, Raleigh*

October 1, Awards Presentation, Governor's Programs of Excellence in Education, Raleigh

October 2, "Live at Noon," WRAL-TV, Raleigh†

October 2, Ice Cream Social, State Employee Appreciation Day, Raleigh

October 3, Presentation of Governor's Business Awards in Math and Science, Greensboro

October 4, North Carolina Senior Games State Finals, Raleigh

October 8, Remarks for Transportation Press Conference [draft], Raleigh*

October 8, Pinning of Charles E. Scott as Adjutant General of North Carolina, Raleigh

October 8, BNR Research Laboratory Announcement, Morrisville

October 9, Department of Transportation Cost Improvement Conference, Raleigh

October 10, Statement at Press Conference, Raleigh†

October 10, North Carolina State Grange, Clemmons

October 14, Opening Session, Southeast United States-Japan Association, Tokyo, Japan

October 31, Statement at Press Conference, Raleigh†
October 31, Local Government Advocacy Council, Raleigh
November 1, I-40 Opening [N.C. 132 and Gordon Rd.], New Hanover
    County*
November 5, Joint Meeting of Charlotte Rotary Clubs, Charlotte
    [dated November 6]
November 4, Myrtle Desk Co. Dedication, Chadbourn [dated
    November 11]
November 7, Governor's Volunteer Awards Ceremony, Raleigh
November 7, North Carolina Sports Hall of Fame Induction
    Ceremony, Raleigh
November 10, Dalton Wing Dedication, Mint Museum, Charlotte
November 14, Statement at Press Conference, Raleigh†
November 15, Proposed Educational Program for Elementary and
    Secondary Education, Raleigh*
November 21, Glaxo, Inc., Headquarters Dedication, Research
    Triangle Park
November 21, Union County Farm-City Week Banquet, Wingate
    [dated November 22]
November 22, North Carolina Awards Presentation, Raleigh
November 25, Mack Trucks, Inc., Plant Dedication, New Bern
November 26, Swearing-in of I. Beverly Lake, Jr., as Superior Court
    Judge, Raleigh†
November 27, Statement at Press Conference, Raleigh†
December 2, March of Dimes Kickoff, Research Triangle Park
December 3, State Employees Combined Campaign Recognition
    Ceremony, Raleigh
December 10, Christmas Tree Lighting Ceremony, Raleigh
December 12, Drexel Burnham Lambert Breakfast, New York City
December 19, Statement at Press Conference, Raleigh†
December 20, BarclaysAmerican Christmas Breakfast, Charlotte
    [unrevised]

1986

January 8, Gaston County Chamber of Commerce [unrevised],
    Gastonia
January 9, Statement at Press Conference, Raleigh†
January 10, Opening of Woodring Indian Art Exhibit and
    Proclamation of Year of the Native American, North Carolina
    Museum of Natural History, Raleigh

January 15, "Improving the Teaching Profession" [notes and handout], State Board of Education, Raleigh*

January 15, Blacks United in State Government Tribute to Martin Luther King, Jr., Raleigh

January 15, Blacks United in State Government Tribute to Martin Luther King, Jr. [revised], Raleigh

January 15, Central North Carolina Section, American Chemical Society, High Point

January 16, Statement at Press Conference, Raleigh†

January 19, Iredell Memorial Hospital Dedication, Statesville

January 19, Iredell Memorial Hospital Dedication [revised], Statesville

January 22, Greensboro Preservation Society, Greensboro

January 23, Shelby Chamber of Commerce, Shelby*

January 24, Annual Meeting of Local Health Directors [draft], Raleigh

January 24, Annual Meeting of Local Health Directors [unrevised], Raleigh

January 24, North Carolina Association of Educators, Raleigh*

January 27, Response to Small Business Council Report [unrevised], Raleigh

January 27, Park Communications Drop-In, Raleigh

January 28, Statement on *Challenger* Space Shuttle Tragedy, Raleigh

January 29, Statement on Union Camp/"Roanoak" Television Series, Raleigh

January 30, Statement on Vocational Education, Raleigh

January 30, Statement on Governor's Council on Alcohol and Drug Abuse among Children and Youth [draft], Raleigh

January 30, North Carolina Press Association Awards Presentation, Chapel Hill

January 30, North Carolina Press Association Awards Presentation [revised], Chapel Hill

February 3, Mt. Airy Chamber of Commerce [notes], Mt. Airy*

February 4, North Carolina Association of Chamber of Commerce Executives, Raleigh

February 4, North Carolina Association of Chamber of Commerce Executives [revised], Raleigh

February 5, Acceptance of Boy Scout Report, Raleigh

February 5, Acceptance of Boy Scout Report [revised], Raleigh

February 5, Joint Meeting, State Goals and Policy Board and North Carolina Education Council, Raleigh*

February 6, Statement on Athletes Against Crime, Raleigh†

February 7, Hanes Converting Co. Dedication, Conover

February 7, Introduction of Governor Pete du Pont, Mecklenburg County Lincoln Day Dinner, Charlotte

February 7, Introduction of Governor Peter du Pont [revised], Mecklenburg County Lincoln Day Dinner, Charlotte

February 10, Bing Crosby Golf Tournament Announcement, New York City*

February 10, Bing Crosby Golf Tournament Announcement, Greensboro†

February 11, Champion International Expansion Announcement [unrevised], Roanoke Rapids

February 12, Groundbreaking for Bryan Research Building, Duke University, Durham

February 12, Groundbreaking for Bryan Research Building [revised], Duke University, Durham

February 13, Statement at Press Conference, Raleigh†

February 14, Governor's New Product Awards Presentation, Professional Engineers of North Carolina, Winston-Salem

February 18, Regency Park/IBM Dedication, Cary

February 20, Presentation of Governor's Award of Excellence for Outstanding Achievement in Waste Management, Raleigh

February 20, Presentation of Governor's Award of Excellence for Outstanding Achievement in Waste Management [revised], Raleigh

February 20, Presentation of Governor's Award of Excellence for Outstanding Achievement in Waste Management [as delivered], Raleigh

February 21, Dedication of Martin Village, University of North Carolina at Charlotte

February 21, Dedication of Martin Village [revised], University of North Carolina at Charlotte

February 21, Concerned Charlotteans [unrevised], Charlotte

February 24, Committee on Criminal Justice and Public Protection, National Governors' Association, Washington, D.C.*

February 25, Introduction of President Gerald R. Ford [unrevised], Elon College

February 27, Town Meeting, Asheville†

March 4, State Employees Association of North Carolina [unrevised], Raleigh

March 5, North Carolina Council on Economic Education, Raleigh

March 5, North Carolina Council on Economic Education [revised], Raleigh

March 6, Driver of the Year Award Presentation, Raleigh†

March 6, Statement on Prison Plan, Raleigh*
March 10, Presentation of Ivey's Commemorative Bowl, Charlotte†
March 13, Indian Unity Conference, Greensboro [dated March 14; unrevised]
March 14, Swearing-in of Governor's Crime Commission, Raleigh*
March 14, Swearing-in of Governor's Crime Commission [revised], Raleigh*
March 14, Carolina Society of Association Executives [unrevised], Raleigh
March 14, Youth Legislative Assembly, Raleigh
March 14, Takeda Plant Dedication, Wilmington
March 15, State Convention of Beta Clubs, Charlotte
March 15, State Convention of Beta Clubs [revised], Charlotte
March 18, Fayetteville Chamber of Commerce, Fort Bragg*
March 20, Statement at Press Conference, Raleigh†
March 21, Arbor Day Ceremony, Raleigh*
March 21, Azalea Planting, Executive Mansion, Raleigh
March 21, Distinguished Woman of North Carolina Awards Presentation, Raleigh
March 21, Distinguished Woman of North Carolina Awards Presentation [revised], Raleigh
March 22, Christening of Cronkite Yacht *Wyntji*, Wrightsville Beach
March 25, Opening of 1986 Carolina Foodservice Expo, Charlotte
March 25, Opening of 1986 Carolina Foodservice Expo [revised], Charlotte
March 27, North Carolina Student Legislature, Raleigh
April 15, Book Presentation, *Sam J. Ervin, Jr., The Man and the Mason*, Raleigh
April 15, Eastern North Carolina Industrial Council, Greenville
April 17, Statement on Roads to the Future Program, Raleigh*
April 17, Presentation, Governor's Business Awards in the Arts and Humanities, Greensboro
April 18, National Guard Association, Greensboro
April 22, Announcement on Economic Development Report for 1985, Raleigh†
April 22, Combined Rotary Clubs, Winston-Salem
April 24, Wake County Business and Education Conference, Raleigh*
April 28, Statement at Press Conference, Marion†
April 29, James E. Holshouser Highway Dedication [U.S. 321], Boone*
April 29, Introduction of Governor Holshouser, Boone†
April 29, Press Availability, Boone†

April 29, Cherokee County Schools Business-Education Partnership, Murphy*

April 30, Main Street Program Awards Presentation, Raleigh

April 30, Preview of Television Series "Roanoak," Raleigh

April 30, Preview of Television Series "Roanoak" [revised], Raleigh

April 30, "Pieces of Gold" Drop-In, Wake County Education Foundation, Raleigh

May 1, Statement at Press Conference, Raleigh†

May 7, Dan K. Moore Freeway-Interstate 40 Dedication, Research Triangle Park

May 7, Dan K. Moore Freeway Dedication Luncheon, Research Triangle Park

May 7, Passing of "Run for Liberty" Relay Torch, Raleigh

May 10, Commencement Address, Shaw University [short text], Raleigh

May 10, Commencement Address, Shaw University [long text], Raleigh

May 11, Commencement Address, University of North Carolina at Chapel Hill

May 13, Town Meeting, Morganton†

May 14, Statement at Press Conference, Raleigh†

May 15, Interstate 77-South Welcome Center Dedication, Mecklenburg County*

May 19, Presentation of North Carolina Public Service Award to C. C. Cameron, Charlotte

May 20, Triad Chambers of Commerce Salute to Small Business, High Point*

May 22, Statement at Press Conference, Raleigh†

May 27, Presentation of Governor's Award for Fitness and Health, Raleigh

May 28, Statement on U.S. Department of Energy High-Level Waste Announcement, Raleigh*

May 29, Statement at Press Conference, Raleigh†

May 29, Acceptance of "Crafted with Pride" Banner, Burlington Industries, Statesville†

June 3, Newspaper Column on Transportation Needs, Raleigh*

June 5, Statement at Press Conference, Raleigh†

June 6, General William C. Lee Memorial Service, Dunn

June 11, Ivie Clayton Roast, Raleigh

June 12, Statement at Press Conference, Raleigh†

June 13, North Carolina Federation of Business and Professional Women's Clubs, Raleigh*

June 13, American Legion State Convention, Raleigh*

June 13, American Legion State Convention [revised], Raleigh*

June 13, Presentation of Distinguished Service Award to William S. Powell, Manteo

June 14, Statement on North Carolina Film Industry, Wilmington*

June 17, Acceptance of Klopman Distinguished Professorship in Textiles for North Carolina State University, Raleigh

June 19, Statement at Press Conference, Raleigh†

June 19, United Negro College Fund Luncheon, Raleigh

June 20, Dedication of Lane's Ferry Industrial Community and International Transit Systems, Ltd./Irizar SEI Announcement, Rocky Point

June 20, Dedication of Lane's Ferry Industrial Community and International Transit Systems, Ltd./Irizar SEI Announcement [revised], Rocky Point

June 21, North Carolina Bar Association, Myrtle Beach, South Carolina*

June 21, Statement on Retirement of Chief Justice Joseph Branch, North Carolina Bar Association, Myrtle Beach, South Carolina

June 26, Statement at Press Conference, Raleigh†

June 26, Greet Future Agriculture Leaders, Raleigh†

July 2, Liston Ramsey Roast [unrevised], Raleigh

July 3, Statement at Press Conference, Raleigh†

July 4, Message in Observance of July 4, Raleigh

July 24, Statement at Press Conference, Raleigh†

August 5, Town Meeting, Albemarle†

August 7, Statement at Press Conference, Raleigh†

August 7, Town Meeting, Taylorsville†

August 11, Introduction of General Alexander M. Haig, Jr., Southern Governors' Association, Charlotte

August 14, 106th Annual Masonic Picnic, Mocksville

August 16, Statement at Press Conference, Salisbury†

August 16, Statement at Press Conference, Albemarle†

August 19, Procordia Group AB, Board of Directors, Raleigh

August 19, Procordia Group AB, Board of Directors [revised], Raleigh

August 21, Statement at Press Conference, Raleigh†

August 21, Welcome Friendship Force to Capitol, Raleigh

August 24, Introduction of Mike Parton, National Governors' Association Panel on International Trade, Hilton Head Island, South Carolina

August 27, Statement on *North Carolina's Blueprint for Economic Development*, Raleigh†

August 29, Stadium Dedication, Thomasville High School

August 30, Somerset Plantation Homecoming, Creswell

September 2, Swearing-in of Robert Orr as Court of Appeals Judge, Raleigh†

September 3, Swearing-in of Rhoda Billings as State Supreme Court Chief Justice, Raleigh†

September 4, Statement at Press Conference, Raleigh†

September 4, Main Street Program National Town Meeting, Winston-Salem

September 13, Presentation of Distinguished Service Awards to Agribusiness, North Carolina Agribusiness Council, Raleigh

September 20, Presbyterian Hospital Fine Arts Auction, Charlotte

September 20, Dedication of Shalom Park and Jewish Community Center, Charlotte

September 22, Governor's Prayer Breakfast, Wake County Fellowship of Christian Athletes, Raleigh

September 23, USS *North Carolina* Silver Anniversary Celebration and Introduction of George F. Will, Wilmington

September 24, State Employees Combined Campaign Kickoff, Raleigh

September 24, Outstanding Volunteer Recognition Ceremony, Raleigh*

September 25, Introduction of Paul Fulton, Crosby Golf Tournament Press Conference, Winston-Salem

September 25, BASF Corp. Agricultural Research Center Dedication, Research Triangle Park

September 25, BASF Corp. Agricultural Research Center Dedication [revised], Research Triangle Park

September 29, Statement at Press Conference, Raleigh†

October 1, Presentation of Governor's Award for Fitness in Public Schools, Raleigh

October 2, Announcement on North Carolina Information Network [draft], Raleigh*

October 2, Recognition of Outstanding State Employees, Raleigh

October 3, Outstanding Volunteer Recognition Ceremony, Asheville*

October 9, Presentation of Conservation Endowment Award, 1986 Farm Family of the Year, J. Page Evans Farm, Alleghany County

October 10, Konishiroku Plant Announcement, Raleigh†

October 14, Southeast United States-Japan Association Session on Trends and Initiatives in International Trade, Hot Springs, Virginia

October 17, North Carolina State Fair Opening Ceremony, Raleigh

October 17, Inauguration of C. D. Spangler, Jr., as University of
North Carolina President, Chapel Hill

October 18, Rededication of Joyce Kilmer Memorial Forest, Graham
County

October 20, Senior Citizens' Day, North Carolina State Fair, Raleigh

October 21, North Carolina League of Municipalities [transcript],
Charlotte

October 22, Textile Volunteers Award Ceremony, Raleigh

October 23, Unveiling of Beirut Memorial, Jacksonville*

October 24, North Carolina Nurses Association, Raleigh

October 25, Richmond Hill Law School Dedication, Boonville

October 25, Physical Activities Complex Groundbreaking, University
of North Carolina at Greensboro

October 29, Broughton Hospital Wellness Trail Dedication,
Morganton

October 29, Royal Insurance Co. U.S. Headquarters Dedication,
Charlotte

October 30, Statement at Press Conference, Raleigh†

October 30, E. I. du Pont de Nemours and Co. Electronics
Development Center Dedication, Research Triangle Park

November 10, Plaque Presentation, State Wildlife Commission,
Raleigh†

November 11, Veterans Day Ceremony, Raleigh

November 11, Acceptance of Certified Items from Space Shuttle
Challenger, from Mrs. Michael Smith, Raleigh

November 11, Groundbreaking, Vietnam Highway Memorial,
Interstate 85-South Rest Area, Davidson County*

November 12, Greensboro Retail Merchants Association,
Greensboro*

November 12, Pinning Ceremony for General Clinton V. Willis, Jr.,
Raleigh

November 13, Statement at Press Conference, Raleigh†

November 13, North Carolina School Boards Association,
Winston-Salem*

November 13, Braxton Bragg Chapter, Association of the U.S. Army,
Fort Bragg

November 15, Z. Smith Reynolds Foundation Fiftieth Anniversary,
Raleigh

November 20, State Employees Combined Campaign Recognition
Ceremony, Raleigh

November 21, North Carolina Awards Presentation, Raleigh

November 24, Statement on DWI Kickoff, Raleigh†

November 24, Northeast North Carolina Legislative Caucus, Elizabeth City*

December 1, Charlotte Chamber of Commerce, Charlotte

December 2, "Building a Legacy of Learning," North Carolina Citizens for Business and Industry, Raleigh

December 4, Statement at Press Conference, Raleigh†

December 4, Dinner for John Medlin, Raleigh

December 8, Panel Moderator, "A Look at the Election and the Future of the GOP," Republican Governors' Association, Parsippany, New Jersey†

December 11, Local Government Advocacy Council [unrevised], Raleigh

December 18, Statement at Press Conference, Raleigh†

1987

[No date], 1987 State of the Environment Report [draft], Raleigh

January 6, Statement at Press Conference, Raleigh†

January 19, Press Conference Announcing Governor's Language Institutes, Winston-Salem

January 20, Dedication, White Memorial Presbyterian Church Activity Center, Raleigh

January 22, Statement at Press Conference, Raleigh†

January 22, North Carolina Job Training Coordinating Council, Raleigh

January 29, Poly-Tech, Inc., Dedication, Battleboro

January 29, North Carolina Press Association Awards Presentation, Chapel Hill

February 4, North Carolina Retail Merchants Association, Pinehurst*

February 5, Statement at Press Conference, Raleigh†

February 6, Governor's New Product Awards Presentation, Professional Engineers of North Carolina, Raleigh*

February 11, Introduction of Governor Michael S. Dukakis, Emerging Issues Forum, Raleigh*

February 12, Statement at Press Conference, Raleigh†

February 13, Veterans of Foreign Wars, Raleigh*

February 18, Press Briefing on Interstate 40 Progress, Winston-Salem†

February 18, Introduction of Peter V. Ueberroth, United Way Volunteer of the Year Award Presentation, Winston-Salem [dated February 22]

February 19, Statement at Press Conference, Raleigh†

February 19, Sampson County Combined Rotary Clubs "Excellence
in Business" Awards Presentation, Clinton
February 20, National Honor Society Induction, Whiteville High
School
February 26, Statement at Press Conference, Raleigh†
February 26, Bravery and Heroism Awards Presentation, Raleigh
February 27, Statement on State Employees' Health Insurance,
[Raleigh]
March 3, Statement at Press Conference, Raleigh†
March 3, Sir Walter Cabinet, Raleigh
March 5, Centennial Founders Day Convocation, Pembroke State
University
March 6, North Carolina League of Middle Level Schools,
Winston-Salem
March 6, Optional Editorial, "Employ the Older Worker," Raleigh*
March 9, Newspaper Column on Teacher Career Ladder, Raleigh
March 10, SAS Institute, Inc., Dedication, Cary
March 10, Centennial Founders Day Dinner, North Carolina State
University, Raleigh
March 10, Centennial Founders Day Dinner [revised], North
Carolina State University, Raleigh
March 11, Swearing-in of James S. Lofton as Secretary of
Administration, Raleigh†
March 12, Statement at Press Conference, Raleigh†
March 12, The Fifty Group, Raleigh
March 13, Driver of the Year Award Presentation, Raleigh†
March 13, North Carolina Association of School Administrators,
Raleigh
March 14, Haywood County Town Meeting, Canton†
March 16, Second Language Conference, Raleigh*
March 17, Town Meeting, Danbury†
March 18, National Conference on Alcoholism Research, Research
Triangle Park
March 19, Press Conference and Azalea Planting, Raleigh
March 20, du Pont Nafion Laboratory Dedication, Fayetteville
March 20, North Carolina Association for the Gifted and Talented,
Wilmington
March 23, Veterans Preference Press Conference, Raleigh
March 23, State Building Construction Conference, Raleigh*
March 23, Louisburg College Bicentennial Torch Relay, Raleigh
March 24, Presentation of WTVD Jefferson Awards [two parts],
Durham

March 26, Statement at Press Conference, Raleigh†

March 26, Introduction of U.S. Transportation Secretary Elizabeth H. Dole, North Carolina Citizens for Business and Industry, Raleigh

March 27, Draft Remarks on Marion Bypass, Marion

March 28, Student Legislature Fiftieth Anniversary, Raleigh

March 30, Western Steer/Mom and Pop's Owners' Convention, Charlotte

March 30, Western Steer/Mom and Pop's Owners' Convention [revised], Charlotte

March 30, Speech at Hunter Huss High School, Gastonia

March 30, Media Availability on School Bond Issue, Gastonia†

March 31, International Conference on Robotics and Automation, Raleigh

April 1, Action Sportswear Ribbon-Cutting, Weldon

April 1, Seaboard Box Co. Ribbon-Cutting, Enfield

April 1, Tillery Manufacturing, Inc., Ribbon-Cutting, Enfield

April 2, Statement at Press Conference, Raleigh†

April 3, Carver Boat Corp. Announcement, Burgaw

April 3, Press Availability on Literacy Commission, Raleigh*

April 6, North Carolina and Virginia Dairy Products Associations, Pinehurst

April 7, Statement at Press Conference, Raleigh†

April 7, Independent Grocers Association, Kenansville*

April 8, First Shipment of DMS-10 Equipment from Northern Telecom to Nippon Telegraph and Telephone Corp., Research Triangle Park

April 8, Swearing-in of David T. Flaherty as Secretary of Human Resources, Raleigh

April 9, Dedication of American Express Regional Operations Center, Greensboro*

April 9, Press Question and Answer on School Bond Issue, Greensboro†

April 10, Kenan Center Dedication, University of North Carolina at Chapel Hill

April 11, Brunswick County Airport Dedication [revised], Southport*

April 13, Governor's Eastern Listening Tour: Elizabeth City, Barco, Camden, Hertford, Gatesville, Murfreesboro, Rigecroft School [Hertford County]†

April 13, Bicentennial Celebration, Murfreesboro

April 14, Commissioning of Department of Correction Honor Guard, Raleigh

April 15, Charlotte Home Builders Association, Charlotte

May 11, Press Statement on Governor's Conference on Travel and Tourism, High Point*

May 12, Garner Senior High School Achievement Awards Program, Garner

May 12, North Carolina Alliance for Public Education, Raleigh

May 13, Konishiroku [Konica] Photo Industries Groundbreaking, Greensboro

May 13, Press Question and Answer on School Bond Issue, High Point†

May 14, Catawba County State Legislative Issues Forum, Raleigh*

May 14, National Genealogical Society, Raleigh

May 15, North Carolina Economic Development Board, Raleigh

May 15, Law Enforcement Memorial Day, Raleigh

May 15, Talent Identification Program Recognition Ceremony, Duke University, Durham

May 15, Lake Norman Medical Center Dedication, Mooresville

May 16, North Carolina State Council, Knights of Columbus, Asheville

May 17, Duke Children's Classic Awards Ceremony, Durham

May 18, Central Cabarrus High School Assembly on Citizenship Training, Concord†

May 19, Joseph Palmer Knapp Bridge Dedication, Coinjock

May 20, Reception for Donna Oliver, National Teacher of the Year, Raleigh

May 21, Statement at Press Conference, Raleigh†

May 21, Graham Outstanding High School Students, Burlington

May 22, Crosby Clambake Comedy Routine, Forsyth County

May 23, North Carolina Jaycees State Convention, Winston-Salem

May 26, Embrex, Inc., Dedication, Research Triangle Park

May 26, Teletec Corp., Dedication, Raleigh

May 27, Official Opening of Executive Mansion Victorian Garden, Raleigh

May 27, I-40 Groundbreaking [draft], Winston-Salem

May 28, North Carolina Association of Realtors, Greensboro*

May 28, Rutherfordton-Spindale Chamber of Commerce, Rutherfordton

June 2, First Official Telephone Call to Cancer Information Service of North Carolina [script], Raleigh

June 4, Press Conference on 1986 Economic Development Annual Report, Raleigh

June 5, North Carolina Disabled American Veterans, Fayetteville*

June 5, Southern Growth Policies Board, Research Triangle Park

June 9, United Durham, Inc., Industrial Park Anniversary, Durham

June 9, News Conference and Groundbreaking, Thirtieth Aviation Battalion Headquarters and Flight Facility No. 1, North Carolina National Guard, Raleigh-Durham Airport, Wake County*

June 9, American Airlines Black-Tie Reception, Raleigh-Durham Airport, Wake County

June 10, United Negro College Fund Reception, Raleigh

June 11, Southern Textile Association, Asheville*

June 11, Press Question and Answer, Morganton†

June 12, Dedication of Ronald E. McNair Engineering Hall, North Carolina A&T State University, Greensboro

June 12, American Legion Boys' State, Wake Forest University, Winston-Salem*

June 12, Triennial Meeting of the Society of Friends, Greensboro

June 13, "Keep North Carolina Clean and Beautiful" Golf Tournament, Pinehurst

June 15, American Airlines Hub Ribbon-Cutting, Raleigh-Durham Airport, Wake County

June 16, Presentation of Governor's Award for Fitness and Health in Business and Industry, Raleigh

June 17, North Carolina Future Farmers of America, Raleigh

June 18, Statement at Press Conference, Raleigh†

June 18, North Carolina School Food Service Association, Raleigh*

June 20, Acceptance Speech as Chairman of Southern Regional Education Board, Atlanta, Georgia

June 22, U.S. Highway 264 Opening Ceremony, Greenville

June 23, Groundbreaking, Franklin Memorial Hospital, Louisburg

June 24, Town Meeting, Sanford†

June 25, Statement at Press Conference, Raleigh†

June 26, Reception Honoring North Carolina Industrial Commission Appointee Harold Davis, Southport

June 26, Southport-Oak Island Chamber of Commerce, Southport*

June 30, Freedom Bell Ceremony, Raleigh

July 1, Executive Mansion Luncheon for Donors of Governor's Office Furnishings, Raleigh

July 1, Ribbon-Cutting Ceremony Celebrating Refurbishing of Governor's Office, Raleigh

July 2, Statement on North Carolina House Bill 589, Raleigh

July 3, Meeting with Centenarians Allie Grubb Hill and Maggie Grubb Lambeth, Denton

July 9, Statement at Press Conference, Raleigh†

July 9, Exhibit Opening, "North Carolina and the Olympics," North Carolina Museum of History, Raleigh

July 9, Exhibit Opening, "North Carolina and the Olympics" [revised], North Carolina Museum of History, Raleigh

July 9, Introduction to Performance of *Strike at the Wind*, Pembroke

July 13, Swearing-in of North Carolina Wildlife Resources Commission, Raleigh

July 13, Town Meeting, Yanceyville†

July 15, Olympic Festival Torch Lighting Ceremony, Greensboro

July 16, Statement at Press Conference, Raleigh†

July 17, U.S. Olympic Festival Opening Ceremony, Raleigh†

July 18, State Department of Commerce Business and Industry Division Breakfast, Raleigh

July 20, Copy for North Carolina Association of County Commissioners' Newsletter, Raleigh

July 23, Presentation of Governor's Award of the Gold Clover, State 4-H Congress, Raleigh

July 23, Statement at Press Conference, Raleigh†

July 25, Appear with North Carolina Symphony, Narrate *Lincoln's Portrait*, Bicentennial Anniversary Celebration, Boone†

July 31, Statement at Press Conference, Raleigh†

August 14, Legislative Wrap-Up Press Availability, Raleigh†

August 14, North Carolina Poultry Federation, Raleigh

August 17, Groundbreaking, Kitchens of Sara Lee, Tarboro

August 17, Statement at Press Conference, Greenville†

August 17, Town Meeting, Williamston†

August 18, Statement at Press Conference, Greensboro†

August 18, Statement at Press Conference, Charlotte†

August 18, Beta Clubs Convention, Asheville†

August 19, Press Availability, Hendersonville†

August 19, Press Availability, Clyde†

August 19, Press Availability, Murphy†

August 19, *Unto These Hills* Performance, Franklin

August 20, Press Availability, Black Mountain†

August 20, Marion Rotary Club, Marion*

August 20, Press Availability, Armstrong Fish Hatchery, McDowell County†

August 20, Press Availability, Burnsville†

August 20, Western North Carolina Arboretum Acceptance Ceremony, Bent Creek

August 20, Press Availability, Bent Creek†

August 24, State Employees Credit Union Groundbreaking,
Statesville
August 24, Crescent Electric Membership Corp. Dedication,
Statesville
August 24, Sheller-Globe Groundbreaking, Grover
August 25, Old-Fashioned Apple Breakfast, Hendersonville
August 25, Motheread Press Conference, Raleigh*
August 25, Motheread Press Conference [revised], Raleigh*
August 27, All-America City Award Presentation, Hickory
August 29, Cannon Mills 100th Anniversary, Kannapolis
September 3, Statement on Superconducting Super Collider,
Raleigh*
September 3, *Inc.* 500 Luncheon, Raleigh
September 8, State Employees Day, Raleigh
September 8, State Employees Award Ceremonies, Raleigh
September 9, WISE Festival, Raleigh
September 10, Semiconductor Industry Association and
Semiconductor Research Corp., Research Triangle Park
September 11, Linn Cove Viaduct Dedication, Blue Ridge Parkway,
Grandfather Mountain
September 12, North Carolina Pickle Festival, Mt. Olive
September 12, University of North Carolina Dental Research Center
Twentieth Anniversary, Chapel Hill
September 14, Tobacco Conference of the States, Raleigh
September 14, Presentation of Farm Family of the Year Award to
Jack Winslow Family, Palmyra
September 14, Champion International No. 4 Paper Machine
Rebuilding Announcement, Roanoke Rapids
September 16, Mitchell County U.S. Constitution Bicentennial
Celebration, Ledger
September 17, Turkey Festival, Raeford
September 17, U.S. Constitution Bicentennial Celebration, Charlotte
September 17, Southern Women's Show, Charlotte
September 17, Volunteer Recognition Ceremony, Raleigh*
September 17, U.S. Constitution Bicentennial Celebration, Raleigh
September 25, Statement at Press Conference, Raleigh†
September 25, University City Celebration, University of North
Carolina at Charlotte
September 25, Katherine and Tom Belk Gymnasium Dedication,
University of North Carolina at Charlotte
September 28, Opening Remarks, Challenge '87, Raleigh*
September 28, Closing Remarks, Challenge '87, Raleigh

September 29, Belk's 100th Anniversary, Charlotte
September 29, Small Business Conference, Raleigh
October 3, "Biotechnological Images and Public Policy" [press copy],
    Yokohama, Japan
October 5, Opening Ceremonies, Southeast United States-Japan
    Association, Tokyo, Japan
October 5, Kimono Exhibit Announcement, Tokyo, Japan
October 6, Closing Ceremonies, Southeast United States-Japan
    Association, Tokyo, Japan
October 20, Statement at Press Conference, Raleigh†
October 21, PLUS [Project Literacy U.S.] II Breakfast, Raleigh*
October 21, Acceptance of Honorary Degree, Catawba College
    Founders Day, Salisbury*
October 21, Jake Alexander Highway Dedication, Salisbury
October 21, Ribbon-Cutting and Open House, IRM Insurance,
    Charlotte
October 22, North Carolina Medal of Honor Memorial Dedication,
    Valley Forge, Pennsylvania*
October 23, Nickels for Know-How Kickoff, Raleigh
October 23, Volunteer Recognition Ceremony, Wilmington
October 26, Town Meeting, Columbia†
October 27, North Carolina Association of Certified Public
    Accountants, Winston-Salem*
October 27, North Carolina Business Committee for Education,
    Winston-Salem
October 27, North Carolina Business Committee for Education
    [revised], Winston-Salem
October 27, Announcement of Signal Processing Project between
    AT&T and Bowman-Gray School of Medicine, Winston-Salem
October 28, Career Day Celebration, East Burke High School, Icard
October 28, Great Pumpkin Bake-Off Awards Presentation, Western
    Carolina Center, Burke County†
October 28, Volunteer Recognition Ceremony, Morganton
November 2, Town Meeting, Goldsboro†
November 5, Statement at Press Conference, Raleigh†
November 5, John Q. Burnette Welcome Center Dedication [I-85],
    Charlotte
November 6, Statement on AIDS Awareness Week [taped message],
    Raleigh
November 6, North Carolina Awards Presentation, Raleigh
November 6, North Carolina Awards Presentation [revised], Raleigh

November 9, News Conference on Northwestern Highways, Winston-Salem*

November 9, Acceptance of Apache Helicopters for North Carolina National Guard, Raleigh-Durham Airport, Wake County*

November 9, Town Meeting, Henderson†

November 10, Entrepreneurial Excellence Luncheon, University of North Carolina at Chapel Hill

November 10, Highway Announcement, Asheville†

November 11, Veterans Day Parade, Charlotte

November 13, Newspaper Column Encouraging Local Bond Issues for School Construction, Raleigh*

November 16, Newspaper Column on Rural Water and Waste-Water Planning, Raleigh

November 20, Statement at Press Conference, Frankfurt, West Germany†

November 23, Press Conference on Red Tide, Wrightsville Beach†

November 23, Press Conference on Red Tide, Sneads Ferry†

November 24, Richard Dobbs Spaight Highway Dedication, New Bern

November 24, Coastal Initiative Presentation, New Bern†

November 25, Wake County American Institute of Bankers, Raleigh†

November 30, Press Opportunity, Gastonia†

November 30, Gaston County Chamber of Commerce, Gastonia†

November 30, Education Town Meeting, Gastonia†

December 1, du Pont Butacite Works Expansion, Fayetteville*

December 3, John P. East Freeway Dedication, Greenville

December 10, Press Conference on Driving While Impaired and Designated Driver Concept, Raleigh

December 16, Governor Morehead School Christmas Party, Raleigh

December 22, Greet White Memorial International Students, Raleigh†

1988

[No date], Announcement of February 4 Public Meeting on Drunken Driving [Greensboro], Raleigh

[No date], Telegram to U.S. Interior Secretary on Oregon Inlet, Raleigh

January 4, Announcement and Filing for Re-Election, Raleigh†

January 7, American Airlines European Flights Announcement, Raleigh-Durham Airport, Wake County

January 11, Statement at Press Conference, Raleigh†

January 12, North Carolina League of Savings Institutions, Research
 Triangle Park
January 14, Western Regional Travel and Tourism Conference,
 Cherokee
January 16, Perdue Co. Zero Defect Day, Williamston
January 18, Wallace Chamber of Commerce, Wallace*
January 20, "Top of the Day," WBTV, Charlotte†
January 20, Statement on Motor Racing's Economic Impact,
 Charlotte Motor Speedway, Harrisburg
January 20, Greensboro Jaycees' Bosses' Night, Greensboro*
January 21, North Carolina Press Association Awards Presentation,
 Chapel Hill
January 22, Natural Resources and Community Development-Take
 Pride in America Awards Presentation, Raleigh
January 22, Press Association Candidates Forum, Chapel Hill†
January 23, Richard Petty Day, Wilson
January 28, Lesson Plan on Superconducting Super Collider, Capitol
 for a Day, Jacksonville Senior High School
February 2, "University Research Park: The First Twenty Years,"
 Charlotte
February 3, Sears Telecatalog Center Announcement, Greensboro
February 4, Driving While Impaired Public Meeting [draft],
 Greensboro*
February 5, Swearing-in of North Carolina Inmate Grievance
 Resolution Board, Raleigh
February 7, First Baptist Church Sanctuary Dedication [notes],
 Charlotte
February 8, Introduction of President Reagan, Conference on
 Substance Abuse in the Workplace, Durham
February 9, Introduction of Lamar Alexander, Real Estate Breakfast,
 Raleigh†
February 12, Human Relations Council Awards Presentation, Raleigh
February 13, American Airlines Reservation Center Ribbon-Cutting,
 Cary
February 16, Ethan Allen Furniture Co. Announcement, Spruce Pine
February 17, Proposal to Consolidate Health, Environmental
 Protection, and Natural Resources Functions of State Agencies
 into a Department of Health and Environment, Raleigh
February 17, Bravery and Heroism Awards Presentation, Raleigh
February 17, Bravery and Heroism Awards Presentation [revised],
 Raleigh

February 18, *Inc.* 500 Conference Announcement, Raleigh
February 18, Farm Credit Luncheon, North Carolina Cooperative
    Council, Greensboro*
February 18, North Carolina Amateur Athletic Union, Greensboro
February 19, Press Availability, Rocky Mount†
February 19, Cities in Schools Press Conference, Rocky Mount
February 19, Fountain Industrial Complex Groundbreaking, Rocky
    Mount†
February 20, North Carolina Black Elected Officials Scholarship
    Banquet, Winston-Salem
February 23, Acceptance of Award from Fund for Renewable Energy
    and the Environment [for surface water protection], Washington,
    D.C.
February 23, North Carolina Health Care Facilities Association,
    Winston-Salem
February 24, Twentieth Anniversary of RTP Federal Credit Union,
    Research Triangle Park
February 25, Statement on Infrastructure Report, Raleigh
February 25, I-40 Opening Ceremony [I-40 and U.S. 70; draft], Garner
February 26, "Midday with Doug Mayes," [broadcast to WSOC-TV,
    Charlotte], WRAL-TV, Raleigh†
March 1, State Employees Association of North Carolina
    Membership Kickoff, Raleigh*
March 2, Acceptance of Boy Scout Annual Reports, Raleigh
March 3, Statement at Press Conference, Raleigh†
March 3, North Carolina Scholars and North Carolina Teaching
    Fellows, Raleigh
March 4, Youth Legislative Assembly, Raleigh
March 7, Press Availability, Fayetteville†
March 7, Fayetteville Area Economic Development Corp.,
    Fayetteville
March 7, Luncheon Meeting with Farmers and Farm Leadership,
    Fayetteville†
March 10, North Carolina Association of Electric Cooperatives,
    Raleigh*
March 10, Emerging Issues Forum, Raleigh†
March 13, Distinguished Citizen Award Reception Honoring Charles
    Raper Jonas, Lincolnton
March 14, Town Meeting, Wadesboro†
March 15, Dedication of Isabel Stallings Holmes Bridge, Wilmington

March 15, Wilmington, Wilmington East, and Cape Fear Rotary
   Clubs, Wilmington
March 15, Cape Fear Boy Scouts, Bladenboro
March 16, North Carolina Citizens for Business and Industry, Raleigh
March 17, Zoo Education Competition Announcement, Raleigh
March 17, Statement on Governor's Award of Excellence for
   Outstanding Achievement in Waste Management, Raleigh
March 18, North Carolina Aggregates Association, Pinehurst
March 19, Carolina Heart Institute Dedication, Charlotte Memorial
   Hospital
March 19, North Carolina Minority Business Association, Pinehurst
March 22, Twenty-first Century Work Force Initiative Conference,
   Raleigh
March 22, Scotland County Literacy Council, Laurinburg*
March 23, North Carolina Council of Engineers, Charlotte*
March 23, Close Up, Union County Schools, Wingate†
March 23, Access Road Ribbon-Cutting for Entrance to East Union
   Elementary School, Marshville
March 23, Foundation for the Carolinas, Charlotte
March 24, "Literacy in the Workplace," Triad Jaycees, Greensboro
March 24, Aging Plan Announcement, Raleigh*
March 25, North Carolina Student Legislature, Raleigh
March 25, North Carolina Association of Independent Colleges and
   Universities, Candidates Forum, Raleigh†
March 25, North Carolina Association of Education Personnel,
   Candidates Forum, Greensboro†
March 28, Azalea Planting, Raleigh
March 29, Jefferson Awards Telecast, WTVD, Durham
March 29, Hoots Memorial Hospital Groundbreaking, Yadkinville*
March 29, Dedication of Yadkin County Senior Center, Boonville*
March 29, Greater Greensboro Banquet, Greensboro
March 30, Distinguished Woman of North Carolina Awards
   Presentation, Raleigh*
March 31, Statement at Press Conference, Raleigh†
March 31, International Council of Shopping Centers, Charlotte
March 31, North Carolina Rural Water Association, Raleigh
April 7, Presentation of Published Papers of Governor James B. Hunt,
   Jr., Raleigh
April 8, Motheread Graduation, Women's Correctional Center,
   Raleigh
April 9, Azalea Festival Queen Coronation, Wilmington
April 11, Sara Lee Distribution Center Announcement, Rural Hall

April 11, Transportation Lesson for History Class, Mineral Springs Middle School, Winston-Salem

April 11, Winston-Salem Merchants Association, Winston-Salem

April 11, Governor's Conference on Travel and Tourism, Greenville*

April 12, KAO Chemical Dedication, High Point

April 12, Inspection of ROTC Battalion, St. Augustine's College, Raleigh

April 13, "International Challenges Facing the South," Center for Public Television, Chapel Hill*

April 14, Driver of the Year Award Presentation, Raleigh

April 15, Inauguration of Chancellor Richard Eakin, East Carolina University, Greenville

April 15, U.S. 264-Bypass Groundbreaking, Farmville

April 16, Christening Ceremonies, Lake Norman

April 18, Announcement on 1987 Economic Development Report, Raleigh

April 18, Dobbins Heights Community Development Block Grant Award [notes], Richmond County

April 18, Town Meeting, Rockingham†

April 20, ASMO Co., Ltd., Announcement, Statesville

April 20, Bank of Iredell Christening, Mooresville

April 21, Allibert, Inc., Dedication Ceremony, Stanley

April 21, Combined Rotary Clubs Meeting, High Point*

April 21, Community General Hospital, Thomasville

April 22, North Carolina National Guard Convention, Greensboro

April 22, Greensboro Civitan Club, Greensboro

April 25, Textile/Clothing Technology Corp. Apparel Technology Center Opening, North Carolina State University, Raleigh

April 26, "Lowell Shumaker Show," WPTF Radio, Raleigh†

April 27, Government Leaders Against Drunk Driving, Raleigh

April 29, Older Americans Month Press Conference, Raleigh

April 29, Rural Fire Districts Thirtieth Anniversary, Hickory

April 30, Murray's Mill Dedication, Catawba County

May 2, Plant Extension Announcement, Kelly-Springfield Tire Co., Fayetteville

May 4, Swearing-in of Kenneth R. Harris to State Board of Education, Raleigh†

May 4, Unveiling, James H. Cromartie Painting of U.S. Capitol, Raleigh

May 6, Statement on Drug Trafficking Laws, Raleigh

May 6, BNR Laboratory Dedication, Research Triangle Park

May 7, Arts 'Round the Square, Graham

May 9, Campbell University Commencement, Buies Creek
May 9, Senior Center Dedication, Coats*
May 9, North Carolina Sports Hall of Fame Silver Anniversary,
     Raleigh
May 12, Statement at Press Conference, Raleigh†
May 13, Special Olympics Opening Ceremonies, Chapel Hill
May 14, Rotary District Governors Conference, Lake Junaluska*
May 16, North Carolina Community College System Silver
     Anniversary, Raleigh
May 17, Champion Products, Inc., Ribbon-Cutting, Dunn
May 17, "Taste of North Carolina," Dunn
May 17, Address to Triton High School Student Body, Dunn
May 18, Premiere of Executive Mansion Documentary, *The Mansion at
     200 North Blount*, Raleigh
May 19, Lexington and Thomasville Chambers of Commerce, Raleigh
May 20, Revolving Loan Announcement, Hickory
May 20, North Carolina Economic Development Board, Hickory*
May 20, Catawba County Chamber of Commerce, Hickory*
May 20, Jaycee Convention, Asheville
May 23, North Carolina Automobile Dealers Association, Asheville
May 23, North Carolina Automobile Dealers Association [revised],
     Asheville
May 23, "Export Now" Press Conference, Raleigh*
May 26, Governor's Conference on Aging, Raleigh
May 26, Governor's Conference on Aging [revised], Raleigh
May 26, Ribbon-Cutting, American Airlines Inaugural Flight to Paris,
     Raleigh-Durham Airport, Wake County†
May 27, Announcement on U.S. 23 and U.S. 25 Construction,
     Asheville
May 27, Asheville Area Chamber of Commerce, Asheville
May 30, Teaching Fellows, Raleigh
May 31, Pinning Ceremony, Brigadier General David L. Jennette,
     Raleigh
May 31, Main Street Program Awards Reception, Raleigh
May 31, Main Street Program Awards Reception [revised], Raleigh
June 1, Statement at Press Conference, Raleigh†
June 3, Eastern Alamance High School Graduation, Mebane
June 6, Exide Electronics Group, Inc., Raleigh
June 7, Superconducting Super Collider Advisory Board, Raleigh*
June 8, Potential Revisions to the Governor's 1988-1989
     Supplemental Budget, Raleigh

June 9, North Carolina Hospital Association Seventieth Anniversary Taping, Raleigh*

June 9, Flag Presentation and Ribbon-Cutting, RTP Marriott Hotel, Research Triangle Park

June 9, Family Support Administration Awards Ceremony, Raleigh

June 9, North Carolina School of the Arts International Music Program Concert, Raleigh

June 15, New Mexico Amigos, Raleigh

June 15, Big Rock Blue Marlin Tournament Fish Fry, Morehead City

June 16, Organon Teknika Announcement, Raleigh

June 17, North Carolina Credit Union League, Pinehurst

June 17, Boys' State, Wake Forest University, Winston-Salem

June 17, Girls' State, University of North Carolina at Greensboro

June 17, Welcoming Remarks, North Carolina State Games, Raleigh

June 18, Eastern Music Festival, University of North Carolina at Greensboro

June 20, Introduction of Governor Ned McWherter, Southern Regional Education Board, Nashville, Tennessee

June 20, Introduction of Dick Riley, Southern Regional Education Board, Nashville, Tennessee

June 20, Introduction of Lamar Alexander, Southern Regional Education Board, Nashville, Tennessee

June 21, Statement Prior to Recognition of Special Achievements in Support of Educational Quality, Southern Regional Education Board, Nashville, Tennessee

June 21, Introduction of Governor Ray Mabus, Southern Regional Education Board, Nashville, Tennessee

June 22, North Carolina Chapter, National Postmasters State Convention, Raleigh

June 23, Statement at Press Conference, Raleigh†

June 23, Burroughs Wellcome Co. Reception, Dinner, and Expansion Dedication, Research Triangle Park

June 27, U.S. Department of Energy Task Force on Superconducting Super Collider [notes], Raleigh

June 27, Inaugural North Carolina Balloon Launch [*Spirit of Kitty Hawk*; notes], Raleigh

June 30, Statement at Press Conference, Raleigh†

July 2, North Carolina Black Leadership Conference, Winston-Salem

July 4, Old Threshers Reunion, Denton

July 4, Fourth of July Parade and Celebration, Harrisburg

July 4, Tanglewood Fourth of July Celebration, Clemmons

July 7, Statement at Press Conference, Raleigh†

July 7, N.C. FREE Conference [notes], Asheville

July 7, Press Availability, Washington, D.C.†

July 8, Dedication of North Carolina Scottish Rite Clinic for Childhood Language Disorders, University of North Carolina at Charlotte

July 8, Valmet Paper Machinery Co. Groundbreaking, Charlotte

July 8, Valmet Paper Machinery Co. Groundbreaking [revised], Charlotte

July 8, Charlotte Outer Loop Groundbreaking [I-485], Charlotte

July 9, North Carolina Home Builders Association, Hilton Head, South Carolina

July 9, North Carolina Home Builders Association [revised], Hilton Head, South Carolina

July 11, Prison Superintendents Meeting, Raleigh

July 12, Inaugural North Carolina-Liaoning Province Economic Cooperation Conference, Raleigh

July 13, Inaugural Meeting, Governor's Rail Passenger Task Force, Raleigh [not delivered]

July 13, National Extension Homemakers Conference, Charlotte

July 14, Press Conference, Lou Harris-Cushman and Wakefield Business Poll, Raleigh

July 16, Farmers' Day Celebration, China Grove

July 18, U.S. 441 Highway Dedication, Cherokee

July 20, Dedication of Cedar Island Rest Area and Visitors' Center, Christening of MV *Carteret*, Beaufort

July 26, Systel Business Equipment Co., Inc., Ribbon-Cutting, Fayetteville

July 27, General Baptist Convention, Winston-Salem

July 27, U.S. 17-Bypass Groundbreaking, Shallotte

July 28, Lee Co. Distribution Center Groundbreaking, Mocksville

July 28, General Conference, African Methodist Episcopal Zion Church, Charlotte

July 29, Press Conference on 1990 U.S. Census, State Highway Fund [transcript], Raleigh*

July 29, Press Conference Statement on State Budget as Approved by 1987 General Assembly, 1988 Short Session, Raleigh*

August 4, Computer Commission, Raleigh

August 4, North Carolina Law Enforcement Officers Association, Asheville*

August 5, Robeson Technical College Graduation, Lumberton

August 6, Alamance County Parent-Child Golf Tournament, Burlington

August 6, Press Availability with Lanny Wadkins, Burlington†
August 6, Domino's Pizza Team Tennis Championship, Charlotte
August 7, Rex Classic Celebrity Pro-Am Golf Tournament, Raleigh
August 9, Caldwell County-Lenoir Southwest Loop Groundbreaking
  [U.S. 18 to U.S. 321], Lenoir
August 9, Alspaugh Dam Bridge Dedication, Millersville
August 11, Statement at Press Conference, Raleigh†
August 11, Alcohol and Drug Resource Center Dedication, Durham*
August 15, National Association of County Agricultural Agents,
  Charlotte
August 15, Sears Telecatalog Center Ribbon-Cutting, Greensboro
August 15, Sears Telecatalog Center Ribbon-Cutting [revised],
  Greensboro
August 16, Winston-Salem Board of Realtors, Winston-Salem
August 19, Elizabethtown Airport Dedication, Elizabethtown
August 29, Drug Eradication News Conference, Raleigh
August 29, Summitville Carolina, Inc., Groundbreaking, Glen Alpine
August 29, Summitville Carolina, Inc., Groundbreaking [revised],
  Glen Alpine
August 29, Governor's First Safety Awards to State Agencies, Raleigh
August 30, NGK Ceramics USA, Inc., Announcement, Mooresville
August 30, NGK Ceramics USA, Inc., Announcement [revised],
  Mooresville
August 30, Ducks Unlimited Pro-Am Golf Tournament, Pinehurst
September 1, Statement at Press Conference, Raleigh†
September 1, Sears Source Award Presentation to Glendale Hosiery
  Co., Siler City
September 2, Statement on Coastal Initiative [draft], Plymouth*
September 2, Statement on Coastal Initiative [draft], Columbia*
September 2, Statement on Coastal Initiative [draft], Edenton*
September 2, Statement on Coastal Initiative [draft], Swansboro*
September 6, Moore's Creek National Battlefield-Highway 210
  Dedication, Currie
September 6, Yang Ming Line Tenth Anniversary, Wrightsville Beach
September 7, Cotton Field Day, Johns Station
September 7, North Carolina Highway Users Conference Annual
  Highway Day, [no place]
September 8, Christa McAuliffe Plaque Presentation to Nancy Severt,
  Raleigh
September 8, State Employees Combined Campaign, Raleigh
September 10, North Carolina Agribusiness Council, Raleigh

September 12, Employment Security Commission Job Service Employer Awards, Raleigh

September 12, *Business Week* Advertising Supplement Announcement, Raleigh

September 13, Volunteer Recognition Ceremony, Greenville

September 14, North Carolina Great American Fly-In, Raleigh

September 15, North Carolina Farm Family of the Year Commemoration, C. Spurgeon and Alene Brooks/Sunnybrook Farms, Inc., Richfield

September 15, North Carolina Farm Family of the Year Commemoration [revised], C. Spurgeon and Alene Brooks/ Sunnybrook Farms, Inc., Richfield

September 15, Charlotte Association of Life Underwriters, Charlotte

September 16, Franklin County Chamber of Commerce, Louisburg

September 16, CPC International, Inc.-Knorr-Best Foods Plant Dedication, Asheboro

September 17, Mary Francis Center Dedication and Opening, Tarboro

September 19, Northeast Tour-U.S. 64 Dedication, Plymouth*

September 19, Groundbreaking, U.S. 158 Widening Project, Jarvisburg

September 20, Smoky Mountain Host Visitors Center and Rest Area Dedication, Franklin

September 20, State Employees Awards Ceremonies, Raleigh [not delivered]

September 20, State Employees Appreciation Day, Raleigh [not delivered]

September 20, Computer Commission, Raleigh

September 22, I-40 Opening Ceremony [New Hope Church Road to U.S. 15-501; draft], Orange County

September 22, Meeting of Raleigh and Wilmington Mayors and Completion of Benson Leg of I-40 [notes], Benson

September 22, Statement on I-40, Wilmington

September 22, C. B. Corp. Dinner, Charlotte

September 24, Mountain Heritage Day, Western Carolina University, Cullowhee

September 24, Celebration of the Arts, Hiddenite

September 28, Alcohol and Drug Professionals Association, Charlotte

September 28, North Carolina Public Health Association, Winston-Salem*

September 29, Mayors Breakfast, North Carolina Seafood Festival, Morehead City

September 29, North Carolina Seafood Festival-North Carolina
    Coastal Boating Guide Announcement, Morehead City
September 29, Presentation of 1988 Textile Citizen of the Year Award
    to Charles Corbett, Raleigh
September 29, Press Conference on North Carolina Boating Guide,
    Highway U.S. 70, and Superconducting Super Collider, Raleigh
September 29, Statement on Americans with Disabilities Act
    [proposed federal law], Raleigh
October 1, Dedication of Refurbished Jamestown School, Greensboro
October 4, Trail of Tears 150th Anniversary Commemoration,
    Cherokee
October 4, Testimonial in Memory of Harry Clarke, Asheville
October 5, Presentation of SSC Proposal to U.S. Energy Secretary
    Herrington, Washington, D.C.†
October 5, Press Availability, Washington, D.C.†
October 5, GLADD Pinning of President Reagan, Washington, D.C.†
October 5, Arthur Smith's Fishing Tournament Banquet, Myrtle
    Beach, South Carolina†
October 6, Presentation of Distinguished Service Medal to North
    Carolina Air National Guardsman Master Sergeant Forrest Earley,
    Raleigh
October 6, Governor's Business Committee for Education, Raleigh
October 6, Volunteer Recognition Ceremony, Greensboro
October 6, North Carolina Forestry Association, Asheville*
October 7, Western Region Volunteer Recognition Ceremony,
    Morganton
October 8, Adopt-A-Highway Program in Gaston County [draft],
    Belmont*
October 9, Oakwood Homes "500" Stock Car Race, Harrisburg†
October 10, Emergency Medicine Today '88, Charlotte
October 10, Division of Motor Vehicles Express Office Opening,
    Charlotte*
October 10, Bahlsen, Inc., Dedication, Cary
October 11, Taiwanese Tobacco Contract Signing, Raleigh
October 11, Athletes Against Crime "Walk Against Crime," Raleigh
October 12, National Rural Economic Development Conference,
    Raleigh
October 12, Installation of Chancellor Paul Hardin, University of
    North Carolina at Chapel Hill
October 13, Leicester Highway [N.C. 63] Groundbreaking, Asheville
    [dated October 12]
October 13, Greensboro Kiwanis Club, Greensboro†

October 13, Division of Motor Vehicles Express Office Opening, The
    Market Place, Winston-Salem*
October 14, North Carolina State Fair Opening, Raleigh
October 15, Woolly Worm Festival, Banner Elk
October 16, All-America City Celebration, Kinston
October 17, Senior Citizens' Fun Festival, North Carolina State Fair,
    Raleigh
October 18, Praxis Biologics, Inc., Dedication, Sanford
October 20, Opening Ceremonies, Southeast United States-Japan
    Association, Charleston, South Carolina [dated October 21]
October 21, PTA Annual Convention, Raleigh
October 22, North Carolina Voice for Child Care, Research Triangle
    Park*
October 22, North Carolina Yam Festival [short text], Tabor City
October 22, North Carolina Yam Festival [long text], Tabor City
October 31, Glaxo, Inc., Expansion Groundbreaking, Research
    Triangle Park
October 31, I-40 Opening Ceremony [Interstate 85 to New Hope
    Church Road], Hillsborough
November 11, USS *North Carolina* Monument Dedication, Wilmington
November 14, Opening Ceremonies, Southeast United States-Korea
    Association Meeting, Williamsburg, Virginia*
November 14, Opening Ceremonies [revised], Southeast United
    States-Korea Association Meeting, Williamsburg, Virginia*
November 14, Investment Issues Panel Discussion, Southeast United
    States-Korea Association, Williamsburg, Virginia
November 14, Investment Issues Panel Discussion [revised],
    Southeast United States-Korea Association, Williamsburg, Virginia
November 17, Statement at Press Conference, Raleigh†
November 17, Murphy Farms Open House and Dedication, Rose Hill
November 18, North Carolina Awards Presentation, Raleigh
November 30, Pinning of Nathaniel H. Robb, Jr., Raleigh†
December 1, Swearing-in of Judge Robert Orr, Raleigh†
December 1, North Carolina Citizens for Business and Industry,
    Raleigh*
December 4, Executive Committee, Council of State Governments,
    Kansas City, Missouri
December 4, President's Dinner, Council of State Governments,
    Kansas City, Missouri
December 5, "Strengthening the American Family," Council of State
    Governments, Kansas City, Missouri

December 5, Introduction of Neal Peirce, Council of State Governments, Kansas City, Missouri

December 5, Presentation of Innovation Award to Governor Gerald L. Baliles of Virginia, Council of State Governments, Kansas City, Missouri

December 6, Corporate Associates Breakfast, Council of State Governments, Kansas City, Missouri

December 8, North Carolina Association of County Commissioners, Research Triangle Park

December 10, Shrine Bowl, Charlotte

December 12, APV Baker FM, Inc., Dedication, Goldsboro

December 13, North Carolina Public School Forum, Raleigh

December 15, Press Conference on Designated Driver Concept and Governor's Task Force on Injury Prevention, Raleigh

December 22, I-40 Opening Ceremony [N.C. 42 to N.C. 210], Johnston County

December 29, Seymour Johnson Air Force Base, Goldsboro

EXECUTIVE ORDERS

[Governor Martin issued seventy-nine executive orders during his first term in office. Although space limitations prohibit the inclusion of each of these items in their entirety in this documentary, a listing of titles has been provided below. Complete texts of Martin's executive orders, promulgated during the period from 1985 to 1989, are located as follows: numbers 1 through 21, *Session Laws of North Carolina, 1985,* 1405-1479; numbers 22 through 25, *Session Laws of North Carolina, 1985, Extra and Regular Sessions, 1986,* 673-685; numbers 26 through 53, *Session Laws of North Carolina, 1987,* II, 2307-2396; numbers 54 through 74, *Session Laws of North Carolina, 1987, Regular Session, 1988,* III, 921-987; and numbers 75-79, *Session Laws of North Carolina, 1989,* II, 3071-3093. These documents are also filed among the Governors Papers, James G. Martin, Archives, Division of Archives and History, Raleigh.]

1985

Executive Order Number 1, established new North Carolina Board of Ethics and superseded Executive Order Number 1 [Hunt], January 31

Executive Order Number 2, established Governor's Efficiency Study Commission, February 12

Executive Order Number 3, established new North Carolina Advisory Council on Vocational Education and superseded Executive Order Number 25 [Hunt], March 27

Executive Order Number 4, restored Social Security disability review procedures and repealed Executive Order Number 97 [Hunt], May 10

Executive Order Number 5, established Governor's Commission on Child Victimization, May 20

Executive Order Number 6, established State Employees' Work Place Requirements Program for Safety and Health, May 20

Executive Order Number 7, established Women's Economic Development Advisory Council, June 28

Executive Order Number 8, established new Governor's Advisory Committee on Travel and Tourism and superseded Executive Order Number 46 [Hunt], June 28

Executive Order Number 9, established new North Carolina Public Transportation Advisory Council and superseded Executive Order Number 29 [Hunt], June 28

Executive Order Number 10, established new North Carolina Small Business Council and superseded Executive Order Number 51 [Hunt], June 28

Amendment to Executive Order Number 10, regarding North Carolina Small Business Council, July 25

Executive Order Number 11, established new Governor's Advisory Commission on Military Affairs and superseded Executive Order Number 80 [Hunt], June 28

Executive Order Number 12, established new Governor's Highway Safety Commission and superseded Executive Order Number 56 [Hunt], June 28

Executive Order Number 13, established new North Carolina Health Coordinating Council and superseded Executive Order Number 91 [Hunt], June 28

Executive Order Number 14, established new Governor's Task Force on Domestic Violence and superseded Executive Order Number 55 [Hunt], June 28

Executive Order Number 15, established membership guidelines for Juvenile Justice Planning Committee, June 28

Executive Order Number 16, established North Carolina Council on the Holocaust and superseded Executive Order Number 63 [Hunt], June 28

Executive Order Number 17, extended through December 31, 1987, Executive Order Number 88 [Hunt] creating county committees on America's Four Hundredth Anniversary, June 28

Executive Order Number 18, statement on state government equal employment opportunity policy, July 1

Executive Order Number 19, established Governor's Commission for Recognition of State Employees, August 7

Executive Order Number 20, established Wellness Improvement for State Employees (WISE) program, September 3

Executive Order Number 21, established State Family Planning Advisory Council, October 3

1986

Executive Order Number 22, imposed hiring freeze on vacant positions in executive branch of state government, January 8

Executive Order Number 23, established Governor's Council on Alcohol and Drug Abuse among Children and Youth, January 29

Executive Order Number 24, established Governor's Program to Strengthen Historically Black Colleges, February 13

Executive Order Number 25, continued Lead Regional Organization policy for North Carolina, February 21

Executive Order Number 76, amended Executive Order Number 18,
     state policy on equal employment opportunity, September 14
Executive Order Number 77, amended Executive Order Number 34
     and established Governor's Program to Encourage Business
     Enterprises Owned and Controlled by Minorities, Women, and
     Handicapped Persons, September 14
Executive Order Number 78, established Governor's Task Force on
     Injury Prevention, November 1

1989

Executive Order Number 79, amended Executive Order Number 10,
     North Carolina Small Business Council, January 5

NOTE ON APPOINTMENTS

During his first administration, Governor Martin named to state boards, commissions, and other bodies many individuals who served through or were reappointed during his final four years in office. To include an appointments section in the volume for each of his two terms would entail repeating much information. Therefore, a list of the governor's designees to statutory entities, 1985-1993, will be published in the documentary chronicling his second administration.

APPENDIX I

PRESENTATION OF UNIVERSITY AWARD TO BILL AND IDA FRIDAY, A DIPLOMATIC TRANSCRIPTION

[Governor Martin often revised the addresses his speech writers generated for him. The clear text editorial method adopted for this volume, however, prevents specific examples of those changes from being shown in the documents reproduced herein. Therefore, this diplomatic transcription of Martin's remarks at the presentation of the University Award to William C. and Ida H. Friday has been prepared in order to demonstrate tangible evidence of his personal imprint.

The following editorial symbols designate changes made to the text as prepared for the governor:

ΛinsertionΛ	passages the governor inserted
<deletion>	passages the governor deleted
<ΛchangeΛ>	passages the governor inserted and later deleted
italic	passages the governor underlined
[editor]	details supplied by the editor

Capitalization, spelling, punctuation, treatment of numbers, paragraph arrangement, the use of ampersands and ellipses, and the heading of the speech have been retained as in the original.

The clear text version of this address appears on pages 224-227.]

Remarks by Governor James G. Martin
Presentation of University Award to Bill and Ida Friday
Wednesday, December 4, 1985: 6:30 P.M.
Morehead Building Banquet Hall
U[niversity of]. N[orth]. C[arolina].-C[hapel]. H[ill].
Chapel Hill, N[orth]. C[arolina].

Thank you all very much. ΛPres[ident] & Mrs Friday (whose careers have outlasted--and outranked?[1]--7 governors so far [)]. Gov[ernor] & Mrs Moore/Scott who can so testify,Λ Chairman Λ& MrsΛ Carson, members of the University Board of Governors, <distinguished platform guests>, officials of the facult<y>ΛiesΛ and administration, Λmembers of our General Assembly whose support has been steadfastΛ[,] and Λmarvelous presenters of tributes,Λ ladies and gentlemen.

Dottie and I are delighted to have the opportunity of sharing Λwith youΛ this evening <with you> Λof the University Awards CeremonyΛ in honor of <Bill and Ida> Λour manΛ Friday Λand our lady Ida . . . Λ, two individuals who have devoted the major part of their lives to this university, to those it has served and, in the spirit of their enterprise, to those it will continue to serve for many future generations.

North Carolina has a long heritage of educational diversity, as represented by the 16 campuses of the Greater University, and this tradition has done much to contribute to our state's greatness. ∧ . . a model of excellence and service that never ceases to win deserved recognition.∧

No one has done more to contribute to the perpetuation of this tradition than Bill Friday. Whether as a student in his undergraduate days or studying for his law degree or, later, as a dean and president of a great institution, Bill Friday has spent a lifetime *taking serious ideas seriously.*

<Next spring> ∧Too soon∧, he will end an outstanding career as President of the University System---a career which spans almost one-third of a century---commemorating the longest tenure ever served by an individual in that position.

Bill, you and your devoted <wife> ∧Ida∧, without whose support and encouragement this distinguished record could not have been achieved, have earned the deep respect and appreciation of all North Carolinians, and < I > ∧we∧ thank you.

You have brought to us an historic challenge. We have the opportunity to prepare North Carolina, not just for the next 15 years, but for the twenty-first century. It is a challenge to keep North Carolina moving forward toward that first shining vision---a state of unprecedented opportunity, where achievement is limited only by how big we dream, how hard we work, and how well we learn.

And we know that the path to that vision is through economic growth and new technologies and renewed excellence in education. ∧And the cycle in which each supports the other.∧

Yet, as important as technology and economic growth are to our future, education is more important still. Bill Friday has instilled that lesson---a lesson which began in 1791 [*sic*] when the University opened its doors for the first time as America's first great adventure in public higher education.

Bill Friday has helped us understand that without education, human advancement and individual achievement are limited. And he has made us aware that without education, we *could* even lose our fundamental values--our beliefs in freedom, hard work, and personal initiative.

Under his leadership, he has created an awareness that if we educate our young people well, ∧(∧grounding them in our values, and teaching them the greatness of spirit,∧)∧ the future will be the best that North Carolina has ever seen.

President Reagan has said that education is the architect of the soul. ∧I say that for all its intellectual grandeur [education?] is the expression of the soul.∧ Bill Friday has helped us search the soul of North Carolina, ∧/∧ and that search has enabled us to build one of the ∧truly∧ great university systems of our nation.

Bill Friday has brought unmatched experience and <expertise> ∧wisdom∧ to his current responsibilities. He has served so long and so faithfully that his presence has almost been taken for granted.

Tonight we acknowledge ∧/∧ for all American education ∧/∧ that he is *indeed* an exceptional individual, a great man and a caring public servant. He has always been immensely dignified, yet never stuffy; always hopeful, and yet ever realistic. <∧I remember well when he kindly hosted an interview during the past year, his real enjoyment of my.∧> [Incomplete]

We are proud, then, to honor him for what he has done and, even more, for what he is.

Tonight, we also honor Ida Friday. It has been the good fortune of North Carolina to have this great lady as one of the major forces at work to enhance the arts, culture, volunteerism, and the spirit of individualism. She has had a profound influence of [*sic*] our quality of life.

ΛAs a part of our team,Λ Ida Friday has been a steady hand guiding her husband in uncertain times, giving reassurance, rearing a family of three daughters Λ(and Betsy, I can tell you that you made a lot of fathers and mothers very happy and proud tonightΛ[).] <and> ΛOur co-honoree hasΛ giv<ing>ΛenΛ of herself without compromise to helping young people find direction and purpose in life.

She has helped to create choices for those who saw none. She has turned failures into successes. She has brought hope where their was despair.Λ . . . a friend for so many who needed one.Λ Together with Bill Friday, she has helped to add a new dimension to our lives.

ΛBill you're a great guy--but we know you married above yourself!Λ

Bill and Ida Friday have given us *strength through* clarity; *security through faith in ourselves*; and *progress through intellect*. They have been innovators who have helped to lead our state forward.

Jonathan Swift, <author of "Gulliver's Travels,"> once wrote, "Who'er excells in what we prize, appears a hero in our eyes."

Well, Bill and Ida Friday are indeed amon[g] the real heroes of North Carolina.

The University Awards which have been bestowed upon them tonight are but a token of our gratitude. The meaning of that gratitude will remain *with* us and, we sincerely hope, with *them* always.

ΛIn truth, you both have *become* . . . the North Carolina University AwardsΛ[.]

---

[1]The governor originally used angle brackets in this instance, rather than dashes, as follows: "outlasted <and outranked?> 7 governors so far."

APPENDIX II

"FIRING LINE: CAN WE REPUBLICANIZE THE SOUTH?"

COLUMBIA, SOUTH CAROLINA, MARCH 25, 1987

["Firing Line," the weekly public-affairs television forum, first aired on April 8, 1966. According to William F. Buckley, Jr., the program "has devoted an hour to examining the thought (sometimes the attitudes, sometimes the stratagems) of a single guest, sometimes two guests, for a full hour. I have been its host since the outset. And, a distinction extremely important, the hour was never conceived of as an 'interview.' It was to be an 'exchange of opinions.'" William F. Buckley, Jr., *On the Firing Line: The Public Life of Our Public Figures* (New York: Random House, 1989), xxxiii, 504.

The edition of "Firing Line" taped March 25 and televised April 5, 1987, was entitled "Can We Republicanize the South?" In it, Buckley questioned three GOP governors—Martin, Guy Hunt of Alabama, and Carroll Campbell of South Carolina—on their roles in and the nature of their party's challenge to the Democratic status quo. The trio's responses, recorded in the following transcript, further illuminate one of the most significant phenomena in the political history of the United States during the final decades of the twentieth century.

"Can We Republicanize the South?" has been reprinted herein with the permission of the Southern Educational Communications Association. As received from SECA, the transcript was unannotated. All footnotes have been supplied by the editor.]

MR. BUCKLEY:[1] We have enough Republican Southern governors here today to launch a counterrevolution, and as a matter of fact, that substantially is what we are here to discuss: namely, can the South be Republicanized? Some statistics are reassuring: Twice as many white Southerners registered Republican in 1984 as in 1980. On the other hand, four Republican senators lost their seats.[2] We have experts on hand who can help us to understand exactly what is going on.

From the south of where we sit, we have the freshman governor of Alabama. Strange things happen in Alabama, but perhaps none stranger than that the successor to George Wallace should be a Republican, the first in 112 years, i.e, since Reconstruction. Governor Guy Hunt, the pros around the Statehouse like to tell you, got in only because there was an internecine fight among the Democrats who wished to succeed Wallace.[3] But there are those others who point to his skills as a public speaker, to his active role as a lay minister, to his length of service as a probate judge as responsible for his election. Governor Hunt was an appointee of the Reagan administration in the Department of Agriculture. He is a veteran of the Korean War, who never attended college. He is surrounded by Democrats who run the state legislature and the courts; and indeed, his lieutenant governor is a Democrat.[4] But he manages to look very cheerful.

Governor James Martin is the senior governor in the room, having been elected governor of North Carolina in 1984. He had served six terms in the

Congress. He was born in Georgia, went to public schools in South Carolina, went to Davidson College in North Carolina for his B.A., and to Princeton University for his Ph.D. in chemistry. He taught at Davidson until he went into politics. I shall, in just a moment, ask him to tell us about the so-called Blackberry Farms meeting of July, 1985, which crystallizes as a historic way station in Republican politics in the South.

And finally, our host here in Columbia, South Carolina, Governor Carroll Campbell, Jr.—like his colleagues, only the second Republican to occupy the Statehouse in more than a century. Mr. Campbell was born and educated in Greenville. He did not have the financial resources to stay in college and went therefore into business, which included a chain of Burger King restaurants, a stud farm of Arabian horses, and in 1978 a seat in Congress. During eight years in Washington, Mr. Campbell returned to his studies, earned an advanced degree in political science at American University, and was inaugurated here last January.

I should like to begin by asking Governor Martin if he would tell us something about the Blackberry Farms meeting and how it has evolved.

Governor Martin: Bill, actually it began with an idea of Lamar Alexander, who, as you know, was governor of Tennessee this immediate past term, and a very distinguished Republican leader. He had thought all along that we needed to address more attention to state issues if we were going to build Republican parties in the southeastern states. He had recognized that very often when we would have our southeastern Republican gatherings, everyone would get together and talk about the national debt and talk about foreign policy issues, which are important, but for governors and legislators and county commissioners there are also issues that need to be dealt with in the South. And he thought if we could focus attention on that we might be able to build a stronger grassroots base. In fact, we invited Carroll Campbell, who participated, Trent Lott of Mississippi, Governors Dick Thornburgh of Pennsylvania and John Sununu of New Hampshire[5]—

Buckley: And that's now an ongoing organization, isn't it, differently named?

Martin: It has now grown into a conference of elected officials from all the southeastern states. This past year we met in Raleigh, North Carolina, and next year we are looking forward to a meeting here in South Carolina.[6]

Buckley: Now, I saw a result of a poll published in connection with your election, which listed the top five and the bottom five concerns of Southern voters. It rather surprised me. The top five in the order given were: Number one, drunken driving; number two, drug abuse; number three, AIDS; number four, education; and number five, crime. The bottom five were: Star Wars,[7] school busing, aid to the Contras,[8] and inflation. Now, does this reconcile with your feel of public sentiment in the South?

Martin: Well, I would have seen education as a higher score in the polls that we have been taking.

Buckley: Well, it's in the top five.

MARTIN: I thought you said that was in the bottom five.

BUCKLEY: No, sir. No, sir.

MARTIN: You read those first ones—

BUCKLEY: No, no, no, that was the top five. The bottom five were Star Wars, school busing, aid to the Contras, and inflation. Or did you mean the school busing part of education?

MARTIN: Well, in response to your question, what that shows, of course, is that people are going to be more concerned about those things that they can perceive as an immediate threat to them and their household and their family and to society in the neighborhood rather than those things which can be perhaps more cataclysmic, but which don't enter into their daily thinking nearly as much.

BUCKLEY: Well—

MARTIN: I have had to train myself to think in those terms of the more personal issues, the community issues, as I began my campaign for governor, because I had been accustomed to thinking on the global scale, on the national scale, which is important when you have a job in Washington.

BUCKLEY: Sure. Well, Governor Hunt, let me ask you this, since you were a probate judge in Alabama for all those years: Why is it that the Republican party should be thought of as having abstract concerns and the Democratic party as having local concerns? Is it because the Democratic party in fact governs in the South? Is that why they are associated with fixing the pothole or getting you a scholarship or whatever, whereas the Republicans are sort of big thinkers?

GOVERNOR HUNT: I think that's been part of it in the past. However, I think that's changed and very much so. I think like Governor Martin and Governor Campbell, we are addressing issues that are considered to be the traditional Democrat issues of the South, and I think that's one of the reasons why that we were elected. We talked about problems with the aged; we talked about problems with the poor; we talk about, as all the governors are, welfare reform; we talk about education and the improvement of education. And of course, even in Alabama recent polls showed that the majority of people were concerned about drunken driving, which we are all addressing. I think the lesson to the Republicans in the South and around the nation is that we have got to be concerned about the issues that face us on an everyday basis. We are interested, of course, in foreign policy and a strong defense, but at the same time, when a person is run off the road with a drunken driver, or they don't have a job, those are the issues that face them, and I think that part of our success in the South has been because we're addressing those issues.

BUCKLEY: Well, Governor Campbell, what excuse have you got for your election? [Laughter.]

MARTIN: He got all the votes.

GOVERNOR CAMPBELL: Oh, hard workers—[laughter]. I think that as Jim Martin said a while ago and Guy Hunt has just reiterated part of, we talked about an agenda of progress. You know, too often Republicans have been "aginners." They have been against everything that comes along. The Republican party in the South is not that way. We understand that we have to have a positive agenda at the state level. We understand very well that the people of the South are very conservative from a fiscal standpoint and that they are concerned about intervention of government. But what we were able to do was to differentiate what the intervention of government might be. They don't want the federal government intervening, but they do want an activist state and local government dealing with problems. And in the past too many times Republicans had applied the principle of nonintervention in problems to state and local government. We went the other way. As Jim said, when we were in Tennessee at the meeting with Lamar Alexander and others, we talked about issues that needed to be addressed—positive issues. We talked about an agenda for reform, for progress, economic development. We spoke of how we could coordinate educational efforts with the efforts to attract industry or jobs or to change the economic base of the South. So when we went to the people, we went with a different message—not just that we'll fix potholes, not just "Send us down there and it will be just the same." But that we have another agenda. We recognize competition, we recognize the fact that in many areas we are not competitive in the South, we want to become competitive, and this is how we want to do it.

BUCKLEY: Now, how does that distinguish you from your Democratic opponent?[9]

CAMPBELL: Primarily, I think it was— His campaign was more of, "Elect me and it will be the same that we had with the incumbent governor," who was a very fine governor. And it was a good way for him to run. And I was running a different direction, not against the incumbent governor, but with a different agenda. He had an agenda of improving public education—absolutely necessary. The campaign of my opponent was, "Elect me and I'll keep that going." My agenda essentially was, "Wonderful. We've got to attract jobs to the tax base, we've got to be able to pay for these things, and here is how we are going to have to do it from a practical standpoint."

BUCKLEY: Well, let me ask whoever wants to reply to this question. Does it tend to pay, if you are running on the Republican ticket in the South, to associate yourself with Ronald Reagan, or does it not tend to pay?

CAMPBELL: I will jump that one in a hurry. I was President Reagan's campaign manager in 1980 and '84. He came in and campaigned for me. I appreciate it. I wish he could have come more often. He was an asset. From a national standpoint, the president still enjoys extremely high ratings; in the South, people see him as doing a job they thought was necessary in Washington, and I can say that from my standpoint he was an asset. Did he get a Southern governor elected? Certainly he helped. But his agenda was not the local agenda that we were running on. And I'm like Jim Martin is. I had a hard time being a congressman, trying to vote in Washington, then come down here and talk about a different agenda. It was hard not to overlap.

BUCKLEY: Yes. You had that problem also, Governor?

MARTIN: The problem of being in Washington and campaigning? Yes, of course. Of course, I had no problem at all with Ronald Reagan. In our campaign of '84, it was a strong boost—I'd say three or four percentage points. I also had the benefit of a fight in the Democratic party where they really tore each other up, and I was able to pick up some of the strength in the backwash there, but in addition, I had an opponent who tried to seize an anti-business theme and tried to make business an ogre and a target for his campaign.[10] And he would accuse me of being in favor of business, which I thought was great. I'd say, "Yes, indeed, I'm for business—"

BUCKLEY: Yes, right. Right.

MARTIN: "—large, small, anything in between." And we're, as Carroll has indicated, all of us throughout here are working to build our economy and that was a good issue for us. We could talk about building jobs for the future and it was a good issue.

BUCKLEY: Well, now, Governor Hunt, Governor Wallace was on this program quite a while ago, before he was wounded, and he was rather defensive at that particular moment about not having rejected the Democratic party, which was going sort of haywire—I mean especially haywire—in that particular period. And he said, "Well, the trouble with the Republicans is that they simply don't care about people"—he used that particular line—and in many ways sort of presaged your own commentary about local concerns. Now, in Alabama, there is, as I understand it, a tradition of a rather paternalistic government, isn't there, and are you able to walk a tight schizophrenic line between paternalism at home—

CAMPBELL: Careful, Guy. [Laughter.]

BUCKLEY: —and a little laissez-faire at the federal level?

[HUNT]: Well, as you know, in Alabama, we've really not been in the mainstream of the Democratic party since 1948 when the state— Carroll had a friend here by the name of Strom Thurmond, who was on the ticket that year.[11] I believe only twice since then have all of our electors really gone to the Democratic party. Three out of the last four presidential elections, we have elected Republicans in the—voted for the Republican presidential candidate. And I think that we still have a distrust of the federal government in the South. I think Governor Wallace, after my election, he had a press conference and told the people that I was a person who had the feelings for the grass-roots Alabamans and feelings for the poor, that I would make a good governor. I think that helped me off to a good start.

BUCKLEY: Right. Right, right. So that you don't find it either—any of you—you don't find it difficult simultaneously to associate yourself with the national position of people like Ronald Reagan and on the other hand in your concerns as governors to be fastidiously interested in all the problems of individuals.

HUNT: Not at all. In fact, I feel very good, as far as the presidential candidates in 1988, that I'm willing to associate myself with those Republicans who are seeking the nomination. And I think I would have a better opportunity to do that than my Democratic counterparts in the state with their candidates.

CAMPBELL: I think there's another thing. Looking at the South and looking at the presidential level. The South has been voting for Republicans at the presidential level with one exception over the last twenty-five years. And that means that the people who are electing officeholders at home had developed a tradition of splitting tickets, recognizing a philosophy at a national level they were comfortable with, maintaining the local ties to their local Democrat party. And most of us have been active in politics. I came out of the General Assembly of South Carolina and then to Washington. The people that I worked with there, Republicans and Democrats, I daresay if you had to go and ask—poll the General Assembly of South Carolina—if they could do it without signing their name, you would find that Ronald Reagan carried a majority of the members of the General Assembly of South Carolina where the Republicans make up less than 25 percent of the membership.

BUCKLEY: Yes. Touching on the point that you make, three or four months ago, Howard Baker[12] and Lamar Alexander were on this program, and the question arose, which almost obsesses Republican thinking, which is, however much progress you are making among white people in the South, why aren't there signs of progress among blacks in the South? Now, there isn't much progress among blacks out of the South, with the exception of New Jersey—what happens there, I just don't understand—but in any event, Howard Baker made the point, and Lamar Alexander tended to agree with him, that so institutionalized is the Democratic habit in the South that that operates very dramatically against the upward mobility of the Republican class of black voters. Is that correct as far as you can see, or is that only a partial explanation?

CAMPBELL: I think it's partial. I think that the future of the Republican party in the black community really rests with the growing black middle class in the South, and it is taking place. In the election that I just finished, we got not a very high percentage of black votes—

BUCKLEY: Higher than 5 percent?

CAMPBELL: Yes, we got close to 8 percent. At the election night they announced 12 percent, and I knew that was wrong. But we didn't get them in the traditional Democrat boxes. We didn't get them in the areas that were what you call the old machine boxes. They still exist. We got them in some of the rural areas. We got the votes in some of the mixed communities, more upwardly mobile communities, and we went after that vote. We went out and held out our hands and said, "Look, here we are, and this is what our agenda is," and I think that we can attract. Quite frankly, the Democrats in the past have been able to marry a constituency that was totally alien to each other. They have been able to marry the hardcore radical or the whites, as well as the black community, into one group of voters. And that's difficult. The middle—as it grows, we'll grow.

BUCKLEY: Well, now, is that your experience also in Alabama? I remember how surprising it was to the whole world when the majority of the black people voted for Mr. Wallace, who was almost a legendary anti-black figure in terms of American history.[13] Did you get a substantial number of black votes?

HUNT: No, I got a small amount of the black vote. My opponent, of course, had been very much aligned with some of the black leadership over the years.[14] However, since the election we've found that we're having very good response from the black community. Just before the march that they held in Montgomery, we had sixteen of the twenty-two black mayors from across the state to meet with me. We're putting together a program to work with them. I also have a black Democrat woman from Birmingham who is one of my floor leaders in the House, and so we feel like, and I think—

BUCKLEY: Had she been in the House before your election?

HUNT: Yes. I think, like Governor Campbell has said, we have an emerging Democrat black leadership in Alabama that's going to, I believe, be more and more Republican as the years roll by.

BUCKLEY: Are there any signs of black intellectual disaffection with the shibboleths of the Democratic party? By which I mean, it seems to me that there is a mountain of empirical evidence that shows that if you really want to help people, they tend to be helped much more exuberantly by a Republican program than by a Democratic program, and some people like Walter Williams and Tom Sowell[15] have—both distinguished black educators—have made that point. But sometimes you think it's only those two. In fact, somebody said that they never ride in the same airplane together.

MARTIN: The two of them?

BUCKLEY: Yes. [Laughter.] But is there a growth of an intellectual critical movement among blacks that looks at the policies of the Democratic party and says, "It's not really helping us as dramatically as an alternative program would help us"?

MARTIN: Well, it's not at a critical mass yet.

BUCKLEY: No, no.

MARTIN: It's just beginning. And we saw some evidence of that in our past campaigns, both for Congress and for governor. We estimate that in my election in '84 I got maybe 15 percent of the black vote.

BUCKLEY: Is that right?

MARTIN: But particularly it was stronger in the areas that are where—those blacks who are in business at a variety of levels, those who are in professions, and those in academic communities live, because those would be the precincts where we would build up a stronger base—never a majority, but enough to offset the precincts where that machine—

BUCKLEY: Right.

MARTIN: —that delivers the votes so dramatically, as you said, has been successful. The Democratic party has been much more effective at that, and yet we believe, and I think this is something you will find throughout the South, that we're going to appeal to the voters, whatever their race, on the basis of the ideas and delivery system and the delivery of good government, getting good government for the money that we can afford, and those kinds of ideas. And to the extent that any voters respond to that, then we are going to be successful.

BUCKLEY: Well, that's kind of a platonic observation that people—

MARTIN: It's a start.

BUCKLEY: What's that?

MARTIN: It's a start.

BUCKLEY: It's a start, but since there is such a heavy presumption among black people that they should vote Democratic, it seems to me you have to accost that as a phenomenon rather than merely that they are attuned to Democratic seductions. So is there in the South a conscious effort to attack the intellectual community among the blacks and say, "Look. Here's really why you ought to think twice before voting automatically the Democratic ticket." Is such an effort being made, or not?

MARTIN: Well, it is, but again, it's a fledgling movement. My secretary of corrections, for example, [Aaron] Johnson, was a member of the City Council of Fayetteville, a black who switched from Democrat to Republican because he felt that the kind of games his former party had [been] playing had been entrapping the black population. This is a movement that we see among a lot of others—

BUCKLEY: He wasn't necklaced for it?

MARTIN: Well, there was some intimidation and reprisals for it.

BUCKLEY: Because that is a factor, isn't it?

MARTIN: Reprisals and intimidations?

BUCKLEY: Yes.

MARTIN: Surely it is.

BUCKLEY: I am told that among undergraduates those blacks who want genuine integration in many cases and don't want to sequester themselves with the other black students and live a completely endogamous existence sometimes are considered to be traitorous to their own race. Now, that may be more a Northern phenomenon than a Southern phenomenon, because paradoxically in the South I have always found that there is an easier relationship between black and white than there is in many parts of the North, whose integrationism tends to be ideological rather than practical.

MARTIN: What I was talking about was just partisan reprisals for someone who switches, black or white.

BUCKLEY: Oh, you're not talking about boycotts or anything like that.

MARTIN: No.

CAMPBELL: But the partisan reprisals are pretty tough. In my campaign we had quite a few people that came out in the black community and they took a lot of flack for it. Peer pressure was applied, and—

BUCKLEY: That's the kind of thing I'm talking about, yes.

CAMPBELL: —and they were willing to stand. They did. Essentially those that were there were the business leaders, the college graduates, the professors, the intellectual community, if you will. And as Jim says, it may be a fledgling movement, but there is a keen understanding that it is a much better program to offer an opportunity to survive, to climb a ladder to success in the free enterprise system that we're offering—

BUCKLEY: Right, right.

CAMPBELL: —than it is to maintain a larger and larger public contribution to a subsistence, and I think that's what we have to sell.

BUCKLEY: Right. Right. Well, now, have you had any experience with black candidates who are running on the Republican ticket?

CAMPBELL: Yes, we have.

BUCKLEY: And how well have they done among their own people?

CAMPBELL: We had a very fine lady, Dr. P. T. Williams, that ran for superintendent of education on the Republican ticket a few years ago. She did extremely well in the white community. She did not do very well in the black community.

BUCKLEY: What percentage would she have gotten?

CAMPBELL: In the black community, a little higher than mine.

BUCKLEY: Was she running against a black or against a white?

CAMPBELL: No, she was running against a white.

BUCKLEY: So that the white opponent—

CAMPBELL: The white liberal—

BUCKLEY: The Democratic opponent, of course, right. Right, right.

CAMPBELL: But we've had several others. We had the head of the NAACP in Columbia—switched and ran for the House of Representatives, ran a fine race. He lost. He carried a very high percentage of the vote in the white community, a substantial vote, but not nearly enough to offset the machine politics that's still there. So we're still there butting our heads against it, and we have good people in the black community that are trying to establish a two-party system. They see the competitive factor more as a long-term advantage than they do maybe just being a Republican.

BUCKLEY: Right.

CAMPBELL: They like our philosophy, but they understand that there has to be competition for the opportunity to be created, and I think that we can build on that and build on it well.

BUCKLEY: Well, let's touch, if I may, on national politics. Just this morning there was an analysis of Super Tuesday, in which it said that—this particular analyst said—that the Democrats may have outsmarted themselves, because all of a sudden they have got a situation in which the same people are going to the poll on the same day on a presidential primary and also where local contests are concerned, and that this might numerically mean that people who are prepared to vote Democratic simply as a matter of habit, other than in presidential races, are going to have to adjust their thinking to make a coherent vote at both levels. Is this a dawning reality among politicians in the South about this Super Tuesday?

HUNT: Well, of course, in Alabama we have our presidential primary at a different time than what the other primaries—

BUCKLEY: Yes, you hold out on that.

HUNT: But in 1980, we came within 20,000 votes voting as many in the presidential preference primary as the Democratic party. And a recent poll shows that—just last week, I believe it was—that only 44 percent of the people in Alabama are even considering voting in the Democratic presidential primary and that—

BUCKLEY: Is that sloth or what?

HUNT: I really don't know. They further showed that Gary Hart[16] was running second to Jesse Jackson among Democratic voters in Alabama.

CAMPBELL: It's an interesting thing in South Carolina. The Republicans have a primary in the presidential preference; the Democrats don't. They stuck with the caucus. So we wound up being the more open party, offering the opportunity to participate, and that puts us in an activist role, and they are kind of holding onto the status quo. We are—

BUCKLEY: The primary will come before the—

CAMPBELL: It will come on the Saturday before the Super Tuesday.

BUCKLEY: I see. I see.

CAMPBELL: And so in our state, we will have a Republican primary, people will not have to choose between the local offices and the national office. When we had the first primary in 1980, as a matter of fact we voted about four times the number that we had ever had participate in a Republican primary in our state. And I think that our opening up the national level of politics in the South has helped us indirectly as we have built at the state level and at the local level.

BUCKLEY: Well, is this something that the Democrats are frightened about, this arrangement?

HUNT: Yes, I would think so.

MARTIN: The Super Tuesday?

BUCKLEY: Yes.

MARTIN: But they were the ones who initiated it—

BUCKLEY: I know.

MARTIN: —and crusaded for it, and in fact some of our Republican leaders in North Carolina felt that they perhaps automatically should oppose that. I had felt, and this is my theory, that it would prove to be a Trojan Horse, to use a classical alliteration suitable to this program—[laughter]—a Trojan Horse for the Democrats, because after all, the same candidates who would have to be appealing to the voters nationwide would be right here in the Southeast with the Republican roster and the Democratic roster side by side and it just seemed to me that no matter how it turns out, that was going to convince a lot of Southern conservatives that they really were Republicans rather than Democrats.

BUCKLEY: Well, purely at an objective—if you like, Machiavellian—level, would it help Republicans for Jesse Jackson to simply run away with the Democratic vote?

MARTIN: Well, I'll let them do whatever they want to do on their side. I wouldn't want to advise the Democratic primary.

HUNT: I think, Bill, as far as we're concerned, in looking over the main front runners in the field on the Democratic side, we'd be very comfortable to have any of those opposing us in 1988. [Laughter.]

BUCKLEY: Right, right, right.

MARTIN: But another good factor, too, in that was the Supreme Court decision that held that if a party organization—let's say the Republican party—wants to allow the independent voters to vote in our primary, the legislature, dominated by the other party, cannot prohibit that.[17] And that means that we are going to have an interesting option to invite those people to join with us and feel very comfortable with us and I think that will be a good, positive—

BUCKLEY: Do I understand you that anybody can vote in the Republican primary so long as he signs up as a Republican the day before, or just cold?

MARTIN: No, under the previous law—

BUCKLEY: Yes.

MARTIN: —that had been in effect, only those who had been registered as Republicans or Democrats thirty days before the primary could in fact participate in their party's primary. The independents were left out entirely.

BUCKLEY: Yes.

MARTIN: They could not— Now, what this will say is that it depends on what the party's rule is, rather than what the state's law is. The state cannot preempt the political party.[18]

BUCKLEY: And what is that rule in North Carolina?

MARTIN: It's not been changed yet, but we're addressing that because it's—

BUCKLEY: Tomorrow.

CAMPBELL: We're different.

MARTIN: Well, over the next few weeks.

CAMPBELL: We don't register by party, and if you want to vote in the Republican primary, you show up as a registered voter and you vote, whether you be Democrat, Republican, or independent.

Buckley: What's to keep you from voting in both primaries?

Campbell: Well, there is a cross-check on it.

Buckley: Because of course in California it was legal for years.

Campbell: Yes.

Hunt: Yes.

Campbell: You cannot vote in the two primaries, but since the Democrats don't have a primary—

Buckley: It doesn't make any difference.

Campbell: —on the day [of] the presidential, it doesn't impact that much. But it's very interesting to see the crossover that's beginning to take place, and in our regular primaries that we have, the same holds true. If someone decides that they want to come in and vote, they can come in and vote. The only prohibition is in voting in a runoff. If you have voted in one primary, you obviously can't switch over and vote in a runoff for another primary.

Buckley: Sure. Sure. Well, let's trace the consequences of something that you said a moment ago. Suppose a year from now Jesse Jackson easily defeats the runner-up, say, Gary Hart. Now, I assume you are familiar with certain polls that have said that the most vocal leaders of the black American community do not adhere to positions that correspond with those of the majority of black Americans. They are much more radical, much more pronouncedly left wing on a whole series of issues. If that is the case, would it then follow that the identification of people like Jesse Jackson with the hard left movements rooting for Castro, cheering Che Guevara, with his eccentric position on the Middle East and so on and so forth, that the South, the Southern voter, will identify the Democratic Southern vote with Jesse Jackson, resulting in a tremendous movement towards the Republican party as the natural opposition?

Hunt: I think it would probably increase that movement. However, I think that movement has already begun, and I don't think even Gary Hart could stop that movement in the South. It might very well be—and I am sure it would be—that if Jesse Jackson received the large percentage of the vote it would cause a great deal of concern with the conservative wing of the Democrat party in Alabama.

Buckley: What would they do about it?

Hunt: I think they would vote for the Republican.

Buckley: Well, would there be any formal schismatic movement to the Republican side?

Hunt: Well, basically, in Alabama, as I have mentioned—and especially, say, the middle of Alabama toward the gulf—basically the Democrat who votes in local primaries for Democrats also end up voting for the Republican presidential candidate. So I think it would just fasten that movement and encourage it.

Campbell: What you would have, forgetting about the black/white side of it all, is you would have a situation that was similar to 1972, where the thing that saved the Democratic party in the South was George Wallace, because he gave them a way to go and still stay local in that vote in the general election.

Buckley: And not go Republican.

Campbell: And not go Republican. Lacking that type person, you would have a race that would be like the McGovern/Nixon race in the South, where if you added up all the votes, you would find that the majority at that time would have moved heavily over [to] the Republican column from the top, which would have given some—obviously some—help down the ladder.[19] And I think that's what you'll find.

Buckley: Well, now, at what point will the Southern[er] who votes for the Republican candidate, presidential candidate, session after session, year after year, at what point does he reason to the logical next step, which is that he should look with more interest at Republican candidates running for lesser offices?

Campbell: It's happening. It happened first at the federal level, in the Senate. We saw it with a number of Southern senators, Republicans, that went in with Reagan. But before that in the Congress. In South Carolina in the early 1980s our congressional delegation had four Republicans and two Democrats.[20] So they were voting there. They were identifying at that next level down. It's begun to happen down into the local level, and there is a local base that is beginning to build, and we are seeing more and more growth at the state level. I left the state senate in 1978, and at the time I left, there were three Republicans in the senate. Today there are nine. There are three special elections—there could be twelve in the next month.[21] So it's that type of growth.

Buckley: Do you have a comparable story in North Carolina?

Martin: It's an astonishing story in regard to the local elections. We have 100 counties in North Carolina. Today almost a third of the county commissioners are Republicans, based on the last two elections. In 1982 we had 11 of those counties with Republican majorities, in 1984 we had 23, today we have 31. Tomorrow we are going to continue to work on it.

Campbell: There's something else—

Martin: We have that growth, and the point where a particular person changes, of course, depends on that person and their lifelong allegiance to the party and their parents and grandparents and so forth, for reasons that are spiritual rather than intellectual.

BUCKLEY: Sure. So sheer superannuation works.

MARTIN: But gradually different ones will make that change, and as they do, they leave behind a party that is more controlled by the liberal leadership and therefore, that becomes an even greater burden on the ones who haven't yet made the change. And it's just a steady erosion, and we're going to do what we can to build a two-party system in the South, not only for the good competitive health of it, but for example, insofar as delivering the services of government. I believe you are going to see a stronger resurgence of public schools and education in the Southeast which for years [we] have been apologizing. We couldn't afford to do what we needed to do for public schools, and yet today, at the very time when you've got a rivalry between two parties now, we are beginning to see stronger commitments made to public education because the two major parties are vying with one another to see who can lead that crusade and put us where we need to be. And I think it's great.

BUCKLEY: Yes. And as this poll indicates, that's one of the top four or five concerns of the Southern people, i.e., the level of education.

MARTIN: And we came on just at the right time for that.

BUCKLEY: Right. Now, what about Alabama? Do you have a comparable story to those of Governor Campbell or Governor Martin?

HUNT: Well, really we do. The recent polls showed that only 45 percent of Alabamans identify themselves as Democrats, which is a tremendous change from just four years ago. We've seen this begin to change since the election of Ronald Reagan and people are identifying themselves with the philosophy that he speaks. We have some counties in Alabama today where all of the board of commissioners, I believe three counties, are Republicans. This is— We've had that in Winston County—the Free State of Winston[22]—for a great number of years.

BUCKLEY: Three out of how many?

HUNT: I think 3 counties out of 67 where all of the commissioners are Republicans. We have Shelby County, which is south of Birmingham, Baldwin County, which is on the gulf, which is all three sections of Alabama. And we have elected quite a few. We only have 21 of the 140 members of the legislature, but that has gone up from 10 or 11 the year before, and so we're making those gains and people are changing. People are beginning to vote on the local and state level for Republicans, and I think it's just a matter of time. I think in Alabama and in the South really, Bill, that Governor Wallace and his great strength over the years has given people an excuse to vote for what was called an Alabama Democrat.

BUCKLEY: Right.

HUNT: And now that that's been taken away, the last presidential election in Alabama was the first time that some of our main state leaders ever campaigned openly for a national Democrat, and it has identified them that they—

BUCKLEY: The national Republicans, you mean.

HUNT: Well, no, they campaigned, some of the Democrat leaders— As an example, the lieutenant governor campaigned for Mr. Mondale—

BUCKLEY: Oh, excuse me. I've got you. Right.

HUNT: —and this was really the first time that leaders in the state, the state of Alabama, would openly campaign for the Democratic candidate for president in the last few years. And I think that identifies that that cut is coming between the Republicans and the Democrats. You cannot be an Alabama Democrat and divorce yourself from the Democratic party, and I think that message has come through well to Alabama people.

CAMPBELL: Bill, there is one other thing taking place. I didn't mean to step on Jim's answer a minute ago. The Republican party has also been concentrating very, very hard at building at the local level, and for the first time we have now reached a point that we can offer candidates for office with experience at all levels. And when we go to recruit, we used to have to go and try to recruit the best-known businessman in town, who had never been in politics, to try to run them for governor or for the top office, and we were trying to build from the top down. Even though the top was switching and the allegiance was there, we didn't have the foundation. There has been a tremendous effort in building a foundation. We have throughout our state, and as you've just heard, the others, an awful lot of local officeholders. And they move from city council to the state legislature and up. And as they do this, they establish their credibility—

BUCKLEY: Right.

CAMPBELL: —and also they attract a crossover much easier.

BUCKLEY: They give you an indigenous feel that you didn't have when you sort of imported somebody to run.

CAMPBELL: Absolutely.

BUCKLEY: Yes, I can see where that makes a big difference. Let me ask you something that is sort of an administrative question. All three of you have lieutenant governors who are Democrats. Is this a national phenomenon, or are there a lot of states outside the South in which you have people from different parties as chief executive and as vice-governor—lieutenant governor?[23]

HUNT: Well, you know, a lot of states, the governor and the lieutenant governor run together as a team—

BUCKLEY: That's what I thought.

HUNT: —but we do not do that in Alabama. However, we have, I think, a good situation in Alabama in that the lieutenant governor was basically supported by the same groups who supported me—the business groups and et cetera. We have a good relationship, of course. My lieutenant governor is the son of former governor "Big Jim" Folsom,[24] and no doubt has political aspirations of his own, but so far we are working well together. Many of the people who are in the Senate who are Democrats are also working with me. So there's been a lot of speculation about it, but I think it's going to work well, because the success of this administration and what we do economically is going to reflect either good or bad on the lieutenant governor. So he has a reason to make this a success.

BUCKLEY: I suppose the extent to which it doesn't work really hasn't had much of a workout, since there hasn't been a Republican governor for 100 years, right? So the inherent paradox, which at the presidential level was settled by a constitutional amendment years ago, isn't something that yet has rubbed in in South Carolina or in Alabama or in North Carolina, right? For instance, would you anticipate organic problems because your second in command is a Democrat?

CAMPBELL: Not at this stage of an administration. As you move towards the end of an administration, especially if you are in a position to succeed yourself, then you are going to begin to develop those types of problems. I ran this time with a colleague from the Congress, and we offered as a team, with the argument that we should be elected that way and that the state should operate that way.[25] It didn't work. It worked in that it elected me, I believe. And I give a lot of credit to the fact that my running mate contributed a great deal to that effort. But the lieutenant governor of the state is a friend of mine, we served on the same delegation from the same county when I was in the General Assembly, and from a personal standpoint, we can work well together.[26] In the long term, from a political standpoint, it is going to create problems. My argument has been, and I guess it will remain, that when people are voting for a chief executive, that it makes sense to have the balance there in case anything happens so that you have the same philosophy within that term of government.

BUCKLEY: Right.

CAMPBELL: And I hold to that, even though we have the split now, and I would like to see my state change to accommodate that someday.

BUCKLEY: Well, do you intend to lead a movement for that reform, or are you just going to hope to see that enthusiasm for it accumulate simply by looking at the situation?

CAMPBELL: I think that as it's discussed over time that it will build. I don't think there is a need to polarize in our state to try to seek it because we have a decent situation with the two individuals there—we get along. That's not necessarily going to be the case time and time again, and when it's not the case, it's the people of the state that are going to suffer by having the constant battle between a governor and a lieutenant governor.

BUCKLEY: So the reform might be a popular reform.

CAMPBELL: I think that the demand will come in time, and I think that it will be probably pushed over time by both parties.

BUCKLEY: Okay, let me—since we only have 10 minutes—I know that our viewers would be interested in a distinctive Southern position, if there is such a thing, on the national Republican ticket. Everybody acknowledges that Mr. Reagan has been hurt, though not everybody acknowledges that his being hurt invalidates any of the principles that made him popular. Would you feel that his successor would have a better chance to carry the South if his positions were congruent with those of Ronald Reagan, or would you be happier with somebody who was viewed as a little bit more to the left?

MARTIN: Well, first of all, you have to recognize that Ronald Reagan is still very popular in the South. There is no question about that.

BUCKLEY: Well, he is still very popular everywhere, actually, even at 45 percent.

MARTIN: But I was pointing to our area that we are trying to address here.

BUCKLEY: Yes, right.

MARTIN: I am talking about very popular in the South.

BUCKLEY: You mean over 55?

MARTIN: It would be stronger than that. People admire him for what he has done to get our nation back on the right track. They grieve with him when he gets off the track and he's got to spend some time and energy and effort to deal with a particular situation like the Iran opportunity, where clearly his motive was to try to salvage for the future a productive relationship with the people of Iran and the people of the United States, on the grounds that we can't forever be sworn enemies to one another. There has to come a time for rapprochement there, and he saw that. It didn't work out very well. It may have been undermined to some extent by other groups within Iran. But our people grieve for that and they sympathize with him and they want him to recover and they are very much in favor of him. So he has a great deal of strength in North Carolina, and I think throughout the Southeast. Now, insofar as the future candidates, I would say that our people are going to be supporting someone who will express those same philosophic commitments and that same grounding that Ronald Reagan has brought to the national scene and which has helped us to move what yet may turn out to be a revolution of movement in the direction of sounder, more conservative principles of government.

BUCKLEY: Would that be true in your state, Governor?

HUNT: Yes, it would be. I know that I would be more comfortable, and I feel like the voters would be more comfortable with a candidate near Ronald Reagan.

BUCKLEY: And that would be true in South Carolina?

CAMPBELL: Oh, I don't think there is any question about it.

BUCKLEY: Okay, well, then let me ask you this question. Assuming that Candidate—let's not name them—assuming that Candidate A is viewed as sort of a traditional liberal Republican, a Rockefeller type,[27] and Candidate B is viewed as sort of a Reaganite. Is it predictable that Candidate B would beat Candidate A unless he is stupid?

MARTIN: I think you could say that, and not having a liberal candidate having announced yet, we don't have that dilemma.

BUCKLEY: No, and one of the reasons we don't have that dilemma is because there has been no call for polarization. That is to say, people aren't saying, "Vote for me—I'm the most liberal man in town." They've been, I think, rather careful not to stress any inchoate differences that they might feel between themselves and Ronald Reagan. But there is a journalistic and intellectual movement that says it's going to happen, this cycle that we keep hearing about. The lead story in *Time* magazine this week is all about just that point: All of a sudden the Republican party coast to coast is waking up and recognizing that the Republican party isn't concerned enough with the little people.[28] I'm not asking an intellectual question, because we all know the answers to it, but if this cycle in fact is swinging, is it likely to swing through the South, or is the South going to be as resistant to it as it has been to the alienation from Reagan that has been general elsewhere?

CAMPBELL: I think that any national cycle affects the South. It affects it to a lesser degree—

BUCKLEY: Yes, right.

CAMPBELL: —a much lesser degree than it might affect another section.

BUCKLEY: Why is that?

CAMPBELL: I think—

BUCKLEY: Is it their historical fortitude? Tenacity?

CAMPBELL: Yes, I think the fact that the Southerners are very steeped in tradition—Jim Martin made a statement a while ago about worshipping ancestors or whatever it might be, but the fact is is that we aren't easily swayed from our basic beliefs as other areas are.

BUCKLEY: Not as trendy, yes.

CAMPBELL: No, we're not.

BUCKLEY: Now, would that be true at the undergraduate level also?

CAMPBELL: Well, I think there you have obviously a lot more volatility, but the interesting thing is, is that all of the polls show that in the colleges, in the undergraduate level, we are attracting the people, and the "we" means the Republican party that is headed by Ronald Reagan, and so it's very interesting if you can equate that. But of course you've got to realize—

BUCKLEY: That's almost a risque thing to do in the undergraduate world, isn't it?

CAMPBELL: Well, it is, but it's happening. It's happening.

BUCKLEY: Yes. Yes. Now, North Carolina would not be typical here, would it, Governor, because one thinks of it sort of as the border state.

MARTIN: With respect to the pattern that he's ascribed?

BUCKLEY: Yes. Yes.

MARTIN: No, I would say it is typical. The same respect for family and for tradition is certainly a hallmark of the Down Home State.

BUCKLEY: And yet over the years one associates with people like Mr. Graham[29] a kind of a populist or even left of center Democratic leadership, which one would never associate with South Carolina.

MARTIN: Or even more recently. But here again, it's the vagaries of politics.

BUCKLEY: Yes.

MARTIN: It's sometimes fickle, and you can't count on every year being exactly what you thought.

BUCKLEY: No.

MARTIN: But over the long haul, I'd say the same principles are there.

BUCKLEY: And in Alabama?

HUNT: Yes. The same principles. Very much strong family, strongly religious, and so I think we would be typical of South Carolina.

BUCKLEY: Incidentally, it is widely supposed that the heavily Baptist element in the South has been pro-Republican. My information is that that is not correct. For instance, the majority of them voted for Jimmy Carter in 1976. Is that so?

HUNT: Yes, I would say so in 1976.

BUCKLEY: But in '80 they switched?

HUNT: I would say in '80 and '84 they switched.

BUCKLEY: Now, is that switch permanent or was that an attraction to an individual?

HUNT: No, I think it's on the issues of abortion, on the family matters, more the traditional values. I think in 1976 they perceived that Jimmy Carter held the views that they held and then by 1980 they were ready to switch.

BUCKLEY: So that the fundamentalists or the evangelical movement is likely to continue to be Republican.

HUNT: I think they will be conservative. I don't know whether you would call them conservative. In Alabama, as an example, we have a large percentage who would call themselves independent. And I think you could say that is a swing vote. And as long as our leaders and our national platforms hold up to the values they believe in, that they will support us and continue to support us.

BUCKLEY: Well, is it likely—let me ask you, Governor, this: Is it likely that the presidential campaign a year from now is going to fortify Republican roots in the South?

CAMPBELL: Yes.

BUCKLEY: It is.

CAMPBELL: Yes.

BUCKLEY: For all the reasons that we have touched on. Are there any reasons we haven't touched on that you want to touch on.

CAMPBELL: Well, no philosophical reason. None of the exact intellectual reasons that we could come up with, but the fact is is that the Republicans are attracting their national candidates into the South and as a result of that—the Democrats, as you know, for years ignored the South, didn't campaign, it was in the bag—it was the Republicans that opened it, brought their candidates in more and more. People became more familiar. This time around we have candidates that go from the vice-president, and we will have eight or nine, all of them well known in some field or fashion, coming in. The attraction will be there. There will be more involvement and more participation. And just by the involvement and participation, we are going to build a much broader and stronger base.

BUCKLEY: Does it matter at all or a great deal that one of the candidates running either for president or vice-president should be from the South?

CAMPBELL: The South is probably going to control who wins the presidency, and I would say at the very least one of the parties has to have a candidate that appeals to the South.

BUCKLEY: Why not both, then?

CAMPBELL: Maybe they are both trying. I don't see anybody on the other side.

MARTIN: You mean both parties or both candidates?

BUCKLEY: Yes, both parties. Both parties. By which I mean, if you want to win the presidency, and if to win the presidency you have to get the South, and if to get the South you have to have a Southerner on the ticket, why wouldn't that reasoning apply equally to the Republicans and to the Democrats?

MARTIN: I don't know that he's saying you have to have a Southerner on the ticket. What he is saying is that you have to have someone who would make a strong appeal to Southerners.

BUCKLEY: I'm sorry. I'm sorry. So therefore it's not important to have a Southerner on the ticket.

CAMPBELL: It's not—

MARTIN: It wouldn't hurt.

CAMPBELL: It wouldn't hurt. I don't think it's an imperative. I think that it is important.

BUCKLEY: Yes. Right, right, right. All right, since we only have—

MARTIN: But let's say that we also expect that our party will have both the candidates for president and vice-president who will be appealing to the South. We can't anticipate that the effect will be as strong as it was with Reagan versus Mondale, for example, but nevertheless, whatever decisions the two parties make are going to be in our favor in the Southeast.

BUCKLEY: Which leads to the paradox that they will have to in effect disavow the largest Southern vote during the Democratic primary if it goes to Jesse Jackson, as long as Jesse Jackson continues with his present attachments.

MARTIN: We'll have to just see what they do with that.

BUCKLEY: Yes. Well, I thank you very much, Governor Martin and Governor Hunt and Governor Campbell, ladies and gentlemen.

---

[1]William Frank Buckley, Jr. (1925-   ), native of New York City; A.B., Yale University, 1950; honorary degrees; U.S. Army, 1944-1946. Noted conservative commentator; associate editor, *American Mercury*, 1952; editor in chief, *National Review*, since 1955; syndicated columnist, since 1962; host of weekly Public Broadcasting System television program, "Firing Line," since 1966; member, U.S. Information Agency Advisory Commission, 1969-1972; author. *Who's Who in America, 1986-1987*, I, 381.

[2]The following United States senators, Republicans representing southern constituencies, failed to win reelection in 1986:

James Broyhill, of North Carolina, lost to Terry Sanford by a 51.8 percent to 48.2 percent margin. Lamis, *Two-Party South*, 286.

Jeremiah Denton (1925-   ), native, resident of Mobile, Alabama; B.A., U.S. Naval Academy, 1946; M.A., George Washington University, 1964. U.S. Naval officer 1946-1977; promoted to rear admiral, 1973; commandant, Armed Forces Staff College, Norfolk, Va., 1973-1977; U.S. senator from Alabama, elected 1980, and chairman, Security and Terrorism Subcommittee of the Judiciary Committee; lost 1986 election to Congressman Richard Shelby by a 50.3 percent to 49.7 percent margin. Barone and Ujifusa, *Almanac of American Politics, 1986*, 9; Lamis, *Two-Party South*, 271.

Paula Hawkins (1927-   ), born in Salt Lake City, Utah; resident of Winter Park, Florida; was educated at Utah State University. Member, Republican National Committee, 1968; member, Special Advisory Committee, Consumer Affairs, Federal Energy Administration, 1968; president, Commission on White House Fellowships, 1968; member, 1973-1979, chairwoman, 1977-1979, Florida Public Service Commission; unsuccessful GOP candidate for Florida lieutenant governor, 1978. Elected U.S. senator from Florida, 1980; chairwoman, Agricultural Credit and Rural Electrification Subcommittee, Committee on Agriculture, Nutrition, and Forestry, and of Subcommittee on Children, Family, Drugs, and Alcoholism, Committee on Labor and Human Resources; lost 1986 election to Governor Bob Graham by a 54.7 percent to 45.3 percent margin. Barone and Ujifusa, *Almanac of American Politics, 1986*, 277; Lamis, *Two-Party South*, 292, 367.

Mack Mattingly (1931-   ), born in Anderson, Indiana; resident of St. Simons, Georgia; B.A., Indiana University, 1957; U.S. Air Force, 1951-1955. Account supervisor, Arvin Industries, 1957-1959; IBM Sales, 1959-1979; president, Mattingly's Office Products, 1975-1980. Elected U.S. senator from Georgia, 1980; chairman, Military Construction Subcommittee, Committee on Appropriations, and of Economic Policy Subcommittee, Committee on Banking, Housing, and Urban Affairs; lost 1986 election to Congressman Wyche Fowler by a 50.9 percent to 49.1 percent margin. Barone and Ujifusa, *Almanac of American Politics, 1986*, 332; Lamis, *Two-Party South*, 272-273.

[3]H. Guy Hunt (1933-   ), born in Holly Park, Alabama; honorary degrees; joined U.S. Army, 1954; served in Korea. Became Primitive Baptist preacher, 1958; cattle rancher; Amway distributor; Cullman County probate judge, 1964-1976; unsuccessful candidate for Alabama Senate, 1962, and governor, 1978; executive director, Agricultural Stabilization and Conservation Service, U.S. Department of Agriculture, 1981-1985; elected Alabama governor, 1986; Republican. Allen H. Neuharth and others, *Profiles of Power: How the Governors Run Our 50 States* (Washington, D.C.: USA Today Books/Ganett Co., Inc., 1988), 25; *Who's Who in America, 1988-1989*, I, 1507.

Contenders for Alabama's 1986 Democratic gubernatorial nomination included Bill Baxley, lieutenant governor, 1983-1987; Charles Graddick, attorney general, 1979-1983, 1983-1987; Forrest (Fob) James, governor, 1979-1983; and George McMillan, lieutenant governor, 1979-1983. The margin of Baxley's victory in the primary over second-place finisher Graddick was insufficient to avert a runoff, a contest that quickly descended into an orgy of mudslinging and thinly veiled appeals to racism. Graddick won the second election, only to be denied the nomination by a panel of federal judges; the candidate, as attorney general, issued a directive bearing on the participation of Republican crossover voters in the runoff that contravened the U.S. Voting Rights Act. Consequently, a subcommittee of the Alabama Democratic party announced Baxley as the nominee. Graddick unsuccessfully appealed the legal decision and launched a write-in campaign for governor that he abandoned five days before the general election. With support from 56.4 percent of the balloters, Guy Hunt defeated Baxley on November 4, 1986; 87 percent of the voters backing Graddick in the runoff opted for Hunt. John Clements, *Taylor's Encyclopedia of Government Officials: Federal and State* (Dallas, Texas: Political Research, Inc., ongoing, multivolume series, 1967-), VIII, 60, X, 60, XI, 60, hereinafter cited as Clements, *Taylor's Encyclopedia of Government Officials*; Lamis, *Two-Party South*, 266-270.

[4]James Elisha Folsom, Jr. (1949-   ), born in Montgomery, Alabama; resident of Cullman; B.A., Jacksonville State University, 1974; Alabama National Guard, 1968-1970. With Alabama Department of Industrial Relations, 1974-1976; public relations representative, Reynolds Metals Co., 1976-1979; Alabama public service commissioner, 1980; Democratic nominee for U.S. Senate, 1980; elected Alabama lieutenant governor, 1986. Clements, *Taylor's Encyclopedia of Government Officials*, XI, 60; *Who's Who in America, 1988-1989*, I, 1005.

[5]Chester Trent Lott (1942-   ), born in Grenada, Mississippi; resident of Pascagoula; B.P.A., 1963, J.D., 1967, University of Mississippi. Attorney; administrative assistant to U.S Representative William M. Colmer, 1968-1972; elected to U.S. House of Representatives, 1972, and returned in subsequent elections; Republican. Lott missed the Blackberry Farms meeting because of a "schedule conflict." *Biographical Directory of Congress*, 1392; *Washington* (District of Columbia) *Post*, July 28, 1985, hereinafter cited as *Washington Post*.

Richard Lewis Thornburgh (1932-   ), born in Pittsburgh; B. Engineering, Yale University, 1954; LL.B., University of Pittsburgh, 1957; honorary degrees. Attorney in private practice, 1959-1969, 1977-1979, 1987; U.S. attorney for western Pennsylvania, 1969-1975; assistant attorney general, Criminal Division, U.S. Justice Department, 1975-1977; elected Pennsylvania governor, 1978, reelected 1982; director, Institute of Politics, John F. Kennedy School of Government, Harvard University, 1987-1988; replaced Edwin Meese III as U.S. attorney general, 1988; author. *New York Times*, July 13, August 13, 1988; *Who's Who in America, 1988-1989*, II, 3887.

John H. Sununu (1939-   ), born in Havana, Cuba; B.S., 1961, M.S., 1962, Ph.D., 1966, Massachusetts Institute of Technology. Founder, chief engineer, Astro Dynamics, 1960-1965; president, J.H.S. Engineering Co. and Thermal Research, Inc., Salem, New Hampshire, 1965-1982; associate professor of mechanical engineering, 1966-1982, dean, College of Engineering, 1968-1973, Tufts University; member, New Hampshire House of Representatives, 1973-1974; elected governor of New Hampshire, 1982, reelected 1984, 1986; became White House chief of staff with inauguration of George Bush as U.S. president, 1989. *New York Times*, November 17, 1988, January 20, 1989; *Who's Who in America, 1988-1989*, II, 3024.

[6]The brainstorming session called to define GOP strategy in state and local elections was held at Blackberry Farms in Tennessee's Great Smoky Mountains. That meeting grew into the Southern Republican Exchange which convened in Raleigh on January 2 and 3, 1987. *News and Observer*, July 28, 1985, January 3, 4, 1987; *Washington Post*, July 28, 1985, August 3, 1986.

[7]Borrowed from a popular George Lucas motion picture, the title "Star Wars" became the common name by which President Reagan's space-based anti-missile program, the Strategic Defense Initiative, was known.

[8]The Contras were U.S.-supported rebels attempting to overthrow the communist-backed Sandinista government of Nicaragua.

[9]Campbell's Democratic opponent in the 1986 South Carolina gubernatorial election was Michael Roland Daniel (1940-   ), born in Gaffney, South Carolina; B.A., 1962, J.D., 1966, University of South Carolina; U.S. Army, 1967-1968. Attorney; member, South Carolina House of Representatives, 1973-1983, speaker pro tem, 1980-1983; South Carolina lieutenant governor, 1983-1987. Daniel lost the contest for governor by a 48 percent to 52 percent margin. *New York Times*, November 6, 1986; *Who's Who in America, 1988-1989*, I, 706.

[10]The 1984 Democratic nominee for governor was Rufus Ligh Edmisten (1941-   ), born in Boone; B.A., University of North Carolina at Chapel Hill, 1963; J.D., George Washington University, 1967. Attorney; member, staff of U.S. Senator Sam J. Ervin, 1963-1974, and deputy chief counsel to Watergate Committee, 1972-1974; N.C. attorney general, 1975-1985, elected secretary of state, 1988. *North Carolina Manual, 1989-1990*, 489, 527. The bruising primary runoff election between Edmisten and Eddie Knox sent Knox and some of his supporters to the GOP, dividing the Democratic party; for a brief description, see Lamis, *Two-Party South*, 251; Luebke, *Tar Heel Politics*, 187, 196-197; and Snider, *Helms and Hunt*, 132-134, 209.

[11]James Strom Thurmond (1902-   ), born in Edgefield, South Carolina; was graduated from Clemson College (later University), 1923; U.S. Army, 1942-1946; U.S. Army Reserve. Schoolteacher, 1923-1929, Edgefield County education superintendent, 1929-1933; attorney; member, South Carolina Senate, 1933-1938; circuit judge, 1938-1942, 1946; South Carolina governor, 1947-1951; States Rights (Dixiecrat) party candidate for U.S. president, 1948; unsuccessful candidate for Democratic U.S. Senate nomination, 1950. Elected to U.S. Senate, 1954, resigned in April, 1956; reelected in November, 1956, and returned in subsequent elections; president pro tem, 1981-1987, and Judiciary Committee chairman, 1981-1987; changed party affiliation from Democrat to Republican, 1964. *Biographical Directory of Congress*, 1939; Lamis, *Two-Party South*, 30.

[12]Howard Henry Baker, Jr. (1925-   ), born in Huntsville, Tennessee; was educated at Tulane University and University of the South; was graduated from University of Tennessee Law College, 1949; U.S. Navy, 1943-1946. Attorney; U.S. senator from Tennessee, 1967-1985; Senate minority leader, 1977-1981, majority leader, 1981-1985; chief of staff to President Reagan, 1987-1988; Republican. *Biographical Directory of Congress*, 566. "Southern Republican Statesmen Look Around" was the theme of the October 17, 1986, "Firing Line" broadcast in which Baker and Alexander participated. "Firing Line: Can We Republicanize the South" (Columbia, South Carolina: Southern Educational Communications Association, 1987), 26.

[13]George Corley Wallace was perhaps best known outside his native state as the populist and segregationist governor who literally "stood in the schoolhouse door" in a futile attempt to prevent blacks from enrolling at the University of Alabama in 1963. However, facing a credible Republican opponent in the 1982 gubernatorial campaign, Wallace publicly embraced integration, assiduously courted blacks, and consequently won 90 perecent of Alabama's black vote and reelection, as well. Lamis, *Two-Party South*, 88-91, 338n; Robert Sobel and John Raimo, *Biographical Directory of Governors of the United States, 1789-1978* (Westport, CT: Meckler Books, 4 volumes, 1978), I, 37-38, hereinafter cited as Sobel and Raimo, *Biographical Directory of Governors of the United States*.

[14]An estimated 69 percent to 73 percent of the whites voting in Alabama's 1986 general election backed Hunt, while approximately 97 percent of the black ballots cast for governor supported his opponent, Bill Baxley. Two rival black organizations, the Alabama Democratic Conference and the Alabama New South Coalition, endorsed Baxley, as did the Alabama Education Association and the Alabama Labor Council. Lamis, *Two-Party South*, 266, 270.

[15]Thomas Sowell (1930-), born in Gastonia; A.B., Harvard University, 1958; M.A., Columbia University, 1959; Ph.D., University of Chicago, 1968; U.S. Marine Corps, 1951-1953. Economist, U.S. Department of Labor, 1961-1962; taught economics at Douglass College, Rutgers University, 1962-1963, Howard University, 1963-1964, Cornell University, 1965-1969, Brandeis University, 1969-1970, and University of California-Los Angeles, 1970-1980; senior fellow, Hoover Institute, Stanford, California, 1977, and since 1980; economic analyst, American Telephone and Telegraph Co., 1964-1965; author. *Who's Who in America, 1988-1989,* II, 2924.

[16]Gary Warren Hart (1936-   ), was born in Ottawa, Kansas; resident of Kittredge, Colorado; was graduated from Bethany Navarene College, 1958, Yale Divinity School, 1961, and Yale University Law School, 1964. U.S. Justice Department attorney, 1964-1965; special assistant to U.S. Interior Department solicitor, 1965-1967; attorney in private practice, Denver, 1967-1974; elected U.S. senator from Colorado, 1974, reelected, 1980; unsuccessful candidate for Democratic presidential nomination, 1984, 1988; author. *Biographical Directory of Congress,* 1145.

[17]*Tashjian, Secretary of State of Connecticut* v. *Republican Party of Connecticut, et al.,* decided on December 10, 1986, was the U.S. Supreme Court case to which Martin referred. See *United States Reports, Volume 479,* 208-237.

[18]"An Act to Allow Unaffiliated Voters to Vote in the Primary Election of the Party which Authorizes that Voter to Vote, so as to Comply with a Decision of the Supreme Court of the United States," *N.C. Session Laws, 1987,* I, c. 408, was ratified June 18, 1987, and became effective January 1, 1988.

[19]George Stanley McGovern (1922-   ), born in Avon, South Dakota; was graduated from Dakota Wesleyan University, 1946; Ph.D., Northwestern University, 1953; U.S. Army Air Force, 1942-1945. History, government professor, Dakota Wesleyan University, 1950-1953; executive secretary, South Dakota Democratic party, 1953-1956; member, Advisory Committee on Political Organization, Democratic National Committee, 1954-1956; U.S. Representative from South Dakota, 1957-1961; unsuccessful candidate for U.S. Senate, 1960; director, Food for Peace Program, 1961-1962; elected to U.S. Senate, 1962, reelected 1968, 1974; unsuccessful candidate for Democratic presidential nomination, 1968; unsuccessful candidate for U.S. president, 1972; unsuccessful candidate for reelection to U.S. Senate, 1980; lecturer; teacher. *Biographical Directory of Congress,* 1465.

[20]South Carolina's 1981 delegation to the U.S. House of Representatives consisted of Campbell, Thomas F. Hartnett, Floyd Spence, and John L. Napier, Republicans; and Democrats Butler Derrick and Ken Holland. Clements, *Taylor's Encyclopedia of Government Officials,* VIII, 152.

[21]The GOP was represented in the South Carolina Senate by Campbell, Thomas F. Hartnett, and Gilbert E. McMillan in 1978. When inaugurated as governor in 1987, Campbell initially could rely on the support of nine Republican state senators: Davis L. Thomas, W. Richard Lee, John E. Courson, Warren K. Geise, Addison G. Wilson, Ryan C. Shealy, William S. Branton, Jr., Glenn F. McConnell, and William E. Applegate III. That spring, the outcome of special elections placed three new Republicans in the upper house. The Democrats lost a pair of seats when H. Samuel Sitwell won the Sixth District, succeeding Nick A. Theodore who was elected lieutenant governor in 1986, and John R. Russell took the Twelfth. Sherry Martschink kept the Forty-fourth District in the GOP fold. Clements, *Taylor's Encyclopedia of Government Officials,* VI, 152, X, 152, XI, 152, XII, 152.

[22]When Alabama seceded from the Union in 1861, the mountain Republican stronghold of Winston County left the Confederacy and established itself as the Free State of Winston. Lamis, *Two-Party South,* 333n-334n.

[23]Of the thirteen states—Alabama, California, Delaware, Idaho, Iowa, Missouri, North Carolina, Oklahoma, Rhode Island, South Carolina, Texas, Vermont, and Washington—having governors and lieutenant governors from opposing political parties in 1987, all but four were outside the South. Clements, *Taylor's Encyclopedia of Government Officials,* XI, 60-174.

[24]James Elisha Folsom (1908-   ), born in Coffee County, Alabama; was educated at University of Alabama, Howard College (Birmingham, Alabama), and George Washington University. District agent, 1937-1940, state manager, 1940-1946, Emergency and Aid Insurance Co.; governor of Alabama, 1947-1951, 1955-1959; Democrat. During Folsom's first term, Ku Klux Klan members were barred from wearing hoods, punishment by flogging in Alabama prisons was banned, and betting was outlawed; enforcement of federal antisegregation measures characterized his second term. Sobel and Raimo, *Biographical Directory of the Governors of the United States*, I, 35.

[25]Thomas Forbes Hartnett (1941-   ), born in Charleston; resident of Mount Pleasant, South Carolina; was educated at College of Charleston; U.S. Air Force Reserve, 1963-1969. President, Hartnett Realty Co., since 1963; member, South Carolina House, 1965-1972, and Senate, 1972-1980; member, U.S. House, 1981-1987. Hartnett initially desired the Republican gubernatorial nomination in 1986, but was persuaded to run for lieutenant governor instead. He lost that race to Nick Theodore. *Biographical Directory of Congress*, 1147; *Charlotte Observer*, November 5, 6, 1986.

[26]Nick Andrew Theodore (1928-   ), native of Greenville, South Carolina; B.A., Furman University, 1952. Member, South Carolina House, 1963-1966, 1969-1978, and Senate, 1967-1968, 1981-1986; president, William Goldsmith Insurance Agency; elected lieutenant governor, 1986; Democrat. Nick Andrew Theodore to Jan-Michael Poff, October 17, 1988; *Who's Who in America, 1988-1989*, II, 3072.

[27]Nelson Aldrich Rockefeller (1908-1979), born in Bar Harbor, Maine; B.A., Dartmouth College, 1930; honorary degrees. Leader of Republican party's moderate-liberal wing and unsuccessful candidate for U.S. presidential nomination, 1960, 1964, 1968; director, 1931-1958, president, 1938-1945, 1948-1951, and chairman, 1945-1953, 1956-1958, Rockefeller Center, Inc.; coordinator, Office of Inter-American Affairs, 1940-1944; assistant secretary of state for American republic affairs, 1944-1945; chairman, International Development Advisory Board (Point 4 Program), 1950-1951; undersecretary, U.S. Department of Health, Education, and Welfare, 1953-1954; special assistant to President Dwight D. Eisenhower, 1954-1955; chairman, President's Advisory Committee on Government Organization, 1953-1958; elected governor of New York, 1958, reelected 1962, 1966, 1970, resigned 1973; U.S. vice-president, 1974-1977. *Encyclopaedia Britannica*, 15th ed., s.v., "Rockefeller, Nelson Aldrich"; Sobel and Raimo, *Biographical Directory of the Governors of the United States*, III, 1105-1106; *Who Was Who in America, 1977-1981*, 487.

[28]See "A Change in the Weather," *Time*, March 30, 1987, 28-37.

[29]Frank Porter Graham (1886-1972), native of Fayetteville; A.B., University of North Carolina at Chapel Hill, 1909; A.M., Columbia University, 1916; honorary degrees; served in U.S. Marine Corps during World War I. Human rights activist; history instructor, later professor, University of North Carolina, 1914-1930; president, from 1930, University of North Carolina at Chapel Hill, and of the Consolidated University of North Carolina, 1932-1949. Served on numerous federal commissions during administration of President Franklin D. Roosevelt; member, 1946-1947, President's Committee on Civil Rights; cofounder and president, 1946-1949, Oak Ridge Institute of Nuclear Studies; U.S. representative to U.N. Committee of Good Offices mediating Dutch-Indonesian dispute, 1947. Appointed to U.S. Senate, 1949, by Governor Kerr Scott to fill unexpired term of Joseph Melville Broughton; defeated by Willis Smith in heated Democratic primary election for U.S. Senate, 1950. Defense manpower administrator, U.S. Department of Labor, 1951; U.N. mediator in India-Pakistan dispute over Kashmir, 1951-1970, and president, U.N. Speakers Bureau. Warren Ashby, *Frank Porter Graham: A Southern Liberal* (Winston-Salem: John F. Blair, Publisher, 1980), 257-303; Powell, *DNCB*, II, 332-333.

INDEX

and Martin's legislative proposals (1988), 53; N.C. Democratic gubernatorial primary (1984), 1021, 1041n; N.C. gubernatorial, (1984) xxiii, xxviii, xxx, 10, 19n, 57, 58, 99, 100-101, 104, 143, 213, 428, 789, 902, 1018, 1019, 1021, 1023-1024, 1041n; (1988) xlii, 42n, 48, 53n, 943, 994, 995, 997; N.C. primary, 1028; presidential, (1972) 1030, (1976) 1037, (1980) 1037, (1984) 1032, 1037, 1038, (1988) 1022, 1028, 1037; Republican presidential primary (1988), 1037-1038; S.C. gubernatorial, (1986) 1020, 1022-1023, 1025, 1033; S.C. primary, 1027, 1028-1029; shift to odd-numbered years proposed for N.C., 283, 284. See also General Assembly, N.C.; Super Tuesday

Elections, State Board of: 61, 63n-64n, 68n, 97, 98n, 102

Electric Cooperatives, N.C. Association of: 727, 996

Elenbaas, Case: 967, 968

Elf Aquitaine: 882

Eliel, Ernest Ludwig: 811, 812n

Elion, Gertrude Belle: 955, 956n

Elizabeth City: 143n, 157, 158, 159, 697, 698, 830, 831

Elizabeth City State University: 159, 976

Elizabethtown Airport: 1002

Elk River Complex: 264-265, 308, 323-324, 326

Elon College: 281

Embrex, Inc.: 989

Emerald Isle: 715, 975

Emergency Feed Program: 515

Emergency Management Division. See Crime Control and Public Safety, Dept. of

Emergency Management Workshop: 973

Emergency Medicine Today: 1004

Emergency Prison Facilities Development Program: 626

Emergency Response Commission, N.C.: 1010

Emerging Issues Forum: 985, 996

Emmrich, Manfred: 649, 654n

Employers: and employee dismissals, 258

Employment: agricultural, 399-400, 789; among blacks, 161; and Champion International Corp., 723-724; and "Communities of Excellence" program, 735n; discussed, 252, 301, 534, 695, 870-871, 959; and education, 782; and female prison inmates, 567, 568; in film making, 720; forest resources, 263, 273; among Indians, 782; job centers, 480; manufac-

turing, 537; mentioned, xlii, 248, 251, 254, 255, 465, 737n, 755, 939, 986, 1010; among military veterans, 858-859; nonmanufacturing, 540; and Rocco, Inc., 782; in Rowan County, 822; by small businesses, 210, 235-236; statistics, xxxii, 23, 174, 209, 235, 339, 400, 456, 481, 483, 537, 559, 616, 630, 649-650, 695, 710-711, 728, 730, 735n, 754, 781, 789-790, 801, 821, 823, 869-870, 883, 909, 919, 937-938, 940, 948; and super collider, 766, 790, 791; textile and apparel, 114, 236, 273, 240, 399, 534, 562; and traditional industries, 134, 135; in Valdese, 821; and WCI, Inc., 931, 932; among women, 840, 959. See also Unemployment

Employment Security Commission: counsels legislature, 650; Dislocated Worker Program, 27, 435, 443, 479, 517-518, 521, 713, 731; and Farm Economy Task Force, 521; federal funds cut, 504; holds workshops, 258; Job Service Employer Awards, 648-649, 1003; Justus sworn in as chairwoman, 988; and military veterans, 502, 858, 859; offices and work force, 651; produces labor market guide, 478; reserve fund, 476-477, 480, 487-488, 504-505, 518, 538, 651

Energy, U.S. Dept. of: and nuclear waste disposal, 264-265, 283-284, 308, 309, 310, 321-323, 324-325, 326, 350, 981; Office of Civilian Radioactive Waste Management, 324; and super collider, 305, 699-700, 740, 743, 745n, 762, 763, 764-765, 791, 792n-793n, 1000, 1004

Enfield: 533, 536n, 987

Engineers, U.S. Army Corps of: 158, 639, 930

England: 400th Anniversary events in, 107, 573, 988

Enloe, Jeff Hailen, Jr.: 504, 507n, 651

Enloe High School: 75, 973, 976

Enterprise zones: 257

Environment, Health, and Natural Resources, Dept. of: created, 54n

Environmental Defense Fund: 881

Environmental health program: 245

Environmental Management, Division of. See Natural Resources and Community Development, Dept. of

Environmental management and protection: and Champion International, 721-725; cleanup of underground storage tanks, xxxix, 34; consolidation of state regulatory agencies, 50, 54n, 749-753, 814-815, 865, 947, 995; discussed, 663-667, 794-795, 796-797; mentioned, xxiv, xlii, 2,

Addresses and Public Papers of James Grubbs Martin, Governor of North Carolina, 1985-1989 documents the first term of the state's sixty-fifth chief executive. Copies of his inaugural address, messages to the General Assembly, and over 230 speeches and press releases, carefully selected from the more than 960 available, present the aspirations and accomplishments of Martin's administration. They explain the governor's policies and programs, discuss the issues confronting the state, disclose the challenges of office, give voice to his opinions, and contain autobiographical elements. Lists of omitted speeches and executive orders further reveal the scope of Martin's official activities.

Jan-Michael Poff is editor of modern governors' documentaries at the Historical Publications Section, Division of Archives and History, North Carolina Department of Cultural Resources.